W9-AZA-352

FIFTH EDITION

Students with Learning Disabilities

Cecil D. Mercer
University of Florida

With contributions by Ann R. Mercer

Merrill,
an imprint of Prentice Hall
Upper Saddle River, New Jersey ■ Columbus, Ohio

In memory of Blaze, our special golden retriever,
who faithfully served our family for fourteen years
as a master teacher of unconditional love.

Library of Congress Cataloging-in-Publication Data
Mercer, Cecil D.
Students with learning disabilities / Cecil D. Mercer, with contributions by Ann R. Mercer. — 5th ed.
p. cm.
Includes bibliographical references and indexes.
ISBN 0-13-477176-1
1. Learning disabilities—United States. 2. Learning disabled children—Education—United States. I. Mercer, Ann R. II. Title.
LC4705.M47 1997
371.9—dc20 95-52497
CIP

Cover photo: © Chip Henderson/Tony Stone Worldwide
Editor: Ann Castel Davis
Production Editor: Linda Hillis Bayma
Design Coordinator: Jill E. Bonar
Photo Researcher: Angela Jenkins
Text Designer: Rebecca Bobb
Cover Designer: Brian Deep
Production Manager: Laura Messerly
Illustrations: Carlisle Communications, Ltd.

This book was set in ITC Cheltenham Light by Carlisle Communications, Ltd. and was printed and bound by Quebecor Printing/Book Press. The cover was printed by Phoenix Color Corp.

Photo credits: Scott Cunningham/Merrill/Prentice Hall, pp. 47, 108, 144, 156, 224, 242, 254, 414, 566; Jean Greenwald/Merrill/Prentice Hall, p. 1; Larry Hamill/Merrill/Prentice Hall, p. 272; Harvey R. Phillips/PPI, pp. 93, 628; Barbara Schwartz/Merrill/Prentice Hall, pp. 56, 143, 291, 460, 576, 601, 622; David Strickler/Strix Pix, pp. 24, 81, 306, 445; Anne Vega/Merrill/Prentice Hall, pp. 2, 13, 36, 70, 118, 126, 165, 186, 201, 210, 324, 342, 358, 367, 394, 413, 431, 470, 497, 512, 533, 547, 660; Todd Yarrington/Merrill/Prentice Hall, p. 330.

Printed in the United States of America

10 9 8 7 6 5 4 3 2

ISBN: 0-13-477176-1

Prentice-Hall International (UK) Limited, *London*
Prentice-Hall of Australia Pty. Limited, *Sydney*
Prentice-Hall of Canada, Inc., *Toronto*
Prentice-Hall Hispanoamericana, S. A., *Mexico*
Prentice-Hall of India Private Limited, *New Delhi*
Prentice-Hall of Japan, Inc., *Tokyo*
Simon & Schuster Asia Pte. Ltd., *Singapore*
Editora Prentice-Hall do Brasil, Ltda., *Rio de Janeiro*

Preface

Learning disabilities is a dynamic and expanding field. Individuals with learning disabilities exist across all ages, socioeconomic levels, and ethnic groups; their problems range from mild to severe. Professionals as well as parents continue to seek greater knowledge about the nature of learning disabilities and proven methods for enhancing academic, social, and vocational success for people with learning disabilities.

This book offers comprehensive coverage of the field. Many theories and practices have developed quickly. Some have been challenged and found to be lacking. Thus, many practices have been refined, whereas others have either waned or grown. In this text, we have tried to present a balanced picture of the varying theories and practices (educational, medical, and psychological), and we hope this allows you to develop your own perspective.

The book has been revised to include recent developments. This fifth edition reflects the latest trends in the field of learning disabilities, including life-span coverage of the individual with learning disabilities (preschool through adulthood), up-to-date teaching technologies, and current issues such as inclusion, identification, and service delivery options. The book is written from a perspective of what the research indicates are the best practices in the field of learning disabilities. Noteworthy changes in this edition include expanded coverage of cultural diversity, learning strategies, social skills training, affective development, phonological awareness development, successful transition factors, and effective assessment and teaching practices in the academic areas. Recent legislation is presented, and descriptions of tests, software, and materials are updated throughout this edition. Each chapter has been refined extensively to provide comprehensive yet timely coverage of pertinent information. In addition to covering topics that facilitate an understanding of learning disabilities, we have included a strong focus on how to teach and manage students with learning disabilities.

Why is the fifth edition of *Students with Learning Disabilities* a worthwhile book for your learning disabilities introductory class? It is as current as possible, and we think you will find the research to be well integrated. While an effort has been made to provide a definitive point of view, we also have tried to treat fairly the many approaches to learning disabilities. We have attempted to describe how schools really function in this country in an effort to assist you in handling situations in your current or future classrooms.

In the field of learning disabilities, there are no easy answers. It is fraught with controversy, ambivalence, and vagueness, and it lacks consensus about many basic issues. We have made every effort to present the best of what we know. It is our hope that this book stimulates you to discover even more about the nature and needs of individuals with learning disabilities.

The completion of this book was the result of the efforts of many people; however, several individuals deserve special acknowledgment for their outstanding contributions. Heartfelt thanks go to my wife, friend, and colleague, Ann. Her writing contributions and work throughout the publication process made this edition a reality. I also am grateful to Ann Davis, administrative editor, for her guidance and support and to production editor Linda Bayma for her skillful services.

Cecil D. Mercer

Contents

PART ONE

Foundations of Learning Disabilities

Definitions and Characteristics

CHAPTER 1

After studying this chapter, you should be able to:

- identify the four phases in the development of definitions of learning disabilities.
- state the 1977 *Federal Register*/IDEA definition.
- identify the components of the definition and identification criteria in the 1977 *Federal Register* and IDEA.
- discuss trends among state departments of education regarding the identification of students with learning disabilities.
- discuss the similarities and differences among the four most influential definitions of learning disabilities.
- list contemporary characteristics of students with learning disabilities.
- discuss the life-span view of learning disabilities in terms of characteristics, assessment, and treatments.
- describe the heterogeneous nature of individuals with learning disabilities.
- discuss the prevalence of learning disabilities.
- present factors related to gender differences in learning disabilities.
- discuss learning disabilities across cultures and the conditions relating to learning disabilities in other countries.

Imagine having strong emotions or important ideas to share but being unable to express them. Think about being in an environment rich in sounds and sights but being unable to focus your attention. Imagine trying to read or compute but not being able to make sense out of the letters or numbers. You may not need to imagine. You may be the parent or teacher of an individual who experiences academic learning difficulties, or you may have someone in your family who has been identified as having a learning disability. Possibly, sometime in your school years you were told that you had a reading problem called *dyslexia* or some other learning disorder.

Although they differ among individuals, these difficulties are part of the daily experiences for many children, adolescents, and adults with learning disabilities. A person with learning disabilities may experience constant or periodic academic failure and low self-esteem. Having these experiences or living with someone who faces these difficulties can generate intense frustration and bewilderment. A parent of a gifted daughter with learning disabilities shared the following essay that her daughter had written on the topic "A Memory About School" while in the 10th grade:

> The last time I cried in front of strangers was in seventh grade. That was the year I had been moved into a gifted class. The final step had been taken. My dyslexia had been cured. (Or so I thought.) I was all set to be an intellectual.
>
> It was the beginning of the year, and we were all busy finding a place to fit in and fitting into it. My English teacher had made us all write our name, phone number, and class schedule so she would know where to find us if she needed us for something, she said. I thought she wanted the schedule to know what kinds of classes we were in, so she would know if we were smart or stupid. I wrote "gifted"in very dark letters to make sure she noticed.
>
> For our first spelling test, the teacher told us a spelling rule and gave us a list of words to use as examples to learn to spell. She told us that if we learned the rule we wouldn't have to learn the words. I was rather shocked with the idea that by remembering things like putting an *i* before an *e* I could spell correctly, because my spelling was (and is) awful. So I learned the rule.
>
> When we got our spelling tests back, mine was given out last. The teacher walked over to my desk and put the test on it. My *i*'s were before my *e*'s, but the rest of the letters were not in such predictable order. She said I was a very lazy girl and should have done much better. She told me that she would be surprised if I got out of seventh grade or was ever let into high school. My insides squeezed into a space much smaller than they were used to, and tears pushed into my eyes. I had no idea what to say; I was nothing but a stupid LD (learning disability) kid. So I cried and spent most of the rest of the day crying. When I came home from school I was still crying. I told my mother what had happened. She called the teacher and the next day I got an apology. (I pretended to forgive her gracefully.)
>
> My English teacher was thought to be one of the best teachers in our district. I am not really able to say, because this is my only complete memory of seventh-grade English. It was then I first realized that I was always going to have dyslexia. It was something that would always be a part of who I am (a non-speller). It is becoming less obvious, but it never will be invisible.

Although students with learning disabilities are likely to have frustrating experiences, an event such as this one can be prevented with knowledge and sensitivity. Because a person with learning disabilities *can learn*, prospects are hopeful. A learning disability usually affects only selected areas of an individual's development. In fact, it is rare that a learning disability is so severe that it impairs a person's potential to earn a living and lead a happy and productive life.

To understand learning disabilities, it is helpful to examine definitions of *learning disabilities* from a historical perspective. The term *learning disabilities* emerged from a need to identify and serve students who continually failed in school, yet eluded the traditional categories of exceptionality. Numerous disciplines have contributed to the field (e.g., medicine, language, psychology, and education), and a number of terms and definitions have arisen from this multidisciplinary base. Hammill (1990) identified 11 definitions that have been popular at some time during the brief history of learning disabilities.

Even though a single accepted definition has been elusive, school districts, clinics, and private schools throughout the nation have managed to develop and operate programs. During the 1992–1993 school year, 51.1% of the students receiving special education services were students with learning disabilities (U.S. Department of Education, 1994). The development of these programs, in large part, has resulted from the work of professionals and laypersons who have been instrumental in defining and identifying these students during the past 50 years. In the next four sections of this chapter, the major work concerning definitions, terminology, and characteristics is organized and presented according to four phases: (a) brain-injured, (b) minimal brain dysfunction, (c) learning disabilities, and (d) Public Law 94-142/IDEA.

BRAIN-INJURED PHASE

The study of learning disabilities began, in part, with the work of Strauss and his colleagues. In the late 1930s and early 1940s, Strauss and Werner joined forces to study children with brain injuries. Their work culminated in the first volume of *Psychopathology and Education of the Brain-Injured Child*, in which Strauss and Lehtinen (1947) theorized that these brain injuries resulted from exogenous rather than endogenous factors. *Exogenous* refers to an injury outside of the genetic structure (e.g., shortage of oxygen during birth, extremely high fever during infancy, or injury to the head). *Endogenous* refers to inherited brain structures or patterns that result in learning impairments. Although both etiologies recognized learning impairments, Strauss and his colleagues differentiated the characteristics of the two groups (i.e., exogenous retardation and endogenous retardation). They established seven criteria for classifying the child with exogenous retardation. Four of them are classified as behavioral criteria:

1. *Perceptual disorders.* When viewing a picture, a child with perceptual problems may see parts instead of wholes or confuse the background with the foreground. For example, a line drawing of a triangle may be viewed as three unrelated lines. Similarly, the child with figure-ground problems may have difficulty following words printed over a background of scenic landscapes.
2. *Perseveration.* Perseveration is the continuation of an activity once it has started, and it is accompanied by difficulty changing to another activity. For example, a child may repeatedly color the same area and have difficulty switching to a new task.
3. *Conceptual or thinking disorders.* These disorders refer to problems associated with organizing information or thoughts.
4. *Behavioral disorders.* A child with behavioral disorders may exhibit uninhibited behavior, which can be manifested in hyperactive, erratic, or explosive behavior patterns.

The remaining three criteria are classified as biological criteria:

1. *Slight neurological signs.* These many subtle neurological abnormalities can take the form of general clumsiness, confusion regarding dominance, awkward gait, or problems with fine motor tasks.
2. *A history of neurological impairment.* This includes evidence in medical records that suggests damage to the nervous system.

No history of mental retardation. This criterion excludes brain abnormalities due to endogenous or genetic factors.

Later, Strauss indicated that a diagnosis of brain injury could be determined by using only the behavioral criteria. Omitting the necessity of the biological criteria for determining brain injury lessened the pressure on diagnosticians for determining organic injury and made *brain injury* more of a pseudomedical term.

Strauss and his colleagues based their research and descriptions on work with children with mental retardation. Their work prompted Cruickshank to initiate studies regarding the effects of brain injury on children with normal IQs. Cruickshank and his colleagues established that the perceptual problems were not unique to children with retardation. Professionals and laypersons began to develop awareness of children at all IQ levels whose learning problems were due primarily to brain injury. Interventions during this period stressed the need to provide structure, reduced stimuli (distractions), and perceptual-motor activities for these children (Cruickshank, 1967).

However, many people objected to the term *brain injury*. Parents viewed the term as being negative and thought it stressed a condition of permanence. Stevens and Birch (1957) delineated four major objections. Specifically, they noted that the term *brain injured* is (a) cause-oriented and does not relate to the behavioral aspects of the condition, (b) associated with such a wide range of conditions (e.g., cerebral palsy and epilepsy) that it has little specific meaning, (c) not useful in planning teaching approaches, and (d) too broad, leading to oversimplification.

Stevens and Birch (1957) recommended that the term *Strauss syndrome* be used to replace *brain-injured*. *Strauss syndrome* now describes those who exhibit many or all of the following characteristics:

1. Erratic and inappropriate behavior on mild provocation
2. Increased motor activity disproportionate to the stimulus
3. Poor organization of the behavior
4. Distractibility of more than ordinary degree under ordinary conditions
5. Persistent faulty perceptions
6. Persistent hyperactivity
7. Awkwardness and consistently poor motor performance (Stevens & Birch, 1957, p. 348)

MINIMAL BRAIN DYSFUNCTION PHASE

During the 1960s, a shift in terminology occurred with the introduction of the term *minimal brain dysfunction* (MBD). This term popularized the concept of minor brain injury, or dysfunction, and linked it with learning problems. Brain injury can be categorized on a continuum from severe to mild. Children with severe brain impairments such as cerebral palsy and epilepsy are identified readily, but children with minimal impairments are affected in more subtle ways. The term MBD not only recognized minimal physical injury that impairs the brain's functioning but also added such areas as brain structure variations, biochemical irregularities, and slow maturation patterns (C. R. Smith, 1994). MBD primarily was advanced by Clements, who was the project director of Task Force I, a national project cosponsored by the National Society for Crippled Children and Adults and the National Institutes of Neurological Diseases and Blindness that was commissioned to study the characteristics of individuals with brain impairments and to suggest identification procedures.

Task Force I: Characteristics and Definition

Task Force I (Clements, 1966) described some of the symptoms by which individuals with MBD could be identified. Because of the lack of useful literature concerning characteristics of individuals with MBD or learning disabilities, this was a difficult task. Characteristics that Task Force I described were obtained primarily through clinical observation rather than precise measure (in other words, systematic measurement of a large and well-defined sample was not used). The 10 most frequently mentioned characteristics, presented in a rank-order listing, are hyperactivity, perceptual-motor impairments, emotional liability, general orientation deficits, disorders of attention, impulsivity, disorders of memory and thinking, specific learning (academic) disabilities, disorders of speech and hearing, and equivocal neurological signs.

Task Force I also concentrated on terminology and identification of minimal brain dysfunction in children. In Clements's (1966) report, MBD was defined as a disorder afflicting children of near average, average, or above average general intelligence with certain learning or behavior disabilities ranging from mild to severe, which are associated with deviations of function of the central nervous system. These deviations may manifest themselves by various combinations of impairment in perception, conceptualization, language, memory, and control of attention, impulse, or motor function. . . . These aberrations may arise from genetic variations, biochemical irregularities, perinatal brain insults or other illnesses or injuries sustained during the years which are critical for the development and maturation of the central nervous system, or from unknown causes. (pp. 9-10)

This was the first formal definition proposed at a national level. The MBD definition, like that of *brain-injured,* never was accepted widely. Diag-nosticians did not like the task of detecting minimal brain dysfunction. Moreover, special educators found that labels connoting a medical etiology were not useful in planning educational interventions. (See Chapter 3 for current perspectives and practices regarding central nervous system damage.)

LEARNING DISABILITIES PHASE

Learning disability terminology began to appear on a small scale both before and concurrently with MBD terminology. Special educators sought terms with greater educational relevance (e.g., *educationally handicapped, language disordered, perceptually handicapped*). Kirk (1962) coined the term *learning disability* 4 years before Clements (1966) published his report using MBD. Bateman (1965) introduced a definition of *learning disorders* that added a new and important dimension. She included a discrepancy clause, which referred to a difference between estimated capacity and achievement:

> Children who have learning disorders are those who manifest an educationally significant discrepancy between their estimated intellectual potential and actual level of performance related to basic disorders in the learning process, which may or may not be accompanied by demonstrable central nervous system dysfunction, and which are not secondary to generalized mental retardation, educational or cultural deprivation, severe emotional disturbance, or sensory loss. (p. 220)

NACHC Definition

When the U.S. Office of Education (USOE) was given the responsibility of funding special education programs for children with learning disabilities, it became apparent that a definition acceptable to educators was needed for funding purposes. The National Advisory Committee on Handicapped Children (NACHC) was formed in 1968 to develop an acceptable definition. Under Kirk's leadership, the committee submitted a definition that was incorporated into Public Law 91-230, the Specific Learning Disabilities Act of 1969:

> Children with special learning disabilities exhibit a disorder in one or more of the basic psychological processes involved in understanding or in using spoken or written languages. These may be manifested in disorders of listening, thinking, talking, reading, writing, spelling or arithmetic. They include conditions which have been referred to as perceptual handicaps, brain injury, minimal brain dysfunction, dyslexia, developmental aphasia, etc. They do *not* include learning problems which are due primarily to visual, hearing or motor handicaps, to mental retardation, emotional disturbance or to environmental disadvantage. (USOE, 1968, p. 34)

This definition, referred to as the NACHC definition or the USOE definition, was used extensively. Unlike earlier definitions, the NACHC definition indicated that the determination of a central nervous system (CNS) dysfunction was arbitrary and not germane to identifying a child with learning disabilities.

Because of the widespread and continued use of the NACHC definition, the components of the definition should be examined thoroughly to understand many practices (e.g., identification, assessment, and programming) in the area of learning disabilities. (Because this definition was adopted in Public Law 94-142 in 1977 without any major revisions, the specific components are discussed in the next section of this chapter.)

PUBLIC LAW 94-142/IDEA PHASE

The U.S. Department of Education (U.S. Office of Education until 1980) is influential in determining directions of the *learning disabilities* definition. At a national level, it disperses and monitors expenditures of many federal monies in special education. With the passage of Public Law 94-142, it was charged with providing leadership and support to the difficult task of defining *learning disabilities* more precisely. It was faced with making crucial decisions in selecting, eliminating, or integrating the various positions on a definition. Unfortunately, this decision had to be made without the benefit of research data, for none existed.

To begin this task, Congress defined children with specific learning disabilities by using a definition (USOE, 1976) almost identical to that of the NACHC. The USOE reported that no legislative recommendations would be made regarding the definition until research indicated the types of changes that were needed. However, to begin the immediate task of defining *learning disabilities* more precisely, the USOE concentrated on (a) outlining the specific criteria for determining a particular disorder or condition, (b) determining appropriate diagnostic procedures, and (c) monitoring procedures for use in determining if states were following (a) and (b).

1977 *Federal Register*/IDEA Definition

After extensive efforts to improve on the definition (including the publication of a formula to determine a discrepancy between expected achievement and ability), the USOE released the 1977 *Federal Register*, which included the regulations for defining and identifying students with learning disabilities under Public Law 94-142. These regulations endorse a definition almost identical to that of the NACHC:

> "Specific learning disability" means a disorder in one or more of the basic psychological processes involved in understanding or in using language, spoken or written, which may manifest itself in an imperfect ability to listen, think, speak, read, write, spell, or to do mathematical calculations. The term includes such conditions as perceptual handicaps, brain injury, minimal brain disfunction, dyslexia, and developmental aphasia. The term does not include children who have learning problems which are primarily the result of visual, hearing, or motor handicaps, of mental retardation, or emotional disturbance, or of environmental, cultural, or economic disadvantage. (USOE, 1977, p. 65083)

Because this definition is incorporated in Public Law 101-476, which retitled the *Education for All Handicapped Children Act* in Public Law 94-142 to the *Individuals with Disabilities Education Act* (IDEA) in 1990, it currently is used for administering programs for individuals with learning disabilities. The following sections present its major components.

Process Component. The 1977 *Federal Register* definition (which also is the IDEA definition) includes the process factor in the phrase "means a disorder in one or more of the basic psychological processes" (USOE, 1977, p. 65083). Although process factors comprise a major part of the definition, they represent a nebulous area. If the intent of the process component in the definition is examined, perhaps it is possible to determine its general nature. On examination of the field, it is reasonable to conclude that the process component has been interpreted primarily within three contexts (i.e., perceptual-motor, psycholinguistic, and cognitive).

The perceptual-motor interpretation stresses that higher-level mental functioning depends on an adequate development of the motor and perceptual system. Visual, tactile, and haptic perception, as well as intersensory organization, are basic in this position. (Several perception and perceptual-motor approaches are presented in Chapter 8.)

In earlier years, the psycholinguistic interpretation of the process disorder was highlighted by the development and widespread use of the *Illinois Test of Psycholinguistic Abilities* (ITPA) (Kirk, McCarthy, & Kirk, 1968). This position focused on the reception, integration, and expressive abilities of a child by presenting stimuli in the auditory-vocal and visual-motor channels. While the use of the ITPA has diminished, many contemporary perspectives regarding modality-based learning styles spring from the fundamental concepts inherent in the test. (Modality-based instructional practices are presented in Chapters 11 to 14.)

Moreover, in earlier years, the cognitive process interpretation focused on attention and memory problems. Selective attention deficits, as well as short-term memory deficits, were viewed as basic psychological process problems that interfere with learning (Chalfant & Scheffelin, 1969; Hallahan, 1975). Several cognitive approaches (e.g., metacognition and maturational lag) have been added for understanding the learning problems of students with learning disabilities (Deshler & Lenz, 1989). (Cognitive teaching approaches are presented in Chapter 8 and in the chapters dealing with specific academic areas.)

Language Component. The language component is introduced in the phrase "involved in understanding or in using language, spoken or written, which may manifest itself in an imperfect ability to listen, think, speak . . . write, [or] spell" (USOE, 1977, p. 65083). (The language problems of students with learning disabilities and several intervention approaches are presented in Chapters 11 and 12.)

Academic Component. The academic component is included in the phrase "which may manifest itself in an imperfect ability to . . . read . . . or to do mathematical calculations" (USOE, 1977, p. 65083). (The academic problems of students with learning disabilities and selected interventions are presented in Chapters 11 to 14.)

Neurological Component. The neurological component includes the consideration of central nervous system dysfunction. The definition includes this component in the statement "The term includes such conditions as . . . brain injury, minimal brain disfunction, dyslexia, and developmental aphasia" (USOE, 1977, p. 65083). From this statement it is inferred that the child with learning disabilities can have neurological deficits. This definition promotes the position that the determination of a central nervous system dysfunction is arbitrary and not germane to identifying a child with learning disabilities. (The medical aspects of learning disabilities are presented in Chapter 3.)

Exclusion Component. The exclusion component is included in the last sentence of the definition: "The term does not include children who have learning problems which are primarily the result of visual, hearing, or motor handicaps, or mental retardation, or emotional disturbance, or of environmental, cultural, or economic disadvantage" (USOE, 1977, p. 65083). Because the word *primarily* is featured in the definition, it is understood that learning disabilities can coexist with these conditions.

Identification Criteria. Because the 1977 *Federal Register*/IDEA definition is almost identical to that of the NACHC, the charge of defining *learning disabilities* more precisely was not accomplished with the *Federal Register*/IDEA definition. However, the regulations do include criteria for identification, which are presented in Table 1.1.

The major differences between the definition and the identification criteria are that (a) basic psychological processes are omitted in the identification criteria, and (b) in the identification criteria, the academic and language problems are interpreted within the context of a discrepancy factor (see Table 1.2). Thus, according to the criteria, the discrepancy factor and the exclusion factor are basic to defining learning disabilities, and the basic psychological process factor remains optional. (See Chapter 5 for a discussion on how each of the components is assessed.)

Definitions Used by State Departments of Education

In light of the many events and issues surrounding the definition, Mercer, Jordan, Allsopp, and

TABLE 1.1
Criteria for Identifying Students with Learning Disabilities

Academic Component, Qualified by Discrepancy Factor

1. A team may determine that a child has a specific learning disability if:
   (a) The child does not achieve commensurate with his or her age and ability levels in one or more of the following areas when provided with learning experiences appropriate for the child's age and ability levels: oral expression, listening comprehension, written expression, basic reading skill, reading comprehension, mathematics calculation, or mathematics reasoning.
   (b) The team finds that a child has a severe discrepancy between achievement and intellectual ability in one or more of the same areas listed in the preceding statement.

Exclusion Component

2. The team may not identify a child as having a specific learning disability if the severe discrepancy between ability and achievement is primarily the result of:
   (a) a visual, hearing, or motor handicap
   (b) mental retardation
   (c) emotional disturbance
   (d) environmental, cultural, or economic disadvantage.

Note: From the *Federal Register*, Thursday, December 29, 1977, *42*(250), 65082–65085. (Incorporated in IDEA.)

TABLE 1.2
Definition Components and Identification Criteria in the 1977 *Federal Register* and IDEA

LD Definition Components	LD Identification Criteria
Process	Omitted (considered optional)
Language	Defined as oral expression, listening comprehension, and written expression. Language component is tied in with the discrepancy factor.
Academic	Defined as basic reading skill, reading comprehension, mathematics calculation, or mathematics reasoning. Spelling is omitted. Academic component is tied to the discrepancy factor.
Neurological	Omitted
Exclusion	Exclusion component is identical to the definition.

Mercer (1995) surveyed all the state departments of education concerning the definition and identification criteria used for learning disabilities. They compared the results with a similar survey conducted earlier by Mercer, King-Sears, and Mercer (1990). As indicated in Table 1.3, the results of the surveys reflect an emerging consensus on the five components included in the definition. The use of all five components has increased. Except for the increase in the process component criteria (from 27% to 33%), these findings are consistent with the content of the 1977 *Federal Register*/IDEA definition and criteria. Moreover, an examination of the two studies of the definitions used indicates an increase (from 57% to 71%) in the use of the IDEA definition or some variation of it. Several states changed the wording or included the discrepancy component or prereferral conditions in their definitions. It is apparent that numerous states embrace the major components of the IDEA definition but are not satisfied with its wording or inclusiveness.

TABLE 1.3
Comparison of Percentages of Definition Components Across Two Studies

	Mercer et al. (1990) Study		Mercer et al. (1995) Study		
Components	Criteria and/or Definition	Criteria Only	Criteria and/or Definition	Criteria Only	Trend
Process	92	27	94	33	Increase
Academic	96	80	100	90	Increase
Neurological	64	4	75	6	Increase
Exclusion	94	76	98	86	Increase
Discrepancy	88	86	98	94	Increase

Note: More than 5% change in either column is reported as an increase.

National Joint Committee on Learning Disabilities Definition

Dissatisfaction with the 1977 *Federal Register*/IDEA definition resulted in the formation of the National Joint Committee on Learning Disabilities (NJCLD) and a proposed definition. The NJCLD consists of representatives from the American Speech-Language-Hearing Association (ASHA), the Association for Children and Adults with Learning Disabilities (ACLD) (now the Learning Disabilities Association of America [LDA]), the Council for Learning Disabilities (CLD), the Division for Children with Communication Disorders (DCCD), the International Reading Association (IRA), and the Orton Dyslexia Society. An NJCLD (1981) position paper lists several criticisms of the 1977 *Federal Register*/ IDEA definition:

1. Because learning disabilities can occur at all ages, the use of the terms *children* in the definition and *child* in the criteria is not appropriate.
2. The term *basic psychological processes* has stimulated extensive and, perhaps, needless debate in the field.
3. Spelling does not need to be included in the definition, because it can be subsumed under "written expression."
4. The wording in the final statement (i.e., the exclusion clause) has led to misconceptions and confusion.
5. Inclusion of the terms *perceptual handicaps*, *brain injury*, *minimal brain dysfunction*, *dyslexia*, and *developmental aphasia* adds confusion.

In 1981, the NJCLD representatives reached agreement (with the exception of ACLD) on the following definition:

> *Learning disabilities* is a generic term that refers to a heterogeneous group of disorders manifested by significant difficulties in the acquisition and use of listening, speaking, reading, writing, reasoning, or mathematical abilities. These disorders are intrinsic to the individual and presumed to be due to central nervous system dysfunction. Even though a learning disability may occur concomitantly with other handicapping conditions (e.g., sensory impairment, mental retardation, social and emotional disturbance) or environmental influences (e.g., cultural differences, insufficient/inappropriate instruction, psychogenic factors), it is not the direct result of those conditions or influences. (Hammill, Leigh, McNutt, & Larsen, 1981, p. 336)

This NJCLD definition eliminates the term *basic psychological processes*, recognizes the existence of learning disabilities in all ages, emphasizes the heterogeneous nature of learning disabilities, and stresses the disorder-medical model position. In 1988, the NJCLD slightly modified its earlier definition to reflect current knowledge and react to the definition developed by the Interagency Committee on Learning Disabilities (presented later in this chapter). The revised definition indicates that the disorders "may occur across the life span" and states that "problems in self-regulatory behaviors, social perception, and social interaction may exist with learning disabilities but do not by themselves constitute a learning disability" (NJCLD, 1988, p. 1).

Association for Children with Learning Disabilities Definition

The leaders of the Association for Children with Learning Disabilities (1986) (now LDA) rejected the NJCLD definition and wrote their own definition:

> Specific Learning Disabilities is a chronic condition of presumed neurological origin which selectively interferes with the development, integration, and/or demonstration of verbal and/or nonverbal abilities. Specific Learning Disabilities exists as a distinct handicapping condition and varies in its manifestations and in degree of severity. Throughout life, the condition can affect self-esteem, education, vocation, socialization, and/or daily living activities. (p. 15)

This definition differs from the 1977 *Federal Register*/IDEA and the NJCLD definitions in several areas. It stresses the lifelong nature of a learning disability, and it extends a learning disability beyond the academic domain by placing emphasis on socialization and self-esteem. This definition reflects the consensus of parents of children with learning disabilities as well as adults with learning disabilities.

The Interagency Committee on Learning Disabilities Definition

In an effort to improve the learning disabilities definition, the federal Interagency Committee on Learning Disabilities (ICLD) proposed a definition to Congress in 1987. This committee consisted of representatives from 12 agencies within the Departments of Education and Health and Human Services. The ICLD (1987) definition represents a modification of the NJCLD definition. It differs from the NJCLD definition in its emphasis on social skills deficits. Specifically, it includes the following statement: "Learning disabilities . . . refers to a heterogeneous group of disorders manifested by significant difficulties in the acquisition and use of listening, speaking, reading, writing, reasoning, or mathematical abilities, or of social skills" (ICLD, 1987, p. 222). Forness and Kavale (1991) note that the wording of this definition allows for an individual who has social difficulties and no academic problems to be diagnosed as having learning disabilities. They claim that this identification practice adds to the confusion of differentiating learning disabilities from emotional disturbance, and they maintain that social skills deficits should not be included as a primary diagnostic criterion of learning disabilities.

Perspectives on Learning Disabilities Definitions

Given the respective definitions proposed by the various organizations, committees, and governmental agencies, it appears that the learning disabilities definition remains in a state of confusion. Closer inspection, however, allows for a more optimistic view. The most influential definitions (i.e., the 1977 *Federal Register*/IDEA, NJCLD, ACLD, and ICLD definitions) have more similarities than differences. They include many of the same major components (e.g., discrepancy, academic, exclusion, and neurological) in defining a learning disability. Hammill (1990, 1993) notes that the most influential definitions are in fundamental agreement on most definition issues. He further states that a strong relationship exists among the definitions, which suggests that consensus is near.

In a study of 761 children with learning disabilities and 901 children without learning disabilities, Wilson (1985) concludes that the 1977 *Federal Register*/IDEA definition and criteria can be used successfully. He reports that the application of both the academic discrepancy and

exclusion components provides an adequate framework for identifying individuals with learning disabilities. Rather than abandoning current components in favor of new ones, Wilson encourages more systematic and intensive study of the current definition. Moreover, from a literature review and a national study of prevalence rates of special education categories, Hallahan, Keller, and Ball (1986) report that "the data do argue for the conclusion that the definition and identification criteria for learning disabilities are at least as well articulated, and perhaps more so, than those for other categories in special education" (p. 13).

Mather and Roberts (1994) express concern that the shift in terminology from *brain injured* and *minimal brain dysfunction* to *learning disabilities* has given impetus to the notion that a learning disability is only a mildly disabling condition. However, any category of disability exists along a continuum from mild to severe. The term *learning disability* was coined as a general designation for a wide range of disabilities and includes students with severe learning disabilities.

Commentary on Learning Disabilities Definitions

Definition Wording. Because the most influential definitions are in agreement about the major components involved in defining *learning disabilities*, many of the current issues and discussions involve wording differences. At this point, the wording of the NJCLD definition appears to do the best job of addressing the major components.

CNS Dysfunction. For educators, the CNS dysfunction emphasis of the NJCLD definition causes some concern. In discussing the CNS component of the NJCLD definition, Hammill et al. (1981) report that "the Committee agreed that hard evidence of organicity did not have to be present in order to diagnose a person as learning disabled, but that no person should be labelled LD [learning disabled] unless CNS dysfunction was the suspected cause. Certainly, cases should not be diagnosed as LD where the cause is known or thought to be something other than CNS dysfunction" (p. 340). The diagnosis of CNS dysfunction remains imprecise, and neurological services are costly. The measurement of neurological processes is improving, and medical advances regarding learning disabilities appear to be on the brink of knowledge breakthroughs. Hynd, Marshall, and Gonzalez (1991) report that postmortem and neuroimaging studies already are enhancing conceptualizations involving the CNS and learning disabilities. At this point, however, educators continue to need some operational guidelines concerning CNS dysfunction in the identification process.

Definition Functions. A definition is expected to provide the parameters for identifying the respective phenomenon. Moreover, it is expected to be flexible enough to generate continued inquiry and new findings. The knowledge bases for diagnosing and defining each of the components of a learning disability are unequal. For learning disabilities, it is expected that some guidelines will be precise and others will lack specificity. Those that lack preciseness present the most pressing challenges for immediate scientific inquiry. In essence, a learning disabilities definition must cover the parameters of learning disabilities and be accompanied by guidelines that allow the components to be operationalized in light of differential knowledge bases.

Discrepancy. The discrepancy component must be inferred from all four of the most influential definitions. Discrepancy appears to be a common denominator of learning disabilities and needs to be stated directly in a definition.

Exclusion. Except for the ACLD (now LDA) definition, the position is inferred that learning disabilities are not caused primarily by any other disabling condition (i.e., visual, hearing, or motor impairments, mental retardation, or emotional disturbance) but may coexist with these conditions. Excluding individuals whose primary learning difficulties are due to economic, cultural, or environmental disadvantage represents some special concerns. Because a disproportionate number of learning disabilities are associated with child abuse, substance abuse, chemical dependency, low socioeconomic status, juvenile delinquency, family instability, and family tragedy, Lorsbach and Frymier (1992) maintain that the exclusion of economic, cultural, or environmental disadvantage should be omitted from the learning disabilities definition. Their position appears sound when one considers the enormous complexity of assessing these environmental factors. Also, many of these factors are associated with the presumed cause of learning disabilities—CNS dysfunction.

Conclusion. The search for a better definition of *learning disabilities* is active and timely. Morsink (1985) puts the controversy in a meaningful perspective:

> Grossman (1978) . . . discusses the observations of science historian Thomas Kuhn. Kuhn has observed that there is a pattern to the development of definitions. Once definitions are accepted, all new data are measured against them. This is the form of quality control that separates astronomy from astrology and chemistry from alchemy. The accepted definitions, then, need to be specific enough to exclude the absurd yet flexible enough to accommodate the creative thought that generates new knowledge. (p. 395)

The definitions offered by the 1977 *Federal Register*/IDEA, the NJCLD, and the ICLD seem to contain both specificity and flexibility. Their tentative nature reflects a changing knowledge base.

CHARACTERISTICS OF LEARNING DISABILITIES

This section presents a brief overview of contemporary thought on the characteristics of learning disabilities. It is important to keep in mind, however, that the population with learning disabilities is a heterogeneous group. Each student is unique and may exhibit difficulty in one area but not in another. The range of combinations is enormous. Moreover, to be considered characteristic of a learning disability, an identifying behavior must *persist over time*. Many students who do not have learning disabilities behave in a way that is characteristic of a learning disability for brief time periods (e.g., hyperactivity because of excitement about a field trip).

The 1977 *Federal Register*/IDEA criteria provide an initial framework for examining characteristics. The list of the disability areas (oral expression, listening comprehension, written expression, basic reading skills, reading comprehension, mathematics calculation, and mathematics reasoning) shows that academic and language difficulties are primary characteristics. The literature in learning disabilities is replete with descriptions of other characteristics (e.g., metacognitive deficits, social skills deficits, attention disorders, memory problems, and motor problems) common among individuals with learning disabilities. In the last few years, the characteristics of college students and adults with learning disabilities have received extensive attention as it has become apparent that many of the characteristics of students with learning disabilities tend to persist into adulthood. Likewise, specific cognitive deficits as well as social and behavioral characteristics of students with learning disabilities are being examined.

Rather than assigning characteristics, some teachers prefer to describe behaviors. For example, "Carla is constantly out of her seat during desk activities" and "Carla fidgets at her desk" tell more about Carla than saying that she is hyperactive. The label *hyperactive* infers a diagnosis and assigns a trait to the student. Teachers usually can defend behavioral observations but have difficulty justifying a label. When reviewing the following characteristics, it is important to consider individual differences, persistence of identifying behaviors, and the merits of behavioral descriptions.

Specific Characteristics

Discrepancy Factor. The discrepancy factor, originally popularized by Bateman (1964), is a key component in the IDEA identification criteria and is present in most definitions (Hammill, 1990). Many authorities consider it to be the common denominator of learning disabilities. A discrepancy exists when the estimated ability and the academic performance of a student differ greatly (see Figure 1.1). Discrepancy, basic to

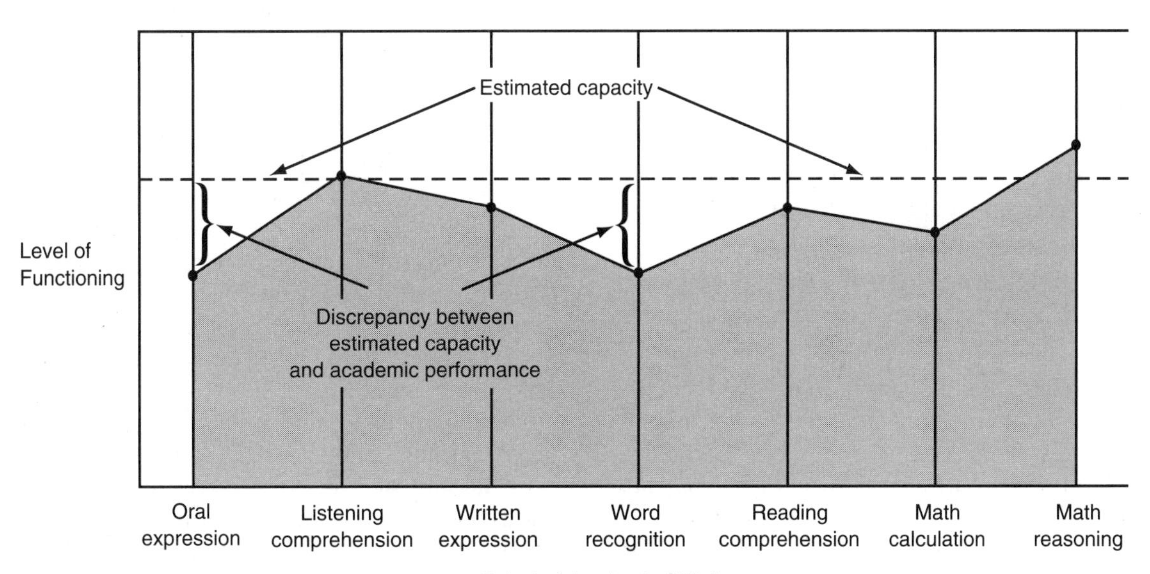

FIGURE 1.1
Discrepancy between estimated capacity and academic performance

the idea of underachievement, can be across one or all skill areas. (Chapter 5 discusses the assessment of discrepancy.)

Academic Learning Difficulty. Academic problems are the most widely accepted characteristic of individuals with learning disabilities. Mentioned in the IDEA identification criteria are basic reading skill, reading comprehension, written expression, mathematics calculation, and mathematics reasoning. Reading problems are the most common. (Chapters 11 to 14 present specific academic disabilities.)

Language Disorders. Language problems, like reading and math difficulties, are interpreted in terms of the discrepancy component. Specifically, the IDEA regulations include deficient skills in oral expression and listening comprehension. The works of Orton (1937), Kirk (1966), Johnson and Myklebust (1967), and, more recently, Wiig and Semel (1984) and Sawyer and Butler (1991), reflect an increasing concentration on language problems. In a study of elementary students, Gibbs and Cooper (1989) found mild-to-moderate language deficits in 90% of 242 students with learning disabilities. Moreover, Mann (1991) notes the indication of research that many students who do not read well suffer from underlying language problems. Because language skills and academic functioning are closely related, it sometimes is difficult to determine the primary disability (i.e., reading or language). (Chapter 11 presents spoken language disabilities.)

Perceptual Disorders. Perceptual problems (inability to recognize, discriminate, and interpret sensation), especially visual and auditory disabilities, traditionally have received much attention from several authorities on learning disabilities. Some common terms in the field include *visual reception*, *visual discrimination*, *visual memory*, *auditory discrimination*, *auditory memory*, and *intersensory integration*. In a recent review of research, Garnett (1992) notes that spatial deficits are a factor in learning math for students with learning disabilities. C. R. Smith (1994) comments on visual-perceptual processes in the following passage:

> Visual-perceptual processes appear to be important to reading and math achievement at young ages and, in very subtle ways, relate to some later spelling, writing, and conceptual difficulties. They do not seem to be a major contributor to the skills needed for higher level academic progress. (p. 143)

An emphasis on perceptual factors is not prominent; however, certain authorities continue to examine perceptual factors with a cautious but curious mindset. IDEA does not include perceptual disorders in the evaluation procedures of learning disabilities. (Chapter 8 discusses perceptual disabilities and includes the reasons for their de-emphasis.)

Metacognitive Deficits. From a knowledge base of 11,000 statistical findings across 28 categories, Wang, Haertel, and Walberg (1993/1994) examined the influence of each category on student learning. The metacognitive and cognitive processes of students ranked second and third on their influence on student learning. Literature suggesting that many students with learning disabilities exhibit metacognitive deficits is accruing (Baker, 1982; Goldman, 1989; Wong, 1991). Basically, metacognition consists of two factors: (a) an awareness of the skills, strategies, and resources needed to perform a task effectively, and (b) the ability to use self-regulatory mechanisms (e.g., planning moves, evaluating the effectiveness of ongoing activities, checking the outcome of effort, and remediating difficulties) to ensure the successful completion of a task (Baker, 1982).

Hresko and Reid (1981) report that the study of metacognitive variables (e.g., predicting, planning, checking, and monitoring) in students with learning disabilities may lead to a better understanding of how these variables function, and this may result in more productive educational interventions. Several researchers (Kulak, 1993; Montague & Applegate, 1993; Swanson, 1990) claim that viewing students with learning disabilities as having metacognitive or cognitive deficits is only partially accurate. They note that many of these students are not deficient in using cognitive strategies but instead apply different strategies. To date, metacognition appears to hold promise for helping practitioners understand individuals with learning disabilities; however, as with other theories, more investigations are needed to determine the extent of its usefulness. (Chapter 8 discusses metacognition.)

Social-Emotional Problems. Frustrated by their learning difficulties, many students with learning disabilities act disruptively and acquire negative feelings of self-worth. Rather than learning and developing attitudes about tasks they can do, youngsters with learning disabilities often learn what they can't do. This lack of positive self-regard often results in poor self-concept and self-esteem. Montgomery (1994) found that some students with learning disabilities have a low self-concept regarding academics but do not differ from their high-achieving peers and peers without disabilities on self-concepts related to other areas (e.g., affect, family, physical, and social). In a study of 790 students with learning disabilities in Indiana, McLeskey (1992) found that about 15% exhibited behavior problems and that the percentage was consistent across grade levels.

Several authorities (Bryan & Bryan, 1986; Gresham & Elliott, 1989; McKinney, 1989) note that youngsters with learning disabilities frequently experience problems in interacting with parents, teachers, peers, or strangers. Bryan (1977) suggests that the social-emotional problems of some youngsters with learning disabilities are the result of social imperceptiveness. Specifically, she reports that many children with learning disabilities lack adequate skills in detecting subtle affective cues. The area of social skills deficits in individuals with learning disabilities has received recent attention. For example, the ICLD definition of learning disabilities includes social skills deficits as a primary disability; this has generated much discussion regarding whether social skills deficits are a primary or secondary disability in learning disabilities (Hammill, 1990). (Chapter 15 discusses social and emotional behavior problems.)

Memory Problems. Hallahan and Kauffman (1988) note that students with learning disabilities usually have problems remembering auditory and visual stimuli. Swanson, Cochran, and Ewers (1990) and Gettinger (1991) found that measures of memory differentiate students with learning disabilities from other students in general classes. Specifically, they note that students with learning disabilities exhibit distinct deficiencies in working memory. Teachers frequently report that students with learning disabilities forget spelling words, math facts, and directions. Torgesen and Kail (1980) provide the following conclusions:

1. Students with learning disabilities fail to use strategies that students without disabilities readily use. For example, in learning a list of words, students without disabilities rehearse the names to themselves or group the words in categories for studying. Generally, students with learning disabilities do not spontaneously use these strategies.
2. Students with learning disabilities may have difficulty remembering because of their poor language skills. Thus, verbal material may be particularly difficult to remember.

Motor Disorders. Students with motor problems may walk with a clumsy gait or have difficulty throwing or catching a ball, skipping, or hopping. Others exhibit fine motor difficulties when cutting with scissors, buttoning, or zipping. Like perceptual disabilities, motor problems received substantial emphasis in research history but have been de-emphasized (Myers & Hammill, 1990). For example, the IDEA definition of learning disabilities mentions motor disabilities only to the extent that basic psychological processes refer to them. (Chapter 8 discusses reasons for the recent de-emphasis of motor disabilities.)

Attention Problems and Hyperactivity. To succeed in school, a student must recognize and maintain thought on relevant classroom tasks and must be able to shift attention to new tasks. Students with attention problems are unable to screen out extraneous stimuli and are attracted by irrelevant stimuli. They may exhibit short attention spans, distractibility, and hypersensitivity. Many researchers have documented the existence of attention problems and related behaviors (Hallahan, Kauffman, & Lloyd, 1996).

Attention deficits and related behaviors received substantial coverage with the introduction of the term *attention deficit disorder* (ADD) in the 1982 *Diagnostic and Statistics Manual of Mental Disorders* (American Psychiatric Association, 1982). Moreover, increased awareness of attention deficits occurred with the revised publication of the manual in 1987 (American Psychiatric Association, 1987), in which the disorder term was changed to *attention-deficit hyperactivity disorder* (ADHD). McBurnett, Lahey, and Pfiffner (1993) describe the 1994 edition of the manual, which includes three subtypes of ADHD: predominantly hyperactive type, predominantly inattentive type, and combined type. They note that the revised symptom list and cut-points have improved reliability and validity for the determination of educational impairment. Silver (1990) notes that the relationship between learning disabilities and ADHD is becoming increasingly clear. (Chapter 3 discusses ADHD and presents the diagnostic criteria.)

As noted, hyperactivity is often mentioned in conjunction with attention problems. Generally, *hyperactivity* refers to an excess of nonpurposeful motor activity (e.g., finger and foot tapping, asking questions incessantly and often repeating the same question, and inability to sit or stand still). As a little-league football coach, I had the opportunity to witness this phenomenon outside of the classroom. William, one of our 10-year-old players, was classified as having learning disabilities. At football practice he constantly picked fights, generally goofed off, talked back to coaches, and used tacky language. After a long practice in which William had been especially difficult to manage, the head coach asked the players to gather in front of him. William obeyed. In no uncertain terms the coach told them to listen to what he was about to say because he did not want to repeat his instructions. After he was assured that everyone was listening, he proceeded to tell them that the next practice was on Monday at 5:30, and that they should wear their helmets and pads. Then he asked if there were any questions. William raised his hand. The coach said, "Yes, William?" William asked, "When's the next practice?" The coach, obviously upset with the question, responded, "William! What was the first thing I said?" William thought for a moment and replied, "Listen." The coaches and players, including William, all enjoyed a good laugh. (Chapter 3 discusses attention problems and hyperactivity.)

Life-Span View of Learning Disabilities

Characteristics must be viewed within the context of an individual's age. In the past, the field of learning disabilities has focused primarily on the elementary school-aged child; however, recent directions stress a life-span view. Figure 1.2 reveals that the number of students identified with learning disabilities increases quickly from ages 6 to 11. Given that academic difficulties are a primary characteristic of learning disabilities, it is not surprising that the number increases during this period, when students are learning to read, compute, problem solve, and communicate through spoken and written language. The percentage gradually decreases from ages 12 to 18. The decrease during the adolescent years probably is related to the high number of students with learning disabilities who drop out of school. For example, during the 1991–1992 school year, 21.3% of students with learning disabilities dropped out of the nation's schools (U.S. Department of Education, 1994). Table 1.4 presents the problem areas, assessment focus, and primary treatment types for each age group.

The Young Child with Learning Disabilities. Two major events have focused attention to serving preschool children who are at high risk for school failure. In 1985, the National Joint Committee on Learning Disabilities and the Preschool Child issued a po-

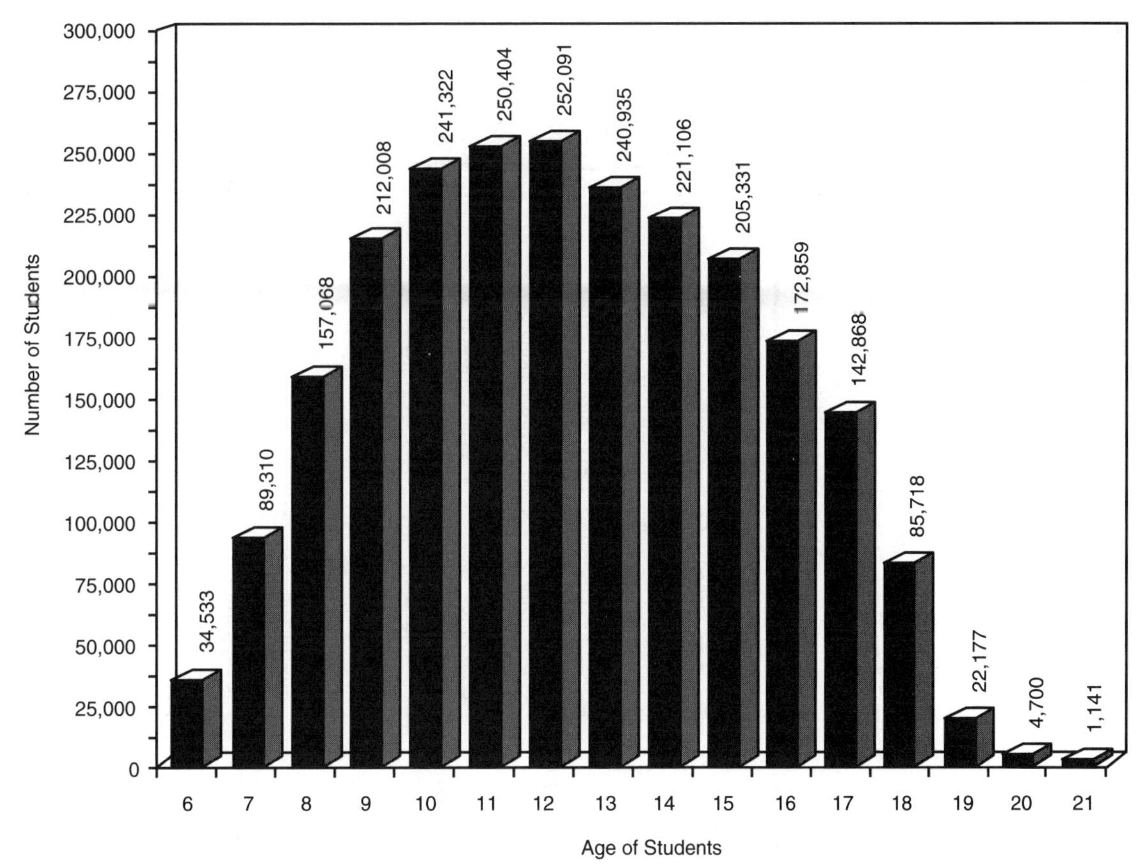

FIGURE 1.2
Number of students with learning disabilities during the 1992–1993 school year, grouped by age
Note: U.S. Department of Education (1994). *To assure the free appropriate public education of all children with disabilities: Sixteenth annual report to Congress on the implementation of the Individuals with Disabilities Education Act.* Washington, DC: Author.

sition paper outlining the needs and issues regarding the identification and treatment of preschool children with learning disabilities. In 1986, the passage of Public Law 99-457 provided legal and economic incentives for serving preschool children with learning or behavior difficulties and established a framework for these services. As Table 1.4 indicates, learning disabilities can affect an individual at any age. Because learning disabilities are primarily an academic learning problem and formal academic instruction usually does not begin until the first grade, the diagnosis of learning disabilities for young children is predictive. Moreover, a preschool or primary-grade child has limited time to become an underachiever, thus making it difficult to apply the discrepancy criteria used to identify students with learning disabilities. Also, the rapid and unpredictable growth rates of young children can complicate the accurate identification of learning disabilities. Educators and diagnosticians must take care not to label a young child prematurely as having learning disabilities (National Joint Committee on Learning Disabilities and the Preschool Child, 1985). Keogh and Weisner (1993) report that aggregated

TABLE 1.4
Life-Span View of Learning Disabilities

	Preschool	Grades K-1	Grades 2-6	Grades 7-12	Adult
Problem Areas	Achievement of developmental milestones (e.g., uses sentences) Receptive language Expressive language Visual perception Auditory perception Attention span Hyperactivity Self-regulation Social skills Concept formation	Academic readiness skills (e.g., alphabet knowledge) Receptive language Expressive language Visual perception Auditory perception Reasoning Motor development Attention span Hyperactivity Social skills	Reading skills Arithmetic skills Written expression Verbal expression Receptive language Attention span Hyperactivity Social-emotional Reasoning Problem solving Self-regulation	Reading skills Arithmetic skills Written expression Verbal expression Listening skills Study skills Metacognition Social-emotional/ delinquency Problem solving Self-regulation	Reading skills Arithmetic skills Written expression Verbal expression Listening skills Study skills Social-emotional Metacognition Vocational skills Life skills
Assessment Focus	Prediction of high risk for later learning problems within ecocultural perspective	Prediction of high risk for later learning problems within ecocultural perspective	Identification of learning disabilities within ecocultural perspective	Identification of learning disabilities within ecocultural perspective	Identification of learning disabilities within ecocultural perspective
Primary Treatment Types*	Preventative Collaborative	Preventative Corrective Collaborative	Remedial Corrective Collaborative Strategic	Remedial Corrective Collaborative Compensatory Strategic Proactive	Remedial Corrective Collaborative Compensatory Strategic Proactive

Treatments with Most Research or Expert Support	Direct instruction in language skills Behavioral management Parent education and involvement	Direct instruction in academic and language areas Behavioral management Parent education and involvement Cooperative learning	Direct instruction in academic areas Behavioral management Parent education and involvement Learning strategies Cooperative learning	Direct instruction: academics, social skills, and learning strategies Tutoring in academics Compensatory instruction Self-instruction training Teaming instruction Curriculum modifications	Direct instruction: academics, social skills, and learning strategies Tutoring in academics or vocational areas Compensatory instruction Self-instruction training Teaming instruction

**Collaborative*, from the teacher's perspective, primarily refers to instruction generated via teachers teaming; from the student's perspective it involves students teaming with each other during the learning process.

Strategic primarily refers to instruction that helps learners identify task demands, set goals, develop plans, coordinate resources, implement the plan, evaluate the plan, and modify the plan. It includes learning strategy instruction in metacognition and problem solving.

Proactive primarily refers to instruction that empowers the learners via self-instruction. The learners use resources and strategies to teach themselves.

data are more valid predictors than single indices. The aggregated data must consist of risk and protective factors gathered within an ecocultural perspective that includes child characteristics, family variables, and social contexts. Whereas risk factors increase the likelihood of a student being at risk for school failure, protective variables influence positively a child's likelihood for school success. These protective factors may include good communication skills, good interpersonal skills, problem-solving ability, family support, and relevant community resources. Thus, professionals and parents must be alert for behaviors and characteristics that are associated with later learning problems and successes. Generally, the importance of perceptual skills in diagnosis and treatment reaches its peak during the preschool years and diminishes as the child ages. Moreover, during the preschool period, developmental milestones and language development are monitored closely. Also, short attention span and hyperactivity represent warning flags to many diagnosticians. The positive influence of parent training as a factor in the treatment of young high-risk children is well documented. (Chapter 9 presents identification and intervention practices for young children with learning disabilities.)

The Elementary-School Child with Learning Disabilities. The elementary-school age range has received the most emphasis in the area of learning disabilities. During second through sixth grade, academic learning problems become apparent, and ability-achievement discrepancies emerge. Social-emotional problems also become more of a factor during the elementary grades. Diagnosis usually is accomplished through ability and achievement tests. As with all ages, direct instruction in the skill areas for this group is an important intervention component.

The Adolescent with Learning Disabilities. Most of the early literature about characteristics of learning disabilities focused on children. Because many differences between children and adolescents exist across physical, mental, and emotional areas, it is not appropriate simply to apply the characteristics of children to young adults. The teenager should be viewed as an adolescent first and then as an exceptional student. Many characteristics of the adolescent period (e.g., puberty, independence, peer group pressures) interact with the learning disability and the demands of the secondary school curriculum to create numerous academic and social-emotional problems.

Many professionals have made a much-needed effort recently to understand the characteristics and needs of the adolescent with learning disabilities (Deshler & Lenz, 1989; Deshler & Schumaker, 1983; Schumaker, Deshler, Alley, & Warner, 1983). The following are some of their most pertinent findings:

1. Most adolescents with learning disabilities exhibit severe academic achievement deficits and typically score below the 10th percentile on achievement measures in reading, written language, or mathematics. Moreover, the majority of adolescents with learning disabilities perform poorly in all achievement areas.
2. The academic skill development of many adolescents with learning disabilities plateaus during the secondary grades, generally by the 10th grade. For example, the average reading and written language achievement of students with learning disabilities in the seventh grade is at the high third-grade level and plateaus at the fifth-grade level in the secondary school.
3. Most adolescents with learning disabilities are deficient in study skills. A majority of the students perform poorly in such areas as test-taking skills, note taking, listening comprehension, monitoring writing errors, and scanning.
4. Many adolescents with learning disabilities exhibit social skills deficiencies. Social skills problem areas include accepting negative feedback, giving feedback, negotiating, and resisting peer pressure.
5. Many adolescents with learning disabilities have deficits related to the demands of settings (e.g., school or work) in which they are required to participate and be successful.

A substantial knowledge base is accruing regarding the adolescent with learning disabilities. As indicated in Figure 1.2, the number of teenagers identified with learning disabilities during the 1992–1993 academic year totaled 1,090,994 (U.S. Department of Education, 1994). (Although this age group is included throughout this book, Chapter 10 specifically addresses the adolescent with learning disabilities.)

The Adult with Learning Disabilities. Traditionally, the adult with learning disabilities has received sparse examination. With the growing realization that individuals with learning disabilities continue to have unique needs as they attend college, enter employment, or begin facing the demands of being self-sufficient citizens, however, information about these individuals is accruing rapidly. In a review of the literature, Gajar (1992) identified more than 200 articles that focused on adults with learning disabilities. Recent articles (Gerber, Ginsberg, & Reiff, 1992; Spekman, Goldberg, & Herman, 1993; Werner, 1993) stress the complexities involved in assessing the relationship of risk factors (e.g., type of learning disabilities, multiplicity of learning disability problems, severity of learning disabilities, age at identification, chronicity, gender, family discord, and poverty) and protective factors (e.g., proactivity, acceptance of strengths and weaknesses, positive outlook, ability to plan, goal setting, work ethic, support from significant others, ability to recruit help, and second-chance opportunities in the community) in determining outcomes for adults with learning disabilities. Researchers agree that the risk and protective factors must be examined within a social and community context if one is to understand the array of conditions that contribute to positive outcomes for adults with learning disabilities.

The following are some pertinent observations from the literature about adults:

1. For most individuals with learning disabilities, academic deficits persist into adulthood (Gajar, 1992; White, 1992).
2. Adults with learning disabilities are somewhat successful in getting jobs. Most studies report rates above 50%. These data often include part-time work (White, 1992).
3. Most adults with learning disabilities are underemployed (Sitlington & Frank, 1993; White, 1992).
4. Most young adults with learning disabilities live with a friend or their family (Sitlington & Frank, 1993).
5. Adults with learning disabilities are the fastest growing group of college students with disabilities receiving services (Gajar, 1992).
6. Females with learning disabilities tend to do better in college than males with learning disabilities, but females have more difficulty obtaining employment after secondary school (Sitlington & Frank, 1993; Vogel, Hruby, & Adelman, 1993).

In studies of 911 secondary school graduates with learning disabilities and 101 dropouts with learning disabilities, Sitlington and Frank (1990, 1993) report that 54% of the graduates and 38% of the dropouts met the following criteria: (a) employed or "meaningfully engaged," (b) living independently or with a relative, (c) paying a portion of their expenses, and (d) involved in more than one leisure activity.

Spekman et al. (1993) emphasize that learning disabilities involve a lifelong process of adaptations and changes. Individuals may do poorly at one stage and be helped to demonstrate resilience, competence, and success at another. After conducting an extensive study of older adults with learning disabilities, Gerber et al. (1992) report the following observation: "It was surprising, however, during data collection to discover the pain and agony, the trials and tribulations, that adults with learning disabilities experienced in order to become successful" (pp. 486–487). (Chapter 10 discusses the college student and adult with learning disabilities.)

Heterogeneity of Learning Disabilities

Most special educators agree that students with learning disabilities are a heterogeneous group. Theoretically, a youngster may qualify as having learning disabilities by exhibiting a discrepancy

between ability and achievement in one or more of the seven areas listed in the IDEA identification criteria and by satisfying the conditions of the exclusion clause. Thus, a student who exhibits just one academic discrepancy problem is labeled as having learning disabilities, and so is one who has discrepancies in all or any combination of the seven. Thus, within the guidelines of the IDEA and other prominent definitions, there are numerous types of learning disabilities (e.g., those in the math group and the written expression group). Moreover, many professionals agree that there is a much broader range of learning disability characteristics beyond those included in the identification criteria. Numerous cognitive and social-emotional characteristics are attributed to individuals with learning disabilities. Cognitive difficulties commonly associated with learning disabilities include deficits in attention, perception, motor functioning, memory, problem solving, and metacognition. Social-emotional difficulties associated with learning disabilities include hyperactivity, low self-concept, learned helplessness, social imperception, distractibility, and disruptive behavior. Theoretically, an individual with learning disabilities could have any one or all of the cognitive or social-emotional problems; thus, more than 500,000 combinations are theoretically possible! When severity or degree of each problem area is considered, the possible characteristics are enormous. According to Keogh (1987),

> The heterogeneity within LD mirrors that of the sponge in its natural surround. . . . Many sponges harbour commensal worms, brittle stars, barnacles, shrimp, crabs, copepods, and amphipods. . . . Over 13,000 animals representing 19 species were found in a single Caribbean sponge. (p. 56)

The heterogeneous nature of learning disabilities does not mean that the area is too nebulous to exist; however, it does indicate the complexity of students with learning disabilities, and it behooves professionals to follow certain guidelines:

1. Outside the common denominator of students with learning disabilities having a discrepancy in an academic area, educators must consider each individual with learning disabilities as having a unique set of cognitive and social-emotional behaviors.
2. Professionals must avoid stereotypic descriptions of individuals with learning disabilities that assign characteristics that may or may not exist.
3. Professionals must delineate the subgroups of learning disabilities. As McKinney (1984) points out, "The emerging literature on LD subtypes supports a multiple syndrome approach to theory in the field and offers a new paradigm for research which seems to accommodate the heterogeneity produced by the complex collection of disorders encompassed" (p. 49).
4. Educators must approach each student with learning disabilities with the viewpoint that no two are exactly alike, and thus, educational and behavioral interventions must be tailored to individual needs.
5. When one examines the characteristics of individuals with learning disabilities, it is common to focus on deficits; however, it is essential to recognize and celebrate the many academic, cognitive, and social-emotional strengths that each person with a learning disability exhibits. These strengths enable professionals, parents, and individuals with learning disabilities to develop and implement plans that enhance the quality of the lives of those with learning disabilities. In her book, *Succeeding Against the Odds*, S. L. Smith (1991) shares powerful stories about individuals with learning disabilities who use their strengths to live productive and happy lives.

Although results are not conclusive, research on subtypes of individuals with disabilities is yielding some preliminary clusters. Basically, three subtypes are emerging: (a) a language deficit group, (b) a visual deficit group, and (c) a behaviorally impaired group (Bender & Golden, 1990). Some researchers (Harnadek & Rourke, 1994; Little, 1993) report the emergence of a nonverbal learning disabilities subgroup. This subgroup has much overlap with the visual deficit group. In addition, several researchers (Lyon, 1985; Swanson et al., 1990; Torgesen, 1988) are examining memory variables in relation to subtypes of students with learning disabilities. Moreover, Lyon and Torgesen suggest remedial reading strategies for a subgroup of students with learning disabilities with serious memory deficits. Kavale and Forness (1987) point out that subtyping research will make meaningful contributions to the degree that it leads to the discovery of educationally relevant subgroups for which effective treatments are identified. Future subtyping research will be followed by many with guarded optimism to see if it leads to more precise identification and treatment of students with learning disabilities.

The heterogeneity of learning disabilities does not imply that a different treatment is necessary for each individual. Explicit instruction, learning strategies, cooperative learning, direct instruction, and behavioral interventions are effective across students with all types of characteristics. Intensity of an intervention as well as differential interventions must be considered as important factors in planning instruction.

PREVALENCE OF LEARNING DISABILITIES

The U.S. Department of Education (1994) reports that 4.09% (2,369,385) of U.S. children and youth ages 6 to 21 were identified as having a learning disability in the 1992–1993 school year. The state percentages range from a high of 6.24% to a low of 2.34%, with variations resulting from differences in identification criteria, policies, programs, economic conditions, and changes in state populations. Table 1.5 presents the percentage of each

TABLE 1.5
Percentage of Students Ages 6 to 21 by Disability Areas During the 1992–1993 School Year

Disability Area	Percentage of Resident Population	Percentage of All Disabilities
Specific learning disabilities	4.09	51.1
Speech or language impairments	1.73	21.6
Mental retardation	0.90	11.5
Serious emotional disturbance	0.70	8.7
Multiple disabilities	0.18	2.2
Hearing impairments	0.10	1.3
Orthopedic impairments	0.09	1.1
Other health impairments	0.11	1.4
Visual impairments	0.04	0.5
Autism	0.03	0.3
Deaf-blindness	0.00	0.0
Traumatic brain injury	0.01	0.1
All disabilities	7.98	100.0

Note: U.S. Department of Education (1994). *To assure the free appropriate public education of all children with disabilities: Sixteenth annual report to Congress on the implementation of the Individuals with Disabilities Education Act.* Washington, DC: Author.

disability area in terms of the resident population and the portion of each disability area as a percentage of all students identified for special education. Table 1.5 reveals that learning disabilities is the largest category and accounts for 51.1% of all disabilities. From the 1991–1992 school year to the 1992–1993 school year, the number of students age 6 through 21 with learning disabilities increased by more than 122,000 students. This increase may be due, in part, to the reclassification of students with other disabilities (e.g., language impairments and mental retardation) into the category of students with learning disabilities.

Although some critics have blamed the rapid increase of learning disabilities on faulty assessment practices, Hallahan (1992) claims that the growth rate is understandable considering the newness of the learning disabilities discipline and the effect of social and cultural factors. He notes that the area of learning disabilities has been under formal study for only 20 to 30 years. Hallahan proposes that during this period professionals and parents have had time to become more sophisticated in understanding and identifying learning disabilities. Specifically, he states that "the increase may be, in part, a reflection of professionals' and parents' growing recognition of the condition of learning disabilities and how to deal with it" (p. 524). Moreover, Hallahan notes that social and cultural influences (e.g., increased poverty, teenage motherhood, and drug abuse) have increased the risk factors associated with CNS dysfunction. Likewise, social and cultural factors involving the family have weakened the social support networks that many students need to succeed in school. In essence, risk factors seem to be increasing and protective factors appear to be diminishing.

Gender Differences

Although studies indicate that males and females are equally intelligent (Aiken, 1987), learning problems occur more among males than females. In a review of the research, C. R. Smith (1994) notes that seven studies report a 2:1 male-to-female ratio, five studies found a 3:1 ratio, four studies found a 4:1 ratio, and one study reports a 6:1 ratio. Researchers offer a variety of medical, maturational, and sociological hypotheses for these sex differences. Medical factors include the following:

1. The male appears to be more biologically susceptible to brain damage during prenatal and postnatal periods than the female.
2. Because males typically have greater birth weights and larger heads than females, they are more at risk for brain insult during the birth process.
3. Males experience one and one-half to three times as many head injuries as females.
4. The left hemisphere, which is associated with language and reading achievement, is particularly vulnerable in the male because abnormalities in the immune system's development are associated with too much testosterone, a male hormone.

Maturational factors include the following:

1. From birth through adolescence, males mature more slowly than females.
2. The male brain's protective sheath tends to mature more slowly than that of the female.
3. The neural maturation of the male's cortical regions associated with attention and language occurs more slowly than that of the female.

Sociological factors include the following:

1. The slow maturity rates of males often translate into a lack of school readiness and poor early-grade-level performance.
2. Because teachers expect males to exhibit more learning problems than females, bias in referring males for assessment and identification results.

Regarding gender differences, Smith concludes that "boys are in greater jeopardy of school failure than girls" (p. 68).

Vogel (1990) found that females with learning disabilities have more severe academic achievement deficits than males in selected aspects of math and reading, whereas males have more difficulty than females in visual-motor abilities, spelling, and mechanics in written language. Several researchers (Shaywitz & Shaywitz, 1988; Vogel, 1990) suspect that females may represent a group of underidentified and underserved individuals who are at risk for long-term academic failure and social-emotional problems.

LEARNING DISABILITIES ACROSS CULTURES

Within the United States, professionals are aware that learning disabilities exist among individuals across cultures. African-Americans, Asians, Hispanics, and Native Americans are the primary ethnic groups represented in U.S. schools. It is recognized that a student is likely to face learning difficulties when the customs or values of the school personnel differ from those of the student. These learning problems are complicated further if the student has a learning disability or if the student's primary language is different from the primary language of the school personnel. Currently, many culturally diverse students are being served in programs for students with learning disabilities in U.S. schools. Some critics (Shapiro, Loeb, & Bowermaster, 1993) maintain that diverse groups actually are overrepresented in special education programs. Problems springing from cultural diversity and learning disabilities, however, are difficult to untangle.

An international perspective regarding learning disabilities reflects that individuals, families, and professionals around the world are striving to understand and secure services for individuals who have learning disabilities. It now is apparent that learning disabilities occur in all cultures and countries, and that there are capable individuals in all cultures and countries who have severe difficulties in learning oral language, reading, written expression, and mathematics.

Reports and research concerning learning disabilities among nations, cultures, and languages are accumulating. The International Academy for Research in Learning Disabilities (IARLD) is dedicated to promoting worldwide research in learning disabilities. Research reports on learning disabilities already have come from many countries including Australia, Canada, Chile, Columbia, Denmark, Germany, Italy, Israel, New Zealand, the Netherlands, and the United Kingdom. Table 1.6 summarizes some of the events and conditions relating to learning disabilities in Canada, Columbia, Germany, Italy, and New Zealand. Inspection of Table 1.6 reveals that countries vary significantly in their recognition, identification, and treatment of students with learning disabilities. For example, the governments of Italy and New Zealand do not recognize the term *learning disabilities*, whereas Canada has a definition similar to those in the United States. Canada and Italy deal with the complexities of official bilingualism in identifying and educating their students with learning disabilities. Lerner (1993) reports that learning disabilities are found both among children learning an alphabet-based written language system (e.g., English) and among children learning a logographic (pictorial) written language system (e.g., Chinese).

PERSPECTIVE

Special education history reflects much concern about assigning labels such as *learning disabilities* to individuals. This concern is well founded when these descriptors provide the labeled individuals with reasons or excuses for failure or result in professionals or parents lowering their positive expectations of the labeled individual. From a different perspective, labels such as *learning disabilities* foster scientific inquiry, advance knowledge, and promote better communications among stakeholders. Terms such as *learning disabilities* give individuals and organizations an identity with a common phenomenon from which to operate to disseminate information and secure better laws, policies, research, funding, and services. Moreover, it gives individuals with learning disabilities an opportunity to learn about learning disabilities and engage in collaborative endeavors with professionals and peers to expand knowledge and needed services.

It is apparent that labels can have positive or negative influences. Most of the negative influences result from people lowering their expectations of labeled individuals or from labeled individuals lowering their own expectations. Thus, people with and without disabilities must maintain outlooks that focus on the strengths and possibilities of individuals with learning disabilities. The person-first terminology (i.e., "individual with learning disabilities" rather than "learning disabled individual") recommended in IDEA represents a national effort to promote positive attitudes about the strengths and capabilities of individuals with disabilities. It is hoped that this change encourages the perspective that individuals with disabilities are people who are quite similar to individuals without disabilities. This orientation embraces the position that the disability is only one of many facets of an individual who has numerous strengths and capabilities.

The following are some of the positive events of the 1990s that are occurring in the field of learning disabilities:

1. A consensus is emerging about the primary components of a definition of *learning disabilities*.
2. Knowledge about cognition (metacognition), neurological development, and social-emotional phenomena is expanding rapidly.
3. Global communication about learning disabilities is emerging.
4. Individuals with learning disabilities are being studied and served across an increasing age span.
5. Organizations and journals pertaining to learning disabilities are increasing, and many parents and teachers know and care enough to be advocates for individuals with learning disabilities.

TABLE 1.6
Learning Disabilities Across Cultures

Country and Source	Definition and Prevalence	Characteristics	Services and Placements	Curriculum
Canada (Wiener & Siegel, 1992)	Similar to U.S. definition Includes heterogeneous, intrinsic CNS problem, exclusion, environmental factors (e.g., poverty) Identifies 11 disability areas including social competence Percent classified as LD range from 1.7% (Saskatchewan) to 10.2% (Quebec)	Diverse culture (French, British, Asian descent) Bilingualism required (English, French) Similar characteristics to U.S. Includes immigrants from Latin America, Russia, Eastern Europe, and the Middle East Similar SES in urban and rural areas	Varied mandated services among provinces; most serve students ages 5–6 to 18–21 years No mandates in three provinces Adult services in preliminary stages Teachers involved in assessment Placement in least restrictive environment required in only two provinces Primarily nonadverserial service provision	Focus on whole child (affective areas and academics) Emphasis on collaboration Emphasis on multidisciplinary involvement Emphasis on informal assessment
Observations and Issues: 1. LDA of Canada is influential. 2. Americans and Canadians share research interests and publish in the same journals. 3. Allophone children come from homes where neither English nor French is the primary language.				
Columbia (de Larrate, 1993)	No government definition No government policies No government guidelines LD referred to as "an alteration of teaching/learning process" (pp. 47–48)		Assistance from centers for individuals with all sorts of mental and physical problems Basic rejection of individuals with LD from public and private schools Segregation of individuals with LD Some assessments provided by CCPDA	No public or private services available No vocational or higher education available CCPDA offers academic tutoring and motor training
Observations and Issues: 1. Recently the Columbian Foundation for LD (CCPDA) was created to foster awareness of LD. 2. CCPDA offers some schooling for a few students with LD.				

continued

TABLE 1.6
continued

Country and Source	Definition and Prevalence	Characteristics	Services and Placements	Curriculum
Germany (Opp, 1992)	Dissimilar to U.S. definition Defined by history of school failure Defined by placement in special school Population classified as LD is 2.3%	Achievement problems Deficits in cognitive functioning—IQ range of 65–85 Processing disorders Sociocultural deprivation Overrepresentation of students of foreign nationalities in LD programs Heterogeneous	Served primarily in special schools Mandated services for students ages 6 to 15 years Certificate (diploma) earned by 43.4% Offered a 3-year apprenticeship and vocational training after earning diploma	Practical content in academics Focus on independent living skills Emphasis on vocational training
Observations and Issues: 1. Ecological perspectives are emerging for viewing students with LD. 2. Self-regulated learning is gaining acceptance. 3. Bilingualism appears related to LD placements.				
Italy (Friul-Venetia-Julia region) (Fabbro & Masutto, 1994)	No official definition in legislation LD term disregarded by legislation but LD often included under "the handicapped" Handicap status determined by local public health services	Reading, math, language, and motor problems described in medical terms Bilingualism contributes to learning problems, especially when Italian is the second language Much of Italy is officially bilingual (e.g., Italian and French)	Lack of standardized tests in the respective languages; valid assessments are difficult Limited services provided in mainstream settings Guaranteed rights to students with disabilities	Remedial programs Limited teacher training Parents of children must secure services from public centers, hospitals, and private institutes
Observations and Issues: 1. Recognition and treatment of LD in Italy differ from region to region. 2. In Italian, there is a regular grapheme-to-phoneme correspondence that tends to reduce dyslexia. 3. Special schools and classes have been abolished.				

TABLE 1.6
continued

Country and Source	Definition and Prevalence	Characteristics	Services and Placements	Curriculum
New Zealand (Chapman, 1992)	No definition recognized by schools Prevalence estimated to be about 7% Some served under provision for educationally retarded	Particular academic difficulties Teachers estimate as many as 15% of students have learning difficulties	Promote mainstreaming and inclusion Resource teachers with limited or no training in remedial methods Most students with learning difficulties struggle in mainstream classes Achievement Initiative policy requires schools to meet needs of students with special needs (limited funding)	Reading Recovery for 6-year-olds with reading difficulties Remedial instruction

Observations and Issues:
1. There is no mention of language, math, attention, or metacognitive problems.
2. New Zealand Federation of Specific Learning Disabilities Associations (SPELD) is a parent group that has battled for decades to have LD recognized.
3. Government of New Zealand maintains a noncategorical perspective regarding students with generic learning problems.
4. SPELD has promoted an outdated view (psychological-processing disorder) of LD.

Given these positive events, it is apparent that stakeholders in the field of learning disabilities are seeking vigorously to understand and help individuals in *old and refined* ways or in *new and improved* ways. As people in the field of learning disabilities continue their efforts to improve the understanding of learning disabilities and the ability to provide individuals with learning disabilities with opportunities to pursue a better quality of life and happiness, it seems appropriate to reflect on the truth of T. S. Eliot's observation: "We shall not cease from exploration and the end of all our exploring will be to arrive where we started and know the place for the first time" (Abrams, 1962, p. 1970). Perhaps all individuals with learning disabilities and their valued others will benefit greatly from a more sensitive and knowledgeable global society.

DISCUSSION/REVIEW QUESTIONS

1. Briefly discuss the development of definitions of *learning disabilities* across the four phases.
2. Compare and contrast the components of the 1977 *Federal Register*/IDEA definition and identification criteria.
3. Discuss the components of the definition that state departments of education use in their identification procedures.
4. Briefly discuss the definitions offered by the NJCLD, the ACLD, and the ICLD.

5. List the disability areas included in the four most influential definitions.
6. Briefly describe the contemporary characteristics of individuals with learning disabilities.
7. Trace the problem areas and treatment approaches for individuals with learning disabilities from preschool to adulthood.
8. Describe the heterogeneous nature of individuals with learning disabilities.
9. Discuss the prevalence of learning disabilities, and list factors related to gender differences.
10. Discuss learning disabilities across cultures, and describe conditions of learning disabilities in various countries.

REFERENCES

Abrams, M. H. (Ed.). (1962). *The Norton anthology of English literature.* New York: W. W. Norton.

Aiken, L. R. (1987). *Assessment of intellectual functioning*. Boston: Allyn & Bacon.

American Psychiatric Association. (1982). *Diagnostic and statistical manual of mental disorders* (3rd ed.). Washington, DC: Author.

American Psychiatric Association. (1987). *Diagnostic and statistical manual of mental disorders* (3rd ed., revised). Washington, DC: Author.

Association for Children with Learning Disabilities. (1986, September–October). ACLD description: Specific learning disabilities. *ACLD Newsbriefs*, pp. 15–16.

Baker, L. (1982). An evaluation of the role of metacognitive deficits in learning disabilities. *Topics in Learning and Learning Disabilities, 2*, 27–35.

Bateman, B. D. (1964). Learning disabilities—Yesterday, today, and tomorrow. *Exceptional Children, 31*, 167.

Bateman, B. D. (1965). An educator's view of a diagnostic approach to learning disorders. In J. Hellmuth (Ed.), *Learning disorders* (Vol. 1, pp. 219–239). Seattle: Special Child.

Bender, W. N., & Golden, L. B. (1990). Subtypes of students with learning disabilities as derived from cognitive, academic, behavioral, and self-concept measures. *Learning Disability Quarterly, 13*, 183–194.

Bryan, T. (1977). Learning disabled children's comprehension of nonverbal communication. *Journal of Learning Disabilities, 10*, 501–506.

Bryan, T. H., & Bryan, J. H. (1986). *Understanding learning disabilities* (3rd ed.). Palo Alto, CA: Mayfield.

Chalfant, J., & Scheffelin, M. (1969). *Central processing dysfunction in children: A review of research* (NINDS Monograph No. 9). Bethesda, MD: U.S. Department of Health, Education, and Welfare.

Chapman, J. W. (1992). Learning disabilities in New Zealand: Where Kiwis and kids with LD can't fly. *Journal of Learning Disabilities, 25*, 362–370.

Clements, S. D. (1966). *Minimal brain dysfunction in children* (NINDS Monograph No. 3, U.S. Public Health Service Publication No. 1415). Washington, DC: U.S. Government Printing Office.

Cruickshank, W. (1967). *The brain-injured child in home, school and community*. Syracuse, NY: Syracuse University Press.

de Larrarte, C. I. K. (1993). Learning disabilities in Columbia, South America. *Journal of Learning Disabilities, 26*, 499–500.

Deshler, D. D., & Lenz, B. K. (1989). The strategies instructional approach. *International Journal of Disability, Development and Education, 36*, 203–224.

Deshler, D. D., & Schumaker, J. B. (1983). Social skills of learning disabled adolescents: Characteristics and interventions. *Topics in Learning and Learning Disabilities, 3*(2),15–23.

Fabbro, F., & Masutto, C. (1994). An Italian perspective on learning disabilities. *Journal of Learning Disabilities, 27*, 138–141.

Forness, S. R., & Kavale, K. A. (1991). Social skills deficits as primary learning disabilities: A note on problems with the ICLD diagnostic criteria. *Learning Disabilities Research & Practice, 6*, 44–49.

Gajar, A. (1992). Adults with learning disabilities: Current and future research priorities. *Journal of Learning Disabilities, 25*, 507–519.

Garnett, K. (1992). Developing fluency with basic number facts: Intervention for students with learning disabilities. *Learning Disabilities Research & Practice, 7*, 210–216.

Gerber, P. J., Ginsberg, R., & Reiff, H. B. (1992). Identifying alterable patterns in employment success for highly successful adults with learning disabilities. *Journal of Learning Disabilities, 25*, 475–487.

Gettinger, M. (1991). Learning time and retention differences between nondisabled students and students with learning disabilities. *Learning Disability Quarterly, 14*, 179–189.

Gibbs, D. P., & Cooper, E. B. (1989). Prevalence of communication disorders in students with learning disabilities. *Journal of Learning Disabilities*, *22*, 60–63.

Goldman, S. R. (1989). Strategy instruction in mathematics. *Learning Disability Quarterly*, *12*, 43–55.

Gresham, F. M., & Elliott, S. N. (1989). Social skills deficits as a primary learning disability. *Journal of Learning Disabilities*, *22*, 120–124.

Grossman, R. (1978). LD and the problem of scientific definitions. *Journal of Learning Disabilities*, *11*, 120–123.

Hallahan, D. P. (1975). Distractibility in the learning disabled child. In W. M. Cruickshank & D. P. Hallahan (Eds.), *Perceptual and learning disabilities in children* (Vol. 2) *Research and theory* (pp. 195–218). Syracuse, NY: Syracuse University Press.

Hallahan, D. P. (1992). Some thoughts on why the prevalence of learning disabilities has increased. *Journal of Learning Disabilities*, *25*, 523–528.

Hallahan, D. P., & Kauffman, J. M. (1988). *Exceptional children: Introduction to special education* (4th ed.). Upper Saddle River, NJ: Prentice Hall.

Hallahan, D. P., Kauffman, J. M., & Lloyd, J. W. (1996). *Introduction to learning disabilities*. Boston: Allyn & Bacon.

Hallahan, D. P., Keller, C. E., & Ball, D. W. (1986). A comparison of prevalence rate variability from state to state for each of the categories of special education. *Remedial and Special Education*, *7*(2), 8–14.

Hammill, D. D. (1990). On defining learning disabilities: An emerging consensus. *Journal of Learning Disabilities*, *23*, 74–84.

Hammill, D. D. (1993). A timely definition of learning disabilities. *Family and Community Health*, *16*(3), 1–8.

Hammill, D. D., Leigh, J. E., McNutt, G., & Larsen, S. G. (1981). A new definition of learning disabilities. *Learning Disability Quarterly*, *4*, 336–342.

Harnadek, M. C. S., & Rourke, B. P. (1994). Principal identifying features of the syndrome of nonverbal learning disabilities in children. *Journal of Learning Disabilities*, *27*, 144–154.

Hresko, W. P., & Reid, D. K. (1981). Five faces of cognition: Theoretical influences on approaches to learning disabilities. *Learning Disability Quarterly*, *4*, 238–243.

Hynd, G. W., Marshall, R., & Gonzalez, J. (1991). Learning disabilities and presumed central nervous system dysfunction. *Learning Disability Quarterly*, *14*, 283–296.

Interagency Committee on Learning Disabilities. (1987). *Learning disabilities: A report to the U.S. Congress*. Bethesda, MD: National Institutes of Health.

Johnson, D. J., & Myklebust, H. R. (1967). *Learning disabilities: Educational principles and practices*. New York: Grune & Stratton.

Kavale, K. A., & Forness, S. R. (1987). The far side of heterogeneity: A critical analysis of empirical subtyping research in learning disabilities. *Journal of Learning Disabilities*, *20*, 374–382.

Keogh, B. K. (1987). Response (to Senf). In S. Vaughn & C. S. Bos (Eds.), *Research in learning disabilities: Issues and future directions*. Boston: College-Hill.

Keogh, B. K., & Weisner, T. (1993). An ecocultural perspective on risk and protective factors in children's development: Implications for learning disabilities. *Learning Disabilities Research & Practice*, *8*, 3–10.

Kirk, S. A. (1962). *Educating exceptional children*. Boston: Houghton Mifflin.

Kirk, S. A. (1966). *The diagnosis and remediation of psycholinguistic disabilities*. Urbana, IL: University of Illinois Press.

Kirk, S. A., McCarthy, J. J., & Kirk, W. D. (1968). *The Illinois Test of Psycholinguistic Abilities*. Urbana, IL: University of Illinois Press.

Kulak, A. G. (1993). Parallels between math and reading disability: Common issues and approaches. *Journal of Learning Disabilities*, *26*, 666–673.

Lerner, J. W. (1993). *Learning disabilities: Theories, diagnosis and teaching strategies* (6th ed.) Boston: Houghton-Mifflin.

Little, S. S. (1993). Nonverbal learning disabilities and socioemotional functioning: A review of recent literature. *Journal of Learning Disabilities*, *26*, 653–665.

Lorsbach, T. C., & Frymier, J. (1992). A comparison of learning disabled and nondisabled students on five at-risk factors. *Learning Disabilities Research & Practice*, *7*, 137–141.

Lyon, G. R. (1985). Educational validation studies. In B. P. Rourke (Ed.), *Neuropsychology of learning disabilities* (pp. 228–253). New York: Guilford.

Mann, V. (1991). Language problems: A key to early reading problems. In B. Wong (Ed.), *Learning about learning disabilities* (pp. 130–163). San Diego: Academic Press.

Mather, N., & Roberts, R. (1994). Learning disabilities: A field in danger of extinction? *Learning Disabilities Research & Practice*, *9*, 49–58.

McBurnett, K., Lahey, B. B., & Pfiffner, L. J. (1993). Diagnosis of attention deficit disorders in DMS-IV: Scientific basis and implications for education. *Exceptional Children*, *60*, 108–117.

McKinney, J. D. (1984). The search for subtypes of specific learning disability. *Journal of Learning Disabilities*, *17*, 43–50.

McKinney, J. D. (1989). Longitudinal research on the behavioral characteristics of children with learning disabilities. *Journal of Learning Disabilities*, *22*, 141–150, 165.

McLeskey, J. (1992). Students with learning disabilities at primary, intermediate, and secondary grade levels: Identification and characteristics. *Learning Disability Quarterly*, *15*, 13–19.

Mercer, C. D., Jordan, L., Allsopp, D. H., & Mercer, A. R. (1995). *Learning disabilities definitions and criteria used by state education departments.* Manuscript submitted for publication.

Mercer, C. D., King-Sears, P., & Mercer, A. R. (1990). Learning disabilities definitions and criteria used by state education departments. *Learning Disability Quarterly*, *13*, 141–152.

Montague, M., & Applegate, B. (1993). Middle school students' mathematical problem solving: An analysis of think-aloud protocols. *Learning Disabilities Quarterly*, *16*, 19–30.

Montgomery, M. S. (1994). Self-concept and children with learning disabilities: Observer-child concordance across six context-dependent domains. *Journal of Learning Disabilities*, *27*, 254–262.

Morsink, C. V. (1985). Learning disabilities. In W. H. Berdine & A. E. Blackhurst (Eds.), *An introduction to special education* (2nd ed., pp. 391–425). Boston: Little, Brown.

Myers, P. I., & Hammill, D. D. (1990). *Learning disabilities: Basic concepts, assessment practices, and instructional strategies* (4th ed.). Austin, TX: PRO-ED.

National Joint Committee on Learning Disabilities. (1981). *Learning disabilities: Issues on definition*. Unpublished manuscript. (Available from The Orton Dyslexia Society, 724 York Road, Baltimore, MD 21204).

National Joint Committee on Learning Disabilities. (1988). [Letter to NJCLD member organizations.]

National Joint Committee on Learning Disabilities and the Preschool Child. (1985, February). *A position paper of the National Joint Committee on Learning Disabilities*. Baltimore, MD: The Orton Dyslexia Society.

Opp, G. (1992). A German perspective on learning disabilities. *Journal of Learning Disabilities*, *25*, 351–360.

Orton, S. T. (1937). *Reading, writing, and speech problems in children*. New York: W. W. Norton.

Sawyer, D., & Butler, K. (1991). Early language intervention: A deterrent to reading disability. *Annals of Dyslexia*, *41*, 55–79.

Schumaker, J. B., Deshler, D. D., Alley, G. R., & Warner, M. M. (1983). Toward the development of an intervention model for learning disabled adolescents: The University of Kansas Institute. *Exceptional Education Quarterly*, *4*, 45–74.

Shapiro, J. P., Loeb, P., & Bowermaster, D. (1993, December 13). Separate and unequal. *U.S. News & World Report*, pp. 46–50, 54–56, 60.

Shaywitz, S., & Shaywitz, B. (1988). Attention-deficit disorder: Current perspectives. In J. F. Kavanagh & T. J. Truss (Eds.), *Learning disabilities: Proceedings of the national conference* (pp. 369–567). Parkton, MD: York Press.

Silver, L. B. (1990). Attention deficit-hyperactivity disorder: Is it a learning disability or a related disorder? *Journal of Learning Disabilities*, *23*, 394–397.

Sitlington, P. L., & Frank, A. R. (1990). Are adolescents with learning disabilities successfully crossing the bridge into adult life? *Learning Disability Quarterly*, *13*, 97–111.

Sitlington, P. L., & Frank, A. R. (1993). Dropouts with learning disabilities: What happens to them as young adults? *Learning Disabilities Research & Practice*, *8*, 244–252.

Smith, C. R. (1994). *Learning disabilities: The interaction of learner, task, and setting* (3rd ed.). Boston: Allyn & Bacon.

Smith, S. L. (1991). *Succeeding against the odds: How the learning-disabled can realize their promise*. New York: L. L. Putnam's Sons.

Spekman, N. J., Goldberg, R. J., & Herman, K. L. (1993). An exploration of risk and resilience in the lives of individuals with learning disabilities. *Learning Disabilities Research & Practice*, *8*, 11–18.

Stevens, G. D., & Birch, J. W. (1957). A proposal of clarification of the terminology and a description of brain-injured children. *Exceptional Children*, *23*, 346–349.

Strauss, A. A., & Lehtinen, L. E. (1947). *Psychopathology and education of the brain-injured child* (Vol. 1). New York: Grune & Stratton.

Swanson, H. L. (1990). Instruction derived from the strategy deficit model: Overview of principles and procedures. In T. Scruggs & B. Wong (Eds.), *Intervention research in learning disabilities* (pp. 34–65). New York: Springer-Verlag.

Swanson, H. L., Cochran, K. F., & Ewers, C. A. (1990). Can learning disabilities be determined from working memory performance? *Journal of Learning Disabilities, 23*, 59–67.

Torgesen, J. K. (1988). Studies of children with learning disabilities who perform poorly on memory span tasks. *Journal of Learning Disabilities, 21*, 605–612.

Torgesen, J. K., & Kail, R. V. (1980). Memory processes in exceptional children. In L. L. Keogh (Ed.), *Advances in special education: Vol. 1. Basic constructs and theoretical orientations*. Greenwich, CT: J.A.I. Press.

U.S. Department of Education. (1994). *To assure the free appropriate public education of all children with disabilities: Sixteenth annual report to Congress on the implementation of the Individuals with Disabilities Education Act.* Washington, DC: Author.

U.S. Office of Education. (1968). *First annual report of National Advisory Committee on Handicapped Children*. Washington, DC: U.S. Department of Health, Education, and Welfare.

U.S. Office of Education. (1976). Education of handicapped children: Assistance to states: Proposed rulemaking. *Federal Register, 41*, 52404–52407.

U.S. Office of Education. (1977). Assistance to states for education of handicapped children: Procedures for evaluating specific learning disabilities. *Federal Register, 42*, 65082–65085.

Vogel, S. A. (1990). Gender differences in intelligence, language, visual-motor abilities, and academic achievement in students with learning disabilities: A review of the literature. *Journal of Learning Disabilities, 23*, 44–52.

Vogel, S. A., Hruby, P. J., & Adelman, P. B. (1993). Educational and psychological factors in successful and unsuccessful college students with learning disabilities. *Learning Disabilities Research & Practice, 8*, 35–43.

Wang, M. C., Haertel, G. D., & Walberg, H. J. (1993/1994). What helps students learn? *Educational Leadership, 51*(4), 74–79.

Werner, E. E. (1993). Risk and resilience in individuals with learning disabilities: Lessons learned from the Kauai longitudinal study. *Learning Disabilities Research & Practice, 8*, 28–34.

White, W. J. (1992). The postschool adjustment of persons with learning disabilities: Current status and future projections. *Journal of Learning Disabilities, 25*, 448–456.

Wiener, J., & Siegel, L. (1992). A Canadian perspective on learning disabilities. *Journal of Learning Disabilities, 25*, 340–350, 371.

Wiig, E. H., & Semel, E. M. (1984). *Language assessment and intervention for the learning disabled* (2nd ed.). Boston: Allyn & Bacon.

Wilson, L. R. (1985). Large scale learning disability identification: The reprieve of a concept. *Exceptional Children, 52*, 44–51.

Wong, B. (1991). The relevance of metacognition to learning disabilities. In B. Wong (Ed.), *Learning about learning disabilities* (pp. 232–261). San Diego: Academic Press.

History

CHAPTER 2

After studying this chapter, you should be able to:

- identify the seven areas that have contributed significantly to the history of learning disabilities.
- identify the three time periods in which historical events related to learning disabilities are organized.
- discuss the primary events in government policy for each time period.
- discuss the major developments in learning disabilities organizations for each time period.
- describe the major theoretical positions and interventions for each type of disorder (spoken language, written language, and perceptual and motor) across each time period.
- describe the primary developments in behavioral theory in each time period.
- describe the primary developments in cognitive theory in each time period.
- discuss contemporary directions in learning disabilities.

Education for students with learning disabilities is a field unequaled in growth by any other area of education for students with special needs. Unknown to most educators before 1965, it was familiar to all special educators by 1970. Most educators used the term *learning disabilities* by 1975, and it since has been regularly used—and misused—by the press, school boards, legislators, and professionals.

To provide an overview of events and individuals that have had a significant impact on the field of learning disabilities, this chapter traces the history of the field across the following areas: government policy, organizations, type of disorder (spoken language, written language, and perceptual and motor), behavioral theory, and cognitive theory. The major events in these areas occurred within three time periods: (a) the foundation period (1800–1960), (b) the emergent period (1961–1974), and (c) the Public Law 94–142 period (1975–1987). The last section of the chapter focuses on contemporary directions.

FOUNDATION PERIOD

During the first 130 years of the foundation period, few significant events concerning learning disabilities occurred in education. However, beginning in 1932, the public slowly became aware of the rights of all children to receive an education, federal involvement was initiated, organizations were formed, and related theories and research were developed.

Government Policy

The history of educational legislation suggests that the current concern for students with learning disabilities was not only improbable before 1960, but also perhaps impossible. It took several hundred years to evolve the social and legislative climate necessary to provide the comprehensive services now taken for granted.

Not until Rhode Island passed a compulsory education law in 1840 did children with special needs have legal precedent for the right to an education. As other states gradually adopted the Rhode Island model, educators were forced to provide for students with disabilities.

There was little federal involvement with special education from 1800 to 1957; however, the establishment of the Department of Special Education in the U.S. Office of Education in 1931 acknowledged that special education was a viable area within the field. Overall, this limited federal involvement impeded the growth of services for students with disabilities.

Organizations

Volunteer groups and professional organizations have been concerned about students with disabilities since the American Colonial period. In most cases, such groups used a specific cause as a rallying point; however, after attaining the goal the organization usually disbanded. Exceptions were professional groups with strong common interests or vocational ties.

As attitudes about responsibility for students with disabilities changed after 1900, these organizations became more numerous and better established. Some have had a lasting effect. The National Society for Crippled Children, organized in 1921, attempted to aid crippled children and adults, educate the public, support research about the causes of crippling conditions, and finance treatment. In 1922, Elizabeth Farrell organized the International Council for the Education of Exceptional Children to promote adequate education for children who were disabled or gifted. From the original 12 members grew the present organization, the Council for Exceptional Children, with more than 900 local chapters.

In the late 1940s and early 1950s, these organizations changed their structure. Operating with greater tenacity, political savvy, and financial independence, they sparked public interest and mobilized support among legislators and administrators at the local, state, and federal levels. The United Cerebral Palsy Association (UCP) grew from a handful of local groups and organizations into a truly national organization by 1949.

Representatives from 20 local parent groups met in 1950 to form the National Association of Parents and Friends of Retarded Children. In 1953, the organization became the National Association for Retarded Children and, more recently, the National Association for Retarded Citizens (NARC). Like the UCP, the NARC vigorously promotes the welfare of all individuals with mental retardation. These groups stimulated favorable legislation and funding from the federal government.

Taking their cue from groups such as the UCP and the NARC, parents of children with learning problems began to organize in the late 1950s. By 1957, two of the earliest local groups had been formed: the Fund for Perceptually Handicapped Children (in Evanston, Illinois) and the New York Association for Brain-Injured Children. Similar local groups later coalesced into a strong national organization and increased their power as voters and pressure groups.

Type of Disorder

Research, theory, and treatment strategies helped to shape the learning disabilities field. Early theory concentrated on three disorders, which were treated primarily by physicians and psychologists: spoken language, written language, and perceptual and motor disorders. Before the late 1950s, researchers emphasized clinical investigations rather than practical school-related topics. They began by studying adults with brain injury, then children with brain injury, and finally, children of normal intelligence.

Investigators focused on process disorders or designed interventions based on the concept of process deficit. *Process* refers to biophysical and psychological conditions (auditory, visual, tactile, motor, vocal, feedback, and memory) that affect learning. The investigators assumed that process integrity was related to appropriate responses and learning.

Disorders of Spoken Language. Most early investigators of spoken language disorders tended to focus on etiology, clinical treatment, and development of models. Specifically, the concepts of localized brain injury and hemispheric dominance received extensive attention. Franz Joseph Gall, a German physician, theorized in 1802 that head injuries were likely to result in mental disorders. Based on his work with adults with brain injury, Gall speculated that specific regions of the brain controlled certain mental activities, and he generated controversy with his position that specific localized brain injury resulted in loss of speech.

Gall's hypothesis was accepted and defined by a well-respected member of the French medical establishment, John Baptiste Bouillaud. In the 1820s, Bouillaud worked to locate the faculty of speech in the frontal anterior lobes of the brain. During the 1860s, Pierre Paul Broca continued Bouillaud's work. Unlike Bouillaud, however, Broca believed that movement and sensation were not located in separate areas of the brain, and that speech disorders were the result of damage to the frontal convolutions of the brain. Broca contributed the hypothesis that the functions of the brain's left and right hemispheres were different. Another researcher, John Hughlings Jackson, attempted to locate speech disorders in the cerebral cortex and developed an entire classification and definition system for speech components.

The medial establishment saw much dissension over these new ideas. The controversy was lessened by Head's (1926) consolidation of theory, which led to wide acceptance of several conclusions about disorders in spoken language:

1. Disorders in language could not be dichotomized as sensory or motor.
2. Motor correlates of language disabilities were not necessarily due to a disturbance in the higher-level brain processes.
3. Brain localization and hemisphere differentiation were valid concepts.
4. Loss of symbolic speech functions did not necessarily include a concomitant loss in mechanical aptitudes.

Two and one-half decades later came the next milestone, Charles Osgood's communication model. Although he drew from the work of many investigators, Osgood was most influenced by clinical neurologists seeking to develop a "schematic diagram" of the communication process (Osgood & Miron, 1963). The Osgood model attempts to explain what happens within an individual between the presentation of an external stimulus and the individual's overt response.

Osgood's contemporary, Helmer R. Myklebust (1955), defined language as symbolic behavior (i.e., using words as symbols for expressing ideas and feelings, and labeling objects). He hypothesized that there were five developmental stages of abstraction: sensation, perception, imagery, symbolization, and conceptualization (Myklebust, 1960), each related directly to experience. He maintained that an unimpaired peripheral and central nervous system was prerequisite to the development of language.

Clinical experience and research with aphasics led Joseph M. Wepman and his colleagues (Wepman, Jones, Buck, & Van Pelt, 1960) to develop a schema of functional organization within the central nervous system. Unlike Osgood, Wepman included memory, internal and external feedback, and modes of transmission in his model.

Wepman postulated that two processes in the central nervous system deal with spoken language: (a) the *transmission* process, which is divided into receptive and expressive modes, and (b) the *integration* process, which provides for the decoding and encoding of previously learned patterns to give meaning to the stimulus. Stimuli transmitted by the two processes are received and stored in the memory as associations. Wepman emphasized the role of recall in spoken language, with the memory bank interconnecting all stages of the perceptual and conceptual levels. While he did not discuss the role of feedback at length, he placed importance on both internal and external feedback as affecting the accuracy and control of response modification. The modality aspects of transmission had direct application to teaching because the child's strengths and weaknesses through visual, auditory, and tactile modes had to be evaluated for planning instruction.

Unlike earlier investigators, Osgood, Myklebust, and Wepman focused on children with suspected brain damage rather than adults. Their contemporaries in the other disorder areas also used this strategy.

Disorders of Written Language. Few investigations of written language disorders were reported before 1900, and then only a few investigators dominated the research. In 1917, a French physician, James Hinshelwood, presented the first well-accepted publication describing etiology and intervention techniques. He defined *word blindness* as a "condition in which, with normal vision and therefore seeing the letters and words distinctly, an individual is no longer able to interpret written or printed language" (Hinshelwood, 1917, p. 2). Such difficulty could be caused by a defect in an area of the brain storing visual memories of words and letters, specifically in a portion of the left hemisphere. Reading proficiency, he believed, could be attained only through intensive practice and the development of the brain's visual memory. Like the investigators of spoken language who paired disorders of language with brain damage, Hinshelwood ascribed disorders of written language to defects in specific areas of the brain.

In the 1930s, Samuel T. Orton, a specialist in neurology and neuropathology, became a dominant voice in the field. After a 10-year study of language acquisition disorders, he speculated that one side of the brain dominated the language processes (Orton, 1937). He thought that children with language disabilities who had no demonstrable brain injury had failed to establish hemispheric dominance. Many of the children Orton examined displayed mixed or confused dominance of the hand, eye, or foot. Orton concluded that this interfered with language functions as well as motor functions and that treatment must address that problem. Orton also believed that mixed dominance could be transferred hereditarily and that the location of a brain injury was more important than the amount of damage.

Little empirical evidence supports Orton's theories concerning brain dominance, but educators continue to use his remediation strategies because they are effective with some children with written language problems. Several investigators developed and publicized these techniques: Marion Monroe, Anna Gillingham, Bessie Stillman, Samuel A. Kirk, Grace Fernald, and Romalda Spalding.

Monroe, Orton's research assistant at the Iowa State Psychopathic Hospital, helped test the efficacy of his theories for education. She published *Children Who Cannot Read* (Monroe, 1932) and credited Orton for calling her attention to children with specific reading disabilities. She also described assessment tests (based on the "dominance" theory) and a teaching strategy called the *synthetic phonetic approach*. This approach begins with pictures mounted on cards from which the child identifies initial consonants and then vowels. Blending begins after a few elements are learned, and gradually the child starts to read selected stories. Drills and the kinesthetic approach (learning through movement exercises such as tracing a word) are used.

Gillingham and Stillman (1936) acknowledged Orton in their book on remedial reading. They focused on developing language-pattern associations among the visual, auditory, and kinesthetic mechanisms in the dominant hemisphere. A multisensory teaching approach was used to build these associations *(linkage)*. Gillingham and Stillman believed that failure to establish any linkage would result in a language disability.

As a result of Kirk's success in 1929 with a delinquent boy with mental retardation, the Chicago Institute for Juvenile Research invited him to confer with Monroe. Monroe agreed to tutor Kirk in the diagnosis and remediation of children with severe cases of reading disabilities. Later, Kirk conducted research at the Wayne County Training School in Northville, Michigan. In 1936, members of the Wayne County Training School research department developed a system to teach phonetic reading (Hegge, Kirk, & Kirk, 1936). Orton, Monroe, and Fernald influenced the system, based on principles of learning from the Chicago school of functional psychology (Kirk, 1976). The second edition of *Remedial Reading Drills* (Hegge, Kirk, & Kirk, 1970) contains the manual and drills for this system.

In 1921, the clinic school at the University of California was established, and Fernald's work influenced the development of many remedial reading programs. She focused on children's problems in reading and writing, without speculating about process, dominance, or brain injury, in her VAKT (visual-auditory-kinesthetic-tactile) approach (Fernald, 1943). She divided reading problems into two general groups, total and partial disability. To Fernald, those with partial disability were more hampered because bad habits interfered with learning.

In 1956, Spalding presented an approach to written language disability called *unified phonics methods*. Acknowledging Orton's influence, Spalding described her approach as follows:

> The core of the method is a technique by which the child learns how to write down the sounds used in spoken English as they are combined into words. Thus, conversely, he can pronounce any printed word. Meaning is thoroughly taught hand-in-hand with the writing and by using new words in original sentences. It begins with correct pronunciation of words and the writing of their component sounds in accordance with the rules of English spelling. By this means the saying, writing, reading, and meaning of words are well learned and understood. (Spalding & Spalding, 1962, p. 8)

As a whole, therefore, these investigators gave rise to multisensory teaching. As a result of their work, clinicians and teachers taught reading with learning activities that involved visual, auditory, kinesthetic, and tactile experiences.

Disorders of Perceptual and Motor Processes. While investigation of perceptual and motor processes related to learning did not gain momentum until after 1900, individuals within this area strongly influenced the learning disability movement. After its establishment, the

Wayne County Training School attracted many outstanding individuals during and after the Depression, and they influenced and interacted with other professionals, thus spreading their influence further.

Kirk Goldstein's work (1936, 1939) provided a partial basis for perceptual-motor investigations. In his adult patients with brain injury, he observed meticulosity, perseveration, figure-ground confusion, forced response to stimuli, and catastrophic reaction.

Goldstein's work influenced Alfred A. Strauss and Heinz Werner to study children with brain injury and mental retardation. These two German professors—Strauss, a neuropsychiatrist, and Werner, a developmental psychologist—had fled Hitler's Germany and within a few years had joined the research staff at the Wayne County Training School. Together they designed and conducted a series of studies (Strauss & Werner, 1942; Werner & Strauss, 1939, 1940, 1941) to investigate children with brain injury and mental retardation. Their findings led to the identification of the *exogenous* subgroup of children with retardation, those whose retardation came from brain injury resulting from non-genetic factors. These children had some unique characteristics, and in a revolutionary statement Strauss and Werner concluded that a standard institutional regimen was inappropriate for them. Strauss and Werner's landmark investigations, educational concepts, and interactions with young scholars continued to establish a foundation for the learning disability movement. Laura Lehtinen, Newell C. Kephart, and William M. Cruickshank tested and expanded their theoretical positions.

Lehtinen, the education director of the Cove School for Brain-Injured Children in Racine, Wisconsin, collaborated with Strauss to develop teaching procedures. They believed that methods could be developed to relieve perceptual and conceptual disturbances and thus reduce symptomatic behavior disorders. In 1947, Strauss and Lehtinen coauthored *Psychopathology and Education of the Brain-Injured Child,* which introduced children with brain injury to the education profession. Strauss and Lehtinen suggested that in such children, various disorders in perception, concept formation, and mental organization seriously interfered with learning. They proposed two interventions: (a) manipulating and controlling the environment, and (b) teaching the child voluntary control. Their specific recommendations for teachers included the following:

1. Teach children with brain injury in small groups.
2. Eliminate visually stimulating material and decorations.
3. Wear plain, unornamented clothes.
4. Establish daily routines.
5. Use instructional materials that are simple and without distractions.

About 8 years after the publication of the Strauss and Lehtinen volume, Strauss and Kephart (1955) coauthored Volume II of *Psychopathology and Education of the Brain-Injured Child.* In this volume, they compared the research on children with brain injury and normal intelligence with the research on children with brain injury and mental retardation. Kephart (1960) later postulated that perceptual-motor development is the basis for all learning. Focusing on practical applications, Kephart developed an assessment scale and specific educational strategies.

Cruickshank, one of the most influential scholars of the Wayne County Training School, first applied Strauss and Werner's findings to youth without mental retardation. In a series of studies beginning with a doctoral dissertation by Jane Dolphin (1950), Cruickshank facilitated the transfer of brain-injury research from children with exogenous retardation to children with normal intelligence.

In the late 1950s, Cruickshank, Bentzen, Ratzeburg, and Tannhauser (1961) designed the Montgomery County Project to study the educational methods that Strauss and Lehtinen had suggested. All the children in the study had normal or near-normal intelligence and exhibited behavior associated with brain injury. Not all the children, however, could be shown to have definite central nervous system impairment. Consequently, it was proposed that perceptual and perceptual-motor problems were not an exclusive function of mental retardation or definite brain injury (i.e., children of normal intelligence with learning problems were also found to have perceptual-motor problems). Today, such children are considered to have learning disabilities whether or not brain injury can be demonstrated.

Behavioral Theory

Behavioral theorists are a subgroup in the larger field of learning theory. When experimenting, they determine a target behavior, carefully and systematically observe and record the specific events that occur before and after the target behavior, and manipulate these events to produce a desired change in the target behavior.

During the foundation period of the field of learning disabilities, relatively little practical application of this theory to schoolchildren was attempted. The contributions of Edward L. Thorndike and B. F. Skinner, however, significantly influenced later investigations.

Thorndike, considered by some (Hilgard & Bower, 1966; Hill, 1963) to be the father of reinforcement theory, believed that the connection between stimulus and response represented all learning. He believed that learning occurs in accordance with the laws of *effect, readiness,* and *exercise.* In the law of effect, a connection becomes stronger or weaker depending on its consequences. A connection is strengthened when it is followed by a satisfying event. The law of readiness refers to the physiological basis for the law of effect. The law of exercise states that practice strengthens a connection. Thorndike influenced many investigators who were applying learning and reinforcement theory to education (Gagné, 1965; Homme, 1969; Skinner, 1963).

Skinner worked with animals to generate a theory of behavior that emphasized observable events (Hilgard & Bower, 1966; Hill, 1963; Skinner, 1953, 1963). He defined two types of learned behavior: respondent and operant. Respondent behaviors are elicited by a stimulus occurring before the behavior, whereas operant behaviors are strengthened or weakened by consequences occurring after the behavior. According to Skinner, only a small part of human behavior is respondent. In his view, *reinforcement* receives an operational definition: the increased probability of a response, resulting from the application of a positive reinforcer or the removal of a negative reinforcer. Skinner rejected the "cause-effect" model and refused to consider "inner causes" to explain behavior. Instead, he described observable events, which occurred together in a particular order. For example, if a child refused to do schoolwork, Skinner would advocate finding events or objects that would increase the frequency of doing schoolwork. His theories received attention from investigators in the 1960s and 1970s and resulted in a variety of applications to educational problems.

Cognitive Theory

In 1956, Jerome Bruner coauthored a book titled *A Study of Thinking* (Bruner, Goodnow, & Austin, 1956) that significantly influenced psychology and education. The authors stressed the importance of studying covert cognitive processes, a viewpoint that received additional support from Noam Chomsky's (1959) writings. Chomsky noted that hierarchically organized associations were not sufficient for understanding complex behaviors and that control and processes are part of complex behavior. Chomsky further maintained that language is not simply stored and reproduced but is reconstructed and recreated in infinite ways.

The relative merits of cognitive theory, which emphasized inner thinking processes, and behaviorism, which emphasized observable behavior and consequent events, were debated extensively during the late 1950s. Overall, both approaches were in their infancy during the foundation period and had little effect on the field of special education.

Summary: Foundation Period

By the 1950s, public attitudes toward education had advanced to the point that most Americans agreed that education should be for all children, thereby establishing a legal foundation for providing such an education. Theories about learning disorders had been developed in three disability areas, and application of educational interventions based on these theories appeared to be effective. Two learning theories, behavioral and cognitive, emerged. At the same time, public pressure for increased services was reaching a critical point. The cumulative effect of these trends produced a 10-year period of radical change in American society, and education for children with learning disabilities emerged and flourished. Table 2.1 presents an overview of events, individuals, and time sequences of the foundation period.

EMERGENT PERIOD

The tempo of significant events greatly increased during the emergent period (1961–1974). The term *learning disabilities* was adopted, public school programs rapidly expanded, federal involvement intensified, organizations solidified and grew, and tests and intervention approaches from various theoretical viewpoints were applied. Moreover, turbulent times emerged as proponents of various theoretical positions began an intense, heated debate.

Government Policy

Before 1957, the federal bureaucracy dealt with education only reluctantly; during the 1960s, it became a pervasive force at all levels. In the mid-1960s, the Department of Health, Education, and Welfare sponsored several task forces to study children with brain injury and learning problems. Largely through the efforts of Clements (1966), the task force director, the term *minimal brain dysfunction* (MBD) was introduced. Although popular with physicians, the MBD terminology, like brain-injury terminology, never was accepted widely by educators. When the U.S. Office of Education (USOE) was given the responsibility for funding special education programs for children with suspected brain injury, it became apparent that terms and a definition acceptable to educators were needed. The National Advisory Committee on Handicapped Children (NACHC) was formed in 1968 to develop a definition. Under Kirk's leadership, the committee developed a definition that was used in Public Law 91-230, the Specific Learning Disabilities Act of 1969.

Organizations

During the late 1950s and early 1960s, many children were referred to special education programs because they were not learning in mainstream settings. These children were permitted to attend school but were not eligible for special classes because they were not diagnosed as being blind, retarded, crippled, or in one of the other recognized "special" categories. Local associations of parents formed to organize classes and provide the services denied by the public schools. The number of local groups and state organizations grew quickly, and by 1963 a national conference had been planned to create a national organization. At this 1963 conference in Chicago, Samuel A. Kirk introduced the term *learning disabilities.* Parents, who had been dissatisfied with the existing terms, received this term enthusiastically and formed the Association for Children with Learning Disabilities (ACLD). Given the extent of parent involvement in education at the time, it seems fitting that the coining of the term *learning disabilities* occurred at a national conference of parent organizations.

In 1964, the ACLD (now the Learning Disabilities Association of America) was established formally. Four years later, the Division for Children with Learning Disabilities (DCLD) (now the Council for Learning Disabilities) was organized as a professional division within the Council for Exceptional Children. Although the ACLD was formed by parents, many professionals

TABLE 2.1
Foundation Period (1800–1960)

	Government Policy	Organizations	Type of Disorder: Spoken Language	Type of Disorder: Written Language	Type of Disorder: Perceptual and Motor Processes	Behavioral Theory	Cognitive Theory
1802			Gall				
1820			Bouillaud				
1840	Compulsory education law						
1860			Broca				
1864			Jackson				
1917				Hinshelwood			
1921		Nat. Society for Crippled Children					
1922		Int. Council for Education of Exceptional Children					
1926			Head				
1930				Orton		Thorndike	
1931	Establishment of Dept. of Special Education in USOE						
1932				Monroe			
1936				Gillingham & Stillman	Goldstein		
				Kirk			
1939					Strauss & Werner		
1943				Fernald			
1947					Lehtinen		

continued

TABLE 2.1
continued

	Government Policy	Organizations	Type of Disorder: Spoken Language	Written Language	Perceptual and Motor Processes	Behavioral Theory	Cognitive Theory
1949		United Cerebral Palsy Association					
1953		Nat. Assoc. for Retarded Children	Osgood			Skinner	
1955			Myklebust		Kephart		Bruner
1956	Minimal federal involvement in special education			Spalding			
1957		Fund for Perceptually Handicapped Children New York Assoc. for Brain-Injured Children		Use of phonics and multisensory remedial reading techniques			
1959							Chomsky
1960			Wepman		Cruickshank		

from a variety of disciplines, such as medicine, psychology, education, and language, joined it. Its focus began as and has remained multidisciplinary. The DCLD was formed primarily by educators, and its emphasis was teacher-oriented.

Type of Disorder

Disorders of Spoken Language. During this period, one of the most significant figures outside the perceptual-motor group was Samuel A. Kirk. Kirk (1972) believed that individual differences in ability had two meanings. First, there could be an interindividual difference (i.e., a comparison of the skills of one child with those of another or of a group). Second, there could be intra-individual differences (i.e., differences in ability within the individual child). Dissatisfied with his early attempts to construct an intra-individual test and convinced that part of the problem was the lack of a theoretical framework, Kirk enrolled in a course taught by Osgood at the University of Illinois. Later, McCarthy and Kirk (1961) produced the *Illinois Test of Psycholinguistic Abilities* (ITPA). Unique among then-current tests, it purported to assess intra-individual differences.

The ITPA and psycholinguistic teaching were by far the most widely used diagnostic and intervention approach in learning disabilities during the 1960s. This diagnostic and intervention approach was based primarily on the notion that youngsters with learning disabilities had modality strengths and weaknesses and that instruction must be planned accordingly.

The ITPA and psycholinguistic teaching continued to dominate the field until the mid-1970s. At that time, several investigators began to raise questions about the efficacy of the ITPA and related training programs. In a review of 39 studies, Hammill and Larsen (1974) concluded that ITPA-based remedial programs had not been validated.

Ysseldyke and Salvia (1974) questioned the ITPA's practicality in showing strengths and weaknesses because of low retest-reliability scores. Thus, the emergent period began with the development and use of the ITPA and related interventions and closed with several investigators raising questions about the usefulness of both the test and related teaching practices.

Disorders of Written Language. Building on the works of Kirk, Monroe, Gillingham and Stillman, and Spalding, educators began to develop teaching strategies. The work of Helmer Myklebust exemplifies the increasing focus on educational strategies during this period. His original work in the 1950s focused on disorders in spoken language; however, by the 1960s, Myklebust had broadened his interest to include disorders of auditory language, reading, written language, math, and nonverbal disorders of learning (Johnson & Myklebust, 1967). Myklebust (1965) considered written language to be an individual's highest verbal achievement.

The investigators of written language helped develop an emphasis on teaching basic academic skills to students with learning disabilities. This approach became the focal point of many commercial materials. By the mid-1970s, commercial academic materials for students with learning disabilities were flourishing.

Disorders of Perceptual and Motor Processes. William Cruickshank, Glen Doman and Carl Delacato, and Marianne Frostig made important contributions in this area. Cruickshank's first major report on the Montgomery County Project (Cruickshank et al., 1961) highlighted the beginnings of a career that promoted intervention strategies based primarily on the theoretical foundations of Werner and Strauss. His highly structured lessons incorporated a multisensory approach in an environment of reduced stimuli. He suggested specific procedures for increasing visual discrimination and eye-hand coordination, auditory training, motor training, a kinesthetic approach to writing, concrete and practical methods for math, and strategies for teaching reading.

Because of his perceptual-motor orientation, the term *learning disability* troubled Cruickshank:

> The appearance of the term *learning disabilities* in 1963 opened a Pandora's box which has resulted in confusion, the phenomenon of the instant specialist, inappropriate definitions of the problem, and a major attempt by many to bring within the definition issues which are far removed from the initial concepts of perceptual disability. (Cruickshank, 1976, p. 109)

As a result of his dissatisfaction, Cruickshank and his doctoral student, Daniel Hallahan, coauthored a historical overview published in 1973 as *Psychoeducational Foundations of Learning Disabilities* (Hallahan & Cruickshank, 1973).

Delacato, an educational psychologist, collaborated in the late 1950s and early 1960s with Doman, a physical therapist, to construct a theory of neurological organization to guide treatment and education of children with brain injury. Doman and Delacato attempted to remediate learning problems by "repatterning" the brain (Delacato, 1963). While the public tends to accept their treatment procedures, professionals strongly criticize them.

Like Werner and Strauss, the Frostigs fled the Nazis in 1938 and settled in the United States. During the early 1950s, Frostig worked part-time with delinquents in Los Angeles. In testing, she noticed indications of perceptual deficits, especially disturbances in body image and spatial orientation, which she had seen earlier while working in Vienna and Poland. After reading Goldstein, Strauss and Lehtinen, and Werner, Frostig concluded that many of the children might be suffering from neurological dysfunction. Her further investigations led to the construction of the *Developmental Test of Visual Perception* (Frostig, Lefever, & Whittlesey, 1961; Frostig, Maslow, Lefever, & Whittlesey, 1964) and training materials for visual perceptual difficulties (Frostig & Horne, 1964).

The use of perceptual-motor tests and training activities flourished in the 1960s and early 1970s. However, in the 1970s, investigators began to question the efficacy of perceptual-motor programs. Hallahan and Cruickshank (1973) noted that little could be concluded about the effectiveness of such programs. Goodman and Hammill (1973) and Hammill, Goodman, and Wiederholt (1974) concluded that perceptual-motor programs did not significantly improve readiness skills, intelligence, academic achievement, or perceptual-motor performance. Likewise, the consensus of reviews of the Frostig materials was that visual perception training alone does not have a significant effect on reading achievement (Hammill et al., 1974; Hammill & Wiederholt, 1973). Thus, this period began with the development and widespread use of perceptual-motor programs and ended with several professionals questioning their usefulness.

Behavioral Theory

The behavioral theorists of this period refined the practical application of what earlier investigators had proposed. Most behavioral theorists assumed that behavior is modifiable, and the development, maintenance, and removal of behavior depends on environmental events or stimuli. Moreover, a lawful, functional relationship exists between behavior and environmental events. Hallahan and Kauffman (1976) suggest two reasons why the growth in the popularity of behavioral theory was related intimately to the interest in learning disabilities: (a) the application of behavioral modification to education can be viewed as an extension of the highly structured, directive approach found by many researchers to be successful with children with brain injury and mental retardation, and (b) the methods of behavior modification had a great influence on the development of educational methodology for all children with disabilities. It is apparent that behavior modification aids the student with learning disabilities and meets the demand for "accountability."

Works by Norris Haring, Ogden R. Lindsley, and Thomas C. Lovitt—three reinforcement theorists active in the 1960s—exemplify the development of reinforcement theory in education. Like the Strauss-Werner dynasty in the area of perceptual-motor research, a cadre of professionals investigated the potential applications of behavior modification. This group, centered primarily in Midwestern universities and the University of Washington, included Richard J. Whelan, Donald M. Baer, Wesley C. Becker, Sidney W. Bijou, Jay Birnbrauer, Florence Harris, R. Vance Hall, Todd R. Risley, and Montrose M. Wolf.

Haring's professional development paralleled the transition of learning disabilities from a focus on clinical investigation to practical educational application. Studying under Cruickshank at Syracuse University, Haring became aware of the need for establishing scientific objectivity in education. The Montgomery County Project (Cruickshank et al., 1961) convinced Haring of three things:

> First, there is a serious lack of procedures, personnel, and facilities for identifying the causes of individual and developmental differences. Second, statistical data and group studies are inadequate as methods of evaluation for instructional program curriculum guides, and psychological and achievement tests. Finally, there is a dichotomy between the philosophy and practice of individual instruction. (Haring, 1974, p. 80)

With E. Lakin Phillips, Haring combined Cruickshank's structured environment and Skinner's work in operant conditioning to develop educational programs for children with emotional disabilities (Haring & Phillips, 1962). As educational director of the Children's Rehabilitation Unit at the University of Kansas Medical Center, he hired the behavioral scientist Ogden R. Lindsley, who had studied with Skinner at Harvard, to develop measurements for classroom behavior. Their 5 years of work resulted in measurement procedures and educational methods more firmly rooted in learning research (Haring & Whelan, 1965; Lindsley, 1964; Whelan & Haring, 1966).

In 1965, Haring moved to the directorship of the Experimental Education Unit at the University of Washington in Seattle. There he formulated experimental techniques that focused on observable and measurable behavior, developed educational procedures based on operant conditioning, and based instructional decisions on behavioral data.

Lindsley successfully had applied operant techniques to the rehabilitation of patients with severe emotional disabilities in Boston. After joining the staff at the University of Kansas, he developed a comprehensive set of measurement procedures, which he called *precision teaching*. The system includes pinpointing behavior, counting and charting performance, and making instructional decisions based on performance data. Equally effective in the measurement of overt behavior and academic performance, it provides systematic procedures for making instructional decisions.

Lovitt's work highlights the use of behavioral theory in learning disabilities. A student of both Haring and Lindsley, he became interested in behavior modification when Haring asked him to report on every operant conditioning study—applied and basic—that had been published. From this review, Lovitt decided to investigate conjugate reinforcement with Lindsley.

Lovitt moved to the University of Washington in 1966 and continued to investigate conjugate reinforcement at the Experimental Education Unit, but his primary assignment was to coordinate the program in learning disabilities. His struggle to reconcile the tenets of behavioral theory and the "disorder" philosophy of learning disabilities (Lovitt, 1976) is representative of the problems that early behaviorists faced. Because Lovitt was close to teachers struggling with problem learners, however, his interests naturally focused on turning the methods of precision teaching and behavior modification toward learning disabilities and curriculum research (Haring & Lovitt, 1967; Lovitt, 1967, 1970).

Work in the 1970s extended the practical applications begun in the late 1960s, but no individual contribution dominated the area. Precision teaching began to move from the university and clinic into the school districts in 1972. The general application of behavioral theory for controlling behavior and teaching academic skills gained popularity with teachers.

During the mid-1970s, the ability-versus-skill issue intensified. The ability position, with its emphasis on correcting inner learning abilities (e.g., perception, and memory), began to lose support when the effectiveness of psycholinguistic teaching and perceptual-motor training was questioned seriously. Conversely, the direct instruction approach of the skill model (e.g., behavioral) began to receive more support. For example, Ysseldyke and Salvia (1974) strongly recommended the skill-oriented approach.

Cognitive Theory

The cognitive approach saw limited activity during the 1960s; however, a few events in the late 1960s and early 1970s had some influence on learning disabilities. Jean Piaget's developmental theory (Piaget, 1970; Piaget & Inhelder, 1969) was interpreted as having some implications for the field of learning disabilities. The theory purports that logical thinking develops in four maturational stages and that the child is capable of learning only selected tasks at each respective stage. According to Piaget's theory, instruction should allow for development of maturational experiences rather than require students to perform skills for which they are not ready.

Although a few investigators applied some cognitive theories to learning disabilities, the overall effect was minimal. Basically, the foundations were being established for cognitive theory to have a future effect.

Summary: Emergent Period

The acceptance of the term *learning disabilities* and the growth of intervention programs came quickly compared with the frequency of events before the 1960s. Significant events include the following:

1. Legislation reflected the mood of society, and federal aid to education was massive and indiscriminate. The public demanded imme-

diate change, regardless of the ability to deliver quality with the change.

2. In the investigation of disorders, theorists examining psycholinguistic and perceptual-motor aspects of learning emerged as the most influential in the learning disability movement. However, the period ended with growing skepticism about both approaches.
3. A label was coined and a definition was accepted to identify the movement and the children it served. While both have been criticized, they represent a beginning in bringing order and direction to the study of children with learning disabilities.
4. The growth, refinement, and acceptance of behavioral theory provided a useful tool for the treatment of learning disability problems. Conflict, however, was generated between proponents of behavioral techniques and advocates of "disorders" in the learning process.
5. The organization and strength of the ACLD and the DCLD provided an effective lobby for service, treatment, and financial aid to the learning disabilities movement. These groups (and others) stimulated research, interdisciplinary cooperation, and legislation on the state and national levels.
6. The cognitive theorists had minimal effect on learning disabilities in this period but developed important theoretical underpinnings.

Table 2.2 provides an overview of the events, individuals, and time sequences of the emergent period.

PUBLIC LAW 94-142 PERIOD

Although the passage of Public Law 94-142 highlights this period (1975–1987), the phenomenal growth in the field of learning disabilities on all fronts also characterizes this era. The learning disabilities movement matured from a few isolated parent groups to several national organizations with thousands of members. In 1978, for example, there were 35,000 dues-paying members of ACLD (now LDA), and in 1980 the DCLD (now CLD) had 9,600 members. The number of students with learning disabilities receiving special education services was not reported until 1969, when 120,000 children were identified (Kirk, 1972). By 1986–1987, the public schools were serving 1,926,097 students with learning disabilities (U.S. Department of Education, 1988). The recently released *Sixteenth Annual Report to Congress on the Implementation of the Individuals with Disabilities Education Act* (U.S. Department of Education, 1994) indicates that the learning disabilities category continues to grow. Gerber and Levine-Donnerstein (1989) report that over the 10-year period of 1977 to 1987, the number of students with learning disabilities represented 43% of all students receiving special education services. Moreover, they note that the number of students with learning disabilities served annually had increased 140% since 1977. Such rapid growth has severely strained education's resources and the ability of researchers to test the growing number of theories, models, and strategies proposed for use with these students.

Government Policy

On November 29, 1975, President Ford signed a landmark piece of federal legislation culminating more than 300 years of education evolution: the Education for All Handicapped Children Act (Public Law 94-142) (now the Individuals with Disabilities Education Act). Unlike most federal laws, this one was specific in its requirements. It ensured the provision of a free, appropriate education to all children with disabilities; established evaluation and assessment policy; guaranteed the right to due process of law; and established a process for financial support of educational services. It also mandated that *learning disabilities* be defined more precisely. Thus, the focus on the definition of the term during the 1975–1977 period was intense and controversial. After hearings, the rules and regulations for Public Law 94-142 were published in 1977 (USOE, 1977), greatly influencing the learning disabilities field. The legislation recognized learning disabilities as a disabling condition,

TABLE 2.2
Emergent Period (1961–1974)

			Type of Disorder				
	Government Policy	Organizations	Spoken Language	Written Language	Perceptual and Motor Processes	Behavioral Theory	Cognitive Theory
1961			McCarthy & Kirk developed ITPA		Cruickshank		
1962						Haring & Phillips	
1963		Kirk introduced term *learning disabilities*			Doman & Delacato		
1964		Assoc. for Children with Learning Disabilities			Frostig	Lindsley	
1965			Widespread use of ITPA and psycholin-guistic teaching		Extensive use of P-M tests and training activities		
1966	Clements reported use of MBD term in task forces sponsored by HEW					Lovitt	

1967				Johnson & Myklebust			
1968	Nat. Advisory Committee on Handicapped Children	Division for Children with Learning Disabilities					
1969	PL 91–230, Specific Learning Disabilities Act						
1970							Piaget
1972						Growing use of precision teaching and behavioral approach	
1973					Value of P-M programs questioned by researchers		
1974			Criticism of psycho-linguistic approach	Development of commercial materials on academics		Criticism of ability model	

eligible for all the services and rights available to other special education categories. In addition, in 1978, five research institutes in learning disabilities received federal funding.

Several investigators (Clark & Amiot, 1981; Iannaccone, 1981) indicate that major shifts in federal policy began in the late 1970s. Some politicians thought education should not be viewed as an arena for national policy initiates and that a return to state and local control (decentralization) of education was needed. The administration of President Reagan and Secretary of Education Terrel Bell took the first steps in this direction by announcing their intention to decrease federal involvement in education. The Reagan administration's attempt to de-emphasize special education (learning disabilities) met much resistance from parents, professionals, and organizations.

The attempt to decrease federal involvement in special education declined significantly in 1980, when Congress established the Department of Education. The Office of Special Education and Rehabilitative Services was created under this department in 1983. Moreover, the Department of Education decided to maintain Public Law 94-142 as a separate categorical program and continue to appropriate special funds to support it. In 1983, Public Law 98-199 reaffirmed the federal role in special education by expanding and including many components of Public Law 94-142. It especially supported better preschool, secondary, and postsecondary programs for students with disabilities, and it promoted special education teacher preparation, early childhood education, parent training, and dissemination of information.

In 1986, Public Law 99-457 was passed, extending the rights and provisions of Public Law 94-142 to infants and preschoolers and requiring the development of an individualized family service plan for these young children. Also Madeleine Will (1986) promoted the Regular Education Initiative (REI), which states that students with learning disabilities (and other exceptionalities) should be educated in the general classroom and maintains that pullout programs are ineffective. Many learning disabilities experts disagree with this position. (Chapter 6 discusses the REI.)

Organizations

Most of the organizations previously discussed continued to gain strength and to influence the direction of the learning disability movement. This growth in influence was accompanied by much professional disagreement and turbulence.

Dissatisfaction with some federal directions (such as the definition of learning disabilities) and the desire to stimulate a forum for discussion of critical issues led to the formation of the National Joint Committee for Learning Disabilities (NJCLD) in 1978. The committee consists of representatives from six organizations, which in 1981 presented a position paper (NJCLD, 1981) that criticized the 1977 *Federal Register* definition and offered a new one. The NJCLD continues to publish position papers on critical issues in the field.

Congress passed the Health Research Expansion Act (Public Law 99-158) in November 1985. Section 9 of this act established the formation of an Interagency Committee on Learning Disabilities (ICLD), which was instructed to review and assess federal research and activities concerning learning disabilities. Silver (1988) reviewed the new definition of learning disabilities recommended by the committee. (Chapter 1 presents the ICLD definition and its ramifications.)

As mentioned previously, the Council for Exceptional Children established a separate division for learning disabilities, the Division for Children with Learning Disabilities (DCLD), in 1968. In the early 1980s, much of the DCLD's membership, under the leadership of Don Hammill and his colleagues, objected to the council's policy of requiring members to join the CEC before they could join a division such as the DCLD. After heated debate among members and organizations, the DCLD membership voted in 1982 to withdraw from the CEC and form an independent organization, the Council for Learning Disabilities (CLD). Also in 1982, a cadre of former DCLD members began a new CEC division called the Division for Learning Disabilities (DLD). By the summer of 1985, membership in DLD had grown to 8,757.

The accomplishments of the ACLD (now the LDA), the CLD, the DLD, and other organizations during this period were significant. They developed and sustained funding for youth, lobbied for passage of Public Law 94-142 and for modification and strengthening of the 1977 federal rules and regulations for its implementation, developed and supported journals and newsletters, developed and published teacher competencies in an effort to improve classroom instruction and teacher training, stimulated and supported the organization of local and state chapters, and sponsored conferences and conventions.

As noted, friction and disagreement accompanied the development of these organizations. During the early 1980s, some of the conflicts among the organizations involved the competition for membership. However, these conflicts likely helped strengthen the field through public review of issues and positions and the respective solutions and findings. In the late 1980s, the organizations appeared to focus more on the issues within the field of learning disabilities (e.g., definition) and less on their individual organizational needs.

Type of Disorder

Disorders of Spoken Language. During the Public Law 94-142 period, professionals in the spoken language area refined their practices and clarified professional roles. The ITPA and psycholinguistic teaching continued to be questioned, and their use decreased significantly. Moreover, primarily through the work of Elisabeth Wiig and Eleanor Semel (1976, 1984), students with learning disabilities were examined and taught within the linguistic model. Also, the responsibility for oral language training shifted from the learning disabilities teacher (with the IPTA influence) to the speech and language specialist.

The 1977 *Federal Register* listed listening comprehension and oral language as two of the seven areas of learning disabilities. The number of commercial language tests dramatically increased, and the area of pragmatics (i.e., functional use of language) became important in the study of learning disabilities. Moreover, a subgroup of learning disabilities—language learning disabilities—became more prominent in the 1980s. Finally, a nationwide concern for students with limited English proficiency emerged. (Chapter 11 discusses the identification and treatment of students with limited English proficiency and learning disabilities.)

Disorders of Written Language. The 1977 *Federal Register* reaffirmed the emphasis on written language disabilities (i.e., disabilities in generating language in written form and decoding and understanding written language) as a primary problem among students with learning disabilities. Moreover, Public Law 94-142 required that an individual educational program (IEP) be developed for each student with learning disabilities. These trends boosted the academic training movement, which included an emphasis on written language disabilities as well as math disabilities. Commercial materials, especially criterion-oriented materials, proliferated in the late 1970s and early 1980s. Materials for adolescents with learning disabilities began to appear in the 1980s, along with literature concerning the adolescent and adult with learning disabilities. Learning strategies developed at the University of Kansas Institute for Research in Learning Disabilities (now the Center for Research on Learning Disabilities) dramatically affected the teaching of adolescents with learning disabilities. The use of microcomputers for teaching academics to students with learning disabilities also mushroomed in the 1980s.

Disorders of Perceptual and Motor Processes. In the 1970s, no major new theories appeared in this area, nor was the area dominated by an individual or group. Yet, early in the decade, commercial programs purporting to aid in perceptual-motor training flooded the market. Most of these materials had little validation, and the professional education literature in the mid-1970s marked a shift from the use of perceptual-motor (ability) models to skill models. Investigators such as Hammill and Larsen (1974, 1978), Vellutino, Steger, Moyer, Harding, and Niles (1977), and Stephens (1977) presented evidence indicating that the perceptual-motor models were of questionable value to educators, and the 1977 guidelines for implementation of Public Law 94-142 minimized their use. Debate ensued, with Kirk, Cruickshank, Frostig, and others strongly defending the ability model.

In the latter half of the 1970s, commercial educational programs began to orient toward criterion measurement, reflecting the shift from ability to skill models. Some attempts to promote the ability model also appeared (Ayres, 1975; Barbe & Swassing, 1979). Barbe and Swassing produced a commercial test designed to assess modality preferences, while occupational therapists began and continue to promote treatment methods based on Ayres's theory of sensory integration. To date, neither approach has presented data to counter the criticisms leveled at earlier ability-oriented treatments. Overall, the perceptual-motor approaches had little effect in the 1980s.

Behavioral Theory

With its emphasis on task analysis, criterion tasks, skill hierarchies, and record keeping of student progress, the behavioral approach was adapted easily to developing the IEPs required by Public Law 94-142. Coupled with the decreased use of perceptual-motor and psycholinguistic training programs, this characteristic made behavioral approaches more popular than ever during the Public Law 94-142 period. Advocates were eager to demonstrate the usefulness of reinforcement and direct instruction (Carnine & Silbert, 1979). Commercial precision teaching programs appeared in 1977–1978, and individuals such as Thomas M. Stephens (1977) demonstrated effective nonprecision teaching approaches based on direct instruction and reinforcement theory. By 1980, teaching strategies based on reinforcement were widespread. Moreover, in 1980, the *Journal of Precision Teaching* was founded. Hughes, Schmid, and Ruhl (1985) conducted a national survey of teacher preparation programs and reported that precision teaching content was included in the majority of the programs. During the late 1980s, the term *applied behavior analysis* gained popularity as a term describing behaviorally oriented approaches. Moreover, curriculum-based assessment (CBA) uses many components of precision teaching and is becoming the prominent data-based system for planning and monitoring instruction.

Although the behavioral approach accrued much research support for its effectiveness in remediating academic problems, several investigators (Poplin, 1984b; Reid & Hresko, 1981) claimed that the behavioral (reinforcement) approach was not sufficient for understanding and treating learning disabilities. These investigators recommended cognitive approaches for learning disabilities.

Cognitive Theory

In a speech at the first national conference of the Division of Children with Learning Disabilities, Don Hammill (1979) stated:

> I suspect that the rampant interest in Skinnerianism, the behavioral objectives, the skills-based problems, and the behavior mod programs has peaked and that we're moving very slowly but very deliberately into an age that is rediscovering cognitive principles. (p. 3)

Hammill and his colleagues continued to foster interest in cognitive approaches throughout the 1980s. In 1981, D. Kim Reid and Wayne P. Hresko published the first major text that stressed the cognitive approach to learning disabilities. Moreover, the entire fall 1984 issue of *Learning Disability Quarterly*, the journal of the Council for Learning Disabilities, was devoted to the cognitive (holistic) approach to learning disabilities. In addition, under the direction of Daniel Hallahan (1980), the University of Virginia Learning Disabilities Research Institute focused on the use of cognitive interventions with students with learning disabilities. Thus, the identification and treatment of students with learning disabilities was influenced by metacognition. In 1987, Wong reviewed metacognition's effect on learning disabilities and predicted continued growth.

During the 1980s, Don Deshler, Jean Schumaker, Keith Lenz, and their colleagues at the University of Kansas Institute for Research in Learning Disabilities (now the Center for Research on Learning) developed the strategies intervention model and prepared a nationwide network of strategy trainers. Their learning strategies, primarily for adolescents with learning disabilities, have become a curriculum component of middle and secondary school programs throughout the nation. Although their learning strategies draw from numerous models, such as the behavioral and ecological models, they primarily are based on cognitive theory and research. During the late 1980s, cognitive-oriented interventions and interventions based on dual orientations dominated the research in learning disabilities and greatly influenced teaching practices. (Chapter 8 discusses the cognitive approach.)

Summary: Public Law 94-142 Period

Poplin (1984a) captures the tremendous growth of this period in her statement "The development of our field has been so explosive that it is difficult to imagine it as it existed even 10 years ago" (p. 2). The passage of Public Law 94-142 and its inclusion of learning disabilities as a disabling condition began this exciting period. The following are some of the main events:

1. Active federal involvement continued throughout the period with the passage of Public Law 94-142 in 1975, the release of the 1977 *Federal Register,* the funding of five learning disabilities research institutes in 1978, the passage of Public Law 98-199 in 1983, and the passage of Public Law 99-457 in 1986.
2. The learning disabilities organizations experienced a stormy but effective period. By 1982, the field was supporting three large organizations: the ACLD (now the LDA), the CLD, and the DLD. These groups were influential in lobbying for supportive legislation and maintaining an active forum for discussion and dissemination of information.
3. The respective disorder areas experienced a movement toward the skill model. The spoken language area became the domain of language specialists. New language tests were published, and pragmatics flourished as an area of language study. The influence of the perceptual-motor area diminished, and its effect continued to be limited.
4. A strong academic emphasis emerged from the written language movement, and commercial materials and computer-assisted instruction appeared.
5. The reinforcement approaches (i.e., direct instruction, precision teaching, behavior modification, and criterion tasks) flourished as viable interventions for students with learning disabilities.
6. In the early 1980s, the cognitive approaches gained significance in the field of learning disabilities. By the late 1980s, cognitive approaches became a major instructional movement in learning disabilities.

Table 2.3 includes individuals and events that were significant during the Public Law 94-142 period.

CONTEMPORARY DIRECTIONS

The area of learning disabilities has made much progress in its brief existence. Public interest has been generated, litigation initiated, legislation written and passed, educational programs developed, and professional organizations established. The field has been active in identifying the issues and confronting them forthrightly. Currently the field of learning disabilities is in a period of transition, and it is difficult to pinpoint the end of the Public Law 94-142 period and the beginning of a new era. Because the field is in an undefined phase, the time period beginning in 1988 is discussed under the title Contemporary Directions.

Many special educators (Hammill, 1993; Kauffman, 1994; Mather & Roberts, 1994; Moats & Lyon, 1993) believe the field of learning disabilities is entering a turbulent transition or reform period. Kauffman maintains that special education and, specifically, learning disabilities is in trouble because special educators have failed to deliver consistent and quality services. Moreover, he believes that many special education leaders have been too timid to respond to the "mugging" that special education has received in the popular press. Moreover, Mather and Roberts note that the movement to include learning disabilities under the umbrella of mild disabilities threatens the existence of the field. Moats and Lyon fear that the needs of students with learning disabilities may begin to seem unimportant in comparison with the issues of crime, poverty, substance abuse, and civil unrest.

Social, political, economic, and professional forces of change are going to have a major effect on the field of learning disabilities in the near future. Fortunately, the field of learning disabilities has an enormous pool of talented professionals, individuals with learning disabilities, and parents of youngsters with learning disabilities who accept challenges and work vigorously to find better answers to complex problems. This section presents some of the latest developments regarding individuals with learning disabilities and the services that are needed to help them.

TABLE 2.3
Public Law 94-142 Period (1975–1987)

	Government Policy	Organizations	Type of Disorder: Spoken Language	Written Language	Perceptual and Motor Processes	Behavioral Theory	Cognitive Theory
1975	PL 94-142		Decreased use of ITPA and psycholinguistic teaching		Shift from use of P-M models to skill models		
1977	Federal regulations for PL 94-142		Listening comprehension and oral language listed as disabilities			Increase in use of precision teaching and direct instruction	
1978	Federal funding of five research institutes in LD	National Joint Committee on Learning Disabilities	Oral language training provided by speech-language specialists	Widespread use of criterion-oriented materials			
1979	Federal de-emphasis of education				Some interest in ability model based on works of Ayres, and Barbe and Swassing		Support of cognitive approach by Hammill
1980	Establishment of Dept. of Education LD category intact at federal level		Importance of pragmatics	Increased emphasis on LD adolescent and adult	P-M is widely criticized	Founding of *Journal of Precision Teaching*	Cognitive interventions stressed by UVa LD Research Institute

continued

TABLE 2.3
continued

	Government Policy	Organizations	Type of Disorder: Spoken Language	Type of Disorder: Written Language	Type of Disorder: Perceptual and Motor Processes	Behavioral Theory	Cognitive Theory
1981		Proposal of new LD definition by NJCLD	Increase in commercial language tests				Publication of Reid & Hresko text on cognitive approach to LD
1982		DCLD withdrawal from CEC and formation of Council for Learning Disabilities Division for Learning Disabilities begun by cadre of former DCLD members	Subgroup of LD–language learning disabilities	Increased use of microcomputers			
1983	Creation of Office of Special Education and Rehabilitative Services PL 98-199						

1984				Learning strategies developed at University of Kansas have major effect on teaching LD adolescents	Minimal effect of P-M approaches	Precision teaching content included in many teacher training programs	Metacognition influences identification and treatment of LD
1985		Interagency Committee on Learning Disabilities					
1986	PL 99-457 Will promotes Regular Education Initiative		Concern for students with limited English proficiency				
1987	Regular Education Initiative becomes major issue Many experts disagree with REI rationale and potential benefits					*Applied behavior analysis* becomes popular term Curriculum-based assessment emerges as a primary assessment system	Wong reviews metacognition in LD and predicts continued growth Cognitive approaches influence teaching practices

Legislation

On October 30, 1990, President Bush signed Public Law 101-476, the Education of the Handicapped Act Amendments of 1990, which changed the name of the law to the Individuals with Disabilities Education Act (IDEA). Throughout the law, the term *handicapped* is replaced with the term *disabilities,* and the general definition of children with disabilities is expanded to include children with autism and traumatic brain injury as separate categories. Attention deficit disorder is not included as a new category, but these youngsters currently may be eligible for services under the Other Health Impairments category or by meeting criteria of existing special education categories. An additional major change involves the specification that states, including state departments of education, are not immune from private lawsuits under IDEA. Also, the new law defines *transition services* as a coordinated set of activities, based upon the individual student's needs, that promotes movement from school to postschool activities including postsecondary education, vocational training, integrated employment, adult services, and community participation. Other changes include (a) greater emphasis on meeting the needs of ethnically and culturally diverse children with disabilities, (b) the development of early intervention programs to address the needs of children prenatally exposed to maternal substance abuse, (c) the continuation of an information dissemination program through the establishment of centers in each state that provide parents with training and materials about special education, and (d) the authorization of funding to continue three national information clearinghouses on children and youth with disabilities. Moreover, in 1991, Public Law 102-119 amended IDEA to provide comprehensive services to infants, toddlers, and preschool children who are eligible through a noncategorical identification (such as developmental delay) or a category of disability. Thus, IDEA and related legislation reflects the current emphasis on providing coordinated services to many individuals with a broad range of disabilities.

Definition

The search for an acceptable definition for *learning disabilities* continues to be an issue in the field. Lyon (1995) maintains that the field of learning disabilities still lacks definitions that are logically consistent, easily operationalized, and empirically validated. Hammill (1993) notes that a consensus is emerging regarding a theoretical definition that frames the conceptual basis of learning disabilities; however, he points out that much work is needed to develop reliable and valid criteria that operationalize definitions of learning disabilities. The definition issue has not received extensive attention for several years, but recent events suggest that significant changes are forthcoming. The emergence of social skills deficits as a major characteristic of students with learning disabilities is causing debate regarding the learning disabilities definition. Moreover, some researchers (Mather & Roberts, 1994; Zigmond, 1993) maintain that intelligence testing is irrelevant to identifying learning disabilities, and they recommend alternative measures. Shaw, Cullen, McGuire, and Brinckerhoff (1995) propose a four-phase model for identifying learning disabilities that omits intelligence testing. Finally, in a survey of 37 educators, Putnam, Spiegel, and Bruininks (1995) found that the respondents predicted that categorical labels (such as *learning disabilities*) will be considered of little value in school settings after the year 2000. If these predictions are correct, the field of learning disabilities will require much restructuring. (Chapter 1 presents detailed coverage of definitions of learning disabilities and related practices, and Chapter 5 presents assessment practices for identifying learning disabilities.)

Heterogeneity of Learning Disabilities

Some students with learning disabilities have reading problems. Others read well but have math problems. Likewise, some youngsters with learning disabilities are hyperactive, and others are reserved and quiet. Clearly, individuals with learning disabilities are not a homogeneous group. Because of the heterogeneity of learning disabilities, numerous researchers have focused on identifying subgroups. These attempts to validate learning disabilities subtypes over the past 30 years have not been successful (Kavale & Forness, 1987). Given the heterogeneity of individuals with learning disabilities, Mather and Roberts (1994) claim that the most useful analysis exists at the individual level through a careful examination of the characteristics and needs of each student. (Chapter 1 covers the characteristics of learning disabilities and discusses the heterogeneity of the population with learning disabilities.)

Assessment

Learning disabilities assessment remains an area of concern, debate, and change. Despite the abundance of standardized commercial tests, reliable, valid, and instructionally relevant tests still are needed, and perhaps some of the recent and forthcoming tests will be helpful. The amount of time and monies allotted to test administration continues to be challenged, and the usefulness of intelligence tests for classifying learning disabilities is being questioned. Many authorities are recommending that more time be devoted to instruction and less time to assessment, and curriculum-based assessment appears to be gaining in use. (Chapter 5 discusses the assessment of learning disabilities, and Chapters 8 to 15 present basic assessment practices in respective areas.)

Life-Span View of Learning Disabilities

Until recently, the field of learning disabilities focused on the elementary-age child. Now professionals are focusing on both the younger (infant to 5 years) and older (adolescent to adult) individual with learning disabilities. Whereas earlier organizations included the word *children* in their titles, more recently formed organizations (CLD, DLD, LDA) do not. Likewise, earlier definitions use the word *children,* while current definitions use *persons* or *individuals.* A recent report to Congress on the implementation of IDEA indicates that preschool, secondary, and postsecondary services are increasing (U.S. Department of Education, 1994). The passage of Public Law 99-457 has resulted in a dramatic increase in programs for children with disabilities from birth to age 5. Likewise, the number of students with disabilities who are 18 to 21 years old and are served by provisions of the law has increased substantially in the last 5 years; in fact, services for students through age 21 are mandated in many states. Some interesting findings are being reported from studies of successful adults with learning disabilities (Reiff, Ginsberg, & Gerber, 1995). Moreover, the development of college programs for individuals with learning disabilities is receiving much attention. (Chapter 1 discusses the life-span view of learning disabilities in more detail. Chapter 9 focuses on early identification and treatment, and Chapter 10 stresses current directions in serving adolescents and adults with learning disabilities.)

Teaching Methodology

Fortunately, the search for improved teaching methods continues to be a major direction in the study of learning disabilities. Researchers are organizing the vast findings about effective instructional practices into pre-instructional factors, interactive instructional factors, and postinstructional factors (Reynolds, 1992). (Chapter 7 features these factors.) Given the heterogeneity of students with learning disabilities and the move to educate more students in general education classes, a variety of instructional practices are required to meet the needs of the diverse learner. Many researchers (Bateman, 1992; Kauffman, 1994; Mather & Roberts, 1994; Moats & Lyon, 1993) claim that the key issue regarding the future of learning disabilities is quality of instruction. To a large extent this quality will depend on the use of a range of instructional choices that empower teachers to teach and students to learn. These choices consist of an array of strategies from holistic and reductionistic paradigms. Thus, direct instruction, explicit instruction, guided discovery, and self-discovery learning will need to exist in the same classroom (Mercer, Lane, Jordan, Allsopp, & Eisele, in press). The fall 1994 issue of *The Journal of Special Education* highlights the need to provide explicit or direct instruction to students with learning disabilities as a function of their prior knowledge and learning needs. Moreover, implicit or holistic instruction appears appropriate for students with extensive prior knowledge. Thus, it appears that the coexistence of instructional strategies from paradigms that traditionally have been at odds will be essential in inclusive classrooms. Philosophical barriers are being removed to create instructional strategies that are effective for a class of diverse learners. (Chapters 7 and 8 highlight this integrated instructional movement.)

Applications of Technology

In addition to providing the teacher with another means of individualizing instruction, computers can perform routine accounting tasks involved in grading, monitoring IEPs, and filing progress reports. Investigators stress that teachers need to be computer-literate if computer applications are to approach their potential for assisting with classroom instruction and management. To help educators develop computer literacy and become acquainted with appropriate software, professional journals (e.g., *Journal of Learning Disabilities, Learning Disabilities Research & Practice,* and *Learning Disability Quarterly*) frequently feature articles on computers. Textbooks, journals, inservice workshops, technology, and courses on technology applications in education are flourishing. Technology has the power to revolutionize the way students with learning disabilities are taught, and it has the potential to individualize instruction to a diverse group of learners simultaneously. (Computer applications in the field of learning disabilities are presented throughout this book. Each chapter either features a section on microcomputing or covers it within the topical content. Chapter 7 provides a detailed discussion of technology applications in teaching students with learning disabilities.)

Service Delivery

The educational placement of students with learning disabilities remains one of the biggest issues of the 1990s. In their survey of 37 educators regarding future directions, Putnam et al. (1995) found that most respondents believe both that inclusive education will continue and that the belief that individuals with disabilities have a right to participate in inclusive settings will increase. Although some professionals are optimistic about inclusion, the movement to educate all students with learning disabilities in general education classrooms continues to be controversial. To some, the inclusion movement represents a reduction of essential instructional services to students with learning disabilities and a threat to the existence of the area of learning disabilities within the educational structure. To others, inclusion represents an opportunity for students with learning disabilities to function successfully in a community of diverse learners without the stigmatization of being segregated. Consultation, or teachers helping teachers, has become a widely endorsed service option. Many researchers and experts have helped develop and refine consultation approaches and techniques. (Chapter 6 presents the inclusion issue and service delivery alternatives.)

PERSPECTIVE

The learning disabilities field never has lacked controversy, change, and, it can be hoped, positive growth. The field faces many important issues (e.g., definition, identification and assessment, heterogeneity, inclusion, and differential instruction) but is embarking on some new and perhaps promising directions (e.g., life-span programming, integrated instructional approaches, and technology applications). Lovitt (1989) captures much of the spirit of controversy and inquiry that characterizes the field of learning disabilities in the following statement:

> The study of learning disabilities is indeed an adventure. . . . It has had its ups and downs, its agreements and controversies and its heroes and villains. It is a frustrating field in that we are today debating some of the issues that were raised two or three decades ago. This is particularly true with respect to definitions and placement. But on the bright side, there are many more options today than there were 20 to 30 years ago. There are certainly more choices when it comes to assessment and curriculum. . . . There is more concern now than there once was with a wider age range of youngsters. . . . These expansions are causes for optimism in our field. (p. 484)

DISCUSSION/REVIEW QUESTIONS

1. Identify each of the seven areas that have had a significant impact on the history of learning disabilities.
2. Identify the three time periods in the history of learning disabilities and the major events in each period.
3. Trace the sequence of governmental events from the foundation period through the Public Law 94-142 period.
4. Trace the primary developments in learning disabilities organizations from the foundation period through the Public Law 94-142 period.
5. Discuss the primary theories and practices in spoken language disabilities across the three time periods.
6. Discuss the primary theories and practices in written language disabilities across the three time periods.
7. Discuss the major positions and practices in perceptual and motor theory across the three time periods.
8. Describe the contributions of behavioral theory across the three time periods.
9. Describe the contributions of cognitive theory across the three time periods.
10. Discuss contemporary directions in learning disabilities.

REFERENCES

Ayres, A. J. (1975). Sensorimotor foundations of academic ability. In W. M. Cruickshank & D. P. Hallahan (Eds.), *Perception and learning disabilities in children* (Vol. 2, pp. 301–358). Syracuse, NY: Syracuse University Press.

Barbe, W. B., & Swassing, R. H. (1979). *Teaching through modality strengths: Concepts and practices.* Columbus, OH: Zaner-Bloser.

Bateman, B. (1992). Learning disabilities: The changing landscape. *Journal of Learning Disabilities, 25,* 29–36.

Bruner, J. S., Goodnow, J. J., & Austin, G. (1956). *A study of thinking.* New York: Wiley.

Carnine, D., & Silbert, J. (1979). *Direct instruction reading.* Upper Saddle River, NJ: Merrill/Prentice Hall

Chomsky, N. (1959). A review of B. F. Skinner's *Verbal Behavior. Language, 35,* 26–58.

Clark, D. L., & Amiot, M. A. (1981). The impact of the Reagan administration on federal education policy. *Phi Delta Kappan, 63,* 258–262.

Clements, S. D. (1966). *Minimal brain dysfunction in children* (NINDS Monograph No. 3, U.S. Public Health Service Publication No. 1415). Washington, DC: U.S. Government Printing Office.

Cruickshank, W. M. (1976). William M. Cruickshank. In J. M. Kauffman & D. P. Hallahan (Eds.), *Teaching children with learning disabilities: Personal perspectives* (pp. 94–127). Upper Saddle River, NJ: Merrill/Prentice Hall.

Cruickshank, W. M., Bentzen, F. A., Ratzeburg, R. H., & Tannhauser, M. T. (1961). *A teaching method for brain-injured and hyperactive children.* Syracuse, NY: Syracuse University Press.

Delacato, C. H. (1963). *The diagnosis and treatment of speech and reading problems.* Springfield, IL: Charles C Thomas.

Dolphin, J. E. (1950). *A study of certain aspects of the psychopathology of children with cerebral palsy.* Unpublished doctoral dissertation, Syracuse University, Syracuse NY.

Fernald, G. M. (1943). *Remedial techniques in basic school subjects.* New York: McGraw-Hill.

Frostig, M., & Horne, D. (1964). *The Frostig program for the development of visual perception: Teacher's guide.* Chicago: Follett.

Frostig, M., Lefever, D. W., & Whittlesey, J. R. B. (1961). A developmental test of visual perception for evaluating normal and neurologically handicapped children. *Perceptual and Motor Skills, 12,* 383–394.

Frostig, M., Maslow, P., Lefever, D. W., & Whittlesey, J. R. B. (1964). *The Marianne Frostig Developmental Test of Visual Perception: 1963 standardization.* Palo Alto, CA: Consulting Psychologists Press.

Gagné, R. M. (1965). *The conditions of learning.* New York: Holt, Rinehart & Winston.

Gerber, M. M., & Levine-Donnerstein, D. (1989). Educating all children: Ten years later. *Exceptional Children, 56,* 17–27.

Gillingham, A., & Stillman, B. (1936). *Remedial work for reading, spelling and penmanship.* New York: Hackett & Wilhelms.

Goldstein, K. (1936). The modifications of behavior consequent to cerebral lesions. *Psychiatric Quarterly, 10,* 586–610.

Goldstein, K. (1939). *The organism.* New York: American Book.

Goodman, L., & Hammill, D. (1973). The effectiveness of the Kephart-Getman activities in developing perceptual-motor and cognitive skills. *Focus on Exceptional Children, 4,* 1–9.

Hallahan, D. P. (Ed.). (1980). Teaching exceptional children to use cognitive strategies. *Exceptional Education Quarterly, 1,* 1–102.

Hallahan, D. P., & Cruickshank, W. M. (1973). *Psychoeducational foundations of learning disabilities.* Upper Saddle River, NJ: Prentice Hall.

Hallahan, D. P., & Kauffman, J. M. (1976). *Introduction to learning disabilities: A psycho-behavioral approach.* Upper Saddle River, NJ: Prentice Hall.

Hammill, D. D. (1979, October). *The field of learning disabilities: A futuristic perspective.* Paper presented at the National DCLD Conference on Learning Disabilities, Louisville, KY.

Hammill, D. D. (1993). A brief look at the learning disabilities movement in the United States. *Journal of Learning Disabilities, 26,* 295–310.

Hammill, D. D., Goodman, L., & Wiederholt, J. L. (1974). Visual-motor processes: Can we train them? *Reading Teacher, 27,* 469–478.

Hammill, D. D., & Larsen, S. C. (1974). The effectiveness of psycholinguistic training. *Exceptional Children, 41,* 5–14.

Hammill, D. D., & Larsen, S. C. (1978). The effectiveness of psycholinguistic training: A reaffirmation of position. *Exceptional Children, 44,* 402–414.

Hammill, D. D., & Wiederholt, J. L. (1973). Review of the *Frostig Visual Perception Test* and the related training program. In L. Mann & D. Sabatino (Eds.), *The first review of special education* (Vol. 1, pp. 33–48). Philadelphia: Journal of Special Education Press.

Haring, N. G. (1974). Norris G. Haring. In J. M. Kauffman & C. D. Lewis (Eds.), *Teaching children with behavior disorders.* Upper Saddle River, NJ: Merrill/Prentice Hall.

Haring, N. G., & Lovitt, T. C. (1967). Operant methodology and educational technology in special education. In N. G. Haring & R. L. Schiefelbusch (Eds.), *Methods in special education* (pp. 12–48). New York: McGraw-Hill.

Haring, N. G., & Phillips, E. L. (1962). *Educating emotionally disturbed children.* New York: McGraw-Hill.

Haring, N. G., & Whelan, R. J. (1965). Experimental methods in education and management. In N. J. Long, W. C. Morse, & R. G. Newman (Eds.), *Conflict in the classroom.* Belmont, CA: Wadsworth.

Head, H. (1926). *Aphasia and kindred disorders of speech* (Vols. 1 & 2). London: Cambridge University Press.

Hegge, T. G., Kirk, S. A., & Kirk, W. D. (1936). *Remedial reading drills.* Ann Arbor, MI: George Wahr.

Hegge, T. G., Kirk, S. A., & Kirk, W. D. (1970). *Remedial reading drills* (2nd ed.). Ann Arbor, MI: George Wahr.

Hilgard, E., & Bower, G. (1966). *Theories of learning.* New York: Appleton-Century-Crofts.

Hill, W. F. (1963). *Learning: A survey of psychological interpretation.* San Francisco: Chandler.

Hinshelwood, J. (1917). *Congenital word blindness.* London: Lewis.

Homme, L. H. (1969). *How to use contingency contracting in the classroom.* Champaign, IL: Research Press.

Hughes, C., Schmid, R., & Ruhl, K. (1985). *National survey of special education teacher preparation programs: Content and methods.* Unpublished manuscript, University of Florida, Gainesville.

Iannaccone, L. (1981). The Reagan presidency. *Journal of Learning Disabilities, 14,* 55–59.

Johnson, D., & Myklebust, H. R. (1967). *Learning disabilities: Educational principles and practices.* New York: Grune & Stratton.

Kauffman, J. M. (1994). Places of change: Special education's power and identity in an era of educational reform. *Journal of Learning Disabilities, 27,* 610–618.

Kavale, K. A., & Forness, S. R. (1987). The far side of heterogeneity: A critical analysis of empirical subtyping research in learning disabilities. *Journal of Learning Disabilities, 20,* 374–382.

Kephart, N. C. (1960). *The slow learner in the classroom.* Upper Saddle River, NJ: Merrill/Prentice Hall.

Kirk, S. A. (1972). *Educating exceptional children* (2nd ed.). Boston: Houghton Mifflin.

Kirk, S. A. (1976). Samuel A. Kirk. In J. M. Kauffman & D. P. Hallahan (Eds.), *Teaching children with learning disabilities: Personal perspectives* (pp. 238–269). Upper Saddle River, NJ: Merrill/Prentice Hall.

Lindsley, O. R. (1964). Direct measurement and prosthesis of retarded behavior. *Journal of Education, 147,* 62–81.

Lovitt, T. C. (1967). The use of conjugate reinforcement to evaluate the relative reinforcing effects of various narrative forms. *Journal of Experimental Child Psychology, 5,* 164–171.

Lovitt, T. C. (1970). Behavior modification: Where do we go from here? *Exceptional Children, 37,* 157–167.

Lovitt, T. C. (1976). Thomas C. Lovitt. In J. M. Kauffman & D. P. Hallahan (Eds.), *Teaching children with learning disabilities: Personal perspectives* (pp. 270–304). Upper Saddle River, NJ: Merrill/Prentice Hall.

Lovitt, T. C. (1989). *Introduction to learning disabilities.* Boston: Allyn & Bacon.

Lyon, G. R. (1995). Research initiatives in learning disabilities: Contributions from scientists supported by the National Institute of Child Health and Human Development. *Journal of Child Neurology, 10*(Suppl. 1), 120–126.

Mather, N., & Roberts, R. (1994). Learning disabilities: A field in danger of extinction? *Learning Disabilities Research & Practice, 9,* 49–58.

McCarthy, J. J., & Kirk, S. A. (1961). *Illinois Test of Psycholinguistic Abilities: Experimental edition.* Urbana, IL: University of Illinois Press.

Mercer, C. D., Lane, H. B., Jordan, L., Allsopp, D. H., & Eisele, M. R. (in press). Empowering teachers and students with instructional choices in inclusive settings. *Remedial and Special Education.*

Moats, L. C., & Lyon, G. R. (1993). Learning disabilities in the United States: Advocacy, science, and the future of the field. *Journal of Learning Disabilities, 26,* 282–294.

Monroe, M. (1932). *Children who cannot read.* Chicago: University of Chicago Press.

Myklebust, H. R. (1955). Training aphasic children. *Volta Review, 57,* 149–157.

Myklebust, H. R. (1960). *The psychology of deafness.* New York: Grune & Stratton.

Myklebust, H. R. (1965). *Development and disorders of written language.* New York: Grune & Stratton.

National Joint Committee on Learning Disabilities. (1981). *Learning disabilities: Issues on definition.* Unpublished manuscript. (Available from The Orton Dyslexia Society, 724 York Road, Baltimore, MD 21204)

Orton, S. T. (1937). *Reading, writing and speech problems in children.* New York: Norton.

Osgood, C. E., & Miron, M. S. (1963). *Approaches to the study of aphasia.* Urbana, IL: University of Illinois Press.

Piaget, J. (1970). Piaget's theory. In P. H. Mussen (Ed.), *Carmichael's manual of child psychology* (Vol. 1, pp. 703–732) (3rd ed.). New York: Wiley.

Piaget, J., & Inhelder, B. (1969). *The psychology of the child.* New York: Basic Books.

Poplin, M. S. (1984a). Research practices in learning disabilities. *Learning Disability Quarterly, 7,* 2–5.

Poplin, M. S. (1984b). Summary rationalizations, apologies and farewell: What we don't know about the learning disabled. *Learning Disability Quarterly, 7,* 129–134.

Putnam, J. W., Spiegel, A. N., & Bruininks, R. H. (1995). Future directions in education and inclusion of students with disabilities: A Delphi investigation. *Exceptional Children, 61,* 553–576.

Reid, D. K., & Hresko, W. P. (1981). *A cognitive approach to learning disabilities.* New York: McGraw-Hill.

Reiff, H. B., Ginsberg, R., & Gerber, P. J. (1995). New perspectives on teaching from successful adults with learning disabilities. *Remedial and Special Education, 16*(1), 29–37.

Reynolds, A. (1992). What is competent beginning teaching? A review of the literature. *Review of Educational Research, 62,* 1–35.

Shaw, S. F., Cullen, J. P., McGuire, J. M., & Brinckerhoff, L. C. (1995). Operationalizing a definition of learning disabilities. *Journal of Learning Disabilities, 28,* 586–597.

Silver, L. B. (1988). A review of the federal government's Interagency Committee on Learning Disabilities Report to the U.S. Congress. *Learning Disabilities Focus, 35,*73–80.

Skinner, B. F. (1953). *Science and human behavior.* Upper Saddle River, NJ: Prentice Hall.

Skinner, B. F. (1963). Reflections on a decade of teaching machines. *Teacher's College Record, 65,* 168–177.

Spalding, R. B., & Spalding, W. T. (1962). *The writing road to reading: A modern method of phonics for teaching children to read.* New York: Morrow.

Stephens, T. M. (1977). *Teaching skills to children with learning and behavior disorders.* Upper Saddle River NJ: Merrill/Prentice Hall.

Strauss, A. A., & Kephart, N. C. (1955). *Psychopathology and education of the brain-injured child: Progress in theory and clinic* (Vol. 2). New York: Grune & Stratton.

Strauss, A. A., & Lehtinen, L. E. (1947). *Psychopathology and education of the brain-injured child.* New York: Grune & Stratton.

Strauss, A. A., & Werner, H. (1942). Disorders of conceptual thinking in the brain-injured child. *Journal of Nervous and Mental Disease, 96,* 153–172.

U.S. Department of Education. (1988). *Tenth annual report to Congress on the implementation of the Education of the Handicapped Act.* Washington, DC: Author.

U.S. Department of Education. (1994). *To assure the free appropriate public education of all children with disabilities: Sixteenth annual report to Congress on the implementation of the Individuals with Disabilities Education Act.* Washington, DC: Author.

U.S. Office of Education. (1977). Assistance of states for education of handicapped children: Procedures for evaluating specific learning disabilities. *Federal Register, 42*(250), 65082–65085.

Vellutino, F. R., Steger, B. M., Moyer, S. C., Harding, C. J., & Niles, J. A. (1977). Has the perceptual deficit hypothesis led us astray? *Journal of Learning Disabilities, 10,* 375–385.

Wepman, J. M., Jones, L. V., Buck, R. D., & Van Pelt, D. (1960). Studies in aphasia: Background and theoretical formulations. *Journal of Speech and Hearing Disorders, 25,* 323–332.

Werner, H., & Strauss, A. A. (1939). Types of visuo-motor activities in their relation to low and high performance ages. *Proceedings of the American Association of Mental Deficiency, 44,* 163–168.

Werner, H., & Strauss, A. A. (1940). Causal factors in low performance. *American Journal of Mental Deficiency, 44,* 163–168.

Werner, H., & Strauss, A. A. (1941). Pathology of figure-background relation in the child. *Journal of Abnormal and Social Psychology, 36,* 236–248.

Whelan, R. J., & Haring, N. G. (1966). Modification and maintenance of behavior through systematic application of consequences. *Exceptional Children, 32,* 281–289.

Wiederholt, J. L. (1974). Historical perspectives on the education of the learning disabled. In L. Mann & D. Sabatino (Eds.), *The second review of special education* (pp. 103–152). Philadelphia: Journal of Special Education Press.

Wiig, E. H., & Semel, E. M. (1976). *Language disabilities in children and adolescents.* Boston: Allyn & Bacon.

Wiig, E. H., & Semel, E. (1984). *Language assessment and intervention for the learning disabled* (2nd ed.). Boston: Allyn & Bacon.

Will, M. C. (1986). Educating children with learning problems: A shared responsibility. *Exceptional Children, 52,* 411–415.

Wong, B. Y. L. (1987). How do the results of metacognitive research impact on the learning disabled individual? *Learning Disability Quarterly, 10,* 189–195.

Ysseldyke, J. E., & Salvia, J. (1974). Diagnostic-prescriptive teaching: Two models. *Exceptional Children, 41,* 181–186.

Zigmond, N. (1993). Learning disabilities from an educational perspective. In G. R. Lyon, D. B. Gray, J. F. Kavanagh, & N. A. Krasnegor (Eds.), *Better understanding learning disabilities: New views from research and their implications for education and public policies* (pp. 251–272). Baltimore: Brookes.

Medical Aspects

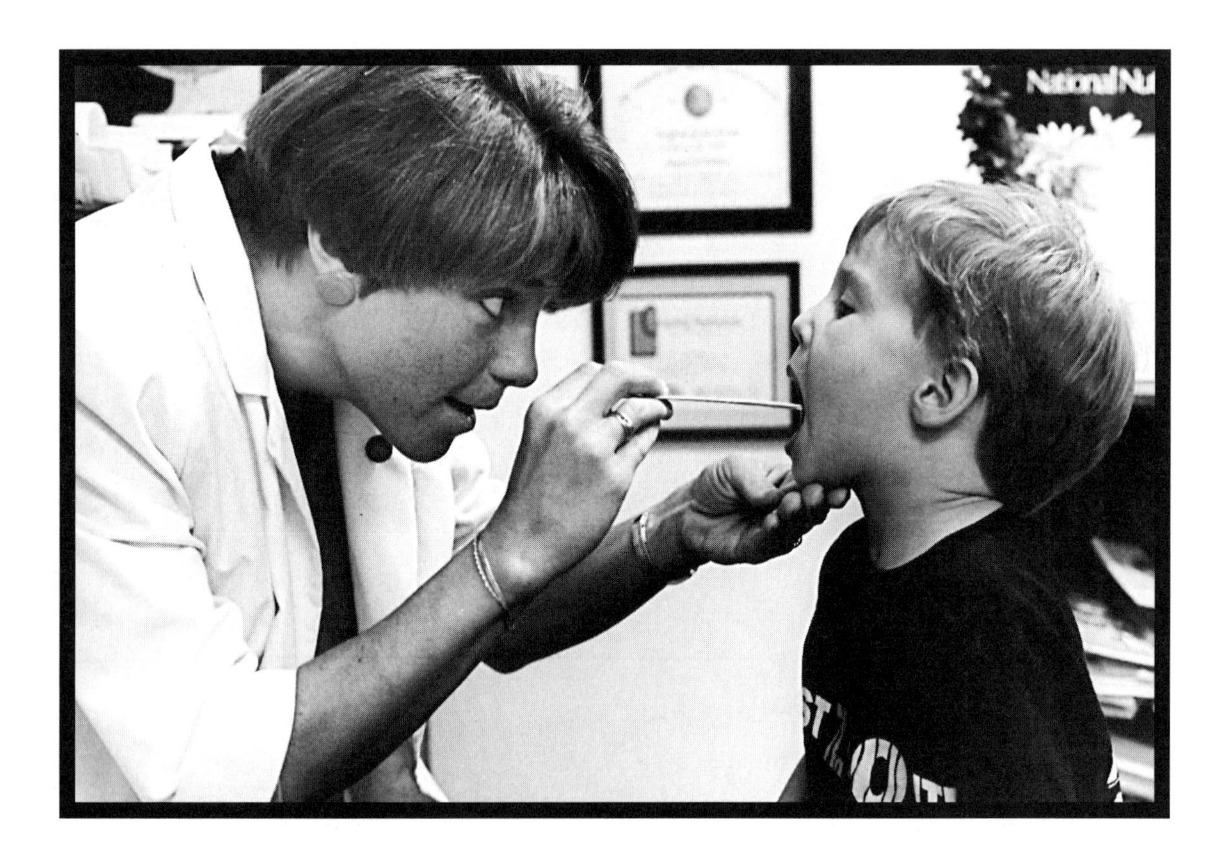

CHAPTER 3

After studying this chapter, you should be able to:

- identify the normal structure and function of the central nervous system.
- discuss neurodiagnostic procedures, and present current neurobiological findings concerning central nervous system dysfunction.
- discuss medically related etiological perspectives of learning disabilities, including acquired trauma, genetic influences, environmental influences, and biochemical abnormalities.
- present diagnostic criteria for attention-deficit hyperactivity disorder.
- discuss pharmacological treatments for learning disabilities.
- describe controversial medical treatments including patterning, vestibular dysfunction approaches, vision training, tinted lenses, megavitamin therapy, and diet modifications.
- describe the primary purpose and components of a neurological examination.
- discuss the reliability and validity of a neurological exam in identifying learning disabilities.
- discuss the roles of the otologist, audiologist, ophthalmologist, and optometrist in treating learning disabilities.

The fields of medicine and learning disabilities are linked closely. As noted in Chapter 2, the works of physicians such as Gall and Broca in the 1800s directly influenced later views of the diagnosis and treatment of individuals with learning disabilities. While a shift toward a more educational view has meant less reliance on neurological explanations, medical research and involvement continues. For example, the Individuals with Disabilities Education Act (IDEA) requires that medical information be part of the multidisciplinary team's assessment of the learner with disabilities when deemed appropriate, and medical services should be provided when necessary. Moreover, the pediatrician is often the first person to notice developmental problems and can be instrumental in early diagnosis and treatment of learning difficulties. In addition, many students labeled as having learning disabilities also receive drugs or other medical treatment regularly.

Because physicians and educators are involved concurrently with students who have learning disabilities, these professionals should understand the practices of both disciplines. Educators should be aware of current medical practices, and physicians should be cognizant of educational interventions. Teachers need to respond knowledgeably to questions from parents and others about medically based treatments such as pharmacology and special diets. Specifically, teachers should know how treatments affect instructional programs and what research reveals about the efficacy of various treatments. This chapter focuses on the role of medicine in the field of learning disabilities. The following areas are discussed: neurology and learning disabilities, etiological perspectives, attention-deficit hyperactivity disorder, pharmacological treatment, controversial approaches to treatment, and medical specialists.

NEUROLOGY AND LEARNING DISABILITIES

All learning occurs in the brain and is facilitated by the nervous system. *Neurology* is the medical specialty that focuses on the structure and function of the nervous system. Based on the theory that subtle or minimal disorders or abnormalities in the nervous system result in learning problems, neurology is the medical specialty most frequently involved with the field of learning disabilities. From a neurologist's point of view, learning disability is the most common neurological disorder among the school-aged population (S. E. Shaywitz, Shaywitz, McGraw, & Groll, 1984). Whereas educators focus on developing appropriate teaching techniques for students with learning disabilities, neurologists seek to diagnose the presence of abnormalities in neurological structure and function.

Central Nervous System Structure and Function

To better understand neurological irregularities and dysfunction and their possible link to learning, it is helpful to understand the normally functioning central nervous system. The nervous system comprises a constantly developing complex system of billions of cells that are created and evolve in biologically preset stages beginning at conception and continuing to adulthood. The basic unit of the nervous system is the nerve cell or neuron. The nervous system consists of many forms of neurons, but a cell body, axon, and dendrites are characteristic of each nerve cell (see Figure 3.1). Electrical or nerve impulses received by the dendrites pass through the cell body and down the axon, where they are picked up by other dendrites. Because of the extensive branching of dendrites, one nerve cell can interact with hundreds of others. Nerve impulses are conducted from one nerve cell to another across a juncture called the *synapse* through the action of chemicals called *neurotransmitters*. Through this relay system, excitory or inhibitory messages regulating behavior are sent throughout the body.

The nervous system has two major regions: the central nervous system (CNS) and the peripheral nervous system (PNS). The CNS consists of the spinal column and the brain. The PNS, made up of nerves and other sensory structures

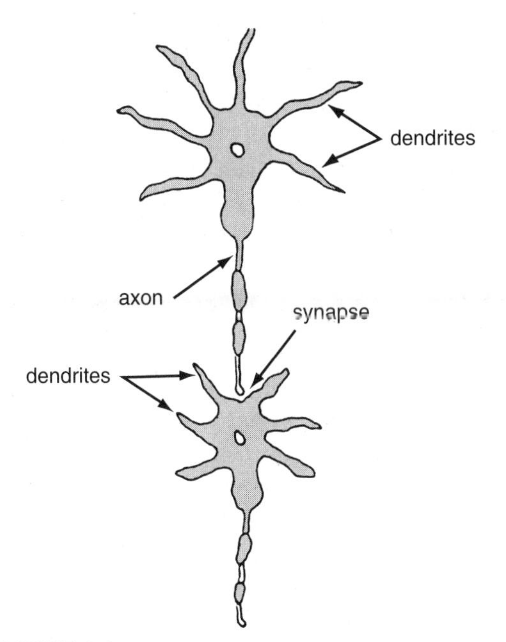

FIGURE 3.1
Nerve cell

that lie outside the CNS, connects the CNS to the rest of the body. The CNS forms the integrative and thinking portions of the nervous system. The spinal column serves as a connecting link between the brain and body, and it either acts on information from sensory nerves or forwards it to the brain.

The brain, as illustrated in Figure 3.2, has three major parts: the brain stem, the cerebellum, and the cerebrum. The *brain stem* consists of the medulla oblongata, pons, midbrain, and diencephalon. It is the oldest, most primitive part of the brain and has changed very little during human evolution. Specifically, the *medulla oblongata* coordinates heart and respiration rates and other reflexive, life-sustaining operations; the *pons* is associated with sensory input and motor outflow to the face; the *midbrain* controls eye movement, the state of brain wakefulness, and possibly attention; and the *diencephalon*, a major relay between the brain stem and the rest of the brain, integrates all sensory systems except smell. The *cerebellum,* in conjunction with other structures, receives and integrates sensory input

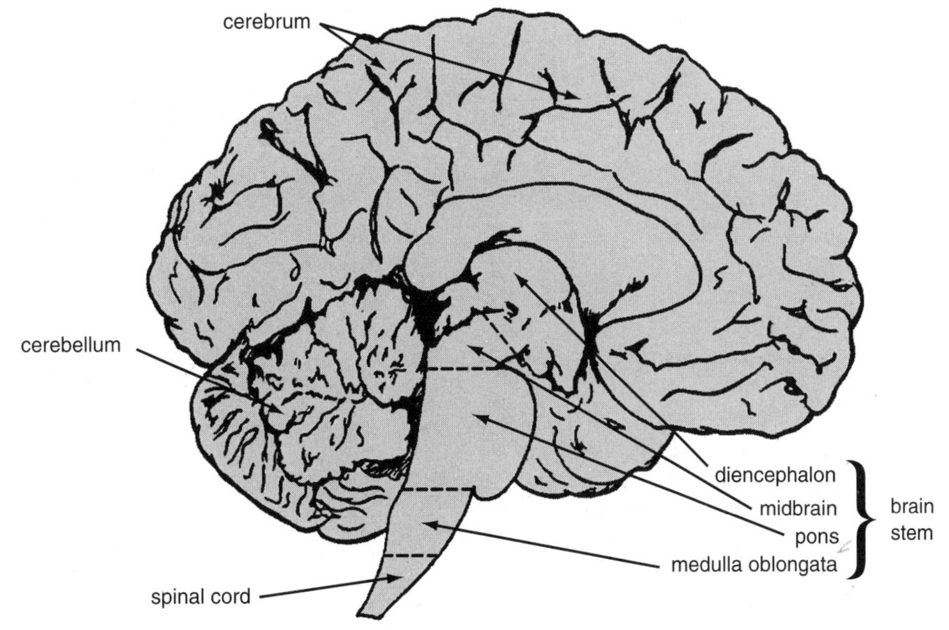

FIGURE 3.2
Regions of the undamaged, mature brain (sagittal section)

to coordinate the voluntary muscle system (e.g., balance, posture, and gait). The *cerebrum* is the largest part of the brain and controls the conscious functioning of the nervous system. The highest levels of neural functioning, including those related to learning, occur in the cerebrum.

The cerebrum has received the most attention from neurologists concerned with learning disabilities. It is divided into two hemispheres: the right and the left (sometimes referred to as the right brain and the left brain). These two hemispheres are connected by the *corpus callosum*, a large tract of nerve fibers that serve as a communication pathway between the right and left hemispheres. Each hemisphere is delineated further into four major regions: the temporal, frontal, parietal, and occipital lobes. The surface of the cerebral lobes is known as the *cerebral cortex* and is covered by convolutions or ridges (gyri) and valleys (sulci). The cerebral cortex receives and integrates all sensory information and controls conscious activity. Each lobe coordinates behavior relating to particular sensory input and functioning (see Figure 3.3). For example, the *temporal* lobe deals with hearing and comprehending what is heard as well as auditory memory. The *frontal* lobe is thought to be the seat of intellectual functions such as abstract thinking and also controls such motor activity as body movement and speech. Tactile sensations for different body parts are located in the *parietal* lobe. The *occipital* lobe deals with vision and visual perception. Nerves from the occipital lobe to other areas allow visual input to acquire meaning and assist in visual processes such as describing and analyzing objects.

The cerebral hemispheres appear to function cross laterally (i.e., they relate, at least with some functions, to opposite sides of the body). For example, the right hemisphere registers sensory information, such as visual, tactile, and auditory, from the left side of the body. Signals for the right hand to perform a function originate in the left hemisphere. The proposed significance of cross laterality has been an integral part the field of learning disabilities. It is hypothesized that learning, especially in the area of reading, is affected adversely if an individual does not establish a

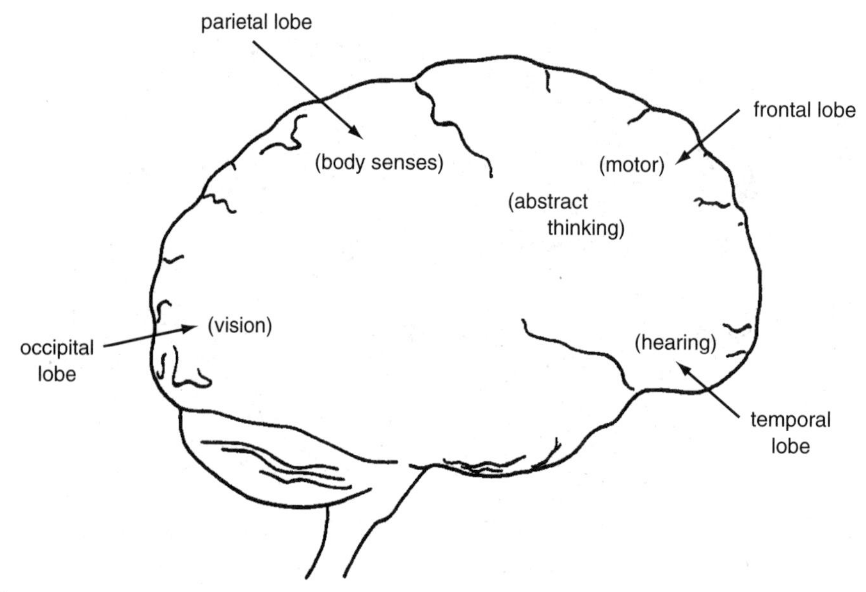

FIGURE 3.3
Hemispherical lobes and their functions

tendency to perform most functions with one side of the body. Therefore, for example, a person who kicks a ball with the left foot but throws a ball with the right hand is said to have *mixed laterality* rather than *established laterality.* Historically, some educators and physicians suggested that mixed laterality caused reading problems; thus, establishing whether laterality is mixed or established was (and still is in many cases) an integral part of a neurological examination. More recently, however, the diagnostic significance of mixed laterality has been challenged seriously. For example, Hiscock and Kinsbourne (1980, 1987) found little difference in the reading abilities of individuals with mixed laterality when compared with individuals who have established laterality.

In addition to the cross-lateral effect, there is evidence that the two hemispheres differ in their roles in learning. For example, the right hemisphere deals with nonverbal stimuli such as visual imagery, visual discrimination, and temporal and spatial orientation. The right brain also has been associated with music and math and, in popular terms, is the center for creative expression. Conversely, the left brain or hemisphere is associated with logic and intellect and appears to be dominant in information processing of words and symbols as well as analytical thinking, sequencing, and other cognitively related processes. In addition, language functions largely are controlled by, or originate in, the left hemisphere regardless of hemispheric dominance (Geschwind, 1968). While people with left hemispheric dominance are normally right-handed and those with right hemispheric dominance are usually left-handed, the left hemisphere controls language functions in almost all right-handed people and in about 70% of left-handed people.

Based on the notion of left-hemispheric dominance for language and reading, Orton (1937) hypothesized that reversal of letters and words was the result of failure to establish the left hemisphere as dominant over the right hemisphere. Orton reasoned that because language functions originate in the left cerebral hemisphere and the left hemisphere is also the center for motor movement on the right side of the body, the language center in the left hemisphere could be strengthened and made dominant by strongly establishing the right-sided motor responses of the body. Orton believed that encouraging right-handed and right-sided activities would reduce the language problems caused by the right hemisphere's interference with the signals of the left hemisphere. Although many left-handed children at that time were encouraged to spend a great deal of time doing things with their right hands, there is now little support for Orton's theories or methods (Myers & Hammill, 1990).

The most dramatic support for differential hemispheric functioning is provided by what has been termed "split brain" research, most of which has been reviewed by Kinsbourne and Smith (1974). These studies describe individuals whose corpus callosums were surgically severed to stop life-threatening seizures, thus discontinuing communication between the two hemispheres. Follow-up studies of these patients indicate that when interactions between the two hemispheres were interrupted, two phenomena occurred: (a) training of one hemisphere no longer resulted in activity or learning in the other, and (b) the two hemispheres functioned differently. Lack of cross-lateral learning between hemispheres was illustrated when a picture was shown to the right brain (i.e., through the left eye), but the patient could not recall having seen it when it was shown to the left brain (i.e., through the right eye). Images shown to the left hemisphere could be described and identified, but the same image projected to the right hemisphere could not.

Finally, it should be noted that although hemispheres may specialize with regard to certain functions, they are not totally independent. Much learning and behavior depends on the interactions of both hemispheres (Hiscock & Kinsbourne, 1987). Thus, laterality and dominance are not as much of a concern as is the overall functioning of the central nervous system.

Neurobiological Origins of Central Nervous System Dysfunction

As previously mentioned, the neurological perspective of learning disabilities is one of subtle CNS disorder or dysfunction. Some individuals theorize that there is an inseparable relationship between the CNS and the process of learning and that, consequently, damage to one or more of the brain's structures may hinder a function specific to that structure (e.g., reading, speech, or language).

The concept of minimal or mild dysfunction when referring to CNS damage is central to the medical perspective of learning disabilities. For an individual to receive a medical diagnosis of learning disabilities, major or gross signs of CNS disorder would be absent, and the dysfunction should be seen as minimal (i.e., obvious signs of trauma or abnormal development of CNS structures are absent). Obvious or major dysfunction does interfere with learning but generally leads to primary labels such as mental retardation or cerebral palsy. Moreover, the emphasis on *minimal* implies that resultant learning problems are not pervasive. Thus, a person with a learning disability performs comparatively well in some areas and poorly in others. Hynd and Semrud-Clikeman (1989) added support to the relationship between learning disabilities and more subtle neurological damage by noting that virtually no studies of neurobiological anomalies in students with reading disorders report signs of gross brain damage or trauma.

In the past, a subtle CNS dysfunction was identified primarily through indirect means. Neurologists relied heavily on tests that measured *soft signs*, which are thought to be behavioral indicators of minimal dysfunction. In other words, the existence of dysfunction had to be inferred rather than proved based on direct examination of the brain. (Soft signs are discussed in more detail later in this chapter in the section Medical Specialists.) Because of problems in the use of indirect methods, neurologists now frequently use procedures and equipment that allow more direct examination of the brain.

Neurodiagnostic Technology and Neurobiological Findings. Today, many procedures use hardware or machines that allow more direct measurement of brain activity and structure. These have been used for diagnosing CNS dysfunction and establishing relationships between neurological abnormalities and learning disabilities. They include the *electroencephalogram* (EEG), *brain electrical activity mapping* (BEAM), *computerized axial tomography* (CAT), *positron emission tomography* (PET), and *magnetic resonance imaging* (MRI). Links between observed abnormalities and the existence of a learning disability are established with these methods by comparing results from persons with a learning disability with results from normally functioning individuals. Findings resulting from such comparisons are only correlational; thus, a causal relationship may be suggested but cannot be established firmly.

The EEG records the electrical activity of the brain through electrodes placed on different parts of the scalp. The electrical impulses of nerve cells on the cerebral cortex are picked up by the electrodes, amplified, and recorded on moving paper. This produces a pattern of electrical activity, which is examined for signs of abnormality (i.e., compared with EEG readings of people without disabilities). The usefulness of the EEG as a diagnostic tool has been questioned seriously. Reviews by Kavale and Forness (1985) and C. R. Smith (1994) indicate only slight differences between the percentages of abnormal EEG readings for normal individuals and for people with learning disabilities. Moreover, Harris (1983) found that only about two-thirds of over 700 students without disabilities had "normal" EEG readings. The EEG is a relatively imprecise instrument, and many things can affect its precision (e.g., movement by the subject). Thus, methods such as BEAM have been developed to enhance the usefulness of EEG results.

BEAM is used to enhance electrical activity information by providing computer-constructed images of brain activity taken from an EEG. Duffy, Denckla, Bartels, Sandini, and Kiessling (1980) used BEAM procedures when studying a group of children who had been diagnosed as having severe reading problems but who had no other problems. BEAM readings were taken on the children while they were performing certain cognitive tasks (e.g., reading and listening), and the readings were compared with those of children without disabilities who performed the same tasks. Students with dyslexia were found to have significantly different brain electrical activity, especially in areas related to speech and reading. While these results offer initial support for this procedure's use in revealing neurological process problems in this population, Hynd and Semrud-Clikeman (1989) urge caution when interpreting these results because of procedural problems within the study.

The CAT scan (sometimes referred to as CT scan) is a radiological technique that allows examination of the brain's structures. The CAT scanner passes multiple X-ray beams at different angles through the brain. Then, through the use of a computer, it generates a composite picture of the brain. This device is also capable of displaying cross-sections of brain structures. The focus of many of the studies using the CAT scan is to ascertain a particular hypothesized abnormality in the brain of persons with dyslexia (Hynd & Semrud-Clikeman, 1989). According to Hynd and Semrud-Clikeman's analysis and summary of these CAT studies, the following tentative conclusions can be made: (a) in most people without disabilities, the left hemisphere is larger than the right hemisphere, resulting in brain asymmetry, (b) most right-handed persons with dyslexia (about 66%) have the same pattern of asymmetry, and (c) many left-handed individuals with dyslexia have reverse asymmetry (i.e., the right hemisphere is larger than the left). As with BEAM studies, problems with the CAT procedure (e.g., lack of precision) and with study design indicate that caution should be used when drawing conclusions.

PET scans involve the introduction of radioactive isotopes to cerebral areas through arteries feeding the cerebrum. The patient is asked to perform different tasks (e.g., respond to visual or auditory stimuli), and blood flow is recorded to determine at what site activation occurs. Like the CAT scan, the PET scan can visualize brain slices, but it also measures metabolism or activity of the brain. Zametkin et al. (1990) used PET imaging to demonstrate that the brains of individuals with attention deficit disorder metabolize glucose at a significantly slower rate than that of normal individuals. However, little research has been conducted using this procedure with individuals with learning disabilities, so the potential of this procedure for precisely identifying CNS dysfunction is undetermined.

The MRI procedure is a nonradiological technique that uses a neuroimaging device. A magnetic field is created that results in measurable changes in brain tissue, and these changes are measured by radio frequencies and computerized enhancement to picture various parts of the brain. Thus, images of multiple sections of the brain are generated, revealing the shape and location of various brain structures. Recent research (Hynd, Semrud-Clikeman, Lorys, Novey, & Eliopulos, 1990; Larsen, Hoien, Lundberg, & Odegaard, 1990) with MRI has been conducted on individuals with dyslexia.

The plana is one of the most obviously asymmetric regions of the normal brain. About 70% of normal brains have asymmetric plana (i.e., with the left being larger than the right), and only 5% of normal brains demonstrate a strong reversal of this asymmetry (Filipek, 1995). Neurobiological theory predicts that individuals with dyslexia, who often have language deficits as well, would exhibit less asymmetry or even reversed asymmetry in regions known to be important to language (e.g., the planum temporale). According to Hynd, Marshall, and Gonzalez (1991), the notion is that at a structural level there is a less-developed neurological system to support the complex process associated with language and reading. In two recent studies, MRI was used to examine the size and patterns of plana asymmetry in individuals with dyslexia. Larsen et al. (1990) found that 70% of the individuals with dyslexia demonstrated symmetry in the region of the plana compared with 30% of the normal subjects. Similarly, Hynd et al. (1990) found that the individuals with dyslexia in their study were characterized by either symmetry or reversed asymmetry (i.e., left smaller or equal to right) of the plana. They found that 90% of the individuals with dyslexia had either symmetric planar length (i.e., right equal to left) or reversed planar asymmetry (i.e., right greater than left). Thus, when careful morphometric measurements are made of regions known to be characterized by asymmetry in most normal brains, significantly less asymmetry is evident in the brains of individuals with dyslexia. However, Filipek (1995) cautions that definition of the borders of the plana temporale is a difficult task in MRI-based morphometry and that measurement of the planum leads itself to potentially high variability among investigators across studies.

Neurodiagnostic technology is developing rapidly and, in the future, may advance knowledge about the relationship between specific areas of CNS dysfunction or abnormalities and learning disabilities, especially dyslexia. Based on current findings, evidence is emerging that in some individuals with dyslexia, (a) hemispheric symmetry is different from that of individuals who do not have dyslexia, (b) structural abnormalities are apparent especially in the left, frontal areas of the brain, and (c) brain electrical activity appears to be more diffuse and less organized. However, methodological limitations (e.g., small numbers of subjects, unclear subject description) existing in studies using these techniques, as well as limited accessibility to school-aged youngsters with learning disabilities (Obrzut, 1989), preclude firm conclusions related to how brain structure and electrical activity affect learning.

Filipek (1995) notes that neuroimaging studies using computed tomographic or MRI scans have yielded inconsistent findings as a result of different methods of image acquisition and analysis. However, technological advances may facilitate the comprehensive study of the brain. For example, techniques have been developed to reformat three-dimensional MRI data into any plane, thus producing virtually identical image planes for morphometric analysis and allowing more accurate cross-anatomic comparisons.

Postmortem Studies. Postmortem examination is another area of medical research that uses more direct procedures for examining brain structure anomaly. These studies are conducted by performing brain autopsies on persons with documented learning disabilities and whose cause of death would not interfere with examination or be a possible reason for brain abnormalities (e.g., severe head injury). Duane (1989) and Hynd, Marshall, and Gonzalez (1991) summarize findings of postmortem studies, many of which were conducted by Galaburda (1988) and his associates at Harvard University. These studies, for the most part, reveal abnormalities in language-related areas of the cerebral cortex. The findings include abnormal hemispheric symmetry and nerve cell anomalies. For example, Galaburda found symmetric plana due to larger areas on the right side in all seven postmortem dyslexic brains studied. The nerve cell anomalies in the postmortem studies involve immature clumps of nerve cells that failed to migrate to another section of the brain, irregularly arranged cells and convolutions, and tiny enfoldings inside the brain that should not be present. In discussing nonmigrating neurons, some researchers (Geschwind & Behan, 1984; Geschwind & Galaburda, 1987) note that this particular clump of cells is formed in the central region of the cerebral cortex but at about 30 weeks is supposed to migrate to the left hemisphere. They suggest that an unusual surge of testosterone (male hormone) inhibits the migration and results in delayed growth of the left hemisphere. While tentative, this finding may explain why there are more males than females labeled as having learning disabilities. When discussing other possible causes of brain structure abnormalities (e.g., abnormal convolutions and immature cells), Geschwind and Galaburda contend that lack of sufficient oxygen supply (anoxia) during critical stages of brain development may have occurred.

Results of postmortem studies are subject to criticisms similar to those of the studies using neurodiagnostic hardware. Also, postmortem studies have included only about eight individuals, and larger numbers of deceased subjects are needed. However, Hynd, Marshall, and Gonzalez (1991) note that the importance of these studies is that they provide direct evidence of the neurodevelopmental factors that may be associated with learning disabilities. Although tentative, these studies offer insights about the brain structures of individuals with dyslexia, and to some extent the findings are in agreement with studies using neurodiagnostic technology. In addition, these findings are interesting because the types of problems found during autopsy occur during specific periods of gestation (usually between 18 and 30 weeks). While this leads to the tentative conclusion that the problems are developmental in nature, rather than due to lesions or trauma, it is not certain whether they are the result of genetic factors or some aspect of the fetal environment.

ETIOLOGICAL PERSPECTIVES

The previous discussion centered on the search for physical evidence of neurological problems and how they may relate to learning disabilities; however, medical researchers also are interested in causes of neurological irregularities and learning problems. They have investigated several possible reasons why a person may experience learning and learning-related problems (e.g., attention deficits and hyperactivity). Four predominant medically related etiologies of learning disabilities include acquired trauma or insult to the CNS, genetic or hereditary influences, environmental influences, and biochemical abnormalities.

Acquired Trauma

Injury to the CNS that originates outside the individual and results in learning disorders is called *acquired trauma* in the medical literature. Acquired CNS damage can occur during gestation, at birth, and after birth. Various pre-, peri-, and postnatal traumas have been shown to be correlated with learning problems.

Prenatal Causes. Complications during pregnancy have been linked empirically with a variety of learning problems. The most common cause associated with these complications and subsequent learning difficulties is maternal drug consumption. These drugs include alcohol, prescription and nonprescription drugs, and chemicals found in cigarette smoke. The unborn child is extremely vulnerable to maternal exposure to these potential toxins because drugs in the bloodstream cross the placenta virtually unobstructed. Once past the placenta, the drugs pass easily into the fetus and tend to concentrate in the still-developing brain. Unlike an adult, the fetus cannot transform toxic substances to nontoxic compounds and, because of immature kidney functions, cannot excrete them readily (Brackbill, McManus, & Woodward, 1985). Adverse effects can vary depending on the amount of toxic exposure, the point in fetal development at which the exposure occurs, and the overall health of the fetus before exposure.

In 1981, the Food and Drug Administration issued a statement warning that pregnant women who consume alcohol may harm the fetus. The term used when a child suffers impairment (e.g., growth impairment, facial disfigurement, and CNS dysfunction) because of excessive maternal alcohol intake is *fetal alcohol syndrome* (FAS). S. M. Smith (1989) describes a milder form of FAS (i.e., one or more forms of impairment are not present) that is called *suspected fetal alcohol effects* (FAE). In 1984, Gold and Sherry reviewed available literature and found a correlation between maternal alcohol consumption during pregnancy and later learning disabilities in the child. For example, S. E. Shaywitz, Cohen, and Shaywitz (1980) assessed 15 children of normal intelligence with fetal alcohol syndrome and found that all had been referred for special education services by the third grade. Among the characteristics observed in these youngsters were academic difficulties, hyperactivity, and attention problems. Van Dyke and Fox (1990) and S. M. Smith note that the incidences of FAS and FAE appear to be on the rise in the United States.

The effect of maternal drug consumption, both prescribed and nonprescribed, has been a related line of research on prenatal factors. In a review of studies examining behavioral effects of obstetric medication on infants, Brackbill et al. (1985) found evidence of adverse behavioral effects in children whose mothers used certain forms of prescribed medication. While these conclusions are disturbing and worth attention, it should be noted that of the 59 studies reviewed, none examined effects after 12 months of age.

In addition to their literature review, Brackbill et al. (1985) conducted a study of the drug consumption of 602 women during pregnancy. They analyzed the drugs ingested and reported on the safety of those drugs with respect to adverse fetal effects. Women in the study consumed an average of 2.16 different drugs during pregnancy, and two-thirds of those drugs lacked published reports of their safety. In addition, almost one-half of the drugs consumed contained one or more ingredients reported to have adverse effects on the fetus.

Recently, both medical and educational researchers have begun to document the growing number of children with learning and behavioral problems associated with prenatal exposure to illicit drugs such as cocaine (usually in the form of crack) and PCP (also called "angel dust"). It is suggested that exposure to cocaine affects the development of neuroreceptors and transmitters and results in a malfunctioning CNS (Van Dyke & Fox, 1990). Infant symptoms include low birth weight, abnormal EEGs, irritability, and low rates of social interaction. Currently, researchers investigating the effects of fetal cocaine exposure report follow-up assessments to about 1 year of age. Long-term studies of these children have not yet been reported; therefore, the full extent of this problem in terms of numbers of children and educational outcomes has not been documented. PCP studies reveal some different infant behaviors from those associated with cocaine. These infants have fine motor problems, and, although their social interactions appear to be unimpaired, language development is delayed. As with the cocaine studies, investigations of infants prenatally exposed to PCP have not included follow-up studies.

Finally, maternal use of tobacco products also has been linked with various aspects of learning disabilities, especially academic problems and hyperactivity (Lovitt, 1989). The two chemicals contained in cigarette smoke, nicotine and carbon monoxide, appear respectively to decrease fetal breathing and the oxygen supply to the fetus (Sparks, 1984).

Fortunately, of all suspected physiological causes of learning problems, those associated with acquired prenatal trauma are the most amenable to prevention. Increased awareness and understanding by parents, physicians, and educators concerning certain substances and their potentially adverse effects certainly could decrease the incidence of disabilities related to their consumption. In 1990, IDEA specified that early intervention programs are to be developed to address the needs of children prenatally exposed to substance abuse.

Perinatal Causes. Events that affect the child during the birth process are referred to as *perinatal traumas* or stresses. Included in this group of acquired causes are prematurity, anoxia, prolonged labor, and injury from medical instruments such as forceps. Birth complications have been associated with later learning disabilities characteristic of minimal brain damage, such as language and motor problems and attention deficits.

In a study of the relationship between birth complications and the later development of learning disabilities, Colletti (1979) reports that children with learning disabilities had more problems at birth (e.g., prolonged labor, induced birth, and forceps delivery) than the national norm (i.e., 96% of the subjects with learning disabilities versus 10% of the normal subjects). Similarly, Sell, Gaines, Gluckman, and Williams (1985) found that 32 out of 74 children who received neonatal intensive care needed special education services in the elementary

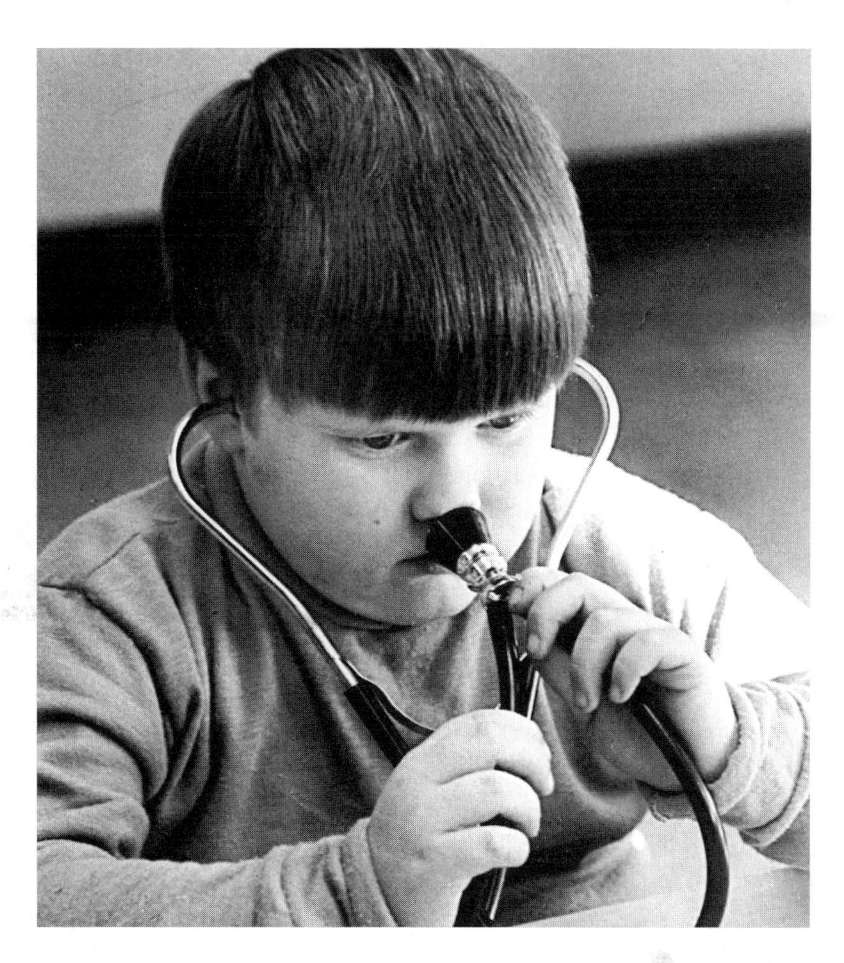

grades. However, while perinatal complications may be more prevalent in the backgrounds of students with learning problems, birth difficulties also occur frequently in the backgrounds of normally achieving students; thus, predicting later school-related problems on the basis of birth complications alone is risky.

Postnatal Causes. Accidents and diseases occurring after birth that are purported to lead to brain damage and concomitant learning problems include stroke, high fever, encephalitis, meningitis, and head trauma. Of these etiologies, the most common is acquired cerebral trauma associated with head injury. Incidence figures estimate that in the U.S., over 1 million children a year sustain a head injury primarily as a result of accidents involving cars, motorcycles, bicycles, and falls (Goldstein & Levin, 1987). Because of medical advances in treatment, more accident victims survive today than in the past; thus, children with head or brain injuries are becoming a growing concern for many professionals in medicine and education. Behaviors due to brain injury vary depending on the extent and location of the injury as well as the age of the victim (i.e., it appears that younger individuals more readily regain cognitive skills than older people because their brains retain their plasticity and are able to compensate for damage by forming new neural connectors). Several behaviors associated with brain injury include distractibility, irritability, maladaptive behavior (e.g., reactions to changes in immediate environment), and impulsivity (Deaton, 1987).

In 1990, IDEA added traumatic brain injury as a separate category for eligibility for appropriate special education and related services. Katsiyannis and Conderman (1994) note that the states are in various stages in developing policies and guidelines for these individuals. Bigler (1990) discusses assessment and intervention for students with traumatic brain injury.

Genetic/Hereditary Influences

Several investigators have examined the relationship between genetics and learning disabilities. Hallgren (1950) studied 276 individuals with dyslexia and their families. The prevalence of reading and language problems among the relatives led him to conclude that learning problems are inherited. After reviewing studies on genetics and reading difficulties, Critchley (1970) concurred. More recently, Decker and Defries (1980, 1981) compared families of 125 children with disabilities and 125 children without disabilities and found greater rates of reading disabilities within the families of the group with disabilities. Finally, in a recent study of four samples of families, S. D. Smith, Pennington, Kimberling, and Ing (1990) found evidence for sex-influenced, major locus transmission of dyslexia in a large proportion of families with dyslexia. Moreover, Pennington (1995) notes that, in studies of familial recurrence of reading problems, sibling recurrence is high and consistent across studies (i.e., ranging from 38.5% to 43%) and parent recurrence is likewise high and generally consistent (that is, ranging from 27% to 49%). Coles (1980), however, questions the conclusions of many of the family studies by noting that they offer little evidence and do not address the issue of environmental effects on learning. The question, then, is to what extent are learner characteristics due to heredity (e.g., genetic transmission) or to environmental influences (e.g., modeling)?

Investigators concerned with the nature versus nurture issue have attempted to control for environmental influences by comparing school performance of identical and fraternal twins. Studies of twins generally indicate that both identical twins (i.e., from the same egg and with identical genetic makeup) are more likely to have reading disabilities than are both fraternal twins (i.e., from different eggs and therefore with different genetic makeup) (Hermann, 1959; Norrie, 1959). Hermann compared 33 pairs of fraternal twins with 12 pairs of identical twins. He found that all members of the identical twin sets had severe reading problems, whereas both siblings exhibited a reading disability in only one-third of the fraternal sets. Pennington (1995) notes that results of a more recent twin study conducted at the Institute for Behavioral Genetics in Boulder, Colorado, indicate that deficits in reading and spelling are substantially heritable, as are deficits in nonword reading. Likewise, results of a twin study conducted in London at the Institute for Psychiatry indicate significant heritability for deficits in spelling.

Other studies have investigated genetic disorders or chromosomal abnormalities. Human genes are found in the nucleus of a chromosome, which is a microscopic unit that determines individual characteristics. Each individual has 23 pairs of chromosomes, one pair of which is called the sex chromosomes (labeled X and Y). Females typically have two X chromosomes (XX), and males have one X and one Y chromosome (XY). Chromosomal aberrations associated with learning disabilities typically relate to abnormal sex chromosome numbers (i.e., either too many or too few). The most frequently found chromosomal variation in males is XXY (i.e., an extra X chromosome) (S. M. Smith, 1989). Males with this condition, called Klinefelter syndrome, typically exhibit reading and language problems as well as poor motor coordination and a tendency to be withdrawn. A less frequent abnormality involves the presence of an extra Y (male) chromosome. Males with this chromosomal variation exhibit some of the same characteristics as those with Klinefelter syndrome but also tend to be more impulsive and hyperactive (S. E. Shaywitz & Shaywitz, 1988; Vogel & Motulsky, 1986). In addition, some research indicates that the fragile X syndrome, a common, inherited form of mental retardation that involves a chromosomal anomaly associated with a breakage of the X chromosome, is linked to learning disabilities, attention deficit disorders, speech and language deficits, and behavior problems in individuals who are mildly affected (Santos, 1992).

Two chromosomal abnormalities are linked with learning problems in females: an extra X (XXX) or a missing X (XO). When one X chromosome is missing (referred to as Turner syndrome), characteristics such as spatial deficits, problems in math, attention deficits or hyperactivity, and poor handwriting often are exhibited. In addition to academic and school-related problems, many females with Turner syndrome have physical abnormalities such as short stature and delayed menstruation. While some of the physical problems can be treated with estrogen (i.e., female hormone), this therapy does not appear to alleviate the cognitive difficulties. Unlike females with Turner syndrome, females with an XXX pattern usually do not exhibit apparent physical problems but they are characterized by a wide range of academic deficiencies.

To date, it is not apparent why irregular numbers of sex chromosomes cause learning problems. Walzer (1985) suggests that neurochemical dysfunction may occur because too many or too few chromosomes result in the production of too much or too little of certain hormones or enzymes.

Environmental Influences

Environmental influences are characterized by disruption of learning processes as a result of exposure to substances found in the environment. Medical research has focused attention on environmental hazards such as exposure to lead and allergic reactions to dietary substances.

Most early research on the effects of lead toxicity focused on individuals exposed to heavy doses of the substance. Large doses have been related primarily to retardation and other major impairments. Currently, some believe that exposure to minimal amounts of lead results in behaviors associated with learning disabilities (e.g., attention and speech problems). Needleman (1983) reports positive correlations between the amount of lead level and low teacher ratings of classroom behaviors (e.g., distractibility and impulsivity). Diagnostic procedures used by medical professionals to determine lead levels in individuals include X rays of bones (especially the knees) and analysis of the teeth (Levine, Brooks, & Shonkoff, 1980). While further research is needed, existing data provide cautious support for a relationship between exposure to lead and some types of learning disabilities.

Allergic reactions to certain foods and food additives also have been linked to learning disabilities. For example, Feingold (1976) proposes that hyperactivity and learning problems in some children may be caused by an allergic reaction to the ingestion of a natural or synthetic compound called *salicylate*, a chemical found in artificial colors and flavors as well as in certain foods (e.g., apples, tomatoes, and berries). Allergic reactions to other foods that do not contain salicylate, such as milk, wheat, sugar, and chocolate, also have been linked to learning disabilities (Crook, 1975; Rapp, 1978, 1986).

While the relationship between dietary influences and learning disabilities has its proponents, the existing evidence is inconclusive. An examination of the efficacy of treatments based on this etiological perspective is included in the section Controversial Approaches to Treatment.

Biochemical Abnormalities

Because some students with learning disabilities have not been diagnosed as having apparent neurological damage or a family history of learning problems, it has been hypothesized that the cause may be biochemical abnormalities at the cellular level. Imbalances in the production of neurotransmitters (e.g., serotonin, dopamine, norepinephrine, acetylcholine, and other chemicals) are assumed to cause difficulties in neural impulse transmission and consequent learning and behavior problems. For example, some attention deficits have been associated with overrapid neural impulses that do not permit adequate time for the brain to process incoming information (B. A. Shaywitz, 1987; Silver, 1988). Most research in this area focuses on the possibility of a chemical basis for this condition and consists of measuring levels of various chemicals in the blood, urine, and cerebrospinal fluid of individuals with learning disabilities. However, results are inconclusive, and specific knowledge about neurotransmitters is in the early stages of development. For example, Brown (1983) points out that 50 neurotransmitters have been identified and another 200 are suspected.

Currently, one area of research that indirectly supports the existence of a chemical imbalance in some individuals with learning disabilities involves the use of psychoactive drugs (e.g., stimulant medication) to improve attention and learning and to decrease hyperactivity. Because of the seemingly positive effects of psychoactive drugs on the learning and social behavior of some individuals with learning disabilities, it is assumed that a chemical imbalance exists and is corrected through administration of drugs. The relationship between learning and chemical alteration of the neurosystem is discussed further in the section Pharmacological Treatment.

ATTENTION-DEFICIT HYPERACTIVITY DISORDER

The term used by the medical community to describe or classify CNS dysfunction related to learning disabilities is *attention-deficit hyperactivity disorder* (ADHD). This current term has evolved through several stages. In the 1950s and 1960s, the term *minimal brain dysfunction* (MBD) was used, and hyperactivity was a major characteristic. In 1968, because of concerns about the usefulness of the MBD term, the American Psychiatric Association presented the term *hyperkinetic reaction to childhood* and described the criteria in their publication, the *Diagnostic and Statistical Manual of Mental Disorders* (*DSM*). In 1980, the term *attention deficit disorder* (ADD) appeared in the third edition of the *DSM* (*DSM-III*) (American Psychiatric Association, 1980) and was presented to reflect the position that attention deficits interfere with learning processes. Moreover, two types of ADD were described: with hyperactivity and without hyperactivity. The diagnostic criteria for ADD with hyperactivity included inattention (e.g., failure to finish tasks and difficulty concentrating), impulsivity (e.g., acting before thinking and difficulty in organizing work), and hyperactivity (e.g., excessive running and climbing, and constant motion). In ADD without hyperactivity, the hyperactive component was excluded and other impairments were not as severe. In 1987, the terminology was changed to *attention-deficit hyperactivity disorder* and was included in the *DSM-III-R* (revised) manual (American Psychiatric Association, 1987).

The *DSM-IV* (American Psychiatric Association, 1994) maintains the term *attention-deficit hyperactivity disorder;* however, subtypes are included: predominantly inattentive type, predominantly hyperactive-impulsive type, and combined type. The diagnostic criteria indicate that the disorder must have persisted for at least 6 months with onset no later than 7 years of age and the symptoms must be present in two or more situations (e.g., school, work, and home). Also, there must be clear evidence of clinically significant impairment in social, academic, or occupational functioning. The *DSM-IV* criteria for ADHD, presented in Table 3.1, emphasize particular behavioral characteristics relating to inattention, impulsivity, and hyperactivity. ADHD, predominantly inattentive type, is diagnosed if Criterion 1 is met, whereas ADHD, predominantely hyperactive-impulsive type, is diagnosed if Criterion 2 is met. Children who have exhibited at least six of the inattentive symptoms and at least six of the hyperactive-impulsive symptoms for the past 6 months fit the ADHD combined type. McBurnett, Lahey, and Pfiffner (1993) note that the revised symptom list and empirical

TABLE 3.1
DSM-IV Criteria for Attention-Deficit Hyperactivity Disorder

Criterion 1: *Inattention*
The individual must exhibit at least six of the following symptoms, with each of the symptoms occurring often for 6 months or more to an extent that is maladaptive and inconsistent with developmental level:

1. Fails to give close attention to details or makes careless mistakes in schoolwork, work, or other activities
2. Has difficulty sustaining attention in tasks or play activities
3. Does not seem to listen when spoken to directly
4. Does not follow through on instructions and fails to finish schoolwork, chores, or duties in the workplace (not due to oppositional behavior or failure to understand instructions)
5. Has difficulties organizing tasks and activities
6. Avoids, dislikes, or is reluctant to engage in tasks that require sustained mental effort (such as schoolwork or homework)
7. Is distracted easily by extraneous stimuli
8. Is forgetful in daily activities

Criterion 2: *Hyperactivity-Impulsivity*
The individual must exhibit at least six of the following symptoms, with each of the symptoms occurring often for 6 months or more to an extent that is maladaptive and inconsistent with developmental level:

Hyperactivity

1. Fidgets with hands or feet or squirms in seat
2. Leaves seat in classroom or in other situations in which remaining seated is expected
3. Runs about or climbs excessively in situations in which it is inappropriate (in adolescents or adults, may be limited to subjective feelings of restlessness)
4. Has difficulty playing or engaging in leisure activities quietly
5. Is "on the go" or acts as if "driven by a motor"
6. Talks excessively

Impulsivity

7. Blurts out answers before questions have been completed
8. Has difficulty awaiting turn
9. Interrupts or intrudes on others (e.g., butts into conversations or games)

Note: Adapted from *Diagnostic and Statistical Manual of Mental Disorders* (pp. 83–84), 4th ed., by American Psychiatric Association, 1994, Washington, DC: American Psychiatric Association. Copyright 1994 by American Psychiatric Association. Reprinted by permission.

determination of symptom cut-points result in increased reliability and predictive validity for educational impairment for the new criteria.

The *DSM-IV* (American Psychiatric Association, 1994) presents some specific features of individuals with ADHD:

> Young children with Attention-Deficit/Hyperactivity Disorder move excessively and typically are difficult to contain. . . . As children mature, symptoms usually become less conspicuous. By late childhood and early adolescence, signs of excessive gross motor activity (e.g., excessive running and climbing, not remaining seated) are less common, and hyperactivity symptoms may be confined to fidgetiness or an inner feeling of jitteriness or restlessness. In school-age children, symptoms of inattention affect classroom work and academic performance. Impulsive symptoms may also lead to the breaking of familial, interpersonal, and educational rules, especially in adolescence. In adulthood, restlessness may lead to difficulty in participating in sedentary activities and to avoiding positions or occupations that provide limited opportunity for spontaneous movement (e.g., desk jobs). (pp. 81-82)

Many educational difficulties are associated with the characteristics of students with ADHD. Zentall (1993) notes that an attentional bias to novelty in students with ADHD can result in achievement deficits in tasks involving selective attention as well as sustained attention. For example, listening tasks, initial exposure to math problems, and learning to spell words involve selective attention requirements, whereas difficulty in sustaining attention to covert thought may explain language production deficiencies or reading comprehension problems in students with ADHD. In addition, excessive verbal and motoric activity in students with ADHD may divert energy from learning, and impulsivity may produce academic errors. Zentall notes that color stimulation (e.g., adding color to increase important task features) may be used as an intervention for selective attention, whereas interventions for sustained attention performance may include the use of color novelty, novel settings for tests and games, music novelty, and psychostimulant medication.

From the medical perspective, the etiology of ADHD is suspected to be a neurotransmitter imbalance or defects in neural connections. For example, a deficiency in the production of the neurotransmitters norepinephrine or dopamine results in decreased stimulation of the brain and a consequent dysfunction of the neural circuits underlying attention (Hynd, Hern, Voeller, & Marshall, 1991). This assumption is based on the effectiveness of stimulant medication on behaviors associated with ADHD as well as the absence of hard signs (i.e., measurements by MRI and CAT scans) for these youngsters. Therefore, some medical researchers hypothesize that the problem exists at the cellular level. Additional evidence of an underlying neurological basis points to morphological differences. Hynd, Semrud-Clikeman, Lorys, Novey, Eliopulos, and Lyytinen (1991) indicate that subtle differences may exist in the brains of children with ADHD. They studied area measurements of the corpus callosum on MRI scans and found that the corpus callosum seems smaller in children with ADHD than in children without disabilities. This finding followed a study by Hynd et al. (1990) that indicated that children with ADHD differed significantly from children without disabilities in the width measure of the right frontal region of the brain, thus pointing to a deviation in the expected pattern of asymmetry: While the right frontal region is larger than the left frontal region in most normal brains, the children with ADHD evidenced symmetry of the frontal region.

Silver (1990) discriminates between ADHD and a learning disability by noting that a learning disability affects the brain's *ability* to learn, while ADHD interferes with an individual's *availability* for learning. Moreover, Cantwell and Baker (1991) note that while there is an association between ADHD and learning disabilities in that students with ADHD are likely to experience academic difficulties and school failure, the nature of the association remains unclear. In a comparison of neuropsychological test profiles of 60 students with either ADHD, learning disabilities, or both, Korkman and Pesonen (1994) found that the students with ADHD were impaired in the control and inhibition of impulses, whereas the students with learning disabilities were impaired in phonological awareness, verbal memory span, and storytelling. Students with both disorders showed additional pervasive attention problems and visual-motor problems, and all students exhibited impaired performance in tasks of visual-motor precision and name retrieval. In addition, in a study that compared parent and teacher behavioral ratings among three groups of children (i.e., those diagnosed as having ADHD with hyperactivity, ADHD without hyperactivity, or learning disabilities), Stanford and Hynd (1994) found that the children with ADHD with hyperactivity were rated as being more disruptive (i.e., shifting tasks, acting without thinking, frequently calling out in class, and having difficulty taking turns), whereas children with ADHD without hyperactivity were described as more withdrawn, prone to daydreaming, underactive, and shy. The behavioral profiles of the group with learning disabilities more closely resembled the profiles of the group with ADHD without hyperactivity. Regardless of the distinction between the disorders, it appears that many students have problems in school that relate to attention and hyperactivity.

ADHD is not identified as a separate disability within IDEA. Advocates of placing ADHD in a separate category of exceptionality claim that students with ADHD are being denied special education services because they do not meet federal criteria for established categories. However, Reid, Maag, and Vasa (1993) challenge the arguments for making ADHD a separate disability category and believe that, because of its subjective nature, doing so could result in overidentification of students with academic and behavior difficulties. Currently, according to a memorandum issued by the Department of Education (Davila, Williams, & MacDonald, 1991), students with ADHD may be eligible for special education services under the Other Health Impairments category if problems of limited alertness negatively affect academic performance. In addition, they may receive services by meeting criteria of existing special education categories (e.g., specific learning disabilities or serious emotional disturbance). Moreover, to study attention deficit disorders and synthesize knowledge about assessment and intervention practices, five research centers have been funded: the University of Miami (Coral Gables, FL), the Arkansas Children's Hospital Research Center (Little Rock, AK), the University of California-Irvine (Irvine, CA), the Research Triangle Institute (Research Triangle Park, NC), and the Federal Resource Center, University of Kentucky (Lexington, KY).

According to the *DSM-IV*, the prevalence of ADHD is estimated at 3% to 5% in school-age children; however, DeLong (1995) notes that up to 9.5% of school children meet the criteria for ADHD. Furthermore, ADHD prevalence rates for students labeled as having learning disabilities range from 41% to 80%, and estimates of learning disabilities in the ADHD population range from 9% to 80% (DeLong, 1995). Barkley (1990) found that the incidence of learning disabilities in students with ADHD was 41% when the criterion for learning disabilities is achievement scores of at least 15 standard score points below the full-scale IQ and 21% when the criterion is achievement scores below the 7th percentile. Thus, there is a strong association or overlap between ADHD and learning disabilities.

Estimates of incidence or prevalence must be viewed with caution because of the assessment methods used to identify ADHD. Various assessment procedures are used, such as direct observation, neurological exams, and rating scales. S. E. Shaywitz and Shaywitz (1988) note that different scales yield different results, and the person who completes the scale also can affect results (e.g., teachers tend to give lower ratings than parents do). One test designed to identify and evaluate attention deficit disorders in persons age 3 to 23 years is the *Attention-Deficit/Hyperactivity Disorder Test* (Gilliam, 1995). The 36 items that describe characteristic behaviors of persons with ADHD are based on the diagnostic criteria in the *DSM-IV*. Teachers, parents, and others knowledgeable about the individual complete the items that comprise three subtests representing the symptoms of hyperactivity, impulsivity, and inattention.

B. A. Shaywitz, Fletcher, and Shaywitz (1995) indicate that there is great diversity embedded within the ADHD diagnosis. They state that ADHD, as it currently is applied, refers to a heterogeneous group of individuals representing a range of behavioral and cognitive characteristics. Fowler (1992) estimates that about 50% of students with attention deficit disorders can be served appropriately within the general education program. An additional 35% can be served in the general classroom by having general and special educators work together as a collaborative team. The remaining 15% may need placement in special classes to receive special intervention strategies. Lerner, Lowenthal, and Lerner (1995) note that four educational approaches currently being used with students with attention deficit disorders include content mastery classes, cooperative learning, peer tutoring, and home-school coordination. In addition, methods of behavior management (e.g., contingency management, cognitive behavior modification, and social skills training) are useful for modifying the behavior of students with attention deficit disorders. Students with ADHD who have coexisting disabilities (e.g., learning disabilities or emotional disturbance) require specialized instruction.

Psychostimulant medications (e.g., Ritalin, Dexedrine, and Cylert) frequently are used to treat youngsters with attention deficit disorders. Lerner et al. (1995) note that psychostimulants appear to (a) increase the arousal or alertness of the central nervous system, (b) stimulate the production of the chemical neurotransmitters needed to send information from the brain stem to parts of the brain that deal with attention, inhibition, and activity, and (c) make youngsters more sensitive to reinforcers in the environment, thus increasing their attention spans and persistence in responding to environmental events. Moreover, in a review of research on the effect of stimulant medications on students with attention deficit disorders, Swanson et al. (1993) note that the basic pattern of expected benefits includes temporary management of overactivity, inattention, and impulsivity as well as temporary improvement in deportment, aggression, social interactions, and academic productivity. They note that many researchers recommend that stimulants always be used in combination with educational and behavioral interventions. Thus, medication should be considered as only one part of a broad treatment program and should be combined with effective instruction, behavior management strategies, and good home management to provide a total interdisciplinary management and intervention program for youngsters with ADHD.

PHARMACOLOGICAL TREATMENT

Pharmacology is the study of the chemical and physical properties of drugs. Pharmacological treatment for learning disabilities and related disorders consists primarily of administering stimulant drugs to improve cognitive and attentional deficits as well as manage hyperactive behaviors. Stimulant drugs fall within the category of psychotropic drugs, which are drugs that influence moods, behavior, and cognition.

The prevalence of the use of stimulant medication with the school-age population varies. It is estimated that 1% to 3% of all elementary-age students receive medication for hyperactivity and attention problems, while there is a sharp decline in use for adolescents (Safer & Krager, 1984). Projected rates are higher for students in special education classes, ranging from 6% to 23%. Aman and Rojahn (1992) suggest that the percentage of students with learning disabilities who are prescribed psychotropic medication may be close to 10% nationwide. Moreover, Bateman (1995) notes that as many as 25% to 50% of students identified as having learning disabilities may be taking medication for attention deficits or hyperactivity. The stimulant drug most commonly prescribed is Ritalin (Gadow, 1986); however, Cylert and Dexedrine also are used (see Table 3.2).

Teachers have increasing responsibility for students who are on medication for the control of their problem behaviors, and they can play an important role in the pharmacotherapy of students. Epstein, Singh, Luebke, and Stout (1991) note that the teacher's role may include supplying the physician with a detailed description of the student's school behavior, giving objective information on drug therapy and treatment alternatives to parents, and reporting to the physician on the side effects of medication or the student's behavior and on changes in behavior that occur during drug-free periods and changes in medication.

Drug Nomenclature

Individuals not trained in medicine may have difficulty understanding the process used for naming a drug. Every drug approved for medical use has four names. First, a chemical name describes the drug's structural formula for pharmacists. Second, an official name is listed in one or the other of two official references for drug standards in the United States: *United States*

TABLE 3.2
Stimulant Drugs Commonly Used with Students Who Have Learning Disabilities

Trade Name	Generic Name	Range of Daily Dose	Onset of Action	Duration of Action	Selected Side Effects	Recommended Age of User
Ritalin	Methylphenidate	5–60 mg (2–3 times a day)	30 minutes	3–5 hours	Nervousness; insomnia; hypersensitivity; fever; anorexia; nausea; palpitations; abdominal pain; weight loss; loss of appetite; drowsiness; skin rash; dizziness; growth reduction	Above 6 years
Cylert	Pemoline	18–112 mg (1time a day)	2–4 hours (may not see results for 2–4 weeks)	long acting	Insomnia; anorexia; weight loss; stomach ache; skin rashes; irritability; mild depression; nausea dizziness; headache; drowsiness; hallucinations	Above 6 years
Dexedrine	Dextroamphetamine	5–40 mg (2 times a day)	30 minutes	3–5 hours	Elevation of blood pressure; overstimulation; restlessness; dizziness; insomnia; euphoria; dryness of mouth; constipation; anorexia; weight loss; tremor; headache; diarrhea	Above 3 years

Pharmacopedia and *National Formulary*. While not officially recognized, the most popular drug reference is the *Physicians' Desk Reference*, which contains summaries of the composition, action, uses, mode of administration, dosage, side effects, and contraindications of commercial pharmaceutical products. Third, a generic name is assigned by the organization that originally develops the drug. Fourth, a trade name is assigned by the drug manufacturer for marketing purposes. For example, the chemical name for Ritalin (trade name) is methyl α-phenyl-2-piperidineacetate hydrochloride; its official name is methylphenidate hydrochloride; and its generic name is methylphenidate. Communication problems about drug names usually stem from one individual using the generic name and another using the trade name.

Drug Action

The human body is composed of elemental atoms combined in various ways to form molecules, which, in turn, form cells. Aggregates of cells form the various tissues and organs of the body. Cells differ because they vary in the chemical combinations of their atoms and molecules (i.e., the specific manner in which certain atoms and molecules are bonded to each other). As a result of medical and chemical research, many of these basic combinations can be described in terms of chemical formulas and equations that represent the action and reaction of atoms and molecules to each other. In humans, altering the chemical bonds among atoms, molecules, and cells changes their interaction and function.

As mentioned earlier, evidence is emerging that children with attention problems and excessive motor behavior may lack certain chemicals responsible for inhibiting neurotransmissions. This deficiency results in an inability to screen out irrelevant stimuli. It is believed that stimulants promote production of these neurochemicals and thus increase the ability to ignore diversions and sustain attention. In a study involving students with documented ADHD, Lou, Henriksen, Bruhn, Borner, and Nielson (1989) found that the students had reduced blood flow to various regions of the brain; however, when Ritalin was administered, the blood flow increased. Thus, it appears that stimulants may affect several physiological systems.

Many professionals note that the reaction to stimulants in students with learning disabilities and students who are hyperactive (i.e., a decrease in restlessness and increase in attention) is the opposite reaction of the response of normal individuals to stimulants (i.e., an increase in restlessness and distractibility). This so-called paradoxical or idiosyncratic reaction is used by some physicians to diagnose hyperactivity. However, as Gadow (1981) notes, the idea of paradoxical reaction as a diagnostic indicator was formulated before studies of the effects of stimulants on normally functioning individuals were conducted. Subsequent research (Rapoport, Buchsbaum, Weingartner, Zahn, & Ludlow, 1978; Weingartner et al., 1980) indicates that normal children react in much the same way as children with hyperactivity do to Dexedrine, a stimulant. Thus, the behavioral effects of stimulants when administered to children with hyperactivity are not paradoxical, as is commonly thought, and the use of the paradoxical effect of stimulant medication in diagnosis has not been substantiated.

Drug Side Effects

Different cell groups (e.g., brain versus liver) have different reactions to the same drug. Consequently, all drugs specify a main effect and side effects. Selected side effects (Forness & Kavale, 1988) of stimulant drugs are listed in Table 3.2. The teacher of a child taking stimulant medication should be aware of drug side effects, especially those that may affect student performance. One side effect that may be of particular concern to parents and the child is suppressed growth. Suppressed growth has been noted as a side effect in children taking stimulants (Gross, 1976; Safer, Allen, & Barr, 1975); however, it appears that growth rebounds to normally projected size after the drug is discontinued. Many physicians prescribe lower doses of medication at nonschool times (e.g., weekends or school vacation days) and recommend periodic trials off the medication to determine continued need.

Drug Main Effects

In the 1930s, Bradley (1937) reported marked improvement in the behavior of children who received the stimulant Benzedrine. Many studies since have been conducted on the effects of stimulants on students with attention and cognition problems as well as associated hyperactivity, and various reviews and summaries (Forness & Kavale, 1988; Kavale, 1982; Pelham, 1986) of these studies have been published. While some researchers question the overall conclusions based on these reviews, there appears to be strong evidence that stimulant medication improves the attention, concentration, and social behavior of many children. However, the effect of stimulants on learning or cognition is less clear and is a subject of some controversy. Hallahan, Kauffman, and Lloyd (1985) maintain that the claim that increased sustained attention contributes to faster acquisition of new skills or improved learning remains unsubstantiated, while others (Forness & Kavale, 1988; Pelham, 1986) report evidence that supports improvement in academic skills for students taking stimulant medication. While this area needs more investigation, teachers should assume that drug therapy alone is not adequate to ensure optimal academic progress.

Another aspect of drug efficacy is that about 25% of children who are hyperactive or have attention deficits do not respond favorably to stimulant medication (Barkley, 1990). Unfortunately, no reliable parameters exist indicating the type of children for whom stimulant drugs are effective. Therefore, some physicians administer stimulants to students who may not benefit by their use or, worse, may respond adversely. Almost all children show an initial positive drug response that lasts up to 1 month (Levine et al., 1980); thus, each child's behavior must be closely monitored, especially during the early months of treatment. DeLong (1995) suggests that a time-limited trial, possibly supplemented by a placebo phase, may be the best way to determine whether a student with a learning disability will benefit from stimulant medication.

Drug Dosage

From his review of the effects of stimulant drugs, Gadow (1981) found a relationship between drug dosage and behavior. When the dosage of stimulants exceeded certain levels, performance on tasks measuring short-term memory and impulsivity was no better than that of subjects taking placebos. Because of inadequate research, overprescribing can happen frequently. Pelham (1981) suggests that high dosages sometimes are prescribed because as dosage increases, social behavior often improves. The student becomes more manageable but at the expense of performance on cognitively related tasks.

Knowledge of effects of dosage level is important for school personnel. For example, because of its short duration of action (see Table 3.2), Ritalin often is administered twice a day, once in the morning and again at lunchtime. In many cases, the midday dose is administered by school personnel. Thus, knowledge of the recommended dosage level and communication with parents about the amount taken in the morning are critical in avoiding overdosage. However, with the development and use of a time-release capsule, many problems associated with overdosage are avoided. Both Cylert and a newer form of Ritalin, called Ritalin SR, are taken once a day. However, Pelham et al. (1987) note that sustained-release forms of Ritalin may be less effective than the standard preparation for elementary-age students.

Close monitoring of student behavior and systematic communication with the physician are necessary to make dosage adjustments that are both behaviorally and cognitively beneficial to the student. Unfortunately, teacher-physician communication is usually rare. For example,

Gadow (1983) states that teachers and physicians communicate directly only in 9% to 27% of cases. This lack of monitoring indicates that dosage adjustments (if any) often are not based on student performance data.

Guidelines

The following guidelines are offered to help the teacher when making decisions or advising parents about pharmacological treatment.

1. Use educationally based interventions (e.g., applied behavioral techniques or cognitive-behavioral approaches) before and during drug intervention. Continue to seek interventions that eventually may replace medication or at least permit a reduction in dosage.
2. Maintain close contact with the parents and the physician about the effects of the drug, especially during the first several months. Record data on both social and academic behaviors, because this information is critical for dosage adjustments.
3. Know the possible side effects, especially as they relate to learning.
4. Because drug effect likely is optimal in the morning, try to teach academics during that period.
5. If you are involved in administering the medication, make sure authorization is documented, dates and times of administration are recorded, and medication is kept in a secure place.

CONTROVERSIAL APPROACHES TO TREATMENT

While the most common medical treatment for learning disabilities is the prescription of stimulants, there are other approaches that are somewhat controversial. Controversial or nontraditional therapies have been characterized by S. E. Shaywitz and Shaywitz (1988) and Golden (1984) as being (a) considered inconsistent with current scientific knowledge, (b) claimed effective for a wide variety of people and problems, (c) described primarily in the popular media rather than in professional journals, or (d) supported by lay groups rather than professional organizations. Moreover, Silver (1995) indicates that a treatment approach can be considered controversial if it (a) is proposed to the public before research or the replication of preliminary research is available, (b) goes beyond what research data support, or (c) is used in an isolated way when a broader assessment and treatment approach is needed. Teachers can be instrumental in providing current information to parents about the efficacy of medically related treatments and should suggest that parents consult a knowledgeable pediatrician for additional help. Parents of children with learning disabilities and related problems such as ADHD are particularly susceptible to unsupported claims made by proponents of various treatment approaches. It should be noted that many of the medical persons who developed or promote some of these controversial approaches have strong personal beliefs in the methods. In the future, additional evidence may support a particular technique; however, at this time the treatment approaches discussed in the following sections are considered controversial.

Patterning

Based on the work of Temple Fay in the 1940s and 1950s, Glen Doman, a physical therapist, and Carl Delacato, an educational psychologist, developed a technique called patterning (Doman & Delacato, 1968). They hypothesize that each individual develops through stages that correspond to human evolutionary stages. Consequently, each child progresses through stages in which the use of specific CNS functions must be mastered sequentially. Doman and Delacato maintain that the human being attains six functions (motor skills, speech, writing, reading, understanding speech, and tactile ability), and that failure to pass through a developmental sequence will result in problems of mobility and communication.

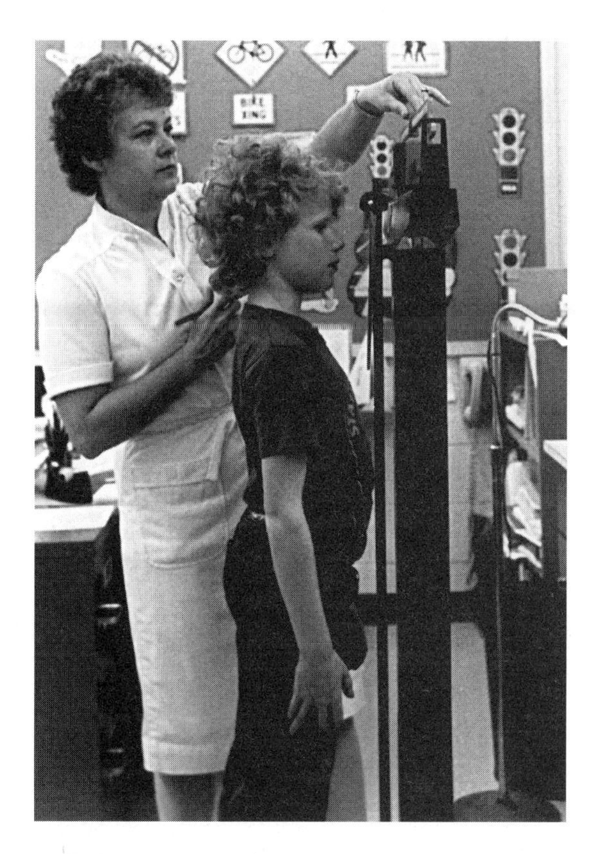

Once a level of unsatisfactory development is identified, an intense regimen of remedial motor activity is imposed. The proposed treatment involves repetitive activities that use specific muscle patterns in the order of normal development. If the individual is physically unable to perform the motor exercises, another person moves the limbs through the prescribed motions. The individual must relearn and properly perform each stage of motor learning: rolling over, sitting, crawling, standing, and walking. Doman and Delacato maintain that by establishing hemispheric dominance through this method, full neurological organization and the elimination of learning problems will result.

While Doman and Delacato report success (Delacato, 1966), others who analyzed the studies or attempted to replicate them have found the theory, specific treatment procedures, and research to be inadequate (Freeman, 1967; Robbins & Glass, 1969; Stone & Pielstick, 1969). Based on a review of relevant literature, the American Academy of Pediatrics (1982) concluded that (a) patterning is of little use, (b) claims about its effectiveness are unsubstantiated, and (c) in some instances the treatment may have deleterious effects on the family because of the extensive demands for implementation. Despite the reservations of professionals in medicine and education, many parents continue to use this difficult-to-implement and somewhat expensive treatment.

Vestibular Dysfunction

Some theorists (Ayres, 1978; Levinson, 1980) hypothesize that poor vestibular functioning results in poor academic performance, especially in reading. This reasoning is due partially to the overlap between some characteristics of learning disabilities and vestibular dysfunction (e.g., poor spatial orientation, faulty eye movements, and poor balance) (Silver, 1995). Consequently, vestibular functioning in individuals with learning disabilities is believed to be substantially poorer than in people without disabilities. In 1984, Levinson published a book on the relationship between dyslexia and vestibular problems in which he promotes the use of anti-motion sickness medication for treating dyslexia.

This treatment approach has been criticized for several reasons. First, many of the tests used to diagnose vestibular dysfunction use procedures that stimulate visual processes rather than vestibular functioning (Silver, 1995). Second, studies on vestibular functioning of persons with learning disabilities report equivocal results at best. For example, Polatajko (1985) compared vestibular functions in children with and without learning disabilities and found no significant difference between the two groups. In addition, no significant correlation was found between vestibular functioning and academic ability. Silver (1995) reports that there is no evidence supportive of the vestibular theories or of the proposed treatment approaches.

Vision Training

Many optometrists practice vision training with children who have learning problems. Vision training is based on perceptual-motor theory and a concept of developmental vision that proposes that vision for complex tasks such as reading is a learned activity involving the CNS as well as the eyes. Vision training activities usually involve some movement that requires fine visual discrimination (e.g., stringing beads or drawing a line between closely spaced lines on the chalkboard). According to Keogh (1974), the basic assumptions of such training are "that vision has motoric and sensory-motor bases; that problems in learning are due to disturbances of underlying functions in terms of visual efficiency and sensory-motor organization; that vision and visual organization can be trained; and that visual training will affect educational performance" (p. 220). Some optometrists believe that ocular malfunctioning can cause learning problems, rather than be merely a symptom.

The controversy regarding the vision training approach centers on whether these methods improve reading skills. Silver (1995) notes that reading is thought to be a complex task involving perception and central language processing, which are considered to be brain processes and not related to the vision functions of the eye. The results of two reviews (Keogh & Pelland, 1985; Metzger & Werner, 1984) indicate little or no support for this treatment. Moreover, the American Academy of Opthalmology (1984) is critical of this approach and indicates that scientific evidence does not support a causal relationship between vision problems and reading disabilities. Thus, there is concern about the use of vision training beyond the treatment of basic visual dysfunction.

Tinted Lenses

Irlen (1983) proposes that tinted colored lenses be used to treat individuals who have a specific type of learning disability (i.e., reading problem) and who also show evidence of scotopic sensitivity syndrome. This syndrome is characterized by photophobia, eye strain, poor visual resolution, a reduced span of focus, impaired depth perception, and poor sustained focus. The colored lenses are designed to reduce print and background distortions, ease strain and fatigue, and improve depth perception. However, Silver (1995) notes that there is no valid and reliable test for scotopic sensitivity syndrome that has been shown to be rater-reliable. Some studies (Blaskey et al., 1990; O'Connor, Sofo, Kendall, & Olsen, 1990; Robinson & Conway, 1990) focus on the use of tinted nonoptical (Irlen) lenses to filter specific light frequencies and minimize a visual-perceptual dysfunction that is believed to adversely affect reading skills; however, Hoyt (1990) notes that these studies do not validate the claim of the effectiveness of the lenses in the treatment of reading disabilities. Moreover, Fletcher and Martinez (1994) found that the use of colored overlays did not significantly affect comprehension in readers with scotopic sensitivity. Thus, these procedures are still experimental and do not have substantiated support.

Megavitamin Therapy

Many people enthusiastically support treatments centering on hypothesized deficiencies in body function. The hypothesis that vitamin deficiencies cause hyperactivity and learning problems underlies megavitamin therapy. Treatment consists of prescribing massive doses of vitamins. While combinations and dosages vary, vitamins commonly used include vitamin C, the B complex, and vitamin E. Vitamins A and D generally are excluded.

Megavitamin therapy originated in the work of Hoffer, Osmond, and Smythies (1954) with schizophrenics. The approach was popularized by a widely quoted article in which Cott (1971) describes a megavitamin treatment for children with learning disabilities. Since Cott's article, the efficacy of this form of therapy with children with learning disabilities has been questioned seriously (Golden, 1984; Silver, 1995), and several studies have failed to show evidence that megavitamin therapy effectively treats learning problems (Arnold, Christopher, Huestis, & Smeltzer, 1978; Haslem, Dalby, & Rademaker, 1984; Kershner, Hawks, & Grekin, 1977). Studies supporting this form of treatment have been criticized for poor experimental control and lack of clear descriptions regarding subjects, treatment, and variables used to measure outcome. In addition, several medical organizations including the American Psychiatric Association and the American Academy of Pediatrics do not support this treatment. Finally, Levine et al. (1980) caution about potential risks of toxicity from large doses of vitamins, especially B vitamins (e.g., nicotinic acid). Other researchers (Eastman, 1978; Golden, 1980) note a possible link between abnormalities in the liver and megadoses of vitamins B_3 and B_6. Golden (1980) reports that large doses of vitamin C and some B vitamins may have deleterious effects such as scurvy, cramps, diarrhea, cardiac arrhythmia, headaches, and fatigue. Although there is no validity to the proposed use of megavitamin therapy to treat learning disabilities, some individuals continue to use this approach to treatment.

Diet Modifications

Some pediatricians and allergists report that many children and adolescents with allergies also have learning disabilities (Silver, 1995). Thus, some treatments for learning disabilities are based on an allergic reaction to food or to other substances. As mentioned previously, Feingold (1973, 1975a, 1975b) proposes that hyperactivity and learning problems in some children may be caused by an allergic reaction to a natural or synthetic compound called salicylate. He purports that some children react adversely to this chemical in food colors and flavors. The chemical occurs naturally in apples, oranges, tomatoes, peaches, cucumbers, berries, and tea. Feingold identified 34 food colors, 1,610 synthetic flavors, and 1,120 other chemicals added to foods. To help control an allergic reaction to salicylates, Feingold prescribes the Kaiser-Permanente diet (K-P), which popularly is referred to as the Feingold diet. This diet eliminates foods containing natural and synthetic salicylates as well as various miscellaneous items such as toothpaste, perfumes, and compounds containing aspirin. Feingold (1976) reports improvement in 30% to 50% of individuals who adhere to the K-P diet. A national association supporting the diet encouraged commercial food processors to provide detailed product labeling and supported the national use of a design that would identify foods free of artificial flavors and colors.

Some professionals express concern about the claimed success of the Feingold diet, and reviews of studies do not show the dramatic improvement promised (Kavale & Forness, 1983; Spring & Sandoval, 1976; Varley, 1984; Wender, 1986). While some support for this treatment exists (Conners, 1980; Mayron, 1979; Rimland, 1983), the general consensus is that the Feingold diet is not effective in treating hyperactivity. A small percentage of children may respond positively to the treatment (i.e., 1% to 2%); however, it is impossible to predict which children will respond favorably.

Rapp (1978, 1986) proposes another diet that eliminates certain foods or food groups (e.g., milk, chocolate, eggs, wheat, corn, peanuts, pork, and sugar) that may cause an allergic reaction in children. In addition, she uses a food extract solution placed under the tongue to test a child's sensitivity to certain foods or to certain chemicals in the environment (e.g., paste, glue, paint, mold, and chemicals in new carpets). These items then are eliminated or avoided. Moreover, Crook and Stevens (1987) suggest a possible allergic reaction to yeast and the development of specific behaviors after a yeast infection. No research studies have confirmed these theories or proposed treatment programs.

Conclusion

Many treatment approaches are presented as being effective but actually lack empirical and professional support. Parents who are seeking help for their child may find it difficult to assess this plethora of unevaluated or unsubstantiated treatments. Teachers should be informed of these controversial therapies so that they can educate parents about what is known concerning these treatments.

Worrall (1990) addressed the topic of detecting health fraud in the field of learning disabilities. He developed a therapy rating scale that can be used by parents, teachers, and medical professionals as a guide to determine whether a claim or therapy represents a reasonable approach to a child's educational problems. Worrall suggests that the following questions be asked to evaluate the treatment approach according to common sense, consistency, and evidence:

1. Does the theory or therapy have a logical connection to the problem or condition being treated? Simply, does it meet common sense standards?
2. Is the theory or therapy consistent with related bodies of knowledge? Does it make sense in light of known facts in areas such as anatomy, psychology, and medicine?
3. How reasonable is the objective evidence? Does the study include control or placebo treatment groups? Is the therapy isolated in the study? Are the groups large enough to make statistical comparisons? How many studies are there?

MEDICAL SPECIALISTS

A variety of medical specialists may become involved in the diagnosis and treatment of learning disabilities. Teachers who are familiar with etiological and treatment perspectives of specialists can interact more easily with them and interpret their diagnostic reports. Bateman (1995) notes that students suspected of having a disability recognized by law are entitled to assessment at no cost in all areas related to the disability. This includes all medical diagnosis and evaluation that may have educational program implications. Medical specialists discussed in this section include the pediatric neurologist, otologist, audiologist, opthalmologist, and optometrist.

Pediatric Neurologist

Parents and school personnel may consult a pediatric neurologist regarding students with unexplained learning problems, especially when physiological involvement is suspected. The pediatric neurologist mainly establishes or rules out the presence of specific nervous system disorders as they relate to learning. Specifically, the neurologist searches for subtle or minor neurological signs that indicate a possible CNS dysfunction. Because the brain cannot be examined directly during the neurological examination, the physician depends on behavioral indicators (i.e., soft signs) to establish dysfunction.

The Neurological Examination. The following components are standard in a neurological examination (Kandt, 1984; Schor, 1983; S. E. Shaywitz & Shaywitz, 1988).

1. *Medical history.* Parents are questioned about any difficulties experienced during pregnancy or birth, or traumas experienced by the child (e.g., high fevers, seizures, or accidents resulting in head injury). In addition, parents are asked about developmental milestones, such as when the child walked and became toilet-trained. A family history also is taken to determine any familial patterns of learning disabilities.
2. *Current health status.* Any available results of recent physical examinations are noted. If necessary, a physical examination is administered.
3. *Examination of cranial nerves.* Various tests are given to ascertain the status of the 12 cranial nerves. The first cranial nerve transmits the sense of smell to the brain, and the patient is asked to identify a variety of smells. The second cranial nerve is the optical nerve, and the neurologist examines the eye for deformities

and checks the pigmentation and blood vessels. Visual acuity is assessed using a Snellen chart. The third, fourth, and sixth cranial nerves are responsible for eye movement, and the patient is asked to track a penlight while the physician monitors for unequal eye movement. Pupilar reflexes also are checked to see if they contract in reaction to bright light. The fifth cranial nerve deals with tactile sensation from the face to the brain and with control of the mouth. The examiner touches different parts of the patient's face and asks the patient to identify the touched areas. The patient also is requested to make chewing motions to assess signals from the brain to the mouth. The seventh cranial nerve controls facial muscles (except for chewing), and function is assessed by having the patient make certain tongue movements and blow the cheeks in and out while the mouth is closed. The examiner administers a simple hearing test when examining the eighth cranial nerve, which affects auditory ability. The ninth through twelfth cranial nerves affect articulation and are assessed by noting speech irregularities and observing abnormal tongue movements.

4. *Test of body sensation.* Sensory nerves running from the body to the brain are assessed by slightly pricking various body sites with a pin and asking the patient to identify the pricked areas. Insensitivity in an area indicates either dysfunctioning nerve pathways or a deficiency in sensory areas of the cerebral cortex.
5. *Motor skill assessment.* Loss of muscle tone, strength, or coordination may be indicative of the brain's failure to send nerve impulses to the muscles. Strength is assessed by having the patient push or pull against the physician's grasp. Hand coordination is tested by having the patient touch, in sequence, the thumb to the fingers in a smooth, rapid manner. Gross motor coordination is checked through movements such as standing on one foot, walking heel to toe, and skipping. Incoordination could indicate disturbances in cerebral functions.
6. *Evaluation of deep tendon reflexes.* Abnormal reflexes may be a sign of neurological damage in the spinal column. Knee and elbow reflexes are tested as well as the Babinski reflex, which is tested by running the thumb along the sole of the patient's foot. Normal reaction is for the foot to curve in as opposed to the toes fanning out.
7. *Assessment of higher processes.* Usually the physician asks the patient to copy designs and perform academic tasks such as math computation, writing, and passage reading. The neurologist also tests for right and left discrimination.

If it is indicated by the results of the neurological exam, the pediatric neurologist may recommend further evaluation using diagnostic hardware (e.g., EEG or CAT scan) discussed earlier in this chapter.

Reliability and Validity of the Neurological Examination. S. E. Shaywitz et al. (1984) note that "in practical terms the significance of a neuromaturational test lies in its ability to differentiate normal and learning-disabled school aged children" (p. 825). The neurological examination theoretically is capable of detecting signs of neurological impairment that may be causing a learning disability. This diagnostic procedure is based on the assumption that individuals with learning disabilities differ neurologically from normally functioning persons and that these differences can be detected. In other words, learning disabilities caused by minor neurological dysfunction should be able to be diagnosed through the identification of a set of symptoms (i.e., soft signs such as mild coordination difficulties or visual-motor disturbances) associated predominantly with learning problems. However, some experts are concerned about the validity and reliability of the neurological examination as a tool for identifying learning disabilities (including ADHD) resulting from CNS dysfunction.

Based on existing literature, the validity of the neurological examination is at best uncertain. Much criticism of this technique results from findings that a wide range of soft signs exist in some students who have no learning problems and that, conversely, some students identified as having a learning disability show no soft signs. In a selected review of the literature, Kavale and Forness (1985) note little support for neurological signs as a means by which to differentiate between students with and without learning disabilities. Other studies on the reliability of the neurological examination are somewhat more positive (Rutter, Graham, & Yule, 1970; S. E. Shaywitz et al., 1984). These studies analyzed performance differences between students with and without learning disabilities and found that, while individual elements of the neurological exam did not differentiate between groups, group differences were found when all elements were computed as a whole.

In spite of many years of research and practice, it remains difficult to diagnose students with learning disabilities as neurologically impaired based on the neurological examination. One reason is that the child's CNS is still maturing, and it is difficult to differentiate between a lag in maturity and an actual disorder. In addition, while some age-normative data exist regarding neurological indices (e.g., motor and sensory functions), further work is needed to increase confidence in the validity and reliability of the neurological examination. S. E. Shaywitz and Shaywitz (1988) strongly suggest that the presence or lack of soft signs never should be used alone as the reason for labeling a child.

When asked by the parent if a child should have a neurological examination, the learning disabilities teacher should recommend that the parent speak to the child's pediatrician. The teacher also can point out that the results of this type of examination should be viewed with some skepticism and that even if the child appears to have CNS problems, the diagnosis has little implication for the treatment of the child, unless ADHD is suspected and medication is suggested. However, subjecting the child to a neurological examination has at least two advantages: (a) it may be helpful emotionally to the parent to try this avenue of investigation, and (b) a neurological exam can eliminate concerns about problems such as tumors or other growths as well as the presence of petit mal seizure activity.

Otologist and Audiologist

Otology is the care and prevention of damage and disease to the ear, and the otologist is a medical doctor who specializes in this area of medicine. An audiologist, on the other hand, is a nonmedical specialist who assesses the extent of hearing loss and prescribes appropriate prosthetic devices, such as hearing aids.

The sense of hearing is crucial for learning. Teachers continuously present material that students must hear. In addition, hearing is essential to language development. While severe losses of hearing are relatively easy to identify, children with slight or mild hearing losses often escape detection. Several informal tests of hearing ability (e.g., conversation at 20 feet, whisper tests, and watch-ticking tests) are used to obtain a rough measure, but the most accurate method uses a pure-tone audiometer. This instrument produces pure tones of known intensity and frequency and permits each ear to be tested separately. *Intensity* refers to the relative loudness (volume) of a sound, while *frequency* refers to the number of vibrations per second of a sound wave (the more vibrations, the higher the pitch). In speech, the most important frequencies are between 500 and 2,000 vibrations per second.

During testing, the child listens to sounds of known intensity and frequency from the audiometer and indicates, by raising a hand or nodding, when a sound is heard. This determines how loud a sound has to be before the child hears it. The volume of a sound is measured in units called *decibels* (dB). If the child must have the volume of a sound increased 30 dB above the level at which it is detected by the normal ear, there is a hearing loss of 30 dB. Paul and Quigley (1990) list the levels of hearing loss as slight (27–40 dB), mild (41–55 dB), moderate (56–70 dB), severe (71–90 dB), and profound

(91 dB or more). A condition associated with slight or mild hearing loss that currently is being examined with respect to its relationship to learning problems is otitis media.

Otitis Media. *Otitis media* is an inflammation of the middle ear caused by allergies or infection. Two types of otitis media are discussed in the medical literature, though they often are hard to distinguish: acute otitis media and otitis media with effusion (OME). The latter condition is investigated most frequently and is associated with increased amounts of fluid that accumulate in the middle ear (Feagans, Blood, & Tubman, 1988). Hearing loss (between 10 to 50 dB) occurs only during episodes of OME. It is hypothesized that this nonpermanent but frequent hearing loss results in developmental delays in language acquisition (Feagans et al., 1988; Hasenstab, 1987). The actual prevalence of OME is difficult to determine because many episodes are "silent" (i.e., there are no accompanying symptoms or discomfort and the incident goes unnoticed).

While the actual effect on verbal development of hearing loss associated with OME still is being debated (Paradise & Rogers, 1986), several studies have been conducted in this area. One longitudinal investigation (Silva, Chalmers, & Stewart, 1986) found that children with bilateral OME performed worse in areas of speech articulation and verbal comprehension and expression than did a control group. A similar study (Friel-Patti & Finitzo, 1990) with young children (6 to 24 months) concluded that language development is affected by hearing loss associated with OME. While more research is needed to establish a causal relationship between OME and developmental delays, it is apparent that a relationship of some nature exists. In a study using students with learning disabilities as subjects, Reichman and Healey (1983) note that otitis media occurred more frequently in the population with learning disabilities than in the school-aged population without disabilities. However, in a longitudinal study of 946 children to determine the relationship between bilateral OME and educational achievement, Peters, Grievink, van Bon, and Schilder (1994) found that in children between the ages of 2 and 4 years, bilateral OME with a duration of at least 3 to 6 months does not appear to affect later reading or arithmetic abilities. Only a small detrimental effect on later spelling and writing abilities was noted.

If a hearing problem is suspected, the teacher may consult with the child's pediatrician and suggest that the parents take the student to an otologist, especially during an episode of OME. In addition, the teacher should monitor closely the student's behavior and provide one-to-one interaction to ensure that the student understands verbal instructions.

Ophthalmologist and Optometrist

Ophthalmology is the care and cure of diseases and injury to the eye and related structures. The ophthalmologist is required to complete medical school, serve an internship in general medicine and surgery, and pursue additional specialized training in the structure, function, and diseases of the eye. The ophthalmologist may prescribe eyeglasses and contact lenses and is permitted legally to diagnose and treat all eye disorders.

Optometry relates to the examination of the eyes, analysis of their function, and use of preventive or corrective measures to ensure maximum vision and comfort. The optometrist pursues a general course of study in college and then enters a graduate school of optometry from which he receives an OD degree. An optometrist is not a physician and cannot treat eye diseases or prescribe medication but can prescribe refractive lenses (eyeglasses and contact lenses) and treat functional aspects of vision.

The Eye. The eye enables the gathering of data necessary for survival and pleasure. Light rays are concentrated so that the image focuses on the tissues of the retina. This is called the *refractive process*, and refractive errors are the most common visual defect. The normal mature eye can focus on an image 20 feet away without muscular effort or refractive changes. When objects are closer or farther than 20 feet, the curvature of the lens alters, so that the image still will focus upon the retina (called *accommodation*). Visual keenness or acuity is expressed as a ratio based upon the basic 20-feet figure: 20/200 indicates that an individual can distinguish at 20 feet what the normal eye can distinguish at 200 feet. Errors in refraction include the following:

1. *Farsightedness* (hyperopia), in which the eye is too short from front to back. The image focuses behind the retina, resulting in a blurred or unclear image of a close stimulus (e.g., reading material).
2. *Nearsightedness* (myopia), in which the eye is too long from front to back. The image focuses in front of the retina, causing blurred vision of a distant stimulus.
3. *Astigmatism*, which results from an irregularity in the cornea or lens of the eye. Light rays cannot focus at the same point on the retina, so some of the image may fall in front of the retina and some behind it, causing blurred vision.

Children sometimes have defective muscular control of the eyes. *Strabismus* (crossed eyes) is caused by a lack of muscle coordination. A defect in muscular balance of the eyes results in *heterophoria*, in which the child cannot integrate the two images, one from each eye, into a single image. While heterophoria is not as noticeable as strabismus, difficulty in visual fusion results from it.

These disorders all are related to the eye as a specific organ. A problem arises with the attempt to define what is meant by *vision*. Should functions of the CNS and the PNS both be included in considerations for a definition, or should one consider the eye alone? Flax (1967) notes that PNS disorders refer to deficiencies of the eye including visual acuity, refractory error, fusion, convergence, and accommodation, whereas CNS disorders involve deficiencies in organizing and interpreting images received by the eyes and sent to the brain.

Assessments for a learning disability center on the presence of problems of visual processing, a CNS function. Children whose eyes do not produce clear vision (a PNS function) are referred to the ophthalmologist or optometrist for further assessment or correction. Vision training, discussed earlier in this chapter, is an example of a controversial treatment approach in which vision specialists become involved in CNS functioning rather than focusing solely on PNS functioning.

Because classroom tasks rely heavily on eyesight, vision problems (e.g., distortion in colors, shapes, letters, and other stimuli) are of concern to the teacher. Often, the teacher is the first person to notice some mild forms of vision problems, such as the child squinting at the chalkboard or a book. The teacher should share these observations with parents or the school nurse and suggest an initial vision screening or an examination by an ophthalmologist.

PERSPECTIVE

Many medical specialties contribute to the area of learning disabilities, and a variety of physiological explanations are being investigated. While an impressive amount of research has been completed to date, many questions about medical diagnosis of learning disabilities remain unanswered. However, new, more precise instrumentation and methods for examining the relationship of the CNS and learning disabilities are encouraging.

Advances have not been as rapid or promising with regard to treatment. Many medically related treatments fall into the category of "controversial." However, teachers should be aware of these approaches so that they can provide parents with up-to-date information and, when appropriate, recommend caution. One notable exception is the use of stimulant medication. While this procedure is controversial, there is substantial support for its use with certain students who have attention problems and hyperactivity. Communication among teachers, parents, and physicians is critical if medication is used, because determining an appropriate dosage level requires trial and error. Teachers also should remember that medication is not a substitute for good teaching and management procedures. In some cases, a combination of medication and behavioral procedures may be more effective than either approach in isolation.

Medical professionals frequently are involved with students with learning disabilities, and teachers should have a general, working knowledge of current medical procedures. This knowledge will help teachers communicate with physicians, give informed advice to parents, and hopefully provide better service to the students who rely on them.

DISCUSSION/REVIEW QUESTIONS

1. Describe the structure of the central nervous system and corresponding functions.
2. List types of neurodiagnostic hardware that are used when examining the structure and function of the brain, and discuss some of the findings of studies that used these procedures as well as the findings of postmortem studies.
3. Discuss four predominant medically related etiologies of learning problems.
4. Present the diagnostic criteria for attention-deficit hyperactivity disorder.
5. Discuss the use of stimulant medications in treating learning disabilities.
6. Discuss controversial treatment approaches, including patterning, vestibular dysfunction, vision training, and tinted lenses.
7. Describe the use of megavitamin therapy and diet modifications in treating learning disabilities.
8. Present the purpose and components of a neurological examination, and discuss its reliability and validity in identifying learning disabilities.
9. Discuss the role of the otologist and audiologist in treating learning disabilities.
10. Describe various disorders of the eye that are treated by the ophthalmologist and optometrist.

REFERENCES

Aman, M. G., & Rojahn, J. (1992). Pharmacological intervention. In N. N. Singh & I. L. Beale (Eds.), *Learning disabilities: Nature, theory and treatment.* New York: Springer-Verlag.

American Academy of Ophthalmology. (1984). *Joint policy statement: Learning disabilities, dyslexia, and vision.* (Available from author, P.O. Box 7424, San Francisco, CA 94120-7424.)

American Academy of Pediatrics. (1982) The Doman-Delacato treatment of neurologically handicapped children: A policy statement by the American Academy of Pediatrics. *Pediatrics, 70,* 810–812.

American Psychiatric Association. (1968). *Diagnostic and statistical manual of mental disorders* (2nd ed.). Washington, DC: Author.

American Psychiatric Association. (1980). *Diagnostic and statistical manual of mental disorders* (3rd ed.). Washington, DC: Author.

American Psychiatric Association. (1987). *Diagnostic and statistical manual of mental disorders* (3rd ed., Rev.). Washington, DC: Author.

American Psychiatric Association. (1994). *Diagnostic and statistical manual of mental disorders* (4th ed.). Washington, DC: Author.

Arnold, L. E., Christopher, J., Huestis, R. D., & Smeltzer, D. J. (1978). Megavitamins for minimal brain dysfunction, a placebo controlled study. *Journal of the American Medical Association, 240,* 2642–2643.

Ayres, A. J. (1978). Learning disabilities and the vestibular system. *Journal of Learning Disabilities, 11,* 18–29.

Barkley, R. A. (1990). *Attention deficit hyperactivity disorder: A handbook for diagnosis and treatment.* New York: Guilford Press.

Bateman, B. (1995). The physician and the world of special education. *Journal of Child Neurology, 10*(Suppl. 1), 114–120.

Bigler, E. D. (Ed.). (1990). *Traumatic brain injury: Mechanisms of damage, assessment, intervention, and outcome.* Austin, TX: PRO-ED.

Blaskey, P., Scheiman, M., Parisi, M., Ciner, E. B., Gallaway, M., & Selznick, R. (1990). The effectiveness of Irlen filters for improving reading performance: A pilot study. *Journal of Learning Disabilities, 23,* 604–612.

Brackbill, Y., McManus, K., & Woodward, L. (1985). *Medication in maternity: Infant exposure and maternal information.* Ann Arbor, MI: University of Michigan Press.

Bradley, C. (1937). The behavior of children receiving Benzedrine. *American Journal of Psychiatry, 4*, 577.

Brown, C. C. (1983). *Childhood learning disabilities and prenatal risk: An interdisciplinary data review for health care professionals and parents.* Skillman, NJ: Johnson and Johnson Baby Products. (ERIC Document Reproduction Service No. ED 242 117)

Cantwell, D. P., & Baker, L. (1991). Association between attention-deficit-hyperactivity disorder and learning disorders. *Journal of Learning Disabilities, 24*, 88–95.

Coles, G. S. (1980). Evaluation of genetic explanations of reading and learning problems. *The Journal of Special Education, 14*, 365–383.

Colletti, L. (1979). Relationship between pregnancy and birth complications and the later development of learning disabilities. *Journal of Learning Disabilities, 12*, 659–663.

Conners, C. K. (1980). *Food additives and hyperactive children*. New York: Plenum Press.

Cott, A. (1971). Orthomolecular approaches to treatment of learning disability. *Schizophrenia, 3*, 95.

Critchley, M. (1970). *The dyslexic child* (2nd ed.). London: Heinemann Medical Books.

Crook, W. G. (1975). Food allergy: The great masquerader. *Pediatric Clinics of North America, 22*, 227–228.

Crook, W. G., & Stevens, L. (1987). *Solving the puzzle of your hard-to-raise child.* Jackson, TN: Professional Books.

Davila, R., Williams, M. L., & MacDonald, J. T. (1991). *Clarification of policy to address the needs of children with attention deficit disorder within general and/or special education* (Memorandum of September 16, 1991). Washington, DC: U.S. Department of Education, Office of Special Education and Rehabilitative Services.

Deaton, A. V. (1987). Behavioral change strategies for children and adolescents with severe brain injury. *Journal of Learning Disabilities, 20*, 581–589.

Decker, S. N., & Defries, J. C. (1980). Cognitive abilities in families of reading disabled children. *Journal of Learning Disabilities, 13*, 517–522.

Decker, S. N., & Defries, J. C. (1981). Cognitive ability profiles in families of reading disabled children. *Developmental Medicine and Child Neurology, 23*, 217–227.

Delacato, C. H. (1966). *Neurological organization and reading*. Springfield, IL: Charles C Thomas.

DeLong, R. (1995). Medical and pharmacologic treatment of learning disabilities. *Journal of Child Neurology, 10*(Suppl. 1), 92–95.

Doman, G., & Delacato, C. (1968). Doman-Delacato philosophy. *Human Potential, 1*, 113–116.

Duane, D. D. (1989). Comment on dyslexia and neurodevelopmental pathology. *Journal of Learning Disabilities, 22*, 219–220.

Duffy, F. H., Denckla, M. B., Bartels, P. H., Sandini, G., & Kiessling, L. S. (1980). Dyslexia: Automated diagnosis by computerization classification of brain electrical activity. *Annals of Neurology, 7*, 421–428.

Eastman, M. (1978). The Eden express doesn't stop here anymore. *American Pharmacy, 40*, 12–17.

Epstein, M. H., Singh, N. N., Luebke, J., & Stout, C. E. (1991). Psychopharmacological intervention. II: Teacher perceptions of psychotropic medication for students with learning disabilities. *Journal of Learning Disabilities, 24*, 477–483.

Feagans, L., Blood, I., & Tubman, J. G. (1988). Otitis media: Models of effects and implementations for intervention. In F. H. Bess (Ed.), *Hearing impairment in children* (pp. 347–374). Parkton, MD: York Press.

Feingold, B. F. (1973). *Introduction to clinical allergy*. Springfield, IL: Charles C Thomas.

Feingold, B. F. (1975a). Hyperkineses and learning disabilities linked to artificial food flavors and colors. *American Journal of Nursing, 75*, 797–803.

Feingold, B. F. (1975b). *Why your child is hyperactive*. New York: Random House.

Feingold, B. F. (1976). Hyperkineses and learning disabilities linked to the ingestion of artificial food colors and flavors. *Journal of Learning Disabilities, 9*, 551–559.

Filipek, P. A. (1995). Neurobiologic correlates of developmental dyslexia: How do dyslexics' brains differ from those of normal readers? *Journal of Child Neurology, 10*(Suppl. 1), 62–69.

Flax, N. (1967). *Visual function in dyslexia*. Paper presented at the annual meeting of the American Academy of Optometry, Chicago.

Fletcher, J., & Martinez, G. (1994). An eye-movement analysis of the effects of scotopic sensitivity correction on parsing and comprehension. *Journal of Learning Disabilities, 27*, 67–70.

Forness, S. R., & Kavale, K. A. (1988). Psychopharmacologic treatment: A note on classroom effects. *Journal of Learning Disabilities, 21*, 144–147.

Fowler, M. (1992). *CH.A.D.D. educators manual: An in-depth look at attention deficit disorders from an educational perspective*. Plantation, FL: CH.A.D.D.

Freeman, R. D. (1967). Controversy over "patterning" as a treatment for brain damage in children. *Journal of the American Medical Association, 202*, 385–388.

Friel-Patti, S., & Finitzo, T. (1990). Language learning in a prospective study of otitis media with effusion in the first two years of life. *Journal of Speech and Hearing Research, 33*, 188–194.

Gadow, K. D. (1981). Effects of stimulant drugs on attention and cognitive deficits. *Exceptional Education Quarterly, 2*(3), 83–93.

Gadow, K. D. (1983). Pharmacotherapy for behavior disorders. *Clinical Pediatrics, 22*, 48–53.

Gadow, K. D. (1986). *Children on medication* (Vols. 1 and 2). San Diego: College-Hill Press.

Galaburda, A. M. (1988). The pathogenesis of childhood dyslexia. In F. Plum (Ed.), *Language, communication and the brain* (pp. 127–138). New York: Raven Press.

Geschwind, N. (1968). Neurological foundations of language. In H. Myklebust (Ed.), *Progress in learning disabilities* (Vol. 1). New York: Grune & Stratton.

Geschwind, N., & Behan, P. (1984). Laterality, hormones and immunity. In N. Geschwind & A. M. Galaburda (Eds.), *Cerebral dominance: The biological foundations* (pp. 211–234). Cambridge, MA: Harvard University Press.

Geschwind, N., & Galaburda, A. M. (1987). *Cerebral lateralization: Biological mechanisms, associations, and pathology*. Cambridge, MA: MIT Press.

Gilliam, J. E. (1995). *Attention-Deficit/Hyperactivity Disorder Test*. Austin, TX: PRO-ED.

Gold, S., & Sherry, L. (1984). Hyperactivity, learning disabilities, and alcohol. *Journal of Learning Disabilities, 17*, 3–6.

Golden, G. S. (1980). Nonstandard therapies in the developmental disabilities. *American Journal of Diseases of Children, 134*, 487–491.

Golden, G. S. (1984). Controversial therapies. *Pediatric Clinics of North America, 31*, 459–469.

Goldstein, F. C., & Levin, H. S. (1987). Epidemiology of pediatric closed head injury: Incidence, clinical characteristics, and risk factors. *Journal of Learning Disabilities, 20*, 518–525.

Gross, M. D. (1976). Growth of hyperkinetic children taking methylphenidate, dextroamphetamine, or imipramine/desipramine. *Pediatrics, 58*, 423–431.

Hallahan, D. P., Kauffman, J. M., & Lloyd, J. W. (1985). *Introduction to learning disabilities* (2nd ed.). Upper Saddle River, NJ: Prentice Hall.

Hallgren, B. (1950). Specific dyslexia: A clinical and genetic study. *Acta Psychiatrica Neurologica, 65*, 1–287.

Harris, R. (1983). Clinical neurophysiology in pediatric neurology. In E. M. Brett (Ed.), *Paediatric neurology* (pp. 582–600). Edinburgh: Churchill Livingstone.

Hasenstab, M. S. (1987). *Language learning and otitis media*. Boston: College-Hill Press.

Haslem, R. M., Dalby, J. T., Rademaker, A. W. (1984). Effects of megavitamin therapy on children with attention deficit disorders. *Pediatrics, 74*, 103–111.

Hermann, K. (1959). *Reading disability: A medical study of word blindness and related handicaps*. Springfield, IL: Charles C Thomas.

Hiscock, M., & Kinsbourne, M. (1980). Individual differences in cerebral lateralization: Are they relevant to learning disabilities? In W. M. Cruickshank (Ed.), *Approaches to learning: Vol. 1. The best of ACLD*. Syracuse, NY: Syracuse University Press.

Hiscock, M., & Kinsbourne, M. (1987). Specialization of the cerebral hemispheres: Implications for learning. *Journal of Learning Disabilities, 20*, 130–143.

Hoffer, A., Osmond, H., & Smythies, J. (1954). Schizophrenia: A new approach: II. Results of a year's research. *Journal of Mental Science, 100*, 20.

Hoyt, C. S., III. (1990). Irlen lenses and reading difficulties. *Journal of Learning Disabilities, 23*, 624–626.

Hynd, G. W., Hern, L., Voeller, K., & Marshall, R. (1991). Neurological basis of attention deficit hyperactivity disorder (ADHD). *School Psychology, 20*(2), 174–186.

Hynd, G. W., Marshall, R., & Gonzalez, J. (1991). Learning disabilities and presumed central nervous system dysfunction. *Learning Disability Quarterly, 14*, 283–296.

Hynd, G. W., & Semrud-Clikeman, M. (1989). Dyslexia and neurodevelopmental pathology: Relationships to cognition, intelligence, and reading skill acquisition. *Journal of Learning Disabilities, 22*, 204–216.

Hynd, G. W., Semrud-Clikeman, M., Lorys, A. R., Novey, E. S., & Eliopulos, D. (1990). Brain morphology in developmental dyslexia and attention deficit disorder/hyperactivity. *Archives of Neurology, 47*, 919–926.

Hynd, G. W., Semrud-Clikeman, M., Lorys, A. R., Novey, E. S., Eliopulos, D., & Lyytinen, H. (1991). Corpus callosum morphology in attention deficit-hyperactivity disorder: Morphometric analysis of MRI. *Journal of Learning Disabilities, 24*, 141–146.

Irlen, H. (1983, August). *Successful treatment of learning disabilities*. Paper presented at the 91st annual convention of the American Psychological Association, Anaheim, CA.

Kandt, R. S. (1984). Neurologic examination of children with learning disorders. *Pediatric Clinics of North America, 31*, 297–315.

Katsiyannis, A., & Conderman, G. (1994). Serving individuals with traumatic brain injury: A national survey. *Remedial and Special Education, 15*, 319–325.

Kavale, K. A. (1982). The efficacy of stimulant drug treatment for hyperactivity: A meta-analysis. *Journal of Learning Disabilities, 15*, 280–289.

Kavale, K. A., & Forness, S. R. (1983). Hyperactivity and diet treatment: A meta- analysis of the Feingold hypothesis. *Journal of Learning Disabilities, 16*, 324–330.

Kavale, K. A., & Forness, S. R. (1985). *The science of learning disabilities*. San Diego, CA: College-Hill Press.

Keogh, B. K. (1974). Optometric vision training programs for children with learning disabilities: Review of issues and research. *Journal of Learning Disabilities, 7*, 219–231.

Keogh, B. K., & Pelland, M. (1985). Vision training revisited. *Journal of Learning Disabilities, 18*, 228–236.

Kershner, J. R., Hawks, W., & Grekin, R. (1977). *Megavitamins and learning disorders: A controlled double-blind experiment*. Unpublished manuscript, Ontario Institute for Studies in Education, Toronto.

Kinsbourne, M., & Smith, W. (Eds.). (1974). *Hemispheric disconnection and cerebral function*. Springfield, IL: Charles C Thomas.

Korkman, M., & Pesonen, A. E. (1994). A comparison of neuropsychological test profiles of children with attention deficit-hyperactivity disorder and/or learning disorder. *Journal of Learning Disabilities, 27*, 383–392.

Larsen, J. P., Hoien, T., Lundberg, I., Odegaard, H. (1990). MRI evaluation of the size and symmetry of the planum temporale in adolescents with developmental dyslexia. *Brain and Language, 26*, 78–86.

Lerner, J. W., Lowenthal, B., & Lerner, S. R. (1995). *Attentive deficit disorders: Assessment and teaching*. Pacific Grove, CA: Brooks/Cole.

Levine, M. D., Brooks, R., & Shonkoff, J. P. (1980). *A pediatric approach to learning disorders*. New York: Wiley.

Levinson, H. N. (1980). *A solution to the riddle of dyslexia*. New York: Springer-Verlag.

Levinson, H. N. (1984). *Smart but feeling dumb*. New York: Warner.

Lou, H. C., Henriksen, L., Bruhn, P., Borner, H., & Nielson, J. B. (1989). Striatal dysfunction in attention-deficit and hyperkinetic disorder. *Archives of Neurology, 46*, 48–52.

Lovitt, T. C. (1989). *Introduction to learning disabilities*. Boston: Allyn & Bacon.

Mayron, L. W. (1979). Allergy, learning, and behavior problems. *Journal of Learning Disabilities, 12*, 32–42.

McBurnett, K., Lahey, B. B., & Pfiffner, L. J. (1993). Diagnosis of attention deficit disorders in *DSM-IV*: Scientific basis and implications for educators. *Exceptional Children, 60*, 108–117.

Metzger, R. L., & Werner, D. B. (1984). Use of visual training for reading disabilities: A review. *Pediatrics, 73*, 824–829.

Myers, P. I., & Hammill, D. D. (1990). *Learning disabilities: Basic concepts, assessment practices, and instructional strategies* (4th ed.). Austin, TX: PRO-ED.

Needleman, H. L. (1983). Environmental pollutants. In C. C. Brown (Ed.), *Childhood learning disabilities and prenatal risk: An interdisciplinary data review for healthcare professionals and parents*. Skillman, NJ: Johnson and Johnson Baby Products. (ERIC Document Reproduction Service No. ED 242 117)

Norrie, E. (1959). Wordblindness. In S. J. Thompson (Ed.), *Reading disability*. Springfield, IL: Charles C Thomas.

Obrzut, J. E. (1989). Dyslexia and neurodevelopmental pathology: Is the neurodiagnostic technology ahead of the psychoeducational technology? *Journal of Learning Disabilities, 22*, 217–218.

O'Connor, P. D., Sofo, F., Kendall, L., & Olsen, G. (1990). Reading disabilities and the effects of colored filters. *Journal of Learning Disabilities, 23*, 597–603, 620.

Orton, S. (1937). *Reading, writing and speech problems in children*. New York: Norton.

Paradise, J. L., & Rogers, K. D. (1986). On otitis media, child development and tympanostomy tubes: New answers or old questions? *Pediatrics, 77*, 88–92.

Paul, P. V., & Quigley, S. P. (1990). *Education and deafness*. White Plains, NY: Longman.

Pelham, W. E. (1981). Attention deficits in hyperactive and learning-disabled children. *Exceptional Education Quarterly, 2*(3), 13–23.

Pelham, W. E. (1986). The effects of psychostimulant drugs on learning and academic achievement in children with attention-deficit disorders and learning disabilities. In J. Torgesen & B. Wong (Eds.), *Psychological and educational perspectives on learning disabilities* (pp. 160–168). New York: Academic Press.

Pelham, W. E., Sturges, J., Hoza, J., Schmidt, C., Biyisma, J. J., Milich, R., & Moorer, S. (1987). Sustained release and standard methylphenidate effects on cognitive and social behavior in children with attention deficit disorder. *Pediatrics, 80,* 491–501.

Pennington, B. F. (1995). Genetics of learning disabilities. *Journal of Child Neurology, 10*(Suppl. 1), 69–77.

Peters, S. A. F., Grievink, E. H., van Bon, W. H. J., & Schilder, A. G. M. (1994). The effects of early bilateral otitis media with effusion on educational attainment: A prospective cohort study. *Journal of Learning Disabilities, 27,* 111–121.

Polatajko, H. S. (1985). A critical look at vestibular dysfunction in learning-disabled children. *Developmental Medicine and Child Neurology, 27,* 283–292.

Rapoport, J. C., Buchsbaum, M. S., Weingartner, H., Zahn, T. P., & Ludlow, C. (1978). Dextroamphetamine: Cognitive and behavioral effects in normal prepubertal boys. *Science, 199,* 560–563.

Rapp, D. J. (1978). Does diet affect hyperactivity? *Journal of Learning Disabilities, 11,* 383–389.

Rapp, D. J. (1986). *The impossible child in school and at home.* Buffalo, NY: Life Sciences Press.

Reichman, J., & Healey, W. C. (1983). Learning disabilities and conductive hearing loss involving otitis media. *Annual Review of Learning Disabilities, 1,* 39–45.

Reid, R., Maag, J. W., & Vasa, S. F. (1993). Attention deficit hyperactivity disorder as a disability category: A critique. *Exceptional Children, 60,* 198–214.

Rimland, B. (1983). The Feingold diet: An assessment of the reviews by Mattes, by Kavale and Forness and others. *Journal of Learning Disabilities, 16,* 331–333.

Robbins, M. P., & Glass, G. V. (1969). The Doman-Delacato rationale: A critical analysis. In J. Hellmuth (Ed.), *Educational therapy* (Vol. 2, pp. 321–377). Seattle: Special Child.

Robinson, G. L. W., & Conway, R. N. F. (1990). The effects of Irlen colored lenses on students' specific reading skills and their perception of ability: A 12-month validity study. *Journal of Learning Disabilities, 23,* 589–596.

Rutter, M., Graham, P., & Yule, W. (1970). *A neuropsychiatric study in childhood.* London: Spastics International Medical Publishers.

Safer, D., Allen, R., & Barr, E. (1975). Growth rebound after termination of stimulant drugs. *Pediatrics, 86,* 113–116.

Safer, D., & Krager, J. M. (1984). Trends in medication therapy for hyperactivity: National and international perspectives. In K. D. Gadow (Ed.), *Advances in learning and behavioral disabilities* (Vol. 3, pp. 125–149). London: JAI Press.

Santos, K. E. (1992). Fragile X syndrome: An educator's role in identification, prevention, and intervention. *Remedial and Special Education, 13*(2), 32–39.

Schor, D. P. (1983). The neurological examination. In J. A. Blackman (Ed.), *Medical aspects of developmental disabilities in children birth to three: A resource for special-service providers in the educational setting* (pp. 173–177). Iowa City, IA: University of Iowa.

Sell, E. J., Gaines, J. A., Gluckman, C., & Williams, E. (1985). Early identification of learning problems in neonatal intensive care graduates. *American Journal of Diseases of Children, 139,* 460–463.

Shaywitz, B. A. (1987). Hyperactivity/attention deficit disorder. In Interagency Committee on Learning Disabilities, *Learning disabilities: A report to the U.S. Congress* (pp. 194–218). Bethesda, MD: National Institutes of Health.

Shaywitz, B. A., Fletcher, J. M., & Shaywitz, S. E. (1995). Defining and classifying learning disabilities and attention-deficit/hyperactivity disorder. *Journal of Child Neurology, 10*(Suppl. 1), 50–57.

Shaywitz, S. E., Cohen, D., & Shaywitz, B. A. (1980). Behavior and learning difficulties in children of normal intelligence born to alcoholic mothers. *Journal of Pediatrics, 96,* 978–982.

Shaywitz, S. E., & Shaywitz, B. A. (1988). Hyperactivity/attention deficits. In J. F. Kavanagh & T. J. Truss (Eds.), *Learning disabilities: Proceedings of the National Conference* (pp. 369–523). Parkton, MD: York Press.

Shaywitz, S. E., Shaywitz, B. A., McGraw, K., & Groll, S. (1984). Current status of the neuromaturational examination as an index of learning disability. *Journal of Pediatrics, 104,* 819–825.

Silva, P. A., Chalmers, D., & Stewart, I. (1986). Some audiological, psychological, educational and behavioral characteristics of children with bilateral otitis media with effusion: A longitudinal study. *Journal of Learning Disabilities*, *19*, 165–169.

Silver, L. B. (1988). A review of the federal government's Interagency Committee on Learning Disabilities report to the U.S. Congress. *Learning Disabilities Focus*, *35*, 73–80.

Silver, L. B. (1990). Attention deficit-hyperactivity disorder: Is it a learning disability or a related disorder? *Journal of Learning Disabilities*, *23*, 394–397.

Silver, L. B. (1995). Controversial therapies. *Journal of Child Neurology*, *10*(Suppl. 1), 96–100.

Smith, C. R. (1994). *Learning disabilities: The interaction of learner, task, and setting* (3rd ed.). Boston: Allyn & Bacon.

Smith, S. D., Pennington, B. F., Kimberling, W. J., & Ing, P. S. (1990). Familial dyslexia: Use of genetic linkage data to define subtypes. *Journal of the American Academy of Child and Adolescent Psychiatry*, *29*, 204–213.

Smith, S. M. (1989). Congenital syndromes and mildly handicapped students: Implications for special educators. *Remedial and Special Education*, *10*(3), 20–30.

Sparks, S. (1984). *Birth defects and speech language disorders.* San Diego: College-Hill Press.

Spring, C., & Sandoval, J. (1976). Food additives and hyperkinesis: A critical evaluation of the evidence. *Journal of Learning Disabilities*, *9*, 560–569.

Stanford, L. D., & Hynd, G. W. (1994). Congruence of behavioral symptomatology in children with ADD/H, ADD/WO, and learning disabilities. *Journal of Learning Disabilities*, *27*, 243–253.

Stone, M., & Pielstick, N. L. (1969). Effectiveness of Delacato treatment with kindergarten children. *Psychology in the Schools*, *6*, 63–68.

Swanson, J. M., McBurnett, K., Wigal, T., Pfiffner, L. J., Lerner, M. A., Williams, L., Christian, D. L., Tamm, L., Willcutt, E., Crowley, K., Clevenger, W., Khouzam, N., Woo, C., Crinella, F. M., & Fisher, T. D. (1993). Effect of stimulant medication on children with attention deficit disorder: A "review of reviews." *Exceptional Children*, *60*, 154–162.

Van Dyke, D. C., & Fox, A. A. (1990). Fetal drug exposure and its possible implications for learning in the preschool and school-aged population. *Journal of Learning Disabilities*, *23*, 160–163.

Varley, C. K. (1984). Diet and the behavior of children with attention deficit disorder. *Journal of the American Academy of Child Psychiatry*, *23*, 182–185.

Vogel, F., & Motulsky, A. G. (1986). *Human genetics.* New York: Springer-Verlag.

Walzer, S. (1985). X chromosome abnormalities and cognitive development. Implications for understanding normal human development. *Journal of Child Psychology and Psychiatry*, *26*, 177–184.

Weingartner, H., Rapoport, J. C., Buchsbaum, M. S., Bunney, W. E., Ebert, M. H., Mikkelsen, E. J., & Caine, E. D. (1980). Cognitive processes in normal and hyperactive children and their response to amphetamine treatment. *Journal of Abnormal Psychology*, *89*, 25–37.

Wender, E. H. (1986). The food additive-free diet in the treatment of behavior disorders: A review. *Journal of Developmental and Behavioral Pediatrics*, *7*, 35–42.

Worrall, R. S. (1990). Detecting health fraud in the field of learning disabilities. *Journal of Learning Disabilities*, *23*, 207–212.

Zametkin, A. J., Nordahl, T. E., Gross, M., King, A. C., Semple, W. E., Rumsey, J., Hamburger, S., & Cohen, R. M. (1990). Cerebral glucose metabolism of adults with hyperactivity of childhood onset. *New England Journal of Medicine*, *232*, 1361–1364.

Zentall, S. S. (1993). Research on the educational implications of attention deficit hyperactivity disorder. *Exceptional Children*, *60*, 143–153.

The Family and Learning Disabilities

CHAPTER 4

After studying this chapter, you should be able to:

- discuss adjustment reactions that parents of a child with learning disabilities typically experience.
- identify some of the factors that contribute to the diversity of families.
- identify informational strategies for use with parents.
- describe counseling strategies for use with parents.
- describe parent involvement programs.
- describe parent training programs.
- discuss home-based services and activities.
- describe home tutoring techniques.
- describe techniques for maintaining positive parent-teacher relationships.
- discuss parent-teacher conferences.
- identify parent rights and advocacy techniques.

Families are interdependent systems and, thus, can be compared with a mobile that hangs over an infant's crib: when one of the objects is touched, all of the objects are affected. Similarly, the presence of a family member with learning disabilities can affect all members of the family intensely. Overall, families that include children with special needs have higher divorce rates and more marital problems than families without children who have special needs (Wright, Matlock, & Matlock, 1985). However, many marriages do remain intact and satisfying in spite of the presence of a child with disabilities (Lambie & Daniels-Mohring, 1993). Family members and the child with learning disabilities need help to create and maintain relationships and structures that foster understanding, support, and acceptance. Given the power of the family to care for its members and influence social policy, educators are encouraged to foster positive relationships with parents.

The influence of parents is prominent through the history of learning disabilities. Parents have formed organizations, started schools, and actively supported legislation, especially in the last decade. Kirk (1984), a distinguished special educator for the past 50 years, recognizes the effect of parents: "If I were to give credit to one group in this country for the advancements that have been made in the education of exceptional children, I would place the parent organizations and parent movement in the forefront as the leading force" (p. 41). Parents of various educational and socioeconomic levels use their respective skills and resources for activities ranging from starting private schools and securing grant monies to volunteering time to public school programs.

Conditions that continue to foster an increased need for parent-teacher partnerships include the following:

1. Legislation (the Individuals with Disabilities Education Act) ensures that parents or surrogate parents may participate in their child's education.
2. Parent advocacy efforts continue to secure special programs, involve more parents, and stimulate legislation.
3. The significant and positive effect of parent involvement is well documented (Eiserman, Weber, & McCoun, 1995; National Center for Education Statistics, 1988).
4. How children with disabilities affect their families is becoming more understood (Lambie & Daniels-Mohring, 1993).
5. Numerous books, materials, and training programs are available to help parents understand and educate their child.
6. The importance of early identification of learning deficits places a responsibility on parents to detect potential problems before school entry.
7. Parents need the partnership of teachers to help them understand the learning needs of their child and provide appropriate support. Likewise, teachers need the partnership of parents to help them understand the emotional and instructional needs of their students.

These conditions indicate that parents and school personnel must work together. McLoughlin, Edge, and Strenecky (1978) encourage parental involvement in each of the five stages of learning disabilities intervention: (a) identification—being alert to early signs of learning disabilities and aware of available services, (b) assessment—gathering observational data at home and supplying relevant information from previous assessments, (c) programming—participating in the selection of the most appropriate educational placement as well as the goals and objectives for the individualized educational program (IEP), (d) implementation—serving as a classroom aide and tutor and performing home-based activities, and (e) evaluation—providing essential information about the generalization of academic skills and judging significant changes in the child's attitude and social behavior. Moreover, Heid and Harris (1989) discuss five types of parental participation that improve student achievement: (a) providing for basic physical and psychological needs, (b) responding to communications from school, (c) participating in school activities, (d) participating in learning activities at home, and (e) participating in educational governance and advocacy.

This chapter discusses the knowledge and skills needed to work effectively with parents. Specifically, it deals with answers to the following questions: What are the common reactions and defenses of such parents? How do you organize a parent conference? What are some ways of reporting the child's progress to the parents? Should parents teach school subjects to their child? Should parents screen and observe their child for learning and behavior problems? What management techniques can parents use at home? What is the parents' role in prevention and remediation? What are some activities and techniques that can help the parents and the child adjust at home? What are the rights of the child and the parents? What are some good resources (e.g., books, parent groups, periodicals, physician, and psychologist) for the parents? What are some ways of comparing teacher and parent attitudes toward the child? Parents as well as professionals may find this chapter helpful in adjusting and securing services for children with learning disabilities.

PARENTAL ADJUSTMENT

Barsch (1969) notes that no parent is ever prepared to be the parent of a child with special needs. The parents primarily learn about the child through the experience of family living, and therefore, professionals working with the parents must focus on these learning experiences. Our society offers a variety of services to support families with normal children: physicians, teachers, counselors, baby-sitters, recreation programs, and friends. These standard resources are not readily available to families of children with disabilities. Thus, the parents of a child with learning disabilities may turn to a medical specialist, counselor, teacher, or another parent of a child with learning disabilities. The individual rendering help must be conscious of his or her potential effect. According to Wolfensberger (1967), "Unless he approaches his task with awe and the willingness to be most cautious and circumspect with his counsel, he is not ready to work with parents" (p. 354).

A. P. Turnbull and Turnbull (1990) identify four factors that influence how a child with special needs affects a family. First, the characteristics of the exceptionality (i.e., nature, severity, and demands of the disability) help shape the family's reactions. J. J. Gallagher, Beckman, and Cross (1983) report that the degree of problems parents experience is highly related to the care-giving demands of the child and the age of the child (i.e., problems intensify as age increases). Second, the characteristics of the family influence the reaction. Size and form, cultural background, socioeconomic status, and geographic location all may affect a family's adjustment to a child with special needs. Third, the personal characteristics of each family member (e.g., family health and coping styles) influence the family's reaction to a disability. Finally, the special challenges of a family (e.g., families in poverty, families in rural areas, families with abuse, or parents with disabilities) may affect their reactions to the disability. Although parents may share common problems and reactions, the combinations of reactions that are possible, the intensity of the reactions, and the duration of the reactions are unique to each family and necessitate that each family be considered individually.

A review of common adjustment problems helps the professional as well as the parent to understand better the unique matrix of reactions that a family may have. For example, parents' reactions to the diagnosis of a learning disability in their child may be similar to feelings of grief and be characterized by shock, denial, blame or guilt, anger, and sorrow. Anderegg, Vergason, and Smith (1992) maintain that the grief cycle

TABLE 4.1
Grief Phases and Behaviors with Related Teacher Interventions

Grief Phases and Behaviors	Teacher Interventions
Confronting	
Shock	Have parents make frequent restatements of the known facts of the child's diagnosis and prognosis.
Denial	
Blame/Guilt	Have parents brainstorm all possible alternatives.
Adjusting	
Depression	Suggest commitment to a short-term goal that requires ongoing cognitive effort to accomplish.
Anger	
Bargaining	Guide parents to seek practical solutions to problems.
Adapting	
Life-style change	Encourage the investigation of alternatives.
Realistic planning	Focus parents' attention on collections of facts.
Altered expectations	Encourage parents to list expectations of each family member.

represents a viable framework for understanding the processes that families experience in dealing with a child with disabilities. Table 4.1 presents the three phases of Anderegg et al.'s model of the grief cycle and includes parent behaviors in each phase as well as related teacher interventions. Anderegg et al. note that various family members are typically at different points in the grieving process and should be supported according to their respective needs.

The following framework is used to further discuss parental adjustment: (a) awareness of a problem, (b) recognition of the problem, (c) search for a cause, (d) search for a cure, and (e) acceptance of the child. A family's adaptation to a child with learning disabilities is multidimensional, and the diversity of adjustment patterns is a result of numerous variables in the individual coping responses. A developmental pattern is not clear-cut, and different parents pass through these areas at different rates. In essence, parents make continual adjustments and readjustments to the individual with disabilities. For example, parents may re-experience various adjustment reactions when their son or daughter with disabilities faces different life experiences (e.g., participating in sporting events, making friends, or planning for college or a career).

Awareness of a Problem

The wide range of characteristics used to describe children with learning disabilities makes a reliable diagnosis difficult. Some children show significant problems in the first few months of infancy, whereas others show no difficulties until they are in school. L. S. Gallagher (1995) reports that parents often feel helpless when their apparently normal child displays such school-related problems as sadness, anger, frustration, sleeplessness, poor self-esteem, mood swings, and unfounded aches and pains. Moreover, Lambie and Daniels-Mohring (1993) note that the longer the child with learning disabilities experiences school problems prior to being diagnosed, the more likely it is that frustration and anger will occur among the child, parent, and teacher.

When the child displays early symptoms, the mother is usually the first to suspect problems. Brutten, Richardson, and Mangel (1973) list some of the usual behaviors or signs that deserve attention:

> Failure to sit by nine months; failure to walk without holding by 18 months to two years; failure to speak understandable single words by three years; any severe spasm or repeated blackouts; any sort

of distant vacant look about the eyes or a lack of recognition and pleasure at familiar voices and faces; exceptional clumsiness with the hands; stumbling gait and much falling; prolonged drooling; unusual and marked emotional reactions; gusts of violent response to *trivial* occurrences; lack of laughter; failure to enjoy ritualized games such as peek-a-boo and pat-a-cake.(p. 58)

When a mother notices some of the early symptoms, she usually expresses her concerns to the father, the pediatrician, or the child's preschool or kindergarten teacher. At this beginning stage of awareness, the parents, relatives, and friends may deny individually or collectively that there is anything wrong. In addition, emotionally healthy parents frequently exhibit temporary denial to lessen the effects of the situation.

When parents have always viewed their child as being normal, a shock reaction may result when they first suspect that their child has a learning disability. Weiss and Weiss (1976) describe their initial reaction: "Initially, we can recall the sense of shock through which we passed when we first became aware of our own child's difficulty in learning according to predictable norms" (p. 59). Other parents who suspect something is wrong may be relieved to learn that there are reasons for the academic or behavior difficulties their child is experiencing. Parents approach problem awareness with difficulty, and their initial concerns must be regarded seriously. In an effort to recognize and cope with the problem, they usually seek and benefit from professional information and support.

Recognition of the Problem

Parents must recognize the nature of the disability, but their hopes for their child's success may make this difficult. They have an image of the ideal child who will achieve great things and surpass or at least attain their own sociocultural level. At the diagnosis of a disability, the parents' worst fears are realized. They cannot cope with the gap between dream and reality. Common reactions include parental conflict, "doctor shopping," and the use of various defense mechanisms to reduce the anxiety generated by guilt, bewilderment, sorrow, anger, grief, and panic.

Parental Conflict. Each spouse differs in perception and reaction to the problem, which frequently leads to conflict. For example, one parent may take the lead as the child's primary caregiver and work with school personnel, monitor the child's progress, discover strengths and weaknesses, and determine when to seek professional advice. The other parent can perceive this attention to the child as unnecessary, too expensive, and promoting learned helplessness. These views create tension between the husband and wife (L. S. Gallagher, 1995). In other cases, guilt and anger occur as parents blame each other for the child's disability or become frustrated with teachers or school personnel as they attempt to locate appropriate services for their child. However, the presence of a child with disabilities is not always associated with parental conflict. J. J. Gallagher et al. (1983) report that in some cases the parents become closer.

"Doctor Shopping." Some parents react to the disability by questioning the accuracy of the diagnosis. A period of "doctor shopping" begins in which the child is rushed from one specialist to another in hopes of repudiating the original diagnosis. This should not be confused with the sound practice of validating a diagnosis. Writing from a parent's perspective, L. S. Gallagher (1995) notes that it is difficult for parents to know when enough is enough regarding diagnosis and related treatments. She points out that during the last 20 years multiple "cures" have come and gone, and there is still no single answer for children with learning disabilities. Learning disabilities, especially milder forms, are often difficult to diagnose during the preschool years. This difficulty provides parents with a valid reason for seeking several evaluations. Parents should be suspected of "doctor shopping" only after several professionals have rendered similar diagnoses, and the parents continue to seek another one.

Defense Mechanisms. Parents often try to reduce their anxiety by using *defense mechanisms*. Some defense mechanisms are effective in reducing anxiety and, thus, their use is reinforced. However, these mechanisms can lead to distortions of reality and can complicate the search for a cause. Some methods work (though they can be destructive in the long run), and thus they reinforce and maintain the behavior. Moreover, they can interfere with the relationship between the parents and the child.

One of the most common defense mechanisms is *denial*, the refusal to believe anything is wrong. Parents may claim that their child is quite capable and insist on making unrealistic demands (e.g., piano lessons, sports, dancing lessons, spelling bees, or oral reading). Conversely, they may overprotect the child by not allowing participation in an activity that the child can do and enjoy. Unrealistic expectations and overprotection interfere with the child's optimum development. Unrealistic expectations often cause the child to feel frustrated and inadequate, and overprotection can result in overdependence. L. S. Gallagher (1995) claims that there is a fine line between overprotection and giving the child the support that is required.

Obviously, recognition of the problem is difficult. Shattered expectations, guilt, anger, parental conflict, and many other aversive states form a kaleidoscope of feelings from which the unique responses of parents emerge. During this grieving process, parents may experience periods of denial, anger, and depression. These reactions can serve a healthy function by enabling the parents to face the problem and its effect and ultimately emerge with thoughtfully considered attitudes. Robinson and Robinson (1976) recommend that this period not be interrupted too quickly with reassurance and comfort from professionals, thus allowing the parents time and opportunity to adjust to the problem. Once they face the issue and are confident of assistance, parents can begin to pick up the pieces and prepare to raise the child. In some situations, however, the parents do not adjust but continue to use defense mechanisms, thus inhibiting the child's optimum development.

Search for a Cause

According to Robinson and Robinson (1976), parents search for a cause of the disability for two reasons: hope for a cure and the removal of guilt. These parents struggle with soul-searching questions. Are they being punished for an act of omission or commission? Did they neglect the child and allow an injury to occur? Is it due to drug usage, alcoholic intake, or sexual practices?

Parents may end up highly frustrated because, in most cases, etiology is elusive. Diagnosis usually is based on behavioral manifestations rather than on precise neurological or genetic findings. Because of the many positions regarding etiology (e.g., maturational lag, problems with metabolism, inner ear impairment, central nervous system dysfunction, diet, and inadequate environment), parents encounter numerous theories of etiology (see Chapter 3). The two most widely espoused etiologies are central nervous system dysfunction and environmental inadequacy.

Search for a Cure

Many parents encounter specialized treatment recommendations from specific etiological viewpoints and latch onto them as a possible cure. Teachers need to be aware of various etiology-intervention approaches (some of which are highly controversial) and their effect on children. Informed teachers can provide the parents with necessary knowledge and, perhaps, direction.

Acceptance of the Child

The final area of parental adjustment is *acceptance*, a term defined in a general way. For example, Robinson and Robinson (1976) describe it as "a warm respect for the child as he is, appreciation of his assets, tolerance for his shortcomings, and active pleasure in relating to him" (p. 420). Wortis (1966) reports two indices of acceptance: (a) the mother maintains her usual acquaintances and continues with her normal activities, and (b) the parents meet the needs both of their normal children and of the child with disabilities. To facilitate acceptance, Brutten et al. (1973) recommend involvement in outside interests and periodic employment of a baby-sitter. Some parents of children with learning disabilities have benefited by baby-sitting for each other, and the independence boosts morale. Also, McWhirter (1976) finds that parents receive emotional support by meeting with other parents of children with learning disabilities.

Weiss and Weiss (1976) discuss some characteristics of accepting parents:

> The most significant characteristic of these parents is that they treat their children as basically normal, emphasizing their strengths rather than becoming preoccupied with their weaknesses. They see these children as independent beings rather than extensions of themselves and thus do not treat each failure as a tragedy. These parents are usually successful human beings who are satisfied with their own lives and don't seem to need their child's successes to fill the void of a failing marriage, declining career, or their own loneliness. (p. 245)

Unlike acceptance, rejection usually is identified readily. J. Gallagher (1956) discusses it as a persistence of unrealistic negative values of the child, which casts a general negative tone over the parent-child relationship and may manifest itself in four ways: (a) underexpectations, (b) maintaining unrealistic goals, (c) escape, and (d) masking the rejection by espousing an exactly opposite viewpoint. Furthermore, J. Gallagher delineates between *primary rejection* and *secondary rejection*. Primary rejection emerges from an unchangeable condition (e.g., ability level) of the child, whereas secondary rejection springs from the child's behaviors. J. Gallagher postulates that most rejection is secondary and quite understandable. Almost anyone would have difficulty adjusting to the persistent and aversive behavior of some children with learning disabilities. In cases of secondary rejection, one should not assume that the negative attitude of the parents is pervasive and that they will not be cooperative.

Most parents of children with disabilities rely on trial-and-error strategies. This technique, coupled with the multitude of parent-child adjustments, makes acceptance a difficult but, it is hoped, obtainable goal. Parents must be careful not to work so hard coping with undesirable behavior that their child learns that love is a reward rather than a constant factor.

Although parenting a child with learning disabilities is challenging, it can be rewarding. L. S. Gallagher (1995) notes that to make it rewarding, parents need help "from the school, the extended family, other professionals, and especially from the physician involved. It is only through this support, encouragement, and the sharing of expertise, that the person with learning disabilities emerges from the school-age years academically, emotionally, and socially intact" (p. 113). One way to ensure this support is for parents and school officials to interact frequently. Research indicates that greater amounts of interactions among teachers and parents increase positive attitudes about others' roles in collaboration (Michael, Arnold, Magliocca, & Miller, 1992).

PARENT COUNSELING AND TRAINING

The term *family* reminds many of a mother, father, and one or more children living together at home. The father works weekdays and spends weekends doing chores and being with the children. The mother keeps house, cooks nourishing meals, and provides constant love. Moreover, grandparents are nearby and ready to spoil the children with gifts, picnics, fishing trips, and plenty of wise counsel (A. P. Turnbull & Turnbull, 1990).

In reality, few American families fit this nostalgic picture (Lambie & Daniels-Mohring, 1993; A. P. Turnbull & Turnbull, 1990). For one thing, more women continue to enter the work force. Current data indicate that the number of women in the work force who are married with children under the age of 6 is substantial. Moreover, about half of all marriages end in divorce

(*Marriage and Divorce Today,* 1987), and about one out of every five families with children under 18 is headed by a single parent (Norton & Glick, 1986). Unfortunately, studies of children from one-parent homes are not encouraging. B. F. Brown (1980) studied more than 3,000 students from one-parent families in three states and found that they had greater problems in school, such as underachievement, tardiness, absence, truancy, discipline problems, suspension, expulsion, and dropping out. These difficulties were independent of economic status. Few people today live in a "traditional" family setting, and the need for support services for existing family structures is extensive.

Families vary in many other ways besides structure. Some key dimensions include ethnic background, education, socioeconomic status, religion, values, and location (i.e., rural, urban, or suburban). Moreover, in a comparison of family backgrounds of elementary students with and without learning disabilities, Toro, Weissberg, Guare, and Liebenstein (1990) found that children with learning disabilities had significantly more family problems than children without disabilities. Specifically, the families of children with learning disabilities provided less educational stimulation at home and had more economic and general family difficulties than families of children without disabilities.

A. P. Turnbull and Turnbull (1990) stress the need for professionals to recognize family differences in their efforts to provide services. Specifically, they state, "Given all the different ways in which families can vary, it is probably safe to say that every family is idiosyncratic, if not unique. . . . The first step in working with families, then, is to understand their diversities. The idea of diversity leads to the conviction that you need to individualize your approach to families" (p. 22).

Divergent cultural perspectives are a part of the diversity among families, and, because these cultural differences can serve as obstacles in establishing school-family relationships, educators should develop culturally sensitive programs to involve parents. In essence, services need to be adjusted according to the family's level of acculturation, prior history with discrimination, and behavioral and developmental expectations (Salend, 1994). Getting to know a student's family is essential for developing sensitive and effective school-family relationships. This can be accomplished through frequent communications, including parent conferences, telephone calls, home visits, and the use of excellent listening and observation skills.

Although the critical role of parents in their child's school success was acknowledged widely as early as the 1920s (Schlossman, 1976), our society has done little to prepare people for parenting. This condition, combined with a society geared to the average (raising normal children), often places the parents of children with disabilities in need of assistance.

Dembinski and Mauser (1977) conducted a survey of parent members of the Association for Children with Learning Disabilities (now the Learning Disabilities Association) to ascertain what parents most want from teachers, psychologists, and physicians. In general, their results indicate that parents would like for professionals to do the following:

1. Use language that is free of jargon.
2. Recognize the importance of including both parents in conferences involving the child.
3. Offer reading material that can help them understand their child.
4. Send copies of written reports involving their child.
5. Have interdisciplinary communication among professionals involved with their child.
6. Offer relevant advice and information concerning management and teaching.
7. Give feedback on both academic and social behavior of their child.

H. R. Turnbull and Turnbull (1985) provide some helpful suggestions to professionals as they prepare to work with parents of individuals with disabilities:

> Professional behavior must be tempered by humility. It is impossible to have all the answers in

> the diagnosis and treatment of problems associated with handicapping conditions. . . . When professionals interact with parents, respect is a necessary ingredient. For too long, the professional-parent relationship has been characterized by a superiority-inferiority interaction. . . . A parent-professional partnership is essential if handicapped children are to be provided with opportunities to reach their full potential. Parents cannot assume all the responsibilities alone. (pp. 131, 133–134)

Parent counseling and parent training must be designed to ensure flexibility in providing individualized treatment programs. Parent-helping strategies are presented under three headings: Informational Strategies, Counseling Strategies, and Parent Involvement and Training Programs.

Informational Strategies

Professionals can serve an important function to parents of children with learning disabilities by providing information about sources, such as parent groups, organizations, readings, specific resource personnel, and workshops. A. P. Turnbull and Turnbull (1990) note that parents frequently request information on the topics of behavior management, homework, educational advocacy, and future planning.

An excellent advocacy resource for parents of children with learning disabilities is the federally funded parent center. These centers are usually staffed by parents of children with special needs. Their primary function is to inform parents of their legal rights and responsibilities in relation to special education. A basic philosophy of these centers is "parents helping parents." Information is shared through newsletters, phone calls, workshops, and letters. A. P. Turnbull and Turnbull (1990) provide addresses of parent centers in various states.

Information sharing can be accomplished in group or individual sessions. Studies of parents who learned behavior-management strategies indicate that parents in group and individual sessions achieve similar positive results (Brightman, Baker, Clark, & Ambrose, 1982). Group sessions enable parents to learn from each other, cost less, and are more time-efficient for the professionals providing the information. Individual sessions, however, allow the professional to develop a close working relationship with the family and focus on its unique needs.

The following resources provide information to parents and families of youngsters with learning disabilities: Brutten et al. (1973), Cordoni (1992), Ingersoll (1988), Lelewer (1994), Silver (1984), Smith (1979, 1991), A. P. Turnbull and Turnbull (1990), Vail (1990), and Weiss and Weiss (1976). Organizations that provide information about learning disabilities are included in Appendix A. In addition to printed materials, the computer has unlimited potential for giving parents helpful information.

Counseling Strategies

Counseling approaches help parents deal with their feelings. Abrams and Kaslow (1977) stress the need for differential treatment based on an examination of family dynamics and the child's problems. They suggest matching family dynamics with one of several different treatment strategies:

1. *Individual therapy only*—for the child whose parents are essentially inaccessible (e.g., parents who are drug addicts, alcoholics, psychotics, or completely rejecting of the child).
2. *Parent group counseling*—for parents who get along well but would benefit from group sessions that focus on solving common problems.
3. *Concurrent therapy of child and parents with different therapists*—for families in which anxiety and feelings are so strained that it would not be beneficial to counsel the child and parents together.
4. *Concurrent therapy of child and parents with the same therapist*—for families in which parents and the child can share the therapist without engaging in power or competitive struggles.

Lambie and Daniels-Mohring (1993) recommend the structural family therapy approach to

helping families adjust and support children with special needs. They maintain that understanding the structural characteristics of a student's family helps educators better understand the student with special needs. Moreover, it provides a framework for assisting the family to identify problems and develop alternative interventions. Family transactional patterns are examined in terms of boundaries, subsystems, and hierarchy. *Boundaries* involve the quality of closeness and distance in a family. *Subsystems* are subgroups within the family and include the spousal, parental, sibling, and extrafamilial subsystems. These subsystems are the building blocks of family interaction. The quality of the interaction among these subsystems determines how well the roles and functions of the family are maintained. *Hierarchy* refers to the distribution of power and decision making within the family system. Once family interaction patterns are understood, a student's behavior can be viewed within the context of the family structure. These contextual family variables assist family members and educators to understand the student and foster academic and emotional development (Lambie & Daniels-Mohring, 1993).

Klein, Altman, Dreizen, Friedman, and Powers (1981a, 1981b) report success with family-oriented psychoeducational therapy in restructuring parental attitudes that negatively influence school behavior. They identify four parental attitudes that hinder students' school progress:

1. *Dysfunctional attitudes toward authority.* The parents undermine the teacher by blaming the teacher and the curriculum for the youngster's school problems. Concurrently, the parents in-

struct the child to go to school and learn. The child, who receives two conflicting messages, becomes confused and unstudious.

2. *Dysfunctional attitudes toward responsibility for learning*. The parents view the child's poor academic performance as "nothing to worry about." The parents believe the child is not responsible for adequate school performance. The message to the child is often "I had some trouble in school just like you, and I made out okay. You will too." The child then views schoolwork as unimportant. On the other hand, some parents view academic achievement as crucial to survival and place unrealistic demands on the child.
3. *Dysfunctional attitudes toward the child*. The parents consider the child intellectually limited when the child is not, or they think it is the child's problem and refuse to get involved. Sometimes they fear that if the child improves, the child will leave them behind and the family structure will collapse. In this latter condition, the child must maintain the learning disorder to receive continued parental love and support.
4. *Dysfunctional attitudes based on cultural factors*. In some subcultures, children postpone academics until after puberty. In other subcultures, parents place a heavy emphasis on work and study and do not recognize the importance of play.

These four attitudes can be seen in parents as well as teachers. In some cases the attitudes warrant therapy, and in others they are good topics for discussion in parent groups and parent-teacher conferences.

Parent Involvement and Training Programs

Most parents want and need information and guidance from their child's school and teachers. Parent involvement programs offer parents and school staff the opportunity to build strong mutually supportive partnerships for enhancing student learning at home and at school.

Parent Involvement. Epstein (1988) notes that successful programs feature several types of parent involvement and include many roles for parents: audience, home tutor, program supporter, colearner, advocate, and decision maker. There are five major types of parent involvement, each of which occurs in different places, requires different materials and processes, and leads to different outcomes (Brandt, 1989).

1. *Parenting*. The school staff can help families establish positive home conditions that support school learning and appropriate behavior. For example, suggestions can be provided for home conditions that support learning, and workshops or videotapes can be offered on parenting and child-rearing issues. These activities may result in increased self-confidence and knowledge of child development for the parent, as well as increased respect on the part of the student for the parent and for the importance of school.
2. *Communicating*. Teachers and administrators must design effective ways to provide information about school programs and student progress to parents, and the form and frequency of communication should be varied (e.g., memos, notices, report cards, and conferences).
3. *Volunteering*. Recruiting parent help and support encourages parents to assist teachers, administrators, and students in the classroom as well as attend student performances, sporting events, and training workshops. As a result, the parent gains an understanding of the teacher's job and school programs and thus becomes comfortable in school interactions; the student receives increased individual attention and develops ease in communicating with adults.
4. *Learning at home*. Teachers should provide ideas to parents on how to assist their child at home with learning activities that are coordinated with classwork. For example, parents may be given calendars with daily topics for discussion or regular homework schedules

that require the student to discuss schoolwork at home. As a result, the parent encourages schoolwork and interacts with the child as a student at home, and the student completes homework and gains increased achievement in practiced skills.

5. *Representing other parents.* Parent leaders can be recruited and trained to participate in parent-school organizations, advisory councils or committees, or independent advocacy groups that work for school improvement. As a result, the parent has input into policies that affect the student's education, the student receives benefits linked to specific policies, and the teacher has an awareness of parent perspectives for policy development.

Williams and Chavkin (1989) present seven elements that are common to successful parent involvement programs:

1. Written policies that legitimize the importance of parent involvement and present a framework for the context of program activities.
2. Administrative support provided through designated funds in the budget for implementing programs, available material and product resources (e.g., communication equipment, computers, or meeting space) to complement program activities, and personnel designated to carry out program efforts or events.
3. Available training for staff and parents that focuses on developing partnering skills.
4. An emphasis on the partnership approach through such activities as joint planning, goal setting, definition of roles, and development of instructional and school support efforts.
5. Frequent, regular, two-way communication between home and school.
6. Networking with other programs to share information, resources, and technical expertise.
7. Regular evaluation activities that enable parents and school staff to revise programs continuously to ensure that activities strengthen the partnership.

Parent Training. The needs of parents should provide the content for training. Generally, training should focus on helping parents (a) interact with professionals involved with their child, (b) promote the emotional, social, and behavioral growth of their child, (c) teach and manage their child effectively, and (d) acquire information relevant to obtaining services for their child. Parents of young children typically are interested in training in child care and development, early intervention, discipline, and school-related expectations. Brotherson, Berdine, and Sartini (1993) note that parents of adolescents usually need training to assist their adolescent in making successful postsecondary transitions. Research during the last decade supports the position that the ongoing involvement of family and friends is significant in helping adolescents make successful postsecondary transitions (Wehman, 1990). Moreover, parents who speak languages other than English may benefit from family-oriented classes in English as a second language as well as in instruction about the policies and practices of the school district.

Two goals frequently stressed in parent training programs are effective communication and behavior management. Table 4.2 presents selected parent training programs that are based primarily on either the behavioral or the Adlerian theory.

The *behavioral* approach is rooted in the premise that behavior is increased, decreased, or maintained by manipulating environmental events. Some of the most popular strategies for managing parent and child behavior include observing and recording behavior (e.g., defining behavior and charting behavior), using techniques for increasing appropriate behavior (e.g., positive reinforcement, contracts, and schedules of reinforcement), and using techniques for decreasing inappropriate behavior (e.g., extinction and punishment). Ehly, Conoley, and Rosenthal (1985) report that behavioral approaches offer several advantages:

1. They enable parents and educators to modify specific behaviors (such as temper tantrums).
2. They focus on observable and measurable behavior.
3. They offer a variety of effective options for changing behaviors.

TABLE 4.2
Parent Training Programs

Program	Theoretical Orientation	Goals	Content	Medium and Materials
Children: The Challenge (Dreikurs & Soltz, 1964; National Education Association, 1976)	Adlerian	Improved family relationships Discipline	Natural and logical consequences Discipline, not punishment Avoidance of power struggles Use of action over words Being consistent	Study groups are conducted with a leader training kit developed by NEA (1976) that includes filmstrips that focus on such topics as listening, discipline, helping your child succeed, and parent-teacher conferences.
Responsive Parenting (M. C. Hall, Grinstead, Collier, & Hall, 1980)	Behavioral	Behavior management	Recording behavior Punishment Time-out Correction Overcorrection Extinction Systematic reinforcement Schedules of reinforcement Contracts	Parent manuals *The Responsive Parent* newsletter Training consists of ten 2-hour weekly sessions. Sessions are conducted by a trained leader, and parents apply techniques at home.
Systematic Training for Effective Parenting (STEP) (Dinkmeyer & McKay, 1989)	Adlerian	Improved family relationships Discipline	Understanding children's behavior and misbehavior Understanding how children use emotions to involve parents Encouragement Communication Developing responsibility Decision making for parents The family meeting Parent confidence	The training kit contains a leader's manual, parent handbooks, audiocassettes or videocassette, posters, and group guideline charts. The program includes nine 2-hour sessions for groups of 10 to 12 parents Parents are encouraged to identify specific concerns and new strategies they have used to change their behavior.

4. They include forms and procedures to document or evaluate the progress of the child.

Research Press publishes a variety of behavior-oriented materials to supplement parent training programs. Their videocassettes include *Parents and Children, Behavioral Principles for Parents,* and *The Practical Parenting Series.*

The behavioral parent training programs have received extensive support (Bergan, Neumann, & Karp, 1983; Forehand & King, 1977; Simpson & Poplin, 1981). For example, the Responsive Parenting Program received national attention (C. C. Brown, 1976) for successfully changing parents' perception of their effectiveness as child managers as well as their ability to manage. M. C. Hall and Nelson (1981) note that single-parent families especially have benefited from the Responsive Parenting Program.

The *Adlerian* parent programs share several common beliefs about children and their behavior. Ehly et al. (1985) report some of these beliefs:

1. The behavior of children is goal-directed, and knowledge of these goals helps professionals and parents understand and deal with children's behavior.
2. A misbehaving child is viewed as a discouraged child (i.e., the child has failed to obtain a positive status in either the family or community).
3. The goals of misbehavior include attention, power, revenge, and an attempt to exhibit inadequacy.
4. Children are more likely to change if they understand that their inappropriate behavior contributes to their difficulties.
5. Discipline is a method of changing behavior, whereas punishment supports continued negative behaviors.
6. Family dynamics are explored by studying relationships between parents and children and between siblings. Democratic family interactions are stressed.

The Adlerian-based approaches have accrued supportive evidence. The National Education Association (1976) developed a two-volume set of materials titled *Briefing for Parents.* These materials are based on the Adlerian-oriented work of Dreikurs and Soltz (1964). Moreover, Dreikurs's study groups have generated long-term benefits for parents (Thorn, 1974).

Ehly et al. (1985) report that educators will find Adlerian and behavioral approaches compatible, and techniques from both can be used successfully. Moreover, both approaches stress consistent responses to children's behavior and nonblaming descriptive understanding of it.

HOME-BASED SERVICES AND ACTIVITIES

Numerous activities are available for parents to foster the social and academic growth of their child. This section presents activities within the areas of parent observation, home management, and parents as teachers. Appropriate activities should be determined according to the unique circumstances of the family's resources and characteristics.

Parent Observation

Because parents spend more time with their child in a wider variety of places than do teachers, physicians, or counselors, they can help by developing observational skills. Once parents confront the issue and are assured of some assistance, they can be accurate judges of their child's level of development.

A physician examining the child may seek information that can be gained by observation. For example, does the child play and get along with brothers and sisters? Does the child get along with other children? What types of games does the child like to play? What are the child's eating and sleeping habits? What are some of the child's interests and fears? Parents can help answer such questions.

When the child reaches school age, the parents must become aware of any behaviors with educational significance. The teacher may give the parents a checklist to guide home observation. Not only can observation provide valuable information, but it also helps foster parental sensitivity regarding the child's strengths and weaknesses. Weiss and Weiss (1976) devised an extensive observational checklist to help parents decide whether their child has learning problems. In addition to motivation, the checklist covers speaking, listening, reading, writing, and math skills. Weiss and Weiss acknowledge that a checklist cannot substitute for professional testing, but it can help parents direct their efforts in specific areas.

Home Management

At home, the child presents numerous management problems. After studying 18 children with learning problems, L. Wilson (1975) discovered that parental indulgence and infrequent punishment are associated with academic difficulties. Compared with a control group, children with learning problems received less physical punishment and completed fewer household tasks. Interestingly, Freund and Elardo (1978) found that the social skills of children with learning disabilities were better in families in which the mother encouraged the child to take on household responsibilities.

Many parents using systematic strategies can manage their child successfully. Weiss and Weiss (1976), parents of two children with learning problems, believe that parents need to deal with their own tension while interacting with the child. Discussing one of their children, they note, "Our calm response often helped him to gain control of himself. If, on the other hand, we became embroiled in his frustrations and responded in anger, we only fed into his problems and made them worse" (p. 73).

Time Management. The establishment of routines can provide essential structure for many youngsters with learning disabilities. Considering the many demands placed on students to complete tasks at specific times and participate in a host of competing activities (such as being with peers, joining clubs, watching television, and listening to music), time management obviously is critical to surviving in school. The child with learning problems usually needs instruction in time management. Activities for teaching time management include making schedules, making time estimates, and establishing priorities:

1. Provide a 5-day schedule of after-school time, and ask the student to record all activities during these time blocks. Next, have the student allocate time blocks for specific activities (see Table 4.3) and follow the schedule as much as possible. Initially, it may help the student to plan a day and then gradually build to a week.

TABLE 4.3
A Student's After-School Schedule

	Monday	Tuesday	Wednesday	Thursday	Friday
3:00–4:00	with friend eat snack	with friend eat snack	with friend eat snack	with friend eat snack	with friend eat snack
4:00–5:00	play ball	play ball	play ball	play ball	play ball
5:00–6:00	play ball	play ball	play ball	play ball	play ball
6:00–7:00	eat dinner	eat dinner	eat dinner	eat dinner	eat dinner
7:00–8:00	study	study	study	go to game	go to movie
8:00–9:00	study	watch TV	study	go to game	go to movie
9:00–10:00	watch TV	watch TV`	play tapes	watch TV	watch TV

Note: From *Teaching Students with Learning Problems* (p. 606), 4th ed., by C. D. Mercer and A. R. Mercer, 1993. Upper Saddle River, NJ: Merrill/Prentice Hall. Copyright 1993 by Prentice-Hall Publishing Company. Reprinted by permission.

2. Provide the student with a calendar to assist in scheduling daily or weekly activities. Notations can be made on the calendar to remind the student of project due dates or test dates. The student also can keep a notebook with all academic assignments and due dates.
3. Remind the student that some flexibility should be allowed in the daily schedule. Occasionally, unexpected events will take precedence over the planned activity. Introduce new events in the daily schedule and explain how adjustments can be made (e.g., if friends invite the student to get a pizza during study time, the student can replace television time with study time). Finally, the student should show the teacher the schedule with written adjustments when applicable.
4. Either provide assignments or have the student list at least four school assignments and estimate how long it will take to complete each task. Then have the student record the amount of time it actually takes to complete the assignments. These times can be written on the student's schedule. For tasks or subject areas in which the student's estimates are consistently inaccurate (off by more than 20%), have the student practice in these areas until the estimates become realistic.
5. Have the student list school assignments and prioritize them. The student can rank the activities in the order they would be completed (i.e., place a *1* beside the first activity, a *2* beside the next activity, and so on). For example:

   _______ Work on social studies project due in 2 weeks.
   _______ Write a lab report in science due in 2 days.
   _______ Complete a math worksheet due tomorrow.
   _______ Practice baseball for the game in 3 days.
   _______ Read 20 pages of a book in preparation for an oral report due in 4 days.

   Discuss the need to consider consequences and time factors in prioritizing lists of things to do. Review the rankings and point out the correct and incorrect rankings in terms of consequences, breaking large tasks into smaller amounts (e.g., subdividing reading material into a number of pages per day), and time factors. Also, have the student practice using value steps in prioritizing activities and tasks by grouping the list into three areas: activities with high value, activities with medium value, and activities with low value.
6. To enhance the efficient completion of academic tasks, encourage the student to work in an environment conducive to studying. Ideally, the study area should be a relatively quiet, unstimulating environment. If noise (e.g., television or classmates) becomes too distracting, the student can consider using earplugs.

Although briefly describing home management strategies generally helps to orient parents and teachers, additional information can guide the beginner to implement a successful management plan immediately. Some helpful sources include Berger (1991), R. V. Hall (1971, 1975), R. V. Hall and Houten (1983), Mercer and Mercer (1993), Patterson (1975, 1976), Ross (1981), A. P. Turnbull and Turnbull (1990), and Weiss and Weiss (1976).

Parents as Teachers

From generation to generation, parents transmit customs, unique family habits, and traditions. Society expects parents to teach values and social skills, but should parents teach academics? The literature is mixed on the general effectiveness of parent tutoring. Some experts claim it is effective, whereas others question it. Basically, it is an individual decision that can be made intelligently if selected guidelines are followed.

Shapero and Forbes (1981) summarize the data from several home tutoring programs with children who have learning disabilities and conclude that the findings generally are positive. Although they found some unsupervised tutoring to be successful, Shapero and Forbes recommend the involvement of the child's teacher in the program. In a study of the effectiveness of parent tutoring in the reading performance of first-grade children in a compensatory education program, Mehran and White (1988) found that long-lasting improvement in reading ability was exhibited in children of parents who had participated consistently in a parent tutoring program that trained them in structured tutoring techniques. Moreover, Thurston and Dasta (1990) conducted studies that demonstrated the positive effects of training parents to use a specific procedure to tutor their children on academic tasks. The procedure involved training in (a) the selection of the tutoring materials, (b) the use of basic instructions (e.g., "Read this problem and give the answer"), (c) the implementation of an error-correction procedure (i.e., read or say correction; have child repeat, reread, or rewrite correction; praise child), and (d) the use of record keeping and charting. The parents successfully used the tutoring procedures after minimal training, and the opportunity for the child to practice academic behavior at home had a positive effect on academic performance in school. Because it has been proven that some parents can tutor their children successfully, one can assume with some confidence that this strategy can be effective.

Eiserman et al. (1995) compared the effects of a clinic-based low parent involvement intervention with a home parent training intervention and found positive results for the home parent training intervention. Children achieved well on measures of speech, language, general development, and family functioning. Eiserman et al. conclude that the "comparable longitudinal effects of the two interventions examined in this study support the stability of programs that offer options to parents and the need for interventionists to be trained broadly enough to be able to assume a variety of roles and to provide a range of services" (p. 20).

Each individual must decide about home tutoring. According to Kronick (1977), the basic consideration is whether tutoring can be accomplished without depriving any family member of the resources (e.g., time, money, and activities) that should be directed toward maintaining a well-balanced life. When determining the feasibility of using parent tutoring, professionals and parents should consider these factors:

1. Are there reasons for deciding against tutoring (e.g., mother-father disagreement over the necessity of tutoring, health problems, financial problems, marital problems, or a large family with extensive demands on parental attention)?
2. Do the parents have the resources of a professional (e.g., a teacher) to assist them? The success of home tutoring may depend on cooperative efforts.
3. Can the sessions be arranged at a time when there is no interruption from siblings, callers, or other demands? These children need sustained attention in order to learn.
4. Will the child become inundated with academic instruction and resent the home sessions or feel overly pressured?
5. Does the parent become frustrated, tense, disappointed, or impatient during the tutorial sessions? These parents may spend their time better with the child in activities that are mutually enjoyable.
6. Do the tutorial sessions create tensions among family members? For instance, do the siblings view the sessions as preferential treatment?
7. Does the parent resent tutoring the child or feel guilty every time a session is shortened or missed? Are the sessions usually enjoyable or rewarding?

In a survey of the 20 variables most highly rated by a 12-member team of experts as being important for learning in children, Reynolds, Wang, and Walberg (1992) list three variables that involve parents. These experts report that to promote learning, parents should show affection for their child, display interest in their child's schoolwork, and expect academic success.

Foremost, parents should provide the child with a home environment of warmth, acceptance, and understanding. The child needs and deserves a comfortable place to retreat from the pressures, demands, and frustrations of daily living. Kronick (1977) captures the essence of this responsibility:

> Our most primary goal must be to insure that the home is a relaxed and pleasant place, a source of strength to the child. It should not shield the child from the world but give courage to cope with it. This means that the child must feel like an accepted, valued member of the family, sharing plans, decisions, special occasions, and concerns. I strongly feel that the home must be the child's anchor and that other considerations are secondary. Therefore, if you have to discard home remediation to create this kind of atmosphere, then discard it. (p. 327)

If the decision is made to engage in parent tutoring, attention must be directed toward doing a good job. Guidelines include the following:

1. Give simple instructions and precisely convey the requirements of the task.
2. Be flexible regarding the length of the session. Sometimes the child will not attend to the work for a concentrated period of time. In these instances, settle for 2 to 5 minutes of concentrated work instead of insisting on completion of the work at the risk of creating frustration and tension (Weiss & Weiss, 1976).
3. Maintain a tutoring log of the child's performance or a written record of observations (e.g., types of errors, questions asked, and rate of responses) made during the tutoring.

These observations can be shared with the teacher and may assist in making future plans. Keeping a record of the child's progress is often helpful.

4. Do not extend formal tutoring indefinitely. Periodically halt the tutoring. Supplement or replace it by incorporating the remedial tasks in everyday chores and games (Kronick, 1977).
5. Make an effort to select the best time for the session. Many parents report that immediately following the evening meal is a good time (Weiss & Weiss, 1976). Also, choose a place for the session that does not restrict the activities of the other family members and is not too distracting. Tutor at the same time and place to establish an expectation for the activity.
6. Identify appropriate levels, and make sure the task is one the child can do. Tutoring sessions should be success-oriented. Work should be challenging but not too difficult.
7. Limit the length of the tutoring session to about 15 minutes for children up to grade six and 30 minutes for older students (Cummings & Maddux, 1985).
8. Use creative techniques in reviewing and teaching new material, and practice activities in ways that reduce boredom (Cummings & Maddux, 1985).
9. Let the child know when a mistake has been made, but do so in a positive or neutral manner. Provide encouragement and praise the learner for trying.
10. Give the child time to become familiar with the task materials. Provide the child with an overview or introduction before beginning formal instruction.
11. Encourage the child to make judgments or choices on the basis of evidence rather than by guessing or appealing to authority. Give the child time to think about the problem.
12. Make sure that the tutoring sessions are pleasant for both the parent and the child. Begin and end each session with an activity that is fun and in which the child is successful (Cummings & Maddux, 1985).

Various instructional activities used in home teaching programs are described by Berger (1991), Brutten et al. (1973), Ring (1980), and Weiss and Weiss (1976).

THE PARENT-TEACHER PARTNERSHIP

As previously mentioned, teachers should work closely with parents to promote learning in school and at home. When parents are involved and cooperative, the home becomes the supportive foundation that the child needs to face the changing demands of school. Teachers and parents should recognize their roles as complementary and supplementary and view their relationship as a partnership to foster the child's progress.

Establishing Cooperation

Teachers and parents often harbor attitudes about each other that inhibit mutual cooperation. These attitudes sometimes manifest themselves through teacher blaming or parent blaming. Such dissonance benefits no one. Its sources should be identified, and strategies should be pursued to promote a cooperative and working relationship.

Initial progress toward cooperation hinges on development of mutual respect. Barsch (1969) suggests that parents prefer a teacher who approaches them as individuals, treats them with dignity, and conveys a feeling of acceptance. A parent does not want to be treated as simply a parent of a child with disabilities. Barsch points out that "As teachers are able to convey a feeling of acceptance of the person, the parent is reciprocally more accepting of whatever counsel the teacher may offer" (p. 11).

Factors threatening cooperation include different educational levels of the parent and teacher, contrasting perceptions of the child's strengths and weaknesses, stereotyping, and terminology (Barsch, 1969). Contrasting attitudes about the child's strengths and weaknesses are a major area of concern that must be confronted. The teacher's perception of the child emerges from experience with similar and different children, the teacher's orientation toward learning disabilities, and observations of the child in the school environment. The parents' perception derives from experiences with the child from infancy across various environmental situations, their orientation toward learning disabilities, experience with the child's siblings, and their stage of adjustment to the child's disability.

Using a Q-sort technique, Kroth (1973) developed an instrument called Target Behavior, which teachers and parents can use to compare their perceptions of the child at home or at school. If they want a comparison of school behavior, the teacher and the parent place 25 behaviors from the school list (see Table 4.4) on a formboard containing 25 squares. The squares on the formboard are arranged so that the behaviors are placed along a continuum, those *most like the child* to those *most unlike the child*. Figure 4.1 shows a typical formboard. Each square on the board has an assigned number from 1 to 9. When all the items have been placed on the board, the teacher and the parent both record the respective number assigned to each of the 25 items. A comparison of the number value for each item is made between the parent sort and the teacher sort. The items on which the number value differs by 4 or more points become target behaviors for parent-teacher planning and discussions. In cases in which a large discrepancy exists (e.g., follows di-

TABLE 4.4
Items on the Behavioral Q-Sort (Elementary Level; School and Home)

School	Home
1. Gets work done on time	1. Does assigned chores
2. Pokes or hits classmates	2. Does homework on time
3. Gets out of seat without permission	3. Goes to bed without problems
4. Scores high in spelling	4. Comes home when should
5. Plays with objects while working	5. Argues with parents
6. Scores high in reading	6. Has friends
7. Disturbs neighbors by making noise	7. Likes school
8. Is quiet during class time	8. Cries or sulks when doesn't get own way
9. Tips chair often	9. Throws temper tantrums
10. Follows directions	10. Likes to watch TV
11. Smiles frequently	11. Likes to read
12. Often taps foot, fingers, or pencil	12. Plays alone
13. Pays attention to work	13. Eats between meals
14. Works slowly	14. Is overweight
15. Throws objects in class	15. Is destructive of property
16. Reads well orally	16. Gets ready for school on time
17. Talks to classmates often	17. Makes own decisions
18. Scores high in English	18. Chooses own clothes
19. Talks out without permission	19. Is unhealthy
20. Rocks in chair	20. Fights with brothers and sisters
21. Scores high in arithmetic	21. Has messy room
22. Asks teacher questions	22. Responds to rewards
23. Uses free time to read or study	23. Does acceptable schoolwork
24. Works until the job is finished	24. Is a restless sleeper
25. Walks around room during study time	25. Stretches the truth

Note: Adapted from *Communicating with Parents of Exceptional Children: Improving Parent-Teacher Relationships* (pp. 46–47) by R. L. Kroth, 1975, Denver: Love. Copyright 1975 by Love Publishing Company. Reprinted by permission.

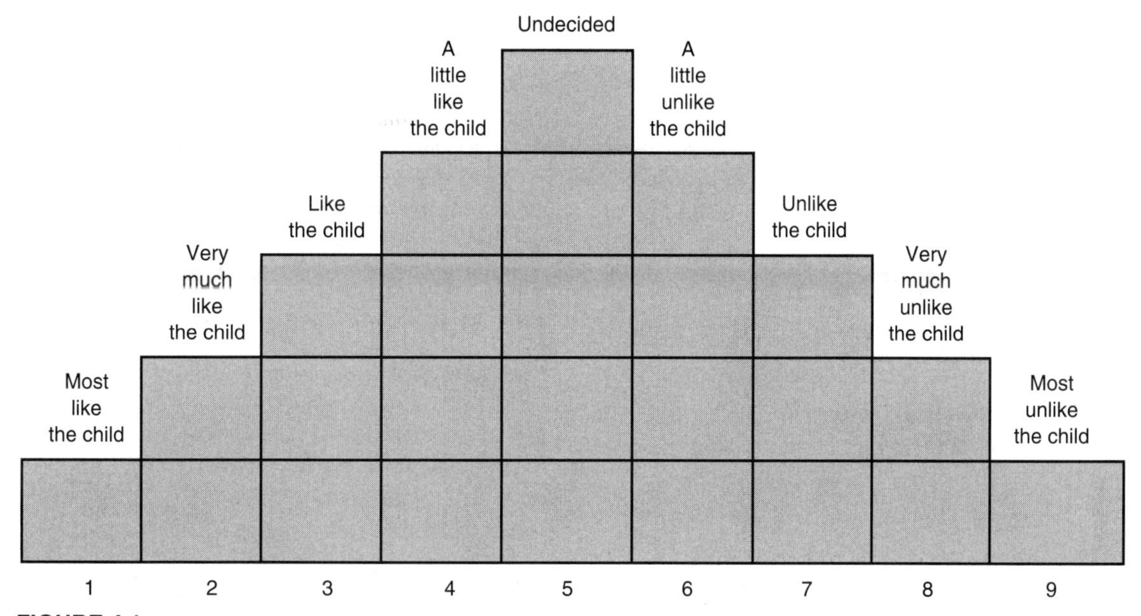

FIGURE 4.1
Behavior formboard
Note: Adapted from *Communicating with Parents of Exceptional Children: Improving Parent–Teacher Relationships* (p. 44) by R. L. Kroth, 1975, Denver: Love. Copyright 1975 by Love Publishing Company. Reprinted by permission.

rections), the teacher can help alleviate the parent's concerns through discussion. The teacher also may plan a program to assist the parent in encouraging the child to behave properly at home (e.g., follow directions).

The *Parent as a Teacher Inventory* (Strom, 1984) is a composite attitude scale that helps educators understand parent perceptions about their child with disabilities. Also, Cone, DeLawyer, and Wolfe (1985) report good results from their instrument, the *Parent/Family Involvement Index* (PFII). The PFII assesses parent participation in 12 categories pertinent to good parent-teacher relationships.

Many obstacles can inhibit cooperative parent-teacher relationships. However, the common goal should enable both to transcend the obstacles and work together. The following selected activities may foster teacher-parent cooperation:

1. Provide parents with training on how to tutor their child (Hudson & Miller, 1993).
2. Invite parents to volunteer in the classroom.
3. Develop an informative and consistent communication system between the teacher and the parents regarding homework. Initiate communication regularly, communicate about a problem early enough to resolve it, follow through on what is said, and communicate clearly (Jayanthi, Nelson, Sawyer, Bursuck, & Epstein, 1995).
4. Communicate frequently through home notes, phone messages, progress reports, parent-teacher conferences, parent nights, e-mail, and at-school events.
5. Ask parents to help with academics by reading to their child, signing homework, asking about their child's school day, helping their child practice math facts or spelling words, and taking their child to the library (National Institute of Education, 1985).
6. Invite parents to go on field trips or visit the classroom.

7. Focus on listening to parents in an effort to gain understanding and show respect.
8. Help parents become informed advocates for their child.
9. Provide transportation and child care services for parents to attend school meetings or events.

O'Shea, O'Shea, and Nowocien (1993) provide a mnemonic device (Co-Advocacy) to support dynamic parent-teacher relationships and mutual interdependence:

CO—*Co-advocates* are individuals valuing, respecting, and accepting each other.

A —*Advocacy* is action by individuals willing to speak up and act.

D —*Discovery* entails seeking mutually satisfying opportunities in home, school, and community settings.

V —*Versatility* means flexibility in cooperating together over time.

O —*Organization* entails resources and materials used to foster mutual success.

C —*Commitment* is mutual cooperation and caring.

A —*Attitude* illustrates co-advocates solving real-life problems together.

C —*Communication* is open discussion promoting dynamic partnerships.

Y —*Y not start now?* is a question promoting co-advocate behavior.

Finally, the changing demography in the United States challenges educators to develop techniques for effectively engaging linguistically diverse parents. C. L. Wilson and Hughes (1994) report that one in seven people speaks a language other than English at home. Some major factors that influence these parents' involvement are length of residence in the United States, English proficiency, availability of support groups and bilingual staff, and prior experience. C. L. Wilson and Hughes offer the following techniques for engaging these parents:

1. Employ an interpreter for parent conferences.
2. Print all signs, school communications, and notes in the language spoken by the family.
3. Send parents a large amount of written and visual information over an extended time.
4. Videotape some class activities and share them with the parents.

Parent-Teacher Conferences

Parent-teacher conferences create an environment in which parents feel they are working in a cooperative partnership with school personnel. Many school districts encourage the special education teacher to meet with the parents before the child begins receiving special education services. Duncan and Fitzgerald (1969) found that early meetings with parents served to prevent or reduce attendance problems, the number of dropouts, and discipline problems. Also, early meetings were associated with higher grades and good future communication.

The initial parent-teacher conference is extremely important. To prepare, the teacher should examine the child's records and review pertinent information such as present status (i.e., chronological age, grade, class, and previous teacher), physical appearance and history, educational status, personal traits, and home and family characteristics. In planning the meeting, the teacher should identify objectives of the meeting and develop an appropriate agenda. The conference time should be convenient for all attending, and the meeting place should be arranged to promote communication.

Successful conferences typically consist of four parts: (a) establishing rapport, (b) obtaining pertinent information from the parents, (c) providing information, and (d) summarizing the conference and planning follow-up activities (Stephens & Wolf, 1989). Starting with neutral topics and providing a comfortable seat help establish rapport. To obtain information, the teacher should state the purpose of the conference, ask open-ended questions, recognize parents' feelings by responding empathetically and avoid irrelevancies (such as marital problems). To provide information, the teacher should start with positive statements about the child's behavior and provide samples of work when possible, avoid educational jargon, and share anticipated plans. To summarize the conference, the teacher briefly should review the main points concerning the student's progress, restate the activities that will be implemented to deal with identified weaknesses and problems, and answer any questions. Finally, the teacher and parents should discuss and agree on follow-up strategies and schedule another meeting, if necessary. The conference should end on a positive note, and the teacher should thank the parents for their input and interest and offer to be available for any future questions concerning their child.

Salend (1994) provides the following helpful parent-teacher conference schedule:

1. Welcome participants.
2. Introduce parents and other school personnel, and include an explanation of the roles of each professional and the services they provide to the student.
3. Discuss the purpose of the meeting and review the agenda.
4. Review relevant information from prior meetings.
5. Discuss the student's needs and school performance, and support statements with work samples, test results, and anecdotal records.
6. Provide the parents with the opportunity to discuss their perspective of their child's progress and needs.
7. Discuss all comments in an attempt to form a consensus.
8. Determine a plan of action.
9. Summarize and review the results of the meeting.
10. Determine appropriate dates for the next meeting.
11. Adjourn the meeting.
12. Evaluate the meeting.

In addition, Kroth and Simpson (1977) and Ehly et al. (1985) discuss various strategies, ideas, and activities to maximize the benefits of parent conferences.

Listening is the key to communication, and both parties must listen. A good listener gains much information that often can help solve problems. Parents like to talk to a teacher who listens in a sympathetic, calm, and nonjudgmental manner. Active listening involves increased levels of responding, body animation, and questioning. Eye contact is a basic component of good listening, whereas fatigue, strong feelings, too much talking, and environmental distractions deter active listening. Simpson (1990) notes that to facilitate the communication process, the effective listener must demonstrate skills in attention, acceptance, and empathy as well as use specific listening strategies (e.g., door-opening statements, clarifying responses, restatements, reflecting silence, and summarization). He states that "the professional who attempts to respond to parents prior to listening to them, or the educator who too hastily assumes the position of 'telling' parents what to do or 'answers' their questions when they simply desire the opportunity to talk, will rarely offer the most satisfactory conferencing relationship" (p. 124).

To evaluate the conference, Simpson (1990) suggests that feedback can be obtained by requesting parents and teachers to respond to various questions such as the following:

1. Was a folder of the student's representative work prepared for the parents?
2. Was sufficient time allotted for the session?
3. Did the teacher provide the parent with an opportunity to ask questions?
4. Was the teacher able to explain the academic remediation strategy to the parents?
5. Was the teacher able to provide an adequate report of social and emotional progress?
6. Was the teacher able to solicit and respond to questions raised by the parents?

Reporting Student Progress

In most school districts, teachers send home progress report cards six times a year, each covering a 6-week period. Parents who receive nothing but these reports cannot reinforce and encourage specific skill development on a daily basis.

In daily report systems, the student's report card usually remains on the student's desk all day. The teacher records the progress or instructs the student to record it during the instructional activities. At the end of the day, the teacher signs each card. Fairchild (1987) notes that use of the daily report card can help to establish communication with parents and can relay various kinds of information such as academic performance, effort, behavior, peer relationships, and homework completion. The daily report card system also allows parents to reinforce their child's improved academic performance or school behavior.

Teachers who use curriculum-based measurement or who chart the student's progress can send the charts home each day. The charts record progress on target skills. The teacher usually measures the progress by the number of correct and incorrect items performed in a 1-minute sample (see Chapter 8). For parents who want to reinforce specific skills, the chart has the advantage of listing the target skill. A teacher can choose to report the student's progress using any metric system (e.g., percentage, rate, number correct, or checklist) that the teacher, parent, and child understand.

Not all students can benefit from the daily system. Some teachers and parents prefer weekly progress reports that give the child the opportunity to recover from a bad day. Such reports take less of the teacher's time. Teachers also should consider making a phone call or sending home notes, "happy-grams," or achievement certificates when the student masters a specific skill.

PARENT ADVOCACY AND PARENT RIGHTS

In their efforts to obtain an accurate diagnosis or secure services, many parents encounter frustrating problems. These experiences have led parents and professionals to join forces (Hallahan & Cruickshank, 1973). Although local coalitions emerged earlier, the organization of the Association for Children with Learning Disabilities (ACLD) in 1964 (now the Learning Disabilities Association) generally is recognized as the first nationwide effort to secure services for students with learning disabilities. ACLD lobbied for the passage of the Learning Disabilities Act of 1969. This act established learning disabilities as a category of exceptionality and provided funds to states for prototype programs, teacher training, information dissemination, and research. Since the passage of this act, some parents have turned to the courts in their quest for public services (Abeson, 1972, 1974; Kuriloff, True, Kirp, & Buss, 1974).

Litigation, coupled with parental and professional concerns, helped to pass the Education for All Handicapped Children Act of 1975 (Public Law 94-142), which was renamed the Individuals with Disabilities Education Act (IDEA) in 1990. This law ensures that all children with disabilities receive a free, appropriate public education. Section 615 of Public Law 94-142 guarantees such children and their parents or guardians rights to various procedural safeguards. In essence, the law actively involves parents in their child's educational program. As indicated in Table 4.5, parents must be informed about their child's referral and assessment for eligibility for special education services and are encouraged to attend and participate in IEP meetings. In addition, parents have the right to due process, which is the right to appeal and contest the decisions made by the placement team concerning the child. In a due process hearing conducted by an impartial hearing officer, the educational agency and the parents of the student attempt to resolve educational disputes. The law also provides parents with the right to confidentiality concerning their child's school records and guarantees that parents can obtain their child's educational records upon request. Moreover, in the 1990 amendments, IDEA specifies that states, including state departments of education, are not immune from lawsuits by private citizens if the law is violated.

TABLE 4.5
Procedural Safeguards According to the Individuals with Disabilities Education Act

I. Protection in Evaluation Procedures
Parents have the right to
1. Review all records related to the identification, evaluation, and placement of the child.
2. Review the procedures and instruments to be used in the evaluation.
3. Refuse consent to the evaluation (subject to the school system's right to a hearing).
4. Be informed of the results of the evaluation.
5. Obtain an independent educational evaluation, which will be considered in any decisions regarding the child.
6. Receive information, upon request, about where an independent evaluation by a certified examiner can be obtained.
7. Upon disagreement with the school system's evaluation (subject to the school system's right to a hearing), obtain an independent evaluation at public expense when ordered by a hearing officer or when agreed to by the School Board in the absence of a formal hearing.

II. Protection in Exceptional Student Education Program Placement
Parents have the right to
1. Receive prior notification of changes in educational placement, including recommendations for assignment, reassignment, or denial of assignment in any exceptional education program.
2. Be notified in their primary language or other primary mode of communication (unless it clearly is not feasible).
3. Refuse consent to initial placement in an exceptional education program (subject to the school system's right to a hearing).
4. Request an impartial hearing if they disagree with the recommendations for educational placement.

III. Protection in Impartial Hearing Procedures
Parents have the right to
1. Be accompanied and advised by counsel and experts in the pertinent areas of exceptionality.
2. Present evidence and confront, cross-examine, and compel the attendance of witnesses.
3. Obtain an independent educational evaluation to be presented as evidence.
4. Examine and reproduce all relevant school records.
5. Prohibit introduction of evidence that has not been disclosed at least 5 days prior to the hearing.
6. Have the child who is the subject of the hearing present, and open the hearing to the public.
7. Obtain a record of the hearing.
8. Appeal the decision of the hearing.

IV. Protection for Confidentiality of Information
Parents have the right to
1. Inspect and review educational records.
2. Receive a response from the educational agency to reasonable requests for explanations and interpretations of the records.
3. Obtain copies of the records.
4. Seek correction of records.
5. Give prior consent for disclosure of personally identifiable information.
6. Request a hearing when there is a problem or question regarding confidentiality of information in their child's records.

The parent-child bond is one of the most permanent and powerful links between individuals. Federal law now recognizes that parents of a child with disabilities are advocates for their child because they are committed personally to their child's cause and are likely to expend their time, resources, and energy to promote their child's welfare (Daniels, 1982). Wolery (1989) states that, as advocates, parents must "understand their rights and the rights of their children, ensure that due process procedures are implemented, identify instances when the best interests of their child and the family are not being met, and initiate appropriate action when their child is not being served appropriately" (p. 10). He also notes that parents can act as advocates by providing support for programs and services, assisting other parents in obtaining appropriate services, and lobbying local, state, and national government officials for services for individuals with disabilities and their families.

Although the assumption that parent participation in their child's educational program has inherent appeal and logic, the formal involvement of parents has not been easy or necessarily productive. Yoshida, Fenton, Kaufman, and Maxwell (1978) conducted a survey of 1,372 members of special education student-planning teams regarding their attitudes toward parental involvement in planning. Yoshida et al. asked members about their attitudes toward parental involvement in 24 activities. Only 2 activities were selected by more than 50% as appropriate for parental participation: presenting information relevant to the case (65.7%) and gathering information relevant to the case (57.4%). Other activities and corresponding percentages include reviewing the student's educational progress (41.1%), reviewing the appropriateness of the student's educational program (36.7%), and judging programming alternatives (34.0%).

A. P. Turnbull and Turnbull (1990) conclude that current findings indicate that parents are passive participants in IEP conferences. Attending and participating in an IEP meeting can be overwhelming for some parents who find themselves facing six or more educators and psychologists who are presenting test results that sometimes are disappointing. However, observations of IEP meetings indicate that, in general, although parents ask few questions and comment or respond infrequently, they usually are satisfied with the meeting outcome and have few questions concerning the resulting decisions (Vaughn, Bos, Harrell, & Lasky, 1988). Morgan (1982) reports that there is still a lack of data that document the benefits of parental participation in the IEP process.

These results indicate that extensive parent involvement in educational planning is not likely and, on occasion, meets opposition. Parents are major stakeholders in their child's educational program, and, because of the emotions involved, it is not uncommon for a teacher to encounter criticism or anger from a parent. Jones and Jones (1995) provide some helpful techniques for teachers to deal with parent criticism and confrontation:

1. Maintain a calm and pleasant manner.
2. Use active listening, and avoid becoming defensive. Look genuinely interested during the process. These behaviors defuse emotions.
3. Ask what the parent wishes to accomplish.
4. Set a time limit if necessary, and give consideration to scheduling another meeting.
5. Ask the parent if the student is aware of the problem of concern.
6. Be honest, and rely on specific data.
7. Let the parent know specifically what will be done to deal with the problem.

Many parents become observers only. On the other hand, Yoshida et al. (1978) point out that schools may view the parents as active participants and encourage parents to assist in making judgments about their child's program. They note that this latter approach "may increase parental support for their child's special education program and promote closer cooperation between school and home in implementing that program" (p. 533). As listed in Table 4.6, A. P. Turnbull and Turnbull (1990) provide suggestions for involving

TABLE 4.6
Suggestions for Involving Parents in the IEP Conference

Preconference Preparation

- Appoint a service coordinator to organize all aspects of the IEP conference.
- Solicit information from the family about their preferences and needs regarding the conference.
- Discuss the meeting with the student and consider the student's preferences concerning the conference.
- Decide who should attend the conference and include the student, if appropriate.
- Arrange a convenient time and location for the meeting.
- Assist families with logistical needs such as transportation and child care.
- Without educational jargon, inform the family verbally or in writing of the following:
    - Purpose of the meeting
    - Time and location of conference
    - Names of participants
- Based on family preferences, share information the family wants before the conference.
- Encourage the student, family members, and their advocates to visit the proposed placements for the student before the conference.
- Facilitate communication between the student and family members about the conference.
- Encourage families to share information and discuss concerns with participants before the conference.
- Gather needed information from school personnel.
- Prepare an agenda to cover the remaining components of the IEP conference.

Initial Conference Proceedings

- Greet the student, family, and their advocates.
- Provide a list of all participants or use name tags.
- Introduce each participant with a brief description of the individual's role in the conference.
- State the purpose of the meeting. Review the agenda, and ask for additional issues to be covered.
- Determine the amount of time participants have available for the conference, and offer the option of rescheduling, if needed, to complete the agenda.
- Ask if family members desire clarification of their legal rights.

Review of Formal Evaluation and Current Levels of Performance

- Provide family members with a written copy of evaluation results if desired.
- Avoid educational jargon as much as possible and clarify diagnostic terminology throughout the conference.
- If a separate evaluation conference has not been scheduled, ask diagnostic personnel to report the following:
    - The tests administered
    - The results of each test
    - Options based on the evaluation
- Summarize the findings including strengths, gifts, abilities, and needs.
- Identify implications of test results for planning purposes.
- Ask family members for areas of agreement and disagreement with corresponding reasons.
- Review the student's developmental progress and current levels of performance in each class.
- Ask family members if they agree or disagree with the stated progress and performance levels.

continued

TABLE 4.6
continued

- Strive to resolve any disagreement with student work samples, and solicit information from family members about collecting further samples.
- Proceed with the IEP only when you and the family members agree about the student's exceptionality and current levels of performance.

Development of Goals and Objectives

- Encourage the student, family members, and advocates to share their expectations for the student's participation in the home, school, and community.
- Collaboratively generate appropriate goals and objectives for all subject areas requiring special instruction consistent with expectations.
- Discuss goals and objectives for future educational and vocational options based on great expectations for the student.
- Identify objectives to expand the positive contributions the student can make to family, friends, and community.
- Prioritize all goals and objectives in light of student preferences and needs.
- Clarify the manner in which the responsibility for teaching the objectives will be shared among the student's teachers.
- Ask family members and advocates if they would like to share in the responsibility for teaching some of the objectives at home or in the community.
- Determine evaluation procedures and schedules for identified goals and objectives.
- Explain to family members and advocates that the IEP is not a guarantee that the student will attain the goals; rather, it represents a good-faith effort on the part of school personnel that they will teach these goals and objectives.

Determination of Placement and Related Services

- Include the student, family members, and advocates in a discussion of the benefits and drawbacks of viable placement options.
- Select a placement option that allows the student to be involved with peers without exceptionalities as much as possible.
- Agree on a tentative placement until the family members can visit and confirm its appropriateness.
- Discuss the benefits and drawbacks of modes of delivery for related services the student needs.
- Specify the dates for initiating related services and anticipated duration.
- Share the names and qualifications of all personnel who will provide services with family members and advocates.

Concluding the Conference

- Assign follow-up responsibility for any task requiring attention.
- Review with the student, family members, and advocates any responsibilities they have agreed to assume.
- Summarize orally and on paper the major decisions and follow-up responsibilities of all participants.
- Set a tentative date for reviewing the IEP document.
- Identify strategies for ongoing communication with the student, family members, and advocates.
- Express appreciation to the student, family members, and advocates for their help in the decision-making process.

Note: Adapted from *Families, Professionals, and Exceptionality: A Special Partnership* (pp. 288–290), 2nd ed., by A. P. Turnbull and H. R. Turnbull, III, 1990, Upper Saddle River, NJ: Merrill/Prentice Hall. Copyright 1990 by Prentice-Hall Publishing Company. Reprinted by permission.

parents in each of the six stages of an IEP conference.

To ensure that appropriate services are provided, parents and professionals must be willing to take action. Several authorities (Biklen, 1982; Ehly et al., 1985) offer guidelines to help parents secure appropriate services for individuals with disabilities:

1. *Form or join a disability rights group.*
2. *Be informed.* Be aware of the services to which parents and their child with disabilities are entitled.
3. *Build a record.* Document activities involving interactions with schools, governmental agencies, and medical personnel.
4. *Monitor the state plan.* Compare the state plan with federal mandates.
5. *Establish a consultant pool.* Identify professional personnel (e.g., educators, psychologists, attorneys, or physicians) that can help.
6. *Litigate.*
7. *Negotiate.* Meet to work out differences.
8. *Identify model programs.*
9. *Engage in active research.* Collect data through surveys and interviews.
10. *Write letters.*
11. *Use the media to inform the public about the needs of individuals with disabilities and their families.*

PERSPECTIVE

The parent-child relationship embodies the range of human emotions. With the trend toward more parent involvement in identification, placement, and educational programming, school personnel must prepare themselves to work more closely and effectively with parents. The teacher must be supportive, sensitive, and informative during crucial parent adjustment periods. Both parties must realize that the optimal growth of the child will emerge only from a pilgrimage of problem-solving ventures. Problem solving is facilitated by identifying the problem, analyzing resources, outlining alternatives, selecting an alternative, and then evaluating its effectiveness. Frustration and hard work surely will accompany the search for services; however, joy likely will accompany the solution. This process beckons the teacher and the parent to develop precise assessment techniques and gather information about resources, techniques, and materials.

School personnel's role is thus "that of consultant to the parents, not as a dominant authority in a transient relationship" (Hobbs, 1975, p. 227). Simches (1975) captures the parent involvement trend in the following passage:

> By assuming new roles, parents are bringing about important changes in the educational system. Through their involvement in the classroom, parents are learning skills that enable them to help their children more effectively. Advising decision-making groups, parents are helping educators find appropriate placements for children. As advocates, parents are protecting the legal rights of the handicapped, and are working to extend and expand the educational opportunities available to all children. From token involvement in the schools, parents are emerging as a potent force capable of constructively changing the entire educational system. (p. 566)

It is hoped that this partnership of parents and school personnel will result in the creation of school and home environments that maximize the pleasures of parenting and teaching and minimize the sorrows and frustrations.

DISCUSSION/REVIEW QUESTIONS

1. Discuss common adjustment reactions that parents of a child with learning disabilities may experience.
2. Identify some of the factors that contribute to the diversity of families.
3. Describe some of the informational strategies that are useful to parents.
4. Discuss the five major types of parent involvement, and present elements that are common to successful parent involvement programs.
5. Discuss behavioral and Adlerian approaches in parent training programs.

6. Describe parent observation, home management, and parent tutoring techniques.
7. Discuss techniques for maintaining positive parent-teacher relationships.
8. Describe techniques for conducting a successful parent-teacher conference.
9. List parent rights according to IDEA.
10. Describe parent advocacy activities.

REFERENCES

Abeson, A. (1972). Movement and momentum: Government and the education of handicapped children—I. *Exceptional Children, 39,* 63–66.

Abeson, A. (1974). Movement and momentum: Government and the education of handicapped children—II. *Exceptional Children, 41,* 109–116.

Abrams, J. C., & Kaslow, F. (1977). Family systems and the learning disabled child: Intervention and treatment. *Journal of Learning Disabilities, 10,* 86–90.

Anderegg, M. L., Vergason, G. A., & Smith, M. C. (1992). A visual representation of the grief cycle for use by teachers with families of children with disabilities. *Remedial and Special Education, 13*(2), 17–23.

Barsch, R. H. (1969). *The parent teacher partnership.* Arlington, VA: Council for Exceptional Children.

Bergan, J. R., Neumann, A. J., III, & Karp, C. L. (1983). Effects of parent training on parent instruction and child learning of intellectual skills. *Journal of School Psychology, 2*(1), 31–40.

Berger, E. H. (1991). *Parents as partners in education* (3rd ed.). St. Louis, MO: C. V. Mosby.

Biklen, D. (1982). *Community organizing.* Upper Saddle River, NJ: Prentice Hall.

Brandt, R. (1989). On parents and schools: A conversation with Joyce Epstein. *Educational Leadership, 47*(2), 24–27.

Brightman, R. P., Baker, B. L., Clark, D. B., & Ambrose, S. A. (1982). Effectiveness of alternative parent training formats. *Journal of Behavior Therapy and Experimental Psychiatry, 13,* 113–117.

Brotherson, M. J., Berdine, W. H., & Sartini, V. (1993). Transition to adult services: Support for ongoing parent participation. *Remedial and Special Education, 14*(4), 44–51.

Brown, B. F. (1980). A study of the school needs of children from one-parent families. *Phi Delta Kappan, 61,* 537–540.

Brown, C. C. (1976). It changed my life. *Psychology Today, 10,* 47–57, 109–112.

Brutten, M., Richardson, S. O., & Mangel, C. (1973). *Something's wrong with my child: A parent's book about children with learning disabilities.* New York: Harcourt Brace Jovanovich.

Cone, J. D., DeLawyer, D. D., & Wolfe, V. V. (1985). Assessing parent participation: The Parent/Family Involvement Index. *Exceptional Children, 51,* 417–424.

Cordoni, B. (1992). *Living with a learning disability.* Carbondale, IL: Southern Illinois University Press.

Cummings, R. E., & Maddux, C. D. (1985). *Parenting the learning disabled: A realistic approach.* Springfield, IL: Charles C Thomas.

Daniels, S. M. (1982). From parent-advocacy to self-advocacy: A problem of transition. *Exceptional Education Quarterly, 3*(2), 25–32.

Dembinski, R. J., & Mauser, A. J. (1977). What parents of the learning disabled really want from professionals. *Journal of Learning Disabilities, 10,* 578–584.

Dinkmeyer, D., & McKay, G. (1989). *Systematic training for effective parenting.* Circle Pines, MN: American Guidance Service.

Dreikurs, R., & Soltz, V. (1964). *Children: The challenge.* Des Moines, IA: Meredith.

Duncan, L. W., & Fitzgerald, P. W. (1969). Increasing the parent-child communication through counselor-parent conferences. *Personnel and Guidance Journal, 47,* 514–517.

Ehly, S. W., Conoley, J. C., & Rosenthal, D. M. (1985). *Working with parents of exceptional children.* Upper Saddle River, NJ: Merrill/Prentice Hall.

Eiserman, W. D., Weber, C., & McCoun, M. (1995). Parent and professional roles in early intervention: A longitudinal comparison of the effects of two intervention configurations. *The Journal of Special Education, 29,* 20–44.

Epstein, J. L. (1988). How do we improve programs for parent involvement? *Educational Horizons, 66,* 58–59.

Fairchild, T. N. (1987). The daily report card. *Teaching Exceptional Children, 19*(2),72–73.

Forehand, R., & King, H. E. (1977). Noncompliant children: Effects of parent training on behavior and attitude change. *Behavior Modification, 1*(1), 93–108.

Freund, J. H., & Elardo, R. (1978). Maternal behavior and family constellation as predictors of social competence in learning disabled children. *Learning Disability Quarterly, 1*(3), 80–86.

Gallagher, J. (1956). Rejecting parents? *Exceptional Children, 22,* 273–276, 294.

Gallagher, J. J., Beckman, P., & Cross, A. H. (1983). Families of handicapped children: Sources of stress and its amelioration. *Exceptional Children, 50,* 10–19.

Gallagher, L. S. (1995). The impact of learning disabilities on families. *Journal of Child Neurology, 10*(Suppl. 1), 112–113.

Hall, M. C., Grinstead, J., Collier, H., & Hall, R. V. (1980). Responsive parenting: A preventive program which incorporates parents training parents. *Education and Treatment of Children, 3*(3), 239–259.

Hall, M. C., & Nelson, D. J. (1981). Responsive parenting: One approach for teaching parents parenting skills. *School Psychology Review, 10*(1), 45–53.

Hall, R. V. (1971). *Managing behavior: Applications in school and home*. Austin, TX: PRO-ED.

Hall, R. V. (1975). *Managing behavior: Basic principles*. Austin, TX: PRO-ED.

Hall, R. V., & Houten, R. V. (1983). *Managing behavior: The measurement of behavior* (Rev. ed.). Austin, TX: PRO-ED.

Hallahan, D. P., & Cruickshank, W. M. (1973). *Psychoeducational foundations of learning disabilities*. Upper Saddle River, NJ: Prentice Hall.

Heid, C., & Harris, J. J., III. (1989). Parent involvement: A link between schools and minority communities. *Community Education Journal, 15*(2), 26–28.

Hobbs, N. (1975). *The futures of children*. San Francisco: Jossey-Bass.

Hudson, P., & Miller, S. P. (1993). Home and school partnerships: Parent as teacher. *LD Forum, 18*(2), 31–33.

Ingersoll, B. (1988). *Your hyperactive child: A parent's guide to coping with attention-deficit disorder*. New York: Doubleday.

Jayanthi, M., Nelson, J. S., Sawyer, V., Bursuck, W. D., & Epstein, M. H. (1995). Homework-communication problems among parents, classroom teachers, and special education teachers: An exploratory study. *Remedial and Special Education, 16*(2), 102–116.

Jones, V. F., & Jones, L. S. (1995). zzz*Comprehensive classroom management: Creating positive learning environments for all students* (4th ed.). Boston: Allyn & Bacon.

Kirk, S. A. (1984). Introspection and prophecy. In B. Blatt & R. J. Morris (Eds.), *Perspectives in special education: Personal orientations*. Glenview, IL: Scott, Foresman.

Klein, R. S., Altman, S. D., Dreizen, K., Friedman, R., & Powers, L. (1981a). Restructuring dysfunctional parental attitudes toward children's learning and behavior in school: Family-oriented psychoeducational therapy. Part I. *Journal of Learning Disabilities, 14,* 15–19.

Klein, R. S., Altman, S. D., Dreizen, K., Friedman, R., & Powers, L. (1981b). Restructuring dysfunctional parental attitudes toward children's learning and behavior in school: Family-oriented psychoeducational therapy. Part II. *Journal of Learning Disabilities, 14,* 99–101.

Kronick, D. (1977). A parent's thoughts for parents and teachers. In N. G. Haring & B. Bateman, *Teaching the learning disabled child*. Upper Saddle River, NJ: Prentice Hall.

Kroth, R. L. (1973). *Target behavior*. Bellevue, WA: Edmark.

Kroth, R. L., & Simpson, R. L. (1977). *Parent conferences as a teaching strategy*. Denver: Love.

Kuriloff, P., True, R., Kirp, D., & Buss, W. (1974). Legal reform and educational change: The Pennsylvania case. *Exceptional Children, 41,* 35–42.

Lambie, R., & Daniels-Mohring, D. (1993). *Family systems within educational contexts: Understanding students with special needs*. Denver: Love.

Lelewer, N. (1994). *Something's* not *right: One's family's struggle with learning disabilities*. Acton, MA: VanderWyk & Burnham.

Marriage and Divorce Today. (1987, July 13). *12*(50).

McLoughlin, J. A., Edge, D., & Strenecky, B. (1978). Perspective on parental involvement in the diagnosis and treatment of learning disabled children. *Journal of Learning Disabilities, 11,* 291–296.

McWhirter, J. J. (1976). A parent education group in learning disabilities. *Journal of Learning Disabilities, 9,* 16–20.

Mehran, M., & White, K. R. (1988). Parent tutoring as a supplement to compensatory education for first-grade children. *Remedial and Special Education, 9*(3), 35–41.

Mercer, C. D., & Mercer, A. R. (1993). *Teaching students with learning problems* (4th ed.). Upper Saddle River, NJ: Merrill/Prentice Hall.

Michael, M. G., Arnold, K. D., Magliocca, L. A., & Miller, S. (1992). Influences on teachers' attitudes of the parents' role as collaborator. *Remedial and Special Education, 13*(2), 24–30, 39.

Morgan, D. P. (1982). Parent participation in the IEP process: Does it enhance appropriate education? *Exceptional Education Quarterly, 3*(2), 33–40.

National Center for Educational Statistics. (1988). *National education longitudinal study of 1988.* Washington, DC: U.S. Department of Education.

National Education Association. (1976). *Briefing for parents.* Washington, DC: Author.

National Institute of Education. (1985, February). *Research in brief.* Washington, DC: Author.

Norton, A. J., & Glick, P. C. (1986). One parent families: A social and economic profile. *Family Relations, 35*(1), 9–17.

O'Shea, D. J., O'Shea, L. J., & Nowocien, D. (1993). Parent-teacher relationships in school renewal and educational reform. *LD Forum, 18*(3), 43–46.

Patterson, G. R. (1975). *Families.* Champaign, IL: Research Press.

Patterson, G. R. (1976). *Living with children: New methods for parents and teachers.* Champaign, IL: Research Press.

Reynolds, M. C., Wang, M. C., & Walberg, H. J. (1992). The knowledge bases for special and general education. *Remedial and Special Education, 13*(5), 6–10, 33.

Ring, B. C. (1980). Training adult tutors for your classroom. *Academic Therapy, 15,* 415–419.

Robinson, N. M., & Robinson, H. B. (1976). *The mentally retarded child: A psychological approach* (2nd ed.). New York: McGraw-Hill.

Ross, B. M. (1981). *Our special child.* New York: Walker.

Salend, S. J. (1994). *Effective mainstreaming: Creating inclusive classrooms* (2nd ed.). Upper Saddle River, NJ: Merrill/Prentice Hall.

Schlossman, S. L. (1976). Before home start: Notes toward a history of parent education in America, 1897–1929. *Harvard Educational Review, 46,* 436–467.

Shapero, S., & Forbes, C. R. (1981). A review of involvement programs for parents of learning disabled children. *Journal of Learning Disabilities, 14,* 499–504.

Silver, L. (1984). *The misunderstood child: A guide for parents of learning disabled children.* New York: McGraw-Hill.

Simches, R. F. (1975). The parent-professional partnership. *Exceptional Children, 41,* 565–566.

Simpson, R. L. (1990). *Conferencing parents of exceptional children* (2nd ed.). Austin, TX: PRO-ED.

Simpson, R. L., & Poplin, M. S. (1981). Parents as agents of change. *School Psychology Review, 10*(1), 15–25.

Smith, S. L. (1979). *No easy answers: Teaching the learning disabled child.* Cambridge, MA: Winthrop.

Smith, S. L. (1991). *Succeeding against the odds: How the learning disabled can realize their promise.* New York: G. P. Putnam's Sons.

Stephens, T. M., & Wolf, J. S. (1989). *Effective skills in parent/teacher conferencing* (2nd ed.). Columbus, OH: School Study Council of Ohio, College of Education, The Ohio State University.

Strom, R. D. (1984). *Parent as a Teacher Inventory manual.* Bensenville, IL: Scholastic Testing Service.

Thorn, P. (1974). *An evaluation of long-term effectiveness of Adlerian study groups.* Unpublished master's thesis, Bowie State College, Bowie, MD.

Thurston, L. P., & Dasta, K. (1990). An analysis of in-home parent tutoring procedures: Effects on children's academic behavior at home and in school and on parents' tutoring behaviors. *Remedial and Special Education, 11*(4), 41–52.

Toro, P. A., Weissberg, R. P., Guare, J., & Liebenstein, N. L. (1990). A comparison of children with and without learning disabilities on social problem-solving skill, school behavior, and family background. *Journal of Learning Disabilities, 23,* 115–120.

Turnbull, A. P., & Turnbull, H. R., III. (1990). *Families, professionals, and exceptionality: A special partnership* (2nd ed.). Upper Saddle River, NJ: Merrill/Prentice Hall.

Turnbull, H. R., III, & Turnbull, A. P. (1985). *Parents speak out: Then and now* (2nd ed.). Upper Saddle River, NJ: Merrill/Prentice Hall.

Vail, P. L. (1990). *About dyslexia: Unraveling the myth.* Rosemont, NJ: Modern Learning Press.

Vaughn, S., Bos, C. S., Harrell, J. E., & Lasky, B. A. (1988). Parent participation in the initial placement/IEP conference ten years after mandated involvement. *Journal of Learning Disabilities, 21,* 82–89.

Wehman, P. (1990). School-to-work: Elements of successful programs. *Exceptional Children, 23,* 40–43.

Weiss, H. G., & Weiss, M. S. (1976). *Home is a learning place: A parents' guide to learning disabilities.* Boston: Little, Brown.

Williams, D. L., Jr., & Chavkin, N. F. (1989). Essential elements of strong parent involvement programs. *Educational Leadership, 47*(2), 18–20.

Wilson, C. L., & Hughes, M. (1994). Involving linguistically diverse parents. *LD Forum, 13*(3), 25–27.

Wilson, L. (1975). Learning disability as related to infrequent punishment and limited participation in delay of reinforcement task. *Journal of School Psychology, 13,* 255–263.

Wolery, M. (1989). Transitions in early childhood special education: Issues and procedures. *Focus on Exceptional Children, 22*(2), 1–16.

Wolfensberger, W. (1967). Counseling the parents of the retarded. In A. A. Baumeister (Ed.), *Mental retardation: Appraisal, education, and rehabilitation.* Chicago: Aldine.

Wortis, J. (1966). Successful family life for the retarded child. In *Stress on families of the mentally handicapped. Proceedings of the Third International Conference of the International League of Societies of the Mentally Retarded.* Brussels, Belgium.

Wright, L. S., Matlock, K. S., & Matlock, D. T. (1985). Parents of handicapped children: Their self-ratings, life satisfactions and parental adequacy. *The Exceptional Child, 32*(1), 37–40.

Yoshida, R. K., Fenton, K. S., Kaufman, M. J., & Maxwell, F. P. (1978). Parental involvement in the special education pupil planning process: The school's perspective. *Exceptional Children, 44,* 531–534.

PART TWO

Assessment and Services

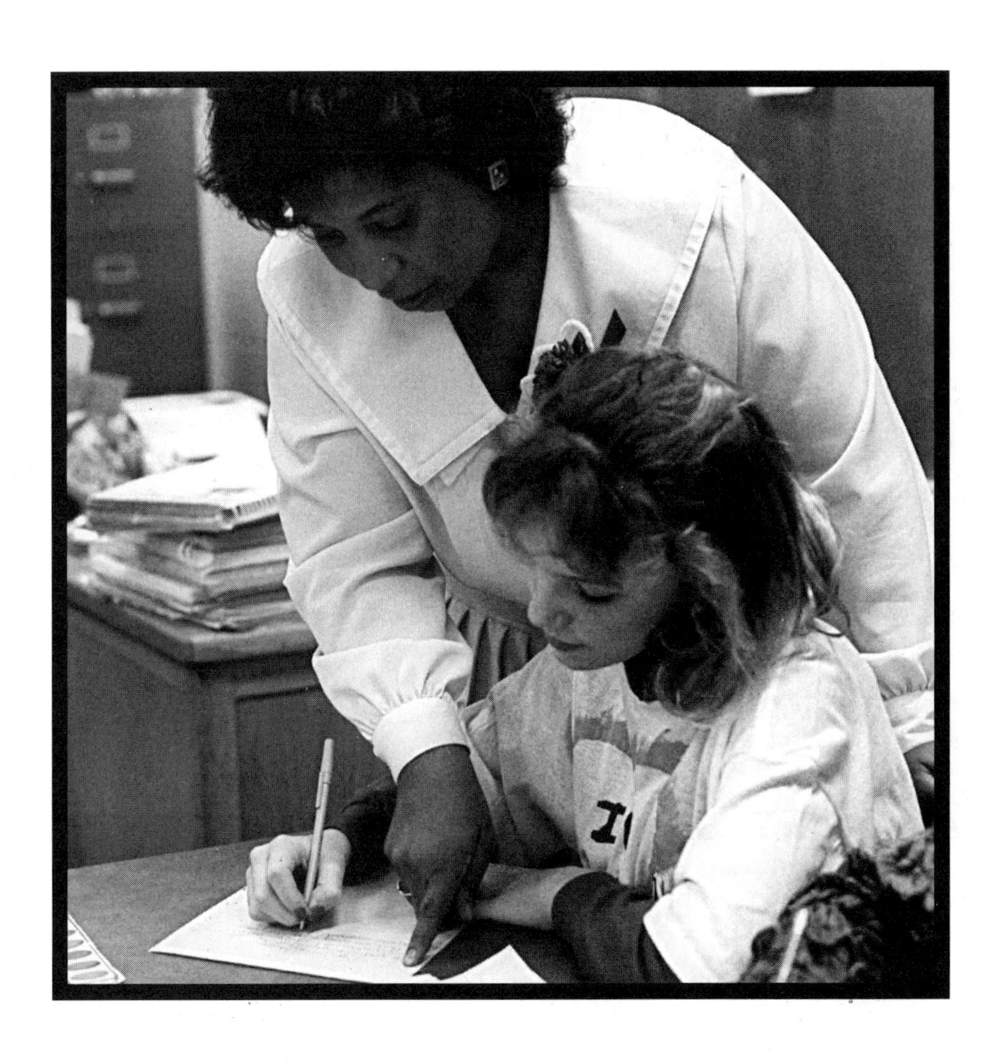

Assessment

3. To stay in your own self space.
4. To not fight or hurt others.
To be kind to others
To feel good and special
3 SPELL
4 COPY
PICTURE
6 WRITE
SPELLING

CHAPTER 5

After studying this chapter, you should be able to:

- identify obstacles that impede the search for better identification practices.
- identify the contents of Public Law 94-142 regarding assessment.
- discuss assessing students from minority cultures.
- discuss formal tests and their advantages and disadvantages.
- identify two tests of intelligence.
- discuss types of informal assessment measures.
- describe curriculum-based assessment and alternative assessment.
- discuss the purposes of assessment.
- present the steps in the assessment process.
- discuss the requirements of the 1977 *Federal Register* in identifying learning disabilities.
- discuss specific components that need to be assessed in identifying learning disabilities.
- discuss procedures used in operationalizing the discrepancy component.
- present the advantages and disadvantages of discrepancy and related practices in identifying learning disabilities.
- present alternative directions for determining a severe discrepancy.
- list guidelines for improving multidisciplinary team functioning.
- present guidelines for assessment of what to teach.
- present assessment areas for determining how to teach.
- discuss the development of an individualized educational program.

Assessment is a complex and somewhat controversial area. The importance of the assessment process, however, is apparent. I once was asked to test a 13-year-old student, Stephanie, who was being seen in a hospital-based pediatric clinic. When I arrived to test, I discovered that Stephanie's folder had been misplaced. So, I proceeded to test her without the benefit of background information. In the beginning of the testing session, Stephanie worked intensely; however, as testing continued, she lowered her head and mumbled incorrect answers. When I asked if she was okay, she did not respond. Through continued efforts to talk with Stephanie, I realized that she stopped trying when the test items became difficult. I explained that the tests covered material through the 12th grade and that it was expected for her to miss some items. I asked her to try to do her best, and I mentioned that we would take a refreshment break periodically throughout the testing. Stephanie liked the idea of taking breaks and promised to do her best. When Stephanie's test responses were scored, she achieved average or above average scores in reading, math, and spelling.

Several days later, I was asked to present the test results at a staffing conference. Much to my dismay, the pediatrician, the psychologist, and the language clinician reported that Stephanie performed at a very low level. In fact, they agreed that she was "trainable mentally retarded" with a full-scale IQ of 37. Furthermore, they noted that she had been in a special class for students with mental disabilities for about 8 years. When I presented Stephanie's scores, I reported average or above-average scores of a 13-year-old individual. The team was puzzled with the results, but discussions revealed that Stephanie had lowered her head and mumbled incorrect responses throughout the testing sessions with all of the other team members. It was agreed that Stephanie's scores in the educational testing were the most valid, and the team recommended that she be placed in a general education class with some temporary support services. Stephanie made appropriate progress in the general education setting.

This experience provides a good example of how the assessment process had a significant effect on the life of a student. Given the important decisions that are based on assessment data, educators need to pay close attention to the assessment process. This chapter focuses on assessment practices and the assessment process in learning disabilities.

THE CHALLENGE OF ASSESSMENT IN LEARNING DISABILITIES

The identification of learning disabilities is a highly debated area. Both under- and overidentification of students with learning disabilities can result in significant problems. Underidentification deprives students of services, whereas overidentification results in inappropriate placements and drains resources from other programs and students. The rapid increase of students placed in learning disabilities programs is a national problem. Adelman (1992) reports that uncontrolled increases in learning disability placements threaten the integrity of the learning disabilities field.

The need for the accurate identification of students with learning disabilities is extensive. Professionals, political groups, and parent groups vigorously are seeking better ways to identify such students, but the following obstacles are impeding the search:

1. Consensus on a theoretical definition of learning disabilities exists; however, much disagreement remains regarding how to operationalize the definition (Hammill, 1990). Even in an attempt to operationalize the same definition (e.g., the federal definition), states vary considerably in the specific criteria used (Mercer, Jordan, Allsopp, & Mercer, 1995). However, the variations should decrease as more experts agree on the major components of a learning disabilities definition.
2. The discrepancy factor, a major component in identifying learning disabilities, has been difficult to operationalize.

3. Many instruments used to identify students with learning disabilities are inadequate. Salvia and Ysseldyke (1995) report that many standardized tests used to diagnose learning disabilities lack adequate reliability or validity.
4. The heterogeneity of the population with learning disabilities makes it difficult to develop a unifying set of identification criteria. One student with learning disabilities may be very different from another, and until learning disability subgroups are better understood, the development of accurate identification criteria will remain complex. Moreover, Mather and Roberts (1994) stress the need for assessment procedures that accurately identify individuals with severe disabilities.
5. Many schools do not provide adequate services to low achievers or disruptive students or give general classroom teachers the support system they need. In an effort to help both general class teachers and low-achieving or disruptive students, such students are referred to the learning disabilities program. Consequently, many students who do not have learning disabilities but who may have other difficulties are placed in learning disabilities programs.
6. In many instances, multidisciplinary team members have not been trained to identify students with learning disabilities. Moore, Fifield, Spira, and Scarlato (1989) report that teams lack group decision-making techniques and have difficulty communicating discipline-specific information. As a result of their study of multidisciplinary team identification of students with learning disabilities, Furlong and Yanagida (1985) strongly encourage professionals to improve the reliability of team decisions.

PUBLIC LAW 94-142 AND ASSESSMENT

Congress enacted Public Law 94-142 in November, 1975. It ensures that all students with disabilities receive a free, appropriate public education. Moreover, it establishes a set of procedures to protect against inappropriate assessment and placement practices. These procedures and safeguards are featured in Table 5.1. Public Law 101-476, the Individuals with Disabilities Education Act (IDEA) of 1990, includes amendments to Public Law 94-142; however, these amendments do not alter the assessment safeguards and practices previously presented in the law (McLoughlin & Lewis, 1994). The regulations promote valid practices in the gathering, interpretation, and use of data in making decisions about students with disabilities. Although these rules continue to receive close scrutiny and may be changed, having such safeguards makes legislative sense as well as educational sense, and they protect due process. In 1977, additional regulations (USOE, 1977) were issued for identification (see the Assessment for Identification section of this chapter).

ASSESSING STUDENTS FROM MINORITY CULTURES

To provide assessment in a nondiscriminatory or unbiased manner, educators must consider sociocultural factors in dealing with students who are culturally and linguistically different. Obviously, an aptitude or achievement test written in English is an invalid measure for students who do not speak English. It is equally discriminatory to assess students from minority cultures with tests based on values, beliefs, and cultural experiences associated with the dominant American life-style (McLoughlin & Lewis, 1994).

Collier and Hoover (1987) discuss the need to consider sociocultural factors in assessing minority students referred for learning disabilities:

> When a minority child is referred for suspected learning disabilities, the child's native culture and language, as well as stage of acculturation, must be considered. Knowledge of sociocultural considerations may help educators reduce unnecessary referrals and bias in making decisions about special education placement. (p. 39)

TABLE 5.1
Assessment and Public Law 94-142

Screening
A child-find program must be developed.

Referral
A referral program must be developed.

Parental Consent for Testing
Due process and procedural safeguards must be followed (see Chapter 4).

Diagnostic Testing
Tests must be nondiscriminatory, administered in the student's native language, and appropriate and valid for their respective uses. No single procedure is to be sole criterion for identification. Student is assessed in all areas related to the disability. Tests must be administered by trained personnel. Assessment is made by a multidisciplinary team or a group of specialists.

Eligibility Staffing
A teacher or other specialist with knowledge in area of suspected disability *must* be on the team.

Planning Educational Program and Determining Placement
An individualized educational program (IEP) must be developed. An IEP meeting must occur within 30 days after eligibility is determined. Placement must occur in the student's least restrictive environment.

Parental Consent for Placement
Parents must be encouraged to participate in designing the IEP (see Chapter 4).

Implementing Program
Services must begin without undue delay after the IEP is written.

Evaluating Program
The IEP must be evaluated at least annually.

Rice and Ortiz (1994) note that over-representation of students from culturally and linguistically diverse backgrounds exists in programs for students with learning disabilities. They point out that these youngsters may exhibit numerous behaviors associated with learning disabilities (e.g., single-word or phrase responses, difficulty with sequence and story retelling, and poor recall, comprehension, and vocabulary); however, these behaviors also are typical of many second-language learners. Rice and Ortiz maintain that the existence of a learning disability may be reasonably suspected when developmentally inappropriate deficits in language exist in both the native and second language and when the examiner can rule out extrinsic variables (such as experiential background, limited English proficiency, loss of native language skills, and lack of opportunities to develop native language skills) as likely causes. (Chapter 11 presents more information on assessing students from culturally and linguistically diverse backgrounds.)

Because appropriate measures for testing minority populations are scarce and agreement is lacking on which measures are nondiscriminatory, it often is difficult to provide a nondiscriminatory assessment. McLoughlin and Lewis (1994) note that the potential for bias can be minimized if several considerations are used:

1. Determine whether the norm group is representative of the student's gender, race, and culture. Ensure that the normative sample of the minority student is large enough to be representative.
2. Review the test for culturally biased items.
3. Use a test that is technically adequate in the student's most fluent language, and have the test administered by an examiner who is proficient in the student's primary language. In a review of pertinent studies, Fuchs and Fuchs (1989) found that examiner familiarity facilitated the performance of Black and Hispanic children. The existence of a common language between examiner and student seems to be an important variable in establishing familiarity and rapport. For limited-English proficient students, Rice and Ortiz (1994) recommend testing students in their primary language as well as in English.
4. Select measures that bypass the limitations imposed by the student's disabling condition. For example, if a student has a reading disability, the examiner should present questions orally or through demonstrations.

TYPES OF TESTING

Although there are numerous ways to collect assessment data, tests are the primary tools used. Haney (1985) states, "Nearly every large education reform effort of the past few years has either mandated a new form of testing or expanded uses of existing testing" (p. 4). Hanley (1995) substantiates the influence of reform efforts on assessment practices. He maintains that the reform movements to educate more or all students with disabilities in general education classes (inclusion) and to develop standards for all students will have a significant effect on curriculum requirements and testing practices for students with disabilities. Hanley recommends the use of computer technology to integrate assessment with instruction and to respond to reform directions.

Educators use both formal and informal types of tests. Formal testing consists of administering standardized tests to help document and identify the particular problem (e.g., learning disability) of a student. Informal testing is classroom-based and uses tests that typically are not norm-referenced. Informal testing often is referred to as *formative assessment* and is used primarily in planning instruction and evaluating student progress on a continuous basis. Many educators prefer informal over formal assessment, and in recent years informal assessment has gained in popularity (McLoughlin & Lewis, 1994).

Assessment in learning disabilities frequently entails the use of tests from several areas (e.g., intelligence, process, language, reading, math, and social-emotional). In a study of 14 Michigan school districts, Perlmutter and Parus (1983) found that an average of three to five tests were administered to each student referred for learning disabilities. Specific tests, both formal and informal, are discussed in a later section of this chapter and in the following chapters: Chapter 8—cognitive and perceptual-motor tests, Chapter 9—tests for early identification, Chapter 11—speech and language tests, Chapter 12—written language tests, Chapter 13—reading tests, Chapter 14—math tests, and Chapter 15—tests of social-emotional skills. Intelligence testing is required in the identification of learning disabilities and is presented in this chapter along with curriculum-based assessment and portfolio assessment.

Formal Evaluation

Most formal evaluation is conducted outside the classroom (except for social assessment, which requires classroom observation) by school psychologists, language clinicians, special educators, and, on occasion, medical or health-related personnel. Formal assessment usually takes place under strict testing conditions.

Most formal tests include a manual that (a) describes the standardization sample, (b) provides reliability information (i.e., refers to how consistent scores are from one administration to another), (c) provides validity information (i.e., refers to the degree that the test measures what it purports to measure), (d) describes procedures for administering and scoring the test, and (e) offers guidelines for interpreting the scores. Because formal tests are norm-referenced, the individual can be compared with others. Data from such tests are reported quantitatively (e.g., age level, grade level, percentile, stanine, scaled scores, or quotient).

Achievement and diagnostic tests frequently are used with students who have learning disabilities. Achievement tests, administered to groups of students, sample content in one area (e.g., math) or several areas (e.g., math, reading, and spelling). These tests can be used for screening, because they provide an overall index of performance. Diagnostic tests are individually administered and focus on evaluating specific skills and abilities in one or more areas. For example, a diagnostic math test probably would include specific subtests in addition, subtraction, multiplication, division, fractions, money, measurement, time, and word problems. Detailed information is obtained about strengths and weaknesses in a particular area. Most diagnostic tests are normed, and thus they usually provide a quantitative score (e.g., percentile, grade, or age level).

Adequacy of Formal Tests. A multitude of formal tests are available; however, many of them are technically inadequate. Generally, the technical aspects have been criticized in three areas: inadequate standardization or norming, poor reliability, and poor validity (Salvia & Ysseldyke, 1995). In addition, the usefulness of the test results frequently is questioned (i.e., test items often are unrelated to classroom tasks or to the purpose of instruction).

Professionals must be aware of the psychometric properties of tests, and several sources are available to help in selecting formal tests:

1. The *Mental Measurements Yearbooks* and *Tests in Print* (available from the Buros Institute of Mental Measurements, 135 Bancroft Hall, University of Nebraska, Lincoln, NE 68588-0348). The 11th *Mental Measurements Yearbook* was published in 1992. The yearbooks are not cumulative; information in each yearbook pertains to new or revised tests, and evaluative reviews of each are included. *Tests in Print* contains a cumulative list of tests in the yearbooks and provides a short description of each one. These sources, along with a computerized data base of the *Mental Measurements Yearbooks,* are available in major libraries.
2. Sweetland, R. C., & Keyser, D. J. (Eds.). (1991). *Tests: A comprehensive reference for assessments in psychology, education, and business* (3rd ed.). Austin, TX: PRO-ED. Keyser, D. J., & Sweetland, R. C. (Eds.). (1984–1994). *Test critiques* (Vols. 1–10). Austin, TX: PRO-ED. *Tests* contains a statement of each instrument's purpose, a concise description of the instrument, scoring procedures, cost, and publisher information. The *Test Critiques* series complements *Tests* and provides crucial information such as practical applications and uses, administration and scoring guidelines, normative data, and validity and reliability information.
3. Hammill, D. D., Brown, L. L., & Bryant, B. R. (1992). *A consumer's guide to tests in print* (2nd ed.). Austin, TX: PRO-ED. This guide provides an extensive evaluation of tests commonly used with students who have learning disabilities.
4. McLoughlin, J. A., & Lewis, R. B. (1994). *Assessing special students* (4th ed.). Upper Saddle River, NJ: Merrill/Prentice Hall. Salvia, J., & Ysseldyke, J. E. (1995). *Assessment* (6th ed.). Boston: Houghton Mifflin. These textbooks provide helpful assessment information.

The use of standardized tests for instructional purposes is receiving substantial criticism. However, their use is required for several other purposes (e.g., screening, identification, and program or school evaluation). Because test results usually are available from referral and staffing procedures for students with learning disabilities, it is helpful for the teacher to be aware of the advantages and disadvantages of formal tests.

Advantages of Formal Tests. An awareness of the advantages and uses of standardized tests enables the teacher to use the information for appropriate purposes. The following are some advantages of formal tests:

1. Students who need further testing or special intervention are identified.
2. The student's major strengths and weaknesses are indicated by content areas, thus suggesting areas that need further assessment.
3. Formal tests show how the student's test performance relates to measured ability, thus helping detect overachievers and underachievers.
4. The student's performance is related to peers or to a standardization sample.
5. Formal tests provide a ready-made, convenient method of providing information about students and model formats for devising informal assessment activities.
6. The student's progress is evaluated over time.

Disadvantages of Formal Tests. A teacher needs to be aware of the numerous disadvantages of formal tests to avoid using them inefficiently or inappropriately. In a review of 27 aptitude and achievement tests, Fuchs, Fuchs, Benowitz, and Barringer (1987) found that developers and publishers provide scant data regarding the appropriateness of their tests for use with students with special needs. Specifically, they report a lack of students with disabilities in the normative sample. Besides standardization, reliability, and validity problems, formal tests have other disadvantages:

1. Formal test results frequently are not related to tasks and behaviors required in the classroom.
2. Test results are influenced easily by the temperament of the student and the examiner. Attention, fatigue, and attitude can influence test results greatly. Because test scores are a function of these and numerous other factors, a student's performance may not be a true measure of achievement or skill mastery.
3. Determining what to teach requires a high degree of specificity. Most formal tests (achievement and diagnostic) yield quantitative data and lack the specificity needed for planning daily instruction. Sometimes it is possible to analyze items and obtain some specificity in an area.
4. The rigid administration procedures of standardized tests prevent the teacher from obtaining some valuable information. For example, a student may respond incorrectly to test items because of failure to follow or understand directions, but administration procedures may prohibit the test administrator from clarifying the directions. To make valid decisions, however, diagnosticians and teachers may need to know whether the student could perform the items if the directions were clarified.

Tests of Intelligence

The goal of intelligence tests is to assess the global ability of an individual's intellectual functioning. It generally is agreed that intelligence tests estimate a person's ability to learn new tasks. They also are used to predict a student's future performance from current performance and reasoning abilities. Salvia and Ysseldyke (1995) remind professionals that regardless of how a person's scores are viewed and interpreted, intelligence tests and their items are simply a sample of behaviors that reflects the test author's concept of intelligence.

In the area of learning disabilities, intelligence tests are used to ascertain a student's general ability level and to rule out mental retardation. In the identification of learning disabilities, an IQ is used as an index of an individual's ability. This measure is then compared with achievement scores to determine whether a discrepancy exists between ability and achievement. If the discrepancy is severe enough, the student is considered to have a learning disability. The practice of using IQ as one of the measures for operationalizing discrepancy is widespread but is receiving some criticism (Mather & Roberts, 1994; Siegel, 1989). Alternatives to using IQ scores to identify students with learning disabilities are discussed in the Assessment for Identification section of this chapter.

The most established intelligence tests include the *Wechsler Intelligence Scale for Children—III* (WISC-III) (Wechsler, 1991) and the *Stanford-Binet Intelligence Scale* (SBIS) (Thorndike, Hagen, & Sattler, 1986). The *Kaufman Assessment Battery for Children* (K-ABC) (Kaufman & Kaufman, 1983) and the *Woodcock-Johnson PsychoEducational Battery—Revised* (WJPEB-R) (Woodcock & Johnson, 1989) also are used to assess intellectual performance. The WJPEB-R contains subtests in the areas of cognitive ability and achievement. The tests of cognitive ability measure seven cognitive factors (long-term retrieval, short-term memory, visual processing, comprehension-knowledge, processing speed, auditory processing, and fluid reasoning), and the tests of achievement provide assessment of reading, mathematics, written language, and knowledge. The WJPEB-R yields grade- and age-equivalent scores, percentile ranks, and aptitude-achievement discrepancies. Other intelligence tests used in assessing students with learning disabilities include the *Slosson Intelligence Test—Revised* (Nicholson & Hibpshman, 1990), a highly verbal test that yields a global IQ score, and the *McCarthy Scales of Children's Abilities* (MSCA) (McCarthy, 1972), which consists of 18 subtests and yields several scores, including a general cognitive score. The WISC-III and the K-ABC are popular tests and are discussed in the following sections.

Wechsler Intelligence Scale for Children-III (WISC-III). The WISC-III is designed to assess students from 6 to 16 years old. It includes verbal and performance subtests.

The verbal subtests require the student to respond orally to verbal (oral) test items. The verbal subtests include the following:

1. *Information.* Measures the ability to answer specific factual questions. The content consists of general information that an individual is expected to have acquired in both formal and informal educational settings.
2. *Comprehension.* Measures the ability to understand verbal directions and make judgments about social situations.
3. *Similarities.* Assesses the ability to detect similarities or commonalities in words that superficially are unrelated.
4. *Arithmetic.* Measures the ability to solve arithmetic reasoning problems within a time limit.
5. *Vocabulary.* Assesses the ability to define spoken words.
6. *Digit Span* (optional). Assesses the ability to remember and repeat a series of orally presented digits.

The performance subtests involve the presentation of a visual stimulus to which the student must respond by performing some task. The performance subtests include the following:

1. *Picture Completion.* Measures the ability to detect missing parts in pictures.
2. *Picture Arrangement.* Requires the student to rearrange a set of pictures in a sequence that displays a logically correct story. It purports to measure comprehension, sequencing, and recognition of relationships.
3. *Block Design.* Measures the ability to arrange blocks in a manner that reproduces a visually presented design.
4. *Object Assembly.* Assesses the ability to put pieces of a puzzle together to form an object.
5. *Coding.* Measures the ability to remember associations between numbers and geometric symbols and record them on paper.
6. *Symbol Search* (optional). Measures the ability to determine whether a match to a shown symbol appears in a row of symbols.

7. *Mazes* (optional). Assesses the ability to find a path through mazes that increase in difficulty.

The WISC-III subtest scores are reported in scaled scores with a mean of 10. Thus, a score of 10 represents average ability on that subtest according to the student's age. The verbal subtests are compiled to yield a verbal IQ, and the performance subtests collectively yield a performance IQ. All subtests are compiled to ascertain a full-scale IQ. A mean score of 100 and a standard deviation of 15 are used for all three scores. The WISC-III has good standardization and adequate reliability and validity (McLoughlin & Lewis, 1994). The use of subtest analysis and verbal-performance discrepancies to identify or differentiate among types of learning disabilities has some support (Holcomb, Hardesty, Adams, & Ponder, 1987; Inglis & Lawson, 1987; Nichols, Inglis, Lawson, & MacKay, 1988). Most authorities, however, discourage the use of subtest analyses for diagnostic and classification decisions (Glutting & Bear, 1989; Kaufman, 1981; Kavale & Forness, 1984).

Kaufman Assessment Battery for Children (K-ABC). The K-ABC is designed to provide a comprehensive measure of intelligence and achievement for children between the ages of 2 years 5 months and 12 years 5 months. The 16 subtests are combined into three scales that are administered regularly and one supplemental scale. The Simultaneous Processing scale, the Sequential Processing scale, and the optional Nonverbal scale measure intelligence. The Simultaneous Processing and the Sequential Processing scales are combined to yield a Mental Processing scale. The test manual indicates that the Nonverbal scale is a good estimate of intelligence for children who have hearing impairments, do not speak English, or have language disorders. Finally, achievement is measured with the Achievement scale, which assesses factual knowledge and skills acquired in school settings or through attentiveness to the environment. The following subtests are in the Sequential and Simultaneous Processing scales:

Sequential Processing Scale

1. *Hand Movements.* The student performs a series of hand movements modeled by the examiner.
2. *Number Recall.* The student recalls a series of digits presented by the examiner.
3. *Word Order.* The student, chronological age of 4 years to 12 years 5 months (CA = 4–0 to 12–5), points to silhouettes of common objects in the sequence named by the examiner.

Simultaneous Processing Scale

1. *Magic Window.* The student (CA = 2–6 to 4–11) identifies a picture that the examiner partially displays in a slotted window.
2. *Face Recognition.* The student (CA = 2–6 to 4–11) recalls a face that has been presented previously by selecting it from a different pose or a group photograph.
3. *Gestalt Closure.* The student completes an inkblot drawing and names or describes it.
4. *Triangles.* The student (CA = 4–10 to 12–5) assembles rubber triangles to match an abstract pattern.
5. *Matrix Analogies.* The student (CA = 5–0 to 12–5) selects a picture or drawing that completes a two-by-two visual analogy.
6. *Spatial Memory.* The student (CA = 5–0 to 12–5) has to remember where pictures were located on a page that is exposed briefly.
7. *Photo Series.* The student (CA = 6–0 to 12–5) must organize photographs to display an event in proper sequence.

Scaled scores (mean = 10, standard deviation = 3) are available for each mental processing subtest. Sequential Processing, Simultaneous Processing, Mental Processing Composite, and Nonverbal scales all are reported with scaled scores (mean = 100, standard deviation = 15). Percentile scores also are available for each subtest and scale. Salvia and Ysseldyke (1995) report that the battery is standardized adequately, and reliability for the composite scales is generally good. They also note that the subtest scores are not reliable, and the validity of the K-ABC is not established.

Informal Evaluation

Teachers conduct informal evaluation to obtain information directly related to instructional planning. Stiggins (1985) points out that teachers need assessment data that are immediate and come from a constantly changing classroom environment. Thus, to keep instruction moving, teachers must rely on assessment procedures provided by instructional materials and tests that they design themselves. Such informal techniques are popular because they help the teacher determine what and how to teach as well as monitor the progress of students.

Advantages of Informal Tests. Advantages of informal tests include the following:

1. Informal tests can be constructed easily from graded curriculum materials or scope and sequence skills lists.
2. The student's tension and anxiety may be reduced through the test's informal nature.
3. Because informal tests can be devised and administered by the teacher, the content relates directly to instruction, and the results can be used to set objectives and monitor progress.
4. The person in the best position to observe the student in a variety of situations can administer the test.
5. Informal tests can be used to evaluate the validity of formal tests.
6. Informal tests can be given frequently and focus on any area.

Disadvantages of Informal Tests. The effort required to devise informal tests is reduced as the teacher gains experience and collects and organizes informal assessment activities. Disadvantages of informal tests include the following:

1. Informal tests are time-consuming to develop.
2. Reliability and validity data are missing from most informal tests; thus, informal tests lack technical adequacy. At a minimum, content validity should be evaluated.
3. Knowledge of the sequence of skills and content to be tested is required.
4. There is considerable judgment involved in selecting a sample of behavior and in scoring and interpreting the test results.
5. Items may be included that are not free of cultural bias.

Informal Assessment Measures

Informal assessment can provide most or all the diagnostic information that the teacher needs. Although formal tests may be useful to the beginning teacher, they usually are not required once the teacher is skilled in observation techniques and is aware of the sequences of skills. This section presents types of informal assessment measures: criterion tests, probes, placement tests, checklists, direct observation, and miscellaneous techniques. (Specific examples are included in Chapters 11 through 15, which focus on specific content disabilities.)

Criterion Tests. The results of some tests are interpreted in terms of an established criterion. Performance is expressed in actual skills or tasks performed, and the student's skill is compared with the criterion (i.e., the student did or did not reach the criterion). In this commonly used method, one student's performance is not compared with the performance of other students. An example would be a spelling test on which the teacher expects the criterion of 80% correct before mastery is assumed. Many such tests are available commercially (e.g., the *Brigance Diagnostic Inventories*). Informal criterion tests are used to assess a student's progress on a span of skills (e.g., scope and sequence of reading) or on a specific skill (e.g., vowel sounds in consonant-vowel-consonant words).

Probes. The use of probes emerged from the field of applied behavior analysis, specifically from precision teaching. Probe sheets, usually on academic tasks, sample the student's behavior for a specified period of time. (Sample probe sheets are featured throughout this book [e.g., in reading and math] but are specifically discussed in Chapter 8.) Typically, the student works on the probe sheet for 1 minute, and the teacher records the rate of correct and incorrect responses and notes any error patterns. Emphasis is placed on rate of responses, which is the major difference between informal criterion assessment and probe assessment. The target behavior is selected on the basis of error patterns and rate of correct and incorrect responses.

Probes are used in daily instruction to determine the student's progress on target skills. From these data the teacher makes strategy decisions (e.g., introduce a new skill, repeat intervention, or drop to a lower skill). Progress over time is recorded on charts (see Chapter 8).

Placement Tests. Some criterion tests or probes help determine where the student should begin instruction in a specific material of graduated difficulty. Such a placement test is made up of samples of items found in the proposed material. If the material is sequenced carefully, student performance on the tasks indicates where the student starts to have difficulty and subsequently where to begin instruction. Some commercial materials provide placement tests.

Checklists. A checklist consists of a series of statements that imply a question about the student's performance or learning characteristics. A checklist may include items such as the following:

_______ 1. The student computes sums involving facts up to 9 quickly and accurately.

_______ 2. The student correctly reads 4th-grade words containing a diphthong.

_______ 3. The student comprehends the main idea of stories in basal level 4.

_______ 4. The student frequently asks for directions to be repeated.

_______ 5. The student frequently is off task during seatwork.

Checklists are flexible and can be used in any area of interest. For example, for recording student progress a checklist may be developed from a scope and sequence skills list or from curriculum material. When the teacher observes that a particular skill has been mastered, that skill statement is checked. In the social skills area the teacher may use the checklist to record whether the student is taking turns in games or playing with others during free time. This information helps the teacher decide what to teach and when to teach it.

Direct Observation. Careful observation of students in class is valuable. However, most teachers do not have the time or energy to observe and record systematically all important events that relate to instruction. Also, because of different student characteristics (e.g., low frustration tolerance), it may be unwise to wait until measurement data reveal that a task is too hard or too easy. When walking around the room, the teacher may note a student performing math seatwork in the following manner:

$$\begin{array}{r} 17 \\ -\,8 \\ \hline 11 \end{array} \qquad \begin{array}{r} 13 \\ -\,4 \\ \hline 11 \end{array}$$

This direct observation points out that the student is having difficulty with regrouping and needs help. Moreover, the teacher must be sensitive to behaviors. For example, a student who becomes tense and anxious while trying to complete seatwork may be trying to work at material that is too difficult, and the teacher can intervene immediately to prevent unnecessary frustration.

Miscellaneous Techniques. Other informal methods include interviews (e.g., with parents and colleagues), anecdotal records, rating scales, classroom quizzes, and various student self-report techniques. Moreover, Salend and Salend (1985) discuss the use of microcomputers to help teachers develop, administer, and score teacher-made tests that focus on the needs of students with learning disabilities. Specifically, they note that presentation and response modes can be adjusted to help students with learning disabilities, and they discuss the motivational factors for using computers in assessment.

Informal Assessment Systems

The traditional procedures of using norm-referenced tests that feature multiple-choice formats to evaluate achievement is being challenged. Critics note that these tests typically have little relevance to the school curriculum and fail to assess higher-order thinking skills (McLoughlin & Lewis, 1994). Because informal assessments are connected to the curriculum and provide more flexible formats, numerous educators suggest that these procedures be employed more to assess student learning. Efforts to improve assessment practices have resulted in two informal assessment systems: curriculum-based assessment (CBA) and alternative assessment.

Curriculum-Based Assessment. CBA refers to any approach that uses direct observation and recording of a student's performance in the school curriculum as a basis for obtaining information to make instructional decisions (Deno, 1987). Although the essential feature of CBA is as old as education itself (e.g., prescriptive teaching), its systematic application is generating some practical tools, novel ideas, and impressive results. CBA is well suited for monitoring the progress of students and providing teachers with data that help them make appropriate instructional decisions. In addition, numerous authorities are finding CBA applicable for other assessment purposes. For example, the use of local norms in CBA decreases the possibility of biased assessment.

Within the CBA model, *curriculum-based measurement* (CBM) refers to the use of specific procedures whereby a student's academic skills are assessed through the use of repeated rate samples using stimulus materials taken from the student's curriculum. The primary uses of CBM are to establish district or classroom performance standards, identify students who need special instruction, and monitor individual student progress toward long-range goals. Marston and Magnusson (1985) report that CBM procedures have proven efficient and effective across a variety of assessment goals: screening, identification, program planning, and monitoring the progress of students with mild disabilities. Moreover, they note that CBM data indicate that special education students are learning in their respective settings.

Peterson, Heistad, Peterson, and Reynolds (1985) describe a computer-based measurement system for monitoring student progress in a reading and math curriculum. Amount of time to complete units of instruction served as the unit of analysis for measuring individual progress and for normative comparisons. A cutoff at the 20th percentile at each grade level identified 100% of the special education students. Peterson et al. discuss a possible implication of this finding: "If this finding holds up in a replication at near-100% level, it could well be argued that a 'progress in curriculum' criterion rather than multifaceted categorical systems . . . is justified and that no child now entitled to special consideration under PL 94-142 . . . would be neglected under this much simpler system" (p. 243).

Bursuck and Lessen (1987) used an expanded version of CBA to assess students with learning disabilities. Their project, titled Curriculum-Based Assessment and Instructional Design (C-BAID), involved a schoolwide assessment of students that promoted cooperative decision making between special and general educators concerning eligibility, placement, and programming for students with learning disabilities. C-BAID consisted of academic skill probes, observation of work habits, and an inventory of the classroom environment. Bursuck and Lessen report that, as a result of C-BAID, curriculum-based measures became a required part of the district's screening process for learning disabilities. Moreover, the quality of learning disabilities referrals improved, data regarding re-entry into general classrooms were modified to include C-BAID data, and multidisciplinary team members began including C-BAID data in their respective assessments.

Deno (1985) and Tindal and Marston (1990) conclude that achievement in basic skills can be measured with reliability and validity by using the school's curriculum to generate test items. They note that CBA holds much promise for the following reasons:

1. It is curriculum-referenced, so that a student's competence is measured in terms of the local school curriculum.
2. It is individual-referenced, so that judgments can be made about an individual student's progress.
3. It is peer-referenced, so that the "normality" of a student's performance can be determined reliably using locally developed peer sampling.

In discussing the legal parameters of using CBA, Galagan (1985) notes that CBA, with its focus on individual needs, is capable of meeting the specific individual needs of students and therefore the legal requirements of Public Law 94-142. Gickling and Thompson (1985) capture the essence of the CBA movement:

> This focus has led to an equally important concern, that of providing low-achieving and mainstreamed children with similar types of learning conditions . . . enjoyed by their more successful peers. This statement is not to imply that they will be able to function at the same ability level as their average and above-average peers, but that they will have similar opportunities for task success in relationship to their own entry skills and that they will begin to make more systematic progress in school. (p. 217)

(Chapter 8 presents expanded applications of CBA for instructional purposes.)

Alternative Assessment. Dissatisfaction with group-administered standardized tests of achievement and the content of traditional test items are two factors that have provided impetus to the alternative assessment movement. The terms (e.g., authentic assessment, direct assessment, outcome-based assessment, portfolio assessment, and performance assessment) used to describe the movement reflect some of the concerns with the artificial nature of traditional tests. Worthen (1993) notes that these approaches are called "alternative assessment" for two reasons: "First, all are viewed as *alternatives* to traditional multiple-choice, standardized achievement tests; second, all refer to *direct* examination of student *performance* on significant tasks that are relevant to life outside of school" (p. 445).

Alternative assessment represents some changes in what is assessed and how assessment takes place. First, authentic tasks are emphasized, and tasks that represent meaningful subskills are minimized. For example, writing a letter is a worthwhile real-life task, whereas completing a worksheet on punctuation is not stressed. Second, student performance is assessed directly across numerous formats including writing, oral discourse, portfolios, or demonstrations. Third, higher-order thinking is stressed by requiring students to explain, demonstrate, or document their thinking processes. This often is demonstrated through portfolio assessment, which is the most widely used alternative assessment.

Portfolio assessment is an attempt to enhance instructional decision making and the evaluation of student progress. According to Paulson, Paulson, and Meyer (1991), "A portfolio is a purposeful collection of student work that exhibits the student's efforts, progress, and achievements in one or more areas" (p. 60). Portfolios are being applied to academic areas for several purposes: (a) to demonstrate student effort, (b) to document student achievement, (c) to enhance assessment information from other sources, and (d) to document the quality of educational programs. From a review of the portfolio literature, Salvia and Ysseldyke (1995) maintain that portfolio assessment consists of six elements:

1. Valued outcomes are targeted for assessment.
2. Authentic tasks (real work) are used for assessment.
3. Selected tasks involve cooperative endeavors among students and between the teacher and the student.
4. Multiple dimensions (e.g., content, strategies, methods of inquiry, and work processes) are used to evaluate learning.
5. The completion of products includes reflection and self-evaluation.
6. Assessment and instruction are integrated.

Portfolios also should be for a specific purpose. Without direction, a portfolio can become a collection of papers or products. The Vermont Portfolio Project developed guidelines for writing portfolios. Abruscato (1993) notes that the writing portfolio includes the following six work samples of writing completed during the school year, as well as the student's response to a formal or standard writing assessment given to all students within a grade level:

> 1. a table of contents;
> 2. a "best piece";
> 3. a letter;
> 4. a poem, short story, play, or personal narrative;
> 5. a personal response to a cultural, media, or sports exhibit or event or to a book, current issue, math problem, or scientific phenomenon;
> 6. one prose piece from any curriculum area other than English or language arts (for fourth-graders) and three prose pieces from any curriculum area other than English or language arts (for eighth-graders); and
> 7. the piece produced in response to the uniform writing assessment, as well as related outlines, drafts, etc. (p. 475)

Salvia and Ysseldyke (1995) caution educators to approach portfolio assessment carefully. They note that many valid concerns surround the use of portfolio assessment and these concerns need to be addressed before this method can become a best practice. Specifically, they summarize their findings in the following passage:

> Despite an initial surge in interest in the use of portfolios, several concerns and limitations have not been systematically addressed: criteria for including work in a student's portfolio, the nature of student participation in content selection, ensuring a sufficient amount of content generated by a student to reach valid decisions, and how portfolio assessment can be made more reliable with consistency of scoring and breadth of sampling of student performances. In addition, there are concerns about biased scoring, instructional utility, and efficiency. Portfolio assessment will remain difficult and expensive for schools, and those who wish to pursue this alternative should give serious attention to how portfolios are assembled and evaluated. Objectivity, less complexity, and comparability are the keys to better practice. (p. 265)

PURPOSES OF ASSESSMENT

Educational assessment is a multidimensional process that involves much more than test administration. Quality assessment is based on the premise that an individual's performance on any task is influenced by the requirements of the task, the individual's background and characteristics, and the factors inherent in the assessment setting. As Salvia and Ysseldyke (1995) define it, "Assessment is the process of collecting data for the purpose of making decisions about students" (p. 5). McLoughlin and Lewis (1994) discuss five primary purposes of educational assessment:

1. *Screening* is an initial stage of data collection used to locate students who may have learning disabilities. During screening, data usually are collected about a group (e.g., 5th-graders), and individuals who exhibit potential problems are identified. These students are referred to as being *at risk*, and frequently

it is recommended that they receive further assessment.

2. *Determining eligibility* involves collecting data that enable diagnosticians to identify a student as having a learning disability. Much of the data used for classification comes from standardized tests. Once identified as having a learning disability, a student is eligible for special education services.
3. *Planning a program* is based on assessment data that are collected and analyzed to make decisions regarding program placement and specific interventions (i.e., what and how to teach). This results in an individualized educational program.
4. *Monitoring student progress* is based on periodic assessment data. Evaluation of student progress involves monitoring daily or weekly progress and evaluating the program's ongoing effectiveness.
5. *Evaluating a program* involves collecting data on the progress of a student to determine the program's effectiveness. This evaluation is required annually.

TESTING GUIDELINES

Many important decisions that affect the lives of students are based on test results; therefore, the examiner has an enormous responsibility in testing an individual. The integrity of the standardized testing procedures must be maintained to ensure reliable and valid results. Moreover, the integrity of the student must be protected to ensure that the test results actually represent the student's abilities, skills, and perceptions. Some factors that help preserve the integrity of the student include (a) rapport between the examiner and student, (b) student motivation, (c) nondiscriminatory items, (d) "best-practice" tests, (e) collaboration of results through other measures and observations, (f) written descriptions of testing conditions that may have affected the results negatively, (g) familiarity with the examiner, and (h) absence of language barriers between the examiner and student. McLoughlin and Lewis (1994) offer some excellent testing suggestions that include pretest information for students, specific administration guidelines, and observations of response style.

THE ASSESSMENT PROCESS IN LEARNING DISABILITIES

Assessment in learning disabilities occurs at numerous points in the continuum of services, which begins with prereferral activities and continues through the monitoring of student progress in an individualized educational program. Generally, the steps follow the sequence outlined in Figure 5.1. The following sections of the chapter discuss each of these stages.

PREREFERRAL

As more students exhibit academic and behavioral difficulties in school, special education is being asked to serve increasing numbers of students under the rubric of learning disabilities. Current funding does not allow serving this increased number of students appropriately. In an effort to decrease the number of referrals to special education and improve services to students with school-related problems, many authorities believe that more efforts need to be directed to the prereferral stage. Gickling and Thompson (1985) report that in attempts to curb the growth

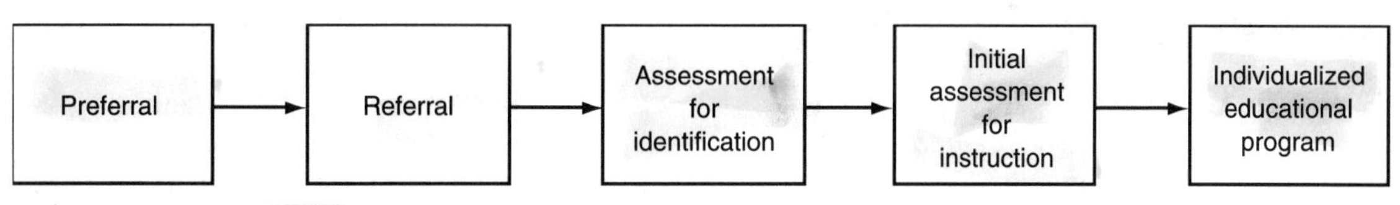

FIGURE 5.1
Steps in the assessment process

of special education, a trend has emerged focusing on developing prereferral strategies that concentrate on interventions in the general classroom.

Prereferral approaches such as teacher support teams and child study teams are gaining wide acceptance. In a survey of state guidelines, Chalfant (1985) reports that 16 states provide some kind of building-based teacher support teams. These teams may consist of general education teachers only or a combination of special and general education teachers. Child study teams allow teachers to analyze individual student cases and find strategies to try before making a referral to special education. Brainstorming is a key technique. Child study teams have been found to alter the nature and rate of referrals (Chalfant, Pysh, & Moultrie, 1979) and broaden the general classroom teacher's tolerance for students with difficulties (Gerber, 1982). Graden, Casey, and Christenson (1985) developed and successfully tested a five-stage prereferral intervention model that features consultation and a child review team.

In a recent survey of the state departments of education, Carter and Sugai (1989) found that prereferral interventions are required in 23 states and recommended in 11 states. Moreover, their survey acknowledges the significant role of the general educator in implementing the prereferral interventions. Finally, the survey reveals the need for training teachers in how to function in teams.

Initially, the purpose of the prereferral process focused on reducing the number of inappropriate placements in special education (Carter & Sugai, 1989). While the goal of reducing inappropriate placements remains viable, prereferral procedures have provided a springboard for expanded goals. Prereferral interventions include extensive use of systematic problem solving and collaborative consultation, which, in turn, have prompted schoolwide changes. What started as special educators acting as consultants to general educators is evolving into a program that fosters the creation of collegial relationships among educators, which promotes full participation of all educators. Through school-based problem-solving teams and collaborative consultation among teachers, schools are concentrating on developing interventions in general classrooms that are more responsive to the needs of students with learning or behavior problems (Graden, 1989). (Chapter 6 further discusses coaching and collaborative consultation procedures.)

REFERRAL

The referral process enables professionals to (a) determine whether a student is a viable candidate for special education services, (b) make contact with the parents to discuss the child's difficulties, (c) begin a screening study to locate problem areas and contributing factors, and (d) meet with the parents and appropriate professionals to determine whether a formal evaluation is needed. During the referral stage, it is important to involve the classroom teacher. Classroom teachers traditionally have been highly accurate in identifying students at risk for school failure and reading problems (Salvesen & Undheim, 1994).

Careful study at the referral level can save much time, effort, and money for parents and school personnel. A well-planned referral process that yields pertinent general information (e.g., motivation factors, home situation, and instructional program) makes the formal evaluation of the student more viable and efficient.

ASSESSMENT FOR IDENTIFICATION

Determination of a learning disability begins with the examination of the parameters that define it. In an examination of these parameters, the heterogeneous nature of the population must be considered. Some investigators primarily consider the students' academic disabilities, whereas others stress attention, memory, perceptual, social-emotional, or motor problems. The debate over the importance of various learning disability characteristics is likely to continue for some time. Meanwhile, one must recognize the identification criteria in the federal regulations and those noted by authorities in the field. The requirements of Public Law 94-142 and its regulations published in the 1977 *Federal Register* (see Table 5.1) provide an initial framework for identification. These are minimal requirements, and additional criteria may be added by individual states or school districts.

Requirements of 1977 *Federal Register*

Multidisciplinary Team. According to the Bureau of Education for the Handicapped (1978), evaluation procedures require a multidisciplinary team that includes the following members:

1. The student's general classroom teacher or a qualified replacement if the student does not have a general classroom teacher.
2. At least one person qualified to conduct individual diagnostic examinations of children (e.g., school psychologist, speech-language pathologist, or reading teacher).
3. A learning disabilities specialist.

Criteria for Determining a Disability. To identify a student as having learning disabilities, the team must determine that the student has a severe discrepancy between achievement and intellectual ability in one or more of the following areas: (a) oral expression, (b) listening comprehension, (c) written expression, (d) basic reading skills, (e) reading comprehension, (f) mathematics calculation, or (g) mathematics reasoning. The team may *not* identify a student as having a specific learning disability if the severe discrepancy between ability and achievement is primarily the result of (a) a visual, hearing, or motor disability, (b) mental retardation, (c) emotional disturbance, or (d) environmental, cultural, or economic disadvantage. Also, the team must document that the student has been provided with learning experiences appropriate for the student's age and ability levels.

Observation. At least one team member other than the student's general education teacher must observe the student's academic performance in class. If the child is younger than school age or out of school, the child must be observed in an environment appropriate for a child of that age. The observation is conducted to determine the relationship of the disability to the educational setting.

Written Report. The *Federal Register* (USOE, 1977) indicates that the team must include the following in reporting the results:

1. Whether the child has a specific learning disability
2. The basis for making the determination
3. The relevant behavior noted during observation
4. The relationship of that behavior to the child's academic functioning
5. The educationally relevant medical findings, if any
6. Whether there is a severe discrepancy between achievement and ability that is not correctable without special education and related services
7. The determination of the team concerning the effects of environmental, cultural, or economic disadvantage (p. 65083)

All team members must certify in writing whether the report reflects their own findings. Any member's discrepant conclusions must be included.

Assessing Specific Components of a Learning Disability

Mercer et al. (1995) report that learning disabilities definitions used by state departments of education usually include statements about process, academic and language achievement, and an exclusion factor. The 1977 *Federal Register* includes the academic, language, and exclusion components but omits the process area. Federal regulations also include a discrepancy factor, which many consider to be the common denominator of learning disabilities. Popularized by Bateman (1964), the discrepancy factor refers to the difference between a learner's estimated ability and actual achievement. Mercer et al. report that

94% of the states include the discrepancy component in their identification criteria. Hammill (1990) notes that consensus concerning the components in the 1977 *Federal Register* exists across the most influential definitions of learning disabilities. The assessment of these basic components is presented next.

Exclusion. The exclusion component is a major component in state criteria for identifying learning disabilities (Frankenberger & Harper, 1987; Mercer et al., 1995). Factors such as hearing and vision should be checked before undertaking an extensive examination. The following exclusions seem appropriate in view of the 1977 federal regulations:

1. Mental retardation, as evidenced by a score of not less than minus 2 standard deviations on an individual test of intelligence, with interpretation of a certified psychologist.
2. Blindness or partial sight, as evidenced by visual acuity in the better eye with best possible correction of 20/70 or better.
3. Deafness or impaired hearing, as evidenced by auditory acuity of no more than a 30 dB loss in the better ear unaided, and speech and language learned through normal channels.
4. Physical disabilities; no evidence of a primary physical disability directly related to the student's problem area.
5. Emotional disturbance so severe that a therapeutic program is needed.
6. Environmental and cultural factors; educators should ensure that the student is being instructed and tested in the student's native language, and it should be determined whether the student has had sufficient experience to benefit from general education.

Exclusion factors 2, 3, and 4 require a physical exam or a check of a recent medical record. Factors 1 and 5 require testing by a psychologist. Factor 6 usually is documented by testing and teaching in the student's native language, reviewing anecdotal records, and conducting interviews and obtaining background information (perhaps with a social worker's help) about cultural factors and experiences. Chalfant (1985) states that the exclusionary criteria for slow learners, the socially and emotionally maladjusted, and the economically disadvantaged should be more precise.

Academic Achievement. The assessment of academic achievement continues to be a major factor in identifying students with learning disabilities. Academic achievement problems usually are interpreted within the ability/achievement discrepancy factor that is included in the 1977 identification criteria (USOE, 1977). Common areas of assessment are reading (word recognition and comprehension), math (calculation and reasoning), and written expression. Although informal measures, curriculum-based assessment, and criterion tests are used extensively in the area of academic achievement, assessment of academic areas for identification purposes primarily involves the use of standardized tests. Scores are reported in a variety of ways (e.g., grade level, age level, percentile, stanine, and scaled score). Many authorities (Salvia & Ysseldyke, 1995) discourage the use of grade-level scores and recommend more use of scaled scores.

Some achievement tests are specific to a select skill area such as reading or math, whereas others include a battery of tests that measure across academic areas. Tests for specific academic areas are discussed in each of the respective content chapters in this text. One of the most widely used battery of tests for identifying students with learning disabilities is the *Woodcock-Johnson Psycho-Educational Battery—Revised.* Because of its large standardization population, its range, and its coverage of academic areas, it is used extensively to test the academic achievement of students with learning disabilities (Cordoni, 1995). The test includes a cognitive battery and an achievement battery. The achievement tests cover writing, reading, math, science, social studies, and humanities.

The learning disabilities literature is replete with concerns about diagnosticians who select technically inadequate tests when better ones are available. Lyon (1995) reports that comprehensive reviews of testing practices indicate that less than one-third of the tests used in the diagnosis of learning disabilities meet criteria for adequate norms, reliability, and validity.

Language Achievement. Language is evaluated by standardized tests in listening comprehension and oral expression. In language assessment it is important to distinguish between the production of oral language (i.e., a student's voice quality and articulation) and the linguistic qualities of oral expression (i.e., the components of morphology, semantics, syntax, and pragmatics). Moreover, language assessment can focus on receptive abilities (listening comprehension) or expressive abilities (oral expression).

The *Goldman-Fristoe Test of Articulation* frequently is used to assess articulation, while the *Test of Language Development—2* and the *Clinical Evaluation of Language Fundamentals—3* are used to measure general language functioning. Because of the recent proliferation of language tests, a variety of tests are used in this area. (Chapter 11 presents a detailed discussion of language tests.)

Process. The process component, which traditionally has been criticized because of nebulous constructs and measurement problems, remains a factor in identifying individuals with learning disabilities. Chalfant (1985) indicates that the process area should be included but that assessment practices in the area need improving. Mercer et al. (1995) report that the process factor is included in 94% of the learning disabilities definitions used by state departments of education; however, only 33% of the states include it in their identification criteria. Moreover, it is not included in the 1977 *Federal Register* procedures on evaluation.

Standardized tests reveal diagnostic data about processing in the following areas:

1. *Visual:* perception (discrimination and closure), memory, association, reception.
2. *Auditory:* perception (discrimination and closure), memory, association, reception.
3. *Haptic:* tactile, kinesthetic.
4. *Sensory-integration:* visual-motor, auditory-motor, auditory-vocal, visual-auditory (vocal).
5. *Motor:* gross and fine motor skills.

Process tests attempt to measure how an individual uses what is heard or seen. Cordoni (1995) notes that one of the best known of these instruments is the *Slingerland Screening Tests for Identifying Children with Specific Language Disability* (Slingerland, 1974). These tests range from preschool through college and measure both auditory and visual processing. Cordoni maintains that processing tests help the examiner better understand how an individual learns. Specifically, she notes that it is helpful for a parent or teacher to know that a child can follow one direction but not three, or that the child finds visual tasks overwhelming so they should be broken into smaller units.

Other commonly used tests include the *Detroit Tests of Learning Aptitude—3* (Hammill, 1991) and the cognitive battery of the *Woodcock-Johnson Psycho-Educational Battery—Revised* as well as the analysis of subtest scores on tests of intelligence or ability (e.g., WISC-III or K-ABC). Chalfant (1985) recommends that the results of standardized tests of process abilities be validated by observations of student performances on classroom tasks that require the process being measured. Unless the observations are consistent with the test results, a process deficit should not be diagnosed. Technically adequate measures must be developed in the process area. (Chapters 8 and 11 present tests and procedures in the process area as well as emerging cognitive approaches that appear to be promising.)

Discrepancy. The discrepancy component is basic to the identification of learning disabilities. As specified in the identification criteria of the federal regulations, a severe discrepancy is defined as an individual's failure to achieve in one of the seven areas (e.g., basic reading skill), commensurate with age and ability. Moreover, the gap between achievement and intellectual ability must be extensive enough to result in a "severe discrepancy." Mercer et al. (1995) and Frankenberger and Harper (1987) found that most states are attempting to operationalize the discrepancy component as part of their criteria for identifying students with learning disabilities.

In the determination of a severe discrepancy according to federal regulations, it is necessary to measure intelligence (ability) and achievement. Individual tests of intelligence such as the WISC-III, the K-ABC, and the *Stanford-Binet Intelligence Scale* are the most recommended and used. Achievement in one or more of the seven areas is assessed through the use of standardized tests. The difference between the ability scores and the achievement scores is analyzed to determine whether a severe discrepancy exists. For determining a severe discrepancy, a multitude of procedures have been reported (Berk, 1984; Chalfant, 1985; Cone & Wilson, 1981; Mercer et al., 1995).

Practices in Determining Discrepancy

Practices in operationalizing the discrepancy component vary across the states and in some cases from one school district to another. Four procedures include the use of deviation from grade level, expectancy formulas, regression analysis, and standard score comparisons.

Deviation from Grade Level. Mercer et al. (1995) report that only a few states use deviation from grade level. This approach includes two variations: constant and graduated deviation. Constant deviation defines severe discrepancy as several years below grade placement (e.g., 2 years below current placement). Some states apply the constant deviation criterion in terms of current age instead of grade placement. In graduated deviation, the degree of deviation between grade placement and achievement varies as a function of current grade placement. The graduated deviation is based on the premise that the higher the grade placement, the more years the student must be behind. For example, a 1-year discrepancy at 2nd grade for an 8-year-old is more severe than a 1-year discrepancy at the 10th grade for a 16-year-old.

Chalfant (1985) notes that the procedures for determining deviation from grade level are administered easily. Unfortunately, he reports that these methods overidentify slow learners and underidentify students with high intelligence scores. Reynolds (1985) reports that grade-level deviation is not an acceptable method for determining a severe discrepancy. Numerous problems exist regarding grade-level scores:

1. Grade equivalents do not account for the dispersion of scores about the mean when the dispersion varies constantly from grade to grade (i.e., variation from the mean score is different from one grade to another). Thus, 2 years below grade level at one grade may be within normal limits, whereas at another grade it may represent a problem (Reynolds, 1985).
2. Grade equivalents are used as, but do not represent, standards of performance. They do not indicate at what level in a reading series a student should be placed. In short, they lack reference to curriculum materials (Reynolds, 1985).
3. Grade-equivalent procedures do not take into account the ability level of the student.
4. Grade equivalents have little meaning in upper grade levels for students who are not taught at those grade levels (Berk, 1982).
5. Grade equivalents are not equal interval measures; thus, they cannot be added, subtracted, multiplied, or divided.
6. Grade equivalents vary markedly from test to test and from subtest to subtest within the same battery (Berk, 1982).

Overall, the grade deviation method is not recommended by authorities in the field (Berk, 1984; Chalfant, 1985; Cone & Wilson, 1981; McLoughlin & Lewis, 1994).

Expectancy Formulas. Expectancy formula methods are based on determining a discrepancy between ability and achievement. Ability and achievement scores usually are converted to age or grade equivalents and evaluated by an expectancy formula.

Forness, Sinclair, and Guthrie (1983) compared eight formulas and concluded that each yielded different results. The percentage of students identified as having learning disabilities ranged from 10.9% to 39% when the eight formulas were applied to a sample of students. Reynolds (1985) reports that formulas that involve grade- or age-equivalent scores can be rejected readily as inadequate or misleading due to the shortcomings of grade- and age-equivalent scores mentioned earlier. Moreover, expectancy formula methods do not consider the respective reliabilities of the tests and the discrepancy score that results. Generally, the expectancy formulas are not recommended for determining a discrepancy for learning disability identification (Berk, 1984; Chalfant, 1985; Cone & Wilson, 1981; Forness et al., 1983; Reynolds, 1985). Moreover, the Council for Learning Disabilities Board of Trustees (1986) has published a strong position statement against the use of discrepancy formulas for identifying students with learning disabilities.

Regression Analysis. Regression analysis is a procedure that includes a statistical correction for the phenomenon of the tendency for scores to regress toward the mean. High or low scores tend to move toward the mean on subsequent testings. These extreme scores introduce sources of error in measurement. Regression analysis uses statistical methods to adjust for this tendency. As a result of this regression phenomenon, the regression method requires a large ability-achievement score difference to define severe discrepancy (Schuerholz et al., 1995). Cone and Wilson (1981) and Shephard (1980) provide some of the various regression models that have been proposed for determining a severe discrepancy.

Numerous investigators (Berk, 1984; Salvia & Ysseldyke, 1995; Shephard, 1980) note that regression analysis is weakened substantially when scores from tests with low reliability are used. Many of the regression techniques do not provide procedures for determining the severity level of the discrepancy score or whether it is reliable (Berk, 1984). McLoughlin and Lewis (1994) maintain that agreement on the most appropriate regression procedures to use are lacking. Finally, regression analysis is difficult for many parents and educators to understand.

Standard Score Comparisons. Reynolds (1985) claims that two conditions must be satisfied to establish a severe discrepancy between a student's two scores. First, the difference between the scores must be reliable enough for one to believe that it is real and not a result of measurement errors. Second, the difference must be great enough to be considered rare among students without learning disabilities. Most authorities (Berk, 1984; Chalfant, 1985; Reynolds, 1992) agree that standard or scaled scores possess the necessary psychometric properties for determining a severe discrepancy. In this method, all scores are converted to standard or scaled scores. This is done by scaling the scores to the same mean and standard deviation. In this manner all scores are expressed in terms of a common metric. A principal advantage of standard scores lies in the comparability of score interpretation across age (Reynolds, 1985). Chalfant (1985) contends that the standard score discrepancy models answer the statistical flaws of expectancy formulas but do not adjust for the regression of IQ on achievement (i.e., over time, IQ scores and achievement scores are likely to become more similar). However, Cone and Wilson (1981) state, "Clearly standard score procedures represent a major advancement in recent attempts to quantify discrepancy or underachievement" (p. 365).

Reynolds (1985) recommends a three-step procedure using standard scores that he claims holds much promise for determining a severe discrepancy. First, the reliability of the discrepancy score must be determined. The difference between the ability and achievement scores must be great enough to indicate with a high degree of confidence (i.e., $p < .05$) that it is not due to chance or to measurement errors. If a discrepancy score is found to be statistically significant ($p < .05$), one can say that such a discrepancy would have occurred by chance only 5 times (or less) in 100. Various formulas are available to test the significance of a discrepancy score (Reynolds, 1985). Second, after reliability has been determined, the frequency of occurrence of the discrepancy must be ascertained. To qualify as severe, it is argued that a discrepancy should be of such magnitude that it occurs relatively infrequently in the normal population. Third, quality input data must be used in computing a severe discrepancy. In essence, test scores must be reliable and valid. No amount of statistical procedures can correct for poor test data. The accuracy of the discrepancy determination ultimately rests with the quality of the data used. Reynolds provides 11 guidelines to ensure high-quality data.

Fortunately, it appears that more states are practicing more reliable and valid procedures for documenting a discrepancy (Ross, 1995). Although procedures for operationalizing the discrepancy component are improving, many issues concerning the validity of discrepancy procedures remain. Some professionals fear that the discrepancy component has become synonymous with the construct of learning disabilities (Mather & Roberts, 1994). Kavale (1987) notes that a severe discrepancy is necessary but not sufficient to identify a student with learning disabilities.

Advantages of Discrepancy and Related Practices. Since Bateman (1964) introduced discrepancy as a component that is basic to defining individuals with learning disabilities, it has been adopted as a key concept in understanding learning disabilities. Some of the advantages of discrepancy and related practices include the following:

1. Learning disabilities is a syndrome with two key components: (a) the presence of a severe discrepancy between age and ability levels versus levels of academic achievement, and (b) the presence of a disorder in a basic psychological process (Reynolds, 1992; Schuerholz et al., 1995). Mather and Roberts (1994) maintain that a salient feature of individuals with learning disabilities is that they do not achieve at an expected level based on their abilities.
2. Discrepancy captures the specific outcome of the learning disabilities condition (Reynolds, 1992).
3. Discrepancy represents the most consensually validated criterion available in identifying individuals with learning disabilities (Reynolds, 1992). Poor practices in the quantification of a severe discrepancy should not be confused with the viable substance of the discrepancy concept (Meyen, 1989).
4. The regulations of Public Law 94-142 for defining and identifying individuals with learning disabilities emphasize the concept of a severe discrepancy.
5. The use of the ability-achievement discrepancy component helps identify students with high IQs whose academic achievement levels are lower than expectations but above average (Shaywitz, Fletcher, Holahan, & Shaywitz, 1992).
6. In a survey of states' practices, Finlan (1992) found that states using a method for determining a severe discrepancy identified fewer students with learning disabilities. Finlan maintains that the use of severe discrepancy methods helps reduce the number of inappropriate placements resulting from the overidentification of students labeled as having learning disabilities.

Disadvantages of Discrepancy and Related Practices. The various severe discrepancy procedures have not produced consistent results in identifying students who have learning disabilities. The differential effects of these procedures coupled with an overreliance on the discrepancy model to identify students with learning disabilities have led to numerous criticisms (Lyon, 1995; Mather & Roberts, 1994). Some of the disadvantages of discrepancy and related practices include the following:

1. The various models for operationalizing a severe discrepancy yield different outcomes. For example, when states or school districts use different models, an individual may be classified as having learning disabilities in one jurisdiction but not in another (Finlan, 1992; Schuerholz et al., 1995; Shaw, Cullen, McGuire, & Brinckerhoff, 1995).
2. Students with lower IQs have trouble demonstrating a discrepancy. When ability (IQ) is used to establish an expected achievement level, it becomes difficult for individuals with low IQs to exhibit a severe discrepancy because the lower IQ predicts lower achievement levels, thus making it difficult to exhibit a large difference between an ability score and an achievement score (Schuerholz et al., 1995).
3. The severe discrepancy model is predicated on school failure. Many severe discrepancy models require that students fall significantly below their predicted achievement potential (based on IQ) before they can be identified and served (Mather & Roberts, 1994; Shaw et al., 1995). Reading problems require intervention when they initially appear. Waiting until reading difficulties become more severe is harmful to the students' chances to improve their reading (Felton & Wood, 1989; Lyon, 1995).
4. Severe discrepancy procedures make it difficult to practice early identification. Many students must reach the threshold of severe failure before they can receive special education services (Felton & Brown, 1991). A system is needed to identify and serve these youngsters prior to extended failure (Lieberman, 1992).
5. Aptitude and achievement measures are not independent. For example, poor reading over

time is likely to lessen an individual's IQ (Siegel, 1992). The degree to which these measures (IQ and achievement) are related undermines the validity of comparing them to compute a discrepancy score. Moreover, the learning disability may be obscured because the aptitude and achievement measures are affected by the individual's learning disability (Swanson, 1993).

6. The identification of learning disabilities through quantifying a severe discrepancy compromises the integrity of the process because of the many factors that can increase or decrease the difference between ability and achievement scores (Lyon, 1995). These factors include the psychometric properties of the tests as well as other variables (e.g., educational support, socioeconomic status, cognitive attributes, and family support) that are not inherent to learning disabilities.
7. Numerous researchers maintain that intelligence tests are irrelevant to the identification of learning disabilities. Some of the concerns about IQ tests are that they do not measure potential, the intercorrelational patterns between IQ and achievement tests are not distinct among ability groups, and they do not yield discerning information about discrepant learners (Fletcher, Francis, Rourke, Shaywitz, & Shaywitz, 1992; Rispens, van Yperen, & van Duijn, 1991; Siegel, 1992; Swanson, 1991).

Alternative Directions for Determining Discrepancy. Given the importance of the discrepancy component to defining and identifying learning disabilities and the problems associated with assessing discrepancy, it is encouraging that several researchers suggest alternative methods for assessing a severe discrepancy. Several options include the following:

1. Assess discrepancies among academic skills (Fletcher, Francis, Rourke, Shaywitz, & Shaywitz, 1993). This procedure stresses the intra-individual differences among skills in instructional domains; thus, an intelligence test is not used. Zigmond (1993) supports this approach because the discrepancy is based on learning tasks that are most important to educators instead of on norm-referenced IQ. Shaw et al. (1995) maintain that this approach is pragmatic and theoretically defensible because it focuses on intra-individual differences that one would expect to find in individuals with learning disabilities.
2. Assess discrepancies among cognitive skills (Fletcher et al., 1993). Several researchers advocate an operational definition of learning disabilities that includes an emphasis on information processing (Levine et al., 1993; Mather & Healey, 1990). Proponents of this approach note that processing deficits are included in the federal definition as well as in other definitions of learning disabilities but have received little attention (Chalfant, 1989). Psychometric sophistication continues to lag behind theoretical developments in cognitive processing, but there is an emerging consensus among cognitive theorists concerning the nature of learning disabilities. Since the dissemination of federal eligibility guidelines in 1977, considerable progress has been made toward including information processing as a criterion for diagnosing learning disabilities (Shaw et al., 1995). For example, Stanovich (1991a, 1991b) notes that there are differences between individuals with reading disabilities and those with general cognitive deficits. Some learners with reading disabilities have a specific cognitive deficit that contributes to the reading difficulty but does not affect other cognitive domains; thus, it becomes important to identify the cognitive deficit.
3. For students with suspected reading problems, consider using the phonological core-variable difference model to identify learning disabilities. Measures related to phonological analysis, especially speech-sound perceptions, auditory closure, and listening comprehension, consistently separate students with and without learning disabilities who have

reading problems (Felton & Brown, 1991; Fletcher et al., 1993; Stanovich, 1991a).

Brinckerhoff, Shaw, and McGuire (1993) offer an operational interpretation of the definition of learning disabilities proposed by the National Joint Committee on Learning Disabilities. It incorporates four levels of assessment to determine a learning disability:

Level 1: *Intra-individual discrepancy.* At this level, significant difficulties and strengths are noted across academic domains, including content areas. This assessment helps identify individuals who have learning problems due to limited cognitive capacities or mental retardation.

Level 2: *Discrepancy intrinsic to the individual.* This level involves assessing central nervous system dysfunction or information-processing problems.

Level 3: *Related considerations.* This level involves an examination of psychosocial skills, physical abilities, and sensory abilities.

Level 4: *Alternative explanations of learning difficulty.* This level involves the examination of factors that contribute to the learning problems but are not intrinsic to a learning disability. These factors, which relate to the exclusion component, include a primary disability other than learning; environmental, cultural, or economic influences; and inappropriate or inadequate instruction.

Brinckerhoff et al. submit this operational definition as a stimulus to help those involved in the field of learning disabilities develop more viable alternatives and move closer to consensus regarding the identification of individuals with learning disabilities.

McLoughlin and Lewis (1994) offer the following recommendations for determining a discrepancy between expected and actual achievement:

1. Use tests with comparable norm groups that are reliable and valid.
2. When using tests with built-in discrepancy analysis systems (e.g., the *Woodcock-Johnson Psycho-Educational Battery—Revised*), examine the measures used to assess aptitude and expected level of achievement. When measures are composite or cluster scores, consider the student's performance on subtests.
3. When test scores indicate a severe discrepancy, confirm the existence of this finding within the school environment.
4. Remember that a severe discrepancy is only one criteria for determining a learning disability. Learning disability is not synonymous with underachievement.

Identification Considerations

The identification of a learning disability is complex and difficult. The severe discrepancy component represents just one of several components that must be assessed. Depending on the definition being used, other components assessed include the exclusion and the process components. As discussed in Chapters 1 and 15, some authorities report that adaptive behavior and social skills represent areas that help diagnosticians identify learning disabilities more precisely. (Chapter 15 presents the assessment and teaching of social skills.) Other investigators (Lyon, 1995; Shaw et al., 1995) claim that the assessment of various cognitive functions (e.g., information processing abilities) offers potential for identifying learning disabilities.

Several authorities (Chalfant, 1985; Hanley 1995; Marston & Magnusson, 1985; Tindal & Marston, 1990) support the use of informal assessment methods in identification of learning disabilities. They claim that informal measures such as curriculum-based assessment hold much promise for assisting in the identification of learning disabilities.

Some states use clinical judgment to determine the existence of a learning disability. Several investigators (Dangel & Ensminger, 1988; McLeskey, 1989) found that numerous students were identified as having learning disabilities without meeting severe discrepancy criteria. In some of these cases multidisciplinary teams likely were exercising clinical judgment. Macmann, Barnett, Lombard, Belton-Kocher, & Sharpe (1989) maintain that the use of clinical judgment is consistent with the spirit of Public Law 94-142 because federal guidelines promote a clinical rather than an actuarial model of classification. This approach is receiving criticism in the literature (Chalfant, 1989; Epps, Ysseldyke, & McGue, 1984). Before too much criticism is leveled at clinical judgment, however, it is important to determine whether its effectiveness has been studied with diagnosticians who actually test or observe the children whom researchers ask them to judge. Studies that obtain data by asking professionals to make decisions about children on the basis of test scores may not be true tests of clinical judgment, because these professionals have not had an opportunity to interact with the children. To date, the literature seems to indicate that many diagnostic specialists and teachers are not well informed about the psychometric properties of tests (Lyon, 1995) or discrepancy procedures (Ross, 1990). It may be true that the uninformed show poor "clinical judgment"; however, does this mean that well-informed diagnosticians also arrive at poor judgments? The major issue may be diagnosticians' skill level rather than the value of clinical judgment. To criticize state personnel department practices and evaluation teams across all settings for using clinical judgment appears, at best, premature. At this time, more inservice training about diagnostic practices may be a better recommendation (Kavale & Forness, 1985; Macmann et al., 1989).

Chalfant (1985) offers the following recommendations for improving multidisciplinary team functioning:

1. *Validate referrals.* The team must determine whether the general school program has tried a variety of instructional interventions before a referral is made for special education services.
2. *Develop an assessment plan.* The team should determine what questions need to be addressed and which team members will address specific questions.
3. *Use diagnostic teaching.* If a student's problem is difficult to assess, the team should recommend a period of diagnostic teaching to assess the student's progress under a variety of interventions.
4. *Determine team composition.* The team should include only professionals who are involved directly with the student.
5. *Offer training in group dynamics and communication.* Training in group dynamics and communication skills is needed to improve group functioning so that quality decisions are made. Communication skills include listening, observing, and interpreting; controlling emotional responses; and thinking before talking.
6. *Train team leaders.* Team leaders must know how to develop characteristics of effective teams: each member is safe, each member's contributions are important, and each team member is valued.

Moreover, Moore et al. (1989) encourage team training in (a) interpersonal communication skills, including the ability to present discipline-specific information, (b) group decision-making strategies, and (c) state-of-the-art formal and informal evaluation procedures. Specifically, they recommend curriculum-based assessment and data-based instructional management.

To help maintain quality data, the team members should be encouraged to examine the strengths and weaknesses of the tests or procedures they use. For example, reliability, validity, and standardization data could be typed on cards and taped to the cover of each test used. As previously noted, the 1977 *Federal Register* requires that a multidisciplinary team determine a student's eligibility. Table 5.2 summarizes an eligibility staffing. Signatures are required, and members who disagree with the decision must sign as such and explain their positions.

Hofmeister and his associates at Utah State University are working with microcomputers to improve assessment procedures for multidisciplinary team members. Hofmeister and Lubke (1986) describe an "expert systems" project in

TABLE 5.2
Specific Learning Disabilities (SLD) Eligibility Staffing Summary

Name ________________ D.O.B. ________ C.A. ________ E.A. ________ Date ________
School ________________ Grade ________ Teacher ________
SLD Resource Teacher ________________ Date of SLD Testing ________

Personnel present: (initials indicate attendance at staffing) SLD Teacher ________
Principal ________ Curriculum Specialist ________ Counselor ________ Social Worker ________
Psychologist ________ Classroom Teacher ________ Speech ________ Other ________

Prerequisites: Prior to referral a parent conference is held and behavior observations are noted. Documentation of alternative strategies attempted and environmental-cultural factors considered: ________________

Criteria for eligibility: To receive SLD service the student must meet *all* of the following criteria.

1. Evidence of academic deficits.
Meets criteria _____ Does not meet criteria _____
PIAT _____ K-TEA _____ Woodcock Reading _____ Key math _____ Other _____
Deficit areas: Reading Recognition/Comprehension ________ Arithmetic ________ Other _____

or

2. Evidence of a language deficit.
Meets criteria _____ Does not meet criteria _____
Specific Language Disability Tests ________________
TOLD-2 _____ CELF-3 _____ Other ________________
Deficit areas: Listening Comprehension ________ Oral Expression ________

and

3. Evidence that learning problems are not due primarily to other disabling conditions.
Intellectual:
Meets criteria _____ Does not meet criteria _____
WISC-III V _____ P _____ FS _____ Stanford-Binet _____ K-ABC _____ Other ________

Physical: (see health records for documentation)
Auditory: Meets criteria _____ Does not meet criteria _____
Visual: Meets criteria _____ Does not meet criteria _____
Motor: Meets criteria _____ Does not meet criteria _____

Emotional:
Meets criteria _____ Does not meet criteria _____
Documentation ________________

Diagnostic prescriptive summary: (Meets, Does not meet) criteria for placement in the program for specific learning disabilities. ________________
Signatures: ________________

which the user interacts with the microcomputer. The expert system presents questions, accepts user responses, matches the responses with a knowledge base, and displays conclusions. In essence, the computer simulates the role of a consultant to the multidisciplinary team members.

INITIAL ASSESSMENT FOR INSTRUCTION

Other than identifying the student for a more appropriate placement, the data gathered in the traditional identification process are not relevant to teaching. This is true especially for the

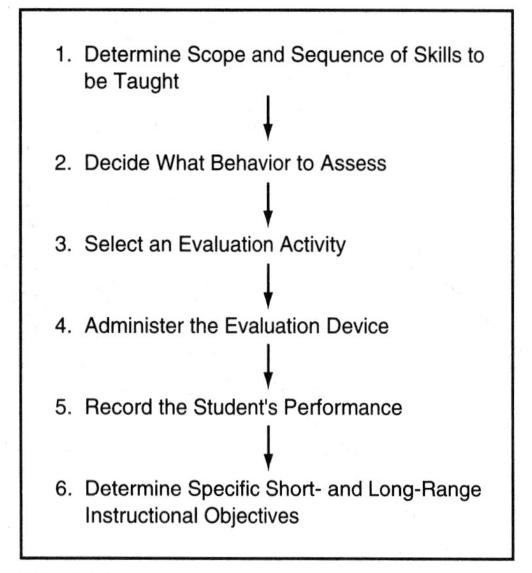

FIGURE 5.2
Assessment model for determining what to teach
Note: From *Teaching Students with Learning Problems* (p. 54), 4th ed., by C. D. Mercer and A. R. Mercer, 1993, Upper Saddle River, NJ: Merrill/Prentice Hall. Copyright 1993 by Prentice-Hall Publishing Company. Reprinted by permission.

standardized test data. Thus, further assessments are needed to determine specifically what to teach and how to teach.

Assessment for What to Teach

Assessment areas for determining what to teach may include academic skills (e.g., science and social studies), motor skills, personal-social skills, and vocationally related skills (e.g., career knowledge and specific vocational training). This type of assessment is required at all grade and age levels.

Assessment Model. The model presented in Figure 5.2 provides guidelines for assessment of what to teach. The model includes six steps:

1. *Determine scope and sequence of skills to be taught.* Teachers frequently are responsible for determining short- and long-range instructional objectives in numerous curriculum areas (such as reading, math, science, and vocational education). To do this effectively, the teacher must understand the scope and sequence or network of skills in the curriculum areas. To be useful, a scope and sequence skills list should organize the sequence into component areas and present the major skills in each area. This type of list helps the teacher to grasp the total content or sequence and to see it in a hierarchical or logical way. For each skill listed in a sequence, the teacher can develop a device or procedure for assessing it.
2. *Decide what behavior to assess.* This step begins at a global level and becomes specific. The process follows four stages: (a) select global area, (b) conduct assessment across a wide span of skills, (c) note problem areas, and (d) conduct specific skill assessment. Performance on a curriculum-based assessment can be used to determine what curriculum skills the student has and has not mastered. Howell, Fox, and Morehead (1993) note that these results are useful in placing students in materials, forming instructional groups, and planning individualized programs.
3. *Select an evaluation activity.* The teacher has many choices in selecting evaluation activities: commercial tests, curriculum tests, portfolios, criterion-referenced skill inventories and checklists, and teacher-made instruments (e.g., a curriculum-based measurement device or an informal reading inventory). As the decision is made, several factors are considered, including purpose, cost, time, and relevance of the activity or test for classroom instruction. Specific skill assessment is used during the initial evaluation to determine instructional objectives. It also is used in daily instruction to evaluate a student's progress in specific skills. (Chapter 8 presents additional information about frequent assessment in the section on data-based instruction.)
4. *Administer the evaluation device.* The teacher usually administers the evaluation device for the initial assessment. As noted previously, the initial assessment involves evaluating both a wide span of skills and specific skills. Because this procedure involves much decision making (e.g., identifying problem areas, noting error patterns, and selecting specific

skills for assessment), it usually is done by the teacher or a diagnostician. After the initial assessment is completed and instructional objectives are determined, procedures for monitoring progress are established.

5. *Record the student's performance.* The teacher needs to record two types of student performance: performance on daily work and mastery of skills. Daily progress usually is recorded by means of teacher-made activities (such as spelling tests, learning charts, and performance on worksheets). Overall skill mastery usually is recorded on individual progress charts. Scope and sequence lists provide a good format for recording skill mastery. In addition, some commercial materials provide individual progress sheets for recording student performance.
6. *Determine specific short- and long-range instructional objectives.* After administering the assessment, the teacher must analyze the data and create instructional objectives. Good objectives specify the target behavior in observable terms, delineate the conditions under which the behavior occurs, and describe the criterion for successful performance. Short-term objectives should contribute directly to the mastery of long-term objectives. For example, the following short- and long-term objectives are related:

   Long-term objective: Given the graphemes of 44 phonemes, the student will say the correct phoneme with 90% accuracy.

   Short-term objective: Given the graphemes for consonant blends, the student will say the phoneme with 90% accuracy.

Chapters 11 through 15 present assessment practices for determining what to teach in various content areas.

Assessment for How to Teach

Knowing how to teach greatly increases the efficiency of instruction. For example, Tony's teacher noticed that Tony completed his seatwork much faster when responses did not require writing small-sized letters or numbers. The teacher then gave him worksheets that provided large spaces for writing responses, and Tony's seatwork performance greatly improved.

Unfortunately, too little emphasis in teacher training and material development has been placed on how to teach. The ability to analyze how a student learns best influences the selection of materials, methods, and procedures used in the intervention program. It is perhaps the foremost skill that distinguishes the professionally trained teacher from other supportive instructional personnel.

The first step in determining how to teach is to identify the major areas of assessment: expectation factors, stimulus events, response factors, and subsequent events. Once these areas are determined, the important factors need to be identified under each of them. Some of the important factors of each major area are outlined in Table 5.3.

In planning instruction, these major areas must be weighted in relation to one another. After each area has been assessed and viewed as a whole, a profile may be written. The profile can display numerous patterns and supply a simple list of do's and don'ts for designing an individual program (see Table 5.4).

Assessment areas guide teacher observation. An instructional plan based on an assessment for determining how to teach should be viewed as a guesstimate. When the right variables are manipulated appropriately, the plan is effective; however, when the assessment is incorrect, adjustments are needed in the plan. All treatment plans should be monitored closely to ensure their efficacy and the student's progress. Thus, assessment for determining how to teach is similar to assessment for determining what to teach in that both are ongoing processes.

Ultimately, teachers determine what and how to teach every day during school. Teachers monitor student progress and adjust both what and how to teach to maintain acceptable progress. Basically, the initial assessment of what and how to teach helps establish the initial teaching plan.

TABLE 5.3
Assessment Areas for Determining How to Teach

Expectation Factors

- Learner Expectations
  - *Negative expectation reactions*
    - Note reactions characterized by negative comments about one's own abilities, avoidance remarks, and comments that reflect the anticipation of failure or problems.
  - *Target of avoidance reactions*
    - By listening, interviewing, or observing the student, ascertain the situations about which the student has negative expectations. The avoidance situation may be a person, place, or activity.
  - *Stated reasons for negative reactions*
- Teacher Expectations
  - *Assignments (too difficult or too easy); interactions (negative/positive)*
- Peer Expectations
  - *Social patterns; peer values*
- Parental Expectations
  - *Negative expectancies in relation to school; unrealistic expectations; too low expectations*

Stimulus Events

- Physical Properties
  - *Noise; temperature; lighting; general physical factors*
- Instructional Arrangements
- Instructional Techniques
- Materials
- Learning Style Preferences
  - *Visual preference indicators; auditory preference indicators; tactile preference indicators; kinesthetic preference indicators*

Response Types

- Verbal
- Verbal-Motor
- Motor

Subsequent Events

- Verbal Praise
- Physical Approval
- Evaluation Events

The Instructional Environment System—II (TIES-II) (Ysseldyke & Christenson, 1993) provides educators with a framework for evaluating and obtaining information about an individual student's instructional environment. The learning environment is examined across 12 instructional-environment components (e.g., motivational factors, relevant practice, and informed feedback) and 5 home-support-for-learning components (e.g., discipline orientation and parent participation) that are considered to be related to instructional outcomes for students. TIES-II can be used to describe the extent to which a student's academic or behavior problems are related to factors in the instructional environment as well as to identify starting points in designing appropriate instructional interventions for individual students. This type of assessment provides educators with a systematic procedure for examining factors that facilitate planning how to teach.

INDIVIDUALIZED EDUCATIONAL PROGRAM

Once it is determined that a student has a learning disability, assessment focuses on instruction. This process is guided by the development and implementation of an *individualized educational program* (IEP) for each student (age 3 to 21) with a disability. According to Public Law 94-142, the IEP must state (a) the student's current performance levels, (b) annual and short-term instructional objectives, (c) the special services and the extent of general classroom participation, (d) the projected date for initiation and anticipated duration of such services, and (e) criteria, evaluation procedures, and schedules for determining progress. Public Law 99-457 provides an *individualized family service plan* (IFSP) for infants and toddlers (birth through age 2) with disabilities. The IFSP documents the early intervention services required by these children and their families.

The IEP and the IFSP both require that the written plan be developed by a multidisciplinary team, which includes the parents, and be based on a multidisciplinary assessment of unique needs. At the IEP meeting, a multidisciplinary team determines at least one short-term objective for each annual goal. The goals are major statements, and parental permission must be given for one to be added or deleted, whereas short-term objectives are steps taken to obtain a stated goal and can be added at the teacher's discretion.

TABLE 5.4
Learning Profile and Treatment Plan

Assessment Area and Findings	Treatment
Learner Expectations	
Thinks teacher dislikes him	Ask for a favor once a day, or ask the student a personal-interest question each day (e.g., "Did you like that football game?").
Senses defeat in reading	Pair reinforcement with effort in reading.
Teacher Expectations	
Assigns work that is too difficult in reading	Provide realistic successes in reading.
Tends to pick on student	Use sensitive responses to incorrect responses.
Peer Expectations	
Is with peers who do not value reading	Seat student near peers who value reading.
Is liked and respected by peers	Use peer teaching with student being tutor or tutee.
Parental Expectations	
Is pushed by parents to work hard	Tell parents not to tutor unless it is a pleasant experience.
Has concerned and cooperative parents	Encourage parents to praise effort as well as correct product.
Physical Properties	
Is allergic to dust	Seat student away from chalk trays.
Prefers cooler areas of room	Allow student to work away from furnace ducts.
Prefers well-lighted areas	Seat student near a window.
Likes to work near other students	Assign work at a table with students who work hard.
Instructional Arrangements	
Dislikes one-on-one with teacher	Make one-to-one instruction pleasant.
Enjoys small-group activities	Use small-group instruction.
Instructional Techniques	
Gets bored with same task	Practice academic skills via tape recorder, instructional games, self-correcting materials, and computer software.
Has low frustration tolerance in reading	Allow student to practice reading on tape recorder before reading orally to the teacher.
Works slowly	Let student work against a timer.
Needs prompts and cues to maintain behavior	Use contingency contracts with a variety of activities.

continued

TABLE 5.4
continued

Assessment Area and Findings	Treatment
Instructional Materials	
Dislikes reading worksheets	Use language experience approach in reading.
Likes games	Use instructional games.
Likes worksheets with only a few items	Use worksheets that are partially completed.
Dislikes cluttered worksheets or materials	Use Language Master or tape recorder.
Learning Style Preferences	
Responds well in all modalities	Present tasks in various modalities.
Response Factors	
Writes slowly and sloppily	Encourage use of a plastic pencil holder.
Prefers short verbal responses coupled with simple motor responses	Use point-and-say responses.
Writes too big for space allowed	Give a lot of room for writing on worksheets or use chalkboard for writing.
Subsequent Events	
Does not respond to one-word praises but enjoys smiles and handshakes	Follow good effort with a smile, touch, and encouraging phrase.
Requests immediate feedback	Use answer keys, peer feedback, and self-correcting materials.
Likes high letter grades	Write big letter grades on good work.
Has difficulty with feedback on incorrect items	Use a variety of sensitive responses for incorrect work.

Note: From *Teaching Students with Learning Problems* (pp. 94–95), 4th ed., by C. D. Mercer and A. R. Mercer, 1993, Upper Saddle River, NJ: Merrill/Prentice Hall. Copyright 1993 by Prentice-Hall Publishing Company. Reprinted by permission.

Table 5.5 shows an IEP format that incorporates the essentials of a plan. Part B-I enables the teacher to outline the short-term objectives for the academic year. Part B-II provides space for short-term objectives but does not segment the objectives into grading periods. The teacher may select either form of Part B, depending on needs and preferences. It is a good practice for the special education teacher to work with a student and their teachers for several sessions before the IEP conference. During this time, the special education teacher can determine realistic objectives and specific teaching techniques.

The IEP is a substantial improvement over past planning strategies used by many educators; however, it is not sufficient for delivering an individualized program. Bateman (1977) compared the components of diagnostic prescriptive teaching (an individualized programming approach) and the IEP. Both require assessment of the student's current level and specification of goals and objectives. However, only prescriptive teaching specifies the teaching tasks inherent in the objectives (such as antecedent events, student responses, consequent events, and daily evaluation for each task).

During the past 15 years, IEPs have undergone few changes. Smith (1990) maintains that in many situations IEPs are not useful documents. In a review of IEPs, Giangreco, Dennis, Edelman, and Cloninger (1994) found that IEPs "did not adequately communicate the individual needs of students, nor did they seem to serve as a useful resource to guide their general education experiences" (p. 295). Given the reform movements in education, it may be an oppor-

TABLE 5.5
Individualized Educational Program

Part A: IEP

Checklist

9-6-96 Referral by Ann Tharin
9-9-96 Parents informed of rights; permission obtained for evaluation
9-16-96 Evaluation compiled
9-17-96 Parents contacted
9-20-96 Total committee meets and subcommitte assigned
9-26-96 IEP developed by subcommittee
9-27-96 IEP approved by total committee

Committee Members

Ann Tharin
Referral Teacher
John Thomas
Other LEA representative
Melissa Williams
Parents
Mary Rivera
Teachers
Joan Beuton
Alice King

Date IEP initially approved 9-27-96

Health Information

Vision: good
Hearing: excellent
Physical: good
Other:

Yearly Class Schedule

	Time	Subject	Teacher
1st semester	8:30-9:20	math	Rivera
	9:30-10:20	language arts	Beuton (Resource)
	10:30-11:20	social studies	Beuton
	11:30-12:20	science	Rivera
		lunch	
	1:10-2:00	art	Shaw
	2:10-3:00	P.E.	King
2nd semester	8:30-9:20	math	Rivera
	9:30-10:20	language arts	Beuton (Resource)
	10:30-11:20	social studies	Beuton
	11:30-12:20	science	Rivera
		lunch	
	1:10-2:00	art	Shaw
	2:10-3:00	P.E.	King

Testing Information

Test Name	Date Admin.	Interpretation
K-TEA	9-10-96	Spelling - standard score 82 Math standard score 104 Reading standard score 78
informal test of phonics	9-12-96	Knows 6 of 20 phonics rules
CBM probe	9-12-96	reads 3rd grade level reader at 84 correct wpm with 70% comprehension
CBM probe	9-16-96	reads 4th grade level reader at 60 correct wpm with 40% comprehension
Social skills check list	9-16-96	Gets along well with others but has difficulty dealing with critical feedback

Identification Information

Name Greg Creswell
School Village Elementary School
Birthdate 5-15-84 Grade 6
Parents' name Ken & Melissa Williams
Address 1300 Johnson Street
Raleigh N.C.
Phone: Home none Office 932-8161

Continuum of Services

	Hours per week
General class	20 hrs
Resource teacher in general classroom	6 hrs
Resource room	4 hrs
Reading specialist	
Speech/language therapist	
Counselor	
Special class	
Transition class	
Others:	

continued

TABLE 5.5
continued

Part B.I.: IEP (Complete for each subject area)

Name: Greg Creswell Subject Area: Reading

Level of Performance: Can identify 6 of 20 phonics rules; reads ~~3rd grade book-84 wpm; 70% comprehension~~; reads 4th grade book-60 wpm; 40% comprehension Teacher: Joan Beuton - Resource Teacher

Annual Goals:
1. Given passages from middle of 4th grade reader, Greg will read 110 wpm correctly with 80% comprehension
2. Greg will identify and use 20 phonics rules.
3.

	First Grading Period Sept. —Oct.	Second Grading Period Oct. —Nov.	Third Grading Period Nov. —Dec.	Fourth Grading Period Jan. —Feb.	Fifth Grading Period Feb. —Apr.	Sixth Grading Period Apr. —June
Objectives	Referred	1. Read initial level 3rd grade passages at 110 correct wpm with 80% comprehension 2. Recognize and use 8 phonics rules	1. Read middle level 3rd grade passages at 110 cprrect wpm with 80% comprehension 2. Recognize and use 11 phonics rules	1. Read upper level (end of book) 3rd grade passages at 110 correct wpm with 80% compre-hension 2. Recognize and comprehend 14 phonics rules	1. Read initial level 4th grade passages at 110 correct wpm with 80% compre-hension 2. Recognize and use 17 phonics rules	1. Read middle level 4th grade passages at 110 correct wpm with 80% compre-hension 2. Recognize and use 20 phonics rules
Agent		Resource Teacher-1 General classroom Teacher-2	Resource Teacher-1 General classroom Teacher-2	Resource Teacher-1 General classroom Teacher-2	Resource Teacher-1 General classroom Teacher-2	Resource Teacher-1 General classroom Teacher-2
Evalu-ation		1. CBM reading probe at 3rd grade level 2. informal test of phonics rules & applications	1. CBM reading probe at 3rd grade level 2. informal test of phonics rules & applications	1. CBM reading probe at 3rd grade level 2. informal test of phonics rules & applications	1. CBM reading probe at 3rd grade level 2. informal test of phonics rules & applications	1. CBM reading probe at 3rd grade level 2. informal test of phonics rules & applications

TABLE 5.5
continued

Part B.II.: IEP (Complete for each subject area)

Student's Name ______________________ Subject Area ______________________

Level of Performance ______________________ Teacher ______________________

Annual Goals: 1. ______________________

2. ______________________

3. ______________________

Date Initiated	Objectives	Materials	Evaluation	Date Achieved	Person Responsible

Note: Adapted from *Developing and Implementing Individualized Education Programs* (pp. 419–420, 430), 3rd ed., by B. B. Strickland and A. P. Turnbull, 1990, Upper Saddle River, NJ: Merrill/Prentice Hall. Copyright 1990 by Prentice-Hall Publishing Company. Reprinted by permission.

tune time to make some major changes in IEPs. Giangreco et al. comment on needed changes in the following passage:

> We suggest that efforts be focused on improving the quality and usefulness of IEPs by, at least in part, reconceptualizing the minimum requirements and extending beyond those minimums. IEP goals, objectives, and supports should be internally and externally congruent and be designed to improve valued life outcomes. That is, . . . content of the IEP should be reflected in what is taught within general education class activities, and student outcomes should be truly meaningful. (p. 295)

Although the IEP is recognized as a major step toward the improvement of educational services for students with learning disabilities, the data management system that accompanies it can be quite burdensome to the teacher. Developing, writing, and monitoring the IEP require a great deal of teacher time, although the microcomputer offers an excellent tool to help educators manage it. Jenkins (1987) compared computer-generated IEPs and handwritten IEPs and found that computer-generated IEPs were of higher quality and took significantly less time to write. A minibibliography of the role of the computer and the IEP appears in the Spring 1988 issue of *Learning Disabilities Focus*.

The following are some of the applications of a microcomputer in IEP management:

1. *Create new IEPs*. A microcomputer can be used to develop an IEP (e.g., store and retrieve demographic data, test scores, annual goals, short-term objectives, and other data).
2. *Monitor procedural safeguards*. A microcomputer can be used to provide the steps in the IEP process (e.g., receipt of parent consent for assessment, notification of IEP meeting, and annual review date) and the respective status regarding each step. Hayden, Vance, and Irvin (1982) provide an example of a computerized procedural safeguard process that features 21 steps.
3. *Update records*. A student's IEP can be displayed readily and modified easily on a microcomputer. For example, progress on short-term objectives can be added. Moreover, the updated or existing record can be printed quickly for parents, teachers, or multidisciplinary team members.
4. *Analyze and interpret test data*. Test results can be scored and analyzed on a microcomputer. Programs are available that include scoring and analysis for the WISC-III, the K-ABC, and the *Woodcock-Johnson Psycho-Educational Battery—Revised*.
5. *Monitor academic progress*. A list of curriculum skills can be programmed, and progress on them can be monitored.

Obviously, applications of the microcomputer to IEP management are extensive. Some school districts have developed their own IEP management programs tailored to their specific needs.

PERSPECTIVE

Chalfant (1985) notes that, unfortunately, educators must follow rigorous and complex procedures to ascertain whether a student is eligible for special services. The number of referrals being made for learning disability programs is disturbingly high. Many school districts report that nearly 25% of the school population is having some type of learning or behavior problem (Chalfant, 1985). It is apparent that the identification of learning disabilities needs more serious review, and local school districts need to be encouraged to produce innovative procedures for identifying or preventing learning disabilities. It also is apparent that general education needs review. Giangreco et al. (1994) claim that improving educational environments with better IEPs represents a viable alternative to the assessment and instructional problems. Chalfant states, "There is a great need for regular education to develop special help alternatives for non-LD students with learning and behavior problems. . . . The identification of LD students . . . is only a small part of a much larger problem in the nation's schools" (p. 19). On a positive note, Reynolds (1985) claims that a viable state-of-the art in assessment is emerging and needs to be implemented. Curriculum-based assessment, computer-assisted assessment, availability of better tests, and a rising consciousness about identification perhaps will provide the impetus and know-how for an improved state of affairs. Ysseldyke and Algozzine (1995) aptly state the basic goal of assessment practices:

> The ultimate goal of assessment is to identify problems with instruction and to lead to instructional modifications. A good share of present-day assessment activities consist of little more than meddling. . . . We must use assessment data to improve instruction. . . . The only way to determine the effectiveness of instruction is to collect data. (p. 198)

DISCUSSION/REVIEW QUESTIONS

1. Discuss some of the problems in identifying learning disabilities.
2. Present the requirements of Public Law 94-142 in identifying learning disabilities.
3. Describe the nature of formal tests and their advantages and disadvantages.
4. Identify two intelligence tests and describe their characteristics.
5. Describe the nature of informal tests and their advantages and disadvantages.
6. Describe curriculum-based assessment and alternative assessment.
7. List the steps in the assessment process for identifying learning disabilities, and discuss the basic components that need to be assessed.
8. Discuss four procedures used in operationalizing the discrepancy component, and present alternative directions for determining a severe discrepancy.
9. Discuss guidelines for assessment of what to teach, and present assessment areas for determining how to teach.
10. Discuss the development of an individualized educational program.

REFERENCES

Abruscato, J. (1993). Early results and tentative implications from the Vermont Portfolio Project. *Phi Delta Kappan, 74*, 474–477.

Adelman, H. S. (1992). LD: The next 25 years. *Journal of Learning Disabilities, 25*, 17–22.

Bateman, B. D. (1964). Learning disabilities—Yesterday, today, and tomorrow. *Exceptional Children, 31*, 167.

Bateman, B. D. (1977). Prescriptive teaching and individualized education programs. In R. Heinrich & S. C. Ashcroft (Eds.), *Instructional technology and the education of all handicapped children*. Columbus, OH: National Center on Media and Materials for the Handicapped.

Berk, R. A. (1982). Effectiveness of discrepancy score methods for screening children with learning disabilities. *Learning Disabilities, 1*(2), 11–24.

Berk, R. A. (1984). An evaluation of procedures for computing an ability-achievement discrepancy score. *Journal of Learning Disabilities, 17*, 262–266.

Brinckerhoff, L. C., Shaw, S. F., & McGuire, J. M. (1993). *Promoting postsecondary education for students with learning disabilities: A handbook for practitioners*. Austin, TX: PRO-ED.

Bureau of Education for the Handicapped. (1978, April). Clarification of evaluation of team requirements for learning disabled children. In *Informal letter to Chief State School Officers, State Directors of Special Education, State Coordinators of Part B of EHA and State Coordinators of the ESEA Title I Handicapped Program* (DAS Bulletin No. 9), Washington, DC.

Bursuck, W. D., & Lessen, E. (1987). A classroom-based model for assessing students with learning disabilities. *Learning Disabilities Focus, 3*(1), 17–29.

Carter, J., & Sugai, G. (1989). Survey on prereferral practices: Responses from state departments of education. *Exceptional Children, 55*, 298–302.

Chalfant, J. C. (1985). Identifying learning disabled students: A summary of the National Task Force report. *Learning Disabilities Focus, 1*(1), 9–20.

Chalfant, J. C. (1989). Diagnostic criteria for entry and exit from service: A national problem. In L. B. Silver (Ed.), *The assessment of learning disabilities: Preschool through adulthood* (pp. 1–26). Boston: College-Hill Press.

Chalfant, J. C., Pysh, M. V., & Moultrie, R. (1979). Teacher assistance teams: A model for within-building problem solving. *Learning Disability Quarterly, 2*(3), 85–96.

Collier, C., & Hoover, J. J. (1987). Sociocultural considerations when referring minority children for learning disabilities. *Learning Disabilities Focus, 3*(1), 39–45.

Cone, T. E., & Wilson, L. R. (1981). Quantifying a severe discrepancy: A critical analysis. *Learning Disability Quarterly, 4*, 359–371.

Cordoni, B. (1995). Psychoeducational assessment for learning disabilities. *Journal of Child Neurology, 10*(Suppl. 1), 31–36.

Council for Learning Disabilities Board of Trustees. (1986). Use of discrepancy formulas in the identification of learning disabled individuals. *Learning Disability Quarterly, 9*, 245.

Dangel, H. L., & Ensminger, E. E. (1988). The use of a discrepancy formula with LD students. *Learning Disabilities Focus, 4*(1), 24–31.

Deno, S. L. (1985). Curriculum-based measurement: The emerging alternative. *Exceptional Children, 52*, 219–232.

Deno, S. L. (1987). Curriculum-based measurement. *Teaching Exceptional Children, 20*(1), 41–42.

Epps, S., Ysseldyke, J. E., & McGue, M. (1984). "I know one when I see one"— Differentiating LD and non-LD students. *Learning Disability Quarterly, 7*, 89–101.

Felton, R. H., & Brown, I. S. (1991). Neuropsychological prediction of reading disabilities. In J. E. Obrzut & G. W. Hynd (Eds.), *Neuropsychological foundations of learning disabilities: A handbook of issues, methods, and practice* (pp. 387–410). San Diego: Academic Press.

Felton, R. H., & Wood, F. B. (1989). Cognitive deficits in reading disability and attention deficit disorder. *Journal of Learning Disabilities, 22*, 3–13, 22.

Finlan, T. G. (1992). Do state methods of quantifying a severe discrepancy result in fewer students with learning disabilities? *Learning Disability Quarterly, 15*, 129–134.

Fletcher, J. M., Francis, D. J., Rourke, B. P., Shaywitz, S. E., & Shaywitz, B. A. (1992). The validity of discrepancy-based definitions of reading disabilities. *Journal of Learning Disabilities, 25*, 555–561, 573.

Fletcher, J. M., Francis, D. J., Rourke, B. P., Shaywitz, S. E., & Shaywitz, B. A. (1993). Classification of learning disabilities: Relationships with other childhood diseases. In G. R. Lyon, D. B. Gray, J. F. Kavanaugh, & N. A. Krasnegor (Eds.), *Better understanding learning disabilities: New views from research and their implications for education and public policies* (pp. 27–55). Baltimore, MD: Paul H. Brookes.

Forness, S. R., Sinclair, E., & Guthrie, D. (1983). Learning disability discrepancy formulas: Their use in actual practice. *Learning Disability Quarterly, 6*, 107–114.

Frankenberger, W., & Harper, J. (1987). States' criteria and procedures for identifying learning disabled children: A comparison of 1981/82 and 1985/86 guidelines. *Journal of Learning Disabilities, 20*, 118–121.

Fuchs, D., & Fuchs, L. S. (1989). Effects of examiner familiarity on Black, Caucasian, and Hispanic children: A meta-analysis. *Exceptional Children, 55*, 303–308.

Fuchs, D., Fuchs, L. S., Benowitz, S., & Barringer, K. (1987). Norm-referenced tests: Are they valid for use with handicapped students? *Exceptional Children, 54*, 263–271.

Furlong, M. J., & Yanagida, E. H. (1985). Psychometric factors affecting multidisciplinary team identification of learning disabled children. *Learning Disability Quarterly, 8*, 37–44.

Galagan, J. E. (1985). Psychoeducational testing: Turn out the lights, the party's over. *Exceptional Children, 52*, 266–276.

Gerber, M. (1982, October). *Reconceptualizing the referral process: A levels of response approach to the identification and assessment of learning disabled students*. Paper presented at the annual meeting of the Council on Learning Disabilities, Kansas City, MO.

Giangreco, M. F., Dennis, R. E., Edelman, S. W., & Cloninger, C. J. (1994). Dressing your IEPs for the general education climate: Analysis of IEP goals and objectives for students with multiple disabilities. *Remedial and Special Education, 15*, 288–296.

Gickling, E. E., & Thompson, V. P. (1985). A personal view of curriculum-based assessment. *Exceptional Children, 52*, 205–218.

Glutting, J. J., & Bear, G. G. (1989). Comparative efficacy of K-ABC subtests vs. WISC-R subtests in the differential classification of learning disabilities. *Learning Disability Quarterly, 12*, 291–298.

Graden, J. L. (1989). Redefining "prereferral" intervention as intervention assistance: Collaboration between general and special education. *Exceptional Children, 56*, 227–231.

Graden, J. L., Casey, A., & Christenson, S. L. (1985). Implementing a prereferral intervention system: Part I. The model. *Exceptional Children, 51*, 377–384.

Hammill, D. D. (1990). On defining learning disabilities: An emerging consensus. *Journal of Learning Disabilities, 23*, 74–84.

Hammill, D. D. (1991). *Detroit Tests of Learning Aptitude—3*. Austin, TX: PRO-ED.

Haney, W. (1985). Making testing more educational. *Educational Leadership*, *43*(2), 4–13.

Hanley, T. V. (1995). The need for technological advances in assessment related to national educational reform. *Exceptional Children*, *61*, 222–229.

Hayden, D., Vance, B., & Irvin, M. S. (1982). Establishing a special education management system—SEMS. *Journal of Learning Disabilities*, *15*, 428–429.

Hofmeister, A. M., & Lubke, M. M. (1986). Expert systems: Implications for the diagnosis and treatment of learning disabilities. *Learning Disability Quarterly*, *9*, 133–137.

Holcomb, W. R., Hardesty, R. A., Adams, A., & Ponder, H. M. (1987). WISC-R types of learning disabilities: A profile analysis with cross-validation. *Journal of Learning Disabilities*, *20*, 369–373.

Howell, K. W., Fox, S. L., & Morehead, M. K. (1993). *Curriculum-based evaluation: Teaching and decision making* (2nd ed.). Pacific Grove, CA: Brooks/Cole.

Inglis, J., & Lawson, J. S. (1987). Reanalysis of a meta-analysis of the validity of the *Wechsler* scales in the diagnosis of a learning disability. *Learning Disability Quarterly*, *10*, 198–202.

Jenkins, M. W. (1987). Effect of a computerized individual education program (IEP) writer on time savings and quality. *Journal of Special Education Technology*, *8*(3), 55–66.

Kaufman, A. S. (1981). The WISC-R and learning disabilities assessment: State of the art. *Journal of Learning Disabilities*, *14*, 520–526.

Kaufman, A. S., & Kaufman, N. L. (1983). *Kaufman Assessment Battery for Children*. Circle Pines, MN: American Guidance Service.

Kavale, K. A. (1987). Theoretical issues surrounding severe discrepancy. *Learning Disabilities Research*, *3*(1), 12–20.

Kavale, K. A., & Forness, S. R. (1984). A meta-analysis of *Wechsler* scale profiles and recategorizations: Patterns or parodies? *Learning Disability Quarterly*, *7*, 136–156.

Kavale, K. A., & Forness, S. R. (1985). *The science of learning disabilities*. San Diego, CA: College-Hill Press.

Levine, M. D., Hooper, S., Montgomery, J., Reed, M., Sandler, A., Schwartz, C., & Watson, T. (1993). Learning disabilities: An interactive developmental paradigm. In G. R. Lyon, D. B. Gray, J. F. Kavanaugh, & N. A. Krasnegor (Eds.), *Better understanding learning disabilities: New views from research and their implications for education and public policies* (pp. 229–250). Baltimore, MD: Paul H. Brookes.

Lieberman, L. M. (1992). Preserving special education . . . for those who need it. In W. Stainback & S. Stainback (Eds.), *Controversial issues confronting special education* (pp. 13–25). Boston: Allyn & Bacon.

Lyon, G. R. (1995). Research initiatives in learning disabilities: Contributions from scientists supported by the National Institute of Child Health and Human Development. *Journal of Child Neurology*, *10*(Suppl. 1), 120–126.

Macmann, G. M., Barnett, D. W., Lombard, T. J., Belton-Kocher, E., & Sharpe, M. N. (1989). On the actuarial classification of children: Fundamental studies of classification agreement. *The Journal of Special Education*, *23*, 127–149.

Marston, D., & Magnusson, D. (1985). Implementing curriculum-based measurement in special and regular education settings. *Exceptional Children*, *52*, 266–276.

Mather, N., & Healey, W. C. (1990). Deposing aptitude-achievement discrepancy as the imperial criterion for learning disabilities. *Learning Disabilities: A Multidisciplinary Journal*, *1*, 40–48.

Mather, N., & Roberts, R. (1994). Learning disabilities: A field in danger of extinction? *Learning Disabilities Research & Practice*, *9*, 49–58.

McCarthy, D. (1972). *McCarthy Scales of Children's Abilities*. San Antonio, TX: Psychological Corporation.

McLeskey, J. (1989). The influence of level of discrepancy on the identification of students with learning disabilities. *Journal of Learning Disabilities*, *22*, 435–438, 443.

McLoughlin, J. A., & Lewis, R. B. (1994). *Assessing special students* (4th ed.). Upper Saddle River, NJ: Merrill/Prentice Hall.

Mercer, C. D., Jordan, L., Allsopp, D. H., & Mercer, A. R. (1995). *Learning disabilities definitions and criteria used by state education departments*. Manuscript submitted for publication.

Meyen, E. (1989). Let's not confuse test scores with the substances of the discrepancy model. *Journal of Learning Disabilities*, *22*, 482–483.

Moore, K. J., Fifield, M. B., Spira, D. A., & Scarlato, M. (1989). Child study team decision making in special education: Improving the process. *Remedial and Special Education*, *10*(4), 50–58.

Nichols, E. G., Inglis, J., Lawson, J. S., & MacKay, I. (1988). A cross-validation study of patterns of cognitive ability in children with learning disabilities, as described by factorially defined WISC-R verbal and performance IQs. *Journal of Learning Disabilities*, *21*, 504–508.

Nicholson, C. L., & Hibpshman, T. M. (1990). *Slosson Intelligence Test—Revised*. East Aurora, NY: Slosson Educational Publications.

Paulson, F. L., Paulson, P. R., & Meyer, C. A. (1991). What makes a portfolio a portfolio? *Educational Leadership*, *48*(5), 60–63.

Perlmutter, B. F., & Parus, M. V. (1983). Identifying children with learning disabilities: A comparison of diagnostic procedures across school districts. *Learning Disability Quarterly*, *6*, 321–328.

Peterson, J., Heistad, D., Peterson, D., & Reynolds, M. (1985). Montevideo individualized prescriptive instructional management system. *Exceptional Children*, *52*, 239–243.

Reynolds, C. R. (1985). Measuring the aptitude-achievement discrepancy in learning disability diagnosis. *Remedial and Special Education*, *5*(3), 19–23.

Reynolds, C. R. (1992). Two key concepts in the diagnosis of learning disabilities and the habilitation of learning. *Learning Disability Quarterly*, *15*, 2–12.

Rice, L. S., & Ortiz, A. A. (1994). Second language difference or learning disability? *LD Forum*, *19*(2), 11–13.

Rispens, J., van Yperen, T. A., & van Duijn, G. A. (1991). The irrelevance of IQ to the definition of learning disabilities: Some empirical evidence. *Journal of Learning Disabilities*, *24*, 434–438.

Ross, R. P. (1990). Consistency among school psychologists in evaluating discrepancy scores: A preliminary study. *Learning Disability Quarterly*, *13*, 209–219.

Ross, R. P. (1995). Impact on psychologists of state guidelines for evaluating underachievement. *Learning Disability Quarterly*, *18*, 43–56.

Salend, S. J., & Salend, S. M. (1985). Implications of using microcomputers in classroom testing. *Journal of Learning Disabilities*, *18*, 51–53.

Salvesen, K. A., & Undheim, J. O. (1994). Screening for learning disabilities with teacher rating scales. *Journal of Learning Disabilities*, *27*, 60–66.

Salvia, J., & Ysseldyke, J. E. (1995). *Assessment* (6th ed.). Boston: Houghton Mifflin.

Schuerholz, L. J., Harris, E. L., Baumgardner, T. L., Reiss, A. L., Freund, L. S., Church, R. P., Mohr, J., & Denckla, M. B. (1995). An analysis of two discrepancy-based models and a processing-deficit approach in identifying learning disabilities. *Journal of Learning Disabilities*, *28*, 18–29.

Shaw, S. F., Cullen, J. P., McGuire, J. M., & Brinckerhoff, L. C. (1995). Operationalizing a definition of learning disabilities. *Journal of Learning Disabilities*, *28*, 586–597.

Shaywitz, B. A., Fletcher, J. M., Holahan, J. M., & Shaywitz, S. E. (1992). Discrepancy compared to low achievement definitions of reading disability: Results from the Connecticut longitudinal study. *Journal of Learning Disabilities*, *25*, 639–648.

Shephard, L. (1980). An evaluation of the regression discrepancy method for identifying children with learning disabilities. *The Journal of Special Education*, *14*, 69–74.

Siegel, L. S. (1989). IQ is irrelevant to the definition of learning disabilities. *Journal of Learning Disabilities*, *22*, 469–478, 486.

Siegel, L. S. (1992). An evaluation of the discrepancy definition of dyslexia. *Journal of Learning Disabilities*, *25*, 618–629.

Slingerland, B. H. (1974). *Slingerland Screening Tests for Identifying Children with Specific Language Disability*. Cambridge, MA: Educators Publishing Service.

Smith, S. (1990). Individualized education programs (IEPs) in special education—From intent to acquiescence. *Exceptional Children*, *57*, 6–14.

Stanovich, K. E. (1991a). Conceptual and empirical problems with discrepancy definitions of reading disability. *Learning Disability Quarterly*, *14*, 269–280.

Stanovich, K. E. (1991b). Discrepancy definitions of reading disability: Has intelligence led us astray? *Reading Research Quarterly*, *26*, 7–29.

Stiggins, R. J. (1985). Improving assessment where it means the most: In the classroom. *Educational Leadership*, *43*(2), 69–74.

Swanson, H. L. (1991). Operational definitions and learning disabilities: An overview. *Learning Disability Quarterly*, *14*, 242–254.

Swanson, H. L. (1993). Learning disabilities from the perspective of cognitive psychology. In G. R. Lyon, D. B. Gray, J. F. Kavanaugh, & N. A. Krasnegor (Eds.), *Better understanding learning disabilities: New views from research and their implications for education and public policies* (pp. 199–228). Baltimore, MD: Paul H. Brookes.

Thorndike, R. L., Hagen, E. P., & Sattler, J. M. (1986). *Stanford-Binet Intelligence Scale* (4th ed.). Chicago: Riverside.

Tindal, G. A., & Marston, D. B. (1990). *Classroom-based assessment: Evaluating instructional outcomes*. Upper Saddle River, NJ: Merrill/Prentice Hall.

U.S. Office of Education. (1977). Assistance to states for education of handicapped children: Procedures for evaluating specific learning disabilities. *Federal Register, 42*, 65082–65085.

Wechsler, D. (1991). *Wechsler Intelligence Scale for Children—III*. San Antonio, TX: Psychological Corporation.

Woodcock, R. W., & Johnson, M. B. (1989). *Woodcock-Johnson Psycho-Educational Battery—Revised*. Chicago: Riverside.

Worthen, B. R. (1993). Critical issues that will determine the future of alternative assessment. *Phi Delta Kappan, 74*, 444–454.

Ysseldyke, J. E., & Algozzine, B. (1995). *Special education: A practical approach for teachers* (3rd ed.). Boston: Houghton Mifflin.

Ysseldyke, J. E., & Christenson, S. L. (1993). *The Instructional Environment System—II*. Longmont, CO: Sopris West.

Zigmond, N. (1993). Learning disabilities from an educational perspective. In G. R. Lyon, D. B. Gray, J. F. Kavanaugh, & N. A. Krasnegor (Eds.), *Better understanding learning disabilities: New views from research and their implications for education and public policies* (pp. 251–272). Baltimore, MD: Paul H. Brookes.

Educational Services

CHAPTER 6

After studying this chapter, you should be able to:

- define *least restrictive environment* and *mainstreaming*.
- discuss severity of learning disabilities and its relationship to placement.
- identify the educational service alternatives for students with learning disabilities.
- describe advantages and disadvantages of service models for students with learning disabilities.
- identify strategies for the reintegration of students with learning disabilities.
- discuss the Regular Education Initiative and the inclusion movement.
- present the rationale for inclusion and the rationale for continuum alternative placements.
- discuss research on mainstreaming.
- discuss the efficacy of inclusion and of special classes and resource rooms.
- present program factors that promote successful mainstreaming.
- discuss team approaches involved in teachers teaching teachers.
- describe the role of the learning disabilities teacher.
- discuss approaches involved in students teaching students.

The Individuals with Disabilities Act (IDEA) of 1990, which incorporates Public Law 94-142, requires that each student with a disability receive a free, appropriate education. To ensure this right, the law mandates that an individualized educational program (IEP) be developed for each student and approved by the parent. (Chapter 5 presents a detailed description of an IEP.) In developing the IEP, educators are faced with the task of placing the student in an educational setting tailored to the student's learning and social-emotional needs. The setting in which services are provided has a strong influence on the student, the teacher, and the family. For years, educational programs for students with learning disabilities were operated by special education teachers in special classes or resource rooms outside the general education class. Under the current law, the general classroom teacher assumes more of the responsibility for educating students with learning disabilities. This chapter discusses the selection of special education services, various service provisions and practices, the movement from mainstreaming to inclusion, and program factors related to the least restrictive environment.

SELECTION OF SPECIAL EDUCATION SERVICES

Selecting the appropriate school setting for serving students with learning disabilities is a complex and important task. This decision affects the quality of instruction provided and determines who does the teaching and who becomes the student's peer group. In essence, the placement decision significantly influences the student's attitude, achievement, and social development. In making the placement decision, educators are required by law to select the setting that represents the student's least restrictive environment.

Least Restrictive Environment and Mainstreaming

According to IDEA, the term *least restrictive environment* (LRE) means that, to the extent appropriate, students with disabilities should be educated with students without disabilities. The IEP committee (typically the student's parents, learning disabilities teacher, school psychologist, school administrator, and other professionals as needed) collectively decides the student's least restrictive environment by determining the setting that best meets the student's social and educational needs. Selecting the student's "most enabling environment" is a more positive way of conceptualizing LRE. Historically, students with disabilities were pulled out of general classrooms and placed in self-contained classes. LRE is based on the premise that placement of youngsters who have disabilities with youngsters who do not results in improved academic and social development for students with disabilities and reduces the stigma associated with being educated in segregated settings. The least restrictive principle stresses the need for using a continuum of services sensitive to diverse needs.

A perspective on this idea is enhanced by examining Deno's (1970) "cascade" system, which describes services in terms of seven levels. As a student moves from Level 1 to Level 7, the degree of segregation from students in general education classes increases:

1. General class assignment with or without supportive services
2. General class assignment plus supplementary instructional services
3. Part-time special class
4. Full-time special class
5. Special school assignment within public school system
6. Homebound instruction
7. Placement in facilities operated by health or welfare agencies

IDEA does not mention the term *mainstreaming*; however, its use is widespread. Mainstreaming springs from the least restrictive environment concept and is used extensively to refer to the practice of integrating students with disabilities socially and instructionally into general education as much as possible. Some authorities debate the similarities and differences of mainstreaming and LRE; however, when both are practiced responsibly, they are similar. When mainstreaming simply involves placing students who have disabilities with normally achieving students without regard for the optimal social and academic growth of the individual student, it is not being practiced responsibly.

EDUCATIONAL SERVICE PROVISIONS AND RELATED PRACTICES

The primary factor in selecting a placement involves determining the best setting for the individual student. Thus, it is necessary to determine the severity of the student's problem(s). Weller (1980) discusses areas that relate to level of severity and placement decisions. Her model (see Table 6.1) focuses attention on criteria that guide educators in selecting placements in which the student is most likely to succeed.

With the numerous placement options available, it often is difficult to select the most appropriate one. About 24.7% of students with learning disabilities receive instruction entirely within general classrooms, 54.2% are served in both resource rooms and general classrooms, 20% are in self-contained classes, and 0.9% are in separate schools (U.S. Department of Education, 1994). Students with learning disabilities have a wide range of needs, and schools vary in the types of resources available. Thus, needs and resources must be examined *student by student* and not be guided by trends or philosophies insensitive to uniqueness.

Figure 6.1 presents a core of necessary alternatives to serve a heterogeneous population of students with learning disabilities. The three major categories of services are general class, special class, and special school. The alternatives are arranged in the figure from bottom to top, and it is in this order that segregation, labeling, and severity of need of the recipients usually increase. In establishing objectives for a student with learning disabilities, it is important to adopt a tentative commitment to a program level and not consider placement in any program as permanent or terminal. Educators must provide these youngsters with programs that continuously will respond to their unique needs. Whenever feasible, a student needs to move from the more restricted setting to the most integrated placement. In addition, placement within a particular program alternative needs to be considered when it appears that a change would be beneficial. For example, a student may be moved from one general classroom to another because a specific teacher has certain qualities or uses an instructional program that is suited specifically to the student.

The appropriate use of the various service alternatives requires careful planning. Table 6.2 presents selected service alternatives with respective advantages and disadvantages.

The General Education Class

More than 78% of students with learning disabilities spend most of their time in general education classes (U.S. Department of Education, 1994). In this placement, the student spends most of the day with youngsters of the same age. Affleck, Madge, Adams, and Lowenbraun (1988) compared the academic achievement of students with learning disabilities in an integrated classroom model with the achievement of students with learning disabilities in a resource room program. No significant differences were found between the achievement scores (i.e., in reading, math, and language) of the students in the respective programs. Affleck et al. note that the integrated classroom model was shown to be less costly than the resource room program but that the two placements achieved similar results. Many issues regarding the general class placement are discussed in this chapter in the section on the movement from mainstreaming to inclusion.

Keogh (1990) notes that the key to success for the student with disabilities placed in the general classroom is the general classroom teacher. Factors that deserve consideration include the teacher's attitude toward having a student with a

TABLE 6.1
Criteria for Severity of Learning Disabilities

Criteria Considerations	Mild	Moderate	Severe
Academic/socialization correspondence	Poor correspondence in the other academic and socialization areas.	Academic problems have some scattered effect on other academic and socialization components but no direct correlation.	Academic problem correlates highly with other academic and socialization skills, rendering the student functionally incapacitated in one area.
Alteration of future life needs	Can function with problem without difficulty after leaving school.	Will experience some problems in an adult world, but can overcome them to live and work normally, if somewhat selectively.	Will need special assistance to be employable or functional in some adult roles. Assistance will need to continue into adulthood.
Remediation vs. compensation	Problem amenable to remediation using standard methods: Results will be proficiency and efficiency the same as others'.	Problem amenable to compensation using standard alternative methods: Results will be proficiency and efficiency slightly less than others'.	Problem requires compensation using prosthetic alternatives or radical teaching methods: Results will be far less efficiency and proficiency than others'.
Effect on social skills with peers and adults	Will be able to solve own problems with peer relationships either in socially acceptable or socially unacceptable ways.	Will tend to exhibit behavior disorders in peer relationships. Teacher must manage behavior through planned intervention in the classroom.	Will need to learn how to cope with normal peers. Teacher becomes a public relations person for the student who must understand the nature of the disability and its limitations.
Avoidance of problem areas	Uses the problem areas to some degree with some efficiency, e.g., will read for information and pleasure.	Uses the problem areas for necessary tasks on demand with impaired efficiency, e.g., will try to read assignments but will avoid pleasure reading.	Will actively solicit areas other than the problem areas in learning, e.g., will use TV or tapes rather than read; will listen rather than take notes.

Note: Adapted from "Discrepancy and Severity in the Learning Disabled: A Consolidated Perspective" by C. Weller, 1980, *Learning Disability Quarterly, 3*(1), p. 88. Copyright 1980 by the Division for Children with Learning Disabilities. Reprinted by permission of the Council for Learning Disabilities.

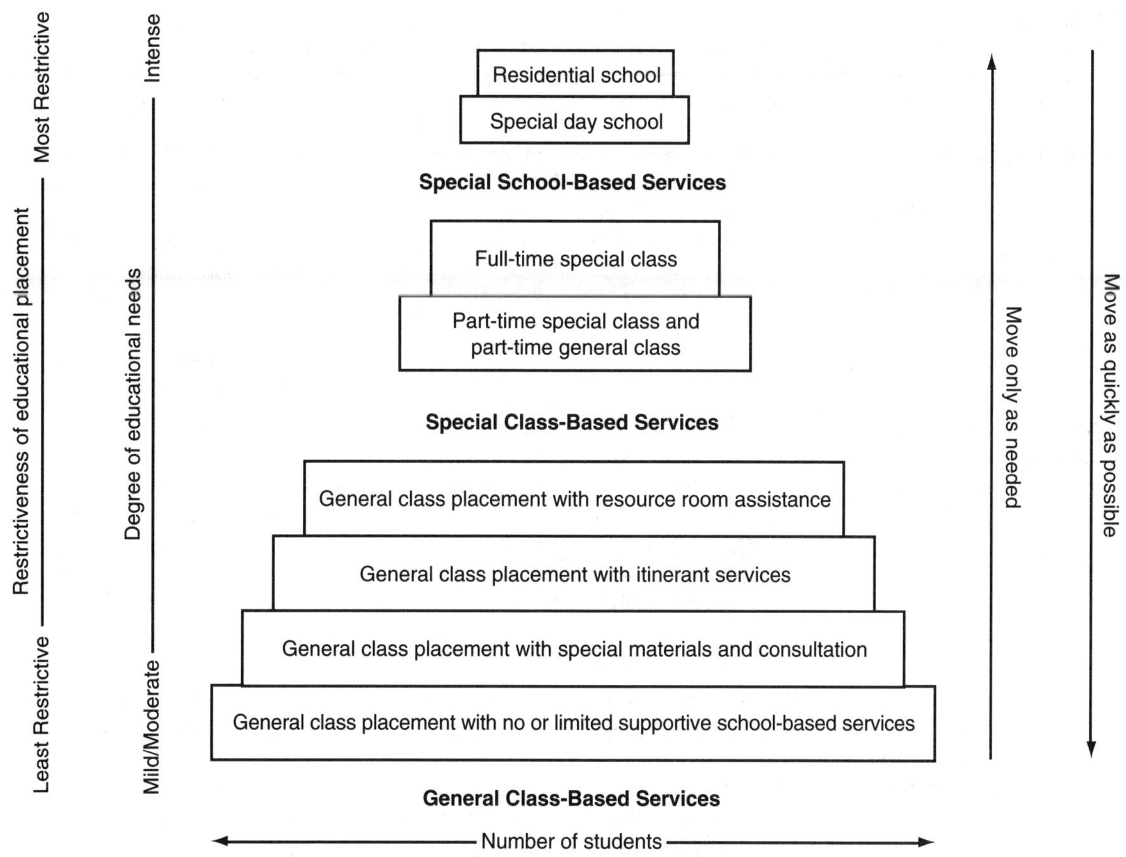

FIGURE 6.1
Continuum of educational placements for students with learning disabilities

disability in the classroom, the teacher's judgment of the student's capacity to make progress, the teacher's ability to deal with peer acceptance problems, and the teacher's skill in dealing with the emotional behavior and problems that may result from the student's inability to compete academically with other students. It is apparent that the general classroom teacher has an enormous responsibility, and it is important that these teachers receive preparation and support. For example, teacher assistance teams and coaching are useful types of support. Moreover, a student with a learning disability should not be placed in a general classroom with a teacher who does not believe that the student will profit.

Special Materials and Consultation. Occasionally, a teacher can manage with the help of additional materials such as a supplementary reading series, learning strategy materials, computer-assisted instruction, content enhancement materials, or manipulative materials for math. To be successful, the teacher must have a reasonable student-teacher ratio (e.g., mid-20s to 1, or lower), especially in the earlier grades (Mueller, Chase, & Walden, 1988). The teacher also may be provided with limited consultation, usually by a learning disabilities teacher. Consultation may consist of demonstrating the use of materials or equipment, performing an assessment, developing specific learning strategies, or providing an inservice

TABLE 6.2
Advantages and Disadvantages of Service Models for Students with Learning Disabilities

Model	Advantages	Disadvantages
General Classroom (LD student remains in general class all day)	Provides for interaction of peers with and without disabilities in least restrictive setting Prevents needless labeling	May compound learning disabilities with instructional factors Includes large number in class population Uses a teacher not specifically trained May not provide small-group or individual instruction
Consultant (Consultant teacher works with general teacher)	Can reach more teachers Can supply specific instructional methods, programs, and materials Can serve more students Influences environmental learning variables Coordinates comprehensive services for students	May not foster inclusion in teaching staff Does not provide firsthand knowledge of students that comes from teaching them Can separate assessment and instruction
Itinerant (Itinerant teacher travels to various schools and consults with general teachers)	Aids in screening and diagnosis Provides some help in area of consulting Offers part-time services Covers needs of students in different schools or areas Is an economical way to address mild problems	Does not provide consistent support for more involved students Does not promote identification with staff Presents difficulty in transporting materials Lacks continuity of program Lacks regular follow-up
Resource Room (LD student spends portion of school day—45–60 minutes—with resource room teacher)	Emphasizes instructional remediation Supplements general classroom instruction Separates students with disabilities from peers without disabilities for limited periods of the school day Provides individualized instruction in problem areas through specially trained teacher May provide consulting services to general teachers Prevents needless labeling Focuses on mainstreaming students	Is not well suited to serve students with severe learning disabilities Presents scheduling problems Tends toward overenrollment Can create misunderstanding of teacher role May inspire conflicts in teacher role Provides no time to observe or consult Provides little time to assess and plan

TABLE 6.2
continued

Model	Advantages	Disadvantages
Special Class (LD student spends majority of school day in special class for LD students)	Constitutes least restrictive setting for some severe cases Provides environmental conditions necessary to meet needs of students with severe disabilities Permits individual or small-group instruction Maintains self-esteem Emphasizes acceptance of the student Provides full-time attention on one teacher Provides full-time highly specialized learning conditions	Is segregated Permits extremely limited interaction with peers without disabilities May stigmatize Has danger of misplacement May become an inappropriate permanent placement Is restrictive for mild and moderate cases May model inappropriate behaviors Fosters low teacher expectation
Special Day School (LD student spends entire school day at a special school)	Permits full use of limited resources of trained personnel and space Accommodates a large number of moderate and severe cases of learning disabilities Centralizes diagnostic, teaching, and consulting services Provides means to develop a model program for later replication Provides special curriculum and environment Provides a special environment while permitting students the advantage of remaining in their homes and communities	Is still self-contained Offers no interactions with peers without disabilities during the school day Is not the least restrictive environment in all cases Can be expensive Removes pressure for the development of local services
Residential School (LD student lives at a special school)	Permits occupational training Allows attention to diet and necessary medical treatment Provides opportunities for involvement in all facets of normal school life within the school program Demonstrates appropriate diagnosis and teaching procedures	Segregates students from mainstream of society Entails financial expense Has high rate of retention Is not the least restrictive environment May lack quality control

Note: Adapted form *Learning Disabilities: Concepts and Characteristics* (pp. 251–253), 3rd ed., by G. Wallace and J. A. McLoughlin, 1988, Upper Saddle River, NJ: Merrill/Prentice Hall. Copyright 1988 by Prentice-Hall Publishing Company. Reprinted by permission.

program. Collaborative consultation is a service that should be inherent in all general class-based service alternatives. (Consultation skills are discussed later in this chapter.)

Itinerant Services. General class teachers sometimes have students in class whose difficulties are not severe enough to warrant resource room instruction or special class placement. In such cases, an itinerant teacher usually visits the schools periodically and focuses on teaching skills and special materials. These consultation services range from daily to biweekly visits, with the classroom teacher still having the basic responsibility for the student. Obviously, the itinerant teacher must be careful in scheduling visits to avoid interrupting the activities of the general classroom teacher. Occasionally, itinerant services are bolstered through the use of volunteers or teacher aides.

Resource Room Assistance. Many students with learning disabilities spend the majority of the day in a general class and go to the resource room for a specified period of time (e.g., 45 to 60 minutes) each day. The resource room teacher, located in the school, works closely with numerous teachers to coordinate the instructional programs of the students. Friend and McNutt (1984) conducted a survey in the 50 states and the District of Columbia regarding the use of the resource room model. Results indicate that in all states and the District of Columbia the resource room is the most frequently used alternative to the general classroom for serving students with mild to moderate disabilities. Friend and McNutt report much variation in the types of services offered within this approach.

Because the resource room teacher provides daily services to about 20 to 30 students with disabilities and their respective teachers, the role demands a highly competent, personable individual. Specifically, Wiederholt (1974) believes it is essential for the resource room teacher to be able to work effectively and harmoniously with teachers and ancillary staff, assess the educational needs of students, and design and implement prescriptive teaching.

Speece and Mandell (1980) surveyed 228 general educators about resource room services. The teachers indicated that resource room teachers should provide these nine support services:

1. Attend parent conferences (74.2%)
2. Meet informally to discuss student progress (74.2%)
3. Provide remedial instruction in the resource room (67.0%)
4. Provide information on behavioral characteristics (54.5%)
5. Provide academic assessment data (53.9%)
6. Schedule meetings to evaluate student progress (52.7%)
7. Provide materials for classroom (52.1%)
8. Suggest materials for classroom (52.1%)
9. Provide written reports of students' activities and progress (51.5%)

Because many of these services require consultation from resource room teachers, Speece and Mandell as well as Idol (1989) encourage more inservice and preservice programs that emphasize the development of consultation skills.

Most students with learning disabilities are served in one of three types of resource room models: categorical, cross-categorical, or noncategorical. Categorical programs serve only students with learning disabilities. Cross-categorical programs serve exceptional students from several categorical areas (i.e., educable mentally retarded, emotionally disabled, and learning disabled). Noncategorical programs meet the educational needs of students with mild learning problems whether they are classified as disabled or not.

Wiederholt and Chamberlain (1989) conducted a critical analysis of resource rooms. Although respective resource room programs vary considerably, they found that resource programs are lumped together in efficacy research. After examining 37 efficacy studies of resource room programs, they report that the results are conflicting and the studies are beset with serious methodological flaws. Wiederholt and Chamberlain recommend improved research efforts before making final judgments about the model. They conclude their analysis with the following passage:

> In sum, the critics of resource programs may be correct in stating that these pull-out programs have failed in many instances to meet the needs of students assigned to these settings. However, the fault may not be with the model itself. Instead, the fault may lie in the fact that these programs are still evolving. Once defined and refined, these programs may well serve as one viable delivery system within the schools for students who are handicapped and those who are at risk for school failure. (p. 25)

Idol (1989) describes a model for improving resource room services. Specifically, she recommends a resource/consulting teacher model that provides direct and indirect services. The direct services consist of assessment and instruction in problem areas relevant to general school success. Indirect services include working with teachers in a consultant role to assist and support teachers in their work with students who have learning or behavior problems.

From a review of the research, Smith (1994) reports that some research supports the effectiveness of resource room services in increasing the attending behavior and academic achievement of the students served. Moreover, she notes that peer acceptance and self-concepts of students attending resource rooms do not appear to diminish. Smith, however, notes that the resource room model has several disadvantages associated with pulling students out of their general classes. The disadvantages of the resource room program include the following:

1. The student may miss valuable lessons in general education while attending the resource room.
2. The student may miss some enjoyable activities (e.g., music, physical education, and art) in the general education class while attending the resource room.
3. The student may feel stigmatized for leaving the general classroom to receive special help.
4. The resource room and general classroom teacher may fail to coordinate instruction.

To deal with these disadvantages, push-in models as opposed to pull-out models are being developed. In the push-in models, the resource room teacher provides instruction in the general education classroom. The resource room teacher's activities may include working with an individual student, team teaching with the general education teacher by teaching the entire class independently or together, and teaching small groups of students in certain content areas. When the resource room teacher works with all the students periodically, it helps decrease the stigma associated with having a teacher only for students who have learning problems. As previously mentioned, these integrated arrangements have yielded equivocal academic gains with less cost than resource room programs.

The Content Mastery Center Program at Corsicanna High School in Corsicanna, Texas, is an example of a resource room in which the general educator has primary responsibility for teaching specific content areas, while the special educator teaches specific strategies or skills to students who need additional instruction. The goal of the Content Mastery Center is to assure that students with disabilities who are enrolled in general classes progress satisfactorily and receive passing grades. The Center is available to students during any class time when they are not receiving direct instruction from the general classroom teacher, and the decision of when to use the Center is made by the student. A Weekly Grade Check Form, filled out by general classroom teachers, reports the grades and performance of each mainstreamed student and alerts the staff of the Center that a student may need to be urged to utilize the Center's services. The Center is staffed full-time by a learning disabilities teacher and an aide, and it offers excellent curriculum resources. All of the school textbooks are available in the Center with important information in each book highlighted. Textbooks and library books on tape, along with audiotape players, also are provided, as well as materials for classroom projects for students who need ideas, materials, and help designing a project. In addition to giving small-group instruction, helping with projects, and keeping in touch with parents on a regular basis, the Center's teachers provide one-to-one tutoring and individualized instruction according to individual student needs.

The Part- and Full-time Special Class

Initially, public schools used special classes for students with learning disabilities. Cruickshank, Bentzen, Ratzeburg, and Tannhauser (1961) provide one of the first descriptions of a special class for students with brain injury and hyperactivity. Their plan features a highly structured program and a reduction of distracting stimuli. In general, these classes consist of 8 to 12 students, a special education teacher, an aide, and the services of supportive personnel (e.g., a speech clinician, physical education teacher, music teacher, and visiting teacher). The students either receive their entire academic instruction within the self-contained class or attend general classes for part of the day.

Because special classes do not provide much integration with other segments of the school, careful consideration should be given to assigning a student to such a class. For years, many educators have questioned the efficacy of using special classes for students with mild disabilities. Dunn (1973) notes the following concerns:

> The self-contained special-class plan has been most severely criticized when used with slow-learning and disruptive children. Too often the plan has been used to put out of sight pupils the regular teachers do not want. It is to be hoped, however, that this practice will not disguise the appropriateness of the plan, especially for children with severe learning disabilities and for younger children. Certain of these children may need an intensive, specialized curriculum to learn specific skills so as to take a greater part in the regular school program later in their school careers. (p. 28)

Beck, Lindsey, and Frith (1981) examined how special class placement affected these students intellectually. While math skills increased over several years, IQ, reading, and spelling scores did not. Beck et al. admit that these results are discouraging to proponents of self-contained service; however, they advise that placement be determined individually.

Special class placement should be considered only for the student with a serious learning disability (e.g., Strauss syndrome, severe dyslexia, or aphasia). When the special class is deemed appropriate, certain criteria are essential:

1. The special class teacher should be trained to teach the type of students in the class.
2. The students should be selected on the basis of learning or social-emotional problems, not on the basis of socioeconomic status or race.
3. The students should receive intensive and systematic instruction tailored to their unique needs.
4. A wide variety of teaching materials and resources should be available to the teacher.
5. The class size should be considerably smaller than that of a general class.
6. A variety of teaching styles is needed to accommodate the different needs of the students.
7. Each student's progress should be monitored constantly. Reintegration into the mainstream should be considered when it appears to be feasible.
8. The class should have administrative support.

Lovitt (1989) reports that much of the research on the efficacy of self-contained classrooms for students with learning disabilities is not conclusive. Most of the research has significant methodological flaws. Moreover, Hallahan and Kauffman (1994) note that most of the efficacy research was conducted from 1960 to 1980 and that special class and mainstreaming practices have improved since these studies. Lovitt notes that the absence of firm conclusions is not surprising when consideration is given to the variability in teacher effectiveness across the studies.

It is reasonable to assume that there are students with learning disabilities in special classes who are receiving an excellent education and there are those who are not. It remains a student-by-student and setting-by-setting decision.

The Special School

Students with severe learning or emotional problems who have difficulty functioning in the regular school may attend a special day school either part-time or full-time. In school systems combining regular and special schools, these students are transported for part of the day to a central school where they receive extra instructional help. Some schools have no services available for students with severe problems, and, in these areas, such students may be educated entirely at a special school. Many educators believe that these settings are too segregated and that all students deserve the opportunity to attend their neighborhood schools.

In some instances, students with learning disabilities attend a private residential school that offers low teacher-student ratios, intensive instruction, and counseling. If the residential school primarily serves exceptional students, it may be viewed as isolated from the mainstream. If it serves all types of students, including those with learning disabilities, it may represent an integrated placement, consistent with the mainstream movement. Some primary considerations involved in a special school placement include (a) severity of the problems, (b) costs to the family, (c) transportation, (d) degree of isolation, (e) home conditions, and (f) parental requests.

Reintegration of Students

To meet the requirements of educating students with learning disabilities in their least restrictive or most enabling environment, it is imperative that educators constantly evaluate each student's needs and progress to determine whether a placement change is appropriate, especially if the student's needs appear to warrant a less restrictive service model. Thus, for students in more restrictive placements, educators frequently must examine the feasibility of reintegrating each student successfully into the general classroom. Critics maintain that too many students with disabilities are identified, labeled, and placed in special education settings without appropriate emphasis given to changing these students' programs or returning them to the mainstream.

Halgren and Clarizio (1993) studied 211 students with learning disabilities from rural schools over a 3-year period to determine the proportion whose classification or degree of services changed. They report that 10% were terminated from special education, 11.4% were reclassified, and 74.6% experienced no classification change. Given that appropriately diagnosed learning disabilities tend to persist into adulthood, it is not surprising that about 75% of the students retained their classification. Program changes for students with learning disabilities involved 25.1% being placed in less restrictive programs, 64% maintained in the same program, and 10.9% being placed in more restrictive programs. Halgren and Clarizio conclude that these program and service changes occurred more frequently than was expected. It is apparent, at least for these students, that their status and programs were monitored and that changes were made to accommodate their needs.

Sabornie (1985) stresses the need for educators to consider the social consequences of integrating students who have disabilities with students without disabilities. Research involving students with learning disabilities indicates that they are not popular in general classes (Horne, 1985). Sabornie concludes that educators must teach essential social skills to students with disabilities to ensure that students without disabilities will not be negative toward them. Salend and Lutz (1984) surveyed general and special educators in elementary schools to ascertain which social skills are considered critical to successful functioning in the mainstream setting. The 15

TABLE 6.3
Student Behavioral Competencies for Success in Secondary Mainstream Settings

Obeying Classroom Rules
Attends class regularly
Obeys class rules
Follows directions
Refrains from cutting classes
Refrains from speaking when others are talking
Exhibits appropriate behavior in large-group settings
Seeks teacher permission before speaking
Avoids distractions

Interacting Appropriately
Avoids getting in fights with others
Respects adults
Refrains from cursing and swearing
Communicates needs
Remembers more than one oral direction at a time
Is aware of the effects of behavior on others
Refrains from boastful comments concerning inappropriate behaviors
Respects the feelings of others
Works well with others

Displaying Appropriate Work Habits
Brings necessary materials to class
Tries to complete a task before giving up
Asks for help when it is appropriate
Completes classwork and homework on time
Demonstrates an adequate attention span
Begins an assignment after the teacher gives it to the class

Displaying Basic Values
Refrains from stealing others' property
Respects the property of others
Tells the truth
Refrains from cheating on tests
Displays proper health and hygiene habits

competencies identified are organized into three categories: (a) interacting positively with others, (b) obeying class rules, and (c) displaying proper work habits. In a later study, Salend and Salend (1986) identified student behaviors needed to be successful in secondary mainstream settings. These behavioral competencies are listed in Table 6.3. Although there are numerous similarities among the competencies needed to succeed in elementary and secondary settings, Salend (1994) notes that the expectations for success in the higher grades are more stringent regarding classroom decorum and behavioral expectations. He also reports that junior high school educators tend to be more stringent than their senior high school counterparts.

Ellett (1993) surveyed secondary teachers to determine student skills and behaviors that they considered necessary for success in general classrooms. She developed the following rank ordering of student competencies (skills or behaviors) important to success in secondary classes:

1. Follows directions in class
2. Comes to class prepared with materials
3. Uses class time wisely
4. Makes up assignments and tests
5. Treats teachers and peers with courtesy
6. Completes and turns in homework on time
7. Works cooperatively in student groups
8. Completes tests with a passing grade
9. Appears interested in content
10. Takes notes in class
11. Scans a textbook for answers and information
12. Volunteers to answer questions in class
13. Writes neatly
14. Is able to give oral reports and speeches

It is apparent that academic and social skills criteria provide placement teams with critical information for determining whether the student is ready to be reintegrated into the mainstream setting.

Anderson-Inman (1986) suggests an excellent four-step transenvironmental programming model for planning and implementing a program to prepare students for success in mainstream settings. The four steps include environmental assessment, intervention and preparation, generalization, and evaluation of target environment. The environmental assessment step entails the determination of the setting demands (e.g., skills and behaviors) of the targeted mainstream setting. The intervention and preparation step involves teaching students the skills and behaviors needed to meet the setting demands. In the generalization step, students are encouraged to use the skills in the general classroom. Finally, the evaluation step involves determining how well the students acquire and use the skills in the mainstream environment. Moreover, Salend and Viglianti (1982) recommend examining the following factors in determining the setting demands of a mainstream classroom: (a) instructional materials and support personnel, (b) presentation formats of content, (c) student response types, (d) student evaluation formats, (e) classroom management, and (f) social interactions and physical design.

Specific guidelines for reintegration include the following:

1. Help students and parents adjust to modifications or a reduction of special education services.
2. Include the respective teachers and solicit their observations of the student in relation to placement decisions.
3. Use fading techniques when changing placements.
4. Be sure the new classroom teacher can make the necessary minor adjustments (Chalfant, 1985; Ellett, 1993).
5. Make certain the exiting criteria include the same variables used in identifying and placing the student (Chalfant, 1985).

In addition, a social comparison method may help determine when reintegration is feasible. First, data are collected on the performances of general classroom peers. When the student performs similarly to peers without disabilities on several critical skills, reintegration is appropriate. Epstein and Cullinan (1979) note that such peer data may be better criteria than teacher intuition or norms on standardized tests.

Obviously, dismissal from a learning disabilities program originates from a re-evaluation of the student's needs and progress. The IEP format offers the teacher an excellent opportunity to examine the possibility of reintegration. If observations indicate that a change is warranted, the teacher can initiate a meeting or re-evaluate the existing IEP.

MOVEMENT FROM MAINSTREAMING TO INCLUSION

When Public Law 94-142 was passed in 1975, it mandated that students with disabilities be provided services in their least restrictive environment. Restriction was interpreted in terms of the amount of time students were educated in classes with their peers without disabilities. The more time students with disabilities spent in settings with peers without disabilities, the less restrictive was the setting. The more time they spent in placements separated from their peers without disabilities, the more restrictive was the setting. Ensuing efforts to educate students with disabilities in classes with their peers without disabilities resulted in an emphasis on mainstreaming.

Mainstreaming emphasized keeping students with learning disabilities in general education classes as much as possible. Mainstreaming was implemented in collaboration with the continuum of special education placement options listed earlier in this chapter. Although some students with learning disabilities remained in part-time and full-time special classes, the most popular service delivery format was the resource room. Most students with learning disabilities attended the resource room for one or two periods a day and remained in general education classes for the remainder of the day. In the resource room, the students received special help as outlined in their IEPs. The dual system of general education placements being supported with selected special education placements continued without serious challenges until 1986. Beginning in 1986, the Regular Education Initiative (REI) promoted the position that students with disabilities be educated in general education classes without pull-out special education services.

The Regular Education Initiative

Madeleine Will, Assistant Secretary for the Office of Special Education and Rehabilitative Services in the Reagan administration, and other educators (Reynolds, 1989; Stainback & Stainback, 1987; Wang, Reynolds, & Walberg, 1986) promoted a system of service delivery to special education students referred to as the Regular Education Initiative (REI). The REI included major revisions in how services are provided to students with learning disabilities. It maintained that a dual system of general and special education is not necessary and that students with learning disabilities can be served more effectively within the general education setting. In essence, the REI recommended that the continuum of special education service alternatives be eliminated and that students with learning disabilities, as well as other special education students, be served totally within the general classroom. REI proponents note that this position is based on the supposition that general education programs can be improved (e.g., through collaborative consultation, effective teaching practices, and curriculum-based assessment) to accommodate students with special needs.

The REI emerged because Will (1986) and several of her colleagues (Wang et al., 1986) maintained that negative consequences occur when special education students are separated from their peers without disabilities to receive instructional services. Specifically, Will offered the following statements as a rationale for the REI:

1. Some students with learning or behavior problems who need special services do not qualify for special education.
2. Students are stigmatized when they are put in special education placements that separate them from their normally achieving classmates.
3. Special education students usually are identified after they develop serious learning problems; therefore, the emphasis is on failure rather than prevention.
4. The special education system, with its eligibility requirements and rigid rules, may not lead to cooperative school-parent relationships.

The REI stimulated much debate and discussion among special educators. There was agreement that general and special educators need to coordinate their services and educate special education students according to the least restrictive environment; however, there was much concern about completely changing the current continuum of services available through special education. During the latter part of the 1980s, the REI position became part of the inclusion movement.

The Inclusion Movement

During the early 1990s, the REI position gained substantial momentum within the context of inclusion. The inclusion movement, however, highlighted the social value of inclusive classes and the need to place individuals with severe disabilities in general education classes (Fuchs & Fuchs, 1994). Also, the inclusion movement stressed strong opposition to the continuum of placements. Likewise, opposition to educating students with and without disabilities in general education classes without the continuum of alternative placements increased. This section examines the relative positions on where students with disabilities should be educated.

The Inclusion Position. Sapon-Shevin notes that inclusion embraces the vision that all students be served in their neighborhood schools in the general classroom with individuals their own age (O'Neil, 1994/1995). These inclusive schools are restructured to be supportive, nurturing communities that meet the needs of all individuals within them, and the schools have substantial resources and support for students and teachers. Sapon-Shevin maintains that little evidence exists to support the education of students in segregated settings. She espouses that inclusive schools are based on the belief that the world is an inclusive community with people who vary not only in terms of disabilities but in race, class, gender, and religious background. To prepare students to live in an inclusive world, it is important for them to learn and grow within communities that are similar to the world they will live in as adults. Sapon-Shevin believes that educators should begin with the assumption that all students are included and their needs will be met in inclusive settings.

The Continuum of Alternative Placements Position. During the mid-1970s, the consensus of advocates for students with disabilities was that students with disabilities should be part of mainstream classes. This viewpoint was incorporated into Public Law 94-142 with the least restrictive environment mandate. This mandate was retained in the Individuals with Disabilities Education Act of 1990. However, Yell (1995) notes that results of litigation show that IDEA supports the continuum of placements rather than forcing the placement of students with disabilities in the general classroom. He states, "At times, the mainstream will be the appropriate placement; however, IDEA and case law interpreting the LRE mandate are clear that for some students with disabilities, the appropriate and least restrictive setting will not be the regular education classroom. . . .The most important placement factor must be the individual needs of the student" (p. 402).

The need for a continuum of alternative placements is based on the assumption that options ranging from full-time placement in general education classrooms to placement in special residential schools or hospitals are essential to meet the diverse needs of students with disabilities. Kauffman notes that educators have to justify every placement decision, inclusive or otherwise (O'Neil, 1994/1995). He states, "Sure, we ought to meet special needs in a regular class when that's possible. But there isn't anything wrong with meeting special needs outside the regular class if that is required. In fact, the law and best practice say we must consider both possibilities" (O'Neil, 1994/1995, p. 7).

In essence, the continuum of alternative placements position rests on the assumption that students with disabilities need optional placements to learn in a manner commensurate with their potential. Prescriptive educations are needed to help them become independent and productive members of society. An inspection of the two positions reveals that both support the idea of educating students in general classes. The inclusion position adopts a general education class placement only, whereas the continuum of alternative placements position recommends the continuation of placement options.

Rationale for Inclusion

Statements of the rationale for inclusion include the following:

1. Many inclusionists believe that placing students in integrated or inclusive settings is morally the correct thing to do. Stainback, Stainback, East, and Sapon-Shevin (1994) state that many educators believe that the practice of grouping students homogeneously based on a common characteristic is inappropriate for moral reasons involving equality. Placing students in settings apart from the mainstream is considered a form of segregation. They note that in the *Brown v. Board of Education* decision, Chief Justice Warren (1954) maintained that segregation produces ill effects and "separate is not equal" (p. 493).
2. The identification and consequent labeling of students within special education categories is harmful to students. Labels lower students' self-esteem and cause others to develop biased viewpoints (e.g., lower expectations) toward them. Inclusion decreases the need to label. Inclusionists (Stainback et al., 1994; Wang, Reynolds, & Walberg, 1994/1995) maintain that instead of labeling and segregating students, educators must find ways to educate all students in inclusive settings that acknowledge individual differences and respond to their needs within a common context.
3. The efficacy of placing students categorically identified in special education placements apart from the mainstream has not been established. Poplin (1988) claims that a major goal of the past 2 decades has been the successful integration of students with learning disabilities into general classes. McLeskey and Pacchiano (1994) state, "Certainly, if any group of students with disabilities should be educated in typical classroom settings, it is students with learning disabilities" (p. 509). Wang et al. (1994/1995) claim that a broad consensus is emerging among educators that

favors abandoning the categorical approach for students with mild disabilities and replacing it with a more inclusive approach.

4. According to Sapon-Shevin, placing students outside the mainstream lessens schoolwide efforts to develop responsible inclusive settings for serving students with disabilities (O'Neil, 1994/1995).
5. Through collaboration among special educators, general educators, parents, and other service providers, the educational needs of all students can be met in general education classes.
6. Placing students with and without disabilities together provides educators with opportunities to teach youngsters to understand and appreciate individual differences. Sapon-Shevin notes that these experiences help prepare students to function in inclusive societies (O'Neil, 1994/1995).

There is a great deal of conviction and passion surrounding the inclusion movement. E. T. Baker, Wang, and Walberg (1994/1995) state, "As schools are challenged to effectively serve an increasingly diverse student population, the concern is not *whether* to provide inclusive education, but *how to implement* inclusive education in ways that are both feasible and effective in ensuring schooling success for all children, especially those with special needs" (p. 34). Moreover, Sapon-Shevin believes that "inclusion is much bigger than special education, much bigger than individual classrooms; it's even much bigger than the school. Inclusion really calls for a fundamental restructuring of the school districts and the schools" (O'Neil, 1994/1995, p. 9).

Rationale for Continuum of Alternative Placements

Statements of the rationale for continuum of alternative placements include the following:

1. The general class placement and the continuum of placements apart from the mainstream are necessary to meet the intense and diverse needs of students with disabilities. Kauffman and Pullen (1989) report that existing service systems need to be maintained and repaired through systematic investigation, and they believe that educators should proceed deliberately. Under the current continuum of special education services, 78% of special education students spend a substantial portion of their time in general class settings (U.S. Department of Education, 1994). This condition provides a rich source of investigation and the opportunity to proceed deliberately.
2. The history of special education documents the enormous efforts that parents, legislators, educators, and organizations have expended in securing these varied and intense service delivery alternatives. Inclusion threatens the loss of service options that advocates have spent years obtaining.
3. The availability of the continuum of alternative placements has been mandated by law since 1975. The mandate reflects the wishes of many parents, educators, and legislators. The position statements of the Learning Disabilities Association of America, the Division for Learning Disabilities, the Council for Learning Disabilities, the American Federation of Teachers, Children and Adults with Attention Deficit Disorders, the Council for Exceptional Children, and many other organizations support the continuum of alternative placements, and the loss of these service options violates the civil rights of students with disabilities (Kauffman & Hallahan, 1995).
4. The efficacy research regarding special classes has serious methodological problems and was conducted so long ago that it has little relevance to current practices in special classes (Hallahan & Kauffman, 1994).
5. The efficacy research regarding resource room programs has serious methodological flaws, is dated, and has inconclusive results (Hallahan & Kauffman, 1994; Wiederholt & Chamberlain, 1989).

6. General education teachers are not prepared to work with students who have disabilities. Keogh (1988) reports that one of the ironies of the REI is the widespread criticism of general education that gained momentum in the 1980s. Specifically, she states, "It is disturbing that the national reports are unanimous in their conclusion that the present system does not provide quality education to regular students. Can we assume that in its present form it will be adequate to incorporate the educational needs of pupils with learning and achievement problems?" (p. 20).
7. Many general educators do not support inclusion. Albert Shanker (1994/1995), President of the American Federation of Teachers, questions how teachers can meet the extraordinary demands of teaching in an inclusive classroom when they already are overburdened with overcrowded classes, persistent social problems, a diversity of learners, and a lack of training to teach students with various disabilities. He states, "Requiring *all* disabled children to be included in mainstream classrooms, regardless of their ability to function there, is not only unrealistic but also downright harmful—often for the children themselves" (p. 18).
8. There is no clear evidence that inclusion is appropriate for all students with disabilities, and evidence of its benefit for average and above-average students is lacking.
9. The charge to help youngsters learn to respect and appreciate individual differences and live at peace with all people who are not infringing on the rights and welfare of others is a noteworthy challenge of all educators. However, because many people believe that most societies in the United States and in the world, in many ways, are not inclusive, the assumption that educators must prepare youngsters through inclusive classroom settings to function in an inclusive society is questionable. People constantly group themselves in a number of ways, such as according to places of worship, neighborhoods, careers, club memberships, socioeconomic status, hobby interests, and university choices. To maintain that the intimate nature of an inclusive classroom community is replicated readily throughout societies of the world is inaccurate. Kauffman comments on the inclusiveness of society: "We're not all included in the same place doing the same or parallel activities; we go to many different places for different purposes. We may go to different places of worship and different places of work, for example, but that doesn't exclude us from being part of other communities outside those places, and it doesn't demean us. We ought to celebrate a diversity of places where we learn and work and play and have friends" (O'Neil, 1994/1995, p. 10).

Research on the Inclusion Versus Continuum of Alternative Placements Issue

One of the reasons that the inclusion versus the continuum of alternative placements issue continues with such intensity is that a solid research base does not exist to guide educators in making decisions about what placements are most appropriate for students with disabilities. Given the differences among communities, schools, students, teachers, curricula, leadership, and funding, it is difficult to compare service alternatives accurately. This section highlights the research on factors related to placements in which students with disabilities should be educated. It is intended to provide a beginning base for helping educators make responsible placement decisions.

Efficacy of Inclusion. The Adaptive Learning Environments Model (ALEM) was developed as a program to demonstrate the feasibility of the REI. The ALEM is a large-scale, full-time mainstreaming program in which students who are nondisabled, disabled, and at risk are integrated in the general classroom. While its advocates (Reynolds, Wang, & Walberg, 1987; Wang &

Zollers, 1990) report that ALEM is successful, other researchers are less positive. Fuchs and Fuchs (1988) and Bryan (1988) evaluated the statistical evidence available in the ALEM research and conclude that support is lacking to call ALEM successful. On the basis of the findings, they note that it is premature to endorse a merger of general and special education. Kauffman and Hallahan (1993) note that it is clear that ALEM has not been effective in meeting the needs of students with mild-to-moderate disabilities.

E. T. Baker et al. (1994/1995) examined three meta-analyses (E. T. Baker, 1994; Carlberg & Kavale, 1980; Wang & Baker, 1985/1986) that addressed the most appropriate placement issue for students with special needs. These meta-analyses yield a common measure called an *effect size.* E. T. Baker et al. report that the effect size for academic and social outcomes favored placement in general education over noninclusive settings by a slight margin.

From 1989 to 1993, the Office of Special Education and Rehabilitative Services supported four research projects to study the education of students with mild disabilities within the general classroom. The four projects were led by the following researchers: Sharon Vaughn and Jeanne Schumm at the University of Miami; Keith Lenz, Jean Schumaker, and Donald Deshler at the University of Kansas; Sue Gordon, Maureen Riley, and Catherine Morocco at the Education Development Center in Newton, Massachusetts; and Lynn Fuchs and Douglas Fuchs at Vanderbilt University. The research teams represented varying philosophical positions, used different research methodologies, and involved hundreds of elementary and secondary teachers from numerous curriculum areas. Amazingly, from this kaleidoscope of differences emerged a common core of vital findings about some of the challenges that teachers face when they attempt to educate a class of academically diverse students. The Joint Committee on Teacher Planning for Students with Disabilities (1995) reports the following four common themes:

Theme 1: *Teachers are sensitive to and concerned about at-risk students in their classes.* These attitudes existed among elementary *and* secondary teachers.

Theme 2: *Specific instructional procedures and tools are workable and effective for most students in general education classrooms.* Teachers were satisfied with the new procedures, and the majority of students, including high, middle, and low achievers, benefited. The instructional procedures included collaboration among teachers, the restructuring of lesson content in learner-friendly formats, and the use of classwide peer tutoring, curriculum-based measurement, and content enhancements.

Theme 3: *Consideration must be given to the complex realities of the general classroom setting when planning a program to meet the needs of students with disabilities.* Instructional procedures that were most readily adopted were those most easily incorporated into the flow of existing routines *and* perceived as benefiting all students in the classroom. Some of the realities facing general education teachers included pressure to cover a lot of content, raise the performance level of learners, teach large groups, prepare for many classes, and work with other teachers and staff.

Theme 4: *Some students with mild disabilities did not benefit from the adjustments made in the general education classroom.* A few students across all projects did not benefit from the instructional procedures. The demands of the inclusive classroom were so extensive that teachers did not have the time or energy to ensure that all students mastered the skills or content.

The researchers from the four projects overwhelmingly reached the following consensus: "In order for students with disabilities to be successfully included in the general education classroom, educators need to think in terms of '*supported* inclusion,' not simply 'inclusion' " (Joint Committee on Teacher Planning for Students with Disabilities, 1995, p. 5). The researchers provide the following set of instructional conditions to implement supported inclusion:

1. Teachers must be philosophically committed to meeting the needs of all students in the general education classroom.
2. Teachers must have time to plan and think about the needs of diverse learners.
3. Teaching practices that meet the needs of all students must be incorporated into the instructional program.
4. General education teachers must collaborate with special education teachers to assess, teach, and monitor student progress.
5. Short-term, intensive instruction from a special education teacher needs to be available for some students with disabilities.
6. Sustained instruction in basic skills or learning strategies that cannot be provided in general education classes must be available to some students with disabilities.

In essence, supported inclusion promotes the process of educating as many students as possible in the general education class, but for those students who fail to make acceptable progress in the general class, short-term and long-term instruction in alternative settings is recommended.

Research on Mainstreaming. Mainstreaming has not been practiced long enough for educators to know its long-term effects. Prior to the REI and inclusion, mainstreaming involved students with learning disabilities spending the majority of their day in general classes and a portion of their day in resource rooms. These dual placements made it difficult to differentiate the respective outcomes of the two placements. Some research findings regarding the mainstreaming of students with learning disabilities include the following:

1. Mainstreamed students with learning disabilities generally need selected support services (e.g., a special education consultant) to hold the gains they made in special education placements (Lieberman, 1985).
2. The academic achievement of mainstreamed students with learning disabilities tends to suffer in comparison with the progress of students in segregated placements (Carlberg & Kavale, 1980). Specifically, Carlberg and Kavale state, " For LD and BD/ED children in special classes . . . an improvement of 11 percentile ranks resulted from their placement. Thus, the average BD/ED or LD student in special class placement was better off than 61% of his/her counterparts in regular class. . . . When exceptional children were placed in special classes on the basis of low IQ, they did not respond as well as their regular class counterparts. The situation was reversed with respect to LD and BD/ED children, who were found to show greater improvement in the special class" (pp. 301–302).
3. General classroom teachers do not tend to individualize instruction for students with learning disabilities. Teachers provide few accommodations (especially at the middle and secondary levels) to respond to the individual needs of students. Whole-class activities or undifferentiated large-group activities are the primary mode of instruction. These activities are guided by teacher manuals that are insensitive to the individual needs of students (J. M. Baker & Zigmond, 1990; McIntosh, Vaughn, Schumm, Haager, & Lee, 1993/1994). Bender, Vail, and Scott (1995) document that mainstream teachers do not use certain strategies (e.g., self-monitoring, behavioral contracts, and advance organizers) that are known to facilitate academic achievement for students with learning disabilities.
4. The popularity of students with learning disabilities tends to be low in mainstream classes. Teacher perceptions, peer perceptions, and social status measures indicate that students with learning disabilities have more social difficulties and occupy a lower status than their normally achieving peers (Bender & Golden, 1988; La Greca & Stone, 1990; Roberts & Zubrick, 1993). (See Chapter 15 for a detailed review of social and emotional behavior.)

5. Mainstream settings do not result necessarily in students with disabilities having greater social interaction with students without disabilities, modeling the behavior of students without disabilities, or having greater social acceptance (Gresham, 1982; Guralnick & Groom, 1988; Jenkins, Speltz, & Odom, 1985). Jenkins et al. maintain that proximity between students with disabilities and students without disabilities is insufficient for promoting the development of students with disabilities beyond that anticipated in segregated settings.
6. According to the research of Vaughn, Schumm, and their associates, students with learning disabilities who are mainstreamed tend to exhibit a passive learner syndrome. Because these students fail to ask questions, seek help, or avail themselves of special help, they, in essence, become inactive learners (McIntosh et al., 1994/1995; Vaughn & Schumm, 1994).

Attitudes of General and Special Educators. In a survey of 94 general class teachers, Coates (1989) found that the teachers did not agree with the basic tenets of the REI. Also, Semmel, Abernathy, Butera, and Lesar (1991) surveyed 381 general and special educators to determine their perceptions regarding issues related to the REI. The researchers report that both general and special educators indicated a preference for pull-out special education services rather than the consultant services model. In general, responses from both groups of teachers reflect concerns that full-time placement of students with mild disabilities in the general classroom could negatively affect the achievement outcomes for all students. These results indicate that teachers believe that full-time placement of students with mild disabilities would not have positive instructional or social effects.

Schumm and Vaughn (1992) surveyed general educators at the elementary, middle, and secondary school levels to determine their attitudes about planning as well as their planning practices for students with disabilities. Some of the findings from their study include the following:

1. Planning practices differ across grade levels. Middle and secondary school teachers frequently responded that mainstreamed students with disabilities should be prepared to cope with the demands of the general curriculum. To illustrate this finding, Schumm and Vaughn include a representative comment from a teacher expressing this belief: "There is absolutely no time for mainstreamed students. . . . They adapt to the program, the program does not adapt to them" (p. 94).
2. Many teachers feel underprepared by their teacher education programs to work effectively with mainstreamed students.
3. Overall, teachers are willing to have mainstreamed students in their classrooms "as long as they do not exhibit emotional or behavioral problems" (p. 96).

Downing, Simpson, and Myles (1990) compared the perceptions of general and special educators concerning nonacademic skills (e.g., obeys class rules, asks for help when it is needed, and interacts appropriately with the teacher) typically expected for successful mainstreaming of students with mild emotional or learning disabilities. The researchers note that, in general, both groups of teachers agree that those nonacademic skills are needed for successful mainstreaming.

Houck and Rogers (1994) surveyed 788 general education and special education administrators and teachers regarding the inclusion of students with learning disabilities. Results indicate efforts to increase the amount of time students with learning disabilities spend in general education settings. However, across all groups, participants doubted the adequacy of general education teachers' skills for making adaptations. The majority of the respondents (56.3%) did not think general education teachers are willing to make needed instructional adaptations for students with learning disabilities. Houck and Rogers note that this requirement is fundamental to building a successful inclusion program.

Attitudes of Students. In a survey of 686 special, remedial, and general students, Jenkins and Heinen (1989) found that the majority of students preferred to receive additional help from their general class teacher. If the students needed help from a specialist, they preferred to be pulled out of class for services. It is apparent that general class teachers and students (general and special) must be involved if the general class becomes the full-time placement of special education students.

Bos and Vaughn (1994) report that research of students' perceptions of teachers' adaptations yield the following results:

1. Students at all grade levels prefer teachers who make adaptations to meet the special needs of students. However, only students with special needs feel that adaptations should be made in the areas of tests, homework, and textbooks.
2. High-achieving students without disabilities are more apt to prefer teachers who make adaptations than are low-achieving students without disabilities. This finding appears to be an altruistic attitude on the part of high-achieving students.

Efficacy of Special Classes and Resource Rooms. As mentioned earlier in this chapter, the findings of the efficacy research remain inconclusive. Inclusionists maintain that special class placement has little or no benefit for students at any level of severity (Gartner & Lipsky, 1987; O'Neil, 1994/1995). Supporters of the continuum of alternative placements, however, maintain that special classes have produced positive outcomes for students with learning disabilities (Hallahan & Kauffman, 1994; Kauffman, 1989). Moreover, numerous researchers acknowledge the serious flaws of research on the efficacy of special classes and its lack of relevance for current practices (Gottlieb, Alter, & Gottlieb, 1983; MacMillan & Becker, 1977).

The findings regarding the efficacy of resource room services also remain inconclusive (Wiederholt & Chamberlain, 1989). Smith (1994) notes that research supports resource room services as a means of increasing on-task behavior and improving achievement. She also acknowledges that pulling students out of their general classes to go to resource rooms has numerous disadvantages.

Perspective on the Movement from Mainstreaming to Inclusion

Although inclusion has theoretical appeal and promising directions, existing realities remind professionals and parents that it is premature to eliminate the continuum of alternative placements. Educators have yet to implement on a broad scale the rapidly accruing knowledge and technology about teaching in general or special education settings. The proverbial gap between research and practices is larger than ever. Singer (1988) states, "Proponents of the [REI] argue that the best solution is to abandon the current system, but in doing so, I fear that we would be throwing out the baby with the bath water" (p. 419). More structural changes are not needed until the quality of instruction in all settings is improved.

There is evidence that students with learning disabilities as well as other students with learning problems are not making acceptable progress. It is apparent that business as usual is not acceptable in either the mainstream or in special education settings. Changes are needed and must be implemented according to a systematic plan that incorporates what is known about the change process in schools. Keogh (1990) highlights the needed focus in this change process in the following passage:

> It is clear that major changes are needed in the delivery of services to problem learners, and that these services need to be the responsibility of

> regular as well as special educators. It is also clear that teachers are the central players in bringing about change in practice. It follows, then, that our greatest and most pressing challenge in the reform effort is to determine how to improve the quality of instruction at the classroom level. (p. 190)

Four years later, Keogh (1994) provides additional insights to the change process:

> We are only 6 years away from the year 2000 and we have a long way to go in a short time. I am reminded again of the observation of Donald Broadbent (1973), an eminent British experimentalist, who summarized a set of studies carried out in his Cambridge laboratory. He then added, "experiment having failed, I decided it was necessary to start thinking" (p. 72). . . . We are now in a time of enormous change, and the potential for progress is real. At the same time, there are many threats to progress, some from social/political and economic conditions, others from conflicts and dissensions within our profession. Real progress requires that we address both policy and research issues. As a start I paraphrase Broadbent and suggest that we are forced to think. (p. 68)

Citizens, educators, and parents all want schools in which every student receives an appropriate education in a safe and caring environment. All individuals also want a society whose diverse members value the rights and cultures of each other. To accomplish these visions, educators must maintain the passion for ideals but retain the wisdom that comes from an awareness of the realities of educating a diverse population with limited funds. It is not a time for segregation through fanaticism and bitterness. Division fueled by antagonism weakens the educational profession and makes it vulnerable to funding cuts and movements not in the best interests of students or teachers. It is time to work together toward the shared goal of educating all students. Also, it is time to realize that many individuals feel strongly about both the inclusion ideas and the need for a continuum of alternative placements. Keogh (1994) challenges educators to stop and think. Thinking is enhanced through listening; thus, educators should listen and then think about what parents and peers are saying during these troubled times in special education. The following quotes deserve attention and thought.

1. According to Kauffman (1994), "Hirschman (1986) observed that many who become impatient with the social welfare programs of government—of which general and special education are examples—offer radical reform or restructuring as the solution to problems that are correctable through patient, deliberate improvements within the current structure. The popular, structuralist approach to reform, however, typically leads to disappointment because only the structure changes; actual treatment, the hardest thing to change, is not modified as the structure changes" (p. 617).
2. Sapon-Shevin states, "I have never, ever met a parent of a child with disabilities who did not hope that the child would someday have friends and connections with the broader community" (O'Neil, 1994/1995, p. 7).
3. Morse (1994) notes, "Special education is declared a caring profession, yet little is said about the rehabilitative function of teacher caring as an essential special education ingredient, even in the discussion of the increasing number of children stultified by not being cared for. . . . Caring by consultation requires even more imaginative extension. Yet caring is what many special children most need" (p. 538).
4. Brandt (1994/1995) concludes, "I endorse the testimony of numerous pioneering educators and satisfied parents that it works—under the right conditions. But I also concede that conditions are often far from right in many schools. Looking at the arguments for and against inclusion . . . I think of Tevya in the musical *Fiddler on the Roof* saying, 'He's right—but she's also right' " (p. 3).
5. Wilmore (1994/1995), an educator and parent of a child with disabilities, states, "Every

committee must think, What if this child were my child? Think about the child's tomorrows. Think about what we do now that will affect those tomorrows. We can't afford to make mistakes" (p. 62).

PROGRAM FACTORS AND LEAST RESTRICTIVE ENVIRONMENT

In school A, the placement of a student with learning disabilities in an inclusive program may be the least restrictive environment, whereas in school B, part-time placement in a resource room would be the least restrictive environment for the same student. This scenario exists because the quality of services varies across districts, schools, teachers, and placements. School A has several general education teachers who are excellent at tailoring instruction to meet the needs of the student with learning disabilities. School B has a learning disabilities resource teacher who does an excellent job of teaching students to achieve academic goals and use learning strategies to become more independent learners. Unfortunately, the general education teachers at school B in this student's grade level are not sensitive to the instructional needs of students with learning disabilities. The variations in mainstream settings led Bender and his associates (Bender & Ukeje, 1989) to research why some mainstream teachers receive students with learning disabilities and tailor instruction appropriately, whereas other teachers respond negatively to mainstreaming. Bender et al. (1995) report that teachers with less positive attitudes toward mainstreaming use effective mainstream instructional strategies less frequently. As noted previously in this chapter, this condition is a core issue concerning the Regular Education Initiative and inclusion.

When the instructional and social needs of students with learning disabilities are met in inclusive settings, it is the most appropriate placement. The question of what constitutes an effective inclusion program is becoming increasingly important. Fortunately, several researchers are investigating the characteristics of effective mainstream environments. Ysseldyke and Christenson (1993) developed *The Instructional Environment System—II* to help educators evaluate learning environments. This scale was developed, in part, on empirically based teaching practices that facilitate positive student outcomes for learners with mild disabilities.

Several researchers (Wang & Baker, 1985–1986; Waxman, Wang, Anderson, & Walberg, 1985) reviewed empirical studies of adaptive instruction used in inclusive settings. They identified the following instructional features as promoting successful mainstreaming:

1. An instructional match is maintained for each student.
2. Individualized pacing for achieving instructional goals is maintained.
3. Student progress is monitored, and continuous feedback is provided.
4. Students are involved in the planning and monitoring of their learning.
5. A broad range of techniques and materials is used.
6. Students help each other to learn.
7. Students are taught self-management skills.
8. Teachers engage in instructional teaming.

This section features program factors that promote the successful inclusion of students with learning disabilities. Topics include teachers teaching teachers, the learning disabilities teacher, students teaching students, and limited teacher-engagement instruction.

Teachers Teaching Teachers

The Individuals with Disabilities Education Act of 1990, which incorporates Public Law 94-142, has had a widespread effect on the identification, instructional, and placement practices in special education. For example, collaboration between special education teachers and general education teachers now is required. It is the responsibility of educators to employ the interactive framework established by Public Law 94-142 to assure that all students are educated in the least restrictive environment. Consequently, researchers have focused on meeting the instructional needs of mainstreamed students in the general education environment (Brady, Swank, Taylor, & Freiberg, 1992; McIntosh et al., 1993/1994; Truesdell & Abramson, 1992). In addition to the need for collaboration among general and special education teachers to meet the diverse needs of students with learning disabilities in general education settings, there are other compelling reasons for working together. Cook and Friend (1991) note that the information explosion necessitates a need for shared expertise. Also, the increasing trend toward site-based management implies that administrators, teachers, parents, and community members must be able to make responsible decisions concerning school quality. Various special education/general education "teaching teams" (Thousand & Villa, 1990) have emerged to meet the challenge of educating students with disabilities in the general classroom.

A teachers-helping-teachers approach focuses on meeting the needs of students with disabilities within the general class before considering formal special education services and more segregated placements. Much of the promise of these activities rests on the assumption that, in a supportive and trusting environment, teachers can support and teach each other to individualize instruction better. Consequently, as teachers become more competent, the general or mainstream setting improves, and referrals to special education decrease.

Strategies for Increasing Consultation Time. Specific strategies for increasing consultation time have been implemented successfully at the elementary, middle, and secondary school levels (West & Idol, 1990). These strategies include the following:

1. Create times when large numbers of students can be brought together for grade-level or schoolwide activities under the supervision of a few teachers.
2. Have the principal teach one period a day on a regular basis.
3. Cluster students working on similar assignments into larger groups under the supervision of a few teachers.
4. Hire a permanent substitute who "floats" from classroom to classroom as needed.
5. Designate a specific time each week for staff collaboration.

6. Designate 1 day each month or 1 day per grading period as "Collaboration Day."
7. Extend the school day for about 20 minutes on 2 days per week to provide collaboration periods for teachers.

West and Idol note that numerous different and creative strategies have been used to support collaborative consultation. Finally, developing strategies to create time for consultation requires more than administrative and logistical support. The collegial problem-solving process must be valued by both teachers and administrators (Phillips & McCullough, 1990; West & Idol, 1990).

Collaborative Consultation. Collaborative problem solving aimed at the prevention of student learning and behavior problems offers a viable alternative to the overused and costly refer-test-place paradigm. The results of a survey of members of the Council for Exceptional Children (1989) on professional development needs illustrate the need for more collaboration. The three top-ranked items from the survey indicate the need for (a) more collaboration with general education teachers and other special program teachers, (b) the coordination of special education with other programs and services, and (c) an improved relationship between special and general education.

West and Idol (1990) point out the differences between consultative and collaborative relationships. In consultative relationships, one professional confers with another to seek guidance. In collaborative relationships, two or more professionals work together with parity and reciprocity to solve problems. When collaborative consultation initially was conceptualized as a special education service model, the following definition emerged:

> Collaborative consultation is an interactive process which enables people with diverse expertise to generate creative solutions to mutually defined problems. The outcome is enhanced, altered, and different from the original solutions that any team member would produce independently. The major outcome of collaborative consultation is to provide comprehensive and effective programs for students with special needs within the most appropriate context, thereby enabling them to achieve maximum constructive interaction with their nonhandicapped peers. (Idol, Paolucci-Whitcomb, & Nevin, 1986, p. 1)

In essence, mutual empowerment is an important goal of educational collaboration.

The major goals of collaborative consultation are to prevent behavior and learning problems, ameliorate learning and behavior problems, and coordinate instructional programs (West, Idol, & Cannon, 1988). For collaborative consultation to be most effective, a formal set of problem-solving stages is recommended. The most commonly accepted stages (Idol et al., 1986; West et al., 1988) include the following:

Stage 1: Goal/Entry. Roles, objectives, responsibilities, and expectations of the consultant and consulter are negotiated.

Stage 2: Problem identification. The problem is defined clearly and discussed until all members have a mutual understanding of the problem.

Stage 3: Intervention recommendations. Interventions are generated and prioritized in the expected order of implementation. Written, measurable objectives are developed to (a) detail specific interventions for each aspect of the problem, (b) establish criteria to determine whether the problem has been solved, and (c) spell out the roles of the student and respective team members and identify appropriate resources needed for delivering interventions.

Stage 4: Implementation recommendations. Implementation is provided according to established objectives and activities. Time lines and respective personnel responsible for selected interventions are specified. In the collaborative model, the consultant and consulter usually have a responsibility. Typically, the consultant assumes a modeling role that phases out as the consulter gains expertise and confidence with the intervention.

Stage 5: Evaluation. The success of the intervention strategies is assessed. This assessment includes measures of student, consultant, consulter, and system change.

Stage 6: Redesign. The intervention is continued, modified, or discontinued on the basis of the evaluation of the intervention strategies.

West and Idol (1990) report that team consensus is reached at each stage before going to the next step. Moreover, they note that adherence to the stages allows for a systematic and efficient approach to solving problems.

Collaborative consultation may occur as a simple problem-solving process in a variety of contexts. Educational reforms are being suggested and demanded to provide learners who have disabilities with appropriate educational programs in their least restrictive environments. Many educators are calling for general and special educators to work together more closely to serve students with learning and behavior problems. Consequently, many team approaches are being developed in which collaborative consultation may occur. Some models being proposed include (a) teacher assistance teams (Chalfant & Pysh, 1989), (b) mainstream assistance teams (Fuchs, Fuchs, & Bahr, 1990), (c) cooperative professional development (Glatthorn, 1990), (d) coaching (Showers, 1985), (e) peer collaboration (Pugach & Johnson, 1988), and (f) cooperative teaching (Bauwens, Hourcade, & Friend, 1989). Teacher assistance teams, coaching, peer collaboration, and cooperative teaching are discussed next.

Teacher Assistance Teams. Kirk and Chalfant (1984) discuss a teacher assistance team (TAT) model that has proven to be effective in helping teachers reduce the number of inappropriate referrals and in resolving many students' problems. Each team consists of three elected teachers, the teacher seeking help, and parents or others as needed. The referring teacher provides information concerning the student's strengths, weaknesses, and interventions that have been tried. Typically, the team conducts a problem-solving meeting by (a) delineating specific objectives with the teacher, (b) brainstorming intervention alternatives, (c) selecting or refining intervention(s), and (d) planning follow-up activities. The teacher leaves the meeting with a copy of the interventions. A follow-up meeting is planned in 2 to 6 weeks to determine whether the suggestions are working.

The TAT model was evaluated in three states for 2 years. Of the 200 students served in the study, the teams helped the classroom teacher resolve the difficulties of 133 students, or 66.5%. Of the 116 students who were underachieving, the teams could meet the needs of 103 (88.7%) without referring them to special education. Moreover, schools with teacher assistance teams cut their diagnostic costs by about 50% (Kirk & Chalfant, 1984). In another study, Chalfant and Pysh (1989) examined the practices of 96 first-year teacher assistance teams in seven states. Results indicate that the TAT model generated interventions that improved student performance, increased the appropriateness of special education referrals, created effective strategies for students without disabilities, and assisted mainstream teachers in serving students with disabilities in their classrooms. Moreover, teacher satisfaction about TAT involvement was positive (i.e., 88% positive statements versus 12% negative statements). Principal support, team attributes, and teacher support were identified as major factors contributing to TAT effectiveness. In addition, Graden, Casey, and Christenson (1985) report success with a prereferral system that uses teacher-to-teacher consultation and group problem-solving sessions.

Coaching. The team approach of coaching also is generating enthusiasm among educators (McREL Staff, 1984–1985; Showers, 1985). Peer coaching involves the formation of a small group of teachers and peer observation. Teachers observe each others' classrooms, get feedback about their teaching, experiment with improved techniques, and receive support (McREL Staff, 1984–1985). Coaching teams of three people engage in a three-phase process involving discussion and planning, observation, and feedback.

In the discussion and planning phase, the teachers focus on the improved technique or strategy they want to learn and outline the specific essential behaviors or actions for implementing the new technique. In the observation phase, Teacher 1 observes Teacher 2, who observes Teacher 3, who observes Teacher 1. A format to guide data collection (e.g., a checklist, log, or tape recorder) helps observation. In the feedback phase, the observer and the teacher meet to discuss the observations. To help maintain the professional nature of coaching, the teachers must never talk to a third person about observations or let a team member draw others into personal problems. Periodically, the coaching teams meet in a support group of 6 to 12 with other coaching teams to plan and offer support for each other. Showers (1985) reports that coaching builds a community of teachers who continuously engage in the study of improved teaching. The coaching process becomes a continuous cycle in which common necessary understandings emerge for improved teaching through collegial study of new knowledge and skills.

The effects of coaching are impressive. Showers (1985) reports that coaching provides the essential follow-up for training new skills and strategies. Also, it is more effective than lecture and demonstration in providing classroom applications (McREL Staff, 1984–1985). In a study in which coached and uncoached teachers received the same training (e.g., theory, demonstration, and practice), Showers (1990) found that 80% of the coached teachers transferred the newly learned skills to their classes, whereas only 10% of the uncoached group transferred the skills. Coaching appears to hold much promise as a technique to help educators develop a broader repertoire of skills for meeting the diverse needs of students in mainstream settings.

Peer Collaboration. According to Pugach and Johnson (1989), there "should always be times when classroom teachers solve problems in the absence of specialists" (p. 235). One way of enhancing classroom teachers' abilities to design and adapt educational interventions for mainstreamed students is through peer collaboration (Pugach & Johnson, 1988). Peer collaboration is based on the assumption that when general education teachers work together using a systematic, problem-solving strategy, they can develop appropriate instructional and behavioral interventions for all of their students.

Peer collaboration involves pairs of teachers who engage in a highly structured dialogue about a problem involving a single student, a group of students, or a whole class. The structured dialogue includes opportunities for self-questioning, summarizing, and predicting with regard to the specific problem concerning the teacher. Each teacher in the dyad has a specific role. The Initiator is the teacher who shares the problem and ultimately solves the problem. The Facilitator guides the partner through each step in the dialogue to arrive at a solution. The peer-collaboration process includes four steps:

1. *Problem description and clarifying questions.* In this step, the Initiator provides the partner with a short, written description of the problem. Next, the Facilitator reads the problem and asks the partner if there are any clarifying questions to be asked. For example, the written problem might be "Robert fails to complete classroom and homework assignments." The Initiator might ask questions such as "When does the behavior occur?" or "Are there any occasions when he does complete his work?" The Facilitator also can guide the process by asking, "Are there questions you could ask yourself about his classroom and homework assignments?" The purpose of this type of probing is to lead the Initiator to a general area of the problem rather than suggest specific areas for examination. The goal is to enable the Initiator to "recognize a pattern of behavior and form a summary" (Pugach & Johnson, 1988, p. 76).
2. *Summarizing.* After the problem is clarified, the Initiator summarizes the problem. The summary includes the clarified behavior pat-

tern of the student, the teacher's response to the behavior, and the relevant factors in the classroom environment under the teacher's control.

3. *Interventions and predictions.* During this step, at least three possible interventions are proposed by the Initiator, and predictions are made regarding potential outcomes for each intervention. The role of the Facilitator is to help the partner arrive at an intervention that is practical and minimally disruptive to the teacher and the class.
4. *Evaluation plan.* During the last step in the process, a reasonably simple plan is developed to document and evaluate the effectiveness of the intervention. For example, in the case of Robert, the Initiator may realize that a check-off sheet for Robert to mark as he completes assignments may help him complete his work. The intervention also can include a special notebook in which Robert records all of his homework assignments. His performance on both tasks should be monitored daily for 2 weeks. Finally, the Initiator and the partner may agree to meet in 2 weeks to discuss whether to continue the intervention or begin the peer collaboration process again.

According to Pugach and Johnson (1988), as this process systematically is repeated, the general format of the dialogue becomes an internalized problem-solving strategy. Peer collaboration can provide general classroom teachers with a strategy to accommodate students with disabilities in the mainstream classroom. In a synthesis of their research on peer collaboration, Pugach and Johnson (1990) report that classroom teachers exhibited the following behaviors as a result of training in the peer-collaboration process:

1. The focus of problem identification shifted away from the students to factors directly under the teachers' control.
2. The teachers generated potential interventions for all problems targeted in a peer-collaboration session.
3. The teachers effectively resolved over 85% of the problems targeted through peer collaboration.
4. The teachers felt significantly more confident in their ability to manage classroom problems.
5. Positive attitudes increased toward their class as a whole.

Cooperative Teaching. West and Idol (1990) note that the term *cooperative teaching* has been used interchangeably with *team teaching*. Cooperative teaching appears to be a viable model for integrating students with disabilities into the mainstream setting. Bauwens and Hourcade (1991) define cooperative teaching as

> an educational approach in which general and special educators work in a co-active and coordinated fashion to jointly teach heterogeneous groups of students in educationally integrated settings (i.e., general education classrooms). In cooperative teaching both general and special education teachers are simultaneously present in the general classroom, maintaining joint responsibilities for specified education instruction that is to occur within the setting. (p. 20)

Using their definition as a framework, Bauwens and Hourcade discuss three different configurations of cooperative teaching. These three instructional arrangements include team teaching, complementary instruction, and supportive learning activities.

In a team-teaching arrangement, two teachers share instructional responsibility for a common body of content-area knowledge. The general and special educator jointly plan and instruct the same academic content to all students. Negotiation is a critical feature of this process. The teachers negotiate how the content will be presented, the time frames for instruction, and specific responsibilities for each part of the unit or lesson. In complementary instruction, the general educator has primary responsibility for teaching specific content areas, while the special educator teaches specific strategies or skills (e.g., note taking, summarizing, or identifying main ideas in reading) to students in need of additional instruction. In contrast to the team-teaching arrangement in which teachers share equal responsibility for the same content, the complementary instruction arrangement features separate but related responsibility for instruction. The instructional roles for the special educator and the mainstream teacher in this model are similar to the roles of the support teacher and the mainstream teacher in the Strategies Intervention Model presented in Chapter 10. Finally, in the supportive learning activities arrangement, the general and special educator collaboratively determine the major content and instructional goals for any lesson. The teachers jointly identify activities to support and extend the lesson. Within the supportive learning activities arrangement, the general educator primarily is responsible for teaching the content; however, the special educator reinforces and enriches the content by implementing supportive learning activities. For example, the special educator may have expertise in the area of computer applications to extend the mathematics unit on decimals and percents. Moreover, the special educator can enrich and support content areas through the use of interest centers.

Communication Skills for Collaboration. In addition to being familiar with various models for collaboration, teachers need to use effective communication skills for successful implementation of collaboration. Parity, shared responsibility, accountability, and mutual goals cannot be mandated. These characteristics result from reciprocal relationships among volunteers who value collaboration and believe it can work to help students and themselves. Idol and West (1991) provide the following principles of successful collaborative consultation skills:

1. Create an atmosphere of mutual trust and respect so that team members feel safe in sharing information.
2. Provide nonevaluative feedback when others are speaking.
3. Use jargon-free language when sharing ideas.
4. Be aware that nonverbal body language can communicate positive or negative messages.
5. Give and receive feedback willingly and effectively, without confrontation.

Adapting and modifying teacher-teacher and teacher-student interactions and teaching repertoires demands considerable risk taking by teachers. General and special educators who share responsibility for modifying their instruction to meet the diverse needs of students with learning disabilities need to establish a trusting relationship to help support their efforts toward change. Moreover, effective changes in how services are delivered to adolescents with learning disabilities take time. Estimates for significant changes within school systems range from 3 to 7 years (Schumaker & Deshler, 1988).

The Learning Disabilities Teacher

Although numerous variables (e.g., funding, support, and cooperation) affect the quality of instructional services provided to students with learning disabilities, the teacher remains the most important influence in program quality. To deliver direct services, the learning disabilities teacher must demonstrate the most effective empirically based assessment and teaching practices (discussed in Chapters 5 and 7). To deliver indirect services, the teacher needs effective consultation skills to work with teachers of mainstreamed students, school-based assistance teams, and parents. Because of the push toward educating more students with learning disabilities in the mainstream environment and the disenchantment with pull-out service delivery options, the trend is moving toward using consultative services to help students succeed in mainstream classrooms. Generally, the research on the outcomes of consultation appears to be promising for reducing referrals to special education and helping students achieve (Heron & Kimball, 1988; Idol, 1988; Polsgrove & McNeil, 1989). Heron and Kimball report that "the data currently available justify consultation as an appropriate service for facilitating the education of all students in the least restrictive environment, and it is clear that the data base regarding the efficacy of specific consultation practices continues to emerge" (p. 27).

Consultation. Collaborative consultation, discussed earlier in this section, represents an increasingly popular process regarding how numerous experts view the dynamics of problem solving in consultation. Learning disabilities teachers as well as mainstream teachers need training to become efficient in the collaborative consultation process. West and Cannon (1988) worked with a 100-member interdisciplinary expert panel to generate consultation competencies needed by learning disabilities and general education teachers to meet the educational needs of students with learning disabilities and other disabling conditions in general classrooms. The panel identified 47 essential competencies in 9 categories. The categories receiving the highest ratings were (a) interactive communication, (b) personal characteristics, (c) equity issues, values, and beliefs, (d) collaborative problem solving, and (e) evaluation of consultation effectiveness. Staff development competencies were rated as important but not essential. Categories that received ratings indicating less importance to the consultation process were (a) consultation theory and models, (b) consultation research, and (c) systems change.

Idol (1988) recommends that a consulting teacher should have completed a supervised practicum experience in school consultation and should have knowledge of (a) all types of exceptional learners, (b) all special education service delivery models, (c) the history of special education, and (d) special education legislation and legal rights of exceptional persons. In addition, Idol notes that a consulting teacher should have demonstrable skills in (a) using assessment techniques (e.g., curriculum-based assessment, criterion-referenced testing, classroom observation, and standardized tests), (b) applying basic remediation techniques for academic skill deficits (e.g., study skill strategies), (c) applying basic behavior management techniques for individuals as well as groups of students, (d) applying accommodation techniques to special needs learners in mainstream settings (e.g., materials modification, principles of reinforcement, and computer-assisted instruction), (e) transferring learned skills from supportive service programs to the classroom, (f) measuring, monitoring, and evaluating academic and behavioral progress in students, and (g) using effective communication and working collaboratively with other adults.

Viable knowledge regarding consultation is increasing, and this knowledge needs to be a part of a learning disabilities teacher's preservice and staff development training. Tindal, Shinn, and Rodden-Nord (1990) provide a model that includes consideration for realistic school-based variables that influence the consultation process. This model includes 11 variables that are organized within three dimensions—people, process, and procedural implementation.

People Variables

1. Consultant background and skills—history, experiences, skills, knowledge, resources.
2. Consulter background and skills—history, experiences, skills, knowledge, resources, teacher tolerance.
3. Client background and skills—history, experiences, skills, knowledge, resources.
4. Administrator background and skills—history, experiences, skills, knowledge, resources.

Process Variables

5. Problem-solving relationship between consultant and consulter—problem identification and problem remediation.
6. Theoretical perspective of consultation—behavioral, organizational, mental health.

7. Stage in consultation—problem identification, problem corroboration, program development, program operationalization, program evaluation.
8. Activity structure—assessment, assessment/direct intervention, assessment/indirect intervention, indirect service to system.

Procedural Implementation Variables

9. Type of data—judgments, observations, tests.
10. Program intervention—context, materials, interactive techniques.
11. Evaluation strategies—qualitative, quantitative (individual-referenced, criterion-referenced, norm-referenced).

Tindal et al. note that the model should be used to help teachers consider important variables as they implement consultation in applied educational settings.

Students Teaching Students

Peer tutoring and cooperative learning are two viable approaches for promoting successful inclusion. These approaches provide the teacher with instructional arrangements that enable students to work independently and free the teacher to instruct other groups or individuals directly. The merits of tutorial instruction include pacing that is tuned to an individual's learning rate, intensive practice for those who need it, and personal benefits to both the tutors and those being tutored. Cooperative learning also is successful with heterogeneous groups of learners and has received support from general and special educators. In inclusive classrooms, the need for effective arrangements that allow students to practice needed skills independently is critical for students to master skills. (Chapter 7 discusses peer tutoring and cooperative learning.)

Limited Teacher-Engagement Instruction

Given the many demands placed on teachers to meet the instructional needs of the diverse group of students who comprise a mainstream class, the teacher needs to develop and use instructional approaches that enhance quality learning for those times when a student must and should work independently. Certainly, peer teaching and cooperative learning provide limited teacher-engagement instructional activities. These activities are suited especially for students to practice skills or review content presented earlier by the teacher. Mastery of skills and content is essential for the school success of students with learning disabilities. Using self-correcting materials, instructional games, and computer-assisted instruction and teaching students to be independent learners are viable approaches to help students work independently in their least restrictive environment. (These approaches are discussed in Chapter 7.)

PERSPECTIVE

Because Public Law 94-142 (incorporated in IDEA) mandates that students with disabilities must be educated in their least restrictive environment, a continuum of services sensitive to various student needs must be available. Service models for students with learning disabilities include programs in general education classes, resource rooms, special classes, and special schools. The resource room remains the most commonly used model for serving students with learning disabilities. Inclusion proponents recommend that special education placement alternatives be eliminated and that students with learning disabilities and students with other disabilities be served totally within the general education class. However, at the present time, there is a lack of data that justify eliminating the special education placement alternatives.

It is important to implement various program factors to promote successful inclusion of students with learning disabilities. Effective teaching practices must be used across educational settings. Collaborative consultation, teacher assistance teams, coaching, peer collaboration, and cooperative teaching are team approaches through which teachers can support and teach each other to individualize instruction. Moreover, to help students with learning disabilities succeed in inclusive settings, the learning disabilities teacher should provide consultation services. An additional program factor for successful inclusion involves the use of students teaching students through peer tutoring and cooperative learning. Educators must provide youngsters who have learning disabilities with programs in their most enabling environment that respond to their unique needs, and the appropriate use of the various special education placement alternatives requires careful planning.

With more than one-third of our nation's youth dropping out of school, it is apparent that many students are experiencing school failure. Many of these youngsters have learning disabilities and face huge obstacles as they strive to become independent and productive members of society. Unfortunately, many of these individuals are from families of intergenerational despair. Edgar (1993) comments on their condition and society's responsibilities in the following passage: "As this group grows, all of us become at risk to have the quality of our lives reduced by their despair. As long as one of us does without, all of us share in the suffering. All the great religions have warned us that 'even as the least fortunate of us suffers, so do we all' " (p. 3).

Given the multitude of society's ills, it behooves both general and special educators to join forces in efforts to help today's students. Students need the help, and general and special educators need each other.

DISCUSSION/REVIEW QUESTIONS

1. Define *least restrictive environment* and *mainstreaming*.
2. Discuss the concept of severity of learning disabilities and its relationship to placement.
3. Identify the general class-based placements and the special class-based placements, and discuss the advantages and disadvantages of each service model.
4. Describe the services of a resource room program.
5. Discuss strategies for the reintegration of students with learning disabilities.
6. Discuss the Regular Education Initiative and the inclusion movement.
7. Present the rationale for inclusion and the rationale for continuum alternative placements.
8. Discuss the efficacy of inclusion and of special classes and resource rooms.
9. Discuss teachers teaching teachers through the use of collaborative consultation, teacher assistance teams, coaching, peer collaboration, and cooperative teaching.
10. Describe the role of the learning disabilities teacher.

REFERENCES

Affleck, J. Q., Madge, S., Adams, A., & Lowenbraun, S. (1988). Integrated classroom versus resource model: Academic viability and affectiveness. *Exceptional Children*, *54*, 339–348.

Anderson-Inman, L. (1986). Bridging the gap: Student-centered strategies for promoting the transfer of learning. *Exceptional Children*, *52*, 562–572.

Baker, E. T. (1994). *Meta-analytic evidence for non-inclusive educational practices: Does educational research support current practice for special-needs students?* Unpublished doctoral dissertation, Temple University, Philadelphia.

Baker, E. T., Wang, M. C., & Walberg, H. J. (1994/1995). The effects of inclusion on learning. *Educational Leadership*, *52*(4), 33–35.

Baker, J. M., & Zigmond, N. (1990). Are regular education classes equipped to accommodate students with learning disabilities? *Exceptional Children*, *56*, 515–526.

Bauwens, J., & Hourcade, J. J. (1991). Making co-teaching a mainstreaming strategy. *Preventing School Failure*, *35*(4), 19–24.

Bauwens, J., Hourcade, J. J., & Friend, M. (1989). Cooperative teaching: A model for general and special education integration. *Remedial and Special Education*, *10*(2), 17–22.

Beck, F. W., Lindsey, J. D., & Frith, G. H. (1981). Effects of self-contained special class placement on intellectual functioning of learning disabled students. *Journal of Learning Disabilities*, *14*, 280–282.

Bender, W. N., & Golden, L. B. (1988). Adaptive behavior of learning disabled and non-learning disabled children. *Learning Disability Quarterly. 11*, 55–61.

Bender, W. N., & Ukeje, I. C. (1989). Instructional strategies in mainstream classrooms: Prediction of the strategies teachers select. *Remedial and Special Education, 10*(2), 23–30.

Bender, W. N., Vail, C. O., & Scott, K. (1995). Teachers' attitudes toward increased mainstreaming: Implementing effective instruction for students with learning disabilities. *Journal of Learning Disabilities, 28*, 87–94, 120.

Bos, C. S., & Vaughn, S. (1994). *Strategies for teaching students with learning and behavior problems* (3rd ed.). Boston: Allyn & Bacon.

Brady, M. P., Swank, P. R., Taylor, R. D., & Freiberg, J. (1992). Teacher interactions in mainstream social studies and science classes. *Exceptional Children, 58*, 530–540.

Brandt, R. (1994/1995). Overview: What is best? *Educational Leadership, 52*(4), 3.

Broadbent, D. E. (1973). *In defense of empirical psychology*. London: Methuen.

Bryan, J. (1988, April). *Perspectives on the regular education initiative*. Paper presented at the meeting of the Council for Exceptional Children, Washington, DC.

Carlberg, C., & Kavale, K. (1980). The efficacy of special versus regular class placement for exceptional children: A meta-analysis. *The Journal of Special Education, 14*, 295–309.

Chalfant, J. C. (1985). Identifying learning disabled students: A summary of the National Task Force report. *Learning Disabilities Focus, 1*(1), 9–20.

Chalfant, J. C., & Pysh, M. V. (1989). Teacher assistance teams: Five descriptive studies of 96 teams. *Remedial and Special Education, 19*(6), 49–58.

Coates, R. D. (1989). The regular education initiative and opinions of regular classroom teachers. *Journal of Learning Disabilities, 22*, 532–536.

Cook, L., & Friend, M. (1991). Collaboration in special education: Coming of age in the 1990s. *Preventing School Failure, 35*(2), 24–27.

Council for Exceptional Children. (1989). Survey of CEC members' professional development needs. *Teaching Exceptional Children, 21*(3), 78–79.

Cruickshank, W. M., Bentzen, F. A., Ratzeburg, F. H., & Tannhauser, M. T. (1961). *A teaching method for brain-injured and hyperactive children*. New York: Syracuse University Press.

Deno, E. (1970). Special education as developmental capital. *Exceptional Children, 37*, 229–237.

Downing, J. A., Simpson, R. L., & Myles, B. S. (1990). Regular and special educators' perceptions of nonacademic skills needed by mainstreamed students with behavioral disorders and learning disabilities. *Behavioral Disorders, 15*, 217–226.

Dunn, L. M. (Ed.). (1973). *Exceptional children in the schools: Special education in transition* (2nd ed.). New York: Holt, Rinehart & Winston.

Edgar, E. (1993, April). *Curricula options at the secondary level: Preparing youth for the twenty-first century*. Paper presented at the Blazing New Trails Specific Learning Disabilities State of Minnesota Conference, Brainerd, MN.

Ellett, L. (1993). Instructional practices in mainstreamed secondary classrooms. *Journal of Learning Disabilities, 26*, 57–64.

Epstein, M. H., & Cullinan, D. (1979). Social validation: Use of normative peer data to evaluate LD interventions. *Learning Disability Quarterly, 2*(4), 93–98.

Friend, M., & McNutt, G. (1984). Resource room programs: Where are we now? *Exceptional Children, 51*, 150–155.

Fuchs, D., & Fuchs, L. S. (1988). Evaluation of the adaptive learning environments model. *Exceptional Children, 55*, 115–127.

Fuchs, D., & Fuchs, L. S. (1994). Inclusive schools movement and the radicalization of special education reform. *Exceptional Children, 60*, 294–309.

Fuchs, D., Fuchs, L. S., & Bahr, M. W. (1990). Mainstream assistance teams: A scientific basis for the art of consultation. *Exceptional Children, 57*, 128–139.

Gartner, A., & Lipsky, D. K. (1987). Beyond special education: Toward a quality system for all students. *Harvard Educational Review, 57*, 367–395.

Glatthorn, A. A. (1990). Cooperative professional development: Facilitating the growth of the special education teacher and the classroom teacher. *Remedial and Special Education, 11*(3), 29–34, 50.

Gottlieb, J., Alter, M., & Gottlieb, B. W. (1983). Mainstreaming mentally retarded children. In J. L. Matson & J. A. Mulich (Eds.), *Handbook of mental retardation* (pp. 67–77). New York: Pergamon Press.

Graden, J. L., Casey, A., & Christenson, S. L. (1985). Implementing a prereferral intervention system. Part I. The model. *Exceptional Children, 51*, 377–384.

Gresham, F. M. (1982). Misguided mainstreaming: The case for social skills training with handicapped children. *Exceptional Children, 48*, 422–433.

Guralnick, M. J., & Groom, J. M. (1988). Peer interactions in mainstreamed and specialized classrooms: A comparative analysis. *Exceptional Children, 54*, 415–425.

Halgren, D. W., & Clarizio, H. F. (1993). Categorical and programming changes in special education services. *Exceptional Children, 59*, 547–555.

Hallahan, D. P., & Kauffman, J. M. (1994). Toward a culture of disability in the aftermath of Deno and Dunn. *The Journal of Special Education, 27*, 496–508.

Heron, T. E., & Kimball, W. H. (1988). Gaining perspective with the educational consultation research base: Ecological considerations and further recommendations. *Remedial and Special Education, 9*(6), 21–28, 47.

Hirschman, A. O. (1986). *Rival views of market society and other recent essays.* New York: Viking.

Horne, M. D. (1985). *Attitudes toward handicapped students: Professional, peer, and parent reactions.* Hillsdale, NJ: Lawrence Erlbaum Associates.

Houck, C. K., & Rogers, C. J. (1994). The special/general education integration initiative for students with specific learning disabilities: A "snapshot" of program change. *Journal of Learning Disabilities, 27*, 435–453.

Idol, L. (1988). A rationale and guidelines for establishing special education consultation programs. *Remedial and Special Education, 9*(6), 48–58.

Idol, L. (1989). The resource/consulting teacher: An integrated model of service delivery. *Remedial and Special Education, 10*(6), 38–48.

Idol, L., Paolucci-Whitcomb, P., & Nevin, A. (1986). *Collaborative consultation.* Austin, TX: PRO-ED.

Idol, L., & West, J. F. (1991). Educational collaboration: A catalyst for effective schooling. *Intervention in School and Clinic, 27*, 70–78.

Jenkins, J. R., & Heinen, A. (1989). Students' preferences for service delivery: Pull-out, in-class, or integrated models. *Exceptional Children, 55*, 516–523.

Jenkins, J. R., Speltz, M. L., & Odom, S. L. (1985). Integrating normal and handicapped preschoolers: Effects on child development and social interaction. *Exceptional Children, 52*, 7–17.

Joint Committee on Teacher Planning for Students with Disabilities. (1995). Planning for academic diversity in America's classrooms: Windows on reality, research, change, and practice. *Effective School Practices, 14*(2), 1–53.

Kauffman, J. M. (1989). The regular education initiative as Reagan-Bush education policy: A trickle-down theory of education of the hard-to-teach. *The Journal of Special Education, 23*, 256–278.

Kauffman, J. M. (1994). Places of change: Special education's power and identity in an era of educational reform. *Journal of Learning Disabilities, 27*, 610–618.

Kauffman, J. M., & Hallahan, D. P. (1993). Toward a comprehensive delivery system for special education. In J. I. Goodlad & T. C. Lovitt (Eds.), *Integrating general and special education* (pp. 73–102). Upper Saddle River, NJ: Merrill/Prentice Hall.

Kauffman, J. M., & Hallahan, D. P. (Eds.). (1995). *The illusion of full inclusion: A comprehensive critique of a current special education bandwagon.* Austin, TX: PRO-ED.

Kauffman, J. M., & Pullen, P. L. (1989). An historical perspective: A personal perspective on our history of service to mildly handicapped and at-risk students. *Remedial and Special Education, 10*(6), 12–14.

Keogh, B. K. (1988). Improving services for problem learners. Rethinking and restructuring. *Journal of Learning Disabilities, 21*, 19–22.

Keogh, B. K. (1990). Narrowing the gap between policy and practice. *Exceptional Children, 57*, 186–190.

Keogh, B. K. (1994). What the special education research agenda should look like in the year 2000. *Learning Disabilities Research & Practice, 9*, 62–69.

Kirk, S. A., & Chalfant, J. C. (1984). *Academic and developmental learning disabilities.* Denver: Love.

La Greca, A. M., & Stone, W. L. (1990). LD status and achievement: Confounding variables in the study of children's social status, self-esteem, and behavioral functioning. *Journal of Learning Disabilities, 23*, 483–490.

Lieberman, L. M. (1985). Special education and regular education: A merger made in heaven. *Exceptional Children, 51*, 513–516.

Lovitt, T. C. (1989). *Introduction to learning disabilities.* Boston: Allyn & Bacon.

MacMillan, D. L., & Becker, L. D. (1977). Mainstreaming the mildly handicapped learner. In R. D. Kneedler & S. G. Tarver (Eds.), *Changing perspectives in special education* (pp. 208–227). Upper Saddle River, NJ: Merrill/Prentice Hall.

McIntosh, R., Vaughn, S., Schumm, J. S., Haager, D., & Lee, O. (1993/1994). Observations of students with learning disabilities in general education classrooms. *Exceptional Children, 60,* 249–261.

McLeskey, J., & Pacchiano, D. (1994). Mainstreaming students with learning disabilities: Are we making progress? *Exceptional Children, 60*, 508–517.

McREL Staff. (1984–1985, Winter). Coaching: A powerful strategy for improving staff development and inservice education. *Noteworthy*, pp. 40–46.

Morse, W. C. (1994). Comments from a biased viewpoint. *The Journal of Special Education, 27*, 531–542.

Mueller, D. J., Chase, C. I., & Walden, J. D. (1988). Effects of reduced class size in primary classes. *Educational Leadership, 45*(5), 48–50.

O'Neil, J. (1994/1995). Can inclusion work? A conversation with Jim Kauffman and Mara Sapon-Shevin. *Educational Leadership, 52*(4), 7–11.

Phillips, V., & McCullough, L. (1990). Consultation-based programming: Instituting the collaborative ethic in schools. *Exceptional Children, 56*, 291–304.

Polsgrove, L., & McNeil, M. (1989). The consultation process: Research and practice. *Remedial and Special Education, 10*(1), 6–13, 20.

Poplin, M. (1988). The reductionistic fallacy in learning disabilities: Replicating the past by reducing the present. *Journal of Learning Disabilities, 21*, 389–400.

Pugach, M. C., & Johnson, L. J. (1988). Peer collaboration. *Teaching Exceptional Children, 20*, 75–77.

Pugach, M. C., & Johnson, L. J. (1989). The challenge of implementing collaboration between general and special education. *Exceptional Children, 56*, 232–235.

Pugach, M. C., & Johnson, L. J. (1990). Meeting diverse needs through professional peer collaboration. In W. Stainback & S. Stainback (Eds.), *Support networks for inclusive schooling: Interdependent integrated education* (pp. 123–137). Baltimore, MD: Paul H. Brookes.

Reynolds, M. C. (1989). An historical perspective: The delivery of special education to mildly disabled and at-risk students. *Remedial and Special Education, 10*(6), 7–11.

Reynolds, M. C., Wang, M. C., & Walberg, H. J. (1987). The necessary restructuring of special and regular education. *Exceptional Children, 53*, 391–398.

Roberts, C., & Zubrick, S. (1993). Factors influencing the social status of children with mild academic disabilities in regular classrooms. *Exceptional Children, 59*, 192–202.

Sabornie, E. J. (1985). Social mainstreaming of handicapped students: Facing an unpleasant reality. *Remedial and Special Education, 6*(2), 12–16.

Salend, S. J. (1994). *Effective mainstreaming: Creating inclusive classrooms* (2nd ed.). Upper Saddle River, NJ: Merrill/Prentice Hall.

Salend, S. J., & Lutz, J. G. (1984). Mainstreaming or mainlining: A competency based approach to mainstreaming. *Journal of Learning Disabilities, 17*, 27–29.

Salend, S. J., & Salend, S. M. (1986). Competencies for mainstreaming secondary level learning disabled students. *Journal of Learning Disabilities, 19*, 91–94.

Salend, S. J., & Viglianti, D. (1982). Preparing secondary students for the mainstream. *Teaching Exceptional Children, 14*, 137–140.

Schumaker, J. B., & Deshler, D. D. (1988). Implementing the regular education initiative in secondary schools: A different ball game. *Journal of Learning Disabilities, 21*, 36–42.

Schumm, J. S., & Vaughn, S. (1992). Planning for mainstreamed special education students: Perceptions of general classroom teachers. *Exceptionality, 3*, 81–98.

Semmel, M. I., Abernathy, T. V., Butera, G., & Lesar, S. (1991). Teacher perceptions of the regular education initiative. *Exceptional Children, 58*, 9–24.

Shanker, A. (1994/1995). Full inclusion is neither free nor appropriate. *Educational Leadership, 52*(4), 18–21.

Showers, B. (1985). Teachers coaching teachers. *Educational Leadership, 42*(7), 43–48.

Showers, B. (1990). Aiming for superior classroom instruction for all children: A comprehensive staff development model. *Remedial and Special Education, 11*(3), 35–39.

Singer, J. D. (1988). Should special education merge with regular education? *Educational Policy, 2*, 409–424.

Smith, C. R. (1994). *Learning disabilities: The interaction of learner, task, and setting* (3rd ed.). Boston: Allyn & Bacon.

Speece, D. L., & Mandell, C. J. (1980). Resource room support services for regular teachers. *Learning Disability Quarterly, 3*(1), 49–53.

Stainback, S., & Stainback, W. (1987). Integration versus cooperation: A commentary on "Educating children with learning problems: A shared responsibility." *Exceptional Children*, *54*, 66–68.

Stainback, S., Stainback, W., East, K., & Sapon-Shevin, M. (1994). A commentary on inclusion and the development of a positive self-identity by people with disabilities. *Exceptional Children*, *60*, 486–490.

Thousand, J. S., & Villa, R. A. (1990). Sharing expertise and responsibilities through teaching teams. In W. Stainback & S. Stainback (Eds.), *Support networks for inclusive schooling: Interdependent integrated education* (pp. 151–166). Baltimore, MD: Paul H. Brookes.

Tindal, G., Shinn, M. R., & Rodden-Nord, K. (1990). Contextually based school consultation: Influential variables. *Exceptional Children*, *56*, 324–336.

Truesdell, L. A., & Abramson, T. (1992). Academic behavior and grades of mainstreamed students with mild disabilities. *Exceptional Children*, *58*, 392–398.

U.S. Department of Education. (1994). *To assure the free appropriate public education of all children with disabilities: Sixteenth annual report to Congress on the implementation of the Individuals with Disabilities Education Act*. Washington, DC: Author.

Vaughn, S., & Schumm, J. S. (1994). Middle school teachers' planning for students with learning disabilities. *Remedial and Special Education*, *15*, 152–161.

Wang, M. C., & Baker, E. T. (1985-1986). Mainstreaming programs: Design features and effects. *The Journal of Special Education*, *19*, 503–521.

Wang, M. C., Reynolds, M. C., & Walberg, H. J. (1986). Rethinking special education. *Educational Leadership*, *44*(1), 26–31.

Wang, M. C., Reynolds, M. C., & Walberg, H. J. (1994/1995). Serving students at the margins. *Educational Leadership*, *52*(4), 12–17.

Wang, M. C., & Zollers, N. J. (1990). Adaptive instruction: An alternative service delivery approach. *Remedial and Special Education*, *11*(1), 7–21.

Warren, E. (1954). *Brown v. Board of Education of Topeka*, 347 U.S. 483, 493.

Waxman, H. C., Wang, M. C., Anderson, K. A., & Walberg, H. J. (1985). Adaptive education and student outcomes: A quantitative synthesis. *Journal of Educational Research*, *78*(4), 228–236.

Weller, C. (1980). Discrepancy and severity in the learning disabled: A consolidated perspective. *Learning Disability Quarterly*, *3*(1), 84–90.

West, J. F., & Cannon, G. S. (1988). Essential collaborative consultation competencies for regular and special educators. *Journal of Learning Disabilities*, *21*, 56–63, 68.

West, J. F., & Idol, L. (1990). Collaborative consultation in the education of mildly handicapped and at-risk students. *Remedial and Special Education*, *11*(1), 22–31.

West, J. F., Idol, L., & Cannon, G. (1988). *Collaboration in the schools: Communicating, interacting, and problem solving*. Austin, TX: PRO-ED.

Wiederholt, J. L. (1974). Planning resource rooms for the mildly handicapped. *Focus on Exceptional Children*, *5*, 1–10.

Wiederholt, J. L., & Chamberlain, S. P. (1989). A critical analysis of resource programs. *Remedial and Special Education*, *10*(6), 15–27.

Will, M. C. (1986). Educating children with learning problems: A shared responsibility. *Exceptional Children*, *52*, 411–415.

Wilmore, E. L. (1994/1995). When your child is special. *Educational Leadership*, *52*(4), 60–62.

Yell, M. L. (1995). Least restrictive environment, inclusion, and students with disabilities: A legal analysis. *The Journal of Special Education*, *28*, 389–404.

Ysseldyke, J. E., & Christenson, S. L. (1993). *The Instructional Environment System—II*. Longmont, CO: Sopris West.

Teaching Practices

CHAPTER 7

After studying this chapter, you should be able to:

- define *individualized instruction*.
- discuss instructional variables related to learning.
- provide strategies for motivating students to learn.
- discuss factors to consider when selecting curriculum materials.
- describe various instructional arrangements.
- discuss peer tutoring, *ClassWide Peer Tutoring*, and cooperative learning.
- describe self-correcting materials and instructional games.
- discuss the use of technological tools.
- discuss research on homework and present guidelines to promote "best practices" in homework.
- discuss learner variables that influence learning and instruction design.
- present interactive teaching competencies from effective teaching research.
- discuss postinstructional activities to improve teaching effectiveness.

Because certain attitudes are important to the success and enjoyment of teaching students with learning disabilities, an individual considering a teaching career in this field should examine relevant thoughts and attitudes. For example, it helps if a teacher thinks that *teachers can make a difference*. This thought frequently appears as a slogan on T-shirts and bumper stickers. Common slogans include "Teachers Touch the Future," "Children Are Our Future: Teach Them Well," "If You Can Read This, Thank a Teacher," and "I Touch the Future: I Teach."

In the following story entitled "Three Letters from Teddy," by Elizabeth Silance Ballard, the teacher discovered that teachers can make a difference:

> Teddy's letter came today and now that I've read it, I will place it in my cedar chest with the other things that are important in my life.
>
> "I wanted you to be the first to know."
>
> I smiled as I read the words he had written and my heart swelled with a pride that I had no right to feel.
>
> I have not seen Teddy Stallard since he was a student in my fifth grade class, 15 years ago. It was early in my career, and I had only been teaching for 2 years.
>
> From the first day he stepped into my classroom, I disliked Teddy. Teachers (although everyone knows differently) are not supposed to have favorites in a class, but most especially they are not to show dislike for a child, any child.
>
> Nevertheless, every year there are one or two children that one cannot help be attracted to, for teachers are human and it is human nature to like bright, pretty, intelligence people, whether they are 10 years old or 25. And sometimes, not too often, fortunately, there will be one or two students to whom the teacher just can't seem to relate.
>
> I had thought myself quite capable of handling my personal feelings along that line until Teddy walked into my life. There wasn't a child I particularly liked that year, but Teddy was most assuredly one I disliked.
>
> He was dirty. Not just occasionally, but all the time. His hair hung low over his ears, and he actually had to hold it out of his eyes as he wrote his papers in class. (And this was before it was fashionable to do so!) Too, he had a peculiar odor about him which I could never identify.
>
> His physical faults were many, and his intellect left a lot to be desired, also. By the end of the first week I knew he was hopelessly behind the others. Not only was he behind; he was just plain slow. I began to withdraw from him immediately.
>
> Any teacher will tell you that it's more of a pleasure to teach a bright child. It is definitely more rewarding for one's ego. But any teacher worth her credentials can channel work to the bright child, keeping him challenged and learning, while she puts her major effort in the slower ones. Any teacher can do this. Most teachers do it, but I didn't, not that year.
>
> In fact, I concentrated on my best students and let the others follow along as best they could. Ashamed as I am to admit it, I took perverse pleasure in using my red pen; and each time I came to Teddy's papers, the cross marks (and they were many) were always a little larger and a little redder than necessary.
>
> While I did not actually ridicule the boy, my attitude was obviously quite apparent to the class, for he quickly became the class "goat," the outcast, the unlovable, the unloved.
>
> He knew I didn't like him but he didn't know why. Nor did I know then or now why I felt such an intense dislike for him. All I know is that he was a little boy no one cared about, and I made no effort in his behalf.
>
> The days rolled on. We made it through the Fall Festival and the Thanksgiving holidays, and I continued marking happily with my red pen.
>
> And as the Christmas holidays approached, I knew that Teddy would never catch up in time to be promoted to the sixth grade level. He would be a repeater.
>
> To justify myself, I went to his cumulative folder from time to time. He had very low grades for the first 4 years, but no grade failure. How he had made it, I didn't know. I closed my mind to the personal remarks.
>
> First Grade: Teddy shows promise by work and attitude, but has poor home situation.
>
> Second Grade: Teddy could do better. Mother terminally ill. He receives little help at home.
>
> Third Grade: Teddy is a pleasant boy. Helpful, but too serious. Slow learner. Mother passed away at end of the year.

Fourth Grade: Very slow, but well behaved. Father shows no interest.

Well, they passed him four times, but he will certainly repeat the fifth grade! Do him good! I said to myself.

And then the last day before the holiday arrived, our little tree on the reading table sported paper and popcorn chains. Many gifts were heaped underneath, waiting for the big moment.

Teachers always get several gifts at Christmas, but mine that year seemed bigger and more elaborate than ever. There was not a student who had not brought me one. Each unwrapping brought squeals of delight, and the proud giver would receive effusive thank you's.

His gift wasn't the last one I picked up: In fact, it was in the middle of the pile. Its wrapping was a brown paper bag, and he had colored Christmas trees and red bells all over it. It was stuck together with masking tape.

"For Miss Thompson from Teddy," it read.

The group was completely silent, and for the first time I felt conspicuous, embarrassed because they all stood watching me unwrap that gift.

As I removed the last bit of masking tape, two items fell to my desk; a gaudy rhinestone bracelet with several stones missing and a small bottle of dime-store cologne, half empty.

I could hear the snickers and whispers, and I wasn't sure I could look at Teddy.

"Isn't this lovely," I said as I tried to place the bracelet on my arm. "Would you help me fasten it?"

He smiled shyly as he fixed the clasp, and I held up my wrist for all of them to admire.

There were a few hesitant oohs and ahhs, but as I dabbed the cologne behind my ears, all the little girls lined up for a dab behind their ears.

I continued to open the gifts until I reached the bottom of the pile. We ate our refreshments, and the bell rang.

The children filed out with shouts of "See you next year!" and "Merry Christmas!" but Teddy waited at his desk.

When they had all left, he walked toward me, clutching his gift and books to his chest.

"You smell just like Mom," he said softly. "Her bracelet looks real pretty on you, too. I'm glad you liked it."

He left quickly. I locked the door, sat down at my desk, and wept, resolving to give Teddy what I had deliberately deprived him of—a teacher who cared.

I stayed every afternoon with Teddy from the end of the Christmas holidays until the last day of school. Sometimes we worked together. Sometimes he worked alone while I drew up lesson plans or graded papers.

Slowly, but surely he caught up with the rest of the class. Gradually, there was a definite upward curve in his grades.

He did not have to repeat the fifth grade. In fact, his final averages were among the highest in the class, and although I knew he would be moving out of the state when school was out, I was not worried for him. Teddy had reached a level that would stand him in a good stead the following year, no matter where he went. He had enjoyed a measure of success, and as we were taught in our teacher training courses, "Success builds success."

I did not hear from Teddy until 7 years later, when his first letter appeared in my mailbox.

Dear Miss Thompson,

I just wanted you to be the first to know. I will be graduating second in my class next month.

Very truly yours,

Teddy Stallard

I sent him a card of congratulations and a small package—a pen and pencil gift set. I wondered what he would do after graduation. Four years later Teddy's second letter came.

Dear Miss Thompson,

I wanted you to be the first to know. I was just informed that I'll be graduating first in my class. The university has not been easy, but I liked it.

Very truly yours,

Teddy Stallard

I sent him a good pair of sterling silver monogrammed cuff links and a card, so proud of him I could burst!

And now today, Teddy's third letter.

Dear Miss Thompson,

I wanted you to be the first to know. As of today I am Theodore J. Stallard, M.D. How about that!!"

I'm going to be married in July, the 7th, to be exact. I wanted to ask if you could come and sit where Mom would sit if she was here. I'll have no family there as Dad died last year.

Very truly yours,
Teddy Stallard

I'm not sure what kind of gift one sends to a doctor on completion of medical school and state boards. Maybe I'll just wait and take a wedding gift, but my note can't wait.

Dear Ted,

Congratulations! You made it, and you did it yourself! In spite of those like me, and not because of us, this day has come for you.

God bless you. I'll be at the wedding with bells on!

Students with learning disabilities bring much more than a label to the learning environment. They exist across all ethnic groups and socioeconomic levels. They come in all sizes and shapes and bring strengths, aspirations, talents, beliefs, fears, sorrows, joys, interests, and hopes with them. To help them use their many resources to learn and experience a positive and productive life, the teacher must think that he or she *can make a difference*. It also helps for the teacher to think that *students are likable and enjoyable*. I once heard a person ask Zig Engelmann "What do you do if you don't like a student?" Without hesitation, he responded, "You do not dislike a student on company time!" Moreover, the teacher should think that *observing a person learn is exciting*. Many successful teachers are thrilled when they witness the "a-ha" effect in learning.

When a teacher thinks that teachers make a difference, that students are enjoyable, and that the teaching-learning process is exciting, preparation for becoming an effective teacher is likely to begin enthusiastically. To start this preparation, it is helpful to view teaching within three domains: planning activities, interactive teaching activities, and postinstructional activities (see Figure 7.1). Because activities in these three domains occur simultaneously and sequentially, they are not bound by time. For example, while providing feedback regarding students' errors (an interactive teaching activity), the teacher may reflect on the students' responses in terms of expected outcomes and use the information to plan the next day's lesson (a postinstructional activity). Also, these domains tend to transcend teaching contexts. Context is important; however, the major difference context makes involves the specific understandings teachers need to explain or model the tasks successfully (Reynolds, 1992). The content does not differentiate the basic teaching practices. Basically, the teaching tasks used to foster learning are similar across contexts and settings.

PLANNING ACTIVITIES

Planning activities include an array of tasks that range from critical thinking to arranging schedules. These activities result in an organizational and action plan that enables the teacher to create a community of learners and provides a framework for making instructional decisions. The following planning activities are discussed: (a) develop empowering beliefs about teaching, (b) consider instructional variables related to student learning, (c) consider the curriculum, (d) consider instructional arrangements, and (e) consider learner variables.

Develop Empowering Beliefs About Teaching

There are many beliefs that empower teachers; however, this section focuses on defining individualized instruction, basing instructional practices on research, and maintaining proactive expectancies of learners. Constructive beliefs in these areas help provide a teaching foundation that is important for teaching students with learning disabilities.

Define Individualized Instruction. Meeting the needs of a diverse group of students with learning disabilities is a formidable task for both gen-

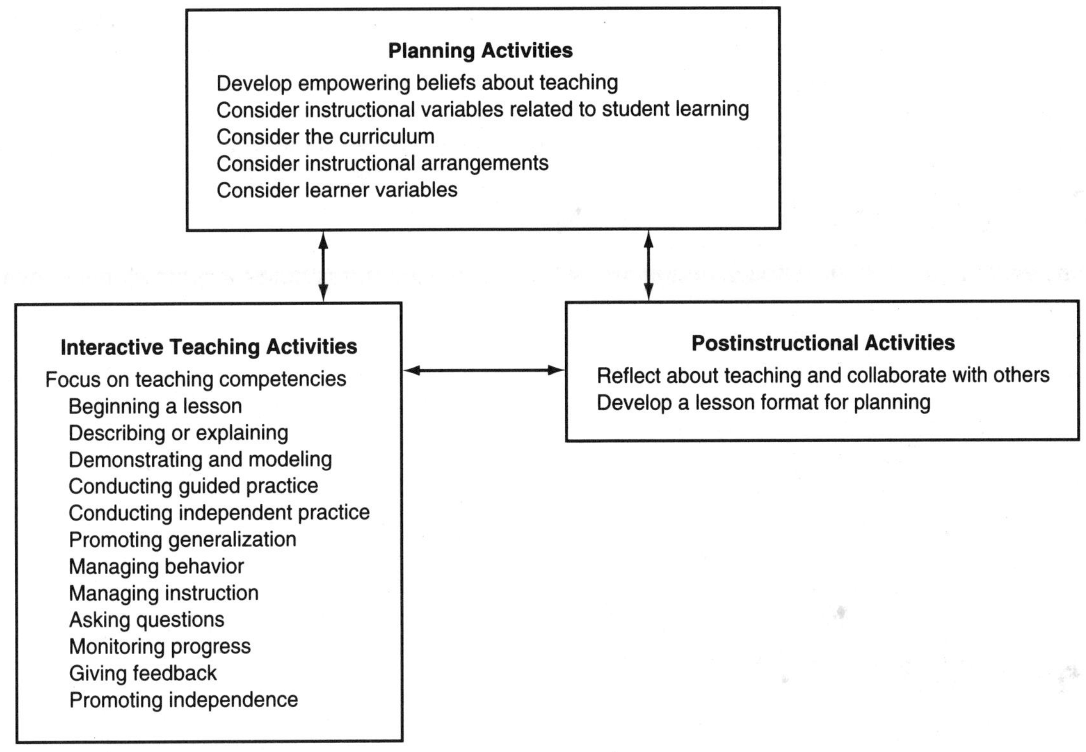

FIGURE 7.1
A framework for structuring teaching activities

eral and special education teachers. Primary and elementary teachers are faced with helping youngsters acquire basic, independent skills and explore careers. While teaching more than 100 students daily, secondary teachers are faced with helping adolescents acquire specific vocational skills, developing dependent strategies, and explore academic knowledge.

These teachers must be able to alter the *type* and *amount* of instruction. Altering the type of instruction may involve putting reading passages on tape or teaching the student a strategy for writing a paragraph. Altering the amount of instruction entails providing more extensive teacher modeling of concepts, using elaborated feedback, or providing more independent practice.

Individualized instruction refers to instruction that enables the student to work on appropriate tasks over time under conditions that motivate. This individualized approach does not imply that each student must be taught one-to-one. It *does* mean, however, that students receive daily instruction tailored to their educational needs. It can occur within various instructional arrangements, including seatwork, small groups, peer teaching, and large groups. The teacher matches the learner, the task, and instructional interventions to ensure optimal student growth.

Some specific components of individualized instruction consist of (a) instructional objectives based on assessment, (b) variable entry points into the curriculum, (c) variable pacing, (d) active participation of the learner in decision making, (e) a variety of instructional arrangements (e.g., large groups, small groups, and cooperative learning) as a function of the task and learning level, and (f) criterion-referenced evaluation of the learner. As noted in

Chapter 5, the individualized educational program (IEP) outlines the plan (i.e., the outcomes, curriculum, teachers' responsibilities, schedule, and settings) that facilitates individualized instruction.

Base Instructional Practices on Research. In selecting a teaching orientation, there are some basic principles that should be followed before interventions are continued with students who have learning disabilities. First, any instructional procedure should be amenable to evaluation. There is evidence indicating that teachers' perceptions of student progress without learner data frequently are incorrect (Miramontes, Cheng, & Trueba, 1984; Utley, Zigmond, & Strain, 1987). It is not sufficient for a teacher to "feel" that an approach is effective. Evaluation results need to document the effectiveness of specific interventions. Second, regardless of one's orientation, an educator must maintain empirical orientation to teaching practices. When research indicates that one approach is more effective than another, the data-supported approach deserves consideration. Third, because the state of knowledge in learning disabilities is tenuous and changing, educators must remain open-minded about best practices. Meaningful breakthroughs are likely to occur across orientations (e.g., medical, cognitive, and behavioral). When these breakthroughs generate empirically supported strategies or techniques, educators should consider incorporating these applications into their teaching practices.

Unfortunately, the history of popular instructional practices reflects wide swings in opinion from decade to decade. For example, the pendulum constantly swings between a teacher-directed, skills-based approach and a student-directed instructional approach. Thus, what are viewed as best practices tend to change about every decade. These instructional shifts are so dramatic that educators frequently use the word *reform* to launch a new teaching practice. Because these recommended reforms usually are tied to opinion rather than to instructional research, educators are constantly in a state of reform. Also, these reforms usually enter the instructional arena in a passionate manner that promotes an attitude of "one size fits all." Constant reform implies that educators are not sure of their knowledge base or that a knowledge base is lacking.

Fortunately, an informative knowledge base is accruing, and it is time for professional educators to adopt a *refinement* rather than a reform posture about instructional practices. In a survey of learning disabilities teachers in Iowa, Kavale and Reese (1991) found that these teachers displayed a sound knowledge base concerning learning disabilities and interventions and appeared to base their practices on their beliefs. Moreover, the learning disabilities teachers seemed willing to modify their practices as new information became available. These gradual modifications need to be anchored in the existing research, and, as additional research provides new information, teaching practices should be refined. Grossen (1993) captures this view in the following passage:

> The state-of-the-art in best teaching practice, as it is defined by scientific educational research, requires balance, not decade-by-decade flip-flopping from one extreme fad to the other extreme fad. It requires a thoughtful, intricate balance. . . . In contrast to this balanced continuum, educational reforms usually promote one extreme and omit or even discredit any attempt to incorporate the other extreme. (pp. 1–2)

Chapter 8 highlights how different theoretical orientations are being used to meet the needs of students with learning disabilities. The good news is that many educators are beginning to recognize the research from various paradigms and integrate the findings into practices that respond to the needs of a diverse population of learners (Englert, Tarrant, & Mariage, 1992).

Maintain Proactive Expectancies of Learners. Although the label *learning disabled* may have general implications for instruction (e.g., the student needs to develop efficient strategies for performing academic tasks), it has limited relevance for daily instruction. No single approach or activity meets the diverse needs of students with learning disabilities. Teachers must enter the instructional arena with an appreciation of each student's uniqueness and a willingness to examine and use a variety of resources. A characteristic thought of effective teachers is that all students are capable of learning. A positive expectancy for each student is a hallmark belief of teachers who succeed in helping students with learning disabilities reach their academic and affective potential.

In addition to the accruing research on what teachers do that promotes student learning, researchers are beginning to examine the influence of what teachers think about learner outcomes. It is estimated that teachers make one decision every 2 minutes (Clark & Peterson, 1986). Teacher thoughts influence teacher decisions and behavior; thus, it is believed that thoughts can be altered to help teachers make more effective decisions.

Consider Instructional Variables Related to Student Learning

Focus on Time for Learning. In their review of teaching research, Stevens and Rosenshine (1981) report that successful teachers maintain a strong academic focus. Effective teachers instruct students to spend more time working directly on academic tasks in texts, workbooks, and instructional materials. They assign and hold students responsible for more homework and test students more frequently.

The importance of an academic focus also receives support from research on engaged time. *Engaged time* is the time a student actually spends performing an academic task (e.g., writing, reading, or computing). An extensive study of teaching activities that make a difference in student achievement was conducted as part of a 6-year Beginning Teacher Evaluation Study funded by the National Institute of Education through the California Commission for Teaching Preparation and Licensing. Denham and Lieberman (1980) report that one of the major contributions of the study is its emphasis on academic learning time—that is, the time a student spends engaged in academic tasks of appropriate difficulty. As expected, the study found that academic learning time is related to student achievement. Specifically, Fisher et al. (1980) report that the time allocated to a content area is associated positively with learning in that area, and the engaged time that students spend successfully performing reading or mathematics tasks is associated positively with learning. Thus, a cornerstone of good teaching is establishing appropriate academic instructional objectives and designing intervention programs that maximize opportunities for the student to work successfully on tasks related to the objectives. Unfortunately, several researchers (Borg, 1980; Larrivee, 1986; Ysseldyke & Algozzine, 1995) report that students' engaged time in many classrooms is relatively low.

Ysseldyke, Christenson, Thurlow, and Skiba (1987) report that the percentage of engaged time in special education classes is about 75% and that engaged time varies across classrooms and among students within a classroom. Haynes and Jenkins (1986) examined the instruction that special education students receive in resource rooms. One of their findings revealed that the amount of reading instruction per day varied from class to class. One class received about 58 minutes a day, and another class received about 17 minutes a day. As expected, the students who spent more time in reading learned more about reading. In an observation of 230 elementary students with mild disabilities, Rich and Ross (1989) found that noninstructional time (e.g., transitions, housekeeping, wait time, and free time) accounted for almost 3 hours of the school day.

Researchers report that achievement gains and academic engagement time are greater during teacher-directed behavior than during independent work (Chow, 1981; Sindelar, Smith, Harriman, Hale, & Wilson, 1986). Some educators (Howell, Fox, & Morehead, 1993) maintain that teachers need to ensure that independent seatwork directly relates to instructional objectives.

The finding that academic learning time is related positively to more student learning is consistent in the research for both general education students and students with learning disabilities (Reynolds, 1992). Maximizing the time that students spend engaged in meaningful academic tasks and minimizing the time off task are extremely important in creating a positive and productive learning environment.

Gettinger (1991) found that students with learning disabilities required significantly more time to achieve mastery on a reading comprehension task than students without learning disabilities. She recommends that students with learning disabilities receive adequate time to achieve and encourages educators to investigate techniques for helping them learn more efficiently and retain the information. In essence, it is helpful when students with learning disabilities are provided with ample time for learning, experience high rates of success, and are taught strategies for how to learn and retain relevant information. Greenwood (1991) used classwide peer tutoring with at-risk elementary students to increase time on academic tasks over a 5-semester period. The peer tutoring group achieved academic gains that were superior to a control group of comparable students.

Researchers claim that achievement is improved in two ways: (a) by increasing the student's learning time and (b) by decreasing the time a student needs to learn. Instructional factors that increase engaged time or decrease time needed for learning a specific skill include relevant learning tasks, effective classroom management, clearly stated learning expectations, timely and specific feedback, teacher-student interaction, reinforcement for learning, and continuous monitoring to meet instructional objectives (L. W. Anderson, 1984; Rieth & Evertson, 1988). The following are some specific suggestions for increasing engaged time overall, during instructional time, and during independent work:

Suggestions for increasing engaged time overall:

1. Schedule more instructional time.
2. Teach students to make transitions quickly.
3. Use effective teaching techniques (see the Interactive Teaching Activities section later in this chapter).
4. Strive to motivate students.
5. Be organized and prepared.
6. Increase teacher instructional interactions with students.
7. Maintain a balance between teacher-led and seatwork time.

Suggestions to increase engaged time during teacher-led instruction:

1. Use signals to remind students to attend (see SLANT in Chapter 15).
2. Be enthusiastic.
3. Maintain a brisk pace.
4. Illustrate content with interesting metaphors or stories.
5. Ask questions frequently and involve all students.
6. Praise students for effort and being on task.
7. Highlight the importance of content and its relation to daily life.

Suggestions to increase engaged time during independent work:

1. Use a variety of seatwork activities, instructional games, self-correcting materials, and computer-assisted instruction.
2. Teach students to work independently.
3. Use peer tutoring pairs and *ClassWide Peer Tutoring*.
4. Make independent work relevant and meaningful.
5. Use cooperative learning groups.
6. Praise students for doing seatwork.
7. Check independent work for progress.
8. Monitor independent work through scanning and moving around the classroom.
9. Give clear and concise directions.
10. Evaluate independent work.

11. Post student work in the classroom.
12. Give independent work at each student's instructional level.

Ensure High Rates of Student Success. The need for students to experience high levels of success has substantial research support. In this research, *success* refers to the rate at which the student understands and correctly completes exercises (Borich, 1992). Success is defined according to the difficulty level of the materials. In high success, the student understands the task and makes occasional careless errors. With moderate success, the student partially understands the material and makes numerous mistakes, and in low success the student does not comprehend the material. Student engagement in academic work is related highly to rate of success (i.e., instruction that produces moderate-to-high success rates results in increased achievement). Apparently, during high success rates more content is covered at the learner's appropriate instructional level. The positive relationship between achievement and high success rate is documented especially when the instruction is didactic or expository.

One of the primary findings of the Beginning Teacher Evaluation Study (Fisher et al., 1980) is that learning improves most when students have a high percentage of correct responses during teacher questioning and seatwork. Furthermore, Stevens and Rosenshine (1981) report that a high percentage of correct responses given rapidly correlates with academic achievement. They suggest that a reasonable success rate appears to be at least 80% during instruction and 90% at the end of a unit. Ideally, the task should maintain an appropriate level of challenge (i.e., require effort to succeed). Fisher et al. highlight this point:

> Common sense suggests that too high a rate of high success work might be boring and repetitive and could inhibit the development of persistence. Probably, some balance between high success and more challenging work is appropriate. Also, we found that older students and/or students who were generally skilled at school learning did not require as high a percentage of time at the high success level. Apparently these students had learned problem solving—how to take a task they did not completely understand and work it out. Such students are able to undertake the challenge of more difficult material, as long as they eventually experience success. . . . When students worked with materials or activities that yielded a low success rate, achievement was lower. (pp. 17–18)

Moreover, Stevens and Rosenshine note that individualization is considered a characteristic of effective instruction if it refers to helping each student achieve a high percentage of correct responses.

Borich (1992) claims that the research suggests that students need to spend about 60% to 70% of their time on tasks that allow almost complete understanding with occasional careless errors. Instruction that promotes high success not only contributes to improved achievement, but also fosters increased levels of self-esteem and positive attitudes toward academic learning and school (Wyne & Stuck, 1982).

In a study of success rates, Rieth and Frick (1983) found that learners with mild disabilities experience 43% high task success, 45% medium task success, and 12% low task success. Fisher et al. (1978) found that normally achieving students experience 45% high task success, 52% medium task success, and 3% low task success. The relative low rates of high success for both groups and the higher rate of low task success for the learners with mild disabilities underscore the need for better instructional matches and the continuous monitoring of student progress (Rieth & Evertson, 1988). The importance of providing the student with success cannot be overemphasized in good teaching. Lack of success can lead to anxiety, frustration, inappropriate behavior, and poor motivation. In contrast, success can improve motivation, attitudes, academic progress, and classroom behavior.

Although many variables contribute to student success, the degree to which an appropriate

TABLE 7.1
Selected Instructional Features That Promote Student Success

Area	Instructional Feature
Content	Is useful or relevant Is clearly specified Is instructionally organized for easy learning
Assessment	Enables appropriate placement Provides frequent feedback regarding programs Leads to the establishment of realistic but high goals
Learning experience	Allows ample time for learning Provides support to facilitate learning Lets students actually experience high rates of progress Reinforces achievements and efforts
Self-regulation	Permits students to work independently Permits students to self-monitor their progress in some lessons Allows students to participate in goal setting and the selection of some activities
Collaboration	Includes peer teaching Includes collaboration in group activities

instructional match is accomplished for each student must be viewed as the cornerstone of teaching that promotes high rates of success. The teacher's ability to diagnose relevant student characteristics (e.g., skill level, prior knowledge, strategy use, interests, and motivation) and task factors (e.g., level of difficulty, time to achieve mastery, and relevance) influences the quality of the instructional match (Christenson, Ysseldyke, & Thurlow, 1989). In essence, the teacher must match the learning task to the student's aptitude (i.e., diagnostic teaching function) to develop an instructional program that ensures student success. As presented in Table 7.1, Wang (1987) highlights some of the features of learning environments that promote successful learning outcomes. Borich (1992) notes that moderate- to high-success rates not only help learners achieve mastery of lesson content but also provide a foundation for students to become independent learners and engage in higher-order thinking. This development becomes more likely when explicit instruction is coupled with strategies or self-directed instruction.

Provide Positive and Supportive Learning Environments. It is well-known that students learn more when the school and classroom environments are positive and supportive (Christenson et al., 1989). For example, Samuels (1986) reports that an academic focus with a humanistic orientation increases student achievement. The teacher is the key individual who influences the tone of a classroom. The teacher arranges physical variables (e.g., lighting, temperature, and seating) and academic variables (e.g., scheduling, method of lesson presentation, test dates, and homework) and establishes the affective nature (e.g., encouragement, competitiveness, and cooperation) of the classroom. Purkey (1978) maintains that the teacher has the power to invite each student to learn. Teacher expectations, encouragements, evaluations, attentiveness, and attitudes greatly influence students' perceptions of themselves as learners. Given that many students with learning disabilities have negative perceptions of their academic abilities, it is important that general and special education teachers create and maintain a supportive classroom setting for them. When the teacher is cheerful, supportive, and enthusiastic, students tend to feel more comfortable and model those actions and attitudes. This can result in a pleasant, productive learning environment for all learners. Teachers easily can notice when things go wrong in the classroom, but *effective* teachers comment on positive classroom happenings. Sprick (1985) notes that learning is greater and behavior is more appropriate in classrooms in which teachers attend more to positive events than to negative events. Specifically, he reports that teachers who maintain a 3:1 ratio of attention to positive over negative events are likely to have a well-managed classroom of high-achieving students. Goodlad (1984) found that teachers with positive styles used about 10% of their time handling behavior problems, whereas teachers with predominantly negative styles spent about 42% of their time managing inappropriate behavior of students. Sprick reports that, unfortunately, most classroom teachers attend to negative events three times more often than they attend to positive events. R. M. Smith, Neisworth, and Greer (1978) convey the importance of the positive approach:

> Liberal amounts of praise, support, and encouragement are found in every good classroom. By emphasizing children's good points, the teacher can build their confidence and desire to tackle more difficult activities. Failure to use such encouragement is a mistake teachers cannot afford to make. The development of a healthy social interaction in the classroom has never been accomplished through criticism and ridicule. (p. 85)

Several educators (Borich, 1992; Brigham, Scruggs, & Mastropieri, 1992) maintain that teacher enthusiasm is an important aspect of teacher effort, is positively correlated to student achievement, and helps establish a positive and supportive learning environment. Brigham et al. examined the effects of teacher enthusiasm on the learning and behavior of junior high school students with learning disabilities. Their results indicate that enthusiastic presentations yield higher academic achievement and lower levels of off-task behavior. They characterize enthusiastic presentations according to eight elements: (a) varied, uplifting, and rapid vocal delivery, (b) dancing, wide-open eyes, (c) frequent, demonstrative gestures, (d) dramatic and varied body movements, (e) varied, emotive facial expressions, (f) varied word usage, (g) ready animated acceptance of ideas and feelings, and (h) exuberant overall energy level. Conversely, they describe unenthusiastic teacher behavior as (a) standing or sitting in the same place, (b) speaking in a monotone or inexpressive voice, (c) making infrequent eye contact, (d) using few animated facial expressions, and (e) generally interacting less with students. Borich maintains that no one can sustain a heightened level of enthusiasm for a long time without becoming emotionally fatigued. He states that a proper level of enthusiasm reflects a balance of gesturing, eye contact, vocal inflections, and movement. Moderate use of these behaviors in combination signals to most students the teacher's enthusiasm (i.e., vigor, involvement, and interest).

Brophy and Good (1986) and Alderman (1990) report that a positive learning environment and student learning are enhanced when teachers believe that *all* students can learn and that teachers can make a difference. Christenson et al. (1989) state that the following factors contribute to a positive learning environment: (a) the use of realistic expectations for student learning, (b) the development of instructional plans that consider student characteristics and needs, (c) the use of reinforcement for student productivity, (d) the use of active monitoring of student progress, and (e) the belief that all students will experience academic success. Alderman notes that in a positive classroom errors are viewed as a natural and important part of the learning process rather than as an indication that the student lacks ability. Moreover, a positive approach is enhanced by the appropriate use of reinforcement for desirable academic, on-task, and social behaviors. The positive effect of reinforcement on academic achievement and work behaviors is well established (Blankenship & Lilly, 1981; Lovitt, 1995). The teacher may consider the following questions to examine his or her potential influence on creating a positive and supportive learning environment:

1. Am I enthusiastic most of the time?
2. What is my attitude toward students?
3. What is my attitude toward peers?
4. Do I support all students?
5. Do I admit mistakes and remain comfortable?
6. Do I change my opinion with new information?
7. Am I happy?
8. Is my job fulfilling?
9. Do I take care of my physical and emotional health?
10. Am I a good listener?
11. Do I laugh and smile much?

Students' descriptions of good teachers (Lovitt, 1977) reflect the importance of being positive. The students in Lovitt's study noted that good teachers compliment students, let students come to them for help, help each student, use good manners, show trust for students, join in class humor, explain more than once, and ask students for help. The students were concerned with fair play, inclusion in the action, and getting work done in a quiet and orderly room. They wanted their teachers to be real people with senses of humor. When the teachers behaved more like this, the academic performance of the students improved: "As the teacher did more things that pleased the students, they did more to please the teacher" (Lovitt, 1977, p. 94).

Strive to Motivate. The initial step in preventing classroom behavior problems is to keep students motivated and, thus, engaged in the learning process. *Motivation* is used to describe what focuses or energizes a student's attention, emotions, and activity. It explains why students choose certain activities over other activities (e.g., do homework or talk on the telephone). Motivators can be internal or external, and they represent things or events that influence choices. Internal motivators come from within the individual (e.g., the desire to read a sports magazine). External motivators come from within the environment (e.g., parental pressure to do homework). When both internal and external sources motivate in the same direction, the impact is powerful. To motivate effectively, the teacher should be aware of a student's internal motivators, such as interests, needs, and aspirations, and external motivators, such as peer influence or teacher approval. Borich (1992) maintains that the key to motivation is to bring internal and external motivators together to engage students in active learning. He encourages teachers to find out students' needs, interests, and aspirations and to use these to personalize learning and, thus, motivate students to learn.

Many students with learning disabilities lose their motivation for learning as a result of a history of frustration and school failure. When teaching students with limited motivation, the teacher should plan systematic procedures to increase motivation. Van Reusen and Bos (1994) examined the effects of motivation strategy instruction on the participation of secondary students with learning disabilities in planning their IEPs. This instruction required the students to examine their strengths and limitations and identify their needs and aspirations. The purpose of the motivation strategy instruction was to involve the learners in key aspects of the learning process and increase the students' commitment to learn. Compared with students with learning disabilities who did not receive the motivation strategy training, the treatment group identified more goals and communicated more effectively during their IEP conferences. These findings highlight the importance of involving students with learning disabilities in the planning of their educational programs. Specifically, the motivation strategy instruction helped the teachers and students recognize needs, interests, and aspirations that were important for motivating these students.

Setting realistic instructional goals and determining specific mastery criteria are important to student motivation (Christenson et al., 1989). Clifford (1990) encourages teachers to establish learning goals that represent a moderate success probability. She notes that students often attribute success with easy tasks to task ease, and they attribute success with extremely difficult tasks to luck. Clifford states, "It is only success at moderately difficult . . . tasks that we explain in terms of personal effort, well-chosen strategies, and ability; and these explanations give rise to feelings of pride, competence, satisfaction, persistence, and personal control" (p. 22). Similarly, Alderman (1990) notes that the linking of success to one's own efforts is critical for the development of motivation in students.

Once goals are established, student motivation is enhanced by the monitoring of progress toward these goals and the delivering of feedback on how to correct errors through learning strategies and study skills (Porter & Brophy, 1988; Wang, 1987). Table 7.2 features strategies for motivating students as suggested by Alderman (1990), Brigham et al. (1992), Brophy (1987), Christenson et al. (1989), Porter and Brophy (1988), and Salend (1994).

Consider the Curriculum

Curriculum primarily involves what is taught in the school and consists of learning outcomes that society considers essential for success. A curriculum is established before students enter the school, and it represents what society values as important for becoming a productive citizen and successful individual. If the curriculum accurately represents what is important, it should not be altered, because students deserve an opportunity to acquire this valued knowledge and skills. To accommodate some students with learning disabilities, it is necessary to prioritize the content to ensure that the most important content is mastered. This position is highlighted in the notion that "less is more." Specifically, it refers to covering highly valued content extensively so that students achieve understanding and mastery of this important content. Another way of accommodating students with learning disabilities is to focus on how to teach the curriculum. Although some curriculum materials simply present objectives and activities, most materials influence how to teach through their organization, sequencing, and activities. Other materials provide extensive directions in how to teach (e.g., teacher scripts). Students with learning disabilities learn better when instruction follows research-supported interactive teaching activities (e.g., explicit modeling, corrective feedback, and monitoring of progress), which are presented later in this chapter. Because only 3% of published curriculum materials are field tested and validated before marketing (Sprick, 1987), educators need to select curriculum materials carefully. This section presents some factors to consider when examining and selecting curriculum materials for students with learning disabilities.

Curriculum Materials Should Promote Best Instructional Practices. The extensive research findings regarding teaching practices (Englert et al., 1992) should be incorporated in curriculum materials. For example, procedures should be included that help the teacher provide good advance organizers, clarify objectives, model concepts explicitly, provide meaningful examples, teach generalization, give helpful feedback, tie the content to something important, and accommodate learner diversity. Teachers deserve to have materials that remind or guide them to use "best practices." Teachers are constantly in a position that requires them to adapt, modify, or restructure curriculum materials to include best teaching practices. For many students with learning disabilities, these teacher procedures represent the difference between success or failure.

Curriculum Materials Should Foster Learner Understanding. Many students have experienced the arduous task of memorizing information (e.g., dates, facts, and math

TABLE 7.2
Strategies for Motivating Students to Learn

Plan for Motivation
Create a supportive and positive environment.
Program for success by maintaining a match between task and student capabilities.
Develop meaningful learning outcomes.
Relate content to students' interests and their daily lives.
Use metaphors, anecdotes, stories, and examples to embellish understanding.

Motivate Through Appropriate Expectations
Communicate positive expectations.
Communicate challenging expectations.
Teach goal setting and help students link efforts to outcomes.

Use Extrinsic Incentives for Students Who Require Them
Praise sincere effort.
Reward good or improved performances.
Point out pragmatic values of learning.
Structure appropriate competitive activities.
Provide students with many opportunities to respond.
Provide immediate feedback to student responses.
Periodically use a game format.

Recognize and Provide Intrinsic Motivation
Teach self-management.
Involve students in planning selected instructional activities.
Provide ample time for students to achieve mastery.
Give students choices in selecting activities or topics.
Allow students to complete products.
Use fantasy or simulation activities.
Challenge students with higher-order thinking activities.
Use cooperative learning and peer tutoring.
Discuss rationales for learning specific skills and content.
Induce students to develop their own motivation.
Encourage students to move from extrinsic to intrinsic motivators.
Use activities that arouse curiosity.

Use Strategies to Promote Motivation
Teach basic social skills.
Model interest in learning.
Project intensity.
Be enthusiastic about content and learning.
Be enthusiastic when presenting and interacting.
Use advance organizers to establish attending and importance.
Use explicit modeling to teach understanding.
Use a variety of independent learning activities (e.g., self-correcting materials and computer-assisted instruction).
Model metacognition through "think alouds" while problem solving.
Minimize anxiety during learning activities.
Monitor progress and adjust instruction accordingly.
Vary grouping arrangements.
Use culturally relevant materials and examples.
Use students' names, experiences, hobbies, and interests in lessons.

formulas) that becomes isolated cognitively (i.e., it does not connect with anything meaningful or relevant). Baker, Simmons, and Kameenui (1994) note that content needs to be presented in relation to "big ideas." These big ideas are concepts or strategies that facilitate efficient learning across a range of examples. The big ideas serve as anchors through which "small ideas" can be connected and understood. Baker et al. suggest that big ideas are especially useful in teaching content areas. For example, they suggest the big idea of using the problem-solution-effect sequence to teach history. This sequence provides a generalizable strategy for understanding historical events and their interrelatedness. When faced with a *problem*, people throughout history have used moving, inventing, dominating, accommodating, or tolerating to *solve* problems. Attempts to solve problems produce *effects* that often produce another problem; thus, the cycle continues. This cyclical look at history helps learners understand history because meaning is clearer and historical events are associated more readily to current events.

Prater (1993) discusses the importance of teaching concepts effectively to students with learning disabilities. She reports that students with learning disabilities have difficulty learning concepts through observation and experience and, thus, need explicit concept instruction to succeed in school and life. Prater presents the following sequence of steps that are well-grounded in theory and empirical evidence for teaching students to understand concepts:

1. Define the instructional objectives.
2. Analyze the task used for demonstrating know- ledge of the concept.
3. Define the concept and label it.
4. Select the number and sequence of examples and nonexamples.
5. Elaborate the defining attributes.
6. Provide immediate feedback.

Materials that feature these steps are noteworthy. Moreover, metaphors, multiple examples, demonstrations, think alouds, and tying content to something relevant also facilitate understanding. For example, Chapter 14 discusses how concrete and graphic representations help students with learning disabilities understand math concepts.

Curriculum Materials Should Guide the Assessment of Relevant Prior Knowledge. The assessment of prior knowledge that is important to learning the new knowledge needs to be featured in curriculum materials. This assessment can guide the review of prerequisite knowledge or the teaching of important prerequisite content. Also, the continuous monitoring of student progress helps the teacher know when it is necessary to reteach, review, or introduce new material. Content chapters in this text present assessment formats and procedures that are useful in assessing prior knowledge and learning progress.

Curriculum Materials Should Guide Mastery Learning. Most students with learning disabilities do not succeed with the spiral curriculum approach of exposing specific content to students and moving on to other content without regard for how well the students learn the content. This "spray and pray" approach usually results in frustration and minimal learning. Curriculum materials that include goal setting and mastery criteria and feature explicit presentations of new content followed by meaningful and varied practice activities help teachers determine whether individual students are achieving mastery. Mastery learning is discussed later in this chapter.

Curriculum Materials Should Promote Generalization. Although teaching for generalization is presented in the Interactive Teaching Activities section of this chapter, it is important to discuss the influence of curriculum materials on generalization. Features such as multiple examples, big ideas, meaningfulness, mastery learning, and application activities that specifically require the learner to connect the new knowledge to daily living foster generalizations.

Recently, much has been written about making content more meaningful through authentic learning and integrated learning. *Authentic learning* refers to learning that is meaningful to the student and is based on the assumption that learners connect prior knowledge with new knowledge to construct meaning (Newmann & Wehlage, 1993). Also, authentic learning assumes that the learner uses a systematic or disciplined strategy to construct meaning that results in discourse, products, or performances that have value beyond success in school. Baker et al. (1994) note that curriculum materials that feature conspicuous strategies (i.e., general steps that students follow when solving a problem) are helpful to students with learning disabilities, especially when they are explicit, concise, and generalizable. Newmann and Wehlage present five standards that are basic to authentic learning: (a) higher-order thinking is required, (b) depth of knowledge is obtained (mastery), (c) learning is connected to the world beyond the classroom, (d) substantive conversation occurs, and (e) social support for student achievement is provided. Integrated or unit instruction helps promote generalization by teaching a concept across subject areas. For example, to teach likenesses and differences among people, students can measure heights and weights of people in math, read stories about individuals with disabilities in reading, and examine the likenesses and differences of people's hair with a microscope in science. A curriculum structure that promotes authentic learning standards or teaches concepts across subject areas enhances generalization.

Curriculum Materials Should Provide Guidelines for Learner Diversity. Curriculum materials that offer viable suggestions for students who learn at different rates help a teacher meet the needs of diverse learners. Materials that include best teaching practices greatly reduce student frustrations and minimize learning diversity. Materials that provide for mediated scaffolding help teachers respond to a wide range of learners. *Mediated scaffolding* refers to personalized guidance, instruction, assistance, and support that a teacher, peer, task, or material provides a learner. It is temporary guided instruction that gradually is removed as the learner acquires skills. Mediated scaffolding may be included in materials through sample teaching scripts, additional examples, metaphors or anecdotes, and meaningful practice activities. Finally, materials that offer suggestions for cooperative learning, computer-assisted instruction, peer-mediated instruction, instructional games, and grouping arrangements help teachers plan and respond to diverse learners. In essence, the curriculum should be designed to reach all students and challenge advanced achievers to higher-order thinking. It appears to be more parsimonious to teach low and average achievers well and challenge high achievers than to frustrate low achievers while focusing primarily on high achievers.

Consider Instructional Arrangements

Five basic instructional arrangements are available to teachers. These include a large group with the teacher, a small group with the teacher, one student with the teacher, students teaching students, and material with the student. The use of a variety of arrangements helps maintain student involvement and attention.

Large-Group Instruction. Teacher presentations to a large group (more than eight students) can be an effective method of instruction. Some major advantages of large-group instruction are that it is time efficient and it prepares students for the type of instruction that primarily is used in secondary schools, community colleges, and universities. The primary disadvantage of lecturing to large groups is that it does not allow for the teacher to deal easily with the diversity in ability levels that is present in most classrooms.

It is apparent that the large-group format is appropriate for such activities as story telling, presenting show and tell, discussing interesting events, taking a field trip, brainstorming, playing a game, and watching a video. If the teacher uses effective presentation strategies (see the Interactive Teaching Activities section) and supplements them with cooperative learning, small-group instruction, or engaging seatwork activities, large-group instruction can be effective for teaching academics and social skills to a range of diverse learners.

Large-group instruction is more likely to accommodate students with learning disabilities if the following guidelines are used:

1. *Keep instructional presentations short.*
2. *Use questions to involve students in the lesson.* Choral or verbal unison responses are good ways to involve all students simultaneously. Positive participation is enhanced if the teacher asks high-ability students the most difficult questions and offers less-demanding questions to low-ability students.
3. *Use lecture-pause routines.* The lecture-pause procedure involves the teacher lecturing for 6 to 12 minutes and then pausing for about 3 minutes to allow students divided into groups of three to follow the RAP procedure:

   R—*Read* your notes or questions.
   A—*Ask* other students about your notes (e.g., spelling, missing information, or questions about the content).
   P—*Put* corrections or answers to questions in your notes.
4. *Use nonverbal unison responding to increase student engagement.* For example, each student can hold up a card with *true* or *false* on it to answer a question.
5. *Use visual aids to promote understanding of lecture material.* Diagrams are useful, especially in helping students understand relationships.
6. *Maintain a lively pace.* Because thinking time always is faster than speaking time, it is important to keep the lecture moving at an appropriate pace to hold interest.
7. *Use frequent "change-ups."* Sprick (1981) notes that "change-ups" are anything the teacher does to vary the presentation. Selected change-up activities include varying voice levels, varying rate of talking, or illustrating a point with a story.
8. *Determine the rules for behavior during presentations.* Mnemonics such as SLANT (presented in Chapter 15) are excellent for reminding students of behavioral expectations during lectures.
9. *Determine the rules for behavior during discussions.* A good rule for discussions is "Raise your hand to request to ask a question or answer a question."
10. *If students misbehave, praise students who follow the rules.* This reinforces students for appropriate behavior, communicates teacher expectations, and provides a model for misbehaving students.

Small-Group Instruction. The small-group arrangement typically consists of three to seven students and represents a major format for teaching academic skills. Although it can be a highly effective arrangement for all students, small-group instruction is recommended especially for students with learning disabilities. In establishing small groups for instruction, the teacher attempts to group students who have similar instructional needs in a specific academic area. Groups can be based on placement in a reader or on need for instruction in selected phonics rules, paragraph writing, or specific math facts. To accommodate different rates of learning, the composition of the groups should remain flexible. If a student makes rapid progress, it may be advisable to place the student in a different group for instruction.

In an examination of general classroom practices, Slavin (1988) reports that little research exists concerning the merits of within-class instructional grouping for reading instruction; however, research on such grouping in mathematics is available and clearly supports grouping for instruction. Specific findings indicate that the effects are greater for low achievers than for average and high achievers. Other research on

this approach also indicates positive benefits (L. M. Anderson, Evertson, & Brophy, 1979; Carnine, Silbert, & Kameenui, 1990). To improve its effectiveness, these researchers recommend placing the students in a semicircle facing the teacher. They note that distractible students tend to perform better when they are in the middle of the group and spaced about 2 feet from the teacher.

One Student with Teacher. Intensive tutorial teaching frequently is used to help students with learning disabilities learn a new skill. One-to-one tutoring is a powerful instructional arrangement. Bloom (1984) states, "We were astonished at the consistency of the findings and at the great differences in student cognitive achievement, attitudes, and self-concept under tutoring as compared with group methods of instruction" (p. 4). In addition, one-to-one teaching can be used spontaneously to prevent or relieve frustration. When teachers observe students having difficulty during group instruction or seatwork, they can give them attention at the first opportunity.

Often, 3 to 5 minutes is just the amount of time needed to help a student understand a concept, receive corrective feedback, understand directions, and feel motivated to continue working. Archer and Edgar (1976) recommend that one-to-one instruction be scheduled daily for students with learning disabilities. The students then know they will have some time with the teacher to ask questions and receive help. Elementary teachers and resource room teachers have fewer students or are with them for a longer time; thus, it is easier for them than for intermediate and secondary level teachers to offer one-to-one instruction.

Students Teaching Students: Peer Tutoring. The students-teaching-students instructional arrangement provides teachers with a viable resource of instructional support and offers students the opportunity for intensive practice on academic tasks tailored to individual needs. It features students working independently and thus frees the teacher to work with other students individually or in small-group sessions. In a mainstream classroom of diverse learners, instructional arrangements that allow students to practice needed skills or learn subject content independently are critical to the academic success of students with learning disabilities. Although students teaching students occurs in a multitude of formats, most peer instructional arrangements feature either peer tutoring or cooperative learning.

Tutorial instruction (e.g., parents teaching their children or older siblings instructing younger siblings) was probably the first pedagogy among primitive societies. As early as the first century A.D., Quintilian, in his *Institutio Oratoria,* discussed teaching settings in which older children tutored younger children. Today, a basic definition of peer tutoring is *an instructional arrangement in which the teacher pairs two students in a tutor-tutee relationship to promote learning of academic skills or subject content.* The teacher determines the academic task and provides the instructional materials. Although peer tutoring is used to foster social skills, positive relationships, and self-esteem for both students, the emphasis is usually on the learning progress of the tutee. To maintain effective peer tutoring, the teacher monitors behavior and praises both students for performing their respective duties.

Several studies have focused on the effectiveness of peer tutoring. Levin, Glass, and Meister (1984) examined the effectiveness of peer tutoring in terms of reading and math outcomes and found that peer tutoring produced more than twice as much achievement as computer-assisted instruction, three times more than reducing the class size from 35 to 30 students, and almost four times more than lengthening the school day by 1 hour. Osguthorpe and Scruggs (1986) reviewed studies in which special education students served as tutors. They found that tutees who received instruction from special education students made academic gains in a variety of content areas. Moreover, many of the tutors benefited academically and socially from being the tutor. These findings provide both mainstream and special education teachers with an opportunity to set up many different tutor-tutee pairs to promote social integration as well as academic gains among students with and without learning disabilities.

Scruggs and Richter (1985) reviewed 24 studies in which students with learning disabilities were involved in tutoring interventions. They note that all investigators favored the use of peer tutoring, and most studies support the continued use of tutoring with students with learning disabilities. Nevertheless, Scruggs and Richter caution against such unqualified endorsements because many tutoring studies have methodological flaws.

Tutor and tutee benefits in academics (i.e., achievement gains across academic and content areas) are reported for students with and without learning disabilities, whereas the effect of peer tutoring on the enhancement of social skills and self-concept remains inconclusive for students both with and without learning disabilities (Cohen, Kulik, & Kulik, 1982; Osguthorpe & Scruggs, 1986). Moreover, the research indicates that peer tutoring program variables are more important to student achievement than are student variables such as age, ability, grade, and training. Relevant program variables include structured settings, lower-order target skills, teacher-developed achievement measures, and programs of shorter longitudinal duration. Also, math achievement appears to be greater than achievement in reading and other subject areas in peer tutoring programs (Cohen et al., 1982). Because of the effect of program variables, it is not surprising that students with learning disabilities as well as students without learning disabilities benefit from peer tutoring programs of similar design and content.

Peer tutoring appears to hold much promise. It can improve academic skills, foster self-esteem, develop appropriate behaviors, and promote positive relationships and cooperation among peers. It benefits both tutor and tutee, and once the program is designed, it requires less of the teacher's time than most instructional arrangements. Also, it is tailor-made for helping

TABLE 7.3
Sample Tutor Checklist

Tutor: ______________________

Date	Date	Date	Date	Date	Date	
						Collects material
						Goes to work space
						Describes lesson to partner
						Praises correct responses
						Shows enthusiasm
						Provides corrective feedback
						Uses positive manner
						Follows directions without assistance
						Speaks in a quiet voice
						Keeps records
						Replaces material at end of session

Note: From *Teaching Students with Learning Problems* (p. 119), 4th ed., by C. D. Mercer and A. R. Mercer, 1993, Upper Saddle River, NJ: Merrill/Prentice Hall. Copyright 1993 by Prentice-Hall Publishing Company. Reprinted by permission.

students with learning disabilities achieve in mainstream settings.

The development and implementation of a successful peer tutoring program require the consideration of numerous factors. The following steps represent best practices from the research and literature regarding the factors involved in planning and implementing peer tutoring:

1. Determine goals of peer tutoring.
2. Target skills or content for the peer tutoring pairs.
3. Select materials.
4. Design procedures for tutor and tutee.
5. Assign tutor-tutee pairs.
6. Train tutors. (Table 7.3 presents a sample tutor checklist for the teacher to use for training and feedback.)
7. Train tutees.
8. Teach social skills used in peer tutoring.
9. Review rules.
10. Schedule the peer tutoring sessions.
11. Conduct a tutoring session.
12. Evaluate the peer tutoring program.

For additional information on implementing these steps, see Mercer and Mercer (1993).

With appropriate planning, student training, and teacher support, peer tutoring can be a viable instructional alternative. Moreover, to maintain the tutors' involvement, it helps for the school to recognize the efforts of the tutors and tutees. Some common activities include displaying pictures of tutors on bulletin boards, allowing tutors to meet before school, offering awards, providing reinforcing events such as meetings with faculty or administrators, publishing articles about the program, and having the principal recognize tutors.

Students Teaching Students: ClassWide Peer Tutoring. One peer-mediated instruction program that deserves consideration from mainstream and special education teachers is *ClassWide Peer Tutoring* (Delquadri, Greenwood, Whorton, Carta, & Hall, 1986; Greenwood, Delquadri, & Carta, 1988). It is designed to help students with mild disabilities improve their basic skills. Maheady, Sacca, and Harper (1988) used *ClassWide Peer Tutoring* in secondary mainstream settings to improve the academic and social performance of students with learning disabilities. Moreover, Maheady, Harper, and Sacca (1988) note that numerous researchers report success with *ClassWide Peer Tutoring* at the elementary school level. The *ClassWide Peer Tutoring* program was developed over an 8-year period and has been field-tested extensively. Research data indicate that *ClassWide Peer Tutoring* improves students' engagement in academic tasks, increases academic achievement gains, and enhances cooperative peer relations (Greenwood et al., 1984; Maheady, Harper, & Mallette, 1991).

ClassWide Peer Tutoring is an integrated behavior management and direct instruction procedure that is based upon reciprocal peer tutoring and group-oriented reinforcement contingencies (e.g., cooperative learning). The method includes three features to increase on-task behavior and amount of practice of academic skills: (a) peers are used to supervise responding and practice, (b) a game format is used that includes points and competing teams to motivate students and maintain interest, and (c) a weekly evaluation plan ensures gains in individual and class progress. The teacher trains students to be effective tutors by carefully explaining and demonstrating error correction procedures and the point system to be followed in the tutoring sessions. Corrective feedback is given during supervised practice opportunities.

The *ClassWide Peer Tutoring* system features the following basic arrangement:

1. Daily tutoring slots of about 30 minutes are required. Each student tutors for 10 minutes and then receives 10 minutes of tutoring. An additional 10 minutes is spent counting points and posting results.
2. On Monday the tutor-tutee pairs for the week are selected. The pair sits next to or across from each other and begins a 10-minute tutoring session. For example, if the task is oral reading, the tutor monitors the reading and awards 2 points for each sentence read correctly. The tutee earns 1 point for correctly rereading a sentence after the tutor has detected an error. The tutor marks points on a Tutoring Point Sheet. At the end of 10 minutes, the tutoring roles are reversed.
3. During the tutoring sessions, the teacher moves among the students and awards bonus points for correct tutoring behavior. The teacher also divides the class into two teams.
4. After the second 10-minute session, each student counts the number of points earned as both tutor and tutee. These point totals are recorded for each student in one of two team columns on a chart. The team earning the highest number of points is the winning team for the day. The composition of the two teams changes periodically.
5. On Friday, the teacher can conduct a more intensive assessment of each student's progress on the skills from that week.

Students Teaching Students: Cooperative Learning. Cooperative learning represents another instructional arrangement in which peers work independently. Because of its success with diverse groups of students (Mainzer, Mainzer, Slavin, & Lowry, 1993) and the independent nature of their work, it represents a viable approach for promoting successful mainstreaming. During the last decade, cooperative learning has enjoyed increasing popularity and enthusiastic support from general and special educators.

There are many forms of cooperative learning, but they all involve students working in teams or small groups to help each other learn (Slavin, 1991). Because cooperative learning provides students with an opportunity to practice skills or learn content presented by the teacher, it supplements teacher instruction. Cooperative learning emphasizes team goals, and team success is achieved only if each individual learns. A basic definition of cooperative learning is *an instructional arrangement in which small groups or teams of students work together to achieve team success in a manner that promotes the students' responsibility for their own learning as well as the learning of others.*

Student Team Learning (STL) techniques represent the most extensive practices used in cooperative learning. STL methods emphasize the position that team goals can be achieved only if each member achieves selected academic objectives. Slavin (1991) notes that the concepts of team reward, individual accountability, and equal opportunities for success are central to all STL methods. Team rewards are earned when a team achieves at or above a predetermined criterion level. Because all teams that achieve criteria are successful (rewarded), teams are not in competition for an all-or-nothing reward. Individual accountability is featured because team success depends on the individual learning of all team members. Team success is evaluated by the composite performances (e.g., scores) of team members on a quiz of material assigned to the group. This relationship of individual performance to team performance fosters activities that involve team members helping each other learn the targeted academic content. Equal opportunities for success are provided because each team member helps the team by improving on past performance. This challenges low, average, and high achievers to do their best because their performances all are valued by the team.

Student Teams-Achievement Divisions (STAD) (Slavin, 1978, 1986) and Teams-Games-Tournament (TGT) (DeVries & Slavin, 1978; Slavin, 1986) are two cooperative learning methods that are adaptable across subject areas and grade levels. In STAD, a heterogeneous group of four students is assigned to a team. After the teacher presents a lesson, the team works together to ensure that all students have mastered the lesson. Then the students take individual quizzes without peer help. The students' quiz scores are compared with their past averages, and points are awarded if their performances meet or exceed their earlier efforts. The points are totaled to yield a team score, and teams that meet criteria are rewarded (e.g., they receive certificates). This cycle of activity usually takes three to five class periods. STAD works best with academic material that has single correct answers (e.g., math computations and map skills). TGT uses the same teacher presentation, group assignment, and teamwork format as STAD. The quizzes, however, are replaced by weekly tournaments. In these tournaments students compete with players from other teams to earn points to add to their respective team scores. Students compete at three-member tournament tables with others who have similar skill levels for the target skills. The winners at the tournament tables each earn the same number of points for his or her team. All students have an equal opportunity for success because low achievers competing with other low achievers can earn as many points as high achievers competing with high achievers. As with STAD, TGT takes three to five classes and is most appropriate with content that features single answers (e.g., math).

In addition to STAD and TGT, two comprehensive curricula exist for specific content and grades. Team Assisted Individualization (TAI) (Slavin, Madden, & Stevens, 1990) is designed for mathematics in third through sixth grade, and Cooperative Integrated Reading and Composition (CIRC) (Slavin, Stevens, & Madden, 1988) is designed for reading in third through fifth grade.

Most of the research on cooperative learning focuses on the STL techniques developed at Johns Hopkins University. In a synthesis of research on cooperative learning, Slavin (1991) reports the following findings:

1. The most successful approaches for improving academic achievement include group goals and individual accountability. In these settings, groups are rewarded on the basis of the performances of the respective team members.
2. In studies that feature group goals and individual accountability, the achievement effects of experimental/control comparisons consistently favor cooperative learning. Specifically, in 37 of 44 studies of at least 4 weeks' duration, the significantly positive effects favor cooperative learning, whereas none favors traditional methods.

3. The positive achievement effects of cooperative learning appear consistent across grades (2 through 12), subject areas, and school settings (rural, urban, and suburban).
4. Effects are equally positive for high, average, and low achievers.
5. The positive effects of cooperative learning are reported consistently in affective areas (e.g., self-esteem, intergroup relations, attitudes toward school, and ability to work cooperatively).

Slavin et al. (1990) report excellent results in math achievement and affective measures with Team Assisted Individualization for students with academic disabilities in mainstream settings. Likewise, Cooperative Integrated Reading and Composition learning groups for reading and writing yield excellent reading and writing outcomes for students without disabilities as well as students with academic disabilities in mainstream settings (Slavin et al., 1988). Slavin (1989/1990) states, "Cooperative learning seems to be an extraordinary success. It has an excellent research base, many viable and successful forms, and hundreds of thousands of enthusiastic adherents" (p. 3).

In the design of a cooperative learning program, it appears that team goals and rewards, individual accountability, and equal opportunities are essential components for many students. Guidelines adapted from those presented in peer tutoring are appropriate for planning and implementing cooperative learning:

1. Determine goals of cooperative learning.
2. Target selected skills or contingent lessons for the teams.
3. Select materials, including quizzes or tournament questions.
4. Design procedures for team members to help each other.
5. Assign students of varying achievement levels to the same teams.
6. Train teams to help each other.
7. Teach social skills for team work.
8. Review classroom rules and teach new rules.
9. Schedule the cooperative learning sessions for 3 to 5 days a week.
10. Conduct a cooperative learning session.
11. Evaluate the cooperative learning program.

Material with Student: Seatwork Activities. From a learning perspective, the material-with-student or independent seatwork arrangement provides the student with opportunities to practice skills that the teacher has presented. Practice helps the student move through the learning sequence that begins with acquisition and progresses to the higher levels of proficiency, maintenance, and generalization. For many students with learning disabilities, the mastery of skills and content requires extensive practice.

From a review of the research on practice, Dempster (1991) offers several suggestions for planning effective practice:

1. Incorporate spaced reviews or practice (including questions from previous and current lessons) into a variety of activities (such as discussions, seatwork, peer tutoring, and homework).
2. Organize lessons so that a brief time is used to review the main points of the previous day's lesson. Include review tasks or questions on seatwork activities.
3. Once or twice a month, conduct a comprehensive practice session that features discussions and seatwork.

From a teacher's perspective, a material-with-student arrangement not only provides students with opportunities to improve achievement but also allows the teacher some freedom to work with small groups or individual students. Although planning seatwork activities and teaching students to work independently is time-consuming, it is worth the effort. Well-designed material-with-student activities can make the school year pleasant and productive. Some guidelines for planning and implementing an effective independent seatwork program follow:

1. *Ensure that the independent work assignments are tailored to the student's instructional level.* Preceding independent practice with demonstration or guided practice is a good way to ensure that the assignment is instructionally appropriate.
2. *Use a variety of independent seatwork activities.* Varying the activities provides the teacher with alternatives and tends to increase student motivation and time on task. Suitable activities include self-correcting materials, instructional games, computer-assisted instruction, Language Master assisted instruction, and tape recorder assisted instruction.
3. *Consider work folders for daily assignments.*
4. *Prepare some cushion activities to accommodate students finishing their work at different times.* Activities include starting another assignment, writing on the computer, working in a learning center, listening to a tape, assisting another student, or reading a book or magazine.
5. *Design procedures that enable students to ask questions while doing independent seatwork.* One procedure includes assigning student helpers to answer questions.
6. *Ensure that students understand the instructions for their seatwork activities before starting small-group instruction.*
7. *Use the direct instruction teaching sequence to teach the behavioral expectations for independent seatwork.*

Material with Student: Self-Correcting Materials. Students spend much classroom time working with instructional materials on their own; thus, it is important that the materials used do not lead to frustration, failure, and the practicing of errors. To some degree, a material serves as a teacher. The more teacher functions it can serve, the more useful is the material. Inexpensive materials can perform the teaching functions of providing instructions, presenting a stimulus or task, and providing feedback about correctness of student responses.

Self-correcting materials provide the student with immediate feedback without the teacher being present. Self-correcting materials are useful especially with students with learning disabilities, who often have a history of academic failure. It is important to reduce their failure experiences, particularly those that take place in public. When the student makes a mistake with a self-correcting material, it is a private event—it happens without anyone else knowing it. Only the student sees the error, and the error can be corrected immediately. Furthermore, if immediate feedback is not provided, mistakes will be practiced until the teacher corrects the student at a later time. With self-correcting materials, the student is corrected immediately and practices only the correct response.

There are many ways to make self-correcting materials, some of which include the use of answer keys, matching cards, puzzles, pocket calculators, and computers (Mercer, Mercer, & Bott, 1984). The materials should be simple in design so that one demonstration enables students to operate them. The best use of these materials is to provide practice or drill on subject matter that the teacher already has introduced.

Finally, students should not be required to use the same self-correcting material for a long time. The teacher should vary the content periodically, exchange materials with another teacher, give students a choice of which material they wish to use, have students make their own content for the self-correcting device, or put away selected materials for a while. By changing self-correcting materials from time to time, the teacher can maintain student interest and involvement. (For extensive coverage of teacher-made and commercial self-correcting materials, see Mercer and Mercer [1993]).

Material with Student: Instructional Games. Once students with learning disabilities understand the concept involved in a new skill or strategy, they need practice to achieve mastery or automaticity. Instructional games help students maintain interest during practice. Familiar game materials such as checkers, cards, dice, spinners, and start-to-finish boards are useful. Game content can be individualized for students by putting questions on cards and requiring the player to answer a question on a card selected from the student's personalized stack (e.g., multiplication facts for one player and word meanings for another player). If the question is answered correctly, the student gets to take a turn (e.g., roll dice or spin a spinner) in the game. Chance factors (e.g., lose a turn, take an extra turn, and skip two spaces) boost interest, and familiar formats (such as a game board) allow students to play independently. To maintain a high level of academically engaged time, students should maintain a good pace during games. A fast pace is facilitated by limiting the number of players to two or three for games in which students take turns or by setting a limit on response time.

Lavoie (1993) notes that some students with learning disabilities do not like games because they are concerned that they do not possess the knowledge or skills needed to win in a game format. He points out that games are only motivating when students think that they have a good chance of winning. Students are more likely to think they can win if the game features content or skills at the students' independent practice level. Also, cooperative game formats should be used until the students have the maturity to handle competitive games. Mercer and Mercer (1993) provide an array of instructional games across content areas.

Material with Student: Technological Tools. Peck and Dorricott (1994) claim that technological tools can improve students' abilities, change the way they work and think, and provide new access to the world. As the information age rapidly continues to emerge, educators need to examine the instructional possibilities of the new technologies for educating students with learning disabilities in the 21st century. Hancock and Betts (1994) discuss the use of technology for instruction according to research-verified applications, emerging applications, and future applications. These applications of technology are featured in Table 7.4.

The computer can be used as a tool for classroom management as well as classroom instruction. Teachers can be released partially from time-consuming tasks through computer-managed instruction (CMI), particularly in developing individualized educational programs and in computer-managed record keeping. Computers can be used to store sequences of instructional objectives and student performance information as well as to track student progress, complete proper forms, and provide required record-keeping data (Fuchs, Fuchs, & Hamlett, 1989).

Computer-assisted instruction, or CAI, refers to software that is designed to provide instruction. The computer offers some unique advantages in instructing students with learning disabilities. Attributes of CAI that appear to be useful in helping students achieve include the following (Fitzgerald, Fick, & Milich, 1986; Lindsey, 1987; Peck & Dorricott, 1994):

1. Instruction is individualized by branching students to items appropriate for them.
2. Tasks are analyzed and presented in meaningful sequences.
3. Progress is at the student's own rate.
4. Reinforcement of individual student responses is immediate.
5. Existing software enables the student to increase the rate of correct responses.
6. The use of animation, sound effects, and game-playing situations makes drill and practice multisensory and motivating.
7. Programs that simulate real-life (authentic) experiences allow the student to make decisions and see the consequences.
8. Strategies related to problem solving can be adapted for the computer through such programs as adventure games and software that teaches how to program.
9. The computer can be made to be user friendly by programming it to use the student's name when giving lessons. A computer

TABLE 7.4
Profile of Technology for Instruction

Applications with Research Verification

Calculators

In addition to arithmetic, algebraic, and trigonometric functions, modern calculators feature plotting and graphing capabilities. These functions enable the student to view computation results in graphic form.

Computer-Assisted Instruction (CAI)/Integrated Learning Systems (ILS)

Select drill and practice programs have yielded small but positive effects on learning. In some schools, CAI that features ILS (including individualized academic tutorials) has produced impressive gains with urban students who are underachieving.

Distance Education

With distance education, learners in remote locations gather at a site that has cable or satellite receivers, phone lines, and video cameras. This equipment allows one- or two-way audio and video contact with a course provider. Hughes Corporation's *Galaxy* is a distance education program that beams daily lessons to schools through satellite.

Laser Videodiscs

Laser videodisc programs enable the learner to interact with print and still or moving images. These programs do not require a computer. Disc players with remote controls and bar-code readers that select and present images are available for a few hundred dollars.

Microcomputer-Based Labs (MBLs)

These labs use microcomputers and probes to sense temperature, pH levels, and light intensity. Computer labs represent a means for providing hands-on science experiences.

Presentation Software

Overhead projectors and other audiovisual technologies effectively support lectures and demonstrations. computer combined with a large-screen monitor or LCD display panel is a powerful medium for presenting visual material. Adding multimedia capability permits enhancements such as sound, graphics, and video images.

Telecommunications

The dissemination of large quantities of information to many people simultaneously is available through telecommunications networks. Students can use telecommunications services for assessing publications, training materials, and collected data.

Applications with Emerging Support

Computerized Adaptive Testing (CAT)

With CAT, the test questions vary according to the test taker's responses. An incorrect answer is followed by an easier question, whereas a correct response generates a more difficult question. Initial studies report that CAT provides more accurate results regarding a person's knowledge level in less time than traditional test formats.

Interactive Multimedia

This computer technology links information from multiple sources and enables the user to interact with program content. Most interactive multimedia programs contain text, line drawings, maps, graphs, animated graphics, voice narration, music, and video clips featuring full motion and color.

TABLE 7.4
continued

Multi-User Dimensions (MUDs)
Using MUDs, individuals with a computer and modem communicate through telecommunications services to play out roles in an imaginary context. MUDs are able to transport the user to any place in any time. MUDs provide opportunities for individuals to pursue collaborative and creative activities that extend beyond typical writing or drama exercises.

Text-to-Speech
Computers can translate text to speech. This function is a popular enhancement for early grades and non-English-speaking populations.

Voicemail
Digital voicemail systems are commonplace and offer an excellent medium for delivering information to students. Each student can be assigned a private mailbox with a personal information number (PIN), and parents, teachers, and other students can access the individual's mailbox from any touch-tone phone.

Word Processing
Word processing programs are used widely in schools to help students develop written expression skills. These programs have been effective especially with students who are low achievers.

Future Applications

Broadband Networks
Through these networks, two-way, delay-free transmissions are delivered to the home through cable or satellite.

Groupware
Groupware allows users in a network to jointly author, share, and disseminate electronic documents, or to join in group decision-making ventures.

Knowbots
Knowbots, which stands for "knowledge robots," are automated systems for collecting, screening, and organizing data.

Pen-Based Computing
Instead of the use of a keyboard, data are entered through pen-based applications that use touch-screen icons and handwriting recognition.

Speech-to-Text
These voice-aware applications enable users to vocally control computer functions.

Virtual Reality
Users wear special goggles connected to a data input device that engulfs the user in a three-dimensional environment emulating the real world.

Wireless Connectivity
Wireless technology, like the cellular phone, enables teachers and students to share information regardless of their location.

also is nonjudgmental and allows the student to make mistakes in a nonthreatening environment.

10. Students need to be proficient in using technology to succeed effectively in the information age.

Educational software can differ in method or mode of delivery as well as in quality. Ellis and Sabornie (1986) discuss six modes of delivery:

1. *Drill and practice.* This common use of computers in education serves as a supplement to other forms of instruction. It is designed to integrate and consolidate previously learned material through practice on the computer.
2. *Tutorial.* The role of teacher is assumed by the computer, and material is presented in a programmed learning format. The student moves from one step to the next by answering questions and can be branched to remedial or review segments as well as to more advanced levels of the program.
3. *Educational games.* Games are designed to develop general problem-solving methods and strategies while maintaining interest and motivation.
4. *Simulations.* Simulations attempt to model the underlying characteristics of a real phenomenon so that its properties can be studied. They can incorporate many game features but primarily are intended to model some reality.
5. *Problem solving.* The computer can be used to solve real-world problems. For example, students may write computer programs to test possible solutions to a variety of real problems.
6. *Word processing.* A word processor is a tool for writing instruction. Ease of correcting errors, availability of spelling and grammar checkers, elimination of the need to rewrite after revisions are made, and use of a printer that produces neat copies are helpful functions in teaching writing to students with learning disabilities.

CAI is promising, but limited information exists concerning how microcomputers can be applied best in the classroom. However, it is apparent that through the use of appropriate software, students with learning disabilities can be motivated through individualized instruction and needed academic practice (Majsterek & Wilson, 1993).

Wiens (1986) suggests three specific criteria for evaluating software to use in teaching students with learning disabilities. First, software should use the computer's capacity to present the materials better than traditional methods. Voice synthesis, interaction, animation, and response monitoring are features of successful CAI. Moreover, Shuell and Schueckler (1988) note that to transcend traditional methods, CAI programs must (a) use the student's knowledge base, (b) provide guided and independent practice, (c) give corrective feedback, (d) present materials in steps that facilitate learning, (e) provide clear lesson overviews and goals, (f) conduct periodic performance evaluations, and (g) finish with a summary and review of the lesson's main points. Wiens's second criterion for good software is that the teacher must be able to modify or adapt the program to develop appropriate instructional matches for individual learners. The third criterion is that the CAI program should include means for collecting student response data so that teachers can monitor student progress. Actually, the teacher should expect software to report graphic representations of progress on easily generated print-outs.

In addition to the many general uses of the computer for students with learning disabilities, several investigators report on specific applications that are suited especially to youngsters with learning disabilities. Grimes (1981) notes that for students who have difficulty maintaining on-task attention, computer programs can promote attention with color cuing, animation, underlining, and varying print sizes. For students who respond impulsively, the computer can provide cues or hints to inhibit impulsive responding. For those who take a lot of time to respond (reflective responders), computer programs can be tailored to allow extra response time.

Research on the use of CAI with students who have learning disabilities appears to be promising but remains inconclusive. Majsterek and Wilson (1993) reviewed several CAI studies that focused on teaching basic skills to students with learning disabilities. They conclude that CAI with well designed software based on sound educational principles and tailored to the learning needs of students with learning disabilities can produce equivalent or slightly less than equivalent learning with less teacher time than traditional instruction. Majsterek and Wilson maintain that teachers should be careful not to assign special attributes to CAI for students with learning disabilities. They state, "At issue in using CAI for these students is less the technology and more the application of effective teaching principles" (p. 21). Other reports of CAI used to teach students with learning disabilities (Ellis & Sabornie, 1986; Hasselbring, Goin, & Bransford, 1988; Woodward & Carnine, 1988) conclude that student achievement usually is greater when CAI supplements rather than replaces teacher-directed instruction. Keefe and Candler (1989) report mixed results on the effectiveness of using word processors with students who have learning disabilities. However, several individual studies report good results for CAI use in teaching students with learning disabilities (e.g., spelling—Fuchs et al., 1989; world geography—Horton, Lovitt, Givens, & Nelson, 1989; reading—Torgesen, Waters, Cohen, & Torgesen, 1988; health—Woodward, Carnine, & Gersten, 1988). The key to future successful technology-assisted instruction depends on a closer working relationship between educators and software manufacturers. (Various software programs for learning strategies, math, reading, spelling, and written expression are presented in their respective chapters.)

Material with Student: Homework. Homework continues to be a widely practiced activity in schools. Many consider it to be an important component for improving the quality of American education (Heller, Spooner, Anderson, & Mims, 1988). Olympia, Sheridan, and Jenson (1994) define *homework* as academic work assigned by teachers that extends the practice of academic skills into other environments. Cooper (1989) notes that homework implies completion during nonschool hours, but in actuality most students have options to do the work during study hall, library time, or subsequent classes. An important aspect of homework includes programming for academic skill generalization through working in numerous environments. Heller et al. outline the components of homework as it relates to special education. They report that a homework activity must (a) be teacher-directed, (b) include only previously taught skills, (c) be an extension of schoolwork, (d) be evaluated, (e) be based on instructional objectives appropriate to the student, and (f) occur outside school hours.

High rates of achievement are related to the amount of time students actively are engaged in academic tasks. Homework represents a viable method to help students with learning disabilities engage in academic tasks and improve achievement. The positive relationship of homework to achievement has been well documented for students with learning disabilities (Jenson, Sheridan, Olympia, & Andrews, 1994). Minimally competent students can compensate for lower ability through increased home study. Specifically, it helps them move through the acquisition, proficiency, maintenance, and generalization stages of learning (Mims, Harper, Armstrong, & Savage, 1991) and provides an opportunity for the teacher to control the temporal aspects of practice (i.e., spaced versus massed practice) that are most effective for learning (Dempster, 1991).

Unfortunately, several characteristics of students with learning disabilities tend to interfere with effective homework completion. Epstein, Polloway, Foley, and Patton (1993) identified the following characteristics of students with learning disabilities as troublesome for completing homework: distractibility, procrastination, need for constant monitoring, failure to complete

work, day dreaming, and inability to work independently. Guidelines presented later in this section help students with learning disabilities overcome some of these troublesome characteristics or habits.

In a synthesis of research on homework in general education, Cooper (1989) reports that homework positively affects achievement but that the effect varies considerably across grade levels. In essence, he notes that the effects of homework are substantial for secondary students and minimal for elementary students. For middle school students, the effects are good but are only about half as beneficial as for secondary students. Cooper also reports that the optimal amount of homework varies across grade levels.

Although there is a limited amount of research on homework practices, Patton (1994) highlights 35 recommended practices from the available research and literature. He discusses practices in the areas of management, assignments, student competencies, and parent involvement. Patton notes that 14 of the recommended practices have empirical validation, 25 have literature-based support, and 5 have field-based support. It is apparent that research is limited, but a validation base for effective practices is emerging.

In a survey of homework practices of 88 teachers of students with learning disabilities, Salend and Schliff (1989) found that most teachers (80%) use homework regularly but fail to use quality practices consistently. They report that 85% of the teachers experience problems in getting students to complete their homework. Salend and Schliff note that the low motivation of students to complete homework may be related to the failure of the learning disabilities teachers to (a) give feedback on homework (43% do not discuss or review homework), (b) incorporate homework into grading policies (42% do not regularly grade homework), or (c) involve parents in the homework process (only 41% solicit feedback from parents). From the limited research on the effects of homework on students with learning disabilities, it appears that quality practices are related to positive student achievement.

Guidelines from the literature (Al-Rubaiy, 1985; Armstrong & McPherson, 1991; Frith, 1991; Mims et al., 1991) and research (Cooper, 1989; Patton, 1994; Rosenberg, 1989) are available to promote best practices in homework:

1. *Assign a reasonable amount of homework.* From his synthesis of the homework research, Cooper (1989) recommends the following amount of homework: 1st through 3rd grade—one to three 15-minute assignments per week; 4th through 6th grade—two to four 15- to 45-minute assignments per week; 7th through 9th grade—up to five 45- to 75-minute assignments a week; 10th through 12th grade—up to five 75- to 120-minute assignments a week. The purpose of homework at the elementary level is to help students develop good study habits, practice newly acquired skills, and realize that learning can take place in nonschool environments. For students in 7th to 12th grade, homework becomes essential to academic achievement and school success. To regulate the amount of time students spend on homework, the teacher periodically should check with students or parents about how much time homework is taking. It is not uncommon for students with learning disabilities to spend twice as much time doing an assignment as students without disabilities (Jenson et al., 1994). Accommodations for students with learning disabilities include the following: (a) separate large assignments into smaller chunks, (b) provide more time to complete the assignment, (c) offer incentives for completing homework to students who are distractible, off task, or impulsive, and (d) organize student groups that can work together. For example, O'Melia and Rosenberg (1994) report good progress on homework completion through cooperative homework teams. Moreover, teachers who work in teams need to plan together on assigning homework. Because students take classes from different teachers in the upper grades, the teachers should work cooperatively to develop appropriate amounts of homework.
2. *Make homework an integral part of the learning process.* Nicholls, McKenzie, and Shufro (1994) compared perspectives of students with and without learning disabilities on the relevance of homework. Most students with learning disabilities viewed homework as an imposition and remotely related to life skills, whereas most students without learning disabilities viewed homework as important and related to life skills. When the teacher discusses the rationale for homework and informs students of the specific objectives (such as mastery of skills) of each assignment, students are able to appreciate the value of homework. Rosenberg (1989) reports that when teachers discuss, review, explain, and evaluate homework assignments with students who have learning disabilities, homework becomes an effective learning activity. Al-Rubaiy (1985) notes that a feeling of ownership of the assignment is promoted when students recognize the value of homework. Homework should not be busy work or used as punishment.
3. *Plan homework assignments at the student's instructional level.* Teachers must ensure that assignments represent an appropriate match between the student's ability or skill level and the difficulty level of the assignment. This instructional match usually is maintained when the teacher assigns homework to practice or review material that the student has been taught.
4. *Make sure the student understands the assignment.* Understanding the purpose and instructions for the assignment is critical (Jenson et al., 1994). When the assignment is similar to classwork, clarity is facilitated. When the assignment is new or different, the teacher should demonstrate the task and provide some guided practice on a portion of the assignment. Understanding also is facilitated when directions are clear and simple and when students are asked to explain the task.

5. *Evaluate homework.* Teachers should evaluate all homework assignments and maintain a cumulative record of the results. Assigning a grade encourages students to complete assignments and develop a sense of responsibility. Moreover, for students who do not test well, homework provides an opportunity to improve their grades and display their skills and knowledge (Mims et al., 1991).
6. *Reinforce the completion of homework.* Teachers should indicate that homework is important to help students learn and develop responsibility. When students complete their homework, encouragement should be provided. Encouragement may be private (verbal praise, note sent home, sticker, or high grade) or public (bulletin-board display of work or display of names with homework stars). Also, the entire class or teams of students may be encouraged when each member has completed the assignment or improved in the number of assignments completed.
7. *Involve parents in homework.* In a study of parents of students with learning disabilities, Kay, Fitzgerald, Paradee, and Mellencamp (1994) examined parent perspectives on homework. They found that parents felt inadequate to help with homework. They desired more information on how to help their children with homework and wanted a two-way communication system that would help them become partners on their child's instructional team. Initially, the teacher should send a letter to parents regarding homework policies and practices. Because letters do not always represent a functional medium of communication to homes, it may be necessary for the teacher to discuss homework in parent conferences, at PTA meetings, during parent nights at school, or on the telephone. Information for parents should include (a) the purpose of homework, (b) the expected frequency of homework, (c) the approximate amount of time assignments should take, (d) homework evaluation procedures, (e) effects of homework on grades, and (f) suggestions for parents on how to help with homework. Some tips regarding parent involvement include the following:
   (a) Schedule a specific time and place for homework.
   (b) Supervise the homework session by periodically checking with the student to determine progress rather than overseeing every task.
   (c) Provide an environment conducive to learning. The area needs to be well lighted and free of things that distract the student.
   (d) Provide the student with appropriate materials.
   (e) Sign and date completed homework assignments.
   (f) Encourage and praise the student for doing homework.
   (g) Share with the teacher any concerns involving the amount of work or the difficulty level of the assignments.
8. *Facilitate homework through effective support systems.* Frith (1991) suggests using the following support systems to support homework activities:
   (a) Use peer tutoring for checking and assessing homework and for giving corrective feedback.
   (b) Use computer-assisted instruction for students who have access to computers.
   (c) Encourage parents to support the value of homework with their actions and words.
   (d) Develop monitoring systems (such as graphs or checklists) for homework.

In his concluding remarks concerning homework, Frith (1991) states,

> For maximum usefulness, homework assignments need to be made in the context of a strong support system that includes assistance from teachers and peers as well as parents. A strong support system will increase positive impressions that students have toward homework, especially when it might appear that these assignments are imposing on their free time. Regardless of perspective, homework is certainly important, and it should be viewed as an integral component of the instructional program—not only in regular education but in special education as well. (p. 49)

Consider Learner Variables

To provide an appropriate education to students with learning disabilities, it is essential to develop an individualized educational program that features an instructional match. To accomplish an instructional match, the teacher must assess the strengths, weaknesses, and needs of a student and design an instructional program based on these assessment results. Given the heterogeneity of students with learning disabilities, the procedures for designing an instructional match must be individualized. After medical factors are considered, the assessment procedures must involve the assessment of a student's present level of achievement, cognitive and metacognitive strategies, social skills, emotional maturity, interests, and motivation. Moreover, the student's support system (i.e., family, friends, advocates, and professional services) must be considered. Throughout this text the characteristics (e.g., academic, social, and cognitive) of individuals with learning disabilities are discussed, and assessment instruments and procedures are featured. This section highlights some generic learner variables that influence learning and instruction design.

Student Aptitudes. In an analysis of research on what helps students learn, Wang, Haertel, and Walberg (1993/1994) discovered a knowledge base comprising 11,000 statistical findings. They organized their findings into a ranking of 28 variables and six categories. The category of student aptitudes was the most influential category on student learning. Specifically, the following student aptitudes ranked high: metacognitive processes (i.e., capacity to plan, monitor, and evaluate during learning) were 2nd, cognitive processes (i.e., academic achievement, IQ, and prior knowledge) were 3rd, social/behavioral attributes (i.e., disruptive behavior highly related to poor school achievement) were 6th, motivational affective attributes (i.e., persistence, effort, and self-regulation) were 7th, and psychomotor skills were 17th.

Because cognitive and metacognitive processes are highly related to learning and applying concepts, it is important to examine instructional procedures for teaching concepts to students with learning disabilities. Prater (1993) notes that concept learning is a fundamental structure for thinking throughout a person's lifetime. Her sequence of steps for teaching concepts (presented earlier in this chapter) has the potential to help students with a wide array of cognitive and metacognitive deficits to acquire, maintain, and apply concepts.

Socioeconomic Status. In their review of variables related to learning, Wang et al. (1993/1994) report that the home environment/parental support variable is highly related to student learning (i.e., it ranked 4th out of 28 variables). Some positive attributes of a home environment include the following: (a) there are high but realistic expectations about schoolwork, (b) an authoritative rather than a permissive or authoritarian approach for discipline is used, (c) the parent-child relationship is positive and supportive, (d) the home environment supports education and is educative, and (e) daily routines and organization facilitate doing homework (Ysseldyke, Christenson, & Kovaleski, (1994). Typically, low socioeconomic home environments have fewer of these positive attributes, and the teacher should consider this when instructing students with learning disabilities who are from low socioeconomic environments. Borich (1992) notes that the following teaching behaviors are important for low- and high-socioeconomic students.

For Low-Socioeconomic Students

1. Be warm and encouraging, and let students know that help is available.
2. Elicit a response from a student each time a question is asked before moving to the next student or question.
3. Present material in small pieces, at a slow place, and with an opportunity for practice.
4. Stress factual knowledge.
5. Monitor student progress.

6. Minimize interruptions by maintaining a smooth flow from one activity to another.
7. Immediately help a student who needs help.
8. Supplement the standard curriculum with specialized material to meet the needs of individual students.

For High-Socioeconomic Students

1. Correct poor answers immediately when a student fails to perform.
2. Ask questions that require associations, generalizations, and inferences.
3. Supplement the curriculum with challenging material.
4. Assign homework and extended assignments.
5. Be flexible.
6. Let students initiate teacher-student interaction.
7. Encourage students to reason out a correct answer.
8. Actively engage students in verbal questions and answers.

Multicultural Differences. Many students with learning disabilities have culturally and linguistically diverse backgrounds. It is important for teachers to value students' cultural differences and provide comfortable ways for these students to share their rich heritage with others. These activities help students respect variations among individuals and provide minority students with events that foster positive self-worth and motivation. Moreover, by becoming acquainted with the cultures of diverse learners, the teacher can adapt curriculum, instruction, and management strategies to accommodate their learning preferences and needs. The chapters throughout this book highlight the needs of culturally diverse learners.

INTERACTIVE TEACHING ACTIVITIES

Focus on Teaching Competencies

Teaching styles are developed individually, but they should not be based on whims, biases, or personal opinions. Teachers and teacher educators have a responsibility to examine the research and apply the findings as they develop teacher practices. Greenwood, Arreaga-Mayer, and Carta (1994) found that students in classrooms in which teachers used research-based interactive teaching practices had higher academic engagement times and achievement scores than students in classrooms in which teachers used other methods. The teaching competencies presented in Table 7.5 highlight the major findings of selected effective teaching research in general and special education and were compiled from the following sources: L. M. Anderson, Brubaker, Alleman-Brooks, and Duffy (1985); L. M. Anderson, Evertson, and Emmer (1980); L. M. Anderson, Raphael, Englert, and Stevens (1991); Bickel and Bickel (1986); Brophy and Good (1986); Christenson et al. (1989); Deno and Fuchs (1987); Ellis, Deshler, Lenz, Schumaker, and Clark (1991); Englert et al. (1992); Fisher et al. (1980); Gage and Needels (1989); Good (1983); Lenz, Bulgren, and Hudson (1990); Rieth and Evertson (1988); Rosenshine and Stevens (1986); Scruggs, Mastropieri, Sullivan, and Hesser (1993); and C. R. Smith (1994). When a teacher incorporates these practices into daily instruction, the likelihood of improving the achievement of students increases.

POSTINSTRUCTIONAL ACTIVITIES

Information regarding the relationship between competent teachers and involvement in postinstructional tasks is limited. However, it is assumed that the following postinstructional activities improve teaching effectiveness: (a) reflecting on one's actions and students' responses, (b) staying current on subject matter and educational issues by reading journals, texts, or professional organization literature, (c) taking advanced education courses, and (d) interacting with colleagues to coordinate teaching plans (Reynolds, 1992). It also is recognized that postinstructional activities combine with planning activities.

TABLE 7.5
Interactive Teaching Competencies from Effective Teaching Research

Competencies for Beginning a Lesson

Gain students' attention through an interesting comment or observation.

Review prior lesson for student understanding and knowledge, and reteach if necessary.

Link current lesson to previous lesson, activities, strategies, or content.

Identify target skill or content of current lesson.

Provide a rationale that relates the importance of learning the skill or content to meaningful contexts (i.e., relate it to events or situations in students' daily lives).

Explain the task in terms of teacher actions and learner expectations.

Competencies for Describing or Explaining

Relate lesson information to other concepts, strategies, and existing knowledge.

Provide an organizational framework to help students organize new information.

Provide step-by-step explanations of the overt and covert processes involved in learning the information, concepts, or strategies.

Describe situations in which the information or strategy is useful.

Encourage goal setting for learning the new information.

Summarize the lesson skill, strategy, or content. Explain how to perform the skill or strategy or use the content. Discuss the contexts for using the skill, strategy, or content and note how it is beneficial and how it can be adapted.

Competencies for Demonstrating and Modeling

Provide step-by-step demonstrations of covert and overt procedures involved in learning new information or applying strategies.

Use think-alouds to model covert processes involved in learning strategies or problem solving.

Provide examples and nonexamples to show distinctive and nondistinctive features of a concept.

Maintain a lively pace while modeling, but allow enough time for students to understand the content or strategy.

Teach with enthusiasm.

Model task-specific learning strategies (i.e., perform the task) and self-instructions (e.g., self-monitoring or problem solving) to help students achieve.

Prompt student involvement, and check understanding during modeling.

Correct student responses, and help students expand responses.

Note organization, relationships, and clues in the new material that elicit learning strategies.

Competencies for Conducting Guided Practice

Provide clear directions and expectations for guided-practice tasks.

Model guided-practice behaviors.

Prompt student participation through questions, and provide additional practice until students stop making errors.

Use prescriptive instructional prompts and cues to guide successful student learning.

Monitor student progress to ensure that students maintain a high success rate (i.e., 70% to 90% accuracy).

Maintain a lively pace.

Provide error-correction procedures through prompting, modeling, or cuing rather than telling the answer.

Use whole-class and small-group instruction.

Summarize the lesson accomplishments of individuals and the group.

Forecast the content of the following lessons.

continued

TABLE 7.5
continued

Competencies for Conducting Independent Practice

Describe the assignment and the criteria (e.g., neatness, accuracy, and promptness) used to evaluate it.
Explain the rationale of the assignment and its importance.
Check to ensure that students understand the assignment through questioning and reviewing homework and previous assignments.
Demonstrate strategies and procedures for completing independent practice activities.
Review tasks in assignments.
Maintain records and graphs of students' performance.
Provide results of evaluations to students.
Provide for error-correction activities during seatwork.
Praise or reinforce students for independent work effort and assignment completion.
Circulate among students to monitor progress and assist students.
Frequently scan the classroom to see if students are working.
Ensure that students experience high rates of success during seatwork.
Hold students accountable for independent work.
Have students complete missed assignments and correct errors.
Ensure that independent work relates to academic goals.
Provide peer tutoring and cooperative-learning grouping arrangements for students mature enough to interact appropriately.
Provide a variety of independent practice activities (e.g., instructional games, self-correcting materials, computer-assisted instruction, tape recorder-assisted instruction, and quality homework practices).
Instruct students to generalize and apply knowledge across settings and situations.

Competencies for Promoting Generalization

Have students discuss rationales for using content or strategy.
Have students identify settings for using content or strategy.
Identify cues in settings that remind students to use content or strategy.
Enlist assistance of other teachers to encourage generalization of content or strategy.
Identify metacognitive processes needed to remember and apply content or strategy.
Set goals to use content or strategy in different contexts.
Teach content or strategy to mastery.
Relate content or strategy use to personal lives of students.
Use a variety of activities in teaching content or strategy (e.g., different teachers, peer instruction, and various practice activities).
Teach content or strategy that is likely to be reinforced or useful in the students' natural environments.
Enlist help of parents to encourage use of content or strategy at home.
Use a variety of formats (e.g., objects, pictures, media, and computer-assisted instruction) to teach content or strategy.
Encourage students to use content or strategy in their daily lives.
Point out to students that successes are related to their own efforts.
Encourage students to engage in self-management through self-recording, self-evaluation, and self-reinforcement activities.
Provide students with problem-solving instruction through metacognitive strategies (e.g., use of mnemonics that key strategy use).
Teach students to set goals and monitor progress toward their goals.

TABLE 7.5
continued

Competencies for Managing Behavior

Establish a positive, expectant, and orderly classroom environment.
Use task-specific and descriptive praise.
Use a hierarchy of reinforcers to adapt to level of student maturity (e.g., food, objects, tokens, points, praise, activity, or sense of mastery).
Maintain a 3:1 ratio of teacher attention to positive classroom events versus negative classroom events.
Provide positive reinforcement for appropriate behavior or effort, successful task completion, and the learning of new or difficult material.
Maintain a positive classroom environment through enthusiasm, encouragement, and a positive disposition.
Ensure that students have the ability or skills to acquire the targeted content or perform the strategy or procedure being taught.
Gradually shift reinforcement from appropriate behavior to learning accomplishments.
Provide students with verbal reminders to follow rules.
Establish rules that involve respect for others.
Correct student behavior in a way that helps them understand the appropriate behavior for the situation.
Clearly state what behaviors are expected and what behaviors are not tolerated.
Introduce and discuss rules, procedures, and consequences for following rules and breaking rules.
Post rules, discuss rules, and provide rationale for rules.
Instruct students to understand and follow rules through demonstrating, modeling, giving examples and nonexamples, providing reinforcement to students for following rules, correcting students for not following rules, and applying consequences for students who break rules.
Use nonverbal signals when feasible to direct students in a manner that does not disrupt the class.
Deliver specific praise contingently.
Foster self-management in students through self-monitoring, self-recording, and self-evaluating.

Competencies for Managing Instruction

Establish classroom routines and procedures to promote flow of activities.
Provide explicit instruction in classroom routines.
Engage in frequent positive and supportive interactions.
Provide more teacher-led instruction than independent work.
Reinforce student accomplishments.
Frequently scan the classroom.
Arrange the classroom to facilitate smooth transitions and ease of student monitoring.
Communicate expectations, and provide structure for learning (e.g., instructional groupings, prescriptive seatwork, accessible materials, and support for working).
Use metaphors, anecdotes, and concrete examples to help students connect new content with their existing knowledge.
Hold students accountable for work, and keep records of progress.
Circulate throughout the classroom to check the accuracy of work and progress of students.
Engage students in talk about their own thinking.
Ask students to interact with each other and collaborate on problem-solving tasks.

continued

TABLE 7.5
continued

Competencies for Asking Questions

Use questions to individualize instruction.
Use questions to increase lesson clarity.
Use questions to check for understanding.
Use rapidly paced questions in basic skill instruction in which short, factual answers can encourage learning.
To maintain group attention, call on a student after, rather than before, a question.
Promote higher-order thinking through questions with more than one correct answer.
Promote higher-order thinking through questions that encourage application (i.e., questions with *apply* and *use*), analysis (i.e., questions with *relate* and *distinguish*), synthesis (i.e., questions with *formulate* and *create*), and evaluation (i.e., questions with *justify* and *appraise*).
Use questions that elicit correct answers about 75% of the time.
Respond to incorrect answers in a sensitive and helpful manner.
Use questions that encourage students to respond with substantive answers (including incorrect, incomplete, and "I don't know" answers) about 25% of the time.
Attend to who is answering questions correctly during discussions.
Call on nonvolunteers, and ask students to elaborate on other students' answers.
Wait or pause for about 3 seconds after asking a question and calling on a student to enable the student to offer a substantive response (e.g., give a correct or incorrect answer, ask for clarification, or say "I don't know").

Competencies for Monitoring Progress

Monitor progress continuously to maintain an instructional match between the instructional task and the student's ability, skill, and existing knowledge.
Monitor to check understanding of task demands by asking the student to perform a sample task.
Monitor to ensure high rates of success.
Use a systematic record-keeping system to monitor progress.
Use the results of monitoring to initiate interventions to improve student learning.
Check homework, grade and comment on homework, and return homework quickly.

Competencies for Giving Feedback

Give frequent positive feedback for student successes.
Provide informative feedback (e.g., note error patterns and highlight positive features) to students in making written or verbal corrections.
Involve students in setting instructional goals, and discuss performance in terms of goals.
View errors as teaching opportunities, and reteach (e.g., provide modeling or guided practice) on the basis of student performance.
Correct errors immediately.
Require students to correct errors so that they remember what to do when they encounter similar problems.
Praise students for error correction.
Use student performance data to make instructional decisions.

TABLE 7.5
continued

Competencies for Promoting Independence
Stress the importance of instructional content (i.e., skills, content, or strategies) and its relevance to daily functioning.
Allow ample time to reach mastery.
Encourage generalization.
Teach effective study skills.
Involve students in goal setting, and point out how their errors relate to goal achievement.
Help students connect their degree of effort to positive and negative consequences.
Encourage students to be proactive about learning.
Provide students with strategies that foster independent learning (e.g., using mnemonics, clustering information to memorize it, and using self-questioning to ensure comprehension).
Model metacognitive or regulatory self-statements to help students self-instruct, self-monitor, and self-evaluate.
Model being a learner.

Reflect About Teaching and Collaborate with Others

One of the primary activities of postinstruction involves the process of reflecting about teaching. Brandt (1991) highlights the importance of reflecting in the following passage:

> Everyone needs opportunities for self-renewal, but those responsible for developing other human beings need them most of all. Thinking deeply about what we are doing leads us to ask better questions, break out of fruitless routines, make unexpected connections, and experiment with fresh ideas. (p. 3)

Reynolds (1992) reports that competent teachers reflect on their teaching to find out what teaching behaviors are successful and unsuccessful with students. This process helps them refine their teaching practices. She notes that reflection occurs during interaction with students as well as after interactions. During interactions, teachers gather information from student comments, actions, and written work to determine levels of student understanding. These multiple forms of assessments provide information that enables teachers to reflect on what practices are effective or ineffective and to improve their teaching. Reynolds notes that as teachers gain experience and become more competent, their reflections change from concerns about classroom management, the quality of their explanations, how they respond to questions, and student participation to concerns about student understanding and instructional events that seem especially noteworthy. It is believed that with experience, teachers develop a system for organizing, understanding, and using the enormous amount of information gained from experience. Because of the learning differences of students with learning disabilities, the focus on student understanding is important in guiding teachers to make adjustments that enable them to succeed.

Journal Writing. One of the primary techniques for fostering teacher reflections is journal writing. Smyth (1989) suggests the following questions to guide reflections that are applicable to teacher journal writing:

1. What do I do? (Elicits description of practice.)
2. What does this mean? (Elicits principles of instruction.)
3. How did I come to be this way? (Elicits awareness beyond the classroom and situates practices in a broader cultural milieu.)
4. How might I do things differently? (Elicits action.)

Collaboration. Although reflection is often a private or individual event, it is facilitated through collaborative activities. Working together with colleagues often helps teachers gain personal insights and create synergistic solutions. (Collaboration is featured in Chapter 6.) The following collaborative questions can foster reflection:

1. Will curriculum-based assessment allow teachers to assess the progress of students in a manner that provides insight into effective instructional activities and learner differences?
2. How can teachers more effectively involve parents in school activities?
3. How can teachers effectively combine elements of whole language instruction with phonological awareness instruction to improve reading instruction?

An additional collaborative/reflective activity involves establishing an educators' forum to focus on school problems.

Research on Teachers' Reflective Teaching. Mohlman, Sparks-Langer, and Colton (1991) report that educators can foster professional growth through performing microteaching followed by writing in reflection journals, conducting self-analysis of video- and audiotapes, conducting action research projects, and collaborating about student learning and teaching. They note that case studies of teaching and learning events that highlight specific context, practices, content, and ethical and moral dilemmas help teachers develop a valuable repertoire of ideas, skills, and attitudes. Finally, Mohlman et al. indicate that teachers need time to understand, interpret, and personalize information from research, theories, and experts.

Develop a Lesson Format for Planning

Elmore (1992) reports that teachers need help to learn and apply the ideas of current research on teaching. He claims that it is unrealistic to expect teachers to accomplish this by themselves. To help teachers model strategies and teach skills, researchers at the University of Oregon (e.g., Doug Carnine, Zig Engelmann, and Russell Gersten) and at the University of Kansas (e.g., Don Deshler, Keith Lenz, and Jean Schumaker) have published materials that include teacher scripts or sample dialogues. The Direct Instruction Model from the University of Oregon is featured in Chapter 8, and the Strategic Intervention Model from the University of Kansas is presented in Chapter 10. These scripts and dialogues provide the teacher with an initial guide on how to model strategies explicitly and how to lead the student to conceptual understanding of content and strategies. As teachers gain confidence with these guided lessons, the content and process of the sample dialogues become a natural part of the teacher's instructional procedures.

Mercer, Jordan, and Miller (1994) present a lesson guide that incorporates much of the effective teaching research and features the following steps: give an advance organizer, describe and model the skill or strategy, conduct guided practice and interactive discourse, conduct independent practice to mastery, provide elaborated feedback, and teach generalization and transfer. The describe-and-model step features explicit teacher modeling of strategies. The guided practice step parallels scaffolding as the teacher guides the student to conceptual understandings and independent work. The independent practice step incorporates working alone and with peers to gain mastery. The elaborated feedback step is used to recognize successes and relate them to learning goals and to use errors for teaching and learning opportunities. The generalization and transfer step encourages the student to reflect on strategy uses. Table 7.6 provides a beginning lesson format for developing sample dialogues and practice activities.

PERSPECTIVE

When teachers examine the many instructional components that are recommended for good teaching, it is understandable if they feel a little

TABLE 7.6
Lesson Format for Developing Sample Dialogues and Practice Activities

Step 1: Give an Advance Organizer
The teacher links the lesson to previous learning or lessons.
The teacher identifies the target skill.
The teacher provides a rationale for learning the skill or strategy and discusses the relevance of the new knowledge.

Step 2: Describe and Model the Skill or Strategy
Procedure 1: The teacher asks a question and provides the answer. The student hears and observes the teacher think aloud while modeling the strategy.
Procedure 2: The teacher asks a question, and the student helps provide the answer. The teacher and the student perform the strategy together, and the teacher continues to provide modeling.

Step 3: Conduct Guided Practice and Interactive Discourse
Procedure 1: The teacher guides the student through the strategy without demonstration unless it is essential. The teacher provides guidance as needed by asking specific leading questions, providing prompts, and providing cues.
Procedure 2: The teacher instructs the student to do the task and reflect on the process and product. The teacher provides support as needed and uses fewer prompts and cues. The student is encouraged to become more independent.

Step 4: Conduct Independent Practice to Mastery
The student is encouraged to reflect and work without teacher assistance. Activities include peer tutoring, cooperative learning, instructional games, self-correcting materials, or computer-assisted instruction.

Step 5: Provide Elaborated Feedback
The teacher gives feedback on correct responses and uses incorrect responses as teaching and learning opportunities. The following procedure regarding feedback routines is based on the research of Kline, Schumaker, and Deshler (1991).
Find the score. Explain the grade.
Enter the score. Use a graph and goal setting and make it meaningful.
Evaluate the score in terms of the goal.
Determine errors by examining the pattern.
Begin error correction. Teacher models similar problem.
Ask students to apply the correction procedure.
Close out the session by giving positive feedback on correction.
Kick back and relax!

Step 6: Teach Generalization and Transfer
The teacher encourages the student to reflect on applications of new knowledge across settings and situations.

overwhelmed. The instructional components related to positive student outcomes represent a formidable list to incorporate into daily teaching practices. Fortunately, the growing knowledge base about effective teaching can enlighten educators about best teaching practices; however, a unifying theory or framework to organize the knowledge base and guide the application of best teaching practices is missing. The examination of teaching in terms of planning, interactive teaching, and postinstructional activities helps organize the many components of teaching into a manageable framework for improving the practice of teaching. If one considers that many of the supported instructional practices are interrelated, the task of effective teaching becomes more reasonable. For example, the competency involving monitoring student progress is inherent in several planning activities (e.g., provide time for learning, ensure success, and strive to motivate), interactive teaching activities (e.g., monitor progress and give feedback), and postinstructional activities (e.g., reflect on student learning and activities that are effective or ineffective).

When examining all the aspects of good teaching, it is nice to remember that students can bring much joy to teaching. As Lovitt (1977) points out, "Youngsters are by definition, fresh. . . . They see life differently. . . . They often develop their own approaches and language systems for dealing with and talking about their lives. . . . Children entertain teachers; they keep them sane, pure in spirit, and incorruptible" (p. 201). It is helpful for the teacher to appreciate students and expect to enjoy their freshness, their humor, their questions, and their ideas.

Perhaps the most important source of knowledge about good teaching is the students. In a paper on "The Good Teacher" presented at a conference titled "Education from Cradle to Doctorate," Clark (1989) notes that students' thoughts and stories about good teachers almost invariably concern four fundamental human needs: (a) to be known, (b) to be encouraged, (c) to be respected, and (d) to be led. Moreover, he discusses the voices of students concerning good teaching:

> In the language of children, their good teachers nurture them by treating them as intelligent people who can become even more intelligent, by taking the time to learn who we are and what we love, treating us fairly by treating us differently, by explaining why he teaches and acts as he does, by telling stories of her own life outside school and listening to ours, by letting me have a bad day when I can't help it. The good teacher is both funny and serious. We can laugh together, and this makes me feel happy and close. She puts thought into surprising us in ways that we will never forget. He draws pictures that show how ideas are connected; we don't feel lost or afraid that we will be sent away or humiliated. The good teacher loves what he is teaching, but does not show off or put distance between us and him. The good teacher sets things up so that children can learn how to learn from one another. She knows how to be a friend while still a responsible adult. . . . The good teacher puts people first, say the children. The good teacher acts from love and caring, and is loved and cared for in return. (pp. 18–19)

DISCUSSION/REVIEW QUESTIONS

1. Briefly discuss three instructional variables related to learning, and list several strategies for motivating students to learn.
2. Discuss factors to consider when examining and selecting curriculum materials.
3. Present guidelines to accommodate students with learning disabilities during large-group instruction.
4. Briefly discuss peer tutoring, *ClassWide Peer Tutoring*, and cooperative learning.
5. Discuss the use of self-correcting materials and instructional games.
6. Discuss the use of technology for instruction according to research-verified applications, emerging applications, and future applications, and present several advantages of using computer-assisted instruction with students with learning disabilities.
7. Present guidelines to promote "best practices" on homework.
8. Discuss learner variables that influence learning and instruction design.
9. List several interactive teaching competencies from effective teaching research.
10. Discuss postinstructional activities to improve teaching effectiveness.

REFERENCES

Alderman, M. K. (1990). Motivation for at-risk students. *Educational Leadership, 48*(1), 27–30.

Al-Rubaiy, K. (1985, Summer). . . . And now for your homework assignment. *The Directive Teacher,* pp. 3–5.

Anderson, L. M., Brubaker, N. L., Alleman-Brooks, J., & Duffy, G. G. (1985). A qualitative study of seatwork in first-grade classrooms. *Elementary School Journal, 88,* 123–140.

Anderson, L. M., Evertson, C. M., & Brophy, J. E. (1979). An experimental study of effective teaching in first grade reading groups. *Elementary School Journal, 79,* 193–223.

Anderson, L. M., Evertson, C. M., & Emmer, E. T. (1980). Dimensions in classroom management derived from recent research. *Journal of Curriculum Studies, 12,* 343–346.

Anderson, L. M., Raphael, T. E., Englert, C. S., & Stevens, D. D. (1991). *Teaching writing with a new instructional model: Variations in teachers' beliefs, instructional practice, and their students' performance.* Paper presented at the annual meeting of the American Educational Research Association, Chicago, IL.

Anderson, L. W. (1984). Instruction and time-on-task: A review. In L. W. Anderson (Ed.), *Time and school learning* (pp. 142–163). New York: St. Martin's Press.

Archer, A., & Edgar, E. (1976). Teaching academic skills to mildly handicapped children. In S. Lowenbraun & J. Q. Affleck (Eds.), *Teaching mildly handicapped children in regular classes* (pp. 15–112). Columbus, OH: Merrill.

Armstrong, S. W., & McPherson, A. (1991). Homework as a critical component in social skills instruction. *Teaching Exceptional Children, 24*(1), 45–47.

Baker, S. K., Simmons, D. C., & Kameenui, E. J. (1994). Making information more memorable for students with learning disabilities through the design of instructional tools. *LD Forum, 19*(3), 14–18.

Bickel, W. W., & Bickel, D. D. (1986). Effective schools, classrooms, and instruction: Implications for special education. *Exceptional Children, 52,* 489–500.

Blankenship, C., & Lilly, M. S. (1981). *Mainstreaming students with learning and behavior problems: Techniques for the classroom teacher.* New York: Holt, Rinehart & Winston.

Bloom, B. (1984). The search for methods of group instruction as effective as one-to-one tutoring. *Educational Leadership, 41*(8), 4–18.

Borg, W. R. (1980). Time and school learning. In C. Denham & A. Lieberman (Eds.), *Time to learn.* Washington, DC: National Institute of Education.

Borich, G. D. (1992). *Effective teaching methods* (2nd ed.). Upper Saddle River, NJ: Merrill/Prentice Hall.

Brandt, R. (1991). Overview: Time for reflection. *Educational Leadership, 48*(6), 3.

Brigham, F. J., Scruggs, T. E., & Mastropieri, M. A. (1992). Teaching enthusiasm in learning disabilities classrooms: Effects on learning and behavior. *Learning Disabilities Research & Practice, 7,* 68–73.

Brophy, J. (1987). Synthesis of research on strategies for motivating students to learn. *Educational Leadership, 45*(2), 40–48.

Brophy, J., & Good, T. L. (1986). Teacher behavior and student achievement. In M. C. Wittrock (Ed.), *Handbook of research on teaching* (3rd ed., pp. 328–375). Upper Saddle River, NJ: Prentice Hall.

Carnine, D., Silbert, J., & Kameenui, E. J. (1990). *Direct instruction reading* (2nd ed.). Upper Saddle River, NJ: Merrill/Prentice Hall.

Chow, S. H. (1981). *A study of academic learning time for mainstream learning-disabled students* (Final Report). San Francisco, CA: Far West Laboratory for Educational Research and Development.

Christenson, S. L., Ysseldyke, J. E., & Thurlow, M. L. (1989). Critical instructional factors for students with mild handicaps: An integrative review. *Remedial and Special Education, 10*(5), 21–31.

Clark, C. M. (1989, October). *The good teacher.* Paper presented at the Norwegian Research Council for Science and the Humanities Conference: "Education from Cradle to Doctorate," Trondheim, Norway.

Clark, C. M., & Peterson, P. L. (1986). Teachers' thought processes. In M. C. Wittrock (Ed.), *Handbook of research on teaching* (3rd ed., pp. 255–296). Upper Saddle River, NJ: Prentice Hall.

Clifford, M. M. (1990). Students need challenge, not easy success. *Educational Leadership, 48*(1), 22–26.

Cohen, P. A., Kulik, J. A., & Kulik, C. C. (1982). Educational outcomes of tutoring: A meta-analysis of findings. *American Educational Research Journal, 19*(2), 237–248.

Cooper, H. (1989). Synthesis of research on homework. *Educational Leadership, 47*(3), 85–91.

Delquadri, J., Greenwood, C. R., Whorton, D., Carta, J. J., & Hall, R. V. (1986). Classwide peer tutoring. *Exceptional Children, 52,* 535–542.

Dempster, F. N. (1991). Synthesis of research on reviews and tests. *Educational Leadership, 48*(7), 71–76.

Denham, C., & Lieberman, A. (Eds). (1980). *Time to learn.* Washington, DC: National Institute of Education.

Deno, S. L., & Fuchs, L. S. (1987). Developing curriculum-based measurement systems for data-based special education problem solving. *Focus on Exceptional Children, 19*(8), 1–16.

DeVries, D. L., & Slavin, R. E. (1978). Teams-games-tournament (TGT): Review of ten classroom experiments. *Journal of Research and Development in Education, 12,* 28–38.

Ellis, E. S., Deshler, D. D., Lenz, B. K., Schumaker, J. B., & Clark, F. L. (1991). An instructional model for teaching learning strategies. *Focus on Exceptional Children, 23*(6), 1–24.

Ellis, E. S., & Sabornie, E. J. (1986). Effective instruction with microcomputers: Promises, practices, and preliminary findings. *Focus on Exceptional Children, 19*(4), 1–16.

Elmore, R. F. (1992). Why restricting alone won't improve teaching. *Educational Leadership, 49*(7), 44–48.

Englert, C. S., Tarrant, K. L., & Mariage, T. V. (1992). Defining and redefining instructional practice in special education: Perspectives on good teaching. *Teacher Education and Special Education, 15,* 62–86.

Epstein, M. H., Polloway, E. A., Foley, R. M., & Patton, J. R. (1993). Homework: A comparison of teachers' and parents' perceptions of the problems experienced by students identified as having behavioral disorders, learning disabilities, or no disabilities. *Remedial and Special Education, 14*(5), 40–50.

Fisher, C. W., Berliner, D. C., Filby, N. N., Marliave, R., Cahen, L. S., & Dishaw, M. M. (1980). Teaching behaviors, academic learning time, and student achievement: An overview. In C. Denham & A. Lieberman (Eds.), *Time to learn.* Washington, DC: National Institute of Education.

Fisher, C. W., Berliner, D. C., Filby, N. N., Marliave, R., Cahen, L. S., Dishaw, M. M., & Moore, J. E. (1978). *Teaching and learning in the elementary school: A summary of the Beginning Teacher Evaluation Study.* San Francisco: Far West Laboratory for Educational Research and Development.

Fitzgerald, G., Fick, L., & Milich, R. (1986). Computer-assisted instruction for students with attentional difficulties. *Journal of Learning Disabilities, 19,* 376–379.

Frith, G. (1991). Facilitating homework through effective support systems. *Teaching Exceptional Children, 24*(1), 48–49.

Fuchs, L. S., Fuchs, D., & Hamlett, C. L. (1989). Effects of alternative goal structures within curriculum-based measurement. *Exceptional Children, 55,* 429–438.

Gage, N. L., & Needels, M. C. (1989). Effects of systematic formative evaluation on student achievement. *Exceptional Children, 53,* 199–208.

Gettinger, M. (1991). Learning time and retention differences between nondisabled students and students with learning disabilities. *Learning Disability Quarterly, 14,* 179–189.

Good, T. L. (1983). Classroom research: A decade of progress. *Educational Psychologist, 18*(3), 127–144.

Goodlad, J. I. (1984). A place called school. New York: McGraw-Hill.

Greenwood, C. R. (1991). Longitudinal analysis of time, engagement, and achievement in at-risk versus non-risk students. *Exceptional Children, 57,* 521–534.

Greenwood, C. R., Arreaga-Mayer, C., & Carta, J. J. (1994). Identification and translation of effective teacher-developed instructional procedures for general practice. *Remedial and Special Education, 15,* 140–151.

Greenwood, C. R., Delquadri, J. C., & Carta, J. J. (1988). *ClassWide Peer Tutoring: Programs for spelling, math, and reading.* Delray Beach, FL: Educational Achievement Systems.

Greenwood, C. R., Dinwiddie, G., Terry, B., Wade, L., Stanley, S. O., Thibadeau, S., & Delquadri, J. C. (1984). Teacher- versus peer-mediated instruction: An eco-behavioral analysis of achievement outcomes. *Journal of Applied Behavior Analysis, 17,* 521–538.

Grimes, L. (1981). Computers are for kids: Designing software programs. *Teaching Exceptional Children, 14,* 48–53.

Grossen, B. (1993). Overview: Toward world class standards. *Effective School Practices, 12*(3), 1–8.

Hancock, V., & Betts, F. (1994). From the lagging to the leading edge. *Educational Leadership, 51*(7), 24–29.

Harris, K. R., & Graham, S. (1994). Constructivism: Principles, paradigms, and integration. *The Journal of Special Education, 28,* 233–247.

Hasselbring, T. S., Goin, L. I., & Bransford, J. D. (1988). Developing math automaticity in learning handicapped children: The role of computerized drill and practice. *Focus on Exceptional Children, 20*(6), 1–7.

Haynes, M. C., & Jenkins, J. R. (1986). Reading instruction in special education resource rooms. *American Educational Research Journal, 23,* 161–190.

Heller, H. W., Spooner, F., Anderson, D., & Mims, A. (1988). Homework: A review of special education classroom practices in the Southeast. *Teacher Education and Special Education, 11,* 43–51.

Horton, S. V., Lovitt, T. C., Givens, A., & Nelson, R. (1989). Teaching social studies to high school students with academic handicaps in a mainstreamed setting: Effects of a computerized study guide. *Journal of Learning Disabilities, 22,* 102–107.

Howell, K. W., Fox, S. L., & Morehead, M. K. (1993). *Curriculum-based evaluation: Teaching and decision making* (2nd ed.). Pacific Grove, CA: Brooks/Cole.

Jenson, W. R., Sheridan, S. M., Olympia, D. E., & Andrews, D. (1994). Homework and students with learning disabilities and behavior disorders: A practical, parent-based approach. *Journal of Learning Disabilities, 27,* 538–548.

Kavale, K. A., & Reese, J. H. (1991). Teacher beliefs and perceptions about learning disabilities: A survey of Iowa practitioners. *Learning Disability Quarterly, 14,* 141–160.

Kay, P. J., Fitzgerald, M., Paradee, C., & Mellencamp, A. (1994). Making homework work at home: The parent's perspective. *Journal of Learning Disabilities, 27,* 550–561.

Keefe, C. H., & Candler, A. C. (1989). LD students and word processors: Questions and answers. *Learning Disabilities Focus, 4,* 78–83.

Kline, F. M., Schumaker, J. B., & Deshler, D. D. (1991). Development and validation of feedback routines for instructing students with learning disabilities. *Learning Disability Quarterly, 14,* 191–207.

Larrivee, B. (1986). Effective teaching for mainstreamed students is effective teaching for all students. *Teacher Education and Special Education, 9,* 173–179.

Lavoie, R. D. (1993, March). *Batteries are not included: Motivating the reluctant learner.* Paper presented at the Learning Disabilities Association International Conference, Washington, DC.

Lenz, B. K., Bulgren, J., & Hudson, P. (1990). Content enhancement: A model for promoting the acquisition of content by individuals with learning disabilities. In T. E. Scruggs & B. Y. L. Wong (Eds.), *Intervention research in learning disabilities* (pp. 122–165). New York: Springer-Verlag.

Levin, H., Glass, G., & Meister, C. (1984). *Cost-effectiveness of four educational interventions.* Stanford, CA: Institute for Research on Educational Finance and Governance, Stanford University.

Lindsey, J. D. (1987). *Computers and exceptional individuals.* Upper Saddle River, NJ: Merrill/Prentice Hall.

Lovitt, T. C. (1977). *In spite of my resistance: I've learned from children.* Upper Saddle River, NJ: Merrill/Prentice Hall.

Lovitt, T. C. (1995). *Tactics for teaching* (2nd ed.). Upper Saddle River, NJ: Merrill/Prentice Hall.

Maheady, L., Harper, G. F., & Mallette, B. (1991). Peer-mediated instruction: A review of potential applications for special education. *Reading, Writing, and Learning Disabilities International, 7,* 75–103.

Maheady, L., Harper, G. F., & Sacca, M. K. (1988). Peer-mediated instruction: A promising approach to meeting the diverse needs of LD adolescents. *Learning Disability Quarterly, 11,* 108–113.

Maheady, L., Sacca, M. K., & Harper, G. F. (1988). Classwide peer tutoring with mildly handicapped high school students. *Exceptional Children, 55,* 52–59.

Mainzer, R. W., Jr., Mainzer, K. L., Slavin, R. E., & Lowry, E. (1993). What special education teachers should know about cooperative learning. *Teacher Education and Special Education, 16,* 42–50.

Majsterek, D., & Wilson, R. (1993). Computer-assisted instruction (CAI): An update on applications for students with learning disabilities. *LD Forum, 19*(1), 19–21.

Mercer, C. D., Jordan, L., & Miller, S. P. (1994). Implications of constructivism for teaching math to students with moderate to mild disabilities. *The Journal of Special Education, 28,* 290–306.

Mercer, C. D., & Mercer, A. R. (1993). *Teaching students with learning problems* (4th ed.). Upper Saddle River, NJ: Merrill/Prentice Hall.

Mercer, C. D., Mercer, A. R., & Bott, D. A. (1984). *Self-correcting learning materials for the classroom.* Upper Saddle River, NJ: Merrill/Prentice Hall.

Mims, A., Harper, C., Armstrong, S. W., & Savage, S. (1991). Effective instruction in homework for students with disabilities. *Teaching Exceptional Children, 24*(1), 42–44.

Miramontes, O., Cheng, L., & Trueba, H. T. (1984). Teacher perceptions and observed outcomes: An ethnographic study of classroom interactions. *Learning Disability Quarterly, 7,* 349–357.

Mohlman, G., Sparks-Langer, S., & Colton, A. B. (1991). Synthesis of research on teachers' reflective thinking. *Educational Leadership, 48*(6), 37–44.

Newmann, F. M., & Wehlage, G. G. (1993). Five standards of authentic instruction. *Educational Leadership, 50*(7), 8–12.

Nicholls, J. G., McKenzie, M., & Shufro, J. (1994). Schoolwork, homework, life's work: The experience of students with and without learning disabilities. *Journal of Learning Disabilities, 27,* 562–569.

Olympia, D .E., Sheridan, S. M., & Jenson, W. R. (1994). Homework: A natural means of home-school collaboration. *School Psychology Quarterly, 9,* 60–80.

O'Melia, M. C., & Rosenberg, M. S. (1994). Effects of cooperative homework teams on the acquisition of mathematics skills by secondary students with mild disabilities. *Exceptional Children, 60,* 538–548.

Osguthorpe, R. T., & Scruggs, T. E. (1986). Special education students as tutors: A review and analysis. *Remedial and Special Education, 7*(4), 15–26.

Patton, J. R. (1994). Practical recommendations for using homework with students with learning disabilities. *Journal of Learning Disabilities, 27,* 570–578.

Peck, K. L., & Dorricott, D. (1994). Why use technology? *Educational Leadership, 51*(7), 11–14.

Porter, A. C., & Brophy, J. (1988). Synthesis of research on good teaching: Insights from the work of the Institute for Research on Teaching. *Educational Leadership, 45*(8), 74–85.

Prater, M. A. (1993). Teaching concepts: Procedures for the design and delivery of instruction. *Remedial and Special Education, 14*(5), 51–62.

Purkey, W. (1978). *Inviting school success.* Belmont, CA: Wadsworth.

Reynolds, A. (1992). What is competent beginning teaching? A review of the literature. *Review of Educational Research, 62,* 1–35.

Rich, H. L., & Ross, S. M. (1989). Students' time on learning tasks in special education. *Exceptional Children, 55,* 508–515.

Rieth, H., & Evertson, C. (1988). Variables related to the effective instruction of difficult-to-teach children. *Focus on Exceptional Children, 20*(5), 1–8.

Rieth, H. J., & Frick, T. (1983). *An analysis of the impact of instructional time with different service delivery systems on the achievement of mildly handicapped students* (Final Grant Research Report). Bloomington: Indiana University, Center for Innovation in Teaching the Handicapped.

Rosenberg, M. S. (1989). The effects of daily homework assignments on the acquisition of basic skills by students with learning disabilities. *Journal of Learning Disabilities, 22,* 314–323.

Rosenshine, B., & Stevens, R. (1986). Teaching functions. In M. C. Wittrock (Ed.), *Handbook of research on teaching* (3rd ed., pp. 376–391). Upper Saddle River, NJ: Prentice Hall.

Salend, S. J. (1994). *Effective mainstreaming: Creating inclusive classrooms* (2nd ed.). Upper Saddle River, NJ: Merrill/Prentice Hall.

Salend, S. J., & Schliff, J. (1989). An examination of the homework practices of teachers of students with learning disabilities. *Journal of Learning Disabilities, 22,* 621–623.

Samuels, S. J. (1986). Why children fail to learn and what to do about it. *Exceptional Children, 53,* 7–16.

Scruggs, T. E., Mastropieri, M. A., Sullivan, G. S., & Hesser, L. S. (1993). Improving reasoning and recall: The differential effects of elaborative interrogation and mnemonic elaboration. *Learning Disability Quarterly, 16,* 233–240.

Scruggs, T. E., & Richter, L. (1985). Tutoring learning disabled students: A critical review. *Learning Disability Quarterly, 8,* 286–298.

Shuell, T. J., & Schueckler, L. M. (1988, April). *Toward evaluating software according to principles of learning and teaching.* Paper presented at the meeting of the American Educational Research Association, New Orleans.

Sindelar, P., Smith, M., Harriman, N., Hale, R., & Wilson, R. (1986). Teacher effectiveness in special education programs. *The Journal of Special Education, 20,* 195–207.

Slavin, R. E. (1978). Student teams and achievement divisions. *Journal of Research and Development in Education, 12,* 39–49.

Slavin, R. E. (1986). *Using student team learning* (3rd ed.). Baltimore, MD: Center for Research on Elementary and Middle Schools, Johns Hopkins University.

Slavin, R. E. (1988). Synthesis of research on grouping in elementary and secondary schools. *Educational Leadership, 46*(1), 67–77.

Slavin, R. E. (1989/1990). Research on cooperative learning: Consensus and controversy. *Educational Leadership, 47*(4), 52–54.

Slavin, R. E. (1991). Synthesis of research on cooperative learning. *Educational Leadership, 48*(5), 71–82.

Slavin, R. E., Madden, N. A., & Stevens, R. J. (1990). Cooperative learning models for the 3 R's. *Educational Leadership, 47*(4), 22–28.

Slavin, R. E., Stevens, R. J., & Madden, N. A. (1988). Accommodating student diversity in reading and writing instruction: A cooperative learning approach. *Remedial and Special Education, 9*(1), 60–66.

Smith, C. R. (1994). *Learning disabilities: The interaction of learner, task, and setting* (3rd ed.). Boston: Allyn & Bacon.

Smith, R. M., Neisworth, J. T., & Greer, J. G. (1978). *Evaluating educational environments*. Columbus, OH: Merrill.

Smyth, J. (1989). Developing and sustaining critical reflection in teacher education. *Journal of Teacher Education, 40*(2), 2–9.

Sprick, R. S. (1981). *The solution book: A guide to classroom discipline.* Blacklick, OH: SRA.

Sprick, R. S. (1985). *Discipline in the secondary classroom: A problem-by-problem survival guide.* West Nyack, NY: The Center for Applied Research in Education.

Sprick, R. S. (1987). *Solutions to elementary discipline problems* [Audiocassette tapes]. Eugene, OR: Teaching Strategies.

Stevens, R., & Rosenshine, B. (1981). Advances in research on teaching. *Exceptional Education Quarterly, 2*(1), 1–9.

Torgesen, J. K., Waters, M. D., Cohen, A. L., & Torgesen, J. L. (1988). Improving sight-word recognition skills in LD children: An evaluation of three computer program variations. *Learning Disability Quarterly, 11,* 125–132.

Utley, B. L., Zigmond, N., & Strain, P. S. (1987). How various forms of data affect teacher analysis of student performance. *Exceptional Children, 53,* 411–422.

Van Reusen, A. K., & Bos, C. S. (1994). Facilitating student participation in individualized education programs through motivation strategy instruction. *Exceptional Children, 60,* 466–475.

Wang, M. C. (1987). Toward achieving educational excellence for all students: Program design and instructional outcomes. *Remedial and Special Education, 8*(3), 25–34.

Wang, M. C., Haertel, G. D., & Walberg, H. J. (1993/1994). Synthesis of research: What helps students learn? *Educational Leadership, 51*(4), 74–79.

Wiens, W. (1986). Computer assisted learning in the learning assistance centre. *B.C. Journal of Special Education, 10,* 17–28.

Woodward, J., & Carnine, D. (1988). Antecedent knowledge and intelligent computer-assisted instruction. *Journal of Learning Disabilities, 21,* 131–139.

Woodward, J., Carnine, D., & Gersten, R. (1988). Teaching problem solving through a computer simulation. *American Educational Research Journal, 25*(1), 72–86.

Wyne, M., & Stuck, G. (1982). Time and learning: Implications for the classroom teacher. *The Elementary School Journal, 83,* 67–75.

Ysseldyke, J. E., & Algozzine, B. (1995). *Special education: A practical approach for teachers* (3rd ed.). Boston: Houghton Mifflin.

Ysseldyke, J. E., Christenson, S., & Kovaleski, J. F. (1994). Identifying students' instructional needs in the context of classroom and home environments. *Teaching Exceptional Children, 26*(3), 37–41.

Ysseldyke, J. E., Christenson, S. L., Thurlow, M. L., & Skiba, R. (1987). *Academic engagement and active responding of mentally retarded, learning disabled, emotionally disturbed, and nonhandicapped elementary students*. Minneapolis: University of Minnesota Instructional Alternatives Project.

Learning and Teaching Theories

CHAPTER 8

After studying this chapter, you should be able to:

- identify the basic tenets of the behavioral approach.
- describe direct instruction.
- discuss the use of task analysis in determining the sequence of skills to be taught.
- discuss the use of curriculum-based measurement to establish performance standards.
- discuss the features of individually referenced data systems.
- present various formats for graphing data.
- discuss the use of data analysis to make instructional decisions.
- list some basic guidelines for implementing data-based instruction.
- identify the stages of learning.
- discuss the basic learning principles of the behavioral approach.
- discuss the cognitive paradigm and the differences between the cognitive and the behavioral approaches.
- discuss the specific abilities approach and the developmental approach.
- discuss the information-processing approach.
- discuss basic components of information-processing models.
- discuss cognitive style and the maturational lag theory.
- discuss teaching methods for cognitive disabilities, including cognitive behavior modification, reciprocal teaching, and the strategies instructional approach.
- present the differences between the reductionist and constructivist paradigms.
- discuss the integration of paradigms and the functionalist approach.

A *paradigm* is a pattern of thinking about a phenomenon. The behavioral and cognitive approaches are the major paradigms for explaining the phenomenon of human learning. Each paradigm consists of theories that are developed to explain how the paradigm works. As research is conducted using specific theories, the theories are modified based on the findings of the research. Theories are dismissed when they repeatedly are not supported by facts or are disproved. The application of untested and poorly tested theories often leads to inaccurate conclusions about a paradigm. However, theories that are supported by facts become the basis for models that demonstrate how the theory can be translated into practice and support a paradigm.

The behavioral paradigm has dominated American education for several decades. In the behavioral approach, success is evaluated according to directly observable changes in an individual's performance in response to the manipulation of factors in the environment, whereas acceptance of the cognitive paradigm rests on the interpretation of mental events that are unobservable and, as a result, unmeasurable. However, research conducted with computer simulations using hypothesized models of human information processing has generated new interest in the cognitive paradigm. Many psychologists argue that the means for objective measurement of mental constructs is forthcoming. Another development that led to renewed interest in cognitive approaches is the use of cognitive principles by behavioral scientists. Many psychologists and educators merged elements of the cognitive and behavioral paradigms to create new educational programs for students. These events led to cognitive-behavioral interventions and a resurgence of research in interventions related to the cognitive paradigm. This chapter presents the behavioral and cognitive paradigms and their implications for students with learning disabilities.

THE BEHAVIORAL APPROACH

The behavioral approach is based on the premise that the environment greatly influences behavior. Terms characteristic of the behavioral viewpoint include *behavior modification, reinforcement theory, operant conditioning, applied behavior analysis, task analysis, data-based instruction, direct instruction, criterion reference,* and *precision teaching.* Most behaviorists share several assumptions, including the following:

1. All behavior is influenced by the principles of learning (e.g., positive reinforcement).
2. Interventions focus directly on the behavior of concern (e.g., reading comprehension, out-of-seat behavior, problem-solving behavior).
3. Teaching objectives are specified, and target behaviors are observable and measurable.
4. Student progress data determine the effectiveness of interventions and guide instructional decisions.

Research reviews on effective teaching (Christenson, Ysseldyke, & Thurlow, 1989; Englert, Tarrant, & Mariage, 1992; Good & Brophy, 1986; Porter & Brophy, 1988; Rosenshine & Stevens, 1986) document the many contributions of the behavioral approach to effective teaching practices. These investigators report that the following instructional components are related to positive student outcomes: setting goals and objectives, providing feedback, monitoring student progress, focusing on academics, teaching to mastery, using explicit step-by-step teaching procedures, ensuring high rates of success, providing many opportunities for student responses, maintaining an instructional match, and using demonstration, modeling, and practice presentation formats. All of these components are fundamental to the behavioral approach to teaching. It is apparent that much of what is known about effective teaching has come from the behavioral orientation.

Because the behaviorists view environment as a critical factor in learning, they place much emphasis on the teacher's role in arranging the classroom for optimal learning. Within this framework, learning failures are not placed readily on the student because of inadequate abilities (e.g., Alex cannot read because of his immaturity and poor memory). Teaching failure is considered a major factor in students' learning difficulties; thus, the responsibility for learning is placed on both the teacher and the learner.

Some educators claim that the behavioral approach does not address ecological relationships or learning characteristics (Iano, 1986; Poplin, 1987). However, Rosenberg and Jackson (1988) note that these areas are viable domains of the behavioral approach. Rosenberg and Jackson encourage more application of behavioral procedures to examine fundamental relationships in ecological contexts. Regarding the study of learner characteristics, they state that "more attention should be devoted to the tasks of (a) developing adequate descriptions of subjects and their presenting skills prior to undertaking a specific intervention and (b) analyzing the relationships between student knowledge systems, defined in terms of observable skills, and applied intervention activities" (p. 33).

Although many terms (e.g., *applied behavior analysis* and *data-based instruction*) are used to describe the behavioral model, certain features consistently characterize the behavioral approach. The essential components of the behavioral approach are presented next and include direct instruction, data-based instruction, stages of learning, and learning principles. Although these components are discussed separately, they usually are interwoven in a behavioral approach.

DIRECT INSTRUCTION

Direct Instruction officially began in 1966 when Bereiter and Engelmann published a book titled *Teaching Disadvantaged Children in the Preschool.* Engelmann maintains that it is more important to develop instructional sequences that systematically teach students essential reading skills, mathematical concepts, and language concepts than to spend time attempting to understand the inner workings of the mind, temperaments, and developmental levels. Because this approach conflicted with the prevailing theories of the 1960s, much controversy resulted, and many educators claimed that Direct Instruction was overly simplistic. Now, as Direct Instruction enters its third decade of practice, many educators (Brophy & Good, 1986; Rosenshine, 1986) have examined the empirical studies of effective instruction and realize the promise and effectiveness of the approach that Engelmann conceptualized. The growing list of extensive studies (Carnine, 1990; Gersten & Keating, 1987; Gersten, Woodward, & Darch, 1986; Kelly, 1993/1994) that document the effectiveness of Direct Instruction across lower- and higher-order skills with at-risk and special education students provides educators with an encouraging data base from which to plan the best instructional practices of the 1990s.

To many educators, *direct instruction* has become a generic term to refer to the structured teaching of academic skills or to a system for effective classroom management. In this text, the University of Oregon model of Direct Instruction is capitalized, and the generic use of the term is not capitalized. Since the 1960s, researchers at the University of Oregon (e.g., Doug Carnine, Zig Engelmann, Wes Becker, Russell Gersten, Ed Kameenui, and John Woodward) have maintained a center for Direct Instruction research, curriculum design, and staff development. The Association for Direct Instruction (P. O. Box 10252, Eugene, OR 97440) operates from Eugene, Oregon, and its members receive *Effective School Practices.* Moreover, several Direct Instruction Conferences are conducted throughout the nation each year. Gersten, Carnine, and Woodward (1987) encourage an understanding of Direct Instruction as defined by researchers at the University of Oregon:

> It is a complex way of looking at all aspects of instruction—from classroom organization and management to the quality of teacher-student interactions, the design of curriculum materials, and the nature of inservice teacher training. . . . The key principle in Direct Instruction is deceptively simple: For all students to learn, both the curriculum materials and teacher presentation of these materials must be clear and unambiguous. While many writers treat curriculum design and effective teaching research as separate strands, practitioners play them in concert.

> Direct Instruction comprises six critical features:
>
> 1. An explicit step-by-step strategy.
> 2. Development of mastery at each step in the process.
> 3. Strategy (or process) corrections for student errors.
> 4. Gradual fading from teacher directed activities toward independent work.
> 5. Use of adequate, systematic practice with a range of examples.
> 6. Cumulative review of newly learned concepts.
>
> Direct Instruction focuses on what many consider mundane decisions: the best wording for teachers to use in demonstrating a skill, the most effective way to correct students' errors, the number and range of examples necessary to ensure mastery of a new concept. (pp. 48–49)

Although the effectiveness of the Direct Instruction approach is well documented and its use is extensive, it is used less than are other programs that have failed to produce positive student outcomes. Authorities at the University of Oregon are redirecting some of their efforts to stimulate more applications of Direct Instruction. Gersten et al. (1987) comment on these directions:

> One priority has become translating research into practice, the development and refinement of sensitive, sensible inservice and professional development activities for teachers and instructional aides. A second emergent priority has been the application of these instructional design principles into technology. In particular, we have begun to explore how technology may assist teachers to implement the more difficult aspects of effective instruction. We believe this research agenda reflects a realism about the kinds of knowledge that can help improve schooling—practical training for teachers, well-conceived and empirically refined instructional materials, and technology to make the teacher's role more manageable. (p. 49)

One line of Direct Instruction research that appears to be encouraging for the 1990s involves the teaching of higher-order skills (e.g., literary analysis, chemistry, legal reasoning, problem solving, critical reading, ratio and proportions, social studies, and syllogistic reasoning) to at-risk and special education students at levels comparable to those of their advantaged peers (Carnine, 1989, 1990). Moreover, Gersten et al. (1987) note that the following principles are emerging for teaching higher-order skills:

1. Before learning cognitively complex skills, students need explicit direct instruction in relevant facts and concepts.
2. The teaching of open-ended processes in which a range of responses is appropriate necessitates clear models of successful solutions, a range of examples, and specific corrective feedback.

Finally, the teaching of these higher-order skills is being implemented successfully through videodisc instruction. Perhaps today's technology will encourage more systematic use of Direct Instruction in school districts across the nation.

Academic Focus

Students with learning disabilities, by definition, exhibit deficits in academic performance. The direct instruction approach concentrates on improving specific academic skills without dealing with inferred process deficits. In a review of the literature, Treiber and Lahey (1983) report success with this orientation. Specifically, they state, "This is not to say that learning disabled children do not have process deficits; rather that direct treatment of these inferred deficits is neither possible nor necessary for academic improvements to occur. This assertion is not a statement of faith, but rather a conclusion based on empirical evidence" (p. 79). Treiber and Lahey discuss literature that indicates the success of direct instruction with individuals with learning disabilities across such academic areas as reading comprehension, handwriting, letter identification, sight-word vocabulary, arithmetic, and oral reading. Moreover, in a review of instructional approaches, Tarver (1986) concludes that strong support exists for direct instruction (DI). Specifically, she states that "current knowledge suggests that DI theory, principles, and programs provide a strong base on which to build effective instructional programs for learning disabled students at the secondary level" (p. 374).

Stevens and Rosenshine (1981) report that the most successful teachers direct the instructional process and play the role of strong leader. Also, they note that the most effective teachers maintain a strong academic focus and typically use an instructional sequence that includes demonstration, controlled practice with prompts and feedback, and independent practice with feedback.

The importance of direct instruction receives support from the literature on engaged time. Findings in this area indicate that academic learning time is related positively to achievement (Englert et al., 1992). Fisher and Berliner (1985) note that students must be engaged in high rates of success in academically relevant tasks to achieve the greatest academic gains. Sindelar, Smith, Harriman, Hale, and Wilson (1986) conclude that time spent on academic tasks is the single best indicator of academic gains among special education students.

Christenson et al. (1989) report that time allocated to academic learning and engaged time vary a great deal across general and special education classrooms and among students within these classes. In an observation study of instructional time use, Rich and Ross (1989) found that nonlearning time (e.g., recess, restroom breaks, transitions, material distribution, and extracurricular programs) account for almost 3 hours of the 6-hour school day in most special education settings. Educators are requesting that more time be allocated to academic instruction and that academic instructional time be used efficiently; that is, student response time to academic tasks should be maximized. The following suggestions are offered to increase the amount of time students are engaged in academic learning:

1. Increase the "opportunity to learn" for students by allocating as much time as feasible for student instruction.
2. Use time scheduled for academic instruction efficiently.
3. Promote student attention and involvement by presenting academic activities that require the student to respond.
4. Plan academic tasks that generate a high percentage of correct responses.
5. Monitor student progress on academic skills and provide daily feedback.
6. Establish an expectancy of work and success in the classroom.
7. Use contingencies to reinforce task completion and student responding.
8. Consider summer or tutoring programs for students who need intense instruction to accomplish important immediate goals (e.g., prevention of learning problems, grade promotion, and graduation).

Unit of Instruction

In direct instruction, the organization and assessment of academic skills are highly structured. Instruction concentrates on either a terminal academic behavior (e.g., reading comprehension) or on subskills considered to be prerequisites for learning the terminal behavior. Task analysis is used for determining or ordering the sequence of skills to be taught.

Task analysis is useful in helping teachers adopt, adapt, or make teaching materials. It consists of dividing a learning project into parts to identify the skills needed. The notion that learning is cumulative—that skills build upon one another—is basic in task analysis.

Task analysis uses precise instructional objectives because they allow the teacher to sequence instruction. A well-formulated objective for a task includes a condition (parameters of the task), a criterion, and a terminal behavior. *Enabling behaviors* are the prerequisite skills for performing the specified behavior. Enabling behaviors are determined by working backwards from the terminal behavior. This process builds a hierarchy of skills. The implication of task analysis for instructional sequencing is clear: teach the easiest skill that the student is unable to perform. The following example illustrates task analysis with the terminal behavior of reading a simple sentence:

Terminal behavior: Read a simple sentence.

Prerequisite skills:

1. Performs left-to-right eye movement.
2. Associates sounds of letters with symbols.
3. Blends sounds into words.
4. Reads words in isolation.
5. Reads words in context.

Frank (1973) outlines four steps in task analysis: (a) clearly state the terminal behavior, (b) identify the subskills of the terminal behavior and sequence them from simple to complex, (c) informally assess to see which subskills the student already can perform, and (d) start teaching in sequential order, beginning with the easiest subskill that the student has not learned.

The task analysis approach to organizing a curriculum frequently is criticized by theorists who believe that the teaching of separate and distinct subskills does not lead to mastery learning of such global skills as reading comprehension. The effect of these criticisms, however, is lessened substantially when one understands the behaviorists' complete perspective on units of instruction. Treiber and Lahey (1983) report that the behavioral approach recommends the teaching of global skills (i.e., oral reading and reading comprehension) when it is successful. When the student does not make adequate progress, then instruction focuses on subskills. Treiber and Lahey state this orientation in regard to reading instruction:

> From a behavioral perspective . . . the target of intervention should at least initially be the functional, or molar, unit of reading. . . . In some cases, however, it may be necessary to also take a more molecular approach to remediation . . . based on a detailed task analysis of the behavior. (p. 100)

Smith (1981) notes that the problem of teaching isolated subskills can be overcome by providing activities that illustrate the use of learned subskills in authentic reading tasks. Idol (1983) provides numerous case studies of successful interventions that involve teaching subskills and molar skills simultaneously. The use of Direct Instruction in teaching higher-order skills (Carnine, 1990) as featured in this chapter demonstrates the successful application of teaching subskills (e.g., facts and concepts) to help students master complex skills (e.g., problem solving).

In essence, the criticism that the behavioral approach focuses only on subskill instruction is not accurate. In many studies, molar or higher-order skills are the unit of instruction in behavioral interventions. What deserves criticism is the practice of teaching isolated skills (e.g., phonics) without activities to illustrate their role in the functional skill (e.g., reading). Moreover, the practice of teaching one subskill after another without regard for the best unit of instruction for the individual should be discouraged.

Sequence of Academic Skills

The hierarchical ordering of academic skills represents a problem area for educators. Although many students have been taught academics successfully through the use of commercial materials that follow a highly specified sequence of skills (e.g., basal reading programs, basal math programs, and special remedial programs such as DISTAR), the best sequence for learning has not been established firmly. Engelmann (1993) maintains that universal hierarchies may never evolve. Specifically, he states,

> The only way we can determine which skills and concepts are prerequisite to future applications is to view the future applications. Since they may occupy different positions in different instructional sequences, and because what students learn is largely limited by what they are taught, the possibility of universal hierarchies is zero. However, this fact does not suggest that programs should be sloppy or nonhierarchical in structure. Rather, they should be designed to anticipate the problems the learner will have and teach all the skills the learner will need to progress smoothly through the particular sequence. (p. 5)

Some subskills may not be necessary for learning a terminal skill. Moreover, the ordering of skills for the most efficient learning has not been determined. These conditions require that teachers remain flexible when selecting and ordering skills to be taught to students with learning disabilities. A continuous record of the student's progress helps determine whether a skill is being learned and generalized to a functional skill.

DATA-BASED INSTRUCTION

Data-based instruction is a widely used approach to teaching that has roots in behavioral theory. It is a direct skill model of instruction that focuses on the direct and continuous measurement of student progress toward specific instructional objectives. Many educators (Alberto & Troutman, 1995; Howell, Fox, & Morehead, 1993) concur that it holds much promise for both current and future teaching practices.

Research in curriculum-based assessment (CBA) has provided a renewed impetus for data-based instruction. *CBA* refers to any approach that uses direct observation and recording of a student's performance in the school curriculum as a basis for obtaining information to make instructional decisions (Deno, 1987). Within this model, *curriculum-based measurement* (CBM) refers to the use of specific procedures whereby a student's academic skills are assessed through the use of repeated rate samples using stimulus materials taken from the student's curriculum. The primary uses of CBM are to establish district or classroom performance standards, identify students who need special instruction, and monitor individual student progress toward long-range goals.

Using Curriculum-Based Measurement to Establish Performance Standards

When CBM is used to establish performance standards, measures are developed from the school curriculum and administered to all the students in a target group (e.g., all fourth graders in a school or district). The results provide data to determine standards of performance. Using CBM to establish standards involves four components: (a) material selection, (b) test administration, (c) performance display and interpretation, and (d) a decision-making framework (Tindal & Marston, 1990).

Material Selection. Selecting the appropriate material from the school curriculum begins the assessment process. An appropriate material is at the level that the teacher expects the student to master by the end of the school year. Appropriate materials could include the following:

1. Reading—200-word passages from a fourth-grade-level basal book without poetry, exercises, or excessive dialogue.
2. Spelling—all words from a fourth-grade spelling curriculum proportionally divided into alternate test forms.
3. Math—alternate forms of 36 randomly selected computation problems that proportionally represent the fourth-grade math curriculum.

The object is to select several samples of the school curriculum in a respective academic area and administer them to all students. A comparison of all students on the same measure provides a norm-referenced data base for making instructional decisions.

Test Administration. Administration procedures include using standardized formats and scoring performance in terms of rate correct per minute. A sample reading administration format includes the following steps:

1. Randomly select a passage from the goal-level material.
2. Place it in front of and facing the student.
3. Keep a copy for the examiner.
4. Provide directions.
5. Have the student read orally for 1 minute.
6. Score the student's performance in terms of number of words read correctly, and note errors for instructional purposes.

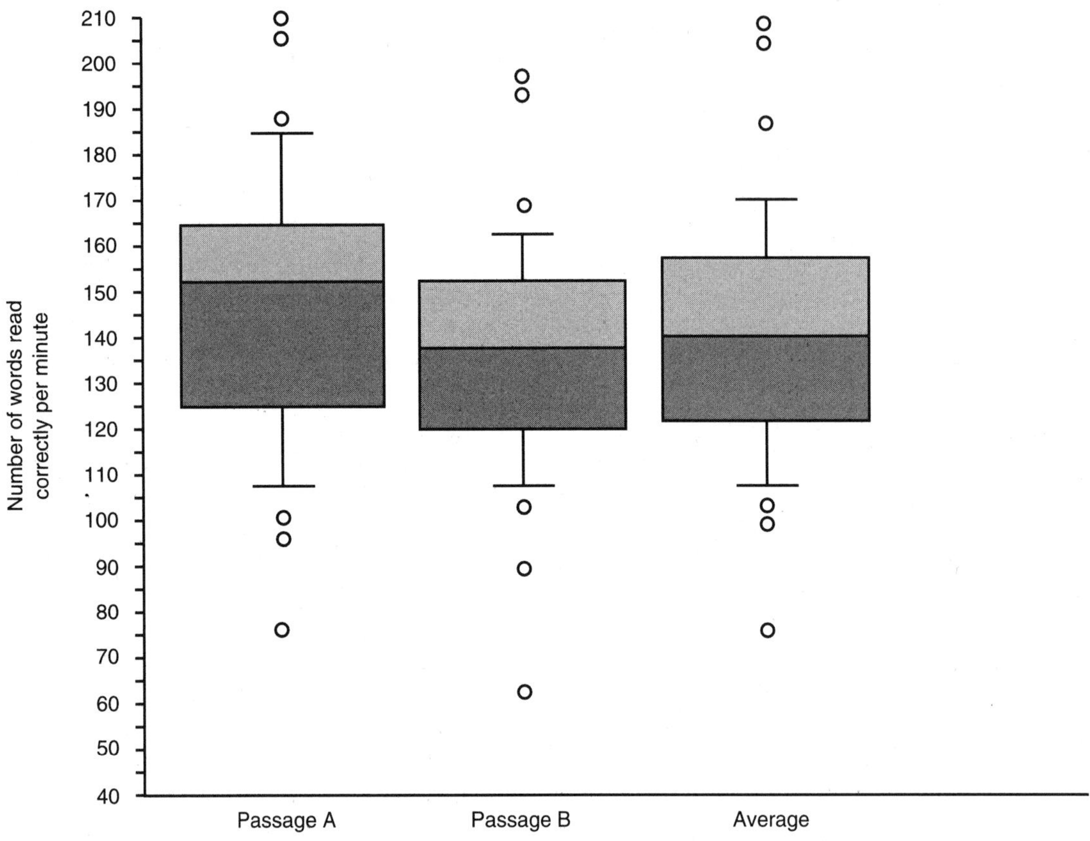

FIGURE 8.1
Box plots of oral reading fluency for a fifth-grade class
Note: From *Teaching Students with Learning Problems* (p. 61), 4th ed., by C. D. Mercer and A. R. Mercer, 1993, Upper Saddle River, NJ: Merrill/Prentice Hall. Copyright 1993 by Prentice-Hall Publishing Company. Reprinted by permission.

It is helpful to administer two or three passages and record the average score.

Performance Display and Interpretation. When all students in the grade or class are tested and the average score for each student is computed, the teacher can develop a plot of the entire group. Figure 8.1 presents sample box plots of 31 fifth-grade students. The top and bottom Ts represent the 90th and 10th percentiles. The box includes the middle 50% of the population with the bottom line representing the 25th percentile, the top line representing the 75th percentile, and the middle line representing the 50th percentile. The circles outside of the 10th and 90th percentiles are individuals with extreme values. The data from this sample reveal that some students read very poorly and probably need to receive specialized services (e.g., Chapter I or special education), whereas other students are extremely fluent in the material. The two passages were selected according to grade-level readability, but the average for Passage A, 152 words read correctly, is significantly higher than the average for Passage B, 137 words read correctly. Thus, an important consideration in using this system is to sample multiple passages to minimize differing levels of difficulty that exist from passage to passage.

Decision-Making Framework. These data enable teachers to (a) identify low performers who need special instruction, (b) divide students into instructional groups, (c) plan instructional programs, and (d) establish long-range goals. T. Hall and Tindal (1989) used this type of assessment to create three reading groups (low group—below 16th percentile, middle group—between 16th and 84th percentile, and high group—above 84th percentile).

For teachers who work with students with learning disabilities, however, the real power of this assessment system is its applicability in establishing a formative evaluation system. By administering successively lower- or higher-level materials from other grade levels and comparing performance with the normative levels for those grades, it is possible to establish both current functioning and appropriate goal-level functioning. Rather than placing students into an instructional material according to the percentage correct, as is done with informal reading inventories, a placement validated through research can be made by placing the student in the level in which the student is most comparable to others. For example, if a fifth-grade student performs most closely to students who are using a third-grade reading material, placement in this material is justified; furthermore, judgments of appropriate goals can be established (e.g., successful performance in fourth-grade material by the end of the school year).

Individually Referenced Data Systems

Since Lindsley (1964, 1971) introduced precision teaching about 25 years ago, many educators have recognized the value of data-based instruction. Other systems that use the methodology of applied behavior analysis to develop data-based instructional procedures include Exceptional Teaching (White & Haring, 1980), Data-Based Program Modification (Deno & Mirkin, 1977), and Individually-Referenced CBA (Tindal & Marston, 1990). The salient features of all of these systems are (a) direct measurement, (b) repeated measurement, (c) graphing data, (d) long-range goal performance monitoring, (e) short-range goal performance monitoring, and (f) data analysis and instructional decisions.

Direct Measurement. One of the most important features of data-based instruction (individually referenced CBM) is its emphasis on direct, continuous, and precise measurement of behavior. Direct measurement entails focusing on relevant classroom behaviors (e.g., oral reading rate or math computation rate).

Repeated Measurement. Repeated measurement requires that a behavior be counted and recorded over a period of time. Howell, Kaplan, and O'Connell (1979) note that performance is a single measure of behavior on one occasion, whereas learning is a change in performance over time. When more than one performance is recorded, the teacher can tell whether the student is staying the same, getting better, or regressing. As more data are gathered, a teacher's perception of learning becomes more accurate. Such continuous data help the teacher make daily instructional decisions.

Kerr and Nelson (1989) provide some practical guidelines for adjusting the frequency of monitoring:

1. Use session-by-session (one or more daily) recording when student progress is rapid through a small-step sequence.
2. Use daily recording when student behavior fluctuates and daily program adjustments are needed.
3. Use daily recording when the daily progress of the student is needed for intervention modifications.
4. Use biweekly or weekly probes when student progress is slow.
5. Use biweekly or weekly probes when general monitoring of behavior is needed and frequent program adjustments are not needed.
6. Use biweekly, weekly, or monthly probes when evaluating maintenance of generalization of previously mastered skills.

Although daily measurement provides the best data for making teaching decisions, research indicates that twice-weekly monitoring of academic performance is as effective as daily monitoring for promoting academic achievement (Fuchs, 1986).

In addition to the most common practice of recording permanent products, a variety of observational recording techniques is available. Recording techniques include event recording, interval recording, time sampling, duration recording, latency recording, anecdotal recording, and permanent product recording. The observation techniques are useful especially in assessing classroom behavior that is related to academic success. (For more detailed descriptions of recording techniques, see Alberto and Troutman [1995]. Howell et al. [1993], or Kerr and Nelson [1989].)

Graphing Data. For data to be useful, the information must be displayed in an easy-to-read format. This involves creating a visual display so that raw data can be analyzed. In data-based instruction, graphing is the most common method of presenting data. Kerr and Nelson (1989) report that graphs serve three important purposes: (a) they summarize data in a manner that leads to daily decision making, (b) they communicate intervention effects, and (c) they provide feedback and reinforcement to the learner and teacher.

Data must be converted into a form that allows for consistent graphing. Basically, this involves reporting three types of data: number correct, percentage (the number of correct responses divided by the total number of responses and then multiplied by 100), and rate (the number correct divided by the time).

The basic format for graphing is a *line graph* that includes two axes. The horizontal axis is the abscissa, or *x*-axis. The vertical axis is the ordinate, or *y*-axis. As shown in Figure 8.2, the *x*-axis is used to record the time factor (i.e., the observation period). The *y*-axis is used to record performance on the target behavior. An example of a line graph on equal-interval graph paper is presented in Figure 8.3.

A *bar graph* uses vertical bars to display data (i.e., vertical bars represent levels of performance). A bar graph is easy to interpret and provides the teacher and student with a clear picture of performance. Figure 8.4 shows some sample bar graphs.

Another type of graph, the *ratio graph,* is suited particularly to charting rate data. Data for ratio graphing are converted into rate per minute and are charted on a semilogarithmic grid. The number of correct and incorrect responses on an instructional pinpoint (such as see word—say word) for a specified time period (frequently 1 minute) provides the data for the graph. Such graphs are a major tool of applied behavior analysis or, more specifically, precision teaching.

Long-Range Goal Performance Monitoring. Individually referenced CBM procedures typically use *performance monitoring charts.* These charts display progress toward a long-range instructional goal. Measurement usually occurs twice weekly from a random sample of a pool of items that measure the same skill. The items represent the goal level the student wants to attain by the end of the semester or year. Figure 8.5 presents a CBM long-range goal-performance monitoring chart. The student's baseline includes the first three data points. The needed rate of improvement is displayed by the broken goal line. It begins at the baseline median at the end of 2 weeks and proceeds to the goal proficiency criterion on the 20th week. The 10 scores after the first vertical intervention line represent the student's progress under intervention A. The trend line superimposed over these scores is an estimate of the student's rate of improvement. When the trend line is compared with the goal line, it is apparent that the student's progress is too slow and an instructional modification is needed. The second vertical line represents a new intervention.

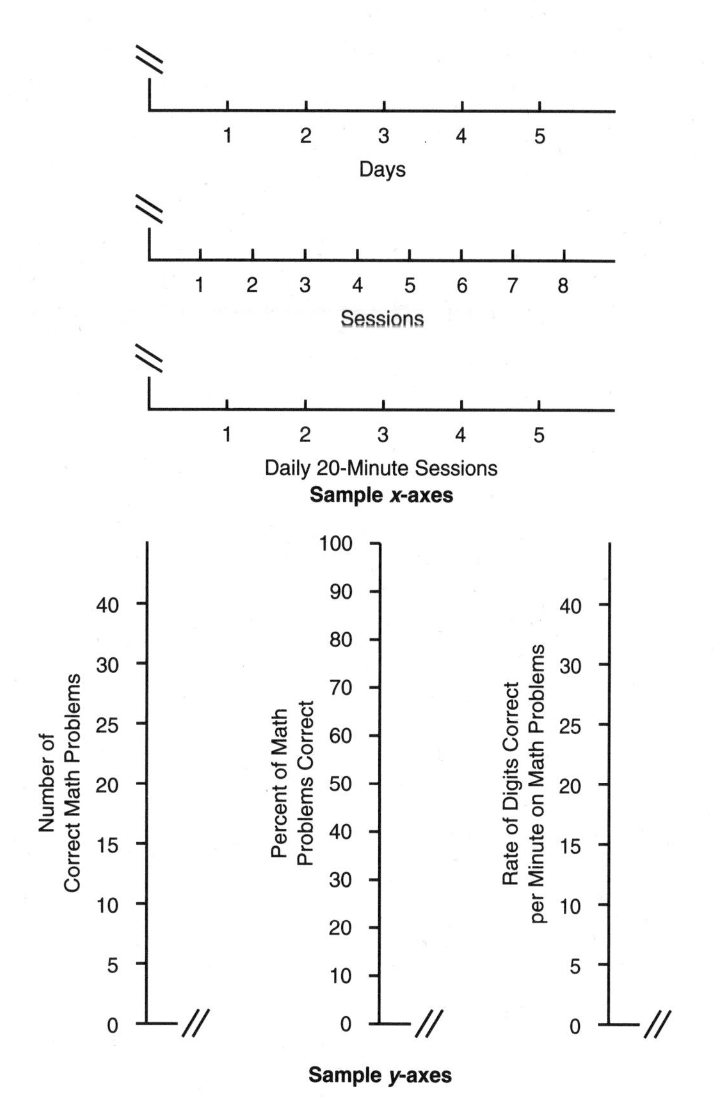

FIGURE 8.2
Sample *x*- and *y*-axes
Note: From *Teaching Students with Learning Problems* (p. 67), 4th ed., by C. D. Mercer and A. R. Mercer, 1993, Upper Saddle River, NJ: Merrill/Prentice Hall. Copyright 1993 by Prentice-Hall Publishing Company. Reprinted by permission.

Because the data points after intervention B display an improved rate of progress consistent with reaching the goal on time, the teacher maintains intervention B. If the trend line is steeper than the goal line, the goal proficiency criterion is increased.

Short-range Goal Performance Monitoring. Another type of chart, a *mastery monitoring chart,* is used to monitor progress on successive short-term goals. When the student masters a short-term goal, a new goal is established, and monitoring continues through a series of short-term goals. The pool of measurement items changes each time the student masters a goal. Although mastery monitoring requires additional teacher work, it has several advantages: (a) the charting system reflects traditional curriculum skill hierarchies, (b) a close tie exists between instruction and measurement, and (c) information is available on

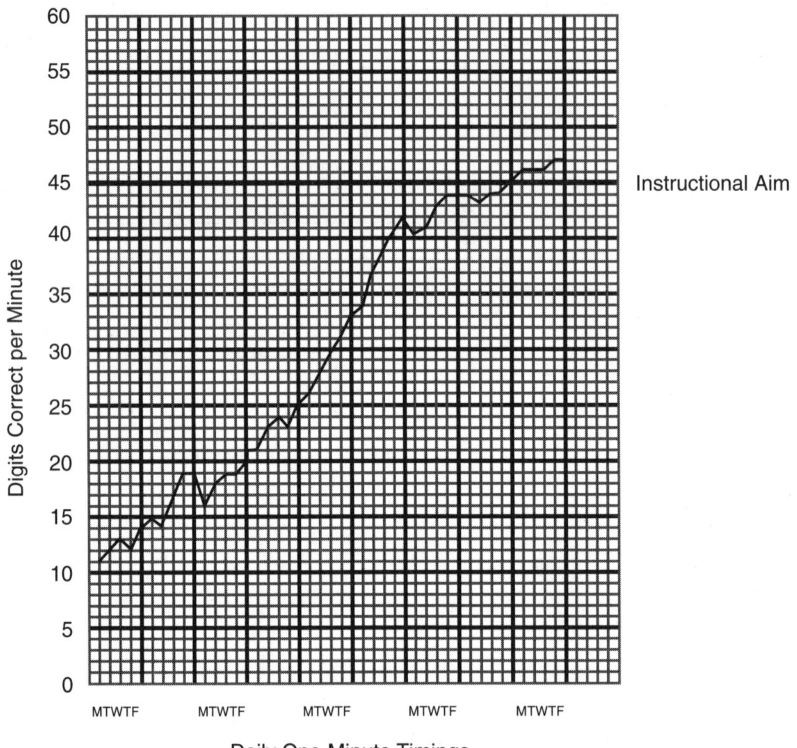

Target Behavior See–Write Multiplication Facts

Student Leon Matthews

Grade 4

FIGURE 8.3

Sample line graph

Note: From *Teaching Students with Learning Problems* (p. 68), 4th ed., by C. D. Mercer and A. R. Mercer, 1993, Upper Saddle River, NJ: Merrill/Prentice Hall. Copyright 1993 by Prentice-Hall Publishing Company. Reprinted by permission.

what to teach. Mastery monitoring is used widely in precision teaching.

Specifically, in precision teaching, the teacher does the following:

1. Selects a target behavior.
2. Develops a task sheet or probe for evaluation of student progress in daily timings.
3. Graphs the data two to five times a week and sets instructional aims that correspond to a standard of fluency.
4. Designs the instructional program.
5. Analyzes data and makes instructional decisions.

Target behaviors usually are determined by administering probe sheets. These sheets include academic tasks and are used to sample the student's behavior. Typically, the student works on the probe sheet for 1 minute, and the teacher records the rate of correct and incorrect responses and notes any error patterns.

FIGURE 8.4
Sample bar graphs
Note: From *Teaching Students with Learning Problems* (p. 69), 4th ed., by C. D. Mercer and A. R. Mercer, 1993, Upper Saddle River, NJ: Merrill/Prentice Hall. Copyright 1993 by Prentice-Hall Publishing Company. Reprinted by permission.

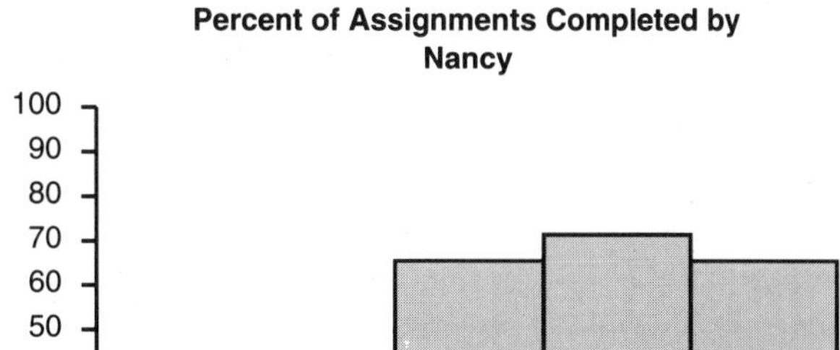
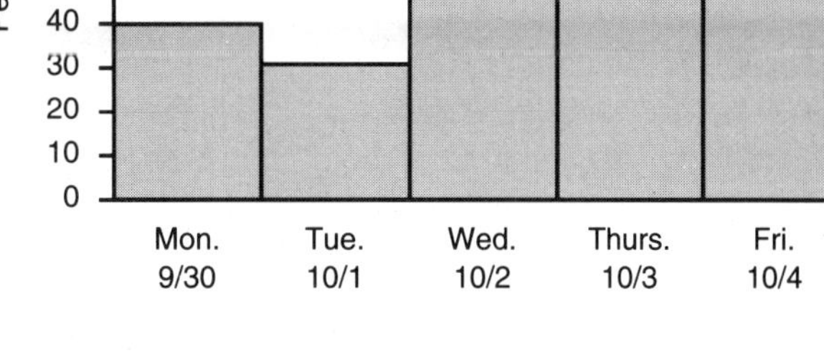

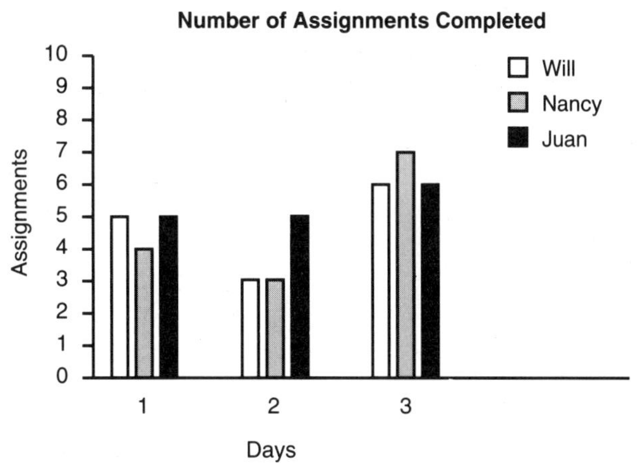

Figure 8.6 displays a probe sheet of a task for assessing addition facts with sums to 9. The instructional objective usually is not established until the student has performed the task on the probe sheet several times. This provides a more reliable index of the student's performance than one test does. The original assessment probe may be used, or a new probe sheet can be designed to stress specific facts (e.g., addition involving zero).

Several materials are available for implementing a precision teaching system. These materials contain an extensive list of academic skill probes that can be used to determine instructional objectives and to monitor student progress. One of these materials is *A Resource Manual for the Development and Evaluation of Special Programs for Exceptional Students* (Volume V-D: Techniques of Precision Teaching), Florida Department of Education, Bureau of Education for Exceptional Students, Tallahassee, FL 32399.

Precision teachers record student performances and graph the results. Teachers who prefer a simple graph can use an equal-interval chart, as previously illustrated in Figure 8.3. This kind of chart can be drawn on square-

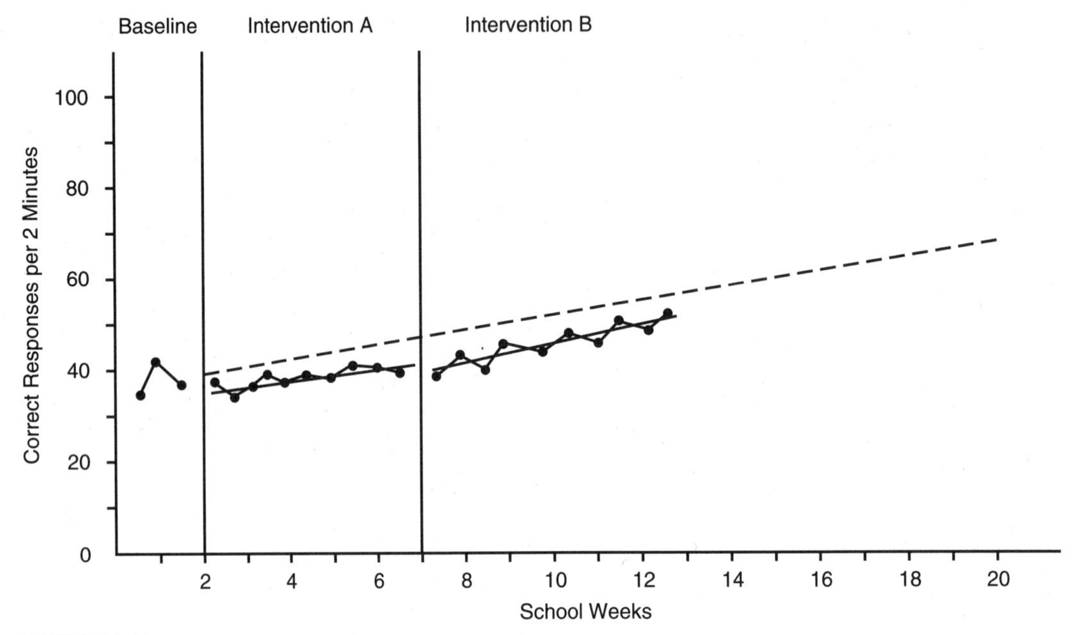

FIGURE 8.5
Long-range goal performance monitoring chart

Name ______________________ Correct ________ Error ________

Date ____________ Comments ______________________

6 + 2	5 + 3	4 + 4	9 + 0	8 + 1	2 + 7	5 + 0
8 + 0	4 + 3	1 + 1	3 + 2	5 + 2	3 + 6	5 + 4
7 + 1	4 + 2	3 + 3	8 + 1	7 + 0	2 + 5	4 + 0
1 + 0	3 + 1	2 + 2	6 + 1	5 + 4	1 + 6	0 + 0
3 + 4	2 + 4	2 + 1	3 + 1	3 + 0	4 + 5	5 + 1
6 + 3	7 + 2	1 + 2	1 + 3	1 + 4	1 + 5	1 + 8

FIGURE 8.6
Probe sheet used to present addition facts—sums to 9

ruled graph paper. The teacher records the frequency of the behavior along the vertical axis and the number of sessions or timings on the horizontal axis. An example of an equal-interval chart on unlined paper is presented in Figure 8.7. Two advantages of equal-interval charts are that they are easy to understand and to obtain.

The value of using graphs is recognized for several reasons:

1. Graphs provide a visual description of data and reduce large amounts of data.
2. Graphs simplify the presentation of results and facilitate communication of program results and student learning.
3. Graphs reflect important characteristics of performance.
4. Graphs facilitate the use of data to plan and modify instruction.
5. Graphs provide informational and, often, motivational feedback.

Moreover, research suggests that achievement is associated with graphed performances. Fuchs and Fuchs (1986) report that when data are charted rather than simply recorded, achievement improves approximately .5 of a standard deviation unit.

Data Analysis and Instructional Decisions. Instructional aims or goals provide the student and teacher with a framework to analyze data and evaluate student progress. When instructional aims are expressed in terms of percent correct, it generally is accepted that 80% correct responses represent mastery. The instructional aim also may be expressed in terms of rate. Rate is equal to the number of movements divided by the number of minutes observed. In precision teaching, the instructional aim usually is defined in terms of rate of correct and incorrect responses per minute. In CBM, it usually is rate of only correct responses per minute. Rate is a sensitive ratio measure that readily reflects the effects of instructional interventions.

Ideally, the aim should represent a mastery level of the skill. Data concerning rates that reflect mastery (i.e., proficiency) in academic tasks have long been lacking. Although disagreement still exists concerning proficiency-level rates, enough data (Howell et al., 1993; Mercer, Mercer, & Evans, 1982) are available to suggest proficiency-level trends on selected academic tasks.

Certain learner characteristics, such as age, grade level, and achievement level, influence the establishment of appropriate aims. Because research has not conclusively determined specific aims for academic tasks, teachers must use their own judgment in setting aims with individual students. One way of facilitating aim selection is to collect rate data from students who are achieving satisfactorily and use their performances as aims (see the section on using CBM to establish performance standards, presented earlier in this chapter). Another way involves the teacher performing the task and using a proportion of this performance as an aim.

Charted data enable the teacher to determine whether the student is making acceptable progress. The analysis of data is enhanced when it is charted to display both baseline data (i.e., present levels of performance) and intervention data (i.e., data gathered during intervention). Each time an intervention change is made, a vertical line is drawn on the chart to indicate the change. Haring (1978) notes that the purpose of charting data is to help the teacher make accurate decisions about teaching strategies (e.g., when to continue or change a procedure). Significant learning patterns often emerge that enable the teacher to find possible reasons for success or failure and make decisions based on data. The most desirable pattern is clear-cut: an increase in the rate of appropriate or correct responses and a decrease in the rate of inappropriate or incorrect responses.

Students with learning disabilities often are identified because they have difficulty keeping

FIGURE 8.7
Equal-interval chart

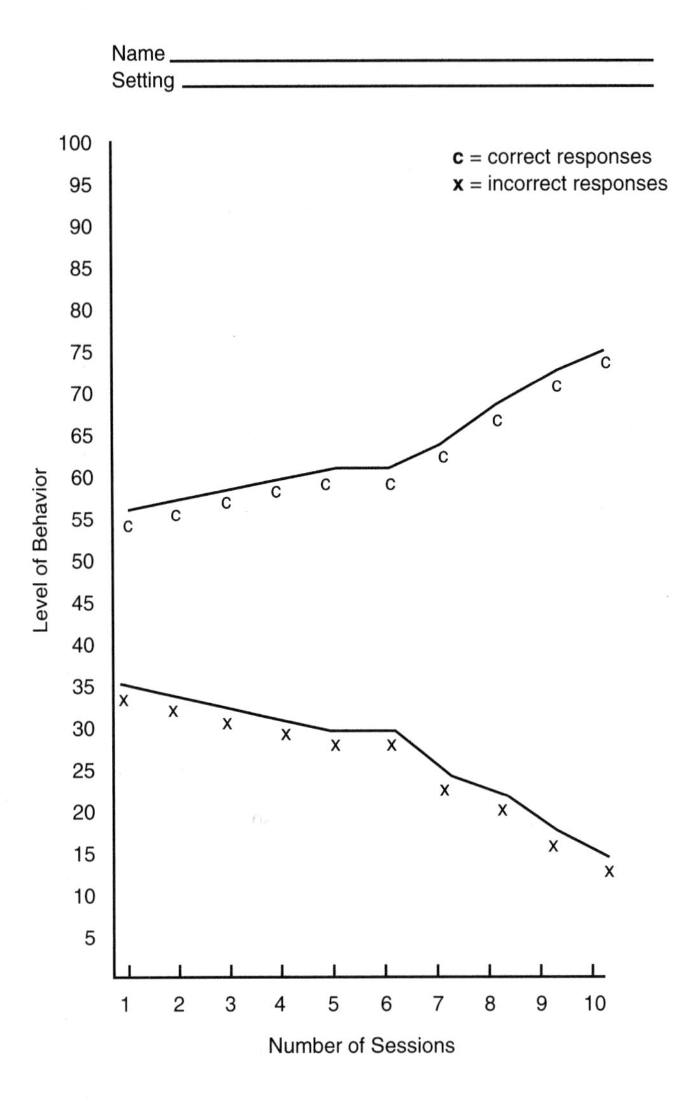

up with instruction. These students fall further and further behind. Analyzing a student's learning pattern can help the teacher identify learning problems and make appropriate decisions about instruction.

Changes in student performance over time can be assessed with several specific measures (see Figure 8.8):

1. Level of performance—refers to immediate changes in level of performance that occur when an intervention is introduced.
2. Slope—refers to the rate of change in a trend line that reflects the values of the data points.
3. Variability—refers to the inconsistency of performance.
4. Overlap—refers to data values that are common across different interventions.

Research supports the use of rules for making decisions when analyzing the data. Fuchs and Fuchs (1986) found that formative evaluation that involves data-utilization rules is associated with an average increase in student achievement

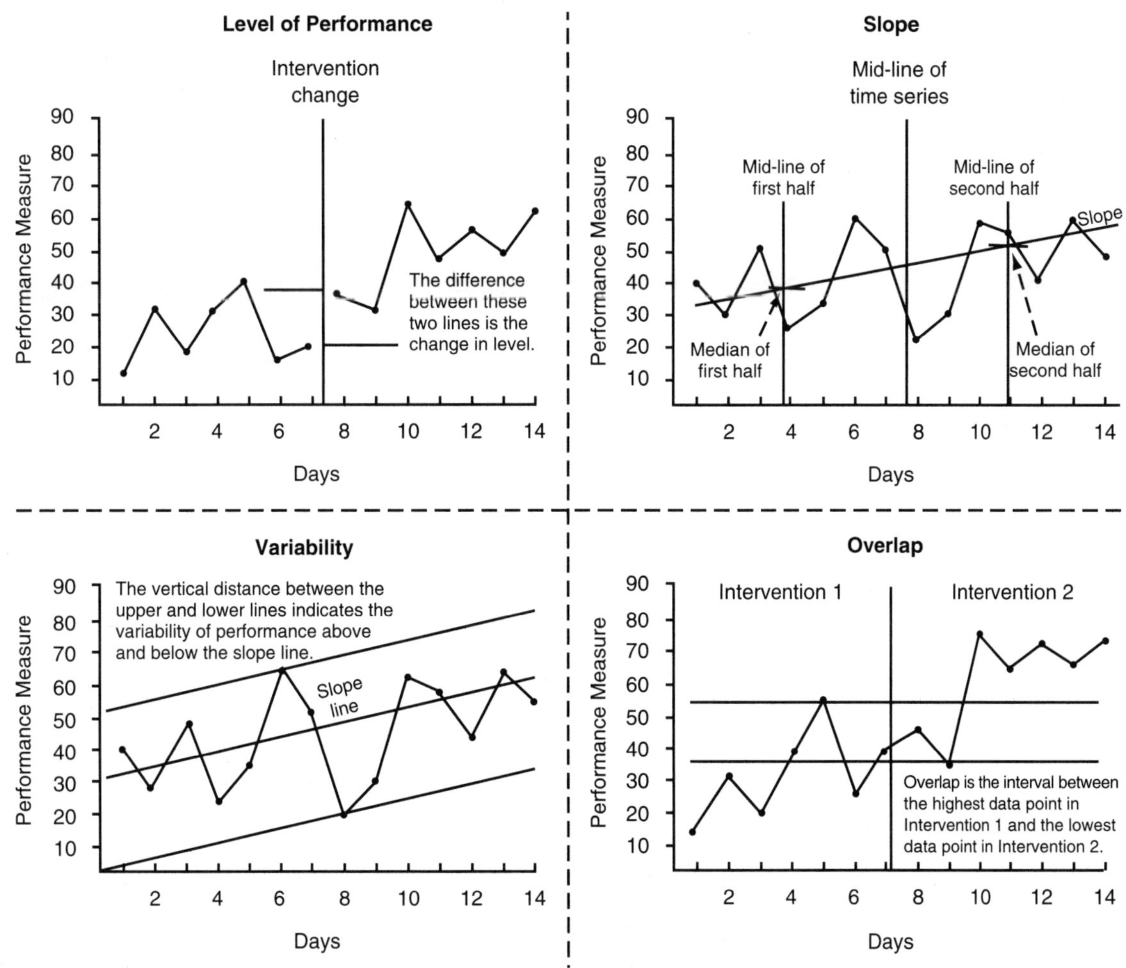

FIGURE 8.8
Four measures of change in student performance over time

of .5 standard deviation over formative evaluation without such rules. An example of a rule is the 3-day rule, in which the teacher makes an instructional modification if the student's progress is unsatisfactory (i.e., below aim) for 3 consecutive days. Fuchs, Fuchs, and Hamlett (1989) found that for CBM to be most effective, teachers must use the data to evaluate instruction and make modifications. Tindal and Marston (1990) provide a detailed discussion of data analysis techniques and decision rules for goal-oriented and treatment-oriented decision making.

Basic Guidelines of Data-Based Instruction

Howell et al. (1979) offer numerous guidelines for implementing data-based instruction. They note that such instruction is most successful when

1. The teacher initially counts only priority behaviors.
2. The teacher identifies strategies to facilitate timing and recording behaviors.
3. The teacher evaluates the recorded data frequently.

4. The teacher uses probes or curriculum-referenced testing.
5. The system remains a tool for teaching rather than a "cause" and is used only as long as it helps the student.

Howell et al. also list the following strategies to facilitate timing and recording behaviors:

1. The teacher can take group timings, especially on written activities. Some teachers, for example, time 1-minute handwriting samples, 1-minute math fact sheets, and 1-minute spelling activities.
2. Students can record time stopped and started. This can be done easily with a rubber stamp of a clock on the students' worksheets.
3. A kitchen timer or prerecorded tape can be used to time sessions.
4. Students can work together and time and record data for each other. This works well with flash-card drills.
5. Students can read into a tape recorder. Teachers later can record correct and error rates for either samples of behavior or the total session.
6. Mechanical counters can be used. Single and dual tally counters as well as beads and golf score counters are available.
7. Counting should be done for a fixed period of time each day. Counting for different intervals confuses the data pattern because such factors as endurance, boredom, and latency of response may enter into the data analysis.
8. Timings for 1 minute can be used because they are easy to chart and no rate plotter is necessary.
9. Aides, peers, student teachers, and volunteers can be trained to help develop materials and to count and record behaviors.

In addition, Wesson (1987) provides time-saving tips in the areas of organization, preparation of materials, administration, scoring procedures, and using the data.

Commentary on Data-Based Instruction

Some highlights of research on data-based approaches include the following:

1. Considerable evidence supports the positive association between data-based monitoring and student achievement gains (Fuchs, 1986; Fuchs, & Fuchs, 1986; Rieth & Evertson, 1988; Tindal & Marston, 1990; White, 1986). In a meta-analysis of formative evaluations, Fuchs and Fuchs found that data-based programs that monitored student progress and evaluated instruction systematically produced .7 standard deviation higher achievement than nonmonitored instruction. This represents a gain of 26 percentage points. Moreover, White reports outstanding gains for students involved in precision teaching programs.
2. CBM measures have good reliability and validity (Fuchs, 1986; Fuchs, Fuchs, & Maxwell, 1988; Howell et al., 1993; Tindal & Marston, 1990).
3. Self-selected goals yield better performance than assigned goals (Fuchs, Bahr, & Rieth, 1989).
4. When teachers establish moderately to highly ambitious goals, students achieve better (Fuchs, Fuchs, & Deno, 1985).

In a national survey of 136 learning disabilities teachers, Wesson, King, and Deno (1984) found that the majority (53.6%) of the 110 teachers who knew of direct and frequent measurement used it; however, those who did not use it felt it was too time-consuming. The position that data-based instruction is time-consuming is prominent among users and nonusers of direct and frequent measurement. However, Wesson et al. report that time involved in direct and frequent measurement does not have to be extensive. Fuchs, Wesson, Tindal, Mirkin, and Deno (1981) report the results of a study in which teachers were trained to reduce by 80% the time they spend in direct measurement (e.g., preparing, directing, scoring, and graphing). Accord-

ing to Wesson et al., "Trained and experienced teachers require only two minutes to prepare for, administer, score, and graph student performance" (p. 48). They also report that direct and frequent measurement is no more time-consuming than other evaluation activities. Wesson et al. sum up the time-consumption issue involving direct and frequent measurement as follows:

> Since related research reveals that frequent measurement involves achievement (Bohannon, 1975; Mirkin et al., 1979), the proposition that direct and frequent measurement is a waste of critical instructional time is without a factual basis. . . . Given its benefits, direct and frequent measurement must be used on a more widespread basis in special education. One implication of the present study is that teachers may need more training and experience in procedures for conducting direct and frequent measurement. . . . Furthermore, experience should improve measurement efficiency. Once these two frequently cited obstacles are minimized, direct and frequent measurement may enjoy more widespread use and may serve to improve the performance of many more students. (p. 48)

STAGES OF LEARNING

Numerous authorities present stages of student learning that are fundamental to designing and implementing effective instruction (Idol, 1983; Smith, 1981). Nelson and Polsgrove (1984) report that a data base is emerging for the practice of matching teaching procedures to the student's stage of learning for a specific skill. Thus, teaching practices for each stage in the learning sequence are being recommended and evaluated.

Although many studies (Nelson & Polsgrove, 1984) demonstrate that academic performance

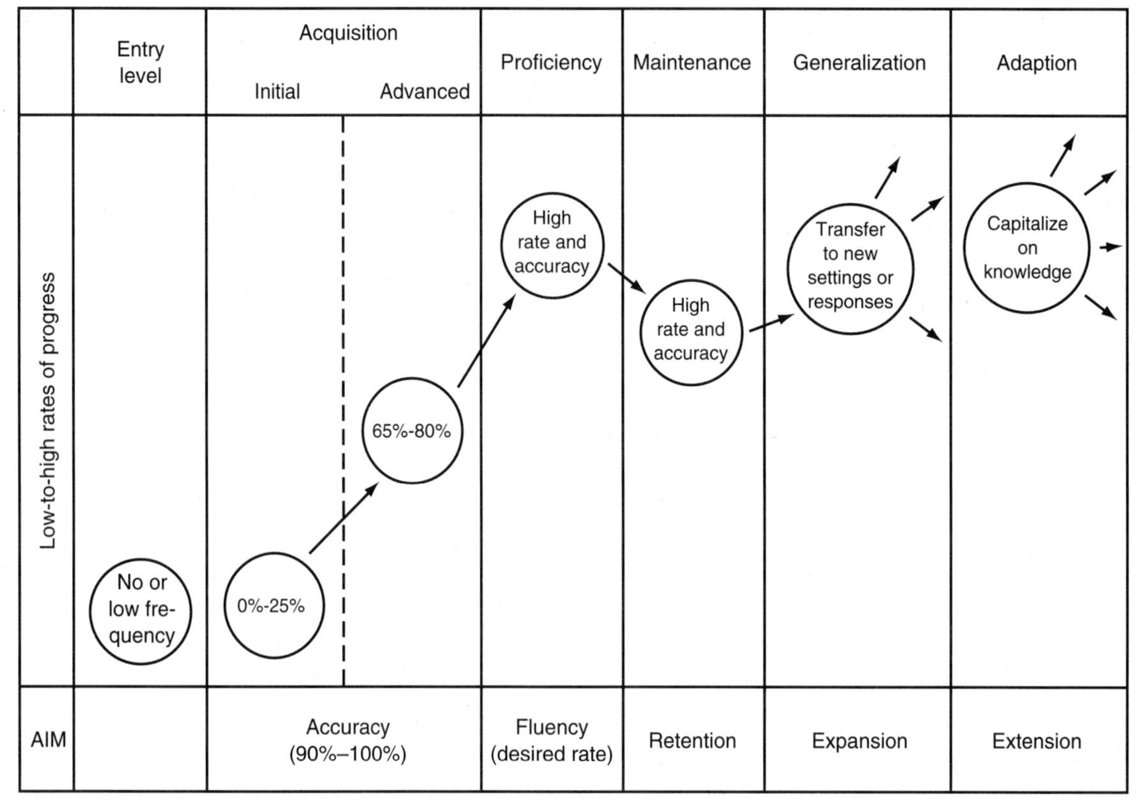

FIGURE 8.9
Stages of learning
Note: Adapted from *Teaching the Learning Disabled* (p. 68), by D. D. Smith, 1981, Upper Saddle River, NJ: Prentice Hall. Copyright 1981 by Prentice-Hall Publishing Company. Reprinted by permission.

can be improved with reinforcement, it is not always the optimal strategy that behaviorists recommend for teaching academics. In fact, several authorities (Ayllon & Azrin, 1964; Smith & Lovitt, 1976) report that reinforcement alone is not always successful in improving academic skills. In instances in which reinforcement was unsuccessful, investigators report that the entry level (i.e., learning stage) of the student was an influential factor. For example, Smith and Lovitt found that reinforcement was ineffective when students were learning how to solve computational math problems but was successful in helping students compute math problems more quickly.

Thus, behavioral authorities believe that the entry-level learning stage is a critical factor in planning teaching activities. Although reinforcement is a viable technique, other strategies (e.g., antecedent changes and stimuli modifications) are needed to promote optimal learning at various learning stages. Smith (1981) presents the stages of learning that are commonly recognized. As featured in Figure 8.9, the stages include initial and advanced acquisition, proficiency, maintenance, generalization, and adaption. This section briefly describes the stages of learning and suggested teaching strategies for each stage.

Acquisition Stage

During the acquisition stage, the learner performance ranges from 0% accuracy (i.e., no knowledge of how to perform the task) to a 90% to 100% range of accuracy. During this stage the instructional goal focuses on helping the student perform the skill accurately.

Smith (1981) recommends some major strategies for teaching a student at the acquisition stage. During initial acquisition, priming tactics are suggested, including rationales for learning a specific skill, physical guidance, shaping, demonstration, modeling, match-to-sample tasks, and cuing and prompting. Also, programming tactics are used during initial acquisition and feature backward and forward chaining and errorless learning. For the advanced acquisition stage, refinement tactics are used and feature feedback, specific directions, error correction, reward for accuracy, and criterion evaluation.

Proficiency Stage

In the proficiency stage, the learner attempts to learn the skill at an almost automatic level. The aim is for the student to perform the task both accurately and quickly. The tactics differ from those used at the acquisition stage. Tactics at this level focus on increasing speed of performance.

Learning at the proficiency stage is enhanced by the use of goal setting, teacher expectations, rationales for increasing rate, positive reinforcement, and progress monitoring. Moreover, for social skill development, self-management is suggested.

Maintenance Stage

After high levels of learning have occurred at the proficiency stage, the student enters the maintenance stage. The goal of instruction here is to maintain the high level of performance. Idol (1983) notes that students at this stage demonstrate the ability to perform the skill at a high level once direct instruction or reinforcement has been withdrawn. Students with learning disabilities frequently encounter much difficulty at this stage because it requires retention (memory) of the skill. Tactics at this stage concentrate on maintaining high levels of learning.

Learning during the maintenance stage involves periodic practice; however, for the student with learning disabilities, practice is not always sufficient and other tactics are necessary. Maintenance and retention also are fostered by overlearning, mnemonic techniques, intermittent schedules of reinforcement, social reinforcement, and intrinsic reinforcement (self-management).

Generalization Stage

During the generalization stage, the learner performs the skill in different times and situations. This means that the student demonstrates proficiency in the skill in different settings (e.g., at home, in the classroom, and at work) and with different people (e.g., the learning disabilities teacher, general classroom teacher, parent, and boss). Generalization is an area of great difficulty for many students with learning problems and, unfortunately, remains an area of limited research (Smith & Luckasson, 1992). Investigators have discovered that one cannot expect generalization automatically to occur with students who have learning disabilities. It must be systematically taught. (Chapter 7 presents competencies for teaching generalization.)

Adaption Stage

In the adaption stage, the learner applies a previously learned skill in a new area of application without benefit of direct instruction or guidance. Simply, this skill may be referred to as problem solving. To illustrate, problem solving occurs when a student who has mastered multiplication facts "discovers" that division is the reverse of multiplication and proceeds to answer division facts accurately and independently. Smith (1981) maintains that although it is important to teach adaption-level skills to students with learning disabilities, this area has been neglected.

Commentary on Learning Stages

It is apparent that behaviorists have given much thought to stages of learning. Implicit in these learning stages is the goal to make the learner an independent, self-motivated thinker. Those who claim that the behavioral orientation focuses on developing passive and dependent learners probably have not considered fully the learning stages within which behaviorists operate. Unfortunately, research documenting successful approaches for developing generalization and problem-solving skills is limited. Some critics have used this lack of research to discount or minimize the effectiveness of the behavioral approach. At best, these critics may stimulate productive research in this needed area. At worst, they may lead some educators to discount the behavioral approach prematurely.

Most behavioral studies document effectiveness only for short-term effects; however, some research in the area of skill generalization appears promising. For example, Idol (1983) reports on eight projects in which generalization occurred through the use of behavioral tactics. Other investigators (Lloyd, Saltzman, & Kauffman, 1981; Schumaker, Deshler, Alley, & Warner, 1983) are using behavioral tactics in teaching rule or strategy learning with positive results regarding generalization.

Several behaviorists recognize shortcomings regarding teaching generalization to students with learning disabilities (Smith, 1981; Treiber & Lahey, 1983). Moreover, combinations of the behavioral approach with other approaches (e.g., cognitive) are being used to teach higher-order skills (Schumaker et al., 1983; Tarver, 1986). Several sources (Howell et al., 1993; Idol, 1983; Smith, 1981) provide detailed coverage of strategies to use at the various stages of learning. (Chapter 10 presents the learning strategies approach.)

LEARNING PRINCIPLES

Behaviorists operate according to a set of learning principles that are based on the premise that behavior is learned and is a function of consequences. Environmental events (antecedent and consequent) are arranged systematically to produce a specific change in observable behavior. Learning principles are applied in a structured manner to increase, decrease, or maintain target behaviors. Reinforcement principles are used to maintain or increase behavior, whereas punishment principles are used to decrease or extinguish a behavior.

In applying these learning principles, the teacher typically collects baseline data on a target behavior and observes events that happen just before the student's behavior (antecedent events) and just after the behavior (consequent events). These events are then manipulated, and various reinforcers or rewards are used to elicit a change in the behavior.

A *reinforcer* is any event that follows a behavior and results in maintaining or increasing the probability or rate of the behavior. Except for primary reinforcers (i.e., reinforcers related to biological needs—food, water, sleep), what is reinforcing varies from student to student. Thus, a reinforcer must be ascertained individually.

Positive reinforcement means adding something pleasurable or positive to the environment (i.e., consequences that increase the probability that the behavior will occur again). In addition to primary reinforcers, positive reinforcers include secondary reinforcers, things that the individual has learned to value, such as social praise. Generally, positive reinforcers are viewed along a continuum that goes from primary events to intrinsic factors: (a) primary rewards (e.g., food), (b) tangible rewards (e.g., toy), (c) activity rewards (e.g., taking a trip or free time), (d) social praise, (e) feedback and success experiences as intrinsic rewards, and (f) self-reinforcement (intrinsic). The goal of most behaviorists is to help the student perform appropriately with reinforcers that occur naturally in the environment. Also, helping students develop intrinsic reinforcement is a major goal. Recent literature in self-management (Alberto & Troutman, 1995) discusses developing and maintaining intrinsic reinforcement. (Chapter 15 discusses reinforcement and punishment in behavior modification and techniques that apply reinforcement principles, such as contingency contracting and token systems.)

PERSPECTIVE ON THE BEHAVIORAL APPROACH

The behavioral approach has been used successfully to teach many students with learning disabilities. Although much research supports the success of the behavioral approach, several issues persist concerning its applications. As noted in this chapter, behaviorists are concerned about documenting long-term effects, increasing the generalization or transfer of learning, identifying the instructional unit and the sequence of tasks that are most efficient for instruction, and improving techniques for developing higher-order learning (e.g., problem solving) and independent motivation. Behaviorists are not complacent regarding these issues but rapidly are developing and testing tactics aimed at these issues and the general improvement of instructional technology (Carnine, 1989).

Some critics in learning disabilities are encouraging professionals in the field to move on to different approaches. Indeed, different approaches that prove to be successful should be encouraged. However, to discount the behavioral approach appears to invite a period of mass experimentation that could result in a loss of skill development for many students with learning disabilities. Given the state of the art in teaching students with learning disabilities, educators must remain open to the contributions of various approaches but remain accountable for the documented progress of students (Carnine, 1992). In the following passage, Rosenberg and Jackson (1988) offer a timely comment on the need for special educators to remain accountable:

> Those intent on cutting special education funds can use theoretical rather than empirical argument to support a range of hypotheses and contentions that assert that special education interventions have little value. At present, special education must continue to prove its worth through rigorous empirical investigations of its activities and practices. A significant shift away from the dominant mechanistic and quantitative perspective would undermine significantly the fundamental notion of educational accountability and leave those advocating an appropriate education for all children with little evidence to support their most powerful assertion—that all children, regardless of handicapping condition, can and do learn. (p. 33)

THE COGNITIVE APPROACH

A cognitive approach to teaching focuses on instruction that is consistent with how a student thinks when learning tasks. Advocates of the cognitive approach to teaching believe that what happens to the learner internally deserves as much attention as what happens externally during the learning process. Many cognitivists also believe that learning is a constructive process. The constructive viewpoint emphasizes that it is the learner who makes learning occur, and materials, teachers, and other external influences are important only if they provide experiences that enable the learner to construct new meanings.

The major implication of the cognitive approach for teachers is that instruction must be based on an understanding of the interaction that takes place between the individual and the environment. The teacher focuses on how the student perceives and interprets the environment, including the instructional process, materials, and situations and settings in which learning and performance are required. Thus, to provide instruction that guides the student in efficient learning, the teacher hypothesizes how a student is identifying, interpreting, organizing, and applying information.

The feature that best distinguishes a cognitive approach from a behavioral approach is the role of the individual in the learning process. Cognitive approaches evolved from the belief that the learner is the critical agent in how information is processed in response to learning demands. If learning does not occur, then the problem rests with the student and, as a result, the student's response to the environment. Behavioral approaches evolved from the belief that the environment (i.e., the teacher, materials, and setting) includes the critical agents in how information is learned and a response is made. If learning does not occur, then the problem is with the environment's response to the student. However, in a cognitive approach the materials, teachers, and other external factors are not as important as the learner in the learning process. These factors provide information on how a student might have to process information to respond to a demand. If there is difficulty in responding, the student may not be ready to learn, may be unable to learn because of cognitive deficits or differences, or may not have developed the appropriate problem-solving strategies to make sense of complex tasks, an ambiguous test, or material presented by disorganized teachers. As a result, in the cognitive approaches the role of the teacher is to help the learner process information from the environment in a manner that leads to generalized learning and performance.

The cognitive paradigm, especially as it is operationalized in the field of learning disabilities, includes a variety of theories and associated instructional models. Unfortunately, many of the theories and associated research that initially guided the field of learning disabilities suffered from the rapid expansion of the field in the late 1960s. As a result, many instructional efforts were based on untested or poorly tested theories. Thus, most professionals lost confidence in the theories and models that were developed within the cognitive paradigm (see Chapter 2). These theories primarily attributed the inconsistent academic performance of individuals with learning disabilities to cognitive processing deficits. Even professionals who accepted the notion of cognitive deficits as the basis for a learning disability rejected the intervention models that were developed for remediation of cognitive deficits. By the mid-1970s, it was apparent that the behavioral paradigm had replaced the cognitive paradigm as the basis for instructional programming. This is clear in the federal mandate of the individualized educational program model, which is based on measurable goals and objectives.

Research initiatives in the mid-to-late 1970s and the 1980s focused on the efficacy of the behavioral and the cognitive paradigms. Extensive research (Hallahan, Kauffman, & Lloyd, 1995; Reid, 1988) documents the various cognitive deficits of students with learning disabilities. Moreover, the application of behavioral methods in learning disability programs provides a general technology for organizing, delivering, and evaluating instruction that was lacking in earlier programming efforts. However, while it is possible to arrange for a change in behavior, many teachers face the problem of durability and generalizability of the behavior change. Concern for these factors probably is the primary reason for the resurgence in interest in the cognitive paradigm. Some researchers now focus their attention on the idea that internal factors may inhibit or explain the differential learning rates of individuals with learning disabilities. As a result, a variety of instructional approaches based on the cognitive paradigm emerged during the 1980s and continue to have an impact on instructional programs.

The following sections present a review of the major intervention approaches that are included within the cognitive paradigm. The initial section presents a brief description of specific abilities training models that are primarily of historical significance but still persist in some research efforts and instructional programs. The developmental approach also is presented, and the remaining sections focus on current and emerging approaches to teaching based on information-processing theory.

SPECIFIC ABILITIES APPROACH

The cognitive approach that has been associated most frequently with learning disabilities and has historical significance in the study of in-

TABLE 8.1
Example of a Process-Oriented Teaching Plan

Process Disability	Observable Classroom Behavior	Teaching Technique
Visual-motor problems (auditory processing is good; assessed via DTVP—2 or VMI*)	Confuses letters and words with similar configurations when writing	*Strength:* Use phonetic reading approach to take advantage of auditory strengths
	Reverses *b, d, p, q, u,* and *n* when writing	*Weakness:* Provide the student with exercises to train visual discrimination and visual-motor abilities

**Note:* DTVP—2 = *Developmental Test of Visual Perception* (2nd ed.)
VMI = *Developmental Test of Visual-Motor Integration*

terventions is the specific abilities approach. This approach is based on the premise that specific abilities serve as the foundation for learning and performance and that attention to deficits in these specific abilities should provide the basis for intervention efforts. From this perspective, the individual with a learning disability is seen as suffering from impairments in the basic processes that are essential to learning.

Deficits related to specific abilities primarily are attributed to dysfunctions in the central nervous system. The central nervous system receives the incoming information from the sense organs, regulates the neural associations, and transmits the signals necessary for an individual's response. Dysfunctions in the central processing system may be due to damage or trauma, genetic or developmental irregularities, or biochemical imbalances or intrusions.

Deficits sometimes are related to poor neurological organization or inadequate development of levels of the brain, and, as a result, remedial treatments are implemented to help individuals progressively develop or integrate the various levels of the brain. In addition, some deficits are connected with specific dimensions of the central nervous system, such as inadequate or delayed development in the motor or perceptual aspects of the nervous system. Because it is difficult to distinguish between the specific processing functions of the perceptual and the motor systems, many of the methods associated with the approaches related to these dysfunctions overlap and often are described collectively as process training, perceptual training, and perceptual-motor training programs.

Numerous recommendations for intervention efforts have been proposed either to remediate deficits or to take into consideration specific deficits in the design of academic programs. Moreover, many tests are designed to help educators isolate deficits in specific processes to enable consideration of such deficits in educational planning activities. To remediate deficits, an attempt is made to identify and isolate specific cognitive functions (e.g., visual memory or spatial relations) and train them. Table 8.1 illustrates the diagnostic-teaching approach of the specific abilities approach. This approach is on the ability side of the "ability versus skill" issue that has generated much controversy in the field.

In a recent review, Kavale (1990) confirmed the lack of empirical support for perceptual, perceptual-motor, and modality training and called for the development of alternative paradigms for developing cognitive training programs in learning disabilities. The lack of research support does not mean that specific abilities of some type may not exist or that they may not play a significant role in the overall development of the individual. It does mean, however, that research has not generated sufficient data from which to build tests that adequately measure such abilities. Sufficient data also are lacking to guide the development of instructional procedures that address such abilities in a manner that leads to more effective academic interventions.

While perceptual and perceptual-motor training seems to be ineffective in increasing academic achievement, some students experience perceptual and perceptual-motor difficulties. The teacher of students with perceptual difficulties must directly teach curriculum skills to foster academic gains, and perceptual-motor activities should be incorporated within academic tasks. When activities designed to promote motor development are incorporated into academic tasks, the purpose of improving such skills should not be confused with teaching perceptual and perceptual-motor skills with the intent of improving academic achievement. Lerner (1993) and Myers and Hammill (1990) provide more in-depth discussions of issues related to the training of perceptual and perceptual-motor abilities.

DEVELOPMENTAL APPROACH

Some professionals approach the education of individuals with learning disabilities from a developmental perspective. Developmentalists are interested in the psychological changes that take place in an individual and parallel biological growth. Researchers in this area focus on how an individual's ability to learn through perceptions expands so that the individual is able to make judgments from experiences and begin to think independently and creatively. This is accomplished by attempting to identify the cognitive capabilities and limits of individuals at various points in development. Also, developmentalists believe that how an individual understands important concepts and integrates prior knowledge with new knowledge at these various stages is important to understanding the development of the ability to learn.

How does developmental theory affect teaching students with learning disabilities? Some developmentalists believe that attempts to speed up the developmental process may cause learning problems. Others believe that individuals with learning disabilities go through the same developmental stages as others but go through these stages differently. Both positions are based on the identification of developmental stages or points that can be used to measure a student's development.

Generally, Piaget (1970, 1972) is most recognized for his theory of the stages of intellectual development of children. Piaget claims that learners pass through specific stages and adapt to the world by structuring new knowledge through assimilation and accommodation. *Assimilation* refers to the process of incorporating new experiences into an already existing cognitive structure. Thus, assimilation strengthens existing cognitive structures. *Accommodation* refers to the process of focusing on the new features of a learning task and results in changing cognitive structures. Learning and cognitive development consist of a succession of changes in cognitive structures by assimilation and accommodation. Contradiction and conflict cause disequilibrium. A youngster possesses certain conceptions, and when new experiences are contradictory, the child becomes puzzled, manipulates the new information, and constructs a new understanding.

The majority of research on Piaget's theory has been conducted with normal children. Research on the application of Piagetian theory to learning disabilities is sparse. The limited research that exists suggests that children with learning disabilities progress through developmental stages in the same order as normally achieving children, but with some delay (Reid, 1978). Information-processing theorists argue that Piagetian theory is inadequate for understanding the development of thought processes because adult models as well as child models of thinking must be studied. They believe that understanding where development is going fosters a better understanding of the development of how children think. Therefore, while the Piagetian model is based on the study of children, information-processing models are based on the study of adults and children.

INFORMATION-PROCESSING APPROACH

The work of most cognitive psychologists in America can be classified under the information-processing paradigm (Gagné, 1985). Information-processing approaches are based on the premise that to understand how students do or do not learn it is necessary to understand the overall system of how the individual processes information. Therefore, in this approach, attention to the overall information-processing system is more important than any specific ability.

The development of information-processing theory resulted from the joining of information theory and computer technology (Loftus & Loftus, 1976). It is not known whether information-processing theory would have evolved without the development of the computer, but the language and concepts that developed around computers and how they operate provided a common analogy and reference point to improve communication and guide research.

Information-processing theory focuses on what and how information is acquired. These theorists examine how people select, extract, maintain, and use information in the environment. While cognitive psychologists may disagree on how information actually is processed, they generally agree that information processing is thinking. To understand thinking it is necessary to explore (a) the nature of the information that an individual must process, (b) the process that is used by the individual to transform the information, and (c) the memory limits that restrict the amount of information that can be processed (Siegler, 1986).

Components of Information-Processing Models

Many information-processing theories and models exist, but most models have the following common characteristics:

1. The processing of information is characterized as being part of a system.
2. The processing of information is accomplished when information is coded and recoded as it enters and moves through the information-processing system.
3. The information-processing system is believed to have structural or capacity features that are not under the direct control of the individual and cannot be changed.
4. The information-processing system is believed to have features that can be changed through experience and training. Some of these features are under the conscious control of the individual, and others are not.

Information-processing models often are represented graphically to illustrate how information might be processed. These representations show possible transformations of information that might comprise the mental events that take place between a stimulus and a response. The graphics are abstract representations of the system of information processing. Some models depict the flow of information, while others depict patterns of how an individual might organize information or make associations regarding information. Most graphic representations depict flow models of information processing.

A simplified model of information processing is presented in Figure 8.10. While this model is simplified, it does provide a framework for discussing some of the major components of common information-processing models and educational implications. This model is based on one proposed by Mellard (1989), of the University of Kansas Center for Research on Learning, that was developed from a synthesis of research studies (Baumeister & Kellas, 1986; Brown & Campione, 1986; Carroll, 1976; Gagné, 1985; Horton & Bergfeld-Mills, 1984; Nation & Aram, 1977; Posner & McLeod, 1982; Pressley, Goodchild, Fleet, Zajchowski, & Evans, 1989; Samuels, 1987; and Swanson, 1987a, 1987b).

The model depicted in Figure 8.10 demonstrates the system characteristics of information

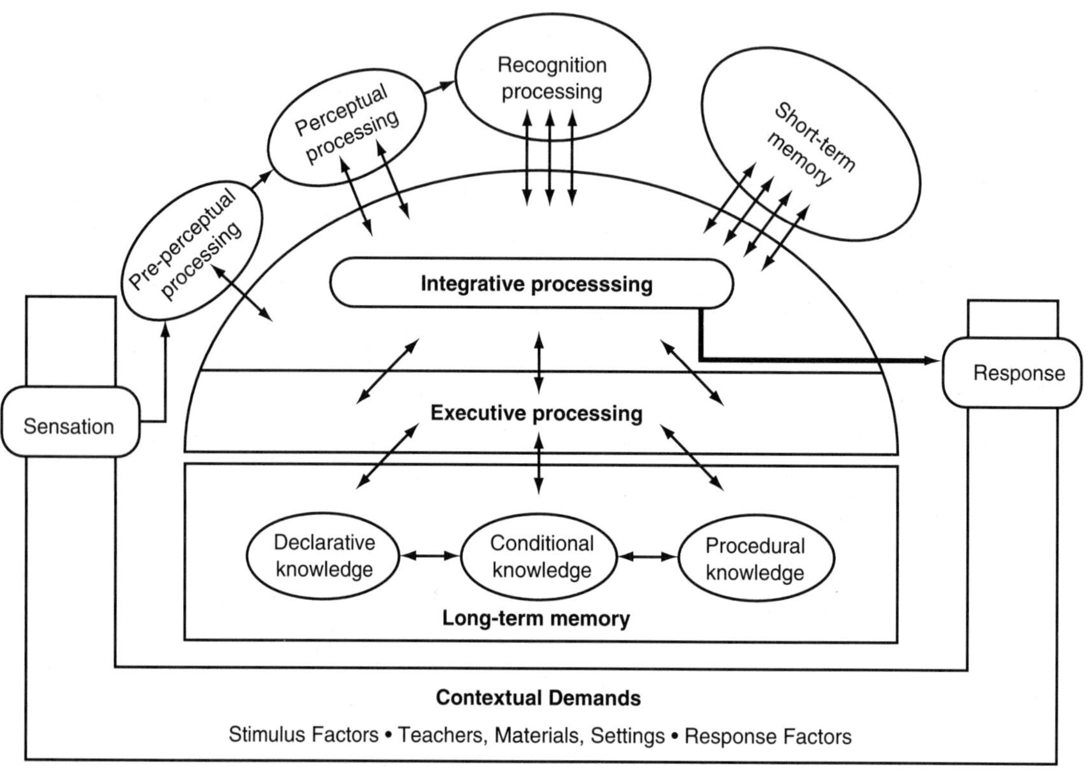

FIGURE 8.10
Simplified model of information processing

processing. The arrows indicate the direction of the hypothesized flow of information processing. As indicated by the arrows that move from left to right, information processing is depicted as primarily a step-by-step process moving from *sensation* to *response,* with a gradual increase in the amount of integrative or higher-order processing required. However, the model recognizes the simultaneous or parallel nature of information processing by depicting the ongoing interaction between the left-to-right flow of processing and the executive and long-term memory aspects of the system. This aspect of the model also represents the integrative and reciprocal relationship among attention, memory, and perceptual functions.

The arrows represent the encoding and recoding transformations that are taking place. The areas that the arrows connect represent the functions or states of the information as it moves through the system. These areas represent activities that either are performed unconsciously and automatically or are consciously generated and directed by the student for learning. The automatic processes often are referred to as lower-order processes. The learner-controlled processes are referred to as higher-order processes. Collectively, these activities are referred to as control processes because they control and decide how learning will proceed. Frequently, they are described as being similar to the software for a computer.

Figure 8.10 also illustrates some of the general proposed relationships between the basic cognitive processes. The flow of information represented by the ovals across the top and moving into the integrative processing area of the figure represents the general stages of information processing and their relationship to long-term memory. Executive processing, which can be thought of as related to maintaining attention and providing feedback to oneself, is considered to be basic to learning and, therefore, is located just below the stages to reflect its foundational role. Long-term memory is placed at the bottom of the figure to indicate that information processing is based on what the individual already knows and believes about the world. This model assumes that all sensory systems are functioning correctly.

Within the information-processing model, basic cognitive processes define each stage of information processing. These processes include pre-perceptual processing, perceptual processing, recognition processing, integrative processing, executive processing, and long-term memory. Researchers attempt to investigate the effect of each of these cognitive processes on the overall information-processing system, but theorists recognize that these cognitive processes function in an interrelated manner to achieve learning.

The following sections provide descriptions of the basic components of information processing. First, the foundational components of the information-processing system (i.e., long-term memory and executive processing) are discussed. Then the linear aspects of the model (i.e., pre-perceptual processing, perceptual processing, and recognition processing) are described. This is followed by the role of integrative processing and short-term memory. Finally, a discussion about the influence of contextual demands on information processing is presented.

Long-Term Memory. The processes associated with long-term memory comprise the search strategies used to retrieve information already learned. This information can be thought of as *acquired knowledge.* However, the individual must be able to call up the knowledge so that it can be used and new information can be included. In general, the better the individual has organized the information in memory, the more efficient will be the search-and-retrieval process. However, the knowledge must be available for retrieval. Some studies indicate that students with learning disabilities differ from students without learning disabilities in the basic information stored in long-term memory (Swanson, 1986). Therefore, on some tasks it is difficult to differentiate between poor performance due to problems in searching and retrieving information and poor performance due to deficits in prior knowledge.

Cognitive psychologists propose that there are three types of knowledge: declarative knowledge, procedural knowledge, and conditional knowledge. *Declarative knowledge* (sometimes called semantic knowledge) describes the information commonly thought of as concepts and facts. This knowledge is memorized for tests, contributed in a conversation, and retrieved to answer questions and solve problems. *Procedural knowledge* describes the steps involved in carrying out activities or performing tasks. Frequently, procedural knowledge is difficult to discuss because it includes fluent operations such as those involved in decoding a word, kicking a soccer ball, tying a shoe, or making an outline. However, once the procedure is understood and can be applied and described, then it is considered to be both declarative and procedural knowledge. *Conditional knowledge* is the information about when and why to integrate procedural and declarative knowledge in the process of learning. Mayer (1987) calls this *strategic knowledge.* Metacognitive strategies or executive strategies are considered to be aspects of conditional knowledge and are a feedback mechanism related to "how things are going" in the learning process. Self-monitoring is one example of the feedback mechanism. The feedback process helps students direct their learning and feelings of competence (Meichenbaum, 1977).

All three types of knowledge are stored in long-term memory and are depicted in Figure 8.10. Long-term memory also can be thought of as background knowledge or prior knowledge.

When presented with a demand, the individual must retrieve knowledge about the task (declarative knowledge), evaluate the critical characteristics of the task in terms of time and purpose to determine the best approach to the task (conditional knowledge), and then complete the task in a planned but fluent manner (procedural knowledge). Therefore, the better the organization of knowledge, the more efficient is the learner.

The ways in which an individual organizes information are called *schemata.* Some cognitive psychologists believe that individuals store relevant or associated information together in schema. Therefore, related declarative, procedural, and conditional knowledge can be thought of as being "packaged" together. For example, when the topic of soccer is discussed, schema are more likely to bring forth knowledge that is associated with soccer rules, concepts, skills, and experiences than knowledge associated with chess. Schema also exist within schema. Soccer may exist within the schema of sports. Within soccer may be schema associated with players, specific games, equipment, rules, and tournaments. Additional schema exist within each of these schema. How well an individual can access this knowledge is an important focus of cognitive approaches to instruction. The search for the perfect example, experience, or analogy that will help the student magically connect new information in the lesson with stored information or experiences can be thought of as the challenge of every teacher.

Hallahan et al. (1995) report that many researchers have studied the memory processes of individuals with learning disabilities by using a visual, short-term memory task. The findings of these researchers have resulted in several conclusions: (a) youngsters with learning disabilities have more difficulty with these tasks than their peers without learning disabilities, (b) the memory problems of individuals with learning disabilities are attributed to the limited use of cognitive strategies (e.g., organization and rehearsal) that others routinely use, and (c) when these cognitive strategies are taught to individuals with learning disabilities, their performances are similar to those of others.

Executive Processing. Another set of processes that serves as a foundation to the information-processing system relates to the individual's ability to monitor, regulate, and evaluate learning and performance. These processes, which are important in making the overall information-processing system work, are stored in long-term memory and are controlled by the learner. The terms *feedback, executive processing,* and *metacognition* often are used synonymously. The use of any of the terms conveys the idea that the learner primarily uses these processes to provide feedback on how learning is progressing. These processes enable the student to focus, select an appropriate task, predict, stay on task, check progress, monitor performance, and evaluate work. Educationally, these processes are thought of as the ability to self-question (e.g., What do I need to do? How did I do that?).

Executive or metacognitive processes are important to information processing because they appear to play a central role in helping to direct learning and feelings of competence (Meichenbaum, 1977). Flavell (1976) notes:

> "Metacognition" refers to one's knowledge concerning one's own cognitive processes and products or anything related to them, e.g., the learning of relevant properties of information or data. For example, I am engaging in metacognition . . . if it occurs to me that I had better scrutinize each and every alternative in any multiple-choice type task situation before deciding which is the best one. . . . Metacognition refers, among other things, to the active monitoring and consequent regulation and orchestration of these processes. (p. 232)

Hallahan et al. (1995) suggest that metacognition can be divided into categories according to specific cognitive processes (e.g., metamemory, metalistening, and metacomprehension in reading). Thus, meta-attention refers to an understanding of the relevant factors that affect an individual's attending behavior.

Of all the processes associated with the executive processing system, the one that has been most studied in the field of learning disabilities is attention. From an information-processing framework, *attention* refers to the ability to be "on target" or ready to learn. Torgesen (1982) notes that attention deficits are actually deficiencies in information-processing behaviors in which there is either a failure to apply efficient strategies and control processes for information processing or a lack of organized cognitive schemes and production systems to direct appropriate information processing for a specific task. Thus, attention is associated closely with executive processing.

Samuels (1987) describes the following different behaviors as aspects of attention.

1. Overt attention (i.e., the use of body language that suggests paying attention, such as looking at a textbook during a reading task).
2. Arousal (i.e., a state of attentiveness that fluctuates from very low arousal, such as during sleep, to high arousal, such as during stress or agitation).
3. Alertness (i.e., readiness to perform).
4. Vigilance (i.e., cognitive endurance or ability to maintain both arousal and alertness over time).
5. Selective attention (i.e., ability to separate background noise or irrelevant, superfluous information from the appropriate stimulus and focus on it).

Learning requires the student to attend to the task. If attention shifts, information or key aspects of information will not be received and processed. Thus, attention is required throughout all stages of information processing.

For years, attention problems have been associated with learning disabilities. Because teachers readily can recall examples of students with learning disabilities who had difficulty paying attention, attention deficits have much face validity. A common term to describe attention problems is *attention deficit disorder* (ADD).

Given the heterogeneity of individuals with learning disabilities, the multidimensional aspects of attention, and the complexity of cognitive processes, it is extremely difficult to ascertain the specific attention deficits of those with learning disabilities. It is apparent that numerous students with learning disabilities have deficits in various aspects of the attention process. The precise reasons (e.g., organization or decision making) for attention deficits remain nebulous. Much of the difficulty in studying attention processes comes from the lack of reliable and valid measures. Recent literature has used on-task behavior as a measure of attention. Cognitive behavior modification (discussed later in this chapter) appears to be a promising means for promoting on-task behavior.

Pre-Perceptual Processing. The preceding discussion of some of the foundational and ongoing processing components is now followed by a discussion of more linear aspects of the information-processing system. These are represented by the ovals in Figure 8.10. The information-processing system is activated when information is received through the senses. Because an information-processing model focuses on how learners think when using information that has been received, it assumes that the senses are not impaired and that information can be processed. Thus, the first step in the process is pre-perceptual processing. Mayer (1987) refers to the most critical activities at this stage as *feature detection.* Feature detection involves identifying the most basic elements or features of the information. Preschool, kindergarten, and early first-grade instruction frequently focuses on teaching the basic visual and auditory elements that are associated with letters, numbers, and shapes. Initially, the learner spends considerable mental energy on learning how to detect the features and groups of features in symbols. Gradually, this process becomes automatic and can be done quickly and effortlessly.

Perceptual Processing. Perception is the second step in the processing of information and occurs when the student is able to recognize information as signs or features that are represented as symbols, numbers, letters, and phonemes. The student must learn how to discriminate between different units of information, and this information then must be stored in long-term memory and be available for immediate retrieval and use. As the learner becomes more skilled, this level of processing gradually should become automatic and not under the conscious control of the learner. Until these processes become automatic, the learner must consciously continue to direct the processing of information.

Recognition Processing. Recognition involves combining the perceptual units and attaching meaning to them as concepts. Mayer (1987) refers to this as *meaning access*. Long-term memory is important especially at this stage because the learner must recognize the unit and its relevant meanings. This information must be part of and retrieved from prior knowledge. Like the processing described in the preceding stages, the recognition process must become automatic and unconscious. The concept of *automaticity* is an important construct in explaining the poor performance of students with learning disabilities in reading and in cognitive processing, and this construct has been investigated by many researchers (LaBerge & Samuels, 1974; Perfetti, 1985; Samuels, 1987; Stanovich, 1986; Swanson, 1987b; Torgesen & Morgan, 1990; Wagner & Torgesen, 1987). Samuels suggests that poor readers have difficulty moving to a more automatic level because all of their attention is focused on word recognition, letter detection, or phonological processing. Thus, they have little mental energy left for higher-order processes such as comprehension. Samuels suggests that reading without expression may characterize this phenomenon.

Integrative Processing and Short-Term Memory. The last stage of information processing involves the integration of automatic and controlled processes that enable learners to respond to specific and general learning demands encountered in various situations and settings. This aspect of information processing is considered to be the most relevant for educators. At this stage, learning is directed based on how the learner is expected to respond from cues in the environment. In other words, the stimulus and the context of the stimulus are evaluated by the learner according to prior knowledge stored in long-term memory. Once information is retrieved from long-term memory, it is held so that it can be manipulated and worked. This "holding tank" is called *short-term memory* and supports integrative processing. Some psychologists do not make a distinction between integrative processing and short-term memory (Gagné, 1985), and the term *working strategies* is then used to convey both ideas.

After information in long-term memory is retrieved and placed in short-term memory, the individual uses this information to construct plans. These plans comprise the working strategies that the student has learned and has retrieved (i.e., remembered). Lower-order processes are used unconsciously as needed, and various types of declarative, procedural, and conditional knowledge are integrated to form the individual's approach to the task. In the field of education, this stage of processing is associated most closely with the term *learning strategies*. However, the processing that takes place in the integrative processing stage requires that the learner retrieve and use multiple cognitive strategies in developing an approach to a task. In addition, the strategies that could be generated might relate to the social and motivational dimensions of a task as well as to the purely academic dimensions.

This stage of information processing often is referred to as *higher-order processing*. Much attention is given to the strategies that the learner employs at this stage because many opportunities exist for teaching students how to approach specific tasks strategically (e.g., how to read a story for better comprehension, listen and take notes from a lecture, or write an interesting story). Some researchers focus on teaching students specific strategies to improve learning. For example, students may be taught how to construct acronyms or other mnemonics to aid in remembering information as a response to a studying task. Some educators raise concerns regarding the isolated training in specific strategies. They argue that such isolated training requires students to integrate the strategy independently into their information-processing system and to know when, where, and how to use the strategy. However, studies indicate that some students are not able or are unwilling to generalize strategies (Ellis, Lenz, & Sabornie, 1987).

Some researchers address the problem of isolated strategy training by conceptualizing this stage of information processing as comprising integrated strategy systems. For example, Swanson (1987a) argues against a focus on isolated strategies as part of information-processing instruction and states that "intelligent performance requires a student to integrate several kinds of mental capabilities rather than merely access an appropriate strategy" (p. 5). From this perspective, processing at this stage is conceptualized as the learner's entire approach to the task, and it includes all of the knowledge, strategies, and substrategies required for the learner to respond effectively and efficiently for generalized learning to occur. Thus, processing at this stage is the result of integrating many aspects of the information-processing system as part of learning as opposed to using a single strategy. This concept of a strategy is reflected in the broad strategy-system definition proposed by Deshler and Lenz (1989). The definition they suggest for conceptualizing training is based on the idea that the term *strategy* should describe a global approach to a task. They argue that "a strategy is an individual's approach to a task and includes how a person thinks and acts when planning, executing, and evaluating performance on a task and its outcomes" (p. 205).

The strategies usually used during this stage of processing can be characterized according to several dimensions. The following strategies are used during integrative processing and appear frequently in the literature:

Cognitive strategies

adding	discriminating	locating	recognizing
associating	dividing	multiplying	recombining
categorizing	elaborating	organizing	rehearsing
chunking	grouping	previewing	repeating
coding	imagining	predicting	rephrasing
combining	justifying	prioritizing	searching
comparing	labeling	quantifying	subtracting
contrasting	listing	reciting	summarizing
counting			

Executive/metacognitive strategies

analyzing	planning	monitoring	choosing strategies
generalizing	reviewing	evaluating	selectively attending

Contextual Demands. The final important aspect of the information-processing model shown in Figure 8.10 is depicted by the box that surrounds the base of the model and frames sensation and response. This dimension relates to the demands placed on the learner to respond. In essence, response demands reflect the challenges posed in the learning task. Information-processing models acknowledge the environmental influences on the learner through this aspect of the model. In other words, information is processed in a context. This component of the model reflects that the learner must evaluate what is required in a learning task to know how to process the information and form the expected response within the context of the situation and setting. Sometimes the expected response is to answer "yes" or "no," whereas at other times the required response may be to read a passage or write a paragraph. Behaviorally, a correct response is the goal. However, from an information-processing perspective, the goal is for the student to process the expectations as a piece of information that helps the learner determine how to process the information and select the correct combination of strategies. Thus, the learning task often defines the types of strategies that are appropriate for a task.

One way to understand how environmental factors are viewed within the information-processing framework is to explore a simple task that a student might face in a classroom. For example, a teacher might present the following assignment to students in a seventh-grade science class:

> Tomorrow there will be a test on the glands in the exocrine system. You need to be able to describe the major glands in the exocrine system and explain how they function and work together. The test will have essay questions, and you will have about 20 minutes to complete it. The information is in your notes.

In this task, many response demands are placed on the learner. The first set of response demands requires the learner to identify the task as an assignment and determine how to remember to do the task. The second set of response demands relates to what the learner must do to study for the test. The third set of response demands relates to how the student actually will respond during the test. However, in all three circumstances, the demands of the task affect the strategies that the learner selects and integrates to complete the task. The demands are the same for all students; however, how each student responds to the demands will vary greatly. In addition, a student's response often is the basis for interpreting the type of strategies that the student employs.

Conclusion. From an information-processing approach, the way an individual processes information is personalized. The types of experiences and knowledge that an individual has acquired determine how information is processed. The processing of information that takes place at the pre-perceptual and perceptual levels usually becomes automatic very early in a person's life, and little integrative processing is involved. For example, in reading, beginning school-age students focus on word meaning and recognition processing. Integrative processing, which is the combination of various knowledge into working strategies, becomes the primary vehicle that enables learning. If the individual continues to create strategies that are not consistent with what is expected, the ability to process information may be questioned. This stage of information processing is given the most attention in learning disabilities research.

Information-Processing Theory and Learning Disabilities

Higher-Order Versus Lower-Order Processing. Many students with learning disabilities have primarily higher-order processing difficulties. They do not seem to apply strategies that lead to effective and efficient responses to demands encountered across settings. Specifically, the strategies that students with learning disabilities seem to use prompt some researchers to describe their responses as passive or inactive (Torgesen, 1977b, 1982). In other words, the control they exert on promoting or guiding their own learning is minimal. Some research indicates that many of the learning problems experienced by individuals with learning disabilities can be explained by deficits in higher-order processes.

However, in addition to the research on higher-order processes, other research focuses on deficits in lower-order processes. For example, some research focuses on specific processing deficits such as phonological processing (Stanovich, 1986; Torgesen & Morgan, 1990). Phonological processing relates to an individual's awareness of and access to the sound structure of language (Torgesen & Morgan, 1990), which takes place in the pre-perceptual and perceptual stages of information processing. Research in this area focuses on the ability to identify individual phonemes in words and to combine the isolated speech sounds into words. Stanovich (1994) notes that explicit instruction in these lower-order processes (e.g., phonological awareness and analysis) produces positive outcomes for students with learning disabilities. Specifically, he states,

> Successful intervention directed at processes of word recognition will more closely resemble exogenous constructivism, in which explicit instruction and teacher-directed strategy teaching are not eschewed. Research has indicated that explicit instruction and teacher-directed strategy training are more efficacious when the focus is developing decoding skill. This is especially true for at-risk children, children with LD, and children with specific needs. In contrast, successful interventions directed at comprehension processes are more likely to have the characteristics of dialectical constructivism—where self-discovery and holistic principles will be more apparent. (p. 270)

(Levels of constructivism are discussed later in this chapter.)

Cognitive Style. Another area within the information-processing theory that is a problem for some individuals with learning disabilities is cognitive style. Cognitive style is purported to have a general influence on learning. A cognitive style that has been used in studying youngsters with learning disabilities involves cognitive tempo or, specifically, a reflectivity-impulsivity dichotomy. If the learner is uncertain about the correct answer, a reflective style is characterized by a careful and deliberate approach in which alternatives are considered before making a response. In contrast, an impulsive style is characterized by quick incorrect responses. Researchers note that many students with learning disabilities tend to be impulsive responders, whereas students without learning disabilities are reflective responders (Epstein, Hallahan, & Kauffman, 1975). Torgesen (1982) suggests that students with learning disabilities become impulsive responders because they lack alternative cognitive strategies. Cognitive behavior modification, presented later in this chapter, has produced the most durable and generalizable results concerning the meaningful improvement of cognitive style (Maker, 1981).

Maturational Lag. Bender (1957) popularized the maturational lag theory to explain learning problems. In this theory, each person has a preset timetable for development. Youngsters who exhibit discrepancies in cognitive abilities do not necessarily suffer from neurological damage or experiential deficits. Instead, their various mental processes are maturing at different rates. Proponents of this theory hypothesize that students with learning disabilities lag behind their normally achieving peers because of different timing, not different ability. According to Ames (1968), this theory leads to the belief that problems in learning are created when students are asked to perform tasks before they are ready.

Research on this theory is limited, but a few studies do exist. Koppitz (1972–1973) conducted a 5-year follow-up study of 177 students with learning disabilities and found that "slow maturation" described many of these youngsters. She concluded that these students are more immature than their normally achieving classmates and need additional time to develop. Koppitz also indicates that when given extra time and help, these students often do well academically.

Because the maturational lag theory suggests that immaturity leads to learning problems, it is reasonable to expect that at a given grade level the younger students would experience more learning difficulties than the older students. Several investigators (Diamond, 1983; DiPasquale, Moule, & Flewelling, 1980) compared the birth month and the percentage of students referred for learning disabilities. They report that the younger students at a grade level were more likely to be referred for learning disabilities than the older students. They labeled this phenomenon the *birthdate effect.*

Silver and Hagin (1966) conducted a follow-up study of youngsters with reading disabilities in a hospital clinic. When these youngsters were young adults (ages 16 to 24), they were re-evaluated. Silver and Hagin claim that through the process of maturation, many learning difficulties such as spatial orientation, auditory discrimination, and left-right discrimination had disappeared.

Overall, the research concerning the maturational lag theory and learning disabilities is incomplete and not conclusive. Well-designed empirical studies with reliable and valid measures are needed before the implications can be applied widely. However, in individual situations it may be useful in helping parents and teachers understand a student's difficulties.

For making intervention decisions, this theory can present some perplexing problems. For example, if a student's immaturity is suspected to be causing learning problems, special intervention may be delayed on the assumption that the youngster will outgrow the problem, and valuable intervention time will be lost. Perhaps a responsible strategy would be to provide sensible interventions when learning difficulties are recognized.

Implications for Use of Information-Processing Theory

Individuals with learning disabilities who seem to have difficulty with higher-order mental functions often are considered to be inactive learners, strategy deficient, or insufficiently strategy oriented during learning (Torgesen, 1977a, 1977b). Much research indicates that many students with learning disabilities have difficulty with this level of information processing. For example, in some studies immature youngsters and students with learning disabilities did not appear to use *active* strategies for learning or problem solving (R. J. Hall, 1980; Lloyd, 1980; Loper, 1980). Several authorities (R. J. Hall, 1980; Lloyd, 1980; McKinney & Haskins, 1980) believe that this failure results, in part, from an inability to generalize a previously learned problem-solving strategy to a new problem. Havertape and Kass (1978) examined the strategies of adolescents with learning disabilities and the strategies of normally achieving adolescents. The students' self-directions were recorded while they attempted to solve problems. From the analysis of these tapes, the researchers conclude that the students with learning disabilities lacked strategies to apply to the problem. For example, 40% of their responses (as opposed to 6% for the control group) consisted of random answers without any relationship to the tasks.

Efforts to train students with learning disabilities to use specific cognitive strategies to improve learning have been successful (Graham & Harris, 1994; Scruggs & Mastropieri, 1994; Stanovich, 1994). However, training paradigms encounter the most success when training is given in both cognitive and metacognitive aspects of the strategy. For example, the student receives training in a strategy as well as in how to generate feedback. This feedback process includes training in self-evaluation, self-monitoring, and goal setting (Palincsar & Brown, 1984). However, debate exists over how these strategies should be taught.

TEACHING METHODS FOR COGNITIVE DISABILITIES

Turnure (1985, 1986) suggests that research on cognitive development should examine interactions among the following dimensions: (a) the characteristics of the learner (e.g., skills, knowledge, and attitudes), (b) the learning activities (e.g., attention, discrimination, and rehearsal), (c) the nature of the criterion task (e.g., recognition, recall, and transfer), (d) the nature of the materials (e.g., sequencing, structure, appearance, and difficulty), and (e) the instructional agent (e.g., how the teacher describes, questions, sequences instruction, and models). Turnure suggests that the teacher is the central organizer of the various dimensions of instruction. A model that emphasizes the teacher's role as the primary "learning situation organizer" places great responsibility on the teacher. Inherent in such a model is the assumption that the teacher has sufficient knowledge and experience to enhance learning and successfully make decisions that provide for an appropriate balance among the instructional dimensions.

Lenz, Bulgren, and Hudson (1990) note that the concept of "information-processing sensitive instruction" refers to instruction with the following characteristics:

1. Is fashioned and differentially delivered based on the teacher's knowledge of the range of information-processing and communication abilities of students (Deshler, Alley, Warner, & Schumaker, 1981).
2. Promotes student attention or reception of incoming information (Lenz, Alley, & Schumaker, 1987; Mayer, 1987).
3. Promotes the activation of strategies that enable the student to access and integrate prior knowledge with to-be-learned information (Ausubel, 1960; Lenz et al., 1987).
4. Promotes the activation of strategies that enable the student to build logical or structural connections between and among incoming ideas and ideas already in memory (Bulgren, Schumaker, & Deshler, 1988; Mayer, 1987).
5. Promotes the active participation of the student in the learning process as a planner, implementor, and evaluator (Brown, 1978; Hughes, Schumaker, Deshler, & Mercer, 1993; Van Reusen, Bos, Schumaker, & Deshler, 1987).
6. Instructs the student in the "why, when, and where" aspects of information related to the use of knowledge (Brown, Day, & Jones, 1983; Lenz & Hughes, 1990).
7. Informs the student of progress and provides appropriate feedback in a manner that improves learning (Kline, Schumaker, & Deshler, 1991; Palincsar & Brown, 1984).
8. Leads the student in the learning process through expert scaffolding and proleptic teaching (Deshler & Schumaker, 1988; Vygotsky, 1978).
9. Takes advantage of the developmental and social contexts of learning by gradually moving from adult guidance and modeling to peer and student guidance and modeling (Allington, 1984; Lenz, Schumaker, Deshler, & Beals, 1984; Palincsar & Brown, 1984; Vygotsky, 1978).
10. Plans for and promotes the acquisition and integration of semantic, procedural, and strategic knowledge throughout all phases and types of instruction (Mayer, 1987).

Translation of Information-Processing Theory into Practice

The process of translating theory into practice must focus on how instructional principles can be organized to affect classroom practice systematically and reliably. Consequently, the identification of pedagogy sensitive to an information-processing perspective requires a practical interpretation of information-processing theory. Ideally, such an interpretation would set the stage for the teacher to monitor and adjust the teaching process as necessary. In other words, a teacher's instructional procedures should be designed to interrupt an existing information-processing sequence, if necessary, and to externally guide or prompt the student's strategic processing of information more effectively and efficiently than would be possible if the learner proceeded alone. As a result, while the learner is processing information, the teacher is attempting to hypothesize how the learner is processing information. This, in turn, leads to the modification of instruction in an attempt to alter how the learner is learning and performing.

The complex nature of information-processing theory must be reduced into a simpler framework while retaining the essential and powerful elements of the information-processing model. Lenz et al. (1990) note that pedagogy accomplishes this when three conditions are met. These conditions deal with the student's awareness that learning is about to occur, the student's active and personal involvement in the learning process, and the student's willingness to use this new knowledge. First, the learner must be oriented to the instructional situation by (a) becoming aware that a learning situation or opportunity exists, (b) attending to the new information, and (c) drawing upon appropriate prior knowledge to contextualize or make logical associations with the new information. Second, the learner begins to understand the information by (a) identifying concepts, (b) identifying similarities between different examples indicating that they do or do not belong to the same concept class, (c) making appropriate associations with prior knowledge regarding these concepts, and (d) distinguishing between important and unimportant pieces of information in the reconstruction of the knowledge base. Third, the learner must act on the new information by (a) testing knowledge and the effect of this knowledge in the real world, (b) exploring the various dimensions of knowledge across situations, settings, and conditions, (c) applying knowledge to solve problems, and (d) using self-practice and memorization activities to ensure that the knowledge is available for later access.

Instructional Paradigms

Educators agree that many students with learning disabilities need to become more strategic in learning; however, they disagree about how strategies should be taught. Two general instructional paradigms promote learning using an information-processing approach: reductionism and constructivism. A discussion of these paradigms indicates how cognitive approaches and instructional methods currently are being implemented in programs for students with learning disabilities.

Reductionist Paradigm. The reductionist paradigm is based on the premise that to understand or explain a complex concept, one must analyze and divide or reduce it to simpler, smaller, or more understandable components. In science, the use of a reductionist research paradigm has led to an understanding of cell biology, neurology, atomic energy, and the nature and cure of diseases. Similarly, reductionism has been applied to the study of human cognition and behavior. For example, behavioral approaches are based on the reductionist principle of behavioral task analysis. In other words, understanding what the individual must do enables the teacher to teach the student how to perform the task. A content analysis involves identifying the component concepts and information that must be acquired in a task. A cognitive task analysis involves identifying the mental steps and states that need to be present for an individual to complete a task. These different types of analyses are based on a reductionist approach to teaching and learning.

In addition to being a central tenet of behavioral approaches, reductionist approaches are embraced by individuals with a cognitive orientation. From a reductionist viewpoint, cognition is reduced to the major components, principles, processes, and structures that might be governing learning. The previous discussion of information-processing theory largely rests on a reductionist paradigm. The identification of strategies and knowledge types is an attempt to organize cognition into components that can be discussed and understood.

Cognitive behavior modification (CBM) is an example of a reductionist approach to cognitive training. Cognitive behavior modification combines behavior modification techniques with self-training methods (e.g., monitoring instruction, evaluation, and verbalization). According to Meichenbaum (1977), the pioneer of cognitive behavior modification, the basic tenet of this approach is that cognitions (of which inner speech is one) influence behavior and that behavior can be changed by modifying cognitions. The steps of a self-instructional program use the following sequence:

1. An adult model performs a task while talking aloud (cognitive modeling).
2. The student performs the same task under the directions of the model's instruction (overt self-guidance).
3. The student whispers the instructions while performing the task (faded, overt self-guidance).
4. The student guides performance through private speech (covert self-instruction).

Essentially, inner speech is viewed as behavior that is subject to the same learning principles as overt behavior. Thus, the student is encouraged to verbalize before acting. Keogh and Glover (1980) discuss the respective roles of cognitive and behavior therapy:

> It is *behavioral* in that it is structured, utilizes reinforcement techniques, is usually focused on particular problems or complaints, and is not concerned with antecedents or etiology of the problem. It is *cognitive* in that its goal is to produce change in the individual by modifying his thinking. (p. 5)

Because of the cognitive deficits of students with learning disabilities, cognitive behavior modification appears to be compatible with their needs. It is multidimensional and includes a variety of strategies, techniques, and programs. To date, most of the work with students with learning disabilities has focused on self-monitoring (Rooney & Hallahan, 1985). Self-monitoring primarily involves the components of self-evaluation and self-recording. For example, in a self-monitoring intervention a student keeps a record of targeted behavior and periodically monitors the progress toward established goals.

Hallahan (1980) and his colleagues at the University of Virginia have conducted much of the research on this approach in teaching students with learning disabilities. Hallahan and Kauffman (1988) found it useful because it stresses self-initiative and helps the student overcome passivity in learning, offers specific methods for solving problems, and seems applicable to treating poor attentiveness and impulsivity. Research suggests that cognitive behavior modification can be used successfully to improve handwriting performance (Kosiewicz, Hallahan, & Lloyd, 1981), attention to task (Kneedler & Hallahan, 1981), reading comprehension (Swanson, 1981; Wong, 1980), and arithmetic productivity (Hallahan, Lloyd, Kosiewicz, & Kneedler, 1979).

It is well documented that, in certain situations, cognitive behavior modification techniques help improve specific behaviors of students with learning disabilities. However, Rooney and Hallahan (1985) note that generalization using cognitive behavior modification has not been established because there is little evidence to suggest that cognitive change is occurring. They indicate that these findings concerning generalization are not surprising because investigators only focused on influencing behaviors on specific tasks or in specific situations. In short, generalization and cognitive changes have not been stressed.

The potential impact of cognitive behavior modification is not likely to be recognized in learning disabilities until a broader intervention focus is developed and studied (Meichenbaum, 1980). Because of the large number of cognitive behavior modification techniques, Rooney and Hallahan (1985) call for a curriculum-oriented view of cognitive behavior modification in which specific interventions are matched to learner needs. They recommend directions for cognitive behavior modification research:

> Research must turn to face a number of substantial concerns. Does CBM result in true cognitive change within the individual? What is necessary

> for the change in cognition to occur? Will the changed cognition . . . be durable? What is necessary for generalizations of the effects of CBM? . . . In theory, CBM has great potential for use with exceptional learners, but the theoretical claims must now be tested in practice to see if the proposed benefits of CBM are real or imaginary. (pp. 49–50)

Constructivist Paradigm. The constructivist approach to understanding learning represents a close approximation to a pure cognitive approach. Constructivism is embraced in both science and psychology to explain complex or traditionally unexplainable phenomena. For example, researchers argue that some phenomena in biology and physics cannot be studied or explained according to a reductionist paradigm. Likewise, cognitive psychologists indicate that learning is too complex to reduce into simple constructs. The constructivist approach is based on the premise that the student is a naturally active learner who constructs new personalized knowledge through linking prior knowledge and new knowledge. Authentic knowledge provides the content for the instructional process, which involves an interactive and collaborative dialogue between the teacher and the student. The teacher orchestrates the instruction within the student's "zone of proximal development" (Vygotsky, 1978) by providing assistance when the learner seems inefficient or frustrated. This zone refers to the instructional area between where the learner has independence (mastery) and what can be achieved with competent assistance (potential).

The nature of teacher-student interactions is viewed differently among constructivists (Harris & Graham, 1994; Moshman, 1982). The endogenous constructivist believes the interaction should be structured so that students discover new knowledge without explicit instruction from the teacher. Students are presented with challenges and then allowed to explore and self-discover new knowledge. The exogenous constructivist believes the teacher engages in more direct instruction. Interactions are characterized by the teacher providing explicit instruction through the use of describing, explaining, modeling, and guiding practice with feedback. The position of the dialectical constructivist is between the endogenous and exogenous constructivists. These interactions are collaborative, with the teacher providing instruction (e.g., offering metacognitive explanations, modeling cognitive processes, asking leading questions, and providing encouragement) as needed to guide student discovery.

Many terms (e.g., *socratic dialogue, collaborative discussions, interaction discourse, reciprocal teaching,* and *scaffolding*) are used to describe these interactions. Reid and Stone (1991) describe scaffolding as a teacher collaborating with a learner to provide the learner with whatever is needed for meaningful participation. Paris and Winograd (1990) maintain that a key feature of scaffolded instruction is a dialogue between teacher and student that provides the learner with just enough support and guidance to enable the student to achieve a goal that would be impossible without the assistance.

Harris and Graham (1994) discuss endogenous, exogenous, and dialectical constructivism in the following comments:

> Moshman (1982) noted the possibility of integrating (but not synthesizing) these views—and the importance of such an integration in furthering our understanding of cognition and its development. . . . [A]t different times or points, endogenous, exogenous, or dialectical considerations can be seen as predominant, thus indicating which . . . is most useful *at that time.* Thus, all three perspectives play a role, yet remain discrete, in this metatheoretical view, which can be applied to both learning and teaching. (p. 237)

Schema theory was proposed to express the dynamic relationship between the learner and the environment. While schema represent the organization of knowledge, the important aspect of schema to the constructivist is that they are generalized, active, and always changing. Therefore, they cannot be reduced to simpler elements.

However, while schema theory emerged as a constructivist response to reductionist methods, the basis for organizing and discussing these structures often relies on reductionist tactics. The difference is that the constructivist is satisfied with organizing understanding of learning into broad and complex structures and working within this understanding to promote learning.

The instructional model that best articulates the basic principles of a constructivist approach to teaching is called *reciprocal teaching*. In most instances, reciprocal teaching is associated with reading instruction; however, the instructional principles that serve as the foundation of this approach frequently are used as the basis for representing the constructivist approach to teaching. Many constructivists argue that the conditions presented in some of the studies of reciprocal teaching represent too many elements of reductionist thinking to reflect a truly constructivist viewpoint. According to Palincsar and Brown (1984, 1986), the reciprocal teaching approach is characterized by the following dimensions:

1. Instruction is viewed as a dialogue between the teacher and the students.
2. Instruction is characterized by a high degree of ongoing interaction between the teacher and students and among students.
3. Instruction is scaffolded; that is, the teacher begins instruction in a strategy at the point where instruction is required to support the students in the next step to complete a task and then fades the support so that students are challenged to use the strategy.
4. Teacher judgment and timing are critical in the process of successfully guiding students to reflect on their performance and learning.
5. The skill level of the students should not affect participation.
6. The purpose of teaching strategies is to answer questions, and the goal of instruction is not to learn to use strategies.

The steps presented by Palincsar and Brown (1984, 1986) indicate the importance of adherence to the following set of procedures for effective instruction:

1. Instruction is initiated by discussing why a task may be difficult, the importance of strategies, and the conditions for using strategies to help in learning.
2. Each strategy is introduced, defined, and discussed with rationales.
3. Practice in the strategy is provided under controlled conditions using familiar and everyday situations.
4. The teacher checks the students' use of key aspects of the strategy to ensure minimal competence in the use of the strategy before the "dialogue" begins.
5. Students are asked to apply the strategy in increasingly difficult aspects of the task and are supported in their attempts to use the strategy by the teacher.
6. The teacher leads a dialogue with students and models the use of the strategies that are to be used by thinking aloud.
7. Students are prompted to comment on the teacher's model, clarify, make predictions, and answer questions that the teacher might have posed about the task.
8. Gradually, the responsibility for the dialogue is shifted from the teacher to the students through guided practice.
9. The teacher monitors the students' performance by praising attempts to use strategies and, when necessary, providing additional instruction and modeling in the use of the strategy.

Studies on reciprocal teaching indicate that it can be effective with some students with learning disabilities (Brown & Palincsar, 1982; Palincsar, 1982). Although few studies include students identified as having learning disabilities, improvement in the performance of students classified as poor readers indicates that this approach may be appropriate for some students with learning disabilities (Palincsar and Brown, 1986). Palincsar and Brown (1984) and Brown and Palincsar (1987) report that students generalize the use of the strategies over time and across settings. For example, they report that students continued to use the strategies in test situations 8 weeks after the training had ended, and generalization of the trained strategies to similar tasks and to general classrooms was observed. However, research has not addressed questions related to the long-term use of the strategies by students with learning disabilities and the degree of expertise required of the teacher in implementing the procedures with these students. Research efforts to validate the use of reciprocal teaching with students with learning disabilities under a variety of learning conditions are under way.

Integration of Paradigms

Many educators are beginning to resist the positions of advocates who maintain that one instructional paradigm fits all learners. The "one size fits all" mentality is too prominent in education today and causes much controversy. It results in groups taking sides and battling (e.g., behaviorists versus constructivists, whole language advocates versus code-emphasis advocates, and direct instruction advocates versus social constructivists). Dixon and Carnine (1994) comment on this condition:

> Every ideology—not just constructivism or behaviorism—has its fringe elements, variously described as radical constructivists or fanatical behaviorists. When the educational fringe groups declare war, the rest of us expend precious resources responding to charges that are, when stripped of rhetorical trimmings, often groundless.
>
> We suspect that when ideological rhetoric is set aside, mainstream educational researchers' (and other educators') best hope for advancing the field might be realized through our commitment to develop and verify the best possible curricular and instructional practices—best in the sense of effectively resulting in well-understood knowledge for all learners, and doing so efficiently, particularly for those children for whom efficiency is no luxury. (p. 364)

Mather and Roberts (1994) note that experience demonstrates that reliance on singular methodologies can result in the system failing particular students. Likewise, Harris and Graham (1994) state,

> We believe that no one intervention or approach can address the complex nature of school success or failure. . . . [F]or students at risk and those challenged by disabilities, we believe that a purposeful, integrated approach to teaching and learning that directly addresses transactional relationships among affective, behavioral, cognitive, developmental, ecological, and social (including family and community) processes of change and outcomes is particularly appropriate and important. (p. 245)

Howell et al. (1993) provide guidelines for choosing an instructional approach. They suggest selecting a more constructivist approach when the student has an adaptive motivational system, has significant prior knowledge of the task, and experiences early success with the task. Moreover, they recommend a more constructivist approach when the task is simple, well defined, conceptual, and able to be completed through a problem-solving strategy. Finally, they note that this approach works best when there is a priority on "learning to learn" and significant time is available.

Howell et al. (1993) recommend a more behavioral approach when the student has a rigid motivational pattern, has limited prior knowledge, and experiences initial failure on the task. Also, they note that the behavioral approach appears to work best when the task is complex, poorly defined, factual, and hazardous; requires a task-specific strategy; is basic to subsequent learning; and must be used with a high level of proficiency. Finally, they note that this approach works best if time is limited and a priority on mastery exists.

Functionalist Approach. The functionalist approach highlights the move toward combining or integrating paradigms to teach learning strategies. The functionalist approach to understanding learning is based on the premise that learning and approaches to promoting learning depend on the individual, the place, and the time. This view of instruction emerged from what Berliner (1989) refers to as "functional psychology." Advocates of a functionalist approach believe that the teacher can "borrow concepts and methods without taking on the ideology of the program of research that is doing the lending" (Berliner, 1989, p. 5). Boring (1957) argues that the functionalist is essentially a pragmatist who takes what works and then uses the most appropriate or available system that best expresses the new general principle.

For the functionalist, effective instruction evolves by attempting to understand the learner at various stages in the acquisition of information and determining when information must be reduced to a simpler form for comprehension. The teacher also must determine when the student should be given the opportunity to explore and construct meaning from experience. As a result, the functionalist attempts to (a) identify the critical strategies that are important for meeting a variety of demands, (b) identify instructional methods that achieve a balance between the role of the teacher and the student at various stages required for acquisition and generalization of strategies and the targeted content or information, and (c) create an instructional environment that guides and supports the student's use of strategies across situations and settings. To accomplish this, the curriculum, instruction, and the environment need to be analyzed, evaluated, and reduced to simple elements to understand them. Subsequently, these components are integrated and the student is immersed in tasks that require natural application and generalization of strategies and the development of belief systems about learning and how to learn.

From the functionalist's viewpoint, neither the reductionist nor the constructivist model can be used as the sole basis for determining instructional practice. As a result, the functionalist may be accused of developing practice without theory. However, the functionalist believes that learning consists of both reductionist and constructivist qualities, and both paradigms are useful in understanding learning and developing instructional programs. Under certain conditions, adhering exclusively to a constructivist or a reductionist approach may be inappropriate for conceptualizing instruction, and such dogmatism may be even harmful to students. However, both paradigms are seen as contributing to the development of instructional practice.

Numerous instructional efforts are based on the functionalist's approach to cognitive instruction, but the most fully developed practices that represent a blend of reductionist and constructivist principles are embodied in the strategies instructional approach (Deshler & Lenz, 1989). The strategies instructional approach first was used as the basis for the development of the Strategies Intervention Model, which was developed by Don Deshler and Jean Schumaker and their colleagues at the University of Kansas Center for Research on Learning. The model was designed for developing a broad range of programs for adolescents with learning disabilities. However, many aspects of the strategies instructional approach are used broadly as the basis for strategy training for both elementary and secondary students. (Chapter 10 describes the Strategies Intervention Model.)

Many features of the strategies instructional approach are based on research from both behavioral and cognitive psychology. Features manifested in cognitive behavior modification and reciprocal teaching also are included directly or are encouraged as part of the model. According to Deshler and Lenz (1989), the approach is based on the premise that the teacher must develop fully three instructional areas for effective instruction. First, the teacher must identify a range of general strategies that can be applied to all content areas as well as specific strategies for learning targeted content (e.g., strategies for learning content and strategies for learning social studies content). This means that the teacher must know the strategies that are most related to success, understand their critical features, and be able to articulate them in meaningful ways to students. These strategies may relate to student motivation, social interactions, or academic performance. Second, the teacher must know how to present information in a manner that induces students to learn when they do not have effective and efficient strategies for acquiring information. The acquisition and generalization of strategies for learning content require explicit instruction that is both intensive and extensive to enhance the time spent teaching strategies to help students learn. Third, the environment in which learning and instruction takes place must facilitate and enhance strategic learning, performance, and competence across all educational settings and interactions.

An underlying principle of the strategies instructional approach is that success is defined by learning important information and not by simply learning a strategy. Instruction in the strategy is seen as a means to more effective and efficient learning and performance. However, initial instruction in some strategies may require the teacher to reduce the demands of learning the content to focus the student's attention on key aspects of the strategy (e.g., practice the strategy on a short segment of content or in high-interest materials). When the student understands the key dimensions of the strategy, the instructional focus immediately centers on applying the strategy to naturally occurring tasks related to learning in the student's environment (e.g., using note-taking strategies for mainstream class lectures or applying test-taking strategies to approach mainstream class tests more efficiently).

Since 1978, at least 60 studies involving more than 1,000 students have demonstrated the appropriateness of various applications of this instructional approach and the benefits that can be achieved for many students with learning disabilities. In addition, ongoing research continues to refine and develop the instructional dimensions of the approach, and current research efforts promise to expand its applications. The critical features of effective strategies instruction exemplify an integrated paradigm approach. (Chapter 10 presents specific instructional procedures and dimensions of this approach.)

Integration Across Academic Areas. Experts in the respective academic areas are promoting the integration or combination of paradigms to meet the needs of diverse learners. In the area of reading, Mather and Roberts (1994) call for combining meaning-emphasis and code-emphasis approaches for teaching students with learning disabilities to read. Kameenui (1993) claims that it is time to abandon the quest for one right method for teaching literacy and to start teaching students to read. Likewise, Stanovich (1994) endorses an integrated reading approach:

> The ideas that self-discovery is the most efficacious mode of learning, that most learning can be characterized as "natural," and that cognitive components should never be isolated or fractionated during the learning process have been useful as tenets for comprehension instruction, but are markedly at variance with what is now known about the best ways to develop word recognition skill. Research has indicated that explicit instruction and teacher-directed strategy training are more efficacious and that this is especially true for at-risk children, children with learning disabilities, and for children with special needs. (p. 259)

In a review of research and practice for teaching communication and language, Warren and Yoder (1994) state,

> We advocate a cross-paradigmatic approach to communication and language intervention because its inherent flexibility fits with what we know at present about the overall process of language acquisition, the relative nature of different intervention approaches, and the nature of human development. This perspective can encompass behavioral approaches (e.g., direct teaching), constructivist approaches (e.g., responsive interaction), and eclectic approaches (e.g., milieu teaching). More importantly, when this approach is guided by empirical, ecologically valid research, we believe it is more likely to lead to optimal intervention than a theoretically cohesive, but narrow or inadequate, approach. (p. 255)

Moreover, in a review of research and practices for teaching writing, Graham and Harris (1994) conclude the following:

> We would like to echo Spiegel's (1992) recommendation that we build bridges between constructivistic programs such as whole language and process writing and "more traditional approaches for the purpose of providing all children with the very best opportunities to meet their literacy needs" (p. 38). . . . As an example, an explicit phonemic awareness training program has been incorporated into Reading Recovery, a popular literacy program based on the principles of constructivism (Juel, 1988). In contrast, it also may be possible to improve the writing of students with special needs by integrating whole language and process writing with skill-oriented instruction. (p. 286)

Finally, in a discussion of research on teaching scientific knowledge to students with mild disabilities, Scruggs and Mastropieri (1994) conclude that the students in the research were capable of engaging in the construction of scientific knowledge (constructivist approach) but the knowledge did not come easily. They report that these students experienced difficulty at all stages of the learning process. Fortunately, these difficulties were overcome through the intensive efforts of special education teachers who worked with the students by using the reductionist approach.

PERSPECTIVE

Once there was a little caterpillar who lived on an Oriental rug. As he crawled around the rug, he heard other caterpillars discussing the relative merits of specific colors and patterns on the rug. Some caterpillars claimed that *red* was the most beautiful color and that it held the key to solving the pattern. Others insisted, "Oh no! *Green* is the key." The discussions became heated, and caterpillars with similar views banded together to exalt their viewpoints and put down other viewpoints. The little caterpillar was confused by all the discussions and unable to decide which group was right. As he nestled in his cocoon he still heard their voices shouting, "Red!" "Green!" "Brown!" Oh, how he wished he knew which group was right!

Soon the little caterpillar became a butterfly. He flapped his wings and began to rise above the rug. As he approached the ceiling, he looked down. He was amazed! On the rug he saw a beautiful mosaic. Although some colors and lines were more prominent than others, all parts were essential to complete the total design.

In the field of learning disabilities, the student, like the rug in the story, is complex. The professionals, like the caterpillars, select different factors to explain or understand the student's problems and generate instructional strategies. The challenge is apparent—educators need to examine the respective paradigms and match the needs of students with the offerings of integrated methodologies. As educators do this, perhaps an integrated mosaic of educational practices will evolve into a vision of practices that are efficient and effective for all students.

DISCUSSION/REVIEW QUESTIONS

1. Describe the basic tenets of the behavioral approach.
2. Identify the major features involved in using curriculum-based measurement to establish performance standards.
3. Discuss the features of individually referenced data systems, and include formats for graphing data.
4. List some guidelines for implementing data-based instruction.
5. Discuss the stages of learning, and present the basic learning principles of the behavioral approach.
6. Discuss the differences between the cognitive and the behavioral approaches.
7. Briefly discuss the information-processing approach, and present the components of an information-processing model.
8. Present the differences between the reductionist and constructivist paradigms.
9. Discuss the use of cognitive behavior modification and reciprocal teaching.

10. Discuss the functionalist approach to understanding learning, and present the strategies instructional approach.

REFERENCES

Alberto, P. A., & Troutman, A. C. (1995). *Applied behavior analysis for teachers* (4th ed.). Upper Saddle River, NJ: Merrill/Prentice Hall.

Allington, R. L. (1984). So what is the problem? Whose problem is it? *Topics in Learning and Learning Disabilities, 3*(4), 91–99.

Ames, L. B. (1968). Learning disabilities: The developmental point of view. In H. R. Myklebust (Ed.), *Progress in learning disabilities* (Vol. 1, pp. 39–74). New York: Grune & Stratton.

Ausubel, D. P. (1960). The use of advance organizers in the learning and retention of meaningful verbal material. *Journal of Educational Psychology, 51,* 267–272.

Ayllon, T., & Azrin, N. H. (1964). Reinforcement and instructions with mental patients. *Journal of the Experimental Analysis of Behavior, 7,* 327–331.

Baumeister, A. A., & Kellas, G. (1986). Process variables in the paired-associate learning of retardates. In N. R. Ellis (Ed.), *International review of research in retardation.* New York: Academic Press.

Bender, L. (1957). Specific reading disability as a maturational lag. *Bulletin of the Orton Society, 7,* 9–18.

Bereiter, C., & Engelmann, S. E. (1966). *Teaching disadvantaged children in the preschool.* Upper Saddle River, NJ: Prentice Hall.

Berliner, D. C. (1989). The place of process-product research in developing the agenda for research on teacher thinking. In J. Lowyck & C. Clark (Eds.), *Teacher thinking and professional action* (pp. 3–21). Belgium: Leuven University Press.

Bohannon, R. (1975). *Direct and daily measurement procedures in the identification and treatment of reading behaviors of children in special education.* Unpublished doctoral dissertation, University of Washington, Seattle.

Boring, E. G. (1957). *A history of experimental psychology.* New York: Appleton Century-Crofts.

Brophy, J., & Good, T. (1986). Teacher behavior and student achievement. In M. C. Wittrock (Ed.), *Third handbook of research on teaching* (3rd ed., pp. 328–375). Upper Saddle River, NJ: Prentice Hall.

Brown, A. L. (1978). Knowing when, where, and how to remember: A problem of metacognition. In R. Glaser (Ed.), *Advances in instructional psychology.* (Vol. 1, pp. 77–165). Hillsdale, NJ: Lawrence Erlbaum.

Brown, A. L., & Campione, J. C. (1986). Psychological theory and the study of learning disabilities. *American Psychologist, 14,* 1059–1068.

Brown, A. L., Day, J. D., & Jones, R. S. (1983). The development of plans for summarizing texts. *Child Development, 54,* 968–979.

Brown, A. L., & Palincsar, A. S. (1982). Inducing strategic learning from texts by means of informed self-control training. *Topics in Learning and Learning Disabilities, 2*(1), 1–18.

Brown, A. L., & Palincsar, A. S. (1987). Reciprocal teaching of comprehension strategies: A natural history of one program for enhancing learning. In J. Borkowski & J. D. Day (Eds.), *Intelligence and cognition in special children: Comparative studies of giftedness, mental retardation, and learning disabilities.* New York: Ablex.

Bulgren, J. A., Schumaker, J. B., & Deshler, D. D. (1988). Effectiveness of a concept teaching routine in enhancing the performance of LD students in secondary-level mainstream classes. *Learning Disability Quarterly, 11,* 3–17.

Carnine, D. (1989). Teaching complex content to learning disabled students: The role of technology. *Exceptional Children, 55,* 524–533.

Carnine, D. (1990). Beyond technique—Direct instruction and higher-order skills. *Direct Instruction News, 9*(3), 1–13.

Carnine, D. (1992). The missing link in improving schools—Reforming educational leaders. *Direct Instruction News, 11*(3), 25–35.

Carroll, J. B. (1976). Psychometric tests as cognitive tasks: A new "structure of intellect." In L. B. Resnick (Ed.), *The nature of intelligence* (pp. 27–56). Hillsdale, NJ: Lawrence Erlbaum.

Christenson, S. L., Ysseldyke, J. E., & Thurlow, M. L. (1989). Critical instructional factors for students with mild handicaps: An integrative review. *Remedial and Special Education, 10*(5), 21–31.

Deno, S. L. (1987). Curriculum-based measurement. *Teaching Exceptional Children, 20*(1), 41–42.

Deno, S. L., & Mirkin, P. K. (1977). *Data-based program modification.* Reston, VA: Council for Exceptional Children.

Deshler, D. D., Alley, G. R., Warner, M. M., & Schumaker, J. B. (1981). Instructional practices for promoting skill acquisition and generalization in severely learning disabled adolescents. *Learning Disability Quarterly, 4*(4), 415–421.

Deshler, D. D., & Lenz, B. K. (1989). The strategies instructional approach. *International Journal of Disability, Development, and Education, 36*(3), 203–224.

Deshler, D. D. & Schumaker, J. B. (1988). An instructional model for teaching students how to learn. In J. L. Graden, J. E. Zins, & M. J. Curtis (Eds.), *Alternative educational delivery systems: Enhancing instructional options for all students* (pp. 391–411). Washington, DC: National Association of School Psychologists.

Diamond, G. (1983). The birthdate effect—A maturational effect? *Journal of Learning Disabilities, 16,* 161–164.

DiPasquale, G., Moule, A., & Flewelling, R. (1980). The birthdate effect. *Journal of Learning Disabilities, 13,* 234–238.

Dixon, R., & Carnine, D. (1994). Ideologies, practices, and their implications for special education. *The Journal of Special Education, 28,* 356–367.

Ellis, E. S., Lenz, B. K., & Sabornie, E. J. (1987). Generalization and adaptation of learning strategies to natural environments: Part 1: Critical agents. *Remedial and Special Education, 8*(1), 6–20.

Engelmann, S. (1993). Priorities and efficiency. *LD Forum, 18*(2), 5–8.

Englert, C. S., Tarrant, K. L., & Mariage, T. V. (1992). Defining and redefining instructional practice in special education: Perspectives on good teaching. *Teacher Education and Special Education, 15,* 62–86.

Epstein, M., Hallahan, D., & Kauffman, J. (1975). Implications of the reflexivity-impulsivity dimension for special education. *The Journal of Special Education, 9,* 11–25.

Fisher, C. W., & Berliner, D. C. (Eds.). (1985). *Perspectives on instructional time.* New York: Longman.

Flavell, J. H. (1976). Metacognitive aspects of problem solving. In L. B. Resnick (Ed.), *The nature of intelligence.* Hillsdale, NJ: Lawrence Erlbaum.

Frank, A. R. (1973). Breaking down learning tasks: A sequence approach. *Teaching Exceptional Children, 6,* 16–29.

Fuchs, L. S. (1986). Monitoring progress among mildly handicapped pupils: Review of current practice and research. *Remedial and Special Education, 7*(5), 5–12.

Fuchs, L. S., Bahr, C. M., & Rieth, H. J. (1989). Effects of goal structures and performance contingencies on the math performance of adolescents with learning disabilities. *Journal of Learning Disabilities, 22,* 554–560.

Fuchs, L. S., & Fuchs, D. (1986). Effects of systematic formative evaluation: A meta-analysis. *Exceptional Children, 53,* 199–208.

Fuchs, L. S., Fuchs, D., & Deno, S. L. (1985). The importance of goal ambitiousness and goal mastery to student achievement. *Exceptional Children, 52,* 63–71.

Fuchs, L. S., Fuchs, D., & Hamlett, C. L. (1989). Effects of instrumental use of curriculum-based measurement to enhance instructional programs. *Remedial and Special Education, 10*(2), 43–52.

Fuchs, L. S., Fuchs, D., & Maxwell, L. (1988). The validity of informal reading comprehension measures. *Remedial and Special Education, 9*(2), 20–28.

Fuchs, L. S., Wesson, C., Tindal, G., Mirkin, P., & Deno, S. (1981). *Teacher efficiency in continuous evaluation of IEP goals* (Research Report No. 53). Minneapolis: University of Minnesota Institute for Research in Learning Disabilities.

Gagné, E. D. (1985). *The cognitive psychology of school learning.* Boston: Little, Brown.

Gersten, R., Carnine, D., & Woodward, J. (1987). Direct instruction research: The third decade. *Remedial and Special Education, 8*(6), 48–56.

Gersten, R., & Keating, T. (1987). Long-term benefits from direct instruction. *Educational Leadership, 44*(6), 28–31.

Gersten, R., Woodward, J., & Darch, C. (1986). Direct instruction: A research-based approach to curriculum design and teaching. *Exceptional Children, 53,* 17–31.

Good, T. L., & Brophy, J. E. (1986). School effects. In M. C. Wittrock (Ed.), *Handbook of research on teaching* (3rd ed., pp. 570–602). Upper Saddle River, NJ: Prentice Hall.

Graham, S., & Harris, K. R. (1994). Implications of constructivism for teaching writing to students with special needs. *The Journal of Special Education, 28,* 275–289.

Hall, R. J. (1980). Information processing and cognitive training in learning disabled children: An executive level meeting. *Exceptional Educational Quarterly, 1,* 9–15.

Hall, T., & Tindal, G. (1989). Using curriculum-based measures to group students in reading. In G. Tindal, K. Essick, C. Skeen, N. George, & M. George (Eds.),

The Oregon Conference '89: Monograph. Eugene: University of Oregon College of Education.

Hallahan, D. P. (Ed.). (1980). Teaching exceptional children to use cognitive strategies. *Exceptional Education Quarterly, 1,* 1–102.

Hallahan, D. P., & Kauffman, J. M. (1988). *Exceptional children: Introduction to special education* (4th ed.). Upper Saddle River, NJ: Prentice Hall.

Hallahan, D. P., Kauffman, J. M., & Lloyd, J. W. (1995). *Introduction to learning disabilities.* Boston: Allyn & Bacon.

Hallahan, D. P., Lloyd, J., Kosiewicz, M. M., & Kneedler, R. D. (1979). *A comparison of the effects of self-recording and self-assessment on the on-task behavior and academic productivity of a learning disabled boy* (Technical Report No. 13). Charlottesville, VA: University of Virginia Learning Disabilities Research Institute.

Haring, N. G. (1978). Research in the classroom: Problems and procedures. In N. G. Haring, T. C. Lovitt, M. D. Eaton, & C. L. Hansen (Eds.), *The fourth R: Research in the classroom* (pp. 1–22). Upper Saddle River, NJ: Merrill/Prentice Hall.

Harris, K. R., & Graham, S. (1994). Constructivism: Principles, paradigms, and integration. *The Journal of Special Education, 28,* 233–247.

Havertape, J. F., & Kass, C. E. (1978). Examination of problem solving in learning disabled adolescents through verbalized self-instructions. *Learning Disability Quarterly, 1*(4), 94–100.

Horton, D. L., & Bergfeld-Mills, C. (1984). Human learning and memory. *Annual Review of Psychology, 35,* 361–394.

Howell, K. W., Fox, S. L., & Morehead, M. K. (1993). *Curriculum-based evaluation: Teaching and decision making* (2nd ed.). Pacific Grove, CA: Brooks/Cole.

Howell, K. W., Kaplan, J. S., & O'Connell, C. Y. (1979). *Evaluating exceptional children: A task analysis approach.* Upper Saddle River, NJ: Merrill/Prentice Hall.

Hughes, C. A., Schumaker, J. B., Deshler, D. D., & Mercer, C. D. (1993). *Learning strategies curriculum: The test-taking strategy* (Rev. ed.). Lawrence, KS: Edge Enterprises.

Iano, R. P. (1986). The study and development of teaching: With implications for the advancement of special education. *Remedial and Special Education, 7*(5), 50–61.

Idol, L. (1983). *Special educator's consultation handbook.* Austin, TX: PRO-ED.

Juel, C. (1988). Learning to read and write: A longitudinal study of 54 children from first through fourth grade. *Journal of Educational Psychology, 80,* 437–447.

Kameenui, E. J. (1993). Diverse learners and the tyranny of time: Don't fix blame; fix the leaky roof. *The Reading Teacher, 46,* 376–383.

Kavale, K. (1990). Variances and verities in learning disability interventions. In T. E. Scruggs & B. Y. L. Wong (Eds.), *Intervention research in learning disabilities* (pp. 3–33). New York: Springer-Verlag.

Kelly, B. F. (1993/1994). Sacrosanctity versus science: Evidence and educational reform. *Effective School Practices, 12*(4), 24–32.

Keogh, B. K., & Glover, A. T. (1980). The generality and durability of cognitive training. *Exceptional Education Quarterly, 1,* 75–82.

Kerr, M. M., & Nelson, C. M. (1989). *Strategies for managing behavior problems in the classroom* (2nd ed.). Upper Saddle River, NJ: Merrill/Prentice Hall.

Kline, F. M., Schumaker, J. B., & Deshler, D. D. (1991). Development and validation of feedback routines for instructing students with learning disabilities. *Learning Disability Quarterly, 14,* 191–207.

Kneedler, R. D., & Hallahan, D. P. (1981). Self-monitoring of on-task behavior with learning-disabled children: Current studies and directions. *Exceptional Education Quarterly, 2*(3), 73–82.

Koppitz, E. (1972-1973). Special class pupils with learning disabilities: A five-year follow-up study. *Academic Therapy, 8,* 133–139.

Kosiewicz, M. M., Hallahan, D. P., & Lloyd, J. (1981). The effects of an LD student's treatment choice on handwriting performance. *Learning Disability Quarterly, 4*(3), 133–139.

LaBerge, D., & Samuels, S. (1974). Toward a theory of automatic information processing in reading. *Cognitive Psychology, 6,* 293–323.

Lenz, B. K., Alley, G. R., & Schumaker, J. B. (1987). Activating the inactive learner: Advance organizers in the secondary content classroom. *Learning Disability Quarterly, 10*(1), 53–67.

Lenz, B. K., Bulgren, J., & Hudson, P. (1990). Content enhancement: A model for promoting the acquisition of content by individuals with learning disabilities. In T. E. Scruggs & B. Y. L. Wong (Eds.), *Intervention research in learning disabilities* (pp. 122–165). New York: Springer-Verlag.

Lenz, B. K., & Hughes, C. A. (1990). A word identification strategy for adolescents with learning disabilities. *Journal of Learning Disabilities, 23,* 149–158, 163.

Lenz, B. K., Schumaker, J. B., Deshler, D. D., & Beals, V. L. (1984). *The learning strategies curriculum: The word identification strategy.* Lawrence: University of Kansas Center for Research on Learning.

Lerner, J. (1993). *Learning disabilities: Theories, diagnosis, and teaching strategies* (6th ed.). Boston: Houghton Mifflin.

Lindsley, O. (1964). Direct measurement and prosthesis of retarded behavior. *Journal of Education, 147,* 62.

Lindsley, O. R. (1971). Precision teaching in perspective: An interview with Ogden R. Lindsley. *Teaching Exceptional Children, 3*(3), 114–119.

Lloyd, J. (1980). Academic instruction and cognitive techniques: The need for attack strategy training. *Exceptional Education Quarterly, 1,* 53–63.

Lloyd, J., Saltzman, N. J., & Kauffman, J. M. (1981). Predictable generalization in academic learning as a result of preskills and strategy training. *Learning Disability Quarterly, 4,* 203–216.

Loftus, G. R., & Loftus, E. F. (1976). *Human memory: The processing of information.* Hillsdale, NJ: Lawrence Erlbaum.

Loper, A. B. (1980). Metacognitive development: Implications for cognitive training of exceptional children. *Exceptional Education Quarterly, 1,* 1–8.

Maker, C. J. (1981). Problem solving: A general approach to remediation. In D. D. Smith, *Teaching the learning disabled* (pp. 132–166). Upper Saddle River, NJ: Prentice Hall.

Mather, N., & Roberts, R. (1994). Learning disabilities: A field in danger of extinction? *Learning Disabilities Research & Practice, 9,* 49–58.

Mayer, R. E. (1987). *Educational psychology: A cognitive approach.* Boston: Little, Brown.

McKinney, J. D., & Haskins, R. (1980). Cognitive training and the development of problem solving strategies. *Exceptional Education Quarterly, 1,* 41–51.

Meichenbaum, D. (1977). *Cognitive-behavior modification.* New York: Plenum Press.

Meichenbaum, D. (1980). Cognitive behavior modification with exceptional children: A promise yet unfulfilled. *Exceptional Education Quarterly, 1,* 83–88.

Mellard, D. (1989). *Assessment of academic processing deficits* (Technical Report). Frankfort, KY: Office of Education for Exceptional Children, Department of Education, State of Kentucky.

Mercer, C. D., Mercer, A. R., & Evans, S. (1982). The use of frequency in establishing instructional aims. *Journal of Precision Teaching, 3*(3), 57–63.

Mirkin, P., Deno, S., Tindal, G., & Kuehnle, K. (1979). *Formative evaluation: Continued development of data utilization systems* (Research Report No. 23). Minneapolis: University of Minnesota Institute for Research in Learning Disabilities.

Moshman, D. (1982). Exogenous, endogenous, and dialectical constructivism. *Developmental Review, 2,* 371–384.

Myers, P. I., & Hammill, D. D. (1990). *Learning disabilities: Basic concepts, assessment practices, and instructional strategies* (4th ed.). Austin, TX: PRO-ED.

Nation, J. E., & Aram, D. M. (1977). *Diagnosis of speech and language disorders.* Saint Louis: C. V. Mosby.

Nelson, C. M., & Polsgrove, L. (1984). Behavior analysis in special education: White rabbit or white elephant? *Remedial and Special Education, 5*(4), 6–17.

Palincsar, A. S. (1982). *Improving reading comprehension of jr. high school students through reciprocal teaching of comprehension-monitoring strategies.* Unpublished doctoral dissertation, University of Illinois, Urbana.

Palincsar, A. S., & Brown, A. L. (1984). Reciprocal teaching of comprehension fostering and comprehension monitoring activities. *Cognition and Instruction, 1*(2), 117–175.

Palincsar, A. S., & Brown, A. L. (1986). Interactive teaching to promote independent reading from text. *The Reading Teacher, 39,* 771–777.

Paris, S. G., & Winograd, P. (1990). Promoting metacognition and motivation of exceptional children. *Remedial and Special Education, 11*(6), 7–15.

Perfetti, C. A. (1985). *Reading ability.* New York: Oxford University Press.

Piaget, J. (1970). Piaget's theory. In P. H. Mussen (Ed.), *Carmichael's manual of child psychology* (Vol. 1, 3rd ed., pp. 703–732). New York: Wiley.

Piaget, J. (1972). Problems of equilibration. In C. F. Nodine, J. M. Gallagher, & R. H. Humphreys (Eds.), *Piaget and Inhelder: On equilibration.* Philadelphia: The Jean Piaget Society.

Poplin, M. S. (1987). Self-imposed blindness: The scientific method in education. *Remedial and Special Education, 8*(6), 31–37.

Porter, A. C., & Brophy, J. (1988). Synthesis of research on good teaching: Insights from the work of the Institute for Research on Teaching. *Educational Leadership, 45*(8), 74–85.

Posner, M. I., & McLeod, D. (1982). Information processing models—In search of elementary operations. *Annual Review of Psychology, 33,* 477–514.

Pressley, M., Goodchild, F., Fleet, J., Zajchowski, R., & Evans, E. (1989). The challenges of classroom strategy instruction. *The Elementary School Journal, 89,* 301–342.

Reid, D. K. (1978). Genevan theory and the education of exceptional children. In J. M. Gallagher & J. A. Easley (Eds.), *Knowledge and development: Vol. 2. Piaget and education.* New York: Plenum.

Reid, D. K. (1988). *Teaching the learning disabled: A cognitive developmental approach.* Boston: Allyn & Bacon.

Reid, D. K., & Stone, C. A. (1991). Why is cognitive instruction effective? Underlying learning mechanisms. *Remedial and Special Education, 12*(3), 8–19.

Rich, H. L., & Ross, S. M. (1989). Students' time on learning tasks in special education. *Exceptional Children, 55,* 508–515.

Rieth, H., & Evertson, C. (1988). Variables related to the effective instruction of difficult-to-teach children. *Focus on Exceptional Children, 20*(5), 1–8.

Rooney, K. J., & Hallahan, D. P. (1985). Future directions for cognitive behavior modification research: The quest for cognitive change. *Remedial and Special Education, 6*(2), 46–51.

Rosenberg, M. S., & Jackson, L. (1988). Theoretical models and special education: The impact of varying world views on service delivery and research. *Remedial and Special Education, 9*(3), 26–34.

Rosenshine, B. V. (1986). Synthesis of research on explicit teaching. *Educational Leadership, 43*(7), 60–69.

Rosenshine, B., & Stevens, R. (1986). Teaching functions. In M. C. Wittrock (Ed.), *Handbook of research on teaching* (3rd ed., pp. 376–391). Upper Saddle River, NJ:Merrill/Prentice Hall.

Samuels, S. J. (1987). Information-processing abilities and reading. *Journal of Learning Disabilities, 20,* 18–22.

Schumaker, J. B., Deshler, D. D., Alley, G. R., & Warner, M. M. (1983). Toward the development of an intervention model for learning disabled adolescents: The University of Kansas Institute. *Exceptional Education Quarterly, 4,* 45–74.

Scruggs, T. E., & Mastropieri, M. A. (1994). The construction of scientific knowledge by students with mild disabilities. *The Journal of Special Education, 28,* 307–321.

Siegler, R. S. (1986). *Children's thinking.* Upper Saddle River, NJ: Prentice Hall.

Silver, A., & Hagin, R. (1966). Maturation of perceptual functions in children with specific reading disabilities. *The Reading Teacher, 19,* 253–259.

Sindelar, P. T., Smith, M. A., Harriman, N. E., Hale, R. L., & Wilson, R. J. (1986). Teaching effectiveness in special education programs. *The Journal of Special Education, 20,* 195–207.

Smith, D. D. (1981). *Teaching the learning disabled.* Upper Saddle River, NJ: Prentice Hall.

Smith, D. D., & Lovitt, T. C. (1976). The differential effects of reinforcement contingencies on arithmetic performance. *Journal of Learning Disabilities, 9,* 21–29.

Smith, D. D., & Luckasson, R. (1992). *Introduction to special education: Teaching in an age of challenge.* Boston: Allyn & Bacon.

Spiegel, D. (1992). Blending whole language and systematic direct instruction. *The Reading Teacher, 46,* 38–44.

Stanovich, K. E. (1986). Mathew effects in reading: Some consequences of individual differences in the acquisition of literacy. *Reading Research Quarterly, 21,* 360–407.

Stanovich, K. E. (1994). Constructivism in reading education. *The Journal of Special Education, 28,* 259–274.

Stevens, R., & Rosenshine, B. (1981). Advances in research on teaching. *Exceptional Education Quarterly, 2*(1), 1–9.

Swanson, H. L. (1981). Modification of comprehension deficits in learning disabled children. *Learning Disability Quarterly, 4,* 189–201.

Swanson, H. L. (1986). Do semantic memory deficiencies underlie learning disabled readers' encoding process? *Journal of Experimental Child Psychology, 41,* 461–488.

Swanson, H. L. (1987a). Information processing theory and learning disabilities: An overview. *Journal of Learning Disabilities, 20,* 3–7.

Swanson, H. L. (1987b). Information processing theory and learning disabilities: A commentary and future perspective. *Journal of Learning Disabilities, 20,* 155–171.

Tarver, S. G. (1986). Cognitive behavior modification, direct instruction and holistic approaches to the education of students with learning disabilities. *Journal of Learning Disabilities, 19,* 368–375.

Tindal, G. A., & Marston, D. B. (1990). *Classroom-based assessment: Evaluating instructional outcomes.* Upper Saddle River, NJ: Merrill/Prentice Hall.

Torgesen, J. K. (1977a). Memorization processes in reading-disabled children. *Journal of Educational Psychology, 79,* 571–578.

Torgesen, J. K. (1977b). The role of nonspecific factors in the task performance of learning disabled children: A theoretical assessment. *Journal of Learning Disabilities, 10,* 27–34.

Torgesen, J. (1982). The learning disabled child as an inactive learner: Educational implications. *Topics in Learning and Learning Disabilities, 2,* 45–52.

Torgesen, J. K., & Morgan, S. (1990). Phonological synthesis tasks: A developmental, functional, and componential analysis. In H. L. Swanson & B. Keogh (Eds.), *Learning disabilities: Theoretical and research issues* (pp. 263–276). Hillsdale, NJ: Lawrence Erlbaum.

Treiber, F. A., & Lahey, B. B. (1983). Toward a behavioral model of academic remediation with learning disabled children. *Journal of Learning Disabilities, 16,* 111–116.

Turnure, J. E. (1985). Communication and cues in the functional cognition of the mentally retarded. In N. R. Ellis & N. W. Bray (Eds.), *International review of research in mental retardation.* New York: Academic Press.

Turnure, J. E. (1986). Instruction and cognitive development: Coordinating communication and cues. *Exceptional Children, 53,* 109–117.

Van Reusen, A. K., Bos, C. S., Schumaker, J. B., & Deshler, D. D. (1987). *The learning strategies curriculum: The educational planning strategy.* Lawrence, KS: Edge Enterprises.

Vygotsky, L. S. (1978). *Mind in society: The development of higher psychological processes.* Cambridge: Harvard University Press.

Wagner, R. K., & Torgesen, J. K. (1987). The nature of phonological processing and its causal role in the acquisition of reading skills. *Psychological Bulletin, 101,* 192–212.

Warren, S. F., & Yoder, P. J. (1994). Communication and language intervention: Why a constructivist approach is insufficient. *The Journal of Special Education, 28,* 148–158.

Wesson, C. L. (1987). Increasing efficiency. *Teaching Exceptional Children, 20*(1), 46–47.

Wesson, C. L., King, R. P., & Deno, S. L. (1984). Direct and frequent measurement of student performance: If it's good for us, why don't we do it? *Learning Disability Quarterly, 7,* 45–48.

White, O. R. (1986). Precision teaching—Precision learning. *Exceptional Children, 52,* 522–534.

White, O. R., & Haring, N. G. (1980). *Exceptional teaching* (2nd ed.). Upper Saddle River, NJ: Merrill/ Prentice Hall.

Wong, B. Y. L. (1980). Activating the inactive learner: Use of questions/prompts to enhance comprehension and retention of implied information in learning disabled children. *Learning Disability Quarterly, 3,* 29–37.

Early Identification and Intervention

CHAPTER 9

After studying this chapter, you should be able to:

- discuss the rationale for early identification and intervention.
- discuss the legislative support for early identification and intervention.
- present key issues in early identification.
- discuss prediction research in early identification.
- discuss early identification guidelines from prediction studies.
- list commonly used screening tests and tests for identification and program planning.
- discuss service delivery options for early childhood special education students.
- present the major curriculum models used in early childhood education programs.
- discuss the types of effective programs in early intervention.
- present guidelines for early intervention programs.
- describe commercial early childhood education programs.
- describe computer software programs in early childhood education.

Young children who exhibit atypical patterns of development in cognition, language, social skills, personal behaviors, or motor abilities in preschool or primary grades are referred to as *at-risk* or *high-risk* children and are considered to be a high risk for later school problems. Many of these high-risk children are referred to special education and eventually become identified as having learning disabilities. During the last decade, the area of early identification and treatment of these children has received substantial support from legislators, parents, and professionals in medicine, psychology, language, and education. It is well documented that a child's development in these early years is critical to cognitive and emotional growth in later years. Most experts believe that many learning, social, emotional, and educational problems can be prevented or corrected if identification and intervention are provided in preschool or kindergarten.

Unfortunately, the need for early identification and intervention is becoming even more critical because of the growing number of infants affected by substance abuse. In a nationwide hospital survey, the National Association for Perinatal Addiction Research and Education (1988) found that at least 11% of all pregnant women surveyed used illegal drugs during pregnancy. Because many of these children display characteristics associated with learning disabilities (Jenks, 1990), they likely will be placed in programs for students with learning disabilities.

SUPPORT FOR EARLY CHILDHOOD EDUCATION

Early intervention significantly benefits high-risk children. Undoubtedly, the now-classic studies of Skeels (1966) and Kirk (1958) initiated the interest in early intervention, which eventually mushroomed into a commitment at the national level. This support is reflected in the federal legislation designed to provide early intervention and related services.

Rationale for Early Identification and Intervention

Before the 1960s, a child's development was viewed primarily as unalterable and fixed by heredity. The beginning of early identification and intervention can be traced to the recognition that intelligence and other human abilities are not fixed at birth. The important conclusion that the development of learning and behavior during infancy and the preschool years can have a substantial influence on intellectual functioning was triggered primarily by two studies and two books.

Skodak and Skeels (Skeels, 1966) conducted a study to determine the effects of early intervention. They selected an experimental group of 13 children under 3 years of age. The average IQ of the group was 64, and 11 of the children were classified as retarded. A contrast group of 12 children under 3 years of age was selected. The average IQ of this group was 86, and 10 were classified as intellectually normal. The contrast group remained in an orphanage and received adequate health and nutritional services. Overall, the environment was not very stimulating. The experimental group was transferred to a state school, where they received care on a one-to-one basis from adolescent patients who were retarded. Each adolescent was given instructions on how to care for the child.

At the end of 2 years, the 13-member experimental group showed a mean gain in IQ of 28 points, and after about 5 years, 11 of them were adopted and placed in good homes. A follow-up after 25½ years revealed highly significant differences in the two groups. For example, 11 members of the experimental group married and had a total of nine children, all of normal intelligence. In the contrast group, two had married and had a total of five children, with one diagnosed as retarded. The experimental group completed a median of 12 grades, whereas the contrast group completed a median of less than 3 grades. All experimental subjects were either self-supporting or functioning as homemakers, and one of them received a bachelor of arts degree. In the contrast group, four members were institutionalized and unemployed. In general, the occupational level for the experimental group was much higher than that of the contrast group. Skeels (1966) concluded that the findings of this study suggest that sufficient knowledge is available to design programs of intervention to counteract the devastating effects of poverty, sociocultural, and maternal deprivation.

In the second major study, Kirk (1958) measured the effects of an enrichment program on the social and mental growth of 81 preschoolers who were retarded. He divided the children into four groups. The experimental children (18 living at home and 15 living in an institution) attended nursery schools, but the control children (26 living at home and 12 in an institution) did not. In a short time, the experimental children achieved IQ gains ranging from 10 to 30 points, whereas the IQs of the control children declined. Over a period of years, the differences between the groups were maintained.

The first book that served as a catalyst to change views about fixed intelligence was *Intelligence and Experience* by J. McVicker Hunt (1961). Hunt presented a comprehensive review of research on intellectual development and environmental influences, and he included two primary recommendations: (a) consider the early years as the most critical stage in human development, and (b) promote environmental stimulation to accelerate the intellectual growth in young children.

The second book that helped change the notion of fixed intelligence was *Stability and Change in Human Characteristics* by Benjamin Bloom (1964). Bloom presented a review of longitudinal studies on human development and provided data to support three premises concerning the critical nature of early experiences: (a) variations in early experiences influence human characteristics, (b) environment and early experience remain important because human growth is cumulative, and (c) initial learning is easier than corrective learning.

McCormick (1994) captures the influence of these classic works in the following passage: "The conclusions of the research and publications of this period regarding the positive impact that early stimulation can have on preventing and reversing developmental deficits may not seem that 'earthshaking' now, but they were startling ideas at the time, and they were extremely important catalysts for changes in attitude" (p. 91).

Moreover, recent research supports the effect of early intervention on improving children's intellectual performance and academic achievement. From a study of three early intervention programs, Ramey and Ramey (1992) found that the benefits of continuous intervention during the first 5 years of life last at least until early adolescence. Also, they note that early intervention reduces the rate of failing a grade in elementary school by almost 50%. In addition, research indicates that if prediction of the onset of reading disabilities is made during the primary grades and leads to early intervention before the third grade, the child's chances of developing appropriate reading skills greatly increase. Lyon (1995) reports that longitudinal studies show that if children with reading disabilities are not identified until the third grade or beyond, about 74% will continue to manifest reading deficits throughout their school and adult years. According to Slavin, Karweit, and Wasik (1992/1993), "Success in the early grades does not guarantee success throughout the school years and beyond, but failure in the early grades does virtually guarantee failure in later schooling" (p. 11). Thus, the importance of early identification and intervention is apparent.

B
early Interv supp

Legislative Support

The Head Start legislation, funded in 1964 and administered through the Office of Economic Opportunity, was the first signal of legislative concern for the education of young children with special needs. Although the original legislation targeted children who were disadvantaged and failed to mention children with disabilities, it was a beginning effort toward federal support for early intervention.

In 1968, the Handicapped Children's Early Education Assistance Act (Public Law 90-538) was passed. This law established funds for demonstration programs for infants and preschoolers with disabilities and their families. The projects funded through Public Law 90-538—the First Chance or Handicapped Children's Early Education Program (now titled the Early Education Program for Children with Disabilities)—continue to facilitate services and research for infants and preschoolers with special needs and their families.

After the enactment of Public Law 90-538, early intervention for children with disabilities received a tremendous boost from the passage of Public Law 92-424 (Economic Opportunity Amendments) in 1972. This law requires Head Start centers to use 10% of their enrollments for preschoolers with disabling conditions.

Public Law 94-142, the Education for All Handicapped Children Act, was passed in 1975 and implemented in 1978. This law mandates that all individuals with disabilities age 3 to 21 years must have access to a free, appropriate public education. Moreover, it includes incentive funds, the Incentive Grant Program, to states for providing preschool programs for children with disabilities. Unfortunately, the Public Law 94-142 requirement for children age 3 to 5 years is too weak to have had a major effect on early intervention programs. States could choose not to serve these children if the mandate was incompatible with existing state laws. Some states used this as a loophole to avoid serving young children with disabilities; however, Public Law 94-142 represents formal endorsement of early intervention efforts and remains an important milestone in the history of early education for individuals with disabilities.

In 1986, Public Law 99-457, which amends Public Law 94-142 and officially extends its rights and provisions to infants and preschoolers, was passed. This law requires a statewide system for comprehensive interdisciplinary services to children from birth through 2 years of age. This statewide system must include a program of public awareness, a central directory of services, and a program of personnel preparation. Public Law 99-457 also extends services for 3- to 5-year old children with special needs. Starting in 1990, this age group began receiving the same services and protections (e.g., full and appropriate education, due process, and court appeals) available to school-age children. A major difference between Public Law 94-142 and Public Law 99-457 is the latter's emphasis on support for families and their involvement in programming.

In 1990, Public Law 101-476 was passed. This law renamed the Education for All Handicapped Children Act as the Individuals with Disabilities Education Act (IDEA), and throughout the text of the law the term *handicapped* was replaced by the term *disabilities*. In reference to young children, the law indicates that early intervention programs are to be developed to address the needs of children prenatally exposed to substance abuse.

Finally, in 1991, Public Law 102-119 was passed. It expands Public Law 99-457 and amends IDEA to provide comprehensive services to preschool children with disabilities and their families. Services are permitted (but not mandated) for infants and toddlers with disabilities (birth through age 2) who are identified with a developmental delay (i.e., a lag in cognitive, physical, communication, social and emotional, or adaptive development) or are at risk for developing a developmental delay, and financial assistance is offered to states to develop plans to meet the needs of these youngsters. Children from birth through age 2 must receive a multidisciplinary evaluation that includes an assessment of the family's strengths and needs related to enhancing the child's development, and an individual family service plan that emphasizes the role of the family must be developed to guide intervention. Moreover, states must serve preschool children, age 3 through 5, who are eligible through a noncategorical identification (such as developmental delay) or a category of disability. Either an individual educational program or an individual family service plan may be used to foster development and preacademic learning skills.

From this brief review of legislation, it is apparent that professionals and our society in general recognize the importance of early intervention for infants and young children with special needs. McCormick (1994) notes that national efforts are under way to ensure that resources are available to maximize the development of infants, toddlers, and preschoolers with special needs.

EARLY IDENTIFICATION

The early identification of a child as *at risk* must be approached cautiously. Identification involves predicting the future development of a child and placing the child in a special program. To date, diagnostic procedures are improving but remain imprecise, and the possibility of inaccurate predictions must be considered. Misdiagnosis can be detrimental to the child and the family. This section presents issues in early identification, prediction research in early identification, perspectives and guidelines from prediction studies, and practices in early identification.

Issues in Early Identification

The early identification of at-risk children is a complex task. Variability in development and maturation is normal across preschoolers without disabilities. Given that variability is common, the determination of discrepancies signaling that a child is at risk for learning problems becomes difficult. Because the early indicators of a learning disability are often subtle, the problem of early identification of these students is even more difficult. These conditions and other factors contribute to several early-identification issues that must be considered. Key issues are discussed within the following topics: (a) tenuous diagnosis, (b) developmental differences, (c) labeling, (d) multiple influences on developmental progress, and (e) miscellaneous factors.

Tenuous Diagnosis. Identification procedures often lack sophistication, especially where youngsters with mild disabilities are concerned. Children with severe disabilities display symptoms and behaviors that enable a diagnostician to identify a very young at-risk child confidently. However, the problem of early detection becomes greater in the field of learning disabilities. The early warning signals of specific learning disabilities may be subtle, vary in degree, and occur within a wide range of behaviors. For example, a child with Strauss syndrome may be identified readily during the preschool years, whereas a child with reading problems may not be identified accurately until the first or second grade.

Developmental Differences. The possibility of maturational lag or developmental imbalances poses another problem in early identification. During the early years of rapid growth, individual children may exhibit unique developmental patterns. For some, the central nervous system develops slowly. These children may exhibit perceptual-motor and attention problems. The central nervous system also may develop in a differential manner, causing the child to demonstrate high ability in one area (e.g., language) but limited skills in another area (e.g., fine motor). However, as the central nervous system matures, such problems may diminish. These unique patterns make it difficult to determine whether a child is high-risk or simply needs more time to mature. The National Joint Committee on Learning Disabilities (1986) reports that at-risk indicators do not always predict which child is in jeopardy of future developmental deficits and at risk for learning disabilities. Consequently, they recommend that these young children be observed over time to ascertain whether growth and development follow expected patterns.

Because it is extremely difficult to evaluate the development of the central nervous system, the best practice is to assist the child whom the diagnostician suspects is high-risk. If the diagnosis is

correct, the child receives the needed educational intervention. If the diagnosis is incorrect, the child usually benefits from the extra instruction.

Labeling. Labeling has become a major issue. Because the accurate detection of high-risk children is difficult, many children are mislabeled. Some authorities believe that labels affect teacher expectations (i.e., a teacher who knows that a child is labeled *learning disabled* will expect certain behaviors). Such expectations may have a negative influence on the child's educational progress. It is purported that the teacher expects less and accepts less from the labeled child in academic performance and social behavior. In addition, labels tend to give children a stigma among peers who may view them negatively and openly say so.

If teachers could avoid developing negative expectancies, the problem of labeling would be reduced greatly. As mentioned, early intervention by a trained teacher likely will benefit any child who receives it. However, without safeguards, early identification has a built-in expectancy phenomenon that may be harmful.

Multiple Influences on Developmental Progress. The National Joint Committee on Learning Disabilities (1986) reports that an effective identification program must be sensitive to the numerous biological and environmental factors that influence a preschooler's development. For example, Kochanek, Kabacoff, and Lipsitt (1990) analyzed child-centered data (from birth to 7 years) and familial factors as predictors of disabilities in adolescence. They found that parental traits (such as maternal education) are better predictors than the child's own behavior from birth to 3 years, whereas child-centered skills evaluated at 4 and 7 years of age are better predictors than familial factors. Kochanek et al. conclude that early identification models that primarily focus on adverse medical events or developmental delay from birth to age 3 are inadequate for predicting later disabilities. They recommend multivariate screening procedures (child and family focused) that account for differential effects of risk factors over time. It is apparent that numerous variables compound the difficulty of identification.

Keogh and Weisner (1993) discuss risk factors (i.e., negative conditions that impede or threaten normal development) and protective factors (i.e., conditions or events that increase the likelihood of a positive developmental outcome despite exposure to risk) that may contribute to the educational and personal-social development of at-risk children. Risk and protective indicators include economic status; child data such as developmental and intellectual level; family data such as configuration and parental employment; measures of the child's educational, social, emotional, and behavior problems and competencies; and family accommodations such as parents' work load and extended family supports. Keogh and Weisner indicate that the ecocultural context (child, family, and social) is an important consideration in predictions about risk conditions and that both risk and protective influences must be taken into account in identification and intervention planning. In addition, they note that identification and prediction based on aggregated data are more valid than predictions based on single indicators.

Because a prediction instrument forecasts whether a child will have later learning problems, the value of the instrument must be considered in terms of the child's environment (e.g., educational program and home support). For example, the accuracy of a high-risk prediction may depend on the type of educational program provided or on teacher differences (Fedoruk & Norman, 1991). If intervention is effective, the child will perform well, and the prediction power of the initial assessment appears to be low. In essence, a high-risk label must be tentative if the multiple influences and interaction possibilities are considered.

Miscellaneous Factors. Several other significant problems exist regarding early identification:

1. The reliability and validity of many prediction instruments remain uncertain; however, research (Lindsay & Wedell, 1982; Miller & Sprong, 1986; Wilson & Reichmuth, 1985) and texts (McLoughlin & Lewis, 1994; Salvia & Ysseldyke, 1995) offer some guidelines.
2. Assessment data used for identification often lack classroom relevance. For example, a poor performance on a *Bender Visual Motor Gestalt Test* does not translate readily into teaching goals.
3. The historical data on preschoolers frequently are inaccurate or unavailable. Parents often cannot recall information (e.g., developmental milestones or infant diseases) essential to clinical evaluation.

Conclusion. Early identification and intervention have enough support to warrant substantial emphasis. Experts (Good, Kaminski, Schwarz, & Doyle, 1990; National Joint Committee on Learning Disabilities, 1986) stress the need to monitor the progress of preschoolers and primary-grade children to ensure the validity of prediction decisions and maintain appropriate programming. Figure 9.1 shows that continuous evaluation is essential for those identified as high-risk to work themselves into the general education program and for low- or no-risk children who do not make adequate progress to receive special intervention. This open-door approach and flexible programming reduce the negative effects on children who are not identified accurately.

The problems involved in early identification and programming behoove professionals to delineate the best practices. In recognition of the need to identify best practices, the following sections review early identification practices and programs.

Prediction Research in Early Identification

Numerous research projects have tried to identify potential learning problems in young children. These studies focus primarily on predicting poor achievement or underachievement rather than predicting a specific condition (e.g., emotional disability, slow learner, or learning disability). Academic underachievement implies objective measurement and encompasses a broader population than usually is implied from the term *learning disabilities*. Early screening identifies children who are likely to perform poorly in school, and not all such children fit the usual definition of learning disability. However, one common characteristic is poor achievement or underachievement. Fortunately, much research exists in the area of predicting poor academic achievement, and this research is beneficial for improving early identification practices. Because practices related to children with moderate or mild disabilities appear to have more implications for learning disabilities than practices related to children with severe disabilities, the moderate/mild area is the focus of this section.

Prediction Techniques. Prediction techniques may be categorized into three areas: *battery of tests*, *single instrument*, and *teacher perception*. A battery of tests may consist of any

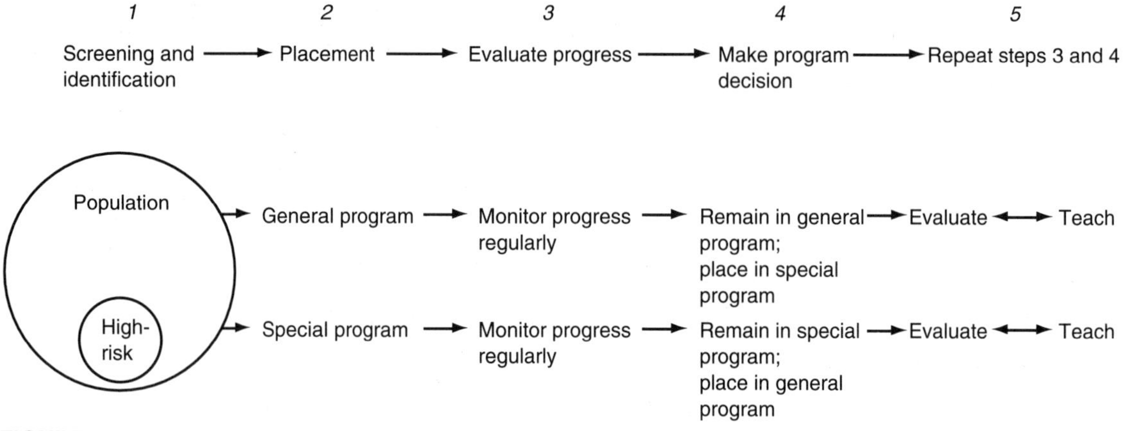

FIGURE 9.1
Steps in programming for high-risk children

combination of tests, subtests, and single-variable measures. A global score or a pattern of scores is used for prediction. For the most part, a teacher administers a battery individually; thus, it requires more time than single instruments.

In the single instrument technique, the teacher uses one instrument or index as a prediction measure. When one instrument (usually a standardized test consisting of several subtests) is used, the total score often becomes the predictor. Also, the teacher can use a single variable for prediction (e.g., an alphabet-recognition score or a subtest of a standardized instrument). Because of time and cost considerations, the teacher must note whether single instruments are administered to groups or to individuals.

Teacher perception involves a teacher identifying high-risk children by observation. The teacher may use a checklist or a scale, or simply be asked to list the high-risk children. Generally, teacher perception requires less time and cost than single instruments and batteries.

Multiple-Instrument Batteries as Predictors. In the establishment of early screening and identification programs, the research on batteries deserves inspection. It provides data about which subtests are most useful in identifying high-risk children. For example, Badian (1988) reports that the language-oriented subtests of the *Holbrook Screening Battery* are good predictors, whereas visual-motor tasks are poor predictors. Moreover, Roth, McCaul, and Barnes (1993) studied the predictive value of a kindergarten screening battery and found that the fine motor modality consistently is a strong predictor of later difficulties in school. Analysis of batteries eventually may yield the delicate combination of variables needed for highly accurate identification of high-risk children during or before kindergarten; however, to date, special predictive batteries have yet to yield high enough predictive validity to compensate for their disadvantages in cost, effort, and time.

Single Instruments as Predictors. The majority of prediction studies use single instruments as predictors. These instruments are categorized as readiness, intelligence, language, or perceptual-motor tests.

1. *Readiness tests*. Hammill and McNutt (1981) discuss the relationship of many single instruments to reading achievement. They found that the Alphabet Knowledge subtest of the *Metropolitan Readiness Test* is a good

predictor. Moreover, Busch (1980) conducted a prediction study and found that the Letters and Sounds subtest (a readiness subtest) of the *Stanford Early School Achievement Test* is a good predictor. Overall, readiness tests appear to be excellent predictors of later reading achievement, with knowledge of letters and sounds being the most critical area.

2. *Intelligence tests*. Group-administered intelligence tests appear to predict reading achievement a little better than individually administered tests. This is an interesting finding when one considers that individually administered intelligence tests require much more training and time to administer. According to Hammill and McNutt's (1981) work, the *Lorge Thorndike* appears to be especially effective. Overall, intelligence tests appear to be good predictors of reading achievement.
3. *Language tests*. Many theorists and researchers contend that adequate language development is a precursor to academic achievement. Language skills develop rapidly during the preschool years. A test for delay in language development might predict later academic failure. Busch's (1980) findings indicate that the *Boehm Test of Basic Concepts* predicts reading achievement well.
4. *Perceptual-motor tests*. The *Bender Visual Motor Gestalt Test* frequently is used to identify high-risk children. Also, Morrison and Mantzicopoulos (1990) examined the use of SEARCH (Silver & Hagin, 1981) to predict reading achievement of kindergartners. SEARCH includes 10 subtests that primarily assess perceptual-motor skills believed to be basic to beginning reading. However, SEARCH yields high error rates, and Mantzicopoulos and Morrison (1994) suggest that factors other than perceptual delays (e.g., behavioral and cognitive characteristics) also may contribute to the development of learning difficulties. Overall, it does not appear that current perceptual or motor tests predict reading achievement.

Teacher Perception as a Predictor. A simple procedure for identifying high-risk children is to ask the teacher. Most studies use a scale or checklist. In the Busch (1980) study of 17 predictors, the *Behavior Rating Scale* (teacher perception) was the second best predictor. Moreover, Coleman and Dover (1993) studied the predictive validity of a rating scale screening measure and found that kindergarten teachers' ratings of their students can be used to predict, with substantial accuracy, the likelihood that children will experience future difficulties in school that require special education services. Also, Mantzicopoulos and Morrison (1994) found that kindergarten teachers' judgments of learning problems are accurate indicators of future reading performance, especially where test-based (SEARCH) misclassifications occurred. Thus, teacher observations may be a key factor in the early identification of learning disabilities. It appears that teacher perception coupled with the use of other instruments may yield high accuracy in screening for potential learning problems.

Commentary on Prediction Research. The prediction research provides professionals with useful information regarding the effectiveness of various screening measures. The inclusion of reliable and valid measures reduces the possibility of identification errors. Screening measures yield an 80% to 90% overall hit rate (i.e., total number of correctly identified children); thus, professionals are able to identify high-risk preschoolers and kindergartners with reasonable accuracy. Appropriate early intervention prevents or corrects the learning or social problems of many high-risk children. This creates an ethical issue regarding prediction studies. Prediction studies typically test and then follow up on students to see if they become good or poor achievers. During this follow-up period, at-risk children receive appropriate interventions. Although these interventions interfere with predictions (e.g., early intervention can help a child who is predicted to do poorly to actually perform well), the choice to wait and see

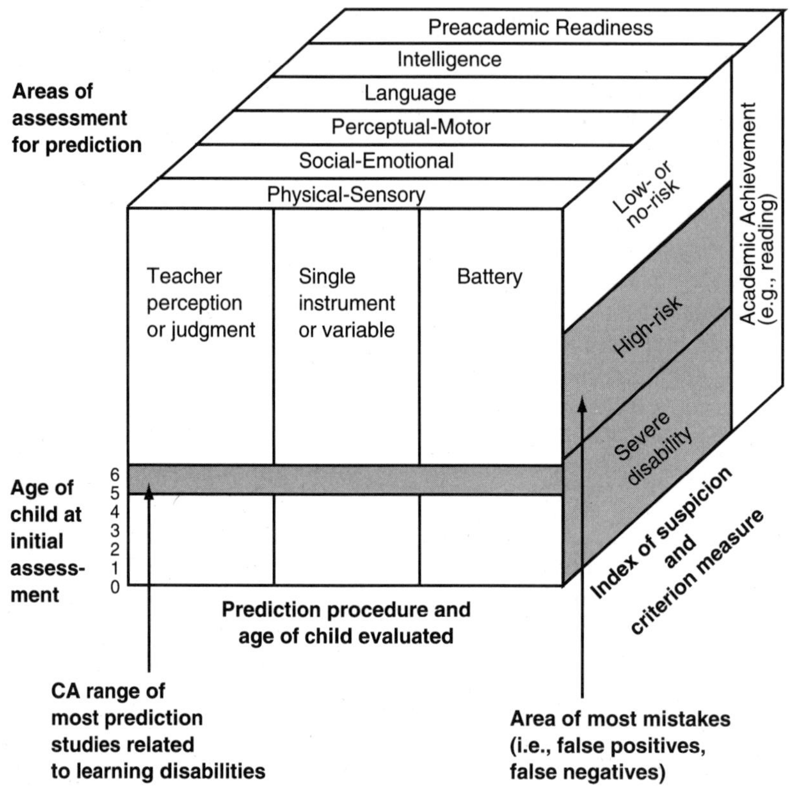

FIGURE 9.2
Components of early screening

if learning problems occur is not an acceptable option when considering that specific early interventions are effective. Thus, identification without follow-up interventions is unethical.

Perspectives and Guidelines from Prediction Studies

It is important to note that early identification without follow-up intervention is useless as well as unethical. Further, as shown previously in Figure 9.1, placement in and out of programs must depend on feedback about children's progress.

Selecting Areas of Assessment. Figure 9.2 presents the major factors that deserve consideration when one is choosing a screening instrument. Initially, one needs to choose which area of assessment will provide relevant information and adequately predict to the criterion measure.

Identification should focus on whether the preschool child has the skills and abilities to succeed in kindergarten or whether the kindergartner has the skills to succeed in first grade. Preacademic skills in reading, math, and language usually are stressed when screening and criterion measures are close in content and time. The recognition of specific skills and abilities provides information that often aids the development of an instructional or prevention program. In addition, the assessment of skills similar to tasks performed in kindergarten or first grade helps determine the child's specific instructional objectives.

Although they are frequently omitted, the social and emotional areas deserve more consideration. High-risk individuals can be detected by the assessment of temperament, attention, self-regulation, and social interaction patterns (National Joint Committee on Learning Disabilities, 1986). All behaviors deserve more study, but existing information provides support for the use of preacademic, language, and intelligence to screen for high-risk children. Other areas (especially social and emotional) may be added if time and resources are available.

Determining Prediction Procedures. The major procedures for selection are teacher perception, single instrument, and battery. All three may be used to assess one or more areas. In addition, a unique battery may be formed using a combination of single measures (which may be combined with teacher perception). Existing data support certain single instruments (e.g., the *Metropolitan Readiness Test* or the *Lorge Thorndike*) and teacher perception.

Beginning Identification. The emphasis of IDEA on providing a free, appropriate public education to the young child with disabilities stresses the need for better identification at younger ages. This area needs more study about physical indices, developmental history, language, and socioeconomic status in the early identification of high-risk infants and preschool children. Karnes, Linnemeyer, and Schwedel (1981) reviewed the limited research on programs for infants with disabilities and generated four conclusions: (a) infancy intervention is helpful, (b) bonding is difficult with an infant with disabilities, and parents need help in this area, (c) multidisciplinary team skills are needed, and (d) parents are the child's first teachers, and they need help with this role.

Choosing a Criterion Measure. The criterion measure, in essence, represents reality; thus, it should be relevant and valid. Prediction studies primarily use reading achievement. Other measures include placement level of a child in a reading group, performance in other academic areas, special education placement, and teacher judgment.

Establishing an Index of Suspicion. Determining the index of suspicion (i.e., degree of disabling condition) is often critical. This factor controls whether or not a child receives special intervention. A major consideration at this step is to establish a cutoff score that provides the desired balance between false positives (those who were predicted to do poorly but actually performed well) and false negatives (those who were predicted to do well but actually performed poorly). False positives may be tolerable when the program is designed to minimize the potential debilitating effects of labeling and allows children the opportunity to work themselves back into general education. False negatives may be tolerable if the no-risk status is not a static decision and children who actually need special intervention are recognized soon by sensitive teachers or measures. In most instances, the exclusion of a child who needs special intervention is a more serious error than the inclusion of a child who does not need it. However, for special education purposes the high-risk child is one who is likely to experience serious learning or adjustment problems.

Practices in Early Identification

Some preschool and kindergarten children who exhibit attention problems, delays in language acquisition, or unusual patterns of visual-motor development are identified as having a developmental delay. During the primary grades, after instruction has been provided in academic areas, additional evaluation is needed to determine whether learning disabilities is the appropriate diagnosis. This section presents the phases of assessment as well as screening instruments and tests for identification and program planning.

Assessment Model. Assessment for early identification and intervention includes numerous phases. Each phase addresses different questions and involves the collection of specific information. Peterson (1987) presents six separate but related phases of the assessment process in an early identification and intervention program. The following sequence includes the assessment types, purposes, and questions to be answered.

1. *Casefinding:* to alert individuals to children who may have special needs and to elicit help in screening. (Does the child exhibit any unusual behavior or development that indicates referral for screening?)
2. *Screening:* to identify children who are not within normal ranges of development and need further evaluation or placement in early intervention programs. (Does the child show evidence of potential problems or abnormalities that indicate a need for further diagnostic evaluations or intervention?)
3. *Identifying:* to determine the nature and severity of the problem through an in-depth evaluation and prescribe treatment or intervention services. (How severe is the problem, and what type of intervention is needed?)
4. *Planning program:* to obtain level of functioning and other performance data for developing an individualized educational program. (In what areas is special instruction needed, and what special services and curriculum should be provided?)
5. *Monitoring performance:* to track the child's mastery of new skills as a result of activities in the intervention program. (Is the child making continuous progress, and are the teaching methods producing the desired learning?)
6. *Evaluating program:* to determine the quality of the intervention program and document its effect on the children or parents it serves. (How effective is the program in regard to the child's performance and developmental gains, and are persons associated with the program satisfied with its services?)

Tests and Procedures. The prediction research discussed earlier in this chapter primarily involves the use of screening instruments. Screening determines overall levels of functioning and identifies children who may have a developmental delay and are potentially at risk for learning and behavior problems. Descriptions of selected screening instruments are presented in Table 9.1.

Once a specific developmental problem is suspected from screening data, the child and family should be referred to qualified professionals for an interdisciplinary team evaluation. Members of this team of professionals assess the child's sensory functions, motor functions, cognition, language, preacademic readiness skills, and social and emotional factors. This interdisciplinary approach is used to obtain and interpret assessment information from various sources to determine the child's specific patterns of abilities and disabilities. In the following passage, the National Joint Committee on Learning Disabilities (1986) provides some important guidelines for this assessment process:

> In some cases, an extended period of assessment and observation is necessary to determine a child's status and needs. Time-limited placement in a diagnostic preschool setting can be a useful means of addressing diagnostic questions, determining the child's developmental age, abilities, and deficits, and evaluating various intervention methods for the individual child. . . . The child's developmental age and accomplishments as well as previous opportunities and experiences will determine the extent to which early academic skills are present on school entry. The variability in a child's readiness for academic learning and instruction reflects cognitive, communicative, social, and emotional growth as well as physical and neurological maturation. Readiness for academic instruction is related more to differential rates of development than chronological age. An integrated perspective on the child's functioning in various areas of growth and development is essential. Such a perspective must be maintained when interpreting assessment results and planning educational placement and instructional approaches appropriate to the child's status and needs. (p. 159)

TABLE 9.1
Selected Screening Instruments

Instrument	Age Level
AGS Early Screening Profiles (Harrison et al., 1990)	2–6 years
This ecological assessment battery uses multiple domains, settings, and sources to identify children who are at risk of experiencing later learning problems. The test is individually administered and consists of three profiles: (a) cognitive/language—reasoning skills, visual organization and discrimination, receptive and expressive vocabulary, and basic school skills, (b) motor—gross and fine motor skills such as walking a straight line, imitating arm and leg movements, and drawing shapes, and (c) self help/social—viewpoints of the child's level of development in the areas of communication, daily living skills, socialization, and motor skills as indicated on a questionnaire completed by the parent or teacher. In addition, four surveys provide information on the child's articulation, behavior, health history, and home environment. The entire battery or portions of it can be administered by nonprofessionals, and administration time ranges from 15 to 40 minutes.	
DABERON—2 Screening for School Readiness (Danzer, Gerber, Lyons, & Voress, 1991)	4–6 years
This individually administered standardized screening scale assesses school readiness and can help identify instructional objectives. The 122 test items sample knowledge of body parts, color and number concepts, gross motor development, categorization, and other developmental abilities that relate to early academic success. The scale can be administered in 20 to 40 minutes and yields a learning readiness equivalency age score that can be used to identify children at risk for school failure. A classroom summary form and a report on readiness form are included.	
Denver Developmental Screening Test—II (Frankenburg et al., 1990)	2 weeks–6 years
This individually administered, norm-referenced instrument is designed to detect delayed development in young children. The 125 items are arranged in a developmental sequence in four general areas: (a) personal-social—ability to relate to other people and to take care of one's self, (b) fine motor-adaptive—ability to draw and manipulate objects, (c) language—ability to perceive, understand, and express language, and (d) gross motor—ability to sit, walk, and jump. Each test item is represented on the test form with an indication of the age at which 25%, 50%, 75%, and 90% of the children in the standardization sample passed the item. A delay in development is considered when the child fails an item that is passed by 90% of younger children. Results of the child's performance also are interpreted as suspect, untestable, or normal. Administration time is 15 to 20 minutes.	
Developmental Indicators for the Assessment of Learning—Revised (DIAL-R) (Mardell-Czudnowski & Goldenberg, 1990)	2–5 years
The *DIAL-R* is an individually administered screening test that assesses motor, conceptual, and language skills and indicates social and emotional development. For ease in screening large numbers of children, the test features a station format in which different examiners administer portions of the test to children who move from one testing area (station) to another. At each of the three stations, the children complete eight items involving age-appropriate tasks using blocks, shapes, a beanbag, and six unique dials that reveal a single stimulus at a time. Percentile ranks and standard scores are provided. The test can be administered in 20 to 30 minutes, and minimal training is required.	

In a survey of teachers in programs funded through the Precise Early Education of Children with Handicaps (PEECH) outreach project, Johnson and Beauchamp (1987) found that the following tests were used most frequently: *Brigance Diagnostic Inventory of Early Development* (46%), *Learning Accomplishment Profile* (39%), and *Systematic Classroom Observation Assessment Programming* (26%). Moreover, from a nationwide survey, Esterly and Griffin (1987) compiled the following list of some of the major assessment instruments: (a) *Basic School Skills Inventory—Diagnostic*, (b) *Kaufman Assessment Battery for Children*, (c) *Test of Early Language Development*, (d) *Test of Early Reading Ability*, (e) *Developmental Indicators for the Assessment of Learning—Revised*, (f) *Learning Accomplishment Profile*, (g) *Inventory of Early Development*, (h) *Bender Visual Motor Gestalt Test*, (i) *Developmental Test of Visual-Motor Integration*, (j) *Bruininks-Osteretsky Test of Motor Deficiency*, (k) *Peabody Picture Vocabulary Test*, and (l) *Denver Developmental Screening Test*.

If screening indicates that a child has a possible problem in readiness for school achievement, the deficit skill area should be examined more closely to help determine objectives for instruction. Table 9.2 presents selected commonly used tests for identification and program planning. Procedures for monitoring progress and evaluating program effectiveness are presented in the data-based instruction section of Chapter 8.

PROVIDING EARLY INTERVENTION SERVICES

Public Law 99-457 and the early childhood amendments (Public Law 102-119) represent the most extensive federal policy ever implemented for early childhood intervention. This legislation increases incentives for states to serve children from 3 through 5 years of age and establishes discretionary programs for services to children from birth through 2 years of age; thus, it is stimulating an unparalleled increase in early intervention programs. The future of early intervention is being shaped by state policies and their respective perceptions of optimal service delivery systems. In a survey of all 50 states and the District of Columbia regarding early intervention policies, Meisels, Harbin, Modigliani, and Olson (1988) found extensive variation among state policies. They report that entitlement is a major variable related to the quality of state early intervention services. An entitlement recognizes the right of all children to avail themselves of a service, whereas a mandate requires only that a service be provided. At the time of the Meisels et al. survey, 16 states had entitlements beginning at age 3, 4 states began at age 4, 17 states began at age 5, and 8 states had no entitlements for services to children below age 6.

Public Law 99-457 mandates the creation of interagency coordinating councils to guide each state's lead agency in the coordination of early childhood services. Karp (1990) identifies difficulties facing these councils and provides strategies to help them operate successfully. Her strategies focus on the following areas: getting membership, defining roles, committing to common goals and consensus building, developing a clear vision of the system, achieving short-term goals, and understanding political strategies.

Service Delivery Options

Generally, three service models commonly are used for early childhood special education services: home-based, center-based, and a combination. In a home-based service model, the child's parent is the primary teacher. For example, in the Portage Project in Portage, WI, a home teacher visits the home once a week to aid parents in assessing the child's present skill level, demonstrate instructional procedures, monitor the child's progress, and set new objectives. Thus, in a home-based program the child is taught in a natural setting and the parent is involved in the child's learning. In contrast, in a center-based model, the child is brought to a facility several times a week for 3 to 5 hours of instruction each

TABLE 9.2
Selected Tests for Identification and Program Planning

Instrument	Age Level
Brigance Diagnostic Inventory of Early Development—Revised (Brigance, 1991)	Birth–7 years
This individually administered criterion-referenced inventory is sequenced by task analysis and determines psychomotor, self-help, communication, general knowledge and comprehension, and academic skill levels. The skill sequences include assessments in developmental, readiness, and early academic skills in 11 content areas: preambulatory motor, gross motor, fine motor, self-help, speech and language, general knowledge and comprehension, social and emotional development, readiness, basic reading, manuscript writing, and basic math. The inventory provides a systematic performance record expressed in developmental ages.	
Test of Children's Language (Barenbaum & Newcomer, 1996)	5–8 years
The test helps in identifying children's strengths and weaknesses in language components and in recognizing youngsters who are at risk for failure in reading and writing. Unit 1 of the test uses a storybook format to ensure children's ability in spoken language and reading. Specific skills include semantics, syntax, and listening comprehension as well as knowledge about print, phonological awareness, and letter knowledge. Additional items assess word recognition and reading comprehension. Unit 2 includes a series of writing tasks divided into three parts: (a) copying, writing from dictation, spelling, and writing vocabulary words, (b) writing a story the student has read previously, and (c) writing an original story about the animal characters in the storybook. The test is designed for use with individuals and can be administered in about 30 to 40 minutes.	
Test of Early Language Development—2 (Hresko, Reid, & Hammill, 1991)	3–7 years
This individually administered test provides information directly related to the semantic (content) and syntactic (form) aspects of language. The items can be administered in about 20 minutes and assess receptive and expressive language using a variety of semantic and syntactic tasks.	
Test of Early Mathematics Ability—2 (Ginsburg & Baroody, 1990)	3–8 years
This test of early math functioning takes about 5 to 10 minutes to administer and measures informal as well as formal (school-taught) concepts and skills. Items in informal mathematics focus on concepts of relative magnitude, counting skills, and calculation, and items in formal mathematics focus on reading and writing numerals, number facts, calculational algorithms, and base-ten concepts. Results are reported as standard scores, percentiles, or age equivalents.	
Test of Early Reading Ability—2 (Reid, Hresko, & Hammill, 1989)	3–9 years
The test measures the actual reading ability of young children through items that focus on knowledge of contextual meaning (print in the environment, relations among vocabulary, and print in connected discourse), alphabet (letter naming, oral reading, and proofreading), and conventions of written language (book handling and other practices). Two alternative forms are available as well as a computer software scoring system.	

continued

TABLE 9.2
continued

Instrument	Age Level
Test of Early Written Language—2 (Hresko, Herron, & Peak, 1996)	3–10 years
The test includes two forms, each with a Basic Writing and a Contextual Writing subtest. The Basic Writing subtest measures a child's ability in such areas as spelling, capitalization, punctuation, sentence construction, and metacognitive knowledge. The Contextual Writing subtest measures a child's ability to construct a story when provided with a picture prompt, and the subtest focuses on such areas as story format, cohesion, thematic maturity, ideation, and story structure. Administration time is 30 to 45 minutes; the test provides standard score quotient, percentiles, and age equivalents.	
Test of Phonological Awareness (Torgesen & Bryant, 1994b)	5–7 years
This test measures young children's awareness of the individual sounds in words and can be used to identify children who may profit from instructional activities to enhance their phonological awareness in preparation for reading instruction. Both the kindergarten version and the early elementary version can be administered either individually or to groups in about 20 minutes.	
Wechsler Preschool and Primary Scale of Intelligence—Revised (Wechsler, 1989)	3–7 years
This standardized measure of intellectual abilities in young children contains 12 subtests. The Verbal Scale subtests are Information, Comprehension, Arithmetic, Vocabulary, Similarities, and Sentences (optional), and the Performance Scale subtests include Object Assembly, Geometric Design, Block Design, Mazes, Picture Completion, and Animal Pegs (optional). The test requires about 1 hour and 15 minutes to administer and yields Verbal, Performance, and Full-Scale IQ scores.	

day. In the Model Preschool Program at the University of Washington, instructional objectives are based on the needs and developmental stages of the child. Finally, home- and center-based models provide flexibility to meet the child's needs. The PEECH Project at the University of Illinois features an individualized educational program that focuses on all areas of development and includes significant family involvement in all program aspects. With all three types of service models, when the child reaches kindergarten, the cascade of service options discussed in Chapter 6 is applicable.

Ramey and Ramey (1992) found that early intervention in center-based programs that is supplemented with home visits to help parents learn how to provide good developmental stimulation is more effective than only center-based or home-based services. Likewise, in a follow-up study of children receiving a home parent training intervention and children receiving a clinic-based intervention, Eiserman, Weber, and McCoun (1995) found that the two groups performed similarly on measures of speech and language functioning, general development, and family functioning. Thus, Eiserman et al. support the importance of offering parents a broad range of role options in their child's early intervention services.

With the proliferation of early intervention programs, two issues have emerged regarding service options (Edmister & Ekstrand, 1987). The question of what is an appropriate program for preschoolers is being debated. Specifically, are half-day programs sufficient or are full-day programs necessary? Edmister and Ekstrand report that research results support the position that for many preschoolers with disabilities, half-day programs meet the requisite for a free, appropriate public education. For kindergartners, Karweit (1992) notes that full-day programs appear to have modest positive effects for at-risk children, but little evidence substantiates long-term positive effects of full-day kindergarten attendance. A second issue concerns inclusion and is discussed in the next section.

Preschoolers in Inclusive Settings. Several barriers exist regarding the placement of preschoolers with disabilities in their least restrictive environment. Because most public school districts do not provide programs for preschoolers, classrooms are not available for integrating preschoolers with and without disabilities in a school setting. Moreover, some confusion exists concerning whether IDEA is being interpreted as requiring the least restrictive environment option for preschoolers. Despite these barriers, it is apparent that the placement of preschoolers with disabilities in inclusive environments has strong support. McCormick (1994) provides some compelling arguments for placing preschoolers in inclusive settings:

1. Maximum exposure to and experiences with peers who do not have disabilities are the primary means by which children with special needs can learn the ways of the normal world.
2. Settings that include only children with disabilities provide limited socialization experiences.
3. Young children with disabilities must have continuous opportunities to observe and imitate normal same-age peers.
4. Early integration encourages positive attitudes and the awareness that children with disabilities are more similar to their peers without disabilities than they are different.

Cole, Mills, Dale, and Jenkins (1991) examined the effects of preschool integration for children with disabilities and found that lower-performing children made greater gains in segregated settings, whereas higher-performing children made greater gains in integrated settings. Cole et al. note that preschool teachers in integrated settings should monitor the instructional and social environment to ensure that lower-functioning students are receiving appropriate simulation. Moreover, Edmister and Ekstrand (1987) report that the documented benefit from the integration of preschoolers with and without disabilities is in the social domain. For example, Jenkins, Odom, and Speltz (1989) investigated the effects of integrating preschoolers with and without disabilities. Their data reveal that structuring social interactions between higher- and lower-performing children can benefit the lower-performing students.

The National Joint Committee on Learning Disabilities (1986) offers the following recommendation regarding program options:

> A continuum of program and service options must be available if preschool children with specific developmental deficits are to be served appropriately. Programs should be mandated through appropriate federal and state legislation. State agencies need to enforce a continuum of service options, provide appropriate funding, and promote interagency cooperation between the public and private section. (p. 160)

Inclusion in the Primary Grades. Unlike the situation of preschoolers, it is apparent that the least restrictive environment requirement of IDEA applies to students with disabilities in the primary grades (i.e., kindergarten to second grade). In a synthesis of the research on interventions for at-risk students, Slavin and Madden (1989) report that pullout special education and Chapter I programs are criticized widely. They note that these programs, at best, keep at-risk students from becoming further behind their age-mates. Moreover, the instruction often is integrated poorly with the general education program. Slavin and Madden report that selected classroom change programs have yielded good achievement with at-risk children. Specific

components of effective classroom change programs are presented later in this chapter.

Curriculum Models

The major curriculum models used in early childhood education programs for children with special needs are developmental, cognitive, behavioral, and combination. (Detailed descriptions of the behavioral and cognitive orientations are presented in Chapter 8.) Moreover, the primary curriculum orientations in early childhood programs stress ecological factors in planning instruction. (The ecological orientation is discussed in Chapter 7.) Brief descriptions of the major models are presented next.

Developmental Model. The developmental model features an enrichment curriculum based on the "whole child" theory of early education. The model stresses all aspects of child growth—physical, emotional, language, social, and cognitive development. The enrichment curriculum is based on the premise that under favorable circumstances the child's inner need to learn will emerge and develop. The curriculum features numerous experiences and learning opportunities. The classroom includes special activity areas and many stimulating materials that promote play and creative expression. Field trips, storytelling, and conversations are encouraged. The teacher orchestrates a flexible schedule of events and capitalizes on opportunities for informal learning. The child development model is used widely in standard nursery school programs. This model has received limited support for use with at-risk children and children with disabilities.

Cognitive Model. Most cognitive-oriented models are based primarily on the work of Piaget. A major focus is on the development of children's cognitive or thinking abilities. Stages of cognitive development are used to plan appropriate instructional activities to facilitate such thinking skills as memory, discrimination, problem solving, concept formation, language, and comprehension. Recently, cognitive theorists have focused on helping children develop metacognitive skills and independent problem-solving skills. For example, Missiuna and Samuels (1989) report excellent learning results when preschool children with developmental problems received mediation instruction. The mediation instruction included teaching general rules and strategies that transcended the specific learning situation. Problem-solving strategies were used, and the children were required to review processes used to derive answers. Moreover, Sainato, Strain, Lefebvre, and Rapp (1990) used a self-evaluation treatment package to help preschoolers with disabilities learn to maintain high levels of appropriate behavior. The Perry Preschool Project (Berrueta-Clement, Schweinhart, Barnett, Epstein, & Weikart, 1984) is an example of the cognitive model for at-risk preschool children.

Behavioral Model. The behavioral model is based on concepts from reinforcement theory and direct instruction. This approach features reinforcement, mastery learning, measurable goals, observable behaviors, direct teaching, and data-based instruction. The teacher arranges instructional environments to facilitate targeted behaviors. This approach has received extensive support for developing preacademic and academic skills with at-risk children and children with disabilities.

Combination Model. Most early intervention programs use elements from several models. A common finding regarding the cognitive and behavioral models is that each has demonstrated success in achieving its respective learning goals. In a nationwide survey of preschool programs for children with learning disabilities, Esterly and Griffin (1987) found that many preschool programs feature a broad range of curriculum goals. For example, they found that major programming elements included preacademic skills, motor skills, socialization, and a high level of structure. Moreover, after conducting a follow-up study of children who participated in two contrasting early intervention programs (i.e., mediated learning and direct instruction), Mills, Dale, Cole, and Jenkins (1995) suggest that children may benefit more from a cognitively based approach during early states of development, whereas as they progress to a higher level of functioning, they may gain more from direct academic instruction. Thus, one particular instructional model may not be the most appropriate for all students.

Because program results tend to match the expectations of specific models, it appears that a well-founded program would include a combination of model objectives and activities. Children can enjoy the best of several approaches if they participate in a program that features some structure, direct academic intervention, daily charting of progress, free-choice activities, developmental task activities, and spontaneous learning experiences.

McCormick (1994) notes that all three curriculum models have expanded to include a more naturalistic perspective. This has resulted in naturalistic curriculum models in which the goal is to increase the young child's control, participation, and interaction in natural environments. In these models, the natural environment is the source of curriculum content, and it provides the settings and criteria for evaluating progress.

Wolery (1987) suggests that preschool programs should engage in evaluating specific activities and their effect on learning outcomes. He notes that outcome studies should focus on specific intervention strategies rather than on curriculum models. Wolery provides guidelines for conducting such studies and points out that they would help answer the question, What interventions are most appropriate for infants and children under specific conditions? Selected intervention strategies used in early programs for at-risk students and students with disabilities are presented in the next section.

Effective Practices in Early Intervention

From an extensive review of the research on early interventions, Slavin and Madden (1989) report on programs that produced significant gains in student achievement. The interventions were provided to at-risk children who exhibited the following characteristics: low achievement, grade retention, behavior problems, poor attendance, low socioeconomic status, and attendance at schools with large numbers of poor students. The research included students in Chapter I, special education, or other remedial services. For a program to be considered effective, Slavin and Madden used the following criteria:

1. The program could be replicated in other school sites.
2. The program was evaluated for at least one semester and was compared with a control group or yielded convincing year-to-year gains. Studies that used fall-to-spring gains were omitted.
3. The program produced effects in reading or math of at least 25% of an individual standard deviation. Essentially, this translates into a minimal effect size of +.25. Slavin and Madden note that this level is both educationally and statistically significant.

The effective programs are discussed in three categories: prevention, classroom change, and supplementary/remedial.

Prevention Programs. Educators have shown an increased emphasis in developing intense early childhood education programs that reduce or eliminate the need for remedial services later. These prevention programs are typically in preschool, kindergarten, or first grade. Slavin and Madden (1989) report that preschool and extended-day kindergarten programs have not produced lasting effects on achievement. Children who are disadvantaged often exhibit immediate improvement in language and IQ scores, but these effects diminish by second or third grade. Overall, these programs help students get a good start, but in isolation they usually are not sufficient to reduce students' risk of school failure.

However, follow-up studies of students who participated in preschool programs are yielding some positive findings. Rothenberg (1990) reports results of an 8-year follow-up study of students who participated in a kindergarten prevention program. The program focused on teaching the students a hierarchy of basic skills. Compared with a control group of at-risk children, the experimental group achieved significantly higher academic gains in first, third, fifth, and seventh grades. Moreover, Berrueta-Clement et al. (1984) note that the longitudinal data from young adults show positive effects of preschool attendance on such outcomes as secondary school graduation and delinquency. Slavin, Karweit, and Madden (1989) report that the programs listed in Table 9.3 are effective kindergarten and first-grade programs.

Classroom Change Programs. A logical way to reduce the number of children who will need remedial services is to provide the best possible classroom instruction in the first place. Teachers should use instructional methods that have proven to be effective in accelerating the achievement of at-risk students. Slavin and Madden (1989) report that almost all programs with convincing evidence of effectiveness fall into two categories: continuous progress models and selected forms of cooperative learning. The effective programs in these categories identified by Slavin et al. (1989) are presented in Table 9.4. In the continuous progress models, students progress at their individual pace through a sequence of instructional objectives. Students are taught in small groups of similar-skill classmates. Frequent assessment guides regrouping decisions. In the cooperative learning models, students work in small teams to master material presented earlier by the teacher. The rewarding of team members based on the achievement of each individual learner is consistently effective in producing positive learning outcomes. The cooperative learning methods combined with continuous progress programs have proven to be highly successful.

Supplementary/Remedial Programs. These programs usually are offered outside the general classroom and are in addition to the regular curriculum. Slavin and Madden (1989) note that the widely used diagnostic-prescriptive pullout special education and Chapter I programs that have produced convincing evidence of effectiveness are categorized into remedial tutoring programs and computer-assisted instruction.

First-grade prevention programs typically use certified teachers or paraprofessionals, whereas remedial tutoring programs tend to involve volunteers or older students. The remedial programs presented in Table 9.5, which Slavin et al. (1989) found to be most effective, all use one-to-one tutoring. Also, remedial tutoring programs are applied across several grades (e.g., first through sixth grade). Programs used in first and second grades are considered to be early intervention programs.

Becker (1987) reports that the quality of computer-assisted instruction varies a great deal and that research has yielded inconsistent results. Slavin and Madden (1989) report that a few computer-assisted instruction models

TABLE 9.3
Kindergarten and First-Grade Prevention Programs

Program	Location	Grade
Alpha Phonics	San Francisco, CA	K
In this reading-readiness program, the letters of the alphabet are introduced one at a time in a 26-week sequence. There are six lessons for each letter, and the student learns to name the letter, write it, and locate uppercase and lowercase examples of the letter. A gamelike presentation is used, and the program features immediate correction and feedback.		
Astra's Magic Math	San Francisco, CA	K
In this math-readiness program, an outer-space theme is used to introduce 22 math concepts in a sequenced manner. A multisensory approach is used, and the self-contained units cover concepts such as shapes, matching, size comparison, counting and recognition of numbers 0–30, number sequences, addition and subtraction of the numerals 0–5, and time in hours.		
Early Childhood Preventative Curriculum	Miami, FL	1
High-risk first graders are put into a special class during first grade where they are provided with an individualized diagnostic-prescriptive program. The individual strengths and weaknesses of each student are identified. Instruction is given in small skill-level groups, and students are allowed to proceed at their own rate.		
Make Every Child Capable of Achieving (MECCA)	Trumbull Public Schools, CT	K
This diagnostic-prescriptive program features daily observation, assessment, and planning for specialized teaching according to students' needs. Additional instruction is prescribed by a team composed of the classroom aide, a learning disabilities specialist, and the classroom teacher and is provided in the classroom based on a task analysis of the learning activity. The specialized instruction is given either individually or in small groups, and the lessons are structured to give children practice in increasingly more difficult skills in the learning activity in which they are experiencing difficulty.		
Multisensory Approach to Reading and Reading Readiness Curriculum (MARC)	Florida Educational Resource	K–1
This continuous-progress reading program for children in kindergarten and first grade focuses on increasing readiness skills in the areas of letter recognition and auditory perception of beginning sounds. When introducing letters, the teacher follows specific steps (called *linkages*) that link the visual, auditory, and kinesthetic approaches.		

continued

TABLE 9.3
continued

Program	Location	Grade
Prevention of Learning Disabilities—New York	New York University Medical Center	1–2
This is a 2-year program in which students are screened for deficits in sensory skills related to reading at the kindergarten or first-grade level. Students who are found to be deficient receive tutoring three to five times a week in small groups (two to three students) with a resource teacher.		
Programmed Tutorial Reading	Farmington, UT	1
Paraprofessionals provide one-to-one tutoring to first graders in the bottom quartile in reading. The highly structured tutoring process features the use of programmed materials based on the basal series used in the school. The tutor is instructed on where to start, what to say, when to praise, and how to respond to errors. In addition to a sight word approach, students are taught word analysis and passage comprehension skills.		
Project TALK	Rockford, IL	K–3
To improve expressive and receptive language skills of children in kindergarten through third grade, a language specialist provides instruction to the class twice a week for 30 minutes over a 6-month period. The classroom teacher observes and participates in demonstration lessons and then conducts follow-up lessons twice a week.		
Reading Recovery	The Ohio State University	1
In this preventative tutoring model, first-grade students who are diagnosed as having reading difficulties receive one-to-one tutoring from a specially trained tutor for 30 minutes a day. Instruction emphasizes having students read aloud from minibooks and write their own stories. The tutor is a certified teacher who is trained over the course of a full school year, and trainers observe sessions and provide detailed feedback.		

have been evaluated as being successful. They note that the most consistently effective programs, as presented in Table 9.6, are products of the Computer Curriculum Corporation's drill-and-practice programs. To date, the positive effects have been moderate, and the costs remain expensive.

Early Education Programs for Children with Disabilities. The findings regarding the effectiveness of early intervention come primarily from studies involving children who are disadvantaged or at risk. The variables of parental involvement, structure, duration, and age of the child (i.e., the younger the child, the more positive the effect) consistently are associated with successful early intervention programs. Casto and Mastropieri (1986) examined the efficacy of early intervention programs involving only preschool children with disabilities. They applied a meta-analysis to 74 studies that were carefully screened for quality. Their findings led to the following conclusions: (a) early intervention with preschoolers with disabilities is effective, (b) longer, more intense programs are associated with positive results, (c) the degree of structure yields mixed results, and data remain inconclusive, (d) involvement of parents can be effective, but their involvement is not essential to success, and (e) the notion of "the earlier, the better" is not supported (i.e., some data indicate that children who start later do better).

Guidelines for Early Intervention

An analysis of specific programs and models used with preschoolers and kindergarten children who are at risk or have disabilities provides

TABLE 9.4
Continuous Progress and Cooperative Learning Programs

Program	Location	Grade
Cooperative Integrated Reading and Composition (CIRC)	Johns Hopkins University Center for Research on Elementary and Middle Schools	3–5
CIRC uses a combination of mixed-ability, cooperative work groups and skill-based reading groups to teach reading, language arts, and writing. Students are assigned to pairs within their reading groups, and the pairs are assigned to four- to five-member teams. Teachers work with reading groups to set a purpose for reading, introduce vocabulary, and discuss story characters, setting, and problems. In their teams, students work in pairs on activities such as predicting story outcomes, identifying elements of story structure, and practicing vocabulary, word lists, and spelling. Teachers provide instruction in reading comprehension skills. Students earn points for their team based on the sum of their individual performances on quizzes. The CIRC language arts program focuses on students working together in their teams to plan, draft, revise, edit, and publish compositions.		
Direct Instructional System for Teaching Arithmetic and Reading (DISTAR)	University of Oregon	K–6
DISTAR features a hierarchical curriculum design, direct instruction, a rapid pace, and a high frequency of student responses. Teachers use highly structured, scripted lessons to teach reading and math and are trained to use specific methods. Students are taught in small groups according to skill level, and progress is assessed frequently to determine whether regrouping is necessary. Research indicates that the positive effects of DISTAR can be long-lasting.		
Exemplary Center for Reading Instruction (ERIC)	Utah	1–6
ERIC focuses on teaching specific word-attack skills, and students proceed through a large number of words in a short time. The program features a rapid instructional pace, specific instructions for the teacher, and frequent assessment of student progress. Students receive instruction in their assigned reading group and work on materials at their own rate.		
Goal-Based Educational Management System (GEMS)	Utah	K–12
In this diagnostic-prescriptive reading program, students proceed at their own rate through 200 skill levels covering kindergarten through 12th grade. Students are placed in instructional groups according to pretests or placement tests. Various teaching strategies are used, and students must attain a score of at least 80% on a posttest to finish a unit. Students who do not meet the criterion are given alternate materials and additional time until they pass. A computer management program indicates student progress.		
PEGASUS	Tuscaloosa, AL	K–8
This classic continuous progress program organizes the reading program into 17 levels from kindergarten through eighth grade. Students are taught in groups according to their current level. A continuum of skills must be mastered at each level, and students progress through the levels at their own pace.		
Project INSTRUCT	Lincoln, NE	K–3
Students are grouped according to skill levels in this continuous progress program. There is cross-grade grouping, and students proceed through a hierarchy of skills at their own rate.		

TABLE 9.4
continued

Program	Location	Grade
Team Accelerated Instruction (TAI)	Johns Hopkins University Center for Research on Elementary and Middle Schools	3–6
In this model, cooperative leaning is combined with a continuous progress approach to mathematics instruction. Students are assigned to skill-level groups as well as to mixed-ability learning teams consisting of four or five members. After teachers instruct the skill-level groups on math concepts, the students return to their teams and work on self-instructional programmed materials. The teammates assist one another by checking work, helping with difficult problems, and preparing for quizzes. When students achieve the mastery score on quizzes, points are added to their team score. At the end of the week, the teams that exceed a pre-established criterion of number of units mastered may earn certificates or rewards. Specific procedures and parallel assessments are provided for students who do not achieve at a mastery level.		
Utah System Approach to Individualized Learning (U-SAIL)	Utah	1–9
In this continuous progress program, students proceed through a hierarchical sequence of objectives at their own pace. There is small-group instruction with some individual work. Students are given exploratory activities with an emphasis on independent reading while the teacher is instructing skill-level groups.		

numerous guidelines for early intervention programs for children with learning disabilities. Early intervention efforts have occurred with students who exhibit characteristics associated with learning disabilities (e.g., academic failure, motor deficits, language deficits, and poor social skills). Some apparent guidelines include the following:

1. Given the emphasis on family involvement and services in Public Law 99-457, it is imperative that quality programs for families be developed. Parent services include identifying the needs of individual parents and providing training and support options to meet their needs as they change over time. However, Casto and Mastropieri (1986) note that parent involvement is not always essential to success. Perhaps a key issue is the desire of the parents to participate and the quality of the experiences available for the parents. Stile, Cole, and Garner (1979) summarize the research and identify more than 30 strategies to improve parent involvement. Some of their strategies include the following: (a) provide a realistic orientation to parents about the program and expected outcomes, (b) clearly delineate their role and use a contract if necessary, (c) provide activities for them to do at home (e.g., keeping records of home progress), (d) conduct training in the home and offer to lend parents toys and equipment, (e) follow up initial contacts with continuous services, and (f) identify successful parents and ask them to serve as trainers for new participants.
2. Academically oriented, structured programs yield the greatest short-term gains in reading and math (Slavin & Madden, 1989; Stallings, 1974). Slavin et al. (1989) present a variety of academic programs that have proven to be effective in producing year-to-year academic gains (see Tables 9.3, 9.4, 9.5, and 9.6). Additional information on

TABLE 9.5
Remedial Tutoring Programs

Program	Location	Grade
School Volunteer Development Project	Miami, FL	1–6
Adult volunteer tutors receive training prior to tutoring in a variety of tutoring skills and use of multimedia materials. Underachieving first through sixth graders are tutored for 30 minutes a day on 4 or 5 days a week. For program evaluation, students were randomly assigned to tutored or nontutored conditions for 1 school year, and those students who received tutoring made higher gains in reading and math than the untutored control students.		
Success Controlled Optimal Reading Experience (SCORE)	San Francisco, CA	1–6
SCORE uses highly programmed materials that feature rapid drill and practice in lists of words grouped to teach specific decoding skills. Students with deficient decoding skills are tutored for 15 minutes a day in a structured tutoring session until they complete the program. Evaluation studies show large gains in word recognition and oral reading accuracy in a variety of settings using older students, parent volunteers, and aides as tutors.		
Training for Turnabout Volunteers	Miami, FL	1–6
Volunteer junior high school students receive training involving a specified structured curriculum to tutor low-achieving first through sixth graders in reading and math. The tutorial materials are not programmed. The students work together for 40 minutes on 4 days a week for 16 weeks. On every fifth day, the tutors receive group supervision in which they are given continuing training in the subject matter being taught and in such tutoring skills as rewarding successes, organizing the work, and refraining from criticizing failures. To evaluate the program, a comparison was made between the gains made by students working with the trained tutors versus the gains made by students working with tutors who did not receive continuing supervision but who worked for similar amounts of time with similar students using the same kinds of materials. The gains were significantly greater for both tutors and tutees when the tutors received continuing training.		

these effective instructional programs is provided by the Joint Dissemination Review Panel in *Educational Programs That Work* (available from Sopris West, 1140 Boston Avenue, Longmont, CO 80501).

3. Intervention initiated with infants has been impressive or helpful (Hayden & Haring, 1976; Karnes, Linnemeyer, & Schwedel, 1981). Hayden and Haring report that the earlier the intervention, the better the results. Studies of birth-to-age-3 interventions indicate that IQ can be modified by changing a child's environment at home or in special center-based programs (Slavin et al., 1992/1993). Intensive intervention must be provided over a period of several years to produce lasting effects on measures of cognitive functioning.
4. In summarizing the results of her Follow Through study, Stallings (1974) states:

> A study of the instructional procedures used in classrooms and the achievement of children indicates that time spent in reading and math activities and a high rate of drill, practice, and praise contribute to higher reading and math scores. Children taught by these methods tend to accept responsibility for their failures but not for their successes. Lower absence rates, higher scores on a nonverbal problem-solving test of reasoning can be attributed in part to more open and flexible instructional approaches in which children are provided a wide variety of activities and materials and where children engage independently in activities and select their own groups part of the time. (p. 9)

TABLE 9.6
Programs Using Computer-Assisted Instruction

Program	Location	Grade
Basic Literacy Through Microcomputers	Salt Lake City, UT	1
This program features the use of electric typewriters or microcomputers to practice and apply phonics skills by typing words, sentences, and stories. When compared with students receiving only regular instruction, positive effects on reading were found for the first-grade students.		
Los Angeles Public Schools: Computer Curriculum Corporation	Los Angeles, CA	1–6 (math) 3–6 (reading; language)
The Computer Curriculum Corporation features the use of a mainframe with terminals linked to a central processing unit by telephone. The computer provides students with appropriate exercises and keeps records of performance and progress. To evaluate the curriculum, students randomly were assigned to receive 10 minutes per day of computer-assisted instruction in math, reading, or language as part of a 30-minute Chapter 1 period. The greatest positive effects were found in math computation, reading vocabulary, and language mechanics.		
Merrimack Education Center	Merrimack, MA	2–9
This program uses the Computer Curriculum Corporation reading materials and supplements 10 minutes per day of computer-assisted instruction with tutorial and small-group instruction from the teacher. An effectiveness study with random assignment of students to computer-assisted instruction and control treatment (Chapter 1 pullout) found positive effects on reading tasks for the students receiving computer-assisted instruction.		
Title I Mathematics Laboratory with Computer-Assisted Instruction	Lafayette Parish, LA	3–6
The Computer Curriculum Corporation curriculum is used, and students receive 10 minutes of computer-assisted instruction in math. For evaluation, students randomly were assigned to Chapter I pullout or to a combination of the pullout model with 10 minutes of computer-assisted instruction. Students receiving computer-assisted instruction made modest gains in math.		

Moreover, a combination of approaches provides for improvements across a variety of objectives (e.g., academic gains, self-regulation, and self-concept). Thus, a curriculum that features a comprehensive program is feasible. A sample early intervention curriculum outline is presented in Table 9.7.

5. For initial achievement gains to be maintained, intervention must continue, and effective teaching across grade levels is the most logical approach for maintaining gains (Slavin & Madden, 1989). Slavin et al. (1992/1993) note that intensive early intervention followed by long-term improvements in instruction and other services can produce substantial and lasting gains.
6. Effective programs are comprehensive. They usually include curriculum materials, lesson guides, and supportive materials. Rather than being a series of workshops to provide teachers with strategies, they are well-defined alternatives to traditional methods (Slavin & Madden, 1989).
7. Effective programs are intensive (Casto & Mastropieri, 1986; Slavin & Madden, 1989). They use much one-to-one tutoring through teachers, peers, paraprofessionals, volunteers, or computer-assisted instruction. Slavin et al.

TABLE 9.7
A Sample Early Intervention Curriculum

Attending and Listening

Perception
Visual perception; visual sequencing and memory; auditory perception and discrimination; auditory sequencing; touch, taste, and smell; gross motor; fine motor (includes prewriting)

Language Development
Listening—receptive language; speaking—expressive language (vocabulary, expressive language, phonology); prewriting; writing; prereading; reading; oral comprehension; literature skills; cognitive language skills

Creative Expression
Art; music; drama

Math
Quantitative ideas; relationship of body and parts to space and objects; geometric ideas; sets; numbers; measurement; relative value and use of coins; ideas of patterns; problem solving

Life Science
Social studies (me, my family, my classroom, my school, my community, work, natural environment); science (matter and energy, space and earth, living things, identifying and classifying objects, beginning measurement, questioning); health; safety; nutrition

Behavior
Social development; self-regulation; self-concept (as an individual, in cultural environment)

Physical Education
Basic movement; rhythmic activities; stunts, tumbling, and apparatus activities; simple games, story games, and dramatic play

(1992/1993) note that effective approaches for preventing early reading failure incorporate one-to-one tutoring of at-risk first graders.

8. Effective programs maintain an instructional match between child and task. This match is achieved through continuous monitoring of progress and changing instruction on the basis of collected data (Slavin & Madden, 1989).
9. Class size is related to effectiveness regarding academic achievement, attitudes, and behavior in early school years. From a review of the class-size research, Robinson (1990) notes that the most positive effect of smaller class size (i.e., classes of 22 students or less) occurs in the primary grades.

COMMERCIAL EARLY CHILDHOOD EDUCATION PROGRAMS

A variety of commercial curriculum materials for early childhood education are available. The following materials may be used to enhance the development of young children who are at risk for learning problems.

Brigance Prescriptive Readiness: Strategies and Practice

Readiness: Strategies and Practice, developed by A. H. Brigance (published by Curriculum Associates), includes over 400 age-appropriate activities to teach and strengthen readiness skills. Skill areas include general knowledge and comprehension; gross motor; fine motor; self-help; visual motor and visual discrimination; general readiness; and early reading, writing, and math. Each skill section includes an objective, rationale, skill sequence, teaching recommendations, and indications of learning difficulties. Parent involvement and enrichment activities are suggested. The activities can be used as a complete early childhood curriculum or to supplement other programs.

2 to 6: Instructional Activities for Children at Risk

Instructional Activities for Children at Risk, developed by C. S. Bos, S. Vaughn, and L. M. Levine (published by SRA), is a complete curriculum that offers a wide range of developmentally appropriate activities. Each activity includes an objective, recommended age range, materials list, teaching procedures, enrichment activities, and upward and downward extensions. The set includes five activity books that focus on early developmental domains (cognitive, social-personal, motor, communication, and adaptive) and two program enrichment books, *Special Times* and *Special Families*.

Phonological Awareness Training for Reading

Phonological Awareness Training for Reading (Torgesen & Bryant, 1994a) is designed to increase the level of phonological awareness in youngsters and can be used with at-risk kindergartners to help prepare them for reading in first grade or with first or second graders who are having difficulty learning to read. The program takes about 12 to 14 weeks to complete if children are taught in short sessions three or four times a week. Children learn to hear the individual sounds in whole words as well as to blend individual sounds into words. All words in the program are presented on picture cards, and game boards are used to provide reinforcing activities. In the final phase of the program, children learn to generalize their acquired phonological awareness skills to reading and spelling simple words. A training manual contains instructions for all phases of the program and includes sample scripts for teaching specific concepts.

COMPUTER SOFTWARE PROGRAMS IN EARLY CHILDHOOD EDUCATION

Computer software programs can help young children develop independence and provide practice in activities that reinforce essential readiness skills. The following programs offer a motivating way of learning and may help at-risk young children master important preacademic skills.

Early Discovery Series

The *Early Discovery Series,* produced by Hartley, includes six interactive programs that provide activities to stimulate early growth and development. *Colors and Shapes* helps children discriminate colors, match color patterns, match shapes, and use shapes to reproduce a model. In *Observation and Classification*, children sharpen their observation skills and classify familiar objects by use and function. *Patterns and Sequence* takes children from simple geometric designs to pairing sequences of three abstract patterns and helps children with part/whole relationships needed to discriminate letters. *Size and Logic* focuses on the ability to discriminate among objects according to size. *Conservation and Counting* includes math-related activities that focus on one-to-one correspondence, conservation of numbers, number/numeral relationships, and matching sets. In *Parquetry and Pictures*, children construct pictures or shapes by assembling given parts. For all programs, only two computer keys are used to operate each lesson, and each learning game contains three levels of difficulty that follow normal stages of development. Supplementary manuals include suggestions for activities to blend the lessons with other experiences.

Stickybear's Early Learning Activities

Stickybear's Early Learning Activities, produced by Optimum Resource, includes six activities to introduce basic skills and prepare children (age 2 through 6) for later academic success. The *Alphabet* activity consists of a word/letter/picture set for every letter of the alphabet and includes a microphone option for pronunciation practice. In *Counting*, animated objects with audio-prompts help children master the numbers *0* through *9*. The *Grouping* activity builds on counting skills and introduces group concepts. In the *Shapes* activity, animated scenes help children become familiar with shapes found in the environment. *Opposites* enhances word recognition and vocabulary skills and reinforces opposite concepts as children differentiate between opposite pairs. In the *Colors* activity, children distinguish different colors and their names. For each activity, two modes of play, structured and nonstructured, allow children to learn through prompted direction or the discovery method.

PERSPECTIVE

In a nation of plentiful resources, rich in energetic and committed people, children must not linger in unstimulating environments. Through the fostering of the cognitive, academic, social, and emotional growth of children, individuals can be assisted in their pursuit of self-fulfillment. Information on early identification and intervention will enhance the development of best practices. As McCormick (1994) states, "Most important as we move toward the year 2000 is the growing consensus that early intervention works. It gives young children with disabilities the impetus they need and deserve to succeed in present and future environments" (p. 111). Slavin and Madden (1989) comment on the use of current knowledge to teach at-risk children: "We know we can do much better with students at risk, that we can begin to consider success in school as the birthright of virtually every child. While there is still more we must learn, we know enough today to take action. We can do no less for our most vulnerable children" (p. 12).

DISCUSSION/REVIEW QUESTIONS

1. Discuss the rationale for early identification and intervention.
2. Present the legislative support for early identification and intervention.
3. Briefly discuss several key issues in early identification.
4. Discuss three types of prediction techniques.
5. Describe guidelines for developing early identification procedures.
6. List several commonly used screening tests and tests for identification and program planning.
7. Discuss service delivery options for early childhood special education students.
8. Briefly discuss the major curriculum models used in early childhood education programs.
9. Discuss the types of effective early intervention programs, and give examples of some effective programs.
10. Present guidelines for early intervention programs, and give examples of commercial programs and computer software programs in early childhood education.

REFERENCES

Badian, N. A. (1988). The prediction of good and poor reading before kindergarten entry: A nine-year follow-up. *Journal of Learning Disabilities*, *21*, 98–103, 123.

Barenbaum, E., & Newcomer, P. (1996). *Test of Children's Language.* Austin, TX: PRO-ED.

Becker, H. J. (1987). *The impact of computer use on learning: What research has shown and what it has not* (Technical Report No. 18). Baltimore, MD: The Johns Hopkins University Center for Research on Elementary and Middle Schools.

Berrueta-Clement, J. R., Schweinhart, L. J., Barnett, W. S., Epstein, A. S., & Weikart, D. P. (1984). *Changed lives.* Ypsilanti, MI: High/Scope.

Bloom, B. S. (1964). *Stability and change in human characteristics.* New York: Wiley.

Brigance, A. H. (1991). *Brigance Diagnostic Inventory of Early Development—Revised.* North Billerica, MA: Curriculum Associates.

Busch, R. F. (1980). Predicting first-grade reading achievement. *Learning Disability Quarterly, 3*(1), 38–48.

Casto, G., & Mastropieri, M. A. (1986). The efficacy of early intervention programs: A meta-analysis. *Exceptional Children, 52*, 417–424.

Cole, K. N., Mills, P. E., Dale, P. S., & Jenkins, J. R. (1991). Effects of preschool integration for children with disabilities. *Exceptional Children, 58*, 36–45.

Coleman, J. M., & Dover, G. M. (1993). The RISK Screening Test: Using kindergarten teachers' ratings to predict future placement in resource classrooms. *Exceptional Children, 59*, 468–477.

Danzer, V. A., Gerber, M. F., Lyons, T. M., & Voress, J. K. (1991). *DABERON—2 Screening for School Readiness*. Austin, TX: PRO-ED.

Edmister, P., & Ekstrand, R. E. (1987). Preschool programming: Legal and educational issues. *Exceptional Children, 54*, 130–136.

Eiserman, W. D., Weber, C., & McCoun, M. (1995). Parent and professional roles in early intervention: A longitudinal comparison of the effects of two intervention configurations. *The Journal of Special Education, 29*, 20–44.

Esterly, D. L., & Griffin, H. C. (1987). Preschool programs for children with learning disabilities. *Journal of Learning Disabilities, 20*, 571–573.

Fedoruk, G. M., & Norman, C. A. (1991). Kindergarten screening predictive inaccuracy: First-grade teacher variability. *Exceptional Children, 57*, 258–263.

Frankenburg, W. K., Dodds, J. B., Archer, P., Bresnick, B., Maschka, P., Edelman, N., & Shapiro, H. (1990). *Denver Developmental Screening Test—II*. Denver: Denver Developmental Materials.

Ginsburg, H. P., & Baroody, A. J . (1990). *Test of Early Mathematics Ability—2*. Austin, TX: PRO-ED.

Good, R., Kaminski, R., Schwarz, I., & Doyle, C. (1990). Identifying at-risk kindergarten and first grade students: Recent developments. *Direct Instruction News, 9*(4), 15–21.

Hammill, D. D., & McNutt, G. (1981). *Correlates of reading: The consensus of thirty years of correlational research* (PRO-ED Monograph No. 1). Austin, TX: PRO-ED.

Harrison, P. L., Kaufman, A. S., Kaufman, N. L., Bruininks, R. H., Rynders, J., Ilmer, S., Sparrow, S. S., & Cicchetti, D. V. (1990). *AGS Early Screening Profiles*. Circle Pines, MN: American Guidance Service.

Hayden, A. H., & Haring, N. G. (1976). Early intervention for high risk infants and young children: Programs for Down's syndrome children. In T. D. Tjossem (Ed.), *Intervention strategies for high risk infants and young children* (pp. 573–607). Baltimore, MD: University Park Press.

Hresko, W. P., Herron, S. R., & Peak, P. K. (1996). *Test of Early Written Language—2*. Austin, TX: PRO-ED.

Hresko, W. P., Reid, D. K., & Hammill, D. D. (1991). *Test of Early Language Development—2*. Austin, TX: PRO-ED.

Hunt, J. M. (1961). *Intelligence and experience*. New York: Ronald Press.

Jenkins, J. R., Odom, S. L., & Speltz, M. L. (1989). Effects of social integration on preschool children with handicaps: *Exceptional Children, 55*, 420–428.

Jenks, S. (1990, February). Drug babies: An ethical quagmire for doctors. *Medical World News*, pp. 39–46.

Johnson, L. J., & Beauchamp, K. D. F. (1987). Preschool assessment measures: What are teachers using? *Journal of the Division for Early Childhood, 12*(1), 70–76.

Karnes, M., Linnemeyer, S., & Schwedel, A. (1981). A survey of federally funded model programs for handicapped infants: Implications for research and practice. *Journal of the Division for Early Childhood, 5*, 25–39.

Karp, J. M. (1990). Strategies for successful early intervention coordinating councils. *Remedial and Special Education, 11*(6), 54–59.

Karweit, N. (1992). The kindergarten experience. *Educational Leadership, 49*(6), 82–86.

Keogh, B. K., & Weisner, T. (1993). An ecocultural perspective on risk and protective factors in children's development: Implications for learning disabilities. *Learning Disabilities Research & Practice, 8*, 3–10.

Kirk, S. A. (1958). *Early education of the mentally retarded: An experimental study*. Urbana, IL: University of Illinois Press.

Kochanek, T. T., Kabacoff, R. I., & Lipsitt, L. P. (1990). Early identification of developmentally disabled and at-risk preschool children. *Exceptional Children, 56*, 528–538.

Lindsay, G. A., & Wedell, K. (1982). The early identification of educationally "at risk" children revisited. *Journal of Learning Disabilities, 15*, 212–217.

Lyon, G. R. (1995). Research initiatives in learning disabilities: Contributions from scientists supported by the National Institute of Child Health and Human Development. *Journal of Child Neurology, 10*(Suppl. No. 1), 120–126.

Mantzicopoulos, P. Y., & Morrison, D. (1994). Early prediction of reading achievement: Exploring the relationship of cognitive and noncognitive measures to inaccurate classifications of at-risk status. *Remedial and Special Education, 15*, 244–251.

Mardell-Czudnowski, C., & Goldenberg, D. S. (1990). *Developmental Indicators for the Assessment of Learning—Revised* (AGS ed.). Circle Pines, MN: American Guidance Service.

McCormick, L. (1994). Infants and young children with special needs. In N. G. Haring, L. McCormick, & T. G. Haring (Eds.), *Exceptional children and youth* (6th ed., pp. 86–112). Upper Saddle River, NJ: Merrill/Prentice Hall.

McLoughlin, J. A., & Lewis, R. B. (1994). *Assessing special students* (4th ed.). Upper Saddle River, NJ: Merrill/Prentice Hall.

Meisels, S. J., Harbin, G., Modigliani, K., & Olson, K. (1988). Formulating optimal state early childhood intervention policies. *Exceptional Children, 55*, 159–165.

Miller, L. J., & Sprong, T. A. (1986). Psychometric and qualitative comparison of four preschool screening instruments. *Journal of Learning Disabilities, 19*, 480–484.

Mills, P. E., Dale, P. S., Cole, K. N., & Jenkins, J. R. (1995). Follow-up of children from academic and cognitive preschool curricula at age 9. *Exceptional Children, 61*, 378–393.

Missiuna, C., & Samuels, M. T. (1989). Dynamic assessment of preschool children with special needs: Comparison of mediation and instruction. *Remedial and Special Education, 10*(2), 53–62.

Morrison, D., & Mantzicopoulos, P. (1990). Predicting reading problems at kindergarten for children in second grade: SEARCH as a screen. *Remedial and Special Education, 11*(4), 29–36.

National Association for Perinatal Addiction Research and Education. (1988, October). Innocent addicts: High rate of prenatal drug abuse found. *ADAMHA News*.

National Joint Committee on Learning Disabilities. (1986, February). *Learning disabilities and the preschool child* (A position paper of the National Joint Committee on Learning Disabilities). Baltimore, MD: The Orton Dyslexia Society.

Peterson, N. L. (1987). *Early intervention for handicapped and at-risk children: An introduction to early childhood-special education*. Denver: Love.

Ramey, C. T., & Ramey, S. L. (1992). *At risk does not mean doomed* (National Health/Education Consortium Occupational Paper No. 4). Washington, DC: National Commission to Prevent Infant Mortality.

Reid, D. K., Hresko, W. P., & Hammill, D. D. (1989). *Test of Early Reading Ability—2*. Austin, TX: PRO-ED.

Robinson, G. E. (1990). Synthesis of research on class size. *Educational Leadership, 47*(7), 80–90.

Roth, M., McCaul, E., & Barnes, K. (1993). Who becomes an "at-risk" student? The predictive value of a kindergarten screening battery. *Exceptional Children, 59*, 348–358.

Rothenberg, J. J. (1990). An outcome study of an early intervention for specific learning disabilities. *Journal of Learning Disabilities, 23*, 317–319.

Sainato, D. M., Strain, P. S., Lefebvre, D., & Rapp, N. (1990). Effects of self-evaluation on the independent work skills of preschool children with disabilities. *Exceptional Children, 56*, 540–549.

Salvia, J., & Ysseldyke, J. E. (1995). *Assessment* (6th ed.). Boston: Houghton Mifflin.

Silver, A. A., & Hagin, R. A. (1981). *SEARCH manual*. New York: Wiley.

Skeels, H. M. (1966). Adult status of children with contrasting early life experiences. *Monographs of the Society for Research in Child Development, 31*(3).

Slavin, R. E., Karweit, N. L., & Madden, N. A. (1989). *Effective programs for students at risk*. Boston: Allyn & Bacon.

Slavin, R. E., Karweit, N. L., & Wasik, B. A. (1992/1993). Preventing school failure: What works? *Educational Leadership, 50*(4), 10–18.

Slavin, R. E., & Madden, N. A. (1989). What works for students at risk: A research synthesis. *Educational Leadership, 46*(5), 4–13.

Stallings, J. A. (1974). *Follow Through classroom observation evaluation 1972-1973* (Executive Summary SRI Project URU-7370). Menlo Park, CA: Stanford Research Institute.

Stile, S. W., Cole, J. T., & Garner, A. W. (1979). Maximizing parental involvement in programs for exceptional children. *Journal of the Division for Early Childhood, 1*(1), 68–82.

Torgesen, J. K., & Bryant, B. R. (1994a). *Phonological awareness training for reading*. Austin, TX: PRO-ED.

Torgesen, J. K., & Bryant, B. R. (1994b). *Test of Phonological Awareness*. Austin, TX: PRO-ED.

Wechsler, D. (1989). *Wechsler Preschool and Primary Scale of Intelligence—Revised*. San Antonio, TX: Psychological Corporation.

Wilson, B. J., & Reichmuth, M. (1985). Early screening programs: When is predictive accuracy sufficient? *Learning Disability Quarterly*, *8*, 182–188.

Wolery, M. (1987). Program evaluation at the local level: Recommendations for improving services. *Topics in Early Childhood Special Education*, *7*(2), 111–123.

Adolescents and Adults

CHAPTER 10

After studying this chapter, you should be able to:

- discuss the demands placed on adolescents in terms of school and employment.
- present the characteristics of adolescents with learning disabilities in the areas of academic deficits, cognitive and metacognitive deficits, social interaction deficits, and motivation deficits.
- discuss program services and premises of secondary programs.
- discuss general secondary curriculum alternatives and types of intervention approaches.
- present models for organizing secondary programming.
- discuss curriculum approaches for promoting motivation, social development, and academic remediation.
- discuss the Learning Strategies Curriculum developed at the University of Kansas Center for Research on Learning.
- describe curriculum approaches for developing functional living skills and promoting career-related instruction.
- present curriculum approaches for promoting transitions from secondary settings.
- present instructional procedures related to the acquisition and generalization of skills and strategies.
- present instructional alternatives pertaining to content enhancements, assignments, peer-assisted instruction, adapting materials, and tutoring.
- discuss collaboration with general classroom teachers as an instructional procedure to maximize learning.
- discuss factors that affect postsecondary adjustments of adults with learning disabilities who have been successful and unsuccessful.
- present suggestions and services for college students with learning disabilities.

Sixteen-year-old Stuart is an enigma to his teachers at Artesia High School. His attention is good, he understands explanations well, and his oral answers usually are precise. Stuart's class standing, however, is low in almost every academic area. His written reports and assignments are incomprehensible, and his handwriting is indecipherable. He reads in a slow, halting, embarrassed manner, and his spelling is atrocious. When asked about the nature of his problem, Stuart shrugs and says, "I dunno. I'm just trying to get along."

During his 2 years at Artesia, Stuart has accumulated only 12 credits, which classifies him as a freshman. There is no doubt that he is intelligent, and his records consistently indicate intelligence test scores in the high-normal range. In the last few years his parents have become frustrated and have developed a pattern of acceptance-rejection. They have been told throughout Stuart's schooling that he is bright, and they cannot understand his lack of performance in school. They tend to think Stuart is lazy, although he does well in his after-school job and home chores.

Stuart must make a choice soon. In 2 years he will be 18, and his state has given 18-year-olds full citizenship. In addition, his state requires that each student pass a minimum competency examination before receiving a secondary school diploma. Frankly, Stuart is intimidated by the thought of being on his own in a world that demands so much independence. In frustration his father has vowed occasionally that if Stuart is not succeeding in school when he reaches 18, he can quit, get a job, and support himself. Stuart is considering the Army as his only solution (although some of his friends are urging him to examine the Job Corps, too), and over the years he gradually has changed his career choice from physician to infantryman. Stuart is well aware of the need for a diploma in today's world. Had he been in this situation a decade ago, Stuart could have dropped out of school, started to work, and readily achieved success. Today, however, an incomplete education may prevent him from even demonstrating what he can do.

With minor variations, Stuart is like many adolescents with learning disabilities. What is an appropriate educational program? What service delivery models are most effective? How can secondary programs best be implemented?

The development of viable secondary and adult programs for individuals with learning disabilities is an essential and difficult task. Based on the assumption that early intervention prevents later learning problems, special and remedial education services and teacher training traditionally have focused on programming for younger children. Although early intervention has helped numerous children with learning disabilities, many adolescents continue to enter secondary school and community life with debilitating learning or behavioral problems. The high dropout rate strongly suggests the need for better secondary programming (Sitlington & Frank, 1993). Levin, Zigmond, and Birch (1985) followed the progress of 51 ninth-grade students with learning disabilities for 4 years. Of this group, 51% dropped out of school. This finding led Levin et al. to conclude that "the 'holding power' of the schools for adolescents with learning disabilities is called into serious question" (p. 6).

Compounding the task of programming for adolescents with learning disabilities is the constant reform in secondary education. Reforms are raising standards for time spent in school, increasing core curriculum demands, and requiring that minimal competency tests be passed. In many situations, curriculum reforms and funding patterns are developed and required without regard for students with special needs. For example, Wang, Rubenstein, and Reynolds (1985) report that a successful secondary program for special education students in a large urban city was terminated because of a quirk in funding procedures. They and other authorities are encouraging special educators to become more involved in reforms and policies in secondary programming to help clear the road to success for adolescents with learning disabilities.

Fortunately, recent efforts in the field of learning disabilities have focused on developing secondary programs. For example, the University of Kansas Institute for Research in Learning Disabilities (now the Center for Research on Learning) was established in 1978 to study the needs of adolescents with learning disabilities and develop appropriate interventions. Under the leadership of Don Deshler, Jean Schumaker, and their colleagues, this institute is having a nationwide impact. Moreover, successful secondary demonstration programs have been developed in many states. Although most programs still are being validated empirically, the recent surge of programs and literature certainly has increased knowledge and hope about secondary and adult programming.

This chapter focuses on the needs of adolescents and adults with learning disabilities and the types of services available to them. It is organized into the following major sections: Demands Placed on Adolescents, Characteristics of Adolescents with Learning Disabilities, Challenges in Secondary Programming, Supportive and Alternative Curriculum Approaches, Instructional Procedures, and Adults with Learning Disabilities.

DEMANDS PLACED ON ADOLESCENTS

The world of most adolescents revolves around the school setting. Adolescents spend most of their day preparing to go to school, getting to school, attending classes, participating in afterschool activities, and completing homework. The home environment gradually has less influence on the adolescent, and peers and adults outside of the home begin to play a greater role in determining how the adolescent behaves. As the adolescent gets older, part- or full-time employment may impose even greater demands. However, the part-time job often is considered a step toward the adult world and greater dependence. In short, the demands placed on adolescents increase and grow in complexity. Across the settings and situations that adolescents must face, the demands placed upon them can be considered as having specific academic, social, motivational, and cognitive dimensions. Coupled with recent reforms in secondary education to increase core curriculum requirements, increase time spent in school, and require that minimum competency tests be passed, these demands are making it extremely difficult for adolescents with learning disabilities to succeed.

School Demands

Gaining Information from Written Materials. Students are expected to acquire information written at the secondary level. However, the readability level of secondary textbooks may exceed the grade level at which they are used (e.g, a text used for a 9th-grade social studies class may be written at a 12th-grade reading level) (Schumaker & Deshler, 1984). Moreover, C. M. Clark and Peterson (1986) note that curriculum planning studies indicate that the textbook is the most important factor in determining what will be taught in a course. As a result, the organization, emphasis, and balance of factual and conceptual information presented in a course may be based completely on textual information.

Gaining Information from Lectures. In an extensive study of the oral language demands of middle and secondary school classrooms, Moran (1980) found that the lecture was the predominant type of listening requirement in secondary school classrooms and that the rate of teacher presentation of information did not differ significantly between 7th-grade and 12th-grade classes. In other words, in the classes that were studied, seventh graders were expected to process information at the same rate as secondary school seniors. Her data clearly demonstrate that to succeed in a secondary school curriculum, all students must possess skills in listening, attending, remembering, note taking, and writing. Some of her specific findings include the following:

1. General class teachers rely heavily on the lecture method and tend to address questions to the whole class rather than to individuals.
2. General class teachers use few advance organizers to help students listen or take notes more effectively.
3. Students are not asked regularly to paraphrase or demonstrate their understanding of materials presented in lectures or readings.
4. General class teachers lecture at a fast pace, and only students with excellent note-taking skills are able to take meaningful notes.
5. The frequency of oral feedback and reinforcement is low.

The frequencies of verbal interactions between teachers and students with and without learning disabilities are reported to be similar (Powell, Suzuki, Atwater, Gorney-Krupsaw, & Morris, 1981). Thus, it is likely that many secondary school teachers do not consider the different learning needs of the students in terms of the oral dimensions of the classroom.

Demonstrating Knowledge Through Tests. The primary method for evaluating learning at the secondary school level is through tests. Classroom tests and quizzes, group-achievement tests, and minimum competency tests are the hallmarks of the secondary school curriculum. In a study of testing demands, Putnam (1992) found that the typical mainstream secondary classroom test includes 34.6 questions written at the 8.9th-grade level. He notes that the multiple-choice format is the most commonly used and the majority of the test responses require memorization of specific information. Thus, students need good test-taking and study skills to cope with testing demands. In addition, teachers expect students to acquire information for tests from textbooks, lectures, and class discussions. Teachers and parents indicate that students with and without disabilities, with few concessions, should be required to meet the same minimum competency requirements (Meyen, Alley, Scannell, Harnden, & Miller, 1982).

Expressing Information in Writing. Moran (1980) reports that the most frequently required writing assignment in the secondary school setting, according to teacher reports, is the short-answer response (e.g., fill in the blank, spell a word, or mark the correct answer). The second most important writing demand reported by teachers is taking notes from lectures or written materials. Writing more than a one-sentence response (e.g., descriptive, narrative, or argumentative writing) is required less frequently, and essay-style writing is not a common significant demand of the secondary school setting. When students are required to write, however, it appears that those who can spell correctly and write long and complete sentences tend to receive the highest grades, even though teachers report that sentence structure and complexity are the most important writing features (Moran & DeLoache, 1982).

Working Independently with Little Feedback. Link (1980) surveyed 44 elementary and 89 secondary teachers concerning essential learning skills. The highest ranking was given to the skill of following oral and written directions. Moreover, basic skills such as reading, mathematics, and spelling were ranked lower than study skills. For example, skimming, locating information in a text, remembering information for a test, and turning in assignments received higher rankings than did more traditional basic skills. The high ranking of study skills indicates a high expectation for students to work efficiently and effectively on their own. In another study directly related to five areas of teacher expectations, Knowlton (1983) separated specific study skills from independent work habits. Subskills associated with independent work habits included bringing materials to class, completing assignments and homework, budgeting time, requesting help, and working independently. Subskills associated with study skills included note taking, using library reference materials, writing reports, test taking, and copying. Knowlton found that general classroom teachers' greatest expectation for students was the demonstration of independent work habits. Socialization skills ranked second, communication skills ranked third, study skills were fourth, and subject-matter skills were fifth. These studies indicate that many general classroom teachers have high expectations for students to develop plans for getting their own work done, monitoring and checking their work, and completing tasks without extra assistance from the teacher. This does not imply that the other areas are unimportant, but rather that teachers consider independent work behaviors to be the trouble spots in delivering organized group instruction, which is the basis for the delivery of the secondary school curriculum.

Demonstrating a Broad Set of Cognitive and Metacognitive Strategies. A strategy is a person's approach to a task, and executive strategies relate to one's ability to reflect and think about one's own thinking processes (or cognitive strategies) and decide how to use them to complete a task effectively and efficiently. For example, students are expected to be able to organize information and resources to promote learning. While students must apply skills to meet these expectations, the process of organizing multiple resources (e.g., notes, text, and worksheets) requires them to manipulate several strategies in a sophisticated manner. Schumaker and Deshler (1984) and Lenz, Clark, Deshler, Schumaker, and Rademacher (1990) conclude that studies on the demands of the secondary school environment clearly indicate that students are required to use higher-order thinking skills in school if they are to be judged successful by general classroom teachers. These skills relate to being an independent problem solver (e.g., trying to solve an assignment-related problem independently before seeking help) as well as being able to apply knowledge across content areas (i.e., a process commonly referred to as *generalization*). Lenz and Mellard (1990) contend that many general classroom teachers assume that these skills automatically will increase, develop, and be applied without special attention as a result of continued exposure to increasingly difficult content-area learning experiences. Thus, explicit instruction in generalized use of skills for application in different classes or materials rarely is provided.

Interacting Appropriately. In a review of studies on the social demands placed on adolescents in the secondary school environment, Lenz, Clark, Deshler, Schumaker, and Rademacher (1990) conclude that for students to meet adult and peer expectations for successful and appropriate social interaction, they must follow rules and instructions in and out of the school setting, participate in group social activities, participate in discussions and conversations with peers and adults, accept criticism and assistance appropriately, recruit assistance appropriately (and only when needed), resist inappropriate peer pressure, and maintain a pleasant manner across social interactions.

Moreover, within the classroom setting, Knowlton (1983) found that across five areas of teacher expectations, socialization ranked second, after independent work habits. In this study, socialization included the subskills of displaying respect for authority, following classroom rules, accepting criticism, and working as a team member. However, Knowlton notes that teachers of nonacademic subjects consider overt conduct classroom behaviors to be more important than do teachers of academic subjects. This may indicate that these classes offer more opportunities for off-task behaviors because of frequent shifts in activities or that the perceived value held by students for these classes is low.

In observational studies of teacher-student and student-student interactions within classroom settings, there is little evidence to indicate that sophisticated social interaction skills are required. Schumaker, Sheldon-Wildgen, and Sherman (1980) found that on the average, only 11% of classroom activities required discussion; however, this percentage decreased as the grade level increased. For example, the average rate of the use of discussion activities in seventh-grade classes was reported to be 18%, in eighth-grade classes it was 11%, and in ninth-grade classes it was only 3%. Many general classroom teachers have begun to infuse the use of cooperative learning activities into classroom activities, but it is unclear whether the introduction of activities related to peer-assisted instruction, such as those employed in cooperative learning, is altering the social demands of secondary school settings.

Demonstrating Motivation to Learn. Teachers expect students to be motivated to learn; however, teachers and students may have different perceptions concerning motivation. Lenz, Clark, Deshler, Schumaker, and Rademacher (1990) report that teachers appear to base their perception of motivation on the student's behavior in planning for timely task completion, setting both short- and long-term goals, putting forth maximum and appropriate effort to achieve goals, and completing educational programs. Should the student or the teacher be responsible for promoting motivation? Teachers appear to believe that students should be motivated to learn secondary school content and that the biggest barrier to their effectiveness relates to student attitudes and the value that they place on academic learning (Lenz, Deshler, & Schumaker, 1991). Lenz, Deshler, and Schumaker conclude that students who appear to be motivated may satisfy a basic criteria that teachers may have for judging the effectiveness of their instruction.

Vocational and Employment Demands

Many adolescents become involved in vocational training programs and part- or full-time jobs during the secondary school years. Attention to career and vocational readiness is appropriate in secondary schools because about 50% of all secondary school students do not continue to higher education (Hamilton, 1986). Significant attention is focused on the creation of career development and vocational training programs in secondary schools, and the actual demands encountered in these settings are similar to those encountered in academic settings. Information must be gained and applied in a social context and motivation must exist to achieve success in school-based vocational training programs and employment settings.

Students are expected to demonstrate oral language, reading, writing, and listening skills in school settings, and research indicates that these same skills are required in employment settings. For example, Mathews, Whang, and Fawcett (1980) identified and validated 13 skills (covering academic and social areas) as being important for obtaining and maintaining employment. The general skills required across the 13 employment skills include reading and writing (e.g., writing a letter to request an interview in response to a help-wanted advertisement, and completing a federal income tax form), listening (e.g., accepting suggestions and criticism from an employer), and oral language (e.g., telephoning to request an interview, participating in an interview, providing constructive criticism to coworkers, explaining a problem to a supervisor, and complimenting a coworker). Students also should to be able to work independently and accept feedback. In addition, in a follow-up study of 284 students with learning disabilities, Fourqurean, Meisgeier, Swank, and Williams (1991) found that math ability was highly related to positive employment outcomes. They reason that the skills needed to solve math problems (i.e., concentration, attention to detail, and verbal abstract reasoning) are important for job success.

Attention to these broad employment demands is critical. Evidence suggests that employee success is highly related to the match between job demands and an individual's characteristics (Siegel & Gaylord-Ross, 1991). The expectation for successful social interactions, academic performance, and independent work habits also is cited by Fourqurean and LaCourt (1990). However, Mithaug, Horiuchi, and Fanning

(1985) argue that students face a broader set of demands when they enter the work force. Mithaug et. al suggest that the real demands placed on employees relate to solving problems, setting goals, and making good decisions and that specific training in job skills will pay off only when these broader skills are learned. Finally, a growing demand of many employment settings is that the employee be drug free. Unfortunately, for many adolescents and young adults, this is a difficult demand to meet.

CHARACTERISTICS OF ADOLESCENTS WITH LEARNING DISABILITIES

The need to adjust to the rapid cognitive, social, emotional, and physical changes makes adolescence a challenging period of development. These rapid changes combined with the increasing demands of secondary school make adolescence a difficult period for many students. Success for adolescents with learning disabilities becomes even more difficult because most of these students enter secondary school with a history of failure and numerous learning problems. This section reviews characteristics of adolescents with learning disabilities and the ability of these adolescents to respond to the demands around them. An understanding of these characteristics provides a framework for delineating and responding to their needs.

Academic Deficits

Poor academic achievement is a primary characteristic of adolescents with learning disabilities. In a study of about 300 students with learning disabilities, Deshler, Warner, Schumaker, and Alley (1983) report a clear trend in achievement levels from 7th to 12th grade. In reading and written language, the average performance of these students began at the high third-grade level for seventh graders and plateaued at the fifth-grade level for the upper grades. In mathematics, average performance began at the fifth-grade level for seventh graders and plateaued at the sixth-grade level in the senior high grades. Also, in a national survey of 810 adolescents with learning disabilities, Gregory, Shanahan, and Walberg (1985) report that students with learning disabilities showed significant deficits in academic areas.

Warner, Alley, Deshler, and Schumaker (1980) report that of the 307 students with learning disabilities whom they studied, the majority scored at or below the 10th percentile in written language, reading, and math. They report that for secondary school students with learning disabilities, achievement scores averaged 5 to 7 years below mental age. They conclude that most of the adolescents with learning disabilities were underachievers and qualified for the severe discrepancy factor prominent in identification criteria. Moreover, they report that these low academic performances differentiated students with learning disabilities from other low-achieving students. Rieth and Polsgrove (1994) maintain that the severe academic deficits of adolescents with learning disabilities are well documented. They note that the deficits are across the areas of reading, spelling, and math. Moreover, many students with learning disabilities fail minimum competency tests even when the tests are modified for them. These deficits in basic skills and the skills measured on minimum competency tests are supported in the literature (Adams, 1990; Algozzine, O'Shea, Stoddard, & Crews, 1988; Vallecorsa & Garriss, 1990). Overall, authorities generally agree that, given most programming practices, basic skills of many adolescents with learning disabilities persist and plateau during the secondary school grades.

Why do the academic skills of adolescents with learning disabilities plateau despite ongoing programming efforts? One explanation is that the secondary setting does not provide sufficient immersion in skill development efforts, and the criterion for success shifts from skill acquisition to content acquisition. The students may work on 4th-grade skills in the learning disabilities program during the fourth period but be faced with 10th-grade-level materials during the fifth period. Thus, the students have no place to apply the skills that they are learning. Another explanation is that adolescents may not be motivated to learn these skills. The continued remediation of skills can lead the students to conclude that their skills are not going to improve and that it is not worth the effort because grades, popularity, and success are based on passing content classes and not on improving skill-oriented test scores. A third explanation may be that the instruction provided in special education programs is not organized or delivered adequately. It may be difficult to modify the secondary school setting sufficiently to increase instructional intensity or time to promote the development of basic skills, and adolescents with learning disabilities may not accept an intensive skill remediation model. Finally, some researchers argue that many adolescents with learning disabilities do not learn specific skills because they do not know how to use and apply them immediately to improve their own learning. Thus, the lack of skill growth may be the result of ineffective or inefficient cognitive and metacognitive strategies.

Cognitive and Metacognitive Deficits

Executive Processing Deficits. Executive strategies relate to one's ability to reflect on one's own thinking processes or cognitive strategies and make decisions about how to use them to complete a task effectively and efficiently. Many information-processing research studies examine how students with learning disabilities approach cognitive tasks (e.g., memory). Several investigators (Hallahan & Bryan, 1981; Torgesen, 1982) report that students with learning disabilities approach tasks passively (i.e., they are less likely to use meaningful grouping of stimuli, mental elaboration, and verbal rehearsal than are their normally achieving peers). Bos and Vaughn (1994) refer to this inactive or passive learning nature that many of these students display as the *passive learner syndrome.* Moreover, Warner, Schumaker, Alley, and Deshler (1982) hypothesize that adolescents with learning disabilities either have delayed or deficit executive functioning (i.e., the component of information processing that selects and coordinates the use of specific processes, such as memorization strategies, according to the demands of the task). Executive functioning processes often are associated with problem-solving ability.

Warner et al. (1982) investigated the executive functioning of groups of several hundred adolescents who either had learning disabilities, were low achievers, and or were normal achievers. The findings indicate that the normally achieving students performed better than the other two groups. Although as a group the students with learning disabilities exhibited poor executive functioning, about 45% of them used an optimal strategy in performing the task. Warner et al. conclude that some but not all adolescents with learning disabilities exhibit excellent executive functioning skills.

The term *executive processing* frequently is used synonymously with the term *metacognition* (which is more popular). However, *executive processing* is used to denote the generation or selection of a strategy related to solving a problem, whereas *metacognition* can be used to denote the ability to plan, self-question, and monitor performance related to a task. In general, metacognition relates to how individuals seek and use feedback from themselves as a task is being completed. Metacognitive strategies monitor and direct the use of specific cognitive strategies.

Ellis, Deshler, and Schumaker (1989) studied 13 adolescents with learning disabilities and investigated the effects of executive strategy training on metacognitive knowledge and the use of executive processes. They found that before training was initiated the students expressed little metacognitive knowledge even when they knew appropriate and specific learning strategies for completing tasks. Thus, the students were not aware of the importance of thinking about their thinking and reflecting on their performance until it was brought explicitly to their

attention. This finding is important because the ability to generalize something learned in one setting to another setting is contingent on one's ability to recognize the relationship and apply the information. The generalization of learning across time and situations is particularly problematic at the secondary level because of the variety of settings that the student must face. Research repeatedly indicates that adolescents with learning disabilities have difficulty generalizing learning across settings (Ellis, Lenz, & Sabornie, 1987a, 1987b; Schmidt, Deshler, Schumaker, & Alley, 1989).

Deficiencies in Learning Strategies and Study Skills. During the past 10 years, research on learning strategies has increased because of interest in the specific strategies that adolescents with learning disabilities use to approach school tasks. Initially, the terms *learning strategies* and *study skills* were used synonymously, but *learning strategies* now has a broader meaning. Nevertheless, in research the terms *study skills* and *learning strategies* are closely associated.

In a survey of secondary learning disabilities teachers, Alley, Deshler, and Warner (1979) found that more than 85% of the students with learning disabilities had significant problems in test taking and study skills. Rieth and Polsgrove (1994) note that deficient skills in note taking, studying, and test taking are well documented among adolescents with learning disabilities.

Numerous studies on the ability of students with learning disabilities to complete specific tasks demonstrate that these adolescents are deficient not only in basic skills but also in the strategies they use to organize the skills they have (F. L. Clark, Deshler, Schumaker, Alley, & Warner, 1984; Lenz & Hughes, 1990; Nagel, Schumaker, & Deshler, 1986; Schumaker, Nolan, & Deshler, 1985). In these studies, students were given typical school tasks under conditions in which the basic skill requirements were reduced to the student's level (e.g., 10th-grade students were given a passage on a social studies topic written at the 4th-grade reading level). A similar task also was given to students under conditions in which the basic skill requirements of the task were at the students' actual grade placement (e.g., 10th-grade students were given a passage to read from the 10th-grade social studies textbook). Regardless of skill ability, the adolescents with learning disabilities in these studies demonstrated ineffective or inefficient strategies, and many even performed poorly on tasks in which the materials or conditions were at the students' level. When students were taught strategies related to meeting the conditions of the task more effectively and efficiently, performance increased on both the student-level task and the grade-level task. These findings demonstrate that the poor performance of many adolescents with learning disabilities on school tasks may be related to the strategies that they use. Overall, research indicates that many adolescents with learning disabilities make little use of learning strategies but that most can learn and apply them successfully (Deshler, Schumaker, & Lenz, 1984; Harris & Pressley, 1991).

Social Interaction Deficits

Schumaker and Hazel (1984) define *social skill* as "any cognitive function [e.g., empathizing with a person's feelings or making inferences about social cues] or overt behavior in which an individual engages while interacting with another person or persons" (p. 422). As noted in Chapter 1, the social skills deficiencies of many individuals with learning disabilities have become so noteworthy that some professionals believe social disabilities should become one of the criteria for identifying learning disabilities.

Perlmutter, Crocker, Cordray, and Garstecki (1983) studied the sociometric status of adolescents with learning disabilities in mainstream settings. Although they found that the students with learning disabilities generally were less well-liked than their peers, a subgroup of the sample of students with learning disabilities was very popular. In another study, Schumaker et al. (1980) found no differences between students with learning disabilities and normal achievers on four indices of peer interactions. Moreover, Schumaker, Hazel, Sherman, and Sheldon (1982) examined the performance of adolescents with and without learning disabilities on eight social variables: accepting negative feedback, giving negative feedback, giving positive feedback, engaging in conversation, following instructions, negotiating, problem solving, and resisting peer pressure. The students without learning disabilities performed significantly better on seven of the eight skills. Further analysis revealed that the social skills of the students with learning disabilities varied. Finally, in a comprehensive review of social skills research on students with learning disabilities, Hazel and Schumaker (1988) report that in the cognitive aspects related to social skills, students with learning disabilities (a) tend to use socially unacceptable behaviors in social situations, (b) are less able than peers to solve social problems and predict the social consequences of their social behaviors, (c) misinterpret social cues, (d) fail to adjust to the characteristics of their listeners, and (e) fail to take into account the thoughts and feelings of other people.

It is apparent that the heterogeneity within the population of adolescents with learning disabilities contributes to the mixed results reported in the social skills research. Some adolescents with learning disabilities have significant social skills deficits, whereas others do not. For those who lack social skills, these deficiencies can be as debilitating as their academic problems (Schumaker & Hazel, 1984). (Chapter 15 features social and emotional aspects of learning disabilities.)

Delinquency and Learning Disabilities. Some researchers link learning disabilities to delinquency because many students with learning disabilities are unable to judge social situations and social consequences. For example, Hazel and Schumaker (1988) report that the performance of social skills such as negotiation and resisting peer pressure is poorer in individuals with learning disabilities than in their normally achieving peers. In fact, the performance of adolescents with learning disabilities on these skills resembles the performance of juvenile delinquents (Schumaker et al., 1982). Moreover, in a study of learning disabilities and persisting delinquency, Waldie and Spreen (1993) found that impulsivity and poor judgment were factors that discriminated between persisting and nonpersisting delinquency. Of the 65 youth with learning disabilities studied (mean age of 18.9 years), 40 continued to have police contact into their mid-20s.

If students with learning disabilities are deficient in cognitive skills related to such areas as resistance, judgment, decision making, goal setting, and social perception, their disability may put them at risk for delinquency. However, some researchers argue that delinquency is a social response to the ongoing problem of general failure across many dimensions of the student's life. In a study of 53 delinquent adolescents, Meltzer, Levine, Karniski, Palfrey, and Clarke (1984) found that many had school problems as early as kindergarten. Moreover, these investigators found that 45% of the delinquents were delayed in reading by the second grade. Some authorities believe that learning problems contribute to an adolescent's sense of failure and frustration, which, in turn, leads to aggressive behavior (Unger, 1978). Preliminary results of a 4-year study of the learning disability/juvenile delinquency link show that the proportion of individuals with learning disabilities is greater among delinquents than among nondelinquents (Keilitz, Zaremba, & Broder, 1979). Keilitz and Dunivant (1986) note that adolescents with learning disabilities are at relatively high risk for delinquency.

While there appears to be a relationship between learning disabilities and juvenile delinquency, no empirical evidence exists to support a theory that learning disabilities cause juvenile delinquency. Lane (1980) states, "Although research has not established that a significant causal relationship exists between learning disabilities and juvenile delinquency, it has uncovered a range of possible relationships between the two variables" (p. 433). Many agree that specialized services should be provided to the delinquent. Crawford (1984) found that after a course of academic remediation (55 to 65 hours during a school year), the delinquent behavior of one group significantly decreased. Likewise, Keilitz and Dunivant (1986) note that some rehabilitation programs are effective in remediating academic deficiencies and reducing future delinquency. In a study of adjudicated youth with learning disabilities, Brier (1994) found that a criminal diversion project (psychosocial, educational, and vocational treatments) was effective in reducing the recidivism rate of participants. Nonparticipants had a recidivism rate of 40%, while project participants had a recidivism rate of 12%.

Motivation Deficits

Many adolescents with learning disabilities have serious motivation problems concerning schoolwork (Deshler, Schumaker, & Lenz, 1984; Rieth & Polsgrove, 1994). The student with learning disabilities has been described as an inactive learner (Torgesen, 1982), as exhibiting learned helplessness (Pflaum & Pascarella, 1982), and as lacking intrinsic motivation (H. S. Adelman & Taylor, 1983). The frustration of a history of limited academic success and the numerous activities (such as driving a car, getting a job, and being with friends) available to the adolescent combine to create substantial motivation problems for some students. Much literature exists that emphasizes the relationship of motivation to problems in learning and performance. H. S. Adelman and Taylor express it simply:

> If a student is motivated to learn something, (s)he often can do much more than anyone would have predicted was possible. Conversely, if a student is not particularly interested in learning something, resultant learning may not even be close to capability. (p. 384)

The teacher expects students to complete tasks, take a proactive approach to facing problems, set goals, demonstrate effort to achieve goals, and remain in school. However, the research indicates that many adolescents with learning disabilities fail to see the relationship between appropriate effort and success, do not realize the benefits of staying in school, have difficulty making a commitment to learn or perform, have few goals or plans for the future, and have trouble setting and attaining goals (Lenz, Clark, Deshler, Schumaker, & Rademacher, 1990). School attendance is cited as a primary example of the failure of the adolescent with learning disabilities to commit to education (Zigmond, Levin, & Laurie, 1985). Consequently, adolescents with learning disabilities are significantly at risk for general school failure and dropping out of school (Owings & Stocking, 1985). In a review of issues related to secondary programming, Zigmond (1990) reports that the dropout rates of students with learning disabilities are greater than for the remainder of the general school population and that this difference is consistent across the United States in both urban and rural school districts. Gregory et al. (1985) report that, in addition to lacking motivation in the school environment, many adolescents with learning disabilities also are less motivated toward work in general. In essence, there are times when motivation, not academic development, becomes the focus of an intervention program.

CHALLENGES IN SECONDARY PROGRAMMING

The characteristics of adolescent development and the settings in which adolescents must participate create a set of conditions that define the context for understanding the adolescent with learning disabilities. Research indicates that these adolescents do not meet many of the demands of either the school or the employment setting and that they are at risk of school failure across academic, cognitive, social, and motivational dimensions of performance. The complex interaction between the demands and expectations that are placed on students and the ability of students is an important factor in the development of secondary programs.

Secondary programming refers to the planning, organization, and implementation of education and services for students with learning disabilities who are enrolled in grades typically found in the middle school through the secondary school settings. Research on secondary programming begins with students who are about 12 years old and in the sixth or seventh grade and includes students who attend school until secondary school graduation or school exit.

Secondary programming for students with learning disabilities is discussed according to a number of parameters: (a) types of program services, (b) premises of programs that determine policy, procedures, and curriculum, (c) general curriculum alternatives that lead to the attainment of program goals and outcomes, and (d) intervention approaches that promote student acquisition and generalization of the targeted content. Secondary programming models also are discussed.

Program Services

The need for a diverse range of services at the secondary level is apparent. An analysis of various programs indicates that seven types of program services are required to accommodate the various needs of secondary students with learning disabilities. These include academic remediation, learning strategies, content instruction, social development instruction, functional living skills, career-related instruction, and transition instruction. These services are provided in a variety of instructional arrangements (e.g., resource room, general class, or self-contained class) by a diverse faculty (e.g., special educators, general class teachers, counselors, and vocational educators).

The heterogeneous nature of adolescents with learning problems underscores the need to offer a variety of services. Some students need one type of service (e.g., academic remediation) in the early stages of their secondary school program and another service later (e.g., career-related instruction or functional living skills). Still others may require only one service (e.g., learning strategies) during their secondary school program, while others need a combination of different services (e.g., academic remediation and content instruction). To date, it appears that no single approach is appropriate for all adolescents with learning problems. The real challenge is not in determining which approach is right or wrong but in ascertaining under what conditions and with whom a given service is most effective.

Premises of Secondary Programs

All secondary programs have several premises that determine policy, procedures, and curriculum. Examination of the literature and site visits indicate six common premises:

1. *Provision is made for students with mild, moderate, and severe learning disabilities.* The implications of this premise include using all curriculum alternatives to meet the diverse needs of adolescents with learning disabilities.
2. *Special education services must become fully integrated into the general education framework.* Special education must be viewed as a specialized part of the general education system designed to meet the needs of a particular population in cooperation with the general educator. This premise embraces philosophical tenets of least restrictive environment and normalization.
3. *Learning is the joint responsibility of the teacher and the adolescent.* Close examination of Public Law 94-142 (incorporated in the Individuals with Disabilities Education Act) reveals a strong implication that much responsibility for learning lies only with the teacher. It appears that if educators properly structure the learning environment with attention to antecedents and consequents, learning invariably will occur. Ideally this may be true; however, in practice educators simply do not control all the necessary antecedents and consequents. Any special educators who expect to "arrange" the environment independently and have learning naturally follow are going to be disappointed. If the adolescent finds street life more exciting than learning and does not attend school (or prefers to goof off when in school), little is going to be accomplished. In the secondary school, the student and teacher must interact intensively if learning is to occur. The student should be involved in the individualized educational program (IEP) planning and in curriculum decisions.
4. *The program orientation will focus on the needs and abilities of each individual student.* The implication is that students' abilities and the demands of their environment will be considered in setting individual program goals. After 10 years of schooling, for example, if a student is reading at second-grade level, it is not realistic to expect the reading level to jump to grade placement in the 9 to 18 remaining months at school. Likewise, a student working part-time as a carpenter's helper has a greater need to learn measurement skills than to master algebra.
5. *The curriculum content of the secondary program will include provisions for effective career, vocational, and transition education.* Some adolescents with learning disabilities have developed career goals, and others are beginning the process of examining career options. Some choices may require a college education, some will require a secondary school diploma, and a few may not require any formal degree. Some adolescents with learning disabilities set unobtainable goals, and others choose realistic careers. Regardless of the circumstances, each student should be encouraged and permitted to select and train for a career.
6. *Any student with learning disabilities placed in a general education class has the skills and motivation to meet the minimum standards for success.* In practice, students with learning disabilities probably are expected to meet the established standards in many classes and modified standards in others. In school systems or states that require a minimum competency test, adolescents with learning disabilities must meet the basic standards to receive a secondary school diploma (Campbell & Olsen, 1994).

General Curriculum Alternatives

An important programming decision at the secondary level is whether the standard secondary curriculum is appropriate for the student or whether an alternative curriculum is required. An alternative secondary curriculum assumes that the disability is severe enough to require a curriculum that is different in difficulty (e.g., basic social studies concepts) or in emphasis (e.g., functional living skills). Graduation requirements may be a factor in this decision. For example, in some states alternative courses cannot be used to earn credits for a standard secondary school diploma. A special diploma or certificate is awarded when approved alternative courses are completed. Usually the selection of an alternative curriculum for a student represents a decision that the student will not be going to a university for an academic degree; however, other postsecondary education and training options are available. Because the selection of an alternative curriculum affects postsecondary options, the student and the family should understand the implications of this decision.

Participation in the standard curriculum assumes that the content of the curriculum represents an appropriate education for the student. The student can participate fully in the secondary curriculum with no additional curriculum content delivered through the learning disabilities program. Thus, the student is not provided with initial skill or content instruction but can seek modifications or tutoring in content or skills that are covered in general classes.

A supportive secondary curriculum may be selected for the student if the standard curriculum is deemed important but additional instruction in skills and content is required. Instruction is provided in a support class setting (e.g., special course, elective course, or resource room), and a special curriculum is identified as being necessary for the student to be successful in the standard curriculum. Instruction is provided in specific academic, strategy, cognitive, social, or motivational areas or in selected topics (e.g., career or vocational education).

Types of Intervention

Another dimension of secondary programming concerns the type of intervention. Three intervention approaches are prominent as instructional emphases across programs for adolescents with learning disabilities: skill-oriented approaches, content-oriented approaches, and strategy-oriented approaches.

Skill-Oriented Approaches. A skill-oriented approach involves teaching students skills that relate to the academic areas in which they are experiencing difficulty. Skills are broken down and taught to the students over time. The two areas frequently emphasized in skill-oriented approaches are basic skills and study skills.

Basic skills remediation is the foundation of learning disabilities programs in the elementary school setting. This approach often focuses on the use of basal reading and math series and corrective programs. Remediation of skills corresponding to the student's achievement level is provided with the goal of sequentially improving the student's skills. Progress in basic skills acquisition is part of almost every schoolwide testing program and generally is used as a major indicator of school success. For example, most essential skills and minimum competency tests focus on reading, writing, and math skills.

Study skills instruction focuses on addressing the organizational and learning problems observed in adolescents with learning disabilities and is designed to promote student success across the content areas. It commonly is characterized by brief instruction in procedures such as taking notes, using a textbook, and studying for a test. Usually a general set of procedures and rules is taught to the student with the emphasis on application of the skill in all classes.

Proponents of skill-oriented approaches attempt to alter the characteristics or skills of the student and argue that instruction in the skills directly addresses the nature of the student's problem. The student must learn the skills to become independent. However, critics claim that adolescents with learning disabilities do not generalize the skills they learn and that progress in learning the skills is so slow that motivation may be destroyed.

Content-Oriented Approaches. A content-oriented approach involves promoting the direct acquisition of content by students. Skill or strategy instruction also is designed ultimately to lead to content-area learning, but the relationship is indirect. In general, content acquisition is promoted by the learning disabilities program through (a) providing tutoring in content areas, (b) offering courses with content that is parallel or equivalent to that of mainstream courses but is delivered differently, or (c) offering alternative content courses that reduce the amount or difficulty of the content to be learned. In a survey of State Departments of Education, McKenzie (1991) found that content instruction by special educators is used extensively throughout the nation.

In the tutorial approach, another teacher is responsible for the delivery of content, but the learning disabilities teacher provides short-term assistance in mastering key aspects of the content in which the student is experiencing difficulty or failure. The support class teacher's major responsibility is to keep the student current in the general curriculum.

Some schools promote content-area learning through the support class by creating specialized content-delivery courses in which the nature of the content is equivalent to that covered in the general classroom. This approach is called an *equivalent-content approach* and involves the total delivery of content by the learning disabilities teacher in a manner that accounts for the student's lack of basic skills, study skills, or strategies. This delivery approach varies in scope but can include such features as the use of audiotaped materials, modified textbooks, expanded study guides and content outlines, alternative test formats, modified pacing, and extended semesters.

The alternate content-delivery approach is based on the selection of an alternative secondary curriculum, and mainstream courses are offered to students as alternatives to participating in the general content class. These courses often use adapted textbooks and limit or reduce the amount of content that is covered. They are not comparable to the content-area courses offered in the general curriculum but provide an alternate content-learning experience that may be more learnable and meaningful to students. However, a student participating in courses offering a watered-down content curriculum is not likely to acquire the background knowledge required to compete in the mainstream curriculum. This concern results from growing evidence that low-achieving students lack sufficient background knowledge, scientific literacy, and cultural or social literacy.

Proponents of content-oriented approaches alter the demands placed on students or change the traditional organization of the environment for instruction. They argue that a focus on content is consistent with the goals of the general secondary curriculum and that students are able to obtain the information that leads to secondary school success (i.e., they will pass their courses). Critics claim that a content focus provides only a short-term solution for students and that when the students graduate they will remain dependent on others for assistance if they have not acquired skills related to being independent.

Strategy-Oriented Approaches. Some educators argue that an instructional intervention that emphasizes only one area or dimension is insufficient to bring about permanent and lasting behavior changes. As a result, many instructional efforts attempt to balance skill and content instruction in an effort to meet a broader range of needs. However, the integration of skill and content approaches usually consists simply of offering both content and skill options but not evaluating the shortcomings of either set of options.

Strategy-oriented approaches focus on helping the student acquire content through instruction in strategies. Deshler and Lenz (1989) define *strategy* as an individual's approach to a task, including how a student thinks and acts when planning, executing, and evaluating performance on a task and its outcomes. However, the goal of instruction is not simply to learn a strategy but to acquire the targeted information. Instruction in strategies should be viewed by students as a vehicle for enabling them to better acquire, store, and express the information.

Strategy-oriented approaches can focus on the acquisition of either specific strategies or integrated strategies systems.

Specific-strategy instruction involves selecting a strategy, such as paraphrasing reading material, and then teaching it directly to students to improve comprehension. The strategy is discussed and practiced, but its application is restricted to the task for which it is targeted. For example, the students may need to memorize lists of information for a test. After instructing them how to create a mnemonic, the teacher may have the students practice the strategy and prompt them to use the strategy across classes; however, the goal of instruction is for the students to use the strategy to respond to immediate and concrete problems they currently are facing. Thus, the students learn the content and also learn and use a strategy to enable them to accomplish this goal.

A more comprehensive approach to strategy instruction for adolescents with learning disabilities is proposed by Don Deshler, Jean Schumaker, and their colleagues at the University of Kansas Center for Research on Learning. They developed the Strategies Intervention Model (SIM) as an intervention approach that serves as the basis for a dual orientation to operationalizing interventions for adolescents with learning disabilities. The underlying framework of the model guides curriculum development, instructional procedures, and organization of the instructional environment across general education classes and classes designed specifically for adolescents with learning disabilities. In addition, the SIM framework guides the development and implementation of instructional programs related to training mentors, promoting a successful school-to-work transition, developing postsecondary support services, working with families of students, and training counselors.

The Strategies Intervention Model is based on the concept of designing instructional programs through an integration of cognitive information-processing theory and behavioral theory. Both teachers and students are viewed as information processors. As a result, strategies and teaching routines are developed that can be used to promote better skill acquisition by students and improved content delivery by teachers. Most curriculum areas (e.g., reading, English, science, career education, and vocational training) are taught using the basic principles of this model. Descriptions of some of the interventions that have been developed as part of this model are presented later in this chapter.

In a multistate study of teachers' and supervisors' perceptions of secondary learning disabilities programs, Cline and Billingsley (1991) found that the primary program components have remained consistent over the past decade but the relative importance of these areas is changing. The four highest-rated program components of teachers and supervisors include direct teaching of content subjects, basic skills remediation, learning/study strategies, and tutorial assistance. The respondents, however, indicate a need to decrease content-area instruction by special education teachers and increase learning strategies instruction. Also, the results highlight a need to provide more consultation to general education teachers.

The context of Cline and Billingsley's (1991) findings regarding the need to provide more consultation to general education teachers becomes more focused when Ellett's (1993) findings are considered. Ellett examined secondary teachers' reactions to 35 intervention strategies suggested for mainstream classes. Results reveal that secondary teachers prefer strategies that can be implemented in their own classroom, can apply to all students, and require little extra time. Their most preferred strategies are to use supplemental resources, simplify instruction, and provide students with support and extra cues. Their least preferred strategies are to facilitate grade improvement, modify the learning environment, teach study skills, and provide positive and cooperative learning environments.

Secondary Programming Models

To implement comprehensive educational services at the secondary level for adolescents with learning disabilities, attention must be given to developing a variety of program components. This is accomplished by identifying the major dimensions of the program and developing each of these areas. Schumaker, Deshler, and Ellis (1986) identify three major areas of program development believed to be critical for developing secondary learning disabilities programs: (a) clearly specifying the nature of the curriculum that is to be taught, (b) identifying the instructional methodologies that will be used to teach the curriculum, and (c) specifying how the instructional environment will be arranged to manage and promote student learning. Table 10.1 represents the dimensions of secondary programming that are addressed in the Strategies Intervention Model of the University of Kansas Center for Research on Learning.

Zigmond (1990) and Polloway, Patton, Epstein, and Smith (1989) also present components for developing secondary programs for students with learning disabilities. These researchers address the same general areas identified by Deshler and his colleagues, but the specific dimension and emphases vary. For example, in addition to renewing attention to the skills students need to learn, increasing the intensity of instruction, and developing stronger ties with general educators, Zigmond proposes two basic models for organizing services. These models are presented in Figure 10.1 and provide useful guidelines for specific program development efforts. Overall, Zigmond's model focuses on four components: intensive instruction in reading and mathematics, training in survival skills, concentration on passing courses needed for graduation, and planning for postschool transitions.

The model for organizing programming presented by Polloway et al. (1989) focuses primarily on delineating the content of the secondary program rather than on specific instructional procedures and management arrangements. They argue that a comprehensive curriculum should be developed that (a) responds to the current needs of individuals, (b) balances the need for maximum interaction with normally achieving peers against critical curriculum needs, (c) integrates related service delivery options, (d) emerges from a realistic appraisal of potential adult outcomes for the student, (e) focuses on transitional needs across the life span, and (f) is sensitive to graduation goals and requirements. Polloway et al. propose a system of tracks in which subgroups of students with learning disabilities may be placed as a way of organizing programming. Their tracks include a functional track for students with severe learning disabilities, a college-preparatory track, and a "tough-to-call" track for students with learning disabilities whose future is difficult to project.

Each of these programming models has a specific emphasis that distinguishes it from the others, but all of the models argue for the identification of well thought-out program components that ensure organized and intensive instruction. These models illustrate the need for the development of comprehensive and multidimensional programs to meet the diverse needs of secondary students with learning disabilities.

SUPPORTIVE AND ALTERNATIVE CURRICULUM APPROACHES

Motivation

Motivation to learn or participate is essential to the success of any intervention approach. The adage "You can lead a horse to water, but you can't make him drink" certainly applies to learning. For an intervention approach to be effective with a student who has learning disabilities, the student must be motivated to participate. For the adolescent with learning disabilities, lack of motivation is often a roadblock to school success. Thus, regarding motivation, the adage may be altered to "Although you can't make a horse drink the water, you can salt the hay."

Several motivation techniques are available to help low-achieving students in secondary school. Deshler, Schumaker, and Lenz (1984) divide these approaches into two broad categories: those that use extrinsic controls and those that focus on developing intrinsic motivation.

TABLE 10.1
Secondary Programming Components of the Strategies Intervention Model

Strategic Curriculum Component

The Strategic Curriculum Component of the Strategies Intervention Model specifies *what* will be taught to low-achieving or at-risk students. This component consists of four types of strategies.

Learning Strategies: designed to teach students how to cope with the academic demands encountered across a variety of school, home, community, and employment settings. These learning strategies teach students how to respond to critical reading, writing, listening, remembering, and test-taking demands.

Social Skills Strategies: designed to teach the student how to interact appropriately across a variety of situations and settings. Strategies such as resisting peer pressure, accepting criticism, negotiating, following directions, and asking for help are included.

Motivation Strategies: consists of strategies that enable students to become active in planning the direction of their lives. Strategies that teach students how to set, monitor, and attain goals related to important areas of their lives and then communicate these goals to others are included.

Executive Strategies: designed to teach students how to solve problems independently and generalize learning. These strategies are taught to students after instruction in three to five learning strategies.

Strategic Instruction Component

The Strategic Instruction Component includes procedures for *how* strategies should be taught to students. In addition, it includes procedures for the effective delivery of content to low-achieving and at-risk students.

Acquisition Procedures: provides teachers with a sequenced set of steps for teaching the strategies to mastery.

Generalization Procedures: provides teachers with a sequenced set of steps for teaching and ensuring generalization and maintenance of newly acquired strategies to other settings and situations.

Strategic Teaching Behaviors: provides teachers with the critical teaching behaviors that should be infused throughout all steps and phases of strategy and content instruction to promote maximum learning by low-achieving and at-risk students.

Content Enhancement Procedures: provides teachers with routines and devices for delivering subject-matter information in a manner that can be understood and remembered by students.

Strategic Environment Component

The Strategic Environment Component deals with how to manage and organize educational settings and programs to promote and prompt strategic learning and performance.

Teaming Techniques: consists of methods related to teaching teachers, students, parents, and other professionals how to work as a team to bring about maximum student learning.

Management Techniques: consists of methods related to how to manage materials, time, instructional arrangements, and student behavior to promote student independence and success.

Evaluation Techniques: consists of systems related to evaluating student performance, program performance, and teacher performance and providing feedback about progress to those involved in a manner that will promote student learning and success.

Development Techniques: consists of methods related to systematically implementing program components and developing strategies responsive to student needs.

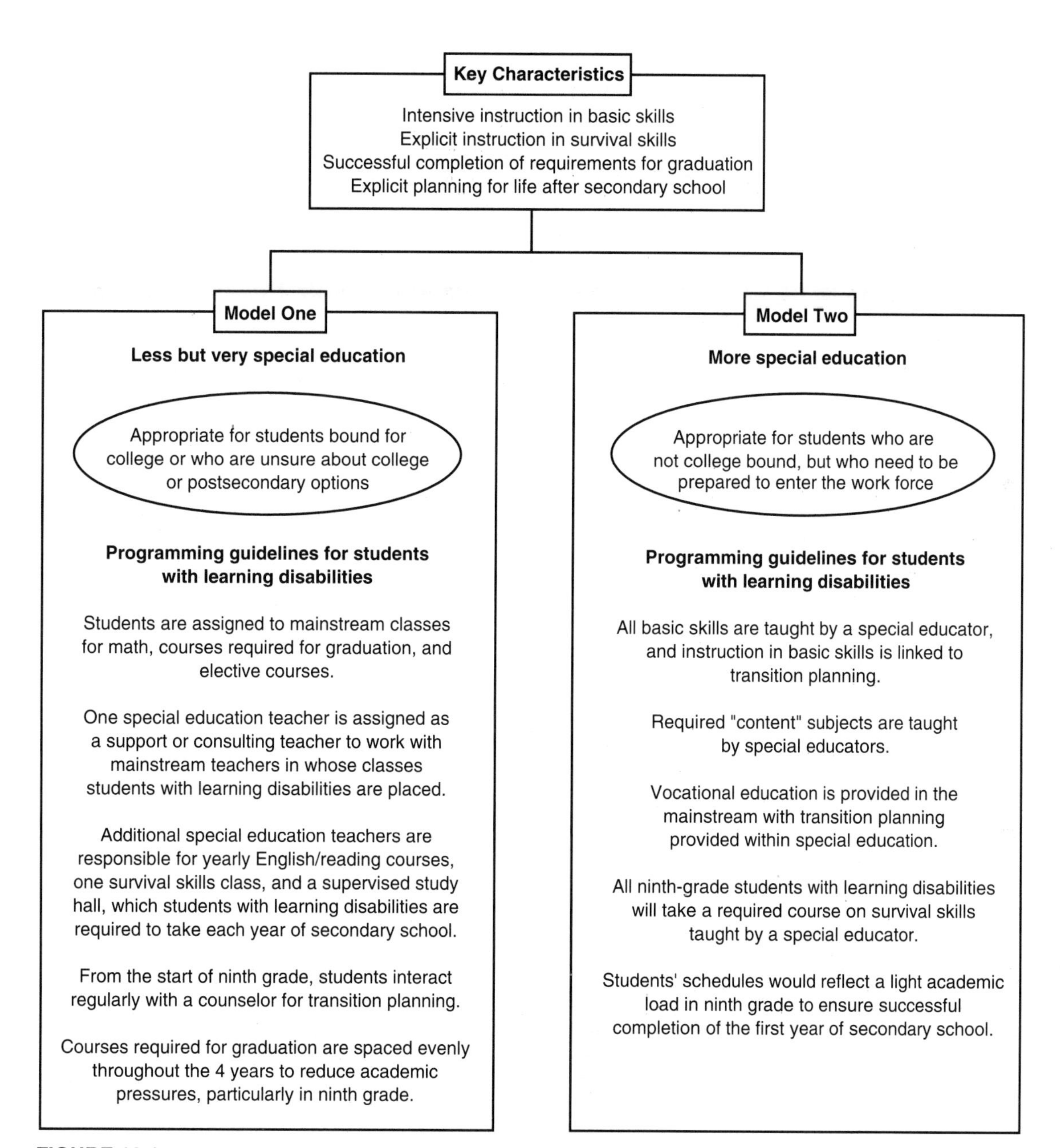

FIGURE 10.1
Secondary school programming guidelines for students with learning disabilities

From their review of motivation studies, Deshler, Schumaker, and Lenz report that several extrinsic control techniques have been used successfully to improve the academic skills of adolescents with learning disabilities. Zigmond, Sansone, Miller, Donahoe, and Kohnke (1986) provide a list of extrinsic reinforcers that appear to be effective with adolescents. The reinforcers include the following:

1. Time for listening to tapes
2. Tokens for progress on academics
3. Charting or self-recording of academic accomplishments
4. Allowances at home tied to grades
5. Time to play games or enjoy a recreational activity
6. Opportunity to participate in scheduling academic activities
7. Tangible reinforcers such as restaurant coupons, magazines, and movie tickets
8. Exemption from some homework or assignments
9. Extra time for a break or lunch

The most useful techniques include token economies, contingency contracting, and verbal feedback (see Chapter 15 for descriptions of these techniques). Techniques aimed at facilitating intrinsic motivation also are receiving support.

Motivation strategies are one of the curriculum components of the Strategies Intervention Model developed at the University of Kansas Center for Research on Learning. Van Reusen and Bos (1994) note that motivation strategies within this model are defined as "techniques and procedures that involve the learner in key aspects of the learning process and are used to increase a student's commitment to learn" (p. 469). Within this context, Van Reusen and Bos examined the effectiveness of IPARS (Van Reusen, Bos, Schumaker, & Deshler, 1987), a motivation strategy designed to foster students' active participation in IEP conferences. They found that students with learning disabilities who received the strategy instruction identified more goals and communicated better during the conferences than did the contrast students. Van Reusen et al. maintain that motivation strategies represent processes that increase the learners' interest in their own learning and foster their ability to gain control over their own performances.

To promote the development of active and independent learners, some motivation strategies are aimed at training self-control skills, including one or more of the following: goal setting, self-recording of progress, self-evaluation, and self-reinforcement. Seabaugh and Schumaker (1981) taught all four of these self-control subskills to adolescents with learning disabilities and had positive results (i.e., the number of lessons completed by the students increased from an average of one-half lesson completed per day to four lessons completed per day). Deshler, Schumaker, and Lenz (1984) report that self-control training holds much promise for helping students with learning disabilities complete their assignments. They note that the training procedures are easy to implement and do not depend on expensive extrinsic reinforcers.

From their review of the motivation literature, H. S. Adelman and Taylor (1983) list tactics for enhancing intrinsic motivation, including the following:

1. Provide some choices in curriculum content and procedures to enhance the student's perception that learning is worthwhile. Also, discussions concerning the relevance (real-life applications) of content are helpful.
2. Through discussion, obtain a commitment to options that the student values and indicates a desire to pursue. Contractual agreements are helpful.
3. Schedule informal and formal conferences with the student to enhance the student's role in making choices and negotiating agreements.
4. Provide feedback that conveys student progress. The student must not perceive the feedback as an effort to entice and control. Self-correcting materials are useful.

A recurring theme in the literature on managing and motivating adolescents with learning disabilities is that of involving the student. For example, in their discussion of secondary classroom management, Kerr and Nelson (1989) state, "We strongly recommend that you encourage pupils to participate in all aspects of the curriculum. Specifically, they should be involved in selecting and ordering their own academic and social goals, in making decisions about the classroom structure, and in setting consequences and contingencies" (p. 157). An example of procedures that teachers can use to teach students how to participate in goal setting and planning is presented by Van Reusen et al. (1987).

Another dimension that may be included in efforts to promote student motivation relates to the beliefs that students have about themselves. Many students do not believe that they can learn or change. Ellis, Deshler, Lenz, Schumaker, and Clark (1991) present four techniques for teachers to use to help students alter their beliefs about their learning and performance:

1. Engineer instructional arrangements to promote and reinforce student independence.
2. Communicate high expectations for students through words and actions.
3. Help students identify and analyze beliefs that underlie their behavior as ineffective learners.
4. Help students discard unproductive beliefs through a variety of activities and interactions.

Social Development

The social skills deficits of many adolescents with learning disabilities are well documented. Numerous authorities (Deshler & Schumaker, 1983; Schumaker & Hazel, 1984; Zigmond & Brownlee, 1980) recommend social skills training for these adolescents. Generally, the development of social skills is believed to help adolescents with learning disabilities in several ways:

1. Social competence helps compensate for academic deficits.
2. Social skills are needed for success in the mainstream and in employment.
3. Social skills training helps adolescents with learning disabilities derive maximum benefit from academic or vocational instruction.
4. Social competence is fundamental to good interpersonal relationships and fosters involvement in leisure and recreational activities.

Zigmond and her colleagues at the University of Pittsburgh and Schumaker and her colleagues at the University of Kansas present social skills curricula for adolescents with learning disabilities. Zigmond's curriculum, the School Survival Skills Curriculum, features three strands: behavior control, teacher-pleasing behaviors, and study skills (Silverman, Zigmond, & Sansone, 1981). The curriculum developed at the University of Kansas Center for Research on Learning, *Social Skills for Daily Living* (Schumaker, Hazel, & Pederson, 1988), focuses on such skills as resisting peer pressure, accepting and giving compliments, asking and answering questions, making friends, responding to teasing, following instructions, apologizing, and joining group activities.

Academic Remediation

The approach of teaching basic academic skills stresses that improved academic skills help the student benefit from course work in all content areas. When academic deficiencies are considered in light of expectancies placed on many students with learning problems to earn a secondary school diploma, the emphasis on academic remediation is understandable.

While the need for academic remediation is apparent, some educators (Deshler, Schumaker, Lenz, & Ellis, 1984) express concern that it is being overused at the secondary level. They claim that many adolescents have difficulty understanding the relevance of academic remediation content. Also, Deshler, Schumaker, Lenz, and Ellis question the effectiveness of this approach in helping students cope with the complex demands of the secondary curriculum. Finally, they report that time spent on remediation may be too limited to have a meaningful effect on academic skills at the secondary level.

In spite of concerns about academic remediation for adolescents with learning problems, many educators promote it. Zigmond (1990) maintains that intensive and efficient instruction in basic academic skills is essential for helping students succeed in employment and in independent living situations. Academic interventions seem especially appropriate for 9th and 10th graders who are achieving below fourth-grade level in one of the basic skill areas. It also appears that academic remediation should be provided in conjunction with other services (e.g., career-related instruction, and functional living skills).

In a review of secondary curriculum content for students with learning disabilities, Rieth and Polsgrove (1994) report several noteworthy findings. In the area of teaching reading to adolescents, they report that phonics instruction appears to be a weak intervention. In the area of spelling, they found that spelling ability appears to improve when spelling instruction is integrated with other meaning-based language arts instruction. In the area of teaching mathematics to adolescents, the use of videodisc technology has yielded impressive achievement gains with adolescents with learning disabilities and has been well received by teachers (Woodward & Gersten, 1992).

Several projects provide academic remediation to secondary students with learning disabilities. For example, the Pittsburgh Child Service Demonstration Center developed a model that is widely used in Pittsburgh secondary schools (Buchwach, 1980). Students attend a resource room (called a learning lab) for no more than two periods daily. The students are removed only from English or math to receive basic skill intervention. A diagnostic systematic approach to skill development is provided, and generalization of newly learned skills is fostered by having students eventually use materials from mainstream classes in the learning lab. A second special education resource teacher functions as a liaison between the students and their mainstream teachers. In addition, this teacher works with the learning lab teacher once a week to provide a school survival skills curriculum (i.e., strands pertaining to behavior, teacher-pleasing behavior, and study skills). Thus, this model demonstrates the use of both academic remediation services and learning strategies intervention.

Because secondary students face numerous curriculum demands and have a limited amount of time to ameliorate deficits, educators are seeking ways to increase the intensity of instruction (e.g., learning labs and high-intensity learning centers). The *Corrective Reading Program*, (published by SRA) is used with adolescents with learning disabilities to increase the level of instructional intensity of academic remediation (Polloway, Epstein, Polloway, Patton, & Ball, 1986). Moreover, summer school programs can provide an opportunity for high-intensity instruction without delaying graduation.

Learning Strategies

As students progress through the grades, the demands for successful performance generally increase. Some educators feel that the complexity of secondary demands contributes as much to adolescent failure as do learning deficits. A learning strategies approach helps students with learning disabilities cope with the complex demands of the secondary curriculum. Deshler and his colleagues at the University of Kansas Center for Research on Learning define *learning strategies* as techniques, principles, or rules that enable a student to learn, to solve problems, and to complete tasks independently. The goal of strategy development is to identify strategies that are optimally effective (i.e., help students meet the demands of both current and future tasks) and efficient (i.e., help students meet the demands of the task in a manner that is appropriate, timely, resourceful, and judicious). The goal of strategies instruction is to teach the strategies effectively (i.e., the strategy is learned and generalized by the student) and efficiently (i.e., the strategy is learned to an optimal level with a minimum amount of effort by the teacher and the student). The goal of this approach is to help students learn course content (such as geography) through instruction in skills necessary to acquire, store, and express content. Basically, it focuses on teaching students how to learn and how to demonstrate command of their knowledge in performing academic tasks. For example, a reading strategy may be used by a student with 4th-grade reading skills to obtain relevant information from a textbook chapter written at the 10th-grade level. As one part of the Strategies Intervention Model, Deshler and his colleagues developed a learning strategies curriculum, whose components have been specified, developed, and validated in classrooms. Field-testing and evaluation data indicate good student progress and a high degree of consumer satisfaction (Deshler & Schumaker, 1986, 1988; Schumaker, Deshler, & Ellis, 1986). Because the strategies included in the Strategies Intervention Model have the longest history of comprehensive research and development for adolescents with learning disabilities, a detailed description of this approach is presented.

The Learning Strategies Curriculum of the University of Kansas Center for Research on Learning includes intervention manuals and support materials. The manuals, available through training, provide guidelines to teachers on how to provide intensive instruction to adolescents with learning disabilities and how to promote the acquisition, storage, and expression of information and demonstration of competence through instruction in learning strategies. The strategies included in the curriculum are listed and described in Table 10.2. Each of the teacher's manuals provides detailed instructional procedures on how to teach the strategy and prompt the student to transfer the strategy across settings. Teachers are trained in the basic concepts of the strategy, which previously has been validated through research, and they are encouraged to tailor strategy instruction according to their personal teaching style to meet the needs of students. Thus, while integrity in the basic features of the strategy and the instructional procedures is necessary to ensure student success, the teacher is given wide latitude to make the intervention meaningful in individual situations.

The learning strategy interventions respond to the specific needs of learning disabilities teachers who need instructional procedures and curricula for adolescents with learning disabilities. Because most learning disabilities teachers provide instruction in a support class setting rather than in the general classroom setting, the curriculum materials are used mainly to teach strategies in one setting and then prompt generalization of the strategies to additional settings (e.g., the general classroom). The student's general classroom materials are used in the process so that the student learns to associate the strategy with success in meeting naturally occurring learning demands. Changes in service delivery options make it possible for general classroom teachers to infuse many dimensions of these strategy interventions into content-area instruction. This allows the student to see the application of the strategy in natural settings. However, additional intensive instruction usually is required by the learning disabilities teacher in a support class setting because many secondary content teachers are not able to provide the explicit or intensive instruction required to overcome the difficulties of students with learning disabilities.

The instructional procedures used in the Strategies Intervention Model can be described best as a direct strategy training approach incorporating planned opportunities for the student to become involved in the instructional process and to discover ways in which the strategy can be personally empowering. Criteria for maximizing the success of strategy instruction include the following:

1. The student should be committed to learn the strategy and fully understand the purpose and benefits of the strategy.

TABLE 10.2
The Learning Strategies Curriculum of the University of Kansas Center for Research on Learning

Acquisition Strand

Strategic Math Series: teaches students problem-solving procedures for acquiring and applying basic math facts. The strategies are designed to help students develop fluency in basic math facts and use strategies for solving word problems.

Word Identification Strategy: teaches students a problem-solving procedure for quickly attacking and decoding unknown words in reading materials, allowing them to move on quickly for the purpose of comprehending the passage.

Paraphrasing Strategy: directs students to read a limited section of material, ask themselves the main idea and the details of the section, and put that information in their own words. The strategy is designed to improve comprehension by focusing attention on the important information of a passage and by stimulating active involvement with the passage.

Self-Questioning Strategy: aids reading comprehension by having students actively ask questions about key pieces of information in a passage and then read to find the answers for these questions.

Visual Imagery Strategy: improves students' acquisition, storage, and recall of prose material. Students improve reading comprehension by reading short passages and visualizing the scene that is described incorporating actors, action, and details.

Interpreting Visuals Strategy: aids students in the use and interpretation of visuals such as maps, graphs, pictures, and tables to increase their ability to extract needed information from written materials.

Multipass Strategy: involves making three passes through a passage to focus attention on key details and main ideas. Students survey a chapter or passage to get an overview, size up sections of the chapter by systematically scanning to locate relevant information that they note, and sort out important information in the chapter by locating answers to specific questions.

Storage Strand

FIRST-Letter Mnemonic Strategy: aids students in memorizing lists of information by teaching them to design mnemonics or memorization aids, and to find and make lists of crucial information.

Paired Associates Strategy: aids students in memorizing pairs or small groups of information by using visual imagery, matching pertinent information with familiar objects, coding important dates, and using a first-syllable technique.

Listening and Note-Taking Strategy: teaches students to develop skills to enhance their ability to learn from listening experiences. Students learn to identify the speaker's verbal cues or mannerisms that indicate important information is about to be given, note key words, and organize notes into an outline for future reference or study.

2. The physical and mental actions covered in the strategy should be described and explained fully.
3. The student should be told how to use the remembering system incorporated in the strategy intervention to facilitate the process of self-instruction.
4. The student should understand the process of learning the strategy and participate in goal-setting activities to anticipate and monitor learning.
5. Multiple models of the strategy should be provided, and an appropriate balance between the physical and mental activities involved in the strategy should be achieved.
6. The student should be enlisted in the model and become a full participant in guiding the strategy instructional process.

TABLE 10.2
continued

Expression and Demonstration of Competence Strand

Sentence Writing Strategy: teaches students how to recognize and generate four types of sentences: simple, compound, complex, and compound-complex.

Paragraph Writing Strategy: teaches students how to write well-organized, complete paragraphs by outlining ideas, selecting a point-of-view and tense for the paragraph, sequencing ideas, and checking their work.

Error Monitoring Strategy: teaches students a process for detecting and correcting errors in their writing and for producing a neater written product. Students are taught to locate errors in paragraph organization, sentence structure, capitalization, overall editing and appearance, punctuation, and spelling by asking themselves a series of questions. Students correct their errors and rewrite the passage before submitting it to their teacher.

Theme Writing Strategy: teaches students to generate ideas for themes, organize these ideas into a logical sequence, write the paragraphs, monitor errors, and rewrite the theme.

Assignment Completion Strategy: teaches students to monitor their assignments from the time an assignment is given until it is completed and turned in to the teacher. Students write down assignments; analyze the assignments; schedule various subtasks; complete the subtasks and, ultimately, the entire task; and submit the completed assignment.

Test-Taking Strategy: teaches students to allocate time during a test and read instructions and questions carefully. A question is either answered or put aside for later consideration. The obviously wrong answers are eliminated from the abandoned questions and a reasonable guess is made. The last step is to survey the entire test for unanswered questions.

7. The strategy should be fully understood and memorized before practice in the strategy is initiated.
8. Practice should begin with controlled guided practice and ultimately conclude with advanced independent practice.
9. A measurement system should provide ongoing information that demonstrates to the student and the teacher that the strategy is being learned and used and that the demands of the setting are being met.
10. While generalization should be prompted throughout the strategy acquisition process, specific efforts to promote generalization should follow strategy acquisition.

The learning strategies, when combined with the motivation and social skills strategies, provide the basis for a solid curriculum for the secondary learning disabilities teacher. The learning disabilities teacher assumes the role of a learning specialist whose goal is to focus on helping students learn to learn. However, simply implementing the specified learning strategies does not necessarily lead to student success. Deshler and Lenz (1989) make the following observation about strategy instruction:

> It could be argued that the key to delivering a truly strategic intervention is to stop conceptualizing strategies instruction as consisting of a single intervention, or several strategy interventions, or even a well developed strategies curriculum. It may be more beneficial to begin thinking about strategy interventions as the creation of a set of environments (e.g., the support classroom, the regular classroom, the home, etc.) in which key activities are done in a strategic manner. Well designed strategies environments should promote, model, guide, and prompt efficient and effective learning and performance across all students, not just those with learning disabilities. (p. 222)

The teaching methods used with students exhibiting learning problems are crucial to the suc-

TABLE 10.3
Functional Living Curriculum Areas

Areas	
1. *Managing family finances*	Clean food preparation areas
Identify money and make correct change	Store food
Make wise expenditures	6. *Buying and caring for clothing*
Obtain and use bank and credit facilities	Wash clothing
Keep basic financial records	Iron and store clothing
Calculate and pay taxes	Perform simple mending
2. *Selecting, managing, and maintaining a home*	Purchase clothing
Select adequate housing	7. *Engaging in civic activities*
Maintain a home	Generally understand local laws and government
Use basic appliances and tools	Generally understand the federal government
Maintain home exterior	Understand citizenship rights and responsibilities
3. *Caring for personal needs*	Understand registration and voting procedures
Dress appropriately	Understand Selective Service procedures
Exhibit proper grooming and hygiene	Understand civil rights and responsibilities when questioned by the law
Demonstrate knowledge of physical fitness, nutrition, and weight control	8. *Using recreation and leisure*
Demonstrate knowledge of common illness prevention and treatment	Participate actively in group activities
4. *Raising children—family living*	Know activities and available community resources
Prepare for adjustment to marriage	Understand recreational values
Prepare for raising children (physical care)	Use recreational facilities in the community
Prepare for raising children (psychological care)	Plan and choose activities wisely
Practice family safety in the home	Plan vacations
5. *Buying and preparing food*	9. *Getting around the community (mobility)*
Demonstrate appropriate eating skills	Demonstrate knowledge of traffic rules and safety practices
Plan balanced meals	Demonstrate knowledge and use of various means of transportation
Purchase food	Drive a car
Prepare meals	

Note: From *Career Education for Handicapped Individuals* (pp. 46–47), 2nd ed., by C. J. Kokaska and D. E. Brolin, 1985, Upper Saddle River, NJ: Merrill/Prentice Hall. Copyright 1985 by Prentice-Hall Publishing Company. Reprinted by permission.

cess of the instruction. These acquisition steps, presented later in this chapter, focus on providing the student with the knowledge, motivation, and practice required to apply a skill or strategy to materials and situations comparable to general secondary classroom demands (Schumaker & Deshler, 1988). Additional information about the Strategies Intervention Model and the Learning Strategies Curriculum can be obtained by contacting the Coordinator of Training, Center for Research on Learning, 3061 Robert Dole Human Development Center, The University of Kansas, Lawrence, KS 66045–2342.

Functional Living Skills

A functional or essential living skills program typically is designed for secondary students whose academic skills are very low (i.e., below fourth-grade level). Functional living skills are essential for successful living in modern society, and for some students with learning problems,

TABLE 10.4
Instructional Areas in Clark and Kolstoe's School-Based Career Education Model

Preparation for Exit for Entry-Level Job If Necessary at Age 16	
Preschool to Grade 2:	Acquisition of job and daily living skills
Grades 2 to 4:	Occupational information
Grades 4 to 6:	Human relationships
Grades 6 to 8:	Values, attitudes, and habits
Grade 9:	Work evaluation or work adjustment program
Preparation for Exit for Entry-Level, Semiskilled, or Specialized Job	
Grade 10:	Cooperative education or work-study program
Grade 11:	Vocational/technical or fine arts program
Grade 12:	College preparatory/general education

they must be taught directly and systematically. Otherwise, the students never may acquire them or may learn them through trial and error that is both costly and time-consuming. Kokaska and Brolin (1985) list nine important areas in planning a functional living curriculum (see Table 10.3). Many of these skills can be taught within the traditional curriculum. For example, Area 1 may be included in math, Areas 3 and 5 in science; Areas 4, 7, and 9 in social studies; Areas 2 and 6 in home economics and shop; and Area 8 in music, art, and physical education.

Career-Related Instruction

The emphasis on career education began in the early 1970s and evolved from dissatisfaction with the educational system's ability to prepare students adequately for the future. In 1988, the U.S. Department of Labor, Education, and Commerce surveyed 134 business representatives concerning their needs, goals, and expectations of education when hiring adolescents. One of their primary findings was that the "basic skills gap" between what businesses need and the qualifications beginning workers possess is widening. Moreover, they report that these skill deficiencies are costing employers a great deal of money in their quest to produce quality products at competitive prices.

Students with learning disabilities often need attractive options in career training. Thus, career education involves a comprehensive educational program that begins in early childhood and continues throughout adulthood. Career-related instruction enables an individual to explore the occupational world, identify with it, and make job decisions that increase self-fulfillment. Moreover, the content places value on all work, regardless of its current social status. Cegelka and Greene (1993) state:

> By emphasizing the relationship of subject matter to various careers and occupations and by developing needed work skills, career education sought to make education more relevant to the economic and employment realities of the day . . . .Career education has been seen as the sum of all experiences through which one learns to live a meaningful, satisfying, and productive work life. (pp. 142–143)

G. M. Clark and Kolstoe (1990) developed one of the most widely accepted models of career development that covers preschool through lifelong learning opportunities. Table 10.4 presents the instructional areas focused on at the elementary and secondary school levels. The emphasis that Clark and Kolstoe's model gives to preparing students for the numerous demands of adulthood reveals that career education is much more than occupational education.

For activities, commercial materials, and computer software programs for teaching academic skills and content, learning strategies, functional living skills, and career-related instruction, see Mercer and Mercer (1993).

Transitions from Secondary Settings

In 1990, a transition mandate was included in the Amendments to the Education of the Handicapped Act, renamed the Individuals with Disabilities Education Act (Public Law 101-476). This law defines *transition* as

> a coordinated set of activities for a student, designed within an outcome-oriented process, which promotes movement from school to post-school activities, including post-secondary education, vocational training, integrated employment (including supported employment), continuing and adult education, adult services, independent living, and community participation. The coordinated set of activities shall be based upon the individual student's needs, taking into account the student's preferences and interests, and shall include: instruction, community experiences, the development of employment and other post-school adult living objectives, and when appropriate, acquisition. (Public Law 101-476, Section 602 [a] [19])

In addition, the law requires that the individualized educational program include

> a statement of the needed transition services for students beginning no later than age 16, and annually thereafter (and, when determined appropriate for the individual, beginning at age 14 or younger), including, when appropriate, a statement of the interagency responsibilities or linkages (or both) before the student leaves the school setting. (Public Law 101-476, Section 602 [a] [20])

Moreover, this law mandates that all students in special education receive transition planning and that each student's need for transition services be determined during the secondary education period. These mandates ensure that the development and delivery of transition services for students with learning disabilities receive serious and overdue consideration (Reiff & deFur, 1992).

Data accrued nationally indicate that 57% of individuals with learning disabilities are employed within 2 years of graduation compared with 62% of the general population (Wagner, 1989). The National Longitudinal Transition Study (Wagner, 1989) reports a graduation rate of 61% for students with learning disabilities and a rate of 71% to 75% for the general population. About 35% of youths with learning disabilities drop out of school, and many of these youngsters leave school at age 16 with minimum academic skills and little or no vocational training.

Although many individuals with learning disabilities become employed shortly after leaving school, inspection of employment adjustments reveals several disturbing findings. Unemployment per se is not the primary issue. Instead, underemployment, low levels of independence, low job status, and low income hinder the successful adjustments of adults with learning disabilities (P. B. Adelman & Vogel, 1993; Okolo & Sitlington, 1988). These follow-up and descriptive data of individuals with learning disabilities readily justify the need for transition planning and services for students with learning disabilities.

A systematic assessment plan is essential for determining the needs of students in relation to their postsecondary goals. Spruill (1993) notes that assessment makes effective secondary planning and programming possible and provides a context for counseling students about career decisions and life plans. She provides a secondary assessment planning chart that covers a range of assessment domains across a 6-year period. Performance areas that may be assessed and appropriate grade levels for evaluation include the following: academic skills (grades 7–10), rate of learning (grades 10–12), critical academic skills (grades 11–12), cognitive abilities (grades 7–10), job-related skills (grades 11–12), motor skills (grades 7–10), job tryouts (grades 11–12), mainstream class performance (grades 11–12), interests (grades 7–11), vocational program tryouts (grades 9–10), and social skills (grades 7–11). Spruill describes some of the primary characteristics of transition-oriented assessment:

1. Assessment is planned and conducted annually for several years.

2. The IEP team consists of a diverse group that addresses academic, social, and vocational skills, and important life skills.
3. In addition to the data generated by the respective professionals, self-assessment data from the student are considered.
4. Informal assessments (e.g., curriculum-based measures) that are relevant to instructional decision making and curriculum planning are featured.
5. Informal data are used to support decisions regarding student eligibility for special education services.
6. The assessment data enhance decisions about postsecondary plans and help facilitate transitions into postsecondary environments.

Some of the domains that are helpful in developing and assessing long-range plans and in preparing individuals with learning disabilities to meet these goals are postsecondary academic education, postsecondary vocational education, employment, independent living, physical health, support group development, personal development, recreation/leisure, use of community resources, and mobility.

Rojewski (1992) reviewed nine transition programs to determine the key components of an exemplary transition program. He identified the following seven components: individualized transition planning, integration of mainstream settings, paid work experience, active family involvement, coordination of data and services, job-seeking and placement, and follow-up and follow-along.

Finally, Durlak, Rose, and Bursuck (1994) note that several affective factors appear to be positively related to the successful postschool adjustments of adults with learning disabilities. Specifically, Durlak et al. identify self-determination skills as being important, and they examined the efficacy of directly teaching self-determination skills to secondary students with learning disabilities. Their results indicate that these students were able to acquire, maintain, and generalize skills of self-advocacy and self-awareness when the skills were taught using explicit instruction, opportunities to practice skills in the training setting and natural environment, and specific feedback. These findings have encouraging implications for developing secondary transition curricula for teaching affective skills.

INSTRUCTIONAL PROCEDURES

Simply identifying the appropriate curriculum for a student does not ensure that the student will learn the targeted information. An additional dimension of secondary programming that must be considered is how the curriculum is acquired by the student. During the development of the total intervention program, the learning characteristics of adolescents with learning disabilities should be considered. The instructional procedures used by the teacher to ensure that the student acquires the skills or content defined by the curriculum must be selected and implemented carefully.

Acquisition and Generalization of Skills and Strategies

Several instructional procedures are used to promote the acquisition of skills by adolescents. These approaches use activities involving guided practice, modeling, peer instruction, provision of feedback, and task analysis. How these instructional procedures are integrated and used to promote adolescent learning has been the focus of research at the University of Kansas Center for Research on Learning since 1978. This research has culminated in a set of instructional procedures that integrate instructional methods into specific stages of instruction. Aspects of this integrated set of instructional procedures are presented in numerous journal articles (Deshler, Alley, Warner, & Schumaker, 1981; Ellis et al., 1987a, 1987b), and a detailed description of instructional issues and the instructional stages is presented by Ellis et al. (1991) and Lenz, Ellis, and Scanlon (1996).

Table 10.5 depicts the instructional stages that are used successfully to teach adolescents with

TABLE 10.5
Stages of Strategy Acquisition and Generalization Developed by the University of Kansas Center for Research on Learning

Stage 1: Pretest and Make Commitments
Purpose: To motivate students to learn a new strategy and establish a baseline for instruction
- Phase 1: Orientation and pretest
  - Give rationales and overview
  - Administer pretest
  - Determine whether strategy is appropriate
- Phase 2: Awareness and commitment
  - Describe:
    - the alternative strategy
    - results others have achieved
  - Ask for a commitment to learn the new strategy

Stage 2: Describe the Strategy
Purpose: To present a clear picture of the overt and covert processes and steps of the new strategy
- Phase 1: Orientation and overview
  - Give rationales for the strategy
  - Describe situations in which the strategy can be used
- Phase 2: Present the strategy and the remembering system
  - Describe the overall strategic processes
  - Explain the remembering system and its relationship to self-instruction
  - Set goals for learning the strategy

Stage 3: Model the Strategy
Purpose: To demonstrate the cognitive behaviors and physical actions involved in using the strategy
- Phase 1: Orientation
  - Review previous learning
  - State expectations
- Phase 2: Presentation
  - Think aloud
  - Self-monitor
  - Perform task
- Phase 3: Student enlistment
  - Prompt involvement
  - Check understanding

Stage 4: Verbal Elaboration and Rehearsal
Purpose: To ensure comprehension of the strategy and facilitate student mediation
- Phase 1: Verbal elaboration
  - Have students describe the intent of the strategy and the process involved
  - Have students describe what each step is designed to do
- Phase 2: Verbal rehearsal
  - Require students to name each of the steps at an automatic level

Stage 5: Controlled Practice and Feedback
Purpose: To provide practice in controlled materials, build confidence and fluency, and gradually shift the responsibility for strategy use to students
- Phase 1: Orientation and overview
  - Review the strategy steps
  - Prompt reports of strategy use and errors
- Phase 2: Guided practice
  - Prompt student completion of activities as teacher models
  - Prompt increasing student responsibility
  - Give clear instructions for peer-mediated practice

TABLE 10.5
continued

Stage 6: Advanced Practice and Feedback

Purpose: To provide practice in advanced materials (e.g., general class or work-related) and situations and gradually shift the responsibility for strategy use and feedback to students

The instructional sequence for Advanced Practice and Feedback is the same as the instructional sequence used for Controlled Practice. However, this level of practice should:
- use grade-appropriate or situation-appropriate materials
- fade prompts and cues for use and evaluation

Stage 7: Confirm Acquisition and Make Generalization Commitments

Purpose: To document mastery and to build a rationale for self-regulated generalization

Phase 1: Confirm and celebrate
- Congratulate student on meeting mastery
- Discuss achievement and attribution for success

Phase 2: Forecast and commit to generalization
- Explain goals of generalization
- Explain phases of generalization
- Prompt commitment to generalize

Stage 8: Generalization

Purpose: To ensure the use of the strategy in other settings

Phase 1: Orientation
- Prompt students to:
- discuss rationales for strategy use
- identify settings in which the strategy may be used
- discuss how to remember to use the strategy
- Evaluate appropriateness of the strategy in various settings and materials

Phase 2: Activation
- Prompt and monitor student application across settings
- Enlist assistance of other teachers
- Prompt students to:
  - apply the strategy in a variety of settings, situations, materials, and assignments
  - set goals for the use of the strategy
- Prompt general classroom teachers to:
  - understand the strategy
  - cue use of the strategy
  - provide feedback on strategy use

Phase 3: Adaptation
- Prompt students to:
  - identify where these processes and strategies are required across settings
  - identify how the strategy can be modified
  - repeat application with the modified strategy

Phase 4: Maintenance
- Prompt students to:
  - discuss rationales related to long-term use of the strategy
  - set goals related to monitoring long-term use
  - identify self-reinforcers and self-rewards

learning disabilities a variety of skills and strategies. A key characteristic of the application of these instructional stages is that they seek to increase the adolescent's role in the instructional process so that the student learns to self-control learning and become empowered. Several important dimensions are built into these instructional stages. While the term *strategy* is used, the same stages are applied to promote the acquisition of many other skills as well (e.g., applying for a job, accepting criticism, outlining, setting goals, identifying words, completing a word problem in math, and writing a paragraph).

The following instructional procedures relate to the acquisition and generalization of skills and strategies:

1. *The student should be committed to learning the strategy and fully understand the purpose and benefits of the strategy.* The student's understanding of the potential effect of the strategy and the consequences of continued use of ineffective and inefficient strategies is the first step in the instructional process. The student must understand that the goal is to learn the content or perform a certain task successfully, rather than simply to learn a strategy. Thus, the teacher is responsible for informing the student of the goals of the strategy and obtaining a commitment from the student to learn the strategy.
2. *The physical and mental actions covered in the strategy should be fully described and explained.* The student must be taught what to do and how to think about each step of the strategy, and the full content of the strategy should be made apparent to the student. Examples and circumstances relevant to the student's experiences should be incorporated into the presentation, and the student should play an active role in exploring and commenting on the strategy and its uses.
3. *The student should be taught how to remember the strategy to facilitate the process of self-instruction.* After the content of the strategy is presented to the student, the teacher should demonstrate how the strategy can be remembered easily. If a mnemonic is used, the teacher explicitly should relate the mnemonic to the intended physical and mental associations and demonstrate how to use the mnemonic to guide the student in the self-instructional process.
4. *The student should understand the process of learning the strategy and participate in goal-setting activities to anticipate and monitor learning.* The student should be informed of the acquisition and generalization process, understand the goals and vocabulary associated with each step, and set goals for mastery of each step. As instruction proceeds, the student should evaluate each step as it is completed to determine whether specified learning goals have been met.
5. *Multiple models of the strategy should be provided, and an appropriate balance between the physical and mental activities involved in the strategy should be achieved.* The heart of strategic instruction is in the think-aloud model in which the teacher presents an accurate and complete demonstration of the application of the strategy. While a complete and thorough initial model is critical, additional modeling episodes should be inserted throughout the instructional process. In each of these models, the physical activities must be demonstrated as the associated mental activities are made apparent in an overt think-aloud depiction of the strategy.
6. *The student should be enlisted in the model and become a full participant in guiding the strategy instructional process.* While the modeling phase of instruction begins with the teacher, it should end with student participation and experience with the modeling process. The teacher gradually should include the student in the model. The student eventually should be able to perform the strategy while providing many of the key mental actions associated with each step.

7. *The strategy should be understood fully and memorized before practice in the strategy is initiated.* Sufficient rehearsal of the strategy steps should be provided before the student is asked to perform the strategy from memory. Before applied practice of the strategy begins, the student should know the remembering system and be able to demonstrate how to use the system to guide the self-instructional process. During the forthcoming practice phase, the student must be confident in knowledge of the strategy and be able to concentrate on applying the strategy rather than focus unnecessary mental effort on remembering aspects of the strategy.
8. *Practice should begin with controlled guided practice and conclude with advanced independent practice.* The goal of the initial practice stage should be mastering the strategy without having to struggle with content or situational demands. Thus, practice should be provided under conditions in which the student feels comfortable or knowledgeable. As the strategy is learned, conditions that approximate actual setting and task demands should be introduced gradually until the student is using the strategy fully to meet actual learning demands.
9. *A measurement system should provide ongoing information that will demonstrate to the student and the teacher that the strategy is being learned and used and that the demands of the setting are being met.* Knowledge of progress and performance is a critical part of the learning process. The measurement system should tell the student whether the strategy is promoting success in meeting a demand. However, the measurement system also should provide information related to the student's mastery of the strategy.
10. *While generalization should be promoted throughout the strategy acquisition process, specific efforts to promote generalization should follow strategy acquisition.* After the strategy has been mastered, the student should commit to focusing on generalizing the strategy. In the generalization stage, the teacher and student must work together to identify where the strategy can be used across settings and conditions, identify modifications in the strategy to make it more generalizable, and program the use of the strategy across settings.

Acquisition and Generalization of Secondary Content

In developing programs for adolescents with learning disabilities, educators face the challenge of determining how students can master the content of the secondary curriculum and, at the same time, develop important skills and strategies (Ellis & Lenz, 1990). In most educational programs, adolescents with learning disabilities spend most of their school day in mainstream classes. Sometimes content-area classes are offered by special education teachers; however, some educators (Deshler & Schumaker, 1988; Ellis & Lenz, 1990)) question the ethics involved in adopting this practice and argue that special educators usually do not have the required knowledge of the subject matter.

In many cases, the general classroom teacher must individualize and modify instruction to accommodate the needs of students with learning disabilities. The accommodations requested from special educators may include altering either (a) how content is delivered or evaluated or (b) the nature or quantity of the content that the teacher expects students to master. Mainstream class teachers use numerous instructional alternatives to help these students. These alternatives often are referred to as accommodation techniques, compensatory techniques, or instructional adaptations. This section presents instructional alternatives in the following areas: content enhancements, assignments, peer-assisted instruction, adapting materials, and tutoring.

Content Enhancements. Research on learning has led to an increase in studies on how content-area teachers can present information that is sensitive to the strategies used by students. When information is presented in a manner that helps students accomplish the goals of organizing, understanding, and remembering important information, the effect of ineffective or inefficient strategies may be minimized. To accomplish this, the teacher delivering the content must select content enhancements that can be used during a presentation to meet specific learning goals and then must guide students in how to use each enhancement successfully. For example, to help students understand something unfamiliar and abstract, the teacher may use an analogy of something that is familiar and concrete. The teacher then must present the analogy so that students see the relationship between the two concepts and the new concept becomes meaningful. Thus, content enhancements are techniques that enable the teacher to help students identify, organize, comprehend, and retain critical content information (Lenz, Bulgren, & Hudson, 1990).

Content enhancements can be used when the content in a lesson appears to demand more manipulation than the teacher predicts the student can handle effectively or efficiently. According to Schumaker, Deshler, and McKnight (1991), the enhancements can be used to (a) make abstract information more concrete, (b) connect new knowledge with familiar knowledge, (c) highlight relationships and organizational structures within the information to be presented, and (d) draw the unmotivated learner's attention to the information. However, simply using a content enhancement as part of a lesson cannot be viewed as an effective practice. Research indicates that the teacher must help the student see how the enhancement is working and enlist each student's active involvement and support in using the enhancement in the learning process. In a review of research on the use of content enhancements, Hudson, Lignugaris-Kraft, and Miller (1993) found the following seven types: advance organizers, visual displays, study guides, mnemonic devices, audio recordings, computer-assisted instruction, and peer mediated instruction.

1. *Advance organizers.* These enhancements help orient and prepare the student for the upcoming lesson. An advance organizer is presented prior to the lesson presentation and can include an array of information about the lesson. Some of the most common features include linking the lesson content to prior lessons or information, introducing the targeted content, explaining tasks to be performed by the teacher and student, providing a rationale for the lesson, and introducing materials and new vocabulary. The teacher can adapt the advance organizer and use the aspects that are appropriate for the delivery of the content and that orient the students to what is being taught. In addition to the advance organizer, the teacher can use lesson organizers that reinforce the critical structure and content of the lesson. To clarify the organization and focus of the content, the teacher can use words and statements such as "first . . ., second . . ., third . . .," and "the most important idea is . . . ." Diagrams, tables, and charts also can help students see the structure of the content. Organizers can be used before an instructional sequence (advance organizer), throughout an instructional sequence (lesson organizer), or at the end of an instructional sequence (post organizer). For example, to help orient students to a learning task, Schumaker et al. (1991) present a teaching routine on introducing a typical chapter. In this routine, the teacher leads the students through an introductory and focused exploration of the chapter before they begin to read the chapter. In the exploration process, the teacher guides the students to discover how the chapter fits in with surrounding chapters, prompts the students to discuss and rephrase the title and subsections of the chapter, and helps the students to identify the critical main ideas and vocabulary presented in the various sections of the text.

2. *Visual displays.* These enhancements feature several formats (e.g., hierarchical/central, comparative, directional, and representative) that graphically display the organization of the content. For example, in this book Table 1.4 features a combination comparative-directional visual display, Figure 5.1 features a directional format, and Figures 3.1 and 3.2 illustrate representative visual displays. Visual displays can be combined to build powerful and sophisticated teaching routines. Concept diagramming (Bulgren, Schumaker, & Deshler, 1988), semantic feature analysis (Bos & Anders, 1987), and semantic webbing (Anders & Bos, 1984) are three routines that help students understand the various parts of concepts. The use of a graphic organizer is included in all of these routines. In the concept diagramming routine, the teacher helps the students brainstorm information about an important concept, and then these characteristics of the concept are organized into three separate lists (i.e., "always present," "sometimes present," and "never present"). The students construct a definition for the concept from the list of characteristics that are always present and then generate examples and nonexamples of the concept based on the definition. The semantic feature analysis routine involves the use of a table in which examples of a concept are listed in a vertical column and important characteristics or features of the concept are listed in a horizontal column. By reading across the table for a given example, students can identify which features of a concept are possessed by the example. Also, students can construct a table by exploring information about an example of a concept and placing a plus or minus sign in the intersection to indicate a positive or negative relationship, a zero to indicate no relationship, or a question mark if the student is unsure of the relationship. The third routine, semantic webbing, involves writing the important term, idea, or concept on the chalkboard and encouraging the students to generate information. The appropriate placement of the information about the concept in relation to the original stimulus concept is discussed, and lines are drawn to indicate coordinate and subordinate relationships, examples, or features.
3. *Study guides.* These enhancements are used to highlight critical information. Study guides usually consist of statements or questions that stress important content; formats include matching, short-answer questions, and framed outlines or fill-in-the-blanks. Thus, guides can consist of outlines or lists of questions that the teacher can use to focus student attention, point out important information, and encourage the student to inspect the material more closely. In guides involving the use of graphics, the student is directed to complete missing parts of constructed diagrams of the content. Both question- and graphic-oriented study guides are more helpful to students than is self-study alone; however, the use of graphics in study guides is perceived as the most effective (Bergerud, Lovitt, & Horton, 1988).
4. *Mnemonic devices.* These enhancements are designed to help students remember content. They feature pictorial or verbal techniques that promote recall of unfamiliar information. Studies on how teachers can help students consolidate information into meaningful chunks of information affirm the premise that students need to understand what they must remember before reducing the memory load with the use of a mnemonic device (Nagel et al., 1986). Thus, the teacher and students should identify what is most important about the information that is presented and then label and organize the information. Studies on the actual manipulations that can help students remember important information consist of a variety of tactics including creating mental images, making familiar associations, using first-letter mnemonics, or using keyword strategies. First-letter mnemonic is the

primary verbal format used to help students with learning disabilities remember information. In this technique, the students learn the first letter of a word, phrase, or sentence to cue them to remember the targeted information. For example, the word EASY is a mnemonic for remembering the following study strategy (Ellis & Lenz, 1987):

E—*Elicit wh* questions to identify important information (who, what, when, where, and why).

A—*Ask* yourself which information is least troublesome.

S—*Study* easy parts first, hardest parts last.

Y—*Yes*—do use self-reinforcement.

Popular verbal formats include keyword, mimetic, and symbolic. The keyword format involves pairing a picture of a familiar object that is phonetically similar to the term to be learned. The mimetic format includes pictorial representations of the targeted information. For example, to remind students of a definition of a lighthouse, a picture of a lighthouse is used. Symbolic mnemonics involve the use of common symbols to represent critical information. For example, doves may be used to symbolize peace.

5. *Audio recordings.* These enhancements include verbatim audiotapes of written materials and key information audiotapes that are used along with other materials.
6. *Computer-assisted instruction.* This enhancement involves delivering instruction through computers. The primary formats include simulations and tutorials, which students usually complete independently. However, Hudson et al. (1993) note that few computer programs, to date, are designed well enough for students with learning disabilities to learn new content independently. In computer simulations, students review and apply facts and concepts previously learned. (Chapter 7 covers computer-assisted instruction.)
7. *Peer-mediated instruction.* This enhancement involves classmates teaching each other. It features peer tutoring, *ClassWide Peer Tutoring*, and cooperative learning. (Chapter 7 presents these strategies.)

Hudson et al. (1993) note that the overall results from the content enhancement research are encouraging. Furthermore, they report that various enhancements can be used effectively at different phases in the instructional cycle. For example, mnemonic devices can be used during a learning set, presentation of new material, and guided practice, whereas peer mediation can be integrated during independent practice and evaluation of student progress. Finally, Hudson et al. emphasize that the research reveals that enhancements are not always effective in helping students with learning disabilities acquire new material.

Assignments. Many special education teachers prefer to have students complete their work in the classroom so that they can observe performance and assist students who cannot complete assignments, Lenz, Ehren, and Smiley (1991) argue that students must be given the opportunity to complete work independently because assignment completion often indicates the independence of a learner in an academic setting. Lenz, Ehren, and Smiley organize assignment completion into completion knowledge and completion management. Completion knowledge involves the academic skills and background knowledge required to finish the assignment. Completion management involves the planning, integration, and organization of time, interests, and resources that facilitate the use of academic skills and knowledge. Lenz, Ehren, and Smiley also identify three basic types of assignments: study, daily work, and project. Study assignments require the students to prepare for a test or some type of class activity, and the focus of the assignment usually is on the process rather than on a permanent product. Daily work consists of assignments (e.g., completion of chapter questions and worksheets) that follow up the content covered in class and are designed to promote practice and understanding of the content. Project assignments take more than 1 or 2 days to complete and often require students to extend or apply content in the form of a report, theme, visual product, or presentation. Depending on the expectations of the teacher, all three assignment types can be completed in the classroom setting (seatwork) or out of the classroom setting (homework) and can be performed either individually or in a group.

Research in the area of homework indicates that the more time a student spends working on homework, the higher the student's achievement (Fredrick & Walberg, 1980; Keith & Page, 1985; Walberg, 1984), even when variables such as socioeconomic status and ability are controlled (Page & Keith, 1981). Harnischfeger (1980) notes that this relationship is consistent across subject-matter areas as early as the fourth grade. Polachek, Kniesner, and Harwood (1978) also report that less-able students can compensate for their lower ability by increasing the amount of homework completed. However, to ensure the positive benefits of homework, Keith and Page (1985) note that the assignments must be appropriate for the student's ability and achievement levels.

Research findings on different types of assignments and the assignment-completion process indicate that creating better-structured and better-organized assignments may not improve the assignment-completion process if the interest or motivation of students is not addressed. Thus, the teacher must attend to the basic nature and quality of the assignments. Lenz and Bulgren (1988) propose the following guidelines regarding classroom assignments to improve the achievement of adolescents with learning disabilities:

1. Assignment requirements must be explicit and clear.
2. Requirements should relate to important learning outcomes.
3. Choices must be provided that enable the students to personalize learning.
4. Over time, choices should include what to learn, how to learn, and how to demonstrate what has been learned.
5. Assignment completion initially should be modeled and guided in class by the teacher with student involvement.
6. Students should know the dimensions of assignments and be prompted to ask questions about assignment completion.
7. The process of learning about assignment completion should be considered as important as learning the content.

8. Discussions regarding the quality of assignments and the outcomes associated with assignment completion should be a regular part of classroom activities.
9. Students should be engaged regularly in setting goals related to improving the completion process and what is being learned as a result of assignment completion.
10. Fewer assignments should be given, and they should emphasize the most important learning outcomes.
11. Assignments should be evaluated rather than graded, and students should revise their work to improve the quality rather than the grade.
12. Peers should be used frequently to promote a variety of learning models.

Peer-Assisted Instruction. Research on the effects of students working together indicates that content learning can be facilitated greatly through the use of peer tutors and student learning teams and the incorporation of cooperative learning activities. For example, some learning disabilities teachers use the pause procedure during lectures to improve the recall of adolescents (Hughes, Hendrickson, & Hudson, 1986). The instructional procedure consists of pausing several times during a lecture (e.g., every 8 to 12 minutes) for students to discuss the content covered. (Chapter 7 presents detailed coverage of peer tutoring.)

Adapting Materials. The difficulty level of texts and materials used in content-area classes may present a problem to secondary students with learning disabilities because the reading level may be several grades above the student's reading level. To assist the student in learning, it often is necessary to modify or adapt the ways in which content is presented. The goal of these modifications is to change the format and mode of presentation while maintaining the basic content.

Wiseman (1980) popularized the Parallel Alternative Curriculum (PAC) by means of a demonstration project. Although the total PAC program has numerous components (e.g., parent involvement and remediation), its heart features the development of curriculum materials that present essential content in ways that help the problem learner organize, practice, and master important information.

Many school districts provide general and special educators with release time or summer employment to write curriculum guides for various courses designed for use with low achievers. Thus, a low achiever receives the standard text and a curriculum guide or booklet. For example, Project PASS (Packets Assuring Student Success) is a mainstream secondary program for students with difficulties in United States history and American government. The instructional packets are written at the third- to fifth-grade reading level and contain vocabulary, a glossary, a pretest and posttest, subject content, activities, and projects. (Information is available from Project PASS, Livonia Public School District, 15125 Farmington Road, Livonia, MI 48154.)

Moreover, some book companies offer adapted textbooks in which the content matches the grade-level textbook but is written at a lower readability level (e.g., *Wonders of Science* and *America's Story*, published by Steck-Vaughn). Other techniques for adapting materials include simplifying and taping texts. Mercer and Mercer (1993) present specific activities for adapting materials.

Tutoring. At the secondary level, earning academic credits is a major instructional concern. Learning disabilities teachers often teach and assign credit for course content or provide tutoring in subject areas required for graduation (Carlson, 1981). Given the tutorial emphasis in secondary grades, Carlson (1985) suggests that guidelines or standards are needed for implementing and evaluating tutoring. He provides three principles for tutoring instruction:

1. *Instruction should be powerful.* To offer powerful instruction, the teacher must know the content well, provide enough time for intensive teaching, and follow the principles of effective instruction (e.g., reinforcement, engaged time, modeling, and feedback).

2. *Instruction should result in long-range benefits to the learner.* Effective instruction should diminish the effect that the learning difficulty may have on future learning or help the student function more adequately. In addition to teaching immediate subject-matter content, the learning of skills (e.g., study skills, and test-taking skills) that increase the student's potential for later learning should be stressed.
3. *Teacher expectations for learner performance should be high.* Success must be maintained, but expected levels of performance should not be reduced unless this is absolutely necessary.

Collaboration with General Classroom Teachers

As the deficiencies of content-area instruction in the support class setting become more apparent (especially those related to students with mild learning and behavior problems), efforts are increasing to infuse appropriate instructional methods into the general class setting. Some educators believe the role of the support class teacher is to teach students the skills and strategies that promote more effective and efficient learning, while the role of the general content-area teacher is to present content in a manner that can be understood and remembered by students (Lenz, Clark, Deshler, Schumaker, & Rademacher, 1990; Schumaker & Deshler, 1988). However, this approach depends on the ability and willingness of general classroom teachers to learn and implement content-area instruction in a manner that achieves this goal.

Several different efforts have been made within the general classroom setting to enhance the success of low-achieving students in the general classroom environment; however, these efforts cannot be compared with the diversity of the approaches associated with content delivery in the support class setting. According to Lenz, Bulgren, and Hudson (1990), efforts to promote maximum learning for low-achieving students must be tempered by several conditions:

1. The content parameters of the general curriculum usually cannot be altered; therefore, efforts to maximize the learning and performance of low-achieving students should not require major modifications of the curriculum.
2. Efforts to promote individual learning should not inhibit, detract from, or have a negative influence on the learning and performance of other students in the class.
3. To the greatest extent possible, efforts should have the potential for benefiting all students in the class.
4. The preparation, implementation, and evaluation of efforts and their results should be integrated easily into ongoing instructional efforts and time frames.
5. The efforts should be powerful enough that their influence on the performance of low-achieving students in the context of the general classroom setting can be directly observed by the general classroom teacher.
6. Efforts made by the general classroom teacher to improve learning and performance should be reinforcing or rewarding to the teacher and should lead to current and future instruction that is personally satisfying.
7. The teacher must perceive that the motivation of students in the class is not lowered when alternative methods are used; in fact, motivation should be increased to the greatest extent possible.

In addition to instructional methods and procedures that may enhance content-area learning in the general classroom setting, increased attention is given to instructional models that promote cooperative teaching, planning, and consultation between the support class teacher and the general education teacher. (Chapter 6 discusses consultation approaches and inclusion techniques and issues.)

ADULTS WITH LEARNING DISABILITIES

The negative effects of learning disabilities persist into adulthood (Spekman, Goldberg, & Herman, 1992; White 1992). These individuals face the same adult issues as others; however, they encounter these issues with more risk because of their learning difficulties and fragile emotional status. The chronic nature of the cognitive, academic, and social difficulties of adults with learning difficulties may affect their ability to function in such adult domains as employment, home and family, leisure, community, health, and relationships (Cronin & Patton, 1993). Studies of adults with learning disabilities are increasing, and overall, the findings affirm that many adults with learning disabilities have difficulties finding quality employment, living independently, feeling good about themselves, and experiencing satisfaction with their lives (White, 1992). Although these findings are discouraging, the studies also indicate that there are a substantial number of adults with learning disabilities who are independent, have quality jobs, enjoy many leisure activities, and are satisfied with their lives (Spekman et al., 1992).

Polloway, Smith, and Patton (1984) note that a study of adults with learning disabilities should begin with an understanding of adult development across the life span. Such a perspective requires that adults not be characterized as having a single fixed set of characteristics. Just as characteristics change between childhood and adolescence, the characteristics of adults change as they move through their adult years. Several researchers (Haring, Lovett, & Smith, 1990; Sitlington & Frank, 1990) promote a lifelong perspective that takes into account the motivational differences in adults with learning disabilities. Their findings indicate that many adults with learning disabilities exhibit prolonged dependence and delayed motivation. Keogh (1993) notes that, given time and intervention, many adults with learning disabilities move through the developmental stages successfully but do so more slowly than adults without learning disabilities. Biological, environmental, historical, and social forces affect who they are, how they function, and what they need. Levinson (1978) identifies three key transitional phases in the life of an adult: early adult transition (ages 17–22), age-30 transition (ages 28–33), and middle-age transition (ages 40–45). Polloway et al. contend that the problems associated with these phases may be of particular importance in identifying potentially problematic periods in the lives of adults with learning disabilities. Spekman, Goldberg, and Herman (1993) highlight the need for a lifelong perspective: "It must be remembered that LD involves a lifelong process of change and adaptation. Individuals doing poorly at one stage can be helped to demonstrate resilience, competence, and success at another" (p. 16).

Young Adults

The years between 18 and 25 are difficult for most individuals. During this time, they are expected to leave the sheltered environment of home and secondary school and enter the "real world." This real-world setting demands more independence and requires the individual to make decisions regarding postschool education, vocational training, employment, and independent living arrangements. Moreover, the transition becomes increasingly difficult when the individual faces higher expectations regarding social maturity, independence, and self-direction.

Although some young adults with learning disabilities make successful postschool adjustments, many of them struggle. An examination of studies and research reviews (Chelser, 1982; deBettencourt, Zigmond, & Thornton, 1989; Fourqurean & LaCourt, 1990; Reiff & deFur, 1992; Sitlington, Frank, & Carson, 1993; Wagner, 1990; White, 1992) on the postsecondary adjustments of individuals with learning disabilities reveals some of the difficulties they experience:

1. *Underemployment.* Many young adults with learning disabilities obtain part-time rather than full-time jobs. Their jobs are mostly at the unskilled or semi-skilled level. They receive low wages and generally work in jobs of low social status.
2. *Job dissatisfaction.* Many young adults with learning disabilities report less job satisfaction than their peers without disabilities.

3. *Dependent living arrangements.* About 60% to 70% of young adults with learning disabilities continue to live with their parents several years after leaving secondary school.
4. *Social skills problems.* Many young adults with learning disabilities have problems with relationships in the work setting. These are manifested in disagreements, misunderstandings, poor communication, and inappropriate appearance.
5. *Poor work habits.* Not working fast enough, experiencing difficulty coping with job pressures, possessing deficient academic skills, and having problems following directions all interfere with the job performance of many individuals with learning disabilities.
6. *Job selection.* Many individuals with learning disabilities have jobs that accentuate their weaknesses. For example, they take jobs that require extensive organization when they have organizational skills deficits.

In an effort to understand what factors contribute to postschool adjustments of individuals with learning disabilities, many researchers study both individuals who have made successful adjustments and those who have not. These studies yield data on conditions or factors that appear to be common to (a) most adults with learning disabilities, (b) individuals with learning disabilities who have been successful, or (c) individuals with learning disabilities who have been unsuccessful. Table 10.6 presents these findings, which have been summarized from the following sources: P. B. Adelman and Vogel (1993), Reiff and deFur (1992), Reiff, Ginsberg, and Gerber (1995); Sitlington et al. (1993); Spekman, Goldberg, and Herman (1993); and Spekman, Herman, and Vogel (1993).

In these studies, risk and protective factors are discussed along with successful and unsuccessful postschool adjustments. Risk factors typically are defined as hazards, adverse circumstances, or negative events that increase the probability of a negative outcome. Protective factors are factors that increase the probability of a positive outcome despite some exposure to risk. Spekman, Herman, and Vogel (1993) point out, however, that the specific determination of a risk or protective factor lacks precision. A multidimensional view is used to determine success in most of the studies. Some common markers of success include age-appropriate activities and thoughts in relation to employment, school attendance, involvement with peers, involvement with family, participation in leisure and social activities, reported satisfaction with life, and description of endeavors in a realistic manner (i.e., perception matches reality) (Sitlington et al., 1993; Spekman et al., 1992). Likewise, a multidimensional view is used to define unsuccessful postschool adjustments and typically includes difficulty with age-appropriate activities and thoughts in the areas of work, school, family, leisure, friendships, satisfaction with life, and aspirations (Spekman et al., 1992).

The risk factors associated with learning disabilities combine with the arduous demands of postsecondary adjustments to make it difficult for young adults with learning disabilities to be successful without substantial support. An examination of factors inherent for success provides a framework for the following services and support that school personnel should provide to these individuals:

1. In assessment, include an examination of protective factors (e.g., communication skills, sense of personal control, proactive tendencies, self-understanding, goal orientation, problem-solving ability, and presence of family and community supports) and risk factors (e.g., severity of learning disabilities, poor relationships, low frustration level, dysfunctional family, and passive learning style). These data provide the information necessary to identify an individual's most relevant strengths and weaknesses and plan accordingly (Spekman, Herman, & Vogel, 1993).
2. Develop strategies and techniques for helping individuals understand their learning disabilities and their respective strengths and weaknesses. Efforts should be made to help

TABLE 10.6
Common Factors of Adults with Learning Disabilities

All adults with learning disabilities tend to
- have learning disabilites throughout adulthood
- face more stress
- be late bloomers
- need a continuing support system
- need help in understanding their disability
- need transition planning
- need to be included in developing their own transition plan
- need assistance with problem-solving strategies

Successful adults with learning disabilities tend to
- understand and accept their learning disabilities
- maintain a proactive approach
- maintain perseverance in dealing with life events
- develop coping strategies and know how to reduce stress
- maintain emotional stability
- set appropriate goals and maintain goal directedness
- have and use support systems (e.g., a history of tutoring and therapeutic and supportive relationships)
- maintain a sense of control in their lives (e.g., make decisions to take charge of their lives and make useful adaptations to move ahead)
- maintain a determination to "make it" (i.e., motivation)
- pursue careers that maximize their strengths and minimize their weaknesses
- develop creative ways to compensate and problem solve
- maintain a positive attitude toward learning
- participate in a family or community ethic that values work and independence
- graduate from secondary school
- exhibit high verbal skills

Unsuccessful adults with learning disabilities tend to
- have higher rates of unemployment if female
- not understand or accept their learning disability
- fail to take control of their lives
- maintain a sense of learned helplessness and fail to assume responsibility
- seek and promote dependent relationships
- pursue careers that accentuate their weaknesses
- have a severe math disability
- have an absence of protective factors (e.g., nurturing home environments) or factors associated with successful adults (e.g., support systems, proactivity, and motivation)
- drop out of secondary school

adults with learning disabilities feel good about themselves (P. B. Adelman & Vogel, 1993; Spekman, Herman, & Vogel, 1993).

3. Teach individuals ways to adapt to their learning disabilities. These entail the development of coping strategies and problem-solving techniques.
4. Encourage individuals to be proactive and take control of their lives through goal setting, goal directedness, persistence, and hard work. Teach students to participate in their own transition plans.
5. Teach individuals how to network and develop support systems (e.g., build relation-

ships) and use supportive persons (such as teachers, employers, therapists, counselors, family members, and friends).

6. Provide each student with learning disabilities with a mentor during the secondary school years. The mentor should be someone who believes in the individual, helps the individual set realistic goals, and provides encouragement during difficult times (Spekman, Herman, & Vogel, 1993).
7. Provide students with learning disabilities with the assistance needed to meet the academic requirements in vocational education. Minskoff and DeMoss (1993) present the Trade-Related Academic Competencies (TRAC) program as a viable alternative for teaching students with learning disabilities the academic skills needed across 26 vocational education areas.
8. Provide students in secondary school and beyond with guidance in selecting vocational courses and careers (P. B. Adelman & Vogel, 1993).
9. Provide ongoing assistance to help students improve their academic and interpersonal skills and their compensatory strategies (P. B. Adelman & Vogel, 1993).
10. Educate more employers about learning disabilities. Employers tend to be more sensitive to individuals with physical disabilities than to individuals with cognitive disabilities (P. B. Adelman & Vogel, 1993; Anderson, Kazmierski, & Cronin, 1995).

College Students with Learning Disabilities

Colleges and universities are experiencing a dramatic increase in the number of students with learning disabilities being admitted. In a survey of 66 state universities and colleges, Spillane, McGuire, and Norlander (1992) found that the academic (e.g., grades, recommendations, and admission tests) and nonacademic (e.g., level of intelligence, motivation, and independence) criteria used to admit individuals with learning disabilities to colleges are similar to the criteria used for applicants without disabilities. Section 504 of the Rehabilitation Act of 1973 and the Americans with Disabilities Act of 1990 state that no individual should be excluded on the basis of a disability. Moreover, the Individuals with Disabilities Education Act (IDEA) states that a "qualified" college person with a disability is someone who with reasonable program modifications can meet the academic requirements. Some reasonable modifications include (a) extended time to finish the program, (b) course substitution, modification, or waiver of a foreign language requirement, (c) part-time study, and (d) extended time for tests. Scott (1994) reviews guidelines for weighing accommodation requests and presents recommendations for determining appropriate academic adjustments for college students with learning disabilities.

Section 504 also states that students must identify or refer themselves and that the university must provide full program accessibility to ensure a fair chance for success. Unfortunately, many college students with learning disabilities do not reveal their learning disability until they are in an academic crisis. Some suggestions for college students with learning disabilities include the following:

1. Talk to your instructors before the semester begins.
2. If you think that you may have a specific learning disability, contact the disabled student services office on campus.
3. Maintain realistic goals and priorities for course work.
4. Keep only one calendar with all appointments and relevant dates (i.e., assignments, tests, and project due dates) clearly marked.
5. Use a tape recorder during lectures, and listen to the tape as soon after class as possible to reorganize your notes.
6. Seek help for any questions you may have so that they can be answered before the next test.

7. Sit near the front of the classroom.
8. Estimate how long a given class assignment will take to complete. Build in breaks from studying because fatigue is a time waster.
9. Obtain a course syllabus, and make sure that course expectations are clear.
10. Ask for reading assignments in advance if you are using books on tape.
11. Use campus support services (e.g., preregistration, assistance in ordering taped books, alternative testing arrangements, specialized study aids, peer support groups, diagnostic consultation, study skills training, and academic tutorial assistance).

In addition, the following selected services may be helpful to college students with learning disabilities: tutors, note takers, books on tape, proctored testing with alternative modes, tape recording, peer pairing, academic remediation, organizational skill remediation, modification in time span of program, course analysis and prescriptive scheduling, early registration, counseling (academic, vocational, and personal), lecture-pause procedure, learning strategies, social skills training, advocacy program, testing and evaluation modifications, support groups, coaching with students and faculty, and self-monitoring training.

Many recent studies focus on the status of students with learning disabilities at the college level in terms of identification and intervention. In a review of the published work on college learning disabilities programs, Hughes and Smith (1990) note that little empirical data exist on young adults with learning disabilities in the college setting. Based on their extensive review of more than 100 studies covering a 20-year period, Hughes and Smith report the following conclusions:

1. The intellectual functioning of college students with learning disabilities can be described as comparable to college students without learning disabilities.
2. College students with learning disabilities score in the average or above-average range on intelligence tests.
3. The reported reading levels vary widely with word-attack skills ranging from the second-grade level to college level. The average reading level for college students with learning disabilities is 10th grade.
4. In studies using self-report measures, college students with learning disabilities most frequently report problems in reading comprehension, reading rate, and retaining information.
5. Empirical evidence indicates that most college students with learning disabilities can identify their own skill problems accurately when compared with measured skill levels on achievement tests.
6. There is a lack of consensus on which measures should be used to evaluate the skill levels of college students with learning disabilities. This presents problems in interpreting data and findings across studies.
7. Many college students with learning disabilities have problems with math computation and application, as well as with more abstract areas of math such as algebra and geometry.
8. Many college students with learning disabilities have severe deficits in written expression areas such as spelling, punctuation, and sentence structure.
9. Learning a foreign language presents a particularly formidable task to many college students with learning disabilities.
10. Few empirical studies focus on the effectiveness of particular interventions or instructional approaches for college students with learning disabilities.

Although the development of college programs for individuals with learning disabilities is receiving much attention, few efforts have been made to validate specific interventions. In an intervention study, Ruhl, Hughes, and Gajar (1990) investigated a pause procedure for enhancing the recall of facts presented through lectures with students both with and without learning disabilities. The pause procedure consisted of providing three 2-minute periods for student discussions and note taking during a standard lecture. The procedure was effective for promoting short-term recall on objective tests for all the students. Ruhl et al. hypothesize that the pausing provides structure and time for extra processing of information presented in a class, and they note that this procedure is simple to implement in the college setting. In another study, Ruhl and Suritsky (1995) found that the pause procedure was more effective than a lecture outline for enhancing the immediate recall of lecture ideas and completeness of recorded notes of college students with learning disabilities.

It is hoped that higher education will respond to the needs of adults with learning disabilities. The Learning Disabilities Association of America (4156 Library Road, Pittsburgh, PA 15234) provides a list of colleges and universities with learning disabilities programs. Also, *The Complete Directory for People with Learning Disabilities* (available from Grey House Publishing, Pocket Knife Square, Lakeville, CT 06039) includes entries about colleges, resources, agencies, transition skills and employment programs, and support services. The *Directory of Facilities for Learning Disabled People,* which includes a list of colleges, universities, and agencies, is available from Bosc, P. O. Box 305, Dept. F, Congers, NY 10920.

General Adulthood

The field of learning disabilities began in the 1960s as the baby-boom generation was growing into puberty; therefore, many individuals of the baby-boom generation missed being identified as having learning disabilities during their school years. As a result, many adults have undiagnosed learning disabilities that currently may be affecting the quality of their lives. Patton and Polloway (1992) report that as individuals with learning disabilities become older, their problems often increase in complexity. Likewise, Gerber et al. (1990) note that the complexity and interaction of variables associated with disabilities are magnified in adulthood.

An emerging focus stresses the need to view adults with learning disabilities from a life-span developmental perspective (Gerber, 1994; Patton & Polloway, 1992). Inherent in this life-span approach is a consideration of mediating variables. These biological, intellectual, social, and experiential variables influence adult functioning as the individual deals with physiological, psychological, social, and vocational changes (Patton & Polloway, 1992). Moreover, the resources to facilitate adjustment to life events vary in a lifetime. Cronin, Patton, and Polloway (1991) note that these mediating variables need to be considered within the contexts of the following adult domains: employment and education, home and family, leisure, community involvement, emotional health, physical health, personal responsibility, and relationships. Gerber (1994) notes that consideration of the mediating variables within these contexts holds promise for more meaningful research on adults with learning disabilities.

In several studies, social deficits are reported as the major area of concern for adults with learning disabilities. Chelser (1982) reports a rank ordering of areas in which 560 adults with learning disabilities felt a need for assistance:

1. Social relationships and skills
2. Career counseling
3. Developing self-esteem and confidence
4. Overcoming dependence; survival
5. Vocational training
6. Getting and holding a job
7. Reading
8. Spelling
9. Managing personal finances
10. Organizational skills

In general, problems such as social relationships of individuals with learning disabilities appear to persist in adolescence, young adulthood, and general adulthood; these individuals must adapt to situations that change over time and often present new challenges and problems. Studies of adults with learning disabilities who have been out of school for several years yield some encouraging findings. For example, Lewandowski and Arcangelo (1994) examined the social adjustment and self-concept of adults both with and without learning disabilities who graduated from secondary school between 1982 and 1988. They found that the adults with learning disabilities were similar to the adults without learning disabilities in terms of social adjustment and self-concept. They conclude, "It appears that any negative effects of a disability classification abate once individuals leave the public school environment, and that previous forecasts of the socioemotional status of adults with learning disabilities may be unnecessarily pessimistic" (p. 598). Likewise, Spekman et al. (1992) maintain that young adults with learning disabilities who are highly dependent on their support systems (i.e., family) tend to become more independent over time. Better jobs, improved wages, and the ability to use community services facilitate independence.

Recent studies involving a different approach to the study of adult learning disabilities may provide insights into understanding all individuals with learning disabilities. Gerber and Ginsberg (1990) studied highly successful adults with learning disabilities to identify alterable patterns of success. After a screening process involving 241 adults with learning disabilities from 24 states and Canada, 46 highly successful adults with learning disabilities and 25 adults with moderate-to-low success rates were identified. Highly successful adults with learning disabilities were more advanced or exceptional in the following ways:

1. They took control of their lives in a manner characterized by adaptability and goal-oriented behavior.
2. They made personal and conscious decisions at points in their lives to (a) succeed, move on, and leave failure behind, (b) set goals, and (c) view problems in a positive manner.
3. They excelled by being persistent and fitting themselves into surroundings where they could succeed and define the terms of success, learn to be creative, surround themselves with supportive people, and create personal improvement programs.

Reiff et al. (1995) studied successful adults with learning disabilities to gain perspectives on teaching. These adults revealed that they had gone through a process of gaining or regaining control in their lives. Many claimed that control was the key to success. Control was viewed as the ability to make conscious decisions (i.e., an internal decision) to take charge of one's life. It also meant that they were able to make adaptations that facilitated ongoing progress (i.e., external manifestations). Reiff et al. present teaching perspectives based on the characteristics of these successful adults to make proactive internal decisions. These characteristics include desire, goal orientation, and reframing (i.e., understanding one's learning disability). Likewise, Reiff et al. offer teaching perspectives based on the external manifestations that these successful adults exhibited: persistence, goodness of fit (i.e., choice of careers that maximized the individual's strengths and minimized weaknesses), learned creativity, and social ecologies (i.e., the ability to develop and maintain social relationships and support systems). Reiff et al. comment on the implications of studying adults with learning disabilities who have succeeded:

> The very existence of adults with learning disabilities who have excelled in a wide gamut of professions should encourage both students and teachers. The media have increasingly popularized the exploits of entertainers and athletes who have learning disabilities, while many organizations salute the achievements of notable historical personages who are purported to have had learning disabilities. Such visibility alone may not encourage realistic and practical career aspirations for students with learning disabilities. Because it draws on the experiences of successful persons with learning disabilities in many different careers, the model of employment success we have discussed has the potential for providing the foundation for a success-oriented curriculum. (p. 37)

Thus, a challenge for educators is to develop educational programs and services that embrace the characteristics that are prevalent in highly successful adults.

PERSPECTIVE

For years adolescents and adults with learning disabilities did not receive much attention from special or general educators. Fortunately, special educators now are recognizing the complex needs of these older individuals and are making progress in designing interventions to meet their diverse needs. However, special educators alone cannot ensure the success of adolescents with learning disabilities in secondary and postsecondary situations. Legislators and policymakers must consider the special needs of this population in reforming secondary education. General and vocational educators must share the responsibility of preparing them for graduation and postschool adjustment. In addition, community services must join forces with educators and employers to provide individuals who have learning disabilities with a continuum of services throughout their life span. Gerber (1986) reports that programs in the Netherlands and Denmark are exemplary and considerably ahead of those in the United States. In reference to adolescents and adults with learning disabilities, the needs are documented, viable interventions exist, and exemplary programs are available. The challenge is apparent.

DISCUSSION/REVIEW QUESTIONS

1. Discuss the school demands and vocational and employment demands placed on adolescents.
2. Describe the characteristics of adolescents with learning disabilities in the areas of academic deficits, cognitive and metacognitive deficits, social interaction deficits, and motivation deficits.
3. Discuss program services and premises of secondary programs.
4. Discuss general secondary curriculum alternatives and types of intervention approaches.
5. Present models for organizing secondary programming.
6. Discuss supportive and alternative curriculum approaches for promoting motivation, social development, academic remediation, and learning strategies.
7. Discuss curriculum approaches for developing functional living skills and promoting career-related instruction and transitions from secondary settings.
8. Present instructional alternatives pertaining to content enhancements, assignments, peer-assisted instruction, adapting materials, and tutoring.
9. Discuss factors that affect postsecondary adjustments of adults with learning disabilities who have been successful and unsuccessful.
10. Present suggestions and services for college students with learning disabilities.

REFERENCES

Adams, A. (1990). The oral reading errors of readers with learning disabilities: Variations produced within the instructional and frustrational ranges. *Remedial and Special Education, 12*(1), 48–55.

Adelman, H. S., & Taylor, L. (1983). Enhancing motivation for overcoming learning and behavior problems. *Journal of Learning Disabilities, 16,* 384–392.

Adelman, P. B., & Vogel, S. A. (1993). Issues in the employment of adults with learning disabilities. *Learning Disability Quarterly, 16,* 219–232.

Algozzine, B., O'Shea, D. J., Stoddard, K., & Crews, W. B. (1988). Reading and writing competencies of adolescents with learning disabilities. *Journal of Learning Disabilities, 21,* 154–160.

Alley, G. R., Deshler, D. D., & Warner, M. M. (1979). Identification of learning disabled adolescents: A Bayesian approach. *Learning Disability Quarterly, 2*(2), 76–83.

Anders, P. L., & Bos, C. S. (1984). In the beginning: Vocabulary instruction in content classrooms. *Topics in Learning and Learning Disabilities, 3*(4), 53–65.

Anderson, P. L., Kazmierski, S., & Cronin, M. E. (1995). Learning disabilities, employment discrimination, and the ADA. *Journal of Learning Disabilities, 28,* 196–204.

Bergerud, D., Lovitt, T. C., & Horton, S. (1988). The effectiveness of textbook adaptations in life science for high school students with learning disabilities. *Journal of Learning Disabilities, 21*, 70–76.

Bos, C. S., & Anders, P. L. (1987). Semantic feature analysis: An interactive teaching strategy for facilitating learning from text. *Learning Disability Focus, 3*(1), 55–59.

Bos, C. S., & Vaughn, S. (1994). *Strategies for teaching students with learning and behavior problems* (3rd ed.). Boston: Allyn & Bacon.

Brier, N. (1994). Targeted treatment for adjudicated youth with learning disabilities: Effects on recidivism. *Journal of Learning Disabilities, 27*, 215–222.

Buchwach, L. (1980). Child service demonstration center for secondary students with learning disabilities. In R. H. Riegel & J. P. Mathey (Eds.), *Mainstreaming at the secondary level: Seven models that work.* Plymouth, MI: Wayne County Intermediate School District.

Bulgren, J. A., Schumaker, J. B., & Deshler, D. D. (1988). Effectiveness of a concept teaching routine in enhancing the performance of LD students in secondary-level mainstream classes. *Learning Disability Quarterly, 11*, 3–17.

Campbell, P., & Olsen, G. R. (1994). Improving instruction in secondary schools. *Teaching Exceptional Children, 26*(3), 51–54.

Carlson, S. A. (1981). *Patterns and trends within exemplary special education programs in the secondary grades.* Washington, DC: National Association of State Directors of Special Education, Project FORUM.

Carlson, S. A. (1985). The ethical appropriateness of subject-matter tutoring for learning disabled adolescents. *Learning Disability Quarterly, 8*, 310–314.

Cegelka, P. T., & Greene, G. (1993). Transition to adulthood. In A. E. Blackhurst & W. H. Berdine (Eds.), *An introduction to special education* (3rd ed., pp. 137–175). New York: HarperCollins.

Chelser, B. (1982). ACLD vocational committee completes survey on LD adult. *ACLD Newsbriefs* (No. 146), pp. 5, 20–23.

Clark, C. M., & Peterson, P. L. (1986). Teachers' thought processes. In M. E. Wittrock (Ed.), *Handbook of research on teaching.* Upper Saddle River, NJ: Prentice Hall.

Clark, F. L., Deshler, D. D., Schumaker, J. B., Alley, G. R., & Warner, M. M. (1984). Visual imagery and self-questioning: Strategies to improve comprehension of written material. *Journal of Learning Disabilities, 17*, 145–149.

Clark, G. M., & Kolstoe, O. P. (1990). *Career development and transition education for adolescents with disabilities.* Boston: Allyn & Bacon.

Cline, B. V., & Billingsley, B. S. (1991). Teachers' and supervisors' perceptions of secondary learning disabilities programs: A multi-state survey. *Learning Disabilities Research & Practice, 6*, 158–165.

Crawford, D. (1984). ACLD-R & D Project summary: A study investigating the link between learning disabilities and juvenile delinquency. In W. M. Cruickshank & J. M. Kliebhan (Eds.), *Early adolescence to early adulthood: Vol. 5. The best of ACLD.* Syracuse, NY: Syracuse University Press.

Cronin, M. E., & Patton, J. R. (1993). *Life skills for students with special needs: A practical guide for developing real-life programs.* Austin, TX: PRO-ED.

Cronin, M. E., Patton, J. R., & Polloway, E. A. (1991). *Preparing for adult outcomes: A model for developing a life skills curriculum.* Unpublished manuscript, University of New Orleans, Louisiana.

deBettencourt, L. U., Zigmond, N., & Thornton, H. (1989). Follow-up of postsecondary-age rural learning disabled graduates and dropouts. *Exceptional Children, 56*, 40–49.

Deshler, D. D., Alley, G. R., Warner, M. M., & Schumaker, J. B. (1981). Instructional practices for promoting skill acquisition and generalization in severely learning disabled adolescents. *Learning Disability Quarterly, 4*, 415–421.

Deshler, D. D., & Lenz, B. K. (1989). The strategies instructional approach. *International Journal of Learning Disability, Development and Education, 36*(3), 203–224.

Deshler, D. D., & Schumaker, J. B. (1983). Social skills of learning disabled adolescents: A review of characteristics and intervention. *Topics in Learning and Learning Disabilities, 3*, 15–23.

Deshler, D. D., & Schumaker, J. B. (1986). Learning strategies: An instructional alternative for low-achieving adolescents. *Exceptional Children, 52*, 583–590.

Deshler, D. D., & Schumaker, J. B. (1988). An instructional model for teaching students how to learn. In J. L. Graden, J. E. Zins, & M. J. Curtis (Eds.), *Alternative educational delivery systems: Enhancing instructional options for all students* (pp. 391–411). Washington, DC: National Association of School Psychologists.

Deshler, D. D., Schumaker, J. B., & Lenz, B. K. (1984). Academic and cognitive interventions for LD adolescents: Part I. *Journal of Learning Disabilities, 17,* 108–117.

Deshler, D. D., Schumaker, J. B., Lenz, B. K., & Ellis, E. S. (1984). Academic and cognitive interventions for LD adolescents: Part II. *Journal of Learning Disabilities, 17,* 170–179.

Deshler, D. D., Warner, M. M., Schumaker, J. B., & Alley, G. R. (1983). The learning strategies intervention model: Key components and current status. In J. D. McKinney & L. Feagans (Eds.), *Current topics in learning disabilities* (Vol. 1, pp. 245–283). Norwood, NJ: Ablex.

Durlak, C. M., Rose, E., & Bursuck, W. D. (1994). Preparing high school students with learning disabilities for the transition to postsecondary education: Teaching the skills of self-determination. *Journal of Learning Disabilities, 2,* 51–59.

Ellett, L. (1993). Instructional practices in mainstreamed secondary classrooms. *Journal of Learning Disabilities, 26,* 57–64.

Ellis, E. S., Deshler, D. D., Lenz, B. K., Schumaker, J. B., & Clark, F. L. (1991). An instructional model for teaching learning strategies. *Focus on Exceptional Children, 24*(1), 1–14.

Ellis, E. S., Deshler, D. D., & Schumaker, J. B. (1989). Teaching adolescents with learning disabilities to generate and use task-specific strategies. *Journal of Learning Disabilities, 22,* 108–119.

Ellis, E. S., & Lenz, B. K. (1987). A component analysis of effective learning strategies for LD students. *Learning Disabilities Focus, 2*(2), 94–107.

Ellis, E. S., & Lenz, B. K. (1990). Techniques for mediating content-area learning: Issues and research. *Focus on Exceptional Children, 22*(9), 1–16.

Ellis, E. S., Lenz, B. K., & Sabornie, E. J. (1987a). Generalization and adaptation of learning strategies to natural environments: Part 1—Critical agents. *Remedial and Special Education, 8*(1), 6–21.

Ellis, E. S., Lenz, B. K., & Sabornie, E. J. (1987b). Generalization and adaptation of learning strategies to natural environments: Part 2—Research into practice. *Remedial and Special Education, 8*(2), 6–24.

Fourqurean, J. M., & LaCourt, T. (1990). A follow-up study of former special education students: A model for program evaluation. *Remedial and Special Education, 12*(1), 16–23.

Fourqurean, J. M., Meisgeier, C., Swank, P. R., & Williams, R. E. (1991). Correlates of postsecondary employment outcomes for young adults with learning disabilities. *Journal of Learning Disabilities, 24,* 400–405.

Fredrick, W. C., & Walberg, H. J. (1980). Learning as a function of time. *The Journal of Educational Research, 73,* 183–204.

Gerber, P J. (1986). Learning disabled adult nexus: Emerging American issues and European perspectives. *Journal of Learning Disabilities, 19,* 2–4.

Gerber, P. J. (1994). Researching adults with learning disabilities from an adult-development perspective. *Journal of Learning Disabilities, 27,* 6–9.

Gerber, P. J., & Ginsberg, R. (1990). *Identifying alterable patterns of success in highly successful adults with learning disabilities* (Executive Summary submitted to the U.S. Department of Education). Washington, DC: National Institute for Disability and Rehabilitation Research.

Gerber, P. J., Schneiders, C. A., Paradise, L. V., Reiff, H. B., Ginsberg, R., & Popp, P. A. (1990). Persisting problems of adults with learning disabilities: Self-reported comparisons from their school-age and adult years. *Journal of Learning Disabilities, 23,* 570–573.

Gregory, J. F., Shanahan, T., & Walberg, H. (1985). Learning disabled 10th graders in mainstreamed settings. *Remedial and Special Education, 6*(4), 25–33.

Hallahan, D. P., & Bryan, T. H. (1981). Learning disabilities. In J. M. Kauffman & D. P. Hallahan (Eds.), *Handbook of special education* (pp. 141–164). Upper Saddle River, NJ: Prentice Hall.

Hamilton, S. F. (1986). Excellence and the transition from school to work. *Phi Delta Kappan, 68*(4), 239–242.

Haring, K. A., Lovett, D. L., & Smith, D. D. (1990). A follow-up study of recent special education graduates of learning disabilities programs. *Journal of Learning Disabilities, 23*(2), 108–113.

Harnischfeger, A. (1980). Curricular control and learning time: District policy, teacher strategy, and pupil choice. *Educational Evaluation and Policy Analysis, 2*(6), 19–30.

Harris, K. R., & Pressley, M. (1991). The nature of cognitive strategy instruction: Interactive strategy construction. *Exceptional Children, 57,* 392–404.

Hazel, J. S., & Schumaker, J. B. (1988). Social skills and learning disabilities: Current issues and recommendations for future research. In J. F. Kavanagh & T. J. Truss (Eds.), *Learning disabilities:*

Proceedings of the national conference (pp. 293-344). Parkton, MD: York Press.

Hudson, P., Lignugaris-Kraft, B., & Miller, T. (1993). Using content enhancements to improve the performance of adolescents with learning disabilities in content classes. *Learning Disabilities Research & Practice, 8,* 106–126.

Hughes, C. A., Hendrickson, J. M., & Hudson, P. J. (1986). The pause procedure: Improving factual recall from lectures by low and high achieving middle school students. *International Journal of Instructional Media, 13*(3), 217–226.

Hughes, C. A., & Smith, J. O. (1990). Cognitive and academic performance of college students with learning disabilities: A synthesis of literature. *Learning Disability Quarterly, 13,* 66–79.

Keilitz, I., & Dunivant, N. (1986). The relationship between learning disability and juvenile delinquency: Current state of knowledge. *Remedial and Special Education, 7*(3), 18–26.

Keilitz, I., Zaremba, B. A., & Broder, P. K. (1979). The link between learning disabilities and juvenile delinquency: Some issues and answers. *Learning Disability Quarterly, 2*(2), 2–11.

Keith, T. Z., & Page, E. B. (1985). Homework works at school: National evidence for policy changes. *School Psychology Review, 14,* 351–359.

Keogh, B. (1993, December). *Viewing learning disabilities through a developmental lens: The importance of time and context.* Paper presented at The Cove School and Cove Foundation meeting, Educational and Psychological Needs of Students with Learning Disabilities, Winnetka, IL.

Kerr, M. M., & Nelson, C. M. (1989). *Strategies for managing behavior problems in the classroom* (2nd ed.). Upper Saddle River, NJ: Merrill/Prentice Hall.

Knowlton, E. K. (1983). *Secondary regular classroom teachers' expectations of learning disabled students* (Research Report No. 75). Lawrence, KS: University of Kansas Center for Research on Learning.

Kokaska, C. J., & Brolin, D. E. (1985). *Career education for handicapped individuals* (2nd ed.). Upper Saddle River, NJ: Merrill/Prentice Hall.

Lane, B. A. (1980). The relationship of learning disabilities to juvenile delinquency: Current status. *Journal of Learning Disabilities, 13,* 425–434.

Lenz, B. K., & Bulgren, J. A. (1988). *Issues related to enhancing content acquisition for students with learning disabilities.* Lawrence, KS: University of Kansas Center for Research on Learning.

Lenz, B. K., Bulgren, J., & Hudson, P. (1990). Content enhancement: A model for promoting the acquisition of content by individuals with learning disabilities. In T. Scruggs & B. Wong (Eds.), *Intervention research in learning disabilities* (pp. 122-165). New York: Springer-Verlag.

Lenz, B. K., Clark, F. C., Deshler, D. D., Schumaker, J. B., & Rademacher, J. A. (Eds.). (1990). *SIM training library: The strategies instructional approach.* Lawrence, KS: University of Kansas Center for Research on Learning.

Lenz, B. K., Deshler, D. D., & Schumaker, J. B. (1991). *Barriers to the planning of instruction for learning disabled adolescents in the regular classroom setting* (Progress Report: The development and validation of planning routines to enhance the delivery of content to students with handicaps in general education settings). Washington, DC: U.S. Department of Education.

Lenz, B. K., Ehren, B. J., & Smiley, L. R. (1991). A goal attainment approach to improve completion of project-type assignments by learning disabled adolescents. *Focus on Learning Disabilities, 6,* 166–176.

Lenz, B. K., Ellis, E. S., & Scanlon, D. (1996). *Teaching learning strategies to adolescents and adults with learning disabilities.* Austin, TX: PRO-ED.

Lenz, B. K., & Hughes, C. A. (1990). A word identification strategy for adolescents with learning disabilities. *Journal of Learning Disabilities, 23,* 149–158.

Lenz, B. K., & Mellard, D. P. (1990). Content area skill assessment. In R. A. Gable & J. M. Hendrickson (Eds.), *Error patterns in academics: Identification and remediation* (pp. 117–145). White Plains, NY: Longman.

Levin, E. K., Zigmond, N., & Birch, J. W. (1985). A follow-up study of 52 learning disabled adolescents. *Journal of Learning Disabilities, 18,* 2–7.

Levinson, D. J. (1978). *The seasons of a man's life.* New York: Knopf.

Lewandowski, L., & Arcangelo, K. (1994). The social adjustment and self-concept of adults with learning disabilities. *Journal of Learning Disabilities, 27,* 598–605.

Link, D. B. (1980). *Essential learning skills and the low-achieving student at the secondary level: A rating of the importance of 24 academic abilities.* Unpublished master's thesis, University of Kansas, Lawrence.

Mathews, R. M., Whang, P. L., & Fawcett, S. B. (1980). Development and validation of an occupational assessment instrument. *Behavioral Assessment, 2,* 71–85.

McKenzie, R. G. (1991). Content area instruction delivered by secondary learning disabilities teachers: A national survey. *Learning Disability Quarterly, 14,* 115–122.

Meltzer, L. J., Levine, M. D., Karniski, W., Palfrey, J. S., & Clarke, S. (1984). An analysis of the learning styles of adolescent delinquents. *Journal of Learning Disabilities, 17,* 600–608.

Mercer, C. D., & Mercer, A. R. (1993). *Teaching students with learning problems* (4th ed.). Upper Saddle River, NJ: Merrill/Prentice Hall.

Meyen, E. L., Alley, G. R., Scannell, D. P., Harnden, G. M., & Miller, K. F. (1982). *A mandated minimum competency testing program and its impact on learning disabled students: Curricular validity and comparative performance* (Research Report No. 63). Lawrence, KS: University of Kansas Center for Research on Learning.

Minskoff, E. H., & DeMoss, S. (1993). Facilitating successful transition: Using the TRAC model to assess and develop academic skills needed for vocational competence. *Learning Disability Quarterly, 16,* 161–170.

Mithaug, D., Horiuchi, C., & Fanning, P. (1985). A report of the Colorado statewide follow-up survey of special education students. *Exceptional Children, 51,* 397–404.

Moran, M. R. (1980). *An investigation of the demands on oral language skills of learning disabled students in secondary classrooms* (Research Report No. 1). Lawrence, KS: University of Kansas Center for Research on Learning.

Moran, M. R., & DeLoache, T. F. (1982). *Mainstream teachers' responses to formal features of writing by secondary learning disabled students* (Research Report No. 61). Lawrence, KS: University of Kansas Center for Research on Learning.

Nagel, D. R., Schumaker, J. B., & Deshler, D. D. (1986). *The learning strategies curriculum: The FIRST-letter mnemonic strategy.* Lawrence, KS: Edge Enterprises.

Okolo, C., & Sitlington, P. (1988). The role of special education in LD adolescents' transition from high school to work. *Learning Disability Quarterly, 11,* 292–306.

Owings, J., & Stocking, C. (1985). *High school and beyond: Characteristics of high school students who identify themselves as handicapped.* Washington, DC: National Center for Education Statistics, U.S. Department of Education.

Page, E. B., & Keith, T. Z. (1981). Effects of U.S. private schools: A technical analysis of two recent claims. *Educational Researcher, 10*(7), 7–17.

Patton, J. R., & Polloway, E. A. (1992). Learning disabilities: The challenges of adulthood. *Journal of Learning Disabilities, 25,* 410–416.

Perlmutter, B. F., Crocker, J., Cordray, D., & Garstecki, D. (1983). Sociometric status and related personality characteristics of mainstreamed learning disabled adolescents. *Learning Disabilities Quarterly, 6,* 20–30.

Pflaum, S. W., & Pascarella, E. T. (1982). Attribution retraining for learning disabled students: Some thoughts on the practical implication of the evidence. *Learning Disability Quarterly, 5,* 422–426.

Polachek, S. W., Kniesner, T. J., & Harwood, H. J. (1978). Education production functions. *Journal of Educational Statistics, 3,* 209–231.

Polloway, E. A., Epstein, M. H., Polloway, C. H., Patton, J. R., & Ball, D. W. (1986). Corrective Reading Program: An analysis of effectiveness with learning disabled and mentally retarded children. *Remedial and Special Education, 7*(4), 41–47.

Polloway, E. A., Patton, J. R., Epstein, M. H., & Smith, T. E. (1989). Comprehensive curriculum for students with mild handicaps. *Focus on Exceptional Children, 21*(8), 1–12.

Polloway, E. A., Smith, J. D., & Patton, J. R. (1984). Learning disabilities: An adult development perspective. *Learning Disability Quarterly,* 179–186.

Powell, L., Suzuki, K., Atwater, J., Gorney-Krupsaw, B., & Morris, E. K. (1981). *Interactions between teachers and learning disabled and non-learning disabled students* (Research Report No. 44). Lawrence, KS: University of Kansas Center for Research on Learning.

Putnam, M. L. (1992). Characteristics of questions on tests administered by mainstream secondary classroom teachers. *Learning Disabilities Research & Practice, 7,* 129–136.

Reiff, H. B., & deFur, S. (1992). Transition for youths with learning disabilities: A focus on developing independence. *Learning Disability Quarterly, 15,* 237–249.

Reiff, H. B., Ginsberg, R., & Gerber, P. J. (1995). New perspectives on teaching from successful adults with learning disabilities. *Remedial and Special Education, 16*(1), 29–37.

Rieth, H. J., & Polsgrove, L. (1994). Curriculum and instructional issues in teaching secondary students with learning disabilities. *Learning Disabilities Research & Practice, 9*(2), 118–126.

Rojewski, J. W. (1992). Key components of model transition services for students with learning disabilities. *Learning Disability Quarterly, 15,* 135–150.

Ruhl, K., Hughes, C., & Gajar, A. (1990). Efficacy of the pause procedure for enhancing learning disabled and nondisabled college students' long- and short-term recall of facts presented through lecture. *Learning Disability Quarterly, 13,* 55–64.

Ruhl, K. L., & Suritsky, S. (1995). The pause procedure and/or an outline: Effect on immediate free recall and lecture notes taken by college students with learning disabilities. *Learning Disability Quarterly, 18,* 2–11.

Schmidt, J. L., Deshler, D. D., Schumaker, J. B., & Alley, G. R. (1989). Effects of generalization instruction on the written language performance of adolescents with learning disabilities in the mainstream classroom. *Journal of Reading, Writing, and Learning Disabilities, 4*(4), 291–311.

Schumaker, J. B., & Deshler, D. D. (1984). Setting demand variables: A major factor in program planning for the LD adolescent. *Topics in Language Disorders, 4*(2), 22–40.

Schumaker, J. B., & Deshler, D. D. (1988). Implementing the regular education initiative in secondary schools: A different ball game. *Journal of Learning Disabilities, 21*(1), 36–42.

Schumaker, J. B., Deshler, D. D., & Ellis, E. S. (1986). Intervention issues related to the education of LD adolescents. In J. K. Torgesen & B. L. Wong (Eds.), *Learning disabilities: Some new perspectives.* New York: Academic Press.

Schumaker, J. B., Deshler, D. D., & McKnight, P. C. (1991). Teaching routines for content areas at the secondary level. In G. Stover, M. R. Shinn, & H. M. Walker (Eds.), *Interventions for achievement and behavior problems* (pp. 473–494). Washington, DC: National Association of School Psychologists.

Schumaker, J. B., & Hazel, J. S. (1984). Social skills assessment and training for the learning disabled: Who's on first and what's on second? Part 1. *Journal of Learning Disabilities, 17,* 422–431.

Schumaker, J. B., Hazel, J. S., & Pederson, C. S. (1988). *Social skills for daily living.* Circle Pines, MN: American Guidance Service.

Schumaker, J. B., Hazel, J. S., Sherman, J. A., & Sheldon. J. (1982). *Social skill performance of learning disabled, non-learning disabled, and delinquent adolescents* (Research Report No. 60). Lawrence, KS: University of Kansas Center for Research on Learning.

Schumaker, J. B., Nolan, S. M., & Deshler, D. D. (1985). *Learning strategies curriculum: The error monitoring strategy.* Lawrence, KS: University of Kansas.

Schumaker, J. B., Sheldon-Wildgen, J., & Sherman, J. A. (1980). *An observational study of the academic and social behaviors of learning disabled adolescents in the regular classroom* (Research Report No. 22). Lawrence, KS: University of Kansas Center for Research on Learning.

Scott, S. S. (1994). Determining reasonable academic adjustments for college students with learning disabilities. *Journal of Learning Disabilities, 27,* 403–412.

Seabaugh, G. O., & Schumaker, J. B. (1981). *The effects of self-regulation training on the academic productivity of LD and NLD adolescents* (Research Report No. 37). Lawrence, KS: University of Kansas Center for Research on Learning.

Siegel, S., & Gaylord-Ross, R. (1991). Factors associated with employment success among youths with learning disabilities. *Journal of Learning Disabilities, 24,* 40–47.

Silverman, R., Zigmond, N., & Sansone, J. (1981). Teaching coping skills to adolescents with learning problems. *Focus on Exceptional Children,* 13(6), 1–20.

Sitlington, P. L., & Frank, A. R. (1990). Are adolescents with learning disabilities successfully crossing the bridge into adult life? *Learning Disability Quarterly, 13,* 97–111.

Sitlington, P. L., & Frank, A. R. (1993). Dropouts with learning disabilities: What happens to them as young adults? *Learning Disabilities Research & Practice, 8,* 244–252.

Sitlington, P. L., Frank, A. R., & Carson, R. (1993). Adult adjustment among high school graduates with mild disabilities. *Exceptional Children, 59,* 221–233.

Spekman, N. J., Goldberg, R. J., & Herman, K. L. (1992). Learning disabled children grow up: A search for factors related to success in the young adult years. *Learning Disabilities Research & Practice, 7,* 161–170.

Spekman, N. J., Goldberg, R. J., & Herman, K. L. (1993). An exploration of risk and resilience in the lives of individuals with learning disabilities. *Learning Disabilities Research & Practice, 8,* 11–18.

Spekman, N. J., Herman, K. L., & Vogel, S. A. (1993). Risk and resilience in individuals with learning disabilities: A challenge to the field. *Learning Disabilities Research & Practice, 8,* 59–65.

Spillane, S. A., McGuire, J. M., & Norlander, K. A. (1992). Undergraduate admission policies, practices, and procedures for applicants with learning disabilities. *Journal of Learning Disabilities, 25,* 665–670, 677.

Spruill, J. A. (1993). Secondary assessment: Structuring the transition process. *Learning Disabilities Research & Practice, 8,* 127–132.

Torgesen, J. K. (1982). The learning disabled child as an inactive learner: Educational implications. *Topics in Learning and Learning Disabilities, 2,* 45–52.

Unger, K. (1978). Learning disabilities and juvenile delinquency. *Journal of Juvenile and Family Courts, 29*(1), 25–30.

U.S. Department of Labor, Department of Education, & Department of Commerce. (1988). *Building a quality workforce.* Washington, DC: U.S. Government Printing Office.

Vallecorsa, A. L., & Garriss, E. (1990). Story composition skills of middle-grade students with learning disabilities. *Exceptional Children, 57,* 48–55.

Van Reusen, A. K., & Bos, C. S. (1994). Facilitating student participation in individualized education programs through motivation strategy instruction. *Exceptional Children, 60,* 466–475.

Van Reusen, A. K., Bos, C. S., Schumaker, J. B., & Deshler, D. D. (1987). *Motivation strategies curriculum: The education planning strategy.* Lawrence, KS: Edge Enterprises.

Wagner, M. (1989). *The transition experiences of youth with disabilities: A report from the national longitudinal transition study.* (USDOE, DSEP Contract #300-87-0054). Menlo Park, CA: SRI International.

Wagner, M. (1990, April). *The school programs and school performance of secondary students classified as learning disabled: Findings from the national longitudinal transition study of special education students.* Paper presented at the meetings of Division G, American Educational Research Association, Boston.

Walberg, H. J. (1984). Improving the productivity of America's schools. *Educational Leadership, 41*(8), 19–30.

Waldie, K., & Spreen, O. (1993). The relationship between learning disabilities and persisting delinquency. *Journal of Learning Disabilities, 26,* 417–423.

Wang, M. C., Rubenstein, J. L., & Reynolds, M. C. (1985). Clearing the road to success for students with special needs. *Educational Leadership, 43*(1), 62–67.

Warner, M. M., Alley, G. R., Deshler, D. D., & Schumaker, J. B. (1980). *An epidemiology study of learning disabled adolescents in secondary schools: Classification and discrimination of learning disabled and low-achieving adolescents* (Research Report No. 20). Lawrence, KS: University of Kansas Center for Research on Learning.

Warner, M. M., Schumaker, J. B., Alley, G. R., & Deshler, D. D. (1982). *An epidemiological study of learning disabled adolescents in secondary schools: Performance on a serial recall task and the role of executive function* (Research Report No. 55). Lawrence, KS: University of Kansas Center for Research on Learning.

White, W. J. (1992). The postschool adjustment of persons with learning disabilities: Current status and future projections. *Journal of Learning Disabilities, 25,* 448–456.

Wiseman, D. E. (1980). The parallel alternative curriculum for secondary classrooms. In R. H. Riegel & J. P. Mathey (Eds.), *Mainstreaming at the secondary level: Seven models that work.* Plymouth, MI: Wayne County Intermediate School District.

Woodward, J., & Gersten, R. (1992). Innovative technology for secondary students with learning disabilities. *Exceptional Children, 58,* 407–421.

Zigmond, N. (1990). Rethinking secondary school programs for students with learning disabilities. *Focus on Exceptional Children, 23*(1), 1–24.

Zigmond, N., & Brownlee, J. (1980). Social skills training for adolescents with learning disabilities. *Exceptional Education Quarterly, 1,* 77–83.

Zigmond, N., Levin, E., & Laurie, T. E. (1985). Managing the mainstream: An analysis of teacher attitudes and student performance in mainstream high school programs. *Journal of Learning Disabilities, 18,* 535–541.

Zigmond, N., Sansone, J., Miller, S. E., Donahoe, K. A., & Kohnke, R. (1986). Teaching learning disabled students at the secondary school level: What research says to teachers. *Learning Disabilities Focus, 1*(2), 108–115.

PART THREE

Specific Learning Disorders

Language and Communication

CHAPTER 11

After studying this chapter, you should be able to:

- discuss general terminology regarding language-learning disabilities.
- discuss the theories of language acquisition.
- discuss approaches to the study of language disorders and present their strengths and weaknesses.
- discuss the components of language and present deficits in each area.
- discuss language difficulties according to various age groups of students.
- discuss issues involving the language skills of bilingual and culturally diverse students.
- describe formal diagnostic language measures.
- present informal language assessment techniques.
- discuss language service delivery models.
- list teaching strategies to enhance language comprehension and production.
- describe commercial language programs and materials.
- describe computer software programs in language.

Oral language is a learned behavior that enables people to transmit their ideas and culture from generation to generation. The ability to communicate through language is perhaps an individual's most vital and complex characteristic. It is through speech and language that people make sense of and respond to their environment. A communication problem can be devastating because it directly affects the individual as well as others in the immediate environment as attempts are made to transmit ideas, facts, feelings, and desires. Language also is related directly to achievement and adjustment in school because language is the basis for formulating questions, extending and clarifying information, and reducing ambiguity in new learning situations (Bashir, 1989). In addition to being part of the academic curriculum, language is a medium through which information is taught and acquired.

Students with severe language impairments usually are identified at an early age and receive speech or language therapy in a prekindergarten or developmental program. A greater number of students possess a more subtle language problem and begin to show difficulties as they grow older. As the curriculum demands increase in about the third or fourth grade, these students lack the language foundation required to build academic skills. Teachers often describe such students as having difficulty maintaining attention, following directions, and using the right words when speaking. Other students are identified when they begin to have difficulties in academic areas such as reading and writing. These students need an informed classroom teacher who is able to identify and understand their language problems and help them receive appropriate intervention.

This chapter is designed to provide a basic understanding of communication, or speech and language, disorders in students with learning disabilities. Basic terminology regarding communication skills is presented, and theories of language acquisition, approaches to the study of language disorders, and the major components of language are discussed. Language difficulties at various stages in a student's life are included, as well as a discussion of issues involving the language skills of bilingual and culturally diverse students. Moreover, assessment techniques, service delivery models, and teaching strategies are provided. Finally, commercial language programs and computer software programs are described.

Although certain language skills are discussed separately in this chapter, they should be understood in the context of their interactiveness and pervasive impact on a student's learning and academic success. Language is viewed as interacting with other cognitive constructs and is best assessed and remediated as a whole in social communication rather than as isolated language skills. To ensure academic success for students with language-learning disabilities, the teacher and language specialist should consult one another and work cooperatively.

PREVALENCE

Students who have a language disorder and academic difficulties in the classroom, such as an inability to read or write, often are identified as having a learning disability. These students, however, also frequently are referred to as having a *language-learning disability*. In addition to the unique educational needs of a student with a learning disability, the existence of a language problem poses further challenges for professionals who work with these students. The teacher should have a basic understanding of how a language-learning disability affects a student's academic, social, and emotional development.

The actual prevalence of students with learning disabilities who also have language problems is difficult to estimate because of the variability in the criteria used to make the diagnosis. Also, students are included in prevalence counts according to their primary disabling condition (learning disabilities) rather than a secondary problem (language). In some cases, students who are initially identified as having speech and language impairments are identified as having learning disabilities later when academic difficulties emerge (Ehren & Lenz, 1989). While students with learning disabilities comprise 51.1% of the population with disabilities and 4.09% of the total population in prekindergarten through 12th grade, students with speech or language impairments are the next largest group (U.S. Department of Education, 1994). They constitute 21.6% of the population with disabilities and 1.73% of the total population. Of the students identified as having learning disabilities, a large portion exhibit a language-learning impairment. Estimates of the prevalence of students with a language-learning disability among students with learning disabilities range from 40% to 60% (Wiig & Semel, 1984). A language-learning disability is characterized by problems in language comprehension, expression, and use; by difficulties in word-finding; and sometimes by problems in auditory processing and speech discrimination. Wiig and Semel note that this language disorder syndrome may combine with an articulatory and graphomotor dyscoordination syndrome or with a visuospatial perceptual deficit syndrome. The articulatory and graphomotor dyscoordination syndrome occurs in 10% to 40% of the population with learning disabilities and is characterized by difficulties in articulation, writing, and drawing. Another 5% to 15% of students with learning disabilities may have visuospatial perceptual deficits characterized by visual discrimination, visual memory, and spatial orientation problems. Although not every student with a learning disability has a problem with language or articulation, students with these problems have unique educational needs and require special attention by teachers and speech and language pathologists.

TERMINOLOGY

Language is defined as "a socially shared code or conventional system for representing concepts through the use of arbitrary symbols and rule-governed combinations of those symbols" (Owens, 1994, p. 45). In contrast, *speech* involves the actual mechanics or motor act of verbal expression. Thus, whereas speech includes spoken utterances to convey meaning, language indicates a person's knowledge of the linguistic concepts on which speech is based. Moreover, language is comprised of receptive skills (understanding) and expressive skills (use) and includes both written and oral forms.

A variety of terms may be used with youngsters who do not acquire language at a normal rate. Terms such as *specific language impairment, language delay,* and *language disorder* generally are used with students who are having difficulty learning language in the absence of any intellectual, sensory, or emotional problems. The American Speech-Language-Hearing Association (1992) provides the following definition of *language disorder*:

> A language disorder is the impairment or deviant development of comprehension and/or use of a spoken, written, and/or other symbol system. The disorder may involve (1) the form of language (phonologic, morphologic, and syntactic systems), (2) the content of language (semantic system), and/or (3) the function of language in communication (pragmatic system) in any combination. (p. 949)

The term *language disorder* generally is used when a student exhibits difficulty learning language or is learning language in a nontypical sequence. However, the initial manifestation of a language disorder is generally a delay in language development (Mogford & Sadler, 1989). Thus, in practice, the distinction is not clear, and the terms *language disorder* and *language delay* often are used interchangeably. As Lahey (1988) states, "It is not always easy to determine whether a child's system is qualitatively different from that of any non-language-impaired child at some point in development" (p. 21).

Another term the teacher may encounter is *aphasia.* This term generally applies to a communication disorder caused by brain damage and is characterized by complete or partial impairment of language comprehension, formulation, and use. It usually excludes disorders associated with sensory deficits, mental deterioration, or psychiatric disorders (Nicolosi, Harryman, & Kresheck, 1978). There are two types of aphasia in youngsters: acquired aphasia and developmental or childhood aphasia. The term *acquired aphasia* is used with youngsters who have normal language development that is disrupted by a cortical lesion, seizure, or stroke that results in a language loss. In contrast, *developmental* or *childhood aphasia* is used with youngsters whose language problems are believed to be caused by central nervous system dysfunction and who exhibit difficulty in their understanding or use of language. Because evidence of central nervous system dysfunction is often highly inferential, this term commonly is replaced by the descriptive term *specific language impairment* (SLI). Thus, youngsters with a specific language impairment are considered to have an isolated language problem with no apparent intellectual, psychological, or sensorimotor basis (Rosenberg, 1984).

By definition, a specific language impairment is similar to a learning disability. As Lahey (1988) states, "Definitions of both learning disabilities and SLI state that the language-learning problems are not the result of sensory impairment, motor problems, mental retardation, emotional problems, or environmental deprivation. In many definitions the two syndromes overlap" (p. 83). In this chapter the term *language disorder* generally is used as a descriptive term that includes students who exhibit language difficulties regardless of etiology.

THEORIES OF LANGUAGE ACQUISITION

Theories of language acquisition fall within three major camps: behavioristic, nativistic (or psycholinguistic), and interactionistic (or cognitive). The behavioristic position (Skinner, 1957) relies on learning principles to explain language acquisition. Braine (1971), Jenkins and Palermo (1964), and Staats (1971) are proponents of the behavioristic position. The behaviorist believes that the infant begins with no knowledge of language but possesses the ability to learn it. The child learns through reinforcement of imitation. Reinforcement of babbling (including parent attention and delight) and the shaping of vocal behavior account for the initial stages of learning. Behaviorists emphasize environmental influences and the universal laws of learning, namely operant conditioning principles. The *DISTAR Language* program (discussed in the section on commercial materials) is based on the behavioral model.

Chomsky (1965), Lenneberg (1967), and McNeil (1970) are proponents of the nativistic position. Chomsky claims that the child possesses an innate capacity for dealing with linguistic universals. The child generates a theory of grammar to help understand and produce an infinite number of sentences. Lenneberg states that the child is biologically predisposed to learn language as the brain matures. In the nativistic position, humans are believed to be "prewired" for language development, and the environment simply triggers its emergence. Language programs that emphasize the teaching of rules for sentence transformations are representative of the nativistic model.

Piaget (1960), the major proponent of the interactionistic position, theorizes that the child acquires language through the interaction of perceptual-cognitive capacities and experiences. The child's environment and neurological maturation determine learning. Language and thought thus develop simultaneously as the child passes through a series of fixed developmental stages requiring more and more complex strategies of cognitive organization. Interactionists consider the capacity for language to be innate; however, unlike the nativist, the interactionist believes the child must internalize linguistic structures from the environment and must become aware of communication's social functions. Thus, language programs in the interactionistic model are based on two ideas: (a) meaning is brought to a child's language through interaction with the environment, and (b) the child uses speech to control the environment. Intervention approaches based on this model emphasize natural language teaching rather than structured exercises and drills.

On the one hand, the biologists (Lenneberg, 1967) and the linguists (Chomsky, 1965) view the child as a product of the maturation process. Biologists and linguists believe that, unless physical or mental complications occur, the child's development is predetermined. This view places heavy emphasis on the child who is considered to be biologically prepared or linguistically preprogrammed to develop language. On the other hand, the behaviorists stress the influence of the environment. The child's role is passive, and development depends largely on the individuals in the child's environment who respond to the child's behavior. The interactionistic position emphasizes the child's active interactions with the environment as the child learns to talk (Bloom, 1975).

Primarily through the work of Wiig and Semel, language intervention has focused on the linguistic model, with direct concern about language functioning through analyzing comprehension and performance according to the components of language (such as phonology) and their rules. The linguistic model has served as the basis for the creation of many language programs. These programs usually focus on a particular language skill that the student should possess. Although the content of these programs is similar (phonemes and morphemes), some have their foundations in behavioral theory, some in nativism, and some in interactionism.

APPROACHES TO LANGUAGE DISORDERS

Two main approaches to the study of language disorders affect how a student is labeled, identified, and treated. These include the etiological-categorical approach and the descriptive-developmental approach. Although not totally incompatible, the two approaches serve different purposes and may have different educational implications. In essence, when considering the two language approaches, the teacher primarily must focus on meeting the needs of the individual student with language disorders. The following includes a brief description of each approach as well as its strengths and weaknesses.

Etiological-Categorical Approach

The etiological-categorical approach focuses on classifying disorders according to their cause or etiology. This approach was common during the 1950s and 1960s in the fields of speech-language pathology and education and continues to be predominant today in the field of medicine. This approach utilizes the medical model (Lahey, 1988) and emphasizes placing youngsters in clinical categories. McCormick and Schiefelbusch (1984) note that the approach focuses on grouping or categorizing youngsters according to similarities or differences and is based upon several assumptions: (a) differential diagnosis is possible, (b) disabilities and aptitudes within a category are consistent, and (c) grouping similar aptitudes together creates more effective programming. Under these assumptions, McCormick and Schiefelbusch describe five general placement groups for youngsters. These include language and communication problems associated with motor disorders, sensory deficits, central nervous system dysfunction, severe emotional-social dysfunction, and cognitive disorders.

Strengths of the Etiological-Categorical Approach. Bernstein (1993b) describes several advantages of the etiological-categorical approach. Perhaps the greatest advantage is convenience, because it is easy to contrast how a student is alike or different from others by discussing categorical characteristics. Second, many states require a diagnostic label for students to qualify for appropriate special education programs such as speech and language therapy and academic resource programs. In some cases, students need a label to participate in programs specifically designed for those with mental, emotional, or learning disabilities.

Some parents and advocacy groups argue in favor of the use of labels because they believe it is better to be labeled and receive services than to not be labeled and receive no special attention. For example, a parent of a young student labeled as having a severe speech-language impairment may continue to fight for the student to retain the label in spite of obvious progress because it ensures the student will receive individualized attention in a self-contained setting. This type of attitude is understandable and perhaps not uncommon from a parent who has struggled to receive help for a youngster with disabilities. A third advantage of the etiological-categorical approach is that it provides a general guideline to the speech and language pathologist and the teacher, who are trying to determine what to expect of the student, which intervention techniques may be beneficial, and which modalities may maximize learning. For example, a student with hearing impairments may immediately receive preferential seating in a classroom, or a student with mental disabilities may receive instructional interventions that provide additional repetition and practice.

Weaknesses of the Etiological-Categorical Approach. Many teachers and speech and language pathologists are critical of the etiological-categorical approach for several reasons. According to McCormick and Schiefelbusch (1984), "It is enough to say that labels, while they may aid placement decisions in the present system, do *not* predict the nature or severity of children's language difficulties. Category labels convey little, if any, instructionally relevant information because children sharing the same classification often exhibit markedly different language and communication abilities" (p. 90). This criticism is echoed by Bloom and Lahey (1978) and Lahey (1988) who note that youngsters rarely fit neatly into one category. Lahey also cautions against the self-fulfilling prophesy, adding that students or teachers may respond according to the given label. For example, a student who is labeled as having a language or communication problem because of a severe emotional-social dysfunction may begin to "act out" or be socially inappropriate. Likewise, a teacher who notes that a student has a language disorder because of a central nervous system dysfunction may use the label to excuse ineffective teaching techniques.

Another disadvantage to the etiological-categorical approach is that students may exhibit different characteristics when interacting with various environments. For example, a student may appear emotionally disabled and aggressive in a nonstructured setting but become compliant and socially appropriate when structure is introduced. Also, different causes may result in the same overt behavior. For example, a youngster who has mild seizures and one who is simply bored may exhibit the same short episodes of staring.

Although the etiological-categorical approach is useful in discovering the possible etiology underlying a particular disability, many teachers criticize it because etiology is difficult to relate to educational interventions. Furthermore, the role of the teacher is to determine appropriate intervention strategies based on the needs of the student, regardless of the etiology.

Descriptive-Developmental Approach

The descriptive-developmental approach focuses on describing students' language strengths and weaknesses rather than classifying them to identify students with a possible language disorder and plan educational intervention. In this approach a student with a language disorder is compared with normally developing peers in terms of ability to understand and use language. According to Lahey (1988), "What a child with a language problem needs to learn about language is precisely what the non-language-impaired child needs to learn about language at some point in development" (p. 89).

The theoretical framework that supports much of the research in the descriptive-developmental approach to language disorders is based on the work of Bloom and Lahey (1978) and is reported by several researchers (Bernstein, 1993b; McCormick & Schiefelbusch, 1984). Bloom and Lahey propose the following five large subgroups of students with language impairments:

1. Delayed language—students whose language and communication skills are similar in every aspect to a younger child with normal development.
2. Content problems—students who exhibit problems formulating and conceptualizing ideas about objects, events, and relations.
3. Form problems—students who exhibit difficulties learning the language code and linking it to what they know about their environment.
4. Use problems—students who have difficulty adjusting their language to meet the listener's needs, expressing a range of communicative functions, or understanding and speaking in certain contexts.
5. Association problems—students who have difficulty integrating content, form, and use.

Strengths of the Descriptive-Developmental Approach. McCormick and Schiefelbusch (1984) note that the primary advantage of the descriptive-developmental approach is the focus on pinpointing specific language deficits, which results in the ability to design effective remediation or intervention. The information is instructionally relevant because it reveals the areas of weakness and the sequence for teaching (Bernstein, 1993b). Furthermore, this approach overcomes some of the limitations of the etiological-categorical approach because it focuses on intervention rather than on finding and categorizing a cause for the disability.

Weaknesses of the Descriptive-Developmental Approach. Bernstein (1993b) presents the following three limitations to the descriptive-developmental approach:

1. It does not provide clear procedures on how to teach or remediate the deficit areas.
2. It disregards the student's age and environment and assumes the disorder is linguistically based. Consequently, older students may receive therapy for skills that are inappropriate for their age or environmental setting.
3. It ignores the labeling requirement for placement in special educational programs.

COMPONENTS OF LANGUAGE

Language refers to "a code whereby ideas about the world are expressed through a conventional system of arbitrary signals for communication" (Lahey, 1988, p. 2). Speakers and listeners both are involved in oral language because language is heard as well as spoken. A speaker's use of this arbitrary vocal system to communicate ideas and thoughts to a listener is referred to as *expressive language,* or *production.* In this process the listener uses *receptive language,* or *comprehension.* Students with expressive language difficulties may be reluctant to participate in verbal activities, whereas students with receptive language problems may have difficulty following directions or understanding content presented orally.

To assess and plan instruction for language problems, the teacher needs to be familiar with the components of language (see Table 11.1). Bloom and Lahey (1978) classify the components of language according to form (phonology, morphology, and syntax), content (semantics), and use (pragmatics). These five components of language are distinct but interrelated and interactive.

Form: Phonology

Phonology is the system of rules that governs sounds and sound combinations, and a *phoneme* is a unit of sound that combines with other sounds to form words. A phoneme is the smallest unit of language and is distinguished from the other language components in that a phoneme alone, such as /s/ and /b/, does not convey meaning. However, when interchanged in a word, phonemes significantly alter meaning (e.g., *sat* to *bat*). The rules that govern phonemes

TABLE 11.1
Components of Language

Component	Definition	Receptive Level	Expressive Level
Phonology	The sound system of a language and the linguistic rules that govern the sound combinations	Discrimination of speech sounds	Articulation of speech sounds
Morphology	The linguistic rule system that governs the structure of words and the construction of word forms from the basic elements of meaning	Understanding of grammatical structure of words	Use of grammar in words
Syntax	The linguistic rule system governing the order and combination of words to form sentences, and the relationships among the elements within a sentence	Understanding of phrases and sentences	Use of grammar in phrases and sentences
Semantics	The psycholinguistic system that patterns the content of an utterance, intent, and meanings of words and sentences	Understanding of word meanings and word relationships	Use of word meanings and word relationships
Pragmatics	The sociolinguistic system that patterns the use of language in communication, which may be expressed motorically, vocally, or verbally	Understanding of contextual language cues	Use of language in context

focus on how sounds can be used in different word positions and which sounds may be combined. For example, standard English does not have a sound for the combination of /zt/.

The English language consists of about 40 phonemes, classified as either vowels or consonants. Vowels are categorized according to where they are produced in the mouth. The tongue may be moved up, down, forward, or backward in producing vowels. These different tongue positions are used to classify vowels as high, mid, or low (i.e., the position of the highest part of the tongue) and front, central, or back (i.e., the location of the highest position) (Owens, 1994). For example, the long /e/ sound is classified as high front because the tongue blade is high in the front of the mouth. The tip of the tongue is down for all vowels. Consonants are classified according to place and manner of articulation. For example, the phoneme /f/ can be described by place (labial) and manner (voiceless stop).

Jacobson and Halle (1956) propose three principles that influence the order of phoneme acquisition:

1. Children learn to distinguish sounds first that have the fewest features in common, such as

oral-nasal (/p/, /m/), labial-dental (/p/, /t/), and stop-fricative (/p/, /f/).
2. Development of front consonants such as /p/ and /m/ precedes the development of back consonants such as /k/ and /g/.
3. Phonemes that occur infrequently among the languages of the world (such as the English short *a* in *bat*), even though they may be frequent in the child's native language, are the last to be acquired.

Owens (1994) notes that vowels are acquired by the age of 3, whereas consonant clusters and blends are not acquired until age 7 or 8. However, there are individual differences, and the age of acquisition for some sounds may vary by as much as 3 years.

Phonological Deficits. Problems in phonology frequently appear as articulation disorders. The most common problem is that of the child who is developmentally delayed in consonant acquisition. The child may omit a consonant (such as saying "oo" for *you*), substitute one consonant for another (such as saying "wabbit" for *rabbit*), or distort a consonant. An example of a consonant distortion is the lateral emission of air in the production of /s/ in which the air escapes over the sides of the tongue (rather than over the tip), resulting in a noticeably slushy quality to the sound.

In addition to problems in expression, problems in reception also can occur, such as discrimination difficulty. For example, the child may hear "Go get the nail" when the command was actually "Go get the mail." The child cannot tell the difference between /n/ and /m/ and, thus, does not respond correctly. Phoneme discrimination errors can occur in comprehension of consonants (/p/ for /b/ and /d/ for /t/), consonant blends (/pr/, /fr/, and /kr/ confused with /pl/, /fl/, and /kl/), and vowels (confusion of vowels produced with the tongue in a forward position as in *pit, pet,* and *pat*) (Wiig & Semel, 1976).

Researchers recently have begun to examine the relationship between phonological disorders and academic reading performance. Ackerman, Dykman, and Gardner (1990) note that students with reading disabilities tend to articulate sequences more slowly than do students without disabilities. Ackerman et al. claim that the slow-speaking student would have greater difficulty sounding out and blending polysyllabic words and comprehending what is read. Pehrsson and Denner (1988) add that many students with language disorders have organization problems, which may inhibit their ability to remember what they have read. Students with a limited phonological repertoire (i.e., unintelligible speech) who are experiencing difficulties in reading, spelling, and writing present concerns for the teacher regarding the priorities and content of appropriate intervention.

Form: Morphology

A *morpheme* is the smallest unit or segment of language that conveys meaning. Two different types of morphemes exist: roots and affixes. Root words are free morphemes that can stand alone (e.g., *car, teach,* and *tall*), whereas affixes are bound morphemes such as prefixes and suffixes that when attached to root words change the meaning of the word (e.g., *car**s***, *teach**er***, and *tall**est***). *Derivational* suffixes change word class; for example, the verb *walk* becomes a noun, *walker,* with the addition of the suffix *er. Inflectional* suffixes change the meaning of a word; for example, the addition of the inflectional *s* to the word *boy* changes the meaning to "more than one boy."

A further distinction can be made between two broad classes of words in a language: content words and function words (Lahey, 1988). Similar to root words, content words convey meaning when they stand alone, and they generally carry the meaning in sentences. Function words or connective words join phrases or sentences together (e.g., pronouns, articles, prepositions, and conjunctions). The meaning of connective words varies according to the context or words that they connect.

Morphological Deficits. Students who are delayed in morphological development may not use appropriate inflectional endings in their speech. An elementary school student may not use the third-person *s* on verbs (e.g., "He walk") or may not use *s* on nouns or pronouns to show possession (e.g., "Mommy coat") or may not use *er* on adjectives (e.g., "Her dog is small than mine"). Older elementary and middle school students who are delayed in morphology may lack more advanced morphemes of irregular past tense or irregular plurals; they may use such forms as *drived* for *drove* or *mans* for *men.* Students such as these exhibit inconsistency regarding morphology usage (i.e., they vacillate in the use of *bringed, brang*, and *brought*).

Students with morphological problems may not acquire and understand the rules for word formation at the same rate and complexity as do their peers with normal language development. Disorders in form or morphology also include difficulties learning the language code and linking it to what already is known about the environment. Wiig and Semel (1984) list the following areas in which specific morphological deficits can be found in many students with language-learning problems:

1. The formation of noun plurals, especially the irregular forms (*-s, -z, -ez,* vowel changes, *-ren,* etc.)
2. The formation of noun possessives, both singular and plural (*-'s, -s'*)
3. The formation of third person singular of the present tense of verbs (*-s*)
4. The formation of the past tense of both regular and irregular verbs (*-t, -d, -ed,* vowel change)
5. The formation of the comparative and superlative forms of adjectives (*-er, -est*)
6. The cross-categorical use of inflectional endings (*-s, -'s, -s'*)
7. Noun derivation (*-er*)
8. Adverb derivation (*-ly*)
9. The comprehension and use of prefixes (*pre-, post-, pro-, anti-, di-, de-*)(p. 303)

Some differences in inflectional endings are observed in students who speak Black English (Baratz, 1969; Bartel, Grill, & Bryen, 1973). The teacher should be aware that some inflectional endings reflect a student's cultural difference rather than a developmental delay. Examples of inflectional differences include "John cousin" in Black English instead of "John's cousin," "fifty cent" instead of "fifty cents," and "She work here" instead of "She works here."

Form: Syntax

Syntax is a system of rules that governs how words or morphemes are combined to make grammatically correct sentences. Rules of syntax specify word order, sentence organization, relationships between words and word classes or types, and other sentence constituents (Owens, 1994). Moreover, syntax specifies which word combinations are acceptable or grammatical and which word classes may appear in noun and verb phrases (e.g., adverbs modify verbs). Thus, syntax frequently is referred to as *grammar.*

Rules of grammar emerge between 18 and 24 months of age, as evidenced in a child's production of two-word sentences. The child does not change abruptly from single words to grammatical two-word sentences. There is a period of transition in which a distinction can be made between two-word utterances and two words in grammatical form. Braine (1976) claims that in this transition period the child often is groping for a pattern that later is replaced by a correct grammatical form.

Wood (1976) outlines six stages in the acquisition of syntax. Stages 1 and 2 are described better with semantic rules of grammar, whereas the last four stages describe syntactic structure. Stage 3 typically begins when the child is 2 to 3 years old. At this age, the child's sentences contain a subject and a predicate. For example, in Stage 2, the child says, "No play," but in Stage 3 says, "I won't play." Stage 4 begins around 2½ years of age and continues to about 4 years of age. In this stage the child begins to perform operations on sentences, such as adding an element to basic sentences through the process of *conjunction*. For example, "where" can be added to the simple sentence "Daddy go" to form "Where Daddy go?" The child also can *embed* (i.e., place words within the basic sentence). For example, the sentence "No glass break" becomes "The glass didn't break." In Stage 4 the word order is changed to ask a question. For example, the question, "Man is here?" is changed to "Is the man here?" During this stage, sentences remain simple in structure. Between 2 and 3 years of age, the child does not combine simple sentences but says them next to each other (e.g., "John bounced the ball; John hit the lamp"). Between 3 and 4 years of age the child combines simple sentences with the conjunction *and* (e.g., "John bounced the ball and hit the lamp").

Stage 5 usually begins between 3½ and 7 years of age. In this stage the child uses complete sentences that have word classes typical of adult language: nouns, pronouns, adverbs, and adjectives. The child also becomes aware of differences within the same grammatical class. This awareness is evident in the child's use of different determiners and verbs with singular and plural nouns. For example, *this* is inappropriate for use in the sentence, "This chairs are heavy." The proper determiner (singular or plural) and appropriate verb for expressing plurality must be used. This same principle applies to prepositional phrases. For example, the sentence "We cried to the movie" is not grammatically correct because an inappropriate prepositional phrase is used. In essence, in this stage the child learns the appropriate semantic functions of words and assigns these words to the appropriate grammatical classes.

Wood's Stage 6 begins when the child is about 5 years of age and extends until 10 years of age. The child begins complex sentence structures and learns to understand and produce sentences that imply a command ("Give me the toy"), a request ("Please pass the salt"), and a promise ("I promise to stop"). Implied commands are the easiest to acquire but often are confused with requests. The premise is difficult for children to understand, and this type of verb may not be mastered until age 10 (Wood, 1976).

Syntactic Deficits. Children who have delay in syntax use sentences that lack the length or syntactic complexity expected for their age. For example, a 6-year-old child who uses a mean sentence length of three words may say, "Where Daddy go?" instead of "Where did Daddy go?" Additional deficits in the processing of syntax include problems in comprehending sentences (such as questions or sentences that express relationship between direct and indirect objects), negation, mood (such as inferences of obligations signified by the auxiliary verbs *must, have to,* and *ought*), and passive sentences (Wiig & Semel, 1976, 1984).

Students with language-learning disabilities may have difficulty processing syntactic structures of increased complexity such as embedded sentences, *wh* questions, interrogatives, and negative sentences. Wiig and Semel (1984) include deficits in memory and recall, difficulties using strategies to enhance memory, and decreased selective attention as being related to deficits remembering spoken messages. Students with language-learning disabilities also may tend to rely on basic sentence structures and exhibit little creativity or use of novel or interesting sentences (Simon, 1985).

Content: Semantics

Semantics refers to language meaning and is concerned with the meaning of individual words as well as the meaning that is produced by combinations of words. For example, the word *cup* has a meaning of a "container from which to drink" and refers to an object in the child's world. An example of meaning attached to combinations of words is the phrase "Daddy's cup." These words add the meaning of possessiveness in relationship to each other (i.e., the cup belongs to Daddy). Receptive semantics refers to understanding language, whereas expressive semantics refers to producing meaningful discourse.

According to Lahey (1988), language content (semantics) has three categories. One category involves objects in general (e.g., cars, ball, Mommy, and juice). The second category involves actions in general (e.g., throwing, hitting, and kicking). The third category involves relations between objects (e.g., Michael and his computer, me and my puppy, and Debbie and her car) and relations between events (such as the causal relation between going swimming and getting wet). The difference between language topic and language content is reflected in the particular message called the topic (e.g., a Power Ranger) and the more general categorization of the message called the content (e.g., toys). Consequently, because youngsters from different cultures talk about different topics, they do not have the same vocabulary even though their content is often the same.

Wood (1976) outlines several stages of semantic acquisition. In Stage 1, a child develops meanings as he or she acquires first words. Wood refers to these first words as one-word sentences. The meanings of these sentences are determined by the context in which they are spoken. An 18-month-old child may use the word *doggie* quite frequently, but the context in which the child says the word may differ and imply different meanings (e.g., "There is a doggie," "That is my doggie," "Doggie is barking," or "Doggie is chasing a kitty").

At about 2 years of age, the child begins to produce two-word utterances with meanings related to concrete actions (such as "Doggie bark" or "My doggie"). In Stage 2, the child conveys more specific information verbally and continues to expand vocabulary and utterance length. However, until about the age of 7, the child defines words merely in terms of visible actions. To a 6-year-old child, a fish is "a thing that swims in a lake" and a plate is "a thing you can eat dinner on." Also, during this stage, the child typically responds to a prompt word (such as *pretty*) with a word that could follow it in a sentence (such as *flower*). Older children, around 8 years of age, frequently respond with a verbal opposite (such as *ugly*) (Brown & Berko, 1960).

In Stage 3, at 8 years of age, the child's word meanings relate directly to experiences, operations, and processes. If a child's neighbor owns a horse, the child may include this attribute in the word meaning of *horse* in addition to the attributes of "animal," "four-legged," and "a thing that can be ridden." When asked where horses live, the child may respond, "At the Kahns'." By an adult definition, this answer is not correct. The child's vocabulary is defined by the child's experiences, not those of adults. At 12 years of age, the child begins to give dictionarylike definitions for words (Wood, 1976). When asked to define *bear,* the child might respond, "a large, warm-blooded animal that hibernates in the winter." At this time the child's word definitions approach the semantic level of adults.

Semantic Deficits. Developmental delay in word meaning (semantics) is observed in youngsters who use or understand a limited number of words. The limited vocabulary may be in specific areas, such as adjectives, adverbs, prepositions, or pronouns. Students may have a longer response time when selecting vocabulary words or have difficulty retrieving or recalling a specific word (dysnomia). The student with retrieval difficulties often attempts to participate in classroom discussions but has no apparent response when called on to answer. Vocabulary difficulties may be evident in an inability to use specific words when describing objects or events (e.g., "that thing over there" or "the thing you use to write with").

Semantics delay also is evident when students assign a narrow set of attributes to each word so that each word has limited meaning. Students with semantic deficits often fail to perceive subtle changes in word meaning that follow from changes in context and may not perceive multiple meanings of frequently used words (Wiig & Secord, 1994). This leads to incomplete understanding and misinterpretations of what is heard or read. In addition, students may have figurative language problems and tend to interpret idioms, metaphors, and proverbs literally (Wiig & Semel, 1984). These problems have important classroom implications when considered with research findings by Lazar, Warr-Leeper, Nicholson, and Johnson (1989). Their study of math, reading, and language arts teachers in kindergarten through eighth grade revealed that 36% of all teacher utterances contained at least one multiple-meaning expression. Indirect requests (27%) occurred most frequently. Moreover, at least one idiom occurred in 12% of the utterances, and the use of idiomatic expressions increased in frequency as grade level increased. Thus, older students with language problems may be at an increased disadvantage when attempting to follow teacher directions or understand classroom discourse. The following middle school classroom discussion exemplifies this problem. The teacher asked the students if the expression "my father hit the roof" meant that the father literally hit the roof. One student, interpreting the nonverbal contextual cues, proudly responded, "No, it doesn't mean he literally hit the roof. It means he hit the roof with his broom or something long!"

Additional semantic difficulties experienced by students with language-learning disabilities include understanding linguistic concepts (e.g., *before/after, if/then, many, some,* and *few*), perceiving logical relationships among words (e.g., comparative, possessive, spatial, and temporal), and comprehending verbal analogies (e.g., sandwich is to eat as milk is to drink) (Wiig & Semel, 1984). Moreover, students may misuse transition words (i.e., conjunctions such as *although* and *if* and phrases such as *in addition*) and avoid making complex sentences and signaling logical relationships among arguments in sentences or sentence sequences (Wiig & Secord, 1994).

Use: Pragmatics

Bruner (1974/1975) defines *pragmatics* as the "directive function of speech through which speakers affect the behavior of others in trying to carry out their intention" (p. 283). In discussing this definition, McLean and Snyder-McLean (1978) distinguish two broad functions: controlling or influencing the listener's action ("Give me the doll") and influencing attitudes ("I think Jane would make a good class president"). These functions also are referred to as the speaker's intent. Bates (1976) notes that the study of meaning in language pragmatics involves how one's communicative intentions are mapped into linguistic forms. The rules then govern how language is used in social contexts to convey a variety of intentions such as requesting, asserting, and questioning. An individual's use of language based on an understanding of how language works in social interactions also is referred to as *communicative competence* (Holland, 1977). Wilcox (1986) describes communicative competence as "the ability to convey effectively and efficiently an intended message to a receiver. . . . This requires not only knowledge of the conventional communicative code, but also knowledge pertaining to socially appropriate communicative behaviors" (p. 644).

One pragmatic function that occurs after 3 years of age is the indirect request or hint (Ervin-Tripp & Mitchell-Kernan, 1977; Leonard, Wilcox, Fulmer, & Davis, 1978). Prutting (1979) notes that these indirect requests frequently are used (e.g., "My mother always lets me have cookies before lunch"). Leonard et al. studied 4-, 5-, and 6-year-old children's understanding of three types of indirect requests: affirmative construction ("Can you shut the door?"), responses with a negative element ("Can't you answer the phone?"), and affirmative construction with a negative intention ("Must you play the piano?"). The 4- and 5-year-old children understood the first two types of requests but not the third type. The 6-year-old children understood the third type of request but made mistakes. Leonard et al. interpret the mistakes to mean that understanding was not complete.

Bloom and Lahey (1978) state that the situation affects the form of the message within the pragmatics of language. The characteristics of the message that increase the likelihood that the message will be accepted as well as understood are referred to as pragmatic presuppositions. In adult speech these presuppositions are apparent in tendencies to be polite and indirect in requests. Children as young as 4 and 5 years of age show these pragmatic presuppositions when they talk politely as they make a request. Pragmatic presuppositions develop as the child matures and learns not to interrupt the speaker, talk at the wrong time, or speak too loudly for the situation.

Pragmatic Deficits. Delay in pragmatics is evident when students do not use functions that are expected for their developmental age. For example, a student with a developmental age above 8 years who seriously answers "Yes" to the indirect request "Must you play the piano?" (instead of ceasing to play the piano) may be developmentally delayed in understanding indirect requests. Moreover, a student may have difficulty determining when the listener does not understand what the student is saying and thus continue with the manner of presentation rather than adapt the speech to the listener's needs. Also, a student may enter conversations in a socially unacceptable fashion or fail to take turns when conversing. The student may either monopolize a conversation or expect the other speaker to do most of the talking with little feedback to indicate listening. Other examples of problems with language use include difficulty staying on a topic during conversation (topic maintenance), inappropriate facial expressions and body posture, immature speech, and difficulty interpreting verbal and nonverbal communication cues (Simon, 1985; Wiig & Semel, 1984). Finally, a student may have difficulty choosing the right linguistic content (i.e., gauging complexity according to the listener), using questioning strategies, and interacting well verbally in a group (Wiig & Semel, 1984). Difficulties with communicative competence are particularly frustrating because they can persist into adulthood and affect the student's academic, vocational, and social performance (Schumaker & Deshler, 1984).

LANGUAGE DIFFICULTIES

Students with language-learning disabilities display a wide variety of difficulties, although many of the deficits initially may be subtle. The teacher should be aware of the potential language difficulties so that students can be identified and receive appropriate services as early as possible. In spite of early intervention, many language problems are long-term and require intervention that changes with the varying needs of the student. This section presents the language difficulties typically found in three age groups of students: preschool and kindergarten, elementary, and secondary. It is important to keep in mind that language is interactive and that many of these difficulties may not occur in isolation. Furthermore, because language difficulties generally do not disappear without intervention, the same deficits may span several age categories.

Preschool and Kindergarten Students

Young students with language-learning problems are a diverse group, so it may be difficult to differentiate them from their normally developing peers. However, various researchers (Bernstein, 1993a; Wiig & Semel, 1984) discuss the difficulties common to this age group. Readiness skills such as counting, naming colors, naming the days of the week, and using scissors often are delayed. The child may be unable to follow simple directions, follow the story line in a book or movie, or enjoy listening to stories. In addition, the period of normal acquisition for articulation and sound development may be delayed, so that the child exhibits immature-sounding speech. The mean length of utterances and vocabulary may be similar to those of a younger child. Word-finding difficulties and an inability to name common objects also may be noted. As a result, the child may exhibit sound substitutions such as "buzgetti" for "spaghetti." The child may produce fewer functionally appropriate and accurate responses, say phrases such as "you know" or "that thing over there," or describe objects rather than name objects. In addition, the child

TABLE 11.2
Characteristics of Young Children with Language-Learning Disabilities

Characteristic Behavior	Example
Poor peer relations	Frequently plays alone
Poor adjustment to change	Becomes upset or confused when routine is altered
Perseveration	Persists in performing a task when not necessary
Poor emotional control	Becomes angry or cries easily
Easily frustrated	Stamps foot or sulks when asked to perform a task
Decreased initiation of communication	Sits quietly rather than requesting to have needs met
Excessive need to touch	Frequently hugs and touches others
Hyperactivity	Has difficulty sitting or standing without excessive movement
Variable performance	Performs well on a task and later appears unable to duplicate performance
Poor task persistence	Has difficulty completing tasks once initiated
Immaturity	Behaves like a younger child
Reduced vocabulary	Lacks understanding and use of object labels
Delayed responses	Needs additional time to understand simple directions
Behavior inappropriate to situation	Laughs and talks excessively to self
Difficulty recalling words (dysnomia)	Knows a particular word but is unable to recall it when needed
Impulsive	Acts or responds quickly without thinking
Difficulty following simple directions	Persists in standing when told to sit unless gestural cues are provided

may be unable to make one-to-one correspondences between letters and sounds and have difficulty discriminating between similar sounds.

Furthermore, young children may have difficulty responding accurately to certain types of questions. Parnell, Amerman, and Harting (1986) note that questions regarding nonobservable persons, actions, or objects are the most difficult for young children. In an evaluation of nine *wh-* forms, *why, when,* and *what happened* were the most difficult.

Young children with language problems also may demonstrate significant deficits in symbolic, adaptive, and integrative play as compared with their linguistically matched peers. They often frequently play by themselves or exhibit more nonplay and parallel play than do their peers (Roth & Clark, 1987). Behaviorally, children with language-learning problems may exhibit a variety of characteristics, as listed in Table 11.2. They often have attention deficits, need additional time to understand information and formulate ideas for expression, and have a poor tolerance for frustration.

Elementary Students

A student with a language-learning disability may exhibit a variety of difficulties in the first grade, such as a limited ability to identify sounds, difficulty analyzing and synthesizing sound sequences, and problems segmenting words into grammatical units. Temporal and spatial concepts, as well as abstract concepts such as *before-after, neither–nor, some, if/then,* and *few,* may pose particular difficulty (Snyder, 1986; Wiig & Semel, 1984). These concepts often are presented in sentences of increased length and complexity that are particularly problematic for students with subtle processing problems. The student may be seen as obstinate or noncompliant, when actually the directions are misunderstood.

In the early elementary grades, the use of manipulatives begins to decrease, and the student must gain information from the teacher's verbal presentation. As the language complexity increases with each grade advance, the student must keep up with the demands of the instructional language as well as absorb the curriculum content. By fourth grade, most of the curriculum content is presented in print, and the student with learning disabilities may have particular difficulty making the transition from narrative to expository writing (Wallach, 1989).

Word finding (retrieval) difficulties still may exist, but the deficits may not be as evident because the student begins to use strategies involving circumlocution (i.e., talking around the word), fillers, and descriptors (Bos & Vaughn, 1994). German (1984) adds the manifestation of secondary characteristics such as tapping and saying "I know it." She claims that students with retrieval problems generally have difficulty with three indices: response time, error index or word selection process, and substitution types. Students generally do not perform similarly across the three areas, and situations often occur in which the student's speed is affected although the correct word eventually is recalled.

Problems stemming from the relationship between phonological disorders and reading achievement begin to emerge in elementary school. Students with reading problems often articulate sequences more slowly than do their peers who do not have reading difficulties. As a result, the slow-speaking student tends to have greater difficulty sounding out and blending polysyllabic words and comprehending what is read (Ackerman et al., 1990). Requirements for comprehension also change because multiple-meaning words emerge and students are required to draw conclusions and make inferences. Deficits in text comprehension lead to problems in reading independence and mastery of content material. Thus, students with language problems may have difficulties participating in group discussions, sharing ideas on a topic, and developing ideas that follow earlier learning (Bashir, 1989).

Students in elementary school also may be deficient in expressive or oral language. In a study that examined children's discourse or ability to tell a story, Merritt and Liles (1987) found that the stories told by students with language disorders contained fewer story episodes and fewer main and subordinate clauses than the stories told by their peers without language disorders. In addition, the students with language disorders had significant difficulty integrating critical parts of a story, and these difficulties continued after maturity and intervention. Merritt and Liles conclude that students with language disorders may have difficulty forming verbal abstractions and performing the logical operations needed to interpret and understand complex concepts. The students also had difficulty formulating and expressing spoken language: such problems often are reflected in academic difficulties.

Finally, elementary students with language disabilities continue to exhibit difficulties in their use of language. In academic settings, this often is reflected in the student's social skills. Students at this age may exhibit some of the same behaviors as they did when they were younger, such as failing to adjust to their listener's needs and having difficulty joining an ongoing conversation. In addition, they may misinterpret social cues, fail to think of others' thoughts and feelings, and be unable to predict the consequences of their behavior. Also, students at this level may be able to formulate a question but have difficulty functionally using requests to obtain new information (Schwabe, Olswang, & Kriegsmann, 1986).

Secondary Students

Adolescents who have language-learning disabilities exhibit a variety of difficulties that tend to become more subtle. These adolescents tend to be passive learners and often appear to lack

the metacognitive strategies necessary to perform complex academic tasks. At the secondary level, the teacher is faced with the challenge of designing interventions to assist students in overcoming or compensating for their language disabilities so that they can meet the increased demands of secondary school.

Many adolescents with language disabilities lack the ability to use and understand higher-level syntax, semantics, and pragmatics in both production and processing (Ehren & Lenz, 1989). Secondary students are expected to organize their time and complete assignments, and, thus, they must follow both oral and written instruction to complete work independently. However, receptive and expressive language difficulties affect their ability to learn effectively. This creates problems in gaining information from class lectures and textbooks, completing homework, following classroom rules, demonstrating command of knowledge through test taking, expressing thoughts in writing, passing minimum competency exams, and participating in classroom discussions (Schumaker & Deshler, 1984). Some adolescents learn strategies to compensate for their language difficulties, whereas others need additional services or support. As students mature, the teacher must be aware of the changing curriculum demands. For example, intervention may change from a content-oriented approach to a functional approach in which the student is taught strategies to deal with everyday situations.

Problems in comprehension of auditory language also are persistent in adolescents and result in short-term memory problems and a decrease in the understanding of linguistic relationships (Riedlinger-Ryan & Shewan, 1984). Frequently, adolescent students with language disabilities have difficulty organizing information and correctly associating or categorizing it for later retrieval. Thus, they often are unable to retain and synthesize complex information because they lack the ability to organize or categorize it. Poor organization and categorization result in other problems, such as poor note-taking, test-taking, and study skills, as well as difficulty integrating information (Schumaker, Deshler, Alley, Warner, & Denton, 1984).

Difficulties also may persist in language use in the areas of awareness of social cues, interpretation of the motives and emotions of others, and use of appropriate language. Because adolescents frequently are aware of their difficulties, behaviors such as aggression, frustration, lack of motivation, withdrawal, and inattention may arise (Hazel & Schumaker, 1988; Seidenberg, 1988; Wiig & Semel, 1984).

BILINGUAL AND CULTURALLY DIVERSE STUDENTS

Bilingual students know and use more than one language. Many bilingual students speak Spanish as their first language and acquire English as a second language. A student who displays inadequate skills in understanding and speaking the English language has limited English proficiency. Unfortunately, some students with limited English proficiency are misdiagnosed as having learning or language impairments because of their poor academic performance or difficulty on standardized tests (Cardoza & Rueda, 1986; Mercer, 1983). As the bilingual population in the United States increases, the teacher is faced with the challenge of distinguishing between students who are unfamiliar with the language and culture and students with a true language problem. Bilingual students with language-learning disabilities may need services somewhat different from those for students whose primary language is standard English. Salend and Fradd (1986) note that bilingual students have the following needs:

1. Access to teachers who are proficient in English as well as in the student's native language.
2. Use of nonbiased assessment and instruction to formulate appropriate individualized educational programs.
3. Exposure to curriculum and alternative instructional strategies that promote the academic and social relevance of instruction.

Several factors should be considered when assessing bilingual students. To determine whether the student has limited English proficiency or a language-learning disability, assessment should be conducted in the student's primary language to examine skills in the areas of writing, reading, listening, and speaking. Language assessments should include the use of both quantitative measures (i.e., formal tests) and qualitative measures (e.g., observations, adapted test instruction, and a language sample). It also is helpful to interview significant people in the student's life with the same cultural background to determine how effectively the student communicates in the primary language. Interviews can yield important information regarding the language spoken at home, attitudes toward the two languages and cultures, the parents' educational level, and a profile of the community in which the student lives (Kayser, 1989).

Gersten and Woodward (1994) discuss two major instructional approaches advocated for bilingual students. In programs with a native-language emphasis, the student receives academic instruction in the primary language, whereas in sheltered English or structured immersion programs, English is used for the majority of the teaching day. Most studies indicate little or no difference in achievement between students taught with these two bilingual approaches. In both approaches, second-language instruction should be relevant rather than only a series of drills on grammar and usage. Gersten and Woodward note that many second-language programs have moved toward the increased use of natural language to promote comprehension and use of English.

Another group of culturally diverse students speaks nonstandard English by using dialects related to geographic regions or race and ethnicity. Dialectical differences may be evident in the student's pronunciation of speech sounds or in variations in morphology and syntax. For example, in Black English the use of the verb *to be* (as in "he be running") is different from its use in standard English. As with bilingual students, language assessment of culturally diverse students should include the collection of spontaneous speech samples in naturalistic settings or interviews with other students who speak the dialect. Thus, the student's cultural background is considered, and the student is compared with others in the same language community to determine the existence of a language disorder.

Students who exhibit normal production of their own primary language or dialect should not be identified as having a language disorder. These students simply are producing an acceptable language variation. However, many students with limited English proficiency or dialectical differences are identified as having a language problem such as a phonological deficiency. For example, a Spanish-speaking youngster may say "cheap" for "chip," and a youngster learning Black English may say "birfday" instead of "birthday." Owens (1991) presents the major variations between standard American English and Black English, Hispanic English, and Asian English in phonology, syntax and morphology, and pragmatics and nonlinguistic features. Adler (1988) raises the following questions regarding these students: Should only standard English be taught to these students? If the dialect is rule-governed and nonstandard, rather than substandard, should the student be taught to speak "correctly" if the dialect is consistent with what is spoken in the community in which the student lives? Finally, should only English be taught to young non-standard-speaking students, or should they be allowed to retain the social dialect of their cultural peers and parents? Alder notes that the current belief appears to support teaching the use of language that is relevant to school talk (standard English) as well as everyday talk (nonstandard English). This is difficult to accomplish, however, because it requires a change in the current system and collaborative interaction between families and teachers in language arts and English. Although changes in the service delivery to bilingual and culturally diverse students are beginning to emerge, the teacher must assume the responsibility of providing quality assessment and intervention to these students to assist in the prevention of instructional problems related to a lack of English proficiency.

ASSESSMENT OF LANGUAGE SKILLS

The heterogeneity of students with language impairments and language-learning disabilities makes the assessment task especially difficult, because no two students exhibit the same strengths and weaknesses. The speech and language evaluator must know not only what areas to assess but also how to interpret the findings and help make the necessary adjustments in the student's curriculum. Although most classroom teachers never conduct an in-depth assessment of a student's language skills, they should understand the implications of a language evaluation because language pervades the curriculum. In the past, speech and language assessments were viewed as separate from the curriculum and the sole responsibility of the speech and language pathologist. However, this trend is changing, and emphasis is being placed on the importance of the teacher and the speech and language specialist sharing the responsibility for diagnosing problems and designing intervention programs to improve a student's receptive and expressive language skills (Nelson, 1989). After becoming familiar with the basic principles of language development, the teacher undoubtedly will identify numerous youngsters who exhibit language problems in the classroom and would benefit from systematic assessment and instruction in the use of spoken language.

Language assessment should be viewed not as a single isolated event but rather as an ongoing process throughout a student's education. The five major reasons for language assessment are as follows:

1. To identify students with potential language problems.
2. To determine a student's language developmental level.

3. To plan educational objectives and design appropriate intervention programs.
4. To monitor the student's progress.
5. To evaluate the language intervention program.

The last three of these assessment functions are most relevant to daily instructional planning. Among these three functions, the first one performed is *planning objectives.* The assessment information describes the student's language. This description is used in planning objectives that relate directly to the problem. The assessment of a morphological disorder, for example, should be specific: "The student does not use *s* on regular nouns to indicate plurality." The teacher then can plan the objective: "The student will use plural *s* on regular nouns with 90% accuracy when naming pictures of plural regular nouns." *Monitoring the student's progress* involves the teacher determining daily or weekly whether the student is reaching short-term instructional objectives. The sample objective of 90% accuracy of plural *s* when naming pictures of plural regular nouns requires an assessment procedure of counting responses. Finally, in *program evaluation,* the teacher assesses the student's progress with the materials and techniques used in the program. This information allows the teacher to determine whether it is necessary to change materials or techniques to achieve the educational objective.

Thus, language assessments of school-age youngsters should be educationally relevant and provide both diagnostic information and intervention strategies. To accomplish this goal, two levels of information should be included in the assessment: the content-oriented level and the process-oriented level. The content-oriented level examines the actual content the student has learned and identifies specific areas that require intervention (e.g., a syntactic deficit in the use of present progressive tense). The process-oriented level examines how skills are learned or acquired (e.g., the use of a strategy such as clustering digits to remember a phone number).

Assessment of language development is an evaluation of the student's receptive and expressive communication skills. The components assessed include phonology, morphology, syntax, semantics, and pragmatics. The teacher can assess all of these components or decide to assess only one or two specific components. An experienced examiner obtains information or observes the student before deciding what to assess. The information gathered can include various observations (e.g., the student is difficult to understand, the student has difficulty understanding what others say, the student uses short sentences, the student uses few words, or the student cannot start and maintain a discussion topic).

The student who is difficult for others to understand, but who understands what others say and uses many words and long sentences, may have problems in phonology. Thus, assessment should begin in this area. The student who uses only a few words needs to be assessed in semantics, and the student who uses short sentences needs assessment in semantic relationships and syntax.

Language assessment includes the use of formal and informal assessment procedures. Quantitative (formal) measures are used when the examiner needs to determine the student's developmental level and obtain a standardized score or classify the student. These measures include observable behaviors and result in a numerical score or an assigned classification. If the examiner wants to determine specific teaching objectives, informal measures are used. Qualitative or naturalistic measures are based on the assumption that behaviors vary across different settings, and their purpose is to determine the relevant behaviors or skills that are evident in the setting being examined. Assessment of both language developmental level and teaching objectives should include both types of tests. School speech and language specialists are experienced in administering and interpreting formal and informal measures of language. The teacher who is unfamiliar with these tests should consider working with the school speech and language specialist in assessing language.

Formal Language Assessment

In a formal language assessment, standardized instruments are used to compare a student's performance with pre-established criteria to determine the existence of a speech or language problem. On these instruments, a student's raw score is con verted to a standardized score, language age or mental age, age equivalent, or, occasionally, a grade equivalent. Students whose scores are much lower than the scores of other students their age usually are referred for additional testing or are placed in speech and language therapy.

Some language tests provide a comprehensive measure of all language functioning. This type of test assesses receptive and expressive language in many components. For example, the *Clinical Evaluation of Language Fundamentals—3* (Semel, Wiig, & Secord, 1995) assesses morphology, syntax, and semantics. Other tests are designed to measure specific components of language. For example, the *Northwestern Syntax Screening Test* (Lee, 1971) assesses receptive and expressive skills in syntax only. Some tests are more specific and measure only receptive or expressive skills in one component. For example, the *Peabody Picture Vocabulary Test—Revised* (Dunn & Dunn, 1981) assesses receptive semantic skills.

Screening Tests. In many school districts, students are given a speech-and-language screening test when they enter preschool or kindergarten. The screening provides a general overview of a student's performance in a particular area, which can be compared with the performance of a student of the same age or grade who is developing normally. Many school districts use standardized or formal screening instruments, whereas other districts devise informal assessment instruments to identify preschool and kindergarten students who may have potential language problems. Students who score below an acceptable level on a screening test usually are referred for a comprehensive evaluation. The *Clinical Evaluation of Language Fundamentals—3: Screening Test* (Semel, Wiig, & Secord, 1996) is an example of a screening test that identifies the need for an in-depth diagnosis of language. It screens receptive and expressive language skills in phonology, morphology, syntax, and semantics in approximately 10 to 15 minutes and is designed for students age 6 through 21.

One advantage of a screening is that it requires little administration time and, thus, allows a large number of students to be evaluated. When all students are screened at the beginning of their formal education, speed is an obvious concern because so many students must be evaluated. However, because of variations in such factors as social and emotional development, participation in a preschool program, family environment, and cultural influences, only a few language skills should be expected to have been mastered by all 4- or 5-year-old children. Thus, a disadvantage to screening young children is that the screenings often are not able to detect subtle language problems. To illustrate, a youngster may receive high scores (80th to 90th percentiles) in both processing and production on a language screening test administered at the beginning of first grade. However, because subtle language problems were not detected at the initial screening and intervention was not made available, the student may experience academic difficulties later, when faced with a more abstract and demanding fourth-grade curriculum. Thus, ideally, several speech and language screenings should be administered (e.g., kindergarten, third grade, sixth grade, and ninth grade); however, time constraints on public school clinicians allow them to give a screening test only one time. Consequently, many students with language disabilities are not identified at an early age.

Diagnostic Tests. Diagnostic tests measure one or more specific language components, including receptive or expressive language. As presented in Table 11.3, comprehensive tests measure a wide range of language skills,

TABLE 11.3
Selected Diagnostic Language Measures

Test	Component Measured	Receptive/ Expressive	Age Norms
Comprehensive Measures			
Clinical Evaluation of Language Fundamentals—3 (Semel, Wiig, & Secord, 1995)	Morphology, syntax, semantics	R, E	6–21 years
This individually administered test consists of five receptive subtests (*Sentence Structure, Concepts and Directions, Semantic Relationships, Word Classes,* and *Listening to Paragraphs*), five expressive subtests (*Word Structure, Formulated Sentences, Sentence Assembly, Recalling Sentences,* and *Word Associations*), and one optional subtest (*Rapid, Automatic Naming*). Each subtest yields standard scores and percentile ranks, and the test also yields receptive, expressive, and total language scores. Dialectical and regional variations that may be present in a student's word and sentence structure are not counted as errors if they are a natural part of the student's language system.			
Oral and Written Language Scales: Listening Comprehension and Oral Expression (Carrow-Woolfolk, 1995)	Syntax, semantics, pragmatics	R, E	3–21 years
Neither scale on this individually administered test requires reading by the student. On the *Listening Comprehension* scale a verbal stimulus is read aloud by the examiner, and the student responds by pointing to one of four pictures. On the *Oral Expression* scale the student is shown a picture while a verbal stimulus is read aloud by the examiner, and the student responds orally by answering a question, completing a sentence, or generating one or more sentences. The test yields standard scores, percentile ranks, and age equivalents.			
Test of Adolescent and Adult Language—3 (Hammill, Brown, Larsen, & Wiederholt, 1994)	Syntax, semantics	R, E	12–24 years
The test includes eight subtests designed to assess receptive and expressive aspects of spoken and written vocabulary and grammar. The composites yield scores in 10 areas: listening, speaking, reading, writing, spoken language, written language, vocabulary, grammar, receptive language, and expressive language. Administration time is 1 to 3 hours, and a software scoring system is available.			
Test of Language Development—2: Primary (Newcomer & Hammill, 1988)	Phonology, syntax, semantics	R, E	4–8 years
Test of Language Development—2: Intermediate (Hammill & Newcomer, 1988)	Syntax, semantics	R, E	8–12 years
The *Told—2 Primary* has seven subtests: *Picture Vocabulary* and *Oral Vocabulary* assess the understanding and meaningful use of spoken words; *Grammatic Understanding, Sentence Imitation,* and *Grammatic Completion* assess differing aspects of grammar; *Word Articulation* and *Word Discrimination* measure the abilities to say words correctly and to distinguish between words that sound similar. The *Told—2 Intermediate* contains six subtests: *Sentence Combinations, Word Ordering,* and *Grammatic Comprehension* assess different aspects of grammar; *Vocabulary, Generals,* and *Malapropisms* measure the understanding and use of word relationships, the knowledge of abstract relationships, and the correcting of ridiculous sentences.			

TABLE 11.3
continued

Test	Component Measured	Receptive/ Expressive	Age Norms
Measures of Specific Components			
Auditory Discrimination Test (Wepman, 1973)	Phonology	R	4–8 years
Forty word pairs are presented to the student for discrimination. Ten of the word pairs are identical, and the others have one differing phoneme in either the beginning, middle, or ending position. The student tells the examiner whether the word pairs sound the same or different.			
Boehm Test of Basic Concepts—Revised (Boehm, 1986)	Semantics	R	5–7 years
Fifty pictorial items, in multiple-choice form, are arranged in approximate order of increasing difficulty and divided into two booklets. The test is read by the teacher, and the students mark their answers in the test booklets. The test measures understanding of basic concepts relating to space, quantity, and time, and it can be administered individually or to small groups in about 30 minutes. A Spanish edition also is available.			
Carrow Elicited Language Inventory (Carrow-Woolfolk, 1974)	Syntax	E	3–7 years
This norm-referenced test diagnoses expressive language deficits by having the student imitate exactly what is heard after listening to the examiner read a sentence. The stimuli range in length from 2 to 10 words with an average length of 6 words. There are 52 oral stimuli including 51 sentences and 1 phrase. Administration time is about 25 minutes.			
Comprehensive Receptive and Expressive Vocabulary Test (Wallace & Hammill, 1994)	Semantics	R, E	4–17 years
The *Expressive Vocabulary* subtest includes 25 items that encourage and require the student to converse in detail about a particular stimulus word. The *Receptive Vocabulary* subtest consists of 61 items in which the student must point to the picture of the stimulus word said by the examiner. The subtest includes 10 plates with six pictures on each plate, and the words associated with each plate relate to a particular common theme and are spaced evenly across all grade levels. Two forms are available, and the test can be individually administered in 20 to 30 minutes.			
Developmental Sentence Analysis (Lee, 1974)	Syntax	E	2–6 years
Spontaneous speech is elicited while the student is in conversation with an adult. A group of 100 phrases is collected, and the Developmental Sentence Types is used to classify these presentence phrases according to diversity and linguistic composition to indicate whether grammatical structure is developing in an orderly manner. Eight grammatical categories are examined: indefinite pronouns and noun modifiers, personal pronouns, main verbs, secondary verbs, negatives, conjunctions, interrogative reversals, and *wh-* questions. The Developmental Sentence Scoring is used to analyze the grammatical structure found in 50 complete sentences. Specific directions are given for scoring syntactic development.			
Goldman-Fristoe Test of Articulation (Goldman & Fristoe, 1986)	Phonology	E	2–16+ years
The first subtest, *Sounds in Words,* consists of 35 pictures that elicit the student's articulation of the major speech sounds in the initial, medial, and final positions. The second subtest, *Sounds in Sentences,* contains two narrative stories that are read by the examiner and illustrated by action pictures. The student is asked to retell each story. The third subtest, *Stimulability,* determines whether misarticulated phonemes are articulated correctly when the student is given maximum stimulation. The student is asked to watch and listen carefully while the sound is pronounced in a syllable, used in a word, and used in a sentence.			

continued

TABLE 11.3
continued

Test	Component Measured	Receptive/ Expressive	Age Norms
Let's Talk Inventory for Children (Bray & Wiig, 1987)	Pragmatics	R*, E	4–8 years
The inventory contains 34 items that each picture a different situation involving peer or adult interactions. The student is asked to formulate a speech act appropriate for the context and the audience. Association items are administered only if the student is unable to respond satisfactorily to the formulation items. Four communication functions are assessed: ritualizing, informing, controlling, and feeling. Drop-back items of a receptive nature are administered to those students who have difficulty with the expressive section.			
Northwestern Syntax Screening Test (Lee, 1971)	Syntax	R, E	3–7 years
Twenty items assess receptive ability by requiring the student to listen to a sentence spoken by the examiner and then select one picture out of four choices that is most appropriate. Also, 20 items assess expressive ability by having the student repeat sentences spoken by the examiner as the examiner points to various pictures.			
Peabody Picture Vocabulary Test—Revised (Dunn & Dunn, 1981)	Semantics	R	2–40 years
Stimulus pictures are presented to the student, who points to the picture (from among four choices) that best represents the corresponding stimulus word spoken by the examiner. There are two forms of 175 items each, and the items are arranged in increasing order of difficulty.			
Test for Auditory Comprehension of Language—Revised (Carrow-Woolfolk, 1985)	Morphology, syntax, semantics	R	3–9 years
The test is individually administered and measures auditory comprehension of word classes and relations, grammatical morphemes, and elaborated sentence constructions. There are 12 test items in which the student looks at a set of three pictures and selects the one that best represents a word or sentence read by the examiner. No oral responses are required, and administration time is about 25 minutes. A computer program is available for scoring and data storage.			
Test of Pragmatic Language (Phelps-Terasaki & Phelps-Gunn, 1992)	Pragmatics	E	5–13 years
The test includes 44 items, each of which establishes a social context, to provide information within six components of pragmatic language: physical setting, audience, topic, purpose (speech acts), visual-gestural cues, and abstraction. After the examiner provides a verbal stimulus prompt and displays a picture, the student responds to the dilemma presented.			
Test of Word Finding (German, 1989)	Semantics	E	6–12 years
Test of Adolescent/Adult Word Finding (German, 1990)	Semantics	E	12–80 years
These two tests contain five naming sections: picture naming—nouns, picture naming—verbs, sentence completion naming, description naming, and naming category words. Each test also includes a comprehension section to determine whether errors are due to word-finding problems or poor word comprehension. The adolescent form also includes a brief test that provides a 10-minute assessment of word-finding abilities.			
Test of Word Knowledge (Wiig & Secord, 1992)	Semantics	R, E	5–17 years
This test evaluates the student's ability to understand and use vocabulary words. Level 1, for students age 5 to 8, includes subtests in expressive vocabulary, word definitions, receptive vocabulary, word opposites, and synonyms (optional). Level 2, for students age 8 through 17, includes core subtests in word definitions, multiple contexts, synonyms, and figurative usage, as well as supplementary subtests in word opposites, receptive vocabulary, expressive vocabulary, and conjunctions and transition words. All stimuli are presented through visual and auditory modes to accommodate students with poor reading skills or auditory memory problems. The test yields standard scores, age equivalents, percentile ranks, and expressive and receptive language scores.			

*if needed

whereas other diagnostic tests assess specific speech and language components. In a comprehensive diagnostic evaluation, it generally is advisable to administer a test that provides an overall view of the student's understanding and use of language. The specific test often is determined by the student's age or level of functioning. If the examiner notices that the student has difficulty formulating words and sentences, an additional test should be administered to measure the student's ability to understand and use words (e.g., the *Test of Word Knowledge*) or apply syntactic skills (e.g., the *Carrow Elicited Language Inventory*). If the student's speech intelligibility is reduced, the examiner may administer a test of phonology to obtain additional information (e.g., the *Goldman-Fristoe Test of Articulation*). The assessment provides an overall view of the student's language skills as well as additional information concerning reported or observed areas of concern.

Although standardized language tests do not provide information regarding academic or therapeutic interventions, they do pinpoint the student's specific strengths and weaknesses. The role of the examiner is to interpret the assessment information and transform it to academically relevant instructional skills and interventions.

Informal Language Assessment

Informal assessment procedures generally are combined with standardized tests to provide descriptive information regarding a student's language ability. Although standardized measures are used widely, the emphasis on including some type of informal assessment is consistent with the theoretically based descriptive approach that is critical to viewing language as a series of independent objectives. Although standardized instruments determine the need for services, they often are too narrow to assess a student's baseline performance or the communicative skills needed for academic achievement in the classroom (Hughes, 1989). Many formal tests use a small number of items to assess a particular skill, and using a small sample can lead to incorrect conclusions about the student's skill level. Thus, informal assessment often is used to affirm or refute the results of formal measures. Also, many formal measures do not give enough specific information to plan educational objectives. Therefore, informal language measures often are used to determine specific instructional objectives. Another common use of informal measures is to monitor a student's daily or weekly progress. Unlike formal measures, which are designed to assess a student over a long period of time, informal measures lend themselves to daily or weekly assessment.

The teacher may wish to interview the student's parents to obtain a case history as a form of informal assessment. This technique gives the teacher insights into the history of the student's language development. In addition, it provides information regarding the student's communicative functioning in environments other than the school setting and can result in suggestions for appropriate assessment and intervention techniques. Larson and McKinley (1995) provide general and supplemental case history forms as well as a learning style questionnaire designed for preadolescent and adolescent students.

The current emphasis in language assessment stresses the informal evaluation of a student's language within the context in which it occurs. The goal of informal language assessment is to provide insight into how the student uses communication from a functional viewpoint in a variety of settings. Specific areas to examine include the intention or purpose of language, the social communicative context, and the physical setting. Various informal techniques that include the use of spontaneous, imitative, or elicited language can be used depending on the type of information desired.

Informal Tests of Phonology. Phonology can be assessed informally by analyzing the student's production of phonemes in single words. The examiner makes a list of all the consonant phonemes and collects pictures to depict words that contain each phoneme. There should be a picture to elicit a word with the consonant in the initial position and a picture to depict the consonant in the final position. For example, a picture of a pot will elicit initial /p/, and a picture of a map will elicit final /p/. The examiner shows the student each picture and says, "Tell me the name of each picture." A notation is made if the student says the word incorrectly, and the results are recorded on a checklist. This type of assessment requires careful, experienced listening for accurate results. Only the error sounds are recorded; for example, a /b/ sound is recorded to indicate that the student said "bot" for *pot.* Also, comments that describe the error are recorded; for example, a substitution of /b/ for /p/ is recorded as an error in voicing. The examiner lists all the phoneme errors and determines which phonemes should have been mastered at the student's developmental age. These phonemes can become target phonemes for the student's educational objectives.

After analyzing the phoneme profile and selecting a target phoneme, the examiner should collect baseline data on the target phoneme in the student's spontaneous speech. The examiner also needs to monitor change in the student's speech after corrective instruction has begun. Informal assessment is the primary tool used to gather baseline data on the target phoneme and to monitor change in the student's speech.

Diederick (1971) recommends direct observation of the production of a phoneme to obtain baseline data and to monitor the student's progress. The examiner engages the student in spontaneous speech with pictures or toys as stimuli to elicit speech from the student. Older students may respond to prompts such as "Tell me about your weekend." The examiner's talking should be kept to a minimum so that the student is allowed to talk. During a 3-minute sample, the examiner counts the student's correct and incorrect productions of the target phoneme. The target phoneme's frequency can be observed by charting the correct and incorrect responses (see Chapter 8 for a discussion on recording data). Accuracy is computed by dividing the number of correct target phonemes the student said by the total number of target phonemes said (correct and incorrect).

One aspect of receptive phonology that is assessed readily by informal measures is auditory discrimination. The examiner may want to verify whether the student has difficulty discriminating between two particular sounds that were confused on a formal measure. For example, the student may have confused /p/ with /b/, and the examiner may assess these sounds further with a criterion measure. The measure can consist of a list of consonant-vowel-consonant words in which only one phoneme is different (e.g., *pin—bin* or *cup—cub*). Two words are said in word pairs, and the student is asked whether the words are the same or different. The examiner records the results on a checklist and scores the responses for accuracy. Accuracy levels can be used to indicate whether the student needs help in learning to discriminate these sounds. Accuracy of 90% or above is a good indication that the student already can discriminate these sounds.

Informal Tests of Morphology. Informal measures of morphology can determine the mastery level of each morpheme in a hierarchy. The examiner can use Brown's (1973) rank ordering of morpheme acquisition to make sentences that assess each morpheme. Pictures are presented with the sentences to assess the use of each morpheme. If the objective is to assess use of the present progressive morpheme *ing*, the examiner may show a picture of girls playing and say, "The girls like to play. Here they are _____." The student says the missing word, "playing." When assessing the use of the morpheme *in*, the examiner may show a picture of a baby sleeping and ask, "Where is the baby? The baby is _____." The student says the missing words, "in bed."

The examiner records the results as correct or incorrect on a checklist. Analysis of the results helps the teacher determine which morphemes are mastered and which morphemes need to be taught. Also, assessing the morphemes in a hierarchical order indicates to the teacher which morpheme to teach first.

Another informal assessment of morphology is a measure of accuracy of a specific morpheme in a student's conversational speech. Mastery of a morpheme is indicated by 90% accuracy in a student's conversational speech (Brown, 1973). It would be time-consuming to obtain a daily or weekly conversational sample with enough occurrences of a specific morpheme to determine accuracy. An informal assessment of a specific morpheme that is less time-consuming is to have the student respond to the prompt, "Tell me about this picture." First the examiner shapes the response by showing the student a picture depicting a person jumping and says, "What is the person doing?" If the student does not describe the action (by saying "jumping" or "jump"), the examiner can prompt the student: "Say *jumping*." After the student gives two correct responses (description of action) to two different pictures and the instructions "What is the person doing?" the instructions can be changed to "Tell me about this picture."The examiner can show a series of 20 pictures, each of which elicits the present progressive *ing* form of a word. As each picture is presented, the examiner says, "Tell me about this picture." The results are recorded on a checklist, and the examiner counts the number of correct and incorrect responses. The accuracy percentage is determined by dividing the correct responses by the total number of pictures. If the accuracy is 90% or above, the morpheme has been mastered and does not need to be taught. Accuracy below 90% indicates that the morpheme is not mastered and may require teaching. The examiner should note whether mastery of the morpheme is expected at the student's developmental age.

An informal measure of receptive morphology is to have the student point to a picture that depicts a morpheme. The examiner says a sentence with a specific morpheme and asks the student to point to the correct picture. For example, to assess the irregular past tense of *eat,* the examiner can show a picture of a girl who has finished eating and a picture of a girl eating. The examiner says, "The girl ate." The student must point to the correct picture of the girl who has finished eating. Sequence picture cards (such as those published by SRA) can be used with this task. The examiner records the results on a checklist by marking each irregular past tense verb as correct or incorrect. The results are analyzed to determine which morphemes the student has mastered receptively. The examiner may recommend that the student master a morpheme receptively before the student is taught to use that morpheme expressively.

Informal Tests of Syntax. Expressive syntax can be assessed informally by analyzing the student's spontaneous speech for use of grammatical forms. Spontaneous speech or language is a student's unrehearsed verbal expression that occurs naturally in real-life settings and situations. The examiner can obtain and record a spontaneous sample of the student's speech using the guidelines presented in the next section on informal tests of semantics. If the sample is used only for grammatical analysis, the guidelines can be modified so that a tape recorder is used without recording the context of each utterance. After recording, the examiner transcribes the sample and lists each utterance on a checklist. Each utterance is analyzed for the grammatical forms used (e.g., possessive *s*, irregular past, *is, not, but,* and *because*), and a list is compiled of the grammatical forms that were not used. Each form is compared with norms for the student's developmental age. If the particular form is expected for the student's developmental age, a teaching objective can be planned to teach it.

An alternative informal assessment of syntax involves sentence repetition. The examiner says each sentence, and the student repeats the sentence. In an imitation task that is long enough to tax the memory, the student frequently translates the adult sentence into the student's own language system and repeats the sentence using those rules (Salvia & Ysseldyke, 1995). Thus, imitation tasks can elicit language forms that the student did not attempt in spontaneous speech. To increase the accuracy of the examiner's judgment, the evaluation session can be recorded on tape so that the student's responses can be checked. The examiner records the student's responses on a checklist and analyzes them for critical syntactic features. Omitted syntactic features should be included in the student's educational objectives.

Informal Tests of Semantics. Some tasks that assess semantics are complex (such as the areas of logical relationships, cause-and-effect relationships, and verbal problem solving) so informal procedures may be difficult to devise. However, for areas such as verbal opposites, categorization, and classification of words, informal testing is useful.

For the assessment of verbal opposites, SRA produces a set of cards that displays pictures of 40 pairs of opposites. When paired correctly, the cards in each set illustrate two opposites (e.g., *near* and *far*). The examiner mixes the cards and asks the student to sort them into sets of opposites. The examiner observes as the student makes set combinations, and the results are recorded on a checklist. Analysis of the incorrect sets helps the teacher determine which opposites to include in teaching objectives for the student.

An informal assessment of word categorization involves having the student say words in the same category. The examiner says a word and asks the student to say as many words as possible in the same category. The words can fall into the category because of similar function or physical attribute. The examiner lists the words on a checklist as the student says them. The results are analyzed to determine whether the student can say several words in a category or whether the student says a word that is an opposite, says a rhyming word, or tends to repeat the stimulus word.

A word association task can be used as a measure of word classification. Young children tend to respond to a stimulus word with a word that precedes or follows the stimulus word according to the rules of syntax. This is called a *syntagmatic* response. For example, if the stimulus word is "apple," the young student may respond with "eat" or "red." Youngsters shift to a response in the same grammatical category around the age of 6 to 8 years. This type of response is called *paradigmatic*. For example, if the stimulus word is "apple," the older student may respond with "orange," "banana," or another word from the fruit category. The examiner says the stimulus word, notes which kind of response the student makes, and records the response under that category (syntagmatic or paradigmatic) on a checklist. The checklist shows whether the student is categorized as a younger child with syntagmatic responses or as an older student with paradigmatic responses. The student may have responses in both categories but have most responses in one category.

Another area of semantics that can be assessed by informal measures is semantic relationships. This area can be assessed if the student's language utterances are composed of three or fewer words. If a student uses more words, a syntactic analysis is more appropriate. Semantic relationships can be assessed informally by analyzing the student's spontaneous speech. The examiner observes the student playing or interacting with someone, codes or transcribes the conversation, and analyzes it according to error pattern. Various objects such as clay, toys, and games can be used to stimulate communication.

McLean and Snyder-McLean (1978) recommend the following guidelines for obtaining a speech or language sample:

1. Set up a partially structured play situation in which the student interacts with a familiar adult.
2. Use toys that the student is familiar with and that are likely to elicit a variety of responses.

3. Record the student's speech on a videotape recorder. Continue the sampling until 50 to 100 intelligible utterances are obtained. If videotape equipment is not available, record the sample on a tape recorder and have an observer record the context of each utterance the student says.
4. Avoid talking excessively or structuring the student's verbal responses by asking questions such as "What is this?" or "What color is the doll's dress?"
5. Transcribe the tape as soon as possible.
6. List each utterance (i.e., any meaningful speech segment preceded and followed by a pause). Analyze each word in the utterance for semantic form (i.e., two-word grammatical, three-or-more-word grammatical, and nongrammatical and one-word utterances), and list each word under the appropriate category: demonstrative (nomination or notice), attribute (recurrence, nonexistence, or descriptive), possession, conjunction, action (agent– action–object), and location (agent–action–object–location). For example, the two-word utterance "milk cookie" is listed under conjunction because it refers to milk *and* cookie, and the three-word utterance "Mommy drink milk" is placed in the action category (agent—Mommy; action—drink; object–milk).
7. After listing each utterance in the appropriate category, analyze the checklist to determine which semantic relationships the student did or did not use. The forms that the student did not use can be included in teaching objectives of semantic relationships. For example, if the student used three-word utterances but did not use action-object-location forms, this may be an appropriate teaching objective.

After the student's language sample is analyzed for semantic grammar, the mean length of utterance in morphemes is computed. Brown (1973) suggests the following guidelines:

1. Transcribe the language sample.
2. Start the analysis on the second page of the transcription, and count the first 100 utterances. Count only fully transcribed utterances, and count utterance repetitions.
3. Count each morpheme in the 100 utterances. Do not count fillers ("mm" or "oh") or repetitions, but do count "no," "yeah," and "hi." Count as single morphemes all compound words, proper names, idiomatic duplications (e.g., *night-night, choo-choo,* and *see-saw*), irregular past tenses of verbs (e.g., *got, did, went,* and *saw*), diminutives (e.g., *doggie*), and catenatives (e.g., *gonna, wanna,* and *hafta*). Count as separate morphemes all auxiliaries (e.g., *is, have, will, can, want,* and *would*) and inflections (e.g., possessive *s,* plural *s,* third-person singular *s,* simple past *ed,* and progressive *ing*).
4. Compute the mean length of utterance by dividing the total number of morphemes by 100.

The mean length of utterance gives the examiner a quick measure of growth over an extended period of time. Many research studies report students' semantic development in terms of this measure rather than chronological age. For example, the agent-action-object semantic form may be reported as occurring in students with a mean length of utterance of three words, rather than in students of any specific chronological age.

Informal Tests of Pragmatics. Pragmatics can be assessed informally by analyzing a sample of the student's spontaneous speech to determine which pragmatic function was used. The first step is to obtain a videotaped language sample from the student. (Guidelines for obtaining a language sample are presented in the semantics section of this chapter.) If videotape equipment is not available, an observer can record what happens just before and just after each utterance. The second step is to transcribe the tape and list each utterance on a checklist according to function (e.g., protest, request, acquire information, label, and answer). The examiner classifies the pragmatic function of an utterance by analyzing the events before and after the utterance. For example, the student's utterance may be "Throw ball." The examiner notes that before the utterance the examiner was holding the ball and the student's arms were extended to catch the ball. It also is noted that the examiner threw the ball to the student after the utterance. The utterance is classified as a request, and a mark is put in the *request* column. The examiner analyzes the checklist for each function the student did or did not use and then lists the functions that the student did not use. For example, it may be noted that the student did not use a protest function, such as "No shoes" to mean "Don't put on my shoes." The teacher can select from the pragmatic functions that were not used to determine appropriate teaching objectives.

In older students, informal assessment of pragmatics includes measures of speaking with inappropriate loudness, talking at inappropriate times, interrupting the speaker, and using indirect requests. These behaviors can be assessed by counting and recording them in several situations and on different days. A teacher may want to count and record these same behaviors in a speaker of the same age who is not delayed in pragmatics. The teacher can select a student who talks to other students and contributes during group activities, rather than a student who is quiet or has little to say. Three situations are chosen, such as group instructional time, independent work time, and lunch or playground time. The teacher counts the number of times each student interrupts other speakers, talks too loudly, and talks when the student should be listening, reading, or working. The results are recorded on charts, and the teacher compares the results of the two students. A significant difference in the two students' behaviors signifies a possible teaching objective. An appropriate objective is to decrease interruptions by increasing skills in determining when a speaker is finished talking.

Indirect requests can be assessed informally in students whose developmental age is 8 years and above by asking the student to restate implied direct requests. For example, the examiner says, "Tell me what I want you to do when I say, 'Can you close the door?' " The student says, "You want me to close the door." The examiner then says, "Tell me what I want you to do in each of the following sentences." The examiner reads indirect requests from a checklist and puts a check in the column indicating whether the student's response is correct or incorrect. The results are analyzed to determine the number of errors made and the forms with which the student is having the most difficulty (i.e., the affirmative: "Can you . . . ?"; the negative: "Can't you . . . ?"; or the affirmative with negative intention: "Must you…?").These forms of indirect requests can become teaching objectives for the student.

Curriculum-Based Measurement. In curriculum-based measurement, curriculum contexts and content are used to determine appropriate language interventions through the identification of activities and skills that may assist the student in developing more effective communicative skills. The goal is to make functional changes relevant to the student's communicative needs within the academic setting. Nelson (1989) suggests that sample language contexts and skills should include expository test comprehension, the ability to follow oral directions, narrative comprehension and production, and use of language to complete math problems. Additional activities may include written expression, silent and oral reading, and listening comprehension of written language. Nelson (1994) discusses the philosophy and methods of curriculum-based language assessment and intervention for students with language-learning disabilities.

LANGUAGE SERVICE DELIVERY MODELS

Pullout Therapy Model

The most common language service delivery model is the pullout therapy model in which the language specialist takes students from their classes and instructs those with similar difficulties in homogeneous groups. Many teachers admit that this model presents various problems and often results in ineffective and

inefficient services. According to Ehren and Lenz (1989), students usually dislike this model because they do not like to be singled out as being different. This becomes particularly important as peer pressure increases during adolescence. Many adolescents also do not want to continue with the same methods and activities as they had during speech instruction in elementary school, and they lack motivation to achieve because speech and language therapy is not a class they register for in their normal schedule.

The pullout method also causes students to miss course work while they are out of the classroom. This is especially devastating to students with language-learning disabilities who can least afford to miss classroom instruction. As attempts are made to formulate a pullout schedule, the language specialist is faced with numerous scheduling concerns, such as from which subject and how often to pull the student as well as how to handle special events, tests, and absences. Scheduling problems are compounded further by the number of students who are identified as needing services and the inability of schools to provide the intensity required by certain students.

A final problem area associated with the pullout model involves fragmentation of services. Because students generally are seen for therapy in a separate classroom, the services often are isolated from general classroom content and, thus, may not be consistent with classroom goals and expectations. Disagreement regarding responsibility for certain content and type of instruction increases when language goals appear to have no relevance to the student's functioning or needs in the general classroom or when the goals are derived without regard to content in the curriculum. This fragmentation of services frequently results in resentment on the part of the general classroom teacher and often hinders students who need instructional consistency to achieve academic success.

Classroom-Based Language Models

Classroom-based models involve a new delivery of traditional services, and some school systems use these models in an attempt to improve the services to students with language disorders and to integrate therapy goals with the student's academic needs. In spite of their differences, all classroom-based models emphasize the need for collaborative consultation between the classroom teacher and the language specialist so that resulting interventions are meaningful and relevant to natural occurrences in the classroom (Damico, 1987; Marvin, 1987). The American Speech-Language-Hearing Association (1991) Committee on Language-Learning Disorders presents a model for collaborative service delivery for students with language-learning disorders. In the collaborative service delivery model, the team members (language specialist, teacher, parents, and student) work together closely to plan and implement each student's educational program. The team devises all treatment goals, assessment methods, intervention procedures, and documentation systems to enhance the student's academic and social functioning in the school environment. The team members share responsibility for educational goals, and all services and instruction take place in the classroom. The five major types of classroom-based language models include team teaching; self-contained classroom teaching; one-to-one intervention; staff, curriculum, or program development; and consultation (Miller, 1989).

Team Teaching. In this classroom-based model, the language specialist teaches with the general or special classroom teacher. The key to this format is that the language specialist actually teaches a portion of the curriculum. The curriculum goals and objectives as well as the methods and materials to be used are established jointly by the members of the professional team. Services can be rendered in a variety of settings, including the general classroom with the general education teacher, or a self-contained classroom or a resource room with a special education teacher.

Self-Contained Classroom Teaching. In this service model format, the language specialist teaches in a self-contained language class. This format is common with younger students, and the language specialist is responsible for teaching content areas including reading, math, science, and social studies to students who need particular interventions in language processing and production. At the middle and secondary school levels, some language specialists offer a separate course that focuses on writing, reading, or other language areas that are difficult for students with language disabilities to deal with in the general curriculum.

One-to-One Intervention. The language specialist can provide one-to-one intervention to particular students in the classroom. In this approach, the language specialist must maintain close contact with the classroom teacher to provide appropriate interventions to each student regarding specific content areas, study skills, writing, and vocabulary. Classroom textbooks and materials are used to maintain relevance to ongoing classroom activities.

Staff, Curriculum, or Program Development. The language specialist can aid students indirectly by providing staff, curriculum, or program development to a school or district. For example, the specialist can plan community programs to increase student and parent awareness of the school's language objectives. The language specialist also can participate in curriculum development and evaluation or present inservice workshops to teachers or parents that focus on the effect of language on academic success. This service delivery format requires a fundamental change in the focus of the language specialist from providing direct service to students to educating those responsible for teaching the students.

Consultation. The language specialist can serve as a consultant to the various professionals who interact with students, such as general or special education teachers, psychologists, physicians, nurses, social workers, and counselors. In this model, the language specialist consults with persons who provide language interventions to the student, and an effort is made through the consultation to determine methods to lessen the student's communication difficulties. An additional benefit of the consultation format is that students who do not qualify for direct services under school district guidelines benefit indirectly from the suggestions of the consultant as they affect educational and social concerns in the classroom (Damico, 1987).

Strategies-Based Model

A strategies-based service delivery model focuses on teaching specific learning strategies to students and is appealing especially to language specialists who work with middle and secondary school students. One of the major differences between the strategy-based model and a classroom-based model is that students are able to register for and receive a grade for the course work. The use of strategies involves increasing the student's understanding and use of metacognitive and metalinguistic skills. These skills focus on improving the student's awareness and use of strategies that enhance learning. In essence, a change is made from teaching students what to learn to teaching students how to learn.

Based on the perspective that many students with language-learning disabilities show delays in metalinguistic maturation and strategic language use, Wiig (1990) discusses the need for emphasizing different reasoning strategies in language intervention. This approach to language intervention is process-oriented rather than product-oriented and is implemented collaboratively between language specialists and classroom teachers. Likewise, Buttrill, Niizawa, Biemer, Takahashi, and Hearn (1989) propose a strategies-based model that considers the learning characteristics of students with language-learning disabilities as well as the demands of the secondary school settings to which they apply.

One of the most widely researched and developed approaches to learning strategies is the Strategies Intervention Model developed by Don Deshler and his colleagues at the University of Kansas Center for Research on Learning. Although this model is quite specific, it is based on principles that have applicability to strategy training in general. Deshler and Schumaker (1986) state that the ultimate goal of learning strategies is to enable students to analyze and solve novel problems in both academic and nonacademic settings. Their approach to teaching learning strategies to adolescents is based on three rationales:

1. The development and application of learning strategies or metacognitive skills are appropriate for older students who are more proficient in these skills.
2. Adolescents who learn how to learn are in a better position to learn new skills in the future.
3. Students should accept responsibility for their learning and progress.

To design relevant instruction, the language specialist must determine what curriculum demands the student is failing to meet. Student involvement and mutual goal setting also should be established to maximize motivation toward learning, and activities should be designed to promote generalization. Motivation can be enhanced by broadening the student's understanding of the skill and its application to a variety of settings. To facilitate generalization, the learning strategies model stresses the importance of cooperative planning and consultation among the language specialist, general and special education teachers, and personnel of other support services.

LANGUAGE TEACHING STRATEGIES

Many teachers who use direct teaching methods for remediation of reading and math problems undoubtedly select this same technique for teaching language skills. With this format, the teacher directs the learning and dictates the content, pace, and sequencing of the lesson. Often the student is allowed little opportunity to engage in spontaneous conversations during this highly structured skills approach. Conversely, some teachers believe that learning should be student centered, with the student dictating the content, pace, and sequencing of the lesson. The teacher controls minimally and emphasizes social interaction so that communication can occur along the lines of normal conversation. To teach new concepts, the responsive interaction approach emphasizes the use of adult expansions or modifications of the youngster's utterances, whereas elicited prompts are used in milieu teaching. Warren and Yoder (1994) suggest that it may be advantageous to use a combination of approaches based on the characteristics of the learner, the instructional context, and the skills being taught. For example, milieu teaching may be effective for teaching early vocabulary, whereas direct instruction can be used for teaching more abstract language skills.

When designing appropriate language intervention, the phonological, syntactic, semantic, and pragmatic aspects should be considered as well as the student's cognitive skills and social environment. Wallach (1989) and Ehren and Lenz (1989) present the following general principles for meeting a student's language needs:

1. The language specialist should be aware of young students with language disorders who have been dismissed from language services, because academic problems may resurface later due to a breakdown in the language system and increased curriculum demands.
2. Language screenings should consist of more than one test and be sensitive to subtle forms of language disorders.
3. Students suspected of having learning disabilities should receive routine language evaluations that emphasize language and auditory processing.
4. School officials should consider service delivery alternatives to the traditional pullout model, and language specialists should focus on both contextualized and decontextualized aspects of language.
5. Professionals should collaborate to devise a coordinated program for students with language-learning disabilities rather than implement a variety of isolated programs.
6. The delivery of instruction in learning strategies should be language sensitive.
7. The curriculum in language intervention should be relevant to the general curriculum, respond to setting demands, reflect areas of academic concern, integrate spoken and written language systems, and focus on generalization.
8. The individual strategy preferences of students with language-learning disabilities should be considered, and students should be encouraged to determine which strategies are successful in a given situation.
9. Intervention should encourage student accountability and responsibility.
10. Effective interventions from other disciplines should be applied.

Moreover, especially when working with young children, the following specific techniques for teaching language may be helpful:

1. Teach language in a context.
2. Follow the sequence of normal language development.
3. Use specific and effective teaching strategies when introducing a new concept.
4. Vocalize thoughts or describe actions.
5. Describe what others are doing using parallel talk.
6. Use modeling to provide practice on a specific language skill.
7. Use expansion to show how an idea can be expressed in a more complex manner.
8. Use elaboration to demonstrate how to provide more information.
9. Use structured programs to provide adequate practice and feedback regarding performance.
10. Use everyday activities to provide practice of skills within a context.

11. Recognize the relationship of comprehension and production.
12. Systematically plan for and teach generalization.

Because language is interactive, the teacher should be creative when implementing teaching methods because an activity designed to focus on a particular skill also may be useful in other areas. The remainder of this section presents strategies for increasing language comprehension, strategies for increasing language production, and imitation and modeling strategies. Parent involvement in language intervention also is discussed.

Strategies for Increasing Language Comprehension

The following strategies may be helpful in improving listening skills and increasing the comprehension or understanding of students with language-learning disabilities:

1. If the student frequently has difficulty following directions or understanding information of increased complexity, establish eye contact and maintain attention prior to presenting information. Cue the student to listen through the use of silent pauses or instructions to listen to or look at the teacher. This helps to establish a mental set for listening.
2. Ask the student to repeat or paraphrase directions or instructions to the teacher or a peer to ensure comprehension.
3. To facilitate listening, arrange classroom seating to limit distractions from doorways and windows and to maximize the use of visual aids.
4. When introducing a new concept or skill, use vocabulary that is familiar to the student and explain new vocabulary words by using familiar terms.
5. Present new concepts in as many modalities as possible (e.g., auditory, visual, and kinesthetic), and use gestures to augment verbal presentations (Bos & Vaughn, 1994).
6. To increase understanding of the relationship between semantic role and word order, encourage young children to act out sentences (e.g., Mommy kiss baby) or manipulate objects and talk about their movement (Connell, 1986).
7. Explain to students that listening is an active process that requires them to behave in certain ways, and teach them to identify specific behaviors associated with good listening (e.g., look, think about what is said, and repeat to yourself). Model effective listening skills by being attentive to students.
8. Use introductory statements (such as "These are the main points" or "Before we begin") to provide an organizational framework and help students prepare for a task.
9. Be sensitive to the linguistic complexity of the students and adjust the rate and complexity of instructional language accordingly. Use structurally simple and relatively short sentences of not more than 5 to 10 words and limit the number of new and unfamiliar vocabulary words presented in a single lesson to 5 or less (Wiig & Semel, 1984).
10. Teach specific memory strategies (e.g., visual imagery, clustering and grouping information, and forming associations) to help students organize, categorize, and store new information for later retrieval.
11. To enhance the student's recall and memorization of new vocabulary, encourage the use of the keyword method, in which familiar words are associated with each new concept or word (Mastropieri, Scruggs, & Fulk, 1990).
12. Engage adolescents in concrete problem-solving activities to identify those who have difficulty thinking symbolically or using reasoning in nonsymbolic events (Moses, Klein, & Altman, 1990).

Strategies for Increasing Language Production

The following strategies focus on improving the production or expressive skills of students with language-learning disabilities:

1. Expect students to speak occasionally in incomplete sentences because this is normal for discourse.
2. Regardless of the effectiveness of a student's communication, convey that the message is important. React first to the content of a student's message because it is most important in the communication process, and then correct the syntax error.
3. When attempting to expand a young child's utterances, provide one or two additional words to the child's spontaneous utterance for the child to repeat rather than impose adult structures that are difficult to imitate. Explain that the reason for the expansion of the utterance is not to correct what the youngster is saying but to give a more complex way of expressing thought (Bos & Vaughn, 1994).
4. Teach language in various natural settings (e.g., the classroom, cafeteria, and playground) rather than only in isolated groups. Also, teach language skills in connection with other curriculum content (Wiig & Semel, 1984).
5. Act as a good language model, and ask students to imitate what they hear. Imitation is frequently a good measure of language skills because students tend to imitate only the forms they know and not necessarily what they hear.
6. Use structured language programs that provide adequate opportunities to practice a new skill as well as interactive activities for applying the skill to relevant contexts (Bos & Vaughn, 1994).
7. Comment or elaborate on students' ideas to demonstrate how more information can be expressed and how concepts can be associated.
8. Use activities such as role playing and Charades to improve a student's use of language in different contexts and to enhance the ability to recognize the importance of nonverbal skills such as eye contact, facial expressions, and gestures. Also, model and reinforce appropriate turn-taking in conversations.
9. When a student has difficulties with word retrieval, examine indices such as response time, error index (word-selection process), and substitution types (German, 1984).
10. Use semantic training to improve a student's word-retrieval skills, and include strategies such as categorizing or classifying words and using associative clues (McGregor & Leonard, 1989).
11. To improve a student's verbal expression, encourage storytelling activities in which the student must name all of the objects or pictures, tell what is happening, and create an ending.
12. Teach generalization of language skills through three phases: an orientation phase in which the student becomes aware of the different applicable contexts, an activation phase in which practice is provided in a variety of situations, and a maintenance phase in which periodic probes are conducted to ensure that proficiency is maintained (Deshler & Schumaker, 1986).

Imitation and Modeling Strategies

Two teaching strategies that frequently are used in teaching language are imitation and modeling. In these strategies, the student gives a response that is similar to that of a model. Courtright and Courtright (1976) distinguish between modeling and imitative behavior that is mimicry. They define *imitative mimicry* as a one-to-one, literal matching response for each stimulus statement. In contrast to mimicry, modeling involves acquiring an abstract language rule without giving an immediate response to the stimulus (Bandura, 1971). For example, the student observes the teacher modeling a rule several times before being required to use the rule. This strategy is apparent in the following method of teaching the use of *s* on singular verbs: The teacher models 20 different singular subject-verb sentences that describe pictures (such as "Dog runs," "Boy walks," "Cat plays"). After the teacher models these sentences, the student is requested to describe the pictures.

Leonard (1975) recommends the use of modeling with a problem-solving set. The teacher uses a puppet as a model. Visual stimuli, such as toys or pictures of objects and people, are placed in front of the model (puppet). The teacher tells the student to listen carefully and determine which sentences earn reinforcers for the model. The model produces 10 to 20 utterances that describe the visual stimuli and deliberately gives 25% of the responses incorrectly. The teacher then presents the same visual stimulus to the student and encourages a response that earned a reinforcer for the model. The student and model take turns responding until the student has produced three consecutive appropriate responses that were presented previously by the model. At this point the student is presented with new visual stimuli and is required to produce unmodeled utterances.

The teacher can use imitative mimicry at one point with a student and gradually move to more spontaneous responses. When using this strategy, the teacher needs to structure the event preceding the student's response (i.e., the antecedent event). The antecedent event can have varying degrees of cuing. A teacher can use *total* cuing in the antecedent event ("What do you want? Tell me, 'I want an apple' ") or *partial* cuing in the antecedent event ("Is this a ball or an orange?"). Partial cuing also can include pointing to or looking at items to help the student make a correct response. *Minimal* cuing can be used when the student is ready to generalize a rule. For example, the teacher can say "What's happening? What's he doing?"

Muma (1978) notes that the expansion model is a modeling technique frequently used by parents for language intervention. With this technique, the youngster's response is expanded by the parent or teacher. For example, the youngster says "Car go," and the parent or teacher immediately gives the expanded model, "The car is going."

Parent Involvement

Parents of students with language-learning disabilities play an important role in language intervention. Tiegerman and Siperstein (1984) note that about 60% of maternal utterances directed toward youngsters with language impairments are not related semantically to the child's vocal, verbal, or nonverbal behavior. However, in a study of social conversational skills of preschoolers, Girolametto (1988) found a significant increase in appropriate language when parent training was involved. In this study, parents received training in three areas: following their child's lead in establishing joint focus on an activity, responding contingently to their child's communicative attempts, and encouraging conversation by taking turns. The training resulted in the parents being less controlling and more responsive to their children. Girolametto notes that following parent training the children initiated more topics, were more responsive to their mother's preceding turn in conversation, allowed more verbal turns when talking, and used a more diverse vocabulary.

COMMERCIAL LANGUAGE PROGRAMS

Numerous commercial language programs and materials are available to help develop language skills of students having difficulty with language. Selection of a program for intervention is influenced by two primary factors: the population the program serves and the theoretical model on which it is based. The theoretical model describes normal language acquisition and includes the content the student learns, the sequence in which the student learns, and how the student learns. There is a close relationship between the language program and the theoretical model of language acquisition (McLean and Snyder-McLean, 1978). Because language is interactive, no single program is appropriate for use alone, and the teacher should select programs based on the language needs of individual students. Thus, the selection of programs and materials for classroom use should reflect the developmental ages of the students for whom they are selected as well as the purpose of the intervention. The following selected commercial language programs may be useful for teaching language skills to students with language-learning disabilities.

Classroom Listening and Speaking

Classroom Listening and Speaking, developed by L. Plourde (published by Curriculum Skill Builders), includes three programs: one for preschoolers, one for students in kindergarten through second grade, and one for students in third through fourth grade. The programs include instructional objectives, a suggested calendar of activities for the year, and pretests and posttests for each grade level. The following specific skills are emphasized: vocabulary, listening, concepts, auditory memory, giving and following directions, categorizing, rhyming, grammar, describing, answering and asking questions, reasoning, and role playing and storytelling. Classroom activities encourage students to listen and communicate carefully, and additional home activities reinforce oral language skills through parent involvement.

Clinical Language Intervention Program

The *Clinical Language Intervention Program* (Semel & Wiig, 1982) focuses on teaching semantics, morphology and syntax, pragmatics, and memory to students in kindergarten through eighth grade. Within each category of language form and content, the materials and tasks are designed to elicit clearly defined intervention targets. The program includes more than 2,000 stimulus pictures, matching verbal stimuli, suggested training methods and strategies, a picture manual to promote acquisition and use of specific language skills or functions, a language activities manual of maintenance and generalization activities, and student progress checklists for recording progress across time.

DISTAR Language

The *DISTAR Language* program, developed by S. Engelmann and J. Osborn (published by SRA), is a highly structured approach to language intervention. It is designed for students in preschool through fourth grade and focuses on expressive and receptive language and cognitive development. In Level I, students practice using complete sentences, answering questions, and following oral directions. In Level II, students learn word and sentence skills and develop questioning and reasoning skills. The structure of spoken and written sentences is analyzed in Level III, and students learn to follow the rules of grammar to communicate information and ideas effectively. Each level includes 160 lessons. The program uses a didactic approach with repetition and group drills to teach language concepts. Following a script, the teacher models, elicits group and individual responses at a fast pace, and either reinforces the correct response or corrects the inappropriate response. Various language skills are taught, such as identity statements, pronouns, prepositions, and multiple attributes.

Let's Talk: Developing Prosocial Communication Skills

The *Let's Talk* program (Wiig, 1982) is designed to develop social communication skills in students from 9 years old through adult age. A communication card game format and structured group interaction activities are used to help teach effective ways to handle everyday social interactions. Students learn to express positive and negative feelings; present, understand, and respond to information in spoken messages; adapt messages to the needs of others; and approach conversations with expectations of what to say and how to say it. The *Communication Intents* package includes card decks pertaining to asking for favors, making dates, sharing feelings, and dating. Card decks in the *Functional Communication* package focus on getting around town, shopping, telephoning, getting a job, and serving people.

Teaching Morphology Developmentally

Teaching Morphology Developmentally, developed by K. G. Shipley and C. J. Banis (published by Communication Skill Builders), is a developmental program for teaching word formation that is designed for students whose language age is between 2½ and 10 years. The 522 color stimulus cards can be used to teach more than 1,000 free morphemes and 700 bound morphemes. Specific morphemes that are focused on include present progressives, plurals, possessives, past tenses, third-person singulars, and derived adjectives (comparative-superlative and irregular forms). Reproducible lists of curriculum items, pretest and posttest forms, and suggestions for developing behavioral objectives are included in the instructional guide.

COMPUTER SOFTWARE PROGRAMS IN LANGUAGE

Computer-assisted instruction can be used to improve students' speech and language skills. As well as enhancing motivation, computers appear to facilitate both social and cognitive interactions (Clements, 1987). Moreover, the use of computers tends to stimulate social use (Lipinski, Nida, Shade, & Watson, 1986), produce more positive and varied facial expressions and smiling (Hyson, 1985), and produce more spoken words per minute when compared with traditional activities such as blocks, art, and games (Muhlstein & Croft, 1986). Also, speech synthesizers such as Echo, DECtalk, and Digispeech provide speech for "talking" programs, and headphones can facilitate individual use. The following programs are examples of types of software that focus on language skills.

Homonyms; Opposites; Antonyms/Synonyms; Roots/Affixes

This vocabulary series (produced by Hartley) includes multilevel lessons appropriate for individualizing instruction. *Homonyms* begins with simple first-level words and progresses to different discriminations. The lessons in *Opposites* begin with 2nd-grade words and increase in difficulty to 10th-grade words. Key words in context help the student when an error is made. *Antonyms/Synonyms* provides practice in identifying and using antonyms and synonyms, and *Roots/Affixes* focuses on the identification of root words, prefixes, and suffixes. A diagnostic test for placement is included.

Nouns/Pronouns; Verbs; Adjectives; Adverbs

The programs (produced by Hartley) in this series on parts of speech present sequenced lessons for students in fourth through sixth grade that give information, ask questions, and provide feedback. Hints and explanations guide the student to the correct answer. The lessons in *Nouns/Pronouns* cover various language concepts such as identifying nouns, selecting correct plural endings of regular and irregular nouns, and choosing the noun that a pronoun represents. *Verbs* focuses on frequently missed identification skills, such as identifying verbs, selecting tenses of regular and irregular verbs, using contractions, and using subjunctive forms. *Adjectives* includes identification of adjectives, possessive nouns and pronouns, adjective endings, and use of adjectives in context. The lessons in *Adverbs* provide practice in identifying and correctly using adverbs that tell how, when, where, and to what extent as well as those that modify other adverbs or adjectives. The content of each program can be modified, and a diagnostic test enables the teacher to determine specific areas of difficulty and prescribe appropriate lessons.

Vocabulary Development

Vocabulary Development (produced by Optimum Resource) is a comprehensive vocabulary-building program for students in third through sixth grade that provides practice in recognizing synonyms, antonyms, homonyms, multiple meanings, prefixes, suffixes, and context clues. The program includes more than 400 words in lessons at six difficulty levels. The student automatically is advanced to the next level upon mastering the previous one. The teacher can create exercises and set difficulty levels to expand the use of the program. Practice sheets and test masters can be printed, and the program keeps records of student progress.

Who, What, Where, When, Why

Who, What, Where, When, Why (produced by Hartley) provides students in first through fourth grade with sequenced practice on question words. The student reads a phrase and selects the appropriate words. When an error is made, feedback includes an explanation of the correct answer. The teacher can modify the lessons to include words and phrases relevant to individual students.

PERSPECTIVE

Language is viewed as interacting with other cognitive constructs and is best assessed and remediated as a whole in social communication rather than as isolated language skills. To ensure academic success for students with language-learning disabilities, the teacher and language specialist should consult one another and work cooperatively as they consider models for language assessment and intervention.

DISCUSSION/REVIEW QUESTIONS

1. Explain the theories of language acquisition, and discuss the etiological-categorical and descriptive-developmental approaches to the study of language disorders.
2. Present the components of the language model proposed by Bloom and Lahey.
3. Discuss phonology, morphology, and syntax, and give several examples of deficits in each area that may occur with students who have language-learning disabilities.
4. Discuss semantics and pragmatics, and give several examples of deficits in each area that may occur with students who have language-learning disabilities.
5. Present the language difficulties of students across three age levels: preschool and kindergarten, elementary, and secondary.
6. Discuss issues involving the language skills of bilingual and culturally diverse students.
7. Describe selected formal language diagnostic measures, and present various informal language assessment techniques.
8. Discuss the pullout therapy model, classroom-based language models, and the strategies-based model as they pertain to service delivery.
9. Present selected teaching strategies to increase students' language comprehension and production skills in the classroom.
10. Describe several commercial language programs and computer software programs for language.

REFERENCES

Ackerman, P. T., Dykman, R. A., & Gardner, M. Y. (1990). Counting rate, naming rate, phonological sensitivity, and memory span: Major factors in dyslexia. *Journal of Learning Disabilities, 23,* 325–327.

Adler, S. (1988). A new job description and a new task for the public school clinician: Relating effectively to the nonstandard dialect speaker. *Language, Speech, and Hearing Services in Schools, 19,* 28–33.

American Speech-Language-Hearing Association. (1991). A model for collaborative service delivery for students with language-learning disorders in the public schools. *Asha, 33*(Suppl. 5), 44–50.

American Speech-Language-Hearing Association. (1992). Definitions for communicative disorders and differences. *Asha, 24,* 949–950.

Bandura, A. (1971). Analysis of modeling processes. In A. Bandura (Ed.), *Psychological modeling: Conflicting theories.* New York: Aldine/Atherton.

Baratz, J. C. (1969). Language and cognitive assessments of Negro children: Assumptions and research needs. *Journal of American Speech and Hearing Association, 11,* 87–91.

Bartel, N. R., Grill, J. J., & Bryen, D. N. (1973). Language characteristics of Black children: Implications for assessment. *Journal of School Psychology, 11,* 351–364.

Bashir, A. S. (1989). Language intervention and the curriculum. *Seminars in Speech and Language, 10,* 181–191.

Bates, E. (1976). Pragmatics and sociolinguistics in child language. In D. Morehead & A. Morehead

(Eds.), *Normal and deficient child language* (pp. 411–463). Baltimore, MD: University Park Press.

Bernstein, D. K. (1993a). Language development: The preschool years. In D. K. Bernstein & E. Tiegerman (Eds.), *Language and communication disorders in children* (3rd ed., pp. 97–122). Boston: Allyn & Bacon.

Bernstein, D. K. (1993b). The nature of language and its disorders. In D. K. Bernstein & E. Tiegerman (Eds.), *Language and communication disorders in children* (3rd ed., pp. 2–23). Boston: Allyn & Bacon.

Bloom, L. (1975). Language development review. In F. D. Horowitz (Ed.), *Review of child development research* (Vol. 4). Chicago: University of Chicago Press.

Bloom, L., & Lahey, M. (1978). *Language development and language disorders.* New York: John Wiley.

Boehm, A. E. (1986). *Boehm Test of Basic Concepts—Revised.* San Antonio, TX: Psychological Corporation.

Bos, C. S., & Vaughn, S. (1994). *Strategies for teaching students with learning and behavior problems* (3rd ed.). Boston: Allyn & Bacon.

Braine, M. (1971). *On two types of models of the internalization of grammar.* New York: Academic Press.

Braine, M. (1976). Children's first word combinations. *Monographs of the Society for Research in Child Development, 41* (Serial No. 164).

Bray, C. M., & Wiig, E. H. (1987). *Let's Talk Inventory for Children.* San Antonio, TX: Psychological Corporation.

Brown, R. (1973). *A first language: The early stages.* Cambridge, MA: Harvard University Press.

Brown, R., & Berko, J. (1960). Word associations and acquisition of grammar. *Child Development, 31,* 1–14.

Bruner, J. S. (1974/1975). From communication to language: A psychological perspective. *Cognition, 3,* 255–287.

Buttrill, J., Niizawa, J., Biemer, C., Takahashi, C., & Hearn, S. (1989). Serving the language learning disabled adolescent: A strategies-based model. *Language, Speech, and Hearing Services in Schools, 20,* 185–201.

Cardoza, D., & Rueda, R. (1986). Educational and occupational outcomes of Hispanic learning-disabled high school students. *The Journal of Special Education, 20,* 111–126.

Carrow-Woolfolk, E. (1974). *Carrow Elicited Language Inventory.* Chicago: Riverside.

Carrow-Woolfolk, E. (1985). *Test for Auditory Comprehension of Language—Revised.* Chicago: Riverside.

Carrow-Woolfolk, E. (1995). *Oral and Written Language Scales: Listening Comprehension and Oral Expression.* Circle Pines, MN: American Guidance Service.

Chomsky, N. A. (1965). *Aspects of the theory of syntax.* Cambridge, MA: MIT Press.

Clements, D. H. (1987). Computers and young children: A review of research. *Young Children, 42*(1), 34–44.

Connell, P. J. (1986). Acquisition of semantic role by language-disordered children: Differences between production and comprehension. *Journal of Speech and Hearing Research, 29,* 366–374.

Courtright, N. A., & Courtright, I. C. (1976). Imitative modeling as a theoretical base for instructing language-disordered children. *Journal of Speech and Hearing Research, 19,* 655–663.

Damico, J. S. (1987). Addressing language concerns in the schools: The SLP as a consultant. *Journal of Childhood Communication Disorders, 11,* 1–16.

Deshler, D. D., & Schumaker, J. B. (1986). Learning strategies: An instructional alternative for low achieving adolescents. *Exceptional Children, 52,* 583–590.

Diederick, W. M. (1971). Procedures for counting and charting a target phoneme. *Language, Speech, and Hearing Services in Schools, 5,* 18–32.

Dunn, L. M., & Dunn, L. M. (1981). *Peabody Picture Vocabulary Test—Revised.* Circle Pines, MN: American Guidance Service.

Ehren, B. J., & Lenz, B. K. (1989). Adolescents with language disorders: Special considerations in providing academically relevant language intervention. *Seminars in Speech and Language, 10,* 192–204.

Ervin-Tripp, S., & Mitchell-Kernan, C. (Eds.). (1977). *Child discourse.* New York: Academic Press.

German, D. (1984). Diagnosis of word-finding disorders in children with learning disabilities. *Journal of Learning Disabilities, 17,* 353–359.

German, D. J. (1989). *Test of Word Finding.* Chicago: Riverside.

German, D. J. (1990). *Test of Adolescent/Adult Word Finding.* Chicago: Riverside.

Gersten, R., & Woodward, J. (1994). The language-minority student and special education: Issues, trends, and paradoxes. *Exceptional Children, 60,* 310–322.

Girolametto, L. E. (1988). Improving the social-conversational skills of developmentally delayed children: An intervention study. *Journal of Speech and Hearing Disorders, 53,* 156–167.

Goldman, R., & Fristoe, M. (1986). *Goldman-Fristoe Test of Articulation.* Circle Pines, MN: American Guidance Service.

Hammill, D. D., Brown, V. L., Larsen, S. C., & Wiederholt, J. L. (1994). *Test of Adolescent and Adult Language—3.* Austin, TX: PRO-ED.

Hammill, D. D., & Newcomer, P. L. (1988). *Test of Language Development—2: Intermediate.* Austin, TX: PRO-ED.

Hazel, J. S., & Schumaker, J. B. (1988). Social skills and learning disabilities: Current issues and recommendations for future research. In J. F. Kavanagh & T. J. Truss (Eds.), *Learning disabilities: Proceedings of the national conference* (pp. 293–344). Parkton, MD: York Press.

Holland, A. L. (1977). Some practical considerations in aphasia rehabilitation. In M. Sullivan & M. S. Kommers (Eds.), *Rationale for adult aphasia therapy* (pp. 167–180). Omaha: University of Nebraska.

Hughes, D. L. (1989). Generalization from language therapy to classroom academics. *Seminars in Speech and Language, 10,* 218–230.

Hyson, M. C. (1985). Emotions and the microcomputer: An exploratory study of young children's responses. *Computers in Human Behavior, 1,* 143–152.

Jacobson, R., & Halle, M. (1956). *Fundamentals of language.* The Hague: Mouton.

Jenkins, J. J., & Palermo, D. S. (1964). Mediation processes and the acquisition of linguistic structure. In U. Bellugi & R. Brown (Eds.), *The acquisition of language. Monographs of the Society for Research in Child Development, 29* (1, Whole No. 92).

Kayser, H. (1989). Speech and language assessment of Spanish-English speaking children. *Language, Speech, and Hearing Services in Schools, 20,* 226–241.

Lahey, M. (1988). *Language disorders and language development.* Boston: Allyn & Bacon.

Larson, V. L., & McKinley, N. (1995). *Language disorders in older students.* Eau Claire, WI: Thinking Publications.

Lazar, R. T., Warr-Leeper, G. A., Nicholson, C. B., & Johnson, S. (1989). Elementary school teachers' use of multiple meaning expressions. *Language, Speech, and Hearing Services in Schools, 20,* 420–429.

Lee, L. (1971). *The Northwestern Syntax Screening Test.* Evanston, IL: Northwestern University Press.

Lee, L. (1974). *Developmental Sentence Analysis.* Evanston, IL: Northwestern University Press.

Lenneberg, E. H. (1967). *Biological foundations of language.* New York: Wiley.

Leonard, L. B. (1975). Modeling as a clinical procedure in language training. *Language, Speech, and Hearing Services in Schools, 6,* 72–85.

Leonard, L. B., Wilcox, M. J., Fulmer, K. C., & Davis, G. A. (1978). Understanding indirect requests: An investigation of children's comprehension of pragmatic meanings. *Journal of Speech and Hearing Research, 21,* 528–537.

Lipinski, J. M., Nida, R. E., Shade, D. D., & Watson, J. A. (1986). The effects of microcomputers on young children: An examination of free-play choices, sex differences, and social interactions. *Journal of Educational Computing Research, 2,* 147–168.

Marvin, C. A. (1987). Consultation services: Changing roles for SLPs. *Journal of Childhood Communication Disorders, 11,* 1–16.

Mastropieri, M. A., Scruggs, T. E., & Fulk, B. J. M. (1990). Teaching abstract vocabulary with the keyword method: Effects on recall and comprehension. *Journal of Learning Disabilities, 23,* 92–96, 107.

McCormick, L., & Schiefelbusch, R. L. (1984). *Early language intervention.* Boston: Allyn & Bacon.

McGregor, K. K., & Leonard, L. B. (1989). Facilitating word-finding skills of language-impaired children. *Journal of Speech and Hearing Disorders, 54,* 141–147.

McLean, J. E., & Snyder-McLean, L. K. (1978). *A transactional approach to early language training.* Boston: Allyn & Bacon.

McNeil, D. (1970). The development of language. In P. H. Mussen (Ed.), *Carmichael's manual of child psychology* (Vol. 2, 3rd ed., pp. 1061–1161). New York: Wiley.

Mercer, J. R. (1983). Issues in the diagnosis of language disorders in students whose primary language is not English. *Topics in Language Disorders, 3*(3), 46–56.

Merritt, D. D., & Liles, B. Z. (1987). Story grammar ability in children with and without language disorder: A story generation, story retelling, and story comprehension. *Journal of Speech and Hearing Research, 30,* 539–552.

Miller, L. (1989). Classroom-based language intervention. *Language, Speech, and Hearing Services in Schools, 20,* 153–169.

Mogford, K., & Sadler, J. (1989). *Child language disability: Implications in an educational setting.* Philadelphia: Multilingual Matters.

Moses, N., Klein, H. B., & Altman, E. (1990). An approach to assessing and facilitating causal language in adults with learning disabilities based on Piagetian theory. *Journal of Learning Disabilities, 23,* 220–228.

Muhlstein, E. A., & Croft, D. J. (1986). *Using the microcomputer to enhance language experiences and the development of cooperative play among preschool children.* Cupertino, CA: De Anza College. (ERIC Document Reproduction Service No. ED 269 004)

Muma, J. R. (1978). *Language handbook: Concepts, assessment, and intervention.* Upper Saddle River, NJ: Prentice Hall.

Nelson, N. W. (1989). Curriculum-based language assessment and intervention. *Language, Speech, and Hearing Services in Schools, 20,* 170–184.

Nelson, N. W. (1994). Curriculum-based assessment and intervention across the grades. In G. P. Wallach & K. G. Butler (Eds.), *Language learning disabilities in school-age children and adolescents* (pp. 104–131). Boston: Allyn & Bacon.

Newcomer, P. L., & Hammill, D. D. (1988). *Test of Language Development—2: Primary.* Austin, TX: PRO-ED.

Nicolosi, L., Harryman, E., & Kresheck, J. (1978). *Terminology of communication disorders.* Baltimore: Williams & Wilking.

Owens, R. E., Jr. (1991). *Language disorders: A functional approach to assessment and intervention.* Boston: Allyn & Bacon.

Owens, R. E., Jr. (1994). Development of communication, language, and speech. In G. H. Shames, E. H. Wiig, & W. A. Secord (Eds.), *Human communication disorders: An introduction* (4th ed., pp. 36–81). Boston: Allyn & Bacon.

Parnell, M. M., Amerman, J. D., & Harting, R. D. (1986). Responses of language-disordered children to wh-questions. *Language, Speech, and Hearing Services in Schools, 17,* 95–106.

Pehrsson, R. S., & Denner, P. R. (1988). Semantic organizers: Implications for reading and writing. *Topics in Language Disorders, 8*(3), 24–32.

Phelps-Terasaki, D., & Phelps-Gunn, T. (1992). *Test of Pragmatic Language.* Austin, TX: PRO-ED.

Piaget, J. (1960). *The psychology of intelligence.* Patterson, NJ: Littlefield, Adams.

Prutting, C. A. (1979). Process \ pra I , ses\n: The action of moving forward progressively from one point to another on the way to completion. *Journal of Speech and Hearing Disorders, 44,* 3–30.

Riedlinger-Ryan, K. J., & Shewan, C. M. (1984). Comparison of auditory comprehension skills in learning-disabled and academically achieving adolescents. *Language, Speech, and Hearing Services in Schools, 15,* 127–136.

Rosenberg, S. (1984). Disorders of first-language development: Trends in research and theory. In E. Gollin (Ed.), *Malformations in development: Biological and psychological sources and consequences.* New York: Academic Press.

Roth, F. P., & Clark, D. M. (1987). Symbolic play and social participation abilities of language-impaired and normally developing children. *Journal of Speech and Hearing Disorders, 52,* 17–29.

Salend, S. J., & Fradd, S. (1986). Nationwide availability of services for limited English-proficient handicapped students. *The Journal of Special Education, 20,* 127–135.

Salvia, J., & Ysseldyke, J. E. (1995). *Assessment* (6th ed.). Boston: Houghton Mifflin.

Schumaker, J. B., & Deshler, D. D. (1984). Setting demand variables: A major factor in program planning for the learning disabled adolescent. *Topics in Language Disorders, 4*(4), 22–40.

Schumaker, J. B., Deshler, D. D., Alley, G. R., Warner, M. M., & Denton, P. H. (1984). Multipass: A learning strategy for improving reading comprehension. *Learning Disabilities Quarterly, 5,* 295–304.

Schwabe, A. M., Olswang, L. B., & Kriegsmann, E. (1986). Requests for information: Linguistic, cognitive, pragmatic, and environmental variables. *Language, Speech, and Hearing Services in Schools, 17,* 38–55.

Seidenberg, P. L. (1988). Cognitive and academic instructional intervention for learning-disabled adolescents. *Topics in Language Disorders, 8*(3), 56–71.

Semel, E. M., & Wiig, E. H. (1982). *Clinical language intervention program.* San Antonio, TX: Psychological Corporation.

Semel, E. M., Wiig, E. H., & Secord, W. (1995). *Clinical Evaluation of Language Fundamentals—3.* San Antonio, TX: Psychological Corporation.

Semel, E. M., Wiig, E. H., & Secord, W. (1996). *Clinical Evaluation of Language Fundamentals—3: Screening Test.* San Antonio, TX: Psychological Corporation.

Simon, C. S. (1985). *Communication skills and classroom success.* San Diego, CA: College-Hill Press.

Skinner, B. F. (1957). *Verbal behavior.* New York: Appleton-Century-Crofts.

Snyder, L. S. (1986). Developmental language disorders: Elementary school age. In J. M. Costello & A. L. Holland (Eds.), *Handbook of speech and language disorders* (pp. 671–700). San Diego, CA: College-Hill Press.

Staats, A. (1971). Linguistic-mentalistic theory versus an explanatory S-R learning theory of language development. In D. I. Slobin (Ed), *The ontogenesis of grammar.* New York: Academic Press.

Tiegerman, E., & Siperstein, M. (1984). Individual patterns of interaction in the mother-child dyad: Implications for the language-disordered child. *Topics in Language Disorders, 4,* 50–62.

U.S. Department of Education. (1994). *To assure the free appropriate public education of all children with disabilities: Sixteenth annual report to Congress on the implementation of the Individuals with Disabilities Education Act.* Washington, DC: Author.

Wallace, G., & Hammill, D. D. (1994). *Comprehensive Receptive and Expressive Vocabulary Test.* Austin, TX: PRO-ED.

Wallach, G. (1989). Current research as a map for language intervention in the school years. *Seminars in Speech and Language, 10,* 205–217.

Warren, S. F., & Yoder, P. J. (1994). Communication and language intervention: Why a constructivist approach is insufficient. *The Journal of Special Education, 28,* 248–258.

Wepman, J. (1973). *Auditory Discrimination Test.* Palm Springs, CA: Language Research Associates.

Wiig, E. H. (1982). *Let's talk: Developing prosocial communication skills.* San Antonio, TX: Psychological Corporation.

Wiig, E. H. (1990). Linguistic transitions and learning disabilities: A strategic learning perspective. *Learning Disability Quarterly, 13,* 128–140.

Wiig, E. H., & Secord, W. A. (1992). *Test of Word Knowledge.* San Antonio, TX: Psychological Corporation.

Wiig, E. H., & Secord, W. A. (1994). Language disabilities in school-age children and youth. In G. H. Shames, E. H. Wiig, & W. A. Secord (Eds.), *Human communication disorders: An introduction* (4th ed., pp. 212–247). Boston: Allyn & Bacon.

Wiig, E. H., & Semel, E. M. (1976). *Language disabilities in children and adolescents.* Boston: Allyn & Bacon.

Wiig, E. H., & Semel, E. M. (1984). *Language assessment and intervention for the learning disabled* (2nd ed.). Boston: Allyn & Bacon.

Wilcox, M. J. (1986). Developmental language disorders: Preschoolers. In J. M. Costello & A. L. Holland (Eds.), *Handbook of speech and language disorders* (pp. 643–670). San Diego, CA: College-Hill Press.

Wood, B. S. (1976). *Children and communications: Verbal and non-verbal language development.* Upper Saddle River, NJ: Prentice Hall.

Written Language

CHAPTER 12

After studying this chapter, you should be able to:

- discuss the assessment of handwriting skills.
- discuss the development of handwriting skills and teaching strategies.
- describe commercial handwriting programs.
- discuss the assessment of spelling skills.
- discuss techniques for teaching spelling skills.
- describe commercial spelling programs.
- discuss the assessment of written expression skills.
- present an overview of the writing stages.
- discuss techniques for teaching written expression.
- describe commercial written expression programs.
- describe computer software programs in written expression.

Written language is a highly complex form of communication. It is both a skill and a means of self-expression. The process of writing integrates visual, motor, and conceptual abilities and is a major means through which students demonstrate their knowledge of advanced academic subjects. Moreover, Hammill and McNutt (1981) report that writing skills are among the best correlates of reading skills. Skills that correlate with reading skills include competence in writing, spelling, punctuation, capitalization, studying, making sound-letter correspondences, knowing the alphabet, and distinguishing one letter from another. Hammill and McNutt conclude that "a strong relationship exists between reading, which is theoretically a receptive form of written language, and almost all other aspects of written language" (p. 35).

Classroom instruction in handwriting usually begins in kindergarten or first grade. Readiness activities such as tracing, coloring, and copying are emphasized at first. The formation of letters, numbers, and words is stressed until about the third grade. After the third grade, more emphasis is placed on writing as a form of meaningful self-expression, and instruction focuses on using grammar and developing the quality of ideas expressed.

Many students with learning disabilities are deficient in writing skills. In a review of research studies on the written composing ability of students with learning disabilities, Newcomer and Barenbaum (1991) report that students with learning disabilities perform significantly lower than their peers on most written expression tasks, especially spelling, punctuation, and word usage (grammar). In addition, in comparison with their peers without disabilities, students with learning disabilities write fewer words per composition (are less fluent), use less effective planning strategies, and produce compositions that possess less organization and coherence. Lerner, Lowenthal, and Lerner (1995) note that handwriting, spelling, and written expression tasks require sustained attention and concentration; thus, students with attention deficit disorders may have difficulty learning to write and producing written products. Many students with learning disabilities and attention deficit disorders need direct, concentrated instruction to become proficient in written communication. This chapter explores three major problem areas: handwriting, spelling, and written expression.

HANDWRITING PROBLEMS

The major objective of instruction in handwriting is legibility. To communicate thoughts effectively through writing, the student first must be taught to write legibly and fluently. Thus, instruction begins by focusing on holding the writing instrument, forming manuscript and cursive letters correctly, and maintaining proper spacing and proportion. Numerous factors contribute to handwriting difficulties: motor problems, faulty visual perception of letters and words, poor visual memory, poor instruction, and lack of motivation.

Fine motor problems also can interfere with handwriting and thus with schoolwork. For example, a student may know how to spell a word but be unable to write legibly or fast enough to keep up with the teacher; thus, the student's spelling may be poor. This same situation may exist in copying material from the chalkboard and working on seatwork. Zentall (1993) notes that students with attention deficit disorders tend to have slower motor and perceptual responses than their peers; thus, these students may have more difficulty than other students with the physical act of handwriting. Unfortunately, many parents and teachers view students as academically slow when, in fact, the real problem is handwriting.

Students show a variety of handwriting problems: slowness, incorrect directionality of letters and numbers, too much or too little slant, spacing difficulty, messiness, inability to stay on a horizontal line, illegible letters, too much or too little pencil pressure, and mirror writing. Newland (1932) examined the cursive handwriting of 2,381 people and found that about 50% of the illegibilities involved the letters *a, e, r,* and *t.* Most commonly, people failed to close letters (such as *a* and *b*), closed top loops (such as writing *e* like *i*), looped strokes that should be non-looped (such as writing *i* like *e*), used straight-up rather than rounded strokes (such as writing *n* like *u*), and exhibited problems with end strokes (not brought up, not brought down, or not left as horizontal). In a study of illegibilities in cursive handwriting of sixth graders, Horton (1970) reports that 12% of all errors were incorrect formations of the letter *r.* Thus, the majority of handwriting errors involve the incorrect writing of a few letters. Common number malformations include writing *5* like *3* (5), *6* like *0* (6), *7* like *9* (7), and *9* like *4* (9).

ASSESSMENT OF HANDWRITING SKILLS

In assessing the young student (8 or 9 years old and younger), the teacher should remember that occasional reversals, omissions, and poor spacing are normal. However, a writing problem exists if such errors continue for a long time and if the student does not improve in simple handwriting tasks. Unlike the other academic skill areas, few standardized tests exist to measure handwriting, and informal procedures are used widely. Minimum standards are difficult to set because activities differ in the emphasis placed on speed, legibility, and character of handwriting.

Published Assessment Devices

To assess a student's overall readiness to learn writing, the writing section of the *Basic School Skills Inventory—Diagnostic* (Hammill & Leigh, 1983) assesses a student's handwriting ability in various tasks: writing from left to right, grasping a pencil, writing first name, maintaining proper writing position, writing letters upon request, copying words, copying from chalkboard to paper, staying on the line, and writing last name. The instrument is norm-referenced for students age 4 years to 7 years 5 months to identify those who are low in handwriting readiness as compared with other students their age. The scale also can be used as a criterion-referenced test to determine what skills need to be taught.

The *Test of Legible Handwriting* (Larsen & Hammill, 1989) is a standardized test of legibility that reports results in terms of standard scores and percentiles. It is designed for students age 7 through 17 and includes an evaluation system that is applied to multiple samples of a student's handwriting. The samples are selected from several themes and settings, such as creative essays, biographical sketches, correspondence, reports, and work samples. Each handwriting sample is matched as closely as possible with one of three scoring guides that feature distinctly different writing styles: (a) a cursive style having a slant to the right or a style that is more or less perpendicular, (b) a cursive style having a slant to the left, and (c) a manuscript or modified manuscript style. The examiner selects the scoring guide that most closely resembles the student's handwriting and uses the examples that range from good to poor in the guide to rate the sample on a scale of 1 through 9. The resulting score is converted to a percentile and standard score; when more than one sample is collected, a composite legibility quotient is obtained.

The *Zaner-Bloser Evaluation Scales* (1984) are based on a national sampling of students' handwriting and frequently are used for assessing manuscript and cursive handwriting. There are scales for first and second grade written in manuscript style and scales for second through eighth grade written in cursive style. Five specimens of handwriting—excellent, good, average, fair, and poor—are provided for each grade level. Each scale contains a sentence or paragraph that the teacher writes on the chalkboard. The students practice writing the model and then copy the sentences in their best handwriting onto a sheet of paper. The teacher compares each paper with the five specimen sentences for the student's grade level and judges the following five elements: letter formation, vertical quality in manuscript and slant in cursive, spacing, alignment and proportion, and line quality. Each student's writing is rated according to the number of satisfactory elements. Through this method a student's handwriting can be compared with that of students in the same grade level; however, a thorough analysis of errors is needed before planning instructional programs.

Various legibility scales traditionally have been used to provide a subjective evaluation of general handwriting competence. However, the objectivity of such scales has been questioned, and they do not highlight specific errors and illegible forms in writing. Thus, handwriting scales may be used best to aid the teacher in rating a writing specimen for screening purposes. To obtain information for instructional purposes, various informal assessment techniques may be helpful.

Informal Assessment Techniques

The teacher can obtain diagnostic information informally through a close visual examination of the student's handwriting. Writing samples can be used to determine problem areas in legibility. Mann, Suiter, and McClung (1992) suggest obtaining three samples: the student's usual, best, and fastest handwriting. The usual writing sample shows the student's work under normal, nonfatiguing conditions. For the best sample, the student is told to take time and write the sentence with best effort. Then a 3-minute timing is given to see how many times the student can write a given sentence. Sometimes a student can write legibly but only when specifically asked to do so. Also, some students write well but at an extremely slow rate. By comparing the three writing samples, the teacher can determine the student's ability with regard to speed and legibility.

While observing the student during handwriting activities, the teacher should note possible problem areas by answering the following questions:

1. Does the student grip the pencil correctly and in a comfortable and flexible manner?
2. Is the student's paper in the proper position on the writing surface?
3. Does the student sit correctly when writing, or is the head too close or too far away from the paper?
4. Does the student consistently use the same hand for writing?
5. Does the student appear to be extremely frustrated, nervous, or emotional when writing?
6. Does the student have a negative attitude toward handwriting and appear bored and disruptive?

Additional instructional information can be obtained by analyzing the student's writing samples for error patterns in the following various aspects of handwriting:

1. *Letter formation:* Letter formation involves the strokes that make up each letter. In manuscript writing, letters are composed of vertical, horizontal, and slanted lines plus circles or parts of circles, whereas cursive letters are composed of slanted lines, loops, and curved lines. To check for legibility, the teacher can use a piece of cardboard with a hole cut in the center that is slightly larger than a single letter. By exposing one letter at a time, the teacher can see more easily which letters are illegible or poorly formed.

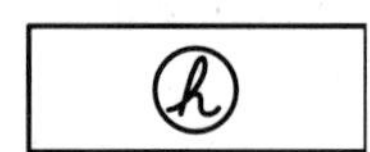

2. *Letter size, proportion, and alignment:* The size and proportion of letters are indicated by their height relationship to one another, and alignment refers to the evenness of letters along the base line, with letters of the same size being the same height. These legibility elements can be measured by using a ruler to draw lines that touch the base and tops of as many letters as possible.

3. *Spacing:* Spacing should be consistent between letters within words, as well as between words and between sentences.

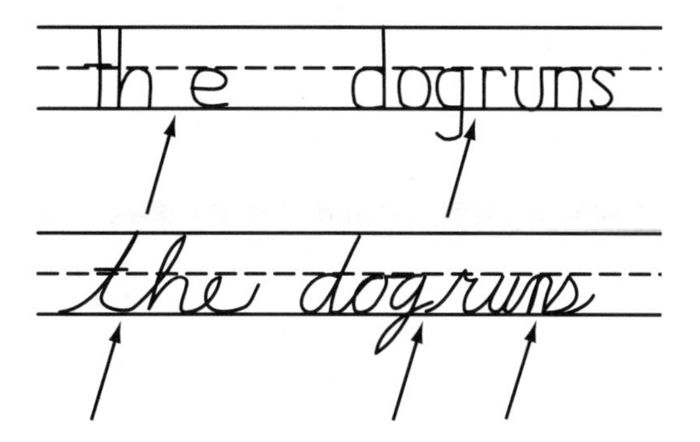

4. *Line quality:* Thickness and steadiness of the lines used to form letters should be consistent. The teacher should mark lines that waver or are too thick or too fine. Incorrect hand or body position or cramped fingers can result in inconsistent line quality.

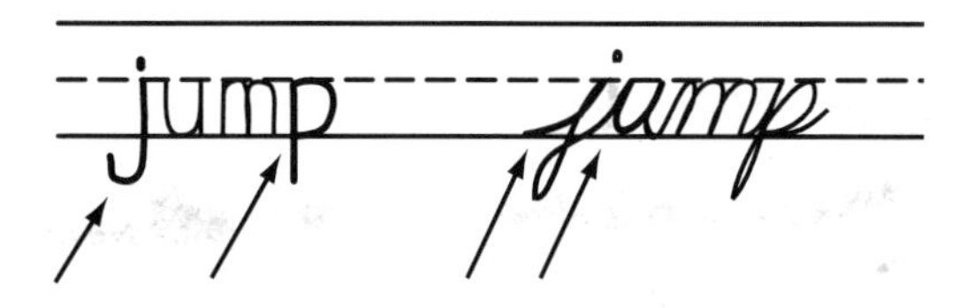

5. *Slant:* The slant of letters should be uniform. In general, manuscript letters are perpendicular to the base line and have a straight up-and-down appearance. In cursive writing the paper is slanted, and strokes are pulled toward the body. Straight lines or lines with a uniform slant can be drawn through the letters to indicate which letters are off slant.

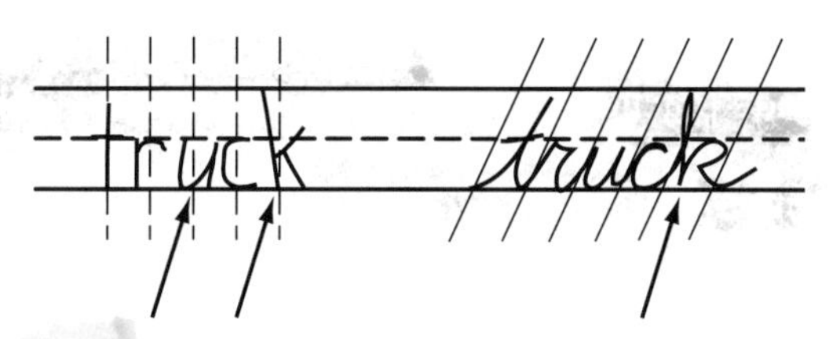

6. *Rate:* Speed of handwriting can be determined on a writing sample by asking the student to write as well and as rapidly as possible. The rate of handwriting—letters per minute (lpm)—is determined by dividing the total number of letters written by the number of writing minutes allowed. Handwriting proficiency rates include the following:

   (a) Zaner-Bloser scales:

   grade 1: 25 lpm
   grade 2: 30 lpm
   grade 3: 38 lpm
   grade 4: 45 lpm
   grade 5: 60 lpm
   grade 6: 67 lpm
   grade 7: 74 lpm

   (b) Larsen and Hammill (1989):

   age 7: less than 20
   age 8: 20–25
   age 9: 26–33
   age 10: 34–40
   age 11: 41–46
   age 12: 47–55
   age 13: 56–65
   age 14+: greater than 65

Probes can be used to assess a specific handwriting skill and determine instructional targets. Handwriting probe sheets can include tasks such as repeatedly writing the same letter, writing first name, writing uppercase letters, writing lowercase letters, and writing words. The student is timed for 1 minute, and daily performance on the probe sheets is charted to monitor progress.

In assessing handwriting difficulties, the teacher also can encourage students to use self-evaluation. Diagnostic charts and evaluation scales can help the students identify their own handwriting inaccuracies. When the students monitor their own writing, they can change their writing performance quickly and easily. Also, positive attitudes may be increased as the students assume some responsibility for learning and improving their handwriting. A commercial material that can be useful in self-evaluation is *Peek-Thru* (Zaner-Bloser). This is a plastic overlay that students place on top of their writing and "peek thru" to check correct letter formation and alignment. A manuscript set is provided for first through third grade, and a cursive set is available for transition, third grade, and fourth grade. For fifth grade and above there are two similar plastic overlay rulers, one in manuscript and one in cursive.

TEACHING HANDWRITING SKILLS

After assessment, the teacher can establish instructional objectives based upon pinpointed errors and the student's overall development of handwriting skills. Skills should be taught through meaningful and motivating real-life writing activities. Repetitious drills and mass practice without supervision should be avoided, and the student should receive immediate feedback. Models should be provided of both good and poor work so that the student eventually can make comparisons to determine necessary changes.

Tompkins and Hoskisson (1991) note that 15- to 20-minute periods of handwriting instruction and practice several times a week are more effective than a single lengthy period. Separate periods of direct instruction and teacher-supervised practice help avoid the development of bad habits and errors in letter formation that may cause problems when the student needs to develop greater writing speed. The teacher should demonstrate the correct way to form letters and should supervise students' handwriting efforts carefully. Wright and Wright (1980) report that observing moving models (i.e., watching the teacher write) is more effective than copying models already written; thus, the teacher should circulate around the classroom to assist individual students and demonstrate a skill while the student is performing the handwriting task. Hofmeister (1981) lists six handwriting instructional errors to *avoid*: (a) unsupervised handwriting practice while skills are being formed, (b) lack of immediate feedback to correct errors, (c) lack of emphasis on student analysis of errors, (d) failure to provide close-range models of correct letter formation, (e) repeated drill of both correct and incorrect letter production, and (f) misplaced emphasis on activities of limited value.

Also, the teacher should help students develop a positive attitude toward handwriting by encouraging progress and stressing the importance of the skill. In upper elementary grades and in secondary classrooms, greater emphasis is placed on identifying and remediating specific deficits revealed in students' daily written work. Students need to diagnose and correct handwriting problems because handwriting difficulties may impede efficient work production and influence teacher evaluation and grading. Markham (1976) found that teachers consistently give higher grades on papers with better handwriting than on papers with poor handwriting, regardless of the quality of the content.

Table 12.1 presents handwriting objectives by suggested grade level. (Note that many handwriting skills can be emphasized at more than one grade level.) The development of handwriting skills and teaching strategies are presented next in the areas of readiness skills, manuscript writing, transitional writing, and cursive writing. Typewriting and keyboarding also are considered as alternatives.

Readiness Skills

Writing requires muscular control, eye-hand coordination, and visual discrimination. The teacher needs to help each student develop skills in these areas before the student is ready to begin handwriting. Muscular coordination can be developed in the young child through manipulative experiences (e.g., cutting with scissors, finger painting, tracing, and coloring). Eye-hand coordination is involved in drawing circles and copying geometric forms. Also, developing visual discrimination of sizes, shapes, and details aids the student's visual awareness of letters and their formation. Chalkboard activities provide practice and give the student the opportunity to use muscle movement of the shoulders, arms, hands, and fingers. Before beginning handwriting instruction, the student should be able to do the following:

1. Perform hand movements such as up-down, left-right, and forward-back.
2. Trace geometric shapes and dotted lines.
3. Connect dots on paper.

TABLE 12.1
Handwriting Objectives by Suggested Grade Level

Grade Level	Objectives
Kindergarten	Begins to establish a preference for either left- or right-handedness Voluntarily draws, paints, and scribbles Develops small-muscle control through the use of materials such as finger paints, clay, weaving fibers, and puzzles Uses tools of writing in making letters, writing names, or attempting to write words Understands and applies writing readiness vocabulary given orally, such as left/right, top/bottom, beginning/end, large/small, circle, space, around, across, curve, top line, dotted line, and bottom line Begins to establish correct writing position of body, arms, hand, paper, and pencil Draws familiar objects using the basic strokes of manuscript writing Recognizes and legibly writes own name in manuscript letters using uppercase and lowercase letters appropriately Uses writing paper that is standard for manuscript writing
Grade 1	Begins manuscript writing using both lowercase and uppercase letters introduced to correlate with the student's reading program Writes with correct posture, pencil grip, and paper position; works from left to right; and forms letters in the correct direction Copies words neatly from near position Writes with firm strokes and demonstrates good spacing between letters, words, and sentences Writes manuscript letters independently and with firm strokes Writes clear, legible manuscript letters at a rate appropriate for ability Arranges work neatly and pleasingly on a page (i.e., uses margins and paragraph indentions and makes clean erasures)
Grade 2	Evaluates writing using a plastic overlay and identifies strengths and weaknesses Writes all letters of the alphabet in manuscript from memory Recognizes the differences in using manuscript and cursive writing Reads simple sentences written in cursive writing on the chalkboard Demonstrates physical coordination to proceed to simple cursive writing
Grade 3	Demonstrates ability to decode cursive writing by reading paragraphs of cursive writing both from the chalkboard and from paper Identifies cursive lowercase and uppercase letters by matching cursive letters to manuscript letters Begins cursive writing with lowercase letters and progresses to uppercase letters as needed Uses writing paper that is standard for cursive writing Writes all letters of the cursive alphabet using proper techniques in making each letter Recognizes the proper joining of letters to form words Writes from memory all letters of the alphabet in cursive form
Grade 4	Slants and joins the letters in a word and controls spacing between letters Uses cursive writing for day-to-day use Begins to write with a pen *if* pencil writing is smooth, fluent, and neat Maintains and uses manuscript writing for special needs, such as preparing charts, maps, and labels Writes clear, legible cursive letters at a rate appropriate for ability
Grade 5	Reduces size of writing to "adult" proportions of letters (i.e., one-quarter space for minimum letters, one-half space for intermediate letters, and three-quarters space for tall lowercase and uppercase letters) Takes pride in presenting neat work
Grade 6	Customarily presents neat work Evaluates own progress in the basic handwriting skills pertaining to size, slant, shape, spacing, and alignment

4. Draw a horizontal line from left to right.
5. Draw a vertical line from top to bottom and bottom to top.
6. Draw a backward circle, a curved line, and a forward circle.
7. Draw slanted lines vertically.
8. Copy simple designs and shapes.
9. Name letters and discern likenesses and differences in letter forms.

Determining the student's hand preference also is important. The teacher should determine which hand the student uses most often in natural situations, such as eating or throwing a ball. Also, the teacher can ask the student to use one hand to take a pencil out of a box, cover one eye, or make a mark on the chalkboard. A youngster who indicates a strong preference for using the left hand should be allowed to do so when writing. A student who uses both hands well should be encouraged to make a choice and consistently use one hand (preferably the right) for writing.

The proper position of paper and pencil also must be taught before extensive handwriting instruction. During writing, the student should be sitting in a comfortable chair, with the lower back touching the back of the seat and both feet on the floor. The desk or table should be at a height that allows the student to place forearms on the writing surface without discomfort. The nonwriting hand holds the writing paper at the top. To prevent elbow bumping, left-handers should be seated in a left-hand desk chair or along the outside at a work table. The pencil should be held lightly in the triangle formed by the thumb and the first two fingers, and the hand should rest lightly on its outer edge. The pencil should be held about an inch above its point by right-handers, and the pencil end should point in the direction of the right shoulder. For left-handers, the pencil should be held about 1¼ inches from its writing point, and the pencil end should point toward the left shoulder. Commercial triangular-shaped pencil grips or masking tape can be placed on the pencil to make it easier to hold.

For manuscript writing the paper should be placed straight on the desk directly in front of the eyes. For some left-handers it may be helpful to slant the paper so that the lower right corner of the paper points to the left of the center of the body. For cursive writing the paper should be tilted. The right-handed student places the paper so that the lower left corner points toward the center of the body and the writing stroke is pulled toward the center of the body. For the left-handed student the paper is slanted north-northeast. The lower right corner points to the center of the body, and the writing stroke is pulled toward the left elbow. Some left-handers begin "hooking" their hand and wrist while writing to see what they have written and to avoid smudging their writing. This practice should be avoided and can be controlled by finding the right slant for the paper and by practicing handwriting on the chalkboard to develop a more natural style.

Manuscript Writing

Manuscript writing usually is taught in kindergarten and first grade and is based entirely on the basic shapes of circles and straight lines. The basic strokes in manuscript writing are the top-bottom line (↓|), left-to-right line (⇄), backward circle (↺), forward circle (↻), and slant lines (↙/ \↖) (Milone & Wasylyk, 1981). The teacher can demonstrate letter forms on the chalkboard, being careful not to block the students' vision. The students should observe the handwriting process as well as the finished product. When writing on the chalkboard, students should write at eye level and stand at arm's length directly in front of the writing.

A multisensory approach often is used in teaching letter forms. The student sees, hears, and traces the letter model. The following steps can be used:

1. The teacher shows the student the letter (or word) to be written.
2. The teacher says aloud the letter name and stroke directions (e.g., "First we go up; then we go down").

3. The student traces the model with a finger and may report the movements aloud while tracing.
4. The student traces the letter model with a pencil.
5. The student copies the letter on paper while looking at the model.
6. The student writes the letter from memory while saying the name of the letter.

A fading model also can be used in teaching handwriting. The letter model is presented at first in heavy, dark lines, and the student traces over the model with a finger and the nonwriting end of a pencil. Gradually, portions of the model are faded, and the student traces the model with a pencil. The model eventually is removed, and the student writes the letter independent of the model.

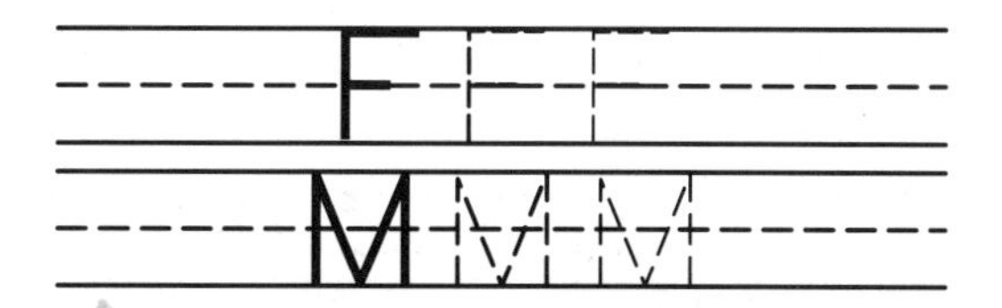

As soon as possible, activities should be provided in which words are used and the writing says something. Copying meaningless letters may result in boredom and negative attitudes toward writing. Also, in copying exercises, the letter or word model should be presented at first on the kind of paper the student uses and be placed on the student's desk. It is more difficult for some students to copy far models (e.g., letters or words written on the chalkboard) than near models because the image of a far model must be transferred through space and from different planes.

Letters that consist entirely of vertical and horizontal strokes (such as *E, F, H, I, L, T, i, l,* and *t*) are learned more easily than letters in which straight and curved lines are combined (such as *b, f, h,* and *p*). Letters with easier strokes may be taught first. The teacher should give more attention to the formation of difficult letter forms. In a study of first graders' errors in the formation of manuscript letters, Lewis and Lewis (1965) made the following observations:

1. Incorrect size was the most common type of error and was seen more often in descender letters (*p, q, y, g,* and *j*).
2. The most frequently reversed letters were *N, d, q,* and *y.*
3. Incorrect relationship of parts occurred most frequently in the letters *k, R, M,* and *m.*
4. Partial omission occurred most frequently in the letters *m, U,* and *I.*
5. Additions often occurred in the letters *q, C, k, m,* and *y.*
6. The most frequently misshaped letter forms were *j, G,* and *J.*

Numerous letters often are reversed, such as *b, d, p, q, s, y,* and *N.* In teaching these letters, the teacher should emphasize the correct beginning point and direction of letters. Students who continue to reverse letters and numbers after the age of 7 or 8 may need direct intervention techniques. As well as receiving immediate corrective feedback followed by practice saying the letter name while tracing and writing it, the student can be instructed to associate the problem letter with another letter that does not cause confusion (e.g., *c* within *d*). In addition to difficulties in formation, some students have problems spacing and aligning manuscript letters. In general, the widest space is left between straight-line letters, and the least amount of space is left between circle letters. Spacing between words equals about the size of one finger or a lowercase *o*, and twice as much space is left between sentences. Poor alignment should be pointed out to the student; however, if the student has extreme difficulty staying on the lines of writing paper, the teacher may choose to provide Right-Line Paper (available from PRO-ED) until the student improves. This paper (both wide- and narrow-rule) has a raised line superimposed on the printed line so that the writer can feel as well as see the base line.

Transitional Writing

The transition from manuscript to cursive writing usually occurs during the second or third grade, after the student has mastered manuscript letters.

However, some controversy exists concerning whether to begin with manuscript or cursive writing. Those who favor manuscript writing (Anderson, 1966; Barbe, Milone, & Wasylyk, 1983; Herrick, 1960) claim that it requires less complex movements and reduces reading problems because most printed pages are in manuscript. In addition, manuscript writing tends to be more legible and has received acceptance in business and commercial contexts. Advocates of cursive writing (Strauss & Lehtinen, 1947) believe that cursive writing results in fewer reversals because of its rhythmic flow and that it helps the student to perceive whole words. Also, transference problems are avoided if writing begins with cursive. Thurber (1983) notes that many students with learning disabilities find it difficult to transfer to cursive writing if they first have learned manuscript writing. However, some educators (Hildreth, 1963; Templin, 1960; Western, 1977) question the need for teaching cursive writing at all and feel that manuscript writing meets the adult needs of speed and legibility. After reviewing research data concerning manuscript versus cursive writing, Graham and Miller (1980) indicate that most evidence supports manuscript instruction; however, the advantages of manuscript writing have yet to be conclusively demonstrated. Because good arguments are presented on all sides, the teacher should assess each individual situation. It may be best to teach students the form of writing used by their peers. Also, many young children want to learn cursive writing because older peers and adults use it. Regardless of the type of writing instruction, the student should be allowed to choose the mode of writing for tests and expressive writing.

Mann et al. (1992) suggest the following method for transitional writing:

1. The word is printed in manuscript.
2. The letters are connected with a dotted line in colored pencil.
3. The student traces over the manuscript letter and the connecting dotted line to form the cursive writing.

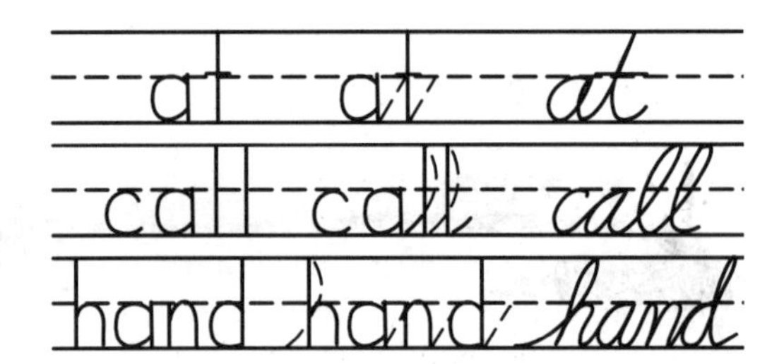

The teacher may begin teaching transitional writing with the easier letters and add more difficult letters one at a time. Certain letters must be taught specifically, such as *b, e, f, k, r, s,* and *z*. Also, when the letter *n* is in the middle or end of a word, enough space must be allowed in front of it for the additional hump needed in the cursive formation of the letter.

Hagin (1983) recommends a simplified handwriting method based on the vertical downstroke rather than the diagonal slant necessary to cursive writing. Manuscript letters are used as a bridge to a simplified writing style with connections between letters made by the natural movement to the next vertical downstroke. Thus, the simplicity of manuscript writing is combined with the speed of cursive writing. In this approach, letter forms are taught through four simple motifs (waves, pearls, wheels, and arrows) that serve as foundations for lowercase letters. After practice at the chalkboard, lessons at the desk include tracing letters on an acetate sheet placed over the printed model, trying to write the letter on the acetate without a model, matching the written letter with the model to determine whether more practice is needed, and providing a permanent record of the letters worked on in that lesson, which later can be compared with previous writing samples during self-evaluation. This approach may be helpful to students who have difficulty learning conventional cursive writing patterns.

Cursive Writing

Instruction in cursive writing usually begins in the second or third grade, depending upon the skill development of the individual student. In cursive writing the strokes are connected, and fine motor coordination is required to perform many precise movements. The basic strokes in cursive writing are the slant stroke (//), understroke (ᴧ/), downstroke (ᵧ/), and overstroke (ᴧ/) (Milone & Wasylyk, 1981). Many of the same techniques used to teach manuscript writing, such as the multisensory approach and fading model, also can be used in cursive writing instruction. The proper slant in cursive writing is achieved by slanting the paper and pulling strokes to the body, as described earlier in the discussion of readiness skills.

Hanover (1983) suggests teaching cursive writing by grouping letters into families based on similar strokes. The letter families include the following:

1. the *e* family (taught first): *e, l, h, f, b, k*
2. the family with a handle to which the next letter is attached: *b, o, v, w*
3. the family that emphasizes the correct formation of hump-shaped letters: *n, s, y*
4. the *c* family: *c, a, d, o, q, g*
5. the hump family: *n, m, v, y, x*
6. the family with tails in the back: *f, q*
7. the family with tails in the front: *g, p, y, z*

Newland (1932) notes that four specific letters—*a, e, r,* and *t*—contribute to a large number of errors in cursive writing. The teacher should give special attention to the proper formation of

TABLE 12.2
Common Illegibilities in Handwriting

a like u	m like n
a like o	n like u
a like ce	o like a
b like li	o like v
be like bl	p like js
b like k	r like n
c like e	r like v
c like a	r like i
d like cl	t like i
e like i	t like l
g like y	u like ee
g like q	u like ei
i like e	w like n
h like li	w like ue
h like k	w like eu
k like ls	x like v
m like w	y like ij

these four letters and also should focus upon the types of errors that result in common illegibilities. Table 12.2 illustrates numerous common illegibilities in forming cursive letters. After students have learned how to form cursive letters accurately, they should be taught to connect letters and to write simple words.

Typewriting and Keyboarding

The typewriter or computer may be a viable alternative for students who have severe fine motor problems or who write very slowly. Polloway and Smith (1992) note that, in addition to simplified motor movements, the advantages of typing include faster speed, the highest degree of legibility, and inherent motivation. Also, the ability to type facilitates the use of computers and word-processing programs, and keyboarding is becoming a basic literacy skill because word processing is a standard method of writing. Selected computer programs available for learning touch-typing and keyboarding include *Kids on Keys* (Spinnaker), *Microtype: The Wonderful World of Paws* (South-Western Publishing), *Stickybear Typing* (Optimum Resource), and *Type!* (Broderbund).

COMMERCIAL HANDWRITING PROGRAMS

Many commercial programs and materials are available to develop or improve handwriting skills. The following selected programs and materials may be helpful to students having difficulty with handwriting.

Better Handwriting for You

Better Handwriting for You, developed by J. K. Noble (published by Noble & Noble), includes a series of eight workbooks and teacher editions. Books 1 and 2 deal with manuscript writing, and Books 3 through 8 present cursive writing. Between Books 2 and 3 is a transitional book that begins with manuscript writing and then introduces cursive writing. Numbers and arrows help teach the sequence and direction of strokes used to write various letters. Students copy models of uppercase and lowercase letters and numbers in the workbooks. The last two books provide devices that allow students to evaluate the quality of their own handwriting. Throughout the program the teacher is provided with instructions on managing left-handed students and determining correct positions for paper and pencil.

Cursive Writing Program

The *Cursive Writing Program* (S. Miller & Engelmann, 1980) consists of 140 developmentally sequenced lessons designed to teach cursive writing to students who have mastered manuscript writing. The program teaches how to form letters, create words, write sentences, and improve writing speed and accuracy. The 20-minute lessons feature a simplified orthography that reduces unnecessary frills, slant arrows to assist in slanting the paper correctly, slant bars to prompt proper spacing, exercises to correct errors, and an emphasis on high-frequency word and letter combinations. Points are awarded following the successful completion of a series of exercises. The materials include a teacher presentation book and a student workbook of practice exercises.

D'Nealian Handwriting

The *D'Nealian Handwriting* program (Thurber, 1987) is designed to simplify handwriting for the readiness student through eighth grade. The forms of most lowercase manuscript letters are the basic forms of the corresponding cursive letters. Each manuscript letter is made with a continuous stroke, except the dotted letters *i* and *j* and the crossed letters *f, t,* and *x*. The transition to cursive writing is simplified because the addition of simple joining strokes is all that is needed for every letter except five (*f, r, s, v,* and *z*). The program includes student workbooks and teacher's editions for each grade level, and alphabet cards and self-sticking alphabet tapes are available.

Handwriting: A Fresh Start

Handwriting: A Fresh Start (Powers & Kaminsky, 1988) is a multisensory remedial program designed to improve cursive writing. The approach links letter forms to guided eye-hand motor skills. Verbal descriptions are paired with letter formations to combine auditory and motor feedback with visual imagery. Horizontal and vertical guidelines (power writing lines) define writing space for proper formation, sizing, and spacing letters. These cues fade gradually in later lessons. Review and reinforcement activities prompt transfer from power writing lines to regular writing lines.

Handwriting: Basic Skills and Application

Handwriting: Basic Skills and Application (Barbe, Lucas, Wasylyk, Hackney, & Braun, 1987) contains a series of nine workbooks for kindergarten through eighth grade. Manuscript is introduced in kindergarten, developed through the second grade, and maintained through all the grades. Primary cursive is introduced in second or third grade and developed in the third and fourth grades, while adult cursive is the focus in the fifth through eighth grades. Letters are introduced systematically: by similarity of stroke in kindergarten through the fourth grade, by size and proportion in the fifth grade, and by rhythmic motion in the sixth grade and up. The elements of legibility are emphasized, and skills can be applied immediately in a practical context. In addition to a teacher's edition for each grade level, there is a supportive materials pack containing such materials as an alphabet wall chart, an evaluation scale, and a peek-through overlay.

SRA Lunchbox Handwriting

SRA Lunchbox Handwriting (produced by SRA) includes two labs for handwriting practice in manuscript and cursive styles for students in kindergarten through fourth grade. Students begin by tracing preletter shapes on plastic overlays, which wipe clean for reuse. Directional dots and arrows show how to complete each stroke. Next, students trace complete letters and then form the letters themselves and compare them with models. Practice includes writing letters, numerals, and sentences. The labs can be used as part of the basic handwriting program or as special aids to individual students. Each lab contains exercise cards, plastic overlays, markers, student progress sheets, and an instruction sheet for the teacher.

DEVELOPMENT OF SPELLING SKILLS

Spelling is the forming of words through the traditional arrangement of letters. Young children developmentally move through stages of invented spelling in which different types of spelling strategies are used. According to Gentry (1982), the five stages include the following characteristics:

Stage 1: *Precommunicative spelling.* The child uses scribbles, letters, and letterlike forms and shows a preference for uppercase letters. There is no understanding of phoneme-grapheme correspondence. This stage is typical of preschoolers, ages 3 through 5.

Stage 2: *Semiphonetic spelling.* The child has some awareness that letters are used to represent sounds and may use abbreviated one-, two-, or three-letter spellings to represent an entire word (e.g., *DA* for *day, LF* for *laugh*). Semiphonetic spellers include 5- and 6-year-old youngsters.

Stage 3: *Phonetic spelling.* The child represents all essential sound features in spelling a word and chooses letters on the basis of sound (e.g., *PEKT* for *peeked, KOM* for *come*). Typically, 6-year-old children are phonetic spellers.

Stage 4: *Transitional spelling.* The child begins to use conventional alternatives for representing sounds and includes a vowel in every syllable (e.g., *AFTERNEWN* for *afternoon, TRUBAL* for *trouble*). Many words are spelled correctly, but words with irregular spellings continue to be misspelled. Transitional spellers generally are around 7 and 8 years old.

Stage 5: Correct spelling. The child spells many words correctly and applies the basic rules of the English orthographic system. The child recognizes when words look incorrect and can consider alternative spellings. Youngsters typically reach this stage by age 8 or 9.

Formal spelling instruction, typically introduced at the beginning of the second grade, facilitates growth in Stage 5. The student extends knowledge of word structure and learns irregular spelling patterns. The ability to spell is essential because it allows one to read written words correctly. In addition, incorrect spelling often results in an unfavorable impression, and the poor speller may be considered uneducated or careless.

The English language presents inconsistent relationships between phonemes (speech sounds) and graphemes (written symbols). There are 26 letters in the alphabet; however, about 44 phonemes are used in English speech. Moreover, there are more than 500 spellings to present the 44 phonemes (Tompkins & Hoskisson, 1991). Thus, differences exist between the spelling of various words and the way the words are pronounced. Many students with learning disabilities have difficulty mastering the regular spelling system, and inconsistent spelling patterns make learning to spell even more complex. Poplin, Gray, Larsen, Banikowski, and Mehring (1980) note that, in general, the spelling skills of students with learning disabilities worsen as they progress through school in relation to the performance of peers without disabilities.

Students who have trouble recognizing words in reading usually have poor spelling skills as well (Carpenter & Miller, 1982; Ekwall & Shanker, 1993). However, some students are able to read words but not spell them. Thus, it appears that spelling a word may be a more difficult task than reading a word. Reading is a *decoding* process in which the reader receives clues (such as context) for word recognition. Spelling is an *encoding* process in which the learner must respond without the benefit of a complete visual stimulus; thus, there are fewer clues. Spelling requires concentration on each letter of every word, while in reading it is not necessary to know the exact spelling of words or to attend to every letter. Some students make the same types of errors in both reading and spelling. For example, a phonetic speller may mispronounce phonetically irregular words when reading. In addition, a student who lacks phonetic word-attack skills in reading may not be able to spell because of poor phonetic skills. Whiting and Jarrico (1980) verified that normal students spell with an accuracy from 70% to 100% at grade level and found that the normal reader tends to make spelling errors that are readable, good phonetic equivalents of the dictated word.

To spell a word correctly, the student must apply various abilities including being able to read the word, possess knowledge and skill in certain relationships of phonics and structural analysis, apply phonics generalizations, visualize the appearance of the word, retrieve the word from memory, and use the motor capability to write the word. Spelling errors may result from confused recall of spelling rules (*takeing* for *taking*) or be related to insertion of unneeded letters (*umberella* for *umbrella*), omission of needed letters (*famly* for *family*), substitution of letters (*kome* for *come*), phonetic spelling of irregular words (*laf* for *laugh*), directional confusion (*was* for *saw*), vowels in unaccented syllables (*cottin* for *cotton*), *r*-controlled vowels (*dert* for *dirt*), letter orientation confusion (*doy* for *boy*), or reversed letter sequences (*aminals* for *animals*) (Poteet, 1980). Thus, spelling difficulties may stem from problems in visual memory, auditory memory, auditory and visual discrimination, attention deficits, or motor skills.

ASSESSMENT OF SPELLING SKILLS

A variety of techniques assess the student's spelling performance. Also, specific patterns of spelling errors can be pinpointed. Spelling assessment can include standardized and criterion-referenced tests as well as informal assessment techniques. In choosing spelling assessment techniques, the teacher should know what the test measures and its limitations, supplement the test when possible with other measures, and use informal evaluation techniques to gain specific information for planning a remedial program.

Standardized and Criterion-Referenced Tests

Achievement tests that contain spelling subtests, such as the *Peabody Individual Achievement Test—Revised* (Markwardt, 1989) and the *Wide Range Achievement Test—3* (Wilkinson, 1993), are designed to provide an estimate of the student's general spelling ability. On achievement tests, spelling is assessed by two procedures: recall and recognition. On tests using recall, the student must write words presented orally and used in sentences. On tests using recognition, the student is required to select the correctly spelled word from several choices. Recall items are related to the writing stage of the writing process, whereas recognition items are essentially proofreading and are related to the editing stage (McLoughlin & Lewis, 1994). Achievement tests yield a single score that is compared with the standardized norms and converted to a grade-equivalent score. Thus, achievement tests provide a general survey measure, and they may be useful for identifying students who need corrective instruction and further diagnosis. In contrast, diagnostic tests provide detailed information about a student's performance in various spelling skills. These tests are aimed at determining the student's strengths and weaknesses.

Whereas standardized norm-referenced tests (achievement and diagnostic) *compare* a student's performance with the scores of those in the norm population, criterion-referenced tests *describe* performance in terms of fixed criteria. The teacher can use criterion-referenced spelling tests to determine whether a student has mastered specific spelling instructional objectives (e.g., *wh* spelling, contractions, or vocational words). The teacher determines what skills the student has learned and what skills still must be taught. Also, an objective measure of progress is provided as the student moves from task to task and current performance is compared with previous performance. Table 12.3 describes several diagnostic and criterion-referenced spelling tests.

Informal Assessment Techniques

The teacher can obtain diagnostic information through structured observation and evaluation of the student's attitudes, written work, and oral responses. Attitudes toward spelling and willingness to use a dictionary may be noted, as well as the student's work habits and ability to handle frustration. Analysis of written work can provide information about handwriting problems that are causing errors (such as letter forms or spacing), specific types of errors, range of the student's vocabulary, and knowledge of spelling rules. In addition, the teacher should observe the student's oral responses and note problems in pronunciation, articulation, and dialect. Oral spelling responses also can indicate phonics ability and method of spelling words orally—for example, as units, by letter, by digraphs, or by syllables. The following informal assessment techniques are discussed: dictated spelling test, informal spelling inventory, curriculum-based measurement, spelling error analysis, cloze procedure, probes, and modality testing.

Dictated Spelling Test. The dictated spelling test is a commonly used procedure for assessing various skills in spelling and determining spelling grade level. Words can be selected from any graded word list; the student's performance indicates the spelling grade level. Stephens, Hartman, and Lucas (1982) present sample assessment tasks that use dictated word lists of increasing difficulty. The instructional level is determined when the student achieves 70% to 90% accuracy. Dictated word lists also can assess skills in areas such as phoneme-grapheme

TABLE 12.3
Diagnostic and Criterion-Referenced Spelling Tests

Diagnostic Tests

Diagnostic Spelling Potential Test (Arena, 1981)

The test measures traditional spelling, word recognition, visual recognition, and auditory-visual recognition. The four subtests of 90 items assess students age 7 through adult and take 25 to 40 minutes. Raw scores from each subtest can be converted to standard scores, percentiles, and grade ratings.

Gates-Russell Spelling Diagnostic Test (Gates & Russell, 1937)

The subtests measure nine areas: spelling words orally; word pronunciation; giving letters for letter sounds; spelling one syllable; spelling two syllables; word reversals; spelling attack; auditory discrimination; and effectiveness of visual, auditory, kinesthetic, or combined methods of study. A grade-level score is obtained for performance in each area.

Test of Written Spelling—3 (Larsen & Hammill, 1994)

This dictated word test for students in 1st through 12th grade consists of 100 words chosen from 10 basal spelling series. The test assesses the student's ability to spell words that have readily predictable spellings in sound-letter patterns as well as words whose spellings are less predictable (spelling demons). The test can be administered individually or to small groups of students in about 20 minutes and yields standard scores, percentiles, spelling ages, and grade equivalents.

Criterion-Referenced Tests

Brigance Diagnostic Comprehensive Inventory of Basic Skills Brigance, 1983)

The test contains a section that assesses spelling skills of students whose achievement is at the kindergarten through ninth-grade level. The skill area is arranged in a developmental and sequential hierarchy. Tests include spelling dictation grade placement, initial consonants, initial clusters, suffixes, and prefixes. Also, the reference skills section contains a test on the skill of dictionary use. The instructional objectives related to each test are defined clearly. In addition to determining the student's level of achievement, the results can help the teacher develop individualized programs.

Diagnostic Spelling Test (Kottmeyer, 1970)

The test measures specific phonics and structural spelling elements (e.g., doubled final consonants, nonphonetic spelling, and *th* spelling). The examiner says a word and a sentence using the word, and the student is required to write the word. One test is for students in second and third grades; another test is for students in fourth grade and above. The 32-item tests are designed so that each item measures a particular spelling element. A grade score is computed from the total number of correct spellings. Specific information on skills not yet mastered is obtained through an analysis of the student's errors.

The Spellmaster Assessment and Teaching System (Greenbaum, 1987)

This series of nonstandardized, criterion-referenced tests includes eight diagnostic tests for measuring the spelling of phonetically regular words, eight irregular-words tests, eight homophone (homonym) tests, and entry-level tests. The tests pinpoint the precise strategies students use and the errors they make when spelling words.

---

association (*like, bike, hike*), spelling generalizations (*stories, cries, tries*), homonyms (*pain, pane; pear, pair*), and functional words (*menu, restaurant, cashier*).

The student's proficiency in spelling frequently used words and words that often are misspelled also can be determined. Horn (1926), after studying 10,000 words, reports that 10 words account for 25% of all words used. In order of most frequent to least frequent, these words include: *I, the, and, to, a, you, of, in, we,* and *for.* He also notes that 100 words account for 65% of the words written by adults. In addition, Kuska, Webster, and Elford (1964) present a list of commonly misspelled words that are linguistically irregular and do not follow spelling rules—for example, *ache, fasten, nickel, scratch,* and *double.*

Informal Spelling Inventory. An informal spelling inventory (ISI) can be used to determine the student's approximate grade level in spelling achievement. An ISI can be constructed by selecting a sample of words from spelling books in a basal spelling series (Mann et al., 1992). About 15 words should be chosen from the first-grade book and 20 words from each book for second through eighth grade. Random selection is obtained by dividing the total number of words at each level by 20. For example, 300 words at each level divided by 20 equals 15; therefore, every 15th word should be included in the ISI. For students in fourth grade and below, testing should begin with the first-level words. For students in fifth grade and above, assessment should start with words at the third level. The test is administered in a dictated-word format. The teacher says the word, uses it in a sentence, and repeats the word. Some students prefer that only the word be given (without a sentence), and M. R. Shinn, Tindal, and Stein (1988) suggest that a 7-second interval between words is sufficient. Testing ends when the student responds incorrectly to six consecutive words. The achievement level is the highest level at which the student responds correctly to 90% to 100% of the items, and the instructional level is the highest level at which the student scores 75% to 89% correct. Various errors made on the ISI can be analyzed to provide additional diagnostic information.

Curriculum-Based Measurement. In curriculum-based measurement of spelling skills, rate samples on words from a given spelling curriculum are used to measure the student's spelling skills. The assessment process begins with the selection of appropriate word lists. Tindal and Marston (1990) note that the word lists can reflect a phonic-regularity base (i.e., words with consistency or generalizability of the grapheme/phoneme relationships) or a frequency base (i.e., words that appear frequently in writing). Wesson (1987) suggests that the words can be from a given spelling curriculum level or from a new-words list for a particular reading series. The words can be selected randomly by printing all words in the test item pool on index cards, shuffling the cards before each measurement, and randomly picking cards to present during the measurement task.

The type of response to the spelling task can be either a selection response or a production response (Tindal & Marston, 1990). In word or sentence editing, an incorrectly spelled word is underlined or a blank space representing a specific word is presented in a phrase, and the student must select the correct word from several options to replace the underlined word or to fill in the blank. When the teacher orally presents words from a list, the student must produce the spelling of the word during the dictation task. The teacher dictates words for 2 minutes by saying each word twice and using homonyms in a sentence. There should be a 7-second interval between words for students in fourth through eighth grade and 10-second intervals for younger students and those with fine motor difficulties. When a production response is required, scoring can be computed in terms of number of words spelled correctly or number of letters in correct sequence. The latter strategy focuses on successive pairs of letters, and the blank spaces preceding the first letter and following the last letter are included in counting the pairs of letter sequences. Thus, for a word spelled correctly, the number of correct letter sequences will be one more than there are letters in the word. Deno, Mirkin, and Wesson (1984) suggest that the long-range goal should be 60 to 80 correct letter sequences for students in the first and second grades and 80 to 140 correct letter sequences for students in third through sixth grade. An individualized analysis of errors can be helpful in establishing appropriate instruction.

The teacher can test all students in a grade or class and develop a plot of the entire group (see Chapter 8 for guidelines for developing a box plot of a group). Students who are performing poorly in spelling (i.e., more than one standard deviation below the mean for the group) can be identified, and instructional planning decisions can be made. A graph of a student's weekly performance can be used to evaluate spelling instruction.

Spelling Error Analysis. A *spelling error analysis* chart can be used to provide a profile of spelling strengths and weaknesses. Each time the student makes a specific error, it is recorded on the chart. Spelling errors can be analyzed in written compositions as well as on dictated tests. Taylor and Kidder (1988) examined the misspellings of first- through eighth-grade students and found that the most frequent spelling error was deleting letters in words (e.g., *hoping* for *hopping; spose* for *suppose*). Selected spelling errors may include spelling the word as it sounds (*doter* for *daughter*), omitting a letter that is pronounced (*aross* for *across*), using the wrong vowel digraph (*speach* for *speech*), reversing letters in words (*croner* for *corner*), using an incorrect vowel (*jab* for *job; anemals* for *animals*), using the wrong homonym for the meaning intended (*peace* for *piece*), inserting an unneeded letter (*ulgly* for *ugly*), doubling a consonant unnecessarily (*untill* for *until*), and omitting a silent letter (*bome* for *bomb*) (Hitchcock, 1989). Moreover, Edgington (1967) suggests that the following specific types of errors should be noted on a spelling error analysis chart: addition of extra letters; omission of needed letters; reversals of whole words, consonant order, or syllables; errors resulting from a student's mispronunciation or dialect; and phonetic spelling of nonphonetic words. Misspellings also can be categorized as phonetic or nonphonetic. Phonetic misspellings occur when the student attempts to use the rules of phonics to spell a word, but either the student applies the rule incorrectly or the word does not adhere to those rules, whereas nonphonetic spellings do not appear to be based on the application of phonics rules (McLoughlin & Lewis, 1994). Burns (1980) notes that most errors occur in vowels in midsyllables of words; 67% of the errors result from substitution or omission of letters, and 20% result from addition, insertion, or transposition of letters. Through a careful analysis of spelling errors, the teacher can focus on consistent patterns of errors and plan appropriate instruction.

Cloze Procedure. The cloze procedure is a visual means of testing spelling. The student may be required to complete a sentence by writing the correct response in the blank; for example, "The opposite of down is _____" (*up*). In addition, the student may be asked to complete a word or supply missing letters: "The clouds are in the s_____" (*sky*), or "Please give me a glass of w_t_r" (*water*). Cartwright (1969) notes that the cloze procedure is useful especially in evaluating the student's knowledge of spelling generalizations. In this case, the student is required to fill in blanks pertaining to a rule, such as doubling the final consonant before adding *ing*; for example, "The man was run_____ to catch the bus" (*ning*). A multiple-choice format also may be used; for example, "Mary needed _______ to pay for her lunch" (*munny, mony, money,* or *monie*). The cloze procedure, which is visual, can be used effectively along with the auditory dictated spelling test.

Probes. Spelling skills can be assessed through the use of probe sheets. The student works on the probe sheet for 1 minute, and the teacher records the rate of correct and incorrect responses and notes any error patterns. The probe task (e.g., see picture—write word, see words—write contractions, hear word—write word, or see partial word—write missing letter) may be administered several times to give the teacher a reliable index of how well the student can perform. Starlin and Starlin (1973) suggest a proficiency rate for students in kindergarten through second grade of 30 to 50 correct letters per minute with two or fewer errors at the independent level and 15 to 29 correct letters with three to seven errors at the instructional level. For third grade through adult, the independent

TABLE 12.4
Spelling Competencies

Competency	Subareas
Auditory discrimination	Ability to discriminate consonant sounds and vowel sounds and use correct word pronunciation
Consonants	Knowledge of consonants in initial, final, and medial positions in words and knowledge of consonant blends
Phonograms	Ability to identify phonograms in initial, medial, and final positions in words and ability to identify word phonograms
Plurals	Ability to form a plural by adding *s,* adding *es,* changing *f* to *v,* making medial changes, and knowledge of exceptions
Syllabication	Ability to divide words into syllables
Structural elements	Knowledge of root words, prefixes, and suffixes
Ending changes	Ability to change ending of words that end in final *e,* final *y,* and final consonants
Vowel digraphs and diphthongs	Ability to spell words in which a vowel digraph forms one sound (*ai, ea, ay, ei, ie*) or a diphthong forms a blend (*oi, ou, ow*)
Silent *e*	Knowledge of single-syllable words that end in silent *e*

level is 50 to 70 correct letters per minute with two or fewer errors, and the instructional level is 25 to 49 correct letters with three to seven errors. In addition, the teacher can collect data from students who are achieving satisfactorily and use their rates for comparison when assessing a student with spelling difficulties.

Modality Testing. Sensory modality preference testing, described by Westerman (1971), assesses the student's performance through combinations of five input/output channels:

1. *Auditory-vocal:* The teacher spells the word aloud, and the student orally spells the word.
2. *Auditory-motor:* The teacher spells the word aloud, and the student writes the word on paper.
3. *Visual-vocal:* The teacher shows the word on a flash card, and the student spells the word aloud.
4. *Visual-motor:* The teacher shows the word on a flash card, and the student writes the word on paper.
5. *Multisensory combination channel:* The teacher shows the word on a flash card and spells it aloud, and the student spells the word aloud and writes it on paper.

In modality testing, 40 unknown words are divided into five sets of eight words each. Two words are taught in each of the five modalities for 4 consecutive days, and the student is tested on a written dictation spelling test at the end of each day. On the 5th day the student is tested on all 40 words. The number of correct responses in each modality indicates whether the student shows a pattern of preference among modalities. This kind of assessment information is useful in planning individualized instruction. For example, students with an auditory-motor preference may learn new spelling words by using a tape recorder and writing each word after hearing it. Similarly, visual learners should be provided with many opportunities to see the word.

TEACHING SPELLING SKILLS

Stephens (1977) notes that nine spelling competencies enable the student to be an effective speller. These nine skills and corresponding subareas are presented in Table 12.4. Ekwall and

Shanker (1993) note that the words most frequently misspelled by nearly all students are those words that are the exceptions to the rules of phonics. They suggest that it may be most helpful to teach students to spell correctly those words that appear most frequently in writing. Moreover, spelling should be emphasized in all subject matter and viewed as a skill that will enable students to be more effective writers.

Vallecorsa, Zigmond, and Henderson (1985) note that educators may need to improve their knowledge of validated methods for teaching spelling to be able to use supported techniques routinely. In a research review of spelling instruction for students with learning disabilities, McNaughton, Hughes, and Clark (1994) suggest that the following strategies may enhance learning of spelling skills: limiting the number of new vocabulary words introduced each day, providing opportunities for self-directed and peer-assisted instruction, directing students to name letters aloud as they are practiced, including instruction in morphemic analysis, providing immediate error imitation and correction, using motivating reinforcers, and providing periodic retesting and review. The following teaching methods and strategies provide alternatives for teaching spelling skills to students with spelling difficulties.

Rule-Based Instruction

Spelling instruction can be based on teaching rules and generalizations. After learning a general spelling rule, the student is able to use it with unfamiliar words. These rules can apply to instruction using both linguistics and phonics.

The linguistic approach to teaching spelling is based on the idea that there is regularity in phoneme/grapheme correspondence. This method stresses the systematic nature of spelling patterns. Spelling rules, generalizations, and patterns are taught that apply to whole words. Spelling words are selected according to their particular linguistic pattern—for example, *cool, fool, pool;* or *hitting, running, batting.*

The phonics approach to teaching spelling stresses phoneme-grapheme relationships within parts of words. The student learns to associate a sound with a particular letter or combination of letters. Thus, phonetic rules can help the student determine how sounds should be spelled. Through phonics instruction the student can learn to spell words according to syllables. The student breaks the word into recognizable sound elements, pronounces each syllable, and then writes the letter or letters that represent each sound.

In rule-based instruction (in both linguistics and phonics), only spelling rules and generalizations that apply to a large number of words and have few exceptions should be taught. The general rule should be applicable more than 75% of the time. Spelling rules can be taught by guiding the student to discover rules and generalizations independently. After analyzing several words that share a common linguistic property, the student is asked to apply the rule to unfamiliar words. After the student can generalize, exceptions to the rules can be discussed. The student should be taught that rules are not steadfast and that some words do not conform to spelling rules.

Although phonetic approaches to teaching spelling are used frequently, Hanna, Hodges, and Hanna (1971) note that only about 50% of spellings follow regular phonetic rules. Dixon (1991) suggests that incorporating morphological analysis into spelling instruction potentially may reduce misspellings due to phonetic irregularities and, thus, facilitate students' problem-solving behavior through focusing on both phonetic and morphemic generalization.

Multisensory Approach

Spelling involves skills in the visual, auditory, and motor sensory modalities. The student must be able to exhibit visual and auditory recognition and discrimination of the letters of the alphabet and must have motor control to write the word. Hodges (1966) notes that "a child who has learned to spell a word by the use of the senses of hearing, sight, and touch is in a good position to recall the spelling of that word when he needs it in his writing because any or all the sensory modes can elicit his memory of it" (p. 39).

Fernald's (1943, 1988) multisensory approach involves four sensory modalities: visual, auditory, kinesthetic, and tactile (VAKT). In this approach, Fernald focuses on the following areas as being important in learning to spell: clear perception of word form, development of a distinct visual image of the word, and habit formation through repetition of writing until the motor pattern is automatic. The following steps are included in learning to spell a new word:

1. The teacher writes and says a word while the student watches and listens.
2. The student traces the word with a finger while simultaneously saying the word. Then the student copies or writes the word while saying it. Emphasis is placed on careful pronunciation, with each syllable of the word dragged out slowly as it is traced or written.
3. Next, the word is written from memory. If it is incorrect, the second step is repeated. If the word is correct, it is put in a file box. Later the words in the file box are used in stories.
4. At later stages the tracing method for learning is not always needed. The student may learn the word by observing the teacher write and say it and then by writing and saying it alone. As progress is made, the student may learn the word by looking at it in print and writing it and, finally, merely by looking at it.

The Gillingham method (Gillingham & Stillman, 1970) uses an alphabetic system with repetition and drill. Letter-sound correspondences are taught using a multisensory approach—visual, auditory, and kinesthetic. Words introduced initially include only those with consistent sound-symbol correspondences. The student is given experience reading and spelling one-syllable words as well as detached regularly spelled syllables. Words of more than one syllable are learned syllable-by-syllable (e.g., *Sep tem ber*). Words whose spellings are not entirely consistent are sequenced carefully according to structural characteristics, and words following a pattern are grouped. The technique used in studying spelling words is called simultaneous oral spelling. When the teacher says a spelling word, the student repeats the word, names the letters, writes the letters while saying them aloud, and reads the written word. Letter names rather than sounds are used in this practice so that the technique can be applied to nonphonetic words. Sentence and story writing is introduced after the student is able to write any three-letter, phonetically pure word. Nonphonetic words are taught through drill. Thus, the Gillingham method differs from the Fernald (1943, 1988) approach in two major respects: words to be taught are selected carefully and sequenced or selected as needed for writing rather than being of the student's own choosing, and instruction focuses on individual letters and sounds rather than on whole words. *How to Teach Spelling* (available from Educators Publishing Service) is a comprehensive resource manual based on the Gillingham approach to reading and spelling.

Kearney and Drabman (1993) used a modified write-say spelling intervention designed to provide immediate feedback to the visual and auditory modalities of students with learning disabilities. Spelling accuracy of the students significantly increased through the use of the following procedure:

Day 1: Students receive the spelling word list and are asked to study on their own.

Day 2: Following a test on the spelling word list and verbal teacher feedback on performance, students simultaneously say aloud and write the correct spelling (letter-by-letter) of any incorrectly spelled word five times.

Day 3: The procedure is repeated, except students simultaneously correctly rewrite and restate incorrectly spelled words 10 consecutive times.

Day 4: The procedure is repeated, except students simultaneously correctly rewrite and restate incorrectly spelled words 15 consecutive times.

Day 5: To assess spelling accuracy, students write words from the list verbally presented by the teacher.

Another multisensory approach that features repetition is the cover-and-write method. The student is taught to spell words through the following steps:

1. The student looks at the word and says it.
2. The student writes the word twice while looking at it.
3. The student covers the word and writes it again.
4. The student checks the spelling by looking at it.

The steps are repeated with the student writing the word as many as three times while looking at it, covering the word, writing it, and checking the spelling.

Test-Study-Test Technique

The test-study-test approach to teaching spelling is used frequently. The student is given a pretest at the beginning of each unit of study. The words the student misspells on the pretest become the study list. After instruction, another test determines the degree of mastery. A progress chart is kept, and words missed on the second test are added to the list of words for the following unit of study.

The study-test plan is similar to the test-study-test approach, except that it does not include a pretest. The student's study list consists of all of the words in the unit of study. The student is tested after completing various spelling activities. Petty (1966) and Stephens et al. (1982) note that the test-study-test method obtains better spelling results than the study-test approach. The pretest helps to identify words that the student already knows how to spell, and with the elimination of these words, the student can focus on the unknown words.

In addition, some studies indicate that added reinforcement procedures can encourage students to study harder to obtain higher test scores. For example, Lovitt, Guppy, and Blattner (1969) noted a substantial increase in the number of perfect spelling papers when students were given the test 4 days a week (Tuesday through Friday) and, after receiving 100% on that week's word list, were excused from spelling for the rest of the week and given free time. Also, Sidman (1979) used group and individual reinforcement contingencies with middle school students. Accuracy increased when free time was provided as a reward for improved test scores. The increase was greater during group contingency conditions.

Graham and Voth (1990) recommend daily testing on new and previously introduced words from a spelling unit, as well as periodic maintenance checks to ensure mastery or to identify words that need to be reincorporated into the instructional sequence. In addition, they suggest that the tests should be corrected, with supervision, by the students themselves. Thus, the students receive immediate feedback about their efforts to learn to spell. Because some students spell the words correctly on the test but misspell them in their writing, the teacher periodically should collect samples of student writing to determine whether the students are applying in their writing what they have learned through spelling instruction. To improve accuracy and fluency, practice on misspelled words should include a variety of high-interest activities and games. In addition, spelling performance can be improved through the use of peer tutoring or cooperative learning arrangements.

Study Strategies. Study techniques provide a structured format for the independent study of spelling words and help students with learning disabilities to organize their spelling study. Graham and Freeman (1986) found that students with learning disabilities who were trained to use an efficient study strategy were able to recall immediately the correct spelling of more words than were students who were allowed to choose their own methods for studying unknown spelling words. The study strategy included the following steps:

1. Say the word.
2. Write and say the word.
3. Check the word by comparing it with a model.
4. Trace and say the word.
5. Write the word from memory and check.
6. Repeat the first five steps.

Moreover, Foster and Torgesen (1983) found that directed study improved the long-term retention of spelling words in students with learning disabilities who had average short-term memory; however, students who had short-term memory deficits continued to experience difficulty in the acquisition of spelling words.

Another approach to help students with learning disabilities facilitate their memory of spelling words is the use of visual mnemonics. Greene (1994) suggests that visual mnemonic stimuli can be incorporated into the student's spelling list or put on flash cards with the mnemonic word on one side and the nonmnemonic form of the word on the other side. For example, the word *look* is presented with the two eyes drawn (L👁👁K) and *great* has the *e* circled and slashed to indicate that it is silent (g r ⓔ a t). With eyes closed, the student visualizes the word, attempts to see the mnemonic aide presented in the word, and then writes the word from memory. Moreover, the student can generate associations to facilitate recall of correct spellings (e.g., princi*pal* is your *pal*, de*ss*ert is *s*omething *s*weet).

When structural word analysis, syllable rules, and spelling patterns are taught, Wong (1986) suggests that the student use the following self-questioning strategy:

1. Do I know this word?
2. How many syllables do I hear in this word? (Write down the number of syllables.)
3. I will write the word the way I think it is spelled.
4. Do I have the right number of syllables?
5. Is there any part of the word that I am not sure how to spell? (If so, underline that part and try spelling the word again.)
6. Does the word look right to me? (If not, underline the questionable part of the word and write it again. Listen to the word to find any missing syllables.)
7. When I finish spelling, I will tell myself that I have worked hard.

Finally, individual and classwide peer tutoring can be a viable instructional alternative to meet the need of intensive one-to-one practice with spelling words. When the tutoring sessions include structured lessons, peers can provide direct, individual instruction.

Fixed and Flow Word Lists

Spelling words frequently are presented and taught in fixed word lists. Generally, a new list of words is assigned each week. The words may be either somewhat unfamiliar or completely unknown to the students. Usually a test on each list is given on Friday. This method seldom results in spelling mastery for all students because misspelled words on the test usually are ignored or left for the students to practice independently. Another procedure using fixed word lists is to have students practice the words at their own rate until they are able to spell all of them correctly on a certain number of tests.

On a flow list of spelling words, words are dropped from each student's list upon mastery (e.g., spelled correctly on 2 consecutive days), and then a new (unpracticed) word is added. Thus, the list is individualized, and the student does not spend time practicing known words. McGuigan (1975) developed a teaching procedure, the Add-a-Word Program, which uses flow word lists. McGuigan found that students ages 7 to 13 and adults learned words more quickly with add-a-word lists than with fixed lists and also showed similar or superior retention of learned words.

Graham and Voth (1990) emphasize that the spelling words taught to students with learning disabilities initially should be limited to high-frequency words and misspelled words from their writing. They recommend that weekly spelling lists be limited to 6 to 12 words (emphasizing a common structural element, if possible), and that 2 or 3 words from the list be introduced daily and practiced until the entire set of words is mastered. Likewise, Burns and Broman (1983) recommend presentation of only 5 to 10 words per week to poor spellers (20 words per week may be presented to adequate spellers). In a study of spelling performance of students with learning disabilities, Bryant, Drabin, and Gettinger (1981) found that a higher failure rate and greater variance in performance may occur when 3 or more new words are presented each day. They suggest that 7 to 8 new spelling words per week may be an appropriate number for these students.

MacArthur and Graham (1987) note that students with learning disabilities incorrectly spell 10% to 20% of the words they write. Thus, Graham, Harris, and Loynachan (1994) developed the Spelling for Writing list of 335 words, ordered from first- through third-grade level. The list includes words students use most often when writing, many of which are "spelling demons" and commonly misspelled words.

Imitation Methods

Stowitschek and Jobes (1977) present a method of spelling instruction that involves imitation. It is designed for students who have failed repeatedly to learn to spell through traditional procedures. The teacher provides an oral and written model of the spelling word, and the student is required to imitate the model by spelling the word aloud and writing it. The student receives immediate feedback and praise for correct responses. Incorrect responses are followed by retraining. The procedure is repeated until the student can spell and write the word without models or prompts. A spelling probe is administered after each training session to determine which words have been mastered and to check retention of learned words.

Kauffman, Hallahan, Haas, Brame, and Boren (1978) tested the effectiveness of showing the student a correct model of a spelling word as opposed to first providing a written imitation of the student's spelling error and then showing the correct model. Kauffman et al. found that including the imitation of the student's error was more effective, especially for nonphonetic words. Kauffman et al. suggest that imitation can be useful particularly in teaching words that do not follow regular phonetic rules—words for which the student must use visual memory. However, Brown (1988) conducted a series of experiments and found that exposures to incorrect spellings can interfere with subsequent spelling accuracy.

Additional Considerations

Different types of correctional procedures should be used with various kinds of spelling errors. Visual image should be emphasized with a student who omits silent letters or misspells phonologically irregular words, whereas incorrect spelling of homonyms indicates a need to stress word meanings. Also, words the student misspells in written compositions may be included in the student's spelling program. This can be motivating because the need to learn to spell those words is apparent.

Spelling also may be taught and reinforced throughout the language arts curriculum. One way to improve spelling is through word study in reading (Templeton, 1986). In oral reading the student gives close attention to the sounds of the entire word. In addition, reading gives the student the meanings of words and thus increases interest in them. The student learns the correct usage of words in sentences and can determine whether the word is written correctly. Thus, learning to spell can accompany learning to read, and a program that stresses both skills may be both effective and motivating. As discussed in Chapter 13, the language experience approach and the whole language approach incorporate reading and spelling. T. K. Shinn (1982) stresses that no student should be forced to learn to spell words that he or she cannot read and understand. Otherwise, the student really is memorizing a nonmeaningful series of letters that will not be retained. Thus, spelling lists should be produced from the student's reading vocabulary. Moreover, to facilitate maintenance and generalization, the student should be encouraged to use learned spelling words frequently in writing.

Training in dictionary usage also should be included in the spelling program. Dictionaries help the student become more independent in locating spellings and provide such information as syllabication, meaning, pronunciation, synonyms, and homonyms. Picture dictionaries can be used in the primary grades. Beginning in the fourth grade, special practice in using the dictionary often is included in the curriculum, and the use of dictionaries may be encouraged during writing tasks. When the correct spelling of a word is not known, the student should predict possible spellings for the word by identifying root words and affixes, considering related words, and determining the sounds in the word. Then the student can check the predicted spelling by consulting a dictionary. *The Dictionary of Essential English* (available from American Guidance Service) contains 5,000 frequently used and essential words and provides short, clearly written definitions as well as sample phrases and definitions showing proper word usage.

In teaching spelling skills at the secondary level, the teacher should help the adolescent understand the social and practical significance of correct spelling. For example, employers place value on accurate spelling on job applications. The student's own interests and various areas of study provide new words whose spellings must be learned. Vocational words also can be emphasized. At the secondary level it may be best to teach spelling in conjunction with other activities rather than to use class time solely for spelling instruction. Practice in reading and other learning activities can help the adolescent learn to spell. Success in spelling has increased in importance with the finding that students' beliefs about their efficacy as spellers may affect not only their spelling performance but their writing performance as well (Rankin, Bruning, Timme, & Katkanant, 1993). Finally, strategies to compensate for poor spelling should be taught to students whose spelling problems may affect their grades in content areas. For example, the teacher can provide such students with a spelling checker, which contains frequently used words and words they often misspell. The *Speaking Ace* (produced by Franklin Learning Resources) pronounces, verifies, and corrects the spelling of over 80,000 words.

COMMERCIAL SPELLING PROGRAMS

The following selected basic developmental programs and corrective materials for spelling instruction may be helpful with students who have spelling difficulties. Spelling calculators, spelling games, and spelling reference books also are available from several producers.

Corrective Spelling Through Morphographs

Corrective Spelling Through Morphographs (Dixon & Engelmann, 1980) is an intensive 1-year program for fourth-grade through adult students. The program includes 140 twenty-minute lessons that cover more than 12,000 words, including problem words. The student is taught basic units of meaning in written language (morphographs) that always are spelled according to specific rules. Thus, the student learns analytic techniques and generalizable rules that can be applied to words not in the program. Also available is a book of blackline masters, *Crossword Puzzles for Corrective Spelling Through Morphographs*, which includes puzzles correlated with the words listed in the review lessons of the program.

Instant Spelling Words for Writing

Instant Spelling Words for Writing, developed by R. G. Forest and R. A. Sitton (published by

Curriculum Associates), is an eight-level series designed for writers of all ages (first grade through adult) who have difficulty spelling and proofreading. The series focuses on 1,500 high-frequency words, which cover 90% of all words used in writing. All spelling words are introduced as whole words in list form, and students practice writing each word at least 10 times in a variety of high-interest exercises. Visual imagery is emphasized through activities involving configuration of word shapes and visual discrimination. The program teaches a multimodality word-study procedure and uses the self-corrected test-study-test method. The last exercise in every lesson is a structured writing activity. Using a total language approach, the review lessons and optional extension activities provide language arts exercises that integrate spelling with listening, speaking, reading, writing, and thinking.

Speed Spelling 1 and *2*

This tutorial, phonetically based spelling program (published by PRO-ED) is designed for students of any age who have not mastered 1st- through 6th-grade spelling skills (Level 1) or 6th- through 12th-grade spelling skills (Level 2). *Speed Spelling 1* focuses on increasing speed and accuracy through a systematic development of sound-to-letter correspondence, while *Speed Spelling 2* teaches irregular spellings. Both programs include lessons in word reading, word writing, and sentence writing, and branching instructions are given for students who may need additional help. One-to-one instruction is given, and each session takes about 20 minutes.

Spelling Mastery

Spelling Mastery (Dixon, Engelmann, Meier, Steely, & Wells, 1989) is a six-level basal spelling series designed to teach spelling and strategies to students in first through sixth grade. The series begins with phonemic (sound-symbol) and whole-word strategies and then shifts to morphemic (meaning-symbol) strategies. The program emphasizes learning to spell by generalization rather than memorization, and the 20-minute daily lessons can be used with an entire class or with small groups.

Stetson Spelling Program

The *Stetson Spelling Program* (Stetson, 1988) introduces the 3,000 words most frequently used in writing, which account for 97% of the total words written by the average adult. The program uses effective teaching and learning strategies including pretesting, immediate feedback and self-correction, visual imagery of the whole word, spelling clusters, mnemonics, and visual memory. The 230 lessons each contain 10 to 16 words, and direct instruction is used to present a five-step spelling drill on each word. Three blackline masters books each include 1,000 words as well as student support materials such as three-column self-corrected test forms.

Target: Spelling

This series of six consumable books (published by Steck-Vaughn) is designed to teach spelling to students with learning problems in first through seventh grade. A systematic, highly ordered format is used in which 1,260 words are presented sequentially and with constant reinforcement throughout the six books. Students are asked to learn only six new words per week, and learning experiences to ensure mastery include activities such as word shapes, word search, visual discrimination, recognition in context, matching words with pictures, sound blending, rhyming, and supplying missing letters.

COMPUTER SOFTWARE PROGRAMS IN SPELLING

Microcomputer software can be used effectively to give students additional learning opportunities to improve or enrich their spelling skills. Many students with learning disabilities prefer to practice spelling words at a computer. Gordon, Vaughn, and Schumm (1993) report that computer-assisted instruction can develop positive attitudes toward spelling drill and practice, decrease spelling errors, promote individualized study strategies, and enhance spelling performance when used with time-delay procedures. Software programs can emphasize awareness of word structure and spelling strategies as well as use time-delay, voice simulation, and sound effects. In addition, to aid in writing activities, some software programs offer a built-in spelling scanner that checks for misspelled words or typographical errors according to a predetermined file of common words. Hasselbring and Goin (1989) recommend that instructional computer programs in spelling should require the use of long-term memory, be limited in the size of the practice set of words, require practice spread over several different times, and emphasize speed as well as accuracy. The following computer programs are described to give examples of types of software that are available to reinforce spelling skills.

Spell It 3

Spell It 3 (produced by Davidson) is designed for spellers of all ages and includes over 3,600 words in 200 word lists divided into six levels of difficulty. The program helps students develop sight vocabulary, learn how to spell words correctly in context, apply spelling rules, distinguish between correct and incorrect spelling, develop short-term recall of spelling words, and develop editing skills for identifying errors. The text-to-speech capability allows students to hear each word read aloud, and the text editor facilitates the creation of customized word lists. The word lists, word search puzzles, crossword puzzles, and certificates are printable, and the program includes record keeping to track student progress.

The Spelling System

The Spelling System (produced by Milliken) is designed to teach the major principles and patterns that occur in the spelling of English words. Many spelling irregularities also are covered. The program gives special attention to sound spellings and teaches more than 1,400 commonly misspelled words. The teacher also can add new words. Each lesson is composed of three separate exercises. First, the student receives a brief introduction to the concept or fact being presented. Then the student works through three practice activities (unscrambling words, deciphering words by determining whether a before-letter or after-letter code is used, and locating misspelled words). Finally, the student's mastery of the lesson words is tested through the presentation of a sentence with a word missing. The student may request a sound spelling clue, but only one chance is given for a correct answer. Four diskettes are available (vowel spellings, consonant spellings, special vowel spellings, and word building) as well as a reproducible activity book for supplementary exercises. The program provides instruction for students in fourth through eighth grade as well as review for older students.

Spelling Wiz

Spelling Wiz is included in SRA's *Arcademic Skill Builders in Language Arts* and assists students in spelling more than 300 words commonly misspelled at the first- through sixth-grade levels. The game features a colorful wizard who uses a magic wand to zap missing letters into words. Game control options for speed of game, difficulty level of content, length of game, and sound effects can be preset according to an individual student's needs. Additional activities for review and reinforcement are provided on blackline masters.

Spelltronics

Spelltronics (available from Educational Activities) uses the letter cloze technique to reinforce correct spelling and build visual memory. The entire program teaches 240 words, and it allows the teacher to add additional words. Each word is presented three separate times with different letters deleted. The student adds the missing letters and must type the word into a sentence. If the student is unable to provide the correct spelling after two opportunities, the correct answer is displayed and the student tries again. Correct answers are rewarded in all drills. Words are grouped according to linguistic, phonics, or spelling concepts. Six programs are included: vowel patterns, long vowel patterns, consonant patterns, word endings, useful words, and unexpected spellings. Each pattern has four units containing 10 programmed words and a review unit. The student advances from simple to more complex patterns. The program is useful for all students who have difficulty spelling.

WRITTEN EXPRESSION SKILLS

Written expression, one of the highest forms of communication, reflects a person's level of comprehension, concept development, and abstraction. It is how an individual organizes ideas to convey a message. Whereas handwriting is primarily a visual-motor task that includes copying, tracing, and writing from dictation, written expression requires complex thought processes.

The skill of written expression usually is not acquired until an individual has had extensive experience with reading, spelling, and verbal expression. Problems in written expression may not be diagnosed until the upper elementary school years, when the student is required to use the various language components in written composition and emphasis is placed upon refining writing skills. Written expression is the most complex of the language arts skills and is based on listening, talking, handwriting, reading, and spelling. Thus, it generally is not stressed in instructional programs for students with learning disabilities. Teachers tend instead to focus on the skills prerequisite to written expression. However, as the student acquires those prerequisite skills, instruction in written expression is warranted.

In a comparison of the written products of students with learning disabilities and their normally achieving peers in 4th, 8th, and 11th grades, Houck and Billingsley (1989) found that students with learning disabilities write fewer words and sentences, write more words per sentence, produce fewer words with seven letters or more and fewer sentence fragments, and have a higher percentage of capitalization and spelling errors. Research indicates that the writing difficulties of students with learning disabilities result from problems with basic text production skills, scant knowledge about writing, and difficulties with planning and revising text (Graham, Harris, MacArthur, & Schwartz, 1991). Additional areas of difficulty may include idea generation, maturity of themes, organization, grammar, and theme development (Smith, 1994).

Christenson, Thurlow, Ysseldyke, and McVicar (1989) contend that written language instruction for students with mild disabilities can be improved by increasing the time allocated for instruction, teaching written language as an integrated process, and coordinating written language activities with different content areas. Students with learning disabilities experience a variety of writing problems, and the treatment of these difficulties in a systematic program requires that teachers at all levels allocate instructional time for writing and the review and editing of written products.

ASSESSMENT OF WRITTEN EXPRESSION SKILLS

Assessment of written expression yields information about a student's skill level and aids in instructional planning. The teacher can assess various components of written expression to determine deficiencies. Assessment techniques are presented in two broad categories: standardized and criterion-referenced tests and informal techniques specifically related to instructional planning.

Standardized and Criterion-Referenced Tests

Many standardized survey tests of academic achievement contain some measure of written language. The most frequently assessed areas include word usage, mechanics, and grammar. However, with the shift in emphasis from the product to the process of writing, newer tests include measures of composition. In the *Metropolitan Achievement Tests—Seventh Edition: Writing Test* (Balow, Farr, & Hogan, 1992), students compose written responses to picture prompts and are encouraged to allocate time for each writing process stage from prewriting through editing. Holistic scoring yields a general statement about the student's writing ability, and analytic scoring focuses on content development, organizational strategies, word choice, sentence formation, usage, and writing mechanics. Likewise, the *Peabody Individual Achievement Test—Revised* (Markwardt, 1989) includes a written expression subtest in which the student is required to write a story about a picture. Also, the *Woodcock Language Proficiency Battery—Revised* (Woodcock, 1991) includes written language subtests in dictation, proofing, writing samples, and writing fluency to assess conventions of written language as well as content.

Standardized diagnostic tests of written expression provide additional basic information useful in planning instruction. Measures of writing skills can focus on composition skills such as organization, vocabulary, style, and originality of ideas as well as mechanical aspects including syntax, usage, capitalization, punctuation, spelling, and handwriting. Table 12.5 describes four diagnostic tests of written expression.

Criterion-referenced tests of writing skills also are useful in instructional planning. The *Hudson Education Skills Inventory—Writing* (Hudson, Colson, Banikowski, & Mehring, 1989) measures a student's present level of basic writing skills according to a sequence of objectives arranged by grade level. The skill areas assessed include capitalization, punctuation, grammar, vocabulary, sentences, paragraphs, spelling, and handwriting. The instructional planning form allows the teacher to record assessment results and instructional planning decisions.

Informal Assessment Techniques

The teacher begins informal assessment of written expression by obtaining representative writing samples from the student and analyzing them to determine specific weaknesses. Five major components of written expression that can be analyzed are fluency, syntax, vocabulary, structure, and content. Also, curriculum-based measurement is an informal assessment technique that uses a set of standardized procedures to assess written expression skills. Finally, portfolio assessment can give the teacher insight into student growth.

Fluency. *Fluency* is defined as quantity of verbal output and refers to the number of words written. Isaacson (1988) notes a significant correlation between fluency and other measures of writing skills. For example, a student who is able to write more words is likely to be more fluent in generating ideas as well. Fluency is related to age and includes sentence length and complexity (McCarthy, 1954; Meckel, 1963). The average sentence length in a composition is determined by counting the number of words and the number of sentences in the composition and dividing the number of words by the number of sentences. Cartwright (1968) found that the average sentence length of an 8-year-old is eight words and that this length increases one word per year through age 13. He suggests that any deviation of more than two words indicates a problem.

Syntax. *Syntax* refers to construction of sentences or the way words are put together to form phrases, clauses, and sentences. Frequent written syntax errors of students with learning disabilities include word omissions, distorted word order, incorrect verb and pronoun usage, incorrect word endings, and lack of punctuation (D. J. Johnson & Myklebust, 1967). Thomas, Englert, and Gregg (1987) found that a large proportion of the syntactic errors of older writers with learning disabilities is attributed to errors in which the student generates a phrase instead of a sentence.

TABLE 12.5
Diagnostic Tests of Written Expression

Test	Age/Grade Level
Picture Story Language Test (Myklebust, 1965)	7–17 years
The student writes a story based upon a presented picture. The teacher evaluates it along three dimensions: productivity, syntax, and meaning. Productivity is the total number of words, sentences, and words per sentence; syntax (correctness) refers to word usage, word endings, and punctuation; and meaning of content is judged along a continuum of abstract to concrete. Scores in these three areas can be converted into age equivalents, percentiles, and stanines.	
Test of Written Expression (McGhee, Bryant, Larsen, & Rivera, 1995)	6–14 years
The test includes a series of items that assess different skills associated with writing. Also, the student reads or hears a prepared story starter and uses it as a stimulus for writing an essay. The essay is scored by evaluating performance across ideation, vocabulary, grammar, capitalization, punctuation, and spelling. The test can be administered to individuals or groups and yields standard scores and percentile ranks.	
Test of Written Language—3 (Hammill & Larsen, 1996)	2nd–12th grade
The test assesses cognitive, linguistic, and conventional components of written language by having the student look at pictures and write a complete story based on the pictures. Subtests with spontaneous formats (essay analysis) include (a) contextual conventions—measures capitalization, punctuation, and spelling, (b) contextual language—measures vocabulary, syntax, and grammar, and (c) story construction—measures plot, character development, and general composition. Subtests with contrived formats include (a) vocabulary—measures word usage, (b) spelling—measures ability to form letters into words, (c) style—measures punctuation and capitalization, (d) logical sentences—measures ability to write conceptually sound sentences, and (e) sentence combining—measures syntax. Two equivalent forms are available, and percentiles and standard scores are provided. The test can be administered to individuals or groups in about 90 minutes, and the PRO-SCORE system allows computer scoring of the test.	
Writing Process Test (Warden & Hutchinson, 1992)	2nd–12th grade
This test assesses both written product and writing process by requiring the student to plan, write, and revise an original composition. On the written product, percentile ranks and standard scores are provided for development (purpose/focus, audience, vocabulary, style/tone, support/development, and organization/coherence) and fluency (sentence structure/variety, grammar/usage, capitalization/punctuation, and spelling). The writing process is assessed by the student's rating of the composition on an analytic scale and the student's responses to questions about use of specific writing strategies. Administration time is 45 minutes plus 30 minutes for the optional revision.	

One method for assessing syntactic maturity is counting the number of sentences that fall into several different categories: incomplete (fragment), simple, compound, and complex. The percentage of usage of the four sentence types in a writing sample can be computed to provide comparisons and a record of the student's progress. Cartwright (1969) suggests that the number of compound and complex sentences increases with age and that the use of incomplete and simple sentences decreases.

Another common measure of syntax is T-unit length (words per terminable unit). A T-unit is the shortest grammatically correct segment that a passage can be divided into without creating fragments (Hunt, 1965). Thus, a sentence consisting of one T-unit may have subordinate clauses, phrases, or modifiers embedded within it, whereas a compound sentence is two T-units because it can be divided into two grammatically complete units without leaving fragments. The ratio of the average T-unit length is a total count of the number of words written divided by the number of T-units present. T-unit length is positively correlated to other measures of written expression (Isaacson, 1988), and a general increase in the average T-unit length occurs throughout the school years (Morris & Crump, 1982).

Vocabulary. *Vocabulary* refers to the originality or maturity in the student's choice of words and the variety of words used in the written task. The student's vocabulary should increase with age and experience; however, Morris and Crump (1982) report that, compared with their normally achieving peers at four age levels, students with learning disabilities use fewer word types in their writing. Wiig and Secord (1994) report that some students with learning disabilities have adequate vocabularies for their age range but have assigned a small number of attributes to each word. The Type Token Ratio (TTR) (W. Johnson, 1944) is a measure of vocabulary that is the ratio of different words used (types) to the total number of words used (tokens). For example, the sentence *The two boys went fishing in Noonan's Lake early yesterday morning* has a high TTR (1.0)—11 total words are used, and all 11 words are different. In contrast, the sentence *The little girl saw the little boy in the little house* has a fairly low TTR (.63)—11 total words are used, but only 7 of these words are different. A low TTR may indicate inadequate vocabulary for the written expression task. This technique also can be used for measuring long compositions; however, the number of different vocabulary words decreases as the total number of words in the composition increases (Carroll, 1938). When comparing several compositions produced by the same student or by different students, the same type of sample should be taken. For example, the first 50 words should be used from each composition instead of selecting the first 50 words from some compositions and the last 50 words from others.

Vocabulary variety also can be assessed by using the index of diversification (Carroll, 1938, G. A. Miller, 1951). This refers to the average number of words between each occurrence of the most frequently used word in the writing sample. Cartwright (1969) suggests dividing the total number of words in the sample by the number of *the*'s or by the number of times the word used most often appears. The higher the value of the index, the more diverse the vocabulary.

Finally, vocabulary can be assessed by measuring the number of unusual words. For this assessment, a sample of the student's written expression should be compared with a list of words frequently used by other students—for example, the Dolch (1955, 1960) word list. The number of words the student uses that do not appear on the list indicates the extent of the student's vocabulary.

Structure. *Structure* includes the mechanical aspects of writing, such as punctuation, capitalization, and rules of grammar. The Grammatical-Correctness Ratio (GCR) (Stuckless & Marks, 1966) can be used to assess structure. The GCR quickly analyzes the total number of the student's grammatical errors. To obtain the GCR, a sample of the student's writing (e.g., 50 words from a composition) is scored by counting the number of grammatical errors. The error count is subtracted from 50, and this difference is divided by 50. To obtain a percentage score, this last number is multiplied by 100. Because the final result can be displayed as a percentage, GCRs can be calculated for any number of words and still yield a score that can be compared with the student's previous scores. A GCR score also can be calculated for one specific type of grammatical error or for errors in punctuation or capitalization.

Structure also can be assessed by tabulating types of errors in the writing sample. The frequency of specific errors can be recorded to pinpoint individual weaknesses. An error analysis chart (presented in Table 12.6) provides a profile of errors in writing structure. Errors in spelling (phonetic and nonphonetic misspellings) and handwriting (problems with letter formation, spacing, consistent slant, line quality, alignment, letter size, and fluency) also can be noted.

TABLE 12.6
Writing Structure Error Analysis Chart

Sample Elicitation Procedure: ________ ________ Date: ________ Students' Names	Verbs		Pro-nouns		Words					Sen-tences		Capitals			Punctuation						Total
	Agreement	Tense	Personal	Possessive	Additions	Substitutions	Modifiers	Negatives	Plurals	Incomplete	Run-on	Beginning sentences	Proper nouns	Inappropriate use	Period	Comma	Question mark	Apostrophe	Colon	Other	

Source: From *Teaching Students with Learning Problems* (p. 559), 4th ed., by C. D. Mercer and A. R. Mercer, 1993, Upper Saddle River, NJ: Merrill/Prentice Hall. Copyright 1993 by Prentice-Hall Publishing Company. Reprinted by permission.

In addition to spontaneous writing samples, teacher-made test items also can be used to analyze specific elements of writing structure. Written compositions may not include enough opportunities for various errors to occur. For example, the student may write only sentences that contain grammatical forms or punctuation the student knows how to use. Thus, to assess punctuation, the teacher can devise several short sentences in which punctuation rules are used. The sentences can be dictated for the student to write correctly or can be presented unpunctuated for the student to correct. For example:

1. School starts at 8 30
2. Twenty two boys are in the class
3. Dr Goodman lives in Richmond Virginia
4. His birthday is January 31 1943
5. Blaze our Golden Retriever had four puppies

Content. *Content*, the fifth component of written expression, can be divided into accuracy, ideas, and organization (Cartwright, 1969). Similarly, Isaacson (1988) indicates that aspects of content that should be considered in assessment include idea generation, coherence of all parts of the composition to the topic or theme, organization or logical sequence, and awareness of audience. The nature of the written assignment determines how the different factors should be weighed. For example, accuracy carries more weight when the written exercise is a presentation of historical facts. Cartwright suggests rating each factor on a scale from 0 to 10. A 10 in ideas would indicate that the ideas were pertinent to the topic and represented a high degree of originality, and a 0 would indicate lack of originality or understanding of the task. Some youngsters with learning disabilities may have limited ideas because of lack of experience, while others may have the ideas but not the ability to sequence them in logical order. Thomas et al. (1987) found that in expository writing (i.e., the ability to explain or provide information on a topic), students with learning disabilities frequently terminate their text prematurely, thus indicating difficulty in producing multiple factual statements about familiar topics. In addition, these students tend to repeat information and generate irrelevant items pertaining to the topic. Wallace, Larsen, and Elksnin (1992) note that evaluation of content is especially difficult because the ideas and levels of abstraction contained in the written product are dependent on the student's intelligence, language experiences, cultural background, and interests.

Profile of Components. By examining a student's writing sample, such as an autobiography, the teacher can determine which skills need to be introduced or remediated and which have been acquired. Poteet (1980) developed the *Checklist of Written Expression Skills,* containing four areas: penmanship, spelling, grammar (capitalization, punctuation, and syntax), and ideation (type of writing, substance, productivity, comprehensibility, reality, and style). Likewise, Weiner (1980) devised the *Diagnostic Evaluation of Writing Skills* (*DEWS*), consisting of the following areas: graphic (visual features), orthographic (spelling), phonologic (sound components), syntactic (grammatical), semantic (meaning), and self-monitoring.

A profile of the assessment of written expression components can be used with an individual student or an entire class to record strengths and weaknesses and student progress. Although some interpretation is required, the use of a profile helps to standardize observations and thus yields a more reliable and valid informal assessment. Also, determining the error patterns associated with each writing component is essential for instructional planning.

Curriculum-Based Measurement. Curriculum-based measurement allows the teacher to collect data routinely and monitor instructional progress. Writing skills are assessed through repeated 3-minute writing samples using stimulus story starters or topic sentences. The use of 3-minute writing samples represents a general assessment of writing skills rather than a diagnostic assessment of specific writing deficits; however, it allows the teacher to base instructional decisions on direct, repeated measurement.

Wesson (1987) notes that 30 story starters are needed for 1 year of measurement. When the story starters are written on note cards, the teacher can write the students' initials on the back so that the story starter is not used by the same student more than three times. The measures can be administered to a group of students rather than on an individual basis. Tindal and Marston (1990) present three evaluation strategies: (a) holistic scoring—raters review compositions within the same distribution to determine an overall impression and assign a value from a rating scale; (b) analytical scoring—writing samples are scored on specific qualities or traits (such as organization, ideas, wording, and punctuation) with operational definitions and criteria to aid the judgment process; and (c) primary-trait scoring—raters focus on the degree of consistency in the purpose of writing according to defined traits (such as creativity and persuasion). Parker, Tindal, and Hasbrouck (1991) indicate that holistic judgments appear to be reliable in a writing process approach when there is no judgment of improvement over time; however, in a subskill mastery instructional approach, the most useful indexes for monitoring writing progress are number of correct word sequences, mean length of correct word sequences, and percent of legible words written.

To implement curriculum-based measurement of written expression, the teacher can use the steps in Table 12.7, which includes the administration and scoring procedures of written expression measures as well as procedures for determining long-range goals and graphing data. Deno et al.

TABLE 12.7
Procedures for Administering and Scoring Written Expression Measures, Determining Long-Range Goals, and Graphing Data

Step 1:	To establish a baseline, provide each student with a lined sheet of paper and the same story starter or topic sentence on any 3 days of a given week. Discuss writing ideas, and then have the students write for a 3-minute period. Collect the papers after 3 minutes.
Step 2:	Count the number of words or letter sequences representing words written after the given story starter or topic sentence. Ignore misspellings, content, punctuation, and organization. Continue with this procedure for 2 more days, giving two new story starters or topic sentences during the week. Plot the student's scores on a graph.
Step 3:	Find the median score from the three baseline scores. This is the middle number when ranked from lowest to highest.
Step 4:	Compute the long-range goal. Count the number of weeks left in the school year or semester. Multiply the number of weeks by 2.0 (rate of growth), and add the median score obtained from the baseline week (e.g., 21 weeks $\times$ 2.0 = 42; 42 + 14 [baseline median] = 56 [goal]).
Step 5:	Plot the goal data point on the graph on the line for the last week. Draw the aim line connecting the baseline median data point to the goal data point. This represents the line that the student's performance should follow as the student progresses through the school year.
Step 6:	Beginning with the first week after the baseline, measure student performance two times each week. On 2 different days in a given week, provide the students with a different story starter or topic sentence. Following a brief discussion of the story starter or topic, tell the students to write for 3 minutes and say "Begin writing."
Step 7:	After the 3-minute period, say "Stop." Collect the papers, and count the number of words or letter sequences representing words written after the given story starter or topic sentence.
Step 8:	Plot each score on the graph in the space corresponding with the day and week. Connect the data points.
Step 9:	Continue with this procedure throughout the year. Analyze student error patterns for information regarding writing deficits of individual students. Use this information in planning instructional lessons. Graphs also can be made to monitor progress on specific skills (e.g., capitalization, punctuation, and subject-verb agreement).

Source: From *Teaching Students with Learning Problems* (p. 562), 4th ed., by C. D. Mercer and A. R. Mercer, 1993, Upper Saddle River, NJ: Merrill/Prentice Hall. Copyright 1993 by Prentice-Hall Publishing Company. Reprinted by permission.

(1984) provide the following mean scores for average students: first grade—14.7 words in 3 minutes, second grade—27.8 words, third grade—36.6 words, fourth grade—40.9 words, fifth grade—49.1 words, and sixth grade—53.3 words.

In addition to increasing student motivation to write, monitoring written expression provides the teacher with information that encourages sensitive and relevant instructional modifications. For example, for a student who has great difficulty with written expression, the following modifications are useful:

1. Allow the student to copy selected words during the 3-minute timing to help get the student started. Selected words may center around a theme (e.g., marine life), word family (e.g., *cat, fat, rat, bat*), or a special interest (such as sports).
2. Provide story starters that include sentences with missing words or letters. Have the student write words or letters for the blanks. Count the number of correct words that student input helped create.
3. Periodically introduce specific written expression interventions (e.g., capitalization,

punctuation, compound words, and contractions), and note if student writings reflect content from instructional lessons.
4. Use experiences (e.g., science project, class visitor, field trip, or movie) for story starters.
5. If the student is unable to produce sentences, have the student generate words. Score the number of legible words.

Portfolio Assessment. The student can compile a collection of self-produced written words to reflect efforts, progress, and achievements in written expression. Writing portfolios may include notes, diagrams, drafts, and the final version of a writing project, as well as diverse entries such as journal writings, letters, poems, or essays (Wolf, 1989). The student's self-assessment of the writings as well as the teacher's notes about the writings and the student as a writer also may be included. Thus, the student is a participant in the assessment process and learns to set goals and evaluate learning in progress. The *Language Arts Assessment Portfolio* (Karlsen, 1992) provides an analysis of student achievement and progress in reading, writing, listening, and speaking. In the writing area, evaluation is included in the writing process and the written product as well as optional evaluations in spelling and mechanics. The student assembles writing samples in portfolio folders and writes comments in self-evaluation booklets on selected work and achievements. Three levels are available: first grade, second and third grade, and fourth through sixth grade. The portfolio folders document student growth throughout the school year and are transferred to the next grade level with the student as a continuing record of achievement.

TEACHING WRITTEN EXPRESSION SKILLS

Written expression primarily is concerned with creative writing but also includes functional writing. *Creative writing* is the personal expression of thoughts and experiences in a unique manner, as in poetry, story writing, and personal narratives. *Functional writing* focuses on conveying information in a structured form, such as writing answers to chapter questions, social and business letters, invitations, reports and essays, or minutes of a meeting. The writing program for students with learning disabilities should include a range of writing experiences in both creative and functional writing. The student must learn to organize thoughts logically and follow the proper mechanics of writing (including punctuation and capitalization) to communicate clearly and accurately.

In teaching writing, the emphasis has shifted from the product of writing to the process involved in creating that product (Graves, 1985). The product approach focuses primarily on grammar, spelling, capitalization, punctuation, and handwriting. The process approach stresses meaning first and then skills in the context of meaning. Students work through various stages (e.g., prewriting, drafting, revising, editing, and publishing) and focus their attention on one stage at a time (Tompkins, 1994). An overview of the writing stages is presented in Table 12.8.

In the process approach, the student independently selects a writing topic and rehearses (brainstorms) before writing. After drafting and redrafting for several days, the student discusses the work with the teacher or peers and then revises and edits. Revising refers to reworking the text in a way that alters its content or structure, whereas editing is the process of correcting errors in grammar, syntax, punctuation, and spelling. Finally, the product is published or shared with the audience for whom the student has written. Thus, the teacher's role has shifted from merely assigning and assessing a product to working with the student throughout the writing process. By working through the writing process, the student develops problem-solving skills, critical thinking skills, and a positive self-image.

Isaacson (1990) discusses four characteristics of the process approach in which the teacher introduces the student to the entire process of writing, from initial idea generation to editing of the final draft:

TABLE 12.8
Overview of Writing Stages

Prewriting Stage
Select a topic for the written piece.
Consider the purpose for writing (e.g., to inform, describe, entertain, or persuade).
Identify the audience for whom the writing is intended (e.g., classmates, parents, business persons, or publishers).
Choose an appropriate form for the composition based on purpose and audience (e.g., story, report, poem, script, or letter).
Engage in rehearsal activities to gather and organize ideas for writing (e.g., drawing, talking, reading, interviewing, brainstorming ideas, and clustering main ideas and details).
Participate in writing a collaborative or group composition with the teacher so that the teacher can model or demonstrate the writing process and clarify questions and misconceptions.

Drafting Stage
Write a rough draft by skipping every other line and allowing adequate space for revising.
Emphasize content rather than mechanics, grammar, and spelling.

Revising Stage
Reread the rough draft and make changes by adding, substituting, deleting, and moving text.
Share the composition in writing groups in which listeners respond with compliments as well as comments and suggestions about how to improve the composition.
Make revisions based on feedback from the writing group by crossing out, drawing arrows, and writing in the space left between the writing lines.

Editing Stage
Focus on mechanics, including capitalization, punctuation, spelling, sentence structure, word usage, and formatting considerations.
Proofread the composition by reading word-by-word and hunting for errors (e.g., spelling, capitalization, and punctuation) rather than reading for meaning, and insert proofreading symbols to indicate needed changes.
Correct as many mechanical errors as possible and, if necessary, use a dictionary or have a conference with the teacher for instruction or a minilesson on a needed skill.

Publishing Stage
Publish the writing in an appropriate form (e.g., make a covered booklet or contribute to a newspaper or magazine).
Share the finished composition with classmates or appropriate audiences by reading it aloud in the class "author's chair" or displaying the writing on a bulletin board.

1. *The process should be modeled.* In a prewriting discussion, the teacher should model planning strategies by raising questions on the topic and demonstrate ways to organize information (e.g., charts or semantic maps). The teacher can model how to convert planning notes into written sentences by thinking aloud while performing the task. Finally, the teacher should model reviewing and revising strategies and show that first drafts differ greatly from the finished copy.
2. *The process can be collaborative.* Collaboration can involve either the teacher or other students in activities such as brainstorming ideas, contributing and organizing information, giving constructive feedback, and editing for mechanical errors. Writing groups can be formed to share writing and develop ideas; a peer team is also a good arrangement for editing written work.
3. *The process can be prompted.* The teacher can provide assistance by prompting the

steps of the writing process or helping with writing decisions. For example, a prompt procedure in the prewriting stage can begin with having students list isolated words related to a topic. In the editing stage the teacher can write a code in the margin for a type of error (e.g., *sp* for spelling, *v.* for verb form, and *cap* for capitalization) to prompt the student to find and correct errors.

4. *The process should become self-initiated and self-monitored.* The teacher can give the student instruction in specific writing strategies and ideas for self-instructional statements, such as a sentence-writing strategy (PENS), a paragraph-writing strategy (PLEASE), an error-monitoring strategy (COPS), and an acronym (TOWER) for use in theme writing, which are presented later in this section.

Graham and Harris (1994) note three advantages of the process writing approach: (a) student writing is frequent and meaningful, (b) environmental conditions are created that foster self-regulated learning, and (c) emphasis is placed on the integrative nature of learning in literacy development. However, they note that these benefits may be weakened "by an overreliance on incidental learning and by a lack of emphasis on the mechanics of writing" (p. 275). Many students with learning problems do not develop effective strategies and skills for writing without careful instruction. Thus, the writing of students with learning problems may be improved by integrating process writing with skill-oriented instruction.

For students with academic learning problems, Kameenui and Simmons (1990) recommend a skills-based approach to expressive writing instruction. This approach focuses on a scope and sequence of basic skills and systematically develops these skills for advanced exercises and applications. In this approach, the instructional emphasis focuses first on the writing and editing phases (teacher-directed), and then the process of planning (student-initiated) is introduced and developed. Thus the student is taught to rely on writing skills when engaging in the process of planning more complex written products.

Graham and Harris (1988) offer 10 instructional recommendations for developing an effective writing program for students with written expression difficulty:

1. *Allocate time for writing instruction.* A sufficient amount of time should be allocated to writing instruction (e.g., four times per week) because students can learn and develop as writers only by writing.
2. *Expose students to a broad range of writing tasks.* Students should participate in writing activities that present highly structured problem-solving situations as well as activities that involve self-selected and expressive writing.
3. *Create a social climate conducive to writing development.* The teacher needs to be encouraging in a nonthreatening environment and should try to develop a sense of community by promoting student sharing and collaboration.
4. *Integrate writing with other academic subjects.* Writing should be integrated with other language arts activities to increase the frequency of writing and to develop skills.
5. *Aid students in developing the processes central to effective writing.* The composition process can be divided into a series of discrete stages (e.g., prewrite, write, and rewrite), and students can be taught appropriate task-specific and metacognitive strategies (e.g., self-instructional strategy training).
6. *Automatize skills for getting language onto paper.* The teacher should provide direct instruction in mechanical skills and sentence and paragraph production, or the mechanical requirements of composing can be removed through the use of oral dictation.
7. *Help students develop explicit knowledge about the characteristics of good writing.* Students should be given exposure to the characteristics of various literary compositions either through reading or teacher presentation of written or live models that incorporate a specific skill or style, or students should receive direct instruction in the structured elements representative of a particular literary style.
8. *Help students develop the skills and abilities to carry out more sophisticated composing processes.* Three methods for the development of more mature composing processes include conferences during which teachers act as collaborators, procedural facilitation in which external support is provided, and self-instructional strategy training.
9. *Assist students in the development of goals for improving their written products.* Goal setting and having students evaluate their own or others' written products according to specific criteria can help students accurately monitor and evaluate progress.
10. *Avoid instructional practices that do not improve students' writing performances.* Skills in grammar and usage should be developed within the context of real writing tasks, and the teacher should give specific, explanatory feedback on only one or two types of frequently occurring errors at any one time.

The first step in writing instruction is to promote a positive attitude to motivate the student to write. The student must feel comfortable expressing thoughts and feelings. The teacher can promote discussion by encouraging the student to share ideas. Writing should be integrated into the entire curriculum, and the teacher should help the student understand that the purpose of writing is to communicate. Writing instruction thus begins with establishing a positive environment and then proceeds to skill development.

One of the most effective means of teaching writing skills to students with learning disabilities is through spontaneous written expression. Each student's writing samples can be used as a base from which to introduce instruction in various writing skills. In other words, the objective of the writing program may be for the student to express ideas and thoughts with ease. The written work then is used as the basis for skill development. Thus, spontaneous writing samples can be used to teach written expression within the context of various instructional programs such as whole language, language experience, or direct skill instruction. The teacher can provide events (e.g., discussions, field trips, and films) that stimulate topics. At first, the student may be most comfortable writing about personal topics, such as family, trips, or holidays. Some students enjoy writing each day in journals about their experiences and reactions to events. Students also enjoy writing stories about pictures or intriguing titles and completing unfinished stories (i.e., story starters or story enders). Books in which the pictures are presented in sequence without text can provide stimuli for writing activities. Commercial materials also are sources of writing assignments—for example, *Creative Story Starters* (published by SRA) and *Story Starters—Primary and Intermediate* (published by Curriculum Associates). In general, students should be responsible for choosing their own topics for writing. When students produce their own stories, the material is meaningful to them, and they are motivated to study it. This may be especially important for adolescents, because the stories they compose are on their level of maturity. Also, writing tasks may become more meaningful when students are allowed to work on the same writing project for an extended period of time. Students' involvement or interest in a given topic influences their ability to write about it.

To begin writing, brainstorming can generate ideas and words to be used. The student lists all words and phrases that come to mind in response to the topic. Clustering or mapping information also can help the student organize ideas for writing. The cluster or map can include main ideas, details, and examples. In these informal writing strategies and as the student begins tentatively to write ideas, the emphasis is on content rather than mechanics.

As the student continues to be encouraged to express ideas well in writing, instruction on the more mechanical aspects of writing begins. In teaching punctuation and capitalization skills, the teacher can call attention to such errors in the student's written work, show the proper use of the skill, and point out how its use enhances meaning. Dowis and Schloss (1992) suggest the use of directed minilessons to teach specific skills during the writing process so that skills and content can develop concurrently. Thus, writing mechanics are explained as needed, and the student becomes aware of their importance.

The teacher should avoid excessive correction of the mechanical aspects of writing, which may discourage the student from trying to express ideas. The student may think that how thoughts are written is more important than what is written and, thus, may begin to limit vocabulary use, write only simple sentences, and avoid expressing complex and creative thoughts. Good writing models should be provided, and reinforcement should be combined with constructive criticism. The teacher should say something positive about the student's work prior to offering correction and give encouragement and praise for whatever amount the student has written. In general, more attention should be given to developing the written expression of ideas than to correcting mechanical errors. Of course, students who learn to use the right punctuation, correct grammar, and good organization are likely to become better writers. Thus, balanced instruction targets both process and mechanics. Some teachers prefer to give two grades for some writing assignments—one for ideas and one for technical skills. Also, the teacher can provide selective feedback directly to a student through oral conferences.

To help improve a student's writing, the teacher should give considerable attention to sentence and paragraph development. The student should be helped to recognize the different syntactic patterns in which ideas can be expressed. Having the student read interesting material at his or her independent reading level will expose the student to good sentences in other people's writing and may help develop a sense of English sentence constructions. Also, through orally reading or tape-recording stories, the student is likely to notice faulty sentence constructions. Learning to write unified, coherent paragraphs can be facilitated by activities in which the student categorizes or classifies ideas or organizes ideas in a logical sequence. An organizational framework can be provided through the use of content charts, semantic maps (or webbings), and pyramid diagrams that present an overview of information and visually represent how items are related (Levy & Rosenberg, 1990). Suggesting the use of transition words (such as *finally* and *in addition to*) may help the student put compositions together.

A sentence-writing strategy designed by Schumaker and Sheldon (1985) can be used to teach the basic principles of sentence construction and expression. The student learns a set of steps and formulas that facilitates the recognition and writing of different kinds of sentences. The acronym PENS helps the student remember the steps to sentence writing:

P—*Pick* a sentence type and formula.

E—*Explore* words to fit the formula.

N—*Note* the words.

S—*Search* for verbs and subjects, and check.

PENS also is used in the paragraph-writing strategy developed at the University of Kansas Center for Research on Learning to help the student write a topic sentence, detail sentences, and a clincher sentence to form a paragraph (Schumaker & Lyerla, 1991). This learning strategy teaches the student to write various types of paragraphs: sequential (narrative or step-by-step), descriptive, expository, and comparison and contrast. Also, *Teaching Competence in Written Language* (Phelps-Terasaki & Phelps-Gunn, 1988) contains highly structured lessons in which the student progresses effectively in a step-by-step fashion from ideas to sentences or paragraphs.

Welch (1992) presents a metacognitive strategy to teach students to write paragraphs. The use of a first-letter mnemonic cues the student how to complete the writing task independently:

P—*Pick* a topic, an audience, and the appropriate textual format (e.g., enumerative, comparison and contrast, or cause and effect).

L—*List* information about the topic to be used in sentence generation, ongoing evaluation, and organizational planning.

E—*Evaluate* if the list is complete and plan how to organize the ideas that will be used to generate supporting sentences.

A—*Activate* the paragraph with a short and simple declarative topic sentence.

S—*Supply* supporting sentences based on items from the list.

E—*End* with a concluding sentence that rephrases the topic sentence, and *evaluate* the written work for errors in capitalization, punctuation, spelling, and appearance.

Welch notes that the intervention increases the student's metacognitive knowledge of the writing process involved in prewriting, planning, composing, and revising, as well as improves the student's attitude toward writing and writing instruction.

As basic writing skills are acquired, the student should learn to proofread and edit. In proofreading, the student reads the written work to identify and correct errors. To edit the work, the student can be guided to look for elements in the writing such as capitalization, sentence sense, punctuation, misspelled words, margins, and paragraph indention. At first it may be helpful for the student to proofread the work several times with a different purpose in mind each time. As the student reads the work aloud, errors such as omitted words, improper punctuation, or poor organization may be noticed. Also, peer critiquing can be used as a revision strategy, and individual conferences with the teacher in a supportive atmosphere can result in constructive editing.

To cue the student to detect four kinds of common errors, the teacher can introduce COPS questions to be used as an error-monitoring strategy (Schumaker, Nolan, & Deshler, 1985). The student is instructed to ask the following questions and look for these errors:

C—Have I *capitalized* the first word and proper nouns?

O—How is the *overall* appearance? (Look at spacing, legibility, indention of paragraphs, neatness, and complete sentences.)

P—Have I put in commas, semicolons, and end *punctuation*?

S—Have I *spelled* all the words correctly?

Periodically the teacher can review COPS and encourage each student to use it daily so that it will become a habit. The teacher can require all papers to be "COPSed" before being accepted.

Because the goal of writing is to communicate ideas, students should be encouraged to share their written work. Notebooks or books of stories the students want to share may be exchanged for reading material. Also, students can be given the opportunity to read their selections voluntarily in front of other students. Through sharing stories, students receive feedback and become more motivated to improve the quality of their work. Also, the students are provided with models to help them improve their writing.

At the secondary level, greater written expression demands are placed on students. Not only are students required to take notes during class lectures and express themselves on written tests, but they also frequently must write themes and reports. Teaching theme writing through the use of the acronym TOWER provides a structured approach:

T—*Think* about content (i.e., title, major subtopics, and details).

O—*Order* topics and details.

W—*Write* the rough draft.

E—Look for *errors* (use COPS).

R—*Revise/rewrite.*

Before writing, the student can be encouraged to fill in a form with the topic at the top and ideas organized according to subtopics or paragraphs. After writing a rough draft, the student can ask COPS questions to edit the work and monitor errors.

Teachers expect written work to be reasonably neat and unconsciously may judge an assignment based on the appearance of the paper. Archer and Gleason (1988) suggest a strategy using the acronym HOW to improve the appearance of written work and remind the student how the paper should look.

H—*Heading* (include name, date, subject, and page number if needed).

O—*Organized* (start on front side of paper, include a left and right margin, have at least one blank line at the top and at the bottom, and space well).

W—*Written neatly* (write words or numbers on the line, form words or numbers clearly, and neatly cross out or erase errors).

MacArthur, Schwartz, and Graham (1991) present a model for writing instruction that integrates word processing and strategy instruction into a process approach to writing. Strategy instruction in writing primarily has been used to help students learn to better internalize and regulate the cognitive activities involved in effective planning, production, and revision of text (Graham et al., 1991). To enhance the quality and quantity of writing, there should be increased focus on thinking as a critical aspect of the writing process, and writing should be practiced and applied in a variety of situations and contexts to foster generalization of these skills.

COMMERCIAL WRITTEN EXPRESSION PROGRAMS

Various published materials and programs are available for developing written expression skills. This section presents selected commercial written expression materials and programs that may be helpful to students with learning disabilities.

Expressive Writing 1; Expressive Writing 2

Expressive Writing 1 and *Expressive Writing 2,* developed by S. Engelmann and J. Silbert (published by SRA), present an effective writing program designed for students who read at or above the third-grade level. The program includes 50 daily 45-minute lessons that integrate sentence writing, paragraph construction, and editing skills. At the completion of the program, students are able to write, punctuate, and edit compound sentences, sentences with dependent clauses, direct quotations in dialogue form, and sentences that list items. The program includes a teacher presentation book and a student workbook, and students participate in self-evaluation activities.

Moving Up in Grammar

Moving Up in Grammar (published by SRA) is a program designed to help students in the elementary and intermediate grades improve their grammar skills. Six independent kits of varnish-coated cards, blackline masters, answer cards, and award certificates provide well-organized practice in various areas. *Sentences* consists of 16 units covering such skill areas as simple and complete subjects and predicates, types of sentences, and compound subjects and verbs. *Nouns and Verbs* contains eight units on nouns (e.g., proper nouns, singular and plural possessive nouns) and eight units on verbs (e.g., linking verbs, the verb *to be*, and irregular past tense verbs). *Capitalization and Punctuation* covers such skills areas as titles of respect and rank, names of relatives, and periods, question marks, exclamation points, quotation marks, and commas. *Word Usage* consists of 16 units covering words such as *accept* and *except, can* and *may, lay* and *lie,* and *sit* and *set. Adjectives and Adverbs* covers eight adjective skill areas and eight adverb skill areas (e.g., comparatives, superlatives, and irregular comparisons). *Pronouns* presents 16 units in areas such as noun substitutes, pronoun/verb agreement, relative pronouns, and demonstrative pronouns.

Reasoning and Writing

Reasoning and Writing (published by SRA) is a real-life writing and thinking program that starts with templates to guide students in the process of writing and progresses to independent writing assignments. Six levels are available for students in kindergarten through sixth grade. The beginning levels develop a foundation for reading comprehension and writing and expand thinking skills. By the third level, students are fully engaged in the writing process, including drafting, revising, and editing for clarity. Knowledge of grammar and complex sentence structure is expanded, and students learn to vary word choice and sentence structure as well as to take notes, paraphrase, and evaluate evidence from various perspectives to form opinions. Editorial checklists allow the teacher to correct errors and provide precise instruction.

Writers at Work

Writers at Work (Morocco & Nelson, 1990) is designed to implement a process writing approach for students in fourth through sixth grade. Units on five types of written composition are included: personal memoir, biography, fables, research, and advertising. The lesson plans give detailed instruction in concepts, procedures, and skills critical to each type of writing, and students engage in prewriting, drafting, revising, editing, and proofreading activities. The program also provides suggestions for additional support, extension activities, and guidelines for assessment. The material has been tested with students with learning difficulties.

Written Expression

Written Expression (Warden, Allen, Hipp, Schmitz, & Collett, 1988) is an instructional program that teaches composition as a three-phase process: prewriting, composing, and editing. In the prewriting stage, the student completes a chart of *wh-* questions and uses graphic organizers such as a vocabulary and sentence chart to create a visual organization of ideas. This phase focuses on teacher-directed, student-interactive exercises. During composing, the student works independently to write a first draft. The *Writer's Guide* includes resources such as a thesaurus, spelling demons, and lists of conjunctions and transition words. In the editing stage, the student develops self-evaluation skills through the direct teaching of editing and proofreading techniques. The *Written Expression* materials are designed for students in 2nd through 12th grade, as well as for adults. They are designated as elementary, intermediate, and advanced, rather than by grade levels, so that the program can be matched to each student's needs and instructional level.

COMPUTER SOFTWARE PROGRAMS IN WRITTEN EXPRESSION

The use of the computer as a word processor can facilitate the teaching of writing. Word processing allows the student to correct, edit, revise, and manipulate text. The ease of changing words in a word processor before printing can motivate the older student to proofread for spelling and mechanical errors as well as to make improvements in other aspects of composition writing. MacArthur (1988) notes that the visibility of writing on a word processor can facilitate interaction between the student and teacher as well as collaborative writing activities among students and sharing of work in progress. In addition, the availability of a spelling checker and the ability to produce a neat, printed copy can be motivating especially to students who typically exhibit spelling or handwriting difficulties. Additional features of some computer-supported writing applications include speech synthesis, pronunciation editing, visually highlighted words, spell checking, spelling assistance, spelling modifications, insertion of correctly spelled words into the document, word dictionaries, word prediction, organizational assistance, and grammar correction and tutoring (Hunt-Berg, Rankin, & Beukelman, 1994).

Outhred (1989) found that the use of a word processor with students with learning disabilities resulted in fewer spelling errors and the production of longer stories. However, research has not confirmed the advantages of word processors for all students with learning disabilities. For example, in a study involving fifth- and sixth-grade students with learning disabilities, MacArthur and Graham (1987) found no differences on several variables (e.g., length, quality, story structure, and mechanical errors) between handwritten stories and those composed on a word processor. Isaacson (1990) notes that for the use of a word processor to contribute effectively to the development of writing skills, the teacher must teach the necessary subskills (such as keyboarding) and self-monitoring strategies for writing that take advantage of the computer's capabilities.

Bank Street Writer Plus (published by Broderbund and available from Learning Lab Software) is a popular word-processing program designed to meet the writing needs of students in 2nd through 12th grade and can be effectively used with students with learning disabilities. The program includes pull-down menus that provide access to all writing functions, and an integrated spelling checker and on-line thesaurus are included for editing and proofreading. *Kidwriter* (produced by Spinnaker) is designed for students in first through fourth grade and includes simple word processing features and graphics (e.g., background scenes, shapes, characters, and objects) for creating illustrated stories. *Write This Way* (produced by Hartley) is a voiced word-processing program for students in 4th through 12th grade that highlights spelling and grammatical errors and guides the student to correct mistakes. Also, user-friendly desktop publishing programs (such as *Print Shop* produced by Broderbund and *The Children's Writing and Publishing Center* produced by The Learning Company) make it possible to publish in a wide range of professional-looking formats. Moreover, numerous software programs are available that focus on specific written expression skills. The following programs are presented as examples of software that may facilitate instruction of students who have difficulty with written expression skills.

Grammar Problems for Practice

Grammar Problems for Practice (produced by Milliken) is divided into three separate modules that provide extensive drill and practice in troublesome grammar and usage areas related to homonyms, verbs, and pronouns. After entering a program, the student takes a pretest on the lesson. If mastery is achieved, the student advances to the next lesson. If mastery is not reached, the student reviews and then works practice exercises pertaining to the failed portions of the pretest. During practice, the student is congratulated intermittently with positive reinforcements. If necessary, the student can branch to "help" screens that provide review of the homonym, verb, or pronoun form, as well as definitions and context sentences. The student can review progress at any time, and a performance summary is given at the completion of the practice exercises. A posttest is given at the end of each lesson. If mastery is not achieved, the student is returned to the practice exercises. The programs focus on skills generally introduced in the third through sixth grade; however, they are appropriate for remediation in the seventh through ninth grade.

Verb Viper; Word Invasion; Word Master

These three programs for students in first through eighth grade are included in SRA's *Arcademic Skill Builders in Language Arts.* In *Verb Viper,* a friendly elastic-necked creature helps the student master subject agreement with regular and irregular verbs in present tense, past tense, and past participle form. *Word Invasion* provides practice in identifying words representing six parts of speech (nouns, pronouns, verbs, adjectives, adverbs, and prepositions) by letting the student control the magic ring of a friendly alien octopus. *Word Master* presents practice in identifying pairs of antonyms, synonyms, or homonyms at three difficulty levels in a race against time and advancing electronic rays. In all three programs, speed, length of the game, content levels, and sound effects can be preset according to the student's needs. A teacher's manual and blackline masters of activities are included for each program.

The Writing Adventure

The Writing Adventure (produced by SRA) provides instructional support while allowing the student to develop stories. In each adventure the student directs the main character through intriguing scenes and takes notes on computer note cards for later reference. The student must make choices and think logically in developing stories and must end the stories by writing the main character out of a trap. When writing a story, the student can review notes on the computer screen or print them. A proofing aid highlights potential errors and displays grammar rules and examples that relate to them. The stories can be printed and shared with other students. The program package is designed for students age 9 and older and consists of two disks: *Story Starter* presents the adventure scenes, brief scene descriptions, note cards, and prompting questions, and *Story Writer* has word processing capabilities for note taking, editing, and printing stories.

The Writing Workshop

The Writing Workshop (produced by Milliken) is designed for students in 3rd through 10th grade and covers the entire writing process from initial concept development through final editing and revision. The prewriting module shows the student how to organize thoughts and plan writing through activities on three disks: *Brainstorming, Branching,* and *Nutshelling.* The word processor allows the student to turn plans and creative thoughts into writing. The postwriting module teaches revising, editing, and proofreading skills and offers assistance with word usage, spelling, style, and sentence completeness. Finally, writing activity files provide exercises on a broad range of writing tasks, and research paper activities lead the older student through a logical sequence of steps for writing a research paper. The activities can be modified to meet student or assignment needs and can be printed to be used as worksheets.

PERSPECTIVE

Written language is a highly complex process of communication that ranges from mastering the motor movements of handwriting to the expression of creative thought. Given the complexities of written language and the heterogeneous nature of learning disabilities, the possible types and combinations of written language problems are enormous. Educators must strive to assess the handwriting, spelling, and written expression skills of individual learners and prescribe interventions that yield a high probability of success. This match of learner needs with effective instruction challenges educators to master many assessment and intervention strategies.

One constant theme throughout the written language literature is the need to maintain a supportive instructional environment free of criticism and rich in encouragement for effort and expression. The following thought-provoking mnemonic was devised by Paul Scammacca, a college student with learning disabilities, to remind his teacher of his difficulty with written language tasks:

P—*Please* realize that writing is difficult for me.

A—*Accept* my limitations but do not allow me to stagnate.

U—*Use* my strengths and help me to build upon them.

L—*Look* beyond my simplicities and imperfections; I could be a Mark Twain in disguise!

This chapter describes many effective practices used in assessing and teaching students with learning disabilities who have written language problems. "Write on!"

DISCUSSION/REVIEW QUESTIONS

1. Discuss the assessment of handwriting skills by listing several published assessment devices and describing informal techniques.
2. Briefly discuss the development of handwriting skills and present teaching strategies in the areas of readiness, manuscript writing, transitional writing, and cursive writing.
3. Describe several commercial handwriting programs.
4. Discuss the assessment of spelling skills by listing several standardized and criterion-referenced tests and describing informal techniques.
5. Briefly discuss several techniques for teaching spelling skills.
6. Describe several commercial spelling programs.
7. Discuss the assessment of written expression skills by listing several standardized and criterion-referenced tests and describing informal techniques.
8. Discuss the stages of the writing process and present techniques for teaching written expression.
9. Describe several commercial written expression programs.
10. Describe several computer software programs in spelling and written expression.

REFERENCES

Anderson, D. W. (1966). Handwriting research: Movement and quality. In T. D. Horn (Ed.), *Research on handwriting and spelling.* Champaign, IL: National Council of Teachers of English.

Archer, A. L., & Gleason, M. M. (1988). *Skills for school success.* Boston: Curriculum Associates.

Arena, J. (1981). *Diagnostic Spelling Potential Test.* Novato, CA: Academic Therapy.

Balow, I. H., Farr, R. C., & Hogan, T. P. (1992). *Metropolitan Achievement Tests— Seventh Edition: Writing Test.* San Antonio, TX: Harcourt Brace Educational Measurement.

Barbe, W. B., Lucas, V. H., Wasylyk, T. M., Hackney, C. S., & Braun, L. (1987). *Handwriting: Basic skills and application.* Columbus, OH: Zaner-Bloser.

Barbe, W., Milone, M., & Wasylyk, T. (1983). Manuscript is the "write" start. *Academic Therapy, 18,* 397–406.

Brigance, A. H. (1983). *Brigance Diagnostic Comprehensive Inventory of Basic Skills.* North Billerica, MA: Curriculum Associates.

Brown, A. S. (1988). Encountering misspellings and spelling performances: Why wrong isn't right. *Journal of Educational Psychology, 80,* 488–494.

Bryant, N. D., Drabin, I. R., & Gettinger, M. (1981). Effects of varying unit size on spelling achievement in learning disabled children. *Journal of Learning Disabilities, 14,* 200–203.

Burns, P. C. (1980). *Assessment and correction of language arts difficulties,* Columbus, OH: Merrill.

Burns, P. C., & Broman, B. L. (1983). *The language arts in childhood education* (5th ed.). Chicago: Rand McNally.

Carpenter, D., & Miller, L. J. (1982). Spelling ability of reading disabled LD students and able readers. *Learning Disability Quarterly, 5,* 65–70.

Carroll, J. B. (1938). Diversity of vocabulary and the harmonic series law of word-frequency distribution. *Psychological Record, 2.*

Cartwright, G. P. (1968). Written language abilities of normal and educable mentally retarded children. *American Journal of Mental Deficiency, 72,* 499–508.

Cartwright, G. P. (1969). Written expression and spelling. In R. M. Smith (Ed.), *Teacher diagnosis of educational difficulties* (pp. 95–117). Columbus, OH: Merrill.

Christenson, S. L., Thurlow, M. L., Ysseldyke, J. E., & McVicar, R. (1989). Written language instruction for students with mild handicaps: Is there enough quantity to ensure quality? *Learning Disability Quarterly, 12,* 219–229.

Deno, S. L., Mirkin, P. K., & Wesson, C. (1984). How to write effective data-based IEPs. *Teaching Exceptional Children, 16,* 99–104.

Dixon, R. C. (1991). The application of sameness analysis to spelling. *Journal of Learning Disabilities, 24,* 285–291, 310.

Dixon, R. C., & Engelmann, S. (1980). *Corrective spelling through morphographs.* Blacklick, OH: SRA.

Dixon, R. C., Engelmann, S., Meier, M., Steely, D., & Wells, T. (1989). *Spelling mastery.* Blacklick, OH: SRA.

Dolch, E. W. (1955). *Methods in reading.* Champaign, IL: Garrard.

Dolch, E. W. (1960). *Better spelling.* Champaign, IL: Garrard.

Dowis, C. L., & Schloss, P. (1992). The impact of minilessons on writing skills. *Remedial and Special Education, 13*(5), 34–42.

Edgington, R. (1967). But he spelled them right this morning. *Academic Therapy Quarterly, 3,* 58–59.

Ekwall, E. E., & Shanker, J. L. (1993). *Locating and correcting reading difficulties* (6th ed.). Upper Saddle River, NJ: Merrill/Prentice Hall.

Fernald, G. (1943). *Remedial techniques in basic school subjects.* New York: McGraw-Hill.

Fernald, G. (1988). *Remedial techniques in basic school subjects.* Austin, TX: PRO-ED.

Foster, K., & Torgesen, J. K. (1983). The effects of directed study on the spelling performance of two subgroups of learning disabled students. *Learning Disability Quarterly, 6,* 252–257.

Gates, A., & Russell, D. (1937). *Gates-Russell Spelling Diagnostic Test.* New York: Teachers College, Columbia University.

Gentry, J. R. (1982). An analysis of developmental spellings in *Gnys at wrk. The Reading Teacher, 36,* 192–200.

Gillingham, A., & Stillman, B. (1970). *Remedial training for children with specific disability in reading, spelling, and penmanship* (7th ed.). Cambridge, MA: Educators Publishing Service.

Gordon, J., Vaughn, S., & Schumm, J. S. (1993). Spelling interventions: A review of literature and implications for instruction for students with learning disabilities. *Learning Disabilities Research & Practice, 8,* 175–181.

Graham, S., & Freeman, S. (1986). Strategy training and teacher- vs. student-controlled study conditions: Effects on LD students' spelling performance. *Learning Disability Quarterly, 9,* 15–22.

Graham, S., & Harris, K. R. (1988). Instructional recommendations for teaching writing to exceptional students. *Exceptional Children, 54,* 506–512.

Graham, S., & Harris, K. R. (1994). Implications of constructivism for teaching writing to students with special needs. *The Journal of Special Education, 28,* 275–289.

Graham, S., Harris, K. R., & Loynachan, C. (1994). The Spelling for Writing list. *Journal of Learning Disabilities, 27,* 210–214.

Graham, S., Harris, K. R., MacArthur, C. A., & Schwartz, S. (1991). Writing and writing instruction for students with learning disabilities: Review of a research program. *Learning Disability Quarterly, 14,* 89–114.

Graham, S., & Miller, L. (1980). Handwriting research and practice: A unified approach. *Focus on Exceptional Children, 13*(2), 1–16.

Graham, S., & Voth, V. P. (1990). Spelling instruction: Making modifications for students with learning disabilities. *Academic Therapy, 25,* 447–457.

Graves, D. H. (1985). All children can write. *Learning Disabilities Focus, 1*(1), 36–43.

Greenbaum, C. R. (1987). *The Spellmaster Assessment and Teaching System.* Austin, TX: PRO-ED.

Greene, G. (1994). The magic of mnemonics. *LD Forum, 19*(3), 34–37.

Hagin, R. A. (1983). Write right—or left: A practical approach to handwriting. *Journal of Learning Disabilities, 16,* 266–271.

Hammill, D. D., & Larsen, S. C. (1996). *Test of Written Language—3.* Austin, TX: PRO-ED.

Hammill, D. D., & Leigh, J. E. (1983). *Basic School Skills Inventory—Diagnostic.* Austin, TX: PRO-ED.

Hammill, D. D., & McNutt, G. (1981). *Correlates of reading: The consensus of thirty years of correlational research* (PRO-ED Monograph No. 1). Austin, TX: PRO-ED.

Hanna, P. R., Hodges, R. E., & Hanna, J. S. (1971). *Spelling: Structure and strategies.* Boston: Houghton Mifflin.

Hanover, S. (1983). Handwriting comes naturally? *Academic Therapy, 18,* 407–412.

Hasselbring, T. S., & Goin, L. I. (1989). Use of computers. In G. A. Robinson, J. R. Patton, E. A. Polloway, & L. R. Sargent (Eds.), *Best practices in mild mental disabilities.* Reston, VA: Division on Mental Retardation, Council for Exceptional Children.

Herrick, V. E. (1960). Handwriting and children's writing. *Elementary English, 37,* 248–258.

Hildreth, G. (1963). Simplified handwriting for today. *Journal of Educational Research, 56,* 330–333.

Hitchcock, M. E. (1989). *Elementary students' invented spellings at the correct stage of spelling development.* Unpublished doctoral dissertation, University of Oklahoma, Norman.

Hodges, R. E. (1966). The psychological bases of spelling. In T. D. Horn (Ed.) *Research on handwriting and spelling.* Champaign, IL: National Council of Teachers of English.

Hofmeister, A. M. (1981). *Handwriting resource book: Manuscript/cursive.* Blacklick, OH: SRA.

Horn, E. A. (1926). *A basic writing vocabulary* (University of Iowa Monographs in Education, First Series No. 4). Iowa City: University of Iowa.

Horton, L. W. (1970). Illegibilities in the cursive handwriting of sixth graders. *Elementary School Journal, 70,* 446–450.

Houck, C. K., & Billingsley, B. S. (1989). Written expression of students with and without learning disabilities: Differences across the grades. *Journal of Learning Disabilities, 22,* 561–567, 572.

Hudson, F. G., Colson, S. E., Banikowski, A. K., & Mehring, T. A. (1989). *Hudson Education Skills Inventory—Writing.* Austin, TX: PRO-ED.

Hunt, K. W. (1965). *Grammatical structures written at three grade levels* (NCTE Research Report No. 3). Champaign, IL: National Council of Teachers of English.

Hunt-Berg, M., Rankin, J. L., & Beukelman, D. R. (1994). Ponder the possibilities: Computer-supported writing for struggling writers. *Learning Disabilities Research & Practice, 9,* 169–178.

Isaacson, S. (1988). Assessing the written product: Qualitative and quantitative measures. *Exceptional Children, 54,* 528–534.

Isaacson, S. (1990). Written language. In P. J. Schloss, M. A. Smith, & C. N. Schloss (Eds.), *Instructional methods for adolescents with learning and behavior problems* (pp. 202–228). Boston: Allyn & Bacon.

Johnson, D. J., & Myklebust, H. R. (1967). *Learning disabilities: Educational principles and practices.* New York: Grune & Stratton.

Johnson, W. (1944). Studies in language behavior. I. A program of research. *Psychological Monographs, 56*(2).

Kameenui, E. J., & Simmons, D. C. (1990). *Designing instructional strategies: The prevention of academic learning problems.* Upper Saddle River, NJ: Merrill/Prentice Hall.

Karlsen, B. (1992). *Language Arts Assessment Portfolio.* Circle Pines, MN: American Guidance Service.

Kauffman, J. M., Hallahan, D. P., Haas, K., Brame, T., & Boren, R. (1978). Imitating children's errors to improve their spelling performance. *Journal of Learning Disabilities, 11,* 217–222.

Kearney, C. A., & Drabman, R. S. (1993). The write-say method for improving spelling accuracy in children with learning disabilities. *Journal of Learning Disabilities, 26,* 52–56.

Kottmeyer, W. (1970). *Teacher's guide for remedial reading.* New York: McGraw-Hill.

Kuska, A., Webster, E. J. D., & Elford, G. (1964). *Spelling in language arts 6.* Don Mills, Ontario, Canada: Thomas Nelson & Sons.

Larsen, S. C., & Hammill, D. D. (1989). *Test of Legible Handwriting.* Austin, TX: PRO-ED.

Larsen, S. C., & Hammill, D. D. (1994). *Test of Written Spelling—3.* Austin, TX: PRO-ED.

Lerner, J. W., Lowenthal, B., & Lerner, S. R. (1995). *Attention deficit disorders: Assessment and teaching.* Pacific Grove, CA: Brooks/Cole.

Levy, N. R., & Rosenberg, M. S. (1990). Strategies for improving the written expression of students with learning disabilities. *LD Forum, 16,* 23–30.

Lewis, E. R., & Lewis, H. P. (1965). An analysis of errors in the formation of manuscript letters by first grade children. *American Educational Research Journal, 2,* 25–35.

Lovitt, T. C., Guppy, T. E., & Blattner, J. E. (1969). The use of free-time contingency with fourth graders to increase spelling accuracy. *Behavior Research Therapy, 7,* 151–156.

MacArthur, C. A. (1988). The impact of computers on the writing process. *Exceptional Children, 54,* 536–542.

MacArthur, C., & Graham, S. (1987). Learning disabled students' composing under three methods of text production: Handwriting, word processing, and dictation. *The Journal of Special Education, 21,* 22–42.

MacArthur, C. A., Schwartz, S. S., & Graham, S. (1991). A model for writing instruction: Integrating word processing and strategy instruction into a process approach to writing. *Learning Disabilities Research & Practice, 6,* 230–236.

Mann, P. H., Suiter, P. A., & McClung, R. M. (1992). *A guide to educating mainstreamed students* (4th ed.). Boston: Allyn & Bacon.

Markham, L. R. (1976). Influences of handwriting quality on teacher evaluation of written work. *American Educational Research Journal, 13,* 277–283.

Markwardt, F. C., Jr. (1989). *Peabody Individual Achievement Test—Revised.* Circle Pines, MN: American Guidance Service.

McCarthy, D. (1954). Language development in children. In L. Carmichael (Ed.). *Manual of child psychology.* New York: Wiley.

McGhee, R., Bryant, B. R., Larsen, S. C., & Rivera, D. M. (1995). *Test of Written Expression.* Austin, TX: PRO-ED.

McGuigan, C. A. (1975). *The effects of a flowing words list vs. fixed words lists and the implementation of procedures in the add-a-word spelling program* (Working Paper No. 52). Seattle: University of Washington, Experimental Education Unit.

McLoughlin, J. A., & Lewis, R. B. (1994). *Assessing special students* (4th ed.). Upper Saddle River, NJ: Merrill/Prentice Hall.

McNaughton, D., Hughes, C. A., & Clark, K. (1994). Spelling instruction for students with learning disabilities: Implications for research and practice. *Learning Disability Quarterly, 17,* 169–185.

Meckel, H. C. (1963). Research on teaching composition and literature. In N. Gage (Ed.), *Handbook of research on teaching.* Chicago: Rand McNally.

Miller, G. A. (1951). *Language and communication.* New York: McGraw-Hill.

Miller, S., & Engelmann, S. (1980). *Cursive writing program.* Blacklick, OH: SRA.

Milone, M. N., & Wasylyk, T. M. (1981). Handwriting in special education. *Teaching Exceptional Children, 14,* 58–61.

Morocco, C., & Nelson, A. (1990). *Writers at work.* Blacklick, OH: SRA.

Morris, N. T., & Crump, D. T. (1982). Syntactic and vocabulary development in the written language of learning disabled and non-learning disabled students at four age levels. *Learning Disability Quarterly, 5,* 163–172.

Myklebust, H. R. (1965). *Development and disorders of written language: Picture Story Language Test* (Vol. 1). New York: Grune & Stratton.

Newcomer, P. L., & Barenbaum, E. M. (1991). The written composing ability of children with learning disabilities: A review of the literature from 1980 to 1990. *Journal of Learning Disabilities, 24,* 578–593.

Newland, T. E. (1932). An analytical study of the development of illegibilities in handwriting from the lower grades to adulthood. *Journal of Educational Research, 26,* 249–258.

Outhred, L. (1989). Word processing: Its impact on children's writing. *Journal of Learning Disabilities, 22,* 262–264.

Parker, R. I., Tindal, G., & Hasbrouck, J. (1991). Progress monitoring with objective measures of writing performance for students with mild disabilities. *Exceptional Children, 58,* 61–73.

Petty, W. T. (1966). Handwriting and spelling: Their current status in the language arts curriculum. In T. D. Horn (Ed.), *Research on handwriting and spelling.* Champaign, IL: National Council of Teachers of English.

Phelps-Terasaki, D., & Phelps-Gunn, T. (1988). *Teaching competence in written language.* Austin, TX: PRO-ED.

Polloway, E. A., & Smith, T. E. C. (1992). *Language instruction for students with disabilities* (2nd ed.). Denver: Love.

Poplin, M. S., Gray, R., Larsen, S., Banikowski, A., & Mehring, T. (1980). A comparison of components of written expression abilities in learning disabled and non-learning disabled students at three grade levels. *Learning Disability Quarterly, 3*(4), 46–53.

Poteet, J. A. (1980). Informal assessment of written expression. *Learning Disability Quarterly, 3*(4), 88–98.

Powers, R., & Kaminsky, S. (1988). *Handwriting: A fresh start.* North Billerica, MA: Curriculum Associates.

Rankin, J. L., Bruning, R. H., Timme, V. L., & Katkanant, C. (1993). Is writing affected by spelling performance and beliefs about spelling? *Applied Cognitive Psychology, 7,* 155–169.

Schumaker, J. B., & Lyerla, K. D. (1991). *The paragraph writing strategy.* Lawrence: University of Kansas Center for Research on Learning.

Schumaker, J. B., Nolan, S. M., & Deshler, D. D. (1985). *Learning strategies curriculum: The error monitoring strategy.* Lawrence: University of Kansas.

Schumaker, J. B., & Sheldon, J. (1985). *The sentence writing strategy.* Lawrence: University of Kansas Center for Research on Learning.

Shinn, M. R., Tindal, G., & Stein, S. (1988). Curriculum-based measurement and the identification of mildly handicapped students: A research review. *Professional School Psychology, 3*(1), 69–85.

Shinn, T. K. (1982). Linguistic and functional spelling strategies. In D. A. Sabatino & L. Mann (Eds.), *A handbook of diagnostic and prescriptive teaching* (pp. 263–295). Rockville, MD: Aspen Systems.

Sidman, M. T. (1979). The effects of group free time contingency and individual free time contingency on spelling performance. *The Directive Teacher, 1,* 4–5.

Smith, C. R. (1994). *Learning disabilities: The interaction of learner, task, and setting* (3rd ed.). Boston: Allyn & Bacon.

Starlin, C. M., & Starlin, A. (1973). *Guides to decision making in spelling.* Bemidji, MN: Unique Curriculums Unlimited.

Stephens, T. M. (1977). *Teaching skills to children with learning and behavior disorders.* Upper Saddle River, NJ: Merrill/Prentice Hall.

Stephens, T. M., Hartman, A. C., & Lucas, V. H. (1982). *Teaching children basic skills: A curriculum handbook* (2nd ed.). Upper Saddle River, NJ: Merrill/Prentice Hall.

Stetson, E. (1988). *Stetson spelling program.* Austin, TX: PRO-ED.

Stowitschek, C. E., & Jobes, N. K. (1977). Getting the bugs out of spelling—or an alternative to the spelling bee. *Teaching Exceptional Children, 9,* 74–76.

Strauss, A., & Lehtinen, L. (1947). *Psychopathology and education of the brain-injured child.* New York: Grune & Stratton.

Stuckless, E. R., & Marks, C. H. (1966). *Assessment of the written language of deaf students* (USOE Cooperative Research Project 2544). Pittsburgh, PA: University of Pittsburgh.

Taylor, K. K., & Kidder, E. B. (1988). The development of spelling skills: From first grade through eighth grade. *Written Communication, 5,* 222–244.

Templeton, S. (1986). Synthesis of research on the learning and teaching of spelling. *Educational Leadership, 43*(6), 73–78.

Templin, E. (1960). Research and comment: Handwriting, the neglected R. *Elementary English, 37,* 386–389.

Thomas, C. C., Englert, C. S., & Gregg, S. (1987). An analysis of errors and strategies in the expository writing of learning disabled students. *Remedial and Special Education, 8*(1), 21–30, 46.

Thurber, D. (1983). Write on! With continuous stroke point. *Academic Therapy, 18,* 389–396.

Thurber, D. N. (1987). *D'Nealian handwriting* (Rev. ed.). Glenview, IL: Scott, Foresman.

Tindal, G. A., & Marston, D. B. (1990). *Classroom-based assessment: Evaluating instructional outcomes.* Upper Saddle River, NJ: Merrill/Prentice Hall.

Tompkins, G. E. (1994). *Teaching writing: Balancing process and product* (2nd ed.). Upper Saddle River, NJ: Merrill/Prentice Hall.

Tompkins, G. E., & Hoskisson, K. (1991). *Language arts: Content and teaching strategies.* Upper Saddle River, NJ: Merrill/Prentice Hall.

Vallecorsa, A. L., Zigmond, N., & Henderson, L. M. (1985). Spelling instruction in special education classrooms: A survey of practices. *Exceptional Children, 52,* 19–24.

Wallace, G., Larsen, S. C., & Elksnin, L, K. (1992). *Educational assessment of learning problems: Testing for teaching* (2nd ed.). Boston: Allyn & Bacon.

Warden, R., Allen, J., Hipp, K., Schmitz, J., & Collett, L. (1988). *Written expression.* San Antonio, TX: Psychological Corporation.

Warden, R., & Hutchinson, T. A. (1992). *Writing Process Test.* Chicago: Riverside.

Weiner, E. S. (1980). Diagnostic evaluation of writing skills. *Journal of Learning Disabilities, 13,* 48–53.

Welch, M. (1992). The PLEASE strategy: A metacognitive learning strategy for improving the paragraph writing of students with mild learning disabilities. *Learning Disability Quarterly, 15,* 119–128.

Wesson, C. L. (1987). Curriculum-based measurement: Increasing efficiency. *Teaching Exceptional Children, 20*(1), 46–47.

Westerman, G. S. (1971). *Spelling & writing.* San Rafael, CA: Dimensions.

Western, R. D. (1977). Case against cursive script. *Elementary School Journal, 78,* 1–3.

Whiting, S. A., & Jarrico, S. (1980). Spelling patterns of normal readers. *Journal of Learning Disabilities, 13,* 40–42.

Wiig, E. H., & Secord, W. A. (1994). Language disabilities in school-age children and youth. In G. H. Shames, E. H. Wiig, & W. A. Secord (Eds.), *Human communication disorders: An introduction* (4th ed., pp. 212-247). Boston: Allyn & Bacon.

Wilkinson, G. S. (1993). *Wide Range Achievement Test—3.* Wilmington, DE: Jastak Associates.

Wolf, D. P. (1989). Portfolio assessment: Sampling student work. *Educational Leadership, 46*(7), 35–39.

Wong, B. Y. L. (1986). A cognitive approach to teaching spelling. *Exceptional Children, 53,* 169–173.

Woodcock, R. W. (1991). *Woodcock Language Proficiency Battery—Revised.* Chicago: Riverside.

Wright, C. D., & Wright, J. P. (1980). Handwriting: The effectiveness of copying from moving versus still models. *Journal of Educational Research, 74,* 95–98.

Zaner-Bloser Evaluation Scales. (1984). Columbus, OH: Zaner-Bloser.

Zentall, S. S. (1993). Research on the educational implications of attention deficit hyperactivity disorder. *Exceptional Children, 60,* 143–153.

Reading

CHAPTER 13

After studying this chapter, you should be able to:

- discuss causal factors related to reading disabilities.
- list types of reading problems.
- discuss the term *dyslexia*.
- discuss the organization of reading skills.
- describe the stages of the development of reading skills.
- describe standardized survey and diagnostic reading tests.
- describe criterion-referenced reading tests.
- discuss informal assessment techniques in reading.
- discuss code-emphasis versus meaning-emphasis programs in teaching reading skills.
- discuss developmental reading approaches.
- discuss remedial reading programs and methods.
- discuss teaching strategies for vocabulary and comprehension development.
- discuss reading and study skills for adolescents.
- describe commercial reading programs.
- describe computer software programs in reading.

Reading is one of the central difficulties of students with learning disabilities. Carnine, Silbert, and Kameenui (1990) suggest that it is the principal cause of failure in school. Reading experiences strongly influence a student's self-image and feeling of competency; furthermore, reading failure can lead to misbehavior, anxiety, and a lack of motivation. Moreover, in American culture, learning to read is important in maintaining self-respect and for obtaining the respect of others.

Reading is a complex task, and numerous definitions exist. In this chapter, *reading* is defined as a visual-auditory task that involves obtaining meaning from symbols (letters and words). Reading includes two basic processes: a *decoding* process and a *comprehension* process. The decoding process involves understanding the phoneme-grapheme relationships and translating printed words into a representation similar to oral language. Thus, decoding skills enable the learner to pronounce words correctly. Comprehension skills enable the learner to understand the meaning of words in isolation and in context.

Whereas 10% to 15% of the general school population experience difficulty in reading (Harris & Sipay, 1990), the majority of all students with learning disabilities have reading problems. Reading disabilities reflect a persistent deficit rather than a developmental lag. According to Lyon (1995), longitudinal studies indicate that of those students who have reading disabilities in the third grade, about 74% continue to have disabilities in the ninth grade. Thus, students who receive effective intervention before the third grade have a greater chance of developing appropriate reading skills.

FACTORS RELATED TO READING DISABILITIES

Why do some students read poorly? Kirk, Kliebhan, and Lerner (1978) organize possible factors into three areas: physical, environmental, and psychological. Table 13.1 lists factors related to reading disabilities and their various components. These factors may contribute to reading problems but do not cause reading disabilities.

TABLE 13.1
Factors Related to Reading Disabilities

Physical Factors
*Neurological dysfunction
*Cerebral dominance and laterality
Visual defects
Auditory defects
*Heredity and genetics

Environmental Factors
*Inadequate teaching
Cultural differences
Language differences
Social and emotional problems

Psychological Factors
*Auditory perception
*Visual perception
*Language disorders
*Selective attention
*Memory
Intelligence

*These factors have received more attention in learning disabilities than the others.

Physical Factors

The work of Hinshelwood (1917) and S. T. Orton (1937) stimulated much research in the area of neurological dysfunction and reading disabilities. Hinshelwood described neurological correlates of reading problems in his book *Congenital Word Blindness*. S. T. Orton claimed that the inability to read is a function of a lack of cerebral dominance. He labeled reversal errors in reading and writing (e.g., *was* for *saw*) *strephosymbolia*, meaning "twisted symbols." Visual and auditory defects also have been studied as physical factors that inhibit reading ability. New developments in neuroimaging reinforce the hypothesis that reading disabilities have a biologic basis (Lyon, 1995). Finally, studies of heredity and genetics indicate that reading disabilities sometimes occur in a family line. Lyon notes that research provides evidence for genetic etiology of reading disabilities, with deficits in phonological awareness reflecting the greatest degree of heritability.

Environmental Factors

Many special educators believe that youngsters fail to read primarily because they are not taught properly. Inadequate instruction may consist partly of inappropriate methods. Heilman, Blair, and Rupley (1994) report that the teacher is a key ingredient in reading success. Additional environmental factors include cultural differences (e.g., students who are disadvantaged or from a minority group), language differences (i.e., the student's language reflects environment), and social and emotional problems.

Psychological Factors

It is not established firmly that reading failure is linked to poor auditory and visual perception (as measured by commonly used perception tests); however, researchers have studied how reading relates to problems in auditory discrimination, sound blending, and visual and auditory memory. In a review of the research, Samuels (1973) found that poor visual memory, intelligence, and language disorders (i.e., the student lacks normal speech and language development even though normal speech and language opportunities exist in a standard environment) are associated with poor reading. Moreover, numerous researchers (Dykman, Ackerman, Clements, & Peters, 1971; Keogh & Margolis, 1976) report that many students with learning disabilities and poor readers have difficulty paying attention, a problem highly correlated to reading difficulty (Samuels & Edwall, 1981).

Combinations of Factors

Probably, combinations of factors interact and contribute to reading problems. According to Rosner, Abrams, Daniels, and Schiffman (1981), "An approach to the disabled reader-learner that takes into consideration the unique interaction of functional and organic factors is most desirable" (p. 439). The student is a physical being, functioning in a social environment in a psychological manner.

However, regardless of cause, the teacher can deal only with factors that can be controlled (e.g., reading method, material, intensity of instruction, and reinforcement). The teacher must determine what the student's problems are and how to provide intervention effectively.

TYPES OF READING PROBLEMS

Because reading problems stem from many causes and the reading process is so complex, many reading difficulties can exist. Bond, Tinker, Wasson, and Wasson (1989) provide the following general classification of the more prevalent reading difficulties: (a) faulty word identification and recognition, (b) inappropriate directional habits, (c) deficiencies in basic comprehension abilities, (d) limited special comprehension abilities (such as inability to locate and retain specific facts), (e) deficiencies in basic study skills, (f) deficiencies in ability to adapt to reading needs of content fields, (g) deficiencies in rate of comprehension, and (h) poor oral reading. Table 13.2 presents some common problems in reading habits, word recognition errors, and comprehension errors.

Some errors are auditory; others are visual. Mispronunciation of a word is considered to be an auditory error if the student is unable to blend sounds or word parts correctly into a complete word. Also considered to be auditory-based is the inability to distinguish easily the difference between phonemic sounds. Moreover, the student may be unable to remember letter sounds (auditory memory) or may distort or omit speech sounds and syllables (auditory sequential memory).

Reversals of letters (*b*, *d*; *p*, *q*) and words (*no*, *on*; *tub*, *but*) are frequent errors. Youngsters who make these errors may be confusing left from right and sometimes top from bottom (*b*, *p*). The student with visual discrimination problems may have difficulty noting fine differences between

TABLE 13.2
Common Reading Problems of Students with Reading Disabilities

Characteristics	Comments
Reading Habits	
Tension movements	Frowning, fidgeting, using a high-pitched voice, and lip biting.
Insecurity	Refusing to read, crying, and attempting to distract the teacher.
Loses place	Losing place frequently (often is associated with repetitions).
Lateral head movements	Jerking head.
Holds material close	Deviating extremely (from 15 to 18 inches).
Word Recognition Errors	
Omissions	Omitting a word (e.g., *Tom saw ⓐ cat*).
Insertions	Inserting words (e.g., *The dog ran* [fast] *after the cat*).
Substitutions	Substituting one word for another (e.g., *The house* ~~horse~~ *was big*).
Reversals	Reversing letters in a word (e.g., *no* for *on, was* for *saw*).
Mispronunciations	Mispronouncing words (e.g., *mister* for *miser*).
Transpositions	Reading words in the wrong order (e.g., *She away ran* for *She ran away*).
Unknown words	Hesitating for 5 seconds at words they cannot pronounce.
Slow choppy reading	Not recognizing words quickly enough (20 to 30 words per minute).
Comprehension Errors	
Cannot recall basic facts	Unable to answer specific questions about a passage (e.g., *What was the dog's name?*).
Cannot recall sequence	Unable to tell sequence of the story that was read.
Cannot recall main theme	Unable to recall the main topic of the story.
Miscellaneous Symptoms	
Word-by-word reading	Reading in a choppy, halting, and laborious manner (e.g., no attempts are made to group words into thought units).
Strained, high-pitched voice	Reading in a pitch higher than conversational tone.
Inadequate phrasing	Inappropriately grouping words (e.g., *The dog ran into* [pause] *the woods*).
Ignored or misinterpreted punctuation	Running together phrases, clauses, or sentences.

letters (*m*, *n*) and words (*pan*, *pat*), whereas a youngster with poor visual memory may be unable to recognize specific letters and sight words. Moreover, some students transpose or scramble letters in words (*clam* for *calm*) and words within sentences (visual sequential memory).

Whereas some word recognition errors have negligible effect on the student's ability to understand, others cause substantial comprehension loss. Students whose errors result in comprehension loss show progress when they learn, with help, to "break the code." A few students with this problem do better on tests of silent reading than oral reading because they use contextual analysis to aid comprehension. Those who cannot easily recall stated facts on a literal level undoubtedly will have difficulty with complex decisions such as predicting outcomes and making value judgments.

DYSLEXIA

The term *dyslexia* refers to severe difficulty in learning to read. Its various definitions include behavioral manifestations of central nervous system deficits or dysfunctions, genetic or inherited causation, maturational lag, and inability to learn to read through general classroom methods. Critchley (1981) defines developmental dyslexia as follows:

> Developmental dyslexia: a learning disability which initially shows itself by difficulty in learning to read, and later by erratic spelling and by lack of facility in manipulating written as opposed to spoken words. The condition is cognitive in essence, and usually genetically determined. It is not due to intellectual inadequacy or to lack of socio-cultural opportunity, or to faults in the technique of teaching, or to any known structural brain defect. It probably represents a specific maturational defect which tends to lessen as the child gets older, and is capable of considerable improvement, especially when appropriate remedial help is offered at the earliest opportunity. (pp. 1–2)

It should be noted that recent neuroscientific research indicates that dyslexia has a genetic basis and that some individuals with dyslexia have a different anatomical brain structure (Filipek, 1995; Pennington, 1995).

Although primarily a medical term, *dyslexia* has an educational perspective. The medical perspective (which originated in Europe) focuses on genetics, brain damage, and central nervous system dysfunction. In comparison, American educators and psychologists consider dyslexia to be simply a reading disability of individuals who have average or above average intelligence. Although the term *dyslexia* still is used today (primarily by medical specialists), most educators prefer the term *severe reading disability*.

The student with dyslexia has persistent difficulty in learning the components of words and sentences. There may be a history of delayed language development, and the student almost always has problems writing and spelling (Bryan & Bryan, 1986). Spatial directional confusion (left-right disorientation) can result in prolonged difficulty in differentiating letters that look similar (*p*, *q*; *b*, *d*). Reversals of letters and numbers (*pan*, *nap*; *71*, *17*) are errors of sequential ordering. Also, the student's oral reading is marked by slow, word-by-word reading. The student may be able to recognize words presented in isolation but miss these same words presented in context. Sometimes a student with dyslexia may misread or mispronounce a word and still know what the text says. For example, in oral reading the student may read *John* for *Jim*, but a comprehension check indicates that the student knows the name is *Jim*. Likewise, the student may misread many words on a given list but be able to pick out the same words when they are presented orally. Thus, what the student says (reading output) is incorrect, but reading input (what is understood) is adequate, and internally the student knows the word correctly. Finally, Bryan and Bryan (1986) indicate that some youngsters with dyslexia also have difficulty learning representational systems such as telling time, directions, and seasons. They confuse time and direction words, such as *up* for *down*, *first* for *last*, and *go* for *stop*.

D. J. Johnson and Myklebust (1967) classify dyslexic problems as either auditory or visual. Individuals with auditory dyslexia cannot perceive discrete sounds of spoken language, have difficulty discriminating consonant and vowel sounds (especially short vowels), and are unable to associate specific sounds with their printed symbols. Thus, they have great difficulty with spelling, and phonics instruction is virtually meaningless. Individuals with visual dyslexia cannot accurately interpret what they see and cannot correctly translate printed language symbols into meaning. The student may see certain letters backward and upside down and also may see parts of words in reverse. Thus, the student becomes frustrated trying to read whole words in the context of a sentence.

Because the student with dyslexia cannot rely on visual and auditory senses to interpret printed symbols accurately, overlearning is imperative. The teacher can involve sense of touch and muscular coordination through tracing, templates, and cutout letters or can provide the object and sound, such as showing the student a shirt to help associate the digraph *sh* and the word *shirt*. In addition, a language enrichment program and the presentation of linguistic skills within the context of reading may be helpful. Thus, various remediation techniques can be adapted according to each student's problem.

ORGANIZATION OF READING SKILLS

To assess or teach reading skills effectively, it is helpful to understand the general organization of reading content and related subskills. As implied in the definition, reading content is divided into word recognition skills and comprehension skills. Figure 13.1 illustrates these skills. Reading approaches differ in the skills they stress and when to introduce them. For example, a phonics approach emphasizes the early introduction of the sound-symbol system, whereas an approach that focuses on meaning stresses learning whole words by sight at first and introduces the sound-symbol system later.

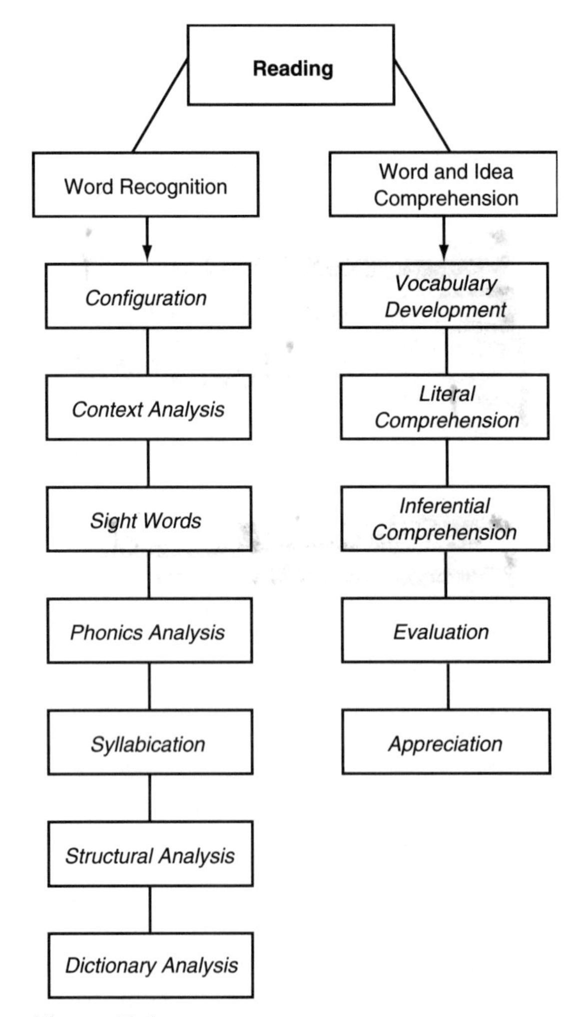

Figure 13.1
An organizational framework of developmental reading skills

Educators commonly use seven strategies of word recognition (Ekwall & Shanker, 1989; Guszak, 1985):

1. *Configuration*—the outline or general shape of a word. Word length, uppercase letters, and letter height can provide some visual cues to the unskilled reader.
2. *Context analysis*—"the use of any surrounding information that may unlock a given word's name or meaning" (Guszak, 1985, p. 72). Semantic and syntactic (grammatical) cues help the reader predict word possibilities according to context. Likewise, pictures can provide context cues.
3. *Sight words*—words the reader recognizes without applying phonetic analysis. Sight words include frequently used words, such as those on the Dolch list (Dolch, 1955), as well as words the reader knows instantly from repeated exposure. Many words in English that have irregular spellings are taught as sight words; that is, they are learned as whole words. In reading approaches that focus on meaning, the whole-word method is used predominantly to introduce printed words.
4. *Phonics analysis*—decoding words by symbol-sound associations. This involves the learning of phonemes and rules concerning the various sounds such as those pertaining to single initial consonants, initial and ending consonant blends, consonant digraphs, silent consonants, short and long vowel sounds, and vowel teams and special letter combinations.

5. *Syllabication*—the process of dividing a word into its component parts. Each syllable contains a vowel sound. Some authorities place syllabication in phonics skills, whereas others include it in structural analysis (Ekwall & Shanker, 1989).
6. *Structural analysis*—the use of meaningful units such as root words, prefixes, suffixes, possessives, plurals, word families, and compound words. Comprehension of these structures permits a faster rate of reading than does analyzing individual sounds.
7. *Dictionary analysis*—the use of a dictionary. Although seldom used for word recognition, it provides an independent means of pronouncing unknown words by using the pronunciation key symbols in a glossary or dictionary.

Five major areas are included in reading comprehension (Ekwall & Shanker, 1989; Smith & Barrett, 1979):

1. *Vocabulary development* is essential for the reader to understand the words a writer has used. A background of meaningful experience (exposure to books, people, and places) and learning words from context (through a variety of reading material) help develop vocabulary.
2. *Literal comprehension* refers to recognition and recall of explicitly stated information. Some of the skills involved in literal reading include reading for the central thought and main ideas, noting and remembering significant details, noting the order or sequence of events, and finding answers to specific questions.
3. *Inferential* (or *interpretative*) *comprehension* requires the reader to make conjectures or hypotheses based on stated information, intuition, and personal experience. Grasping cause-effect relationships, anticipating the remainder of a story, and forming opinions are inferential comprehension skills.
4. *Evaluation* or *critical reading* deals with judgments based on the reader's experiences, knowledge, or values. Evaluation focuses on qualities of accuracy, acceptability, worth, or probability of occurrence. It includes determining validity and judging the difference between reality and fantasy or fact and opinion. It also involves making value (moral) judgments and analyzing the intent of the author.
5. *Appreciation* deals with being emotionally and aesthetically sensitive to the written selection. To function at this level, the student identifies with characters and incidents and verbally can express emotional feelings about the work (e.g., excitement, fear, or boredom).

In functional reading, the student reads to obtain information. Whereas developmental reading (word recognition and comprehension) involves *learning to read*, functional reading involves *reading to learn*. Functional reading sometimes is called *study skills* because it includes locating information (using indexes, tables of contents, and encyclopedias), comprehending data (technical vocabulary, maps, and tables), outlining and summarizing, researching, and developing study patterns for specific content areas.

DEVELOPMENT OF READING SKILLS

Chall and Stahl (1982) discuss three reading models that differ in the amount of importance they attach to text and meaning. The *bottom-up* model emphasizes that readers proceed from text to meaning; that is, letters and words are perceived and decoded and then the text's meaning is comprehended. In contrast, the *top-down* model emphasizes that readers rely on prior knowledge and comprehension of the meaning of the textual material rather than on word recognition and decoding of individual text elements. In essence, in the bottom-up model, reading depends primarily on the reader's skill in sound-symbol association and word recognition, whereas in the top-down model the focus is on the reader's ability to question, hypothesize, and comprehend rather than on decoding individual text elements. The *interactive* model emphasizes both text and meaning by proposing that readers shift between attending to the text (i.e., specific letters and words) and what is in their mind (i.e., predicting or hypothesizing). For example, a reader may use a top-down approach when the material is familiar but change to a bottom-up approach when confronted with unfamiliar text.

Reading content has a structure in which the student first constructs simple relationships (such as grapheme-phoneme) and then progresses to more complex tasks (such as critical reading). Thus, the interactive model may describe the reading process most adequately, especially in the early stages of learning to read. As the reader becomes more proficient, attention to comprehension is increased and less attention is given to scrutinizing individual letters and words. Many authorities (Chall, 1983b; Kirk et al., 1978) feel that growth in reading skills occurs in several stages. Knowing the stages helps the teacher select assessment tasks, develop instructional goals, and choose instructional approaches. In addition, carefully monitoring student progress helps determine when the student moves from one level to the next. Chall (1983b) divides reading development into six stages, from 0 to 5, covering prereading to highly skilled reading: (0) prereading, (1) initial reading or decoding, (2) confirmation, fluency, and ungluing from print, (3) reading for learning the new, (4) multiple viewpoints, and (5) construction and reconstruction.

Stage 0: Prereading

During the prereading stage, from birth to about age 6, children gradually and unsystematically accumulate understandings about reading. Most children acquire some knowledge and insight into print and learn to recognize letters, common signs, and common words. Many children can print their own names and pretend they can read a story that has been read frequently to them. Prereading activities should include parents' reading to children (especially reading that involves the child actively through discussing stories and learning to identify letters and words), experiences with environmental print (e.g., fast-food restaurant signs, food labels, and traffic signs), and children's art and play activities.

The relationship of mental age to reading readiness has received much attention. Some educators maintain that a minimum of 6 to 6 ½ years is essential, but this position—primarily based on studies conducted in large classrooms in the 1930s (Gates, 1937)—is being viewed critically. Educators now realize that difficulty of material, pace of instruction, method used, amount of individualized help, and the child's specific abilities affect the minimum mental age required for efficient learning. Harris and Sipay (1990) note that reading readiness activities, now begun in kindergarten in some schools, are viewed not as distinct from reading and preparing the way for it but as the teaching of specific prereading skills that merge gradually into reading.

Stage 1: Initial Reading or Decoding

The initial reading stage (first to second grade) involves learning to use letter-sound relationships to decode printed words not recognized immediately. Children learn to recognize words and understand material in their books; however, what they can read at this stage is considerably below what they can understand in speech. Often the student reads slowly, word-by-word, trying to break a detailed, complicated code. Some students experience difficulty acquiring beginning decoding skills due to problems with the phonological aspects of language (Perfetti, 1985). A basic phonological problem of poor readers is lack of awareness that words have parts (i.e., phonemes, syllables, and morphemes). (Phonological awareness is discussed later in this chapter.) For many students, adequate phonics instruction involving the sequencing and blending of sounds to form words is necessary for the acquisition of basic decoding skills; however, students who have difficulty with phonics analysis may use context analysis, syllabication, or structural analysis to aid in word identification.

Much controversy exists among researchers concerning this stage in relation to the *code-emphasis* approach versus the *meaning-emphasis* approach. The code approach stresses the early introduction of the sound-symbol system and teaching phonics. The meaning approach stresses the initial learning of whole words and sentences by sight, with phonics instruction introduced later.

Stage 2: Confirmation, Fluency, and Ungluing from Print

In the second and third grades, what students previously have learned is consolidated in the recognition of words and the use of decoding skills to help them comprehend easy and familiar texts. At this stage, students automatically begin to use the tools acquired previously, attain fluent reading, and are able to read grade-level material in the range of 100 to 140 words per minute with two or fewer errors. By using their decoding skills along with repetitions inherent in the language and stories read, students gain competence in using context and, consequently, improve in fluency and reading rate. Perfetti (1985) notes that when the decoding process becomes automatic (accurate and rapid), attention is freed for higher-level reading comprehension skills. Most students develop rapid word recognition as a result of the familiarity that develops from extended practice; however, students with reading problems require additional practice and repetition to reach automaticity. The transition from the initial stage to the fluency stage is similar to the transition experience of a baby who at first must concentrate intensely on learning to walk and then can walk automatically without thinking about it. Students at the initial stage read automatically until an unknown word is encountered, and then they try a variety of word-attack approaches. By the end of this stage, students have developed fluency and can quickly recognize familiar words, sound out words they do not recognize, and predict other words according to context. Measures of reading speed and reading accuracy should be included in reading assessment to determine which students are ready to move to the next stage of reading instruction (Perfetti, 1985).

Stage 3: Reading for Learning the New

This stage, which begins in fourth grade and continues through eighth grade, marks the beginning of reading to learn, as opposed to learning to read in earlier stages. Reading is used to gain new knowledge, experience new feelings, and learn new ideas and attitudes. Thus, students acquire a rich base of information and vocabulary concepts by reading a wide variety of materials. At this stage, silent reading is done in large units (e.g., a complete story or selection), and word study is concerned more with meanings than with recognition or decoding because the reading materials contain more unfamiliar abstract, technical, and literary words. Snider and Tarver (1987) suggest that students with learning disabilities who read with slow and inaccurate decoding skills may fail to learn many of the concepts that typically are acquired during this stage by inference from the context and by analogical reasoning from prior knowledge. In other words, students with learning disabilities may be limited in learning from usual reading experiences because poor decoding skills present a barrier to the acquisition of knowledge. The resulting impoverished knowledge base may be insufficient for comprehension of more complex reading material. Thus, because of the cumulative effects of deficiencies at earlier stages, students with learning disabilities are especially in need of effective and efficient instruction at this stage.

Stage 4: Multiple Viewpoints

Reading at the secondary school level requires students to deal with a variety of viewpoints and to compare and evaluate information from a variety of sources. Secondary students are expected to read complex texts in advanced content areas. Through reading and studying materials that vary widely in type, content, and style, students practice acquiring difficult concepts and learning new concepts and points of view through reading. At this level, metacognitive processes play an important role through monitoring and evaluating one's understanding of the text while reading. Instruction in comprehension monitoring should be followed by instruction in study skills and use of reference materials. The failure of a student with learning disabilities to monitor understanding of the text may be due to an inability to decode rapidly and efficiently or to a lack of necessary information to understand the topic. To facilitate the use of textbooks with students who have difficulty reading them, Ciborowski (1995) presents a textbook teaching-learning model that focuses on activating prior knowledge, helping students become more active comprehenders and thinkers, and consolidating and extending textbook usage. Moreover, Snider and Tarver (1987) suggest that supplemental materials emphasizing vocabulary and background information should be developed to accompany content-area textbooks to help students with learning disabilities profit from reading in the content areas.

Stage 5: Construction and Reconstruction

At the college level, students read books and articles in the detail and depth that they need for their own purposes. From reading what others write, students construct knowledge for their own use. At this stage, the reader synthesizes information and forms hypotheses that usually are restricted to a specific area of study at an advanced level. Thus, reading at this stage requires extensive background knowledge in highly specialized content areas. The acquisition of the highly specialized knowledge in this stage is dependent upon the rich base of information acquired in Stages 3 and 4, which, in turn, is dependent upon accurate decoding and fluency skills developed in Stages 1 and 2.

ASSESSMENT OF READING SKILLS

Once the teacher recognizes the decoding and comprehension processes of the reading task and is aware of the network of reading skills and their general developmental sequence, reading assessment can be undertaken in a meaningful manner. In addition to indicating the student's current reading ability, assessment can point to specific strengths and weaknesses and aid in planning instructional objectives. Both commercially prepared instruments and informal measures are useful.

Many commercial tests have been standardized on large groups of students. Such norm-referenced tests enable the teacher to compare each student's performance with the population upon which the test was standardized. Scores from standardized reading tests are reported in several ways (such as reading grade level, reading age score, percentile, and stanine score). However, the use of norm-referenced tests requires following strict procedures in administration, scoring, and interpretation. In addition to norm-referenced tests, some published reading measures are criterion-referenced. These tests describe performance, rather than compare it, and can be used to determine whether the student has mastered specific instructional objectives. In addition, informal assessment techniques often are used.

To obtain a valid assessment of the student's reading abilities, the teacher should use a variety of assessment procedures—standardized tests, observations, and informal inventories. The information the teacher wants to obtain should help determine the type of assessment device used. For example, a group-administered reading achievement test yields information on the level of reading of the entire class, whereas more specific information about certain skills of one student can be obtained from an individually administered diagnostic reading test or through informal assessment.

Standardized Tests

Achievement and Reading Survey Tests. General achievement tests assess a student's ability in various academic areas. Achievement tests with reading subtests often are used to obtain an overall measure of reading achievement. These tests are norm-referenced and thus yield objective results that can be compared with the norms of the standardization sample. Reading survey tests measure reading skills only and also are used frequently to indicate a student's general range of reading abilities. Achievement and reading survey tests are basically screening measures and can help determine which students are experiencing reading difficulties and need further assessment. Reading survey tests and achievement tests with reading subtests include the following:

1. *Gates-MacGinitie Reading Tests—Third Edition* (MacGinitie & MacGinitie, 1989). Assesses vocabulary and comprehension.
2. *Iowa Tests of Basic Skills* (Hoover, Hieronymus, Frisbie, & Dunbar, 1993). Assesses word analysis, vocabulary, and reading comprehension.
3. *Kaufman Test of Educational Achievement* (Kaufman & Kaufman, 1985). Assesses reading decoding and comprehension.
4. *Metropolitan Achievement Tests—Seventh Edition* (Balow, Farr, & Hogan, 1992). Assesses word recognition, reading vocabulary, and reading comprehension.
5. *Woodcock-Johnson Psycho-Educational Battery—Revised* (Woodcock & Johnson, 1989). Assesses letter-word identification, word attack, reading vocabulary, and passage comprehension.

Diagnostic Tests. In contrast to achievement and general reading survey tests, which yield broad information, diagnostic reading tests provide a more precise, comprehensive analysis of specific reading abilities and disabilities. Diagnostic tests differ from achievement tests in that they generally have more subtests and test items related to specific reading skills. The teacher finds out *how* the student attempts to read. By pinpointing the student's specific strengths and weaknesses in various subskills of reading, diagnostic tests yield detailed, useful information for planning appropriate individual educational programs.

Diagnostic reading test batteries are designed to measure many reading subskills. They often include multiple subtests that sample performance in areas such as word analysis, word recognition, comprehension, and various reading-related skills. In contrast to test batteries, some diagnostic reading tests are designed to measure the student's ability in a specific skill area. Table 13.3 lists selected standardized diagnostic reading test batteries and tests of specific skills.

Criterion-Referenced Tests

Whereas norm-referenced tests compare a student's performance with the scores of others, criterion-referenced tests describe performance according to fixed criteria. The teacher finds out what skills the student has learned, what is being learned now, and what skills still must be taught. The teacher uses criterion-referenced reading tests to determine whether the student has mastered specific objectives, such as recognition of *ed* endings or use of the *ch* consonant digraph. Test items are presented in a hierarchy to assess a sequence of reading skills. If performance on each skill does not reach the established criterion of success (e.g., 95% level of proficiency), the teacher provides instruction specifically for that skill. A student who demonstrates mastery of a skill according to the determined criterion progresses to the next skill in the sequence. Thus, criterion-referenced tests focus on the student's ability to master specific skills, and the assessment relates to curriculum content and instructional objectives. The student's progress is determined by comparing current performance with previous performance. Table 13.4 includes four criterion-referenced reading assessment measures.

TABLE 13.3
Selected Standardized Diagnostic Reading Tests

Test	Grade Levels	Areas Assessed
Test Batteries		
Diagnostic Reading Scales (Spache, 1981)	1–7	Oral reading errors, silent reading comprehension, auditory comprehension
Three word recognition lists and 22 reading passages of increasing difficulty are included. The student's performance on the word lists, which increase in difficulty, indicates the level at which the reading passages should begin. As the student reads orally from the reading passages, the teacher notes reading errors and then checks comprehension by asking several questions following each passage. Instructional, independent, and potential reading levels are determined. Twelve supplementary phonics and word analysis tests also are included to assess such areas as consonant and vowel sounds, blending, initial consonant substitution, and auditory discrimination.		
Durrell Analysis of Reading Difficulty (Durrell & Catterson, 1980)	1–6	Oral reading, silent reading, listening comprehension, word recognition and word analysis
Oral reading passages and accompanying comprehension questions are included, as well as paragraphs for silent reading and listening comprehension. Additional subtests are included in listening vocabulary, sounds in isolation, spelling, visual memory of words, identifying sounds in words, and prereading phonics abilities. The battery assesses a wide variety of specific skills and requires about an hour to administer. In addition to providing a profile of grade-level scores, the test includes a checklist of instructional needs on which the teacher can note particular reading difficulties. Also, the test manual contains helpful information concerning corrective instruction and program planning.		
Gates-McKillop-Horowitz Reading Diagnostic Tests (Gates, McKillop, & Horowitz, 1981)	1–6	Oral reading (with error analysis), flash presentation of words, knowledge of word parts, recognition of visual forms representing sounds, auditory blending, auditory discrimination, written expression
This comprehensive diagnostic reading battery assesses a wide range of word analysis skills. The teacher may choose to administer only certain subtests, depending on the student's age and level of skill development. The test lacks a subtest assessing reading comprehension, but the battery can be quite useful when used with a student experiencing severe difficulties in word analysis.		
Stanford Diagnostic Reading Test—Fourth Edition (Karlsen & Gardner, 1995)	1–13	Phonetic analysis, vocabulary, comprehension, scanning
This group-administered test is both norm-referenced and criterion-referenced. There are six levels, identified by color, and several subtests of the four skill areas are not included at all six levels; for example, phonetic analysis is included only in the first three levels, and scanning is assessed in the last three levels. Two forms are available for the last three levels. In addition to yielding percentile ranks, stanines, grade equivalents, and scaled scores, the test results can be used to identify strengths and weaknesses in specific reading skills.		

TABLE 13.3
continued

Test	Grade Levels	Areas Assessed
Woodcock Reading Mastery Tests—Revised (Woodcock, 1987)	K–college and adult	Visual auditory learning, letter identification, word identification, word attack, word comprehension, passage comprehension
This battery of tests yields cluster scores (in readiness, basic skills, and comprehension) and a total reading score, as well as derived scores (age- and grade-based percentile ranks and standard scores, and age and grade equivalents). The test contains two forms (one of which omits visual-auditory learning and letter identification). A microcomputer scoring program can be used to assist the examiner in computing scores and providing score printouts.		
Tests of Specific Skills		
Formal Reading Inventory (Wiederholt, 1985)	1–12	Silent reading comprehension, oral reading miscues
The four separate forms of the inventory each include 13 developmentally sequenced passages with five multiple-choice comprehension questions following each story. On two forms the student silently reads the paragraphs and answers the comprehension questions, and on the other two forms, which are identical to the forms of the *Gray Oral Reading Test—Revised*, the student orally reads the passages while the examiner notes miscues. Each form takes about 15 minutes to administer, and the inventory yields a silent reading comprehension quotient, a percentile score for silent reading comprehension, and a classification of oral reading miscues.		
Gray Oral Reading Tests—Third Edition (Wiederholt & Bryant, 1992)	1–12	Reading miscues, reading rate, comprehension
This test includes two forms, each of which contains 13 developmentally sequenced passages with five comprehension questions. As the student reads aloud, the teacher notes reading characteristics, errors, and time elapsed in reading each paragraph. Comprehension questions are asked after each paragraph is read. A system for performing a miscue analysis of reader performance yields information in four areas: meaning similarity, function similarity, graphic/phonemic similarity, and self-correction. Standard scores, percentile ranks, and grade equivalents are provided. The *Gray Oral Reading Tests—Diagnostic* (Bryant & Wiederholt, 1991) can be used as a supplement to the GORT—3. The student reads passages orally and responds to comprehension questions. If performance on the paragraph reading is poor, additional subtests are administered in decoding, word identification, word attack, morphemic analysis, contextual analysis, and word ordering. Thus, information is provided about graphic-phonemic, function, and meaning cues that the student uses to decipher words in print and comprehend words and ideas.		
Test of Reading Comprehension—3 (Brown, Hammill, & Wiederholt, 1995)	2–12	General vocabulary, syntactic similarities, paragraph reading, sentence sequencing
This test includes eight subtests and can be administered to either groups or individuals. In addition to the four general comprehension core subtests, there are four diagnostic supplementary subtests in mathematics vocabulary, social studies vocabulary, science vocabulary, and reading the directions of schoolwork. Standard scores, grade and age equivalents, and reading comprehension quotients are provided.		

TABLE 13.4
Selected Criterion-Referenced Reading Tests

Test	Grade Levels	Areas Assessed
Brigance Diagnostic Comprehensive Inventory of Basic Skills (Brigance, 1983)	K–9	Word recognition, oral reading, word analysis, reading comprehension
This inventory is used primarily to establish educational objectives and monitor progress toward these objectives. Student record books show at each testing the point of competence to which the student has progressed. Also, a class record book is provided for the teacher to keep a record of each student's progress.		
Hudson Education Skills Inventory—Reading (Hudson, Colson, & Welch, 1989)	K–12	Readiness, sight word vocabulary, phonics analysis, structural analysis, comprehension
This curriculum-based inventory provides a criterion-referenced measure of reading skills for use in planning instruction. A test-down/teach-up model is used in which the teacher ends the test at the student's actual level of performance and then can simply teach up the curriculum skills sequence. The teacher can administer any part of a test as needed for instructional planning. An optional computerized program provides an instructional planning form that includes student goals and objectives.		
Standardized Reading Inventory (Newcomer, 1986)	K–8	Oral and silent reading, word recognition, reading comprehension
This instrument is designed like an informal reading inventory, with each of its two forms consisting of 10 word lists and 10 graded reading passages. The word lists and passages include typical words found in five popular basal reading series. After reading words in isolation on the word lists until three or more words are misread, the student reads passages aloud while the examiner records errors in oral reading. Then the student reads the same passages silently and responds to comprehension questions. The scoring of the inventory indicates whether the student's word recognition skills and reading comprehension are at an independent, instructional, or frustration level. This criterion-referenced instrument is standardized in that it includes set administration procedures, objective scoring criteria, and guidelines for interpreting results.		
Wisconsin Tests of Reading Skill Development (1977)	K–6	Word attack, comprehension, study skills
A total of 38 short tests at four levels of difficulty assess word-attack skills commonly taught in kindergarten through third grade. The student demonstrates mastery of a specific skill by responding correctly to at least 80% of the items on any given test. Also, comprehension tests are available in five levels used in kindergarten through sixth grade. The tests assess the comprehension skills of establishing cause-and-effect relationships, using context clues to derive word meanings, drawing conclusions, and judging relevance. The results indicate which skills have not yet been mastered and can be used to plan instruction as well as monitor student progress.		

Informal Assessment

Informal assessment involves examining the student's daily work or administering teacher-constructed tests by which the teacher can assess any measurable reading skill. The teacher also can determine specific strengths and weaknesses by analyzing reading errors. Informal procedures usually offer two advantages: they require less time to administer than formal tests, and they can be used with classroom materials during regular instruction periods (Kirk et al., 1978).

An experienced teacher can obtain diagnostic information through careful, day-to-day observations. The teacher has many opportunities to observe and informally assess the student's reading skills and can obtain information about the student's reading interests and attitudes, as well as word analysis and comprehension skills, by observing oral reading, seatwork assignments, instructional sessions, testing sessions, and recreational reading periods. Several informal observations during a period of time also can confirm or supplement the results of formal assessment tests.

Teacher observations can be recorded on a checklist of reading skills and behaviors. Table 13.5 presents a reading diagnosis checklist devised by Ekwall and Shanker (1993) consisting of 28 reading or related abilities. The teacher is to check each ability three times. Thus, specific

TABLE 13.5
Reading Diagnosis Checklist

NAME ______________________ TEACHER ______________________

GRADE ______________________ SCHOOL ______________________

Category	No.	Item	1st check	2nd check	3rd check
Pre-reading	1	Lacks Knowledge of the Alphabet			
Oral Reading	2	Word-by-Word Reading			
	3	Incorrect Phrasing			
	4	Poor Pronunciation			
	5	Omissions			
	6	Repetitions			
	7	Inversions or Reversals			
	8	Insertions			
	9	Substitutions			
	10	Guesses at Words			
	11	Voicing-Lip Movements, Finger-Pointing, and Head Movements			
Decoding	12	Basic Sight Words Not Known			
	13	General Sight Vocabulary Not up to Grade Level			
	14	Phonics Difficulties: Consonants			
	15	Phonics Difficulties: Vowels			
	16	Phonics Difficulties: Blends, Digraphs, or Diphthongs			
	17	Structural Analysis Difficulties			
	18	Contractions Not Known			
	19	Inadequate Ability to Use Context Clues			
Comprehension	20	Vocabulary Inadequate			
	21	Comprehension Inadequate			
Study Skills	22	Low Rate of Speed			
	23	Inability to Adust Reading Rate			
	24	High Rate of Reading at the Expense of Accuracy			
	25	Inability to Skim or Scan			
	26	Unable to Locate Information			
Other	27	Undeveloped Dictionary Skills			
	28	Written Recall Limited by Spelling Ability			

The items listed above represent the most common difficulties encountered by pupils in the reading program. Following each numbered item are spaces for notation of that specific difficulty. This may be done at intervals of several months. One might use a check to indicate difficulty recognized or the following letters to represent an even more accurate appraisal:

D—Difficulty recognized
P—Pupil progressing
N—No longer has difficulty

Source: From Locating and Correcting Reading Difficulties (p. xxii), 6th ed., by E. E. Ekwall & J. L. Shanker, 1993. Upper Saddle River, NJ: Merrill/Prentice Hall.

strengths and weaknesses are noted, and progress is charted.

Teacher observation is continuous and permeates all types of informal assessment. This section presents the following informal assessment techniques: graded word lists, informal reading inventory, curriculum-based measurement, portfolio assessment, reading miscue analysis, cloze procedure, and teacher–made tests.

Graded Word Lists. Graded word lists examine the student's word recognition skills. Word lists can be useful in informal diagnosis to indicate the student's sight vocabulary, to estimate the level at which the student can read with fluency and has little difficulty with word attack, and to reveal basic weaknesses in word-attack skills as the student confronts unknown words (Otto & Smith, 1980).

The teacher can develop word lists by randomly selecting 20 to 25 words for each level from the glossaries of graded basal readers. To obtain a random sample of 25 words for each level, the teacher would divide the total number of words for each level by 25. For example, 250 total words divided by 25 would mean that every 10th word is included. The teacher should check to make sure that the words represent various phonics skills (such as consonant and vowel sounds in different positions, consonant blends, and digraphs). The words also should include prefixes, suffixes, and compound words. The words for each grade level can be typed on separate cards for the student to read, but the teacher should have a list of all the words.

Word lists can be presented in two ways. A timed flash exposure (1 second) can be given to assess the student's instant recognition or sight word vocabulary. Second, words the student is unable to recognize at first can be presented untimed to test ability to apply word-attack skills to unknown words. The teacher also can obtain additional information by giving prompts, such as providing an initial sound or covering part of the word.

The teacher can determine a word recognition grade level score—indicating the student's ability to identify words—by an untimed presentation of graded word lists. In general, the level at which the student misses none or only one word is the *independent level*. At the *instructional level* the student identifies two words incorrectly, and when three or more words are missed, the student has reached the *frustration level*. As well as using word lists to determine grade-level placement in word recognition, the teacher also should note specific errors in word attack. When the student mispronounces a word, the teacher should write down the mispronunciation to analyze the method of word attack and look for error patterns. For example, the student may recognize only initial consonant sounds and guess at the remainder of the word or may not be able to blend individual sounds into whole words. The student who reads *month* as *mouth* or *long* as *large* may be responding to configuration cues, whereas a response of a completely dissimilar word, such as *after* for *field*, may indicate a lack of phonetic word-attack skills. In addition, the teacher should note the student's skill in structural analysis—knowledge of prefixes, roots, and endings.

Informal Reading Inventory. An informal reading inventory provides information about the student's general reading level. It uses reading passages of increasing difficulty from various graded materials, such as selections from a basal reading series with which the student is unfamiliar. In general, the passages should consist of about 50 words (at preprimer level) to 200 words (at secondary level). The student begins reading passages aloud at a level at which word-attack and comprehension tasks are handled easily. The student continues reading passages of increasing difficulty until the passages become too difficult for the student to read. As the student reads aloud, the teacher records errors and asks five to eight questions about each passage. Questions of many kinds should be used: recall of facts (who, what, or where), inference (why), and vocabulary (general or specific meanings). To assess literal comprehension, the student can be asked to state the main idea of the passage, propose a title, recall details, present a series of events or ideas, or explain the meaning of vocabulary words. Inferential comprehension can be evaluated by asking questions that force the student to go beyond the information provided in the passage. For example, the student can be asked to draw conclusions, make predictions, evaluate ideas or actions, or suggest alternative endings. The student should be allowed to reread or inspect the passage before answering comprehension questions. Otherwise, it is possible that *memory* rather than comprehension is being tested. The percentage of words read correctly for each passage is computed by dividing the number of correctly read words by the number of words in the selection. The percentage of comprehension questions answered correctly is determined by dividing the number of correct answers by the number of questions asked.

Through this method the teacher can estimate ability at three levels: independent, instructional, and frustration (M. S. Johnson, Kress, & Pikulski, 1987). At the *independent level,* the student can read the graded passage with high accuracy, recognizing 99% to 100% of the words and answering the comprehension questions with 90% to 100% accuracy. The reading is fluent and natural, and there is no finger pointing or hesitation. At this level, the teacher can hand out supplementary materials for independent or enjoyment reading. The level at which the student needs some help is the *instructional level.* The student can recognize about 95% of the words and comprehends about 75% of the material. The material is challenging but not too difficult, and the student reads in a generally relaxed manner. The teacher should provide directed reading instruction at this level. At the *frustration level,* the student reads with considerable difficulty. Word recognition is 94% or less, and comprehension is less than 70%. The student is tense and makes many errors or reversals. Reading material at this level cannot be used for instruction.

According to Carnine et al. (1990), one of the major purposes of an informal reading inventory is to help the teacher place the student at the appropriate instructional level in a basal series. Lovitt and Hansen (1976) offer guidelines for placement in a basal series: a correct reading rate of 45 to 65 words per minute with 8 or fewer errors and 50% to 75% comprehension. Deno and Mirkin (1977) suggest that curriculum placement decisions be based on a reading rate of 50 to 99 correct words per minute with 3 to 7 errors, whereas Starlin (1982) recommends a correct reading rate of 70 to 149 words per minute with 6 to 10 errors.

In addition to using an inventory to record oral reading word recognition and comprehension, the teacher should note various types of reading errors such as omitting words or parts of words, inserting or substituting words, reversing a word or its letters, and repeating words. Spache and Spache (1986) note that types of reading errors can have particular meanings. Omissions may indicate that the student is skipping unknown words or is reading quickly without attention. Insertions of words that do not appear in the passage may suggest a superficial reading, a reliance on context for assistance, or a lack of interest in accuracy. Whereas omissions and insertions are more characteristic of older students, reversals are common at the primary age level or with students for whom English is a second language. Repetitions may indicate that the reader is tense and nervous or is delaying to gain time to attack the next unknown word. Mispronunciations are common among students who attempt to sound out words without knowing exceptions to phonetic rules and also may occur in students who have low levels of listening vocabulary and are unable to use context clues. Self-corrections indicate that the reader is attempting to read more accurately and rely upon information from the context of the sentence, whereas no attempt at decoding and the need for the teacher to supply the unknown word is suggestive of a dependent reader.

An informal reading inventory also can be used to assess silent reading. Whereas in oral reading the focus is on word-attack skills, in silent reading the emphasis is on comprehension. The student silently reads each passage and answers comprehension questions. The percentage of correct responses indicates the student's silent reading level: independent (90% to 100%), instructional (75%), or frustration (50%). While the student reads silently, the teacher can note whispering, lip movements, finger pointing, facial grimaces, and fidgeting. The student also may have difficulties such as low rate, high rate at the expense of understanding, poorly organized recall, and inaccurate recall. Comprehension errors can be classified according to an analysis of skills including recall of factual details, comprehension and summary of main ideas, understanding of sequence, making inferences, and critical reading and evaluation. The teacher can compare the student's oral and silent reading performances to determine whether there is a great difference.

In addition, the material in an informal reading inventory can be read to the student to determine listening or hearing capacity level, which is the highest level at which the student can comprehend 75% of the material. This provides an estimate of the student's reading potential or what the level would be if the student had no problems with the mechanics of reading.

Although it is time-consuming to use informal reading inventories because they are individually administered, they are used widely. They help the teacher to plan needed corrective instruction and to provide reading materials suited to the student's abilities. An informal reading inventory can be administered from time to time to check the student's reading progress. Several published informal reading inventories are available that contain graded word lists and graded passages. Three widely used inventories are the *Analytical Reading Inventory* (Woods & Moe, 1995), the *Burns/Roe Informal Reading Inventory* (Roe, 1993), and the *Classroom Reading Inventory* (Silvaroli, 1990).

Curriculum-Based Measurement. Curriculum-based assessment includes any approach that uses direct observation and recording of a student's performance in the school curriculum as a basis for obtaining information to make instructional decisions. Within this model, *curriculum-based measurement* refers to a specific set of standardized procedures in which rate samples are used to assess a student's achievement in academic skills (Deno, 1987, 1989). In curriculum-based measurement of reading skills, basal reading passages are used to measure oral reading fluency. The student reads passages under timed conditions, the examiner counts the number of words read correctly and incorrectly, and student performance is summarized as the rate correct.

Materials for reading include passages of about 200 words—excluding poetry, exercises, and excessive dialogue—from the reading curriculum used in the school. In selecting this material, four to six sample passages are helpful because this provides the teacher with enough material for several administrations. All passages should reflect similar difficulty (possibly based on their readability). Once materials are selected, they can be prepared by creating a student copy retyped to eliminate picture distractions and a teacher copy that has the cumulative number of words on successive lines printed along the right margin. When administering a reading passage, the teacher instructs the student to read at a comfortable rate during the 1-minute timing. The teacher follows the reading on the teacher's copy and crosses off the following incorrectly read words: (a) misread words (such as *house* for *horse*), (b) words the student cannot read in about 3 seconds, (c) words not read (omissions), and (d) reversals of letters within words (such as *saw* for *was*). The following miscues are not counted as errors: (a) proper nouns that are mispronounced more than once, (b) self-corrections, and (c) words added into the text by the student (additions or insertions). The rate correct (i.e., cumulative number of words minus the number of errors) indicates the student's performance, and errors are examined to ascertain error patterns. It is helpful to administer two passages of similar readability and record the average score. Mercer and Mercer (1993) provide procedures for administering and scoring reading passages, determining long-range goals, and graphing data.

Potter and Wamre (1990) note that the use of oral reading rate measures in curriculum-based measurement is proving to be a viable measure of general reading skill and is consistent with developmental reading models such as Chall's (1983b) stages of reading development. Moreover, research indicates that students who read more fluently also perform higher on comprehension tasks (Tindal & Marston, 1990).

Portfolio Assessment. A reading portfolio consists of a collection of materials that reflect the student's personal reading history and accomplishments as a reader. The student should participate in the selection and evaluation of the materials chosen to be included in the portfolio. The materials can vary widely depending on the function of the portfolio assessment, which may include providing information for the teacher to use in assessing student achievement and making instructional decisions, documenting a record of student progress, and demonstrating student accomplishments to parents. Reading logs that indicate the number and variety of books read can be included as well as checklists made from student observations and questionnaires completed by the student on reading interests and attitudes toward reading. Audiotapes of the student's best oral reading also can be collected at regular intervals. Reviews of the student's portfolio can provide information for teacher assessment as well as self-assessment by the student to evaluate reading progress and plan future activities to enhance reading achievement.

Reading Miscue Analysis. Reading miscue analysis, based on the work of K. S. Goodman (1969, 1973), is a method of analyzing the student's oral reading strategies. The selection read by the student should be a complete story or passage (i.e., have a beginning, middle, and end) that is one grade level above the material used by the student in class. It also should be unfamiliar to the student and of sufficient length and difficulty to generate a minimum of 25 miscues. Following the oral reading, the student retells the story.

Although comprehension is considered in an informal reading inventory, it is the major consideration in reading miscue analysis. Emphasis is placed on the nature of the reading errors (miscues), rather than on the number of errors made. Miscues can be classified in the following categories:

1. *Semantic*—the miscue is similar in meaning to the text word. Some miscues indicate that the student comprehends the passage; thus, the simple substitution of a word is not important (e.g., substitution of *dad* for *father*).
2. *Syntactic*—the miscue is the same part of speech as the text word. Some miscues show that the student fails to comprehend the meaning but at least substitutes a word that makes grammatical sense.
3. *Graphic*—the miscue is similar to the sound/symbol relationship for the initial, medial, or final portion of the text word (such as *find* for *found*). Some miscues indicate the student's knowledge of phoneme-grapheme relationships.

It must be determined whether each miscue changed or interfered with the meaning of the information conveyed in the sentence or phrase in which it occurred. The most acceptable miscue is semantically correct, whereas less acceptable errors are grammatically correct but semantically incorrect or fit the graphic or phonic characteristics of the text but are semantically and grammatically incorrect. Basically, the seriousness of miscues depends on whether they form a consistent pattern that alters the meaning of the written passage and thus affects the student's comprehension.

Some oral mistakes reveal that the student is reading with meaning (K. S. Goodman, 1969, 1973). These errors are not very serious if one believes that the purpose of reading is understanding. Fry (1977) suggests that the three types of linguistic errors—semantic, syntactic, and sound-symbol—can be useful to the classroom teacher in informal observation of any oral reading. For the teacher who wants to pursue a systematic diagnosis of meaning-clue deficiencies, the *Reading Miscue Inventory* (Y. M. Goodman & Burke, 1972; Y. M. Goodman, Watson, & Burke, 1987) is helpful. Each oral reading miscue is scored according to nine categories: dialect, intonation shift, graphic similarity, sound similarity, grammatical function, correction, grammatical acceptability, semantic acceptability, and meaning change. A short form of the *Reading Miscue Inventory* also is available (Burke, 1976).

Cloze Procedure. The cloze procedure can be used as an informal method to measure reading levels and comprehension (Bormuth, 1968). It allows the teacher to estimate the difficulty the student will have with a specific reading material and thus helps determine whether a book is appropriate. The teacher presents an unfamiliar reading passage of about 250 words to the student. The first sentence is typed completely, but in subsequent sentences every fifth word is replaced with a blank. The blanks should be of uniform length. The remainder of the selection is typed as it appears in text. The student reads the passage and fills in the missing words or synonyms. Thus, the student must rely on context clues within the passage to make meaningful responses.

A variation of the cloze procedure is the maze procedure, in which the student is presented with a vertical array of choices for each omitted word. This changes the task from completion to multiple-choice or recognition. Another modification includes having the student select words from an answer key. Also, the teacher may choose to delete only every 10th word, or other appropriate words can be omitted to avoid the inadvertent continuous omission of articles or proper names.

A reading passage using the cloze procedure can be administered either individually or in groups. Reading levels are determined by changing the number of correct responses to percentages. Bormuth (1968) suggests the following scoring of cloze passages: *independent reading level,* above 57% correct responses; *instructional reading level*, 44% to 57% correct responses; and *frustration reading level*, below 44% correct responses. When the maze procedure is used, because identification of a correct word is easier than production of a correct word, the criterion is higher (e.g., about 60% to 85% correct for instructional level). For additional information the teacher should attempt to analyze why the student makes certain errors. Hafner (1965) notes that cloze errors can be examined according to linguistic components, cognitive types, and reasoning skills.

Teacher-Made Tests. The teacher can devise an informal test to obtain a quick estimate of a specific skill. Probe sheets can be developed to assess a particular reading objective, such as consonant sounds, vowel sounds, blends, or compound words. The probe is administered for a 1-minute period; then the correct and incorrect responses are tallied. Suggested proficiency reading rates for words in a list range from 50 to 100 correct words per minute, and suggested proficiency reading rates for words in text range from 100 to 200 words per minute with two or less errors (Mercer & Mercer, 1993).

Teacher-made tests can be constructed by using items in standardized tests and workbook exercises as guides. A variety of items that measure a specific skill can be used (e.g., multiple-choice, true/false, completion, or matching). The teacher should be careful to include enough items to sample the skill adequately. Short-form word analysis tests can be devised to measure specific skills. Items also can be developed to assess specific comprehension skills, such as stating the main idea, noting details, and understanding cause-and-effect relationships. Teacher-made tests often deal with reading skills the student must use daily, and they provide a measure of student progress over a specific period of time.

TEACHING READING SKILLS

Many approaches and materials have been developed to teach reading. Methods of beginning reading instruction can be divided into two major approaches: the bottom-up or code-emphasis approach and the top-down or meaning-emphasis approach. The primary difference between the two approaches is the way decoding is taught. This is reflected in the debate over the relative importance of text versus meaning or decoding versus comprehension. In the bottom-up sequential approach, decoding skills are taught first and instruction in comprehension follows. Beginning reading programs that stress letter-sound regularity are *code-emphasis* programs. The top-down model is the basis for the spontaneous approach to reading instruction, and reading for meaning is emphasized in the first stages of instruction. Programs that stress the use of common words are *meaning-emphasis* programs.

Code-emphasis programs begin with words consisting of letters and letter combinations that have the same sound in different words. The consistency in the letter-sound relationship enables the reader to read unknown words by blending the sounds together. For example, the word *sit* is sounded out as "sss-ii-tt" and pronounced "sit." The word *ring* is sounded out as "rrr-ii-nng" and pronounced "ring." The letter *i* has the same sound in both words. Moreover, a new word is not introduced unless its component letter-sound relationships have been mastered. Some major code-emphasis programs include *Basic Reading* (J. B. Lippincott), *Reading Mastery* (SRA), *Merrill Linguistic Reading Program* (SRA), *Palo Alto Reading Program* (Harcourt Brace Jovanovich), and *Programmed Reading* (Phoenix Learning Resources). The phonics, linguistic, modified alphabet, phonological awareness training, and programmed programs also are classified as code-emphasis programs.

Meaning-emphasis programs begin with words that appear frequently, based on the assumption that these words are familiar to the reader and thus easier to learn. Students identify words by examining meaning and position in context and are encouraged to use a variety of decoding techniques, including pictures, context of story, initial letters, and word configuration. Words are not controlled so that a letter has the same sound in different words. For example, the words *at*, *many*, and *far* may occur, though the *a* represents a different sound in each word. Some of the major meaning-emphasis programs include *Ginn 720* (Ginn & Company); *Houghton Mifflin Reading Series* (Houghton Mifflin); and *Basics in Reading*, the *New Open Highways*, and *Reading Unlimited* (Scott, Foresman). Moreover, the whole language, language experience, and individualized reading approaches generally are classified as meaning-emphasis programs.

Code-emphasis programs are considered to be more effective in teaching students to decode (Bleismer & Yarborough, 1965; Bond & Dykstra, 1967; Chall, 1983a; Diederich, 1973; Dykstra, 1968). Early systematic instruction in phonics provides the skills necessary for becoming an independent reader earlier than is likely if phonics instruction is delayed and less systematic (Dykstra, 1974). Many researchers contend that the foundation of comprehension is accurate word recognition, which is attained through careful decoding and practice over time (Chall, 1989; Perfetti, 1985). Thus, decoding or facility with phonics is viewed as a necessary step in the acquisition of reading comprehension and other higher-level reading processes.

Those who support the meaning-emphasis approach agree that code-emphasis programs have an advantage in teaching decoding, but they maintain that meaning-emphasis programs have an advantage in teaching comprehension. Whole language instruction, which is the current meaning-emphasis approach to beginning reading, tends to be associated with a natural, self-directed or developmental, and open view. Some whole language proponents stress that skills (including phonics) should not be taught directly but acquired from more natural reading and writing activities. Carbo (1987) stresses that most primary students are global learners who need to learn to read with holistic reading activities such as reading books of their own choosing, engaging in choral reading, writing stories, and listening to tape recordings of interesting, well-written books.

Though the meaning- versus code-emphasis debate continues, Carnine et al. (1990) strongly recommend the code-emphasis approach, especially for students with learning problems. They note that the results of almost 4 decades of research on beginning reading indicate that phonics programs are superior to meaning-emphasis approaches in the early grades. In a review of research on beginning instruction in reading, Adams (1990) notes that instructional approaches that include systematic phonics lead to higher achievement in both word recognition and spelling, especially in the early grades and for students who are slower or economically disadvantaged. She advocates an eclectic instructional program that includes phonics skills as well as practice reading connected text. Beginning reading instruction should stress decoding but not ignore comprehension (Carnine et al., 1990). Accurate and automatic habits in decoding lead to reading fluency, which allows attention to be directed to higher-level reading comprehension. Lyon (1995) notes that slow and inaccurate decoding is the best predictor of deficits in reading comprehension. Because successful reading requires proficiency in word identification as well as comprehension, competency is required in both areas. Thus, there needs to be a proper balance between systematic decoding instruction and attention to developing reading comprehension.

Harris and Sipay (1990) state that teacher skill is more important than reading methodology and that "efforts should concentrate on determining which aspects of a program are most effective for particular children when used by certain teachers under given conditions and, what is more important, why" (p. 90). Thus, a teacher must know several instructional practices in reading to teach students with reading disabilities. Heilman, Blair, and Rupley (1994) state:

> No single approach to teaching literacy [i.e., learning to read and reading to learn] works best for all students. In a sense, no set of materials or instructional procedures is foolproof. By knowing when to modify or use different materials and instructional procedures to address students' needs, the teacher is the major factor in determining the success of a literacy program. . . . Effective reading teachers integrate features associated with different philosophies and materials to match the needs of their students. (p. 269)

The teacher must consider each individual case to determine which skills need corrective instruction and then select the approach most likely to be effective.

DEVELOPMENTAL READING APPROACHES

Developmental reading approaches emphasize daily, sequential instruction. Most are programmed according to a normative pattern of reading growth. The basic material for instruction is usually a series of books (such as basal readers) that directs what will be taught and when. A well-developed program provides supplementary materials such as workbooks, skillpacks, wall charts, related activities, learning games, and filmstrips. To teach students with learning disabilities it often is necessary to adapt developmental programs to meet their needs by changing the sequence, providing additional practice activities, and modifying the input-output arrangements of selected tasks. Moreover, combinations of programs often are superior to single approaches (i.e., using supplemental phonics or adding language experiences to any kind of reading). The following developmental approaches are discussed: basal, phonics, linguistic, whole language, language experience, and individualized reading.

Basal Reading Approach

Many teachers use a basal reading series as the core of their program. Most series include a sequential set of reading texts and supplementary materials such as workbooks, flash cards, placement and achievement tests, and filmstrips. In addition, a comprehensive teacher's manual explains the purpose of the program and provides precise instructional plans and suggestions for skill activities. The teacher's manual usually is highly structured and completely outlines each lesson, perhaps including skill objectives, new vocabulary words, motivational activities, and questions for checking comprehension on each page of the text.

The readers usually begin with preprimers and gradually increase in difficulty through the eighth grade. Some basals are changing their progression from grade-level readers to levels corresponding to stages in development. The content is based upon common student experiences and interests. Materials designed for student groups that are multiracial or disadvantaged sometimes feature settings and content to appeal to a variety of backgrounds and ethnic groups. Basals may use either a meaning-emphasis or a code-emphasis approach. Some basals feature a whole language approach and focus on whole-word recognition and comprehension through the reading of children's literature stories. Others focus on word decoding strategies such as phonics. A basal series systematically presents reading skills in word recognition, comprehension, and word attack, and it controls the vocabulary from level to level. The reader, manual, and student workbook provide activities that help teach word-attack skills (including phonics), develop comprehension, and increase reading rate steadily.

Most basal readers recommend a *directed reading activity* procedure for teaching a reading lesson. The steps include:

1. Motivate the student to learn the material.
2. Prepare the student by presenting new concepts and vocabulary.
3. Guide the student in reading the story by asking questions that give a purpose or goal for the reading.
4. Develop or strengthen skills relating to the material through drills or workbook activities.
5. Assign work to apply the skills acquired during the lesson.
6. Evaluate the effectiveness of the lesson.

This guided reading approach can be used to increase comprehension skills. Basal readers contain stories with many details and often are divided into small parts. Thus, location exercises can be given to find the main idea or main characters as well as specific words, phrases, sentences, and paragraphs.

An alternative to the directed reading lesson is the *directed reading-thinking activity* (Stauffer, 1981). In this thought-provoking strategy, the student largely determines the purposes for reading and must generate questions about the selection, read the selection, and then validate the answers to the questions through group judgment. The teacher acts as a catalyst and provides thoughtful questions in directing the process: "What do you think?" "Why do you think so?" and "Can you prove your conclusion?"

The basal reading approach is used in most reading programs in the United States; however, Schumm, Vaughn, Haager, and Klinger (1994) note that many widely used basal reading programs offer none or only a few teaching suggestions for planning and implementing instruction for students with reading disabilities in inclusive settings. The teacher must adjust or supplement the materials to meet the individual needs of students with reading problems. Modifications to enhance the base lesson include teacher modeling, additional examples, control of the learning set, gradual movement to discrimination exercises, and additional phonological awareness activities (e.g., word segmentation exercises) (Simmons, Chard, & Kameenui, 1994). Also, for supplemental reading, high-interest low-vocabulary books offer a relatively easy vocabulary while maintaining an interest level appropriate for the more mature reader. Mercer and Mercer (1993) provide a listing of numerous high-interest low-vocabulary reading materials that cover a wide variety of topics.

Phonics Approach

The phonics approach teaches word recognition through learning grapheme-phoneme associations. After learning vowels, consonants, and blends, the student learns to sound out words by combining sounds and blending them into words. Thus, the student learns to recognize unfamiliar words by associating speech sounds with letters or groups of letters. Table 13.6 presents the sounds stressed in a phonics program. The emphasis on phonics (or decoding) in the primary grades has become an almost universal practice in beginning reading programs (with the exception of whole language programs).

The teacher can use the synthetic method or the analytic method to teach phonics. In the *synthetic* method, the student learns that letters represent certain sounds (e.g., *b—buh*) and then finds out how to blend, or *synthesize*, the sounds to form words. This method emphasizes isolated letter sounds before the student progresses to words. The *analytic* method teaches letter sounds as integral parts of words (e.g., *b* as in *baby*). The student must learn new words on the basis of phonics elements similar to familiar or sight words. Carnine et al. (1990) note that synthetic phonics appears to yield better results in beginning reading than does an analytic phonics approach. Phonics methods and materials differ on details, but the main objective is to teach the student to attack new words independently.

Phonics instruction builds on a foundation of phonemic awareness and can be integrated into a total reading program. Kirk, Kliebhan, and Lerner (1978) note that instruction in phonics may be added effectively to the basal reader or language experience approach after the student has acquired a basic sight vocabulary of 50 to 100 words. Phonics is helpful with beginning readers in a developmental program or as a remedial technique for students who have a strong

TABLE 13.6
Sounds Stressed in a Phonics Program

Vowel Sounds

Short Sounds		Long Sounds	
a	bat	a	rake
e	bed	e	jeep
i	pig	i	kite
o	lock	o	rope
u	duck	u	mule

W is sometimes used as a vowel, as in the *ow* and *aw* teams. *W* is usually used as a vowel on word endings and used as a consonant at the beginning of words.

Y is usually a consonant when it appears at the beginning of a word and a vowel in any other position.

Three consonants usually affect or control the sounds of some, or all, of the vowels when they follow these vowels within a syllable. They are *r, w,* and *l*.

r (all vowels)	*w* (*a, e,* and *o*)	*l* (*a*)
car	*law*	*all*
her	*few*	
dirt	*now*	
for		
fur		

Consonant Sounds

b	bear	*k*	king	*s*	six
c	cat	*l*	lake	*t*	turtle
d	dog	*m*	money	*v*	vase
f	face	*n*	nose	*w*	wagon
g	goat	*p*	pear	*x*	xylophone
h	hen	*q*	queen	*y*	yellow
j	jug	*r*	rat	*z*	zebra

The following consonants have two or more sounds:

c	cat	*g*	goat	*s*	six	*x*	xylophone
c	ice	*g*	germ	*s*	is	*x*	exist
				s	sure	*x*	box

When *g* is followed by *e, i* or *y*, it often takes the soft sound of *j*, as in *gentle* and *germ.* If it is not followed by these letters, it takes the hard sound illustrated in such words as *got* and *game.*

When *c* is followed by *e, i,* or *y*, it usually takes the soft sound heard in *cent.* If it is not followed by these letters, it usually takes the hard sound heard in *come.*

Qu usually has the sound of *kw;* however, in some words such as *bouquet* it has the sound of *k*.

continued

TABLE 13.6
continued

Consonant Blends

Beginning

bl	b*l*ue	*pr*	p*r*etty	*tw*	t*w*elve
br	b*r*own	*sc*	s*c*ore	*wr*	w*r*ench
cl	c*l*own	*sk*	s*k*ill	*sch*	s*ch*ool
cr	c*r*own	*sl*	s*l*ow	*scr*	sc*r*een
dr	d*r*ess	*sm*	s*m*all	*shr*	sh*r*ink
dw	d*w*ell	*sn*	s*n*ail	*spl*	sp*l*ash
fl	f*l*ower	*sp*	s*p*in	*spr*	sp*r*ing
fr	f*r*om	*st*	s*t*ory	*squ*	squ*ash
gl	g*l*ue	*sw*	s*w*an	*str*	st*r*ing
gr	g*r*ape	*tr*	t*r*ee	*thr*	th*r*ow
pl	p*l*ate				

Ending

ld	wi*ld*
mp	la*mp*
nd	wi*nd*
nt	we*nt*
rk	wo*rk*
sk	ri*sk*

Consonant and Vowel Digraphs

Consonant

ch	*ch*ute	*sh*	*sh*ip
ch	*ch*oral	*th*	*th*ree
ch	*ch*urch	*th*	*th*at
gh	cou*gh*	*wh*	*wh*ich
ph	gra*ph*	*wh*	*wh*o

Vowel (Most common phonemes only)

ai	p*ai*n	*ie*	p*ie*ce	(A number of other phonemes are common for *ie*.)
ay	h*ay*			
ea	*ea*ch	*oa*	*oa*ts	
or		*oo*	b*oo*k	
ea	w*ea*ther	*oo*	m*oo*n	
ei	w*ei*ght	*ou*	t*ou*gh	(*ou* may be either a diagraph or diphthong.)
or				
ei	*ei*ther	*ow*	l*ow*	(*ow* may be either a digraph or a diphthong.)
		or		
		ow	c*ow*	

Diphthongs

au	h*au*l*	*oi*	s*oi*l
aw	h*aw*k*	*ou*	tr*ou*t
ew	f*ew*	*ow*	c*ow*
ey	th*ey*	*oy*	b*oy*

*Some may hear *au* and *aw* as a digraph.

Source: From *Locating and Correcting Reading Difficulties* (pp. 311–313), 6th ed., by E. E. Ekwall & J. L. Shanker, 1993. Upper Saddle River, NJ: Merrill/Prentice Hall. Copyright 1993 by Prentice-Hall Publishing Company. Reprinted by permission.

sight vocabulary but are unable to analyze unfamiliar words. Some commercial phonics programs used with students with learning disabilities include *Cove School Reading Program* (SRA), *Merrill Phonics Skilltext Series* (SRA), and *Phonic Remedial Reading Lessons* (Kirk, Kirk, & Minskoff, 1985).

Linguistic Approach

Most linguistic approaches to reading stem from the ideas of various linguists. Linguists, who mainly are concerned with oral communication, have provided important information about the nature and structure of language. Bloomfield and Barnhart (1961) and Fries (1963) provide such a framework, which emphasizes decoding—changing the printed words into verbal communication.

Many linguistic reading materials use a *whole-word* approach. Instead of using exercises in sounding and blending, words are taught in word families and only as wholes. In beginning reading, words are introduced that contain a short vowel and consist of a consonant-vowel-consonant pattern. The words are selected on the basis of similar spelling patterns (such as *cab, lab, tab*), and the student must learn the relationship between speech sounds and letters (i.e., between phonemes and graphemes). The student is not taught letter sounds directly but learns them through minimal word differences. Words that have irregular spellings are introduced as sight words as the student progresses. After the words are learned in the spelling patterns, they are put together to form sentences.

The linguistic approach differs from the phonics approach in that linguistic readers focus on words instead of isolated sounds. It differs from the basal reading approach in that linguistic instruction emphasizes breaking the written language code before considering meaning and comprehension. Thus, many linguistic series contain no pictures or illustrations that may provide clues and tempt the student to guess rather than decode the printed word. Although the frequent repetition of words in this approach may be helpful to students with learning disabilities, the use of nonsense words and phrases for pattern practice detracts from reading for comprehension. Some commercial materials using the linguistic approach are *Basic Reading Series* (SRA), *Let's Read* (Educators Publishing Service), *Merrill Linguistic Reading Program* (SRA), and *Palo Alto Reading Program* (Harcourt Brace Jovanovich).

Whole Language Approach

The whole language concept (K. S. Goodman, 1986) involves the use of students' language and experiences to increase their reading and writing abilities. Reading is taught as a holistic meaning-oriented activity and is treated as an integrated behavior rather than being broken into a collection of separate skills. According to Altwerger, Edelsky, and Flores (1987), the main consideration regarding classroom reading and writing within the whole language framework is that there be *real* reading and writing rather than exercises in reading and writing. Thus, the emphasis is on reading for meaning rather than learning decoding skills, and the student is taught to break the code in reading within the context of meaningful content. In a classroom with a whole language orientation, the curriculum is organized around themes and units that increase language and reading skills, and reading materials consist of various relevant and functional materials such as children's literature books and resources the students need or want to read. Whole language relies heavily on literature or on printed matter used for appropriate purposes (e.g., a recipe used for making a dessert rather than for finding short vowels) and on writing for varied purposes. In this approach, reading is immersed in a total language arts program, and teachers develop the curriculum to offer instructional experiences relating to real problems and ideas. The underlying concept is that all language arts are related and should not be taught as if they were separate subjects. The premise is that students learn naturally from exposure and use rather than from isolated instructional drills.

Advocates of the whole language reading approach oppose teaching phonics in any structured, systematic way and believe that students will develop their own phonetic principles through exposure to print as they read and write. Students initially start to read meaningful, predictable whole words and then use these familiar words to begin to learn new words and phrases. To develop comprehension skills and for reading to make sense, it is believed that students must begin with a meaningful whole, and they initially are given familiar, predictable material. A constructive process is used in which students recognize familiar parts in unfamiliar written matter, and their reading is monitored to ensure it is making sense to them. While learning to read, students also are learning to write and are encouraged to write about their experiences. K. S. Goodman (1986) suggests that to implement a whole language approach in the classroom, the teacher should establish a center for reading and writing and encourage students to participate in activities such as dictating stories to an adult and then reading them or following along while listening to audiocassettes of books. The teacher also can read to students and provide them with an opportunity to predict events within the story. In addition, the teacher can plan sustained silent reading and reading activities in which students read independently and are guided by reading conferences.

According to Chiang and Ford (1990), "Integrating the whole language strategies with other effective methods such as direct instruction can bring about a more balanced perspective with equal emphasis on fostering LD [learning disabled] students' positive attitudes toward reading and on facilitating a more functional and purposeful use of printed materials" (p. 34). They offer the following guidelines for implementing whole language programs with students who have learning disabilities:

1. Read aloud to students regularly.
2. Devote a few minutes each day to sustained silent reading.
3. Introduce students to predictable books with patterned stories.
4. Use writing activities that provide opportunities for the teacher to model writing strategies and skills.
5. Include journal writing as part of the students' individualized educational programs.
6. Provide meaningful printed materials in the instructional setting (e.g., simplified dictionaries and categorized lists of words).
7. Establish a network to communicate with other teachers using holistic techniques in working with students with learning disabilities.

One aspect of the whole language approach that has found acceptance is the integration of the language arts program, especially in the area of writing. This approach minimizes a fragmented curriculum, and students see writing as a complement of reading. However, the whole language approach to reading lacks direct instruction in specific skill strategies, and students with learning disabilities may need a more systematic approach to decoding and comprehension than the whole language approach provides. Heymsfeld (1989) and Mather (1992) suggest that because both whole language and skill-based instruction have strengths, the teacher should create a combined approach. Likewise, Gersten and Dimino (1993) suggest that aspects of both whole language and direct instruction should be implemented to teach reading so that all students, including students at risk and with learning disabilities, can succeed. Chall (1987) notes that research indicates that better results are achieved when young children are taught skills systematically and directly and use them in reading. In addition, research shows that being read to and reading and writing stories and selections in which newly gained skills are applied also contribute to reading development. In a review of research on the whole language approach, Stahl and Miller (1989) note that the whole language approach may be most effective when used early in the process of learning to read (i.e., kindergarten) and for teaching functional aspects of reading such as print concepts and expectations about reading. However, more direct approaches may be better at helping some students master word recognition skills prerequisite to effective comprehension. Finally, research indicates that the whole language approach may have less of an effect with populations that are disadvantaged and have a lower socioeconomic status (Stahl & Miller, 1989).

Pressley and Rankin (1994) provide support for reading instruction that balances decoding instruction with authentic literary experiences and note that "reading instruction strictly consistent with whole language precepts is probably not the most effective instruction for students who are at risk for reading difficulties, including students with learning disabilities, those who are economically and socially disadvantaged, and those who are culturally and linguistically diverse" (p. 164). Thus, until whole language has been found to be effective at various levels with students who have learning disabilities, it should be used cautiously, especially in light of the success that teachers have had in using direct instruction.

Two commercial programs based on the use of literature for students with learning disabilities are *Learning Through Literature* (Dodds & Goodfellow, 1990/1991) and *Victory!* (Brigance, 1991). Also, Norton (1992) discusses selecting literature for a literature-based reading program and provides sources for children's literature. An example of a model program that integrates whole language with direct instruction and precision teaching is B.A.L.A.N.C.E. (Blending All Learning Activities Nurtures Classroom Excellence) (Hefferan & Parker, 1991), developed in Orlando, Florida (FDLRS/Action, 1600 Silver Star Road, Orlando, FL 32804). B.A.L.A.N.C.E. stresses direct instruction but encourages the use of writing, quality literature, and integrated subjects to enhance the application of skills. In addition, the use of precision teaching helps the teacher make decisions about students' learning and enhance their fluency.

Language Experience Approach

The language experience approach integrates the development of reading skills with the development of listening, speaking, and writing skills. The materials are made up of what the student is thinking and saying. According to Lee and Allen (1963), the language experience approach deals with the following thinking process: what students think about, they can talk about; what students say, they can write (or someone can write for them); and what students write (or others write for them), they can read.

The language experience approach stresses each student's unique interests. The approach is based not upon a series of reading materials but upon the student's oral and written expression. The student's experiences play a major role in determining the reading material. The student dictates stories to the teacher. These stories may originate at first from the student's own drawings and artwork. The teacher writes down the stories, and they become the basis of the student's initial reading experiences. Thus, the student learns to read the dictated written thoughts. In this approach the language patterns of the reading materials are determined by the student's speech, and the content is determined by experiences. The teacher tries to broaden and enrich the base of experiences from which the student can think, speak, and read. Eventually, with help, the student can write stories. Thus, according to Hall (1981), the approach is based on the concept that "reading has the most meaning to a pupil when the materials being read are expressed in his language and are rooted in his experiences" (p. 2).

At first the teacher guides students in writing an experience chart. The story in the chart derives from the students' experiences as they share information through group discussion. Experience charts may comprise several topics:

narrative descriptions of experiences, reports of experiments or news events, or fictional stories the students create. The teacher writes the ideas in a first draft on the chalkboard, guides the students' suggestions and revisions, and discusses word choice, sentence structure, and the sounds of letters and words. Specific skills such as capitalization, punctuation, spelling, grammar, and correct sentence structure can be taught as needed during the editing and revising of the chart. Thus, the teacher provides skill development at the appropriate time instead of following a predetermined sequence of training in reading skills. Because the students create the content, motivation and interest are usually high.

In the language experience approach, students are encouraged to proceed at their own rate. Progress is evaluated in terms of each student's ability to express ideas in oral and written form and to understand peers' writing. Progress or growth in writing mechanics, spelling, vocabulary, sentence structure, and depth of thinking is evident in the student's written work. The stories each student writes can be illustrated and bound in an attractive folder, and students can trade story notebooks.

The language experience approach is similar to whole language in that both emphasize the importance of literature, treat reading as a personal act (i.e., accept language varieties of individual students), and advocate an abundance of books written by youngsters about their own lives. However, language experience presumes that written language is a secondary system derived from oral language, whereas whole language sees oral and written language as structurally related without one being a rendition of the other (Altwerger et al., 1987). The teacher frequently may take dictation from students in the language experience approach, but dictation is less frequent in a whole language curriculum because it deprives the learners of making meaning through the act of writing. Moreover, in the language experience approach, a student's dictation often is used to teach word-attack or phonics skills, whereas whole language theory disputes that fragmented exercises can lead to comprehensive knowledge of language.

The language experience approach is mainly a way of teaching beginning reading. However, it may be just as effective in the intermediate grades and often is used with older students for corrective instruction and motivation. When teacher organization and instruction in word-attack and comprehension skills are provided, the language experience approach can be used effectively to teach students with learning disabilities. It also can be used to improve comprehension skills of older students who have developed basic decoding skills or to maintain interest and motivation. Research, however, indicates that the language experience approach may produce weaker effects with populations labeled specifically as disadvantaged (Stahl & Miller, 1989).

Individualized Reading Approach

In an individualized reading program, students select their own reading material according to interest and ability and progress at their own rate. A large collection of books should be available at different reading levels, with many subjects represented at each level of difficulty. After the students choose reading materials, they pace themselves and keep records of their progress. The teacher teaches word recognition and comprehension skills as each student needs them.

Each student meets once or twice a week with the teacher, at which time the teacher may ask the student to read aloud and discuss the reading material. The teacher can note reading errors and check the student's sight vocabulary, understanding of word meanings, and comprehension. Also, the teacher can guide the student with regard to the next reading selection, although the choice is made by the student. From these conferences the teacher keeps a record of the student's capabilities and progress to plan activities to develop specific skills. The teacher's role is to diagnose and prescribe, and success of the program depends on the teacher's resourcefulness and competence. Individual work can be supplemented with group activities using basal readers and workbooks to provide practice in specific reading skills.

Self-pacing and self-selection can be considered advantages of the individualized reading approach. Self-pacing builds self-confidence, and self-selection satisfies personal interests and promotes independent reading. Individualized reading also eliminates "high" and "low" reading groups and avoids competition and comparison. However, the value of the individualized reading approach for students with learning disabilities is questionable, because it involves self-learning and lacks a systematic check of developmental skills in the reading process (Kirk et al., 1978).

REMEDIAL READING PROGRAMS AND METHODS

Remedial programs are designed to teach reading to the student who has, or would have, difficulty learning to read in the general classroom reading program. In addition, several remedial methods are designed for students with moderate to severe reading problems—for example, nonreaders or students who are more than 1 year behind in reading achievement. The remedial programs and methods discussed in this section include *Reading Mastery* and the *Corrective Reading Program, Reading Recovery,* phonological awareness training, programmed reading instruction, multisensory reading method, modified alphabet method, neurological impress method, and glass analysis.

Reading Mastery and the *Corrective Reading Program*

Reading Mastery (Engelmann & Bruner, 1995) is an intensive, highly structured programmed instructional system. There are six levels for students in first through sixth grade; however, Levels I and II (formally known as DISTAR) and Fast Cycle are designed to remediate below-average reading skills of students through third grade. The students are grouped according to their current abilities, with no more than five students in a group. They sit in chairs in a quarter-circle around the teacher. Each day, one 30-minute lesson is presented. The manual specifies the sequence of presentation as well as statements and hand movements. Each student receives positive reinforcement (praise or points) for correct responses. A student who masters skills (indicated by performance on tests) changes groups.

The program uses a synthetic phonics approach and emphasizes basic decoding skills, including sound-symbol identification, left-to-right sequence, and the oral blending of sounds to make words. The program includes games to teach sequencing skills and left-to-right orientation, blending tasks to teach students to spell words by sounds ("say it slow") and to blend quickly ("say it fast"), and rhyming tasks to teach how sounds and words relate. Take-home sheets are used to practice skills. The program teaches students to concentrate on important sound combinations and word discriminations and to use a variety of word-attack skills. In Level I, students learn how to read words, sentences, and stories, both aloud and silently, and to answer literal comprehension questions about their readings. Level II expands basic reading skills, and students learn strategies for decoding difficult words and for answering interpretive comprehension questions. The program also teaches basic reasoning skills, such as applying rules and completing deductions.

In this direct instruction approach, emphasis is placed on learning specific skills, and the method of teaching is characterized by (a) teacher modeling or demonstration of important skills, (b) frequent student responding, (c) appropriate, direct feedback to students (including correction), (d) adequate provisions for practice, and (e) student mastery. *Reading Mastery* is fast-paced, providing immediate feedback and correction procedures for various student errors. Repetition is built into the program, and the library series reinforces skills developed in the program and provides opportunity for independent reading. Research indicates that the program has been highly effective in teaching reading to young students with learning problems (Carnine et al., 1990; Stallings, 1974). However, Kirk et al. (1978) note that the rigidity of the instructional program and its emphasis on auditory skills may be considered disadvantages.

The companion *Corrective Reading Program* (Engelmann, Becker, Hanner, & Johnson, 1988, 1989) is an advanced remedial reading program designed for students in 4th through 12th grade who have not mastered decoding and comprehension skills. The program is divided into two strands, decoding and comprehension, and each strand includes 315 lessons. Each lesson lasts 35 to 45 minutes and provides teacher-directed work, independent applications, and tests of student performance. The decoding strand follows the *Reading Mastery* format and includes word-attack basics, decoding strategies, and skill applications. The comprehension strand presents real-life situations and includes thinking basics, comprehension skills, and concept applications. The presentation book for the teacher specifies the teacher's role in each lesson. The program gives the student immediate feedback and provides a built-in reinforcement system.

Reading Recovery

Reading Recovery, an early intervention program developed in New Zealand for young children experiencing difficulty in beginning reading (Clay, 1985; Pinnell, DeFord, & Lyons, 1988), combines writing and reading and helps children learn phonics within meaningful written contexts. In this intervention, which combines whole language with tutoring in specific skills, low-achieving first-grade students are provided with one-to-one tutoring for 30 minutes each day in addition to classroom reading instruction. In the daily individual lessons, students read aloud from minibooks and write their own one- or two-sentence messages, and each child's progress is monitored consistently. The tutor is a certified teacher who is trained over the course of a full school year at a teacher training site (available in various school districts and universities). Lesson components include easy and fluent reading, challenging reading, and writing, during which the teacher works alongside the student and intervenes to teach appropriate strategies. Thus, this highly structured model emphasizes direct teaching of metacognitive strategies, learning to read by reading, teaching of phonics in the context of students' reading, and integration of reading and writing. Although implementing a high-quality *Reading Recovery* program is difficult and time-consuming due to required training and one-to-one intervention, research indicates that it has both immediate and long-term effects in helping low-achieving students learn to read and write (Pinnell, 1990).

Phonological Awareness Training

The ability to read and comprehend depends on rapid and automatic recognition and decoding of single words, which is dependent on the ability to segment words and syllables into phonemes. Phonological awareness is an insight that words are composed of smaller units, and deficits in phonological awareness reflect a core deficit in students with reading disabilities (Lyon, 1995). According to Torgesen, Wagner, and Rashotte (1994),

> Phonological awareness is generally defined as one's sensitivity to, or explicit awareness of, the phonological structure of the words in one's language. It is measured by tasks that require children to identify, isolate, or blend the individual phonemes in words. (p. 276)

Thus, phonological awareness includes the ability to perceive spoken words as a sequence of sounds as well as the ability to consciously manipulate the sounds in words (Adams, 1990). Although the relationship is reciprocal, phonological awareness precedes skilled decoding. Rather than being the ability to make letter-sound correspondences or to sound out words (as in phonics), phonological awareness refers to an awareness that comes intuitively before such abilities. Of the components of phonological awareness, auditory blending and segmenting correlate strongly with reading acquisition (Adams, 1990) and appear to be critical dimensions in prereading instruction.

Some experts (Adams, 1990; Stahl, Osborn, & Lehr, 1990) indicate that the phonological awareness of children entering school may be the single most powerful determinant of reading success or failure. Individual differences in phonological awareness prior to school entry are highly related to and predictive of the ability to learn to read in the first grade (Mather, 1992). Research indicates that children who are strong in phonological awareness in kindergarten usually learn to read more easily than children with relatively delayed development in this area. Results of a longitudinal study (Torgesen et al., 1994) indicate that inefficient development of phonological awareness in kindergarten is causally related to difficulties in acquiring alphabetic reading skills in first and second grade.

Simmons, Gunn, Smith, and Kameenui (1994) note that children who are lacking in phonological awareness may not be able to (a) identify sounds in words, (b) represent the separate sounds in a word, (c) detect and manipulate sounds within words, (d) perceive a word as a sequence of sounds, and (e) isolate beginning, medial, and ending sounds. Because these children are unable to infer the underlying alphabetic relationships that are essential to generalized word reading skills, they experience difficulty in reading programs that do not provide explicit instruction in phonological decoding. Thus, there is a need for early and explicit instruction in phonological awareness as an oral language skill as well as a need for instruction in the alphabetic principle as an aid to the development of independent word reading skills (Adams, 1990; Liberman & Liberman, 1990). Children who are at risk for reading problems can be identified accurately even before they begin the process of learning to read (Hurford, Schauf, Bunce, Blaich, & Moore, 1994), and preventive interventions can be introduced to increase their phonological awareness.

Fortunately, phonological awareness in young children can be developed, and training in phonological awareness produces improved performance in reading. When phonemic skills do not develop naturally or children enter school with limited language backgrounds, systematic instruction may be required. Phonological awareness training prior to reading instruction may reduce the incidence of reading disabilities significantly among young children and, thus, should be included in preventive or remedial programs for children who are at risk or identified with reading disabilities.

Simmons et al. (1994) present four recommendations to enhance the effectiveness of phonological awareness instruction:

1. *Focus first on the auditory features of words.* When asking the student to blend the sounds of a word together or to identify the individual sounds in a word, instruction initially should occur without alphabetic symbols.
2. *Move from explicit, natural segments of language to the more implicit and complex.* Initial segmenting instruction should proceed from segmenting sentences into words, words into syllables, and syllables into phonemes.
3. *Use phonological properties and dimensions of words to enhance performance.* Task complexity can be controlled by initially selecting words with fewer phonemes and words in which consonant and vowel configurations can be distinguished easily (e.g., words with vowel-consonant or consonant-vowel-consonant patterns). Also, words with discrete phonemes (e.g., *rug*) are segmented more easily than those beginning and ending with consonant blends, and words that begin with continuous sounds (e.g., *sun*, *mat*) facilitate sound blending activities.

4. *Scaffold blending and segmenting through explicit modeling*. Strategies should be modeled by the teacher and practiced over time to make the blending and segmenting processes obvious and explicit.
5. *Integrate letter-sound correspondence once learners are proficient with auditory tasks.* Blending and segmenting skills should be applied to realistic reading, writing, and spelling situations.

Phonological Awareness Training for Reading (Torgesen & Bryant, 1994) is a program designed to increase children's awareness of the phonological structure of words and help them understand how spoken language is represented by the alphabetic system. In the program, various activities are practiced across different word sets. Warm-up rhyming activities focus attention on sounds in words. In blending activities, words are presented segmented into two parts called the onset and rime sounds (e.g., /d/-og), and the child is taught to blend the sounds together to say the correct word (*dog*). Then the child is taught to blend all the individual sounds in a word (e.g., /d/-/o/-/g/) to say the word. In segmenting activities, the child identifies words that have similar beginning, ending, or middle sounds. The child also is trained to indicate the position in a word that a given phoneme occupies and to pronounce individual phonemes that occur at the beginning and ending of words. In addition, the child practices identifying the mouth and tongue positions required for the production of each consonant phoneme. Finally, activities are included in which the child uses letters to represent the phonemes in words so that there is generalization of the phonological awareness skills to tasks required when learning to read.

Torgesen et al. (1994) note that programs designed to train phonological awareness in young children generally have been successful; however, they suggest that explicit and intense training procedures may be required to have a substantial effect on the phonological awareness of children with severe reading disabilities. (Chapter 9 includes an assessment instrument and commercial material for phonological awareness.)

Programmed Reading Instruction

Programmed reading materials can be in either a workbook format or a teaching machine. The materials are designed to be self-teaching and self-correcting. Subject matter is presented in small steps or frames in a systematic, logical sequence. The student must respond to the question in each frame and then check the response by sliding down a marker. Question forms can be true/false or multiple-choice, completing a sentence, writing a word, or completing a word by filling in letters. When working with a machine, the student responds by pulling a lever or knob, pushing a button, or turning a crank. With all programmed materials, the student receives immediate feedback. In workbooks the answers often are in the margin, whereas on teaching machines a light or sound can give feedback, the answer can be uncovered, or the response can appear on the screen. In a *linear* program, the student must correct a wrong response before continuing. In a *branching* program, after an incorrect response, the student is referred to another page where the mistake is explained; thus, the student progresses at the student's own rate and receives positive reinforcement or correction at each step.

Repetition and feedback are important when using programmed materials with students who have learning disabilities. The success of the approach depends on providing students with materials suited to their needs. Two commercially available programmed reading materials are *Programmed Reading* and *Programmed Reading for Adults* (Phoenix Learning Resources).

Multisensory Reading Method

The multisensory method is based on the premise that some students learn best when content is pre-

sented in several modalities. Frequently, kinesthetic (movement) and tactile (touch) stimulation is used along with the visual and auditory modalities. The multisensory programs that feature tracing, hearing, writing, and seeing often are referred to as VAKT (visual-auditory-kinesthetic-tactile). To increase tactile and kinesthetic stimulation, sandpaper letters, finger paint, sand trays, raised letters, and sunken letters are used. The Fernald (1943, 1988) and the Gillingham (Gillingham & Stillman, 1970) methods highlight VAKT instruction. The Fernald method stresses whole-word learning, and the Gillingham method features sound blending.

The Fernald Method. Vocabulary is selected from stories the student has dictated, and each word is taught as a whole. In the Fernald approach there is no attempt to teach phonics skills. The teacher identifies unknown words, and the student writes the words to develop word recognition. Each word is learned as a whole unit, and it immediately is placed in a context that is meaningful to the student. Success is stressed to help maintain a high level of motivation.

The method consists of four stages. In Stage 1, the student selects a word to learn, and the teacher writes it with a crayon in large letters. The student then traces the word with a finger, making contact with the paper (tactile-kinesthetic). While tracing, the student says each part of the word aloud (auditory). In addition, the student sees the word (visual) while tracing it and hears the word while saying it (auditory). This process is repeated until the student can write the word correctly without looking at the sample. If an error is made when tracing or writing, the student must start over so that the word always is written as a unit. If the word is correct, it is filed alphabetically in a word bank. The student writes a story using the learned words, and the story is typed so that the student can read the words in print.

In Stage 2, the student no longer is required to trace each word but now learns each new word by looking at the teacher's written copy of the word, saying it, and writing it. The student continues to write stories and keep a word file.

In Stage 3, the student learns new words by looking at a printed word and saying it before writing it, thus learning directly from the printed word; the teacher is not required to write it. At this point the student can begin reading from books. The teacher continually checks to see that the student is retaining learned words.

Finally, in Stage 4, the student can recognize new words by their similarity to printed words or parts of words already learned and thus can apply reading skills and expand reading interests.

The Fernald approach uses language experience and tracing (kinesthetic) techniques. Progress is slow, and to sustain interest the student chooses the material. Success is stressed to help maintain a high level of motivation. The student never is encouraged to sound out word parts or to copy words that have been traced. Each word is learned as a whole unit and is placed immediately in a context that is meaningful to the student. The four stages must be mastered in sequence. This remedial approach generally is used with students with severe reading problems. However, Otto and Smith (1980) note that the tracing technique alone can be used effectively to help students learn frequently used words with which they are having difficulty.

The Gillingham Method. The Gillingham method (Gillingham & Stillman, 1970) is a highly structured, phonetically oriented approach based on the theoretical work of S. T. Orton (1937). The method requires five lessons a week for a minimum of 2 years. Each letter sound is taught using a multisensory approach. Consonants and vowels with only one sound are presented on drill cards (consonants on white cards and vowels on salmon-colored cards), and letters are introduced by a key word (e.g., *fun* for *f*). *Associative* processes are used, beginning with the student associating (linking) the name and sound of a letter with its printed symbol. The method involves the following procedures:

1. A drill card showing one letter is shown to the student. The teacher says the name of the letter and the student repeats it. When this has been mastered, the teacher says the sound of the letter, and the student repeats the sound. Then the card is exposed and the teacher asks, "What does this letter say?" The student is to give its sound.
2. Without presenting the drill card, the teacher makes the sound represented by the letter and says, "Tell me the name of the letter that has this sound." This strategy is essentially oral spelling.
3. The teacher carefully writes the letter and explains its form, thus instructing the student in cursive handwriting. The student traces the letter over the teacher's lines, copies it, writes it from memory, and writes it while looking away. Finally, the teacher makes the sound and says, "Write the letter that has this sound."

After mastering the first group of 10 letters, (*a, b, f, h, i, j, k, m, p,* and *t*), the student is taught to blend them into words. The letters are combined to form simple consonant-vowel-consonant words (e.g., *bit*, *map*, and *jab*). Spelling is introduced after blending. When the teacher says a word, the student repeats the word, names the letters, writes the letters while saying them (simultaneous oral spelling), and reads the written word. Sentence and story writing is introduced after the student is able to write any three-letter, phonetically pure word. Nonphonetic words are taught through drill. Consonant blends are taught after the student can read, write, and spell the words in the short stories. Also, syllabication, dictionary skills, and additional spelling rules are introduced. Thus, the Gillingham method emphasizes repetition and drill, and spelling and writing skills are taught in conjunction with reading skills.

Instructional materials developed for the Gillingham method include phonics drill cards or phonetic word cards, syllable concept cards, diphthong cards, and little stories. Lessons and instructions on using the materials to teach various skills are provided (Gillingham & Stillman, 1970; J. L. Orton, 1976). The procedure is highly structured and rigid, and no other reading or spelling materials may be used. Two adaptations of the Gillingham method include *Recipe for Reading* (Traub & Bloom, 1978) and A *Multi-Sensory Approach to Language Arts for Specific Language Disability Children* (Slingerland, 1981). Also, the *Phonic Remedial Reading Lessons* (Kirk et al., 1985) uses a VAKT phonics approach.

Modified Alphabet Method

Some beginning reading programs use a special alphabet that features consistent symbol-sound associations. Two modified alphabet methods are the initial teaching alphabet and the diacritical marking system.

Initial Teaching Alphabet. The initial teaching alphabet (Downing, 1965) was proposed to simplify beginning reading. It uses a modified alphabet to ensure a consistent correspondence between sound and symbol. Letters in the traditional 26-letter alphabet do not always have just one sound apiece. However, because the initial teaching alphabet presents one symbol for each sound, a clear relationship exists between each of the characters and its sound. This pattern helps reduce confusing irregularities in spelling. There are 44 characters, including all the letters of the traditional alphabet except *x* and *q*, and 20 other letters that either look like traditional letters joined together or are new symbols. These additional letters represent special phonemes, such as the *th* sound. In addition, a larger version of the letter indicates uppercase letters. Some examples of words in the initial teaching alphabet include *larj* (large), *laf* (laugh), *askt* (asked), and *wun* (one). The initial teaching alphabet is used only in the beginning stages of reading. As soon as students are fluent in the initial teaching alphabet (usually by the end of the first grade), they transfer to the traditional alphabet.

Diacritical Marking System. In the diacritical marking system (Fry, 1964), phonetic marks are added to the letters in the traditional alphabet. For example, long vowels have a bar over them, silent letters have a slash mark through them, and digraphs have a bar under both letters (e.g., fivȩ, wi<u>th</u>, <u>ch</u>icks). Short vowels and regular consonants are not changed, because these are the most common usages of the letters. In this beginning reading system, nearly every word the student sees (in reading books, on worksheets, and on the chalkboard) is marked according to the diacritical marking system. As the student's reading skill progresses, the use of the marks diminishes.

Neurological Impress Method

The neurological impress method (Heckelman, 1969; Langford, Slade, & Barnett, 1974) was developed to teach reading to students with severe reading disabilities. The method consists of joint oral reading at a rapid pace by the student and the teacher. It is based on the theory that students can learn by hearing their own voice and someone else's voice jointly reading the same material. The student is seated slightly in front of the teacher, and the teacher's voice is directed into the student's ear at a close range. There is no special preparation of the material before the joint reading. The objective is simply to cover as many pages as possible in the allotted time, without tiring the student. At first, the teacher should read slightly louder and faster than the student, and the student should be encouraged to maintain the pace and not worry about mistakes. The teacher's finger slides to the location of the words as they are being read. As the student becomes capable of leading the oral reading, the teacher can speak more softly and read slightly slower, and the student's finger can point to the reading. Thus, the student and teacher alternate between leading and following.

Instruction begins at a level slightly below that at which the student can read successfully. No attempt is made to teach any phonics skills or word recognition, and no attention is given to comprehension of the material being read. The basic goal is for the student to attain fluent reading automatically. The neurological impress method emphasizes rapid decoding and can be most effective with students age 10 or older who spend too much time sounding out words and do not read fluently (Faas, 1980). Reading phrases rather than isolated words reveals progress, as does learning to pause for punctuation previously ignored.

A variation of the neurological impress method is the method of repeated readings (Samuels, 1979). This method requires the student to reread a short, meaningful passage several times until a satisfactory level of fluency (e.g., 80 to 100 correct words per minute with three to six errors) is reached. The procedure then is repeated with a new passage. Repeated readings thus emphasize reading rate on a single passage rather than single words, and identification of words in context must be fast as well as accurate. In a study of students with learning disabilities in fifth through eighth grade, O'Shea, Sindelar, and O'Shea (1987) found that repeated readings (three and seven times) combined with attentional cues were effective in increasing fluency (i.e., number of words correctly read per minute) and comprehension (i.e., percentage of story propositions correctly restated following the final reading). Likewise, Weinstein and Cooke (1992) found that repeated readings is an effective instructional strategy to help students achieve fluency, and they suggest the use of three fluency improvement criteria rather than a fixed-rate criterion. O'Shea and O'Shea (1988) indicate that the method can be used in a variety of learning arrangements, such as small-group instruction with choral reading, peer reading with pairs of reading partners, and learning centers with the use of Language Masters and tape recorders. Comprehension practice can be provided through activities involving the cloze and maze procedure (i.e., reading the passage and filling in the blanks for omitted words with the words that complete phrases or sentences correctly). Although not complete alone, either the neurological impress method or the method of repeated readings can be used effectively to improve reading fluency (Henk, Helfeldt, & Platt, 1986).

Glass Analysis

Glass analysis is a procedure for teaching reading that uses letter clusters as a decoding strategy (Glass, 1973). Letter clusters are two or more letters in a word that represent a relatively consistent sound (e.g., in *crab* the clusters are *cr* and *ab*). Through intensive auditory and visual training, the student is guided to perceive patterns of specific letter clusters that are related to particular sounds. Teaching a word involves five steps: (a) the teacher identifies the whole word as well as the letters and sounds of the clusters; (b) the teacher pronounces the sound of the letter(s) and asks the student what letter(s) represent the sound; (c) the teacher says the letter or letters and asks the student for the sound(s); (d) the teacher takes away letters and asks the student what sound is left; and (e) the teacher asks the student to read the whole word. The student's attention to the word is essential, and the entire word always is presented. Portions of the word never are covered, nor are meaningful letter clusters broken apart. Miccinati (1981) notes that through this method, students with reading disabilities can be taught to perceive distinctive features in words. By visually and auditorily responding to redundant letter clusters, the student begins to recognize the distinctive features and synthesize the clusters to form a word.

TEACHING STRATEGIES IN READING

Many reading approaches and instructional techniques are available for teaching students with learning disabilities. Although the research indicates that reading is taught most effectively through direct instruction (i.e., teaching reading skills directly rather than through process skills), none of the approaches (basal, phonics, linguistic, whole language, language experience, or others) has emerged as superior. Each approach has been successful with some students, and selected teaching strategies can be incorporated within each approach. Because each student with learning disabilities is unique, a combination of approaches and various teaching strategies are needed to meet the needs of these students. The keyword method, reciprocal teaching, and mapping strategies all are effective teaching techniques.

Keyword Method

To teach new vocabulary words and the initial learning and retention of facts, Mastropieri (1988) suggests the use of the keyword method, which is a memory-enhancing technique that relies strongly upon visual imagery. The method uses three steps: (a) recoding—changing a vocabulary word into a word (keyword) that sounds like part of the vocabulary word and is easy to picture (e.g., *ape* as a keyword for *apex*); (b) relating—integrating the keyword with its definition by imagining a picture of the keyword and its definition doing something together (e.g., an ape sitting on the highest point [apex] of a rock), and (c) retrieving—recalling the definition by thinking of the keyword and the picture or interactive image of the keyword.

In teaching abstract and concrete vocabulary words to students with learning disabililities, Mastropieri, Scruggs, and Fulk (1990) found that keyword mnemonic instruction resulted in higher levels of recall and comprehension than a rehearsal condition. Students were shown mnemonic pictures for each new vocabulary word in which the keyword was pictured interacting with its definition in a line drawing or interacting with an instance of the definition. For example, for the word *oxalis*, meaning "a cloverlike plant," an ox (keyword for oxalis) was pictured eating a cloverlike plant, and for *chiton*, meaning "a loose garment," a kite (keyword for chiton) was shown in a picture of people making kites out of loose garments. In addition, when using the keyword method, the teacher can enhance fluency and application by presenting practice exercises that require students to use the new words in sentences and in oral communication.

Reciprocal Teaching

To improve reading comprehension, reciprocal teaching is an interactive teaching strategy that promotes both comprehension of text and comprehension monitoring through active participation in discussions of text (Palinscar & Brown, 1986, 1988). The teacher and students work together to comprehend text through the use of a dialogue structured by four strategies:

1. *Predicting*: Students are taught to make predictions about upcoming content from cues in the text or from prior knowledge of the topic. They can use text structure such as headings, subheadings, and questions embedded in the text to hypothesize what the author will discuss. This gives students a purpose for reading (i.e., to confirm or disprove their hypotheses).
2. *Question generating*: Through teacher modeling and practice in generating main idea questions about the text, students learn to identify information that provides the substance for a good question. Students become more involved in the reading text when they are posing and answering questions rather than responding to teacher or text questions.
3. *Summarizing*: The teacher guides students in integrating the information presented in the text. For example, the students can identify or invent topic sentences, name lists with appropriate labels, and delete unimportant or repeated information. This provides students with an opportunity to monitor their own understanding of the text.
4. *Clarifying*: The students' attention is given to reasons why the text may be difficult to understand (e.g., unfamiliar vocabulary, unclear referent words, or disorganized text). They are taught to reread or ask for help to restore meaning.

In reciprocal teaching, the teacher initially leads the dialogue and models the use of the four strategies while reading. Through guided practice, the responsibility for initiating and maintaining the dialogue is transferred to the students. Thus, there is interplay among the teacher and students, and the teacher uses explanation, instruction, and modeling with guided practice to help students independently apply the strategies and learn from text. When using the strategies or thinking skills, students are forced to focus on the reading material and, at the same time, monitor for understanding.

Englert and Mariage (1991) present a comprehension procedure that includes the reciprocal teaching format as well as semantic mapping to improve students' recall of information in expository text. In POSSE, students apply the following strategies:

P—*Predict* text ideas based on background knowledge.

O—*Organize* the predicted textual ideas and background knowledge based on text structure into a semantic map.

S—*Search* for the text structure in the expository passage by reading.

S—*Summarize* the main ideas and record the information in a semantic map.

E—*Evaluate* comprehension by comparing the semantic maps, clarify information by asking questions, and predict what information will be in the next text section.

In this procedure students take turns leading the comprehension dialogue, and there is group interaction to promote internalization of the reading strategies. In addition, the teacher constructs a semantic map of students' ideas to visually represent the text structure and organization of ideas. Thus, text structure mapping and reciprocal teaching within the reading process are combined. In a study on the effectiveness of the intervention, Englert, Tarrant, Mariage, and Oxer (1994) report that POSSE produced powerful effects on the comprehension abilities of students with learning disabilities and was found to be a highly effective procedure for comprehension instruction regardless of students' age levels.

Mapping Strategies

Story-mapping procedures can be used to improve reading comprehension through a schema-building technique (Idol & Croll, 1987). A pictorial story map is used as an organizer for readers, and the students are asked to fill in the map components as they read. The map components of a narrative story include the setting (characters, time, and place), problem, goal, action, and outcome. The teacher initially models the story-mapping procedure by pointing out information related to the story-map components and having the students write the correct answer on the story-map outline. Then students independently complete the story map with prompting from the teacher as needed. Improved comprehension results as students build a structural schemata (the story-map components) that are applied to a narrative story. Story mapping brings the reader's attention to important and interrelated parts of a story and provides a framework for understanding, conceptualizing, and remembering story events.

Idol (1987) notes that a mapping strategy designed for use with expository material can result in improved comprehension. A critical thinking map is used that highlights the major aspects of a passage, including (a) the important events, points, or steps that lead to the main idea, (b) the main idea itself, (c) other viewpoints and opinions of the reader, (d) the reader's conclusion upon reading the passage, and (e) any relevancy the reader perceives for contemporary situations. The reader completes the map components either during or after reading a passage in the text.

READING AND STUDY SKILLS FOR ADOLESCENTS

Most secondary course work requires a relatively large amount of reading, because textbooks and supplementary materials are the major sources of information. In expository materials, the vocabulary is often more difficult to decode and pronounce than that found in narrative material, and the general content is frequently beyond the reader's experiences. According to Roe, Stoodt, and Burns (1995), "Content teachers can help students comprehend content materials by teaching them the meanings of key vocabulary terms. . . . Content area teachers need to be familiar with the types of writing patterns encountered frequently in their particular disciplines, so that they can help students to better understand these patterns" (p. 9). The secondary teacher also should be aware that older students often need to develop study skills and reading rate, in addition to increasing decoding and comprehension skills.

Increasing reading rate and adjusting reading rate according to purpose should help the adolescent read more efficiently in numerous content areas at a higher academic level. Also, setting a purpose for reading through the use of study guides or the SQ3R method can improve the older student's comprehension. Finally, learning strategies can be used to enhance adolescents' word identification and reading comprehension.

Reading Rate

The adolescent may need to increase reading speed to finish assignments on time and keep up with older classmates. Roe et al. (1995) note that secondary students should be made aware of poor reading habits that may decrease their reading rate, including forming each word as it is read, sounding out all words (familiar and unfamiliar), rereading material, and pointing to each word with the index finger. Another technique for increasing rate, which often is used in a reading laboratory, is to present words and phrases with a tachistoscope and gradually reduce the presentation time, thus speeding up the student's responses. The teacher can have the student practice timed readings with stopwatches or egg timers. Progress should be reinforced and charted continuously. Timed readings should be accompanied by comprehension checks, and the teacher should encourage rate increases only if comprehension does not suffer.

Rupley and Blair (1989) note that successful reading in the content areas requires the ability to adjust one's rate of reading to the type of material being read. Three types of reading are required: skimming, scanning, and studying. Skimming refers to covering a selection to get some of the main ideas and a general overview of the material without attending to details. In skimming, the student should read the first paragraph line-by-line; read bold print headings as they appear; read the first sentence of every paragraph; examine pictures, charts, and maps; and read the last paragraph. Skimming practice may involve giving the student a short amount of time to skim a content chapter and write down the main ideas or having the student skim newspaper articles and match them to headlines. *Scanning* refers to reading a selection to find a specific piece of information. When scanning, the student should use headings to locate the pages to scan for the specific information; run eyes rapidly down the page in a zigzag or winding S-pattern; note uppercase letters when looking for a name, numbers for dates, and italicized words for vocabulary items; and read only what is needed to verify the purpose. Scanning activities may include having the student find the date of a particular event by scanning a history chapter or locate a specific person's number in a telephone directory. In *study-type reading*, the goal is total comprehension, and reading is deliberate and purposeful. Rupley and Blair state that students must have these three types of reading explained to them, practice them under teacher supervision, and be given opportunities for independent practice.

Study Skills

As students learn to study various content areas, they should develop effective study skills. The

SQ3R method, developed by Robinson (1961), is used widely, especially for social studies and science. This method can be useful to students with learning disabilities in providing a systematic approach to better study skills. The method involves the following steps:

1. *Survey*: To get an overview of the reading material, the student scans the entire assignment, glancing at headings to see the major points that will be developed and reading introductory statements and summaries. The student also should inspect graphic aids such as maps, tables, graphs, and pictures. This survey provides a framework for organizing facts in the selection as the student progresses through the reading.
2. *Question*: To give a purpose for careful reading of the material, the student devises questions that may be answered in the selection. Questions can be formed by rephrasing headings and subheadings.
3. *Read*: The student reads the material with the intent of finding the answers to the questions. Also, the student may take notes during this careful reading.
4. *Recite*: The student looks away from the reading material and notes and briefly recites the answers to the questions. This checks on what the student has learned and helps set the information in memory.
5. *Review*: The student reviews the material and checks memory of the content by rereading portions of the selection or notes to verify answers given during the previous step. The student also can note major points under each heading. This review activity helps the student retain the material better by reinforcing the learning.

Another strategy to increase students' comprehension is for the content teacher to provide a reading guide or study organizer containing questions and statements on the content of the text material. The student should receive it beforehand and complete it while reading. A study organizer summarizes the main ideas and important concepts of the material in a factual style or in a schematic form such as a flowchart, diagram, or table.

Learning Strategies

Lenz and Hughes (1990) present a word identification strategy, DISSECT, that is effective in reducing common oral reading errors such as mispronunciations, substitutions, and omissions made by adolescents with learning disabilities. The seven steps of the strategy include the following:

D—*Discover* the content: Skip a difficult word and read the remainder of the sentence to guess the word by using the meaning of the sentence.

I —*Isolate* the prefix: Look at the beginning of the word to see if it is possible to box off the first several letters that create a phoneme that can be pronounced.

S —*Separate* the suffix: Look at the end of the word to see if it is possible to box off ending letters that form a suffix.

S —*Say* the stem: If able to recognize the stem (what is left after the prefix is isolated and the suffix is separated), say the prefix, stem, and suffix together.

E—*Examine* the stem: If unable to name the stem, apply one of two rules:

(a) If a stem, or any part of a stem, begins with a vowel, separate the first two letters from the stem and pronounce. If a stem, or any part of a stem, begins with a consonant, separate the first three letters from the stem and pronounce. Apply the rule until the end of the stem is reached and then pronounce the stem by saying the dissected part. Add the prefix and suffix and reread the whole word.

(b) If the first rule cannot be used, isolate the first letter of the stem and try to apply the first rule again. When vowels appear together in a word, pronounce both vowel sounds and then make one vowel sound at a time until it sounds right.

C—*Check* with someone: If unable to pronounce the word after applying the first five strategy steps, obtain assistance by checking with someone (such as a teacher, parent, or better reader) in an appropriate manner.

T—*Try* the dictionary: If personal assistance is unavailable, look up the word in the dictionary, pronounce it by using the pronunciation guide, and read the definition.

Students with learning disabilities also can be taught to use learning strategies designed to increase their reading comprehension (Clark, Deshler, Schumaker, Alley, & Warner, 1984). For example, the visual imagery strategy requires the student to read a passage and create representative visual images. The self-questioning strategy helps maintain interest and enhance recall by teaching the student to form questions about the content of a passage as the student reads. The use of learning strategies involves the student more actively in the reading process. The reader is asked to formulate questions, take notes on the content, or verbally paraphrase critical information. Thus, the student is engaged in information rehearsal and practice involving either reciting or writing down critical information.

To improve reading from content-area texts, Grant (1993) suggests a mnemonic strategy, SCROL, to help students use text headings:

S—*Survey* the headings and subheadings in the text selection to determine what information is being presented.

C—*Connect* the segments by writing key words from the headings that show how the headings relate to one another.

R—*Read* the heading segment and pay attention to words and phrases that express information about the heading.

O—*Outline* the major ideas and supporting details in the heading segment without looking at the text.

L—*Look* at the heading segment to check the outline for accuracy and correct inaccuracies.

COMMERCIAL READING PROGRAMS

Many commercial reading programs and materials are available for use with students who have learning disabilities. These materials can supplement one of the basic reading approaches to develop or improve specific skills, such as word attack or comprehension. This section presents several well-known commercial reading materials.

Learning Strategies Curriculum

The Learning Strategies Curriculum of the University of Kansas Center for Research on Learning is designed to improve a student's ability to cope with specific curriculum demands and to perform tasks independently. The learning strategies in the acquisition instructional strand enable students to gain information from written material. The *Word Identification Strategy* (Lenz, Schumaker, Deshler, & Beals, 1984) is aimed at quick decoding of multisyllabic words. The strategy teaches students a problem-solving procedure for quickly attacking and decoding unknown words in reading materials. The *Paraphrasing Strategy* (Schumaker, Denton, & Deshler, 1984) is designed to improve comprehension by focusing attention on the important information of a passage. It directs students to read a limited section of material, ask themselves the main idea and the details of the section, and put that information in their own words. Additional acquisition learning strategies are being developed. The *Visual Imagery Strategy* improves reading comprehension by having the student form mental pictures of the events described in a passage. In the *Self-Questioning Strategy* students form questions about key pieces of information in a passage and then read to find answers to these questions. The *Interpreting Visuals Strategy* increases the ability to obtain information from visuals such as pictures, diagrams, charts, tables, and maps. Finally, *Multipass* is a strategy for attacking textbook chapters that involves making three passes over the chapter to survey it, obtain key information from it, and study the key information.

Phonic Remedial Reading Lessons

Phonic Remedial Reading Lessons (Kirk et al., 1985) is a program designed to teach phonetic reading and word-attack skills to students who are reading below the third-grade level and need remedial assistance. The 77 lessons are divided into six parts and consist of words with a consistent phonic pattern. Part I introduces the most frequent sounds, including sounds of short vowels and consonants. Part II consists of two- and three-letter sequences that have a single sound. Part III includes integration of known symbols into consonant blends and common syllables. Part IV presents new configurations of sound-symbol associations. Part V provides exercises that cover exceptions to sounds previously taught. Part VI covers grammar concepts such as plurals, possessives, and past tense. The lessons emphasize learning the sounds of letters and blending letters together, and students are instructed to visualize, write, say, and hear the sounds simultaneously as each phoneme is introduced.

Specific Skill Series

The *Specific Skills Series* (Boning, 1990) includes exercise booklets designed to provide practice in reading comprehension skills for students reading at the prefirst- through eighth-grade level. The series includes nine separate skill strands: identifying inferences, getting the facts, using the context, drawing conclusions, getting the main idea, working with words, detecting the sequence, following directions, and locating the answer. The skill strands feature integrated language activities and emphasize critical reading and thinking skills. Students are allowed to work at their own pace, and the strands continue upward in sequential levels. Placement tests in each of the nine areas of reading comprehension are available in book format or computer software.

TR Reading Comprehension Series

The *TR Reading Comprehension Series* (published by SRA) features a structured framework for teaching comprehension skills to remedial students in third through seventh grade who are reading two to three grades below level. The program consists of eight worktexts (readability level—low-first grade to high-fourth grade) that can be used with phonics/decoding programs and with graded readers. Each worktext contains 42 lessons that focus on the following areas of skill development: vocabulary, genres, topic and main idea, details, sequence, spatial relationships, contrast and comparison, cause and effect, critical and interpretive thinking, and study skills.

Victory!

Victory! (Brigance, 1991) combines skill-based reading and whole language activities in a newspaper format for at-risk pre-adolescents through adults (third- through sixth-grade reading level). The literacy-cued, newspaper-style stories include current topics with an interest level of fourth grade through adult, and the vocabulary is controlled for readability. For each grade level, there are two semester workbooks, each with 35 student lessons and progress charts, that develop reading skills through critical thinking and word analysis practice. Students participate in written, verbal, and interactive activities, are shown patterns for word analysis, and learn about life through reading.

COMPUTER SOFTWARE PROGRAMS IN READING

Microcomputer programs can be used effectively to develop basic skills in reading by providing varied drill and extra practice. Word identification skills as well as comprehension skills can be reinforced. Numerous software programs are available to reinforce sight words, expand vocabularies, provide drill in phonics, analyze words according to structural analysis, and test comprehension. Also, the teacher can use a microcomputer to develop language experience lessons, store individual reading vocabulary tests, and produce cloze tests.

With recent technological advances, some currently available programs offer speech feedback and allow the reader to select any word on the screen for pronunciation by synthetic speech, and CD-ROM equipment allows the availability of "talking books" that provide graphic images as well as digitized speech. In addition, hypermedia computer-based reading materials offer definitions and spoken pronunciation of unfamiliar words, animation and zoom-ins, full-motion graphics and video, and links to data bases of related information (Boone, Higgins, Falba, & Langley, 1993). MacArthur and Haynes (1995) present a software system (Student Assistant for Learning from Text) for developing hypermedia versions of textbooks designed to help students compensate for their reading disabilities. Support features that enhance comprehension include speech synthesis, ready access to a glossary, highlighting of main ideas, questions embedded in the text at appropriate places, and summaries of important points.

Torgesen and Barker (1995) note that computer-assisted instruction and practice in reading can help students with learning disabilities learn to read more effectively by assisting them in acquiring accurate and fluent word identification skills. They describe computer programs that provide training in phonological awareness, specific context-free word identification, and reading of connected text. The following programs provide examples of available software that focus on reading skills.

Cloze-Plus

Cloze-Plus (produced by Milliken) develops reading comprehension skills and vocabulary through the use of structured cloze and context analysis activities. A factual reading selection with one word omitted is presented along with five possible word choices. The student reads the paragraph and types the letter of the best word choice. Context clues in which pertinent information is underlined can be requested. After two incorrect responses, the correct answer is displayed along with explanatory information. After a correct response, a positive reinforcement appears. Upon completion of a selection or session, the student receives a summary of performance. The cloze exercises focus on meaning completion, vocabulary in context, or syntax completion. They reinforce skills of interpretation and association, identifying same or opposite meaning, identifying definitions, making comparisons and contrasts, identifying pronoun antecedents, and noting similarities and differences. Eight levels are available with vocabulary controlled from the second- to ninth-grade level. The programs also can be used for remediation with older students.

Comprehension Power

Comprehension Power (produced by Milliken) is designed to build comprehension skills of students reading at the 4th- through 12th-grade level. In addition to the nine individual levels, there are three programs for middle and secondary school students who are reading at extremely low levels. The programs consist of three activities: preparation (new vocabulary words used in context), preview (key sentences from the reading selection), and comprehension reading. Stories are presented on a wide range of high-interest topics including adventure, sports, contemporary issues, and career awareness. The reading selection is presented either one line at a time at a preassigned rate (from 50 to 650 words per minute) or page-by-page with the student advancing the page manually. After each segment, the student answers comprehension questions. Responses are followed by immediate feedback and positive reinforcement. The student may reread the segment, if necessary, and also may adjust the reading rate. At the end of the session, the student receives an overall summary of performance. Each level provides practice and measurement of 25 commonly accepted reading comprehension skills in the areas of literal understanding, analysis, appreciation, interpretation, and evaluation. Thus, this software provides the opportunity to practice major comprehension skills and increase reading speed at the same time.

DLM Reading Fluency

DLM Reading Fluency (published by SRA) consists of four programs that build on one another to develop automatic decoding skills. *Hint and Hunt I* and *II* focus on vowels and vowel groups to teach basic decoding skills. The words and sounds contained in the programs are correlated to those introduced in basal reading series. The instructional phase, *Hint*, features a realistic voice stimulus and animated graphics. The practice phase, *Hunt*, is designed in a fast-action game format. *Construct-a-Word I* and *II* help the student read words more quickly and accurately by increasing knowledge of consonants, consonant clusters, and phonograms. The words and sounds presented in the programs are the same as those introduced in basal reading series. The student creates words by selecting appropriate word beginnings and endings. *Syllasearch I, II, III,* and *IV* provide the student with intensive practice in seeing and hearing multisyllable words. Each level has three phases: (a) meet the words (pronunciation of each word in a given level), (b) yank the syllables (analyzing the whole words to find particular syllables), and (c) collect the words (synthesizing syllables to form words). Finally, *Word Wise I, II,* and *III* help the student build comprehension through the development of vocabulary. The student matches words to definitions, explanations, and examples on an electronic game board. All of the software programs require the use of a speech output system to provide actual human speech for instruction, feedback, and correction.

SuperSonic Phonics

SuperSonic Phonics (produced by Curriculum Associates) is an intensive phonics program that is designed for new readers and readers who need to strengthen their phonics skills. The program helps the student develop critical symbol-to-sound and decoding skills to enhance automatic word recognition and phonics application. The student receives clearly pronounced computer audio instructions and uses the computer mouse to complete each exercise. A repeat button allows the student to hear a sound or word as often as needed. Based on performance, the student automatically is branched to reinforcement activities (such as a reward game) or to more challenging activities. Level 1 focuses on consonants and short vowels; Level 2 includes short vowels, long vowels, silent *e*, consonant digraphs, and consonant blends; and Level 3 features short and long vowel review, vowel *r* words, vowel combination words, and two-syllable words. A management system is included that provides student performance reports.

Word Man; Word Radar

These two programs for students in first through eighth grade are included in SRA's *Arcademic Skill Builders in Language Arts. Word Man* uses a game format that consists of a tricky maze of rectangular tracks with groups of letters placed along the rows. As a consonant moves past the letter combinations, the student must decide when a word is formed. Thus, the student practices basic phonetic patterns by forming words with the consonant-vowel-consonant or consonant-vowel-consonant silent *e* patterns. Only words with one syllable and three to four letters are used. *Word Radar* provides practice in matching basic sight words by having the student role-play a control tower operator who scans words that increase in length. In both programs, the speed and length of the game can be altered, as well as content and difficulty level.

PERSPECTIVE

Reading is a complex learning task, and many students with learning disabilities have reading disabilities. Educators must have an understanding of reading development, assessment procedures, and instructional approaches to meet the complex needs of students with reading disabilities. It is difficult to match the best instructional approach with a learner. Research indicates that reading is taught most effectively through teaching reading skills directly; however, none of the direct approaches (basal, phonics, linguistic, language experience, and so on) has emerged as superior, and each approach has been successful with some students. Moreover, Stanovich (1994) discusses the merits of different approaches for word recognition and comprehension. Specifically, he states,

> The ideas that self-discovery is the most efficacious mode of learning, that most learning can be characterized as "natural," and that cognitive components should never be isolated or fractionated during the learning process have been useful as tenets for comprehension instruction, but are markedly at variance with what is now known about the best ways to develop word recognition skill. Research has indicated that explicit instruction and teacher-directed strategy training are more efficacious and that this is especially true for at-risk children, children with learning disabilities, and for children with special needs. (p. 259)

Each student with learning disabilities is unique, and a combination of approaches is needed to meet the needs of these students. The growing research base in phonological awareness highlights the need to intervene early to ensure that students have certain implicit awareness regarding sound/symbol structures and relationships (Lyon, 1995). To date, the most valid way to match a reading approach to a learner is to trial-teach with various approaches and monitor the student's progress. When an approach produces effective learning, it should be considered appropriate. These procedures necessitate that a teacher be familiar with a variety of reading approaches and techniques.

DISCUSSION/REVIEW QUESTIONS

1. Discuss physical, environmental, and psychological factors related to reading disabilities.
2. Discuss the term *dyslexia*.
3. Discuss the organization of reading skills by presenting strategies of word recognition and areas included in reading comprehension.
4. Discuss the stages of the development of reading skills.
5. Describe several standardized and criterion-referenced reading tests.
6. Briefly discuss informal assessment techniques in reading including graded word lists, informal reading inventory, curriculum-based measurement, reading miscue analysis, cloze procedure, and teacher-made tests.
7. Briefly discuss developmental reading approaches including basal, phonics, linguistic, whole language, language experience, and individualized reading.
8. Briefly discuss remedial reading programs and approaches including *Reading Mastery* and the *Corrective Reading Program*, *Reading Recovery*, phonological awareness training, and programmed reading instruction.
9. Briefly discuss remedial reading methods including multisensory, modified alphabet, neurological impress, and Glass analysis.
10. Describe several commercial reading programs and computer software programs in reading.

REFERENCES

Adams, M. J. (1990). *Beginning to read: Thinking and learning about print*. Cambridge, MA: MIT Press.

Altwerger, B., Edelsky, C., & Flores, B. M. (1987). Whole language: What's new? *The Reading Teacher*, *41*, 144–154.

Balow, I. H., Farr, R. C., & Hogan, T. P. (1992). *Metropolitan Achievement Tests—Seventh Edition*. San Antonio, TX: Harcourt Brace Educational Measurement.

Bleismer, E. P., & Yarborough, B. H. (1965, June). A comparison of ten different beginning programs in first grade. *Phi Delta Kappan*, 500–504.

Bloomfield, L., & Barnhart, C. L. (1961). *Let's read—A linguistic approach.* Detroit, MI: Wayne State University Press.

Bond, G. L., & Dykstra, R. (1967). The cooperative research program in first-grade reading instruction. *Reading Research Quarterly, 2,* 5–142.

Bond, G. L., Tinker, M. A., Wasson, B. B., & Wasson, J. B. (1989). *Reading difficulties: Their diagnosis and correction* (6th ed.). Upper Saddle River, NJ: Prentice Hall.

Boning, R. A. (1990). *Specific skill series* (4th ed.). Blacklick, OH: SRA.

Boone, R., Higgins, K., Falba, C., & Langley, W. (1993). Cooperative text: Reading and writing in a hypermedia environment. *LD Forum, 18*(3), 29–37.

Bormuth, J. R. (1968). The cloze readability procedure. *Elementary English, 45,* 429–436.

Brigance, A. H. (1983). *Brigance Diagnostic Comprehensive Inventory of Basic Skills.* North Billerica, MA: Curriculum Associates.

Brigance, A. H. (1991). *Victory*! East Moline, IL: LinguiSystems.

Brown, V. L., Hammill, D. D., & Wiederholt, J. L. (1995). *Test of Reading Comprehension—3.* Austin, TX: PRO-ED.

Bryan, T. H., & Bryan, J. H. (1986). *Understanding learning disabilities* (3rd ed.). Palo Alto, CA: Mayfield.

Bryant, B. R., & Wiederholt, J. L. (1991). *Gray Oral Reading Tests—Diagnostic.* Austin, TX: PRO-ED.

Burke, C. L. (1976). *Reading Miscue Inventory—Short form.* Bloomington, IN: Indiana University.

Carbo, M. (1987). Matching reading styles: Correcting ineffective instruction. *Educational Leadership, 45*(2), 55–62.

Carnine, D., Silbert, J., & Kameenui, E. J. (1990). *Direct instruction reading* (2nd ed.). Upper Saddle River, NJ: Merrill/Prentice Hall.

Chall, J. S. (1983a). *Learning to read: The great debate* (Updated edition). New York: McGraw-Hill.

Chall, J. S. (1983b). *Stages of reading development.* New York: McGraw-Hill.

Chall, J. S. (1987). Reading and early childhood education: The critical issues. *Principal, 66*(5), 6–9.

Chall, J. S. (1989). *Learning to Read: The Great Debate* 20 years later—A response to "Debunking the great phonics myth." *Phi Delta Kappan, 70,* 521–538.

Chall, J. S., & Stahl, S. A. (1982). Reading. In H. E. Mitzel (Ed.), *Encyclopedia of educational research* (5th ed., pp. 1535–1559). New York: Free Press.

Chiang, B., & Ford, M. (1990). Whole language alternatives for students with learning disabilities. *LD Forum, 16*(1), 31–34.

Ciborowski, J. (1995). Using textbooks with students who cannot read them. *Remedial and Special Education, 16,* 90–101.

Clark, F. L., Deshler, D. D., Schumaker, J. B., Alley, G. R., & Warner, M. M. (1984). Visual imagery and self-questioning: Strategies to improve comprehension of written material. *Journal of Learning Disabilities, 17,* 145–149.

Clay, M. M. (1985). *The early detection of reading difficulties* (3rd ed.). Auckland, New Zealand: Heinemann Educational Books.

Critchley, M. (1981). Dyslexia: An overview. In G. Pavlidis & T. Miles (Eds.), *Dyslexia research and its application to education* (pp. 1–11). New York: John Wiley.

Deno, S. L. (1987). Curriculum-based measurement. *Teaching Exceptional Children, 20*(1), 41–42.

Deno, S. L. (1989). Curriculum-based measurement and special education services: A fundamental and direct relationship. In M. R. Shinn (Ed.), *Curriculum-based measurement: Assessing special children* (pp. 1–17). New York: Guilford Press.

Deno, S. L., & Mirkin, P. (1977). *Data-based program modification: A manual.* Reston, VA: Council for Exceptional Children.

Diederich, P. I., II. (1973). *Research 1960-70 on methods and materials in reading.* Princeton, NJ: Educational Testing Service.

Dodds, T., & Goodfellow, F. (1990/1991). *Learning through literature.* Blacklick, OH: SRA.

Dolch, E. W. (1955). *Methods in reading.* Champaign, IL: Garrard.

Downing, J. (1965). *The initial teaching alphabet reading experiment.* Chicago: Scott, Foresman.

Durrell, D. D., & Catterson, J. H. (1980). *Durrell analysis of reading difficulty* (3rd ed.). San Antonio, TX: Harcourt Brace Educational Measurement.

Dykman, R. A., Ackerman, P. T., Clements, S. D., & Peters, J. E. (1971). Specific learning disabilities: An attentional deficit syndrome. In H. R. Mykelbust (Ed.), *Progress in learning disabilities* (Vol. 2). New York: Grune & Stratton.

Dykstra, R. (1968). Summary of the second-grade phase of the cooperative research program in primary reading instruction. *Reading Research Quarterly, 4,* 49–70.

Dykstra, R. (1974). Phonics and beginning reading instruction. In C. C. Walcutt, J. Lamport, & G. McCracken (Eds.), *Teaching reading: A phonic/linguistic approach to developmental reading*. Upper Saddle River, NJ: Prentice Hall.

Ekwall, E. E., & Shanker, J. L. (1989). *Teaching reading in the elementary school* (3rd ed.). Upper Saddle River, NJ: Merrill/Prentice Hall.

Ekwall, E. E., & Shanker, J. L. (1993). *Locating and correcting reading difficulties* (6th ed.). Upper Saddle River, NJ: Merrill/Prentice Hall.

Engelmann, S., Becker, W., Hanner, S., & Johnson, G. (1988). *Corrective reading—decoding*. Blacklick, OH: SRA.

Engelmann, S., Becker, W., Hanner, S., & Johnson, G. (1989). *Corrective reading—comprehension*. Blacklick, OH: SRA.

Engelmann, S., & Bruner, E. C. (1995). *Reading mastery*. Blacklick, OH: SRA.

Englert, C. S., & Mariage, T. V. (1991). Making students partners in the comprehension process: Organizing the reading "POSSE." *Learning Disability Quarterly, 14,* 123–138.

Englert, C. S., Tarrant, K. L., Mariage, T. V., & Oxer, T. (1994). Lesson talk as the work of reading groups: The effectiveness of two interventions. *Journal of Learning Disabilities, 27,* 165–185.

Faas, L. A. (1980). *Children with learning problems: A handbook for teachers*. Boston: Houghton Mifflin.

Fernald, G. (1943). *Remedial techniques in basic school subjects*. New York: McGraw-Hill.

Fernald, G. (1988). *Remedial techniques in basic school subjects*. Austin, TX: PRO-ED.

Filipek, P. A. (1995). Neurobiologic correlates of developmental dyslexia: How do dyslexics' brains differ from those of normal readers? *Journal of Child Neurology, 10*(Suppl. 1), 62–69.

Fries, C. C. (1963). *Linguistics and reading*. New York: Holt, Rinehart & Winston.

Fry, E. A. (1964). A diacritical marking system to aid beginning reading instruction. *Elementary English, 41,* 526–529.

Fry, E. (1977). *Elementary reading instruction*. New York: McGraw-Hill.

Gates, A. I. (1937). The necessary mental age for beginning reading. *Elementary School Journal, 37,* 497–508.

Gates, A. I., McKillop, A. S., & Horowitz, R. (1981). *Gates-McKillop-Horowitz Reading Diagnostic Tests*. New York: Teachers College Press.

Gersten, R., & Dimino, J. (1993). Visions and revisions: A special education perspective on the whole language controversy. *Remedial and Special Education, 14*(4), 5–13.

Gillingham, A., & Stillman, B. (1970). *Remedial training for children with specific disability in reading, spelling, and penmanship* (7th ed.). Cambridge, MA: Educators Publishing Service.

Glass, G. G. (1973). *Teaching decoding as separate from reading*. Garden City, NY: Adelphi University Press.

Goodman, K. S. (1969). Analysis of oral reading miscues: Applied psycholinguistics. *Reading Research Quarterly, 5,* 9–30.

Goodman, K. S. (1973). *Miscue analysis: Applications to reading instruction*. Urbana, IL: National Council of Teachers of English.

Goodman, K. S. (1986). *What's whole in whole language?* Portsmouth, NH: Heinemann.

Goodman, Y. M., & Burke, C. L. (1972). *Reading Miscue Inventory: Manual of procedure for diagnosis and evaluation*. New York: Richard C. Owens.

Goodman, Y. M., Watson, D. J., & Burke, C. L. (1987). *Miscue Inventory: Alternative procedures*. New York: Richard C. Owens.

Grant, R. (1993). Strategic training for using text headings to improve students' processing of content. *Journal of Reading, 36,* 482–488.

Guszak, F. J. (1985). *Diagnostic reading instruction in the elementary school* (3rd ed.). New York: Harper & Row.

Hafner, L. (1965). Importance of cloze. In E. T. Thurstone & L. E. Hafner (Eds.), *The philosophical and social bases for reading: 14th yearbook*. Milwaukee: National Reading Conference.

Hall, M. (1981). *Teaching reading as a language experience* (3rd ed.). Columbus, OH: Merrill.

Harris, A. J., & Sipay, E. R. (1990). *How to increase reading ability: A guide to developmental and remedial methods* (9th ed.). New York: Longman.

Heckelman, R. G. (1969). The neurological impress method of remedial reading instruction. *Academic Therapy, 4,* 277–282.

Hefferan, M., & Parker, S. (1991). *B.A.L.A.N.C.E.: Blending all learning activities nurtures classroom excellence*. Orlando, FL: FDLRS/Action.

Heilman, A. W., Blair, T. R., & Rupley, W. H. (1994). *Principles and practices of teaching reading* (8th ed.). Upper Saddle River, NJ: Merrill/Prentice Hall.

Henk, W. A., Helfeldt, J. P., & Platt, J. M. (1986). Developing reading fluency in learning disabled students. *Teaching Exceptional Children, 18,* 202–206.

Heymsfeld, C. R. (1989). Filling the hole in whole language. *Educational Leadership, 46*(6), 65–68.

Hinshelwood, J. (1917). *Congenital word blindness.* London: H. K. Lewis.

Hoover, H. D., Hieronymus, A. N., Frisbie, D. A., & Dunbar, S. B. (1993). *Iowa Tests of Basic Skills.* Chicago: Riverside.

Hudson, F. G., Colson, S. E., & Welch, D. L. H. (1989). *Hudson Education Skills Inventory—Reading.* Austin, TX: PRO-ED.

Hurford, D. P., Schauf, J. D., Bunce, L., Blaich, T., & Moore, K. (1994). Early identification of children at risk for reading disabilities. *Journal of Learning Disabilities, 27,* 371–382.

Idol, L. (1987). A critical thinking map to improve content area comprehension of poor readers. *Remedial and Special Education, 8*(4), 28–40.

Idol, L., & Croll, V. J. (1987). Story-mapping training as a means of improving reading comprehension. *Learning Disability Quarterly, 10,* 214–229.

Johnson, D. J., & Myklebust, H. R. (1967). *Learning disabilities: Educational principles and practices.* New York: Grune & Stratton.

Johnson, M. S., Kress, R. A., & Pikulski, J. J. (1987). *Informal reading inventories.* Newark, DE: International Reading Association.

Karlsen, B., & Gardner, E. F. (1995). *Stanford Diagnostic Reading Test—Fourth Edition.* San Antonio, TX: Harcourt Brace Educational Measurement.

Kaufman, A. S., & Kaufman, N. L. (1985). *Kaufman Test of Educational Achievement.* Circle Pines, MN: American Guidance Service.

Keogh, B. K., & Margolis, J. (1976). Learn to labor and wait: Attentional problems of children with learning disorders. *Journal of Learning Disabilities, 9,* 276–286.

Kirk, S. A., Kirk, W. D., & Minskoff, E. (1985). *Phonic remedial reading lessons.* Novato, CA: Academic Therapy.

Kirk, S. A., Kliebhan, J. M., & Lerner, J. W. (1978). *Teaching reading to slow and disabled learners.* Boston: Houghton Mifflin.

Langford, K., Slade, K., & Barnett, A. (1974). An explanation of impress techniques in remedial reading. *Academic Therapy, 9,* 309–319.

Lee, D. M., & Allen, R. V. (1963). *Learning to read through experience* (2nd ed.). New York: Appleton-Century-Crofts.

Lenz, B. K., & Hughes, C. A. (1990). A word identification strategy for adolescents with learning disabilities. *Journal of Learning Disabilities, 33,* 149–158, 163.

Lenz, B. K., Schumaker, J. B., Deshler, D. D., & Beals, V. L. (1984). *Learning strategies curriculum: The word identification strategy.* Lawrence: University of Kansas Center for Research on Learning.

Liberman, I. Y., & Liberman, A. M. (1990). Whole language vs. code emphasis: Underlying assumptions and their implications for reading instruction. *Annals of Dyslexia, 40,* 51–76.

Lovitt, T. C., & Hansen, C. L. (1976). Round one—Placing the child in the right reader. *Journal of Learning Disabilities, 9,* 347–353.

Lyon, G. R. (1995). Research initiatives in learning disabilities: Contributions from scientists supported by the National Institute of Child Health and Human Development. *Journal of Child Neurology, 10*(Suppl. No. 1), 120–126.

MacArthur, C. A., & Haynes, J. B. (1995). Student assistant for learning from text (SALT): A hypermedia reading aid. *Journal of Learning Disabilities, 28,* 150–159.

MacGinitie, W. H., & MacGinitie, R. K. (1989). *Gates-MacGinitie Reading Tests—Third Edition.* Chicago: Riverside.

Mastropieri, M. A. (1988). Using the keyword method. *Teaching Exceptional Children, 20*(2), 4–8.

Mastropieri, M. A., Scruggs, T. E., & Fulk, B. J. M. (1990). Teaching abstract vocabulary with the keyword method: Effects on recall and comprehension. *Journal of Learning Disabilities, 23,* 92–96, 107.

Mather, N. (1992). Whole language reading instruction for students with learning disabilities: Caught in the cross fire. *Learning Disabilities Research & Practice, 7,* 87–95.

Mercer, C. D., & Mercer, A. R. (1993). *Teaching students with learning problems* (4th ed.). Upper Saddle River, NJ: Merrill/Prentice Hall.

Miccinati, J. (1981). Teach reading disabled students to perceive distinctive features in words. *Journal of Learning Disabilities, 14,* 140–142.

Newcomer, P. L. (1986). *Standardized Reading Inventory.* Austin, TX: PRO-ED.

Norton, D. E. (1992). *The impact of literature-based reading.* Upper Saddle River, NJ: Merrill/Prentice Hall.

Orton, J. L. (1976). *A guide to teaching phonics*. Cambridge, MA: Educators Publishing Service.

Orton, S. T. (1937). *Reading, writing, and speech problems in children*. New York: W. W. Norton.

O'Shea, L. J., & O'Shea, D. J. (1988). Using repeated reading. *Teaching Exceptional Children, 20*(2), 26–29.

O'Shea, L. J., Sindelar, P.T., & O'Shea, D. J. (1987). The effects of repeated readings and attentional cues on the reading fluency and comprehension of learning disabled readers. *Learning Disabilities Research, 2,* 103–109.

Otto, W., & Smith, R. J. (1980). *Corrective and remedial teaching* (3rd ed.). Boston: Houghton Mifflin.

Palinscar, A. S., & Brown, A. L. (1986). Interactive teaching to promote independent learning from text. *The Reading Teacher, 39*(8), 771–777.

Palinscar, A. S., & Brown, A. L. (1988). Teaching and practicing thinking skills to promote comprehension in the context of group problem solving. *Remedial and Special Education, 9*(1), 53–59.

Pennington, B. F. (1995). Genetics of learning disabilities. *Journal of Child Neurology, 10*(Suppl. 1), 69–77.

Perfetti, C. (1985). *Reading ability*. New York: Oxford University Press.

Pinnell, G. S. (1990). Success for low achievers through *Reading Recovery. Educational Leadership, 48*(1), 17–21.

Pinnell, G. S., DeFord, D. E., & Lyons, C. A. (1988). *Reading Recovery: Early intervention for at-risk first graders*. Arlington, CA: Educational Research Service.

Potter, M. L., & Wamre, H. M. (1990). Curriculum-based measurement and developmental reading models: Opportunities for cross-validation. *Exceptional Children, 57,* 16–25.

Pressley, M., & Rankin, J. (1994). More about whole language methods of reading instruction for students at risk for early reading failure. *Learning Disabilities Research & Practice, 9,* 157–168.

Robinson, F. P. (1961). *Effective study*. New York: Harper & Row.

Roe, B. D. (1993). *Burns/Roe Informal Reading Inventory* (4th ed.). Boston: Houghton Mifflin.

Roe, B. D., Stoodt, B. D., & Burns, P. C. (1995). *Secondary school reading instruction: The content areas* (5th ed.). Boston: Houghton Mifflin.

Rosner, S. L., Abrams, J. C., Daniels, P. R., & Schiffman, G. B. (1981). Dealing with the reading needs of the learning disabled child. *Journal of Learning Disabilities, 14,* 436–448.

Rupley, W. H., & Blair, T. R. (1989). *Reading diagnosis and remediation: Classroom and clinic* (3rd ed.). Upper Saddle River, NJ: Merrill/Prentice Hall.

Samuels, S. J. (1973). Success and failure in learning to read: A critique of the research. *Reading Research Quarterly, 8,* 200–239.

Samuels, S. J. (1979). The method of repeated readings. *The Reading Teacher, 32,* 403–408.

Samuels, S. J., & Edwall, G. (1981). The role of attention in reading with implications for the learning disabled student. *Journal of Learning Disabilities, 14,* 353–361, 368.

Schumaker, J. B., Denton, P. H., & Deshler, D. D. (1984). *Learning strategies curriculum: The paraphrasing strategy*. Lawrence: University of Kansas Center for Research on Learning.

Schumm, J. S., Vaughn, S., Haager, D., & Klinger, J. K. (1994). Literacy instruction for mainstreamed students: What suggestions are provided in basal reading series? *Remedial and Special Education, 15,* 14–20.

Silvaroli, N. J. (1990). *Classroom Reading Inventory* (6th ed.). Dubuque, IA: William C. Brown.

Simmons, D. C., Chard, D., & Kameenui, E. J. (1994). Translating research into basal reading programs: Applications of curriculum design. *LD Forum, 19*(4), 9–13.

Simmons, D. C., Gunn, B., Smith, S. B., & Kameenui, E. J. (1994). Phonological awareness: Applications of instructional design. *LD Forum, 19*(2), 7–10.

Slingerland, B. (1981). *A multi-sensory approach to language arts for specific language disability children: A guide for elementary teachers*. Cambridge, MA: Educators Publishing Service.

Smith, R. J., & Barrett, T. C. (1979). Teaching reading in the middle grades (2nd ed.). Reading, MA: Addison-Wesley.

Snider, V. E., & Tarver, S. G. (1987). The effect of early reading failure on acquisition of knowledge among students with learning disabilities. *Journal of Learning Disabilities, 20,* 351–356, 373.

Spache, G. D. (1981). *Diagnostic Reading Scales*. Monterey, CA: CTB McGraw-Hill.

Spache, G. D., & Spache, E. B. (1986). *Reading in the elementary school* (5th ed.). Boston: Allyn & Bacon.

Stahl, S. A., & Miller, P. D. (1989). Whole language and language experience approaches for beginning reading: A quantitative research synthesis. *Review of Educational Research, 59,* 87–116.

Stahl, S. A., Osborn, J., & Lehr, F. (1990). *Beginning to read: Thinking and learning about print—A summary.* Urbana-Champaign: University of Illinois Center for the Study of Reading.

Stallings, J. A. (1974). *Follow Through classroom observation evaluation 1972-1973* (Executive Summary SRI Project URU-7370). Menlo Park, CA: Stanford Research Institute.

Stanovich, K. E. (1994). Constructivism in reading education. *The Journal of Special Education, 28,* 259–274.

Starlin, C. (1982). *On reading and writing.* Des Moines, IA: Department of Public Instruction.

Stauffer, R. G. (1981). Strategies for reading instruction. In M. P. Douglas (Ed.), *Reading: What is basic? 45th yearbook. Claremont reading conference.* Claremont, CA: Center for Developmental Studies.

Tindal, G. A., & Marston, D. B. (1990). *Classroom-based assessment: Evaluating instructional outcomes.* Upper Saddle River, NJ: Merrill/Prentice Hall.

Torgesen, J. K., & Barker, T. A. (1995). Computers as aids in the prevention and remediation of reading disabilities. *Learning Disability Quarterly, 18,* 76–87.

Torgesen, J. K., & Bryant, B. R. (1994). *Phonological awareness training for reading.* Austin, TX: PRO-ED.

Torgesen, J. K., Wagner, R. K., & Rashotte, C. A. (1994). *Longitudinal studies of phonological processing and reading. Journal of Learning Disabilities, 27,* 276–286.

Traub, N., & Bloom, F. (1978). *Recipe for reading.* Cambridge, MA: Educators Publishing Service.

Weinstein, G., & Cooke, N. L. (1992). The effects of two repeated reading interventions on generalization of fluency. *Learning Disability Quarterly, 15,* 21–28.

Wiederholt, J. L. (1985). *Formal Reading Inventory.* Austin, TX: PRO-ED.

Wiederholt, J. L., & Bryant, B. R. (1992). *Gray Oral Reading Tests—Third Edition.* Austin, TX: PRO-ED.

Wisconsin Tests of Reading Skill Development: Word attack, study skills, and comprehension. (1977). Madison, WI: Learning Multi-Systems. (Developed by the Evaluation and Reading Project Staffs at the Wisconsin Research and Development Center for Cognitive Learning)

Woodcock, R. W. (1987). *Woodcock Reading Mastery Tests—Revised.* Circle Pines, MN: American Guidance Service.

Woodcock, R. W., & Johnson, M. B. (1989). *Woodcock-Johnson Psycho-Educational Battery—Revised.* Chicago: Riverside.

Woods, M. L., & Moe, A. J. (1995) *Analytical Reading Inventory* (5th ed.). Upper Saddle River, NJ: Merrill/Prentice Hall.

Mathematics

CHAPTER 14

After studying this chapter, you should be able to:

- describe concepts basic to understanding numbers.
- present problem areas of students with learning disabilities and their relationship to math performance.
- describe specific common error patterns.
- explain the levels of learning in math.
- describe standardized survey and diagnostic math tests.
- describe criterion-referenced survey and diagnostic math tests.
- discuss informal assessment of math.
- discuss the major components of effective math instruction.
- present guidelines for the use of manipulative objects and for planning and implementing basic fact instruction.
- explain low-stress algorithms.
- present problem-solving interventions.
- describe commercial math programs.
- describe computer software programs in math.

I recently had the opportunity to work on a math project with second-grade teachers and their students in a rural Florida school. During the last week of school I attended the end-of-the-school-year picnic. I was sitting at a table enjoying an ice cream cone when I heard a confident but quiet voice say, "I know 99 times 0." Standing beside the table was a second grader named Matt, with his hands in his pockets, waiting for my response. I decided to have some fun. I said, "How could you possibly know 99 times 0 and still be in the second grade? That must be at least a third-grade skill." Matt quickly replied, "99 times 0 is 0!" With a surprised expression, I said, "Lucky guess!" Matt looked directly at me and said, "I'll be back." Then he turned and walked away. A few minutes later, Matt approached me with several of his second-grade friends. Upon their arrival, one of Matt's friends said, "I know 1,000 times 1." I responded, "You're kidding. That problem is impossible for a second grader." The friend blurted out, "1,000!" More second graders joined our discussion. They continued to share with me their knowledge of multiplication—1,000,000 times 1, 6,000 times 0, 9 times 8, and so on. The group of 8 to 10 students consisted of normally achieving students and students with learning disabilities. They displayed their knowledge of rules, multiplication facts, and problem-solving skills. I praised them for their knowledge and smartness. I was surprised that the students continued to discuss math when they had the opportunity to be playing. That afternoon while driving home, I realized that I had learned a lesson about empowered students.

Unfortunately, this scenario of students excited about their math learning is uncommon. For many students, math problems often result in school failure and lead to much anxiety. Although deficiencies in reading are cited most often as a primary characteristic of students with learning disabilities, Mastropieri, Scruggs, and Shiah (1991) note that deficits in math are as serious a problem for many of these students.

The National Research Council (1989) claims that mathematics represents "the invisible culture of our age" that affects our daily lives. From a *practical* perspective, math knowledge influences many decisions, including the calculation of the effects of a salary increase, the comparison of interest rates on loans, and the figuring of unit prices. From a *civic* perspective, math concepts relate to public policies such as helping individuals understand taxation, debt, and statistics involving health, crime, ecology, and institutional budgets. In terms of *professional* parameters, math knowledge provides many individuals with the tools to succeed on the job. From a *recreational* perspective, math knowledge can be a source of relaxation and fun, including playing strategic games, keeping score in various card or sport games, and understanding probabilities in games. Finally, from a *cultural* viewpoint, math can be appreciated for its power to solve problems and predict outcomes.

Research confirms that many students with learning disabilities are unable to compute basic number facts (Fleischner, Garnett, & Shepherd, 1982; Goldman, Pellegrino, & Mertz, 1988). Fleischner and her colleagues found that sixth-grade students with learning disabilities computed basic addition facts no better than third graders without learning disabilities. Other studies indicate that math deficiencies of students with learning disabilities emerge in the early years and continue throughout secondary school. Cawley and Miller (1989) report that the mathematical knowledge of students with learning disabilities progresses approximately 1 year for each 2 years of school attendance. Warner, Alley, Schumaker, Deshler, and Clark (1980) found that the math progress of students with learning disabilities reaches a plateau after 7th grade. The students in their study achieved only 1 more year's growth in math from 7th through 12th grade. Both studies report that the mean math scores of students with learning disabilities in the 12th grade are at the high 5th-grade level.

In a survey of students with learning disabilities in the sixth grade and above, McLeod and Armstrong (1982) found that two of every three students are receiving special math instruction. Moreover, in a survey of elementary and secondary teachers of students with learning disabilities, Carpenter (1985) found that teachers use one-third of their instructional time to teach math.

The importance of providing quality instruction for students with math problems is apparent; however, the challenge intensifies when the reforms being considered in math education are examined. The *Curriculum and Evaluation Standards for School Mathematics*, published in 1989 by the National Council of Teachers of Mathematics (NCTM), is shaping current reform efforts in math education. Spurred by poor performances of American youth on national math tests, this document urges professionals to adopt the NCTM standards. Specifically, the NCTM calls for practitioners and researchers to embrace problem solving as the basis for math instruction and minimize meaningless rote drill and practice activities.

Upon initial inspection, the NCTM standards are very appealing. The goals of the standards enjoy widespread acceptance. Closer inspection, however, reveals some serious limitations of the standards as they pertain to the education of students with learning disabilities. The following limitations center around the modest attention given to student diversity and the rigid adherence to select instructional paradigms:

1. The standards make only modest reference to students with disabilities (Giordano, 1993; Hofmeister, 1993; Hutchinson, 1993b; Rivera, 1993).
2. The standards are not based on replicable, validated, instructional programs. Research-supported instructional programs for students with moderate to mild disabilities are especially lacking (Hofmeister, 1993; Hutchinson, 1993b; Rivera, 1993). For example, Hutchinson states that there is "no evidence to support the claim that exposure to the proposed content and experiences will result in mathematical power for students with disabilities" (p. 20).
3. The standards promote an endogenous constructivist approach (self-discovery) for teaching math to all students. This position ignores the wealth of teaching practices generated from the process-product research (Englert, Tarrant, & Mariage, 1992) that have proven to be effective with students who have moderate-to-mild disabilities. Moreover, strict adherence to endogenous constructivism does not recognize the promising findings being generated from constructivists who promote a directed discovery (exogenous) approach or constructivists who advocate a guided discovery (dialectical) approach.

Mercer, Harris, and Miller (1993) recommend that mathematical reform be guided by contributions across paradigms. Specifically, they encourage educators to recognize the contributions of various paradigms. (For detailed reactions to the NCTM standards regarding students with disabilities, see the November/December 1993 issue of *Remedial and Special Education*.)

Reforms that produce higher standards are certain to frustrate teachers and students who are struggling with current standards and traditional curricula. For example, some states already have raised their secondary school diploma requirements to include the successful completion of Algebra I. Given that traditional mathematics instruction is failing many students (Carnine, 1991; Cawley, Miller, & School, 1987), not just those with learning disabilities, and that higher standards are being implemented, the reason for concern is apparent. Without better math instruction, these individuals will continue to face debilitating frustration, anxiety, and failure. Fortunately, the amount of research on teaching math has increased dramatically in the last decade, and it now is clear that an appropriate curriculum and effective teaching behaviors can result in positive mathematical outcomes for students with learning disabilities.

General and special educators must work together to ensure that students with learning disabilities receive adequate instruction and that the instructional reforms are sensitive to their unique learning and emotional needs. Cawley and Miller (1989) report that students with learning disabilities are capable of making progress in math throughout the school years, and comprehensive programming is essential to ensure their progress.

DEVELOPMENT OF MATH SKILLS

Mathematics has a logical structure. The student first constructs simple relationships and then progresses to more complex tasks. As the student progresses in this ordering of math tasks, the learning of skills and content transfers from each step to the next. Hierarchies of math skills that are useful in planning specific interventions are provided by Evans, Evans, and Mercer (1986), Silbert, Carnine, and Stein (1990), and Underhill, Uprichard, and Heddens (1980). The following skill introduction sequence indicates what commonly is stressed at each grade level: addition and subtraction—first and second grades, multiplication and division—third and fourth grades, fractions—fourth and fifth grades, and decimals and percent—fifth and sixth grades. These skills also apply to many adolescent students with learning disabilities because their problems usually involve skills taught in the upper elementary grades.

Several cognitive factors are needed for a student to progress in mathematics. To begin formal math instruction, the student should be able to form and remember associations, understand basic relationships, and make simple generalizations. More complex cognitive factors are needed as the student progresses from lower-level math skills to higher-order skills. Moreover, the mastery of lower-level math skills is essential to learning higher-order skills; thus, the concept of *learning readiness* is important in math instruction. In their *Twelve Components of Essential Mathematics*, the National Council of Supervisors of Mathematics (1988) highlight the need for students to be knowledgeable of basic facts and proficient in basic operations. Many authorities (Kirby & Becker, 1988; Underhill et al., 1980) claim that failure to understand basic concepts in beginning math instruction contributes heavily to later learning problems. Unfortunately, students with learning disabilities often fail to achieve an understanding of basic math facts or to develop fluency in using these initial skills.

Readiness for Number Instruction

Piaget (1965) describes several concepts basic to understanding numbers: classification, ordering and seriation, one-to-one correspondence, and conservation. Mastering these concepts is necessary for learning higher-order math skills.

Classification is one of the most basic intellectual activities and must precede work with numbers (Piaget, 1965). It involves a study of relationships, such as likenesses and differences. Activities include categorizing objects according to a specific property. For example, children may group buttons according to color, then size, then shape, and so on. Most children 5 to 7 years old can judge objects as being similar or dissimilar on the basis of properties such as color, shape, size, texture, and function (Copeland, 1979).

Ordering is important for sequencing numbers. Many children do not understand order until they are 6 or 7 years of age (Copeland, 1979). They first must understand the *topological* relation of order. When counting objects, students must order them so that each object is counted only once. The teacher can display objects in a certain order and ask the students to arrange identical objects in the same order. Ordering activities include sequencing blocks in a certain pattern, lining up for lunch in a specific order, and completing pattern games—for example, students are given a series such as X-O-X-O-X-O-X- __ and then must determine what goes in the blank.

Topological ordering involves arranging a set of items without considering a quantity relationship between each successive item. The combination of *seriation* and *ordering*, however, involves ordering items on the basis of *change* in a property, such as length, size, or color. An example of a seriation task would be arranging items of various lengths in an order from shortest to longest with each successive item being longer than the preceding item. Children 6 to 7 years old usually master ordering and seriation (Copeland, 1979).

One-to-one correspondence is the basis for counting to determine how many and is essential for mastering computation skills. It involves understanding that one object in a set is the same number as one object in a different set, whether or not characteristics are similar. If a teacher places small buttons in a glass one at a time and the students place the same number of large buttons one at a time in a glass, the glass containing the large buttons soon displays a higher stack. If students respond "Yes" to the question, "Does each glass have the same number of buttons," they understand one-to-one correspondence. If they respond "No, because the buttons are higher in one glass," they are not applying one-to-one correspondence and instead are judging on the basis of sensory cues. Most children 5 to 7 years old master the one-to-one correspondence concept. Initial activities consist of matching identical objects, whereas later activities should involve different objects. Sample activities are giving one pencil to each child, matching each head with a hat, and matching a penny to each marble.

Piaget (1965) considers the concept of *conservation* fundamental to later numerical reasoning. Conservation means that the quantity of an object or the number of objects in a set remains constant regardless of spatial arrangement. Copeland (1979) describes two types of conservation: quantity and number. Conservation of quantity is illustrated in the familiar Piagetian experiments of pouring identical amounts of water into a tall, thin glass and a low, wide glass and rolling a piece of clay into a ball and a long roll. Students who recognize that the amount of water or clay remains constant probably understand conservation of quantity. Conservation of number involves understanding that the number of objects in a set remains constant whether the objects are close together or spread apart. The teacher can ask students to select a spoon for each of seven plates and have them check their work by putting a spoon on each plate. The teacher then can remove the spoons, put them in a stack, and ask the students if there is still the same number of spoons and plates. If they respond "Yes," they probably understand the concept of conservation of number (Copeland, 1979). Most children master conservation between the ages of 5 and 7.

Several authorities consider an understanding of Piaget's concepts to be a prerequisite for formal math instruction. Many teachers in preschool through first grade directly teach to help students understand these concepts. Moreover, some authorities recommend that teachers in later grades spot deficits in these concepts and provide remedial instruction.

Readiness for More Advanced Mathematics

Once formal math instruction begins, students must master operations and basic axioms to acquire skills in computation and problem solving. Operations are well-known: addition, subtraction, multiplication, and division. Basic axioms are less familiar. Some axioms that are especially important for teaching math skills to students with learning disabilities are the commutative property of addition, commutative property of multiplication, associative property of addition and multiplication, distributive property of multiplication over addition, and inverse operations for addition and multiplication.

Commutative Property of Addition. No matter what order the same numbers are combined in, the sum remains constant:

$$a + b = b + a$$

$$3 + 4 = 4 + 3$$

Commutative Property of Multiplication. Regardless of the order of the numbers being multiplied, the product remains constant:

$$a \times b = b \times a$$
$$9 \times 6 = 6 \times 9$$

Associative Property of Addition and Multiplication. Regardless of grouping arrangements, the sum or product is unchanged:

Addition

$$(a + b) + c = a + (b + c)$$
$$(4 + 3) + 2 = 4 + (3 + 2)$$

Multiplication

$$(a \times b) \times c = a \times (b \times c)$$
$$(5 \times 4) \times 3 = 5 \times (4 \times 3)$$

Distributive Property of Multiplication over Addition. This rule relates the two operations:

$$a(b + c) = (a \times b) + (a \times c)$$
$$5(4 + 3) = (5 \times 4) + (5 \times 3)$$

Inverse Operations. These axioms relate operations that are opposite in their effects. The following equations demonstrate inverse operations:

Addition and Subtraction

$a + b = c$ $5 + 4 = 9$

$c - a = b$ $9 - 5 = 4$

$c - b = a$ $9 - 4 = 5$

Multiplication and Division

$\mathrm{a} \times \mathrm{b} = \mathrm{c}$ $9 \times 3 = 27$

$\mathrm{c} \div \mathrm{a} = \mathrm{b}$ $27 \div 9 = 3$

$\mathrm{c} \div \mathrm{b} = \mathrm{a}$ $27 \div 3 = 9$

MATH DISABILITIES

Specific Learning Disabilities in Math

Many educators believe that too many students are failing to acquire essential mathematical concepts, skills, and problem-solving strategies. Unfortunately, students with learning disabilities represent a sizeable number of students who are failing to make acceptable progress in mathematics (Cawley & Miller, 1989; Scheid, 1990). The Individuals with Disabilities Education Act (IDEA) lists mathematics calculation and mathematics reasoning as two areas in which a student can have a learning disability. Since the passage of Public Law 94-142 in 1975, knowledge about the characteristics of students with learning disabilities that relate to mathematics learning has expanded rapidly. An examination of these characteristics provides an improved understanding of math disabilities and insights into how to plan better mathematics instruction.

Peterson, Carpenter, and Fennema's (1989) finding that the teacher's knowledge of an individual student's problem-solving skills predicted math achievement better than the teacher's knowledge of problem solving or number fact strategies underscores the need for teachers to be aware of the learning characteristics of their students. This learner-specific knowledge was positively correlated with the teacher presenting problems for students, questioning students about methods they used to solve problems, and listening to students. Thus, knowledge of a student enables the teacher to interact more prescriptively with a student to enhance achievement and motivation (e.g., asking appropriate questions, modeling cognitive processes, monitoring progress, and providing feedback and encouragement).

General Characteristics. Although each student is unique, an examination of the characteristics of students with learning disabilities alerts the teacher or researcher to learning factors that deserve inspection when planning and teaching. Some students with learning disabilities have achievement problems across academic domains, whereas others have specific learning problems (e.g., reading disabilities, written expression disabilities, or math disabilities). Many of these individuals have histories of academic failure and have developed a *learned helplessness* about math (Parmar & Cawley, 1991). It is postulated that learned helplessness in math results from youngsters trying to solve problems when they have little or no understanding of mathematical concepts (e.g., when students practice computing multiplication facts but do not understand what multiplication means). This lack of understanding fosters the student's dependency on the teacher and thus promotes the notion that external help is needed to compute problems correctly. Repetition of this scenario promotes and strengthens learned helplessness. Likewise, it helps create *passive learners*, a term that frequently is used to describe students with learning disabilities and refers to students who are cognitively passive because they typically do not participate actively or self-regulate their own learning (Parmar & Cawley, 1991). Given their experiences, it is not surprising that many of these students are characterized as having motivational deficits. Attention deficits (Zentall & Ferkis, 1993), memory deficits (Zentall & Ferkis, 1993), visual-spatial deficits (Garnett, 1992), transfer problems (Brownell, Mellard, & Deshler, 1993), and information-processing deficits (Torgesen, 1990) traditionally have been cited as learning processes that contribute to poor math achievement. These and other factors combine in intricate ways to produce students with learning disabilities who fail to develop automaticity with basic math facts or operations, to use efficient strategies for computing answers or solving word problems, and to transfer their knowledge across settings or math problems (Garnett, 1992; Kulak, 1993; Woodward, 1991).

Table 14.1 presents problem areas derived from the characteristics of students with learning disabilities and their implied relationship to math performance. Traditionally, perceptual, attention, memory, motor, and language problems have received the most attention in examinations of the math deficiencies of students with learning disabilities. Currently, the focus has shifted to the study of cognitive problems as they relate to math disabilities. Specifically, the study of metacognitive weaknesses is receiving much attention.

Cognitive and Metacognitive Processes. From a knowledge base of 11,000 statistical findings across 28 categories, Wang, Haertel, and Walberg (1993/1994) examined the influence of each category on student learning. The metacognitive and cognitive processes of students ranked second and third on their influence on student learning. *Metacognition* refers to a student's awareness of the skills, strategies, and resources that are needed to perform a task and the ability to use self-regulatory mechanisms to complete the task (Baker & Brown, 1984). Within a metacognitive perspective, students with learning disabilities are described as having difficulty in (a) assessing their abilities to solve problems, (b) identifying and selecting appropriate strategies, (c) organizing information to be learned, (d) monitoring problem-solving processes, (e) evaluating problems for accuracy, and (f) generalizing strategies to appropriate situations (Cherkes-Julkowski, 1985; Goldman, 1989).

Several researchers (Kulak, 1993; Montague & Applegate, 1993; Swanson, 1990) claim that viewing students with learning disabilities as having metacognitive or cognitive deficits is only partially accurate. They note that many of these students are not deficient in using cognitive strategies but apply different strategies. For example, many students use numerous strategies with word problems (e.g., reading, checking, and computing strategies); however, they do not have working knowledge of strategies associated with representing problems (Montague & Applegate, 1993). Problem representation involves converting linguistic and numerical information (via paraphrasing, visualizing, and hypothesizing) into mathematical equations and algorithms. This finding that students with learning disabilities have problems with representation strategies has been documented consistently (Hutchinson, 1993b; Montague & Applegate, 1993; Montague, Bos, & Doucette, 1991; Zawaiza & Gerber, 1993). Moreover, students with learning disabilities have responded well to strategy interventions that are sensitive to

TABLE 14.1
Common Difficulties That Affect Math Performance of Students with Learning Disabilities

Learning Difficulty		Math-Related Performance
Visual Perception	Figure-ground	loses place on worksheet does not finish problems on a page has difficulty reading multidigit numbers
	Discrimination	has difficulty differentiating between numbers (e.g., *6,9; 2,5;* or *17,71*), coins, the operation symbols, clock hands
	Spatial	has difficulty copying shapes or problems has difficulty writing across paper in a straight line has confusion about before-after concepts (e.g., has difficulty with time or counting) has difficulty relating to directional aspects of math, which can be noted in problems with computations involving up-down (e.g., addition), left-right (regrouping), and aligning numbers puts decimals in the wrong place has difficulty spacing manipulatives into patterns or sets has difficulty using number line has confusion about positive and negative numbers (directional)
Auditory Perception		has difficulty doing oral drills has difficulty doing oral word problems is unable to count on from within a sequence has difficulty writing numbers or assignments from dictation has difficulty learning number patterns
Motor		writes numbers illegibly, slowly, and inaccurately has difficulty writing numbers in small spaces (i.e., writes numbers that are too large)
Memory	Short-term	is unable to retain math facts or new information forgets steps in an algorithm is unable to retain the meaning of symbols
	Long-term	works slowly on mastering facts over time performs poorly on review lessons or mixed probes forgets steps in algorithms
	Sequential	has difficulty telling time does not complete all steps in a multistep computation problem has difficulty solving multistep word problems
Attention		has difficulty maintaining attention to steps in algorithms or problem solving has difficulty sustaining attention to critical instruction (e.g., teacher modeling)

TABLE 14.1
continued

Learning Difficulty		Math-Related Performance
Language	Receptive	has difficulty relating math terms to meaning (e.g., *minus, addend, dividend, regroup, multiplicand,* and *place value*) has difficulty relating words that have multiple meanings (e.g., *carry* and *times*)
	Expressive	does not use the vocabulary of math has difficulty performing oral math drills has difficulty verbalizing steps in solving a word problem or an algorithm
Reading		does not understand the vocabulary of math word problems
Cognition and Abstract Reasoning		has difficulty converting linguistic and numerical information into math equations and algorithms has difficulty solving word problems is unable to make comparisons of size and quantity has difficulty understanding symbols in math (e.g., $>$, $<$, $\times$, and $=$) has difficulty understanding the abstract level of mathematical concepts and operations
Metacognition		is unable to identify and select appropriate strategies for solving computation and word problems has difficulty monitoring the problem-solving process in word problems and multistep computations is unable to generalize strategies to other situations
Social and Emotional Factors	Impulsive	makes careless mistakes in computation responds incorrectly and rapidly in oral drills corrects responses frequently when asked to look at or listen to a problem again does not attend to details in solving problems
	Short attention/ Distractibility	does not complete work in assigned time has difficulty doing multistep computation starts a problem and does not finish it but goes on to next problem is off-task
	Passivity/Learned helplessness	omits computation problems omits word problems appears disinterested lacks strategies
	Self-esteem	lacks confidence gives up easily
	Anxiety	becomes so tense during math test that performance is impaired avoids math to reduce anxiety

their deficit in using representational strategies (Hutchinson, 1993b; Montague, Applegate, & Marquard, 1993).

Given that many students with learning disabilities use qualitatively different strategies in math from students who are high achievers, it is important for teachers to ascertain the strategies that students are using. This information is critical to designing instruction because evidence indicates that different students need different types of strategy instruction (Swanson, 1990). Learning strategy instruction can help students become successful self-regulated and motivated learners. Perhaps the promise of these potential outcomes will encourage educators to examine student thought processes and design strategies that are most parsimonious for individual student success.

Social and Emotional Factors. The affective domain also is recognized as an important variable in the math performances of students with learning disabilities. For example, it is believed that repeated academic failures frequently result in low self-esteem and passivity in mathematical learning (Cherkes-Julkowski, 1985). The emotional reaction of some individuals to math is so negative that they develop *math anxiety.* This condition is believed to stem from a fear of school failure and low self-esteem and causes students to become so tense that their ability to solve, learn, or apply math is impaired (Slavin, 1991). *Arousal deficit theory* provides a tentative explanation for math anxiety. This theory maintains the existence of a biological arousal system that regulates alertness across situations. A low-level arousal is associated with relaxing among friends, whereas perceiving a threat to one's safety engenders a high level of arousal. The arousal deficit theory suggests that the arousal system of certain individuals with learning disabilities, especially those with attention deficit disorder, fails to function properly. Specifically, it is postulated that their arousal system generates too much arousal during pressure situations. If this happens during a math test or lesson, the excessive arousal leads to anxiety and results in confused thinking, disorganization, avoidance behavior, and math phobia (Conte, 1991; Zentall & Zentall, 1983).

Perspectives on Math Disabilities

An examination of the literature suggests that many individuals with learning disabilities have learning, social, or emotional characteristics that predispose them for mathematical disabilities. Although some students with learning disabilities have a learning disability *only* in mathematics, many others have a combination of academic disabilities (e.g., reading disability and math disability). Lovitt (1989) notes that other disabilities represent correlates of failure in math; for example, reading, language, and handwriting disabilities can have a strong negative influence on math performance. The heterogeneity of students with learning disabilities as discussed in Chapter 1 is apparent with math disabilities. For example, Cawley et al. (1987) examined the responses of students with learning disabilities on problem-solving tasks (word problems) and recorded 97 different responses to a single item. In a study of responses to multiplication and division problems, Miller and Milam (1987) found that students with learning disabilities made 98 different responses to multiplication problems and 93 different responses to division problems. These incorrect responses were classified into 35 different error categories. The heterogeneity becomes more of an issue when students without disabilities, at-risk students, and students with learning disabilities and mild retardation participate continuously in the same math lessons. Recently, Parmar, Cawley, and Miller (1994) found that students with learning disabilities and mild retardation perform differently and require differentiated instruction. Moreover, Kavale, Fuchs, and Scruggs (1994) report that students with learning disabilities and low achievers have differential learning characteristics. The complexity of math disabilities and learning characteristics is enormous, but several perspectives make it less intimidating to the educator.

The increased interest and research in mathematics are resulting in a better understanding of math disabilities and, perhaps, will lead to some meaningful subtyping among students with learning disabilities. Much of the poor math performance of students with learning disabilities has occurred within instructional programs that do not represent best practices in math instruction. Many authorities (Carnine, 1991; Cawley et al., 1987; Kelly, Gersten, & Carnine, 1990; Scheid, 1990) believe that poor or traditional instruction is a primary cause of the math difficulties of many students with learning disabilities. Numerous studies support the position that students with math disabilities can be taught to improve their mathematical performance (Kirby & Becker, 1988; Mastropieri et al., 1991; Mercer & Miller, 1992b; Rivera & Smith, 1988; Scheid, 1990).

It is encouraging that these successful interventions do not require instructional adaptations for each type of math disability or error pattern. In many cases, successful interventions represent procedures that teachers readily can implement. It is plausible that the widespread use of best practices in math instruction would greatly reduce the number of students who have math disabilities. This, in turn, would decrease the heterogeneity resulting from error patterns, inefficient or ineffective strategies, and faulty algorithms that originate from limited or no understanding of math concepts. Specific interventions are presented later in this chapter.

ASSESSMENT OF MATH SKILLS

The assessment of math concepts and skills follows a general-to-specific format. As presented in Figure 14.1, assessment begins with an evaluation of general math skills. At this level, a span of skills (e.g., operations, word problems, and measurement) is tested. Standardized or informal survey tests typically are used to assess general math skills. The primary goal of assessment at this level is to identify the overall strengths and weaknesses of the student. Also, standardized scores frequently are used to identify math disabilities and qualify students for learning disabilities services. Specific skill

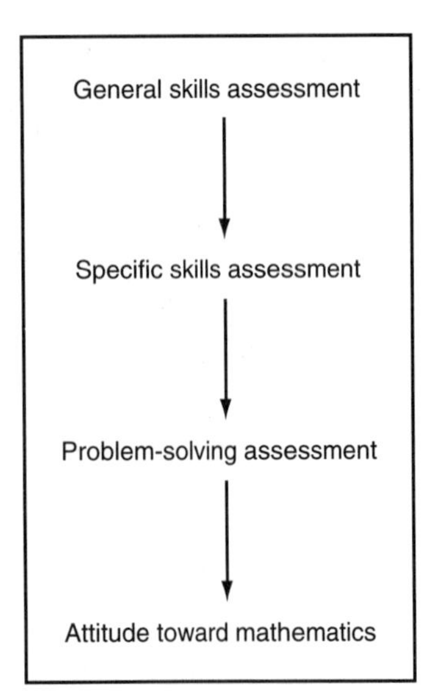

FIGURE 14.1
Math assessment progression

assessment usually involves the use of standardized diagnostic tests or informal tests; however, informal tests are the preferred instruments for evaluating specific math skills. At this level, the purpose of assessment is to determine specific teaching objectives. The assessment of problem-solving skills involves examining the student's ability to solve word problems. This assessment tests the student's ability to apply mathematical concepts and operations to real-life problems and to determine problem-solving instructional objectives. Finally, diagnostic interviews and informal testing are used to evaluate the student's attitudes and feelings about learning math. These affective factors frequently provide essential insights into planning math instruction. Throughout the math assessment process (general skills to attitude assessment), it is important to examine types of errors, level of understanding, and mastery learning.

Examining Math Errors

Although the specific error patterns of each student must be considered individually, it is helpful to examine some of the research regarding types of errors made by many students at different grades.

Computation. In a study of third graders, Roberts (1968) reports that careless numerical errors and poor recall of addition and multiplication facts were found with the same frequency in all levels of ability. Random responses accounted for the most errors of low-ability students, and defective algorithm techniques accounted for the most errors of students in the other three ability levels. An algorithm includes the specific steps used to compute a math problem. An algorithm is defective if it does not deliver the correct answer. For example, the student who adds $24 + 16$ by adding each number without regard for place value (i.e., $2 + 4 + 1 + 6 = 13$), is using a defective algorithm.

Cox (1975) conducted a study of error patterns across skill and ability level among students with and without disabilities. In a comparison with students without disabilities, she found that the average percentages of systematic errors in multiplication and division were much higher for the special education students. The majority of errors for all students occurred because of a failure to understand the concepts of multiplication and division. Moreover, Cox found that without intervention many of these youngsters persisted in making the same systematic errors for a long period of time.

In a study of multiplication and division errors made by 213 students with learning disabilities, Miller and Milam (1987) found that the majority of the errors were caused by a lack of prerequisite skills. Errors in multiplication primarily were the result of a lack of knowledge of multiplication facts and inadequate addition skills. Errors in division included many subtraction and multiplication errors. The most frequent error in division was the failure to include the remainder in the quotient. According to Miller and Milam,

> Many of the errors discovered in this study indicated a lack of student readiness for the type of task required. Students were evidently not being

> allowed to learn and practice the skills necessary for higher order operations. The implications are obvious: Students *must* be allowed to learn in a stepwise fashion or they will not learn at all. (p. 121)

Kelly et al. (1990) examined the error patterns that secondary students with learning disabilities made in adding and multiplying fractions. They found that the errors of students instructed in a basal program primarily involved a confusion of the algorithms for addition and multiplication of fractions. However, an effective curriculum design decreased error patterns and resulted in better achievement. Kelly et al. conclude that a strong relationship exists between the number and types of errors and the curriculum.

The determination of a specific error is important because corrective intervention is influenced by the type of error. For example, the type of error can influence whether the student receives place value instruction or specific algorithm instruction. K. W. Howell, Fox, and Morehead (1993) provide the following guidelines for conducting an error analysis:

> 1. Collect an adequate behavior sample by having the student do several problems of each type in which you are interested.
> 2. Encourage the student to work and talk aloud about what she is doing, but do nothing to influence her responses.
> 3. Record all responses the student makes, including comments.
> 4. Look for patterns in the responses.
> 5. Look for exceptions to any apparent pattern.
> 6. List the patterns you have identified as assumed causes for the student's computational difficulties.
> 7. Interview the student. Ask her to tell you how she worked the problem to confirm suspected patterns. (pp. 334, 336)

The following common error patterns in addition, subtraction, multiplication, and division illustrate some of the computational problems of students with learning disabilities:

1. The sums of the ones and tens are each recorded without regard for place value:

$$\begin{array}{r} 83 \\ +\ 67 \\ \hline 1410 \end{array} \qquad \begin{array}{r} 66 \\ +\ 29 \\ \hline 815 \end{array}$$

2. All digits are added together (defective algorithm and no regard for place value):

$$\begin{array}{r} 67 \\ +\ 31 \\ \hline 17 \end{array} \qquad \begin{array}{r} 58 \\ +\ 12 \\ \hline 16 \end{array}$$

3. Digits are added from left to right. When the sum is greater than 10, the unit is carried to the next column on the right. This pattern reflects no regard for place value:

$$\begin{array}{r} {\scriptstyle 21}\ \\ 476 \\ +\ 851 \\ \hline 148 \end{array} \qquad \begin{array}{r} {\scriptstyle 37} \\ 753 \\ +\ 693 \\ \hline 1113 \end{array}$$

4. The smaller number is subtracted from the larger number without regard for placement of the number. The upper number (minuend) is subtracted from the lower number (subtrahend), or vice versa:

$$\begin{array}{r} 627 \\ -\ 486 \\ \hline 261 \end{array} \qquad \begin{array}{r} 861 \\ -\ 489 \\ \hline 428 \end{array}$$

5. Regrouping is used when it is not required:

$$\begin{array}{r} {\scriptstyle 6}\ \ \\ 1\not{7}5 \\ -\ 54 \\ \hline 1111 \end{array} \qquad \begin{array}{r} {\scriptstyle 7}\ \ \\ 1\not{8}5 \\ -\ 22 \\ \hline 1513 \end{array}$$

6. When regrouping is required more than once, the appropriate amount is not subtracted from the column borrowed from in the second regrouping:

$$\begin{array}{r} {\scriptstyle 5}\ \ \ \ \\ \not{6}\not{3}2 \\ -\ 147 \\ \hline 495 \end{array} \qquad \begin{array}{r} {\scriptstyle 4}\ \ \ \ \\ \not{5}\not{2}3 \\ -\ 366 \\ \hline 167 \end{array} \qquad \begin{array}{r} {\scriptstyle 4}\ \ \ \ \\ \not{5}\not{6}3 \\ -\ 382 \\ \hline 181 \end{array}$$

7. The regrouped number is added to the multiplicand in the tens column prior to performing the multiplication operation:

```
   2      4
  17     46
 × 4    × 8
 128    648
```

8. The zero in the quotient is omitted:

```
     21
 6)1206
   1200
      6
      6
```

Many computational errors stem from an inadequate understanding of place value. Lepore (1979) analyzed the computational errors of 79 youngsters age 12 to 14 with mild disabilities. The type of error they made most frequently involved regrouping, a procedure that requires understanding of place value. Place value is introduced in the primary grades; however, students of all ages continue to make mistakes because they do not comprehend that the same digit expresses different orders of magnitude depending on its *location* in a number. Many of the error patterns presented earlier reflect an inadequate understanding of place value.

Ashlock (1994) provides a thorough listing of computational error patterns. In addition to analyzing the student's work, one of the best ways to determine error patterns is to ask the student to show how the answer was computed. The response may offer immediate insight into the error pattern and its cause.

Problem Solving. Recently, the problem-solving skills of students with learning disabilities have received much attention. Problem-solving skills primarily are assessed by means of word problems. Research indicates that many students with learning disabilities have trouble solving word problems, especially those categorized as more difficult (Russell & Ginsburg, 1984; Scheid, 1990). One way to vary the difficulty level of word problems is to vary what is unknown. For example, the following word problems increase in difficulty as a function of what is unknown.

1. Tom has 5 stickers. Pam gave him 3 more. How many stickers does Tom have now? (Result unknown)
2. Tom has 5 stickers. How many more does he need to have 7? (Change unknown)
3. Tom had some stickers. Pam gave him 3 more. Now he has 7. How many stickers did Tom have to start with? (Start unknown)

Cawley et al. (1987) found that students with learning disabilities experienced difficulty with problems that include extraneous information. Montague and Bos (1990) report that students with learning disabilities have difficulties predicting operations (such as multiplication or subtraction), choosing correct algorithms for multistep problems, and correctly completing problems. As mentioned earlier in this chapter, many students with learning disabilities experience difficulty in transforming word problems into mathematical representations. Fortunately, several researchers (Cawley et al., 1987; Goldman, 1989; Hutchinson, 1993a; Montague, 1993) indicate that strategies exist to help students with learning disabilities be successful problem solvers.

Determining Level of Understanding

Students frequently memorize a fact or algorithm without understanding the concept or operation involved in the computation. This process leads to the rote memorization of information that is not comprehended. In reading, it is analogous to word calling without comprehension. An understanding of the information to be learned improves memorization and the manipulation of math concepts, operations, and axioms to solve computation and word problems. Thus, knowledge of the levels of understanding in mathematics is vital to math assessment and instruction. Underhill et al. (1980) report that there are several basic levels of learning in mathematical learning experiences. These levels are *concrete, semiconcrete,* and *abstract.*

Concrete Level. The concrete level involves the manipulation of objects. This level can be used to help the student relate manipulative and computational processes. At this level the learner concentrates on both the manipulated objects and the symbolic processes (e.g., 6×3) that describe the manipulations (Underhill et al., 1980). For example, in assessing or teaching multiplication, the teacher presents the problem 5×3 and instructs the student to display the problem using objects. The student looks at the first number, *5,* and forms five groups using paper plates. The student then looks at the second number, *3,* and places three objects on each plate. The student counts or adds the number of objects on the plates and says "5 groups times 3 objects equals 15 objects." This procedure illustrates that the student understands at a concrete level that 5×3 means "5 groups of 3 objects equals 15 objects." Some students demonstrate their need for concrete-level activities by counting on their fingers when requested to complete simple computational problems. Concrete experiences are important for teaching and assessing skills at all levels in the math hierarchy.

Semiconcrete Level. The semiconcrete level involves working with illustrations of items in performing math tasks. Items may include dots, lines, pictures of objects, or nonsense items. Some authorities divide this level into semiconcrete and semiabstract (Underhill et al., 1980). *Semiconcrete* refers to using pictures of real objects, whereas *semiabstract* involves the use of tallies. In this book, *semiconcrete* refers to both pictures and tallies. A worksheet that requires the learner to match sets of the same number of items is a semiconcrete-level task. One way to assess a student's understanding at this level is for the teacher to present a problem (such as 5×3) and ask the student to use drawings (i.e., lines and tallies) to solve the problem. The student looks at the first number, *5,* and draws five horizontal lines. The student then looks at the second number, *3,* and draws three tallies on each line. The student counts or adds the number of tallies on the lines and says "5 groups times 3 tallies equals 15 tallies." This procedure illustrates that the student knows at a semiconcrete level of understanding that 5×3 means "5 groups of 3 items equals 15 items." Most commercial math programs include worksheets of tasks at this level. Many students with math learning problems need practice at this level to master a concept or fact. Often students demonstrate their reliance on this level by supplying their own graphic representations. For example, the problems $5 + 4 = \_$ and $3 \times 2 = \_$ can be approached in the following manner:

5	/////	3	//
+ 4	////	× 2	//
9		6	//

At the semiconcrete level, the emphasis is on developing associations between visual models and symbolic processes.

Abstract Level. The abstract level involves the use of numerals. For example, in computation this level involves working only with numerals to solve math problems. Students who have difficulty in math usually need experience at the concrete and semiconcrete levels before they can use numerals meaningfully. Traditionally, assessment has focused on the abstract level; however, assessment should not be limited to this level. The goal of assessment involves determining the learner's ability to relate to math computation in a meaningful way. To do this, tasks are needed at each of the levels. Sample activities for assessing levels of understanding are presented later in this chapter.

Determining Mastery Learning

Many educators use percentage scores to determine a mastery level for a skill. In many cases these scores are a valid measure of a student's mastery learning. For some students, however, percentage scores are not sufficient for assessing mastery. Many students with learning disabilities produce accurate answers at a slow rate and use tedious procedures (such as counting on fingers and drawing tallies for large numbers) to compute answers without understanding the math concept or operation. (I once tested a youngster who started drawing tallies for the problem 75 × 75.) Several authorities (Kirby & Becker, 1988; Lovitt, 1989) report that slow rates of computation are a primary problem of students with learning disabilities or math problems. Wood, Burke, Kunzelmann, and Koenig (1978) examined the math rates of successful students, unsuccessful students, and community workers. In nearly every comparison, the rates of unsuccessful students were lower than the rates of successful students. Also, the rates of successful students were about the same as those of community workers.

As noted in Chapter 8, rate is an excellent measure of mastery learning. In addition to helping with retention and higher math performance, high rates of correct responses help students complete tests on time, finish homework quickly, and keep score in games. Math rate assessment involves the use of probes (i.e., a sheet of selected math problems) that are administered under timed conditions (usually 1 minute). Scores are computed by counting the number of correct and incorrect digits written per minute. A sample probe is presented later in this chapter.

Formal Math Assessment with Standardized Tests

Standardized math tests are norm-referenced and provide many kinds of information. They usually are classified into two categories: survey or achievement, and diagnostic. Most achievement tests include sections covering specific academic areas, such as reading, spelling, and math. Each of these specific academic areas is divided into skill areas. For example, a math section can be divided into numerical reasoning, computation, and word problems. Survey tests cover a broad range of math skills and are designed to provide an estimate of the student's general level of achievement. They yield a single score, which is compared with standardized norms and converted into standard scores or a grade- or age-equivalent score. Survey tests are useful in screening students to identify those who need further assessment. Several commonly used survey tests are listed in Table 14.2.

Diagnostic tests, in contrast, usually cover a narrower range of content and are designed to assess the student's performance in math skill areas. Diagnostic tests aim to determine the student's strengths and weaknesses. No single diagnostic test assesses all mathematical difficulties. The examiner must decide on the purpose of the assessment and select the test that is most suited to the task. Because quantitative scores are not very useful in developing a systematic instructional program, most diagnostic tests are criterion-referenced. However, four standardized diagnostic math tests are included in Table 14.2.

Formal Math Assessment with Criterion-Referenced Tests

Standardized tests compare one individual's score with norms, which generally does not help diagnose the student's math difficulties. However, criterion-referenced tests, which describe the student's performance in terms of criteria for specific skills, are more suited to assessing specific difficulties. Like standardized tests, criterion-referenced tests are divided into survey and diagnostic tests.

Criterion-referenced achievement or inventory tests usually cover several academic areas. Each of these areas is further subdivided into skill categories. Selected criterion-referenced survey tests are listed in Table 14.2. Whereas survey tests locate general problem areas, diagnostic tests focus on more specific difficulties. Of all available published tests, criterion-referenced diagnostic tests are the most suited for identify-

TABLE 14.2
Selected Standardized and Criterion-Referenced Math Tests

Test	Norm- or Criterion-Referenced	Grade Levels	Areas Assessed
Survey Tests			
Brigance Diagnostic Comprehensive Inventory of Basic Skills (Brigance, 1983)	Criterion-referenced	K–9	Numbers (readiness skills), number facts, computation of whole numbers, fractions and mixed numbers, decimals, percents, word problems, metrics, and math vocabulary
Brigance Diagnostic Inventory of Essential Skills (Brigance, 1981)	Criterion-referenced	6–12	Minimal academic and vocational competencies (stresses functional and applied math skills)
The *Brigance Inventories* provide instructional objectives and include a record-keeping system for monitoring the progress of individual students. Also, placement tests are included that yield an age and grade equivalent. These levels are not based on norms but were determined by examining the hierarchial content of commercial materials.			
California Achievement Tests—Fifth Edition (1992)	Norm-referenced	K–12	Computation, concepts, and applications
This group-administered test has a locator test to identify the level of the test that is most appropriate. There are two forms of the test, and criterion-referenced objectives are available.			
Diagnostic Achievement Battery—2 (Newcomer, 1990)	Norm-referenced	1–9	Mathematics reasoning and mathematics calculation
The Mathematics Reasoning subtest consists of 30 items, in each of which a mathematical problem is presented orally and the student must solve the problem without paper or pencil. In the Mathematics Calculation subtest the student works directly on a math calculation worksheet of 36 problems that become progressively more difficult.			
Kaufman Test of Educational Achievement (K-TEA) (Kaufman & Kaufman, 1985)	Norm-referenced	1–12	Applications and computation
This individually administered test includes 60 items on math concepts and applications in practical situations as well as 60 items on computation involving basic operations, exponents, symbols, abbreviations, and algebraic equations. A brief form also is available. K-TEA *ASSIST* software provides quick score conversion and error analysis.			
Metropolitan Achievement Tests—Seventh Edition (Balow, Farr, & Hogan, 1992)	Norm-referenced	K–12	Concepts and problem solving and procedures
Many of the concepts and computation items in the mathematics section of this group-administered test are presented in contexts that are meaningful and relevant to students. Reading is controlled to below-grade level except for the lower levels, in which the items are dictated. The problem-solving strategy questions assess critical-thinking skills, and many of these questions are constructed to elicit an actual performance on the part of the student. An optional test measures the ability to apply math procedures to solve computation problems both with and without context.			
Peabody Individual Achievement Test—Revised (PIAT-R) (Markwardt, 1989)	Norm-referenced	K–12	Skills ranging from matching and recognizing numbers to solving geometry and trigonometry problems
This individually administered test features an easy-to-use easel kit. Sometimes scores are inflated because the student response always involves selecting the correct answer from among four choices. Reading is not required, and the math subtest of 100 multiple-choice items takes 10 to 15 minutes to administer. PIAT-R *ASSIST* software is available for scoring ease.			
Woodcock-Johnson Psycho-Educational Battery—Revised (Woodcock & Johnson, 1989)	Norm-referenced	K–college	Calculation and applied problems
This individually administered test has two forms and examines basic math skills and application of those skills. The supplemental battery includes a subtest in quantitative concepts. Software programs are available for scoring and report writing.			

continued

TABLE 14.2
continued

<table>
<tr><th>Test</th><th>Norm- or Criterion-Referenced</th><th>Grade Levels</th><th>Areas Assessed</th></tr>
<tr><td colspan="4">Diagnostic Tests</td></tr>
<tr><td>Diagnostic Mathematics Inventory/Mathematics System (Gessell, 1983)</td><td>Criterion-referenced</td><td>K–8</td><td>Whole numbers, fractions and decimals, measurement and geometry, and problem solving and special topics</td></tr>
<tr><td colspan="4">This diagnostic-prescriptive inventory contains a grade-level based and an ungraded, objectives-based system. The four major content areas are divided into 29 categories containing 82 instructional objectives that are cross-referenced to mathematics textbooks and commercial instructional materials. The inventory takes approximately 1 hour to administer and is designed to identify math performance levels, determine areas of specific strengths and weaknesses in math, prescribe appropriate intervention activities, and monitor student progress.</td></tr>
<tr><td>Diagnostic Test of Arithmetic Strategies (Ginsburg & Mathews, 1884)</td><td>Criterion-referenced</td><td>1–6</td><td>Setting up problems, number facts, written calculation, and informal skills</td></tr>
<tr><td colspan="4">This individually administered test is designed to elicit information about the procedures the student uses to perform calculation in addition, subtraction, multiplication, and division. The results are descriptive and identify the calculational strategies used and the types of errors that consistently occur. The manual provides suggestions for formulating remedial teaching procedures based on the test results.</td></tr>
<tr><td>Enright Diagnostic Inventory of Basic Arithmetic Skills (Enright, 1983)</td><td>Criterion-referenced</td><td>4–adult</td><td>Computation of whole numbers, fractions, and decimals</td></tr>
<tr><td colspan="4">This test determines the exact math skill at which to begin instruction and provides a clear explanation of computation errors. Four types of tests are included: (a) basic facts tests determine mastery of all basic facts in addition, subtraction, multiplication, and division; (b) wide-range placement tests establish a starting point for the skill placement test; (c) skill placement tests assess skills in each computation area and determine the appropriate skill test for error analysis; and (d) skill tests identify specific computation problems for corrective instruction. The inventory is based on a task analysis of basic computation skills, and error analysis for 144 math computation skills indicates the student's process errors. The test can be administered individually or in groups.</td></tr>
<tr><td>Hudson Education Skills Inventory—Mathematics (Hudson & Colson, 1989)</td><td>Criterion-referenced</td><td>K–12</td><td>Numeration, addition, subtraction, multiplication, division, fractions, decimals, percentages, time, money, measurement, statistics, graphs, tables, geometry, and word problems</td></tr>
<tr><td colspan="4">This inventory provides a curriculum-based assessment of math skills for use in planning instruction. A test-down/teach-up model is used in which the examiner ends the test at the student's actual level of performance and then simply can teach up the curriculum skills sequence. An optional computerized program provides a printed instructional planning form for each student that includes goals and objectives in the basic skill area.</td></tr>
<tr><td>Key Math-Revised: A Diagnostic Inventory of Essential Skills (Connolly, 1988)</td><td>Norm-referenced</td><td>K–9</td><td>Basic concepts, operations, and applications</td></tr>
<tr><td colspan="4">Key Math-Revised is based on a comprehensive content scope and sequence and is composed of 13 subtests in three areas. Spring and fall norms are given, and two parallel forms are available. Derived scores for the three area composites and total test include standard scores, grade and age equivalents, percentile ranks, and stanines. Key Math-R ASSIST software is available to provide quick derived score conversion as well as suggestions for remedial instruction.</td></tr>
<tr><td>Sequential Assessment of Mathematics Inventory (SAMI) (Reisman, 1985)</td><td>Norm-referenced</td><td>K–8</td><td>Mathematics language, ordinality, number and notation, measurement, geometric concepts, computation, word problems, and mathematical applications</td></tr>
</table>

TABLE 14.2
continued

Test	Norm- or Criterion-Referenced	Grade Levels	Areas Assessed
The classroom survey tests provide a profile of student performance in math concepts and skills, and the individual assessment battery gives an in-depth evaluation. The test covers 300 objectives organized into eight strands, and items are sequenced from easy to difficult. In addition to the norm-referenced items, SAMI provides follow-up probes to test the student's grasp of the material at various cognitive levels, including the concrete level. Manipulative materials included in the concrete materials kit can be used with the probes for diagnosing concrete representation. SAMI offers three types of test activities (paper/pencil, oral interview, and concrete representation) to provide a well-rounded picture of the student's strengths and weaknesses in math skills.			
Stanford Diagnostic Mathematics Test (Beatty, Madden, Gardner, & Karlsen, 1995)	Norm-referenced	1–13	Concepts and applications and computation
This group-administered test is divided into six separate levels, identified by color, and two forms are available for the upper three levels. Each level provides both multiple-choice and free-response formats to reveal the problem-solving process and product. In addition to yielding percentile ranks, stanines, grade equivalents, and scaled scores, the test results can be used to identify strengths and weaknesses in specific math skills.			
Test of Mathematical Abilities (Brown, Cronin, & McEntire, 1994)	Norm-referenced	3–12	Story problems and computation
In addition to information about a student's skills in two major areas (story problems and computation), the test provides related information regarding expressed attitudes toward mathematics, understanding of mathematical vocabulary used in a mathematical sense, and the application of mathematical concepts in real life.			

ing specific math problems. Several of the most recommended tests are listed in Table 14.2.

Unfortunately, commercial instruments for diagnosing understanding at the three levels are sparse. Only the *Sequential Assessment of Mathematics Inventory* (Reisman, 1985) includes a concrete materials kit containing manipulative materials for test activities involving concrete representation. Most available tests, which have test items only at the abstract level, are useful mainly in helping to determine the student's level of achievement and general area of weakness. Once the problem area is identified, the teacher can use informal assessment techniques to determine the levels of instruction necessary for teaching specific concepts and facts.

Informal Math Assessment

Informal assessment involves examining the student's daily work samples or administering teacher-constructed tests. Informal assessment is essential for the frequent monitoring of student progress and for making relevant teaching decisions regarding individual students. Such assessment enables teachers to sample specific skills through the use of numerous test items that are related directly to the math curriculum. Because the content of standardized math tests and the content of math curriculum texts have a low degree of overlap (Tindal & Marston, 1990), the practice of assessing each student's achievement within the curriculum becomes essential. With informal techniques the teacher also can determine the student's understanding of math concepts at the concrete, semiconcrete, and abstract levels. By asking appropriate questions and listening to students' responses, teachers can assess not only whether a student can solve a particular problem but *how* the problem is solved. Informal assessment thus is the most efficient way of determining the instructional needs of individual students.

Curriculum-Based Measurement. When progress is assessed within the curriculum to measure achievement, the teacher is assured that what is being assessed is what is being taught. Curriculum-based measurement (CBM) offers the teacher a standardized set of informal assessment procedures for conducting a reliable and valid assessment of a student's achievement within the math curriculum.

Curriculum-based measurement begins by assessing an entire class with a survey test of a span of appropriate skills. From the results of a survey test, a box plot (see Chapter 8) is developed for making instructional decisions. Five steps are required in developing and administering a survey test:

1. *Identify a sequence of successive skills included in the school curriculum.* Many curriculum unit tests or review tests provide a source of sequenced skills and corresponding test items.
2. *Select a span of math skills to be assessed.* For a beginning fourth-grade class, it may be appropriate to administer a survey test of the computation skills covered in the third grade. This third-grade survey test would help identify students with math problems and provide some normative information to facilitate goal setting.
3. *Construct or select items for each skill within the range selected.* A survey test may be used to assess computation and problem-solving skills. To maintain an adequate sample, it is a good practice to include a minimum of three items per specific skill.
4. *Administer and score the survey test.* The teacher instructs the students to work successive problems during the 2-minute timing. In scoring, the teacher counts all correct digits. Table 14.3 provides detailed CBM administration directions and scoring procedures.
5. *Display the results in a box plot, interpret the results, and plan instruction.* To increase the accuracy of the results, it helps to develop an alternate form of the survey test and administer both survey probes of the same skills. The results should be interpreted to help with the placement of students in instructional groups and for planning individual programs.

From an analysis of student performances on a span of skills, the teacher develops probes of specific skills for monitoring individual student progress. Specific skill monitoring usually involves a single skill until mastery is achieved. Selected research on rates that reflect mastery or proficiency on specific math skills indicates that, generally, a rate of 40 to 60 correct digits per minute is appropriate for most students on math computation problems (Mercer & Mercer, 1993).

Teacher-Constructed Tests. Teacher-constructed tests are essential for individualizing math instruction. They enable the teacher to identify problems, determine level of understanding, and monitor progress. The type of test the teacher selects depends, in part, on the purpose of the assessment. To identify specific problem areas, the teacher may construct a survey test with items at several levels of difficulty. There are four steps to developing and using this type of test:

1. *Select a hierarchy that includes the content area to be assessed.* This hierarchy may come from a math program series, a curriculum guide, or a textbook.
2. *Decide on the span of skills that needs to be evaluated.* Because a hierarchy includes a wide range of skills, the teacher must select which range of skills needs to be evaluated with an individual student. This is done by examining the student's performance on published tests and by analyzing the math curriculum by grade level. In deciding on the span, begin with items that are easy for the student and proceed to more difficult ones.
3. *Construct items for each skill within the range selected.* A survey test is designed to assess the student's computation (abstract) performance within a hierarchy; thus, all items are

TABLE 14.3
Curriculum-Based Measurement Administration Directions and Scoring Procedures for Math

Administration Directions

The following steps are recommended for administering 2-minute timings to individuals or groups:

1. Select the appropriate measurement (i.e., survey test or specific skill probe) and pass it out to students face down.
2. Give standardized directions at the beginning of the administration. Also, use specific instructions for different parts of some tests.

   "The sheets I just passed out are math problems." If a single skill probe is used, tell the students the operation: "All problems are _____ (addition, subtraction, multiplication, or division)." If a multiple skill probe is used, say: "There are different types of problems on the sheet. There are some addition, subtraction, and multiplication problems. Look at each problem closely before you compute it."

   "When I say 'Begin,' turn the sheet over and answer the problems. Start with the first problem at the beginning of the first row. Touch the problem. Work across the sheet and then go to the beginning of the next row. If you are unable to do a problem, mark an X on it and go to the next problem. If you finish one page, go to the next page. Do you have any questions?"

   "Ready, start."
3. Monitor student work to ensure that students are following the directions (i.e., working in successive rows). Watch for students who want to skip around and do the easy problems.
4. When 2 minutes have elapsed, say: "Stop. Put your pencils down."

Scoring Procedures

1. Underline each correct digit.
2. Score numerals written in reverse form (for example, Ɛ for 3) as correct.
3. Score a correct digit in the proper place (column) as correct.
4. Award full points (number of digits used in solving a problem) when the student has a correct answer even if the work is not shown.
5. If the student displays work and the answer is incorrect, give credit for each digit done correctly.
6. Do not count numerals written for regrouping purposes (i.e., carried numbers).
7. Do not count remainders of zero.
8. When an X or a zero is placed correctly as a place holder, count it as one digit correct.
9. Give credit for any correct digits even if the problem has not been completed.
10. Count the number of digits correct in each row and write that number at the end of the row.
11. Total the number of correct digits and record it on the paper.

Source: Adapted from *Teaching Students with Learning Problems* (pp. 252–253), 4th ed., by C. D. Mercer & A. R. Mercer, 1993, Upper Saddle River, NJ: Merrill/Prentice Hall. Copyright 1993 by Prentice-Hall Publishing Company. Reprinted by permission.

at the abstract level. If an untimed criterion approach is used, the teacher should include three items for each skill and set 67% or 100% as a passing criterion (Underhill et al., 1980). Most commercial tests do not adequately sample a specific skill. Including three items per skill helps to control the factor of carelessness and provides an adequate test sample. The use of probes is helpful in assessing mastery of specific skills. To use timed probes, the teacher should construct one for each skill and establish the criterion in terms of correct and incorrect responses per minute. To obtain a valid performance, each probe should be administered at least three times. The highest rate from the three samples is used for determining the criterion. From analyzing proficiency rates, Mercer and Mercer (1993) suggest that a useful criterion is a score of 40 to 60 correct digits per minute

TABLE 14.4
Survey Test: Division with Whole Numbers

Skill	Criterion (score in %)
1. Identify symbols for division by circling problems that require division.	
$\begin{array}{r}4\\+4\\\hline\end{array}$ 6 × 3 6 ÷ 2 7 − 4 $\frac{6}{2}$	
4)16 7 × 4 8 ÷ 2 $\frac{9}{3}$ $\begin{array}{r}13\\\times 7\\\hline\end{array}$	
4×1 $\begin{array}{r}6\\-2\\\hline\end{array}$ 8)64 6 + 2 9 = 3	☐
2. Compute basic division facts involving 1.	
1)8 1)7 1)1	☐
3. Compute basic division facts.	
4)36 7)42 8)56	☐
4. Compute division of a nonzero number by itself.	
7)7 29)29 1)1	☐
5. Compute quotient of a one- or two-place dividend and a one-place divisor with a remainder.	
3)7 4)7 2)9	☐
8)74 6)39 3)17	☐
6. Compute quotient with expanding dividend.	
3)9 3)90 3)900	
2)6 2)60 2)600	
4)8 4)80 4)800	☐
7. Compute quotient of a three-place dividend with a one-place divisor.	
8)638 6)461 3)262	☐
8. Compute quotient of a many-place dividend with a one-place divisor.	
7)47,864 6)2783 3)578,348	☐
9. Compute quotient of a three-place dividend and a two-place divisor where divisor is multiple of 10.	
40)681 30)570 10)874	☐
10. Compute quotient when divisors are 100, 1000, and so on.	
100)685 100)4360 100)973	☐
1000)6487 1000)99,490 1000)7430	☐
11. Compute quotient of a three-place dividend and a two-place divisor.	
27)685 39)871 14)241	☐
12. Compute quotient of a many-place dividend and a many-place divisor.	
649)78,741 3641)100,877 247)8937	☐

Note: When this test is administered, the directions for items 2–12 should simply state: Solve the following division problems.

Source: From *Teaching Students with Learning Problems* (pp. 257–258), 4th ed., by C. D. Mercer & A. R. Mercer, 1993, Upper Saddle River, NJ: Merrill/Prentice Hall. Copyright 1993 by Prentice-Hall Publishing Company. Reprinted by permission.

with no errors. Rate, however, can vary as a function of age, motor (handwriting) skills, and difficulty level of the task.

4. *Score the test, and interpret the student's performance.* The teacher starts with the easiest skill items and applies the two-out-of-three (67%) criterion or the criterion of rate correct per minute. At the point where the criterion is not achieved, the teacher analyzes the student's performance (i.e., errors, basic fact deficit, and understanding) to determine what skill to teach. The test also can be used to monitor student progress.

The division test presented in Table 14.4 is based on a math scope-and-sequence skills list. The skills become progressively more difficult, and three items are presented for each skill. It is sometimes less threatening for the student if the items in each skill area are written on index cards. In using the test, the teacher scores the student's responses under each skill and determines if the 67% criterion has been obtained. Failure to reach the criterion on a skill alerts the teacher to a specific area of difficulty. These areas can become the target of instruction and further assessment. It is common practice to use the type of survey test presented in Table 14.4 to determine what to teach. However, after becoming more skillful in assessment and teaching, the teacher can construct other diagnostic tests to determine the student's level of understanding.

Teacher-constructed tests can include a number of formats. The following are sample skills and related assessment items:

1. Identifies before and after for numbers to 10.

   Fill in the spaces:

   1 ___ 3 ___ 5 ___ 7

   What numbers are missing?

   __ 2 __ __ 5 __ 7 __ 9

2. Identifies the greater or smaller number for numbers 0 to 100 and uses > and <.

   Circle the greater number:

   [87 100] [35 53] [19 10]

   [40 26] [1 6] [33 44]

   Put > or < in the ◯:

   23 ◯ 32 8 ◯ 19 94 ◯ 76

   13 ◯ 43 43 ◯ 29 65 ◯ 59

3. Identifies place value with ones and tens.

   State the face value and the place value of the underlined digit:

$4\underline{6}3$	$2\underline{8}$	$48\underline{4}3$
face value __	face value __	face value __
place value __	place value __	place value __

   Complete the following:

   7 ones, 3 tens = __
   5 tens, 4 ones = __
   0 tens, 3 ones = __

4. Computes three two-digit numerals, sum of ones column greater than 20.

   Add:

26	57	29
18	38	47
+ 47	+ 49	+ 36

5. Identifies unit fraction inequalities.

   Circle the numeral that represents the smaller number of each pair:

   $\frac{1}{2}$ $\frac{1}{3}$ $\frac{1}{6}$ $\frac{1}{2}$ $\frac{1}{4}$ $\frac{1}{3}$

6. Identifies fraction names for 1.

   Fill in each ☐:

   $1 = \frac{\square}{8}$ $1 = \frac{\square}{77}$ $1 = \frac{\square}{689}$

Teacher-made probes also can be used to identify problem areas. Mixed probes are used to locate areas that need further assessment or instruction. Figure 14.2 presents a mixed probe in addition. Each of the following categories has nine items: basic addition facts of sums to

4 + 3	22 + 41	33 + 6	9 + 7	6 + 2	36 + 62	41 + 3	6 + 5	8 + 0
53 + 44	78 + 1	5 + 8	7 + 2	43 + 36	82 + 5	7 + 4	5 + 3	61 + 37
42 + 4	8 + 7	4 + 5	33 + 52	31 + 8	9 + 9	6 + 0	24 + 53	65 + 24
7 + 6	5 + 2	82 + 13	37 + 2	6 + 6	4 + 4	31 + 18	57 + 32	7 + 9

Name ________________________ Date ______________

Correct Digits: ________

Incorrect Digits: ________

Patterns: 0–9 facts ______/9

2D + 2D ______/9

2D + 1D ______/9

0–18 facts ______/9

Comments: ________________________________

FIGURE 14.2 Mixed addition probe with no regrouping

Source: From *Teaching Students with Learning Problems* (p. 260), 4th ed., by C. D. Mercer & A. R. Mercer, 1993, Upper Saddle River, NJ: Merrill/Prentice Hall. Copyright 1993 by Prentice-Hall Publishing Company. Reprinted by permission.

9 (first item and then every fourth item), two-digit number plus two-digit number with no regrouping (second item and then every fourth item), two-digit number plus one-digit number with no regrouping (third item and then every fourth item), and basic addition facts of sums to 18 (fourth item and then every fourth item). On this probe, the student can obtain a maximum score of 63 correct digits with no errors. After three timings, a high score of 40 or more correct digits per minute with no errors is a reasonable criterion for diagnostic purposes. (See Mercer and Mercer [1993] for a more thorough discussion of rate criteria across skills and ages.) If the student fails to reach the criterion on a mixed probe, it is important to analyze the responses and locate the items being missed. This analysis provides the teacher with information for further assessment with specific skill probes (such as 0 to 9 facts). Also, specific skill probes can be used to monitor the daily progress of the student.

Assessment at the Concrete, Semiconcrete, and Abstract Levels. As discussed earlier, learning math facts and concepts progresses through three levels of understanding: concrete, semiconcrete, and abstract. Most published tests consist of abstract-level items; therefore, they do not yield information on the student's understanding at the semiconcrete and concrete levels. The student's level of understanding determines whether manipulative, pictorial, or abstract experiences are appropriate. To obtain the type of information required for effective instructional planning, the teacher can construct analytical tests that focus on both identifying difficulties and determining level of understanding. Items at the concrete level involve real objects, items at the semiconcrete level use pictures or tallies, and numerals are used in items at the abstract level.

Assessment at the concrete level can begin either with a written problem (such as 5 + 3 = __), with a display of objects, or with both numerals and objects. When assessment begins with a written problem, the student is instructed to read the problem and then solve it by using objects. When assessment begins with objects, the student is instructed to look at the display of objects (e.g., °°°°° + °°° = __) and then write the problem and solve it. When assessment begins with both numerals and objects (e.g., 5 °°°°° + 3 °°° = __), the student uses the objects (i.e., counts, removes, or groups) to solve the problem. The preferred sequence is to (a) use both numerals and objects, (b) use only objects and have the student write the problem, and (c) use only written problems and have the student arrange objects to solve them. Assessment at the semiconcrete or representational level can begin with a written problem, with drawings (i.e., pictures or tallies), or with both numerals and drawings (e.g., 5 ///// + 3 /// = __). When assessment begins with a written problem, the student is instructed to solve the problem by drawing tallies. When assessment begins with pictures or tallies, the student is instructed to write the problem and solve it. When assessment begins with both numerals and drawings, the student uses the pictures or drawings to solve the problem. The preferred sequence in assessing at the semiconcrete level is to (a) use both numerals and drawings, (b) use only drawings and have the student write the problem, and (c) use only written problems and have the student generate the drawings (tallies). Sometimes it is not feasible to present the problem through the use of objects or drawings because the operation is not implied. For example, in arranging the objects for subtraction, only the objects or drawings for the minuend are used in beginning the problem. The subtrahend involves taking away objects from the minuend; thus, the subtrahend is not part of the original stimulus. At the abstract level only numerals are used in presenting and solving problems.

The examples that follow should help the reader develop analytical math tests in specific skill areas. For a more detailed discussion of this type of assessment, the reader is referred to Underhill et al. (1980).

1. Skill: Addition facts (0 to 9)

   Concrete level: Write problem and sum.

   □ □ □ □ □ + □ □ □ =

   ____ + ____ = ____

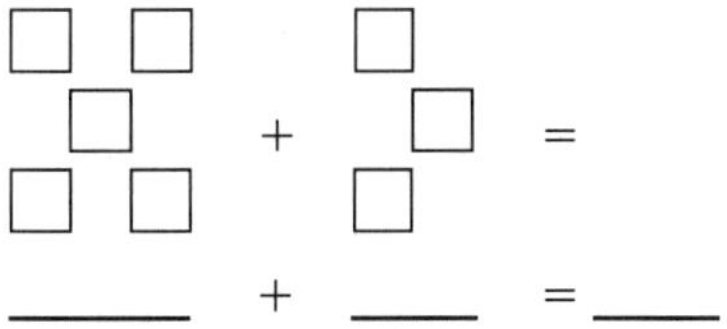

   Semiconcrete level: Write problem and sum.

   ```
     /////      +   ___
   +  ///           ___
                    ___
   ```

   Abstract level: Write sum.

   ```
     5
   + 3
   ```

2. Skill: Addition operation without regrouping

   Concrete level: Let ▭ = 1 ten and □ = 1 one. Write problem and sum.

   ```
     ▭ □ □               ____
   + ▭ □ □ □ □     +     ____
                         ____
   ```

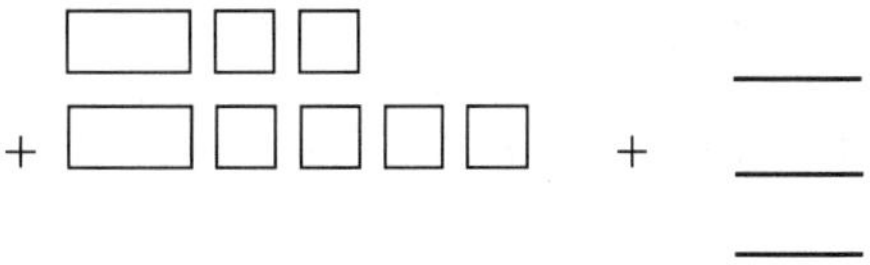

   Semiconcrete level: Let ○ = 1 ten and ∘ = 1 one. Write problem and sum.

○∘∘
+○∘∘∘∘ + ___ ___ ___

Abstract level: Write sum.

$$\begin{array}{r} 12 \\ +\ 14 \end{array}$$

Evans et al. (1986) provide a detailed discussion of math assessment that features guidelines for conducting periodic and continuous assessment in math. Periodic assessment includes an initial testing that generates instructional objectives; periodic evaluations include checkups of general progress and in-depth evaluations of students experiencing difficulty. Continuous assessment focuses on monitoring the student's progress. It involves daily, weekly, or biweekly assessments. Silbert et al. (1990) highlight the importance of continuous assessment:

> The importance of careful monitoring cannot be overemphasized. The sooner the teacher detects a student's skill deficit, the easier it will be to remedy. For each day that a student's confusion goes undetected, the student is, in essence, receiving practice in doing something the wrong way. To ameliorate a confusion, the teacher should plan to spend 2 days reteaching for every day the student's confusion goes undetected. Thus, careful monitoring is a critical component of efficient instruction. (p. 12)

Diagnostic Math Interviews. As a curriculum area, math is quite different from reading, language, or written communication. One major difference is that skill in math is not reflected in global tasks such as oral reading, language samples, or written passages. A student may have extensive knowledge about math but perform poorly on a math test that does not cover that specific material. Thus, to perform a functional math assessment, the evaluator needs to know what the student has been taught and is expected to know. Moreover, K. W. Howell et al. (1993) remind evaluators that basals vary dramatically in their sequences and coverages of math content and that grade-level scores from math tests are not comparable. In summing up the issue of grade-level scores, they state that "given the variability in sequencing among tests and programs—the grade level statements from all math tests are useless" (p. 224). Thus, placing students in math programs based on grade-level scores is strongly discouraged.

Because of growing dissatisfaction with math tests, a move toward "authentic" math assessment is evolving. This movement involves portfolio assessments that are typified by open-ended performance measures (California Mathematics Assessment Advisory Committee, 1990). This approach emphasizes that math is more than the language of numbers. Assessment procedures that ask students only to look at and write numbers are too limiting to reflect current views of math instruction. Given the lack of consistency across programs and tests, and the evolving portfolio approach, it is highly recommended that student interviews be used when assessing math at specific levels. Interviews can provide insights into mathematical strategies, processes, products, and social-emotional reactions to math.

The diagnostic interview provides information to determine what math skills to teach the student and how to teach them. In this technique the student expresses thought processes while solving math problems. This technique often is used in administering diagnostic math tests. Moreover, the diagnostic interview enables the teacher to identify specific problems, error patterns, or problem-solving strategies in math. A sample interview illustrates how the procedure can yield important information:

> The teacher gave Mary three multiplication problems and said, "Please do these problems and tell me how you figure out the answer." Mary solved the problems in this way:

$$\begin{array}{r} {}^{2}27 \\ \times\ 4 \\ 168 \end{array} \qquad \begin{array}{r} {}^{4}36 \\ \times\ 7 \\ 492 \end{array} \qquad \begin{array}{r} {}^{3}44 \\ \times\ 8 \\ 562 \end{array}$$

For the first problem, Mary explained, "7 times 4 equals 28. So I put my 8 here and carry the 2. 2 plus 2 equals 4, and 4 times 4 equals 16. So I put 16 here." Her explanations for the other two problems followed the same logic.

By listening to Mary and watching her solve the problems, the teacher quickly determined Mary's error pattern: she adds the number associated with the crutch (the number carried to the tens column) *before* multiplying the tens digit. Mary explained that she had been taught to add the number being carried when regrouping in addition. After identifying Mary's error pattern and its origin, the teacher could plan instruction for teaching the correct algorithm and developing an understanding of the multiplication process. Without the interview, the teacher incorrectly may have planned instruction in the basic multiplication facts.

Clinical interviews also offer an excellent technique for identifying negative emotions and attitudes toward math. Knowledge of these feelings helps teachers adjust math instruction (e.g., using graphic cuing, prompts, reinforcement, and charts) to alter a student's feelings. Several activities can be used in an interview session to assess attitudes:

1. Instruct the student to solve some math problems and observe the student's behavior (e.g., makes negative statements, becomes upset, or gives up quickly).
2. Have the student respond to some oral sentence-completion tasks. The teacher starts a sentence and the student responds aloud. Sample starters include:
   (a) Math is very . . .
   (b) My best subject is . . .
   (c) During math lessons I feel . . .
3. Ask the student direct questions. The following are some sample questions:
   (a) What is your favorite subject?
   (b) Do you like to do math?
   (c) What is your favorite thing about math?
   (d) What do you not like about math?
   (e) Do you use math outside school?
   (f) What would you do to make math more interesting?

The validity of the diagnostic findings depends on the quality of the exchange between teacher and student. The teacher must establish a rapport and ensure that the student feels free to respond honestly. Some general guidelines for conducting an interview include the following:

1. Establish rapport and be alert to the student's attitudes toward math throughout the session. It often is helpful to start with items that are easy for the student to complete.
2. Focus only on the student's problem area that is the lowest on the skill sequence. Limit each session to one area of difficulty (e.g., two-column addition with regrouping).
3. Allow the student the freedom to solve the problem in his or her own way.
4. Record the student's thinking processes, and analyze for error patterns and problem-solving techniques.
5. Once an error pattern or faulty problem-solving technique is discovered, introduce diagnostic activities for assessing the student's level of understanding. These activities should include tasks at the semiconcrete and concrete levels. (For more detailed discussions of diagnostic math interviews, see Ginsburg [1987] and Stenmark [1989].)

RESEARCH ON EFFECTIVE MATH INSTRUCTION

The amount of research on teaching math has increased substantially in the last decade, and it is now clear that both curriculum design and teacher behavior directly influence the math achievement of low-achieving students and students with learning disabilities (Hutchinson, 1993a; Kameenui & Simmons, 1990; Kelly et al., 1990; Mastropieri et al., 1991; Mercer, Jordan, & Miller, 1994; Mercer & Miller, 1992b). Although much remains to be learned about teaching math, educators need to examine existing research and literature to determine *what* should be taught in a math curriculum and the best practices for *how* to teach it. Only through the systematic examination and application of what is known about math instruction can educators ensure that the achievement levels of students with learning disabilities are commensurate with their potential. The components of effective math instruction are presented next.

Selecting Appropriate Mathematics Content

Mathematics educators are recommending reforms in the content of the mathematics curriculum. Although computation remains a vital component, experts agree that obtaining answers through the use of written work is not sufficient. Estimating answers and cross-checking with alternative methods are stressed in the current recommendations. Moreover, the ability to think critically and the understanding of concepts, operations, and real-life applications are important goals of a mathematics curriculum. The official 1988 statement of the National Council of Supervisors of Mathematics, *Twelve Components of Essential Mathematics*, has implications for planning math instruction for students with learning disabilities.

1. *Problem solving*. Learning to solve problems by applying previously acquired information to new and different situations is one of the primary reasons for studying math. Problem solving involves solving verbal (text) problems as well as nonverbal problems. Skills involved include using trial and error, asking relevant questions, selecting an operation, illustrating results, analyzing situations, and translating results.
2. *Communication of mathematical ideas*. Students must learn the language and notation of math. They should present math ideas through the use of manipulative objects, drawings, written work, and speech.
3. *Mathematical reasoning*. Students must learn to conduct investigations of math concepts. These skills include making tentative conclusions, recognizing patterns, and using math knowledge to support conjecture.
4. *Application of mathematics to everyday situations*. Students should be encouraged to translate daily experiences into mathematical representations (i.e., graphs, tables, diagrams, or math expressions) and interpret the results.
5. *Alertness to the reasonableness of results*. Students must be able to examine results against viable conjecture. The use of calculators and computers makes this an essential skill in society.
6. *Estimation*. Students must be able to perform rapid mental approximations to establish the reasonableness of a math solution. In addition to approximating purchase costs, these estimations involve measurements such as length, area, volume, and weight.
7. *Appropriate computational skills*. Students must gain proficiency in using operations (i.e., addition, subtraction, multiplication, and division) with whole numbers and decimals. Knowledge of basic facts is essential, and mental arithmetic is important. Competence in using common fractions and decimals is necessary, and knowing when to use a calculator also is helpful.
8. *Algebraic thinking*. Students must learn to use letters to represent math quantities and expressions and to represent mathematical relationships and functions with graphs, tables, and equations. Students need to understand how one quantity changes as a function of another.
9. *Measurement*. Students must learn the basic concepts of measuring (i.e., distance, weight, time, capacity, temperature, and angles) through concrete experiences.
10. *Geometry*. Students must learn geometric concepts to function in a three-dimensional world. Parallelism, perpendicularity, congruence, similarity, and symmetry are im-

portant concepts. These concepts should be explored in situations that involve measurement and problem solving.

11. *Statistics.* Students must learn to collect and organize data to answer daily questions. Measures of central tendency and variance are important as well as interpreting tables, maps, graphs, and charts.
12. *Probability.* Students must understand the basic notions of probability to predict the likelihood of future events that are important in their lives.

Many experts recommend that math instruction focus on problem solving within an authentic context. One way to accomplish this is to introduce math concepts and operations within the context of a word problem. For example, solving division equations in algebra could be introduced with the following word problem: "Cindy plans to give 30 coupons for free pizza to 6 of her friends. How many coupons will each friend receive?" The teacher explains that this can be represented and solved through the use of simple division: 30 coupons ÷ 6 friends = __ coupons per friend. Then the teacher also demonstrates how the problem can be solved through the use of algebra by giving the unknown a letter name and moving it to the left side of the equation: 30 coupons ÷ 6 friends = __ becomes 6 friends × c (coupons per friend) = 30 coupons. Furthermore, the teacher uses the students' prior knowledge about the multiplication and division relationship to solve the problem (i.e., What number multiplied by 6 equals 30?). As the lessons progress the teacher guides and encourages the students to create their own word problems that can be solved through the use of division equations.

If mathematical content is to be authentic to learning, it is imperative that it be presented in a real-world context. For example, if the instructional content fails to relate $6y + 2y + 6 = 48$ to a pragmatic word problem, then students are memorizing meaningless procedures for obtaining answers. In a study of technological math interventions with students with learning problems, Bottge and Hasselbring (1993) found that contextualized learning was a key factor.

Another consideration for determining what mathematics content to teach involves a student's prior learning. As noted earlier in the discussion on readiness, mathematics is a logical interrelated system of concepts and operations that are hierarchically ordered. Numerous experts (Bley & Thornton, 1995; Kameenui & Simmons, 1990; Miller & Milam, 1987; Silbert et al., 1990) stress the importance of teaching students skills for which they have the necessary preskills. For example, students should know some addition facts before learning subtraction facts. The instruction of students in skills in which they lack the necessary preskills often leads to a limited amount of fragmented or rote learning and much frustration. A best teaching practice clearly involves teaching students the preskills that are germane to learning a new skill or beginning instruction with a skill in which students possess the essential preskills. Finally, educators must ensure that students with learning disabilities receive math instruction on relevant or practical math skills. For example, the teaching of Roman numerals appears to lack relevance.

Teaching the Acquisition of Math

Follow Teaching Steps. A viable plan for teaching the acquisition of computation or problem-solving skills includes the following activities:

1. Assess the student's math skills and identify an appropriate instructional objective. To promote success, the objective should be relevant and one in which the student has the essential preskills.
2. Obtain a commitment from the student to learn the math skill and set goals. Discussions regarding the applications of the targeted skill help the student establish a desire to learn. Moreover, goal setting provides the student

and teacher with instructional expectations and fosters motivation. Goal setting is enhanced by identifying the expected time period for reaching a mastery criterion. In their synthesis on research on good teaching, Porter and Brophy (1988) report that good teachers are clear about instructional goals and communicate expectations and why the specific expectations exist. In presenting goals, effective teachers explain what the student needs to do to achieve the goal and what the student will learn in achieving the goal (Christenson, Ysseldyke, & Thurlow, 1989). There is growing support for the premise that teachers tend to make goals too easy for students with learning problems (Anderson & Pellicer, 1990; Clifford, 1990; Fuchs, Fuchs, & Deno, 1985). Clifford reports that students need challenge rather than easy success and that tasks involving moderate risk-taking provide the best level of difficulty in setting goals. She recommends that instructional environments should feature error tolerance and reward for error correction. A substantial research base (Locke & Latham, 1990; Locke, Shaw, Saari, & Latham, 1981) documents the premise that difficult but attainable goals lead to higher effort and achievement than do easier goals.

3. Use effective teaching steps to teach the math skill. These teaching steps are presented in Table 14.5, which provides a format for developing sample dialogues across teaching steps. Numerous researchers have used these steps and variations of these steps to produce excellent math achievement in students with learning disabilities. Also, during the learning of new material, it is important for the student to maintain a high success rate.

Use Teacher Modeling of Explicit Strategies. A promising feature from the recent literature entails the *substance* of teacher modeling. Instead of the traditional teacher modeling of mathematical algorithms in a meaningless context, researchers are exploring the modeling of problem-solving strategies (i.e., cognitive and metacognitive) to solve meaningful problems and develop self-regulation processes. Woodward (1991) notes that cognitive task analyses are being conducted to enable teachers to model thinking processes involved in math problem solving. Explicit teacher modeling of cognitive and metacognitive strategies in solving word problems has yielded encouraging results in teaching students with learning disabilities (Hutchinson, 1993a; Montague, 1992).

Hutchinson's (1993a) intervention for teaching adolescents with learning disabilities included explicit teacher modeling of strategies for solving algebra word problems. The strategies consisted of self-questions for representing and solving algebra word problems. The intervention also featured scripts to guide instruction, teacher prompts, encouragement, corrective feedback, student think-alouds, guided practice, independent practice, and the use of graphs to monitor student progress. Selected self-questions for representing algebra word problems included the following: (a) Have I read and understood the sentence? (b) Do I have the whole picture, a representation, for this problem? and (c) Have I written the representation on the worksheet? The students displayed improved performance on algebra word problems, and maintenance and transfer of the problem-solving strategy were evident.

To teach problem solving strategies to middle school students with learning disabilities, Montague (1992) used explicit modeling of cognitive and metacognitive strategies. The intervention also included verbal rehearsal, corrective and positive feedback, guided practice, and mastery checks. The specific cognitive strategies included (a) *read* for understanding, (b) *paraphrase* in your own words, (c) *visualize* a picture or diagram, (d) *hypothesize* a plan to solve the problem, (e) *estimate* or predict the answer, (f) *compute* or do the arithmetic, and (g) *check* to make sure everything is right. Montague reports that the students readily learned these strategies and applied them successfully in solving word

TABLE 14.5
Format for Developing Sample Dialogues Across Teaching Steps

Step 1: Give an Advance Organizer

Link the lesson to previous learning or lessons.
Identify the target skill.
Provide a rationale for learning the skill or strategy and discuss the relevance of the new knowledge.

Step 2: Describe and Model the Skill or Strategy

Procedure 1: The teacher asks a question and the teacher answers the question. The students hear and observe the teacher think aloud while modeling metacognitive strategies.

Procedure 2: The teacher asks a question and students help provide the answer. The students participate by answering the questions and solving the problem. The teacher and the students perform the strategy together, and the teacher continues to provide modeling.

Step 3: Conduct Guided Practice and Interactive Discourse

Procedure 1: The teacher guides the students through problem-solving strategies without demonstration unless it is essential. Guidance is provided as needed and the following supportive techniques are used:

(a) The teacher asks specific leading questions and models if necessary (e.g., What is the first step in solving a problem?).
(b) The teacher provides prompts regarding declarative knowledge (e.g., Use a variable [letter] to represent the unknown in the word problem).
(c) The teacher provides cues regarding procedural knowledge (e.g., Remember to isolate the variable in solving the equation).

Procedure 2: The teacher instructs the students to do the task and reflect on the process and product. The teacher provides support on an as-needed basis and uses fewer prompts and cues. The students are encouraged to become more independent.

Step 4: Conduct Independent Practice to Mastery

The students are encouraged to reflect (i.e., estimate, predict, check, and create) and work without teacher assistance. Activities include peer tutoring, cooperative learning, instructional games, self-correcting materials, and computer-assisted instruction.

Step 5: Provide Elaborated Feedback

This procedure guides the teacher to give feedback on correct responses and use incorrect responses as teaching and learning opportunities.

F—*Find* the score. Explain the grade.
E—*Enter* the score. Use a graph and goal setting and make it meaningful.
E—*Evaluate* the score in terms of the goal.
D—*Determine* errors by examining the pattern.
B—*Begin* error correction. Teacher models similar problem.
A—*Ask* student to apply the correct procedure.
C—*Close* out the session by giving positive feedback on correction.
K—*Kick* back and relax!

Step 6: Teach Generalization and Transfer

Reflect on applications of new knowledge across settings and situations.
Encourage the students to create meaningful math word problems related to new knowledge.

problems. Because some of the students failed to maintain and generalize the strategies, she encourages the use of techniques to promote generalization. Specifically, she suggests mnemonics and verbal rehearsal as techniques to help students remember and gain access to procedural math knowledge. Finally, Montague concludes that this type of strategy instruction holds much promise for helping students with learning problems achieve in math.

These preliminary findings (Hutchinson, 1993a; Montague, 1993) suggest that specific strategy instruction in math holds significant promise for students with learning disabilities. These findings support Zawaiza and Gerber's (1993) position that "successful strategy instruction . . . requires modeling of competent strategy use, sufficient and appropriate exemplar problems, ample opportunity to practice and receive correction on strategy use, and adequate opportunities for students to describe and evaluate how effectively they are employing newly learned strategies" (p. 67).

Focus on Teacher-Student Interactions. A focus on teacher-student interactions provides a timely opportunity for educators to improve the quality of instructional discourse for teaching math. Earlier research mainly stressed the role of the teacher in providing instruction to cover content, whereas recent research focuses on the dynamic nature of the dialogue between the student and the teacher to develop conceptual understandings. In this dynamic process the teacher constantly adapts the dialogue according to student needs. Teachers are encouraged to time their interactions prescriptively so that they know when it is appropriate to provide direct instruction, give guided instruction, ask questions, challenge, offer corrective feedback, encourage, let the student work independently, reflect with the student, set instructional goals, model a cognitive or metacognitive strategy, discuss rationales for learning new declarative or procedural knowledge, or discuss transfer. When teachers prescriptively interact (i.e., base interactions on student behavior) during instruction to ensure that students develop conceptual understandings, students are treated as active agents in their own learning.

Elmore (1992) notes that teachers need extensive help to learn and apply the ideas of current research on teaching. He claims that it is unrealistic to expect teachers to accomplish this by themselves. Apparently, teacher education and commercial materials have not helped teachers to teach conceptual understandings. Most materials present information that describes how to use algorithms to solve math problems. This algorithm-driven approach provides little or no help to teachers who desire to teach the conceptual underpinnings implicit in math.

To help teachers model strategies and teach understanding of math concepts, several researchers have provided scripts or sample dialogues (Hutchinson, 1993a; Mercer & Miller, 1992b; Montague, 1993). These scripts or sample dialogues provide the teacher with an initial guide on how to model metacognitive strategies explicitly and how to lead the student to conceptual understandings of math concepts (declarative knowledge) and apply declarative and procedural knowledge to solve word problems and math equations. The scripts serve as a springboard for helping teachers engage in productive teacher-student discourse. As teachers gain confidence and experience with these interactions, the sample dialogues are not needed. Researchers (Harris, Miller, & Mercer, 1995; Mercer, Enright, & Tharin, 1994) are field testing a sample dialogue that guides the teacher through the teaching steps. The describe-and-model step features explicit teacher modeling of strategies. The guided-practice step parallels scaffolding as the teacher guides the students to conceptual understandings and independent work. The independent-practice step incorporates working alone and with peers to gain mastery. The elaborated-feedback step is used to recognize successes and relate them to learning goals and to use errors in math for teaching and learning opportunities. The generalization-and-transfer step encourages the students to reflect on strategy uses and create their own word problems. Table 14.5 provides a beginning format for developing sample dialogues and practice activities.

Use the Concrete-Semiconcrete-Abstract Sequence. During the acquisition of a computational or problem-solving skill, it is essential that the student be instructed in such a way that understanding is assured. Many authorities believe that the use of the concrete-semiconcrete-abstract (CSA) sequence is an excellent way to teach students with learning disabilities to understand math concepts, operations, and applications. Several research studies (Harris, Miller, & Mercer, 1995; Mercer & Miller, 1992b) reveal that the CSA sequence is an effective way to teach math to students with learning disabilities. Results indicate that students with learning disabilities do not need large numbers of formal experiences at the concrete and semiconcrete levels to understand the basic facts. In this research, within six 30-minute lessons (three concrete and three semiconcrete), students with learning disabilities demonstrated an understanding of the respective operation and generalized their learning to abstract-level (numbers only) problems. Moreover, the students retained the targeted skills during follow-up testing. The CSA sequence especially seems to be useful in helping students who have deficits in *representing* or *reformulating* math from word problems to equations, equations to objects, pictures or drawings to equations, and vice versa. Because the CSA sequence requires students to represent math concepts and operations with objects and drawings, math concepts (such as addition, place value, multiplication, fractions, and equations) are understood. Examples of CSA teaching are presented later in this chapter.

Teach Concepts and Rules. The learning of concepts and rules also is germane to facilitating a student's understanding of math. A student who memorizes that $8 + 6$ is 14 but sees $6 + 8$ as a new problem to memorize needs to understand a basic concept (in this case, the commutative property of addition) to learn addition effectively. Likewise, the learning of subtraction is facilitated if a student understands the inverse relationship of addition and subtraction (i.e., $a + b = c$; $c - b = a$). Also, the concept of place value is difficult for many students and deserves much teacher attention. Finally, rules such as *any number times zero is zero* help students learn multiplication facts. Concrete and semiconcrete experiences are excellent ways to demonstrate concepts and rules to students.

Monitor Progress and Provide Feedback. The research is replete with the positive effects of monitoring the math progress of students with learning disabilities and giving feedback (Fuchs, 1986; Lloyd & Keller, 1989; Miller & Milam, 1987; Robinson, DePascale, & Roberts, 1989). Monitoring progress through the use of charts has yielded some excellent results regarding student achievement (see Chapter 8). Gersten, Carnine, and Woodward (1987) report that teachers who provide immediate corrective feedback on errors produce higher student achievement. Robinson et al. found that feedback helped students with learning disabilities complete more problems and improved accuracy from 73% to 94%. They stress the importance of feedback in the following passage:

> Feedback is potentially even more important for learning disabled (LD) children, who may be less attentive, participate less in academic work, and make more errors than higher achieving learners. Academic environments that maximize LD students' opportunities to learn under direct teacher supervision with timely feedback are essential. (p. 28)

Kline, Schumaker, and Deshler (1991) developed and evaluated an elaborated feedback routine with students with learning disabilities. Their results indicate that the elaborated feedback routine helps students achieve learning goals quickly and efficiently. A major factor in this routine stresses that errors represent learning opportunities for the students and teaching opportunities for the teacher. Clifford (1990) recommends that instructional environments feature error tolerance and reward for error correction. The essential features of elaborated feedback are included in the mnemonic FEEDBACK presented in Table 14.5. The letters *D, B, A,* and *C* stress error correction procedures.

Maintain Flexibility. Given the heterogeneity of students with learning disabilities, it is important for the learning disabilities teacher to use some flexibility in teaching math. From the numerous learning disabilities characteristics that can affect math learning, it is apparent that a variety of teaching activities or procedures is needed. If a specific teaching activity does not result in student learning, it may help to try another. Low-stress algorithms, specific modality-oriented instruction, visual and auditory cuing, prompting, and reinforcement represent a few instructional alternatives that can be manipulated readily.

Teaching Mastery

In this discussion, *mastery learning* refers to teaching a skill to a level of automaticity. Individuals usually reach a level of automaticity when they continuously respond to math problems without hesitating to compute the answer. Most people operate at a level of automaticity when responding to questions such as What is your phone number? or What is 6 plus 2? Rate of responding is regarded as an effective measure of automaticity (Hasselbring, Goin, & Bransford, 1987; Kirby & Becker, 1988; Lovitt, 1989). Reaching mastery on a skill provides numerous benefits, including improved retention and ability to compute or solve higher-level problems. Other benefits include finishing timed tests, completing homework faster, receiving higher grades, and developing positive feelings about math.

Before mastery instruction or techniques are used, the students must possess the preskills and understand the concept related to the targeted skill. Once they understand a skill, they can be instructed at mastery level. Students with learning disabilities vary considerably on the number of trials they need before achieving automaticity. Independent practice is the primary instructional format used to acquire mastery. Because practice can become boring, the teacher must try to make practice interesting or fun. Instructional games, peer teaching, computer-assisted instruction, self-correcting materials, and reinforcement are helpful in planning practice-to-mastery activities.

Several techniques are available to improve speed in math computation:

1. Reinforce high rates of correct responses.
2. Set a rate goal.
3. Chart performances and terminate daily practice once the goal is achieved.
4. Tell students to work faster.
5. Challenge students to beat their last rate score.
6. Teach students to use rules (e.g., any number times 2 is double that number).
7. Teach efficient algorithms (such as counting up in addition).
8. Drill difficult problems with flash cards.
9. Play instructional math games.
10. Provide rate practice in small intervals (10 to 20 seconds).
11. Teach students the relationships between addition and subtraction or multiplication and division when they are learning the respective facts.

In establishing mastery rate levels for individuals, it is important to consider the learner's characteristics (such as age, academic skill, and motor ability). For example, oral responses may be more appropriate for a student who has handwriting difficulties. For most students, a rate of 40 to 60 correct digits written per minute with two or less errors is appropriate; however, for younger students (kindergarten through second grade), it often is necessary to lower the digits-per-minute criterion. Once a mastery level is achieved, the teacher and student are able to move to the next skill level with appropriate preskills and more confidence.

Teaching Problem Solving

Problem solving has received more attention since the National Council of Teachers of Mathematics (1980) made a statement noting that problem solving should be a top priority in math instruction. Although problem solving has received a decade of attention from educators, its exact nature remains ambiguous. The National Council of Teachers of Mathematics (1989) describes problem solving as it relates to word problems and computation problems. It seems reasonable that a problem-solving activity is needed for any task that is difficult for the student. Thus, computation and word problems both could require problem-solving procedures. For skills in which automaticity has been achieved, problem solving is probably not a necessary procedural process.

Most authorities (Cawley et al., 1987; Fleischner, Nuzum, & Marzola, 1987; Kameenui & Simmons, 1990) interpret problem solving within the context of word problems. From an analysis of the problem-solving literature on students with learning disabilities, several components that are germane to problem solving are evident. These components include that to problem solve, the student needs to (a) have a mathematical knowledge base, (b) apply acquired knowledge to new and unfamiliar situations, and (c) actively engage in thinking processes. These thinking processes involve having the student recognize a problem, plan a procedural strategy, examine the math relationships in the problem, and determine the mathematical knowledge needed to solve the problem. Then the student needs to represent the problem graphically, generate the equation, estimate the answer, sequence the computation steps, compute the answer, and check the answer for reasonableness. The student self-monitors the entire process and explores alternative ways to solve the problem. Problem solving is a complex procedure, and these descriptors are offered as a frame of reference to promote understanding and appreciation of the numerous components involved in it.

Fortunately, in spite of the complexity of the concept, the problem-solving emphasis is generating research that provides insights into how to teach students with learning disabilities to solve word problems. Paralleling the emphasis on problem solving has been a focus on strategy instruction. In strategy instruction, students learn a strategy that helps them engage in the appropriate steps needed to recognize and successfully solve a word problem. Numerous learning strategies are being developed and evaluated to teach problem-solving skills to students with learning disabilities. For example, mnemonics helps students with memory problems acquire, remember, and apply specific math content and procedures. The following are some guidelines for problem-solving instruction:

1. Link instruction to students' prior knowledge and help them connect what they know in learning new information. For example, to help students learn division facts, point out the relationship between multiplication and division (i.e., $9 \times 7 = 63$; $63 \div 9 = 7$; $63 \div 7 = 9$).
2. Teach students to understand concepts and operations.
3. Provide students with problems that pertain to daily living.
4. Teach word problems simultaneously with computation skills.
5. Concentrate on helping students develop a positive attitude toward math.
6. Teach students learning strategies that help them become independent learners.

Cawley et al. (1987) present the following list of do's and don'ts for teachers:

Do:

1. Begin problem solving the day a child enters school.
2. Make problem solving the reason for computation.
3. Develop long-term programs of problem solving.
4. Conduct problem solving as a multimodal activity.
5. Partial out the effects of one variable on another. If the child cannot read the problem, rewrite it. If the computation is too complex, make it simpler.
6. Have children prepare or modify problems.
7. Differentiate between process and knowledge.
8. Prepare problems in such a way that children must act upon the information. Prepare a set of problems in which all problems have the same question.
9. Present problems dealing with familiar subject matter.
10. Constantly monitor progress and modify problems to fit the child's weaknesses and progress.

Don't:

1. Use cue words to signal an operation.
2. Teach children to use computational rules to solve problems. That is, do not tell children to add when they see three different numbers.
3. Use problem-solving activities as an occasional wrap-up to computation.
4. Mark a child wrong if he/she makes a computational error in problem solving if the operation is correct.
5. Train teachers to treat problem solving as secondary to computation.
6. Assume that because the child is able to perform an arithmetic operation that he/she can automatically solve problems that use that operation.
7. Conclude that an incorrect answer automatically indicates lack of facility in problem solving.
8. Fail to realize that problem solving is the most important aspect of mathematics for daily living.
9. Fail to seize the opportunities for training in problem solving in conjunction with other subject areas.
10. Present problem solving in a haphazard manner. Order and careful planning are essential. (pp. 91–92)

Specific interventions for teaching problem-solving skills are presented later in this chapter.

Teaching Generalization

As discussed in Chapter 8, *generalization* refers to the performance of the targeted behavior in different, nontraining conditions (i.e., across subjects, settings, people, behaviors, or time) without arranging the same events in the conditions that were present in the training conditions (Stokes & Baer, 1977). Students with learning disabilities typically have difficulty generalizing skills. A lack of instruction aimed at teaching students with learning disabilities to generalize math skills has contributed to their generalization problems. Ellis, Lenz, and Sabornie (1987a, 1987b) report that generalization must be taught prior to, during, and subsequent to instruction. Instructional practices to help students generalize math skills include the following:

1. Develop motivation to learn. It is believed that students who desire to learn a skill or strategy are most likely to generalize it. Motivation helps students feel responsible for their own learning and helps establish the independence needed to apply the new skill in settings without teacher support.
2. Throughout the instructional process, have periodic discussions with students about the rationale for learning the math skill and in which situations it is useful (e.g., homework, recreational activities, and shopping).
3. Throughout the instructional process, provide students with a variety of examples and experiences. For example, vary the manipulative objects (such as cubes, checkers, and buttons) in concrete activities, and use a variety of graphic representations (i.e., different pictures, drawings, and tallies) in semiconcrete activities. Likewise, vary the format in abstract computation or word-problem activities (e.g., present computation problems in verbal and horizontal formats). Also, vary the person doing the instruction (e.g., aide, peer, and parent).
4. Teach skills to a mastery level so that students can concentrate on using and not just remembering the skill.
5. Teach students strategies for solving multistep math problems. When students possess a strategy for solving difficult problems, they are more likely to develop independent behavior and to actively engage in the problem-solving process. Mnemonic devices frequently are used to help students retrieve appropriate strategies.
6. Teach students to solve problems pertinent to their daily lives. This connects the skill to functional uses and promotes motivation and the need to generalize. Students also can be instructed to create their own word problems.
7. Use reinforcement contingencies that are likely to occur in the natural environment. In this way, students are not dependent on artificial contingencies (i.e., reinforcers available only in the classroom) to maintain and use the learned skill.
8. Once the skill is established, move the teaching situation from a highly controlled format (i.e., teacher-led) to a more loosely controlled format (such as independent work).
9. Encourage students to generalize.

Promoting a Positive Attitude Toward Math

Many students with learning disabilities have a history of math failures. Consequently, they often develop negative attitudes toward math learning and feel insecure about their capabilities to succeed in math. Attitudes, beliefs, and motivation play an important role in the learning of math. The National Council of Teachers of Mathematics (1989) and the National Council of Supervisors of Mathematics (1988) stress the need to focus on the affective side of mathematics instruction. Bley and Thornton (1995) present this emphasis in the following passage:

> Students' feelings about themselves as learners and about their experiences with mathematics can greatly influence the level of their efforts and eventual success. By providing an environment that is accepting, encouraging, stimulating, and enjoyable, a program can foster a strong self-image and a positive attitude toward mathematics. (p. 5)

Clearly, math instruction must be designed to ensure success and promote positive attitudes. Many instructional techniques for promoting success and motivation are presented in Chapter 7. In addition, selected guidelines for promoting positive attitudes toward math learning include the following:

1. Involve students in setting challenging but attainable instructional goals. Goal setting has a powerful influence on student involvement and effort (Locke & Latham, 1990).
2. Provide students with success by building on prior skills and using task analysis to simplify the instructional sequence of a math skill or concept. Use charts to give students feedback on how well they are doing.
3. Discuss the relevance of a math skill to real-life problems. Use word problems that are part of a student's daily life.
4. Communicate positive expectancies of students' abilities to learn. Students need to sense that the teacher believes they will achieve in math.
5. Help students understand the premise that their own effort affects outcomes regarding achievement. Constantly point out that what they do influences both success and failure. This premise helps students realize that their behavior directly influences what happens to them. In turn, they realize that they are in control of their own learning.
6. Model an enthusiastic and positive attitude toward math and maintain a lively pace during math instruction.
7. Reinforce students for effort on math work and stress that errors are learning opportunities.

SPECIFIC MATH INTERVENTIONS AND ACTIVITIES

Concrete-Semiconcrete-Abstract Activities

The concrete-semiconcrete-abstract (CSA) sequence is appropriate for teaching the understanding of math throughout the span of math concepts, skills, and word problems. The use of manipulative objects requires some specific guidelines to ensure effective results. Dunlap and Brennan (1979) offer the following guidelines:

1. Before abstract experiences, instruction must proceed from concrete (manipulative) experiences to semiconcrete experiences.
2. The main objective of manipulative aids is to help students understand and develop mental images of mathematical processes.
3. The activity must accurately represent the actual process. For example, a direct correlation should exist between the manipulative activities and the paper-and-pencil activities.
4. More than one manipulative object should be used in teaching a concept.
5. The aids should be used individually by each student.
6. The manipulative experience must involve the moving of objects. The learning occurs from the student's physical actions on the objects rather than from the objects themselves.

Moreover, Thornton and Toohey (1986) suggest that the teacher (a) continuously ask students questions about their actions as they manipulate objects, (b) encourage students to verbalize their thinking, (c) have students write out the problem being solved through the use of objects, and (d) have students use objects to check answers.

The following sample procedures can assist the teacher in developing instructional tasks at all three levels for subtraction with regrouping and for multiplication facts. (See Mercer and Mercer [1993] and Underhill et al. [1980] for examples of other operations.)

Subtraction with Regrouping.

Concrete level: 33 − 18 = __

The student looks at the first number and counts that many objects and groups them as the appropriate number of tens and ones. The student looks at the second number and takes away the appropriate number of objects from the ones and from a renamed group of ten. The student counts the remaining objects for the answer.

Example:

Change to:

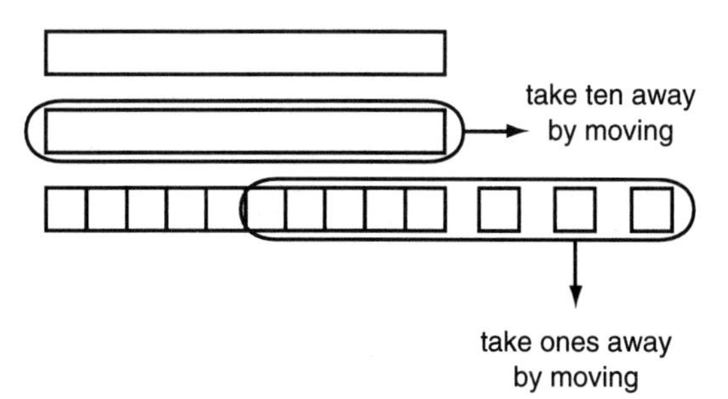

answer = 1 ten and 5 ones or 15

Semiconcrete level: 33 − 18 = __

The student looks at the first number and draws tens and ones. The student looks at the second number and crosses out the appropriate number from the ones and a renamed group of ten. The student counts the remaining tens and ones for the answer.

Example:

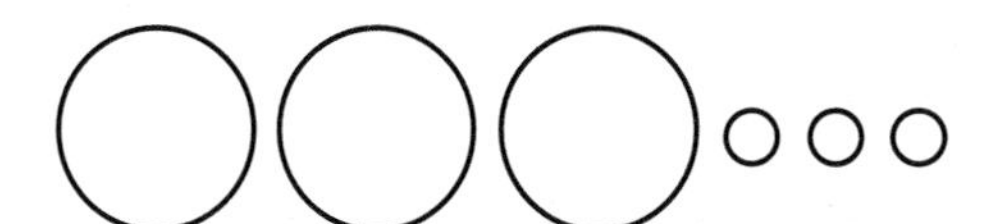

Change to:

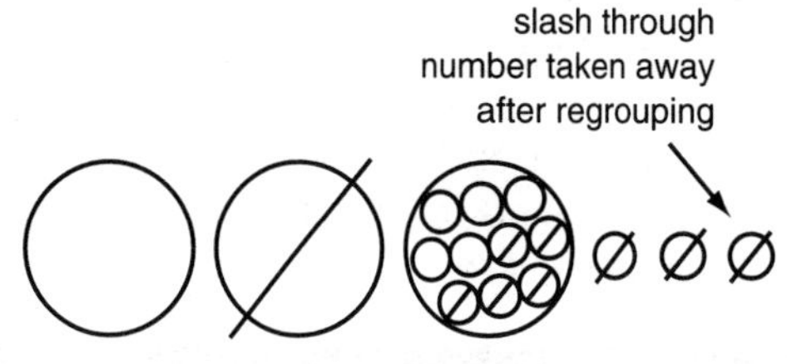

answer = 1 ten and 5 ones or 15

Abstract level: 33 − 18 = __

The student uses an algorithm to solve the problem.

Example:

$$\begin{array}{r} 33 \\ -\,18 \\ \hline 15 \end{array} \quad \text{or} \quad 33 - 18 = 15$$

Multiplication.

Concrete level: 3 × 4 = __

The student looks at the first number and selects that many containers to represent groups. The student looks at the second number and puts that many objects in each container (group). The student counts or adds objects across the groups for the answer.

Example:

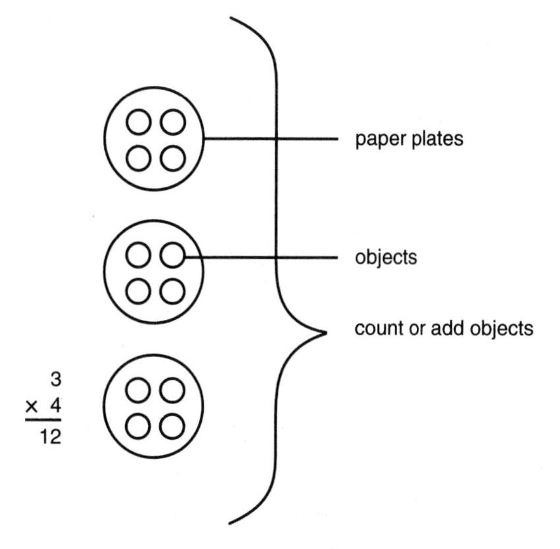

Semiconcrete level: $3 \times 4 =$ __

The student looks at the first number and draws that many groups using horizontal lines. The student looks at the second number and draws that many tallies in each group (i.e., horizontal line). The student counts or adds the tallies across the groups for the answer.

Example:

```
  3     ______
× 4     ______   groups
___     ______

  3     ////  4 ⎫
× 4     ////  4 ⎬ add tallies
 12     ////  4 ⎭
```

Abstract level: $3 \times 4 =$ ____ (learned primarily from memory)

The student answers the problem from memory or uses an algorithm.

Example:

```
  3    or   3 × 4 = 12
× 4

 12
```

When the abstract level is reached and memorization of facts is required, it may be helpful to teach the following multiplication rules, which minimize the amount of memorizing required.

1. *Order rule:* The order of the numbers to be multiplied does not affect the answer ($6 \times 3 = 18$; $3 \times 6 = 18$).
2. *Zero rule:* Any number times 0 is 0 ($8 \times 0 = 0$; $647 \times 0 = 0$).
3. *One rule:* Any number times 1 is the number ($9 \times 1 = 9$; $78 \times 1 = 78$).
4. *Two rule:* Any number times 2 is double the number (i.e., $4 \times 2 = 4 + 4$ or 8) ($8 \times 2 = 8 + 8$ or 16; $12 \times 2 = 12 + 12$ or 24).
5. *Five rule:* Any number times 5 involves counting by 5s the number of times indicated by the multiplier (i.e., 5×6 means counting "5, 10, 15, 20, 25, 30") ($3 \times 5 = 5 + 5 + 5$ or counting 5, 10, 15).
6. *Nine rule:* When multiplying any number by 9, subtract 1 from the multiplier to obtain the tens digit and then add enough to it to make 9 to obtain the ones digit ($9 \times 4 = 36$—3 is one less than 4 and $3 + 6 = 9$).

If these rules are used, there are only 15 facts left to be memorized:

$3 \times 3 = 9$	$4 \times 8 = 32$
$3 \times 4 = 12$	$6 \times 6 = 36$
$3 \times 6 = 18$	$6 \times 7 = 42$
$3 \times 7 = 21$	$6 \times 8 = 48$
$3 \times 8 = 24$	$7 \times 7 = 49$
$4 \times 4 = 16$	$7 \times 8 = 56$
$4 \times 6 = 24$	$8 \times 8 = 64$
$4 \times 7 = 28$	

Some teachers report that these facts are learned faster by grouping the doubles ($3 \times 3 = 9$, $4 \times 4 = 16$, and so on), thus leaving only 10 facts.

Thornton and Toohey Math Facts Activities

Thornton and Toohey (1985) report that substantial literature indicates that modifying the *sequence* and *presentation* of learning tasks can improve basic fact learning among students with learning disabilities. They offer guidelines that are supported by the literature for planning and implementing basic fact instruction for students with learning disabilities. These guidelines form the basis for MATHFACT, which was developed and used successfully in Queensland, Australia (Thornton & Toohey 1982–1985). An American miniversion is used in the United States (Thornton, 1984, 1985; Thornton & Toohey, 1984). Their guidelines include the following:

1. *Modify the sequence in which facts are presented for learning.* Traditional fact instruc-

tion sequences addition facts by the size of the sum. Thornton and Toohey (1985) maintain that other sequences are more effective for various learners. For example, for immature students or those with serious deficits, they recommend beginning instruction with the easiest addition facts: count-ons (+1, +2, +3) (45 facts), zeroes (19 facts), and doubles (6 facts not previously encountered).

2. *Before drill, teach students strategies for computing answers to unknown facts.* Many students with learning disabilities need to be taught specific strategies to help them solve problems independently. For example:

7 + 2	6 + 3	Start BIG and count on.
6 + 0	0 + 8	Plus zero stays the same.
8 + 6	6 + 8	Order of addends does not affect sum

Overall, the following sequence is suggested: (a) easy addition facts, (b) easy subtraction facts, (c) other addition facts, and (d) other subtraction facts.

3. *Modify the presentation of activities to fit the learning style of each student.* Students with learning disabilities are a heterogeneous population with many different learning styles and preferences. Some procedures for taking advantage of various modality preferences include the following:

For Auditory Learners
1. Precede all actions and demonstrations with spoken instructions. Each step may have two parts: (a) oral instructions only; (b) oral instructions closely followed by a visual stimulus, concrete manipulation, or demonstration.
2. Provide a verbal summary of each step.
3. If necessary use key words to focus the child's attention (e.g., "listen").
4. Remove extraneous visual stimuli.

For Visual Learners
1. Precede all oral instructions by concrete manipulations or mimed demonstrations. Each step may have two parts: (a) presentation of the visual stimulus only; (b) visual presentation in conjunction with verbalization.
2. Have children describe mimed or demonstrated actions, pictures, or concrete manipulation.
3. Provide a visual summary of each step.
4. Encourage children to make mental images of visual stimuli. Provide opportunity for them to reproduce these images (verbally, pictorially).
5. Use cue cards to focus children's attention.
6. Try a silent lesson.

For Kinesthetic/Tactile Learners
1. Precede all instructions by the physical manipulation of objects by the child. The teacher should guide all manipulations. Each step may have two parts: (a) physical manipulation only; (b) physical manipulation in conjunction with oral instruction.
2. Remove visual stimuli if distracting. Have children close their eyes or place objects in their hands behind their backs.
3. Provide a summary (physical manipulation of each step).
4. Use a cuing system to focus the child's attention.
5. Use textured material (pipe cleaners, sandpaper, plasticine, sandtrays, and magnetic boards). (Thornton & Toohey, 1985, pp. 52–53)

4. *Ensure provisions for overlearning.* Once facts are mastered, emphasis shifts to activities that help students with learning disabilities store them in long-term memory. This usually requires a variety of drill activities and performances on tasks at a high criterion level. Instructional games, self-correcting materials, computer-assisted instruction, peer teaching, and periodic review are a few of the activities appropriate for developing overlearning.

Selected Low-Stress Algorithms

Addition Algorithms. After the student knows addition facts through sums to 18, an adaptation of the *tens method* (Fulkerson, 1963) may be a useful algorithm. To illustrate:

```
  2 2 2
  8 6 7
  5 7 4
  6 4 7
+ 7 8 6
 2 8 7 4
```

Beginning at the top right in the example, 7 + 4 = 11, which can be renamed as 1 ten and 1 one. A horizontal line is drawn through the 4 to represent the ten, and the ones number is written on the extension of the line. Because the line represents the ten, the student no longer needs to hold it in mind. The student uses the 1 (ones digit) that is left over to begin adding until another ten in obtained. In this example, 1 + 7 = 8; then 8 + 6 = 14. Thus, a line is drawn through the 6 to represent the ten, and the 4 ones are written on the line. Because all numbers in the ones column have been added, the 4 is recorded as the ones digit at the bottom of the column.

The two lines drawn in the ones column represent 2 tens; thus, addition in the tens column begins by carrying the 2 tens by writing *2* above the tens column. These 2 tens are added to the 6 tens, and this continues until there is a sum greater than or equal to 10 tens: 2 tens + 6 tens = 8 tens; 8 tens + 7 tens = 15 tens. A line is drawn across the 7 to represent 10 tens, and the remaining 5 tens are written on the line. Then, 5 tens + 4 tens = 9 tens; 9 tens + 8 tens = 17 tens. A line is drawn across the 8, and the 7 is recorded on the line extension and as the tens digit at the bottom. In the tens column each line represents 10 tens or 1 hundred. Thus, the two lines in the tens column are carried by writing *2* at the top of the hundreds column to begin addition there. The 2 hundreds are added to 8 hundreds, and addition proceeds in a similar manner.

Another addition algorithm is referred to as *partial sums*. To illustrate:

```
  47
+ 28
  15
+ 60
  75
```

In this algorithm, when the sum of the ones column is greater than or equal to 10, it is written as a two-digit number at the bottom of the ones and tens columns. In the given example, 7 + 8 = 15, so 15 is written at the bottom on the columns. Next, the tens column is added and the sum is written below the ones column sum. In this case, 4 tens + 2 tens = 6 tens or 60. Then the two partial sums are added.

Multiplication Algorithm. One multiplication algorithm is the *partial products* algorithm. This algorithm reduces the regrouping requirement in multiplying multidigit numbers by one-digit numbers. For example:

```
  27
× 6
  42    (7 × 6) partial product
 120    (20 × 6) partial product
 162
```

```
  362
×   4
   08    (2 × 4)
  240    (60 × 4)
 1200    (300 × 4)
 1448
```

Fraction Algorithm. Ruais (1978) describes a low-stress algorithm for teaching the addition and subtraction of fractions. The algorithm is called *ray multiplication* and consists of the following steps:

1. An overhead projector is used to drill the student on the location of geometric shapes and numbers: $\frac{\circ}{\triangle}\ \frac{\square}{\diamond}$ are model items used to show locations of bottom right, bottom left, top right, and top left.
2. The student is instructed to draw three rays (↗): from bottom right to top left, from bottom left to top right, and from bottom left to bottom right. Thus, $\frac{\circ}{\triangle}\ \frac{\square}{\diamond}$ would look like $\frac{\circ}{\triangle}\!\times\!\frac{\square}{\diamond}$
3. On a sheet that has pairs of numerical fractions, the student is directed to draw the three rays and multiply along the

rays. The student writes the answers to these multiplicaiton tasks. After the rays are multiplied, the student writes the operation sign between the fractions in a pair. For example:

$$^{3}\frac{1}{2} \times \frac{1}{3}^{2}_{6}$$

4. In this step the student writes a new fraction for each pair. The new numerator is formed by performing the correct operation on the products of the diagonal ray mutliplications. The new denominator for both fractions is the product of the horizontal ray multiplication. For example:

$$\frac{3}{6} + \frac{2}{6}$$

5. Now the student computes the sum or difference of the numerators and writes the result over the denominator. For example:

$$\frac{3}{6} + \frac{2}{6} = \frac{(3 + 2)}{6} = \frac{5}{6}$$

Ruais reports that this ray multiplication algorithm leads to reduced stress, reduced teaching time prior to mastery, and increased computation power.

Problem-Solving Interventions

In word problem solving, math problems are presented in the context of social situations, and information needed to solve each problem must be identified and then used. In some problems extraneous information is included, and the number of operations may vary from one to several. Selected problem-solving strategies are presented earlier in this chapter under the heading Teaching the Acquisition of Math. This section presents additional strategies.

Interventions That Use Sequential Steps. RIDE is a mnemonic strategy that identifies the steps needed to solve story problems successfully:

R—*Read* the problem correctly.

I—*Identify* the relevant information.

D—*Determine* the operations and unit for expressing the answer.

E—*Enter* the correct numbers and calculate and check the answer.

Fleischner et al. (1987) discuss a study in which they used a strategy-based intervention with a cue card to help students with learning disabilities successfully solve addition and subtraction word problems. The cue card presents the following sequence:

1. Read: What is the question?
2. Reread: What is the necessary information?
3. Think: Putting together? = add; Taking apart? = subtract; Do I need all the information? Is it a multistep problem?
4. Solve: Write the equation.
5. Check: Recalculate, label, and compare.

In the study, during the *Read* step, the students highlighted the question and wrote the metric pounds, inches, and so on. In the *Think* step, the students were instructed to circle the largest number and write it. Then they were asked to see what happened to the number (i.e., did it get smaller or larger?) Finally, the students used calculators to compute the answer so that they could focus on problem solving rather than on computation.

Montague and Bos (1986) present an eight-step cognitive strategy to help students with learning disabilities solve verbal math problems. In a study of this strategy, they found that students were able to maintain and generalize the strategy. The steps include the following:

1. Read the problem orally.
2. Paraphrase the problem orally.
3. Visualize or graphically display the problem.
4. State the problem.
5. Hypothesize.
6. Estimate.
7. Calculate.
8. Self-check.

Interventions That Use the CSA Sequence. S. C. Howell and Barnhart (1992) developed a concrete-semiconcrete-abstract instructional sequence for teaching young students to solve word problems. The concrete stage features six steps and involves the systematic manipulation of objects to represent equations. The following activity is included in the sixth step. The student reads (or has someone read aloud) the problem "There are three blue circles and two orange circles. How many circles are there?" The student places the correct numbers and colors of circles on the display boards. The student states, "I placed three blue circles on one side and two orange circles on the other side. To find out how many circles there are, I place the groups together, so three circles plus two circles equals five circles." If this activity is done correctly, the student goes to the next stage.

In the semiconcrete stage the student is guided through six steps in which manipulative objects are replaced with pictures or drawings. In the sixth step the student represents a story problem by drawing tallies, writing the equation, and calculating the answer.

In the abstract stage a series of five questions are presented to promote a thinking strategy for solving word problems (Eicholz et al., 1985):

1. What is the question?
2. What are the numbers in the problem?
3. What do I do to the numbers?
4. What is the answer?
5. Do I need to check the answer by drawing tallies?

The final step at the abstract stage involves having the student independently write a story problem. For example, the number sequence $7 - 4 = 3$ may be written as the following story problem: "My dog had 7 puppies. There are 4 male puppies and the rest are females. How many puppies are females?"

Mercer and Miller (1992a) present a learning strategy approach to teach students with learning problems multiplication facts and word problems simultaneously. The word problems, as presented in Table 14.6, feature a graduated sequence of difficulty in which students learn to solve problems with extraneous information and create their own word problems. This CSA sequence guides the student to understand and apply multiplication to real-life word problems. Field-test results indicate excellent acquisition of multiplication facts, generalization, and problem-solving skills.

Calculators

Calculators are used widely in our society, and their use makes computation accurate and easy. The National Council of Teachers of Mathematics (1980) recommends that calculators be routinely available to students in elementary school. Because effective math instruction stresses understanding, problem solving, and computation, the instructional role of calculators needs clarification. Suydam (1980) believes that calculators should be used primarily with problems that students are capable of doing by hand. Paper and pencil may be most effective with simple addition and subtraction problems, whereas calculators are better suited for doing long-division problems (Lovitt, 1989). Fleischner et al. (1987) report that the use of calculators when solving word problems allows students with learning disabilities to focus on problem solving rather than becoming bogged down in computations. Moreover, some experiences with calculators can promote interest in other math areas. Finally, calculators provide a means for students to check their work.

COMMERCIAL MATH PROGRAMS

Numerous published programs and materials are available for teaching math concepts and skills. The following selected programs and materials are useful for teaching math skills to students with learning disabilities.

Connecting Math Concepts

The *Connecting Math Concepts* curriculum, developed by S. E. Engelmann, D. Carnine, O. Engelmann, and B. Kelly (published by SRA), es-

TABLE 14.6
Multiplication Problem-Solving Sequence

Description	Example
A computation problem is presented with the word *groups* written to the right of the first number and blanks beside the second number and the answer space.	6 groups of 3 _____ _____
The student writes the name of the manipulative objects used in the lesson in the blanks, solves the problem, and reads the statement. "Six groups of 3 checkers is 18 checkers."	6 groups of 3 checkers 18 checkers
A computation problem is presented with the word *groups* written to the right of the first number and blanks beside the second number and the answer space.	6 groups of 3 _____ _____
The student writes the name of the drawings used in the respective lesson in the blanks, solves the problem, and reads the statement. "Six groups of 3 circles is 18 circles."	6 groups of 3 circles 18 circles
A computation problem is presented with the word *groups* written to the right of the first number and common words written to the right of the second number and the answer space.	6 groups × 3 apples apples
The student solves the problem and reads the statement. "Six groups of 3 apples is 18 apples."	6 groups × 3 apples 18 apples
A computation problem is presented with a noun or phrase (adjective-noun) written to the right of the first and second numbers and the answer space.	6 brown bags × 3 red apples red apples
The student solves the problem and reads the statement. "Six brown bags of 3 red apples is 18 red apples."	6 brown bags × 3 red apples 18 red apples
A computation problem is presented with words on both sides of the numbers and the answer space. The numbers remain lined up in a vertical format.	Susan has 6 bags of 3 apples. She has _____ apples.
The student solves the problem and reads the statement.	Susan has 6 bags of 3 apples. She has 18 apples.
A regular sentence-style word problem is presented in which the numbers are not aligned.	Susan has 6 bags. There are 3 apples in each bag. How many apples does Susan have?
The student solves the problem and writes the equation.	$6 \times 3 = 18$
A sentence-style word problem including extraneous information is presented.	Susan has 6 bags. There are 3 apples in each bag. Bill has 2 pet turtles. How many apples does Susan have?
The student crosses out the extraneous information, solves the problem, and writes the equation.	Susan has 6 bags. There are 3 apples in each bag. ~~Bill has 2 pet turtles.~~ How many apples does Susan have? $6 \times 3 = 18$

TABLE 14.6
continued

Description	Example
The student is instructed to write or dictate his or her own multiplication word problem.	______ ______ ______
The student writes or dictates a multiplication word problem, solves the problem, and writes the equation.	There are 3 puppies. Each puppy has 2 spots. How many spots are there altogether? $3 \times 2 = 6$
Three types of word problems are presented: one problem without extraneous information; one problem with extraneous information; one problem to be created by the student	
The student writes or dictates the created problem, solves the problem, and writes the equation.	

tablishes relationships among math concepts and their application. The basal program includes Levels A through F for students in first through sixth grade, and skills are organized in tracks for the ongoing development of a particular topic. Suggestions are provided for problem-solving activities, games, cooperative learning activities, and the use of manipulative materials.

Corrective Mathematics

Corrective Mathematics (Engelmann & Carnine, 1982) is a remedial series in basic math for students in fourth grade through adult age who have not mastered basic skills. The basic facts are taught in addition, subtraction, multiplication, and division. The program includes the concepts of carrying and borrowing as well as translating story problems into numerical statements. Each lesson (65 in each operation area) takes 25 to 45 minutes and includes both teacher-directed instruction and independent review activities. Additional mathematics modules developed by S. E. Engelmann and D. Steely are available in basic fractions; fractions, decimals, and percents; and ratios and equations.

Cuisenaire Manipulative Starter Kit

The Cuisenaire Manipulative Starter Kit, produced by Cuisenaire Company of America, includes 12 widely used manipulative materials to offer a hands-on approach to learning mathematics. The kit includes color cubes, two-color counters, fraction circles, a set of Cuisenaire rods, mirrors, dice, a tangram, and a geoboard. Materials for use on an overhead projector include transparent spinners, circular counters, pattern blocks, and a set of base-ten blocks. In addition, a resource book, *Start with Manipulatives,* gives an overview of each manipulative and indicates which math concepts are taught most appropriately with each model. Various manipulative materials also are available from Educational Teaching Aids, Dale Seymour Publications, and SRA.

DISTAR Arithmetic

These math kits, developed by S. E. Engelmann and D. Carnine (published by SRA) for students in preschool through second grade, stress direct instruction within a highly systematic, intensive framework. Each kit includes a teacher's guide, teacher's presentation books, take-home workbooks for students, and group progress indicators. *DISTAR Arithmetic* is designed primarily for use with students in small groups, but suggestions are included for teaching large groups. The 160 lessons in each kit are fast-paced, and the teacher's guide specifies what the teacher should say and do. Simple skills are presented first, followed by more complex skills. Oral responses are used extensively; however, written work also is required. *DISTAR Arithmetic I* focuses on facts and fact derivation, story problems, rote counting, symbol identification, equality, addition, subtraction, and multiplication. *DISTAR Arithmetic II* broadens knowledge of basic math facts and includes strategies for problems in columns, multiplication, fraction operations, length and weight measurement, and negative numbers. The *DISTAR* programs have been field tested and evaluated extensively. The results indicate that *DISTAR Arithmetic* is effective in teaching math skills to economically disadvantaged children (Becker & Engelmann, 1976; Stallings & Kaskowitz, 1974).

Key Math Teach and Practice

The *Key Math Teach and Practice* program (Connolly, 1991) provides activities for the diagnosis and remediation of math difficulties. It includes essential concepts covered in kindergarten through eighth grade, and the three packages of basic concepts, operations, and applications are linked directly with the *Key Math—Revised: A Diagnostic Inventory of Essential Mathematics.* Math inventories and probes are used to pinpoint a student's strengths and weaknesses. Instructional intervention follows a sequence of foundation steps (reviewing prerequisite skills, introducing concepts and skills, and demonstrating application), learning activities (moving from the use of manipulatives to pictorial to symbolic representations), and drills, games, and extensions (including exercises of estimation and problem solving). A teacher's guide, a student progress record, and a scope and sequence chart also are included. In addition, *Key Math Activity Pacs* are available that include manipulatives (such as attribute blocks, cubes, chips, tumblers, and trays) to provide hands-on learning experiences to enrich the math program.

Strategic Math Series

The *Strategic Math Series,* developed by C. D. Mercer and S. P. Miller (published by Edge Enterprises), is designed to enable students with math difficulties to understand, acquire, remember, and apply math concepts and skills. The program is based on research in effective teaching, learning strategies, memory, mastery learning, applied behavior analysis, generalization, and student motivation. Eight instructional stages are included: pretest, concrete, representational, DRAW (mnemonic), abstract, posttest, practice to mastery, and periodic review. All lessons include scripts to guide the teacher through the instructional components of advance organizer, demonstrate/explain, guided practice, independent practice, problem solving (i.e., students learn to create their own story problems), and lesson feedback. Manuals are available for addition facts 0 to 9, subtraction facts 0 to 9, place value, addition facts 10 to 18, subtraction facts 10 to 18, multiplication facts 0 to 81, and division facts 0 to 81.

SOLVE: Action Problem Solving

The *SOLVE: Action Problem Solving* program, developed by B. E. Enright (published by Curriculum Associates), is designed for students in fourth grade through adult age. The three skillbooks for word problems develop problem solving for whole numbers, fractions, and decimals and percents. The program teaches a five-step blueprint for problem solving:

S—*Study* the problem.

O—*Organize* the facts.

L—*Line* up a plan.

V—*Verify* your plan with computation.

E—*Examine* your answer.

The program provides students with a variety of problem-solving strategies and includes both guided and independent practice. In addition, three scripted teacher guides provide presentation ideas and extension activities.

COMPUTER SOFTWARE PROGRAMS IN MATH

Computer software programs in math can be used to provide drill and practice activities in a motivating manner. Some programs present game-playing situations, and others effectively use animation and sound effects to maintain student interest. The computer also can provide self-correcting feedback so that the student does not practice errors. R. D. Howell, Sidorenko, and Jurica (1987) examined the effects of computer use on the learning of multiplication facts by students with learning disabilities. They found that it was necessary to combine direct teacher instruction with tutorial and drill-and-practice software for effective results. The following software programs present various math skills and can help the student understand and master these skills.

Arcademic Skill Builders in Math

Arcademic Skill Builders in Math (produced by SRA) is a software series designed to motivate students of all ages to learn fundamental math skills through the fast action and colorful graphics of arcade games. Six individual programs provide practice and drill in the four basic math operations and combinations of operations. *Alien Addition* uses an alien invasion theme to provide practice in basic addition facts. *Minus Mission* offers practice in basic subtraction facts as the student uses a robot that fires laser beams to target correct answers. Practice in basic multiplication facts is provided in *Meteor Multiplication*, in which the student must disintegrate meteors moving toward a star station. *Demolition Division* gives the student the opportunity to practice basic division facts as tanks move toward cannons that the player can fire. In *Alligator Mix* the student feeds hungry alligators while increasing skill in both addition and subtraction facts. *Dragon Mix* provides practice in multiplication and division facts as a large dragon protects the city behind it from invading forces. In all the programs the range of numbers can be changed to practice basic facts with the numbers 0 through 3, 0 through 6, or 0 through 9. Also, there are nine speed options, and game time can range from 1 to 5 minutes. Blackline masters and flash cards are included with each program.

SRA also produces three programs that provide excellent drill-and-practice vehicles for intermediate students. *Decimal Discovery* helps students improve their skills in adding, subtracting, multiplying, and dividing with decimals ranging from tenths to thousandths. *Fast-Track Fractions* incorporates the excitement of car racing as students add, subtract, multiply, and divide with fractions. *Fraction Fuel-Up* uses an educational space game to help students learn how to solve fraction word problems.

Computer Drill and Instruction: Mathematics

Computer Drill and Instruction: Mathematics (produced by SRA) includes 500 major skills from the first- through ninth-grade math curriculum and permits each student to practice specific skills independently. The four levels include lessons in number readiness, whole numbers, addition, subtraction, multiplication, division, fractions, decimals, computation, number and numeration, ratio and percent, measurement, prealgebra, and applications. The program includes an interactive tutorial that breaks a problem into small steps and leads the student through each step. An electronic blackboard feature allows the student to work multistep problems directly on the screen. The Seatwork Generator prints tests and additional skill exercises for use in class drill or take-home assignments. An additional three-level program,

Computer Drill and Instruction: Word Problems, provides 82 lessons in effective problem-solving strategies for students in first through sixth grade.

Math Blaster

The *Math Blaster* software series (produced by Davidson & Associates) covers various math curriculum skills. *In Search of Spot,* for students in first through sixth grade, features an adventure theme and covers addition, subtraction, multiplication, division, fractions, decimals, percents, estimation, and number patterns. *Secret of the Lost City,* for students in third through eighth grade, builds on math skills learned in the previous program and teaches more advanced basic math concepts. The two software programs in *Math Blaster Mystery,* for students in fifth grade and above, use a detective theme to focus on problem solving, critical thinking skills, and word problems with positive and negative numbers, fractions, decimals, percents, ratios, and proportions. *Alge-Blaster 3* helps students master the basic steps in solving equations, translate word problems into algebraic equations, and practice graphing skills, whereas *What's My Angle* teaches basic geometry concepts and demonstrates how geometry applies to real-life situations. The *Math Blaster* series of software includes such features as digitized speech, sound effects, and music as well as various levels of math difficulty and record keeping to track progress.

Math Sequences

Math Sequences (produced by Milliken) consists of 12 diskettes that provide a comprehensive, objective-based mathematics curriculum with structured drill and practice designed for students in first through eighth grade or as remediation for older students. Topics covered include number readiness, addition, subtraction, multiplication, division, laws of arithmetic, integers, fractions, decimals, percents, equations, and measurement formulas. The range of problem levels (from 16 to 64) within a sequence makes it possible to place students according to level of understanding. The work (such as carrying, borrowing, and canceling numbers) for each problem is completed on the screen. Graphic or textual reinforcements are given for a correct response. When a problem is missed more than once, the correct solution is displayed, step-by-step, for the student to study. The student is advanced by a level after specific achievement criteria are met or moved back a level until mastery is achieved. The management program maintains records for each student and allows the teacher to establish personalized performance levels and make individual and class assignments.

WordMath

The *WordMath* programs (produced by Milliken) provide students with individualized instruction and practice in solving word problems. The lessons for students in second and third grades in *Primary WordMath* focus on addition, subtraction, and basic facts and include tutorial messages for all errors. Computation is completed on the screen, and, if the student has difficulty, a step-by-step solution is given. *WordMath I* and *II* for students in fourth through eighth grade include modules in basic problems, forward/reverse order, extra numbers, hidden numbers, key words, dictionary, mixed practice, and advanced mixed practice. Graphic reinforcement supports correct answers, and tutorial error messages provide immediate assistance on the kind of error made and the particular problem worked. The program includes two levels of difficulty on each disk as well as a comprehensive management system. Supplemental workbooks are provided. The program can be used for supplemental instruction or remediation.

PERSPECTIVE

Many students with learning disabilities experience math difficulties. As reforms occur in math education, the changing times must be viewed as an opportunity to provide students with learning disabilities with more comprehensive math programs. Teacher educators and academicians must stop advocating math reform prior to gathering supportive and generalizable findings. As a profession, math education would be better served by the adoption of a refining rather than a reforming posture. Reform implies that the prior knowledge in the profession has been unacceptable, whereas refinement implies that prior knowledge can be connected with new knowledge to construct new and improved knowledge. Perhaps research-driven changes would decrease the need to have a major reform movement in math every 20 years (Carnine, 1992) and result in a growing knowledge base about how to learn and teach math.

Math assessment that covers sequence, understanding, mastery, and error analysis needs to be followed by instruction that features best practices in acquisition training, mastery training, problem solving, and generalization training. Algorithm-driven instructional materials must be replaced with math materials that (a) have been validated and replicated in various school settings prior to publishing; (b) correspond to the academic school year (i.e., many materials have 40 to 60 more daily lessons than there are days in the school year); (c) guide the teacher to use authentic content, model explicit metacognitive strategies, use instructionally prescriptive interactive dialogues, use elaborated feedback, and use transfer of learning techniques; and (d) recognize the strengths of various paradigms. Moreover, instruction must occur in a supportive environment that promotes positive attitudes toward math. Calculators and computers must be viewed as valuable resources in helping students with learning disabilities understand, compute, and apply math concepts and operations. In addition, university educators and staff development personnel need to stay informed about the ongoing projects and research so that the growing number of effective techniques reach students with learning disabilities quickly.

If educational researchers scientifically can tap the potential benefits of research-driven principles and if teacher educators and publishers of commercial materials can place the products of these findings in the hands of teachers, educators will have an opportunity to improve significantly the math learning of students and the math instruction of teachers. Perhaps student beliefs about learning math will change, and more math teachers will be sitting quietly on a playground and experience the satisfaction and joy of having a student approach them and say, "I know how to solve $9x$ minus $6x$ plus 12 equals 24". . . and the fun begins.

DISCUSSION/REVIEW QUESTIONS

1. Discuss the development of math skills by describing the concepts basic to readiness for number instruction and explaining basic math axioms.
2. Present problem areas of students with learning disabilities and their relationship to math performance.
3. Explain the levels of learning in math and present a sample procedure for teaching understanding of multiplication facts.
4. Describe several standardized and criterion-referenced survey and diagnostic math tests.
5. Discuss informal math assessment and give sample skills and related assessment items.
6. Discuss the major components of effective math instruction.
7. Present guidelines for the use of manipulative objects and for planning and implementing basic fact instruction.
8. Explain low-stress algorithms in addition, multiplication, and addition and subtraction of fractions.
9. Describe several commercial math programs.
10. Describe several computer software programs in math.

REFERENCES

Anderson, L. W., & Pellicer, L. O. (1990). Synthesis of research on compensatory and remedial education. *Educational Leadership, 48*(1), 10–16.

Ashlock, R. B. (1994). *Error patterns in computation* (6th ed.). Upper Saddle River, NJ:Merrill/Prentice Hall.

Baker, L., & Brown, A. (1984). Cognitive monitoring in reading. In J. Flood (Ed.), *Understanding reading comprehension* (pp. 21–44). Newark, DE: International Reading Association.

Balow, I. H., Farr, R. C., & Hogan, T. P. (1992). *Metropolitan Achievement Tests—Seventh Edition.* San Antonio, TX: Harcourt Brace Educational Measurement.

Beatty, L. S., Madden, R., Gardner, E. F., & Karlsen, B. (1995). *Stanford Diagnostic Mathematics Test—Fourth Edition.* San Antonio, TX: Harcourt Brace Educational Measurement.

Becker, W. C., & Engelmann, S. E. (1976). *Technical report 1976–1.* Eugene, OR: University of Oregon.

Bley, N. S., & Thornton, C. A. (1995). *Teaching mathematics to students with learning disabilities* (3rd ed.). Austin, TX: PRO-ED.

Bottge, B. A., & Hasselbring, T. S. (1993). A comparison of two approaches for teaching complex, authentic mathematics problems to adolescents in remedial math classes. *Exceptional Children, 59,* 556–566.

Brigance, A. H. (1981). *Brigance Diagnostic Inventory of Essential Skills.* North Billerica, MA: Curriculum Associates.

Brigance, A. H. (1983). *Brigance Diagnostic Comprehensive Inventory of Basic Skills.* North Billerica, MA: Curriculum Associates.

Brown, V. L., Cronin, M. E., & McEntire, E. (1994). *Test of Mathematical Abilities—2.* Austin, TX: PRO-ED.

Brownell, M. T., Mellard, D. F., & Deshler, D. D. (1993). Differences in the learning and transfer performances between students with learning disabilities and other low-achieving students on problem-solving tasks. *Learning Disability Quarterly, 16,* 138–156.

California Achievement Tests—Fifth Edition. (1992). Monterey, CA: CTB McGraw-Hill.

California Mathematics Assessment Advisory Committee. (1990). *Guidelines for the mathematics portfolio: Working paper.* Sacramento: California Assessment Program, California State Department of Education.

Carnine, D. (1991). Curricular interventions for teaching higher order thinking to all students: Introduction to the special series. *Journal of Learning Disabilities, 24,* 261–269.

Carnine, D. (1992). The missing link in improving schools—Reforming educational leaders. *Direct Instruction News, 11* (3), 25–35.

Carpenter, R. L. (1985). Mathematics instruction in resource rooms: Instruction time and teacher competence. *Learning Disability Quarterly, 8,* 95–100.

Cawley, J. F., & Miller, J. H. (1989). Cross-sectional comparisons of the mathematical performance of children with learning disabilities: Are we on the right track toward comprehensive programming? *Journal of Learning Disabilities, 23,* 250–254, 259.

Cawley, J. F., Miller, J. H., & School, B. A. (1987). A brief inquiry of arithmetic word-problem solving among learning disabled secondary students. *Learning Disabilities Focus, 2,* 87–93.

Cherkes-Julkowski, M. (1985). Information processing: A cognitive view. In J. Cawley (Ed.), *Cognitive strategies and mathematics for the learning disabled* (pp. 117–138). Austin, TX: PRO-ED.

Christenson, S. L., Ysseldyke, J. E., & Thurlow, M. L. (1989). Critical instructional factors for students with mild handicaps: An integrative review. *Remedial and Special Education, 10*(5), 21–31.

Clifford, M. M. (1990). Students need challenge, not easy success. *Educational Leadership, 48*(1), 22–26.

Connolly, A. J. (1988). *Key Math—Revised: A Diagnostic Inventory of Essential Mathematics.* Circle Pines, MN: American Guidance Service.

Connolly, A. J. (1991). *Key Math teach and practice.* Circle Pines, MN: American Guidance Service.

Conte, R. (1991). Attention disorders. In B. Wong (Ed.), *Learning about learning disabilities* (pp. 60–103). San Diego: Academic Press.

Copeland, R. W. (1979). *Math activities for children: A diagnostic and developmental approach.* Columbus, OH: Merrill.

Cox, L. S. (1975). Diagnosing and remediating systematic errors in addition and subtraction computations. *The Arithmetic Teacher, 22,* 151–157.

Dunlap, W. P., & Brennan, A. H. (1979). Developing mental images of mathematical processes. *Learning Disability Quarterly, 2*(2), 89–96.

Eicholz, R. E., O'Daffer, P. G., Fleenor, C. R., Charles, R. I., Young, S., & Barnett, C. S. (1985). *Addison-Wesley mathematics 1-3 components.* Menlo Park, CA: Addison-Wesley.

Ellis, E. S., Lenz, B. K., & Sabornie, E. J. (1987a). Generalization and adaptation of learning strategies to natural environments: Part I: Critical agents. *Remedial and Special Education, 8*(1), 6–20.

Ellis, E. S., Lenz, B. K., & Sabornie, E. J. (1987b). Generalization and adaptation of learning strategies to natural environments: Part II: Research into practice. *Remedial and Special Education, 8*(2), 6–23.

Elmore, R. F. (1992). Why restructuring alone won't improve teaching. *Educational Leadership, 49*(7), 44–48.

Engelmann, S. E., & Carnine, D. (1982). *Corrective mathematics.* Blacklick, OH: SRA.

Englert, C. S., Tarrant, K. L., & Mariage, T. V. (1992). Defining and redefining instructional practice in special education: Perspectives on good teaching. *Teacher Education and Special Education, 15,* 62–86.

Enright, B. E. (1983). *Enright Diagnostic Inventory of Basic Arithmetic Skills.* North Billerica, MA: Curriculum Associates.

Evans, S. S., Evans, W. H., & Mercer, C. D. (1986). *Assessment for instruction.* Boston: Allyn & Bacon.

Fleischner, J. E., Garnett, K., & Shepherd, M. J. (1982). Proficiency in basic fact computation of learning disabled and nondisabled children. *Focus on Learning Problems in Mathematics, 4,* 47–55.

Fleischner, J. E., Nuzum, M. B., & Marzola, E. S. (1987). Devising an instructional program to teach arithmetic problem-solving skills to students with learning disabilities. *Journal of Learning Disabilities, 20,* 214–217.

Fuchs, L. S. (1986). Monitoring progress among mildly handicapped pupils: Review of current practices and research. *Remedial and Special Education 7*(5), 5–12.

Fuchs, L. S., Fuchs, D., & Deno, S. L. (1985). The importance of goal ambitiousness and goal mastery to student achievement. *Exceptional Children, 52,* 63–71.

Fulkerson, E. (1963). Adding by tens. *The Arithmetic Teacher, 10,* 139–140.

Garnett, K. (1992). Developing fluency with basic number facts: Intervention for students with learning disabilities. *Learning Disabilities Research & Practice, 7,* 210–216.

Gersten, R., Carnine, D., & Woodward, J. (1987). Direct instruction research: The third decade. *Remedial and Special Education, 8*(6), 48–56.

Gessell, J. K. (1983). *Diagnostic Mathematics Inventory/Mathematics System.* Monterey, CA: CTB McGraw-Hill.

Ginsburg, H. P. (1987). *Assessing the arithmetic abilities and instructional needs of students.* Austin, TX: PRO-ED.

Ginsburg, H. P., & Mathews, S. C. (1984). *Diagnostic Test of Arithmetic Strategies.* Austin, TX: PRO-ED.

Giordano, G. (1993). Fourth invited response: The NCTM standards: A consideration of the benefits. *Remedial and Special Education, 14*(6), 28–32.

Goldman, S. R. (1989). Strategy instruction in mathematics. *Learning Disability Quarterly, 12,* 43–55.

Goldman, S. R., Pellegrino, J. W., & Mertz, D. L. (1988). Extended practice of basic addition facts: Strategy changes in learning disabled students. *Cognition and Instruction, 5,* 223–265.

Harris, C. A., Miller, S. P., & Mercer, C. D. (1995). Teaching initial multiplication skills to students with disabilities in general education classrooms. *Learning Disabilities Research & Practice, 10,* 180–195.

Hasselbring, T. S., Goin, L. I., & Bransford, J. D. (1987). Developing automaticity. *Teaching Exceptional Children, 19*(3), 30–33.

Hofmeister, A. M. (1993). Elitism and reform in school mathematics. *Remedial and Special Education, 14*(6), 8–13.

Howell, K. W., Fox, S. L., & Morehead, M. K. (1993). *Curriculum-based evaluation: Teaching and decision making* (2nd ed.). Pacific Grove, CA: Brooks/Cole.

Howell, R. D., Sidorenko, E., & Jurica, J. (1987). The effects of computer use on the acquisition of multiplication facts by a student with learning disabilities. *Journal of Learning Disabilities, 20,* 336–341.

Howell, S. C., & Barnhart, R. S. (1992). Teaching word problem solving at the primary level. *Teaching Exceptional Children, 24*(2), 44–46.

Hudson, F. G., & Colson, S. E. (1989). *Hudson Education Skills Inventory—Mathematics.* Austin, TX: PRO-ED.

Hutchinson, N. L. (1993a). Effects of cognitive strategy instruction on algebra problem solving of adolescents with learning disabilities. *Learning Disability Quarterly, 16,* 34–63.

Hutchinson, N. L. (1993b). Second invited response: Students with disabilities and mathematics education reform—Let the dialogue begin. *Remedial and Special Education, 14*(6), 20–23.

Kameenui, E. J., & Simmons, D. C. (1990). *Designing instructional strategies: The prevention of academic learning problems.* Upper Saddle River, NJ: Merrill/Prentice Hall.

Kaufman, A. S., & Kaufman, N. L. (1985). *Kaufman Test of Educational Achievement.* Circle Pines, MN: American Guidance Service.

Kavale, K. A., Fuchs, D., & Scruggs, T. E. (1994). Setting the record straight on learning disability and low achievement: Implications for policymaking. *Learning Disabilities Research & Practice, 9,* 70–77.

Kelly, B., Gersten, R., & Carnine, D. (1990). Student error patterns as a function of curriculum design: Teaching fractions to remedial high school students and high school students with learning disabilities. *Journal of Learning Disabilities, 1,* 23–29.

Kirby, J. R., & Becker, L. D. (1988). Cognitive components of learning problems in arithmetic. *Remedial and Special Education, 9*(5), 7–15, 27.

Kline, F. M., Schumaker, J. B., & Deshler, D. D. (1991). Development and validation of feedback routines for instructing students with learning disabilities. *Learning Disability Quarterly, 14,* 191–207.

Kulak, A. G. (1993). Parallels between math and reading disability: Common issues and approaches. *Journal of Learning Disabilities, 26,* 666–673.

Lepore, A. (1979). A comparison of computational errors between educable mentally handicapped and learning disability children. *Focus on Learning Problems in Mathematics, 1,* 12–33.

Lloyd, J. W., & Keller, C. E. (1989). Effective mathematics instruction: Development, instruction, and programs. *Focus on Exceptional Children, 21*(7), 1–10.

Locke, E. A., & Latham, G. P. (1990). *A theory of goal setting and task performance.* Upper Saddle River, NJ: Prentice Hall.

Locke, E. A., Shaw, K. N., Saari, L. M., & Latham, G. P. (1981). Goal setting and task performance: 1969–1980. *Psychological Bulletin, 90,* 125–152.

Lovitt, T. C. (1989). *Introduction to learning disabilities.* Boston: Allyn & Bacon.

Markwardt, F. C., Jr. (1989). *Peabody Individual Achievement Test—Revised.* Circle Pines, MN: American Guidance Service.

Mastropieri, M. A., Scruggs, T. E., & Shiah, S. (1991). Mathematics instruction for learning disabled students: A review of research. *Learning Disabilities Research & Practice, 6,* 89–98.

McLeod, T., & Armstrong, S. (1982). Learning disabilities in mathematics—Skill deficits and remedial approaches. *Learning Disability Quarterly, 5,* 305–311.

Mercer, C. D., Enright, B., & Tharin, M. A. (1994). *Solving division equations: An algebra program for teaching students with learning problems.* Unpublished manuscript, University of Florida, Gainesville.

Mercer, C. D., Harris, C. A., & Miller, S. P. (1993). First invited response: Reforming reforms in mathematics. *Remedial and Special Education, 14*(6), 14–19.

Mercer, C. D., Jordan, L., & Miller, S. P. (1994). Implications of constructivism for teaching math to students with mild to moderate disabilities. *The Journal of Special Education, 28*(3), 290–306.

Mercer, C. D., & Mercer, A. R. (1993). *Teaching students with learning problems* (4th ed.). Upper Saddle River, NJ: Merrill/Prentice Hall.

Mercer, C. D., & Miller, S. P. (1992a). *Strategic Math Series: Multiplication facts 0 to 81.* Lawrence, KS: Edge Enterprises.

Mercer, C. D., & Miller, S. P. (1992b). Teaching students with learning problems in math to acquire, understand, and apply basic math facts. *Remedial and Special Education, 13*(3), 19–35, 61.

Miller, J. H., & Milam, C. P. (1987). Multiplication and division errors committed by learning disabled students. *Learning Disabilities Research, 2*(2), 119–122.

Montague, M. (1992). The effects of cognitive and metacognitive strategy instruction on the mathematical problem solving of middle school students with learning disabilities. *Journal of Learning Disabilities, 25,* 230–248.

Montague, M. (1993). Student-centered or strategy-centered instruction: What is our purpose? *Journal of Learning Disabilities, 26,* 433–437, 481.

Montague, M., & Applegate, B. (1993). Middle school students' mathematical problem solving: An analysis of think-aloud protocols. *Learning Disability Quarterly, 16,* 19–30.

Montague, M., Applegate, B., & Marquard, K. (1993). Cognitive strategy instruction and mathematical problem-solving performance of students with learning disabilities. *Learning Disabilities Research & Practice, 8,* 223–232.

Montague, M., & Bos, C. S. (1986). The effect of cognitive strategy training on verbal math problem solving performance of learning disabled adolescents. *Journal of Learning Disabilities, 19,* 26–33.

Montague, M., & Bos, C. S. (1990). Cognitive and metacognitive characteristics of eighth grade students' mathematical problem solving. *Learning and Individual Differences, 2,* 371–388.

Montague, M., Bos, C., & Doucette, M. (1991). Affective, cognitive, and metacognitive attributes of eighth-grade mathematical problem solvers. *Learning Disabilities Research & Practice, 6,* 145–151.

National Council of Supervisors of Mathematics. (1988). *Twelve components of essential mathematics.* Minneapolis, MN: Author.

National Council of Teachers of Mathematics. (1980). *An agenda for action: Recommendations for school mathematics of the 1980's.* Reston, VA: Author.

National Council of Teachers of Mathematics. (1989). *Curriculum and evaluation standards for school mathematics.* Reston, VA: Author.

National Research Council. (1989). *Everybody counts: A report to the nation on the future of mathematics education.* Washington, DC: National Academy Press.

Newcomer, P. L. (1990). *Diagnostic Achievement Battery—2.* Austin, TX: PRO-ED.

Parmar, R. S., & Cawley, J. F. (1991). Challenging the routines and passivity that characterize arithmetic instruction for children with mild handicaps. *Remedial and Special Education, 12*(5), 23–32, 43.

Parmar, R. S., Cawley, J. F., & Miller, J. H. (1994). Differences in mathematics performance between students with learning disabilities and students with mild retardation. *Exceptional Children, 60,* 549–563.

Peterson, P. L., Carpenter, T., & Fennema, E. (1989). Teachers' knowledge of students' knowledge in mathematics problem solving: Correlational and case analyses. *Journal of Educational Psychology, 81,* 558–569.

Piaget, J. (1965). *The child's conception of number.* New York: W. W. Norton.

Porter, A. C., & Brophy, J. (1988). Synthesis of research on good teaching: Insights from the work of the Institute for Research on Teaching. *Educational Leadership, 45*(8), 74–85.

Reisman, F. K. (1985). *Sequential Assessment of Mathematics Inventory.* San Antonio, TX: Psychological Corporation.

Rivera, D. M. (1993). Third invited response: Examining mathematics reform and the implications for students with mathematics disabilities. *Remedial and Special Education, 14*(6), 24–27.

Rivera, D. M., & Smith, D. D. (1988). Using a demonstration strategy to teach midschool students with learning disabilities how to compute long division. *Journal of Learning Disabilities, 21,* 77–81.

Roberts, G. H. (1968). The failure strategies of third grade arithmetic pupils. *The Arithmetic Teacher, 15,* 442–446.

Robinson, S. L., DePascale, C., & Roberts, F. C. (1989). Computer-delivered feedback in group-based instruction: Effects for learning disabled students in mathematics. *Learning Disabilities Focus, 5*(1), 28–35.

Ruais, R. W. (1978). A low-stress algorithm for fractions. *Mathematics Teacher, 71,* 258–260.

Russell, R., & Ginsburg, H. (1984). Cognitive analysis of children's mathematical difficulties. *Cognition and Instruction, 1,* 217–244.

Scheid, K. (1990). *Cognitive-based methods for teaching mathematics to students with learning problems.* Columbus, OH: LINC Resources.

Silbert, J., Carnine, D., & Stein, M. (1990). *Direct instruction mathematics* (2nd ed.). Upper Saddle River, NJ: Merrill/Prentice Hall.

Slavin, R. (1991). *Educational psychology.* Upper Saddle River, NJ: Prentice Hall.

Stallings, J. A., & Kaskowitz, D. H. (1974). *Follow Through classroom observation evaluation.* Menlo Park, CA: Stanford Research Institute.

Stenmark, J. K. (1989). *Assessment alternatives in mathematics.* Berkeley: EQUALS, Lawrence Hall of Science, University of California.

Stokes, T. F., & Baer, D. M. (1977). An implicit technology of generalization. *Journal of Applied Behavioral Analysis, 10*(2), 349–367.

Suydam, M. N. (1980). *Using calculators in precollege education: Third annual state-of-the-art review.* Columbus, OH: Calculator Information Center.

Swanson, H. L. (1990). Instruction derived from the strategy deficit model: Overview of principles and procedures. In T. Scruggs & B. Wong (Eds.), *Intervention research in learning disabilities* (pp. 34–65). New York: Springer-Verlag.

Thornton, C. A. (1984). *Basic mathematics for the mildly handicapped: First year report* (Grant No. G008301694, Project No. 1029JH30133). Washington, DC: U.S. Department of Education, Office of Special Education and Rehabilitative Services.

Thornton, C. A. (1985). *Basic mathematics for the mildly handicapped: Second year report* (Grant No. G008301694, Project No. 1029JH40016). Washington, DC: U.S. Department of Education, Office of Special Education and Rehabilitative Services.

Thornton, C. A., & Toohey, M. A. (1982–1985). *MATH-FACT: An alternative program for children with spe-*

cial needs (A series of four kits: *Basic Addition Facts; Basic Subtraction Facts; Basic Multiplication Facts; Basic Division Facts*). Brisbane, Australia: Queensland Division of Special Education.

Thornton, C. A., & Toohey, M. A. (1984). *Matter of facts: Addition; Matter of facts: Subtraction; Matter of facts: Multiplication; Matter of facts: Division.* Oak Lawn, IL: Creative Publications.

Thornton, C. A., & Toohey, M. A. (1985). Basic math facts: Guidelines for teaching and learning. *Learning Disabilities Focus, 1,* 44–57.

Thornton, C. A., & Toohey, M. A. (1986). Subtraction facts hide-and-seek cards can help. *Teaching Exceptional Children, 19,* 10–14.

Tindal, G. A., & Marston, D. B. (1990). *Classroom-based assessment: Evaluating instructional outcomes.* Upper Saddle River, NJ: Merrill/Prentice Hall.

Torgesen, J. (1990). Studies of children with learning disabilities who perform poorly on memory span tasks. In J. K. Torgesen (Ed.), *Cognitive and behavioral characteristics of children with learning disabilities* (pp. 41–58). Austin, TX: PRO-ED.

Underhill, R. G., Uprichard, A. E., & Heddens, J. W. (1980). *Diagnosing mathematical difficulties.* Columbus, OH: Merrill.

Wang, M. C., Haertel, G. D., & Walberg, H. J. (1993/1994). What helps students learn? *Educational Leadership, 51*(4), 74–79.

Warner, M. M., Alley, G. R., Schumaker, J. B., Deshler, D. D., & Clark, F. L. (1980). *An epidemiological study of learning disabled adolescents in secondary schools: Achievement and ability, socioeconomic status and school experiences.* (Report No. 13). Lawrence: University of Kansas Center for Research on Learning.

Wood, S., Burke, L., Kunzelmann, H., & Koenig, C. (1978). Functional criteria in basic math skill proficiency. *Journal of Special Education Technology, 2*(2), 29–36.

Woodcock, R. W., & Johnson, M. B. (1989). *Woodcock-Johnson Psycho-Educational Battery—Revised.* Chicago: Riverside.

Woodward, J. (1991). Procedural knowledge in mathematics: The role of the curriculum. *Journal of Learning Disabilities, 24,* 242–251.

Zawaiza, T. R. W., & Gerber, M. M. (1993). Effects of explicit instruction on math word-problem solving by community college students with learning disabilities. *Learning Disability Quarterly, 16,* 64–79.

Zentall, S. S., & Ferkis, M. A. (1993). Mathematical problem solving for children with ADHD, with and without learning disabilities. *Learning Disability Quarterly, 16,* 6–18.

Zentall, S. S., & Zentall, T. R. (1983). Optimal stimulation: A model of disordered activity and performance in normal and deviant children. *Psychological Bulletin, 94,* 446–471.

Social and Emotional Behavior

CHAPTER 15

After studying this chapter, you should be able to:

- discuss the social development of students with learning disabilities.
- discuss emotional characteristics that may be present in students with learning disabilities.
- describe behavior problems that may be exhibited by students with learning disabilities.
- discuss prominent hypotheses concerning etiology of social and emotional behavior problems.
- list commercial instruments that involve teacher or parent ratings for the assessment of social and emotional behavior.
- list commercial measures of adaptive behavior.
- describe commercial self-report instruments and informal self-report techniques.
- explain sociometric assessment techniques.
- discuss naturalistic observations as an assessment technique.
- discuss general techniques for promoting social, emotional, and behavior development.
- discuss the concept of behavior modification and the use of contingency contracts and token systems.
- discuss social skills training.
- discuss specific techniques for promoting emotional development.
- discuss techniques for promoting behavior development.
- describe commercial programs for social and emotional behavior.

Historically, learning disabilities have been recognized primarily as cognitive or academic disabilities; however, many educators maintain that the noncognitive aspects of learning disabilities deserve more attention (Bender, 1994). Experts maintain that it is not sufficient to treat academic deficits in isolation and that educational plans must consider the social and emotional characteristics and needs of students with learning disabilities.

The social and emotional aspects of learning disabilities are receiving substantial attention. For example, Gresham (1988) reports that 75% of all published articles on social skills were published between 1983 and 1988. Moreover, the number of articles in this area continues to flourish in special education journals. As reported in Chapter 1, the Interagency Committee on Learning Disabilities (1987) formulated a definition of learning disabilities that includes social skills deficits as a specific learning disability. While educators agree that social skills deficits are important in planning intervention programs, controversy exists over whether they should be included among the criteria for identifying a learning disability (Bender, 1994; Gresham & Elliott, 1989b). Regardless of how the definition issue is resolved, social and emotional factors clearly must be considered to better understand and educate students with learning disabilities. Bender (1994) comments on the growing importance of social and emotional factors in the following passage:

> I believe that social/emotional development will be the next major area from which meaningful change will come for students with learning disabilities. At the very least, studies of these areas are appropriate, considering the national trend toward inclusive classrooms. Specifically, when mainstream and special education teachers share a single inclusive classroom, the classroom behavior, organizational skills, and social acceptance of students with LD will be major challenges. (p. 251)

Studies regarding certain social and emotional variables (e.g., self-concept, distractibility, and social imperceptions) have appeared in the learning disability literature since the 1970s. Recent studies, however, have focused on variables previously not examined (e.g., depression and suicide, anxiety, temperament, and loneliness). Findings from these recent studies have generated new concerns regarding the social, emotional, and behavior development of individuals with learning disabilities. The next three major sections of this chapter present findings and perspectives regarding variables concerning the social development, emotional development, and behavior development of individuals with learning disabilities. Table 15.1 includes profiles of students and related interventions for selected social, emotional, and behavior characteristics that may be present in some students with learning disabilities.

SOCIAL DEVELOPMENT

Problems with peer relationships at an early age are strong predictors of difficulties later in life. Given the importance of effective social functioning and the tendency for many students with learning disabilities to have problems with social functioning, it is imperative that educators understand social development and related interventions. The social status of students with learning disabilities has received considerable attention because it is considered to be a reliable predictor of maladjustment, criminality, and school dropout (Vaughn, McIntosh, Schumm, Haager, & Callwood, 1993). Unfortunately, many factors impede the development of positive social relationships for individuals with learning disabilities (e.g., information-processing difficulties, immaturity, inattentiveness, hyperactivity, poor self-esteem, difficulty expressing feelings, and reactions to failure experiences) (Smith, 1994). Because of the interrelatedness of the numerous factors that influence social development, it is difficult to identify discrete variables for study and discussion; however, after reviewing the research on the social development of students with learning disabilities, it appears log-

TABLE 15.1
Profiles of Students and Related Interventions for Selected Social, Emotional, and Behavior Characteristics

Social Skills Deficits

Nobody seems to like Barry. He often is called rude or inconsiderate. For example, he may continue to relate the details of a neighborhood rumor even though the face of one of his classmates is red with embarrassment, or he thoughtlessly may interrupt a serious conversation between two adults. He cannot tell when his listeners have lost interest. To help Barry identify critical social and nonverbal cues, his teacher involves him in role playing and games such as Charades. A social skills curriculum also is used.

Poor Self-Concept

Melanie, a secondary school student, has faced repeated failure and frustration throughout her school years. She has few friends and seldom initiates social interactions or takes part in school activities. When given an academic task, Melanie frequently responds, "That's too hard for me. I can't do it." Melanie's English teacher, who has taken an individual interest in her, has minimized her anxiety about failure through the use of support and success techniques. The teacher is helping Melanie attribute her failures to insufficient effort and praises her for effort regardless of the accuracy of her responses. She also uses Melanie as a peer tutor to enhance her feelings of self-worth.

Dependency

As a young child, Brad was very dependent on his mother. She gave him excessive attention and assistance. Now, he frequently turns to his teacher with requests such as "Help me" or "Show me how." Brad's teacher is trying to provide him with appropriate academic tasks and success experiences and is reinforcing him for effort. Brad also works independently with self-correcting materials and computer software programs that provide him with immediate feedback without the teacher being present.

Loneliness

Tessa usually works, plays, and eats alone. She sits quietly at her desk, staring into space, rather than working or participating in discussions. She seldom willingly joins group activities or even initiates a conversation. She does not share and frequently makes negative comments that reduce the likelihood of further interaction (e.g., "You sure are dumb. Don't you know how to do anything right?"). Tessa's teacher is providing her with much support and praise and gradually is encouraging various interpersonal relationships. Peer teaching and instructional games in which Tessa is paired with a competent, accepting student are providing Tessa with appropriate peer contact. The teacher systematically reinforces any group participation or positive social interaction.

Disruptive Behavior

Larry is often out of his seat or yelling across the room. He starts fights over minor incidents, such as tripping or butting in line. Larry's teacher is using social skills training and behavior modification techniques to reduce his disruptive behavior. She reinforces and praises him for appropriate behavior and ignores him as much as possible when he is being disruptive. When she must reprimand him, she does so quietly so that others cannot hear.

Hyperactivity

Richard's mother describes her son as having been in a state of perpetual motion since he was very young. It seems impossible for him to sit still for even a few minutes. At mealtime, he quickly stuffs his food in his mouth and is then once again on the go. In the classroom Richard also is easily excitable and constantly in motion. For example, he frequently is out of his seat, shuffling papers, moving his feet or legs, or tapping his pencil on his desk. Richard's activity level causes him to have frequent accidents (e.g., while riding his bicycle), and he sometimes unintentionally hurts a classmate when playing too rough on the playground. Richard takes Ritalin every morning under his doctor's prescription, and his classroom teacher structures Richard's daily work schedule according to his attention span, reinforces him when he is less active, and frequently allows him to perform tasks that permit him to move about the room.

Distractibility

According to her teacher, Amy is highly distractible and has a short attention span. She can work on an assignment for a short time, but she is diverted quickly by any noise or motion in the room. She stares out the window or daydreams, and her assignments go uncompleted. Her teacher uses a carrel to isolate Amy from potentially distracting auditory and visual stimuli. She also encourages Amy to use verbal mediation (i.e., quietly talking to herself about what she is doing) while performing a task and gives her praise for on-task behavior.

Impulsivity

Jane's impulsivity is evident in class. She is usually the first person to complete and hand in a worksheet, always without checking the accuracy of her responses. Jane's grades in math especially have been affected by her tendency to respond impulsively, even though she usually can correct a wrong response when given the opportunity. She talks out of turn and without thinking says things that may hurt someone's feelings. Jane's teacher is encouraging her to pause before acting or speaking. In math her teacher has Jane estimate the answers and check her work. Also, through contingency contracts Jane is reinforced according to an accuracy criterion (percent correct) for each task.

ical to discuss social development in terms of social skills, social acceptance, and social competence.

Social Skills

The social skills deficits of students with learning disabilities are receiving extensive attention. In comprehensive reviews, Gresham (1988) and Smith (1994) support the position that many students with learning disabilities clearly exhibit social skills deficits. Some examples of social skills in which students with learning disabilities lack competence include greeting someone, accepting criticism, receiving compliments, saying no, and giving positive feedback. Tur-Kaspa and Bryan (1994) compared the social information-processing skills of students with learning disabilities with the skills of students who were low achievers and average achievers. Basically the task involved listening to vignettes and offering solutions to presented social situations. The students with learning disabilities performed significantly less competently than the average-achieving students in generating quality solutions. Moreover, the students with learning disabilities exhibited unique problems in the encoding of social information and in their inclination to recommend incompetent self-generated solutions. Tur-Kaspa and Bryan note a developmental trend in the processing of social information and report that the social information-processing deficits of students with learning disabilities cannot be attributed solely to low academic achievement or weaknesses in receptive or expressive vocabulary.

Many educators claim that problems in social skills are as debilitating as academic problems to students with learning disabilities. The low social status of students with learning disabilities and the rejection they encounter in inclusive settings have stimulated the surge of interest in their social skills deficits (Roberts & Mather, 1995). In a survey of 299 learning disabilities resource room teachers, Baum, Duffelmeyer, and Geelan (1988) report that teachers believed that 38% of the 1,478 students they served had deficits in social functioning. The results were consistent across age groups. Because most students studied in research on learning disabilities are male, Ritter (1989) examined the social competence of adolescent females with learning disabilities. He found that girls with learning disabilities, like boys with learning disabilities, exhibit significantly poorer social competence than youngsters without disabilities of the same age and gender.

The social skills deficits of some students with learning disabilities are caused by their inability to understand social cues. For example, they do not react appropriately to others' facial expressions, hand and arm gestures, posture, tone of voice, or general moods. Research (Bryan & Bryan, 1986) indicates that these students often do not grasp the significance of nonverbal communication (i.e., judging emotions or assessing affective expressions). For example, the child with learning disabilities may confuse the emotion of embarrassment with that of joy and thus be viewed as insensitive toward another individual's feelings. Minskoff (1980a, 1980b) offers ways to help teach these social perceptions. Moreover, Gresham and Reschly (1986) note that some students with learning disabilities exhibit social skills deficits in task-related behaviors (e.g., completing tasks, on-task behavior, and following directions) and in interpersonal and self-related behaviors (e.g., helping others, expressing feelings, and having a positive self-attitude).

Social Acceptance

Social acceptance involves being welcomed by peers and is an important issue when students with learning disabilities are placed in general education classes. Social acceptance is highlighted when peers invite students with learning disabilities to sit with them at lunch or play together during recess. If a student consistently is rejected from social activities and the rejections are unrelated to the student's ability in that specific area, social isolation results. Social isolation often leads to poor self-concept or sadness. Another negative outcome of social isolation is its effect on the victim's academic performance. The recipient may not be chosen to participate in debates or may be left out of cooperative learning activities. Finally, social isolation differs from social rejection. Social isolation is a passive condition in which a student goes unnoticed, whereas social rejection is an aggressive event in which the student may be rejected actively because of annoying behaviors or poor hygiene.

The most popular and accurate measure of social acceptance is peer ratings. This measure provides actual data on the frequency with which students without disabilities accept students with disabilities in classroom and extracurricular activities. Ochoa and Olivarez (1995) conducted a meta-analysis of 17 peer-rating sociometric studies of students with learning disabilities. They note that 20 years of peer-rating sociometric research unequivocally show that individuals with learning disabilities have lower social acceptance than their peers without disabilities. These findings also are supported by ratings from teachers and parents. Research on social status supports several findings:

1. Low social acceptance of students with learning disabilities occurs across all grade levels and across work and play settings (Bender, 1995; Ochoa & Olivarez, 1995).
2. Low social acceptance does not exist for all students with learning disabilities. For example, Conderman (1995) found that attractiveness and athletic prowess positively influenced the social acceptance of students with learning disabilities. Kistner and Gatlin (1989) found that most of the students with learning disabilities in their study were accepted by their classmates. Moreover, in a comparison of students with learning disabilities with other achievement groups of peers, Vaughn et al. (1993) found that students with learning disabilities and students with higher academic achievement did not differ significantly on the number of reciprocal friendships.
3. Low social acceptance of students with learning disabilities appears to be stable with different classmates across time and continues into adulthood.

Several researchers discuss some of the primary reasons that students with learning disabilities experience low social acceptance. Kistner and Gatlin (1989) found that acting-out behavior and withdrawal are variables that lead to low social acceptance of students with learning disabilities. La Greca and Stone (1990) report that low academic achievement is a factor in the low social acceptance of some students with learning disabilities. Moreover, Swanson and Malone (1992) maintain that immaturity, aggression, and personality problems are factors that influence the low social acceptance of students with learning disabilities. It appears that the behavior characteristics of students with learning disabilities need to be examined within the context of five social acceptance groupings: popular, rejected, neglected, controversial, and average (Ochoa & Olivarez, 1995).

The collective findings of peer perceptions of students with learning disabilities indicate that enough students with learning disabilities experience low social status to warrant further study. However, not all youngsters with learning disabilities experience peer group rejection. The finding that achievement and IQ appear unrelated to social status (Kistner & Gatlin, 1989) suggests that many students with learning disabilities exhibit social and emotional problems that damage peer relations. For example, the relationship of rejection to withdrawal and acting-out behaviors is germane to understanding peer relations and planning interventions. Moreover, the need to further explore gender differences in social status is apparent. Gender differences appear to exist, but clear patterns are not present across research studies. Many researchers claim that the social status data have implications for identifying

subgroups of students with learning disabilities. Finally, the heterogeneity of the population with learning disabilities is apparent in the peer perception data. Perhaps future research will help identify meaningful subgroups of students with learning disabilities and facilitate the development and use of more effective interventions.

Several researchers (Bender, 1995; Ochoa & Olivarez, 1995; Roberts & Mather, 1995) maintain that the anticipated benefits of social integration or inclusion have not been achieved for students with learning disabilities. Interventions are needed to facilitate the integration and social acceptance of students with learning disabilities in inclusive settings.

Social Competence

Social competence is a global construct that involves the interaction of personality development variables and social interaction factors (Bender, 1995). Rosenthal (1992) claims that psychological development depends on successful interactions with others and that many of the emotional factors (e.g., self-concept, learned helplessness, and dependency) exhibited by students with learning disabilities evolve as a function of social interactions. Because social competence is multidimensional, researchers use an array of measures to define and assess it. Vaughn and Haager (1994) provide one of the most advanced conceptualizations of social competence. They maintain that social competence represents an interaction and an interrelationship among four components: (a) peer relations as measured by social acceptance, (b) social cognition as measured by self-concept, (c) behavior problems as measured by a reputable behavior problem checklist, and (d) social skills as measured by a respectable social skills rating scale for teachers.

In the area of learning disabilities, social competence has been researched extensively during the past 15 years. Bender and Wall (1994) found 75 studies since 1984 regarding the social competence of individuals with learning disabilities. In a longitudinal study, Vaughn and Haager (1994) compared social competence of students with learning disabilities, low-achieving students, and average- and high-achieving students over a 6-year period. They found that over time students with learning disabilities displayed the same trends on all aspects of social competence as students without disabilities. Students with learning disabilities and low-achieving students were similar on all measures of social competence; however, they had significantly lower social skills and more behavior problems than the average- and high-achieving students. Self-concept or peer acceptance scores were similar for all groups.

Overall, a substantial body of research indicates that many students with learning disabilities have deficits in social competence (Bender & Wall, 1994). Moreover, Mellard and Hazel (1992) note that social competence deficits become more acute during the preadolescent years and that social incompetence is an important factor in postsecondary maladjustments of students with learning disabilities. In spite of these general conclusions regarding the social incompetence of individuals with learning disabilities, a growing body of research indicates that social incompetence is not implicit in learning disabilities. Numerous studies have found more similarities than differences among students with and without learning disabilities. This finding has been especially indicative of adolescents with learning disabilities (Coleman & Minnett, 1992/1993; Sabornie, 1990; Tur-Kaspa & Bryan, 1995).

In comparison studies of social competence among students with and without learning disabilities, Coleman and Minnett (1992/1993) and Haager and Vaughn (1995) found that social competence is not a defining characteristic of learning disabilities. Coleman and Minnett state, "We must guard against allowing the disproportionately high rate of social rejection among children with LD to lure us into the generalization that LD and social deficits are linked causally" (p. 245). Haager and Vaughn maintain that academic underachievement may be the only common characteristic of individuals with learning disabilities. Given the heterogeneous nature of learning disabilities, extensive efforts are needed to identify the subgroups that experience inherent social incompetence (Haager & Vaughn, 1995; Tur-Kaspa & Bryan, 1995). These youngsters need to be understood, and a portion of instructional time should be devoted to improving social competencies. Selected interventions are provided later in this chapter.

EMOTIONAL DEVELOPMENT

Emotional factors involve a person's perception or thoughts about oneself and include such variables as self-concept, anxiety, depression, and self-efficacy. Learning disabilities can influence emotional development negatively by causing the student to face excessive academic failure and frustration. While not all students with learning disabilities have problems in emotional development, many may exhibit one or several of the characteristics discussed in the following sections.

Self-Concept

In a review of 27 studies, Bender and Wall (1994) conclude that students with learning disabilities exhibit lower self-concepts and lower perceived academic competence than peers without disabilities. Moreover, they note that research suggests that lower overall self-concept affects social and academic achievement. Because students with learning disabilities suffer repeated academic failure, disappointments, and frustrations, it is not surprising that many of them have low feelings of self-worth. Some students may even refuse to try a task due to fear of failure.

Bryan (1986) discusses self-concept in terms of academics and general self-worth. She found that the self-concepts of students with learning disabilities regarding academic performance are more negative than those of their peers without disabilities, whereas their general feelings of self-worth are equivalent to their peers without disabilities. The position that many students with learning disabilities have positive overall self-concepts but negative self-concepts regarding their academic competence has received substantial support. Montgomery (1994) and Kloomok and Cosden (1994) found that students with learning disabilities exhibited equivalent self-concepts to students without disabilities in nonacademic areas (i.e., appearance, social, and family) but had significantly more negative self-concepts in the areas of academics and competence. These studies underscore the need to consider the multidimensional nature of self-concept in studying students with learning disabilities.

Kistner, Haskett, White, and Robbins (1987) found a subgroup of students with learning disabilities who hold unrealistically negative or positive opinions of themselves. In general, research findings are encouraging in that many students with learning disabilities express positive views about their overall self-worth. The possibility of a subgroup of students who are overly negative or positive about their self-worth needs more study. Given the heterogeneity of learning disabilities, some variances in self-perceptions are expected across subgroups of students.

Motivation

In a review of 14 studies on motivation, Bender and Wall (1994) report that elementary students with learning disabilities have less academic self-regulation and lower motivation for on-task behavior than their peers without disabilities. Furthermore, they report that college students with learning disabilities exhibit the capacity to use coping strategies to compensate for their processing and skill deficits. Bender and Wall note that college students' use of compensations suggests that motivation variables may exist along a maturation continuum.

Given the repeated academic failure that many students with learning disabilities experience, it is not surprising that they are less motivated to perform than their peers without disabilities. When early attempts to succeed in school meet with failure, it is common for students to believe that success is beyond their abilities and efforts. Consequently, they develop a learned helplessness and lose their intrinsic motivation to prove their competence. Thus, they become externally motivated because they believe that success is dependent upon external factors and beyond their control (Smith, 1994).

Learned helplessness and external motivation may lead to dependency behavior. Many students with learning disabilities exhibit overdependence on parents, teachers, and others by requiring excessive help, reassurance, and assistance in various activities. When such students are confronted with difficulties in performing tasks they see others do or that the social environment requires of them, they may revert to helplessness and dependency as strategies of coping. Children can learn to be excessively dependent if adults continue to do things for them or encourage them to get help even with things that they could do or learn to do. Lack of academic success also can lead to an excessive need for assistance and reassurance. One indication of the dependency of students with learning disabilities is their vulnerability to peer pressure. Several studies indicate that students with learning disabilities are more willing than their normally achieving classmates to succumb to peer pressure to engage in antisocial actions (Bryan, Pearl, & Fallon, 1989).

Anxiety

The concept of anxiety that concerns psychologists is trait anxiety, which involves a persistent feeling of anxiousness that is unrelated to environmental events or hazards (Bender, 1995). Research indicates that students with learning disabilities have higher scores on measures of anxiety, worry, and oversensitivity than their peers without disabilities, and they have lower scores on autonomy levels (Margalit & Shulman, 1986). Also, Margalit and Raviv (1984) found a higher prevalence of minor somatic complaints among students with learning disabilities. Bender notes that the limited number of studies in the area of learning disabilities and anxiety precludes any definitive positions. Moreover, because of the preliminary nature of the results, no theorists report specific intervention recommendations for trait anxiety among students with learning disabilities.

Loneliness

Given the affective differences (e.g., locus of control, self-concept, and anxiety) of individuals with and without learning disabilities, researchers are beginning to examine more emotional variables such as loneliness, depression, and suicide. Only a few studies on loneliness are reported, but they highlight the need to examine the relationship of loneliness and learning disabilities (Bender & Wall, 1994). Existing studies (Margalit & Ben-Dov, 1992; Sabornie, 1994) suggest that children as well as adolescents with learning disabilities exhibit more loneliness than their peers without disabilities.

In a meta-analysis of 25 studies that compared students with learning disabilities with their normally achieving peers, Bender and Smith (1990) report that students with learning disabilities exhibit significantly more shy and withdrawn behavior than do their normally achieving peers. Social withdrawal may result from the student's previous failures at interaction or a feeling of incompetence because of academic failure. Some students may become so socially isolated that they are unable to interact in a positive manner with peers or adults. Because loneliness frequently appears within the context of depression and suicide, it is essential to develop interventions and preventive strategies. In a review of the research, Bender and Wall (1994) were unable to find intervention studies that targeted loneliness.

Depression and Suicide

An examination of depression in students with learning disabilities is important for two reasons. First, a depressed state of existence is a miserable condition for an individual to endure. Second, depression is highly related to suicide. Estimates indicate that depression is a factor in 60% of suicide cases (Wright-Strawderman & Watson, 1992). Some symptoms of depression in children include somatic complaints, withdrawal, lying, aggression, poor self-concept, and poor peer interactions, whereas symptoms in adolescents and adults include helplessness, suicidal ideation, drug abuse, somatic complaints, and social withdrawal (Wright-Strawderman & Watson, 1992). Other symptoms across ages include change in appetite or weight, fatigue, guilt, decreased concentration, agitation, sleep disturbance, and loss of energy (Emslie, Kennard, & Kowatch, 1995).

Overall, most researchers maintain that depression is higher among individuals with learning disabilities than individuals without disabilities (Bender & Wall, 1994; Huntington & Bender, 1993; Wright-Strawderman & Watson, 1992). However, the prevalence of depression among individuals with learning disabilities varies considerably among studies (i.e., from 10% to 36%) (Maag & Reid, 1994; Wright-Strawderman & Watson, 1992). The variations appear due to (a) different measures of depression, (b) heterogeneity of learning disabilities, (c) different self-perceptions of academic competence, and (d) interrelatedness of depression with behavior disorders and self-concept (Heath, 1995; Maag & Reid, 1994). In a study of students with learning disabilities with similar achievement levels, Heath found that depressed students with learning disabilities had more negative and realistic perceptions of their academic competence than nondepressed students with learning disabilities. Because the negative self-perceptions about academic competence among students with learning disabilities appear to reflect a reality rather than a distortion, this cognitive variable should be considered in assessing and treating depression.

Bender (1995) notes that suicide and suicide attempts among individuals with learning disabilities is disheartening. For example, in a study of children under age 15 who committed suicide during a 3-year period, Peck (1985) found that 50% were identified as having learning disabilities, compared with 5% to 8% in the general population. Other studies indicate that suicide ideation (i.e., thoughts of suicide) and parasuicide (i.e., unsuccessful suicide attempts) appear to be more common among students with learning disabilities (Huntington & Bender, 1993). Depression and suicidal thoughts must not be ignored. Suggestions for helping students at risk of suicide are presented later in this chapter.

Temperament

Research indicates that certain personality traits are relatively stable in very young children. For example, it appears that task persistence and responses to various stimuli are established in late infancy (Goldsmith & Gottesman, 1981). These temperament variables typically are measured by teacher or parent ratings regarding how a child responds in specific settings. Current research supports the position that children with learning disabilities show less task persistence and exhibit less social flexibility than their peers without disabilities (Bender, 1995; Keogh, 1983).

BEHAVIOR DEVELOPMENT

Teachers consistently rate students with learning disabilities as exhibiting more problem behaviors than students without learning disabilities; however, the problem behaviors are similar to those of students who are low achievers. These problem behaviors frequently interfere with academic achievement and social relationships and contribute to social incompetence. This section presents behavior characteristics across the following domains: adaptive behavior, disruptive behavior, hyperactivity, inattention and distractibility, impulsivity, and substance abuse.

Adaptive Behavior

Adaptive behavior or *adaptivity* "is a proactive process through which individuals organize their lives in purposeful, flexible, and advantageous ways to meet the demands of multiple environments" (Weller, Watteyne, Herbert, & Crelly, 1994, p. 282). Because adaptive behavior is a multidimensional variable, Weller and Strawser (1981) divide it into four domains: social coping, relationships, pragmatic language, and production (i.e., how one produces work). In a literature review, Bender and Wall (1994) found 15 studies conducted since 1984 on adaptive behavior and learning disabilities. They note that the existing research clearly indicates that individuals with learning disabilities exhibit adaptive behavior deficits that are related to underachievement and maladaptive behavior. The adaptive behavior deficits of individuals with learning disabilities continue into adulthood and interfere with postsecondary education and quality employment (Mellard & Hazel, 1992; Weller et al., 1994).

Bender and Golden (1988) examined mainstream teacher ratings of children with and without learning disabilities on the *Weller-Strawser Scales of Adaptive Behavior* (Weller & Strawser, 1981) and the *Walker Problem Behavior Identification Checklist* (Walker, 1983). (These two measures are discussed later in Tables 15.2 and 15.3.) Ratings on both measures revealed that students with learning disabilities had significantly less desirable adaptive behavior than their peers without disabilities. On adaptive behavior, the students with learning disabilities rated less desirable in all subtests (i.e., social coping, relationships, pragmatic language, and production). Because adaptive behavior includes measures of social coping and the pragmatic use of language in social situations, Bender and Golden note that it may be a broader construct than classroom behavior, and they suggest that it be considered in the learning disabilities identification process. In another study, Bender and Golden (1989) found that teacher rating scores of students with learning disabilities on the Weller-Strawser scales and the Walker checklist were highly correlated. They note that this finding suggests that teachers view the problem behaviors of students with learning disabilities as a major determinant of adaptive behavior in the classroom.

Disruptive Behavior

Disruptive behavior generally includes acts that interrupt or interfere with appropriate activities. Disruptive behavior inhibits the learning or work of others and requires the teacher or supervisor to stop productive events and deal with the disruption. The behavior problems of numerous students with learning disabilities are well documented (Bender & Smith, 1990; McKinney & Feagans, 1984). Some students display disruptive aggressive behavior toward others (e.g., fighting and acting out). Their low tolerance for frustration often leads to outbursts that include name calling, sarcasm, or swearing. The disruptive behavior may be the result of social skills deficits or frustration over lack of academic success. These behavior problems frequently lead to disruptive events in inclusive classrooms and prompt educators to view the behavior difficulties of students with learning disabilities as serious deterrents to their school success.

Bender and Wall (1994) note that the disruptive behavior of young students with learning disabilities typically is limited to mild inappropriate behaviors; however, the disruptive behavior of some students with learning disabilities becomes more severe (i.e., overt hostility, delinquency, or violence) immediately prior to adolescence. Pearl and Bryan (1992) maintain that the misperception of social cues and the desire for relationships combine with the susceptibility of adolescent students with learning disabilities to give in to peer pressure and result in more severe disruptions. Disruptive behavior patterns cause students with learning disabilities to be at higher risk for delinquency than higher-achieving students.

Hyperactivity

Hyperactive individuals engage in excessive motor activity or lack self-control (Bender & Wall, 1994). Many have short attention spans and are easily distracted, restless, clumsy, and irritable. These youngsters may show unusually high levels of motor activity when asked to perform a specific structured task; however, in unstructured situations in which the child is not required to be task oriented, activity levels may be similar to those of nonhyperactive children. Thus, the hyperactive behavior may be situationally specific and is more likely to involve difficulties in sustaining attention rather than gross motor problems.

The comorbidity of attention-deficit hyperactivity disorder and learning disabilities is prevalent in the literature. DeLong (1995) reports that estimates of the rate of attention-deficit hyperactivity disorder in the population labeled as having learning disabilities range from 41% to 80%. Because of the heterogeneity among individuals with attention-deficit hyperactivity disorder and learning disabilities, numerous researchers (Lyon, 1985; Riccio, Gonzalez, & Hynd, 1994) point out the need to examine the subtypes that are emerging among this population. An examination of the subtypes enhances understanding of these individuals and reduces the heterogeneity.

Attention-deficit hyperactivity tends to increase until age 3 and then gradually diminish until adolescence. Although hyperactivity decreases in many adolescents with learning disabilities, other manifestations may include inattentiveness, low self-esteem, behavior problems, or depression (Shaywitz, 1987).

Among the theories concerning the cause of hyperactive behavior are central nervous system dysfunction (Hynd, Hern, Voeller, & Marshall, 1991; Shaywitz, 1987), genetic factors (Stewart, 1970), biochemical imbalances (Silver, 1971), diet (Feingold, 1974), and social-cultural changes in the environment (Block, 1977). Because the causes of hyperactivity vary among individuals, numerous remediation techniques have been offered. The two most widely used approaches include medical management (i.e., the use of stimulant drugs such as Ritalin) and behavior management (e.g., the use of applied behavior analysis techniques). (Chapter 3 discusses the medical aspects of hyperactivity.)

Inattention and Distractibility

The majority of the research on attention and learning disabilities indicates that students with learning disabilities are deficit in each aspect of attention (i.e., time on task, focus of attention, and selective attention) and frequently are perceived as being distractible (Bender, 1995). McKinney, McClure, and Feagans (1982) indicate that students with learning disabilities spend less time on their work and more time in nonproductive behavior than do their peers without disabilities. Thus, many students with learning disabilities have difficulty maintaining concentration on a target stimulus or activity when competing stimuli or activities are in the same setting. The students become easily distracted by irrelevant or inappropriate stimuli. In a meta-analysis of 25 studies in which the classroom behavior of students with learning disabilities was compared with the behavior of students without disabilities, Bender and Smith (1990) report that students with learning disabilities are significantly more distractible and off task than their peers without disabilities. In addition, they note that the distractibility of students with learning disabilities decreases with age (i.e., distractibility is lower in secondary school students). Distractibility also is a prominent factor in students with attention-deficit hyperactivity disorder.

Impulsivity

Many students with learning disabilities react quickly without thinking about alternative ways of responding. From a review of the research, Bender and Wall (1994) report that impulsivity includes attention skill deficits and impulsive responding. They found that students with learning disabilities exceed normative ranges of impulsivity on measures of impulsivity and exhibit attention deficits on attention measures. Keogh (1977) suggests that this impulsive style is detrimental to successful school performance. Moreover, Waldie and Spreen (1993) found that impulsivity and poor judgment were factors in discriminating persisting from nonpersisting delinquency in youth with learning disabilities.

Torgesen (1982) notes that impulsive responding may be caused by a lack of alternative cognitive strategies that provide the student with other ways of coping with learning tasks. An impulsive student talks or acts quickly without considering the consequences. For example, on multiple-choice test items, the impulsive student may immediately select one response without reflecting on the other available answers. Also, an impulsive child may rush to be first in line without realizing that someone could be knocked down. Thus, such children may exhibit poor academic and social skills.

Substance Abuse

The degree of alcohol and other drug use among America's youth is greater than in any other industrialized nation in the world (Johnston, O'Malley, & Bachman, 1989). Substance abuse among adolescents is a national issue. Karacostas and Fisher (1993) maintain that students with learning disabilities display many of the demographic, academic, and socio-psychological characteristics (e.g., male, low socioeconomic status, low achievement, misconduct, low self-esteem, and adaptive behavior problems) associated with substance abuse. Yet substance abuse among individuals with learning disabilities has received scant attention only recently. For example, Karacostas and Fisher compared chemical dependency among students with and without learning disabilities. They report that the presence or absence of a learning disability was a better predictor of chemical dependency or nonchemical dependency than gender, family composition, socioeconomic status, age, or ethnicity. Specifically, they found that 30 students out of 191 adolescents (88 with learning disabilities; 103 without disabilities) were chemically dependent and that 70% of these were youngsters with learning disabilities. Moreover, Maag, Irvin, Reid, and Vasa (1994) compared substance use among students with and without learning disabilities and found that tobacco and marijuana use were higher for adolescents with learning disabilities; however, no differences were found for alcohol use. These preliminary findings alert educators to seek more information about substance use among individuals with learning disabilities and to develop effective "just say no" intervention strategies.

ETIOLOGY OF SOCIAL AND EMOTIONAL BEHAVIOR PROBLEMS

Bryan and Bryan (1986) discuss several hypotheses about the cause of social difficulties of students with learning disabilities. They note that these students violate the rules governing social behavior and, while they may be knowledgeable about social norms, they may not conform to them. They lack awareness or ability to understand the emotions, motives, and intentions of other people. They are deficient in role-taking abilities and have difficulty understanding and taking the viewpoints of other people. Some are poorer communicators than their peers. They may lack appropriate classroom behavior and not focus as much on academic tasks as do their normally achieving classmates.

Interacting factors make it difficult to determine an exact causal relationship between learning disabilities and social and emotional behavior problems. Several of the most prominent hypotheses concerning etiology are primary cause, secondary cause, and social learning theory (Gresham & Elliott, 1989b).

Primary Cause

The primary cause position maintains that social and emotional behavior problems are caused by organic factors. This position is apparent in the definition of *learning disabilities* put forth by the Interagency Committee of Learning Disabilities (1987). The definition states that social skills deficits are presumed to result from central nervous system dysfunction. To date, the central nervous system dysfunction theory remains speculative. Gresham and Elliott (1989b) report that little evidence exists to suggest that altered central nervous system dysfunctions result in a deficit area as specific as social skills. Moreover, they note a lack of studies to support the position that localized brain dysfunctions cause specific social skills deficits.

Weinberg, Harper, and Brumback (1995) note that computerized brain imaging has enabled researchers to localize cerebral cortical lesions accurately and correlate these with specific communication and behavioral dysfunctions in adults. Currently, researchers are able to hypothesize the location of select social and emotional dysfunctions of individuals with learning disabilities. These brain localizations include areas that seem to control mood states such as mania and depression. Keogh and Bernheimer (1995), however, caution researchers about the uncertainty of the neurological and learning disabilities relationship. They note that neurological indices continue to lack accuracy in predicting individual learning disabilities.

Various theories have been advanced that propose that social and emotional behavior problems are organically based. Biochemical disturbances, nutritional irregularities, allergies, and genetic factors are some of the organically oriented positions applied to individuals with learning disabilities. (Chapter 3 discusses these positions and the controversies concerning them.)

Secondary Cause

The secondary cause position views social and emotional behavior problems as being "side effects," or secondary to academic problems.

According to this position, students with learning disabilities find themselves in situations in which they continually are frustrated with academic work, and their failure to achieve creates secondary social and emotional behavior problems. Correlational data between academic achievement and social skills are mixed. Some studies report a positive relationship, whereas others report no significant relationships. Moreover, correlational data do not allow for cause-effect claims. For example, it is reasonable to consider that academic problems result in social and emotional behavior problems and vice versa. Finally, it is plausible to assume that academic problems result in social and emotional behavior problems for some students with learning disabilities but not for others. This position gains credence when the heterogeneous nature of students with learning disabilities is considered.

Social Learning Theory

The social learning theory maintains that social skills deficits result from the failure to acquire or perform social behaviors. This view draws from Bandura's (1977) position that a distinction exists between acquisition and performance deficits. Within this orientation, Gresham (1981) separates social skills problems into social skills deficits and social performance deficits. Social skills deficits result from a failure to learn a social skill because of limited opportunities to acquire it or to view models of appropriate social behavior. Social performance deficits result from limited opportunities to perform social skills or from a lack of reinforcement for socially appropriate behaviors. Students with social performance deficits are not motivated to perform appropriately. Likewise, Gresham (1988) makes similar distinctions between self-control skill deficits and self-control performance deficits.

Some advantages of the social learning theory position to social and emotional behavior problems include the following:

1. Social and emotional behaviors are treated as an important class of behaviors and are not viewed as being secondary or related to questionable causes.
2. Social learning theory allows for a functional approach to understanding and treating social skills deficits. Much data support the position that social behavior is influenced strongly by environmental events (i.e., antecedent, sequential, and consequent events). An analysis of environmental events enables the practitioner to target events that precede or follow socially skilled or interfering behaviors and manipulate these events to influence their occurrences in the appropriate direction.
3. In social learning theory, there is a direct link between assessment of social behavior and interventions (Gresham & Elliott, 1989b).

Causes and Treatments

Social and emotional behavior problems clearly are likely to result from the interaction of the student with learning disabilities and society. However, behaviors seen as problems in one context may not be viewed as such in another situation by a different observer. Thus, the existence of a problem may be the result of the reactions of others. Treatment must emphasize changing the behavior as well as the reactions to the behavior.

Whereas medical treatments often are applied for organically based problems, treatments for psychological and social causative factors can include such environmental interventions as the systematic use of applied behavior analysis or the provision of supportive surroundings. Social and emotional behavior problems of students with learning disabilities are likely the result of various interacting causes. Thus, it can be difficult to determine a specific cause for a particular problem. Many social and emotional behavior problems, regardless of their cause, will respond to several treatment strategies. Various techniques for improving social skills, emotional well-being, and behavior are presented later in this chapter.

ASSESSMENT OF SOCIAL AND EMOTIONAL BEHAVIOR

Assessment of social and emotional behavior involves the use of various types of measurement and evaluation procedures. In addition to student behavior in the classroom, a thorough assessment of social and emotional behavior factors considers student self-concept and attitudes as well as behavior outside the classroom. To provide a broad and natural picture of the student, an ecological assessment includes an evaluation of the student's behavior and status in various environments in which the student functions. Currently, no single test is sufficient to yield a comprehensive, reliable, valid, and useful assessment of social skills or emotional problems. Thus, several instruments and procedures are required to assess social and emotional behavior. Helpful information may be obtained from teachers, parents, students, and peers as well as from records of social, developmental, and educational history.

During assessment of social and emotional behavior, the type of behavior and its frequency, intensity, and duration should be considered. Assessment procedures help the teacher identify social and emotional behavior problems that require immediate attention. This section presents several techniques and measures available to assess social and emotional behavior. Included are commercial observer-rater instruments, commercial measures of adaptive behavior, self-report instruments, sociometric techniques, and naturalistic observations.

Commercial Observer-Rater Instruments

With these instruments an observer (teacher, guidance counselor, social worker, school psychologist, or family member) completes either a checklist or a rating scale. Checklists generally are used to record the presence or absence of specific characteristics or behaviors. Rating scales are designed to indicate the frequency of a particular behavior or the degree to which certain characteristics are present. Teacher ratings frequently are used to assess behavior problems in classrooms. These ratings usually are conducted through the use of published checklists, scales, or questionnaires. These formats are most useful for general screening and initial identification of student behavior problems as well as for measuring student progress over time. Inspection of Table 15.2 reveals 10 instruments for use in assessing social, emotional, and behavior problems.

Traditionally, teacher ratings of social skills have received less attention than emotional and behavior problems. Recently, however, interest in teacher ratings of social skills is receiving more attention. For example, Gresham and Elliott (1990) and Walker and McConnell (1988) authored instruments that involve teacher ratings of social skills (see Table 15.2). The teacher version of the *Social Skills Rating System* (Gresham & Elliott, 1990) features items that represent a broad range of behaviors (e.g., positive behaviors such as sharing, giving compliments, and following rules, as well as problem behaviors such as aggression, hyperactivity, and social withdrawal). Another dimension of the *Social Skills Rating System* involves the teacher specifying whether each behavior is critical, important, or unimportant for the classroom system. These ratings indicate which behaviors are priorities for social skills intervention. Gresham and Elliott (1989a) note that an important feature of the *Walker-McConnell Scale of Social Competence and School Adjustment* (Walker & McConnell, 1988) is its reliability and validity. Maag (1989) indicates that teacher ratings are valuable for identifying students and problematic behaviors that can be assessed further through naturalistic observations.

Parent ratings also have been used extensively to rate children's atypical behaviors and adaptive behavior. Included in Table 15.2 are five behavior rating instruments suitable for parent use. Parent ratings of social skills have received limited attention, but Gresham and Elliott (1990) recently developed the parent version of the

TABLE 15.2
Observer-Rater Instruments

Instrument	Age/Grade	Respondent
Behavior Assessment System for Children (Reynolds & Kamphaus, 1992)	4–18 years	Teacher, parent, student
The system provides teacher, parent, and self-reports, as well as a structured developmental history and observed classroom behavior of the student. The teacher rating scale includes items (such as "Bullies others" and "Adjusts well to new teachers") related to adaptive and problem behaviors in school settings, whereas the parent rating scale pertains to behaviors exhibited in community and home settings. The self-report measure of personality includes short true/false statements concerning personal thoughts and feelings. The teacher and parent scales use a 4-point rating scale of frequency, and all three scales yield composite scores of problem behaviors. Additional student information is obtained on the development history survey of social, psychological, developmental, educational, and medical areas, and during a 15-minute classroom observation maladaptive and adaptive behaviors are coded and recorded. Two computerized formats for easy scoring are available.		
Behavior Evaluation Scale—2 (McCarney & Leigh, 1990)	Kindergarten–12th grade	Teacher
The scale yields behavioral information about students according to five subscales: learning problems, interpersonal difficulties, inappropriate behavior, unhappiness/depression, and physical symptoms/fears. The 76 items are stated in observable and measurable terms, and raw scores are weighted according to severity and frequency of observed behaviors.		
Behavior Rating Profile—2 (Brown & Hammill, 1990)	1st–12th grade	Teacher, parent, student, peers
Six independent measures of behavior are included: teacher rating scale, student rating scale (school), parent rating scale, student rating scale (home), sociogram, and student rating scale (peer). The three student rating scales are embedded in a 60-item true/false format, and the parent and teacher rating scales each contain 30 items that the respondents classify on a 4-point scale. The sociogram provides information about the student's sociometric status within the classroom. The results of the profile can be used to identify students whose behavior is perceived to be deviant and to identify specific settings in which behavior problems are prominent. Also, the profile can be useful in identifying persons whose perceptions of a student's behaviors are different from those of other respondents.		
Comprehensive Behavior Rating Scale for Children (Neeper, Lahey, & Frick, 1990)	6–14 years	Teacher
The teacher uses a 5-point scale to indicate how descriptive each of 70 statements is of the student. Nine scales are included: inattention-disorganization, reading problems, cognitive deficits, oppositional-conduct disorder, motor hyperactivity, anxiety, sluggish tempo, daydreaming, and social competence. Thus, the scale focuses on cognitive as well as emotional and behavioral dimensions.		

TABLE 15.2
continued

Instrument	Age/Grade	Respondent
Devereux Behavior Rating Scale—School Form (Naglieri, LeBuffe, & Pfeiffer, 1993)	5–18 years	Teacher, parent
The scale is effective especially as a screening device to identify the existence of behaviors that fall within the normal range and behaviors that indicate a severe emotional disturbance. Two 40-item versions, one for children age 5 through 12 years and one for adolescents age 13 through 18 years, feature separate sets of appropriate items. The four subtests focus on interpersonal problems, inappropriate behaviors/feelings, depression, and physical symptoms/fear. Administration time is about 5 minutes, and item-level scores help identify specific problem behaviors.		
Revised Behavior Problem Checklist (Quay & Peterson, 1987)	Kindergarten–8th grade	Teacher, parent, anyone familiar with the student
A rating system distinguishes among behaviors not observed, observed but mild, and observed and severe. Problem behaviors are classified according to six domains: conduct disorder, socialized aggression, attention problems or immaturity, anxiety or withdrawal, psychotic behavior, and motor excess.		
Social-Emotional Dimension Scale (Hutton & Roberts, 1986)	5–18 years	Teacher
The 32-item norm-referenced rating scale can be used to assess students who are at risk for conduct disorders, behavior problems, or emotional disturbance. Student performance is assessed in six areas: physical/fear reaction, depressive reaction, avoidance of peer interaction, avoidance of teacher interaction, aggressive interaction, and inappropriate behavior.		
Social Skills Rating System (Gresham & Elliott, 1990)	3–18 years	Teacher, parent, student
There are three rating forms (teacher, parent, and student) that evaluate a broad range of behaviors. The social skills scale (on all three forms) evaluates positive social behaviors (such as cooperation, assertion, responsibility, empathy, and self-control). The problem behavior scale (on the teacher and parent forms) measures behaviors that can interfere with the production of social skills (such as aggression, anxiety, and hyperactivity). The academic competence scale (on the teacher form) is an index of academic functioning. Items on each scale are rated according to perceived frequency and importance. SSRS *ASSIST* software provides computerized scoring and reporting as well as behavioral objectives and suggestions for planning intervention.		
Walker-McConnel Scale of Social Competence and School Adjustment (Walker & McConnell, 1988)	Kindergarten–6th grade	Teacher
A 5-point scale format is used to measure teacher-preferred social behavior, peer-preferred social behavior, and adjustment to the behavioral demands of the classroom. The 43-item scale takes about 5 minutes per student to complete and is useful to screen and identify social deficits among elementary-age students.		
Walker Problem Behavior Identification Checklist (Walker, 1983)	Preschool–6th grade	Teacher
The checklist takes about 15 minutes to administer and consists of 50 statements describing behaviors that may interfere or compete with successful academic performance. The items are designed to measure five behavioral factors: acting out, withdrawal, distractibility, disturbed peer relations, and immaturity.		

Social Skills Rating System for parents to rate children's social skills on items in the areas of cooperation, assertion, self-control, and responsibility. An important feature of the instrument is the inclusion of a frequency dimension and an importance dimension for each social skill rated. According to Gresham and Elliott, the parent instrument differentiates children with mild disabilities from children without disabilities.

Commercial Measures of Adaptive Behavior

Adaptive behavior refers to the way an individual adjusts to the demands and changes in the physical and social environment. The interview technique frequently is used to obtain information from parents about the student's current nonacademic functioning, whereas teachers typically respond on written questionnaires concerning the student's social and emotional behavior. Adaptive behavior assessment scales generally include items for measuring personal self-sufficiency, independence in the community, and personal and social responsibility. Four measures of adaptive behavior are presented in Table 15.3.

Self-Report Instruments

Self-report techniques allow students to report on their own specific behaviors. Self-report procedures obtain information directly from the students; thus, the information is totally subjective. Its validity depends on the willingness of students to report the information and on their ability to understand and perform the task. Some commercial self-report instruments have built-in lie scales to screen for defensiveness and unrealistic levels of social desirability. Commercial self-report instruments are presented as well as the Q-sort technique and various informal techniques.

Commercial Instruments. Self-report measures are the primary means for assessing students' self-concepts and for identifying areas that cause students anxiety or concern. The students respond directly to test items concerning themselves. Table 15.4 includes seven commercial self-report instruments for assessing self-concept. Self-report instruments have several weaknesses because of the potential for bias, the desire to give responses that please, social desirability, and reading-level difficulties (Gresham & Elliott, 1989a). Because of these weaknesses, self-report measures of students' social skills are not used as widely as sociometrics, teacher ratings, and other measures. However, the self-report version of the *Social Skills Rating System* (Gresham & Elliott, 1990) represents an attempt to develop a reliable and valid self-report measure of social skills. It includes one version for 3rd through 6th grade and another for 7th through 12th grade. The scales yield scores in the areas of cooperation, assertion, self-control, and empathy. Gresham and Elliott (1990) report that the student version discriminates students with disabilities from students without disabilities.

Q-Sort Technique. The Q-sort technique is a procedure for investigating self-concept that can be used to identify areas for behavior modification (Kroth, 1973). The technique focuses on determining the degree of discrepancy between an evaluation of the "real" self and the "ideal" self. The procedure, as presented in Chapter 4, offers a way to select specific social and emotional behaviors for intervention.

The student is given a set of cards containing statements that must be sorted onto a pyramid formboard. The formboard contains nine categories that form a continuum from *most like me* to *most unlike me*. The student is given the same number of descriptor cards as there are squares in the pyramid. In sorting the items, the student must arrange the cards so that each square is used and none is left blank or used twice. First the student is asked to complete a *real sort* by sorting the items onto the formboard to best reflect the student's own beliefs about the student's classroom behavior. After the responses of the

TABLE 15.3
Measures of Adaptive Behavior

Instrument	Age/Grade	Respondent
AAMR Adaptive Behavior Scale—School (Lambert, Nihira, & Leland, 1993)	3–21 years	Teacher, parent, anyone familiar with the student
The school edition covers social and daily living skills and behaviors. Part I evaluates personal independence in daily living (e.g., independent functioning, self-direction, and responsibility). Part II measures social maladaptive behaviors (e.g., conformity, trustworthiness, and self-abusive behavior). The scale domains are grouped into five factors: personal self-sufficiency, community self-sufficiency, personal-social responsibility, personal adjustment, and social adjustment. The responder must circle the highest level of functioning demonstrated by the student, answer "yes" or "no" to a series of statements, or rate the statements in each item as occurring never, occasionally, or frequently. The scale yields standard scores and percentiles for each domain, and a software scoring and report system is available.		
Scales of Independent Behavior (Bruininks, Woodcock, Weatherman, & Hill, 1984)	Infant–adult	Teacher, parent, student, anyone familiar with the student
The instrument provides a noncognitive measure of adjustment in social, behavioral, and adaptive areas. It assesses functional independence and adaptive behavior in motor skills, social and communication skills, personal living skills, and community living skills. Also, an optional problem behavior scale focuses on general, externalized, internalized, and asocial maladaptive behaviors. Because the instrument is linked conceptually and statistically to the *Woodcock-Johnson Psycho-Educational Battery*, adaptive behavior can be measured based on cognitive ability. Administration time is 45 to 60 minutes, and a Spanish version and a computer scoring program are available.		
Vineland Adaptive Behavior Scale (Sparrow, Balla, & Cicchetti, 1984)	Birth–18 years (survey and expanded forms); 3–12 years (classroom edition)	Teacher, parent, anyone familiar with the student
Three versions are available: (a) interview edition, survey form—aids in screening or classification decisions, (b) interview edition, expanded form—provides specific prescriptive information that can be used for educational programming, and (c) classroom edition—allows for direct observation of adaptive behavior of students and uses a checklist format. The scale assesses adaptive behavior in four areas: communication, daily living skills, socialization, and motor skills. The survey and expanded forms also measure maladaptive behavior. Standard scores and percentiles are available for each area and subarea as well as total adaptive behavior, and *Vineland ASSIST* software provides helpful score conversion.		
Weller-Strawser Scales of Adaptive Behavior (Weller & Strawser, 1981)	6–12 years (elementary scale); 13–18 years (secondary scale)	Teacher
The adaptive behavior of elementary and secondary students with learning disabilities is assessed in four areas: social coping, relationships, pragmatic language, and production. Each scale consists of 35 items that present pairs of descriptions of an adaptive behavior characteristic, and the teacher marks the alternative that best describes the student's behavior. A profile is obtained of either mild-to-moderate or moderate-to-severe adaptive behavior problems in each of the areas. Recommendations for programming and environment modifications are included for each possible profile.		

TABLE 15.4
Self-report Instruments

Instrument	Age/Grade
Coopersmith Self-Esteem Inventories (Coopersmith, 1981)	8–15 years
The self-report questionnaires consist of short statements (e.g., "I'm a failure" and "I can usually take care of myself") to be answered "like me" or "unlike me." The inventories are designed to measure attitudes toward the self in social, academic, and personal contexts. The school form contains 58 items that produce a total score, a lie score, and attitude scores toward social self/peers, home/parents, and school/academics.	
Culture-Free Self-Esteem Inventories—2 (Battle, 1992)	5 years and older
The inventories contain a 60-item form (or a 30-item brief form) that measures self-esteem of students in five areas: general, peers, school, parents, and lie (defensiveness) scales. The 40-item adult form includes four areas: general, social, personal, and lie scales. Yes/no responses can be either written or spoken. The test screens for possible intervention and yields percentiles for total and subtest scores.	
Multidimensional Self-Concept Scale (Bracken, 1992)	5th–12th grade
The instrument includes six 25-item scales in the following areas: social, competence, affect, academic, family, and physical. Each area can be assessed independently. The test yields standard scores and can be administered in about 20 minutes. The manual provides specific recommendations for improving self-concept.	
Piers-Harris Children's Self-Concept Scale (Piers & Harris, 1984)	4th–12th grade
The scale covers many areas of self-concept, among which are physical appearance, social popularity, and happiness-satisfaction. The student responds with "yes" or "no" to 80 declarative statements (e.g., "I am good looking" and "My classmates make fun of me"). The items are written on a third-grade reading level, and both positive and negative statements are included. Suggested administration time is 15 to 20 minutes.	
Self-Esteem Index (Brown & Alexander, 1991)	7–18 years
This norm-referenced measure indicates how individuals perceive and value themselves. The index includes four scales: academic competence, family acceptance, peer popularity, and personal security (physical appearance and personal attributes). The student classifies each item on a scale ranging from *always true* to *always false*. In addition to a global self-esteem score, the four scales yield standard scores and percentile ranks.	
Student Self-Concept Scale (Gresham, Elliott, & Evans-Fernandez, 1992)	3rd–12th grade
The scale includes 72 items that relate to the perceived confidence and importance of specific behaviors influencing the development of a student's self-concept. The student rates items on three dimensions (self-confidence, importance, and outcome confidence) to measure self-concept in three areas: academic (e.g., reading skills and listening to teacher), social (e.g., playing with others and sharing), and self-image (e.g., general self-concept and global self-perception). The scale can be individually or group-administered in about 20 to 30 minutes.	
Tennessee Self-Concept Scale (Fitts & Roid, 1988)	13 years and older
The scale is designed to measure self-concept and includes eight general categories: identity, behavior, self-satisfaction, physical self, moral-ethical self, personal self, family self, and social self. There are 100 descriptive statements (e.g., "I have a healthy body" and "I have a lot of self control"), and each item is answered on a 5-point scale from *completely false* to *completely true*. The scale is written at a fourth-grade reading level and requires about 10 to 20 minutes to complete.	

real sort are recorded, the student is asked to complete an *ideal sort* in which the same items are arranged on the formboard to indicate how the student would *like* to be in daily classroom activities. During sorting, the student may rearrange the cards as many times as needed. The teacher compares the student's responses on the real sort with the responses on the ideal sort and notes items that differ greatly—that is, by 4 points or more. These items can become target behaviors for intervention.

The behavioral Q-sort also can be administered to parents or teachers. Thus, comparisons can be made between others' perceptions of the student's school behavior (both real and ideal) and the student's own perceptions. The teacher's rating of the student's behavior can be compared with the student's own rating. When the comparisons on a specific behavior (such as "Pays attention to work") are very different, that behavior can be selected for examination and intervention.

Informal Self-Report Techniques. Informal self-report techniques provide a general idea of a student's problems. Each student who participates should be assured that the information provided is confidential and that only honest answers are helpful to the teacher. Wallace, Larsen, and Elksnin (1992) note that teacher-developed measures of self-concept have reliability and validity levels that are similar to those of widely used research instruments to assess students' self-concepts. Four frequently used informal self-report techniques are checklists, questionnaires, interviews, and autobiographies.

In a teacher-made checklist, students are asked to indicate which behaviors or descriptions they believe apply (such as "Has a lot of friends," "Finishes classwork," and "Gets mad quickly"). Checklists are easy to administer and can give the teacher some insights concerning how the students view themselves. For example, students are presented with a list of adjectives and are instructed to check all words they consider to be descriptive of themselves. Sample items include the following:

_______absent-minded	_______noisy
_______athletic	_______friendly
_______lonely	_______cooperative
_______intelligent	_______quiet
_______likable	_______happy

Several kinds of questionnaires are designed to obtain information about a student's personal, social, and emotional behaviors. The yes/no or true/false format is useful and easy to administer:

1. Are you usually very friendly? Yes No
2. Do you get mad often? Yes No
3. I usually like to be by myself. True False

Questionnaires using open-ended questions or sentence completion require students to complete the statements. Thus, students express themselves in their own words. Such a format requires more time and ability on the part of the students, but it often yields more meaningful information than the yes/no or true/false format. Sample items from a sentence completion questionnaire include the following:

1. I work best when ____________________.
2. I get angry when ____________________.
3. When I feel lonely I __________________.

Specific information also can be obtained from students through interviews. They provide an opportunity for students to express opinions and feelings about themselves and others. Interview techniques even can be extended into daily conversations, providing a flexible and ongoing source of information. In an interview, the teacher should relate the discussion questions to the student's particular area of difficulty. The interview is most effective when conducted in private and rapport is established that reflects an honest interest in the student. Interview questions should be kept to a minimum and should be broad instead of specific; in this way, the student is required to develop a topic or express an opinion. If the teacher receives proper consent, the interview can be recorded so that it is available for later study. If recording is not possible, note taking during the interview should be minimal but immediate.

In autobiographies, students give a written account of their lives or reveal their feelings about themselves and others. Personal experiences, ambitions, or interests can be described. Students who have difficulty in expressive writing can record oral presentations. The type of autobiography depends upon the age and maturity of the student. Students can be asked to respond to specific questions or be given a topic, such as "Things That Upset Me." Autobiographical material then can be analyzed for present or potential problem areas.

Sociometric Techniques

Sociometric techniques are among the most commonly used methods for assessing social skills and related problems (Maag, 1989). Sociometric methodology typically is grouped into three categories: peer nominations, peer ratings, and peer assessment. A sociogram provides a visual record of the group's social structure.

Peer Nominations. This procedure involves asking students to nominate peers according to *nonbehavioral* criteria (such as preferred work partners, best friends, or preferred play partners). These criteria are viewed as nonbehavioral because they refer to activities (e.g., play) or attributes (e.g., best friend) rather than specific behaviors (e.g., asks for the opinion of others). Thus, nominations assess attitudes and preferences for engaging in selected activities with peers. Peer nominations can be fixed-choice (i.e., the student nominates a limited number of peers) or unlimited choice (i.e., the student nominates as many peers as desired). It helps when a printed list of the names of all class members is provided, and responses should be kept secret. Nominations can be weighted (i.e., the order of nominations is considered with weights assigned in a rank-order manner) or unweighted (McConnell & Odom, 1986). Peer nominations also can be keyed to negative criteria (e.g., least preferred play partner). Research suggests that positive and negative nominations are not at opposite ends of the same continuum but measure two distinct dimensions of sociometric status (Gresham & Reschly, 1988; McConnell & Odom, 1986).

Coie, Dodge, and their associates (Coie, Dodge, & Coppotelli, 1982; Dodge, 1983) have generated empirical support for the peer nomination approach. Coie et al. provide a classification system for peer nominations that identifies five sociometric status groups: popular, neglected, rejected, controversial, and average. These groups are then evaluated in terms of *liked most* and *liked least.* These techniques provide a detailed description of the social status of a student with learning disabilities in a peer group. Moreover, behavior correlates are being identified for each sociometric group. For example, rejected students exhibit high rates of aggressive and disruptive behaviors and low rates of cooperative, peer reinforcing behaviors, whereas neglected students display high rates of shy, withdrawn, and fearful behaviors and low rates of positive social interactions (Dodge, 1983).

Peer Ratings. In a peer rating, *all* students in a classroom rate each other on a Likert-type scale according to *nonbehavioral* criteria. These criteria are similar to peer nominations in that areas such as *play with* and *work with* preferences are used. A student's score on a peer rating is the average rating received from peers. Gresham and Elliott (1989a) note that these ratings tend to indicate a student's overall acceptance level within the peer group. Peer ratings feature several advantages over peer nominations. First, every student in the class is rated rather than only a few students. Second, a student's rating scores are more reliable because they are based on a large number of raters. Third, peer ratings typically do not involve the use of negative criteria, thereby reducing ethical objections to sociometric assessments. Disadvantages of peer ratings include stereotypical ratings (i.e., giving many peers the same rating) and central tendency errors (i.e., rating peers in the middle of the scale) (McConnell & Odom, 1986).

Peer Assessment. In peer assessment, students are asked to nominate or rate peers on several *behavioral* characteristics. Students hear or read behavioral descriptions and then nominate or rate individuals according to the descriptions. One of the more popular peer assessment techniques with learners who have mild disabilities is the *Guess Who?* technique (Kaufman, Agard, & Semmel, 1985). Students nominate peers who fit behavioral descriptions involving such dimensions as disruptive behavior, smartness, dullness, and quiet/good behavior.

Sociogram. Responses from a sociometric questionnaire indicating the number of times each student is chosen may be recorded on a tally sheet, or a *sociogram* can be constructed to provide a visual record of the social structure within the class. Figure 15.1 shows a sociogram of 10 fourth-grade students who were asked to write the names of two classmates with whom they would most like to play. In this example, for the most part, girls preferred to play with girls, and boys with boys. Among the girls, Alice, Debby, and Judy seemed to have a close relationship. None of these girls chose other classmates. Joan did not receive any choices, and Kim was selected as first choice only by Joan. Kim was the only girl to choose a boy. Among the boys, Bob and Steve were mutual choices, as were Ken and John. Adam received no choices, and John was the only boy to choose a girl.

The information obtained from the sociogram can help to identify isolates as well as leaders and can give the teacher a basis for congenial, effective group activities. In addition, the social preferences discovered provide insight about which social patterns should be changed and which should be encouraged. In this example, activities involving Adam and either Ken or Steve may be a positive for Adam, who in general is an isolate. Among the girls, situations should be planned to foster relationships outside of the clique. Different patterns probably will be revealed for different activities or settings. A student may be selected by several classmates as their choice for a study partner but may receive no choices for social activities.

Information also can be provided through peer nomination techniques, in which each student responds to statements about attitudes or behavior by naming classmates (e.g., "Which students are very popular?" or "Which students are selfish?"). Sociograms can be scored (rather than mapped) based on combinations of positive and negative nominations, and the social status of students can be identified as popular (high number of positive nominations and low number of negative nominations), rejected (high number of negative nominations and low number of positive nominations), controversial (high numbers of positive and negative nominations), and neglected (no evaluations).

Overall, sociometric assessment can be an important component in evaluating students with learning disabilities. To date, Gresham and Elliott (1989a) maintain that the Coie et al. (1982) system offers the best reliability and validity.

Naturalistic Observations

Direct observation provides an in-depth study of possible problem behaviors identified by rating scales, checklists, and interviews. Moreover, defining target behaviors, observing and recording their frequency in the natural environment, and analyzing the data represent the most direct and ecologically valid assessment of students' social skills and related behaviors (Elliott, Gresham, & Heffer, 1987). Naturalistic assessment allows for a functional analysis of the antecedent events, behavioral sequence, and consequences that may be operating to influence inappropriate social behavior or decrease prosocial behaviors (Maag, 1989). This approach promotes the use of operationally defined social skills or behaviors and the development of systems for measuring and recording target behav-

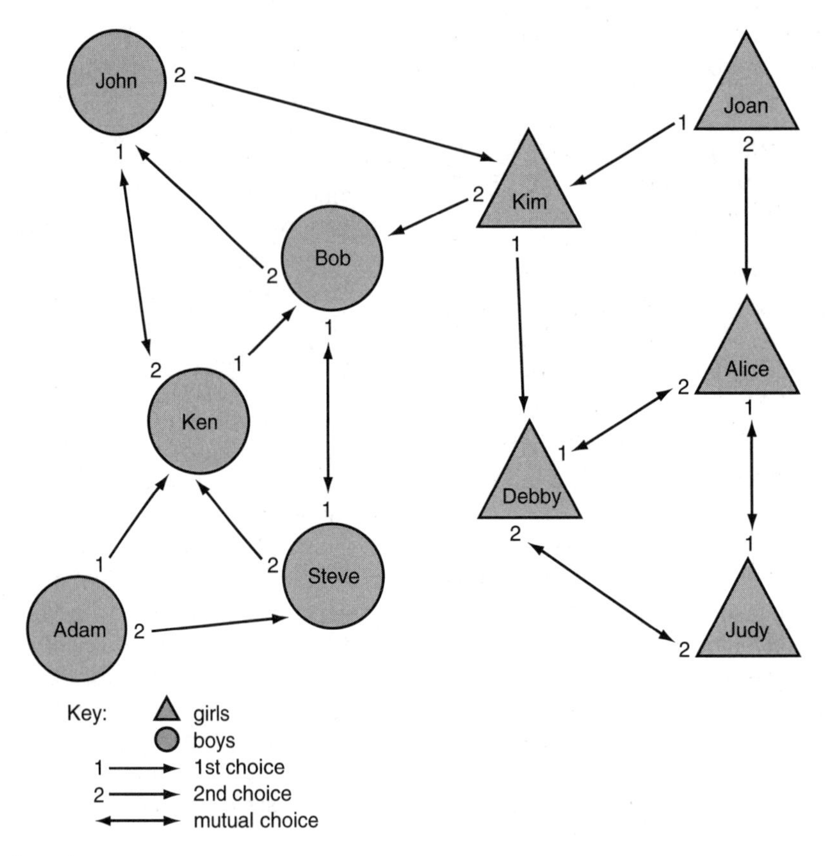

FIGURE 15.1 A sociogram

Source: From *Teaching Students with Learning Problems* (p. 195), 4th ed., by C. D. Mercer and A. R. Mercer, 1993, Upper Saddle River, NJ: Merrill/Prentice Hall. Copyright 1993 by Prentice-Hall Publishing Company. Reprinted by permission.

iors. The collection of frequent data provides a sensitive index to variations in student behavior. Direct observation of social and emotional behavior includes observing the behavior, the teacher-student interaction, and the environment. The primary difficulty with naturalistic observation is that the student might not act naturally in the context in which observation occurs. If the observer suspects that the student is not behaving naturally, role-play assessment may be useful.

Observation of Behavior. Direct, systematic observation of student behavior can provide information and insights about the student's social and emotional skills. Many teachers have training in personality development and work with students for several hours each day in different situations; therefore, they usually are highly qualified to observe and assess behavior. If behaviors are *described* and reported as responses seen or provided (such as "Gets out of seat," "Butts in the cafeteria line," or "Calls Bill a sissy during math seatwork") instead of as interpretations (such as "hyperactive," "disruptive," or "impulsive"), the validity of teacher observations increases. The teacher should observe the conditions under which the behavior occurs and record the frequency of occurrence. Careful observation may reveal, for example, that out-of-seat behavior occurs only during math, or that singing in class occurs when the student is sitting near Maria. The target behavior also can be measured by duration—how long the student exhibits the behavior—or by a time sampling, in which the student is observed during certain periods for specified lengths of time.

In addition to the behavior itself, the teacher also should note the events that occur immediately before and immediately after the behavior and serve to reinforce the behavior. Information about the surrounding conditions may enable the teacher to choose management strategies. For example, a student's swearing might receive the reinforcement of attention from peers (laughter). The teacher could concentrate on eliminating peer reinforcement and encouraging peer attention to desirable responses. Finally, daily measurement of behavior can provide feedback on the success of strategies used to resolve the behavior.

Observation of Teacher-Student Interaction. Flanders (1970) presents the *interaction analysis system* for measuring the interactions between the teacher and the students in the entire class. Flanders specifies 10 behavior categories: seven involve the teacher's verbal behavior (e.g., praising or encouraging students, asking questions, and criticizing); two involve students' verbal behavior (e.g., responding to the teacher); and one is for silence or confusion. Teacher-student interactions are observed, and behaviors are recorded every 4 seconds. Data are collected for several days during short observation periods. A simplified version of the Flanders technique involves the use of a videotape or audiotape recorder instead of a trained observer. The teacher can interpret the recordings made during the day and can categorize the verbal interactions according to Flanders' 10 categories. By using this assessment device, the teacher can identify verbal patterns of student-teacher interactions in the classroom.

Sprick (1985) developed a system for monitoring teacher-student interactions that focuses on the frequency of teacher responses to negative events and positive events. He suggests that a 3:1 positive-to-negative ratio is needed for effective interaction and classroom management. Other variables noted include bias toward different students (e.g., low achievers or males) and how often inappropriate behavior is reinforced.

In teacher-student interactions, a teacher occasionally may overact to a certain behavior. Teachers must show understanding and awareness to control inappropriate reactions.

Observation of Environment. In assessing social and emotional behavior, the teacher should observe the student in different environments. The teacher then can consider the environment's influence in starting or maintaining the problem behavior. Some observation can be made outside the school setting; however, the teacher mainly should observe in-school environments (such as art class, physical education class, lunchroom, and playground). Perhaps the target behavior surfaces only in certain settings or instructional conditions. The student may become disruptive when required to remain seated for long periods of time during a lecture; however, when allowed to move about or participate in class discussions, the student's behavior may be acceptable. Also, a student may exhibit anxiety and withdraw when required to read orally in front of the class or to compute timed math problems, but be quite comfortable when working alone in untimed situations or in small-group activities. Thus, teacher observation of various environments can help determine the adjustments needed to improve the student's instructional program.

Role-Play Assessment. With this approach, a student's behavior is elicited in response to staged social interactions (such as receiving criticism), and the student's performance is recorded. Advances in role-play methodology (Dodge, Pettit, McClaskey, & Brown, 1986) have improved their generalizability to naturalistic observations. Moreover, role-play assessments enable the observer to determine whether the student has a social skill acquisition deficit (i.e., does not possess the skill) or a social skill performance problem (i.e., does not desire to perform the skill).

Perspective on Assessment

The assessment of social and emotional behavior traditionally has lacked reliable and valid assessment instruments and procedures. Fortunately, substantial progress has been made regarding the assessment of these important domains, and many psychometrically sound instruments are now available for use. Also, Gresham and Elliott (1989a) note that improvements have been made in the measurement of social behavior, and now there are norm-referenced teacher, parent, and self-report rating scales with adequate psychometric properties. Moreover, when assessment consists of a combination of various methods, contexts, and sources of data, the social and emotional behavior problems of students can be identified and lead to appropriate educational interventions.

GENERAL TECHNIQUES FOR PROMOTING SOCIAL, EMOTIONAL, AND BEHAVIOR DEVELOPMENT

The development of social, emotional, and behavior attributes is complex because these affective domains are interdependent. Improvement in one domain frequently has a positive effect on the other areas. For example, positive reinforcement can help a youngster behave more appropriately, and when other students respond positively and accept the youngster, this improves the individual's self-concept. Fortunately, several techniques are appropriate for developing positive attributes in social, emotional, and behavior domains. The general techniques featured in this section include teach for success, focus on promoting proactivity, promote cooperation, teach self-management, model target behaviors and attributes, and focus on motivation through behavior modification.

Teach for Success

Many students with learning disabilities have low self-concepts, attention deficits, social skills deficits, or emotional problems. Because these types of affective problems can lead to aggressive, disruptive, or withdrawal behavior, students with learning disabilities may become difficult to manage in the classroom. Moreover, it appears that subgroups of these students are overly negative about themselves. Sprick (1981) notes that acting out, misbehaving in a manner to get caught, and giving up or withdrawal are common manifestations of a poor self-concept. Educators agree that effective behavior management must begin with preventive techniques and that these techniques start with good teaching. It is highly likely that most behavior problems of students with learning disabilities can be prevented with effective instruction. The development of positive social, emotional, and behavior attributes through teaching is fundamental to a student's school success, motivation, and future learning.

Teach Effectively. Effective teaching leads to academic progress, and this success is critical if a student with learning disabilities is to develop a positive self-concept. Sprick (1981) states, "There is nothing more important for any student than believing he or she is able to learn, grow, and be successful. When in doubt about what to do to improve a child's self-concept, teach!" (Book E, p. 9) Chapter 7 of this text presents a framework for making instructional decisions, including instructional variables related to student learning. Although all the variables likely would lead to improvements in the social, emotional, and behavior attributes of students with learning disabilities, the ones that are especially noteworthy are (a) ensure high rates of student success, (b) monitor progress and provide feedback, and (c) provide positive and supportive learning environments.

Provide Feedback. The importance of feedback to success is well documented; however, the type of feedback that improves a student's social, emotional, and behavior development needs examination. First, positive feedback or reinforcement should be contingent on student performance (i.e., students should be praised for accomplishing tasks that require a reasonable amount of effort). Second, noncontingent feedback or praise can signal to students that the teacher thinks they cannot do better work; thus, the students receive the message that they lack ability, and this lowers their opinion of their learning capabilities. Third, students often view criticism or corrective feedback as positive when high achievers receive it (Weinstein, 1982). This feedback indicates that the teacher believes the students can do better; thus, it communicates a positive opinion about the teacher's view of a student's potential. Consequently, Bryan (1986) reports that the use of corrective feedback is a viable strategy to help improve the self-concepts of students with learning disabilities. Furthermore, corrective feedback may communicate that the teacher cares about a student.

Plan Instruction. Rieth and Evertson (1988) provide an excellent framework for planning instruction for difficult-to-teach students. Their review of the research and subsequent guidelines for effective teaching, presented in Table 15.5, are organized according to preinstructional variables, instructional delivery variables, and postinstructional variables. (Chapter 7 discusses these variables.)

Focus on Promoting Proactivity

Many students with learning disabilities live a reactive existence and maintain an external locus of control. Essentially, they believe that they have little control over what happens to them. Thus, fate, bad luck, and good luck are guiding forces in their lives. This reactive existence causes individuals to believe that the conditions in their lives are out of their control, and this in many ways is a terrible way to live. These students need to learn that they can control many of the events or consequences in their lives. Proactivity is based on the following belief: I can control events in my life through my own efforts (e.g., I study and I get good grades; I behave appropriately and people treat me well). A proactive or internal locus of control is much more empowering than a reactive existence. The following techniques promote proactivity: (a) set goals, (b) give responsibility, and (c) engage in self-appreciation.

Set Goals. When a student reaches goals that require considerable effort, self-worth is improved. Individuals feel good about themselves when they work hard to achieve a worthwhile goal. Goal ambitiousness is related positively to school success. In contrast, goals that are too easy often lead students to believe that the teacher thinks they are not capable of higher-level achievements. Consequently, these low teacher expectations frequently lower students' beliefs about their learning potential. It is important for the teacher to point out how the students' efforts were essential in reaching a goal. The teacher should constantly pair effort with positive or negative consequences.

Give Responsibility. Students with poor affective attributes often are pleased when the teacher thinks they can accept responsibility. Giving students responsibility demonstrates a level of trust in their ability to act maturely. Some responsibilities include (a) caring for a class pet, (b) taking messages to the office or other classes, (c) conducting a lunch count, (d) tutoring other students, (e) leading the line, (f) making a bulletin board, (g) using equipment, and (h) grading papers.

Engage in Self-Appreciation. Self-depreciation tends to lower a student's self-worth. Conversely, self-appreciation or positive self-talk can help improve self-worth. The teacher should reinforce students for making appropriate positive comments about themselves. Students can make lists of their positive attributes and periodically refer to them.

Promote Cooperation

To develop positive social, emotional, and behavior attributes, students should work in a community of cooperative learners. The following

TABLE 15.5
Variables Related to Effective Instruction of Difficult-to-Teach Students

Instructional Variables	Specific Emphasis
Preinstructional Variables	
Arrangement of classroom space	Arrange classroom to facilitate smooth transitions and ease of student monitoring.
Rules and procedures	Communicate expectations and provide structure for learning.
Managing student academic work	Hold students accountable for work and keep records of progress.
Assessment	Use criterion-referenced measures to match tasks to students and monitor performance in terms of instructional objectives.
Communication of learning goals	Communicate rationales for academic tasks and clearly state learning goals.
Pacing decisions	Maintain a lively instructional pace but allow enough time for much practice. Presentation-demonstration-practice-feedback cycles appear to be most effective.
Time allocations	Plan as much time as possible for academic learning.
Instructional Delivery Variables	
Engagement time	Maintain substantive interactions with students and provide feedback. Reinforce students for being on task and for work completed.
Success rate	Maintain high rates of success because success is related to student achievement and motivation.
Academic learning time	Facilitate the amount of time students are engaged in high rates of success or appropriate goals.
Monitoring	Circulate throughout the room to check the accuracy and progress of students.
Postinstructional Variables	
Testing	Regularly administer informal criterion-referenced measures (e.g., curriculum-based assessment) to assess student progress or plan instruction.
Academic feedback	Provide immediate feedback on academic work to promote learning. Praise and corrective feedback are most effective when used together.

techniques promote cooperation: (a) promote positive interactions among students, (b) use peer tutoring, and (c) use cooperative learning.

Promote Positive Interactions Among Students. Sprick (1981) notes that teaching students to be positive with each other benefits individual students. If the students can learn to interact positively, they will receive pleasant and friendly reactions in return. The teacher can pair students with learning disabilities with popular students for social group activities or on teams in instructional games so that the paired students share positive and pleasant experiences. Fox (1989) paired students with learning disabilities with normally achieving students to perform a mutual-interest activity. The activity resulted in improved ratings for the students with learning disabilities. Sprick recommends three techniques for promoting positive interactions: (a) modeling positive interactions in daily teaching, (b) practicing positive interactions through role playing specific situations, and (c) reinforcing positive interactions as they occur throughout the school day.

Use Peer Tutoring. Peer tutoring typically involves pairing a competent student with one who has difficulty in a particular academic area. Peer tutoring also can be used to improve social skills. If assessment reveals that a student has no friends or is not accepted by peers, peer tutoring can be a strategy for enhancing social growth. Using information from a sociometric device, such as a sociogram, the teacher can pair a student with a preferred tutor. The student thus will be likely to model the appropriate behavior. The teacher should train the student tutor in teaching and reinforcement techniques. Tutoring sessions should have easy-to-use materials and a set routine. Self-correcting materials and instructional games provide excellent materials for peer teaching arrangements.

Paine, Radicchi, Rosellini, Deutchman, and Darch (1983) provide guidelines for establishing and maintaining a peer tutoring program: (a) determine the roles of the tutors, (b) select the tutors, (c) train the tutors, and (d) supervise and reinforce peer teaching arrangements. In addition to improving academic skills, a successful peer tutoring program can enhance self-esteem, encourage appropriate behavior, and foster positive and cooperative relationships among peers. Moreover, peer tutoring is appropriate for helping students with learning disabilities achieve in inclusive settings. (Chapter 7 discusses peer tutoring.)

Use Cooperative Learning. Cooperative learning is an instructional arrangement in which small groups or teams of students work together to achieve team success in a manner that promotes the students' responsibility for their own learning as well as the learning of others. In cooperative learning, team goals are emphasized, and team success is achieved only if each individual learns. Slavin (1991) reports the following research findings on cooperative learning: (a) positive achievement effects are consistent across grades, subject areas, and school settings; (b) effects are equally positive for high, average, and low achievers; and (c) positive effects are reported in affective areas (e.g., self-esteem, intergroup relations, and ability to work cooperatively). (Chapter 7 discusses cooperative learning.)

Teach Self-Management

A problem common to many youngsters with learning disabilities is their inability to solve problems and make decisions effectively. Difficulties in these areas can affect their performance adversely at school, home, or work. Issues related to problem solving, interpersonal relations, and generalization learning can be viewed within the context of self-management skills (Shapiro, 1989). Self-management typically is divided into three components: self-monitoring, self-evaluation, and self-reinforcement. Each component requires specific instruction.

Several researchers report success using self-management training with students who have mild disabilities. Brigham, Hopper, Hill, De Armas, and Newsom (1985) report that self-management training helped disruptive students improve their behavior. Likewise, Hughes, Ruhl, and Peterson (1988) used the demonstration-guidance-practice-feedback sequence to teach self-management skills to learners with mild disabilities. Hughes et al. found a differential effect to the training: Self-monitoring only or self-monitoring and self-evaluation were sufficient for some students to accomplish at criterion level; however, other students needed self-monitoring, self-evaluation, and self-reinforcement to achieve a criterion. Moreover, several researchers (Sander, 1991; Shapiro, 1989) have found self-management to be effective for helping adolescents with learning disabilities to improve their motivation to stay on task. In a 3-year study, Shapiro compared the performance of students with learning disabilities who received self-management training with the performance of students with and without learning disabilities who did not receive self-management training. The students who received the training showed significant improvements on measures of problem solving and job-related social skills. Shapiro concludes that self-management instruction appears to be a promising approach for teaching students with learning disabilities to be more independent learners and citizens.

Model Target Behaviors and Attributes

The saying, "Don't do what I do, do what I say," is not appropriate for helping youngsters with learning disabilities to develop social, emotional, and behavior attributes. These youngsters need models to imitate and emulate regarding social skills (e.g., listening, giving encouragement, and saying "no"), emotional states (e.g., being positive and proactive), and appropriate behavior (e.g., being considerate of others and respecting property). Cognitive behavior modification is a procedure that frequently involves modeling to help youngsters internalize appropriate thinking processes related to affective behavior.

Teach Cognitive Behavior Modification. Cognitive behavior modification analyzes the thinking processes involved in performing a task. Meichenbaum (1977) discusses self-instructional training as a method to encourage appropriate responses and discourage inappropriate responses. The following sequence can be used:

1. Instruction by another person (e.g., an adult model such as the teacher performs a task while talking aloud).
2. Overt self-instruction (e.g., while performing a task, the student speaks or whispers self-instructions).
3. Covert self-instruction (e.g., the student guides performance through private speech).

Thus, inner speech is considered to be an aspect of the thinking process, and the student is encouraged to verbalize before acting. Language is thought to enhance thinking and, in turn, affect behavior. In the classroom the student can be taught to use the following self verbalizations: (a) questions about the task ("What does the teacher want me to do?"), (b) answers to the question ("I'm not supposed to talk out in class"), (c) self-instruction to guide the student through the task ("First I raise my hand and wait for the teacher to call on me"), and (d) self-reinforcement ("I really did well that time!").

In cognitive modeling, the teacher not only should model strategies for performing a task but also should model actions and language appropriate for dealing with frustrations and failures. In addition to self-instruction, the student can be taught to use images (e.g., thinking of sitting in the classroom during recess as an image to reduce out-of-seat behavior).

Set Up Models in the Classroom. In modeling, students learn appropriate behaviors by observing and imitating others. When students observe one of their peers being rewarded for desirable behavior, they tend to follow the example of the model. Thus, they learn behaviors that have positive consequences. Likewise, unacceptable behavior can be discouraged when students watch others receive punishment for such behavior. In addition, the teacher can call attention to behavior that should be modeled: "I like the way Jimmy raised his hand instead of talking out, so I will answer his question first."

In using modeling to influence a specific behavior, the following steps are helpful: (a) select the behavior, (b) select the model, (c) give the model and the observer directions concerning their roles, (d) reinforce the model for exhibiting the behavior, and (e) reinforce the observer for imitating the behavior. The modeling process can have three effects on students: (a) new behaviors may be learned from the model, (b) previously acquired behaviors may be strengthened as the students observe similar desirable behaviors of the model being reinforced, or (c) previously acquired behaviors may be weakened as the students observe the model receiving punishment for similar unacceptable behaviors.

Focus on Motivation Through Behavior Modification

Given their failure experiences and difficulties in processing information, it is understandable that many students with learning disabilities lack motivation to work in school. Whereas many normally achieving students are motivated to achieve for intrinsic reasons (e.g., mastery, task completion, and enjoyment of learning new information), students with learning disabilities often need extrinsic reinforcers to help motivate them to work and behave. Some students with learning disabilities even require punishment or negative consequences to help them reduce off-task and disruptive behavior. Although external reinforcers and negative consequences are needed to help some students work and behave, the goal of effective teachers is to help these youngsters become mature or intrinsically motivated learners. This section covers some of the behavior modification techniques that can be used to help motivate and manage students with learning disabilities.

The basic premise of behavior modification is that behavior is learned and is a function of behavior's consequences. According to Wallace and Kauffman (1986), "Behavior modification refers to any systematic arrangement of environmental events to produce specific changes in observable behavior" (p. 21). Thus, it is a highly structured and systematic approach that results in strengthening, weakening, or maintaining behaviors.

After identifying and collecting baseline data on a target behavior, the teacher must observe events that happen just before the student's behavior (antecedent events) and just after the behavior (subsequent events). These events are then manipulated, and various reinforcers or rewards are used to elicit a change in the behavior. A *reinforcer* is any event that follows a behavior and results in maintaining or increasing the probability or rate of the behavior. *Positive reinforcement* means adding something pleasurable or positive to the environment (i.e., consequences that increase the probability that the behavior will occur again), whereas *negative reinforcement* means withdrawing something unpleasant or negative from the environment (i.e., avoidance of a negative consequence by performing a behavior). Reinforcement results in strengthening or increasing the target behavior.

Various social or tangible reinforcers can be used (e.g., praise, hugs, treats, and free time). The following hierarchical order of the level of reinforcers moves from extrinsic reinforcers (reinforcement from outside the performance of a task) to intrinsic reinforcers (reinforcement directly from performing a task):

Extrinsic Reinforcers

1. Primary reinforcers (e.g., sleeping, eating, and drinking—necessary for survival)
2. Tangible reinforcers (e.g., food items, pencils, and certificates)
3. Token reinforcers with backup items or activities (e.g., chips that can be exchanged for a preferred item or activity when a certain amount is earned)
4. Social approval (e.g., gestures, touch, and verbal expressions)
5. Project or activity (e.g., running errands, being a line leader, getting free time, or playing a game)

Intrinsic Reinforcers

6. Task completion
7. Feedback or result
8. Acquisition of knowledge or skill
9. Sense of mastery or accomplishment

Extrinsic reinforcers initially can be used to encourage a student to exhibit appropriate behavior or perform a task. The teacher gradually should withdraw material reinforcers and stress activities and events. Eventually, as competence in a task increases, the need for extrinsic reinforcement will decrease, and intrinsic reinforcers will provide motivation.

Praise is one of the most effective and convenient positive reinforcers for teachers to use in managing student behavior. Paine et al. (1983) report that effective praise has several important features:

1. Good praise adheres to the "if—then" rule, which states that *if* the student is behaving in the desired manner, *then* (and *only* then) the teacher praises the student.
2. Good praise frequently includes students' names.
3. Good praise is descriptive.
4. Good praise conveys that the teacher really means what is said (i.e., it is convincing).
5. Good praise is varied.
6. Good praise does not disrupt the flow of individual or class activities.

In using reinforcement techniques, the teacher must remember that reinforcement immediately following the behavior is most effective. In addition, attention can act as a reinforcer for inappropriate behavior. For example, when the teacher frowns or speaks sharply, the student may interpret this as reinforcing attention. Thus, the teacher should be careful not to reinforce inappropriate behavior with attention. The teacher should shift from reinforcing everyday appropriate behavior to reinforcing academic effort as soon as possible. Behaviors such as raising a hand to talk or appropriate lining up for lunch eventually should become routine and be maintained without a great deal of teacher praise. Contingent reinforcement of academic learning promotes a higher level of functioning and improves achievement.

The *schedule of reinforcement* (i.e., the plan of conditions under which reinforcement occurs) can be either continuous or intermittent. On a *continuous schedule*, the desired behavior is reinforced every time it occurs. On an *intermittent schedule*, reinforcement is given according to either an *interval* (reinforcers given at certain times) or a *ratio* (reinforcers given after a specific number of responses).

Shaping refers to reinforcing steps toward the target behavior. The goal is broken down into an ordered sequence of steps or tasks, and reinforcement is given to those behaviors that come close to the desired behavior. The desired behavior thus is shaped by gradually increasing the requirement for reinforcement until the target behavior is obtained.

Punishment, as opposed to reinforcement, refers to presenting something negative or withdrawing something positive following the behavior. This results in decreasing the undesirable response. Before punishment is used, the teacher should explore alternatives to punishment such as (a) discussing the problem with the student, (b) ignoring the misbehavior when feasible, and (c) reinforcing students who are acting appropriately. Once punishment is selected, Sprick (1981) recommends the following guidelines:

1. Punishment must change the behavior in the desired direction.
2. Punishment always should be used in conjunction with a reinforcement plan.
3. Punishment always should be administered calmly.
4. Punishment should be used discriminately.
5. Once a punishable behavior is targeted, it should be punished consistently.

One procedure frequently used to decrease undesirable behavior is *time out*. *Time out* is a short period of time during which no reinforcement is available. Thus, the student is removed from a positively reinforcing situation. Time out can be used while the student is seated in the classroom simply by removing the opportunity for reinforcement (e.g., avoiding any contact with the student for 30 to 60 seconds) or by not allowing the student to participate in a reinforcing activity for a certain amount of time. Also,

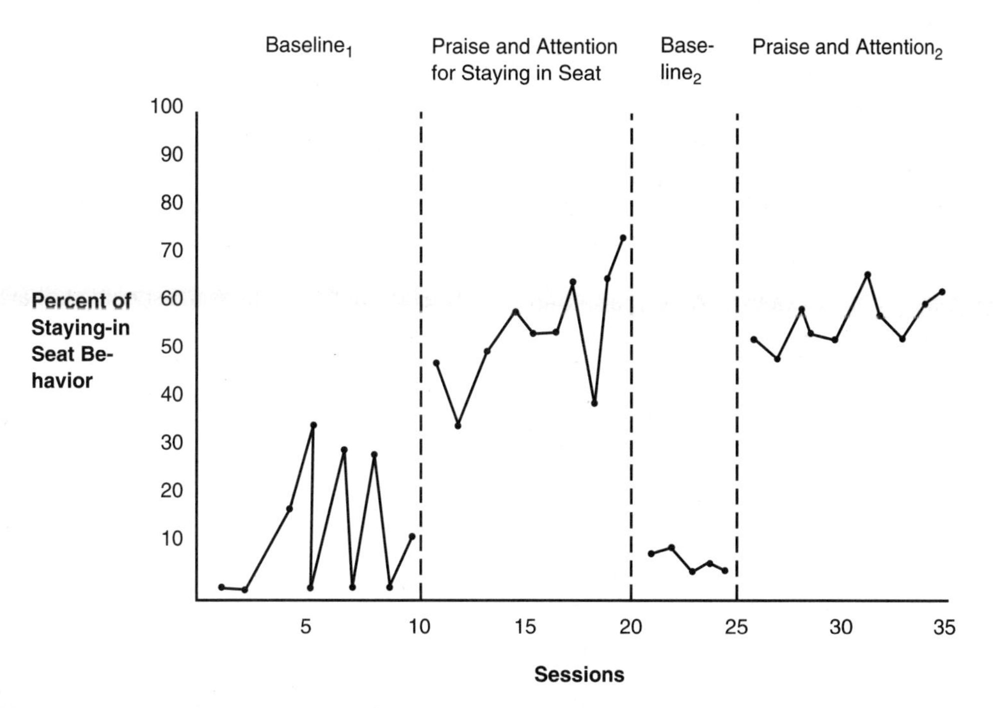

FIGURE 15.2 Record of a behavior modification plan to increase staying-in-seat behavior
Source: From *Teaching Students with Learning Problems* (p. 205), 4th ed., by C. D. Mercer and A. R. Mercer, 1993, Upper Saddle River, NJ: Merrill/Prentice Hall. Copyright 1993 by Prentice-Hall Publishing Company. Reprinted by permission.

time out can be used by isolating the student in a specific time-out area for a brief period (3 to 5 minutes). Time out is based on the premise that behaviors followed by no reinforcement tend to decrease in frequency.

Response cost is another punishment technique that involves the loss of a reinforcer contingent on inappropriate behavior. The consequent loss can be an activity, points, a privilege, or a token. Kazdin (1972) reports that response cost has been used successfully without the undesirable side effects (such as escape, avoidance, and aggression) sometimes observed with other forms of punishment. Although punishment and negative reinforcement are sometimes necessary to manage behavior, the teacher should strive to maintain a positive reinforcement system. When it is necessary to use aversive techniques, they are most effective when combined with positive techniques.

Knowledge and application of reinforcement principles are helpful in managing a classroom. Many teachers apply these principles in a natural way, without taking the time to write a behavior modification plan specifying the target behavior, consequent events, schedule of reinforcement, and so forth. However, the behavior of some students does not change unless a highly systematic behavior modification plan is developed and applied.

Figure 15.2 presents a record of a behavior modification plan to increase staying-in-seat behavior. The teacher used a time-sampling technique to record whether the student stayed seated during seatwork activities. Observation sessions were 30 minutes long, and the teacher used a recording sheet marked off with a row of 10 squares. The teacher looked at the student every 3 minutes and recorded a "+" if the student was seated and a "−" if the student was not. As Figure

15.2 shows, the student's percentage of staying-in-seat behavior was low during baseline$_1$. However, when the teacher began giving the student praise and attention for appropriate in-seat behavior (in sessions 11 through 20), the level of the desired behavior increased greatly. When praise and attention were withdrawn in baseline$_2$ (sessions 21 through 25), the student's staying-in-seat behavior sharply diminished. However, when praise and attention were provided again (in sessions 26 through 35), the level of the appropriate behavior quickly increased. Thus, the teacher was able to note the effects of teacher attention on modifying the student's out-of-seat behavior.

Use Contingency Contracting. Contracts between a student and the classroom teacher can help to motivate the student toward desirable behavior changes. A *contract* is an agreement—verbal or written—between two parties. The term *contingent* means that there is a relationship between what one does and the consequences. In behavior modification, contingency contracting is based on the Premack Principle (Premack, 1959). This principle states that the frequency of a less-preferred activity increases when it is followed by the opportunity to engage in one that is preferred. For example, if the student would rather play outside than sit quietly in the classroom, the contingency contract might state that sitting quietly for a certain amount of time will be followed by outside play.

The following steps are involved in writing a contingency contract:

1. The teacher outlines the specific behavior required of the student.
2. The teacher identifies the reinforcement for which the student will work. This reinforcement should be available to the student *only* for performing the specified behavior. The required behavior or the consequent reinforcement can be determined through student-teacher discussions.
3. The teacher specifies the terms of the contract, which should include the amount or type of behavior required and the amount or type of reward.
4. The teacher watches for the specified behavior to occur and then rewards the student according to the terms of the contract.

A sample contingency contract is presented in Figure 15.3.

FIGURE 15.3
A sample contingency contract
Source: From *Teaching Students with Learning Problems* (p. 206), 4th ed., by C. D. Mercer and A. R. Mercer, 1993, Upper Saddle River, NJ: Merrill/Prentice Hall. Copyright 1993 by Prentice-Hall Publishing Company. Reprinted by permission.

CONTRACT

Beginning date: 10/21

Ending date: 10/25

STUDENT: I agree to finish my math seatwork during math period on Monday Tuesday, Wednesday, and Thursday.

Signed: Timmy

TEACHER: I agree to give Timmy free time during math period on Friday

Signed: Mrs. Jackson

A contingency contract should represent agreement between the student and the teacher. The terms should be stated clearly in a positive manner and should be fair for both the student and the teacher. After both parties have signed the contract, the conditions should be monitored frequently to assess progress. In addition, all parts of the contract should be followed systematically, and the student should receive reinforcement as soon as the contract is completed.

Various types of contracts can be used. The agreement may or may not specify a time limit within which the required behavior must be performed. Intermittent reinforcers can be used in long-term contracts, and steps toward the desired behavior can be rewarded. Contracts also can include agreements between the student and other school personnel or parents. Group contracts can be used in which the entire class agrees to behave in a certain manner or perform a specified task by a designated date, and the teacher agrees to reward the students who fulfill the agreement. Contingency contracting thus can promote desirable actions (social or academic) by involving students in managing their own behavior.

Use Token Systems. Token reinforcement systems are used widely in behavior modification. These systems have three basic characteristics: (a) behaviors to be reinforced are stated clearly, (b) procedures are devised for giving out a reinforcing stimulus (token) when the target behavior occurs, and (c) a set of rules is explained to govern the exchange of tokens for reinforcing objects or events.

A *token* is an item given to a student immediately after a target behavior occurs. Usually the tokens have little intrinsic value, but they acquire value when they can be exchanged for a desired object or activity. Tokens can consist of play money, trading stamps, poker chips, stars, or any other object that is easy to dispense and store. These tokens can be accumulated and then exchanged for a desired object or activity. A classroom store can be established where, at designated times, each student may purchase reinforcers by trading in earned tokens. Objects (balloons, comics, jewelry, sports trading cards, pennies, coloring books, and magazines) and activities (playing a game, listening to records, coloring, and watching a filmstrip) can be available in the store. A reward menu can be posted, listing the store items and their costs (e.g., listening to records for 10 minutes = 10 tokens, and purchasing a baseball trading card = 15 tokens).

Token systems have several advantages. First, they avoid boredom because tokens can be traded for a variety of reinforcing objects or events. Second, a token system is useful with students who generally do not respond to social reinforcement. Third, tokens are administered easily, and the number can be adjusted to reflect the time and energy required to perform the target behavior. Fourth, token systems help students appreciate the relationship between desirable behavior and reinforcement. Students learn that behavior has consequences, and this is likely to enhance self-control.

Blackham and Silberman (1980) stress that a token system must be developed and applied thoughtfully. They also report that problems should be expected at first, and the teacher will have to refine the system. Blackham and Silberman suggest guidelines for planning and using a token system:

1. The target behaviors that earn tokens should be specified clearly. For example, individual behaviors can be posted on a student's desk. Rules governing group behavior contingencies should be reviewed frequently.
2. The reinforcers that the tokens are exchanged for must be appealing and available *only* within the token system.
3. The number of tokens earned must match the effort required for performing the target behavior. If a student has great difficulty staying on task during math seatwork, the reward for staying on task must be sufficient to encourage on-task behavior.

4. If possible, the teacher should keep a record of the number of tokens each student and the group earn. This type of record often provides an additional incentive to students.
5. If *response cost* (token fines) is used, the conditions under which tokens are earned and lost must be specified clearly. Awarding and taking away tokens always must be related to student *behavior*. Arguments about token loss should be avoided.
6. A scheduled token exchange for the end of the day usually works best.
7. The system should be devised so that there is self-competition rather than competition with others.
8. A well-planned token system gradually should withdraw material reinforcers and stress reinforcing activities and events. Also, praise should be combined with the tokens so that social reinforcement eventually can be used alone to maintain desirable behaviors.
9. The token system should be simple, functional, and not distracting to the learning process. In school, check-mark tokens are often the easiest to use. Each student is given a card, and the teacher puts checks on it as they are earned. A special pen can be used to distinguish these checks. Other students cannot use a student's card, whereas tangible tokens might be traded or stolen.

Apply Consequences with Adolescents. In managing secondary students, Kerr and Nelson (1989) report that structure and consistency are essential. The likelihood of power struggles and defiance of authority is greater with adolescents. Thus, both teacher and student must function in a structured environment in which expectations (rules), consequences, and routines have been established clearly. Techniques that have been effective with secondary students include token economies, contingency contracting, verbal feedback, mutual goal setting, and self-control training (Deshler, Schumaker, & Lenz, 1984; Polsgrove, 1979). Moreover, the importance of involving adolescents in curriculum and management decisions is stressed throughout the literature.

Some suggestions for managing consequences with adolescents include the following:

1. Stress the natural consequences of behavior. For example, the natural consequence for stealing is arrest, for being tardy is detention, and so on. Thus, if a rule is broken, the stated consequence is applied. This helps reduce power struggles between the student and teacher because the student is likely to view the teacher as a person who follows rules rather than as an authority figure who maliciously applies punishment (Kerr & Nelson, 1989).
2. Use conditioned reinforcers (such as points) with adolescents. They are administered easily or withheld with a minimum of teacher verbalization (Kerr & Nelson, 1989).
3. Consider using peer interactions as reinforcers for adolescents.
4. Develop a continuum of consequences for managing inappropriate behaviors. Public reprimands should be avoided because they increase the probability of further conflict. Use little verbal interaction and eye contact when administering a negative consequence. Response cost is a good beginning step in dealing with inappropriate behavior. Time out is another effective consequence with adolescents.

SPECIFIC TECHNIQUES FOR PROMOTING SOCIAL DEVELOPMENT

Among affective domains social competence has received the most attention in the learning disabilities literature (Bender & Wall, 1994). Given the low social competence of many individuals with learning disabilities and the extensive social demands of adult living, it is apparent why social competence receives so much attention. Social skills, a component of social competence, has been the focus of many intervention studies involving students with learning disabilities (Mellard & Hazel, 1992).

Social Skills Training

Several procedures have been used to improve the social skills performance of students with learning disabilities (Hazel & Schumaker, 1988; Schumaker & Hazel, 1984). One technique involves the manipulation of antecedent and consequent events associated with the target social behavior. For example, environmental events can be changed in an effort to increase the probability of future occurrence of appropriate social behaviors while decreasing the probability of occurrence of inappropriate behaviors. Approaches of this technique include the use of cooperative goal structures, the delivery or the withholding of particular consequences contingent upon the occurrence of social responses, the application of group contingencies, and the use of home-based contingency management systems. Another technique that has been used to reduce the rate of inappropriate social behaviors is cognitive training aimed at teaching self-control of personal behaviors (e.g., self-recording and self-evaluation of behaviors).

Also, interpersonal social skills can be increased through direct instruction. Schumaker and Hazel (1984) discuss four types of instructional interventions that have been used to facilitate the acquisition of social skills:

1. Description—primarily oral techniques in which the teacher describes how to perform a skill appropriately.
2. Modeling—demonstrations of the social skill either by live models or by film, audiotape, or pictorial models.
3. Rehearsal—verbal rehearsal of required skill steps to ensure that students have memorized the steps in sequence and can instruct themselves in what to do next, and structured practice (e.g., role-play activities) whereby the learner attempts to perform the skill.
4. Feedback—verbal feedback following rehearsal to inform the students what steps they performed well and what behaviors need improvement.

Frequently, combinations of these procedures are included in social skills training interventions.

A social skills curriculum also can be used. Cartledge, Frew, and Zaharias (1985) and Maag (1989) note that a basic principle of social skills instruction is that behaviors chosen for instruction should be those valued by persons important in the learner's environment. In an analysis of social behaviors selected for individualized educational programs, Pray, Hall, and Markley (1992) found that academically related social skills (e.g., task-related skills such as following directions or being on task) were much more prominent than interpersonal skills (e.g., making conversation or accepting authority). In a similar vein, Mellard and Hazel (1992) maintain that nonacademic characteristics may have more effect than academics on the employment of an individual with learning disabilities. Thus, Pray et al. and Mellard and Hazel recommend more emphasis on interpersonal skills for students with learning disabilities. To foster peer interaction, attention should be given to areas such as informal conversation and play skills. The following social skills curriculum consists of four main areas:

1. Conversation skills—using body language, greeting others, introducing oneself, applying active listening, answering questions, interrupting correctly, asking questions, saying good-bye, and conversing.
2. Friendship skills—making friends, saying thank-you, giving compliments, accepting thanks, accepting compliments, joining group activities, starting activities with others, and giving help.
3. Skills for difficult situations—giving criticism, accepting being told "no," accepting criticism, following instructions, responding to teasing, resisting peer pressure, and apologizing.
4. Problem-solving skills—negotiating, giving rationales, persuading, problem solving, getting help, and asking for feedback.

Sugai and Fuller (1991) provide an excellent decision model for examining a social skills curriculum. Their model addresses background, assessment, and instruction and features insightful questions to ask in each area.

Bender and Wall (1994) note that the research indicates that social skills training has been successful in helping students with learning disabilities. Unfortunately, most of this research has focused on short-term outcomes. Research is needed to demonstrate that social skills training generalizes to the daily settings of employment, significant other relationships, and recreation (Bender & Wall, 1994; Mellard & Hazel, 1992).

SPECIFIC TECHNIQUES FOR PROMOTING EMOTIONAL DEVELOPMENT

The emotional development of individuals with learning disabilities has not received much attention. Fortunately, as noted earlier in this chapter, this domain is being recognized as an area that warrants study and the development of related interventions. This section features selected interventions to promote emotional development and includes bibliotherapy, attribution retraining, life-space interviewing, reality therapy, and techniques for improving mood states.

Bibliotherapy

Bibliotherapy is a teaching technique that uses reading materials to help students better understand themselves and their problems. Characters in the books learn to cope with problems and situations similar to those faced by the students. Through identifying with the character, students release emotional tensions and achieve a better understanding of themselves and their problems. Also, characteristics, attitudes, values, and situations in reading selections can serve as models for the students.

Hoagland (1972) notes that for bibliotherapy to be effective, students must move through three phases during or immediately after reading a book: (a) *identification*—the students must become personally involved and must identify themselves or see a situation similar to some of their own situations, (b) *catharsis*—the students must release emotional tensions regarding the problems, and (c) *insight*—through empathizing with the character or plot, the students must reach a better understanding that tempers their emotional drives.

Cianciolo (1965) suggests the following steps for discussing a book with a student:

1. Retell the story and emphasize incidents, feelings, relationships, and behavior.
2. Discuss changes of feelings, relationships, and behaviors.
3. Identify similar events from the student's life or other reading selections.
4. Explore the consequences that occurred.
5. Generalize about the consequences or helpfulness of alternative behaviors.

The student should begin to realize that many other people have experienced the same problem and that there is more than one way to solve a problem.

Books chosen for a bibliotherapeutic program should focus on a particular need and should be written on the student's level. The selections also should depict realistic approaches and have lifelike characters. Suitable books can be selected from various bibliographies that are cross-indexed by theme and age level. Russell and Russell (1979) provide various activities to be used in conjunction with bibliotherapy. Although research on bibliotherapy is minimal, Lenkowsky and Lenkowsky (1978) note that the approach seems to help some students with learning disabilities by providing them with reading materials relevant to their own social and emotional needs.

Attribution Retraining

Attributions refer to a person's beliefs concerning the causes of events. Students differ in their ideas concerning the causes of their successes and failures. Those who believe in an internal locus of control explain the outcomes of their actions on the basis of their abilities or efforts. In contrast, persons with an external locus of control believe that factors outside their control, such as luck or task difficulty, determine their fates.

Students with learning disabilities are more likely than normally achieving students to believe that their successes are a function of external factors (Chapman & Boersma, 1979; Pearl, Bryan, & Donahue, 1980). Bryan (1986) notes that it would seem advantageous to induce students with learning disabilities to have more positive and self-serving expectations of their academic successes. As students with learning problems experience many academic failures, they are likely to lack confidence in their intellectual abilities and doubt that anything they do will help them overcome their difficulties. Thus, these students may lessen their achievement efforts, especially when presented with difficult material. In other words, repeated failure can lead students to believe that they are not capable of overcoming their difficulties, and students' beliefs about their abilities can affect their achievement efforts and accomplishments.

Attribution retraining studies (Schunk, 1981; Shelton, Anastopoulos, & Linden, 1985) have found that teaching students to attribute their failures to insufficient effort can result in increased persistence and improved performance when confronted with difficulty. In these studies, students are engaged in academic tasks and are given feedback that emphasizes the importance of their effort. In a review of attribution retraining research, Bryan (1986) reports that attribution retraining sessions have been shown to be somewhat successful in changing attributions and persistence behavior. Fowler and Peterson (1981) found that prompting and reinforcing students for verbalizing the appropriate effort attributions can be more effective than simply telling students when they fail that they need to try harder. In addition to stressing effort as a determinant of a student's difficulties, it also can be helpful to teach students to attribute their failures to ineffective task strategies (Licht, 1984). Bryan notes that teachers should convey to students with learning disabilities that they are learning new skills and that determined application of the new skills can help them overcome their difficulties.

Ellis, Lenz, and Sabornie (1987) suggest the following instructional sequence in attribution retraining:

1. Teach students to make statements that reflect effort.
2. Teach students to attribute difficulty to ineffective strategies.
3. Arrange for students to have success with newly learned strategies.

Life-Space Interviewing

Life-space interviewing is a verbal strategy for intervention that can be used in the classroom to manage a crisis or an everyday problem. This technique attempts to structure a situation so that the student works out the problem independently. The interview is designed to be free of judgment. The teacher is simply a listener and helper as the student makes decisions about how to handle the problem.

Morse (1971) outlines the steps in life-space interviewing:

1. All students involved in the specific incident are allowed to give their own impressions of the occurrence without interruption.
2. The teacher listens and, without casting judgment, asks questions to determine the accuracy of each student's perception.
3. If the students cannot resolve the problem agreeably, the teacher may have to suggest an acceptable plan to deal with the problem.
4. The students and the teacher work together to develop a plan for solving similar problems in the future.

The classroom teacher may use life-space interviewing best to provide emotional first aid at times of unusual stress. Thus, the technique is used to (a) reduce students' frustration and anxiety by giving them support during an emotional situation, (b) change behavior and reinforce behavioral and social rules, (c) enhance self-esteem, and (d) assist students to solve their own everyday problems by expanding their understanding and insight into their own and others' behavior and feelings. For example, after a fight on the playground, the teacher can engage in life-space interviewing to allow the students to release frustration and anger. The teacher provides support and helps the students in viewing all sides of the situation and the rights of others.

Wood and Long (1991) use the term *life-space intervention* to emphasize that a crisis always evokes verbal intervention. They note that the key to success or failure in obtaining a therapeutic outcome of a crisis is the quality of the adult's verbal intervention. The teacher's attitude and behavior as interviewer influence the effectiveness of life-space interviewing. The teacher should be polite to the student and should maintain eye contact. Asking *why* questions should be avoided, and the interviewer should try to reduce any apparent guilt feelings. In addition, the teacher should encourage the student to communicate and ask questions as they work together to develop a plan of action for present or future use. The life-space interview technique is time-consuming and requires sensitivity and emotional control from the teacher. However, it can help students see the consequences of behavior and find ways to deal with a problem.

Reality Therapy

Reality therapy, developed by Glasser (1965), is used to manage behaviors by teaching students to behave responsibly and to face reality. An interview technique similar to life-space interviewing is used in an attempt to help students make sound decisions when they are confronted with a problem. In reality therapy all students are assumed to be responsible for their own behavior, and inappropriate behaviors are not excused on the basis of unconscious motivations. During interviews the student is provided with emotional support, and no judgments are made of the present behavior. The teacher and the student jointly develop a plan to increase the student's responsible behavior, and the student is encouraged to make a commitment to carry out the plan. The student is expected to realize the consequences of irresponsible behavior, and no excuses are accepted. Thus, the morality of behavior is emphasized, and the student is taught socially accepted ways to handle problems.

Glasser (1965) presents a three-step format for applying reality therapy. The first step is to help the student identify the problem. This is accomplished by asking questions such as "What happened?" and "Where are you going?" The second step is to help the student develop a value judgment, asking questions such as "Is the behavior helping you?" or "Is the behavior against the rules?" The third step is to involve the student in carrying out a plan to correct the inappropriate behavior (e.g., "What can you do about it?").

Techniques for Improving Mood States

In their review of the affective research since 1984 regarding individuals with learning disabilities, Bender and Wall (1994) found no intervention studies for treating depression and suicide, anxiety, temperament, and loneliness. However, Bender (1995) offers some tentative suggestions for dealing with temperament, suicide, and general personality variables.

Temperament. Some students with learning disabilities have a temperament that predisposes them to be less task persistent or display less social flexibility; thus, educators should strive to develop interventions that lessen the negative effects of their temperament. Because little intervention research exists in this area, the following suggestions should be regarded as tentative:

1. Reward on-task behavior, and discuss the positive consequences of completing tasks.
2. Teach the student to self-monitor on-task and off-task behavior.
3. Include the student in selecting some tasks to do.
4. Lessen social inflexibility by helping the student make transitions among activities (e.g., periodically cue the student about a transition prior to its occurrence).
5. Reward smooth transitions and discuss their positive outcomes.
6. Involve the student in role-play games or situations in which students must take turns.

Suicide. The following suggestions are offered for dealing with suicide concerns:

1. Take suicide-related drawings and comments (such as "I hope I die") seriously, and keep records of their occurrence.
2. Elicit confirmation regarding a student's suicidal signals (e.g., "Do you think about hurting yourself often?").
3. Affirm a commitment to life when responding to a student's concerns (e.g., "I see how that can upset you, but isn't it nice that you have your friend to enjoy each day?").
4. Have the student stay with someone if the student's thoughts or actions seem serious.
5. Seek professional help in dealing with the student.

Personality Variables. The following suggested interventions focus on dealing with personality variables:

1. Separate the student's problem from the person, and do not criticize the student personally.
2. Provide opportunities for the student to be proud (e.g., encourage the sharing of a special interest or talent when the content or situation is appropriate).
3. Constantly point out the relationship between the student's efforts and outcomes, and encourage the student to set goals for learning. These activities may help the student develop a more internal locus of control.
4. Display the student's work on bulletin boards, and arrange situations in which outsiders (such a principal or other teachers) are able to encourage or praise the student.

TECHNIQUES FOR PROMOTING BEHAVIOR DEVELOPMENT

If the techniques featured in this chapter in the sections on interventions (i.e., general techniques for promoting social, emotional, and behavior development; specific techniques for promoting social development; and specific techniques for promoting emotional development) are applied, inappropriate behavior should diminish to the extent that it is not a problem. In essence, when applied within a classroom community that values cooperation, feelings, and property, the use of the techniques listed in this chapter and in Chapter 7 should diminish or eliminate chronic disruptive behavior. The primary techniques include (a) academic success through good teaching, (b) the use of motivation techniques, (c) the occasional use of mild consequences, (d) social skills instruction, and (e) sensitivity to personality variables. If these techniques are unsuccessful, the individual may have an organically based problem and need medication (see Chapter 3). Bender (1995) offers the following general techniques for promoting adaptive behavior:

1. Create an environment that encourages work completion.
2. Provide students with opportunities to engage in persuasive arguments.
3. Use role playing to problem solve and enhance understanding of others' feelings.
4. Use gentle verbal reminders to help students stay on task.
5. Provide areas of minimal distractions for students to think or work.

COMMERCIAL PROGRAMS FOR SOCIAL AND EMOTIONAL BEHAVIOR

Various programs and materials are designed to help students understand themselves better and get along with others. The following programs and materials can be used to enhance self-concept and general social and emotional growth.

Developing Understanding of Self and Others

The *DUSO* kits (Dinkmeyer & Dinkmeyer, 1982) are designed to encourage the social and emotional growth of students in kindergarten through fourth grade. *DUSO I,* for students in kindergarten through second grade, is used to develop appreciation of individual strengths and acceptance of limitations, beginning of social skills, and awareness of feelings, priorities, and choices. *DUSO II,* for third and fourth graders, helps develop a greater understanding of the purposive nature of behavior, more effective communication skills, a greater understanding of feelings and empathetic behavior, and skill in recognizing and making choices. The central character of both programs is a puppet, Duso the Dolphin. A problem situation and a story are presented and followed by role-playing and puppet activities. The kit provides hand puppets, posters, activity cards, and audiocassettes of stories and songs.

Getting Along with Others

Getting Along with Others: Teaching Social Effectiveness to Children (Jackson, Jackson, & Monroe, 1983) presents a direct intervention approach with systematic instructional methods. A tell-show-practice model of social skills training is used in which the students participate in role-playing activities and learn adaptive coping responses. A notebook of skill lessons and activities presents 17 core social skills (e.g., following directions, giving and receiving positive feedback, and saying "no" to stay out of trouble). The program guide provides teacher scripts and offers 32 training activities and 5 main teaching strategies as well as 9 additional techniques to enhance the learning potential in any interaction. It also includes a built-in behavior management system for reducing or eliminating problem behaviors.

Skillstreaming the Elementary School Child; Skillstreaming the Adolescent

These two manuals provide a program for teaching prosocial skills based on a structured learning method that involves teacher modeling (demonstrating the behavioral steps that make up specific skills), student role playing (reviewing, rehearsing, and performing each of the skill steps), group performance feedback (evaluating the role-play), and transfer training (developing assignments for using the skills in real-life situations). In *Skillstreaming the Elementary School Child* (McGinnis, Goldstein, Sprafkin, & Gershaw, 1984), 60 specific prosocial skills (such as apologizing, dealing with anger, and responding to teasing) are presented within the content areas of dealing with feelings, classroom survival skills, alternatives to aggression, friendship-making skills, and dealing with stress. *Skillstreaming the Adolescent* (Goldstein, Sprafkin, Gershaw, & Klein, 1980) presents 50 prosocial skills (such as maintaining a conversation, setting a goal, and standing up for oneself or a friend) within the content areas of beginning and advanced social skills, dealing with feelings, alternatives to aggression, dealing with stress, and planning skills. A video program is available that illustrates the concepts and training procedures contained in the books.

Social Skills for Daily Living

Social Skills for Daily Living (Schumaker, Hazel, & Pederson, 1988) provides a curriculum for students age 12 through 21 that teaches 30 social skills organized in three categories: conversation and friendship skills, skills for getting along with others, and problem-solving skills. An instructional sequence gives students the opportunity to understand the skill, memorize the skill steps, practice the skill, and apply the skill in real-life situations. The program is designed according to the interests and capabilities of secondary-level students and has a fourth-grade reading level. In addition to skill books and student workbooks, the program includes comic books that present science fiction stories to illustrate the use of skills, cards that provide role-play situations to practice skills, and blackline masters that include activities requiring students to apply skills.

The Solution Book

The Solution Book (Sprick, 1981) is a teacher resource material, packaged in a looseleaf binder, that presents a positive approach to discipline and gives practical, simple solutions to common classroom behavior problems. The first section contains nine topic booklets (e.g., Effective Reinforcement, Effective Punishment, and Establishing a Discipline Plan) that help the teacher establish an environment that minimizes misbehavior and maximizes learning. The second section consists of 100 solution sheets that each present a specific problem (such as fighting, talking out, and failing to complete work) and suggest a specific solution. The final section contains reproducible materials such as awards, certificates, and notes to parents that can be used effectively with elementary students to motivate and reinforce appropriate behavior.

The Walker Social Skills Curriculum

The ACCEPTS Program (Walker et al., 1983) is a social skills curriculum that teaches classroom and peer-to-peer social skills to students in kindergarten through sixth grade. The 28 classroom competencies and social skills are presented in five areas: (a) classroom skills (e.g., listening to the teacher and following classroom rules), (b) basic interaction skills (e.g., eye contact, listening, and taking turns talking), (c) getting-along skills (e.g., using polite words, sharing, and assisting others), (d) making friends skills (e.g., good grooming, smiling, and complimenting), and (e) coping skills (e.g., when expressing anger, when being teased, and when things don't go right). *The ACCESS Program* (Walker, Todis, Holmes, & Horton, 1988) teaches peer-to-peer skills, skills for relating to adults, and self-management skills to students at the middle and secondary school levels. The 30 social skills are presented in three areas: (a) relating to peers (e.g., interacting with the opposite sex, being left out, and handling group pressures), (b) relating to adults (e.g., disagreeing with adults, working independently, and developing good study habits), and (c) relating to oneself (e.g., being organized, using self-control, and feeling good about oneself). The curriculum is designed for use by both general and special education teachers and can be taught in one-to-one, small-group, or large-group instructional formats.

PERSPECTIVE

Academic difficulties clearly cause frustration, anxiety, low self-concept, and mood swings. The degree to which these academic learning problems contribute to social and emotional aberrations is difficult to ascertain. An understanding of academic and social and emotional behavior problems is complicated further by the position that social and emotional behavior problems can interfere with academic learning. Certain educators continue to debate the academic deficiency/behavior disorder relationship. Which one occurred first? Which one caused the other? Does the student primarily have emotional disabilities or primarily have learning disabilities? Moreover, some students exhibit social or emotional disabilities yet maintain excellent academic progress. These conditions and their related questions are complex, and until precise causes and valid diagnostic procedures are developed, they will continue to generate controversy. Meanwhile, perhaps the best strategy involves the direct treatment of target behaviors and the placement of youngsters in settings that provide earned success, reasonable structure, and sensitive support. This chapter offers information (i.e., characteristics, assessment practices, and intervention procedures) aimed at facilitating an appropriate education for students with learning disabilities who also have social, emotional, or behavior problems.

The disintegration of the family and its supportive structures combine with increasing crime, violence, child abuse, and substance abuse to remind educators that perhaps at no other time in the history of civilization has it been more important for school personnel to provide safe and caring environments for students. Thus, in concluding this chapter on the social, emotional, and behavior development of students with learning disabilities, it seems appropriate to give an example of how the kind act of one teacher had a major effect on the lives of her students. Helen Mrosla, a teacher from Morris, Minnesota, shares a heartwarming story that illustrates the power of a caring classroom environment.

Helen was a third-grade teacher at St. Mary's School in Morris, Minnesota. She notes that all of her students were dear to her but that Mark was "one in a million." Mark had a neat appearance and a happy-to-be-alive attitude. He was occasionally mischievous and talked incessantly. When Helen corrected him for talking without permission, he would say in a serious and endearing manner, "Thank you for correcting me!" Helen grew accustomed to hearing his "thank-you" response many times a day.

One day, when her patience was thin and Mark continued to talk without permission, Helen made the mistake of telling Mark, "If you say one more word, I'm going to tape your mouth shut!" Of course, Mark spoke within 10 seconds. Helen went to her desk, opened a drawer, got out the masking tape, and walked to Mark's desk. She tore off two pieces of tape and placed them in the shape of an X over Mark's mouth. Helen returned to the front of the classroom. When she glanced at Mark to see how he was doing, he winked at her, and she immediately started laughing. The entire class cheered as she walked back to Mark's desk, removed the tape, and shrugged her shoulders. His first words were "Thank you for correcting me, teacher!"

At the end of the year, Helen was asked to teach math in the junior high school. The years passed, and Mark became a student in her class again. He was just as polite, talked less, and was more handsome than ever.

One Friday, Helen noted that the class seemed tense and edgy. The students had been working diligently on some new math concepts, and several of the students were frustrated. Helen decided to stop the irritable atmosphere before it became a problem. She told her students to stop what they were doing and get out two sheets of paper. She asked them to write the names of all the other students in the class and leave space between each name. Then Helen told them to think of the nicest thing they could say about each classmate and write it down. This activity took the entire period. As the students left the room, each student handed Helen the paper. Some smiled. Mark said, "Thank you for teaching me. Have a good weekend."

During the weekend Helen wrote the name of each student on a separate sheet of paper and listed all the things everyone wrote about that individual. On Monday, she gave each student his or her list. Some students smiled and whispered some of the things on their lists, and others made statements such as "I didn't know others liked me so much!" The papers were not mentioned again; however, the exercise was successful in bringing a positive atmosphere back to the class.

Several years later, Helen returned from a vacation. On the way home from the airport her parents told her that Mark's parents had called. Her father told Helen that Mark was killed in Vietnam, and his parents wanted her to attend the funeral. Helen remembers being the last person to bless Mark's coffin. While she stood there, one of the soldiers who was serving as a pallbearer approached her and asked, "Were you Mark's math teacher?" She nodded. He said, "He talked about you a lot." (The remainder of the story is best captured in Helen Mrosla's [1993] own words.)

> After the funeral most of Mark's former classmates headed to Chuck's farm for lunch. Mark's mother and father were there, obviously waiting for me. "We want to show you something," his father said, taking a wallet out of his pocket. "They found this on Mark when he was killed. We thought you might recognize it."
>
> Opening the billfold, he carefully removed two worn pieces of notebook paper that had obviously been taped, folded and refolded many times. I knew without looking that the papers were the ones on which I had listed all the good things each of Mark's classmates had said about him. "Thank you so much for doing that," Mark's mother said. "As you can see, Mark treasured it."
>
> Mark's classmates started to gather around us. Chuck smiled rather sheepishly and said, "I still have my list. It's in the top drawer of my desk at home." John's wife said, "John asked me to put his in our wedding album." "I have mine too," Marilyn said. "It's in my diary." Then Vicki, another classmate, reached into her pocketbook, took out her wallet and showed her worn and frazzled list to the group. "I carry this with me at all times," Vicki said without batting an eyelash. "I think we all saved our lists."
>
> That's when I finally sat down and cried. I cried for Mark and for all his friends who would never see him again. (p. 128)

DISCUSSION/REVIEW QUESTIONS

1. Discuss the social development of students with learning disabilities.
2. Discuss emotional characteristics that may be present in students with learning disabilities.
3. Describe behavioral problems that may be exhibited by students with learning disabilities.
4. Discuss the most prominent hypotheses concerning etiology of social and emotional behavior problems.
5. Briefly discuss the assessment of social and emotional behavior problems in the areas of teacher ratings, parent ratings, measures of adaptive behavior, self-report instruments, sociometric techniques, and naturalistic observations.
6. Discuss general techniques for promoting social, emotional, and behavior development.
7. Discuss the concept of behavior modification, and describe the use of contingency contracts and token systems.
8. Discuss the use of social skills training.
9. Briefly discuss bibliotherapy, attribution retraining, life-space interviewing, reality therapy, and techniques for improving mood states.
10. Briefly describe several commercial programs for social and emotional behavior.

REFERENCES

Bandura, A. (1977). *Social learning theory.* Upper Saddle River, NJ: Prentice Hall.

Battle, J. (1992). *Culture-Free Self-Esteem Inventories—2.* Austin, TX: PRO-ED.

Baum, D. D., Duffelmeyer, F., & Geelan, M. (1988). Resource teacher perceptions of the prevalence of social dysfunction among students with learning disabilities. *Journal of Learning Disabilities, 21,* 380–381.

Bender, W. N. (1994). Social-emotional development: The task and the challenge. *Learning Disability Quarterly, 17,* 250–252.

Bender, W. N. (1995). *Learning disabilities: Characteristics, identification, and teaching strategies* (2nd ed.). Boston: Allyn & Bacon.

Bender, W. N., & Golden, L. B. (1988). Adaptive behavior of learning disabled and non-learning disabled children. *Learning Disability Quarterly, 11,* 55–61.

Bender, W. N., & Golden, L. B. (1989). Prediction of adaptive behavior of learning disabled students in self-contained and resource classes. *Learning Disabilities Research, 5*(1), 45–50.

Bender, W. N., & Golden, L. B. (1990). Subtypes of students with learning disabilities as derived from cognitive, academic, behavioral, and self-concept measures. *Learning Disability Quarterly, 13,* 183–194.

Bender, W. N., & Smith, J. K. (1990). Classroom behavior of children and adolescents with learning disabilities: A meta-analysis. *Journal of Learning Disabilities, 23,* 298–305.

Bender, W. N., & Wall, M. E. (1994). Social-emotional development of students with learning disabilities. *Learning Disability Quarterly, 17,* 323–341.

Blackham, G. J., & Silberman, A. (1980). *Modification of child and adolescent behavior* (3rd ed.). Belmont, CA: Wadsworth.

Block, G. H. (1977). Hyperactivity: A cultural perspective. *Journal of Learning Disabilities, 10,* 236–240.

Bracken, B. A. (1992). *Multidimensional Self-Concept Scale.* Austin, TX: PRO-ED.

Brigham, T. A., Hopper, C., Hill, B., De Armas, A., & Newsom, P. (1985). A self-management program for disruptive adolescents in the school: A clinical replication. *Behavior Therapy, 16,* 99–115.

Brown, L. L., & Alexander, J. (1991). *Self-Esteem Index.* Austin, TX: PRO-ED.

Brown, L. L., & Hammill, D. D. (1990). *Behavior Rating Profile—2.* Austin, TX: PRO-ED.

Bruininks, R. H., Woodcock, R. W., Weatherman, R. F., & Hill, B. K. (1984). *Scales of Independent Behavior.* Chicago: Riverside.

Bryan, T. H. (1986). Self-concept and attributions of the learning disabled. *Learning Disabilities Focus, 1,* 82–89.

Bryan, T. H., & Bryan, J. H. (1986). *Understanding learning disabilities* (3rd ed.). Palo Alto, CA: Mayfield.

Bryan, T., Pearl, R., & Fallon, P. (1989). Conformity to peer pressure by students with learning disabilities: A replication. *Journal of Learning Disabilities, 22,* 458–459.

Cartledge, G., Frew, T., & Zaharias, J. (1985). Social skill needs of mainstreamed students: Peer and teacher perceptions. *Learning Disability Quarterly, 8,* 132–140.

Chapman, J. W., & Boersma, F. J. (1979). Learning disabilities, locus of control, and mother attitudes. *Journal of Educational Psychology, 1,* 250–258.

Cianciolo, P. J. (1965). Children's literature can affect coping behavior. *Personnel and Guidance Journal, 43*(9), 897–903.

Coie, J., Dodge, K., & Coppotelli, H. (1982). Dimensions and types of social status: A cross-age perspective. *Developmental Psychology, 18,* 557–570.

Coleman, J. M., & Minnett, A. M. (1992/1993). Learning disabilities and social competence: A social ecological perspective. *Exceptional Children, 59,* 234–246.

Conderman, G. (1995). Social status of sixth- and seventh-grade students with learning disabilities. *Learning Disability Quarterly, 18,* 13–24.

Coopersmith, S. (1981). *Coopersmith Self-Esteem Inventories.* Palo Alto, CA: Consulting Psychologists Press.

DeLong, R. (1995). Medical and pharmacologic treatment of learning disabilities. *Journal of Child Neurology, 10*(Suppl. 1), 92–95.

Deshler, D. D., Schumaker, J. B., & Lenz, B. K. (1984). Academic and cognitive interventions for LD adolescents: Part I. *Journal of Learning Disabilities, 17,* 108–117.

Dinkmeyer, D., & Dinkmeyer, D., Jr. (1982). *Developing understanding of self and others* (Rev. ed.). Circle Pines, MN: American Guidance Service.

Dodge, K. (1983). Behavioral antecedents of peer status. *Child Development, 54,* 1400–1416.

Dodge, K. A., Pettit, G. S., McClaskey, C. L., & Brown, M. M. (1986). Social competence in children. *Monograph of the Society for Research in Child Development, 51*(2, Serial No. 213).

Elliott, S. N., Gresham, F. M., & Heffer, R. W. (1987). Social-skill interventions: Research findings and training techniques. In C. A. Maher & J. E. Zins (Eds.), *Psychoeducational interventions in the schools* (pp. 141–159). New York: Pergamon.

Ellis, E. E., Lenz, B. K., & Sabornie, E. J. (1987). Generalization and adaptation of learning strategies to natural environments: Part 2: Research into practice. *Remedial and Special Education, 8*(2), 6–23.

Emslie, G. J., Kennard, B. D., & Kowatch, R. A. (1995). Affective disorders in children: Diagnosis and management. *Journal of Child Neurology, 10*(Suppl. 1), 42–49.

Feingold, B. F. (1974). *Why your child is hyperactive.* New York: Random House.

Fitts, W. H., & Roid, G. H. (1988). *Manual: Tennessee Self-Concept Scale.* Los Angeles: Western Psychological Services.

Flanders, N. (1970). *Analyzing teacher behavior.* Menlo Park, CA: Addison-Wesley.

Fowler, J. W., & Peterson, P. L. (1981). Increasing reading persistence and altering attributional style of learned helpless children. *Journal of Educational Psychology, 73,* 251–260.

Fox, C. L. (1989). Peer acceptance of learning disabled children in the regular classroom. *Exceptional Children, 56,* 50–59.

Glasser, W. (1965). *Reality therapy: A new approach to psychiatry.* New York: Harper & Row.

Goldsmith, H. H., & Gottesman, I. I. (1981). Origins of variation in behavioral style: A longitudinal study of temperament in young twins. *Child Development, 52,* 91–103.

Goldstein, A. P., Sprafkin, R. P., Gershaw, N. J., & Klein, P. (1980). *Skillstreaming the adolescent.* Champaign, IL: Research Press.

Gresham, F. M. (1981). Social skills training with handicapped children: A review. *Review of Educational Research, 51,* 139–176.

Gresham, F. M. (1988). Social competence and motivational characteristics of learning disabled students. In M. Wang, M. Reynolds, & H. Walberg (Eds.), *The handbook of special education: Research and practice* (pp. 283–302). Oxford, England: Pergamon Press.

Gresham, F. M., & Elliott, S. N. (1989a). Social skills assessment technology for LD students. *Learning Disability Quarterly, 12,* 141–152.

Gresham, F. M., & Elliott, S. N. (1989b). Social skills deficits as a primary learning disability. *Journal of Learning Disabilities, 22,* 120–124.

Gresham, F. M., & Elliott, S. N. (1990). *Social Skills Rating System.* Circle Pines, MN: American Guidance Service.

Gresham, F. M., Elliott, S. N., & Evans-Fernandez, S. (1992). *Student Self-Concept Scale.* Circle Pines, MN: American Guidance Service.

Gresham, F. M., & Reschly, D. J. (1986). Social skill deficits and low peer acceptance of mainstreamed learning disabled children. *Learning Disability Quarterly, 9,* 23–32.

Gresham, F. M., & Reschly, D. J. (1988). Issues in the conceptualization, classification, and assessment of social skills in the mildly handicapped. In T. Kratochwill (Ed.), *Advances in school psychology* (pp. 203–247). Hillsdale, NJ: Erlbaum.

Haager, D., & Vaughn, S. (1995). Parent, teacher, peer, and self-reports of the social competence of students with learning disabilities. *Journal of Learning Disabilities, 28,* 205–215, 231.

Hazel, J. S., & Schumaker, J. B. (1988). Social skills and learning disabilities: Current issues and recommendations for future research. In J. F. Kavanagh & T. J. Truss (Eds.). *Learning disabilities: Proceedings of the national conference* (pp. 293–344). Parkton, MD: York Press.

Heath, N. L. (1995). Distortion and deficit: Self-perceived versus actual academic competence in depressed and nondepressed children with and without learning disabilities. *Learning Disabilities Research & Practice, 10,* 2–10.

Hoagland, J. (1972, March). Bibliotherapy: Aiding children in personality development. *Elementary English,* pp. 390–394.

Hughes, C. A., Ruhl, K. L., & Peterson, S. K. (1988). Teaching self-management skills. *Teaching Exceptional Children, 20*(2), 70–72.

Huntington, D. D., & Bender, W. N. (1993). Adolescents with learning disabilities at risk? Emotional well-being, depression, suicide. *Journal of Learning Disabilities, 26,* 159–166.

Hutton, J. B., & Roberts, T. G. (1986). *Social-Emotional Dimension Scale.* Austin, TX: PRO-ED.

Hynd, G. W., Hern, L., Voeller, K., & Marshall, R. (1991). Neurological basis of attention deficit hyperactivity disorder (ADHD). *School Psychology, 20*(2), 174–186.

Interagency Committee on Learning Disabilities. (1987). *Learning disabilities: A report to the U.S. Congress.* Bethesda, MD: National Institutes of Health.

Jackson, N. F., Jackson, D. A., & Monroe, C. (1983). *Getting along with others: Teaching social effectiveness to children.* Champaign, IL: Research Press.

Johnston, L. D., O'Malley, P. M., & Bachman, J. G. (1989). *Drug use, drinking and smoking: National survey results from high school, college, and young adult populations,* 1975–85 (DHHS Publication No. ADM 89-1638). Washington, DC: U.S. Government Printing Office.

Karacostas, D. D., & Fisher, G. L. (1993). Chemical dependency in students with and without learning disabilities. *Journal of Learning Disabilities, 26,* 491–495.

Kaufman, M., Agard, J., & Semmel, M. (1985). *Mainstreaming: Learners and their environment.* Cambridge, MA: Brookline Books.

Kazdin, A. E. (1972). Response cost: The removal of conditioned reinforcers for therapeutic change. *Behavior Therapy, 3,* 533–546.

Keogh, B. (1977). Research on cognitive styles. In R. Kneedler & S. Tarver (Eds.), *Changing perspectives in special education.* Columbus, OH: Merrill.

Keogh, B. K. (1983). Individual differences in temperament: A contributor to the personal-social and educational competence of learning disabled children. In J. D. McKinney & L. Feagans (Eds.), *Current topics in learning disabilities* (Vol. 1). Norwood, NJ: Ablex.

Keogh, B. K., & Bernheimer, L. P. (1995). Etiologic conditions as predictors of children's problems and competencies in elementary school. *Journal of Child Neurology, 10*(Suppl. 1), 100–105.

Kerr, M. M., & Nelson, C. M. (1989). *Strategies for managing behavior problems in the classroom* (2nd ed.). Upper Saddle River, NJ: Merrill/Prentice Hall.

Kistner, J. A., & Gatlin, D. (1989). Correlates of peer rejection among children with learning disabilities. *Learning Disability Quarterly, 12,* 133–140.

Kistner, J., Haskett, M., White, K., & Robbins, F. (1987). Perceived competence of self-worth of learning disabled and normally achieving children. *Learning Disability Quarterly, 10,* 37–44.

Kloomok, S., & Cosden, M. (1994). Self-concept in children with learning disabilities: The relationship between global self-concept, academic "discounting," nonacademic self-concept, and perceived social support. *Learning Disability Quarterly, 17,* 140–153.

Kroth, R. (1973). The behavioral Q-sort as a diagnostic tool. *Academic Therapy, 8,* 317–329.

La Greca, A. M., & Stone, W. L. (1990). LD status and achievement: Confounding variables in the study of children's social status, self-esteem, and behavioral functioning. *Journal of Learning Disabilities, 23,* 483–490.

Lambert, N., Nihira, K., & Leland, H. (1993). *AAMR Adaptive Behavior Scale—School* (2nd ed.). Austin, TX: PRO-ED.

Lenkowsky, B., & Lenkowsky, R. (1978). Bibliotherapy of the LD adolescent. *Academic Therapy, 14,* 179–185.

Licht, B. G. (1984). Cognitive-motivational factors that contribute to the achievement of learning-disabled children. *Annual Review of Learning Disabilities, 2,* 119–126.

Lyon, G. R. (1985). Identification and remediation of learning disabilities subtypes: Preliminary findings. *Learning Disabilities Focus, 1*(1), 21–35.

Maag, J. W. (1989). Assessment in social skills training: Methodological and conceptual issues for research and practice. *Remedial and Special Education, 10*(4), 6–17.

Maag, J. W., Irvin, D. M., Reid, R., & Vasa, S. F. (1994). Prevalence and predictors of substance use: A comparison between adolescents with and without learning disabilities. *Journal of Learning Disabilities, 27,* 223–234.

Maag, J. W., & Reid, R. (1994). The phenomenology of depression among students with and without learning disabilities: More similar than different. *Learning Disabilities Research & Practice, 9,* 91–103.

Margalit, M., & Ben-Dov, I. (1992). *Kibbutz versus city comparisons of social competence and loneliness among students with and without learning disabilities.* Paper presented at the annual IARLD Conference, Amsterdam.

Margalit, M., & Raviv, A. (1984). LD's expressions of anxiety in terms of minor somatic complaints. *Journal of Learning Disabilities, 17,* 226–228.

Margalit, M., & Shulman, S. (1986). Autonomy perceptions and anxiety expressions of learning disabled adolescents. *Journal of Learning Disabilities, 19,* 291–293.

McCarney, S. B., & Leigh, J. E. (1990). *Behavior Evaluation Scale—2.* Columbia, MO: Hawthorne Educational Services.

McConnell, S., & Odom, S. (1986). Sociometrics: Peer-referenced measures and the assessment of social competence. In P. Strain, M. Guralnick, & H. Walker (Eds.), *Children's social behavior: Development, assessment, and modification* (pp. 215–284). Orlando, FL: Academic Press.

McGinnis, E., Goldstein, A. P., Sprafkin, R. P., & Gershaw, N. J. (1984). *Skillstreaming the elementary school child.* Champaign, IL: Research Press.

McKinney, J. D. (1989). Longitudinal research on the behavioral characteristics of children with learning disabilities. *Journal of Learning Disabilities, 22,* 141–150, 165.

McKinney, J. D., & Feagans, L. (1984). Adaptive classroom behavior of learning disabled students. *Journal of Learning Disabilities, 16.* 360–367.

McKinney, J. D., McClure, S., & Feagans, L. (1982). Classroom behavior of learning disabled children. *Learning Disability Quarterly, 5*(1), 45–52.

Meichenbaum, D. (1977). *Cognitive-behavior modification: An integrative approach.* New York: Plenum Press.

Mellard, D. F., & Hazel, J. S. (1992). Social competencies as a pathway to successful life transitions. *Learning Disability Quarterly, 15,* 251–271.

Minskoff, E. H. (1980a). Teaching approach for developing nonverbal communication skills in students with social perception deficits. Part I: The basic approach and body language clues. *Journal of Learning Disabilities, 13,* 118–124.

Minskoff, E. H. (1980b). Teaching approach for developing nonverbal communication skills in students with social perception deficits. Part II: Proxemic, vocalic, and artifactual cues. *Journal of Learning Disabilities, 13,* 203–208.

Montgomery, M. S. (1994). Self-concept and children with learning disabilities: Observer-child concordance across six context-dependent domains. *Journal of Learning Disabilities, 27,* 254–262.

Morse, W. C. (1971). Worksheet on life space interviewing for teachers. In N. J. Long, W. C. Morse, & R. G. Newman (Eds.), *Conflict in the classroom: The education of emotionally disturbed children* (2nd ed.). Belmont, CA: Wadsworth.

Mrosla, H. P. (1993). All the good things. In J. Canfield & M. V. Hansen, *Chicken soup for the soul* (pp. 125–128). Deerfield Beach, FL: Health Communications. (Originally appeared in *Proteus: A Journal of Ideas,* Spring 1991)

Naglieri, J. A., LeBuffe, P. A., & Pfeiffer, S. I. (1993). *Devereux Behavior Rating Scale—School Form.* San Antonio, TX: Psychological Corporation.

Neeper, R., Lahey, B. B., & Frick, P. J. (1990). *Comprehensive Behavior Rating Scale for Children.* San Antonio, TX: Psychological Corporation.

Ochoa, S. H. & Olivarez, A., Jr. (1995). A meta-analysis of peer rating sociometric studies of pupils with learning disabilities. *The Journal of Special Education, 29,* 1–19.

Paine, S. C., Radicchi, J., Rosellini, L. C., Deutchman, L., & Darch, C. B. (1983). *Structuring your classroom for academic success.* Champaign, IL: Research Press.

Pearl, R., & Bryan, T. (1992). Students' expectations about peer pressure to engage in misconduct. *Journal of Learning Disabilities, 15,* 582–585, 597.

Pearl, R., Bryan, T., & Donahue, M. (1980). Learning disabled children's attributions for success and failure. *Learning Disability Quarterly, 3*(1), 3–9.

Peck, M. L. (1985). Crisis intervention treatment with chronically and acutely suicidal adolescents. In M. Peck, N. Farbelow, & R. Litman (Eds.), *Youth suicide* (pp. 1–33). New York: Springer-Verlag.

Piers, E. V., & Harris, D. B. (1984). *The Piers-Harris Children's Self-Concept Scale.* Los Angeles: Western Psychological Services.

Polsgrove, L. (1979). Self-control: Methods for child training. *Behavioral Disorders, 4,* 116–130.

Pray, B. S., Jr., Hall, C. W., & Markley, R. P. (1992). Social skills training: An analysis of social behaviors selected for individualized education programs. *Remedial and Special Education, 13*(5), 43–49.

Premack, D. (1959). Toward empirical behavior laws: I. Positive reinforcement. *Psychological Review, 66,* 219–233.

Quay, H. C., & Peterson, D. R. (1987). *Revised Behavior Problem Checklist.* Coral Gables, FL: University of Miami.

Reynolds, C. R., & Kamphaus, R. W. (1992). *Behavior Assessment System for Children.* Circle Pines, MN: American Guidance Service.

Riccio, C. A., Gonzalez, J. J., & Hynd, G. W. (1994). Attention-deficit hyperactivity disorder (ADHD) and learning disabilities. *Learning Disability Quarterly, 17,* 311–322.

Rieth, H., & Evertson, C. (1988). Variables related to the effective instruction of difficult-to-teach children. *Focus on Exceptional Children, 20*(5), 1–8.

Ritter, D. R. (1989). Social competence and problem behavior of adolescent girls with learning disabilities. *Journal of Learning Disabilities, 22,* 460–461.

Roberts, R., & Mather, N. (1995). The return of students with learning disabilities to regular classrooms: A sellout? *Learning Disabilities Research & Practice, 10,* 46–58.

Rosenthal, I. (1992). Counseling the learning disabled late adolescent and adult: A self-psychology perspective. *Learning Disabilities Research & Practice, 7,* 217–225.

Russell, A. E., & Russell, W. A. (1979). Using bibliotherapy with emotionally disturbed children. *Teaching Exceptional Children, 11,* 168–169.

Sabornie, E. J. (1990). Extended sociometric status of adolescents with mild handicaps: A cross-categorical perspective. *Exceptionality, 1,* 197–209.

Sabornie, E. J. (1994). Social-affective characteristics in early adolescents identified as learning disabled and nondisabled. *Learning Disability Quarterly, 17,* 268–279.

Sander, N. W. (1991). Effects of a self-management strategy on task-independent behaviors of adolescents with learning disabilities. *B. C. Journal of Special Education, 15,* 64–75.

Schumaker, J. B., & Hazel, J. S. (1984). Social skills assessment and training for the learning disabled: Who's on first and what's on second? Part II. *Journal of Learning Disabilities, 17,* 492–499.

Schumaker, J. B., Hazel, J. S., & Pederson, C. S. (1988). *Social skills for daily living.* Circle Pines, MN: American Guidance Service.

Schunk, D. H. (1981). Modeling and attributional effects on children's achievement: A self-efficacy analysis. *Journal of Educational Psychology, 73,* 93–105.

Shapiro, E. S. (1989). Teaching self-management skills to learning disabled adolescents. *Learning Disability Quarterly, 12,* 275–287.

Shaywitz, B. (1987). Hyperactivity/attention deficit disorder. In Interagency Committee on Learning Disabilities, *Learning disabilities: A report to the U.S. Congress* (pp. 194–218). Bethesda, MD: National Institutes of Health.

Shelton, T. L., Anastopoulos, A. D., & Linden, J. D. (1985). An attribution training program with learning disabled children. *Journal of Learning Disabilities, 18,* 261–265.

Silver, L. B. (1971). A proposed view on the etiology of the neurological learning disability syndrome. *Journal of Learning Disabilities, 4,* 123–133.

Slavin, R. E. (1991). Synthesis of research on cooperative learning. *Educational Leadership, 48*(5), 71–82.

Smith, C. R. (1994). *Learning disabilities: The interaction of learner, task, and setting* (3rd ed.). Boston: Allyn & Bacon.

Sparrow, S. S., Balla, D. A., & Cicchetti, D. V. (1984). *The Vineland Adaptive Behavior Scale.* Circle Pines, MN: American Guidance Service.

Sprick, R. S. (1981). *The solution book: A guide to classroom discipline.* Blacklick, OH: SRA.

Sprick, R. S. (1985). *Discipline in the secondary classroom: A problem-by-problem survival guide.* West Nyack, NY: The Center for Applied Research in Education.

Stewart, M. A. (1970). Hyperactive children. *Scientific American, 222,* 94–98.

Sugai, G., & Fuller, M. (1991). A decision model for social skills curriculum analysis. *Remedial and Special Education, 12*(4), 33–42.

Swanson, H. L., & Malone, S. (1992). Social skills and learning disabilities: A meta-analysis of the literature. *School Psychology Review, 21,* 427–443.

Torgesen, J. K. (1982). The learning-disabled child as an inactive learner: Educational implications. *Topics in Learning and Learning Disabilities, 2,* 45–52.

Tur-Kaspa, H., & Bryan, T. (1994). Social information-processing skills of students with learning disabilities. *Learning Disabilities Research & Practice, 9,* 12–23.

Tur-Kaspa, H., & Bryan, T. (1995). Teachers' ratings of the social competence and school adjustment of students with LD in elementary and junior high school. *Journal of Learning Disabilities, 28,* 44–52.

Vaughn, S., & Haager, D. (1994). Social competence as a multifaceted construct: How do students with learning disabilities fare? *Learning Disability Quarterly, 17,* 253–266.

Vaughn, S., McIntosh, R., Schumm, J. S., Haager, D., & Callwood, D. (1993). Social status, peer acceptance, and reciprocal friendships revisited. *Learning Disabilities Research & Practice, 8,* 82–88.

Waldie, K., & Spreen, O. (1993). The relationship between learning disabilities and persisting delinquency. *Journal of Learning Disabilities, 26,* 417–423.

Walker, H. M. (1983). *Walker Problem Behavior Identification Checklist.* Los Angeles: Western Psychological Services.

Walker, H. M., & McConnell, S. R. (1988). *Walker-McConnell Scale of Social Competence and School Adjustment.* Austin, TX: PRO-ED.

Walker, H. M., McConnell, S., Holmes, D., Todis, B., Walker, J., & Golden, N. (1983). *The Walker social skills curriculum: The ACCEPTS program.* Austin, TX: PRO-ED.

Walker, H. M., Todis, B., Holmes, D., & Horton, G. (1988). *The Walker social skills curriculum: The ACCESS program.* Austin, TX: PRO-ED.

Wallace, G., & Kauffman, J. M. (1986). *Teaching students with learning and behavior problems* (3rd ed.). Upper Saddle River, NJ: Merrill/Prentice Hall.

Wallace, G., Larsen, S. C., & Elksnin, L. K. (1992). *Educational assessment of learning problems: Testing for teaching* (2nd ed.). Boston: Allyn & Bacon.

Weinberg, W. A., Harper, C. R., & Brumback, R. A. (1995). Neuroanatomic substrate of developmental specific learning disabilities and select behavioral syndromes. *Journal of Child Neurology, 10*(Suppl. 1), 78–80.

Weinstein, R. S. (1982). *Expectations in the classroom: The student perspective.* Invited address, Annual

Conference of the American Educational Research Association, New York.

Weller, C., & Strawser, S. (1981). *Weller-Strawser Scales of Adaptive Behavior for the learning disabled.* Novato, CA: Academic Therapy.

Weller, C., Strawser, S., & Buchanan, M. (1985). Adaptive behavior: Designator of a continuum of severity of learning disabled individuals. *Journal of Learning Disabilities, 18,* 200–204.

Weller, C., Watteyne, L., Herbert, M., & Crelly, C. (1994). Adaptive behavior of adults and young adults with learning disabilities. *Learning Disability Quarterly, 17,* 282–295.

Wood, M. M., & Long, N. J. (1991). *Life space intervention: Talking with children and youth in crisis.* Austin, TX: PRO-ED.

Wright-Strawderman, C., & Watson, B. L. (1992). The prevalence of depressive symptoms in children with learning disabilities. *Journal of Learning Disabilities, 25,* 258–264.

APPENDIX A

Organizations and Journals

ORGANIZATIONS

American Speech and Hearing Association, 9030 Old Georgetown Road, Washington, DC 20014

Association for Supervision and Curriculum Development, 1250 North Pitt Street, Alexandria, VA 22314

Children with Attention Deficit Disorders, 499 N.W. 70th Avenue, Suite 308, Plantation, FL 33317

Council for Exceptional Children, 1920 Association Drive, Reston, VA 22091

Council for Learning Disabilities, P.O. Box 40303, Overland Park, KS 66204

Division for Learning Disabilities, Council for Exceptional Children, 1920 Association Drive, Reston, VA 22091

International Reading Association, 800 Barksdale Road, P.O. Box 8139, Newark, DE 19711

Learning Disabilities Association, 4156 Library Road, Pittsburgh, PA 15234

Orton Dyslexia Society, Chester Building, Suite 382, 8600 LaSalle Road, Baltimore, MD 21286

JOURNALS

Asha, American Speech and Hearing Association, 9030 Old Georgetown Road, Washington, DC 20014

Bulletin of the Orton Society, Orton Society, Chester Building, Suite 382, 8600 LaSalle Road, Baltimore, MD 21286

Educational Leadership, Association for Supervision and Curriculum Development, 1250 North Pitt Street, Alexandria, VA 22314

Exceptional Children, Council for Exceptional Children, 1920 Association Drive, Reston, VA 22091

Exceptional Parent, 1170 Commonwealth Avenue, Boston, MA 01234

Focus on Exceptional Children, 6635 East Villanova Place, Denver, CO 80222

Intervention in School and Clinic, PRO-ED, 8700 Shoal Creek Boulevard, Austin, TX 78757

Journal of Applied Behavior Analysis, Department of Human Development, University of Kansas, Lawrence, KS 60045

Journal of Learning Disabilities, PRO-ED, 8700 Shoal Creek Boulevard, Austin, TX 78757

Journal of Precision Teaching, Plain English Publications, P.O. Box 7224, Kansas City, MO 64113

Journal of Reading, International Reading Association, 800 Barksdale Road, Newark, DE 19711

The Journal of Special Education, PRO-ED, 8700 Shoal Creek Boulevard, Austin, TX 78757

LD Forum, Council for Learning Disabilities, P.O. Box 40303, Overland Park, KS 66204

Learning Disabilities Research & Practice, Division for Learning Disabilities, Council for Exceptional Children, 1920 Association Drive, Reston, VA 22091

Learning Disability Quarterly, Council for Learning Disabilities, P.O. Box 40303, Overland Park, KS 66204

Reading Research Quarterly, International Reading Association, 800 Barksdale Road, Newark, DE 19711

The Reading Teacher, International Reading Association, 800 Barksdale Road, Newark, DE 19711

Remedial and Special Education, PRO-ED, 8700 Shoal Creek Boulevard, Austin, TX 78757

Teaching Exceptional Children, Council for Exceptional Children, 1920 Association Drive, Reston, VA 22091

Topics in Early Childhood Special Education, PRO-ED, 8700 Shoal Creek Boulevard, Austin, TX 78757

APPENDIX B

Publishers of Books, Tests, and Materials

Academic Therapy Publications, 20 Commercial Boulevard, Novato, CA 94949
Adapt Press, 808 West Avenue North, Sioux Falls, SD 57104
Addison-Wesley Publishing Company, 2725 Sand Hill Road, Menlo Park, CA 94025
Adston Educational Enterprise, 945 East River Oaks Drive, Baton Rouge, LA 70815
Allied Education Council, P.O. Box 78, Galien, MI 49113
Allyn & Bacon, 160 Gould Street, Needham Heights, MA 02194
American Association on Mental Deficiency, 5201 Connecticut Avenue, Washington, DC 20015
American Book Company, 450 West 33rd Street, New York, NY 10001
American Guidance Service, 4201 Woodland Road, P.O. Box 99, Circle Pines, MN 55014
Appleton-Century-Crofts, 440 Park Avenue South, New York, NY 10016
Arista Corporation, 2 Park Avenue, New York, NY 10016
Aspen Publishers, 7201 McKinney Circle, P.O. Box 990, Frederick, MD 21701
Clarence L. Barnhart, Box 250, Bronxville, NY 10708
Behavioral Research Laboratories, P.O. Box 577, Palo Alto, CA 94302
Benefic Press, 10300 West Roosevelt Road, Westchester, IL 60153
Biological Sciences Curriculum Study, P.O. Box 930, Boulder, CO 80306
Bobbs-Merrill Company, 4300 West 62nd Street, Indianapolis, IN 46206
Bowmar/Noble Publishers, 4563 Colorado Boulevard, Los Angeles, CA 90039
Paul H. Brookes Publishing Company, P.O. Box 10624, Baltimore, MD 21285
Brooks/Cole Publishing Company, 511 Forest Lodge Road, Pacific Grove, CA 93950
William C. Brown Publishers, 2460 Kerper Boulevard, P.O. Box 539, Dubuque, IA 52004
C. C. Publications, P.O. Box 23699, Tigard, OR 97223
Childcraft Education Corporation, 20 Kilmer Road, Edison, NJ 08817
Communication Skill Builders, 3830 East Bellevue, P.O. Box 42050-CS4, Tucson, AZ 85733
Consulting Psychologists Press, 3803 East Bayshore Road, P.O. Box 11096, Palo Alto, CA 94303
Continental Press, 520 East Bainbridge Street, Elizabethtown, PA 17022
Council for Exceptional Children, 1920 Association Drive, Reston, VA 22091
CTB/McGraw-Hill, 20 Ryan Ranch Road, Monterey, CA 93940
Cuisenaire Company of America, P.O. Box 5026, White Plains, NY 10602
Curriculum Associates, 5 Esquire Road, North Billerica, MA 01862
Dale Seymour Publications, P.O. Box 10888, Palo Alto, CA 94303
Devereux Foundation Press, 19 South Waterloo Road, Devon, PA 19333

Dormac, P.O. Box 752, Beaverton, OR 97075

EBSCO Curriculum Materials, Box 11542, Birmingham, AL 35201

Economy Company, P.O. Box 25308, 1901 North Walnut Street, Oklahoma City, OK 73125

Edge Enterprises, 708 West 9th, Suite R4, P.O. Box 1304, Lawrence, KS 66044

Edmark Corporation, P.O. Box 3218, Redmond, WA 98073

Educational Achievement Systems, P.O. Box 7449, Delray Beach, FL 33484

Educational Activities, P.O. Box 392, Freeport, NY 11520

Educational Performance Associates, 600 Broad Avenue, Ridgefield, NJ 07657

Educational Progress Corporation, P.O. Box 45663, Tulsa, OK 74145

Educational Service, P.O. Box 219, Stevensville, MI 49127

Educational Teaching Aids, 620 Lakeview Parkway, Vernon Hills, IL 60061

Educational Testing Service, P.O. Box 6108, Princeton, NJ 08541

Educators Publishing Service, 31 Smith Place, Cambridge, MA 02138

Enrich, Mafex Associates, 90 Cherry Street, Johnstown, PA 15907

Exceptional Education, P.O. Box 15308, Seattle, WA 98115

Fearon Publishers, 6 Davis Drive, Belmont, CA 94002

Field Educational Publications, 2400 Hanover Street, Palo Alto, CA 94302

Fox Reading Research Company, P.O. Box 1059, Coeur D'Alene, ID 83814

Franklin Learning Resources, 122 Burrs Road, Mt. Holy, NJ 08060

Garrard Publishing Company, 1607 North Market Street, Champaign, IL 61820

General Learning Corporation, 250 James Street, Morristown, NJ 07960

Ginn and Company, 191 Spring Street, Lexington, MA 02173

Grosset and Dunlap, 51 Madison Avenue, New York, NY 10010

Grune and Stratton, 111 Fifth Avenue, New York, NY 10003

Gryphon Press, 220 Montgomery Street, Highland Park, NJ 18904

Guidance Associates, 1526 Gilpin Avenue, Wilmington, DE 19806

H and H Enterprises, 946 Tennessee, Lawrence, KS 66044

Harcourt Brace Educational Measurement, 555 Academic Court, San Antonio, TX 78204

Harcourt Brace Jovanovich, 6277 Sea Harbor Drive, Orlando, FL 32821

Harper and Row Publishers, 10 East 53rd Street, New York, NY 10022

Haworth Press, 12 West 32nd Street, New York, NY 10010

Hawthorne Educational Services, 800 Gray Oak Drive, Columbia, MO 65201

D. C. Heath and Company, 125 Spring Street, Lexington, MA 02173

Heinemann, 361 Hanover Street, Portsmouth, NH 03801

Holt, Rinehart and Winston, 301 Commerce Street, Fort Worth, TX 76102

Houghton Mifflin, 222 Berkeley Street, Boston, MA 02116

Hubbard, P.O. Box 104, Northbrook, IL 60062

Human Development Training Institute, 1081 East Main Street, El Cajon, CA 92021

Human Sciences Press, 72 Fifth Avenue, New York, NY 10011

Ideal School Supply Company, 11000 South Lavergne Avenue, Oak Lawn, IL 60453

Incentive Publications, P.O. Box 12522, Nashville, TN 37212

Initial Teaching Alphabet Publications, 6 East 43rd Street, New York, NY 10017

International Reading Association, 800 Barksdale Road, Newark, DE 19711

Interstate Printers and Publishers, 19 North Jackson Street, P.O. Box 50, Danville, IL 61834

Janus Books, 2501 Industrial Parkway, West, Hayward, CA 94545

Jastak Associates, 1526 Gilpin Avenue, Wilmington, DE 19806

Learning Concepts, 2501 North Lamar Boulevard, Austin, TX 78705

Learning Skills, 17951-G Sky Park Circle, Irvine, CA 92707

LinguiSystems, 3100 4th Avenue, P.O. Box 747, East Moline, IL 61244

J. B. Lippincott Company, Educational Publishing Division, East Washington Square, Philadelphia, PA 19105

Little, Brown and Company, 34 Beacon Street, Boston, MA 02108

Longman, 95 Church Street, White Plains, NY 10601
Love Publishing Company, 1777 South Bellaire Street, Denver, CO 80222
Lyons and Carnahan, 407 East 25th Street, Chicago, IL 60616
Mafex Associates, 90 Cherry Street, Box 519, Johnstown, PA 15907
Mayfield Publishing Company, 1240 Villa Street, Mountain View, CA 94041
McGraw-Hill Book Company, 1221 Avenue of the Americas, New York, NY 10020
Media Materials, 1821 Portal Street, Baltimore, MD 21224
Melton Book Company, 111 Leslie Street, Dallas, TX 75207
Melton Peninsula, 1949 Stemmons Freeway, Dallas, TX 75207
Milton Bradley Company, 74 Park Street, Springfield, MA 01101
Modern Curriculum Press, 13900 Prospect Road, Cleveland, OH 44136
Modern Education Corporation, P.O. Box 721, Tulsa, OK 74101
William C. Morrow, 105 Madison Avenue, New York, NY 10016
C. V. Mosby Company, 11830 Westline Industrial Drive, Saint Louis, MO 63141
New Readers Press, 1320 Jamesville Avenue, Box 131, Syracuse, NY 13210
Newby Visualanguage, Box 121-E, Eagleville, PA 19408
Noble and Noble Publishers, 1 Dag Hammarskjold Plaza, New York, NY 10017
Numark Publications, 104-20 Queens Boulevard, Forest Hills, NY 11375
Open Court Publishing Company, 1039 Eighth Street, Box 599, LaSalle, IL 61301
Opportunities for Learning, 20417 Nordhoff Street, Chatsworth, CA 91311
Parker Brothers, P.O. Box 900, Salem, MA 01970
Phoenix Learning Resources, 2349 Chaffee Drive, St. Louis, MO 63146
Phonovisual Products, 12216 Parklawn Drive, Rockville, MD 20852
Prentice Hall, One Lake Street, Upper Saddle River, NJ 07458
PRO-ED, 8700 Shoal Creek Boulevard, Austin, TX 78757
Psychological Corporation, Harcourt Brace Jovanovich, 555 Academic Court, San Antonio, TX 78204
Rand McNally and Company, P.O. Box 7600, Chicago, IL 60680
Random House/Singer School Division, 201 East 50th Street, New York, NY 10022
Reader's Digest Services, Educational Division, Pleasantville, NJ 10570
Reading Joy, P.O. Box 404, Naperville, IL 60540
Research Press, Box 9177, Champaign, IL 61826
Riverside Publishing Company, 8420 Bryn Mawr Road, Chicago, IL 60031
Scholastic Magazine and Book Services, 50 West 44th Street, New York, NY 10036
Scott, Foresman and Company, 1900 East Lake Avenue, Glenview, IL 60025
Selchow and Righter, 505 East Union Street, Bay Shore, NY 11706
Select-Ed, 117 North Chester, Olathe, KS 66061
L. W. Singer, A Division of Random House, 210 East 50th Street, New York, NY 10022
Slosson Educational Publications, 140 Pine Street, East Aurora, NY 14052
Society for Visual Education, 1345 Diversey Parkway, Chicago, IL 60614
Sopris West, 1140 Boston Avenue, Longmont, CO 80501
South-Western Publishing Company, 5101 Madison Road, Cincinnati, OH 45227
Special Child Publications, 4635 Union Bay Place, Northeast, Seattle, WA 98105
Special Learning Corporation, 42 Boston Post Road, Guilford, CT 06437
SRA, P.O. Box 543, Blacklick, OH 43004
Steck-Vaughn Company, P.O. Box 27010, Austin, TX 78755
Stoelting Company, 620 Wheat Lane, Wood Dale, IL 60191
Syracuse University Press, 1011 East Water Street, Syracuse, NY 13210
Teachers College Press, Teachers College, Columbia University, 1234 Amsterdam Avenue, New York, NY 10027
Teaching Strategies, P.O. Box 5205, Eugene, OR 97405
Texas Instruments, 2305 University Avenue, Lubbock, TX 79415
Thinking Publications, 424 Galloway Street, P.O. Box 163, Eau Claire, WI 54702
Charles C Thomas Publisher, 2600 South First Street, Springfield, IL 62794
Trend Enterprises, P.O. Box 43073, Saint Paul, MN 55164

Troll Associates, 320 Route 17, Mahwah, NJ 07430
University of Illinois Press, 54 East Gregory Drive, Champaign, IL 61820
University Park Press, 233 East Redwood Street, Baltimore, MD 21202
VORT Corporation, P.O. Box 60132, Palo Alto, CA 95306
Wadsworth Publishing Company, 10 Davis Drive, Belmont, CA 94002
George Wahr Publishing Company, 316 State Street, Ann Arbor, MI 41808
Walker Educational Book Corporation, 720 Fifth Avenue, New York, NY 10019
Warner Educational Services, 75 Rockefeller Plaza, New York, NY 10019
Wayne Engineering, 1825 Willow Road, Northfield, IL 60093
West Publishing Company, 50 West Kellogg Boulevard, P.O. Box 64526, Saint Paul, MN 55164
Western Psychological Services, 12031 Wilshire Boulevard, Los Angeles, CA 90225
Wilcox & Follett Book Company, 1000 West Washington Boulevard, Chicago, IL 60607
John Wiley and Sons, 605 Third Avenue, New York, NY 10016
B. L. Winch and Associates, 45 Hitching Post Drive, Building 29, Rolling Hills Estates, CA 90274
Xerox Education Publications, 245 Long Hill Road, Middletown, CT 06457
Zaner-Bloser Company, 1459 King Avenue, P.O. Box 16764, Columbus, OH 43216
Richard L. Zweig Associates, 20800 Beach Boulevard, Huntington Beach, CA 92648

PRODUCERS AND DISTRIBUTORS OF EDUCATIONAL COMPUTER SOFTWARE

Academic Software, c/o Software City, 22 East Quackenbush Avenue, Dumont, NJ 07628
American Educational Computer, 525 University Avenue, Palo Alto, CA 94301
American Micro Media, P.O. Box 306, Red Hook, NY 12571
Avant-Garde Creations, P.O. Box 30160, Eugene, OR 97403
BMI Educational Services, Hay Press Road, Dayton, NJ 08810
Borg-Warner Educational System, 600 West University Drive, Arlington, IL 60004
Broderbund, P.O. Box 6125, Novato, CA 94948
Cambridge Development Laboratory, 86 West Street, Waltham, MA 02154
Charles Clark Company, 168 Express Drive South, Brentwood, NY 11717
Classroom Consorta Media, 28 Bay Street, Staten Island, NY 10301
COMPU-TATIONS, P.O. Box 502, Troy, MI 48099
Computer Courseware Services, 300 York Avenue, Saint Paul, MN 55101
Computer Curriculum Corporation, P.O. Box 3711, Sunnydale, CA 94088
Computer-Ed, 1 Everett Road, Carmel, NY 10512
Cross Educational Software, 1802 North Trenton, Box 1536, Ruston, LA 71270
Davidson & Associates, P.O. Box 2961, Torrance, CA 90509
Dilithium Software, P.O. Box 606, Beaverton, OR 97075
Dorsett Educational Systems, Box 1226, Norman, OK 73070
Educational Activities, P.O. Box 392, Freeport, NY 11520
Educational Computing Systems, 106 Fairbanks, Oak Ridge, TN 37830
Educational Micro Systems, P.O. Box 471, Chester, NJ 07930
Educational Software Consultants, P.O. Box 30846, Orlando, FL 32862
Educational Systems Software, 23720 El Toro Road, P.O. Box E, El Toro, CA 92630
Educational Teaching Aids, 159 West Kinzie Street, Chicago, IL 60610
Edu-Ware Services, 28035 Dorothy Drive, Agoura, CA 91301
Encyclopaedia Britannica Educational Corporation, 425 North Michigan Avenue, Chicago, IL 60611
Follett Library Book Company, 4506 Northwest Highway, Crystal Lake, IL 60014
Gamco Industries, Box 1911, Big Spring, TX 79720
J. L. Hammett Company, Box 545, Braintree, MA 02184
Harcourt Brace Jovanovich, 6277 Sea Harbor Drive, Orlando, FL 32821
Hartley, 3451 Dunckel Road, Suite 200, Lansing, MI 48911
Houghton Mifflin, 222 Berkeley Street, Boston, MA 02116
Humanities Software, P.O. Box 950, 408 Columbia Street, Hood River, OR 97031
Huntington Computing, P.O. Box 1297, Corcoran, CA 93212
K-12 Micromedia, 172 Broadway, Woodcliff Lake, NJ 07675

Krell Software, 1320 Stony Brook Road, Stony Brook, NY 11790

The Learning Company, 4370 Alpine Road, Portola Valley, CA 94025

Learning Lab Software, 21000 Nordhoff Street, Chatsworth, CA 91311

Learning Systems, P.O. Box 9046, Fort Collins, CO 80525

Little Bee Educational Programs, P.O. Box 262, Massilon, OH 44648.

Love Publishing Company, 1777 South Bellaire Street, Denver, CO 80222

Magic Lantern Computers, 406 South Park Street, Madison, WI 53715

MARCK, 280 Linden Avenue, Branford, CT 06405

MECC, 6160 Summit Drive North, Minneapolis, MN 55430

Media Materials, 1821 Portal Street, Baltimore, MD 21224

Mercer Systems, 87 Scooter Lane, Nicksville, NY 11801

Merry Bee Communications, 815 Crest Drive, Omaha, NE 68046

The Micro Center, P.O. Box 6, Pleasantville, NY 10570

Microcomputer Workshops, 103 Puritan Drive, Port Chester, NY 10573

MICROGRAMS, P.O. Box 2146, Loves Park, IL 61130

Midwest Visual Equipment Company, 6500 North Hamlin, Chicago, IL 60645

Milliken Publishing Company, 1100 Research Boulevard, P.O. Box 21579, Saint Louis, MO 63132

Milton Bradley Educational Division, 443 Shaker Road, East Longmeadow, MA 01028

MindPlay, 82 Montvale Avenue, Stoneham, MA 02180

Opportunities for Learning, 20417 Nordhoff Street, Department 9, Chatsworth, CA 91311

Optimum Resource, 5 Hiltech Lane, Hilton Head, SC 29926

Orange Cherry New Media Schoolhouse, P.O. Box 390, 69 Westchester Avenue, Pound Ridge, NY 10576

Queue, 5 Chapel Hill Drive, Fairfield, CT 06432

Quicksoft, 537 Willamette, Eugene, OR 97401

Random House School Division, 201 East 50th Street, New York, NY 10022

Reader's Digest Services, Educational Division, Pleasantville, NY 10570

Right On Programs, Division of Computeam, P.O. Box 977, Huntington, NY 11743

Scholastic Software, 2931 East McCarty Street, Jefferson City, MO 65102

Scott, Foresman and Company, 1900 East Lake Avenue, Glenview, IL 60025

Society for Visual Education, 1345 Diversey Parkway, Department CC-1, Chicago, IL 60614

Southwest EdPsych Services, P.O. Box 1870, Phoenix, AZ 85001

South-Western Publishing Company, 5101 Madison Road, Cincinnati, OH 45227

Spinnaker Software, 201 Broadway, Cambridge, MA 02139

SRA, P.O. Box 543, Blacklick, OH 43004

Sunburst Communications, 39 Washington Avenue, Box 40, Pleasantville, NY 10570

Teacher Support Software, 1035 Northwest 57th Street, Gainesville, FL 32605

Texas Instruments, P.O. Box 10508, Mail Station 5849, Lubbock, TX 79408

Author Index

Subject Index

ABOUT THE AUTHOR

Cecil D. Mercer is a professor of education at the University of Florida. He received his Ed.D. in special education from the University of Virginia in 1974. Cecil has written numerous articles and books on educating exceptional students. One of his major works is *Teaching Students with Learning Problems*, and he is coauthor of the *Strategic Math Series*, a math strategies curriculum. Cecil remains involved in the educational programs of exceptional students through his participation in inservice and classroom activities in public and private schools, and he is a featured keynote and workshop speaker at many national and international conferences. Cecil is a member of the Learning Disabilities Association of America Professional Advisory Board, and he has been awarded the College of Education Teacher of the Year award three times at the University of Florida. Cecil and his wife, Ann, have three sons—Kevin, Greg, and Ken—and a golden retriever named Buckley.

Shirley R Hartwell
13317 Playa Terrace
Apt #135
OKC, OK 73120